10/01

College and University Business Administration

SIXTH EDITION

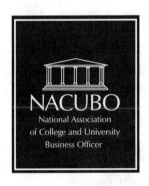

NACUBO
National Association
of College and University
Business Officer

Book design and typeset by AAH Graphics, Inc.

Senior Editor: Caroline M. Grills

Publications Director: Donna Klinger

Production Manager for Print and Electronic Media: Judith Castagna

ISBN: 1-56972-014-2 (book)
ISBN: 1-56972-013-4 (CD-ROM)

Contents

Contents

Foreword

THE TURN OF THE MILLENNIUM SERVES AS AN IMPORTANT METAPHOR FOR THE publication of the sixth edition of *College and University Business Administration*. For those of us who bear responsibility for the financial health and operational effectiveness of this nation's colleges and universities, this is arguably the most fascinating and challenging time in the history of American higher education.

Our institutions have grown more complex—whether large or small, public or independent, two-year, four-year, or research institution. Our revenue sources have become more diverse and more difficult to predict. The remarkable and sustained pace of economic growth over recent years has helped to raise revenues from many sources, including tuition, government funding, private fund-raising, endowments that have benefited from escalations in the stock market, patent royalties, and numerous new manifestations of university technology transfer. Yet we know these trends do not reflect a permanent condition. Reallocation of resources, requirements to achieve increased productivity, and growing competition from new higher education providers are immediately on the horizon. Successful pursuit of productivity improvements and innovative strategies for cost containment are becoming a way of life in all effective organizations.

In the meantime, the expenditure side of higher education budgets has also swelled. The need to invest in information technology is one of the most significant imperatives. Competition for faculty will continue to require increases in their salaries. Modernization and retrofitting of infrastructure and buildings from science labs to residence facilities will keep pressure on capital budgets. The public understands that higher education is the *sine qua non* of the future prosperity of their families. However, parents remain anxious about whether their children will have access to the college of their choice, even while they are distressed about the increasing cost of college attendance.

Powerful forces of change are impacting every sector of our society and our economy. Higher education will not be immune to these megatrends, nor to their transformational effects on the college and university enterprise. A brief description of some of these major forces of change and their potential implications follows:

Population demographics: Rising demand for higher education will derive from population growth and from the increasing importance of higher education to our economic viability. Growth in higher education enrollments will come, not only from those in the "Baby Boom Echo," but increasingly from workers pursuing additional education throughout their productive lives.

Knowledge economy: As knowledge and skill become the source of this nation's competitive strength, education is becoming our most important national resource. The strong correlation between level of education and lifetime income emphasizes that higher education is the best strategy to get a job, keep a job, or get a better job.

Information technology: The digital revolution is transforming the way business is conducted throughout the economy. Since an increasing portion of our gross domestic product comes from information technology industries, jobs in those industries command higher salaries. These trends have significant implications for expanding and altering our academic programs. Just as investment in transportation infrastructure helped build a strong United States economy in the 20th century, the infrastructure of the 21st century is information technology. The consequences for higher education are profound and are transforming the way we carry out teaching, research, and public service. Information technology, which has already become the basic scaffolding on which modern science and research are conducted, is playing an increasing role in the teaching/learning process and is challenging the traditional business model of colleges and universities.

Knowledge explosion: The accelerating pace at which the frontiers of knowledge expand is altering the skills that college and university graduates need to be competitive. At the same time, the knowledge explosion creates obsolescence and unrelenting pressure to continuously renew our education.

Globalization: As the global economy takes shape, the knowledge, innovation, and skill of our workforce is becoming the most important competitive advantage of this country. Yet talent pools developing in other parts of the world will place increasing pressure on corporations to expand operations—including their research and development centers—outside the United States. These trends will, in turn, place even greater pressures on our colleges and universities.

Taken together, these external forces of change will require higher education to reframe its response to emerging possibilities. Business and financial officers must play a central role in defining these new relationships and in developing the strategies to meet these new challenges. As I listen to campus business officers across the University of North Carolina, I know that they expect that those entering and advancing in this field will have broad expertise beyond accounting and financial management. The breadth of operations in the colleges and universities of today and tomorrow extends into many new areas of management, new forms of contracting, and new policy issues.

The Internet and the prospect of a networked world exemplify the power in the forces of change, as well as the demand for both skills and strategies to seize the opportunities at hand. The digital world is spawning new educational providers in what has been our protected marketplace. These providers are taking advantage of the reduction in barriers to entry and in the barriers of distance and time. If our established colleges and universities lose significant ground to these new providers in the high-volume, lower-cost courses and programs, then the challenge of sustaining other important but high-cost programs will become formidable. Successfully navigating in this digital world will require business and financial officers who can support institutional and academic leadership with the expertise to guide new implementation strategies. This could mean addressing challenging new dimensions of intellectual property policies and implementing joint ventures and contractual arrangements of various types—all while keeping a watchful eye on the financial health and fiscal integrity of the institution.

American colleges and universities are among the most complex organizations in the world, with operational and governance structures that do not easily adapt to rapid change. Among the most challenging dimensions of higher education's organizational complexity is the array of important constituencies that must be served. The interests of internal constituencies (faculty, students, staff, and board members) are not always aligned with one another. The interests of external constituencies (such as governors, legislatures, alumni, and the press) are not always uniformly aligned either, or even complementary with the interests of internal groups. Collegial forms of governance, while providing many important advantages that have been the source of great strength over many years, are not as compatible with rapid change as are hierarchical forms of governance.

As partners in the success of the overall enterprise, business and financial officers must contribute to leadership development, team building, and productive collaboration with these many important constituencies. Effective administrative leaders must be able to work broadly across this organizational complexity. Building consensus out of conflict is an important part of successful leadership.

As we look to the future, organizational boundaries are likely to become even less well defined. Strategic alliances are likely to develop on many fronts. Already, academic centers and institutes are emerging that cut across multiple disciplines and multiple campuses and that require new ways of budgeting, managing, decision making, and ensuring accountability. New forms of strategic alliances with business and industry present legal and financial challenges to be overcome. Yet these innovative approaches to collaboration with the private and government sectors offer great promise that technology transfer, for example, will proceed expeditiously, bringing with it great potential for economic development. Imagining ways to organize, contract, and operate these alliances will take deep knowledge of higher education, as well as knowledge of the principles of good management.

Higher education is built upon academic values and exists to carry out the three-part mission of teaching, research, and public service. Our abiding commitment is to the free flow of information and to the advancement of scholarship. As innovative new strategies and joint ventures are considered, these academic values must serve as first principles that cannot be compromised. Only by faithful commitment to these values and goals will higher education keep the support and good will of the larger public. As we seek regulatory relief and increased flexibility to respond to the forces of change, we must ensure appropriate accountability. Financial and business officers must play an important role in the development of metrics to demonstrate that accountability.

Given the rising importance of advanced learning to the success of our society and our economy, higher education could find itself as the centerpiece of an increasingly important domestic policy of our nation. Higher education's business and financial leaders can choose from among an extraordinary array of innovative opportunities to help their institutions serve the needs of learners of all ages. At the same time, these administrative leaders face daunting challenges. *College and University Business Administration* will be a strategically important tool to assist them in understanding best practices, in making wise choices, and in building effective strategies.

Molly Corbett Broad
President
The University of North Carolina

Sponsors

Official Sponsor

KPMG

Supporters

AT&T
COLLEGIS
Commonfund
J.P. Morgan
Oracle Corporation
PeopleSoft, Inc.
Siemens Building Technologies, Inc.

Contributors

Access Group, Inc.
Adams Consulting Group
Association for Financial Professionals (AFP)
Blackboard, Inc.
Campus Pipeline
CARS Information Systems
College Now
Credentials, Inc.
Educational Management Network/a division of Witt/Kieffer
Eduprise
Follett Higher Education Group
George K. Baum & Co.
HigherMarkets, Inc.
Johnson Controls, Inc.
Jones Lang LaSalle
Key Education Resources
Lehman Brothers
Morgan Stanley Dean Witter
National Association of Campus Card Users (NACCU)
National Association of College Stores (NACS)

NCS
Nicholas-Applegate Capital Management
Salomon Smith Barney Consulting Group
The College Board
The Document Company Xerox
The Vanguard Group
TIAA-CREF
United Educators Insurance Risk Retention Group, Inc.
University Risk Management & Insurance Association (URMIA)
Wallace's Bookstore, Inc.
Windstar Technologies, Inc.

Preface

THE SIXTH EDITION OF *College and University Business Administration* (CUBA 6) has been completely revised since the fifth edition was published in 1992. The environment in which colleges and universities operate has changed dramatically over the past eight years. Greater management and leadership skills than ever before are now required of higher education administrators.

This authoritative reference for higher education administration has evolved over 50 years. In addition to growing to nearly 1,400 pages, the publication is now available on CD-ROM, making searches and direct links to information on the Internet possible.

College and University Business Administration addresses primarily financial and business officers, but other persons involved in higher education administration, including legislators, presidents, provosts, and governing board members, will also benefit from its expertise. It presents theory, policy, and practice; it is not a procedures manual.

College and University Business Administration, sixth edition (CUBA 6), is a product of wide-ranging input, thoughtful review, and consensus building on the part of hundreds of people and is based on the sound foundation provided by the fifth edition. A large cadre of authors wrote the new material and adapted text from the fifth edition. The CUBA 6 Advisory Committee and numerous volunteers who are experts in their fields reviewed each chapter. The large number of contributors and reviewers—and their consensus—provides the authority for the sixth edition.

The CUBA 6 Advisory Committee provided guidance for this edition, particularly in determining its scope and level and in confirming its intended audience. Countless hours of effort brought this revision to fruition. Members of the committee are:

Benjamin F. Quillian, California State University, Fresno (Chair)

Susan Stetson Clarke, Unconventional Wisdom

William Gauthier, State University of West Georgia

Barbara Gitenstein, The College of New Jersey

Virginia Gregg, Rensselaer Polytechnic Institute

Rhonda I. Gross, Lehigh University

Judith Palmer, Indiana University

Steven Relyea, University of California, San Diego

Therese Sampson, Atlantic Community College

Michael Shirley, Elgin Community College

James F. Sullivan, California State University, Northridge

G. Richard Wynn, Haverford College

It is notable that G. Richard Wynn has served on the advisory committee for three consecutive editions of *CUBA*. Similarly, this is the second consecutive edition for which Susan Stetson Clarke has served as an advisory committee member. Their long-term commitment to this endeavor is commendable.

While recognizing the hundreds of experts who provided and reviewed material, the CUBA 6 Advisory Committee also acknowledges the many people who gave more than was expected of them and spent a great deal of time and effort on this edition, including:

Mary Bachinger, NACUBO

Christopher Campbell, NACUBO

Mary L. Fischer, University of Texas at Tyler

Anne Gross, NACUBO

David A. Lieberman, University of Miami

Richard Mooney, University Procurement Consulting Group

Diane Oakley, TIAA-CREF

Laurie Quarles, NACUBO

Julia A. Rudy, EDUCAUSE

Paul Stromgren, California State University System

Abbott Wainwright, who played a large and pivotal role in the three previous editions, deserves special recognition for the part he played in the sixth edition. He served as primary advisor and reviewer. Mr. Wainwright's expertise and careful consideration of the material were enormously valuable. He helped shape both the form and the content of each edition. NACUBO is indebted to him for his continued involvement in this publication.

Many NACUBO staff members also worked on this edition. Anna Marie Cirino directed the development of the manuscript, as she did in 1992. Larry Goldstein and Carla Balakgie provided leadership throughout the undertaking. Donna Klinger and Caroline Grills provided editorial leadership. Brent Mundt led the successful sponsorship campaign. Judith Castagna saw the manuscript through production. Andrea Richards designed the CD-ROM and was involved in the preliminary book production process. Christopher Brown, Mark Campbell, and Lisa James assisted with administrative tasks throughout the long and arduous process of development, editing, and production, as well as the sponsorship campaign. Maryann Terrana assisted in text development. Karen Bandy, Diana Blessinger, Ann Hunter, Stephen Hunter, Anne Kendrick, Hillary Price, Cynthia Tinsley, Allyson Walker, and Michele West also assisted in the editorial process. Clearly, many additional staff members across the organization played a part in this major endeavor. Their assistance, as well as that of those named above, is gratefully acknowledged.

The fifth edition constituted a break from previous editions in that it provided only an overview of financial reporting. This edition does likewise. *The Financial Accounting and Reporting Manual for Higher Education* (NACUBO, 1990) offers an updated and vastly expanded presentation of the material contained in Part 5 of *College and University Business Administration*, fourth edition, and supersedes it as the authoritative reference on this subject. The purpose of *The Financial Accounting and Reporting Manual for Higher Education*, which is updated bimonthly, is to equip business and financial officers with the information needed to address complex and changing financial and accounting requirements.

In addition to *The Financial Accounting and Reporting Manual for Higher Education*, NACUBO has since developed several other subscription services, which offer comprehensive and detailed information on specific subject areas. These include: *Federal Auditing Information Service for Higher Education; Managing Federal Grants;* and *A Guide to Federal Tax Issues for Colleges and Universities.*

In the preface of the third edition of *College and University Business Administration*, Neal Hines wrote that the profession would face more demands in the future. He was absolutely right; the profession of higher education administration has seen a great deal of change and expansion in the years that have passed since that edition was published. Despite the enormous challenges presented in the 1990s, it is possible that they may pale in comparison to those in this current decade. The principles and practices discussed in the sixth edition are commended for use by all higher education business and financial administrators.

Benjamin F. Quillian
Chair
CUBA 6 Advisory Committee

James E. Morley Jr.
President
National Association of College and
University Business Officers

Acknowledgments

MANY PEOPLE AND ORGANIZATIONS WERE INVOLVED IN THE SIXTH EDITION OF *College and University Business Administration*; their contributions are acknowledged on these pages. Many hours of effort are represented by the names that follow. Unfortunately, some reviewers cannot be recognized individually because they were called upon by others. To these anonymous reviewers, as well as to those whose names are listed below, NACUBO expresses deep appreciation. Mention of reviewers by name does not necessarily indicate their approval of the published chapter, but only that they had a part in the development of the material.

Chapter 1: The Role of the Chief Financial and Business Officer

Janice Abraham, United Educators Risk Retention Insurance Group, Incorporated; Greg J. Baroni, KPMG; Craig Bazzani, University of Illinois University Administration; Lawrence W. Broomall, Washington and Lee University; C. Joseph Carter, Western Carolina University; Susan Stetson Clarke, Unconventional Wisdom; L. Edwin Coate, Mira Costa Community College District; John A. Falcone, SUNY Institute of Technology at Utica/Rome; Patricia Farris, California State Polytechnic University, Pomona; Jose Garcia, Texas A&M International University; William Gauthier, State University of West Georgia; Barbara Gitenstein, The College of New Jersey; Rufus Glasper, Maricopa Community College; Larry Goldstein, National Association of College and University Business Officers; Virginia Gregg, Rensselaer Polytechnic Institute; Rhonda I. Gross, Lehigh University; Janet C. Hamilton, University of California, Davis; Caspa Harris; Mernoy E. Harrison Jr., Arizona State University; David G. Healy, The Milton Academy; Herman D. Johnson; Gina A. Kranitz, Paradise Valley Community College; Mary M. Lai, Long Island University; Beverly E. Ledbetter, Brown University; David A. Lieberman, University of Miami; Roger D. Lowe, Wichita State University; Walter McCarthy, College of New Rochelle; John McDonald, California State University, Chico; Judith Block McLaughlin, Harvard University; Orie E. Meyers Jr.; James E. Morley Jr., National Association of College and University Business Officers; Jack D. Mulholland, Indiana University; Diane Oakley, TIAA-CREF; Judith G. Palmer, Indiana University; John A. Palmucci, Loyola College in Maryland; John D. Patterson, Pittsburg State University; Benjamin F. Quillian,

California State University, Fresno; Steven Relyea, University of California, San Diego; Therese Sampson, Atlantic Community College; Michael Shirley, Elgin Community College; R. Eugene Smith, University of Memphis; Joe Smolskis, Trinity College; Paul Stromgren, California State University; James F. Sullivan, California State University, Northridge; Maryann Terrana, National Association of College and University Business Officers; Abbott Wainwright; Barry Walsh, Indiana University; G. Richard Wynn, Haverford College.

Chapter 2: Planning

Christopher K. Ahoy, Iowa State University of Science and Technology; Greg J. Baroni, KPMG; Will Barratt, Indiana State University; L. Edwin Coate, Mira Costa Community College District; Albert A. Dekin Jr., Binghamton University; John Eldert, Babson College; William Gauthier, State University of West Georgia; Larry Goldstein, National Association of College and University Business Officers; Virginia Gregg, Rensselaer Polytechnic Institute; Rhonda I. Gross, Lehigh University; Patricia R. Gustavson, John Brown University; David G. Healy, The Milton Academy; K. Scott Hughes, K. Scott Hughes Associates; Weldon E. Ihrig, University of Washington; Katherine Johnston, University of Minnesota, Twin Cities; David A. Lieberman, University of Miami; Patrick Sanaghan, The Napier Group; Andreea Serban, Santa Barbara City College; Gerard Shaw, Shaw Gardner Group; James F. Sullivan, California State University, Northridge; Timothy R. Warner, Stanford University; Abbott Wainwright; Michael Whalen, Cornell University.

Chapter 3: Implementation Strategies and Outcomes Assessment

Janice M. Abraham, United Educators Risk Retention Insurance Group, Incorporated; Greg J. Baroni, KPMG; Will Barratt, Indiana University; Susan Stetson Clarke, Unconventional Wisdom; L. Edwin Coate, Mira Costa Community College District; John Eldert, Babson College; Larry Goldstein, National Association of College and University Business Officers; Virginia Gregg, Rensselaer Polytechnic Institute; Rhonda I. Gross, Lehigh University; Ethelynda Harding, California State University Fresno Center for Enhancement of Teaching and Learning; Weldon E. Ihrig, University of Washington; David A. Lieberman, University of Miami; Richard Norman, Miami University of Ohio; Gerard Shaw, Shaw Gardner Group; James F. Sullivan, California State University, Northridge; Suzanne H. Summers, Miami University of Ohio; Maryann Terrana, National Association of College and University Business Officers; Abbott Wainwright.

Chapter 4: Budgeting

Susan Stetson Clarke, Unconventional Wisdom; Nathan Dickmeyer, Mercy College; William Gauthier, State University of West Georgia; Sarah A. Gillman, The Stillwater Group; Larry Goldstein, National Association of College and University Business Officers; Virginia Gregg, Rensselaer Polytechnic Institute; Rhonda I. Gross, Lehigh University; Patricia R. Gustavson, John Brown University; David Hornfischer, Berklee College of Music; Harvey H. Kaiser, Harvey H. Kaiser and Associates; John Swiger, Our Lady of the Lakes University; Abbott Wainwright; Stephanie Woodfork, National Association of College and University Business Officers.

Chapter 5: Financial Reporting

Greg J. Baroni, KPMG; Craig Becker, New York Institute of Technology; Joe Blythe, Governmental Accounting Standards Board; Susan E. Budak; Mary L. Fischer, The University of Texas at Tyler; Robert T. Forrester, PricewaterhouseCoopers; Robert Gallo, KPMG; Larry Goldstein, National Association of College and University Business Officers; Joe Gorman, Sinclair Community College; K. Scott Hughes, K. Scott Hughes Associates; Janice Krogen, National Association of College and University Business Officers; John R. Kroll, University of Chicago; Richard Larkin; David J. Lyons, Rockefeller University; Kathleen McNeely, Indiana University; John S. Ostrom, Cornell University; Judith G. Palmer, Indiana University; Raymond P. Pipkin, University of Memphis; Pauline Roberts, National Association of College and University Business Officers; John R. Shipley, Purdue University; Ingrid S. Stafford, Northwestern University; Phil Tahey, KPMG; Charles Tegen, Clemson University; Abbott Wainwright; Richard P. West, California State University; G. Richard Wynn, Haverford College.

Chapter 6: Managerial Reporting

Greg J. Baroni, KPMG; Susan E. Budak; Nathan Dickmeyer, Mercy College; Robert T. Forrester, PricewaterhouseCoopers; Joe Gorman, Sinclair Community College; K. Scott Hughes, K. Scott Hughes Associates; Janice Krogen, National Association of College and University Business Officers; Michael Kulig, KPMG Consulting; Kathleen McNeely, Indiana University; Paul Nacon, KPMG; John A. Palmucci, Loyola College in Maryland; Roger Patterson, University of North Carolina at Chapel Hill; Yoke San L. Reynolds, Cornell University; Pauline Roberts, National Association of College and University Business Officers; John R. Shipley,

Purdue University; Charles Tegen, Clemson University; Abbott Wainwright; Barbara Walsh, Georgia Institute of Technology.

Chapter 7: Information Technology and Services

Greg J. Baroni, KPMG; Susan Stetson Clarke, Unconventional Wisdom; James Cross, Michigan Technological University; William Gauthier, State University of West Georgia; Eric Gerlach, The University Center; Barbara Gitenstein, The College of New Jersey; Janet C. Hamilton, University of California, Davis; Polly McClure, Cornell University; Mick McKellar, Michigan Technological University; Anthony Mordosky, Bradley University; Shirley C. Payne, University of Virginia; Margaret F. Plympton, Bucknell University; Steven Relyea, University of California, San Diego; Jeri Semer, Association of College and University Telecommunications Administrators; Charlotte Sullivan, University of Texas at Austin; Anthony Tanzi, Brown University; Maryann Terrana, National Association of College and University Business Officers; Abbott Wainwright.

Chapter 8: Treasury Management

Donna Sue Broadstreet, Indiana University Bloomington; Larry Goldstein, National Association of College and University Business Officers; Julie Karns, Rider University; Steven C. Snyder, Commonfund Treasury, Inc.; Abbott Wainwright.

Chapter 9: Endowment Management

Mary L. Fischer, The University of Texas at Tyler; Virginia Gregg, Rensselaer Polytechnic Institute; Janice Krogen, National Association of College and University Business Officers; John R. Kroll, University of Chicago; Louis R. Morrell, Wake Forest University; Abbott Wainwright; G. Richard Wynn, Haverford College.

Chapter 10: Debt Financing and Management

Herman R. Charbonneau, Roosevelt and Cross, Incorporated; James E. Costello, Lehman Brothers; R. Michael DeSalle, Columbia College; Nathan Dickmeyer, Mercy College; Michael E. Finnerty, Lehman Brothers; Rhonda I. Gross, Lehigh University; Patrick J. Hennigan, Morgan Stanley Dean Witter; Thomas Nedell, St. John's University; John C. Nelson, Moody's Investors Service; Mary Peloquin-Dodd, Standard and Poor's Corporation; Raymond P. Pipkin, University of Memphis; William S. Reed, Wellesley College; Naomi G. Richman,

Moody's Investors Service; Judith Van Gorden, University of Colorado; Abbott Wainwright; G. Richard Wynn, Haverford College.

Chapter 11: Taxation

Mary Bachinger, National Association of College and University Business Officers; Greg J. Baroni, KPMG; Bonnie B. Cauthon, University of Florida; John Copoulos, University of Massachusetts, Treasurer's Office; Anne E. Davenport, Miami University of Ohio; Kelly D. Farmer, Arizona State University; Bertrand Harding, Law Offices of Bertrand Harding; Joseph R. Irvine, Ohio State University; Steve Katz, California State University, Fresno; James J. McGovern, KPMG Washington National Tax; Diane Oakley, TIAA-CREF; Gerald Siegert, University of Cincinnati; Abbott Wainwright; Barbara Warren, Johns Hopkins University.

Chapter 12: Human Resources and Benefits Administration

Mary Bachinger, National Association of College and University Business Officers; Susan Stetson Clarke, Unconventional Wisdom; Barbara Gitenstein, The College of New Jersey; Virginia Gregg, Rensselaer Polytechnic Institute; Rhonda I. Gross, Lehigh University; Patricia R. Gustavson, John Brown University; Diane Oakley, TIAA-CREF; Mary Peloquin Dodd, Standard and Poor's Investment Services; Jackie R. McClain, California State University System; Benjamin F. Quillian, California State University, Fresno; Jeannine Raymond, California State University, Fresno; Gerard Shaw, Shaw Gardner Group; James F. Sullivan, California State University, Northridge; Abbott Wainwright; Maureen Young, Rensselaer Polytechnic University.

Chapter 13: Facilities Management

Herman Bulls, LaSalle Partners; William Daigneau, University of Texas, MD Anderson Cancer Center; Brian Donnelly, Southern Illinois University at Edwardsville; William Gauthier, State University of West Georgia; Anne Gross, National Association of College and University Business Officers; Thomas L. Lussenhop, University of Pennsylvania; Benjamin F. Quillian, California State University, Fresno; Daniel J. Rodas, Duke University; Therese Sampson, Atlantic Community College; Roger Smith, Jones Lang LaSalle Americas, Inc.; Maryann Terrana, National Association of College and University Business Officers; Abbott Wainwright.

Chapter 14: Environmental Health and Safety

Janice M. Abraham, United Educators Risk Retention Insurance Group, Incorporated; Anne Gross, National Association of College and University Business Officers; Julaine Kiehn, University of Missouri; Roger D. Lowe, Wichita State University; Judith A. Merritt, Campus Safety Health and Environmental Management Association; William R. O'Connell, National Association of Student Personnel Administators, Inc.; Fay M. Thompson, University of Minnesota; Paul A. Uravich, University of South Florida; Abbott Wainwright; Barry Walsh, Indiana University.

Chapter 15: Security and Law Enforcement

Janice M. Abraham, United Educators Risk Retention Insurance Group, Incorporated; Asa T. Boynton, University of Georgia; Max Bromley, University of South Florida; Eugene R. Ferrara, University of Cincinnati; William Gauthier, State University of West Georgia; Anne Gross, National Association of College and University Business Officers; Rhonda I. Gross, Lehigh University; Jules C. Jacquin, Rensselaer Polytechnic Institute; Thomas J. Mackel, State University of West Georgia; Elizabeth M. Nuss, Goucher College; Benjamin F. Quillian, California State University, Fresno; Steven Relyea, University of California, San Diego; Therese Sampson, Atlantic Community College; R. Eugene Smith, University of Memphis; Everett H. Stevens, University of Florida; Paul A. Uravich, University of South Florida; Abbott Wainwright.

Chapter 16: Risk Management and Insurance

Janice M. Abraham, United Educators Risk Retention Insurance Group, Incorporated; William Gauthier, State University of West Georgia; Anne Gross, National Association of College and University Business Officers; James E. Morley Jr., National Association of College and University Business Officers; Benjamin F. Quillian, California State University, Fresno; Steven Relyea, University of California, San Diego; Therese Sampson, Atlantic Community College; R. Eugene Smith, University of Memphis; Abbott Wainwright.

Chapter 17: Procurement

Arnold Combe, University of Utah; Ray T. Jensen, Arizona State University; Richard L. Mooney, University Procurement Consulting Group; Therese Sampson, Atlantic Community College; Ronald Santi, Iowa State University; Abbott Wainwright.

Chapter 18: Research and Sponsored Programs

Greg J. Baroni, KPMG; Tony DeCrappeo, Council on Government Relations; Bill Kirby, KPMG; Peggy S. Lowry, Murray State University; David Mears, University of California System; Kate Phillips, Council on Government Relations; Steven Relyea, University of California, San Diego; Andrew B. Rudczynski, University of Pennsylvania; Abbott Wainwright; Mareda Weiss, University of Wisconsin, Madison.

Chapter 19: Student Financial Aid

Greg J. Baroni, KPMG; Christopher Campbell, National Association of College and University Business Officers; Joe Paul Case, Amherst College; Mary Farrington, U.S. Department of Health and Human Services; Anne Gross, National Association of College and University Business Officers; Kay H. Hanson, Consortium on Financing Higher Education; Todd Harmening, National Association of College and University Business Officers; Laurie Quarles, National Association of College and University Business Officers; Joseph Russo, University of Notre Dame; Joe Smolskis, Trinity College; Abbott Wainwright; G. Richard Wynn, Haverford College.

Chapter 20: Auxiliary Enterprises and Other Activities

Diana Bakkom, Western Washington University; Larry L. Barrett, University of California, San Diego; Nick J. Bruno, Southeast Louisiana University; Cheryl Callahan, The University of North Carolina-Greensboro; Jim Carruthers, University of California, San Diego; Cynthia D'Angelo, National Association of College Stores; Alan B. Davis, National Association for Campus Activities; Gwendolyn J. Dungy, National Association of Student Personnel Administrators, Inc.; William Gauthier, State University of West Georgia; Frank X. Gladu, Vanderbilt University; Mernoy E. Harrison Jr., Arizona State University; Pamela D. Hayes, Association of Collegiate Licensing Administrators; James L. Isch, National Collegiate Athletics Association; Julaine Kiehn, University of Missouri; George Masforroll, Broward Community College; Deb Naughton, Sodexho Marriott; William R. O'Connell, National Association of Student Personnel Administrators, Inc.; Joseph G. Pietrantoni, Duke University; Therese Sampson, Atlantic Community College; Gerard Shaw, Shaw Gardner Group; R. Eugene Smith, University of Memphis; Joseph H. Spina,, National Association of College and University Food Services; James F. Sullivan, California State University, Northridge; Paula L. Swinford, University of Southern California; Maryann Terrana, National

Association of College and University Business Officers; Abbott Wainwright; Stephanie Woodfork, National Association of College and University Business Officers; Dean A. Wright, Brigham Young University; Dennis Yesalonia, Sullivan Weinstein and McQuay, P.C.

Chapter 21: Legal Issues

Mary Bachinger, National Association of College and University Business Officers; Anne Gross, National Association of College and University Business Officers; Rhonda I. Gross, Lehigh University; Bertrand Harding, Law Offices of Bertrand Harding; David G. Healy, The Milton Academy; Janette Redd-Williams, California State University; Therese Sampson, Atlantic Community College; R. Eugene Smith, University of Memphis; Abbott Wainwright; G. Richard Wynn, Haverford College.

Chapter 22: Auditing

Greg J. Baroni, KPMG; Diana Biggs, University of Southern Indiana; Robert T. Forrester, PricewaterhouseCoopers; Robert Gallo, KPMG; Larry Goldstein, National Association of College and University Business Officers; Joe Gorman, Sinclair Community College; Cynthia Harris, Crowe, Chizek & Co. LLP; Jules C. Jacquin, Rensselaer Polytechnic Institute; Janice Krogen, National Association of College and University Business Officers; Kathleen McNeely, Indiana University; John S. Ostrom, Cornell University; Richard Peper, Bowling Green State University; Terry Radke, Indiana Unversity; Chris Robinson, California State University, Fresno; Warren H. Spruill, University of Alabama System; Phil Tahey, KPMG; Charles Tegen, Clemson University; Abbott Wainwright.

Authors

REBECCA L. ADAIR (CHAPTER 16, RISK MANAGEMENT AND INSURANCE) HAS BEEN the university risk manager at Iowa State University since 1991. Ms. Adair is an active member of the University Risk Management and Insurance Association (URMIA). She is currently chair of the Association Relations Committee, on the Board of Directors, and the organization's representative to the Council on Higher Education Management Associations (CHEMA). She is also past president of the Iowa Chapter of the Risk and Insurance Management Society. She serves as a faculty presenter at the College Business Management Institute and is a frequent speaker on risk management issues. Ms. Adair is a graduate of Iowa State University with degrees in English and speech communications.

DAVID ANILOFF, C.I.S.A., (Chapter 22, Auditing) is an information systems auditor for the University of Pennsylvania. He specializes in information security audits of computer networks and Windows NT and UNIX systems. He is a member of the Information Systems Audit and Control Association, the Association of College and University Auditors, and the Institute of Internal Auditors. Mr. Aniloff has a B.S. degree from Pennsylvania State University.

JOHN H. AUGUSTINE (Chapter 10, Debt Financing and Management) managing director, leads the higher education finance group for Lehman Brothers. He joined Lehman Brothers in 1986 and is responsible for the firm's services to clients in higher education. Mr. Augustine has 18 years of experience in university and investment banking positions, including three years on the faculty of Yale University. A Fulbright Scholar at Oxford University, Mr. Augustine holds a B.A. from Wheaton College, a Ph.D. from the University of Minnesota, and an M.B.A. in finance from Yale University.

THERESA A. BACHMANN (Chapter 6, Managerial Reporting) is KPMG's national manager for Higher Education, Research, and Other Not-for-Profits. She helps coordinate professional services to their premier higher education clients. Having served in the nonprofit community for 10 years, Ms. Bachmann also helps develop training programs for KPMG not-for-profit professionals in specialized products for the higher education community. She graduated from Georgetown University.

CAROLE A. BARONE (Chapter 7, Information Technology and Services) is vice president of EDUCAUSE, where her responsibilities include a focus on the National Learning Infrastructure Initiative (NLII). She currently is a member of the New Media Centers Board and recently served on the National Policy and Planning Council of the University Corporation for Advanced Internet Development. She was also on the boards of CAUSE and Educom prior to their consolidation to form EDUCAUSE. Dr. Barone is the 1995 recipient of the CAUSE ELITE Award for Exemplary Leadership and Information Technology Excellence. She holds master's and doctorate degrees from the Maxwell School of Citizenship and Public Affairs at Syracuse University. She speaks and writes extensively on the impact of information technology on organizations.

GREG J. BARONI (Chapter 4, Budgeting) is a senior vice president at KPMG, responsible for the Public Services practice focused on higher education, academic medical centers, research institutions, and other not-for-profits. He has national experience providing financial management, transformation, and technology services. Mr. Baroni manages the relationship with the National Association of College and University Business Officers as KPMG assumes administration of the Higher Education Benchmarking Program. He is currently a member of NACUBO and the National Association of Business Economists. Mr. Baroni has M.S. and B.S. degrees in economics from the University of Southern California.

WILHEMENA BLACK (Chapter 12, Human Resources and Benefits Administration) is director of Affirmative Action Programs, ADA compliance officer, and Title IX coordinator at the University of Miami. Ms. Black has been with the University of Miami for 20 years and has been a lecturer in the School of Business at the University of Miami. Ms. Black is an active member of several civic and professional organizations including the Women's Network, Association of Affirmative Action Professionals, Society for Human Resources Management (SHRM), and the College and University Personnel Association (CUPA). She received her undergraduate degree from Metropolitan State College and her master's degree in human resources from St. Thomas University.

MOLLY CORBETT BROAD (Foreword) is president of the University of North Carolina. She has an extensive leadership background in the areas of administration, finance, and operations. Ms. Broad is active with several organizations as well as occupying board seats with several institutions. She has earned a bachelor's degree in economics from Syracuse University and a master's degree in the same field from Ohio State University. Currently, she is pursuing her doctorate degree in economics from Syracuse.

MARY LEE BROWN, C.I.A., (Chapter 22, Auditing) is the executive director for University and Information Systems Audit at the University of Pennsylvania. With over 22 years experience in higher education, she has served in several leadership roles, including director of accounting services in a controller's office, project leader for a major financial systems implementation, and assistant director and EDP audit manager. Ms. Brown is a member of the Information Systems Audit and Control Association (ISACA), Association of College and University Auditors (ACUA), and the Institute of Internal Auditors (IIA).

ELIZABETH CARMICHAEL, C.P.C.U., (Chapter 16 Risk Management and Insurance) provides risk management services for Amherst, Hampshire, Mount Holyoke, and Smith colleges, and consults with the University of Massachusetts at Amherst as requested. As the risk manager for Five Colleges Incorporated, she has worked in the insurance and risk management industry for 20 years, including underwriting and brokerage. She places the colleges' property and casualty insurance policies and student health policies and handles claims management, litigation management, and safety. Ms. Carmichael speaks frequently on risk management issues and is the coauthor of a book on liability and vehicle safety.

JOHN CARPENTER (Chapter 15, Security and Law Enforcement) has been the director of public safety at San Diego State University for the past 25 years. Mr. Carpenter has a bachelor's degree in sociology and secondary education and a master's degree in public administration from San Diego State University. He is a graduate of the FBI National Academy and has provided expert witness services for a variety of public and independent universities throughout the United States. He is a past president of the International Association of Campus Law Enforcement Officers (IACLEA).

JOCELYN CEASAR (Chapter 11, Taxation) is a senior tax consultant with the tax-exempt organizations group at the PricewaterhouseCoopers Boston office. Specializing in tax-exempt organizations, Ms. Ceasar's clients include colleges, universities, hospitals, and other charitable organizations. She graduated from Vanderbilt University in 1993 with a B.A. degree and from Vermont Law School in 1997 with a J.D. degree.

SUSAN STETSON CLARKE (Chapter 2, Planning) is a partner in Unconventional Wisdom, a consulting firm specializing in services for educational and cultural institutions. She was formerly vice president for administration at Rensselaer Polytechnic Institute and later associate vice president for operations at New York Medical College. Ms. Clarke earned an M.B.A. degree from Boston University and a B.A. from Wheaton College.

STEPHEN G. COLICCI (Chapter 22, Auditing) is the director of the office of

Audit & Management Advisory Services at Syracuse University. He has 25 years of internal auditing experience, including 15 years conducting and supervising annual athletics compliance audits at Syracuse University. He has participated as a peer reviewer of the NCAA's Athletics Certification Program and presented athletics compliance training sessions at several ACUA annual conferences and mid-year seminars. Mr. Colicci received a bachelor's degree in accounting from Utica College of Syracuse University.

J. STEPHEN COLLINS, C.P.A., (Chapter 19, Student Financial Aid) is an associate professor of accounting in the College of Management at the University of Massachusetts at Lowell, where he teaches courses in financial and managerial accounting. He is the author of the NACUBO publication *Audits of Student Financial Aid Programs*. He is also a consultant to colleges and universities and public accounting firms. Dr. Collins holds a Ph.D. from Boston College.

WALTER CONWAY (Chapter 8, Treasury Management) manages Visa USA's merchant and industry marketing programs. He has worked with education institutions nationwide to implement payment card acceptance for tuition and fees. Mr. Conway speaks at regional and national seminars sponsored by NACUBO and The Commonfund, among others. He is also an alumni advisor to Purdue's Krannert School of Management. He received his B.S. degree with honors from Purdue University, and holds an S.M. in management from the Massachusetts Institute of Technology's Sloan School of Management.

JOHN R. CURRY (Chapter 4, Budgeting) joined the Massachusetts Institute of Technology (MIT) as executive vice president in November 1998. He is responsible for the overall leadership, management, and organization of MIT's administrative and financial affairs, including operations, financial management and planning, human resources management, information systems, resource development, and facilities. Mr. Curry holds a B.A. in physics and an M.A. in mathematics from West Virginia University. He completed course work for a Ph.D. in mathematics from Carnegie Mellon University, where he served as an instructor in mathematics from 1965 to 1967.

LAWRENCE DAVIS (Chapter 14, Environmental Health and Safety) is the registered sanitarian with environmental health and safety at the University of Massachusetts at Amherst. He is involved with food, housing, swimming pool, and lead paint inspections. Mr. Davis has been in the field of public health for more than 18 years. He has been on the advisory committee for Massachusetts Public Health Swimming pool regulations. He has also served as a sanitarian for the Amherst, Massachusetts Board of Health.

MICHAEL T. DIESCHBOURG, C.I.M.A., (Chapter 9, Endowment Management) is national director of institutional consulting at Salomon Smith Barney Consulting Group. He delivers consulting services to institutional clients in asset/liability analysis, asset allocation strategy, investment policy development, manager research and performance evaluation, and measurement. Mr. Dieschbourg holds a B.B.A. degree from Loyola University.

VICTORIA S. ESCALERA, C.I.A., C.P.A., C.E.E., (Chapter 22, Auditing) has directed the internal audit function at Brown University since 1988. Her duties as university auditor include staffing the governing board's audit committee, administering contracts for external audit services, and monitoring sub-recipients of federal awards. Ms. Escalera served on NACUBO's Accounting Principles Committee for several years during the 1990s and has been a contributing author and editor for other NACUBO publications. She has been active in the Association of College and University Auditors (ACUA), the Institute of Internal Auditors (IIA), and the advisory council for the University of Rhode Island's accounting program. Ms. Escalera is a graduate of Wellesley College, and she received master's degrees from Salve Regina University and the University of Rhode Island.

KAYE B. FERRITER, C.P.A., (Chapter 11, Taxation) is the tax director for the Healthcare, Higher Education and Not-for-Profit group in PricewaterhouseCoopers Tax Service. She provides tax services to the firm's tax-exempt clients. Ms. Ferriter has over 20 year of tax consulting experience with PricewaterhouseCoopers. She is a member of the American Institute of Certified Public Accountants (AICPA), the Massachusetts Society of CPAs, and the American Bar Association (Tax Section). She is also the chair of the AICPA's tax-exempt organization committee. Ms. Ferriter holds a bachelor's degree in psychology from Brown University and earned a law degree and a master's in law in taxation from Boston University.

MATTHEW FINUCANE (Chapter 14, Environmental Health and Safety) is the director of the University of Pennsylvania's Office of Environmental Health and Radiation Safety and a health and safety consultant to research and development, and biotechnology firms. He is responsible for safety in 2,000-plus laboratories, in which more than $460 million of sponsored research is conducted annually. Mr. Finucane supervises a staff of over 45 professional, technical, and administrative personnel. He is certified by the American Board of Industrial Hygiene and is active in the American Industrial Hygiene Association. He also serves on the board of the Campus Safety Health and Environmental Management Association (CSHEMA) as a member at large.

HERBERT K. FOLPE (Chapter 5, Financial Reporting) is a lecturer at the Yale School of Management and serves as a consultant on financial accounting and reporting matters to various not-for-profit industry groups. He has written extensively on the not-for-profit sector and has been the editor since 1992 of the *Financial Accounting and Reporting Manual for Higher Education*, published by the National Association of College and University Business Officers. He has also served on numerous committees and task forces of the AICPA, FASB, and GASB involved in the development of financial accounting and reporting standards for private and public not-for-profit organizations.

ROBERT FORREST, C.H.P., (Chapter 14, Environmental Health and Safety) is the senior medical health physicist in the University of Pennsylvania's Office of Environmental Health and Radiation Safety. He is also a radiation safety consultant to hospitals, academic institutions, and biotechnology firms. He is responsible for all clinical radiation safety aspects of a large broad scope medical license. Mr. Forrest is certified by the American Board of Health Physics. He is also an active member of the Health Physics Society and past president of the Delaware Society for Radiation Safety.

JAMES P. FOX (Chapter 14, Environmental Health and Safety) is the manager, Hazardous Waste Management Services, Environmental Health and Safety at the University of Massachusetts Amherst. He is primarily responsible for hazardous waste management, and other environmental and occupational safety areas. Mr. Fox is a member of the American Institute of Chemical Engineers, the Massachusetts Licensed Site Professional Association, and the Air and Waste Management Association. He received his B.S. (cum laude) in environmental science from the University of Massachusetts and his M.S. in environmental science/engineering from the University of Texas.

ROBERT F. GERMAN JR. (Chapter 7, Information Technology and Services) has been the director of policy and strategic planning in the Office of Information Technologies at the University of Virginia since 1993. Previously he was chief of staff to University of Virginia President John Casteen and assistant to President Robert M. O'Neil, and he served as director of the university's news office and its publications office. He is also a member of the Commonwealth of Virginia's Council on Technology Services. Mr. German holds a bachelor's degree in biology and English and a master's degree in English from the University of Virginia.

BETSY HOBSON (Chapter 19, Student Financial Aid) is the associate director of financial aid at Williams College. She began her financial aid career at the University of Colorado, Boulder. Ms. Hobson is responsible for the successful implementation of the Direct Loan program at Williams. She is a member of the Midwest Association of Student Financial Aid Administrators (MASFAA) and the Eastern Association of Student Financial Aid Administrators (EASFAA).

JULES C. JACQUIN (Chapter 16, Risk Management and Insurance) is the senior director of risk management and internal auditing at Rensselaer Polytechnic Institute. He is a member of the board of directors of Genesis Limited, a reinsurance company owned by Rensselaer and 14 other leading colleges and universities. He has served as adjunct associate professor in Rensselaer's Lally School of Management and Technology. He is a member of the board of directors of the Association of College and University Auditors and serves on the editorial advisory board of the Institute of Internal Auditors. He received an M.B.A. degree from Rensselaer, an M.S. degree from the Massachusetts Institute of Technology, and a B.S. from Texas A&M University.

LEIGH A. JONES, (Chapter 9, Endowment Management) B.B.A., M.B.A., C.P.A., is retired vice president for business and finance, Berea College. His undergraduate degree is from the University of Minnesota, while his master's degree is from Eastern Kentucky University. He received national recognition on the certified public accountant examination. He has served as chairman of the NACUBO Investment Committee and as a member of the Accounting Principles Council. Mr. Jones received the Rodney H. Adams award for exceptional contributions to professional development and research activities in the field of college and university endowment and investment management. He has authored several articles on accounting for college and university investments and accounting for split interest agreements and has frequently served on the faculty for NACUBO seminars and workshops.

HARVEY H. KAISER (Chapter 13, Facilities Management) is president of Harvey H. Kaiser and Associates, a firm providing architecture, facilities management, and master planning services. He has provided services for higher education, health care, governments, foundations, and private corporations worldwide. Dr. Kaiser has written many books and articles and has spoken frequently on facilities management, higher education administration, and preservation of historic architecture. He received a B.Arch. degree from Rensselaer Polytechnic Institute and an M.Arch. and a Ph.D. in social science from Syracuse University.

STEPHANIE KARGER, C.P.A., (Chapter 19, Student Financial Aid) is the controller's office project coordinator for financial systems redesign and software implementation at Brandeis University. She has focused on improving higher education and administrative operations at Wellesley College, Harvard University,

North Shore Community College, and Coopers & Lybrand. Ms. Karger earned a B.A. in history from Brandeis University, an M.A. from Ohio State University, and B.S. and M.S. degrees in business administration and accounting from the State University of New York.

RICHARD N. KATZ (Chapter 7, Information Technology and Services) is vice president of EDUCAUSE. He is responsible for developing and delivering much of the association's educational program through a variety of publications and conferences and workshops, as well as for member and corporate relations, research and development, and outreach. Mr. Katz is the author or editor more than two dozen books, monographs, and articles on a variety of management and information technology topics.

BILL KIRBY (Chapter 6, Managerial Reporting) is a consultant to KPMG Consulting, LLC, specializing in university research administration and grants management issues. He focuses on the assessment and improvement of research administration strategy and operations, best practices, and the application of technology to improve research administration and other higher education processes. Mr. Kirby is an active member of a number of research management associations, and is a past president of the National Grants Management Association (NGMA). He holds a B.S. in business administration from Georgetown University and an M.A. in public administration from the American University.

EVA KLEIN (Chapter 10, Debt Financing and Management/Chapter 13, Facilities Management), president of Eva Klein & Associates, is known for her expertise in strategic management and financing for higher education and not-for-profit organizations, and for her international work in knowledge-based economic development. Ms. Klein has an M.B.A. from The Wharton School, University of Pennsylvania; an M.A. from New York University; an M.S. from the Graduate School of Education, University of Pennsylvania; and a B.A. from Douglass College, Rutgers University.

GLENN KLINKSIEK, A.R.M., (Chapter 16, Risk Management and Insurance) is director of risk management and audit at the University of Chicago. Since 1988, he has been responsible for coordinating the university's risk management programs and managing internal audit for the campus, medical center, and health system. He is immediate past president of the University Risk Management and Insurance Association (URMIA) and a director of United Educators Insurance Risk Retention Group, Inc. and School, College and University Underwriters Holdings, Ltd. Mr. Klinksiek is a chartered property and casualty underwriter and holds an M.B.A. in finance from Indiana University.

ROBERT LAFORD (Chapter 14, Environmental Health and Safety) is campus safety officer with environmental health and safety at the University of Massachusetts at Amherst. He is involved in occupational injury management, employee safety training, and emergency planning and response for the university. Mr. Laford is an 18-year fire service veteran currently serving as captain with the Petersham, Massachusetts Fire Department. He is the author of a guide for emergency services planning and operations, as well as a number of articles that have appeared in fire safety publications.

BEVERLY E. LEDBETTER (Chapter 21, Legal Issues) is the vice president and general counsel at Brown University. She has received many distinguished honors and awards such as Minority Counsel Award (ABA), Order of the COIF (University of Colorado Law School), and the National Association of College and University Attorneys's Distinguished Service Award. She earned her bachelor's degree in chemistry from Howard University and her law degree from the University of Colorado. She also graduated from the Institute for Educational Management at Harvard University. She is a member of the NACUBO Board of Directors.

PHILIP E. LONG (Chapter 7, Information Technology and Services) is director of ITS Academic Media & Technology at Yale University. Long has worked in various technical and management positions in information technology at Yale for 29 years, developing infrastructure and facilitating the use of technology in support of academic programs. He is an active consultant working on strategic planning with colleges, universities, and university systems. Mr. Long presents regularly at regional and national conferences on academic technology and networking and is currently serving as an advisor to EDUCAUSE's NSF-sponsored project supporting Advanced Networking for Minority Serving Institutions. He holds a bachelor's degree in psychology from Yale University.

JEAN F. MACCORMACK (Chapter 3, Implementation Strategies and Outcomes Assessment) is interim chancellor of the University of Massachusetts Dartmouth. She has more than 20 years of experience in educational administration at the secondary and higher education levels. Dr. MacCormack earned a bachelor's degree in literature and fine arts from Emmanuel College, and a master's and doctorate in education from the University of Massachusetts Amherst. She continues to publish, teach, advise students, and serve on doctoral committees.

BETH MALRAY (Chapter 12, Human Resources and Benefits Administration) has been associated with the University of Miami for more than 28 years. As director of the Professional Development and Training Office, she is responsible for designing and conducting training and development programs that enhance university employees' skills and capabilities. She works as a consultant to various educational, social, political, and religious organizations, governmental agencies, and private businesses across the United States and in the Caribbean. Ms. Malray has a bachelor's degree from Grambling State University, and a master's degree from the University of Massachusetts at Amherst.

EDWARD MIENTKA, (Chapter 14, Environmental Health and Safety) C.S.P., is the program manager of Campus Safety and Fire Prevention Services with Environmental Health and Safety (EH&S), University of Massachusetts at Amherst. He is a former loss control representative with Liberty Mutual Insurance Co. Mr. Mientka is also a certified American Red Cross CPR instructor, a Massachusetts registered EMT, and the deputy chief of the Amherst Fire Department Call Force. He received his bachelor's degree from the University of Massachusetts at Amherst in 1977.

JOSEPH D. MURPHY (Chapter 16, Risk Management and Insurance) is currently treasurer of Northeastern University. He is responsible for the university's endowment fund, all capital financing, cash management and banking relations, as well as all property and casualty insurance programs. Mr. Murphy holds a bachelor's degree from the College of the Holy Cross. He has also done graduate work in the M.B.A. program at Northeastern University.

JULIE T. NORRIS (Chapter 18, Research and Sponsored Programs) is director of the Office of Sponsored Programs at the Massachusetts Institute of Technology (MIT). Her responsibilities include management of both pre- and post award activities in the area of sponsored programs, including preparation and negotiation of MIT's indirect cost proposal and other cost analysis activities. Ms. Norris is a member of the Council on Governmental Relations (COGR). She served on COGR's board from 1982 to 1988, 1989 to 1990, and 1992 to 1998. She is also a member of the National Council of University Research Administrators (NCURA) and has served that national organization as treasurer, vice president, and president.

J. MICHAEL PEPPERS, C.P.A., C.I.A., (Chapter 22, Auditing) is the director of audit services at the University of Texas Medical Branch at Galveston. His professional experiences have included public accounting and directing internal auditing functions in higher education. Mr. Peppers is on the board of the Association of College and University Auditors and has served as president and a member of the board of a chapter of the Institute of Internal Auditors. He is an active public speaker in the field of internal auditing and is a Distinguished Faculty

Member for the Institute of Internal Auditors. Mr. Peppers received B.S. and M.Acc. degrees from the University of South Florida.

DENNIS REEDY (Chapter 8, Treasury Management) is managing director of cash and investment management for the Indiana University system. He has 25 years experience in cash management, investments, and bank relations. Mr. Reedy is a past president and a current director of the Treasury Management Association of Indiana (TMAI). He is also active with NACUBO and the AFP (formerly the Treasury Management Association) serving as a faculty member for various programs and on numerous committees and task forces.

JOHN F. RILEY, C.P.M., (Chapter 17, Procurement) is the associate director of purchasing and business services at Arizona State University. He has more than 30 years experience in purchasing for and managing business related activities for public agencies, including managing recreation programs for the Department of Defense at various overseas locations. Mr. Riley is a graduate of Rutgers and Troy State universities. He is currently completing his Ph.D. in public administration at Arizona State University. He also holds a lifetime certified purchasing manager designation from the National Association of Purchasing Managers.

DONALD A. ROBINSON (Chapter 14, Environmental Health and Safety) is director of the Environmental Health and Safety division of the University of Massachusetts at Amherst, where he is also a faculty member in the College of Engineering and in School of Public Health and Health Sciences. He serves as the vice president of the National Safety Council for the Campus Safety, Health and Environmental Management Association. Dr. Robinson is a registered professional engineer and a certified safety professional. He received a B.S. from the University of Massachusetts, an M.S. from Northeastern University, and a Ph.D. in industrial engineering and operations research from the University of Massachusetts.

RONALD E. SALLUZZO (Chapter 6, Managerial Reporting) is responsible for emerging issues in KPMG's Higher Education practice. He has over 28 years of experience in advising boards and senior management of major not-for-profit institutions across the country and meets with the top leaders of universities and other major philanthropic organizations on issues of institutional vision, transformation, and performance improvement. Mr. Salluzzo has also represented KPMG and its clients with federal regulatory agencies that influence the tax-exempt arena, including the Department of Education, the Internal Revenue Service, and the Department of Health and Human Services. He is a recognized leader in translating business concepts and corporate best practices into the unique environments of charitable institutions.

JON SPEARE (Chapter 8, Treasury Management) has 14 years experience in institutional financial services emphasizing treasury management. He currently is a coexecutive director of The Treasury Institute for Higher Education. Mr. Speare is also a faculty member of NACUBO professional development programs and has written articles for Robert Morris Associates, NACUBO, and The AFP Journal of Cash Management. He has a B.A. from The Colorado College and an M.B.A. from Villanova University.

GWEN SPENCER (Chapter 11, Taxation) is a manager in the tax-exempt organizations practice at PricewaterhouseCoopers's Boston office. Specializing in tax-exempt organizations, her clients include colleges, universities, hospitals, and other charitable organizations. She graduated from The University of Connecticut School of Law in 1995 with a J.D. degree and from Boston University School of Law in 1997 with an LL.M. degree.

VALERIE I. STEINBERG (Chapter 14, Environmental Health and Safety) is the biological and chemical safety officer in the Environmental Health and Safety Division at the University of Massachusetts at Amherst. She has conducted research on persistent viral infections. Dr. Steinberg is a member of the American Society for Microbiology and the American Biological Safety Association. She received a B.A. from the University of Rochester and a Ph.D. in microbiology from the University of Kansas.

MICHAEL STRAUSS (Chapter 8, Treasury Management) has been a managing director at Commonfund Treasury since 1998. He has 19 years of institutional financial services and investment experience. Mr. Strauss has been a speaker on CNN and CNBC and, over the years, has been quoted by several prominent publications. He has been a faculty member at the National Association of College and University Business Officers (NACUBO) Treasury Conference. Mr. Strauss has a B.S. degree with distinction from Cornell University and an M.B.A. with distinction from New York University.

MICHAEL SWAIN (Chapter 14, Environmental Health and Safety) is the campus fire prevention officer with Environmental Health and Safety at the University of Massachusetts Amherst. He is involved with building inspections, fire safety training, and plan reviews. Mr. Swain has worked in fire safety at the university for 16 years, and he is also a lieutenant in the Greenfield (Massachusetts) Fire Department. He also serves as second vice-president of the Fire Prevention Association of Massachusetts.

ROOSEVELT THOMAS, JR. (Chapter 12, Human Resources and Benefits Administration) serves as vice president for human resources and affirmative action and adjunct faculty in the School of Business Administration at the University of Miami. He is responsible for human resources, benefits administration, affirmative action, and professional development and training programs. Dr. Thomas is a member of several national and local organizations including the College and University Personnel Association (CUPA) and the Society for Human Resource Management (SHRM). He received his B.A. from Texas College, M.Ed. from the University of Massachusetts, and Ed.D. from the University of Miami.

JOAN K. THOMPSON (Chapter 8, Treasury Management) is treasurer of Iowa State University. She is responsible for planning, directing, and coordinating the university's cash management and investment programs, managing master lease and internal lease borrowings, and acting as paying agent and registrar for the Iowa State University Board of Regents bonds. Ms. Thompson speaks at regional and national seminars sponsored by NACUBO, CardTech SecurTech (CTST), and Professional Development Group (PDG). She received her B.S. degree with honors from Drake University and her M.B.A. from Iowa State University.

WILLIAM J. WALSH (Chapter 12, Human Resources and Benefits Administration) has been executive director, benefits administration, at the University of Miami in Coral Gables since 1992. Prior to his current employment he worked for 10 years at Pennsylvania State University. Walsh holds a master's degree in education with a major in educational administration. He also has a law degree.

BARRY WALSH (Chapter 7, Information Technology and Services) received his electrical engineering degree from University College Dublin, Ireland and his M.B.A. in finance from Indiana University. Since 1984, he has been at Indiana University, where he currently has appointments in both the information technology and finance organizations. Mr. Walsh is the coauthor of a book on implementing financial information systems in organizations and a frequent speaker at conferences and seminars dealing with emerging technologies. He is a member of the NACUBO Board of Directors.

JOHN WATSON, C.I.C., A.R.M., (Chapter 16, Risk Management and Insurance) has been Pepperdine University's director of insurance and risk management since 1987. His responsibilities include the procurement and administration of the property, casualty, workers' compensation, and athletic medical insurance programs for the university. He also facilitates the university's loss control programs, including catastrophe management. Mr. Watson currently serves on the University Risk Management and Insurance Association (URMIA) Board of Directors and the Risk Management Advisory Council of United Educators Insurance Company. He received his bachelor of business administration degree from Loyola

Marymount University and is currently pursuing the certified risk manager designation.

RICHARD WERTZ (Chapter 20, Auxiliary Enterprises and Other Activities) is in charge of business affairs at the University of South Carolina. He is responsible for the bookstore, trademark and licensing, purchasing, consolidated services and inventory, risk management and insurance, health and safety, and food service on campus. Dr. Wertz is a tenured faculty member in the College of Education where he regularly teaches courses on the financial aspects of higher education. He has also served as a consultant for higher education institutions for auxiliary services and in the area of privatization and outsourcing of campus services. He received his bachelor of science and master of education degrees from Pennsylvania State University, and his doctorate of education from Columbia University.

RICHARD P. WEST (Chapter 1, The Role of the Chief Financial and Business Officer) is the executive vice chancellor and chief financial officer for the California State University (CSU) system. As a key member of the Chancellor's Office, he has overall primary responsibility for directing the development of the budget, allocating fiscal resources to campuses, and managing the elements of financial accountability necessary to accomplish the CSU's mission. Mr. West also has responsibility in providing general advice on the business and finance of the system. He received a B.A. degree in economics from the University of California, Santa Cruz and an M.B.A. from the University of California at Berkeley.

RICK N. WHITFIELD (Chapter 22, Auditing) is vice president for audit and corporate compliance at the University of Pennsylvania and the University of Pennsylvania Health System. His professional experiences include public and independent higher education and health care accounting and internal auditing and public accounting. Mr. Whitfield is the immediate past president of the Association of College and University Auditors (ACUA).

PHILIP G. WICK (Chapter 19, Student Financial Aid) was most recently the director of financial aid at Williams College where he worked for 35 years. In 1979, he developed an admission/financial aid data-sharing instrument for which the Consortium on Financing Higher Education (COFHE) assumed responsibility in 1985. Mr. Wick has been involved in various association activities regionally and nationally. He is also a member of the Society for the Advancement of Financial Aid Management in Higher Education.

JOHN ZANYK (Chapter 12, Human Resources and Benefits Administration) has served with the University of Miami for 22 years as director of human resources of the Coral Gables/Marine Campuses and currently is executive director of human resources on the University Medical Campus. He has been a member of the Society of Human Resources Management (SHRM), American Mensa Society, Independent Colleges and Universities of Florida, College and University Professional Association for Human Resources (National and Florida Chapter), and the South Florida Healthcare Human Resources Association. Mr. Zanyk has a bachelor's degree in industrial relations from Kent State University and has obtained a certificate of human resources management awarded by the University of Miami/Society of Human Resource Management.

A History of College and University Business Administration

THE FOLLOWING IS EXCERPTED FROM THE PREFACE TO THE THIRD EDITION OF *College and University Business Administration*.

A Glance at the Beginnings

The effort for improved business administration of colleges and universities in the United States is an outgrowth of several developments: (1) the movement toward efficiency, which affected all aspects of organizational activity, beginning about 1890; (2) the increased interest and activities of business professionals in higher education; (3) the growth of the accounting profession; and (4) the survey movement, which evolved into the "self-survey" and the modern, introspective "management by objectives." Since the 1890s, certified public accountants have been active in higher education, and many have been active in seeking "generally accepted standards" in colleges and universities.

Two very successful businessmen were outstanding in their continuing interest and philanthropy: John D. Rockefeller Sr., and Andrew Carnegie. Mr. Rockefeller was especially interested in the second University of Chicago, beginning in the 1890s. As a result, that university was one of the first to have a "business manager"; it also had one of the first "auditors." This was Trevor Arnett, who published the first unit costs in higher education. He also wrote what is considered the first generally accepted book in the field, *College and University Finance*, published by the General Education Board in 1922. Copies were sent to every college and university in the country.

Mr. Rockefeller developed a practice of inviting the officers of the University of Chicago to discuss the university's plans for the following year: what funds were expected, their sources, and their purposes. This was one of several forerunners of budgeting as it is practiced today in colleges and universities. The General Education Board, created by Mr. Rockefeller, provided the funds to write and publish the interim and final reports of the Morey Committee (1930–1935). Later, the Rockefeller Foundation provided funds to support the work of the committee that compiled and published the first *College and University Business Administration*

("Volumes I and II"). The various Rockefeller foundations have steadily supported the efforts of colleges and universities to achieve better business administration.

Andrew Carnegie, in the early 1900s, developed the Carnegie Foundation for the Advancement of Teaching, and selected Dr. Henry S. Pritchett, president of the Massachusetts Institute of Technology, as the president of this foundation. One of Dr. Pritchett's first steps was to seek a definition of a "college or university," and soon after this he initiated one of the first efficiency studies of such an institution. Morris Llewellyn Cooke, one of the outstanding "efficiency experts" of that time, administered the program, which included a cost study. About the same time, Dr. Pritchett provided his auditor, Harvey S. Chase, C.P.A., of Boston, with a number of financial reports of colleges and universities in an effort to develop a standard form for reporting the financial facts of these institutions; pamphlets resulting from this study were published in 1910 by the Carnegie Foundation as "Standard Forms for Financial Reports of Colleges, Universities, and Technical Schools." This foundation thus sponsored the first endeavor toward standard reports, as well as the first survey.

The Carnegie Foundation supported the Educational Finance Inquiry Commission of the American Council on Education in 1921, resulting in the 13-volume publication in 1925. It supported the Morey Committee, beginning in 1930, the work of the Council's Financial Advisory Service in the late 1930s, and together with the Rockefeller Foundation, it furnished funds to the National Committee on the Preparation of a Manual on College and University Business Administration (known as the Manual Committee).

Since the 1890s there have been many studies, published and unpublished, on college and university administration and costs. Beginning in 1913, the U.S. Office of Education was a leader in the survey movement, from which numerous cost studies were developed. One of these, in 1929, was the monumental survey of land-grant colleges and universities. This led Dr. Arthur J. Klein, who was chief of the Division of Higher Education of the U.S. Office of Education, to press for something resembling standard practices in accounting for colleges and universities.

As a result, and in response to growing demands from colleges and universities for authoritative guidance in the accounting and reporting field, the American Council on Education organized in 1930 a National Committee on Standard Reports for Institutions of Higher Education (the Morey Committee, mentioned above). Chairman of the committee was a man widely acknowledged as a leader in the profession, Lloyd Morey, comptroller (and later president) of the University of

Illinois, who in that same year published his own pioneering textbook, *University and College Accounting*.

Dr. Morey appointed Thad L. Hungate, comptroller of Teachers College, Columbia University, who had worked with Trevor Arnett, to examine approximately 100 financial reports from higher education institutions. This work was published by the committee, and also served as Mr. Hungate's master's thesis at Teachers College. The committee then issued a series of pamphlets on various aspects of college and university accounting. One listed as author W.B. Franke, C.P.A., who had a large practice among colleges and universities. This pamphlet, "Suggested Forms for Internal Financial Reports of Colleges and Universities," was Bulletin No. 5, published by the National Committee in 1932. Three other C.P.A.s joined Mr. Franke in this study: Lloyd Morey; Gail A. Mills, who had helped Dr. Morey write his book, and who later was to be the long-time comptroller at Princeton University; and F.L. Jackson, who for many years was vice president and treasurer at Davidson College.

As the committee worked, it was increasingly in consultation with representatives of the Association of American Colleges, the American Association of Collegiate Registrars, and other organizations. The committee's final report, *Financial Reports for Colleges and Universities*, was published by the University of Chicago Press in 1935. The editorial committee of this publication was composed of Lloyd Morey; E.S. Erwin, of Stanford University; and George E. Van Dyke, then a graduate student at the University of Chicago and a former student-employee of Dr. Morey's. The committee not only produced the first set of "standard" guidelines, but pointed to other ways in which professional guidance might be provided.

Following publication of *Financial Reports*, the American Council on Education established a Financial Advisory Service, a consultative and reference project (mentioned above in reference to the Carnegie Foundation). First administrator of the service was George Van Dyke, who was followed by J. Harvey Cain, comptroller of the Catholic University of America, and others. Twenty-one pamphlets were published under the auspices of the service, which operated until the advent of World War II.

Much of the impetus for improvement of management practices during this period came from the two regional associations of college and university business officers then existing: the Central Association (then the Association of Business Officers of the State Universities and Colleges of the Middle West), organized in 1912, and the Eastern Association (then the Association of University and College Business Officers of the Eastern States), organized in 1920. The members of these associations were drawn together by a common need to discover generally accept-able ground rules for conducting business and financial affairs. Such interests, thus germinating, would grow in the ensuring years into the far more elaborate and sophisticated professional programs that would be required to cope with problems of management in an entirely new age. In this movement the American Council was a centralizing force. Long before there was a national organization of business officers, the Council was the rallying point for those leaders of the profession who, sharing their knowledge and experience, contributed voluntarily to developing the studies of management principle of which the Council was sponsor and pub-lisher.

The Search for Management Principle

It was in this period that *College and University Business Administration* was conceived. The authority of *Financial Reports* was unquestioned. But the success of that guide suggested that there might be developed a publication of similar authority, but broader in scope, touching all major areas of business and financial administration. The question was discussed at the 1937 meeting of the Central Association of College and University Business Officers. In 1938 representatives of four regional associations—the Central and the Eastern, the Southern, which had been organized in 1928, and the Western, organized in 1936—met in Pitts-burgh to form a body called the National Committee on the Preparation of a Man-ual on College and University Business Administration. The chairman was J.C. Christensen, of the University of Michigan. The movement thus begun continued during World War II with the support of grants to the American Council, in 1942 and 1943, by the Carnegie Foundation. The four regional associations also contributed to the fund, as did the Association of Business Officers in Schools for Negroes (later the American Association of College and University Business Offi-cers) that had been organized in 1939. Through such an essentially informal mobi-lization the groundwork was laid for activities that would follow World War II.

In 1946 Thad L. Hungate's doctoral dissertation, *Financing the Future of Higher Education*, was published by Columbia University. Included in this work was a new unit: cost of professional instruction. In 1950 Harvey Sherer's master's thesis, under the direction of Lloyd Morey, was published at Urbana. This was a comparative study of the Morey Committee's recommendations and the financial reporting practices in 1948. Also in 1950, Mr. Sherer was appointed by the Man-ual Committee to revise the 1935 volume *Financial Reports* in the light of his findings; his work for the committee ended with Volume I of *College and University Business Administration*.

The Original "Volumes I and II"

The work of the National Committee on the Preparation of a Manual proceeded from the date of the first grant, 1942, until publication of *College and University Business Administration* had been completed by the American Council in 1955. The manual was in two volumes, the first, published in 1952, covering the principles of financial accounting and reporting and the second those other aspects of college and university management clearly within the realm of the business officer's interest and responsibility. Not surprisingly, the publication was universally referred to in the profession as "the manual" or "Volumes I and II."

Associated with the development of Volumes I and II were persons who had achieved or would attain positions of professional leadership. Thomas E. Blackwell, then vice chancellor and treasurer of Washington University, was appointed editor in 1946. Arthur W. Peterson, vice president for business and finance at the University of Wisconsin, represented the American Council as chairman of the executive committee. The original membership including Lloyd Morey and E.S. Erwin; L.H. Foster Jr., Tuskegee Institute; A.M. Graham, Winthrop College; and A.S. Johnson, Rutgers University. Later, during the preparation of Volume II, the membership included E.S. Erwin, and L.H. Foster Jr.; John F. Meck, Dartmouth College; W.T. Middlebrook, the University of Minnesota; and Clarence Scheps, Tulane University. Ralph S. Johns headed a special committee of five from the American Institution of Accountants (now the American Institute of Certified Public Accountants) that provided consultation on accounting and auditing. Mr. Blackwell's Editorial Committee for Volume II included Mr. Middlebrook, Mr. Peterson, and George Van Dyke, then assistant comptroller of the Rockefeller Foundation, who would himself serve as editor when the time came to revise the volumes. (Far more comprehensive acknowledgments of all who contributed to these efforts will be found in the prefaces of the volumes.) Expenses were defrayed by the Commission on Financing Higher Education, an organization sponsored by the Association of American Universities and financed by grants from the Rockefeller Foundation and the Carnegie Corporation.

The First Revision "CUBA (1968)"

The time for revision arrived shortly. There had come into existence in 1951 the National Federation of College and University Business Officers Associations, predecessor to the National Association, and by 1959 the board of the Federation formally recognized the need to create a mechanism for revision. In 1960 a national committee was established under the chairmanship of Dr. Scheps, but it was not until 1964, when financing finally was obtained by the American Council, that the new group could proceed. Financing during the course of the project came from the American Council itself, from the American and regional associations of business officers, the U.S. Office of Education, the Teachers Insurance and Annuity Association, the International Business Machines Corporation, and the General Electric, Shell, and United States Steel Foundations.

The Scheps group was called the National Committee to Revise Volumes I and II, *College and University Business Administration*. Mr. Van Dyke was appointed full-time editor, serving until his retirement in 1966, when he was succeeded briefly by John M. Evans, of the University of Connecticut, who was throughout the chairman of the Editorial Subcommittee. Members of the subcommittee were Kenneth R. Erfft, Duquesne University; Robert B. Gilmore, California Institute of Technology; R. W. Kettler, State University of New York; Bruce J. Partridge, Johns Hopkins University; Fred S. Vorsanger, American Council on Education; and Dr. Scheps. The national committee itself was composed of some 30 business officers, consultants, and representatives of other organizations including the American Institute of Certified Public Accountants and the U.S. Office of Education.

An early decision of the national committee was to combine into a single volume the new revision of Volumes I and II. Many business officers provided drafts of chapters and scores of others contributed readings and comments. This work went forward for three years. The Editorial Subcommittee, handling drafts and manuscripts, met monthly on weekends from May 1964 to March 1967, and while the costs of operations were covered by outside support, the time and effort were volunteered by committee members. The single-volume revision was published by the American Council in 1968. It became known almost at once as "*CUBA (1968)*." About 17,000 copies were sold before the book went out of print in 1973.

The Second Revision: "CUBA (1974)"

The National Association's office was established in Washington in 1967, some months before the 1968 revision was published. Already it was clearly recognized that further revision should be anticipated, perhaps in five years, and that the national office now provided an operating base of a kind that had not existed before. Even then there was the hope that the National Association could become the publisher of future revisions, but the professional machinery first had to be organized. Accordingly, National President James J. Ritterskamp Jr., appointed a new Committee on the Revision of the Manual under the chairmanship of Robert B. Gilmore, vice president for business and finance at Caltech.

By 1971, the Manual Revision Committee had developed certain general procedures for the preparation of materials. The drafting of preliminary texts was given to those professional associations or National Association committees having primary interest, experience, or authority in the various management fields. These associations or committees were invited to assign authors to produce draft texts. When the drafts were submitted, they were given a preliminary evaluation by voluntary groups appointed to serve as short-term subcommittees of the Manual Revision Committee, each to deal only with its particular subject, and many including in their membership a consultant from outside the college and university field, also participating voluntarily. When the manuscripts were further revised, the texts then were exposed to 60 to 80 business officers. Manuscripts completing such exposure were adjusted as necessary and forwarded, finally, to the National Association's Board of Directors for approval for publication.

Because of the central importance of the financial accounting and reporting functions, there had been, since the time of Volumes I and II, close liaison between the college and university business professional and members of organizations representing certified public accountants. By 1970, the National Association had established its Accounting Principles Committee, designed to become in the college and university field the equivalent of the AICPA's former Accounting Principles Board. This committee, headed first by Gilbert L. Lee Jr., of the University of Chicago, and later by W. Harold Read, of the University of Tennessee, performed a most important early service by establishing a close working relationship with the AICPA's Committee on College and University Accounting and Auditing which, under the chairmanship of Daniel D. Robinson, of Peat, Marwick, Mitchell & Co., was developing a new AICPA guide, *Audits of Colleges and Universities*. Through the Accounting Principles Committee and through its liaison representatives to AICPA, Dr. Scheps and Mr. Gilmore, the National Association participated in the early drafting of the guide, and in 1972 assisted directly in the exposure of the draft text. When the AICPA guide was published in 1973, the text so closely reflected the general professional consensus that copies of the publication were distributed by the National Association to its members.

In preparing to assume responsibility for publication of *College and University*

Business Administration, the National Association faced first the challenge of mobilizing professional resources, then the less familiar tasks of organizing staff, procedures, and support for publication itself. In each of these fields it had truly magnificent assistance and cooperation.

Professional participation was very broad. All of the Association's "program" committees—those dealing with specific areas of management concern or levels of institutional interest—were deeply involved in the processes of developing or evaluating manuscripts. The four original associations were similarly engaged, not only in the exposure of manuscripts but in organizing discussions at annual meetings and workshops of substantive issues related to accounting and auditing. Further, 14 associations having interest in the field of college and university business were directly engaged in the preparation of manuscripts or in evaluating or exposing the manuscripts finally produced.

From 1969 until 1973, the responsibility for developing and recommending publication plans rested primarily upon the Manual Revision Committee under the chairmanship of Mr. Gilmore with the counsel of the Publications Committee under the chairmanship of Vincent Shea, of the University of Virginia. In 1973 these two committees were combined into an enlarged Publications Committee headed by Kurt M. Hertzfield of Amherst College. It was this committee that pushed to conclusion the review of manuscripts and the final act of publication.

The long process of preparation was one necessitating special support, financial and otherwise, that the Association was ill-equipped to provide. The financial support came in the form of special awards by the Ford Foundation, the United States Steel Foundation, Inc., and the General Motors Corporation, and for this assistance the association and its member institutions continue to be grateful. This gratitude will be shared, certainly, by all who find in *College and University Business Administration* the management assistance it is designed to offer.

Neal O. Hines (1974)

College and University Business Administration

SIXTH EDITION

Chapter 1

The Role of the Chief Financial and Business Officer

by

Richard P. West
California State University System

Sponsors

KPMG
Contact: Greg J. Baroni
1676 International Drive
McLean, VA 22102
703-747-3004
www.kpmg.com

With over 30 years of serving higher education, KPMG offers a broad range of services that helps our clients analyze their businesses with true clarity, raises their level of performance and delivers the strategic and infrastructural components to support highly dynamic E-business models in colleges, universities, and academic medical centers.

ACCESS GROUP, INC.
Contact: School Services
1411 Foulk Road
P.O. Box 7430
Wilmington, DE 19803-0430
800-227-2151
www.accessgroup.org

The Access Group is a nonprofit organization that offers federal and private loans for students enrolled in law, medical, dental, business, health, and other graduate programs.

Contents

No topic in higher education can be fully understood without addressing a central theme: change. The drivers of change—new technology, shifting demographics, rising costs, increasing regulation, changing workforce needs, and, perhaps most significantly, the advent of competition—have been well documented. These external forces are predicted to transform the entire educational enterprise fundamentally over the next decade. Thus, understanding the role of the chief financial or business officer (abbreviated here to CFO) requires us to look beyond what the position is today and to consider how it is being shaped by, and must respond to, the forces driving change in every aspect of higher education.

The CFO's responsibilities may include business and financial affairs, planning and budgeting, investments, facilities, real estate, legal affairs, technology, public safety, procurement/purchasing, human resources, labor relations, equal opportunity, and auxiliary enterprises such as housing and food services. In large organizations, some of these functions may be assigned to one or more other administrators. The CFO provides the critical business, financial, and administrative support, as well as professional guidance that allows the institution to realize its academic mission of teaching, research, and public service. To best understand these responsibilities and their relationship to change, it is helpful to view the position of the CFO through the perspective of three different roles: *advisor, manager,* and *change leader.*

Until relatively recently, the function of the CFO essentially involved only the two roles of advisor and of manager. In the advisor role, the CFO essentially performs as an expert in technical matters relating to the institution's financial and physical assets. In the second traditional role, manager, the CFO oversees often large and complex administrative functions that provide essential campuswide business and financial services. These two roles continue to be the mainstay of the position. However, even these traditional roles have been affected by the rapidly changing world that universities and colleges now confront. As a result, the advisor and manager roles have been expanded and reshaped to encompass new information, new tools, and new technologies.

But there has been an even greater impact of change. Beyond incremental modifications to the CFO's traditional roles, an entirely new role is emerging: the change leader. In this third role the CFO moves beyond the traditional functions to a role that is proactive and aims to facilitate the transformation of the institution while maintaining continuity with its mission. In the advisor and manager role, the CFO adds value to the institution through sound business practices. As universities and colleges face a time of fundamental and transformational change, CFOs will be asked to expand the dimension of their roles as leaders and facilitators of change.

Roles are not played in isolation. The three CFO roles occur in an institutional context. Historically, colleges and universities were a collection of scholars loosely joined in a highly decentralized organization. They were a partnership organization, an organization of peers not unlike a modern-day law practice or medical group. Only as the organization grew and increased in size and complexity was the need for professional business and financial management recognized. The result is an organization that is often portrayed as having two "sides": the business side and the academic side. For the CFO this means that he or she presides over a part of the organization that is generally seen by the largest group of people in the organization, the faculty, as different. In fact, there is a real values tension between the business function, with its emphasis on pragmatic accountability, and the academic function, with its emphasis on knowing, teaching, and learning. To play the three roles effectively, the CFO must learn to manage this dynamic tension. As the representative and personification of one side of this polarity, the CFO must strongly represent and even advocate for the business aspects of the institution while, as a representative of the institution's broader aims, he or she must step outside the polarity to engage the faculty in a dialogue designed to integrate the two perspectives.

This chapter presents a broad overview of the position of CFO. It first locates the CFO in the governance and organizational structure of the institution. It then defines the three key roles played by the CFO and the critical competencies needed to master each of these roles. Finally, it describes preparations and qualifications for the position.

THE GENERIC POSITION

The specific tasks CFOs perform are as diverse as the institutions that employ them. In this chapter, the descriptions are necessarily generic and will not apply precisely to any specific position or institution. The exact accountabilities and responsibilities will depend on such factors as the size, organization, complexity, mission, history, culture, and strategic direction of a particular institution.

THE ORGANIZATIONAL CONTEXT

With more than 3,000 institutions of higher education in the United States, there is no one correct structure for a college or university. In general, they are functionally organized with relatively clear divisions of responsibility, such as academic, business and financial management, student services, and institutional advancement. The key is that each institution's organizational structure must be tailored to meet its mission in the most productive, efficient, and cost-effective manner.

The Governing Board

Every higher education institution—large or small, college or university, public or independent, two-year or four-year—requires some type of governing body, a president, and a team of senior administrators. Although many states have higher education commissions that coordinate certain activities of public colleges and universities and, in some cases, independent institutions as well, they ordinarily do not affect an institution's basic organization.

The president typically reports to the governing board, or if the board governs multiple institutions, the campus CEO may report to the system CEO. The board's powers are contained in the college or university's charter or in legislative acts establishing the institution. In public institutions, the governor and/or legislative bodies commonly appoint board members; in some cases they are elected by popular ballot. In many independent institutions the board is self-perpetuating, although alumni or other constituent groups may elect some members. In church-related institutions, all or some of the members may be elected by the legislative body of the religious denomination or appointed by its executive officers.

The governing board generally has full and final responsibility for ensuring that the institution remains viable and true to its mission, but many public institutions are subject to state-mandated rules and procedures that dilute or supersede this authority. The board's specific responsibilities range from selecting the president and other key employees to approval of major policies and budgets, incurrence of debt, and major capital improvements. At public institutions, authority and responsibility may also be shared with state coordinating boards; in some states, such boards have full and final authority, not the institution's governing board. Many variations (on shared authority, ultimate authority, and roles and responsibilities) exist, both within states that have multiple systems and between states. State intervention in the institutional management process varies from a little to a great deal and, where it is great, introduces a complex environment for institutional management.

Most institutions vest executive authority and responsibility only in the president. In these unitary organizations the president in turn delegates authority to officers responsible for the major functional areas. These officers report to the president, who alone reports to the board. Normally, these officers attend and participate in board meetings. As one of these officers, the CFO works closely with board committees, such as those responsible for the budget, investments, finances, buildings and grounds, long-range planning, and construction. As with any other officer who works directly with the board in the unitary form of organization, the CFO does so as a representative of the president and at his or her delegation.

In contrast to the unitary form of organization, in the multiple form of organization, the governing board delegates authority to the president and other officers, each of whom also reports to the board. For example, under this model the CFO would be directly responsible to the governing board for the institution's business and financial affairs.

Another form of organization is the modified unitary form, in which the CFO is responsible directly to (and may be a member of) the governing board only in a fiscal or investment capacity. For all other functions, he or she reports to the president.

In large state university systems with multiple campuses, a central administrative unit frequently reports directly to the governing board. The administrative unit generally sets systemwide policy and may provide certain services such as accounting, payroll, technology, program approval, investment management, and legal counsel to the campuses. Within the established policies and procedures, administrators on each campus provide day-to-day management and services. In multicampus systems, there is typically a CFO on each campus. In these instances, the system CFO reports to the system president and the governing board. In some smaller systems, the "main campus" may also serve as the central administrative unit, thus making a separate, board-related staff unnecessary.

The President

A college or university chief executive officer usually has the title of *president* or *chancellor*. The president provides overall institutional leadership and assembles a senior management team, the central administration, to manage the institution's day-to-day operations. The visionary president also provides leadership for defining the institution's mission and goals, establishing priorities, and long-range planning.

At both public and independent institutions, in addition to his or her internal responsibilities, the president typically spends much time cultivating friends and funds for the institution. He or she is the principal link between the administration and the governing board. In public institutions, the president also serves as the primary link to the governor, legislature, and state agencies, as well as to a system office where it exists.

The Senior Management Team

The CFO is a member of the senior management team, which is typically made up of the heads of each of the institution's major functional areas. These major functional areas—academic, business and financial management, student services, and institutional advancement—are interrelated and interdependent, making a team approach to their management essential.

Though there are some exceptions, most institutions designate a single officer to head each of these areas:

- a *chief academic officer*, whose title usually is vice president for academic affairs, dean, provost, or something similar;

- a *chief financial and/or business officer;*

- a *chief student services officer*, whose title usually is vice president for student services, dean of students, or something similar; and

- a *chief advancement (or development) officer*, whose title is vice president for advancement (or development), director of development, or something similar.

Smaller institutions may combine the responsibilities for several functions in one position. Larger institutions may have additional major officers for other functional areas, such as research, graduate programs, medical affairs, planning and budgeting, external affairs or community relations, physical plant, housing, human resources, legal affairs, legislative affairs, continuing education, and information technology and services. The authority delegated to each officer is determined by the president and approved by the governing board, or it may be prescribed by the institution's charter.

Responsibilities of the Various Officers

Chief Academic Officer

The chief academic officer's responsibilities include managing the academic units (colleges, schools, and departments), formulating academic missions and goals for the institution, and coordinating academic support services, such as the library and the academic computer center. He or she also has primary responsibility for admissions, student academic records, and student financial aid as they affect the academic stature of the institution.

The chief academic officer focuses on the faculty, and with rare exceptions, has followed a career path that began in the faculty ranks. He or she serves as the key link between the administration and the faculty. It is important, therefore, to understand the role of the faculty in relation to the chief academic officer. In general, faculty are organized by departments (disciplines) and by schools or colleges that comprise broadly related disciplines. Through a governance structure, whether a broadly constituted senate or a narrower elected body, faculty members exercise considerable authority in determining curricula and pedagogy, and they have strong influence in matters related to academic freedom, academic personnel, and educational policy. Faculty members also render institutional service through membership on boards and committees to address issues such as strategic planning, enrollment management, or technology investments. The governing board determines the extent of the faculty's decision-making authority. However, faculty typically are awarded thoughtful consideration by the president and the senior management team on virtually all aspects of the institution's operations.

Chief Student Services Officer

The student services officer may be responsible for activities such as nonacademic counseling, health services, social programs, student activities and organizations, student government, student publications, career placement, and, in many instances, student housing. In some cases he or she is also responsible for administering admissions, student financial aid, and student records.

The chief student services officer focuses on students and prospective students. He or she represents the extracurricular, cocurricular, and personal development concerns of students, including social, financial, and residential issues.

Students also participate in the governance of the institution. Their role in academic affairs is subordinate to that of the faculty, but they have considerable influence on non-academic, student life issues that affect them directly. The chief student services officer often plays a role in supporting student governance activities.

Chief Advancement Officer

The primary responsibility of the advancement officer is private fund raising; in many institutions, he or she is also responsible for public relations, publicity, and alumni relations. These functions may include media relations, both print and broadcast, and institutional publications. The advancement officer is often called on to interpret and represent the institution beyond the campus.

The advancement officer represents the institution's external stakeholders, especially alumni and other donors. These groups are important to the overall financial well being of the institution and often have specific expectations of the institution that must be managed, if not met.

Other Officers

The number of persons reporting directly to the president may be more or fewer than the officers responsible for the major functional areas identified above. For example, an institution with sizable intercollegiate athletic programs typically has a director of athletics who is responsible for these programs and who usually reports directly to the president. In smaller institutions, the director of athletics may report to the student services officer or to another officer.

Senior administrators are generally appointed on a continuing basis, even though they serve at the pleasure of the president. They may hold tenure in an academic department by virtue of prior academic experience and credentials. However, they are not normally granted tenure in their administrative positions.

THE THREE ROLES OF THE CFO

The Advisor Role

The advisor is probably the most traditional role played by the CFO. In the process of exercising and offering advice on accounting and reporting practices, budget administration, regulatory compliance requirements, treasury management, investment strategies, issuance and management of debt, maintenance of reserves, and the like, the CFO facilitates fiscally sound and prudent business decisions.

As an advisor the CFO must attend to legal and ethical as well as functional aspects of decision making. Colleges and universities increasingly encounter federal, state, and local regulations governing every aspect of their operations. In the advisor role it is the CFO's responsibility to ensure that the institution complies with all relevant regulations, whatever their source. Failure to follow regulations can create both institutional and personal liability, with attendant severe financial penalties.

Beyond the law and regulations, the work of the CFO must also be guided by ethical considerations. Ethical behavior is of particular concern because the CFO is responsible for funds that are a public trust, whether they are state appropriations or gifts from private donors. Furthermore, the general public and institutional constituents expect and assume that a high ethical standard prevails in higher education institutions. The institution must—in its treatment of students, faculty, employees, community members, and other stakeholders—deal fairly, honestly, and honorably. The CFO bears responsibility for ensuring that all of the institution's business practices satisfy the highest ethical requirements, as must his or her own behavior.

The CFO most critically performs the role of advisor in working with the president and the governing board. Here the CFO is relied on to advise on a wide range of financial issues. By long-standing practice, these include:

Finance

The CFO often acts as the financial executive for the president and the financial advisor to the governing board. He or she is responsible for protecting the president and the board through diligent efforts to ensure that business transactions are legally permissible, properly conducted, and accurately accounted for, while playing the role of the "prudent spender," who is deliberative and cautious about commitments of institutional resources. The CFO seeks to maintain sufficient financial reserves to handle unforeseen contingencies as well as to provide for some very important flexibility, and he or she should keep the president apprised of the reserve.

Sometimes the CFO serves as an officer of the board as treasurer. Under such arrangements, certain fiduciary responsibilities of the institution may be delegated by the board to the treasurer. Typically, the CFO presents major contractual matters and fiscal policy recommendations to the board for approval. He or she may also work closely with board committees that have oversight responsibility in areas such as investments, budget, facilities, and audit.

Investments

The CFO may be responsible for advising on the investment of the endowment fund (endowment management) and the operating fund (treasury management). For the endowment, institutions generally employ one or more outside investment managers and give them discretion to make specific investment choices consistent with the board's approved asset allocation. The CFO provides leadership in selecting the investment managers and then monitors their performance relative to benchmarks agreed to by the managers and the governing board.

Another approach is to manage the investment of endowment funds internally with an investment staff and the assistance of one or more outside investment advisors. In this approach, the CFO assumes the role of chief investment officer and may be responsible for making the final investment decisions, which are then implemented by members of the investment staff.

In both approaches, the CFO's role is affected by the degree of board involvement. The board usually has an investment committee that makes, or recommends to the full board, investment policies applicable to acceptable degrees of risk, permissible forms and styles of investment, allocation of assets among these various forms and styles, spending rates for endowment income, selection of external investment managers, and the like. If investments are managed internally, the investment committee may make individual investment decisions or may charge the CFO with making them, consistent with approved policies. In either approach, the CFO is the key liaison between the administration and the board in matters related to endowment management. (For a full discussion of this subject, see chapter 9, Endowment Management.)

In the area of treasury management, the CFO and staff generally make investment decisions on a day-to-day basis. The board investment committee usually monitors the performance of investments relative to certain benchmarks that are established as part of the investment guidelines. (For a full discussion of this subject, see chapter 8, Treasury Management.)

The CFO should also be responsible for coordinating financial interactions with separately incorporated, affiliated organizations such as foundations. Some public universities, in particular, have relationships with one or more such foundations. College- or university-related foundations can serve a number of useful roles by receiving gifts and trusts, soliciting research grants and contracts, managing patents and copyrights, and acquiring and selling real estate. An affiliated organization may be helpful as an alternative legal entity through which such activities can be conducted free of procedural constraints by state governments.

Legal Affairs

When the institution does not have legal counsel on staff, the CFO may provide a leadership role to ensure proper oversight of legal matters or institutional compliance with federal, state or local law. The CFO must recognize that legal advice and services are usually needed for:

- ensuring that operating decisions anticipate compliance with the various federal, state, and local laws and regulations and that legal problems are avoided through careful planning;
- performing all documentation involved in business transactions such as land acquisition and bond issues; and
- defending the institution against lawsuits and charges of discrimination, environmental violations, and contract disputes.

The CFO must see that the legal services are provided when needed but not overused from either a cost or managerial standpoint. Legal counsel should serve as an advisor to management and not become a substitute for management. Some institutions maintain in-house attorneys, while others, particularly smaller institutions, find it cost-effective to contract for legal services with one or more outside law firms. (For a full discussion of this subject, see chapter 21, Legal Issues.)

Debt Management

Most debt financing for facilities and major equipment is carried out in the name of the governing board. The CFO provides leadership in negotiating terms of borrowing with financial institutions and in bringing debt issuance to market. These responsibilities involve a few of the institution's key financial staff members and a number of outsiders, such as legal counsel (if not on staff), bond counsel, underwriters, bond trustees, and sometimes a financial advisor and a credit insurance firm. Bond financing requires authorization by the governing board and its approval of the bond indenture and related bond documents. In addition, bond financing usually requires certain approvals at the state or local government level for both public and independent institutions that utilize a public financing authority. (For a full discussion of this subject, see chapter 10, Debt Financing and Management.)

Making the Advisor Role Work

The advisor role has changed over the years in two ways. First, as an integral part of the institution's leadership team, the CFO increasingly is asked to apply his or her expertise to specific problems or projects that other senior management team members are facing. An example would be working closely with the chief academic officer and chief student services officer in anticipating and managing the consequences of proposed student fee increases. Such "peer to peer" advising makes the CFO more a collaborative problem solver than someone who only provides financial advice to the board or the president. As the scope of advising expands, the need for effective communication with all of the institution's stakeholders, especially faculty, also increases. Of special importance is the collaborative relationship between the CFO and the chief academic officer in planning and budgeting. Another area where this relationship is so important is in human resources legal matters in academic affairs, especially tenure, promotions, and discipline. For this relationship to be productive, the CFO must learn as much as possible about the academic enterprise and the administration of academic departments.

In many large institutions there is a trend to decentralize authority and responsibility for many business functions to business officers in the academic units (colleges, schools, and departments). Much of the administrative cost and activity now occurs in these units rather than in the central administration. This has important implications for the relationship between the CFO and the business officers in the academic units, especially with regard to training, accountability, and communications. Some institutions even have a formal line relationship between the CFO or controller and the key business officers in the academic units.

Being an effective collaborative problem solver requires the CFO to go beyond the more technical knowledge of business affairs to a fuller understanding of institutionwide issues and functions. Business considerations must be translated in a nontechnical way that makes their present and potential significance clear and that builds common commitment to the institution's best interests.

The second change in the advising role is an increase in its scope. It has expanded from a fairly narrow focus on fiscal controls and accounting to broader concerns such as technology, outsourcing, and marketing. For example, if an institution selects new administrative computer systems, the CFO must have knowledge of these systems and their strategic role in the institution, as well as the implementation issues they pose and the demands they bring for ongoing support. As institutions move toward new technologies for conducting their business affairs, like intra- and Internet-based approaches and E-commerce, the CFO must be conversant with these technologies, and may, in fact, be the leader in their implementation. Likewise, as competitive pressures grow, the CFO may be the only senior manager with the business skills to head up projects in these areas and the only one with major project management experience. He or she may also be called on to provide leadership in bringing new technologies to bear on institutional marketing, service accessibility, and operational efficiency.

The Manager Role

Beyond being an expert advisor, the CFO manages an area that provides wide-ranging institutional support services. The functions reporting to the position can be numerous and diverse. Generally, they include three areas of responsibility: business and financial services, physical facilities, and auxiliary services. Among the functions in the business and financial services area may be accounting, financial reporting, budgeting, contract administration (including research contracts and grants), administrative computing, non-academic human resources and benefits, labor relations, procurement, student financial aid, debt management, receipts and disbursements, calculation and payment of taxes, investments (treasury and endowment management), legal affairs, risk management, payroll, and cashiering. In the area of physical facilities, the CFO usually manages facilities planning (design, construction, renovation, and repair), facilities upkeep (operation and maintenance), utilities (heating, cooling, power, and telephone), energy conservation, waste management, recycling, grounds maintenance, safety and security, parking and traffic control, motor pool, and environmental health and safety. Finally, in the auxiliary services area, the CFO frequently, in conjunction with student services, has administrative responsibility for campus residences, college unions, bookstores, printing and copying services, vending operations, rental properties, conferences and other summer activities, and food service operations.

The size and complexity of the CFO's organization directly correlate to the overall size and complexity of the institution. Regardless of size, however, the areas under the CFO tend to be functionally organized. Furthermore, most of the functions are the same regardless of institutional size; the variance is in the number of people involved and their degree of specialization. The demands of functions like those found in a major graduate/research operation, a multicampus operation, or a medical school and related teaching hospital can also affect the numbers and specialization of the CFO's staff, as well as the assignment of responsibilities among senior administrators.

In some institutions, especially larger ones, the CFO sometimes carries the title of senior vice president, executive vice president, or vice chancellor. He or she may then have several senior staff members who are responsible for the various functional areas and carry titles descriptive of those functions, such as:

- vice president for business affairs or business manager;
- vice president for facilities or director of physical plant;
- vice president for auxiliary services or director of auxiliary services;
- vice president for human relations;
- budget officer;
- director of investments, trusts, and real estate; and
- chief financial or business officer of a campus in a multicampus system.

Typically, these staff members manage large offices or departments and are deeply involved in day-to-day operations.

In smaller institutions, the CFO may have the title of vice president for business and finance, director of business affairs, or business manager. Those who report directly to the CFO may carry such functional titles as:

- associate or assistant vice president;
- controller;
- director of procurement or purchasing agent;
- director of personnel or human resources;
- director of physical plant; or
- director of auxiliary services (in some institutions, part of student services).

The degree to which the functional areas are separately headed or combined under individuals with these titles is generally determined by size and complexity. The key staff members listed immediately above are involved in the hands-on operation of their areas.

Beyond the formal organization and its direct reporting relationships, the CFO may have shared responsibility, on a "dotted-line" basis, for decentralized business functions located in schools, departments, or institutes. Some institutions have found it effective to move elements of the business function out of a central unit in order to better serve their internal customers. In these arrangements the CFO usually maintains responsibility for coordinating the business function campuswide, while facing the challenge of not having direct authority over the people who actually do the work.

Regardless of staff size, in the manager role the CFO takes on responsibilities common to all managers, such as organizing and structuring the work that must be performed through clear definition and delegation of job responsibilities. Equally critical is capable and effective supervision of the workforce, including team building. The CFO has an obligation to select well-qualified people, develop their skills, inspire their commitment, evaluate their performance and reward them fairly. The manager must stress accountability; in doing so, it is more productive to impart positive tactical and strategic reasons for doing something than to rely on threats. Failure to manage employees effectively will ultimately result in poor performance of the CFO's area, no matter how well structured the unit is from an organizational perspective. The CFO must set the standard and the example for personnel in his or her administrative area.

The CFO must provide supervisors with opportunities to learn how to motivate and retain staff and to develop a strong service orientation in their work. It is also important that the CFO actively seek to bring talented minorities and women into the organization and provide equal opportunities to develop their skills and abilities to the fullest. Among the benefits of diversity in the workplace are that people of multiple backgrounds can give richness of perspective and insights not possible otherwise.

Of particular value are the wide variety of professional development activities available through on-campus and off-campus classes, seminars, conferences, and workshops. In addition, the Internet and video conferencing open a vast array of training and professional development opportunities. At the regional and national level, specialty-specific professional organizations provide many programs satisfying both people-oriented and technically oriented needs.

Changes in the Manager Role

Pressures on higher education to manage cost, quality, and productivity have steadily increased. Institutions are being held more accountable than in the past for measured performance in both administrative and academic outcomes such as graduation and retention rates. These and other outcomes are also accreditation issues. In this environment it is often expected that the CFO will lead efforts to improve institutional effectiveness. Satisfying this expectation has been greatly eased by the adoption of tools from the business world that target improvement opportunities. Some examples of the kinds of tools that have been used include the following:

- *Business process improvement:* involves evaluating the flow of work across the institution, often across traditional functional lines, with the aim of streamlining basic business processes.

- *Continuous quality improvement:* uses certain principles and practices to continuously identify and implement improvements in the way the institution does business, involving everyone in the institution with making improvements in programs and services.

- *Benchmarking:* compares the institution to similar institutions on key performance indicators to identify the best way—the "best practice"—to perform a particular business or financial function. Once identified, these best practices, typically focused on more production-oriented functions like procurement or accounts payable, are then implemented across the campus.

- *Balanced scorecard:* a management tool that translates institutional strategy into a set of related performance measures that assess progress toward attaining strategic objectives.

Regardless of which tools are used, the CFO should look to effective business practices both within and outside of higher education administration, including new models and those that are tried and true to assure prudent, contemporary, and efficient management.

Customer or client service initiatives involving assessment, goal setting, and training in customer service skills continue to grow in use. Because the units headed by the CFO are generally service units whose customers are internal to the institution, the ethic of providing the highest quality service to attain the highest levels of customer satisfaction is particularly relevant. All improvement initiatives involve eliminating rework and other non-value-added steps in a process to reduce transaction processing time and costs. A special challenge is balancing the service/satisfaction ethic with the responsibilities that finance and business units typically have for regulatory compliance, accountability, and cost efficiency. While there may be some tension between these commitments, the CFO can ensure that staff members have opportunities to acquire and enhance their skills in customer service, conflict resolution, and communication. These are skills that enable both ends to be met.

The Change Leader Role

Colleges and universities constantly undergo change. For example, curricula are always being redesigned, new instructional materials are being introduced, and new computer systems are installed. The question is: with all of this change going on, why is a separate change leader role needed? The answer concerns the nature of the changes being made. These day-in-day-out changes are generally local and incremental—they reflect a specific improvement in a specific department or function. But there is another class of changes—those that are fundamental, affecting basic values and assumptions, and pervasive, affecting the entire institution— that calls for a new CFO role.

But what is meant by fundamental change? One example comes from the growing number of for-profit schools that are based on a centralized model of curriculum. Instead of following the long-standing tradition of having individual faculty members develop their own courses, these schools develop courses in central curriculum development groups. Course content becomes more standardized and quality control more consistent. While this may or may not be an appropriate model for most higher education institutions to follow, the point is that traditional colleges and universities are facing direct competition in the marketplace from schools following approaches that differ radically from tradition.

The changing marketplace is but one driver of change that institutions must address; there are many others. Responding effectively to these multiple external drivers of change creates the challenges of the change leader role.

Personally Coming to Terms with Change

Fundamental change is difficult for everyone. Challenging basic perspectives and modifying long-held beliefs do not come easily. Therefore, the first task of change leadership involves coming to terms with our own beliefs and feelings about change—exploring how we will be affected by change, examining our own attitude toward change, and evaluating our personal investment in pushing for change. Beyond looking at our reactions to change, it is also useful to consider our own contribution to creating or sustaining the situation that produces the need for change in the first place; to begin facing our own accountability. It is easier for others to accept their accountability when we acknowledge our own first.

Shifting Our Mindset

Leading fundamental change goes against the grain of normal CFO thinking. CFOs are technical problem solvers and implementers: they learn how to quickly move to solve problems that have relatively well-defined answers. However, in the arena of fundamental change, clear answers do not exist. The task involves setting the stage for working collaboratively around difficult issues—to have a different conversation about the issues than we have in the past. Providing easy answers and quickly reducing the distress people may feel, natural to the CFO as technical expert and manager, conflicts with the need to engage people from across the institution. Effectiveness, then, requires working against this natural tendency, a tendency that is actually rewarded in some parts of the CFO's position.

Moving into New Arenas

Presidents, by nature of their position, and chief academic officers, by nature of their direct connection with the faculty, generally play the lead role in any institutionwide change efforts. It requires both courage and political skills for the CFO to move into this arena. Having the support of the president in creating fundamental change is obviously very helpful, but this support alone will not eliminate all difficulties. Organizations resist change and maintain their equilibrium by pushing back against those who try to create change. As the spokesperson for the "business side" of the university, any attempt by the CFO to lead change may well be greeted with skepticism by the faculty.

With these challenges, one might question the desirability of even assuming the change leader role. After all, being a change leader sounds demanding, intimidating and, perhaps, not very rewarding. The temptation is always to take the easier path and focus on one's own areas, departments, and units. However, perfecting one's own operation while ignoring the greater challenges that face the institution represents a classic case of rearranging deck chairs. True accountability for the CFO can come about only through a willingness to put the well being of the institution first, and that of his or her unit, or self, second. Working through these conflicts creates both the ultimate personal test for a CFO as well as the ultimate opportunity for personal learning and development.

Strategic planning can be an important tool for the change leader. Used effectively, it provides a way to identify the institution's change agenda. However, the key is to use the strategic plan as a place to begin a dialogue about change rather than simply as a way to sell a preconceived notion of what the institution should become. A well-crafted strategic plan, one that does more than justify the status quo, can help guide the difficult resource allocation decisions that must be made. Furthermore, since many business and finance functions, such as capital planning and budgeting, have a long time horizon, it is particularly important to have a strategic plan in place. For example, the capital planning process often involves anticipating enrollments, academic program developments, and student support needs five to 10 years in the future. Depending on the institution, the CFO participates in the strategic planning process or may actually guide and implement the process and provide the link between planning and budgeting. In either case, it is essential that the CFO become an advocate for strategic planning. (For a full discussion of this subject, see chapter 2, Planning, and chapter 3, Implementation Strategies and Outcomes Assessment.)

As a change leader the CFO is challenged to devise new strategies for accomplishing institutional goals. He or she must be innovative and entrepreneurial. An example is seen in the rise in outsourcing as an expense control strategy. In outsourcing, an organization focuses on its mission and competencies, and relies on contracted services to perform functions that are not integral to its core values. In higher education, the core competencies are teaching, research, and public service. Institutions may consider that certain business services such as facilities management, food service, and bookstore management are not core competencies. Rather than manage and staff these activities internally, as has traditionally been the case, more and more institutions are reviewing internal versus external providers of services. In some cases this will require the CFO to shift from being a service manager to being a service negotiator and contract administrator. If it is objectively determined that outsourcing is appropriate for the institution, through a comparison of cost and quality of internally versus externally produced services, then the CFO can take steps to lead the institution in that direction. The result for the campus should be services of higher quality at reasonable cost.

Aware of how businesses transform themselves to enhance competitiveness, and knowledgeable about business tools that enable these transformations, CFOs are in a key position to help their institutions succeed in the increasingly competitive environments of higher education. Thus, the modern CFO will often be involved in arrangements with business corporations, government agencies, public interest organizations, and consortia of institutions of higher education, to tap knowledge, strategies, and technologies that may be transferred and used to enhance the institution's performance, resources, and competitive position.

COMPETENCIES REQUIRED FOR SUCCESS

Each of the three roles that the CFO plays requires different competencies to perform at the highest level. Each role, in fact, tends to draw on a different cluster of competencies.

For the advisor role the CFO must have sound technical skills and knowledge. Less obvious, perhaps, is the need to continually update and expand that technical expertise. Because the half-life of knowledge is shorter today than ever before, reliance on obsolete information and understanding produces obsolete advice. Therefore, the CFO must continually update and expand his or her knowledge and acquire new knowledge. This calls for staying current on the latest in business thinking, as well as the latest developments in technology and their potential for enhancing institutional effectiveness.

A second competency in the advisor role is the ability to build teams and improve relationships. As the CFO advises on a wider range of issues to a more diverse set of stakeholders on campus, collaboration and the ability to build effective relationships across organizational lines become critical. The CFO must understand issues from multiple perspectives, must build relationships effectively, and must think synergistically to become a highly effective member of the institution's leadership team.

For the manager role, the competencies move from the technically oriented to the people-oriented realm, where leadership and communication skills are vital to effectiveness. The CFO must have strong people skills: the ability to select, develop, and empower the people who are part of the team—people whose skills complement those of the CFO. An appreciation of workforce diversity is a principal goal in building an inclusive organization. Research has shown that respect for all individuals has a demonstrable effect on bottom-line performance. So it is in higher education. The CFO must invest in people in order to enhance their performance in a predictable and positive way.

In the role of change leader, the CFO must master a complex set of more abstract competencies: ability to think "out of the box," anticipating opportunities, creating a shared vision, and embracing change. These skills are central to crafting a strategic agenda—a long-term, big-picture direction for change. They must be complemented by interpersonal skills and emotional intelligence to involve others in, and gain their commitment to, the CFO's goals. Regardless of the role—advisor, manager, or change leader—the ability to communicate effectively and the sensitivity to recognize when communication is needed are vital attributes. The CFO must be able to deal with diverse audiences and constituencies—faculty, students, parents, alumni, donors, legislators, and the local community—in advancing the institution's mission, often under circumstances that are stressful or unfamiliar for the people involved. Skillful and considerate communication by the CFO then becomes a key instrument for serving both the institution and its constituents' interests. More and more, CFOs are involved in local and regional projects as colleges and universities reach out to their surrounding communities for mutual support and filling of needs. These activities bring to bear other sets of political and communications skills.

PREPARATION AND QUALIFICATIONS

Mapping out the preparation process for becoming a CFO is difficult. As mentioned above, the role is complex, involving many different competencies, and is, if anything, increasing in complexity. At the same time, there is no clear career path for the CFO—movement "up the ladder" is often as much a question of opportunity and initiative as it is smoothly advancing from one position to the next. Nonetheless, some general patterns can be identified.

Some CFOs advance from within the profession, acquiring experience and passing performance tests along the way. This career progression through increasing levels of responsibility may be obtained within the same institution, by moving to another, similar one, and/or by moving to successively more complex institutions, having once attained the level of CFO. In public institutions, it is particularly important that a future CFO acquire experience working with agencies of the state's legislative and executive branches.

The downside of a career limited to higher education can be the risk of being unacquainted with techniques and perspectives from other settings that might be constructively brought to higher education administration.

When outstanding candidates are not developed from within or recruited from other well-managed institutions, a person with a state or federal government background or from private business may be a viable candidate for CFO. When this happens, the new officer must learn the institution's history and culture and be able to understand and appreciate the unique role that faculty play in the institutional environment—and how things get done. Under these circumstances, a seasoned CFO from a similar institution can be of immeasurable help as a mentor and role model.

Whatever the source, it is important that the future CFO gain a wide variety of experiences to match the job's diverse challenges. This points to some advantage in moving across different areas in business services rather than spending one's early career in a particular specialization or functional "silo" in the organization. Work experience that combines both for-profit business as well as higher education experience is an advantage. Many people in higher education administration come from other backgrounds.

In earlier years of the profession, it was common for the CFO to be an accountant by training, because financial aspects of the position were such an important part of the officer's total responsibilities. While this aspect remains important, other responsibilities have increased in both depth and breadth, so that the accounting function no longer dominates. An undergraduate degree in accounting, finance, business, or management is the most common educational background for business officers. Many also hold a master's degree in business administration (M.B.A.) and/or a certified public accountant (C.P.A.) certification, while a Ph.D. or other advanced degree is becoming increasingly frequent. An advantage of the Ph.D. is that it can help establish a peer relationship with the faculty and thus help to bridge the gap between administration and faculty.

CONCLUSION

Driven by competition and other external forces, colleges and universities are experiencing rapid and fundamental change. The traditional work of the CFO, as an advisor and manager, has focused on providing fiscal and operating stability to the institution. Without diminishing the important and continuing need for those functions, in times of great change, reliance on maintaining the status quo can be counterproductive or even damaging. New visions combined with effective change processes are needed.

Institutions *will* change. Whether that change represents a threat or an opportunity for renewal depends, to no small extent, on the quality of institutional leadership. As a key member of the leadership team, one who brings a unique set of knowledge and skills to the institution, the CFO must move into a new role, one that actively promotes and leads change. By doing so, he or she will be positioned to guide the changes that the institution must make to grow and prosper.

REFERENCES AND RESOURCES

Management Process

Balderston, Frederick E. *Managing Today's University: Strategies for Viability, Change, and Excellence.* San Francisco: Jossey-Bass, 1995.

Buckingham, Marcus, and Coffman, Curt. *First, Break All the Rules: What the World's Greatest Managers Do Differently.* New York: Simon and Shuster, 1999.

Lapovsky, Lucie, and McKeown-Moak, Mary P. (editors), "Roles and Responsibilities of the Chief Financial Officer (New Directions for Higher Education, 107)", San Francisco: Josey Bass, 1999.

Lenington, Robert L. *Managing Higher Education as a Business*. Phoenix: Oryx Press, 1996.

Rayport, Jeffrey and Sviokla, John J. "Managing in the Marketspace." *Harvard Business Review* (November/December 1994).

Van Der Werf, Martin. "A Vice President from the Business World Brings a New Bottom Line to Penn." *The Chronicle of Higher Education* (September 3, 1999): A72–A75.

Management Tools

Brelin, Harvey, Jennings, L. P., Davenport, K. S., and Murphy, P. F. *Focused Quality: Managing for Results*. New York: Wiley, 1995.

Dickerson, Robert C. *Prioritizing Academic Programs and Services*. San Francisco: Jossey-Bass, 1999.

Dougherty, J. D., and Associates. *Business Process Redesign*. Washington, D.C.: NACUBO, 1994.

Epstein, Marc J., and Birchard, Bill. *Counting What Counts: Turning Corporate Accountability to Competitive Advantage*. New York: Perseus Books, 1999.

Heifetz, Ronald A., and Laurie, Donald L., "The Work of Leadership." *Harvard Business Review* (January–February 1997).

Kaplan, Robert S., and Norton, David P. *The Balanced Scorecard: Translating Strategy into Action*. Boston: Harvard Business School Publishing, 1996.

Norman, C. L., Nolan, T. W., Provost, L. P., Nolan, K. M., and Langley, G. J.. *The Improvement Guide: A Practical Approach to Enhancing Organizational Performance*. San Francisco: Jossey-Bass, 1996.

Oster, Sharon. "An Analytical Framework for Thinking About the Use of For Profit Structures for University Services and Activities." Forum for the Future of Higher Education, Stanford University, 1997.

Higher Education Futures

Davis, Stanley, and Botkin, Jim. *The Monster Under the Bed: How Business Is Mastering the Opportunity of Knowledge for Profit*. New York: Simon and Shuster, 1995.

Drucker, Peter F. "The New Society of Organizations." *Harvard Business Review* (September/October 1992).

Heterick, Robert C., and Twigg, Carol A. "Interpolating the Future." *Educom Review* (January/February 1997).

Karabell, Z. *What's College For?* New York: Perseus, 1999.

Katz, Richard N., and Associates. *Dancing With the Devil.* San Francisco: Jossey-Bass, 1999.

Munitz, Barry. "Managing Transformation in an Age of Social Triage." In Johnson, Sandra L. and Rush, S. C. (eds.) *Reinventing the University: Managing and Financing Institutions of Higher Education.* New York: Wiley, 1995.

Twigg, Carol, and Miloff, Michael. "The Global Learning Infrastructure." In Tapscott, Don (ed.) *Blueprint for a Digital Economy: Wealth Creation in an E-Business Era.* New York: McGraw-Hill, 1998.

Change Management

Collis, David. *When Industries Change: Scenarios for Higher Education.* New Haven, CT: Forum Publishing (1999): 47–70.

Collis, David. *"When Industries Change" Revisited: New Scenarios for Higher Education.* Paper presented at the Forum for the Future of Higher Education, September 1999 annual symposium.

Drucker, Peter F. "The Theory of the Business." *Harvard Business Review* (September/October 1994): 95–104.

Eckel, Peter, Hill, Barbara, and Green, Madeleine. "On Change: En Route to Transformation." The ACE Project on Leadership and Institutional Transformation, Washington D.C.: The American Council on Education, 1998.

Eckel, Peter, Hill, Barbara, Green, Madeleine, and Mallon, Bill. "On Change: Reports from the Road: Insights on Institutional Change." The ACE Project on Leadership and Institutional Transformation, Washington D.C.: The American Council on Education, 1999.

Mahoney, Richard J. "Reinventing the University: Object Lessons from Big Business." *The Chronicle of Higher Education* (October 17, 1997): B4.

Oblinger, Diana G., and Katz, Richard N. (eds.) *Renewing Administration: Preparing Colleges and Universities for the 21st Century.* Bolton, Mass.: Anker Publishing, 1999.

Rogers, R. W., Hayden, John. W., Ferketish, B. Jean, and Matzen, Robert. *Organizational Change That Works: How to Merge Culture and Business Strategies for Maximum Results.* Pittsburgh: DDI Press, 1997.

Chapter 2

Planning

by

Susan Stetson Clarke
Unconventional Wisdom

Sponsors

COLLEGIS
Contact: Melissa Meridith
2300 Maitland Center Parkway, Suite 340
Maitland, FL 32751
800-800-1874
www.collegis.com

COLLEGIS is higher education's strategic technology partner—aligning technology resources and investments with institutional goals. COLLEGIS manages institutional administrative, academic and communications technology functions.

Contents

Planning is the process of identifying, quantifying, and developing goals and action plans for accomplishing the mission of an institution. The process enables the institution to understand external and internal conditions and trends, to look broadly at internal programs and means of support, to consider various options, to forecast the financial and other effects of different courses of action, and to make choices to enable the institution to reach its goals. Planning can be dynamic and ongoing, a way of seeking the best use of assets to serve the institution's mission and community. While the outcome of planning is generally a plan to achieve major changes, planning may also result in validation of current directions and confirmation of maintaining stability.

Colleges and universities have three primary purposes: transmission of knowledge to students; research to create new knowledge; and public service through application of that knowledge. Such purposes result in differing (and often conflicting) perspectives and decision making that is decentralized, diverse, and complex, driven by values and human considerations as much as by academics, technology, and economics. Major institutional decisions must be acceptable to the governing board as well as to wide segments of the faculty, staff, and other constituencies. To be effective in planning, campus leaders need to understand their particular institutional situations and to work cooperatively with their various constituent groups.

Planning processes can vary widely. Each one is a function of the institution's culture, the personal styles of its leaders and governing board, its internal organization, the strength of its traditions, and its relationships with multiple constituents. Some institutions work well with extensive and formal planning processes. Others do not wish to have regular re-examination of their fundamental direction. The arrival of a new president frequently gives rise to strategic planning. Impetus can also come from the governing board and/or a need to assess the current situation and to consider new directions. Planning can have the beneficial effects of looking broadly at various options and of unifying a community within plans for action. It can also be perceived less positively, particularly in institutions where changes occur frequently and participants may feel exhausted by planning processes that seem repetitious of earlier actions and take people away from their pri-

◆

mary work. A planning process should be appropriate for the circumstances of the individual institution.

This chapter describes some basic factors and steps for a centralized and widely inclusive process that involves many elements of the institution. The process is intended to result in a strategic plan that provides direction for the institution. Decentralized, individual unit planning can occur within this framework and be linked and related to the overall planning process. The steps suggested can be expanded or compressed according to the needs of the individual institution.

Major steps involved in planning include process design, vision and mission, information gathering, data analyses, making choices, plan creation, and implementation. Major factors involved in planning include leadership support, constituent engagement, positive communication, integration of cultures, and institutional research.

The timetable for completion of the major planning processes fits best within an academic year, both to keep attention focused on what is happening and to incorporate the results into the annual budgeting cycle. Projections and financial plans should extend over a longer period, perhaps five years.

Once the strategic plan has been determined and implementation begun, management generally monitors and assesses the outcomes of the plan. Planning can be a continuous process, with provision for assessment, evaluation of completed actions, and creation of new initiatives. Implementation of the results of the planning process is the subject of chapter 3.

MAJOR ELEMENTS OF THE PLANNING PROCESS

An effective community-based planning effort calls for acknowledgement and inclusion of multiple perspectives. It follows a process that should enable the community to move from vision and mission statements to goals and action plans. Results are stated in a plan that can be implemented through changes in processes, organization, facilities, staffing, and resource allocation.

Planning should apply the important major factors shown in figure 02-01 to each of the major planning steps, so that each step incorporates and reflects the factors in appropriate ways. Expanding this matrix to include greater detail and specific actions would form the beginning of a process design.

Major Planning Factors

Leadership Support

Inclusive planning reflects a total institutional commitment and will involve many constituents as key players—the governing board, faculty, staff, students, alumni, legislators and other elected officials, and local community members.

Leaders of the process must be the same as the leaders of the institution—members of the governing board, the head of the institutional system, the president, senior administrators, and faculty members. A planning coordinator reporting to the president generally helps to design and facilitate the process, assuring consistency with the established framework and keeping the process on schedule. This person plays a key role in understanding the concerns of the president and helping achieve a successful planning outcome. Some of the administrative staff may help support the process for the entire institution. Those engaged in institutional research provide data, identify trends, perform analyses, and otherwise provide substance. (See below for more on this topic.) While planning is not an outsourced activity, outside consultants may be engaged to help shape, focus, and direct the process. Overall, the vision, motivation, and real leadership for planning must come from the president and the rest of the leadership team.

Those involved should be willing to consider risks, to be innovative, and to communicate clearly and broadly about planning expectations. They need to behave in ways that encourage cooperation, reward creative ideas, recognize

Figure 02-01

Major Planning Steps and Factors

	1 Process Design	2 Vision & Mission	3 Information Gathering	4 Data Analysis	5 Making Choices	6 Plan Creation	7 Imple- mentation
Leadership support	•	•	•	•	•	•	•
Constituent engagement	•	•	•	•	•	•	•
Positive communication	•	•	•	•	•	•	•
Integration of cultures	•	•	•	•	•	•	•
Institutional research	•	•	•	•	•	•	•

Major Planning Factors

accomplishments, and challenge limited perspectives—all of which can be reflected in the planning outcomes.

Constituent Engagement

An inclusive process involves as many constituent players as possible and offers opportunity for receipt of information, for participation, and for comment and feedback. While some members of the community may choose not to become engaged, the process should be broadly inclusive and should encourage participation at many levels.

Positive Communication

It is helpful to publicize and communicate the status of the planning process at all stages, as part of emphasizing the importance of planning and providing everyone with the same information. Communication methods should be appropriate to the size and culture of the institution. For example, leaders can make reports on and references to planning activities in daily interactions, in meetings, and at ceremonial occasions. Open communication sessions may be set up that can be attended by any member of the community and that provide opportunity to deal with the high levels of fear and/or aspiration that frequently arise. A Web site can be set up to describe the planning process and its objectives and to make reports on progress during the various stages. Regular bulletins can be distributed electronically, via paper mail, and in campus publications.

Throughout the process, it is important to celebrate achievements and to reward participants with formal thanks from the leadership, with honoraria or extra compensation, with celebration parties, or all of the above.

Integration of Cultures

The inclusion of multiple perspectives also calls for understanding of the differences in various cultures on campus, particularly between faculty and staff, and ways to help bridge those differences. Figure 02-02 describes some of the qualities of faculty and staff that relate to planning.

Getting faculty and staff to think in similar ways on behalf of the institution early in the planning process calls for a clear, nonjudgmental, and respectful acknowledgement of the value and contribution of each of the two very different approaches to defining and carrying out the business of the institution. It also requires creativity and modification of the working style of each. Strategies need to be developed to enable participants to benefit from understanding the strong

Figure 02-02

Faculty Qualities That Relate to Planning

- Loyal to their academic discipline, divisions, or other working groups, some of which often have their own endowments and external supporters.
- See themselves as the heart and central driving force of the institution, as a community of scholars.
- Committed to a process of challenging, discussing, and debating the status quo and new ideas.
- Protected by tenure and some may be self-supporting through research contracts.
- Comfortable with a bottom-up approach to new idea creation and development.
- See change as a creative process subject to the individualistic movement of the interests of the scholar.
- Encourage change from within, fostered by collegial persuasion rather than external pressures or administrative direction or compliance.
- Evaluate outcomes based on flexible, subjective peer judgments that may not be measurable.

Staff Qualities That Relate to Planning

- Comprise a workforce of different expertise and roles.
- Feel their work is important to the functioning of the institution and the well being of students, faculty and staff.
- Expect to respond to changes required or dictated by others.
- Expect centralized planning and regular administrative supervision, as well as quantitative outcome standards in making evaluative judgments.

---

qualitative impetus to the visionary goals as well as appreciate the practical quantitative challenges to achieving them.

Separation of these two cultures in the planning process can result in strategic goals developed by faculty and alignment of resources to meet those goals carried out by staff. The result can be delays or inability to meet goals in the way they were envisioned. Faculty may see staff as obstructionist and staff may see faculty as unrealistic.

Institutional Research

Institutional researchers may contribute to the improvement of academic planning and evaluation processes by developing the following:

- a comprehensive, analytical view of program mission and environmental factors;
- a broader understanding of programs based on appropriate trend data;
- an array of critical internal and external indicators;
- an appropriate format and timely provision for desired information; and

- new ways to link academic and fiscal planning.

Institutional research is the collection, analysis, and transformation of data, including relevant exterior trends, into information in support of the institution's planning, policy formulation, and decision making. Whatever the organizational structure, many institutions have persons engaged in research, analysis, assessment, policy formulation, data administration, and planning. Functions can be labeled "enrollment management," "budgeting and accounting," "outcomes assessment," "planning and analysis," "program evaluation," or some combination of those terms. Institutions that do not have people engaged in such functions may look to other methods for gathering data, such as engaging consultants, assigning individuals, or appointing task forces to work on data gathering and analysis.

Effective institutional researchers must understand the institution, the decision makers involved, and the nature of the issue under consideration. Great care must be taken to assure that analyses are as objective and systematic as possible and to avoid any perception of conflict of interest.

Major Planning Steps

Process Design

The planning process should have clear objectives and a design, structure, and milestones. The design is a series of strategies and events to accomplish the planning and to make best use of available resources. It should include methods for addressing the objectives, accountability, timetables, and expected products or outcomes. The president may appoint an oversight steering committee of campus representatives to manage the process and to make final recommendations. Task forces or similar groups may be appointed to deal with the various goals. Leaders should be those who will generate respect within the campus community, especially from the faculty.

Support staff may be assigned to the task force to assure that processes are followed, that outcomes are realistic in terms of resource requirements, to alert coordinators of the need for mid-course adjustments, and to see that deadlines are met. Planning takes time, and participants may slack off before closure unless techniques are in place to facilitate reaching milestones, especially when their engagement in planning is additional to other functions. Consultant fees, support for conferences and meeting, costs for distribution of information, and other out-of-pocket expenses are generally the primary elements of institutional planning budgets.

As new topics or ideas emerge, the structure should be flexible enough to include them for consideration. All parts of the process should encourage innovative participation.

Vision and Mission

An institution's strategic vision is a guiding concept as to what the institution should be like in the future and the role it will play in the long term. Strategic vision sets the course for the institution over an extended period of time and is the basis from which more detailed individual unit mission statements and thus long- and short-term goals are derived.

Various forces shape the strategic vision: the current character and role of the institution; outside forces (competition such as commercial enterprises that provide courses only online, opportunities and costs from new technologies, demographic shifts, and economic decline or opportunity); and the values, aspirations, and styles of the leadership. While in an ideal situation the strategic vision should be sustainable over leadership changes, a new president, board chair, chief academic officer, or system head is likely to pursue new goals and to approach issues differently from what has gone on in the past. In some cases, changes in the strategic vision may emerge from a series of short-range decisions. They may also be tested and refined in the planning process after having been initially articulated.

The strategic vision must be shared widely and should be understood, shared, and openly supported by other key decision makers at the institution.

The mission statement grows out of and articulates the strategic vision. Legislatures or public systems may require formal mission statements for each institution. Mission statements are useful to express in a concise way the purpose and character of an institution as well as of individual offices or departments. For the institution as a whole, it may indicate its place in an educational system and its relationships to other institutions or communities. For individual departments and offices, it usually describes the nature of the program by scope and level, the people to be served, and the type of service provided. Actions taken with regard to changes in programs should relate to the mission statement.

Information Gathering

In terms of information needed for a strategic plan, data are important to identify or confirm trends and to give participants measures for goal setting and implementation. Information is also important to help reverse unrealistically held opinions. Planning processes look at many key trends both within and outside the institution.

Environmental scanning is the systematic gathering and analysis of information on the technological, demographic, environmental, political, economic, and other environments in which a higher education institution operates. Figure 02-03 shows some environmental scanning and other categories of the types of issues on which data may be gathered in planning.

Data Analyses

Compiling many different types of information and considering the effect of different actions call for analyses beyond the budget model and its line-item structure. Analyses that enable determination of the financial effects of different approaches, given specified assumptions, are those that are most generally used. For example, models can be constructed to project costs and benefits of offering online courses and administrative applications. Consideration can be given to projected enrollment at various rates of student retention and/or tuition. Anticipated employee costs can be examined with alternate assumptions on salary increases, benefit changes, and retirement rates. Other aspects can involve different scenarios for revenue streams, including new donations at different amounts, increased levels of research, and other factors. Benchmarking, the use of comparisons with other institutions of resources used for specific functions, can identify standards used in modeling. The most realistic of those models can then be selected and financial projections based on the outcome of those analyses.

Data and analyses must be accessible to those engaged in planning. Participants benefit from having such data readily available and, in some cases, to be able to perform their own analyses on it, including various possible scenarios. Constituents may review such scenarios and use group decision-making processes to agree on the implications of some scenarios.

Making Choices

Once the strategic vision has been documented in the mission statement and disseminated, and major questions and scenarios reviewed, planning becomes a "focusing-in" process, intended to make a strategic vision work for the long and short term. The responsible team members draw all ideas together for simultaneous and systematic consideration. Since ideas for change reflect priorities from many sources, some will be inconsistent with others. Other ideas may be politically impractical. The team is to prioritize independent streams of activity and

Figure 02-03

Types of Issues and Questions
On Which Data May Be Gathered in Planning

Environmental scanning

- Comparison of programs, resources and effectiveness with competing institutions
- New technologies: current and potential applications
- Markets
- Demand for programs
- Demographics

- Economic trends
- Cultural trends
- Community and regional attitudes, trends, and needs

Culture and values

- Reasons for the founding of the institution
- Changes in mission, if any, from founding to the present

- Significant people and events in the institution's history

Student attributes

- Student enrollment and retention
- Enrollment in different academic programs

- Student demographics, backgrounds, and attitudes

Program quality

- Faculty background changes or aspirations

- Customer survey reviews

Relationships

- Distinctive affiliations or associations to be preserved or abandoned

- Service provider relationships, within and outside the institution

Resources

- Sources of revenue and patterns of expenditures
- New revenues from donations and sponsored programs
- Personnel costs for salaries and benefits
- Faculty and staff workload measures
- Desired capital projects

- Need and opportunity for campus expansion
- Land, expertise or unusual industries that can be developed
- Opportunities for collaboration with regional institutions

ideas, review elements for internal consistency, and assess them against internal and external realities.

The institutional budget structure can help deal with this focusing-in process. All capital commitments and prospects are contained in a draft capital budget. A draft operating budget should include continuing commitments and estimates of both new revenues and new costs. The operating budget should also contain the consequences of the capital budget, such as costs of debt service and maintenance needs of new construction. Both budgets should reflect long-range guidelines.

Which elements to continue, which to give up, and what new ideas to put in place are the questions faced in the focusing-in process. No institution has unlimited revenue sources and some ongoing elements must be dropped or de-emphasized in order to introduce new programs or projects. While the annual budget review contains many of the same processes, in strategic planning many more questions and issues are under consideration and the process is often more public and visible than the budget review. The capital and operating budgets must be compared with political and economic reality and established priorities. Various items must be dropped from or added to the budgets as the process continues until a workable solution is achieved.

A key part of planning is to motivate and inspire participants to be creative and to be willing to consider risks. The focusing-in process should retain and develop the creative ideas and methods for new initiatives that have emerged from the process.

The decisions made at this level of planning are important to be reviewed, justified, and supported by the leadership and shared widely. The values and principles that these decisions reflect must be articulated and emphasized.

Plan Creation

The outcomes of the choices made, values articulated, and goals established constitute the strategic plan. Plans can have many formats and organizational structures, depending on the needs of the institution. The initial strategic plan may be presented at briefings for all parts of the community. A draft may be made available via the Web or other electronic means and/or distributed on paper for input and comments. All constituencies of the institution should have had opportunity to participate in the discussions about the plan and to provide input. Once finalized, the strategic plan should be widely disseminated and referred to, since it will become the framework for the institution's activity at many levels.

Implementation

Implementation converts the strategic plan into specific steps and actions, preferably with measurable standards for success. Implementation depends on the participation of many parts of the institution and on decision making at various levels. Some institutions implement their planning via annual or performance plans that state the actions and define the methods to be used by each major division for achieving the institution's goals. The financial effects of those actions and their measures are incorporated into the annual operating budget and the five-year financial plan. Accountability for achieving goals may also be incorporated into the budgeting process, with support linked to performance and success in reaching goals. Tracking achievements and communicating positively about the results demonstrate the progress made in plan implementation.

The Value of Planning

In a journey, the travel experience itself can have as much value as reaching the destination. In planning, the process itself contributes to the accomplishment of goals as much as the outcomes of the strategic plan. The conduct of a planning effort can be an opportunity to motivate, challenge, and engage individuals. It can empower all parties to think creatively and broadly about future possibilities for their roles in relation to the institution. It provides a forum for addressing issues and concerns and generates feedback from all stakeholders. Planning provides a method for actively seeking best practices and encourages teamwork and new partnerships within and outside the institution. Planning can create new ways of looking at things, thereby encouraging risk taking and testing new ideas. Ultimately, planning serves to commit participants to accomplishing the goals they have helped to identify and determine.

Major Considerations in Planning

Academic Program Planning

Most institutions are forced to look at the effectiveness of the curriculum as part of their planning processes. Motivations for such reviews include:

- *Responding to interest in outcomes by accrediting agencies and by the public.* Public representatives are increasingly interested in knowing what competencies graduates should acquire and what should be the outcomes of their learning. Accrediting agencies are likewise using standards related to what is learned and assessment of outcomes. Emphasis has been shifting to integrate the curriculum, the resources, and the process of learning in order to produce clearly conceived learning outcomes. (See Figure 02-04 for important conditions for curriculum improvement and learning assessment.)

- *Taking advantage of new technologies for presentation of material.* Most institutions have added to the traditional lecture presentations such approaches as team problem-solving projects, small group discussions, computers in the classroom, and online teaching, both on the campus and off campus via distance learning.

- *Needing to find the dollars for new initiatives.* Instructional costs are generally the largest portion of the institutional budget, aren't covered, and are sometimes the logical place to find the desired funds. (See Figure 02-05 for the types of questions being asked at one university as a way of reallocating funds.)

- *Reorganizing the curriculum offerings in the face of proliferation.* In some institutions, the variety of curriculum offerings may cause the educational process to be seen as disjointed and unstructured. Students may perceive that their degrees have more do to with accumulation of credits than with the purposeful pursuit of knowledge.

Such changes in curriculum and teaching methods can be expected to have consequent effects on economic and business matters: improved retention, fewer courses, different classroom designs and uses, new registration procedures, different uses of computers and the Internet, and so on.

In dealing with the consequences of such changes for planning, the chief academic officer and chief business officer and their staffs must work together to recognize and plan for the changes that can be anticipated in services, space usage,

Figure 02-04

Important Conditions for Curriculum Improvement and Learning Assessment

- Faculty ownership of the process and responsibility for teaching and academic content[1]
- Support and resources for the activities
- Priorities established, projects selected, and resources allocated
- Assessment as an integral part of the process and the success of all instructionally related projects measured on the basis of changes in student performance

Figure 02-05

"What If" Questions About the Curriculum Asked at One University[2]

- What if the university optimized class sizes so that appropriate increases could subsidize appropriate reductions?
- What if the university reduced the number of underenrolled course sections?
- What if the university created a schedule to reduce costs for summer school?
- What if the university brought disproportionately expensive programs into line with peer institutions?
- What if the university reduced its reliance on full-time, tenure-track faculty?
- What if the university increased the number of credit hours produced by faculty utilizing technology?
- What if the university salvaged at-risk students?
- What if the university reduced the number of students graduating with excessive credit hours?

---

technology support, and other systems. In some cases, they may be dealing with uncertainties and conjecture about the effects of curriculum changes, but all parties should work at trying to quantify and forecast the results to the extent possible.

Relationships with Constituents; Development and Fund Raising

Independent institutions have traditionally relied on donations for major portions of support. Public institutions benefit from funds from foundations and other mechanisms that generate private support for the institution. Development programs have roles in planning beyond estimating the amount of private funds to be generated to help meet financial goals. The strategic plan incorporates the vision, mission, and goals that can inspire donors to associate themselves with the institution and participate in its future. During the planning process, relationships with donors have implications for the strategic plan, including capital planning and new partnerships.

Development efforts are designed to generate donations as the end result of long-term, mutually beneficial relationships with individuals, corporations, foundations, and government and community partners. While governing boards have the responsibility to set the direction of the educational institution, at independent institutions they are also expected to lead financial support efforts through their own generosity and through their willingness to involve and ask others for donations. Generous alumni and other volunteers who participate in the life of the institution want to see a reflection and demonstration of their ideas. Corporations that provide donations, equipment, research support, and jobs for graduates may have expectations of benefits from their relationships with the institution, such as implied product promotion, provision of graduates whose training matches their needs, or programs for retraining their employees. Donors for new buildings or other capital programs may want to name the building or have other benefits from the gift.

Coordination and cultivation of such relationships is the role of the senior leadership, the chief development officer, the development staff, and many others. Relationships include knowing the individuals involved and understanding their interests and reasons for giving. Such interests can influence the design of an academic program or selection of a particular type of building. The ideas and views of current and potential donors should be included in the strategic plan, since those people will be asked to support the financial goals contained in the plan. A strategic plan that encompasses both the needs of the institution and the interest of donors is of paramount importance.

Enrollment Planning and Management

Estimates of the numbers of students to be recruited and enrolled are a fundamental factor in long-term planning. When institutions have fewer or greater numbers of students than planned, the result can be a major upheaval in either reducing costs to cover the shortfall in revenue, or increasing costs to provide the services needed for larger numbers of students.

Whether at a public or independent institution, enrollment projections are important. Accurate projections and management of enrollment to stay as close to those projections as possible calls for appropriate pricing and financial aid, effective communication with state representatives, enthusiastic recruiting, careful monitoring of students throughout their time at the institution, and provision of academic and other support to promote retention.

Institutions may develop their own strategies and policies or have guidelines imposed by systems or legislatures. They may deal with total enrollment or relate to specific programs or units. Some specialized programs may generate unexpected enrollment patterns that provide opportunities or call for examination.

Most institutions rely heavily on the experience and judgment of their admissions staffs, who review the demographic, environmental, political, economic, and other environments that affect recruitment of new students. In public systems, institutions must frequently work with state mandates regarding numbers of students to be admitted and use of factors like race, gender, minimum academic criteria, family background, and quality of high school.

The pricing of tuition, fees, room and board, and other charges should include the active participation of both the president and the chief business officer. They are responsible for adherence to legal requirements and consistency with financial policies established by the governing board and the administration. Pricing decisions should be rational and made in a context of understanding the various costs charged within the institution.

Student Affairs Changes

Today's students are consumer oriented and expect high levels of customer service. Many of them have come to know life with computers as basic equipment and the Internet as a part of everyday life. They and their families are concerned with costs, quality and learning outcomes, location, opportunities for international experiences, athletic and recreational facilities and programs, and prospects for personal growth. Many students today are creating academic programs from multiple educational providers. Many institutions have found new markets with part-time and adult students, distance education, online courses, and other new approaches.

Contemporary learners are mature and diverse. Many of them are concerned with competing demands on their time. Adults, most of them with jobs, comprise 44 percent of those pursuing undergraduate or graduate degrees, often as part of retraining for new stages in their careers. Only 25 percent of all students are "traditional" 18–22-year-old residential students attending college full-time.[3]

While many new forms of learning institutions are growing or emerging, such as two-year and/or proprietary for-profit educational institutions, the more traditional four-year residential institutions are concerned with using new technologies for effective learning and for taking advantage of linkages with other institutions. They also want to offer expanded life experiences as students look for more opportunities for personal development.

Technology Changes

New technologies have changed the world of higher education and how it operates in terms of both teaching and management. The rapid expansion of ways to make information available is resulting in profound changes in how institutions function. Planning processes should be geared to recognizing those changes and anticipating their impact on all aspects of college and university life.

Lectures and other educational tools provided via the Internet, which can reach thousands of new students, have great potential for new revenue. They also create situations of new competition and the need for new policies. Expanded access to information and business processes modeled after commercial innovations have the potential to dramatically change the business of higher education. Some of the related considerations to be explored in planning include the following:

- Proprietary, for-profit educational institutions and educational institutions that provide education only online are being created, often with a competency-based focus. Competencies for certification and, in some cases, for degrees, are being defined in collaboration with consortia on an industry-by-industry basis. For example, Western Governors University (WGU), founded in 1997, directs students to online courses offered by other colleges and universities and adds an administrative fee. WGU offers competency exams covering specific educational domains, which can lead to a degree in the required number of competencies. Other organizations are being created to aggregate distance learning courses, particularly on a state level, to provide clearinghouses for courses from various educational institutions.

- Entrepreneurship may result in faculty receiving revenues from online courses under noninstitutional auspices without recognition of the role of the college or university. Institutions need to be aware of these activities, to develop policies to deal with such prospects, and to factor anticipated outcomes into their planning.

- The future of the residential campus and the role and importance of nonacademic aspects of college life in individual development are raised as questions in the face of distance learning. What goes on in the classroom or at the computer is only part of the total instructional experience. Current trends in technological learning tend to de-emphasize the premise that learning is best accomplished in a positive physical, cultural, and social milieu that includes interaction with faculty and staff. Planning should make some estimates of the impacts on their campuses of the trends in distance learning.

- Expectations for communication speed and information dissemination have been increased as a result of the Internet and its potential. The role of libraries has been extended to assistance in gaining electronic access to information beyond the campus and in helping students select and organize such information. There is a desire for new and improved software and hardware, including interactive accounting systems, communications, and improved Internet access and applications. Planning for technological improvement calls for new funding and for upgrades and improvements.

Figure 02-06

Critical Issues Pertinent to Capital Planning[4]

- Land use and potential acquisition
- Enrollment and staffing projections
- Facilities condition—deferred and anticipated needs
- Academic, support, research, and service space, and anticipated changes
- Transportation—vehicular and pedestrian traffic
- Infrastructures—roads, walks, parking, utilities, and services

- Building and site design guidelines
- Historic preservation
- Regulatory standards and codes
- Campus and local community issues
- Energy sources

Many institutions find that completion of new installations whets the institutional appetite for more and improved information technology and services.

- New classroom configurations are desirable based on computers as a tool in the classroom for class team projects, analyses, writing, and note taking. Requirements exist for different types of spaces, such as small group discussion rooms and more computer laboratories.

All of the above factors can have profound effects in terms of new initiatives identified in the planning process.

Capital Planning

Capital planning is used for projects that call for major infusions of capital and that could bring major changes to an institution's asset or expense structure. While it has traditionally involved new facilities and building improvements, capital planning can also can be used for major equipment and information technology investments.

Capital planning integrates uneven capital needs with fund raising, financing, and budget planning for debt service and changes in operating and maintenance budgets.

Physical facilities are key assets to be appropriately utilized and protected. Facilities changes should be considered in the context of the overall institutional plan. Figure 02-06 shows critical issues pertinent to facilities planning. A strategic plan for capital development includes the following:

- *A campus master plan* is a plan for future campus development including physical improvements, additions, and changes. It identifies the existing and preferred institutional land uses, buildings, landscape, and open space features, and pedestrian and vehicular circulation systems. It is based on assumptions about basic campus characteristics drawn from projections of institutional plans, future land use, building locations and use, traffic circulation and parking, and infrastructures.

- *The assumptions* are articulated, in part so that they can be examined in the planning process to incorporate changes anticipated in overall institutional direction, such as the desire of a donor to provide a new facility or improvement.

- A *facilities information database* contains compilations of space inventory and facilities documentation; a facilities condition audit quantifying the current building renewal conditions and needs; and a space utilization study. Such information is valuable to the planning process and in performing various analyses, such as reallocation of space to accommodate new programs and methods. The database should incorporate meaningful financial data and integrate fragmented information about capital projects, their costs and their revenues, so that data and analyses are presented in a cohesive manner.

- *Capital improvement plan.* The plan is a summary of all capital projects anticipated for a five-to-ten-year period. It provides opportunity for integrated planning by projecting annual expenditures on capital changes and includes information on possible sources of funding.

Debt and Capitalization Policies

Capital budgets and the large expenses they represent can be paid for in a variety of ways (see figure 02-07), including various types of borrowing. Debt financing can be an addition or alternative to internal financing or capital gifts. Institutions generally consider how debt, in combination with internal resources and aggressive fund-raising programs, can enable the acquisition or maintenance of capital investment. The payback on such debt must be integrated into the annual operating budget. Exploration of borrowing calls for review of the institution's debt capacity and choices among different types and conditions of debt instruments.

The prospect of borrowing may appear so daunting that leaders may consider foregoing capital spending. Such a decision should include an analysis of the comparative costs of borrowing with the potential hidden costs of not doing the project. For example, if research funds or tuition revenues are not attracted, the value of unrealized revenues over time might exceed the cost of financing the improvements essential to realization of the revenues.

Figure 02-07

Options Available for Funding

- Appropriations
- Internal/operating funds (pay as you go)
- Internal borrowings from unrestricted reserves or funds functioning as endowment
- Focused fund-raising or capital campaigns

- Bank debt
- Tax-exempt debt in public markets
- Taxable debt in public markets
- Private-sector development, via ground leases or joint ventures with a real estate developer

---

Debt capacity, the level of debt an institution can reasonably manage, depends on legal and financial management policy factors. A state government, governing board, or management may determine a debt limit, which then defines the institution's debt capacity. In the absence of such set limits, institutional debt management policy and the decisions of rating agencies in the market effectively determine debt capacity. Debt ratings determine interest rates; so the more debt contemplated in relation to capacity, the higher the interest rate.

An institution may consider borrowing from its own endowment, since the process is simple and does not involve outside entities. However, full exploration of the alternatives should be made and consideration given to the opportunity cost that may be incurred if the institution uses invested funds that are earning higher rates of return than would be paid on debt. Tax-exempt financing may offer very attractive financial conditions.

Considerations in reviewing and determining debt depend on the options available in terms of types of borrowing, forms of security, credit ratings, assessment of the market, transaction costs, underwriter's spread, and management of existing debt. An effective debt management program can expand options and offer opportunities for facilities or other major acquisition not available by other financing methods. Projects that are financed by debt can be accomplished within a short time frame and the cost is distributed over a period of time, generally related to the project's useful life. The decision to incur debt, however, increases the costs in the operating budget, incurs restrictions, and includes administrative requirements.

A strong, ongoing strategic planning process tied to operating and capital budgeting processes can be important in enabling an institution to evaluate debt opportunities and build them successfully into a broad capital development plan. (See chapter 10, Debt Financing and Management.)

Human Resources: Employee Compensation and Professional Development and Training

Workforce changes; recruitment and departure incentives. Changes in focus and restructuring at many levels may call for recruitment of new types of faculty and staff and/or reductions in the workforce. The cost and methods of attracting and retaining staff and faculty with the new expertise sought are important factors to be quantified. Elimination or redirection of staff jobs may be due to reorganization, outsourcing, or other decisions. Retraining, easing the transition to finding work elsewhere, or retirement are available options. Programs to deal with this issue include voluntary departure and early retirement incentives, fixed-term contracts, and phased-in retirement—all of which should be quantified and considered in planning.

Programs vary among institutions, but they must be developed in the context of human resources guidelines, be consistent and nondiscriminatory, and apply to all employees within certain definitions, such as length of institutional service, age, or a combination of factors.

Faculty tenure adds to the complexity of redirection of the institution's workforce. Since 1994, when mandatory retirement for faculty was eliminated, faculty retirement rates for ages 70 and older have declined to 33 percent from 100 percent.[5] The consequences for planning have included continuing commitments for relatively high salaries and reduced recruitment of newer faculty.

The type of retirement program benefit provided by the institution can also have an effect on the age of retirement. Those institutions with defined benefit plans, in which the expected value of future benefits begins to decline once a certain age is passed, find that employees, especially faculty, tend to retire earlier. Those with defined contribution plans find the tendency is to retire later.[6]

Salary planning. A part of human resource planning is projection of salary expense and its relationship to the institution's goals. Institutions generally set compensation goals for themselves, such as a percentile of the relevant faculty category at peer and competing institutions or a percentage of the salaries of comparably skilled staff in the recruitment area. Salary surveys prepared by the College and University Personnel Association, the American Association of University Professors, and other professional groups, can be helpful in quantifying goals. The assumptions in salary planning should be reviewed in the context of overall institutional planning and adjusted to reflect changes in strategy.

Benefits. Colleges and universities generally offer part of employee compensation in the form of programs that provide retirement, health insurance, long-term disability, life insurance, child care, vacations, paid sick time and personal time, and tuition benefits. Benefits are a cost to the institution beyond the mandated costs of Social Security, workers' compensation, and other programs. Costs of all benefits need to be considered in planning.

Professional development and training programs. Assisting employees with professional development and training and enabling them to grow and move to new or higher levels within the institution are important in creating a capable and loyal employee base. In times of workforce realignment, retraining for staff can be an important component in assuring stability and positive morale. Such programs must be consistent with the goals of the institution and their costs considered in planning efforts.

Sponsored Programs

Institutions may need to establish funding for a number of areas that are part of a desired long-range plan. Such matters may include sponsored programs or expanded research programs to attract and retain faculty.

Sponsored programs are those financed by external funds with a non-donative intent. They may support the instructional, research, or public service function of an institution, including funding salaries of tenured faculty. Such external support may be significant, even critical, to the achievement of goals and objectives. Contracts, grants, and other instruments can add spending capability and enhancements and can be a marketing opportunity by generating recognition and prestige for the institution.

Issues to be considered in accepting outside funds include the relationship of the project to the institution's overall goals, incentives to encourage attraction of new funds, and the conditions imposed for managing such funds. Potential negative public relations consequences must be reviewed in light of types of research and social responsibility patterns of some corporations.

Current and potential sources of funds should be reviewed as part of the planning process. Funding sources and subject areas for research or other programs should be identified in terms of their inclusion in the strategic plan and their ability to further the institution's goals. Consideration should also be given to the consequences of not receiving anticipated funding. Planning should recognize the possibility of a "soft money trap," in which an institution depends on grants or contracts to support research or programs important to its mission, but may have to find alternate funds to run the programs if outside sources fail to provide the expected support.

While outside funding has many benefits, it must be recognized that contracts are awarded not to an individual, but to the institution, which assumes full legal responsibility for the programs and for fulfilling sponsor requirements. Acceptance of funds from outside sources is accompanied by a requirement for strict accountability and imposes demands on staff and facilities. (See figure 02-08 for elements of administration of sponsored programs.)

Direct costs include salaries and benefits of those working on the project, travel, materials, supplies, and other expenses specifically identified with the project. Indirect costs are those not easily identifiable with the program but are real costs. They generally include a share of operation and maintenance expense, library, technology support, and central administration of sponsored research. Unless institutions are reimbursed by sponsoring agencies for such costs, they must use their own resources, which diverts support from other objectives. Indirect cost rates are computed annually and are often expressed as a percentage of modified total direct cost or of salaries and wages.

Sponsored programs are awarded because of special expertise and accomplishments of the faculty. Many institutions encourage faculty to generate new or additional funding and offer incentives and rewards to do so. Such items include expanded space allocation, enhanced compensation, and returning to the faculty member a portion of the indirect costs generated by the contract. Such a strategy may have the benefit of an incentive, but may also cause the institution to find

Figure 02-08

Elements of Administration of Sponsored Programs

- Preparation, approval and submission of proposals
- Negotiation of grants and contracts
- Development and negotiation of indirect cost rates
- Purchasing according to specified guidelines
- Audit and maintenance of accounts and records
- Management of inventions and copyrights
- Controls related to property and human and animal subjects

- Federally mandated social programs
- Technical and financial reports preparation and submission
- Billing, collecting, and reporting contract and grant revenues
- Compliance with all other conditions

other sources for the funds to cover the full indirect costs. (For a more complete discussion on this topic, see chapter 18, Research and Sponsored Programs.)

Pricing and Financial Aid Strategies

The pricing of tuition, fees, room and board, and other charges are important in planning and achievement of goals. Both the president and the chief business officer should actively participate in setting prices, since they are responsible for adherence to legal requirements and consistency with financial policies established by the governing board and the administration. They should also assure that pricing decisions can be rationally justified and are made with an understanding of various costs within the institution.

Types of tuition include undergraduate tuition, tuition for professional schools, and tuition for graduate schools. Tuition can be expressed in terms of a single course, a specific degree, or a specific time frame. For some online learning applications, tuition may be a per-use, point-of-sale payment.

Undergraduate tuition. Tuition usually refers to undergraduate tuition, and attention tends to focus on the published price rather than discounted prices paid by many students with grants and scholarships. Some independent colleges and universities charge a comprehensive fee, rather than separating tuition from room and board charges, which is intended to encourage students to use institution-owned student housing and food services. Such institutions must also offer an alternative tuition-only choice for off-campus residents and part-time students.

Tuition for professional degrees and graduate studies. Multiple levels of tuition are more prevalent among professional schools, which develop prices based on underlying cost differentials, the institution's competitive position, and the fact that these degree programs are often offered by independent entities within a college or university.

Tuition per course, per degree, and for special periods. Tuition expressed in terms of dollars per credit hour or per course is useful for large numbers of part-time students and adult learning programs such as continuing education.

Miscellaneous fees. Educational and general fees may be charged for a variety of services and purposes, such as laboratory and athletic fees, as well as various educational and ancillary purposes. They may include fees for personal computers, to help defray building loans, or to support parking facilities and plant renovations. Critics assert that some fees charged by colleges and universities represent a form of disguised tuition.

Factors influencing tuition policy. Those responsible for pricing should be aware of their institution's rank among peer institutions. Public relations and the anticipated reaction of students and their families must be considered, along with opinions of state legislators. The budget is closely dependent on tuition revenues and prices set, and analysis must be made of anticipated enrollment.

The changing structure of enrollments calls for recognition that, while tuition can be estimated based on enrollment by academic levels, it should also be considered based on net tuition revenues after student aid grants. Such institutionally funded student aid reflects the fact that some students whom the institution wishes to enroll can or will matriculate only at a reduced price. Institutions need to consider how well financial aid policies and their implementation support objectives and the long-term effects of student aid practices. Other factors that can affect tuition policy include anticipated changes in tuition receivables and student loans that may go into default.

Innovation. In reviewing tuition policies, as in other planning matters, innovation and new approaches should be encouraged. Institutions should use analysis capabilities to investigate the potential advantages and pitfalls of tuition refinements. Properly managed, innovative tuition plans can be rewarding both in their financial and their public relations impact, and they may enhance student retention.

Break-even or full-cost pricing. There are services where break-even or full-cost pricing are taken for granted, including student housing, food services and catering, and college stores, which are generally understood to be self-supporting. On a full-costing basis, the phrase "self-supporting" means that current and long-run revenues equal long-run costs. However, institutions differ in their treatment of certain costs, such as allocations for space, utilities, and housekeeping services. A percentage of current general administrative expenditures is charged to auxiliary enterprises, but the specific percentage varies greatly.

The adequacy of auxiliary enterprise prices can be judged only after determining the specific short- and long-run costs that these prices enable the institution to cover.

Some programs, such as reading and speech laboratories, nursery schools, and theaters operated for student instruction may be considered "sales and services" activities and are often priced on the basis of direct average or marginal costs. The planning process should review these costs to assure a consistent approach and official sanction.

Revenues of intercollegiate athletic activities may include season ticket sales, gate receipts, student activity fees, receipts from merchandise, food and beverage sales, guarantees, radio and television royalties, program sales, parking income, and gifts and grants for current operations. These types of revenues also involve pricing decisions that must be made in an overall institutional context and should include public perception issues in terms of relationships with sponsors and advertising.

Endowment Investment and Payout Policy

An important part of institutional planning and budgeting is the annual revenue realized from endowment earnings, which reflects the institution's investment and payout policy. How to invest the endowment of an institution (or of a foundation set up for the benefit of a public institution) is the function of an investment committee of the governing board, or the governing board itself. The board is responsible for determining the investment policies, which are carried out by the chief financial officer and staff and frequently by one or more fund managers.

Educational endowments have unique features that include exemption from taxation, a very long-term (in theory, perpetual) investment horizon, and the need to create earnings for current operations. Ideally, such earnings should grow in real or inflation-adjusted terms or at minimum should remain stable, but not decline. Investment committees, governing boards, and officers should always take maximum advantage of their fund's tax-exempt and perpetual life status.

Spendable return is the amount of endowment income or earnings (yield plus appreciation) allotted on a regular, periodic basis by the institution for current expenditures. Spending policies are intended to create current income as well as preserve the purchasing power of endowment principal.

The amount of endowment return to be spent should be equal to but not exceed the expected long-term real or inflation-adjusted rate of return. To determine a fund's expected real rate of return, certain assumptions must be made about the endowment's long-term asset mix, which is dependent on the fund's total return objectives or desired spending rate. The higher a fund's long-term return objective, the more aggressively its assets must be invested. Most governing boards make defensible assumptions about sustainable spending rates based on capital market history. Later in the planning process, they review and possibly revise spending policies, after appropriate long-term asset mixes have been identified. (For more on this subject, see chapter 9, Endowment Management.)

Service Provider Relationships and Joint Ventures

A fact of life has become the continuous reevaluation and reengineering of support services as part of the effective delivery of the institution's core mission and fulfillment of its goals. Before decisions are made as to whether services are better provided in-house or through outsourcing, reviews must be made of the services themselves.

Success of such reviews depends on an environment of trust and honesty with the affected staffs, communications to keep them involved in the larger picture, and sessions to address their anxieties. The staffs who do the work every day may have an understandable reaction of not appreciating close scrutiny and not accepting reviews as constructive criticisms. Effective and comprehensive review is generally not limited to an individual office or service unit. Reviews are likely to involve other related services and interdependent processes.

Once the reviews of the service provider relationships have been completed, the process moves to consideration of having the service provided in-house or by an outside entity. Higher education has increasingly moved to work with external providers to bring in expert resources at lower costs that will blend well with the current management and institutional culture. Essential steps in completing this review include defining the measures for evaluating the providers, (which forms the basis for a request for proposal), assessment of responses (including issues beyond perceived quality and price), and selection of the vendor.

Employment of an outside vendor can have risks. Costs may increase and/or there may be public criticism about using institutional funds to support a corporation. Vendor personnel may need special training in order to behave appropriately within the higher education environment. The vendor may go out of business or fail to perform properly, leaving the institution with the difficult task of having to terminate the contract and find another service provider, most likely on short notice. All such considerations must be taken into account in evaluating the prospect of working with an external provider.

On the other hand, relations with external providers frequently move beyond the traditional vendor-client relationship to new arrangements that benefit both parties. For example, a vendor may work with an institution to develop customer satisfaction surveys or new definitions of quality of services in specified areas, resulting in a fresh approach for the institution and the basis for marketing to other higher education customers for the vendor. A computer manufacturer may agree to donate equipment to a specified level over a period of time in return for the institution's exclusive use of that equipment in certain programs. A staff job may be filled with the services of a corporation. A real estate developer may take over the operation of some campus properties, resulting in an arrangement that may provide a profit to the developer, achieve improvements in the facilities, relieve the institution from the expenses of the property, and enable reallocation of resources to educational or other missions.

CONCLUSION

This chapter has described a centralized strategic planning process that engages members of the community and helps them commit to the actions to be taken. The considerations discussed illustrate the wide range of topics and the many aspects of institutional operation that may be examined in planning. The strategic plan thus created becomes a framework for operational planning by each unit within the institution and for implementation. Implementation converts planning into daily actions and evaluates their results.

Ongoing planning incorporates evaluation and feedback. It should also be flexible enough to adjust to change and new considerations, such as different leadership and unanticipated crises. While such changes sometimes have the effect of moving away from previous goals, the planning process should not be discontinued but be adjusted to incorporate new priorities. Ongoing planning can be used to recognize previous conclusions and to carry out a re-examination of an institution and a timely updating of its goals.

NOTES

1. Diamond, Robert M. *Designing and Assessing Courses and Curricula: A Practical Guide.* San Francisco: Jossey-Bass Publishers, 1998, 14.

2. Klinger, Donna and Roberts, Pauline. "The Newlywed Game," *Business Officer*, January 2000, 34.

3. Oblinger, Diana G. "Hype, Hyperarchy, and Higher Education," *Business Officer*, October 1999, 22–31.

4. *College and University Business Administration,* fifth edition. Washington, DC: NACUBO, 1992, pp 841, 829.

5. Wyatt, Edward. "Tenure Gridlock: When Professors Choose Not to Retire," *New York Times*, February 16, 2000, 11.

6. Ibid.

REFERENCES AND RESOURCES

Publications and Articles

Balderston, Frederick E. *Managing Today's University: Strategies for Viability, Change, and Excellence.* San Francisco: Jossey-Bass Publishers, 1995.

Carnevale, Dan. "Assessing the Quality of Online Courses Remains a Challenge, Educators Agree," *Chronicle of Higher Education,* February 18, 2000, A59.

Carr, Sarah. "As Distance Education Comes of Age, the Challenge Is Keeping the Students," *Chronicle of Higher Education*, February 11, 2000, A39.

Diamond, Robert M. *Designing and Assessing Courses and Curricula: A Practical Guide.* San Francisco: Jossey-Bass Publishers, 1998.

Gearhart, G. David. *The Capital Campaign in Higher Education: A Practical Guide for College and University Advancement*, Washington, D.C.: NACUBO, 1995.

Gose, Ben. "Tuition Discounting May Rankle, but It Has Become Widespread," *The Chronicle of Higher Education*, February 18, 2000, A62.

Grace, Kay Sprinkel. *Beyond Fund Raising: New Strategies for NonProfit Innovation and Investment.* New York: John Wiley & Sons, 1999.

Klinger, Donna, and Roberts, Pauline. "The Newlywed Game," *Business Officer*, January 2000, 32.

Levine, Arthur. "The Soul of A New University." *New York Times*, March 13, 2000, OP-ED.

London, Manuel. *Achieving Performance Excellence in University Administration: A Team Approach to Organizational Change and Employee Development.* Westport, CT: Praeger, 1995.

McTague, Michael J., and Meskill, Victor P. "Avoiding the Land Mines: Keys to Successful Outsourcing," *Business Officer*, June 1997, 31.

Nedwek, Brian P., editor. *Doing Academic Planning: Effective Tools for Decision Making.* Ann Arbor: Society for College and University Planning, 1997.

Norris, Donald M., and Olson, Mark A. "Future E-Business Applications in Education," *Business Officer*, July 1999, 32.

Oblinger, Diana G. "Hype, Hyperarchy, and Higher Education," *Business Officer*, October 1999, 22–31.

Scherrens, Maurice W. *Maximizing Service Provider Relationships: Best Practices Through Blended Management,* Washington, D.C.: NACUBO, 1999.

Stenberg, Jacques, and Wyatt, Edward. "Boola, Boola: E-Commerce Comes to Quad," *New York Times,* February 13, 2000, Section 4.

Wyatt, Edward. "Tenure Gridlock: When Professors Choose Not to Retire," *New York Times,* February 16, 2000, 11.

Organizations

The Society for College and University Planning (SCUP)
4251 Plymouth Road, Suite D, Ann Arbor, MI 48105-2785
Voice (313) 998-7832   Fax (313) 998-6532
Email: scup@mich.edu . . . . www.umich.edu/scup

Chapter 3

Implementation Strategies and Outcomes Assessment

by

Jean F. MacCormack
University of Massachusetts, Dartmouth

Sponsors

KPMG
Contact: Greg J. Baroni
1676 International Drive
McLean, VA 22102
703-747-3004
www.kpmg.com

With over 30 years of serving higher education, KPMG offers a broad range of services that helps our clients analyze their businesses with true clarity, raises their level of performance and delivers the strategic and infrastructural components to support highly dynamic E-business models in colleges, universities, and academic medical centers.

COLLEGIS
Contact: Melissa Meridith
2300 Maitland Center Parkway, Suite 340
Maitland, FL 32751
800-800-1874
www.collegis.com

COLLEGIS is higher education's strategic technology partner—aligning technology resources and investments with institutional goals. COLLEGIS manages institutional administrative, academic and communications technology functions.

PEOPLESOFT, INC.
Contact: Karen Willett
4460 Hacienda Drive
Pleasanton, CA 94588
925-694-5453
www.peoplesoft.com/highered

PeopleSoft delivers E-business solutions for higher education management needs, including student administration, grants management, finance, human resources, E-procurement, advancement, and more. PeopleSoft also provides comprehensive customer service, consulting, education, and technical support services.

SIEMENS BUILDING TECHNOLOGIES, INC.
Contact: Sylvia Rainey
1000 Deerfield Parkway
Buffalo Grove, IL 60089-4547
847-215-1050 ext. 5586
www.sbt.siemens.com/SmartU

Siemens Building Technologies is a world leader providing cost effective, facility performance solutions for the comfort, life safety, security, and energy efficiency of your campus.

Contents

Planning and budgeting are a continuum, the tangible and necessary outcomes being the operating budget and the capital budget. Interwoven among them, and essential to effecting them, are implementation strategies, tactics, and tasks, along with the measurement of their outcomes.

The separation, for practical purposes, of (1) planning, (2) implementation strategies and outcomes assessment, and (3) budgeting into three discrete chapters of this book may be artificial, as they are so entwined. Elements of the subject of each of these chapters will be found in the other two, but the whole should provide a comprehensive overview of decision making in higher education.

There are three phases or levels of decision making in institutional planning. The first, or "strategic," phase involves the actual development or subsequent modification of a vision for the institution. A vision is an expression of the institutional mission in the anticipated future; there are different possible futures, and thus different possible visions. This strategic vision, ultimately expressed as a plan, outlines a sense of the institution's primary roles, values, mission, and special character. Strategic vision shapes the institution over an extended period of time. To do this effectively, it also influences the shorter cycle of decisions made each year about practical functions like operating and capital budgets. The outcomes of strategic planning (expressed in a strategic plan) are themselves strategies, which include programs, projects, and processes, each having specific objectives. If these strategies are sound, then reaching objectives achieves goals (or subgoals); if the strategies are wrong, then reaching objectives will *not* achieve goals.

The process of making a strategic vision work for the long and short run moves decision making to a second, more "tactical," phase where strategies focus and direct ongoing and evolving resource, organization, and spending decisions. In this phase, independent streams of activity or ideas are prioritized, reviewed for internal consistency, subjected to detailed costing, and assessed against internal and external realities. Out of this process comes a series of activities or projects approved for "implementation," expressed as tactical or line-item budgets, each of which has its own specific shaping decisions. Implementation is the third, or "operational," phase of institutional decision making[1].

Implementation decisions in higher education, as in other organizations, are essentially about making strategic vision and tactical plans come alive. Assuming a vision that resonates with the broader campus community, and careful and inclusive tactical planning, the critical implementation task is to align various essential operational functions toward making the plan(s) into reality. Some common implementation tasks are managing enrollment, setting pricing and financial aid policies, doing revenue projections and operational budgeting, handling capital asset management, monitoring and maximizing endowment investment and payout, directing employee compensation and development policies, raising funds, and coordinating administrative service delivery systems and approaches. These key activities must be shaped and structured in ways that support the visionary and tactical change agenda set by a larger campus or system plan.

Incremental Implementation Decisions

Describing implementation this way makes it sound like a very linear and structured set of large, sequenced activities. In fact, many implementation decisions in institutions involve minor incremental change strategies and rolling adjustments. They do not change the nature of the core activity but may involve marginal changes in resources utilized, personnel involved, audience served, or programs delivered. About 95 percent or more of an institution's budget, programs, and staffing patterns will be the same from one year to the next. The implementation decisions that result in these incremental changes usually evolve in a relatively consistent fashion over time without any special attention to process.

Many of these "evolving" implementation decisions are handled in a decentralized way. Decisions about the selection of faculty members, program structure and delivery, and student affairs are made at the departmental or divisional level. As plans and budgets are approved for the year, courses are scheduled, teaching roles are assigned, equipment is purchased, space is secured and vacant positions are filled or held open. These marginal adjustments are important implementation decisions to the people directly involved but, except in small colleges, usually have little institutionwide impact. In each of these areas, specific individuals or groups are charged with the decision-making responsibility, usually subject to some administrative review. Because most of the activities are repeated often enough to become routine, in many institutions standardized review and approval of procedures to govern these implementation activities are developed.

Formal Implementation Planning

What does require special attention and some process management is when a new direction is set by strategic or nonincremental changes. These usually require noticeable changes in allocation of resources, in program mix, in space needed, or in other key dimensions of the institutional mission. Most institutions look to formal long-range plan development to identify and deal with these shifts in direction on five- or 10-year cycles.

But over the last decade many institutions have also experienced dramatic changes as a result of external forces—shifting of funding parameters, public challenges of their effectiveness, closer scrutiny and demands for accountability—or governing board, legislative or state standards group's initiatives[2]. The requirement by some states and boards for posttenure review, the demand for higher graduation standards, the desire to curb the rising costs of attending college, and the push to focus greater attention on teaching versus research are examples of these types of externally initiated strategic or tactical changes that require a more deliberate and conscious implementation strategy. Very practical and focused implementation decisions must be made to ensure appropriate responses to these "new" demands.

These kinds of external challenges as well as deliberate or even unanticipated internal shifts require that a new strategic plan be developed or an existing tactical plan be adjusted, resulting in changes at the implementation level. Well-managed institutions expect these types of changes. They see their visions and tactical documents not as rigid, step-by-step game plans, but more like road maps that set the destination but often require arrival by alternate routes. Many of the difficulties higher education institutions have experienced in implementing strategic plans have not been because of this need to adjust periodically, but more because of notable inconsistencies between the assumptions underlying planning approaches and the operational reality of academic institutions[3]. The failure to link planning and budgeting is the most notable cause of failure[4].

Although this chapter deals with the nature of strategic and tactical phases of planning and decision making in higher education and provides an overview of the major areas in an institution where long-range planning is required and significant, its intent is to focus primarily on the third phase—implementation decision-making strategies. It outlines critical factors, or tactical issues, to be considered in setting the stage for effective implementation. It describes the key components of change management in higher education and the critical implementation decision areas. Finally, it deals with measuring the effectiveness of implementation strategies through outcomes assessment.

SETTING THE STAGE FOR IMPLEMENTATION DECISION MAKING

If form follows function, implementation comes after the big-picture goals and directions are set or, alternately, challenged or questioned. It assumes there is shared vision and agreed-upon tactical guidelines. Arriving at this outcome is not an easy task in higher education. Many factors complicate college and university decision making, both in the planning and implementation stages. Unlike businesses, which can key their major efforts to a single goal such as net profit, colleges and universities are complex entities and by their very nature pursue a variety of goals. They are committed to transmitting knowledge to students, creating knowledge, and providing public service through application of that knowledge. Each of these goals is integrally and distinctively linked in every college and university's mission. At the tactical stage, where focusing-in is required, it is essential to understand the balance necessary to meet all these diverse primary mission goals. Focusing on one strategic goal always affects the others.

Identifying Individual and Group Decisions

Another complication is that decision-making authority in colleges and universities is typically decentralized. One person—the named leader—is often not the only person involved in critical decisions. Many decisions in a college or university are group decisions rather than individual decisions. A responsible individual—president, dean, department head—"makes" decisions, but that individual's freedom to make decisions is limited by two factors: he or she has to depend on others for information needed and to carry out the decisions.

Taking into Account Consensus and Collegiality

In a collegial culture, major institutional decisions must be acceptable to wide segments of the faculty and staff and to off-campus constituencies, such as boards and legislators. This limits any leader's ability to independently change direction radically or rapidly. It often takes some time for an institution's constituents to recognize and agree on a major change. Higher education leaders also share the constraints of other types of organizations. They must contend with time pressures, partial information, and unarticulated and perhaps unconscious values. When change is mandated by external conditions to happen very quickly, it often takes a great deal of time for a collegial campus culture to recover and adjust to a sense of loss of control and to understand the rational process for the decision.

There are clear limits to the ability of an institution to absorb significant changes rapidly[5].

Dealing with Campus Climate and Institutional "Culture" Differences

Colleges and universities differ widely in their internal cultures, their areas of real autonomy, the personal styles of their leaders and governing boards, their internal organizational structure, and the strength of their traditions. All of these have an impact on how decision making actually takes place. The above notwithstanding, a general overview of the major shared context for implementation decision making is both possible and useful.

Internally, colleges and universities of many different types usually support two or more basic "cultures" or ways of doing business to meet goals[6]. One culture, the community of scholars—largely the faculty—sees itself as the heart and central driving force of a university. It is a community of disciplinary experts, committed to a process of discussion and debate, strongly rooted in a bottom-up approach to new idea creation and development. Change in this culture, identified more as a creative process, is intentionally slowed, incremental, and subject to the individualistic movement of the interests of the individual scholar. The impetus to significant change must come from within and is fostered by collegial persuasion rather than external pressures or administrative direction or compliance. Evaluation of outcomes is based on flexible, professional peer judgments that are most frequently qualitative rather than quantitative. There is something of a sacred quality to the way this culture views its mission and academic decision-making rights, more similar to that in religious communities than that of industry and corporations.

This first culture recognizes, however, that another exists in the institution. Finances, enrollments, physical plant management, planning, marketing, student recruitment, technology delivery, and many other functions are the work of other, "nonacademic" personnel. These roles are viewed by the first culture as necessary but not a core set of activities. But those who are part of this "nonacademic" culture—the more corporate part of colleges and universities—although not often feeling empowered in a hierarchical structure, see their roles as critical for keeping the institution functioning on a day-to-day basis. This culture has a highly differentiated workforce of experts—accountants and finance personnel, human resource professionals, psychological counselors, institutional researchers, admissions recruiters and evaluators, construction and maintenance supervisors, alumni relations coordinators, purchasers, fundraisers, athletic coaches, and computer programmers, to name only a few. None have direct responsibility for teaching, research, or public service. Because of the interface of their service tasks with both an internal and external world, this part of the college or university is used to responding to changes required or dictated by others. In this culture, continuous and sometimes rapid change and adaptation are regular and expected. Sometimes form dictates rather than follows function. Centralized planning and regular administrative supervision are, however, normal ways of doing business in this culture. Though they vary from one administrative function to another, quantitative outcomes standards set by professional organizations are used often in making evaluative judgments.

Accepting and Understanding Various Points of View

When an institution moves to the implementation phase of decision making with its strategic or tactical plans, these two cultures—these two ways of seeing the world—*must* agree on a collaborative plan of action. However, past practice in institutions has kept most planning tasks highly segregated and hierarchical. Faculty usually do strategic goals and some level of tactics with senior, nonfaculty leaders. Once this task is complete, other nonfaculty are asked to align the operational resources and support to achieve goals. Very often they are also required as operational managers to motivate and lead support staff in implementation activities without the benefit of complete understanding of the full rationale for action.

In a resource-rich environment—people, dollars, and things—whatever mismatches exist between the goals and operational realities because of this typically segregated process have usually been solved with a further resource realignment effort. But for most institutions this is not a realistic option. Lacking the necessary resources puts greater strain on an institution's ability to fix planning miscalculations with additional resources. Planning now frequently is focused on making the maximum use of resources for strategic initiatives.

Old, disjointed planning strategies, if they cause delays and rework, can mean that goals will not be achieved in the anticipated timeframe or at all. When they cannot be achieved in the way they were envisioned or have to be modified to meet fiscal or operational realities that were not anticipated, frustration and skepticism about the value of planning at all levels is generated. If this is the case, faculty see staff as obstructionary and staff see faculty as unrealistic. Implementation is stymied precisely at a time when the institution needs it to work more efficiently and effectively. Getting everyone on the same wavelength early in the strategic and tactical phases is necessary.

Developing Cross-boundary Approaches to Decision Making

Inclusionary planning processes that foster broader communication and exchange of required perspectives have demonstrated significant efficacy[7]. Involving the CFO and other key operational managers in development of the strategic vision has been shown to enhance the likelihood that implementation decisions will be more closely aligned to goals and be effective[8]. Doing this well requires a clear and nonjudgmental but respectful acknowledgment of the value and contribution of the two cultures described above—resulting in two very different approaches to defining and carrying out the business of the institution. It also requires creativity, given the different learning and working styles of the various campus groups. Operational types do not like endless conceptual discussion, and faculty do not like precipitous action.

But the key premise is simple. If both cultural groups have the opportunity to benefit from understanding the strong qualitative impetus to the visionary goals or tactics selected, and appreciate the challenges or practical quantitative impediments to achieving them, the opportunity for creative and practical problem solving is enhanced. While external constituencies urge higher education to be "more like businesses," there is growing evidence that the preferred route is to take a more integrative approach, taking advantage of the diversity and richness of the two cultures to develop a better, more integrative model for doing "academic business[9]."

Encouraging Innovative Leadership

Given the territorial and hierarchical nature of most academic institutions, setting the proper working environment for new models to develop is a real challenge. Leadership that is willing to take risks and be innovative in meeting these challenges is very important, particularly at the implementation stage. Some suggest that higher education may require a new form of leadership for these kinds of "cultural" transformations[10]. Whether it is a new style of leadership or a renewed commitment to real collegiality, what is clear is that leaders do need to communicate clearly and broadly about plan expectations and about who ultimately has responsibility for assuring that outcomes anticipated from various implementation activities actually happen. Setting the climate to encourage cooperation across units, to reward creative ideas, to recognize accomplishment, and to challenge limited perspectives is critical. This clearly requires several assigned leadership roles in implementation activities beyond the senior leader responsible for the activity. Identifying the key people who need to be involved in a leadership capacity and getting them engaged early on in the project-shaping process is essential.

Active Communication, Consultation, and Consensus Building

At the very least, it is clear that an institutional communication strategy is needed and a serious attempt must be made to build consensus around implementation decisions. Commitment starts with mutual understanding and acceptance of the issue(s) being solved or strategic direction(s) being taken. Moving ahead without fully vetting issues will be counterproductive. Large numbers of campus constituents may not be participants in formal planning processes or be aware of the need for small but important incremental process changes, but they may be required to be involved in or be affected by implementation activities. Keeping these people informed about intents and strategies at the implementation phase is critical. Setting the stage will ideally be about breaking down institutional "cultural" boundaries and having the right people working together. But if the impediments to this are too formidable at a particular institution at a particular time, at the very least there must be clear written communication and, whenever possible, sufficient dialogue and discussion to ensure productive activity.

Providing Decision and Implementation Support Tools

A final requirement for setting the stage for productive implementation decision making is having adequate decision support tools to model various options and to project and analyze significant data. Very often these tools are needed in the tactical phase before an implementation activity is selected. But many times they are also needed to shape the details of the implementation and, later, to assess outcomes. One implementation product is timely, accurate, and useful reporting of the results of implementation. Most implementation support information is internal and produced by the institutional research office or the planning and budget group. But more and more, institutions are looking to peer comparison data, national standard databases, benchmarking projects and surveys, and consultant-generated survey reviews to inform all phases of decision making. When there is more than one acceptable path to a goal, being able to weigh options with relevant data is critical.

The types of information usually needed include revenue projections;

resource allocation patterns; databases of major information points like enrollment, personnel, and faculty workload; capital project costs and pricing; and qualitative assessments and customer survey reviews. But having the data is not enough: it also needs to be accessible to those who need it. There needs to be the capacity to link databases and to manipulate and model "what if" options in shaping implementation activities. Institutional researchers and budget personnel often worry about protecting "their" data, but new, easy-to-use data warehouse and Web-interfaced tools make it possible to provide access in ways that can be specified to units and individuals without impact on larger, historical databases.

An institution may have an abundance of data, but such data may not be accessible. Creating useful information from the data requires a wide variety of tools. For higher education, where knowledge development is a primary business, providing full information and data-use tools to inform its own business decisions should be a high priority. Some of this data is strategic, for example, environmental scanning; some is tactical, for example, best practices; and some is implementation-related, for example, results of current activities.

IMPLEMENTATION: MANAGING CHANGE

People and organizations deal with change all the time. Programs change and evolve, students enroll and graduate, financial aid rules get rewritten, and state legislators shift funding priorities. Most organizations are prepared to manage change that is incremental and part of the normal course of doing business. But some changes are dramatic—a fire on a campus, making an all women's college coed, adding professional programs to a primarily liberal arts college, suddenly losing 20 percent of anticipated revenue. Sometimes institutions simply cope with dramatic change rather than seize it as an institutional opportunity. Although every institution has its own cycle for making small and large changes, preparing for or coping with dramatic changes requires special attention.

External Context for Managing Change

The context in which institutional change is being managed must also be taken into consideration. Some say the external changes higher education is experiencing now are different from past changes, describing the current forces as causing "tectonic shifts deeply under the ground on which American higher education stands[11]."

Shifting Economic Realities

Which ground is shifting? The first shift seems to be in the economic ground. The economy is characterized by robust global competition, expansion of multinational corporations, massive foreign investment, instantaneous global communication, growth in service and technology-related industries, reductions in defense-related industries, automation of manufacturing, and across all business sectors pressure for continuous improvement in quality and productivity. Some analysts have suggested that the change in the nature of work worldwide has destabilized both national autonomy and each individual's sense of security. These changes are directly affecting society's expectations of the necessary and appropriate role of higher education institutions in preparing people for this new economic world of identity and work. This should not be a surprise. In previous economic shifts, from agriculture to industry and from unitary to multicultural inclusion, there have been related shifts in the perceived role to be taken by higher education institutions. The question is whether the size and substance of this economic shift is greater than those experienced in the past. Many suggest it is a sea change.

There is no question that this shifting economic ground has already substantially affected the financing of higher education. There are several reasons for this: the cost of higher education is perceived by the public as growing out of proportion to any justifiable rationale; higher education is being seen increasingly as a private gain rather than a public good; payment for education is being recrafted to meet a perceived need for lifelong learning; policymakers wish to move to a higher education delivery system that responds to the competitive marketplace; and higher education is seen by political leaders as not adaptable, not serving long-range social needs, incapable of restructuring because of outmoded governance and vested faculty interests, and not competitive in its ability to prepare for the knowledge society.

Economic and competitive conditions have forced widespread re-engineering and downsizing across a broad range of private sector markets, industries, and enterprises. These actions in response to economic realities have often generated incredulity and impatience with higher education's sense of entitlement to regular increases in funding—public or through tuition increases—without dramatic restructuring. Some suggest that higher education will replace health care as the major economic re-engineering task of the 21st century.[12]

Public distress over the burgeoning cost of higher education at the same time the economy demands educated workers translates into pressure to maintain affordable access to the opportunities higher education provides.[13] Most knowledgeable analysts suggest that in the future the funding for the basic operations of higher education institutions will be less, and it will be targeted to institutions whose missions are clearly identified and supported—and whose successes can be demonstrated by outcome measures.

As higher education becomes more precious, expectation for its value and usefulness also become more salient. Consumer satisfaction is becoming a benchmark of good performance. Now as never before, the public distrust of many of society's institutions, particularly public ones, has created an environment that requires clear information about the return on any taxpayer investment. Driven by economic concerns, the public is demanding evidence that higher education can serve it well.

Shifting Social, Political, and Policy Realities

The second shift seems to be in the social, political, and policy ground. At the same time as new economic challenges for higher education emerge, the public has been increasingly critical of higher education for not doing well what it professes to do best: educate students to become informed citizens and productive members of an emerging, changing, global workforce. Institutions are perceived to graduate too many students who cannot read and write well, think critically and creatively, or adapt effectively to the rapid changes in the world of work. Faculties are perceived as being overly committed to individual research agendas and insufficiently attentive to the learning of their students. Administrative staff is perceived to be out of touch with the latest and most effective business practices.

In the last few decades, higher education visibly engaged in creating access to education for a broader range of students and in building first-class research enterprises. These were perceived to be in accordance with the national agenda, and higher education institutions were seen as effective partners in these public ventures. Although these goals may not yet be fully accomplished, the public now seems to be asking for new partnerships, but perhaps without real clarity on a shared national agenda.

Eighty-five percent of the workforce for the year 2010 is already at work in the year 2000. Many of these workers can expect to be displaced by vigorous international competition and the impact of emerging technologies. The public is not only asking colleges and universities to train the workforce of tomorrow, but also to help retrain displaced workers of tomorrow. It seems clear that higher education institutions must take some initiative in defining the new public partnership agenda and participating actively in it.

Public opinion polls are unambiguous with respect to recognition of the essential and critical role of higher education in creating the nation's economic, social, and cultural future. The public embraces the notion that Whitehead offers—education is the discipline for the adventure of life—but asks that the freshness and soundness of educational approaches be examined.[14] The "just trust us" maxim offered in the past will not do.

There is a profound concern that colleges and universities are not focusing on what society needs and expects for its citizens.[15] Those who assume debt to earn a degree demand assurances that the degree is relevant to the job market and will equip the graduate with competitive technological skills. More and more, other groups are providing training targeted to particular employment opportunities, offering alternatives to traditional degrees, and setting new benchmarks for evaluating learning outcomes. Higher education is no longer the only show in town.

New Technological Options

The third shift is not really in the ground but perhaps in cyberspace. Emerging technology is already changing the world of work, and it will change the way higher education fulfills its teaching role. The options available to students for accessing and processing information, developing skills, evaluating performance, and communicating without respect to time or distance will reshape the teaching and learning enterprise. Will the human dimensions of educational process disappear? No, but perhaps current pedagogy can be enriched, supplemented, improved, and transformed by the addition of technology. There is a new generation growing up with technology options to learning. Certainly higher education needs to be able to include and welcome them in the future.

The definition of the *campus* as the locus of instruction may change from a geographical location to a group of individuals connected through electronic networks—networks where one can see and hear—and perhaps touch. Certainly the definition of instructional resources is changing to include electronic media and global databases.

Information technology has the potential to rearrange not only the boundaries of disciplines but also the approaches to knowledge as discovery. As the world is impacted by this modality, the way higher education institutions do their teaching and research will change.

Internal Responses to External Forces

These are not minor changes: these are rumblings that could foreshadow an earthquake.[16] They have created dramatic change opportunities for higher education. The first wave of rumblings felt in the late 1980s and early 1990s has been characterized as being about costs and expenditures—administration and efficiency. Without question, in higher education there has been a rush to examine cost effectiveness, to streamline administrative services, to be more responsive on accountability issues.[17] Hardly any recent institutional planning has not taken into account a changed financial climate.

Crisis Opportunities

Many institutions report that, under fiscal pressure, they are often able to implement changes—close facilities, consolidate low-enrollment programs, inaugurate substantial fundraising initiatives—which they had long recognized as needed but were unable to accomplish. External pressures created the crisis that they were able to turn into institutional opportunity. Some rules of doing business are suspended in a crisis, which allows for alternative actions.

Transformational Opportunities

But the impacts of the far deeper rumblings about purpose and productivity, about learning outcomes, about the quality of research, about diversity and about connections, collaborations, and social engagement are receiving a slower response.[18] Perhaps because these rumblings challenge institutional mission and core strategic visions, they provoke anxiety and fear. These rumblings can affect structure, if not causing a crumbling, at least introducing cracks. Some institutions have opted for shoring up. Others have decided that may not be enough, but have begun to think of recreating themselves from the foundation up—a much more arduous process.

Managing Fear and Aspiration

Psychiatrists say that major changes—like the ones being suggested for higher education—are undertaken by human beings either motivated by fear or pulled by aspiration.[19] Either a current path becomes too painful to continue to pursue because of internal or external pressures or because it never results in the outcomes intended, or one is inspired to pursue another path that appears attractive and rich with possibilities for meeting newly identified needs.

Any major implementation activity that sets a major new direction for an institution, whether internally motivated or externally provoked, will necessarily generate high levels of fear and aspiration. Leaders have to manage these activities with deliberate change strategies in mind and these strategies need to be directed and matched to the "change stress levels" of the people in the organization. Creating too much worry and fear can be paralyzing, and encouraging too much imaginative dreaming that is actually unachievable can be debilitating. Using each reaction as a potential motivator to productive change is what is required. Each "culture" of the institution sees change differently and, therefore, has to be managed differently. It requires recognizing and achieving a healthy balance between fear and aspiration.

Change Strategies

The literature is rich with potentially effective change strategies, and most may seem like common sense approaches.[20] All of them deal with both process and productivity—how something must be done and by whom it needs to be done, and what must be accomplished and who has to know about it and will be affected by it. Knowing which strategy to use for a particular implementation task is key. Crisis opportunities require different strategies than aspirational stretching opportunities. Specific tasks may require specific approaches, for example, using an engineering or architectural consultant to assist in determining full costing on a construction project may be the most appropriate strategy for a large building project. It would not be the right approach for deciding on new learning outcomes standards that require faculty consensus. Making the match and also having the ability to use a broad array of strategies is required for successful implementation.

Some of the most common change management strategies follow.

Creating Task Forces. Given the collegial culture in higher education, this is a strategy often employed. A group is appointed, given a leader or asked to select a leader from the group, given a charge, a timeline, and a task, and asked to meet a deadline. Task forces can be very effective as an empowering strategy for employees and as a way to integrate differing perspectives. It is essential, however, that it be the right group, that they have all the information and expertise they need, that they understand the outcomes expected, that they know who else they must communicate with, and that the task can be accomplished in the time allotted. While this is an attractive approach for an environment that politically expects involvement in decisions, setting the parameters is often not done well in higher education and implementation task forces can take too long, be either "too conceptual"

or "too practical" if the group mix is not right, not consider key resource requirements, or not take into account internal or external realities. Task forces work best
when the right group is put together, know what they are to do, and have the
resources they need to work on the issue. Task forces seem well matched to curriculum reform implementation activities, major resource allocation shifts, service
improvement projects, and other similar tasks. They are usually not a good choice
for very practical and expertise-specific assignments like redesigning space, technology projects, or responding to demanding crisis issues.

Critical Mass Decision Making. Some major transformative changes require
large-scale participation and agreement in order to be successful. Broad affirma-
tion of a critical implementation direction is required before other sub-tasks can
get underway. Some institutions have very successfully mastered putting this
"whole-systems thinking" approach into practice with managed town meeting
style activities.[21] It is essential that these be well organized, professionally facilitated, time sensitive, and focused on broad implementation directions. Decisions
about how to get consensus, measure buy-in, and communicate follow-up to the
participants need to be made before the process begins.

Consultants. Sometimes an outsider is needed to introduce new perspectives or
broach initially unpopular ideas. Consultants offer the opportunity to open up the
discussion of options in implementation and can bring expertise and best-practice
information from other related settings. When a topic or activity has the potential
for setting off "hot spots," it can be very useful to have the outsider be the
flashpoint and even the inititiator of the most radical view, which can later be
adjusted and modified internally. The large external rumblings referred to above
also indicate that linking with others—businesses, other institutions, legislative
bodies, and so on—can offer the opportunity to break down campus insularity and
expand the possibilities for support for important implementation activities. Let-
ting others into the institution's business can have both risks and benefits. Again,
matching the strategy to the task is key.

Outsourcing. Some implementation tasks may best be done by others outside the
institution. Many higher education institutions are like cities: they deliver mail,
sell things, provide food services, run sports and entertainment facilities, provide
housing and hotels, run bookstores, and maintain streets and facilities. None of
these are the primary business of higher education. Some institutions are deciding
that others with more expertise should perhaps run these operations in order to
save money or improve services. As a change management strategy, outsourcing

may be a viable option, but coming to the decision is usually highly political and must take into consideration the impact on current employees and costs. Outsourcing is discussed in more detail as it applies to the subject matter of the individual chapters in this volume.

TQM and/or Re-engineering Approaches. While these two approaches share the goal of improving responsiveness and effectiveness of services to the various "customers" of an enterprise, they have two very different dynamics as change strategies. Total Quality Management strategies focus on empowering employees and creating teams to make effective implementation decisions. An institution must be sure that it wants to delegate decision making in this way because giving the team the power and task and then vetoing the outcomes will be counterproductive. Re-engineering approaches focus on process redesign or structural changes in the way institutions do business. Both have excellent potential relative to creating cross-boundary teams as discussed earlier. Both approaches require significant investment of time and effort, as well as training and expertise for the leaders and members of the various work teams. Both require buy-in from the top because those who become involved need to know that the approaches and tools learned will be sustained over time. Re-engineering approaches seem to have been embraced more widely than TQM initiatives in higher education.[22]

Creating Internal Expertise or "Champions of Change." Another strategy that is often adopted is creating a cadre of "champions of change." This is often the process used when the implementation tasks are pushing toward stretch goals or new initiatives. Empowering leaders whose time is specifically dedicated to the implementation tasks, and giving them full authority to drive a project to completion has worked very well for activities that are being introduced for the first time. Technology implementations, new academic programs, fundraising drives, and revenue enhancement initiatives are examples of activities that work well with this model.

This approach is usually combined with a professional developmental strategy in institutions where new leaders are trained and developed through regular or special professional development programs, and where skill gaps are filled for a broad array of employees through regular opportunities for improvement and experimentation. Creating a culture where individuals feel the institution will support their efforts to try new things with conceptual and practical skill training enhances the ability of the champions of change to get projects supported across the institution. This is especially important when implementation efforts require the engagement and support of both middle managers and the front line staff.

Deciding which of these or other available change strategies to adopt is probably best informed by assessing whether this is to be a short-term change or one that is critical to institutionalize. Changes that are meant to last need to be looked at in two important dimensions—compatibility and profitability.[23] The first, compatibility, describes the degree to which norms, goals, and values of the change are congruent with those of the institution. If compatibility is low, there must be much more investment in a major transformational strategy technique like critical mass meetings to ensure that next steps will lead to lasting change. If the compatibility is high, then many strategic approaches will work. The second dimension, profitability, describes the extent to which individuals or organizational units are motivated to adopt and maintain the change. It describes the extent to which people perceive the change as beneficial. If the proposed implementation activity is seen as having value to those affected, again, many different change management strategies will work. If it is initially perceived as having no real benefit, strategies addressing that factor will be necessary.[24]

IMPLEMENTATION TASKS

Having adopted effective change management strategies, the institution has important implementation tasks to undertake for every specific project. The following sections describe these tasks.

Costing and Pricing

After clarifying the goals and scope of a project, the first step in implementation is the adoption of an appropriate approach to costing and pricing to translate ideas and programs into operating and capital budgets.

Decisions regarding which of several costing approaches to use—such as full, variable, or standard costing—are usually determined as tactical considerations. For example, strictly speaking, "full costing" means that all costs are considered, direct and indirect, including depreciation. To the extent that operating and capital budgets incorporate full-costing principles, they raise revenue requirements. Conversely, to the extent they relax their full-costing stance, revenue requirements will be reduced. Thus, if in the long run full costing is applied to project, activity, and program costing, but not to budgeting and long-range planning, there is a fundamental policy discrepancy. Such inconsistency could damage an institution's long-term financial condition.

Reporting of cost data provides essential information for evaluating the financial performance of management and the institution. The critical analysis of information about costs is essential in determining how efficiently financial, human, and material resources are being deployed. Cost information is central to pricing, sound budget planning, formulating effective financial controls and policies, and carrying out the trusteeship function of the governing board. It is also essential to long-range financial and program planning.

Because of the complexity and frequent misunderstanding of costing and its effects, those charged with budgetary and resource allocation responsibilities should be well-informed about costing principles in both theory and practice and should be able to communicate these principles to others in implementation working groups.

Pricing in higher education must be seen in a broad context. Colleges and universities depend consistently on non-price-based revenues. In addition, they are engaged in a variety of pricing situations because of the multiple services they render. In this sense, higher education institutions resemble multiproduct or multiservice firms in the for-profit environment. Institutions need to use appropriate cost indices for their various functions and need to present their financial data with appropriate inflationary adjustments identified and included. (For a full discussion of this subject, see chapter 4, Budgeting.)

Operational and Capital Budgeting

Operational budgeting is one of the tools management uses to shape the institution and move it toward its goals. It refers to the budgets set for day-to-day expenditures and revenues, as opposed to those for capital and other longer-term expenditures and inflows. Operational budgeting focuses on the control of financial resources and the evaluation of financial performance. Operational budgets are made by calculating and ratifying expectations for revenues and expenditures. Because college and university personnel set policies and make daily decisions that bring in revenues and cause expenditures, the budget can be used as a mechanism to manage these expectations. In this way administrators know in advance the institution's realistic projection of revenues and expenditure limits.

Like operational budgeting, capital budgeting is also a planning and control process, but is concerned with planning for expenditures too large and too irregular to be easily made part of the operational budgeting process. The size and unusual nature of the activities being budgeted require greater involvement of the governing board than does the operating budget. The activities involved are complex, last longer than a single fiscal year, and commonly require specialized assistance.

Institutions have different budget design systems and different budgeting processes. No matter what style of budgeting an institution selects, the process must be managed. The institutional budget requires assumptions, priorities, and the context of a long-range view of the institution. Few institutions can proceed into budgeting without prescribed assumptions about inflation and energy costs, priority decisions about salary and tuition increases, priority decisions about program additions, and a financial projection mode.

A good system relies on firm budget decision-making responsibilities carefully apportioned to administrators, who keep the system responsive to the ideas of all those affected by budgets. (For a full discussion of this subject, see chapter 4, Budgeting.)

Key Appointments

Implementation activities are certainly affected by leadership changes. The most important implementation planning decisions made in a college or university are those involving the selection of leaders—the president or chancellor and key deans and vice presidents, as well as senior functional area leaders. An opportunity to select a leader is an opportunity to assess what critical skills are needed at the time. If an institution has an active strategic plan, it will look to match its leadership to the direction it is pursuing. If it needs to develop a plan, it will look to attract a leader who has the necessary skills to accomplish that task. An institution should regard these appointment processes not just as formalistic searches, but as planning opportunities. Search committees should consider the nature and character of the activity for which they are seeking a leader, how the activity should develop, the environment in which it operates, and its challenges and opportunities. Then they can seek the best person to help the institution move in the desired direction. Talking with candidates is an invaluable opportunity for insiders to learn how the institution and its programs are viewed from outside and how leaders in the field would bring about needed changes.

Major Academic Program Changes

The start-up, significant reorientation, consolidation, or phase-out of an academic program represents a multiyear commitment and requires special attention.

For a new program, for example, an in-house team, often with help from consultants or visiting faculty, identifies the focus of the program and the specific areas and degrees of expertise required. Approvals must be sought from within the institution and sometimes from external agencies. Preliminary capital and operating budgets must be developed and approved. An initial core faculty must be appointed. These new faculty will proceed to design the curricula and clarify with the admissions office the qualifications of students to be sought. Admissions in turn will identify a recruiting strategy; the academic department or school will provide classrooms, labs, equipment, and other supporting resources, and so on. The entire process may take six months or three or four years before the first students are admitted, and it may be five or ten years before the program is operating at full strength.

To end a program or perhaps consolidate and refocus is no less a challenging activity. Significant tasks include making sure that students in programs that are ending have completed their work, that faculty who are tenured are realigned in areas appropriate to their expertise, that department support staff are either outplaced or reassigned, and that records, documents, and instructional resources are realigned. Getting agreement on program realignments or termination is very difficult in a collegial setting, where there is often heavy investment in current initiatives. Faculty will usually exercise their governance rights strongly on these programmatic issues, but since their deliberations and recommendations are advisory, the leader ultimately will be required to make the difficult political decision.

Facilities Planning and Construction

Facility implementation projects also follow a complex course. Once a decision is made to construct or renovate a facility, a building program must be developed with prospective users, a capital budget must be developed, operating costs identified, and a designer selected. As the design moves forward, improved cost estimates and bid documents must be prepared, the construction firm must be selected, and work must begin. Although the phases of facilities planning and construction are relatively clear, a set of institutional decisions is required at each stage. (For a full discussion of the subject, see chapter 13, Facilities Management.)

Information Technology

While most information technology changes in the past have been incremental, such as replacement of a computer with a more high-powered one to accomplish the same work, the current rapid pace of technology change and the embedding of technology features in the way institutions are carrying out instruction and regular business make decisions about new information technology complex. Having sufficient expertise and being able to communicate it effectively to nontechnological decision makers is key. Decisions to centralize or decentralize responsibility for data collection and management have major implications for the integrity of this information and the effectiveness with which it can be used. Centralization versus decentralization issues also must be addressed (and the resulting decision implemented) with regard to system maintenance and development. Other implementation issues are the necessity of doing process re-engineering first and of running old and new systems in parallel before relying on the new one. Campus networking systems, major software packages, and operating cost implications will affect budgets over several years. (For a full discussion of this subject, see chapter 7, Information Technology and Services.)

Capital Campaigns

Many colleges and universities seek substantial donations from the private sector for capital needs such as buildings or endowment and for support of current operations. The planning for a capital campaign is often as complex as that involved in a new academic program or construction project. The first step is the development of a list of needs; these needs often arise directly from the gaps between the strategic vision and current reality. Prospective sources of support must be identified and their levels of interest and giving potential assessed. A campaign strategy must be developed, matching need with potential sources. The institution will likely need staff or an external consultant to conduct research and develop campaign literature.

Resource Development

The development and maximization of institutional resources is an especially significant challenge in the current context but is always an ongoing challenge. At most institutions, the traditional sources of revenue include tuition and fees, endowment income, charitable gifts, state appropriations, sponsored research, and auxiliary enterprise income. However, as many of these traditional revenue sources reach their limits, colleges and universities have undertaken a variety of activities designed to augment existing revenue streams. Often called revenue enhancement initiatives, these programs vary widely and should be carefully assessed before being undertaken. Areas such as mission compatibility, legal liabilities, investment requirements, and taxes on unrelated business income must be fully considered before launching any revenue enhancement activity. Revenue enhancement, by its very nature, requires institutional creativity and entrepreneurship. It involves linking institutional assets and capabilities to the needs of a particular market.

The Need for Revenue Enhancing Programs

As revenues become constrained and costs continue to rise, many institutions need enhanced resources. Virtually every college and university faces pressure on its traditional revenue sources. Demographic changes have caused enrollment declines at many institutions, leading to losses of tuition and fees, and room and board revenue. Increased attention to the cost of higher education will mean that future tuition growth will be slower than in the past, limiting the sources of revenue. Most colleges and universities lack endowments of sufficient size to support their programs during times of decreasing demand and increasing tuition price sensitivity. Tax law changes and economic conditions can negatively affect trends in charitable giving. Market conditions and stringent spending rules can limit the income available from endowment. Few institutions have large enough unrestricted cash reserves to meet emergency needs.

While the downward pressure on revenue increases, institutions also face upward pressure on their cost structures. Salaries, wages, benefits, goods and services, and capital needs are increasing at rates higher than inflation and the available revenues of most colleges and universities. The financial imbalance caused by these revenue and cost pressures requires that institutions seek ways of curtailing costs as well as finding new sources of revenue, or achieving some combination of both.

Assessing Potential for Revenue Enhancement

Colleges and universities should systematically review their assets, programs, and operations to assess their potential for generating supplemental revenue. In many cases, institutional assets offer opportunities to generate revenue. Some examples of revenue enhancement activities include:

- real estate development in the form of housing, shopping centers, hotels, and research and development parks;
- leasing dormitory and classroom space during the summer months for seminars and conferences;
- technology patenting and licensing programs in which technology

developed by campus researchers is transferred to the corporate world, providing a financial benefit to the researcher and the institution;

- swimming and tennis clubs for alumni and community members;

- licensing of institutional logos and emblems to generate income on the sales of clothing and memorabilia;

- sales of software developed for academic or administrative purposes;

- contract operation of another institution's bookstore or dining service;

- day-care centers and nursery school programs; and

- "dinner theaters," which combine the programs of the theater arts and food service departments.

Some activities are large and obvious, such as real estate development and summer conference programs, while others are more subtle. Less obvious revenue enhancement activities include self-operation of campus vending machines rather than relying on an outside contractor, opening small snack stands in heavily utilized student areas, or charging individuals from the local community for use of the institution's athletic facilities. These latter activities may seem small, but they can mean that two or three additional personal computers can be obtained for the student computer center or that an extra scholarship can be provided to a student.

Institutional Assets for Revenue Enhancement

The process of identifying and developing appropriate areas of revenue enhancement varies with the institution's circumstances. The location, culture, size, and mission of an institution, as well as its willingness to assume risk, have a direct effect on the range and depth of revenue enhancement opportunities. When considering revenue enhancement programs, a useful starting point is to survey the institution's asset base. The term "asset" is used broadly to include not only financial assets but also the physical, programmatic, reputational, and intellectual assets of the institution. In the early stages of considering a revenue enhancement program, it is not useful to assess financial, legal, operational, or mission risk; rather, unconstrained thinking is necessary to foster creativity in assessing institutional assets. In terms of asset categorization, it may be useful to think along the following lines.

Financial assets include cash and endowments that should be managed in the best long-term interests of the institution. Given the scarcity of financial resources for most institutions, revenue enhancement in this area should attempt to maximize the return on cash and endowments within prudent limits of risk. (See chapter 8, Treasury Management, and chapter 9, Endowment Management.)

Physical assets are represented by land, buildings, and equipment.

Reputational assets are the institution's image as perceived by the outside world in terms of its history, its academic stature, and its distinction in related fields such as research, publishing, and athletics.

Intellectual assets represent the quality of faculty and students and the intellectual property developed through faculty research and discoveries, particularly in scientific areas.

It is useful to survey these institutional assets for revenue enhancement opportunities, but decision makers should remember that many opportunities span several categories. A thorough asset review will create questions and opportunities. Each opportunity must be systematically evaluated in terms of practicality and risk.

It is also useful to consider whether there are joint venture opportunities to be explored that draw on the assets of other organizations. Some institutions have explored ways to maximize service provider relationships with current vendors, whether outsourcing completely or trying some forms of blended management. There may also be the possibility to enhance consortia arrangements with other institutions, for example, interlibrary sharing programs or interinstitutional facilities use. The potential for leasing arrangements for technology enhancements or facilities done through public/private arrangements or with other institutions is another way to potentially enhance available revenue. The point is: rather than simply thinking only about one's own assets, there may be some utility in thinking more broadly, to include other organizations.

Opportunities, Risks, and Other Considerations

An institution should not undertake revenue enhancement activities lightly. A number of financial, legal, and operational risks are associated with any new venture. Most important, there should be clear agreement at the senior management and board levels that such activities are in the best interests of the college or university. An activity that seems to be an obvious and simple opportunity to supplement revenues may have long-term implications, and there could be the taxation consequences of unrelated business income.

When considering a potential revenue-enhancing activity, decision makers should ask a variety of questions, several of which concern *mission*. How compatible is the proposed activity with the mission of the institution? Will the proposed venture compromise or dilute the primary mission? Will it change or conflict with the value system of the institution? Are more mission-centered opportunities being missed? Will it commercialize the institution in an unacceptable manner? Will it affect town-gown relations?

Another set of issues concerns *management* capability. Does the institution have the management capabilities and capacity to manage the activity? What management skills are required and do they currently reside in the institution? If not, from where will those skills come? If they do exist in the institution, do individuals have the time to manage the activity? Will their attention be diverted from their primary responsibilities? Has a market assessment been conducted? What is the demand for the service? Who requires the service? What advertising and promotion will be required to reach these individuals? Is the demand sustained or will it change in the future? Who are the competitors for that same market?

Obviously, there will be a set of *financial considerations*. Are sound business and financial plans in place? What are the capital investment requirements in terms of facilities, information systems, equipment inventory, and working capital? What are the ongoing operating costs in terms of salaries, wages, benefits, supplies, utilities, and others? Has the indirect cost impact on institutional support areas been determined and included as a cost? Has a realistic three- to five-year income and expense statement, including monthly cash flow projections, been prepared? What is the source of start-up capital? What is the pricing strategy? What is the return on investment? How long is the payback period?

There will also need to be some *risk management* assessment. What is the institution's risk posture? If the venture is not successful, how will financial losses be handled? Given a "worst-case scenario," what effect will that financial loss have on the institution? Will the quality of the activity or service be commensurate with the quality of the institution? Will poor service quality erode the image of the institution? Will the proposed endeavor compete with local merchants and businesses? How will they react? Are they donors to the institution? How strong is the institution's relationship with the local community? Will the proposed activity jeopardize this relationship? Are there any federal, state, or local legal or regulatory issues that prohibit or constrain the institution from undertaking the activity? Is the institution prepared to pay taxes on unrelated business income (depending upon the activity)? Has an opinion been obtained on whether the activity is related or unrelated to the primary mission of the institution? Have liability issues been adequately considered? Will existing insurance coverage be adequate for this activity? What additional provisions should the college or university make? What safety and security issues need to be considered? Can existing services support the new venture?

And finally, there will be facilities and maintenance issues. Has facility wear and tear been considered? Will sufficient facility downtime be available to allow maintenance crews to prepare the facility for the coming academic year? This question is most appropriate for summer utilization of classrooms and residence halls.

Although some of the questions may not pertain to a particular venture, all should be asked and answered in evaluating any revenue enhancement activity. Criteria should be established to define institutionally appropriate and inappropriate activities and then used in systematically reviewing the opportunities available to the institution. It may be prudent for an institution to retain external business advisors to help it assess the management skills and capabilities required to operate any new venture. Many financially pressed colleges and universities may be tempted to exploit near-term revenue enhancement activities. However, these opportunities must be carefully balanced against the long-term goals, values, and viability of the institution.

OUTCOMES ASSESSMENT

Outcomes, the consequences of the teaching, research, or public service experience at an academic institution, are ultimately measured against the stated and distinct goals of that institution. What did the plan say would happen and did it happen? Many current indicators—typically graduation and retention rates, knowledge gained, or changes in attitudes and behaviors—are outcomes measures. But other outcomes, such as job performance after graduation or a student's contribution to community and society, await the development of more appropriate contextual and analytical approaches.

Many significant questions can be addressed through outcomes assessment. But institutions seriously thinking about conducting assessment activities must ask themselves: What is the purpose of the assessment? (Why are assessment activities being designed?) What is the level of assessment? (Who is to be assessed?) What is to be assessed? This is another "form follows function" issue.

There is no question that although higher education regularly evaluates itself in many ways—mostly on inputs—more successful outcomes measures are necessary both to respond to public questioning and to help shape future planning directions. It is necessary to have better data to know whether a particular implementation task to accomplish a stated goal was successful. If not, why not? Outcomes assessment is clearly the kind of accountability standard that boards, legislators, and the public insist are necessary to measure higher education's ultimate educational, knowledge development, and civic contribution and value.

Program evaluation via outcomes assessment of student learning can have both formative (program improvement) and summative (accountability) functions. How the balance is struck between those functions impacts the degree of centralization of assessment practices and the types of assessment activities that are carried out. On some campuses, a central assessment office participates in data collection and reporting (perhaps with a commitment of confidentiality to the department or program), while on others, outcomes assessment is decentralized to the program level, and departments and programs may not even be required to report the results of their assessment activities. Questions of the purposes of assessment, who carries out the assessment activities, who owns the data, and who is the audience for assessment results are key to implementing an outcomes assessment program.

Emerging Directions

Outcomes assessment rose in prominence in the mid-1980s, primarily because of the actions of state governments and accrediting authorities. Reports published in 1984 and 1985 called for higher education institutions to embark on local programs for assessing student learning as a guide for program improvement and planning. In 1986, more reports called for outcomes assessment to provide greater accountability in higher education, ensuring "consumer protection" to potential students regarding collegiate claims of academic effectiveness and attempting to steer state-level resource allocation processes toward the programs and institutions deemed most "effective."

About two-thirds of the 50 states require public higher education institutions to engage in some form of outcomes assessment. But state-level approaches to assessment vary widely.[25] A few states mandate common testing across institutions; the majority require institutions to develop their own outcomes assessment approach, consistent with their instructional missions and student clientele. Regional accrediting bodies are increasingly requiring evidence about institutional assessment strategies and student learning outcomes.

Emerging practice in outcomes assessment tends to be both faculty centered and highly decentralized because the focus is on learning outcomes. The hallmarks of successful initiatives seem to be a clearly articulated purpose for outcomes assessment, visible and active leadership, and sufficient time for and attention to faculty participation.[26] This also means that outcomes assessment information is being used more at the local unit or department level than institutionwide. Individual departmental approaches to data gathering, interpretation, and use tend to be difficult to compare across organizational units. Recently, again, through external pressures, institutionwide needs for outcomes assessment information have begun to surface and be addressed.

Significant questions that have surfaced as the potential focus of future institutional assessment efforts include: Who applies to and enrolls in the college or university and how well prepared are these students? What do students learn? What do students value? Who is dropping out? What is the quality of undergraduate teaching? What is the quality of the curriculum? How effective is the advising students receive? How do students feel about their undergraduate experiences? How effective are student support services? What happens to students after they graduate?

The greatest institutional benefit of outcomes assessment certainly comes from the process itself and the issues it generates. By its nature, outcomes assessment mandates a clearly stated goal: the design of performance measures requires precisely stated objectives. It also raises critical issues of interdependency and connectedness that are frequently overlooked in the typical department-centered organizational structure of a college or university. Outcomes assessment is suggesting new institutional accountability measures and linkages.

Assessment: Organization of the Function

There is no clear consensus regarding the proper organizational location of the assessment function. One approach involves creating a freestanding function directed and staffed by professionals. But this type of office may potentially duplicate existing student testing, academic planning, or institutional research operations. A more common solution is to create an institutional oversight committee to serve as liaison with these various functions. Assessment is often undertaken by a subcommittee of a curriculum or academic program review committee. Because of this approach, however, the organizational home for the assessment function almost invariably has been in academic affairs.

Primary considerations in organizing the assessment function tend to be available resources, institutional culture, and links to decision making. Establishing assessment as an entity of the institutional research function may provide enhanced external and internal visibility. However, available resources may dictate that assessment is best handled through existing functions, because many "assessment" activities, such as student alumni surveys, placement testing, or employer follow-up are already in place on most campuses. A coordinated approach, moreover, may also be most consistent with institutional culture—particularly if existing academic planning and institutional research offices are functioning well and enjoy high credibility. The most important long-term organizational consideration in assessment is ensuring that it is clearly linked to strategic, tactical, and implementation decision making.

Student Assessment Surveys

Assessment efforts do require a redirection of emphasis in terms of institutional data collection from resource allocation and utilization to attainment of educational outcomes. Among the common types of student assessment surveys most often conducted by persons in centralized offices of institutional research or by decentralized student affairs research offices are follow-up surveys of nonreturning students, surveys of student perceptions of the college environment, and surveys designed to assess student satisfaction with their academic majors, institutions, and student services.

Many surveys are undertaken to discover answers to current issues, whatever they may be. While the ability to develop responses to current issues is important, a well-conceived program of studies conducted systematically over a long period is more likely to yield significant long-term benefits. In this regard, comprehensive outlines of areas under consideration for survey will become valuable because they will encourage awareness of the totality of assessment efforts as well as communication and coordination across a number of organizational units.

Current Tools for Outcomes Assessment

A comprehensive campus assessment plan uses a combination of techniques or tools. Relying upon assessment results based on a single technique has been shown to be too limiting and ultimately not effective in terms of pointing out potential areas for improvement or enhancement. Most practitioners attempt to bring together results drawn from widely different approaches before developing any meaningful policy implications. Sources of information useful for assessment may already be present on many college and university campuses. Examples include existing student surveys, accreditation self-study reports (both institutional and special program accreditation), results of program reviews and local departmental follow-up studies, alumni and placement studies, and results from placement testing, certification/licensure, and graduate school admissions testing. A good first step when undertaking institutional assessment is to assemble the existing sources, evaluate their strengths and weaknesses, and determine what kind of information is missing in the scope of a comprehensive design. A number of institutions have developed comprehensive longitudinal data files on student outcomes that can serve as the basis for research on marketing, attrition, program evaluation, and other areas.

Current tools widely used in outcomes assessment generally fall into one of four broad categories:

Standardized Tests. A range of standardized tests that attempt to assess the outcomes of general education and student majors is offered by organizations such as the Educational Testing Service and the American College Testing Service. The primary advantage of these instruments is that they have high reliability, high external credibility, and ready availability, and that they provide access to comparative results among institutions. The primary disadvantages include cost, low student motivation to perform well on examinations that do not directly affect them, and lack of congruence between test coverage and what is taught.

Faculty-Developed Techniques. A major alternative to standardized examinations is the range of specific techniques developed by faculty. These can vary from specially designed comprehensive techniques to "course-embedded" techniques that use existing course papers and final examinations to review specific course-based knowledge and fundamental intellectual achievement. These techniques are tailored to the institution's particular curriculum, result in far more useful and detailed information than do standardized alternatives, and, because of their authenticity, have high internal credibility with the faculty. However, their intellectual complexity and political sensitivity mean that some of these techniques may require a long time and, possibly, a high cost to develop; they do not lend themselves to comparative information; and they can fail to achieve external credibility. On the other hand, faculty can also use data on performance on projects, internships, culminating experiences, and other learning activities; these may be the most valuable assessment tools available to departments and programs. (This is an example of collecting information that is already being gathered for another purpose (to assign a grade to each student) and using it to determine program strengths and weaknesses.

Surveys. A third approach—generally used to supplement both standardized and faculty-developed tests—is the use of student surveys and other self-reporting techniques. In addition to the institution's own surveys, nationally administered surveys that provide comparative data are available. Generally, surveys are administered to entering students, currently enrolled students, graduating seniors or other program completers, and alumni. The surveys embrace student goals and goal fulfillment, evaluate the services provided and the campus environment, and entail a range of self-reported cognitive and attitudinal outcomes. Such surveys often are administered as part of a systematic longitudinal study design. Many kinds of outcomes can be investigated with the same instrument. Moreover, surveys allow considerable administrative flexibility, and they can be conducted at generally low cost. However, there is high probability of incomplete (and therefore biased) responses and some difficulty interpreting and believing self-reported information.

Student Records. The final approach relies on existing sources of student information, assembled from a range of campus offices and services. Primary sources include registration records, grades, course evaluation data, library utilization statistics, and participation statistics drawn from such services or activities as learning assistance centers, advisement centers, student clubs and organizations, and campus cultural events. Though indirect, these statistics can be used to establish patterns of typical student experience that can account for obtained outcomes. For example, studies have been conducted that determine the relationships between patterns of courses completed and measures of student academic success.

Using Assessment Information

Information on learning outcomes provides departmental and program faculty with feedback on program functioning so that they can make appropriate changes. Other outcomes information supplies external constituencies, such as state governments, accrediting agencies, and potential "customers," with accountability information, and generates information on program strengths and weaknesses for the institution's academic planning and decision making. Although the full benefit of more coordinated institutionwide assessment information is not yet known, it is anticipated to have value for specific internal and externally responsive change management initiatives. Three current uses of assessment information follow.

Academic Planning and Policy Making

Outcomes information is being applied to determine appropriate placement and prerequisite policies (course sequences), clarifying the effects of admissions and academic good-standing policies, and determining the appropriateness of current curriculum and degree requirements. Groups that use these results include campus or school curriculum committees, academic councils, and faculty senates or similar governance bodies.

Academic Program Review

Formal program review processes are also a natural destination for assessment information. Program reviews typically include information on such indicators as employment placement rates, graduate school and/or transfer rates, passing rates on certification and licensure examinations, and other easily gathered statistical indicators. For in-depth periodic reviews, more detailed information drawn from cognitive assessment, current student and alumni surveys, and course-taking behaviors are typically included. Outcomes results of this kind are increasingly used with more traditional information about program goals, resources, and activity levels to determine priorities for program expansion or investment.

Budgeting and Resource Allocation

Outcomes information has directly entered into institutional resource allocation. Under "performance funding" alternatives, results in excess of standard or expectations are rewarded according to an established performance schedule. More commonly, this kind of information is used to identify areas of particular need to direct targeted investment. In both cases, relatively modest marginal reallocations are usually involved, but generally no more than 5 to 7 percent of base.

Decision makers should treat outcomes information with proper caution, however. If information is used as the sole basis for "high stakes" decisions, for example, as the primary basis for program discontinuance or to justify substantial reallocations, program managers may focus their efforts on achieving the best performance indicator scores rather than on improving the program being measured. At the same time, if no visible consequences are associated with results, faculty and academic administrators may become reluctant to collect and take performance indicators seriously.

Currently, organizational deficiencies, such as lack of access to outcomes information, lack of appropriate organizational frameworks or structures for reviewing the results of assessment activities, minimal incentives for using information, and lack of linkages between those who develop, manage, and use information, negatively affect the impact of assessment efforts. Technical factors that inhibit the use of information include unnecessarily lengthy reports, reports that are driven by data rather than real issues, lack of data integrity, unclear data, and lack of timely delivery of data and assistance in interpreting data to users.

Self and Peer Evaluation

Colleges and universities also engage in a wide range of evaluation activities for purposes of external accountability or as a part of internal planning and decision processes. Among the most common are accreditation (both institutional and program-specific), program review, and support-unit evaluations. Peer comparison performed within federal antitrust guidelines also plays a role in many types of institutional decisions. Among the most prominent are setting faculty and staff salaries and determining the program mix and curriculum coverage.

Institutional evaluation activities differ in three ways.

- *Level of Analysis:* Some evaluations are institutionwide, for example, institutional self-study undertaken for purposes of reaccreditation, and some are focused on specific units, for example, academic program review.

- *Role of External Bodies:* Evaluations may be undertaken at the discretion of the institution or may be required by external bodies, such as state governing authorities and regional or professional accrediting bodies.

- *Role of Standards and Peer Comparisons:* Some evaluation processes involve only self-study; others consist of a comparative assessment of performance against an established standard or against the historical performance of units of like type.

These three dimensions embrace a wide range of often-overlapping evaluation processes.

The Concept of Institutional Effectiveness

The concept of institutional effectiveness emphasizes the performance of the total institution in relation to the institution's mission and goals. It encompasses the strategic aspects of enrollment management, student outcomes assessment, and assessment for accountability. Because the concept of institutional effectiveness may include a number of elements, institutional leaders are responsible for identifying the meaning of "effectiveness" in the institution.

Institutional effectiveness criteria require an institution to state its goals (strategic phase), develop methods by which the achievement of its goals may be evaluated (assessment phase), and demonstrate that the information developed (in the implementation phase) is utilized in the planning process (strategic and tactical phases). Planning and evaluation are not merely acknowledged but are actually implemented at all levels of an institution. The primary focus is not only on institutional resources and processes but also on the results of those processes and the use of evaluation results for institutional improvement.

Regional Accreditation

Virtually all public and independent colleges and universities engage in a regular reaccreditation process in association with regional accrediting bodies. Typically, the process occurs once every five to 10 years and involves an extensive self-study by the institution, followed by a site visit by a team drawn from peer institutions. Although "standards" are used, the majority are process standards; for the most part, institutions are judges against their own mission and clientele. Because of its periodic nature, self-study is usually organized as an ad hoc activity coordinated by a specially created institutionwide committee and supported by such offices as institutional research, academic planning, and registration and records.

In most cases, institutions "reinvent" the reaccreditation process each time it occurs, often at the price of temporary upheaval and disorganization. Because of its comprehensive nature, institutional accreditation provides a rare opportunity to review, reorganize, or establish an effective institutional planning process. When undertaking a self-study, administrators should fully document the ways in which data are collected and compiled.

It may be helpful to maintain a subset of data on an ongoing basis as a planning data set for future use. Careful attention to self-study as a "rehearsal" for establishing a formal institutional planning and evaluation function can increase effectiveness. At the same time, it makes the reaccreditation process easier to accomplish the next time it occurs. Institutional self-study committees can sometimes be the basis for institutional planning committees (and also for financial credit reviews), because they are already familiar with institutionwide issues.

Special Program Accreditation

The Council for Postsecondary Accreditation recognizes more than 50 professional and programmatic accreditation bodies in fields as diverse as nursing, engineering, and business. Each accreditation body attempts to stimulate and ensure the quality of programs within its discipline or professional domain by undertaking periodic reviews of institutional programs that wish to remain accredited.

Processes used in special program accreditation vary greatly, but virtually all involve a self-study followed by a site visit. Preparation for both is a department or unit responsibility—supported, if appropriate, by institutionwide offices that provide necessary data. Although it is not as comprehensive as the institutional accreditation process, program-level accreditation is often far more prescriptive. The process may involve the application of detailed external standards for curriculum, resources invested, and the program's organization and governance. Furthermore, program accreditation reviews can recur as often as annually. It is not unusual for a large institution to be engaged in several accreditation studies each year.

Special or professional program accreditation may raise important strategic questions for an institution. On the one hand, accreditation may enhance a program's attractiveness and credibility. On the other, the requirements set by external bodies may not reflect the institution's historic mission or match the curricular and instructional attributes that are most appropriate for the institution's primary clientele. Lest program accreditation become an end in itself, institutions must take care not to abrogate their responsibility to set appropriate programmatic priorities; each program should fit the needs and plans of the institution as a whole.

Academic Program Reviews

Many independent colleges and universities engage in formal, periodic internal reviews of their academic programs. Many public systems of higher education require formal statewide reviews. When formally established, academic program reviews are usually periodic; all programs must undergo review on a rotating basis on a five- to seven-year cycle. Generally, the review process resembles that of program accreditation; it involves a self-study by program faculty, a statistical profile of the department, and a collective determination of the program's strengths and weaknesses. In many cases, the review involves a site visit by "peer reviewers," who are usually faculty drawn from the same discipline at other institutions. The review covers such factors as student demand, curriculum, faculty quality and productivity, resources, and program outcomes. Review results are communicated to the central administration or to an institutionwide program review committee and are used to determine future program priorities.

Academic program reviews commonly serve as the basis for reallocation decisions and processes. They may be part of an institutional self-study in conjunction with state-level program reviews, part of externally inspired program-level accreditation reviews, or part of internal reallocation or retrenchment processes. Information developed by institutional research may serve as a foundation for school or departmental planning and program reviews.

Major issues involved in academic program review center on the degree to which results are tied to decision making. A common complaint is that many results are "paper processes," involving considerable investment to produce but yielding little payoff for program faculty. Like all internal planning and evaluation processes, program review involves an implicit bargain between those who administer the process and those who participate: both must agree to be broadly bound by the results in subsequent decision making. At the same time, the processes themselves should be thoroughly and regularly reviewed. If they are not working as intended, they should be revised or abolished.

Support-Unit Evaluation

Though far more infrequent than academic program review, formal evaluation of institutional support units is established at many colleges and universities. This is an internal process, often managed in parallel with program review, and generally involves self-study, data collection on unit effectiveness, and, in some cases, peer review. Where appropriate, a users' survey to indicate levels of "customer satisfaction" and analysis of staffing, resources, activity and demand levels, and outcomes is also required. Wherever appropriate, "industry standards" set by professional bodies can be applied.

Institutions that engage in formal academic program review but that do not simultaneously examine support units should consider doing so. The existence of such a process helps ensure the continued cooperation of program faculty in the academic review process. Formal review also helps avoid "budgetary tyranny" often exercised by support units when appropriate external benchmarks for investment are unknown or unclear.

Performance Audits

Public colleges and universities have seen an increase in performance audits undertaken by legislative or executive audit bodies or an institution's internal audit department. This is partly a result of increasing concerns about public accountability across higher education and partly a result of increasing interest in assessment and other techniques that promise answers to questions about institutional and program effectiveness.

Performance audits go beyond financial matters to examine specific areas of program functioning and outcomes. They resemble state-mandated program or unit reviews, and institutions that use such processes have been well served by them when they have been audited. A primary issue, however, has been the ability and willingness of audit agencies to understand unfamiliar qualities of the academic enterprise, particularly in areas such as governance and academic "productivity." Generally, an institution benefits considerably if it can work with the audit agency ahead of time, providing data at an early point and actively explaining its assumptions and limits.

The Role of Institutional Research

Institutional researchers may contribute to the improvement of academic planning and evaluation processes by:

- providing a comprehensive, analytical view of an institution's program mission and environmental factors;

- developing a broader understanding of an institution's programs by providing appropriate trend data;

- developing an array of critical internal and external indicators affecting program planning and institutional survival;

- providing desired information in an appropriate format and in a timely fashion; and

- developing means of linking academic and fiscal planning.

This evaluation information can contribute effectively to institutional planning and management decisions.

Any plan for institutional evaluation presupposes that a diverse array of activities and processes will be examined and that institutional research will play a major role in evaluating such activities and processes. Depending on institutional structure and staff background, institutional researchers may act as implementation team coordinators, institutional planners, departmental activity facilitators, or assessment data gatherers.

Participation of institutional researchers in the program review process is not limited to the provision of data. They may develop meaningful measures of departmental resource needs, departmental centrality, and resource allocation priorities; oversee the consolidation of planning data from various databases and distribute appropriate data schedules, forms, and instructions to departments and schools; collect, analyze, and summarize departmental and school evaluations, plans, and budget requests; and work closely with administrative and faculty groups in recommending and implementing further refinements in evaluation processes, statistical schedules, and instructions as a result of feedback from schools and departments in prior evaluation cycles.

The examination of specific curriculum and instruction or faculty staffing issues may have important implications for programming. Using the Induced Course Load Matrix (ICLM) often facilitates the projection of student credit hours by level for schools and departments for program planning purposes. The ICLM is especially useful in demonstrating probable staffing requirements if enrollment increases or decreases in specific majors because it indicates the volume of student credit hours taken by students in a major as well as the majors of students taking courses offered by a department. Institutional research may assist in the evaluation of instruction as well as in the evaluation of instructional media, methods, or processes designed to improve instruction.

Questions concerning the size, composition, and quality of faculty are frequently the subjects of institutional research. Institutional research contributes to the development of models that may be used to project the effects of policies on future faculty profiles. The assessment of probable effects that incentives may have in encouraging early retirement is a topic of increasing interest. As the official source of data and institutional analysis, institutional researchers may become more involved in litigation on issues of salary equity and affirmative action. (See also chapter 21, Legal Issues.)

Use of Peer and Comparative Information

It is often useful in evaluation processes to compile comparative data. Generally, this is done through the use of peer institutions sufficiently like the subject institution in mission, structure, function, and material condition that valid conclusions about comparative performance can be drawn. Once peer groups are chosen, comparative data can be aggregated, either through public sources or through data-sharing arrangements.

The choice of appropriate peer institutions for comparison is a delicate one. Different peer groups may appropriately be chosen for different purposes. A college or university may resemble one set of institutions with respect to its faculty and research characteristics but resemble another with respect to its undergraduate instructional program. As a result, peers for purposes of faculty salary comparison may be different from peers for reviewing curricula. At the same time, some peer groups may reflect current realities while others reflect institutional aspirations. Both are legitimate, but it is critical to keep their purposes clear.

Comparative peer information is best assembled using a range of institutional characteristics. Most common are enrollment size, faculty size (and characteristics), expenditure levels and expenditure mix across functions, control (public or independent), type (such as Carnegie classification), program mix (generally assessed by proportion of degrees granted by field), selectivity, retention rates, and other student enrollment characteristics such as percentage part-time and geographic location. Many other variables are possible. Most commonly, group comparisons are made on a base of 15 to 20 comparative institutions, with data aggregated to create a comparison group average.

Though powerful in evaluation, comparative peer information must be used with caution. The results obtained are highly reflective of the choice of peers, which is a political choice. Institutional decision makers should be fully aware that there is no correct way to choose peer institutions and that results should be used as benchmarks only. In addition, peer averages reflect current practice, not best practice. Comparative expenditure data, for instance, tell only what others have spent, not what they should be spending.

NOTES

1. George Keller, *Academic Strategy: The Management Revolution in Higher Education,* (Baltimore, MD: John Hopkins University Press, 1983).

2. "Higher Education Must Change." *Journal of the Association of Governing Boards of Universities and Colleges* (May/June 1992): 7–23.

3. F.A. Schmidetelein and T.H. Milton. "College and University Planning Perspectives from a Nation-Wide Study," *in Planning for Higher Education* 17 (1988): 1–19.

4. Marshall E. Drummond, Douglas Vinzant and Wayne Prader. "Paying for Your Vision-Integrating the Planning and Budget Process," *Cause/Effect* 14 (Fall 1991): 21–27.

5. R. Birnbaum, "The Cybernetic University: Towards an Integration of Governance Theories," (College Park, MD: National Center for Postsecondary Governance and Finance, University of Maryland, 1990).

6. R. Newton, "The Two Cultures of Academe: An Overlooked Planning Hurdle," *Planning for Higher Education* 21 (Fall 1992): 8–14.

7. David Leslie and E.K. Fretwell, *Wise Moves in Hard Times: Creating and Managing Resilient Colleges,* (San Francisco: Jossey-Bass Publishers, 1996).

8. Jean MacCormack and Sherry H.Penney. "Managing on the Edge; Massachusetts After the Miracle. " *Journal of Higher Education Management,* 7 (Winter/Spring 1992): 23–53.

9. Louis R. Desfosses, " Strategies for Hard Times in Higher Education, " *CUPA Journal,* (Spring 1996): 13–19.

10. Barry Munitz, "Wanted: New Leadership for Higher Education," *Planning for Higher Education* 24 (Fall 1995): 9–16.

11. James B. Appleberry, "The Future Challenges for Higher Education, " Speech to Annual Meeting of American Association of State College and Universities, Washington, DC, Fall, 1995.

12. Sandy Baum. "Will Higher Education Affordability Be the Health Care Issue of the Twenty-First Century? "*The College Board Review* 173 (Fall, 1994): 8–14.

13. Robert H. Atwell, *Higher Education's Unfinished Business,* (Washington, DC: American Council on Education, 1996), p. 1–10.

14. Alfred North Whitehead, *Aims of Education,* (New York: Free Press/MacMillan, Inc., 1929).

15. James Harvey and John Immerwahr. "Public Perceptions of Higher Education: On Main Street and in the Boardroom," *Educational Record* (Fall, 1995): 51–55.

16. "Rumbling," *Special Issue: Pew Policy Perspectives*7 (November 1996): 1–12.

17. David W. Breneman. "Higher Education: On a Collision Course with New Realities," Boston, MA: American Student Assistance, 1993.

18. "Rumbling," *Special Issue: Pew Policy Perspectives* 7 (November 1996): 1–12.

19. Aaron Lazare, "Shame and Humiliation in the Medical Encounter," *Archives of Internal Medicine* 147: 1653–1658, 1987.

20. Jeanie Daniel Duck, "Managing Change: the Art of Balancing," *Harvard Business Review* (November-December 1993): 109–118.

21. Robert Filipczak. "Critical Mass: Putting Whole-Systems Thinking into Practice," *Training* (September 1995): 33–38.

22. Brian P. Nedwek, "Linking Quality Assurance and Accountability: Using Process and Performance Indicators." in *Doing Academic Planning: Effective Tools for Decision Making,* (Ann Arbor, MI: Society of College and University Planning, 1996), p. 137–144.

23. R. M. Kanter, B. Stein and T.D. Jick. *The Challenge of Organizational Change: How Companies Experience It and Leaders Guide It,*(New York: The Free Press).

24. Price Prichett. *Firing Up Commitment During Organizational Change: A Handbook for Managers,* Monograph. (Dallas, TX: Prichett Associates, 1995), p. 1–30.

25. Sandra S. Ruppert. *Charting Higher Education Accountability: A Sourcebook on State-level Performance Indicators,* (Denver, CO: Education Commission of the States, 1994).

26. Henry Levin (edited by Wendy Schwartz), "Raising Productivity in Higher Education," *Higher Education Extension Service Review* 4 (Summer 1993): 1–9.

REFERENCES AND RESOURCES

Publications and Articles

Alstete, Jeffrey W. "Adapting Best Practices to Improve Quality." In *95-5 Benchmarking in Higher Education*, ASHE Higher Education Reports. Colombia, MO: ASHE, 1995.

Askkenas, Ron, Ulrich, Dave, Jick, Todd, and Kerr, Steve. *The Boundaryless Organization*. San Francisco: Jossey-Bass Publishers, 1995.

Bengquest, William H. *The Four Cultures of the Academy*. San Francisco: Jossey-Bass Publishers, 1992.

Bernard, Clark L., Johnson, Sandra, et al., (Ed.). *Reinventing the University: Managing and Financing Institutions of Higher Education*. New York: John Wiley & Sons, 1998.

Dickeson, Robert C. Prioritizing Academic Programs and Services: *Reallocating Resources to Achieve Strategic Balance*. San Francisco: Jossey-Bass Publishers, 1999.

Dougherty, Jennifer D., Kidwell, Jillinda, J., Knight, Donna M., Hubbell, Loren L., and Rush, Sean C. *Business Process Redesign for Higher Education*, Washington, DC: NACUBO, 1994.

Dunn, John A., et al. "Decision Processes," *ASHE Reader on Finance in Higher Education/D, Quinn, Needham, MA, 1993.*

Eckel, Peter. "Making Change Stick." Research Report for the Project on Leadership and Institutional Transformation. Washington, DC: American Council on Education, 1996, p. 15.

Fuhrman, Barbara S. and Jez, Evelyn A. "Implementation: The Missing Link in University Planning." *Metropolitan Universities* (Winter 1995): 129–138.

Hodgkinson, Harold L. "Who Will Our Students Be? Demographic Implications for Urban and Metropolitan Universities." *Metropolitan Universities*, (Winter 1996): 25–39.

Honan, James P. "Monitoring Institutional Performance." *AGB Priorities* 5 (Fall 1995): 1–15.

Keller, George. "Planning, Decisions, and Human Nature." *Planning* 26 (Winter 1997-98) p. 18–23.

Kidwell, Jillinda J. and Long, Laura. *Performance Measurement Systems for Higher Education*. NACUBO: Washington, DC, 1994.

Kotter, John P. *Leading Change*. Boston: Harvard Business School Press, 1996.

Lewis, Ralph, and Smith, Douglas H. *Total Quality in Higher Education*. Delray Beach, FL: Lucie Press, 1994.

Mancini, Cesidio G. "On Rugged Ground—Managing Change in the Academic Enterprise." *NACUBO Business Officer* (June 1997): p. 26–30.

Peterson, Marvin W., Dill, David, and Mets, D. and Lisa A. *Planning and Management for a Changing Environment: A Handbook on Redesigning Post Secondary Institutions*. San Francisco: Jossey-Bass Publishers, 1997.

Phipps, Ronald. "Square One in the Restructuring Process."*Trusteeship,* (March/April 1996): 21–25.

Ramaley, Judith. "Large-Scale Institutional Change to Implement an Urban University Mission: Portland State University." *Journal of Urban Affairs* 18 no. 2: 139–151.

Rowly, Daniel J., Lujan, Herman D., and Dolence, Michael G. *Strategic Change in College and Universities: Planning to Survive and Prosper*. San Francisco: Jossey-Bass Publishers, 1997.

Schoenfeld, Clay. "Campus Cultures in Conflict." *CUPA Journal* (Winter 1994): 29–33.

Shaw, Kenneth A., and Lee, Kathryn E. "Effecting Change at Syracuse University: The Importance of Values, Mission and Vision." *Metropolitan Universities* (Spring, 1997).

———. "To Dance with Change." *Pew Policy Perspectives* 4 no. 2, Section A (March 1992): 1A–8A.

Organizations

Association for Institutional Research (AIR)
Florida State University
114 Stone Building, Tallahassee, FL 32306-4462
850-644-4470 . . . . http://www.airweb.org

Association of Governing Boards of Universities and Colleges (AGB)
One Dupont Circle, Suite 400, Washington, DC 20036
202-296-8400 . . . . http://www.agb.org

National Center for Higher Education Management Systems (NCHEMS)
P.O. Box 9752, 1540 30th Street RL-2, Boulder, Colorado 80301-9752
303-497-0301 . . . . http://www.nchems.org

Society for College and University Planning (SCUP)
311 Maynard Street, Ann Arbor, MI 48104-2211
734-998-7832 . . . . http://www.scup.org

Chapter 4

◆

Budgeting

by

John R. Curry
Massachusetts Institute of Technology

with contributions by

Greg J. Baroni, KPMG

Sponsor

KPMG
Contact: Greg J. Baroni
1676 International Drive
McLean, VA 22102
703-747-3004
www.kpmg.com

With over 30 years of serving higher education, KPMG offers a broad range of services that helps our clients analyze their businesses with true clarity, raises their level of performance and delivers the strategic and infrastructural components to support highly dynamic E-business models in colleges, universities, and academic medical centers.

Contents

Thirhis chapter is a guide to developing and managing college and university budgets through the eyes of a budget officer from a research university perspective, whether the officer is responsible for the budget of the entire institution or that of a department or school. The budget officer is sometimes the chief academic officer or provost and sometimes the chief financial officer. Typically there is a specific officer in the title role, perhaps the director (or vice president) of budget (or sometimes budget and planning). Within departments and schools, the title may be something like "business officer." Regardless of the title, all these players are budget officers relative to their spans of authority and need to know most of the subject matter we discuss here. All of them will work together in the process of developing all the departmental budgets into a coherent whole for the institution.

The first section discusses what budgets are and why they are important. The second section considers academic planning briefly, primarily to introduce those interactions between budgeting and planning that are intended to achieve desirable and feasible future states. These two sections are intentionally short and generic, and will be elaborated in context throughout the sequel.

The third section is devoted to the building blocks of budget development, with relatively detailed presentations of forecasting and budgeting the major sources of revenues and the major components of expenditures. The fourth section looks at capital budgets and their integration with operating budgets. These two sections are more technical than procedural. They discuss the substance of specific revenues and expenditures and begin to elucidate relationships between them. Critical iterations among plans, market conditions, revenue estimates, and management initiatives will emerge.

The fifth section explores the primary architectures of budgeting—from highly centralized to highly decentralized—in effect at colleges and universities today. Section six considers the behaviors and procedures of budget development, implementation, and management to achieve both the academic and financial goals that become agreements during budget negotiations. These two sections bring together all the issues introduced earlier. In particular they show how budgets are developed and managed quite differently depending on the underlying budget architecture.

The seventh section examines the roles of governing bodies (primarily trust-ees and regents). The eighth section offers some observations on philosophy and best practices.

WHAT ARE BUDGETS?

Budgets are complex. Like diamonds, they have many facets. They are plans: expectations of deliverables, with revenues spent to achieve specific purposes. They are controls: mechanisms that authorities use to monitor revenues and expenditures, and curtail spending in excess of authorized levels. Budgets are com-mitments: agreements to deliver enrollment levels or research funds, to hire cer-tain kinds and numbers of faculty, to provide a service to faculty and students at a specified quality level, to develop management information systems, or to con-struct buildings for specific amounts of money and time. Budgets are fiduciary enablers: they are assurances to boards of trustees or state authorities that revenues and expenditures will be kept in balance and that institutional assets—financial and physical—will be appropriately conserved or will grow proportional to future needs. Budgets are performance measures: depending on variances around the bottom line, they measure whether management is delivering expected financial performances; depending on whether revenues earned and expenditures incurred are in accordance with intentions informing budget development, they measure whether management (at all levels) is delivering expected academic and admin-istrative performance.

The penultimate report card on the efficacy of a budget is the audited annual financial statement. Indeed, the financial statement is the primary document by which fiduciary responsibility, creditworthiness, and overall financial viability are judged. Consequently, whether or not it is explicitly stated, a major objective of budgeting is predicting the audited financial statement. A fiduciary wants finan-cial statements to exhibit a long-term trend of increasing net assets. Thus, ideal annual budgets have several features across time. They would not deplete net assets through operations (that is, they would balance operating expenditures to revenues); they would use only as much total return on endowment as would leave enough return invested to preserve future years' purchasing power; and they would increase capitalizable physical assets beyond annual depreciation of those assets. Budgets should be leading indicators of financial statements.

The ultimate report card on the efficacy of a budget is whether the academic plan and academic vitality of the institution are advanced.

PLANNING AND BUDGETS

Academic institutions plan their futures. They aspire to having better students, better faculty, better facilities, better reputations, uniqueness. They aspire in different ways: some may want a more diverse student body; others may want to hire new faculty to establish prowess in an emerging academic field; still others have a vision for the overall functionality and aesthetic of the physical campus. Many aspire to all of these, and more. First order academic plans formalize aspirations of faculties and administrations.

Plans become strategic, and less universally ambitious, when constrained by resources. Budgets, among other things, codify resource limitations. Some aspirations become more important than others when constraints of operating revenues and access to capital enter budget negotiations. Constraints extract priorities from wish lists. Consequently, planning and budgeting go hand in hand.

For example, plans can influence revenues. Hiring new faculty in key research areas who will bring or attract outside sponsorship of their work can increase research revenues. Reducing enrollment to improve the academic quality of first-year students and reduce average class size can also decrease tuition revenues. Plans can require reallocation of expenditure budgets from low priority on-going activities (already in the budget) to new, higher priority activities. Then, too, there just may not be enough money (budget) to implement lower priority initiatives called for in an academic plan.

All this is to say that plans influence budgets and budgets influence plans. In the flow diagram shown in figure 04-01, the left branches of the flow relate plans to annual operating budgets; the right branch relates them to capital budgets. The flows are joined by the question of whether the operating budget can afford debt service on debt capital—hence the double arrow.

Planning and budgeting are dynamic, within annual planning cycles and across years. Indeed, Dwight D. Eisenhower once said: "Plans are nothing. Planning is everything." External conditions change and affect plan assumptions. Federal budget priorities change, affecting research sponsorship; student career interests change, affecting graduate and professional school enrollments; investment markets change, affecting the value of financial assets and thus endowment income and the ability to procure debt financing. Internal conditions change as well—changes in leadership, for example—and similarly can affect the ability to implement key aspects of a plan. Plans mediate environments and intentions, and budgets enable plans. Consequently, plans and budgets must be adaptable. Plans and

Figure 04-01

Interactions between Plans and Budgets

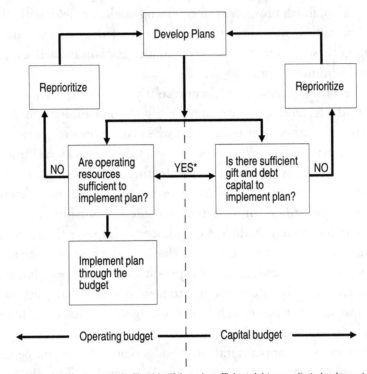

*The double arrow works like this: If there is sufficient debt capacity to implement the plan, the question of whether operating resources are sufficient is really the question of whether operating resources can cover debt service.

budgets are like one frame in a movie: a snapshot of a moment in time. Planning and budgeting are dynamic: two interlocking movies, continuously produced and directed by academic leaders, yet each frame dependent on the preceding ones.

DEVELOPING THE OPERATING BUDGET

Budget development begins by estimating annual revenues. The process continues by determining spending priorities, typically through examining those programs that the prior year's budget funded, along with proposed increments (decrements) for the upcoming year. It ends by balancing (or approximately balancing) expenditures to expected revenues. Operating revenues derive from the day-to-day operations of a college or university. They are the consequence of core transactions: teaching classes, doing research, and providing business services. Operating expenses are the flip side: they enable the transactions that generate the revenues.

Revenues

To budget revenues for a given time period is to forecast and plan them. There are many forecasting methodologies, but the modal and most reliable extrapolates the near future from the recent past. While there is usually considerable inertia in revenues, well-laid plans and dedicated management actions can cause the future to deviate from the past, as can volatile external environments. The following looks systematically at approaches to budgeting by examining the major items comprising a college's or university's revenue budget.

Tuition and Fees

Students pay tuition to enroll in courses. They typically pay either so much per credit hour or per course, or they pay a lump sum for a specific range of credit hours, say 12 to 16 per semester, the bottom of the range being the full-time enrollment threshold. Students pay fees for additional goods and services: laboratory materials, activity books containing tickets to athletic contests or concerts, access to intercollegiate sports competitions, health insurance, and access to campus medical services and counseling offices.

This section concentrates only on tuition, since the subject is more complex than fees, and almost everything said about tuition applies to fees. Moreover, some colleges and universities imbed fees for services into one comprehensive tuition charge: they bundle instruction and noninstructional services.

Enrollment. The basic algorithm for undergraduate tuition revenues is this: estimate total headcount enrollment, that is, the total number of enrolled undergraduate students; multiply by the average total credit hours generated per student; then multiply this product by the tuition price per credit hour. Start at the beginning with first-year enrollment and proceed as follows:

1. Estimate the size of the applicant pool, i.e., the number of applications for admission, by looking at historical data early in the budget development cycle, then looking periodically at the applicant accumulation rate as the fall semester preceding the fiscal year whose budget is being developed unfolds;

2. Estimate the admissibility rate, i.e., the fraction of the applicants who

meet the institution's academic qualifications (SAT or ACT scores, high school class standing, participation in extracurricular activities, essay writing panache, etc.);

3. Estimate yield, i.e., the fraction of admitted students who will actually enroll. (*Note:* yield data are functions of students' intended majors and typically proportional to the reputation and quality ranking of the programs to which the students seek admission.) Finally, there may be some prior-year's students returning to the first-year class, and the institution may enroll first-year transfer students between terms. All of these components must be considered in the estimation of yield.

Enrollment forecasting and planning are iterative. If there are planning goals for the size, quality, and mix of the class, then management attempts to influence the size of the applicant pool, the admissibility rate, and yield among majors to deliver the desired enrollment—all subject to applicant academic quality measures. As the quality of the applicant pool increases, so does the admissibility ratio; also, the greater the institution's academic quality and ranking in a given field, the higher the yield among those applying for admission. Managing all these variables to meet a given enrollment plan cuts across many departments of an institution and requires understanding of the "enrollment marketplace" as well as one's institutional place in it. The budget officer's job is to bring all the issues together in estimating tuition revenues for the fiscal year being planned. Thus the final steps in developing the first-year enrollment budget are:

4. Determine the "right" balance point between plan goals and enrollment market conditions.

5. Adjust numbers of admitted students by intended major, subject to institutional quality tolerances, and multiply by the appropriate yields to estimate the enrolled class.

To estimate the second-year or sophomore class enrollment, one first needs to know the history and recent trends for first-year students returning for their second year: the fraction of first-year matriculants who become sophomores is called the returning enrollment ratio or the persistence rate. In addition, one needs to estimate new transfer students and the numbers of prior-year sophomores returning as sophomores.

These same estimation procedures are used to determine the remaining upper class sizes, with graduation and/or exit rates applicable at the end of the senior and "fifth" undergraduate years. Knowing returning enrollment ratios and exit rates by major can increase the accuracy of upper division tuition revenue budgets; they are even more important for expenditure budgeting. Indeed, as students redistribute themselves among majors, either through successful institutional enrollment management or through their own individual volition, demands for courses and academic advising—as well as for physical space reallocation—change. Consequently, a process that starts as estimating tuition revenues evolves into enrollment planning and space management; ultimately it evolves into planning for course offerings and faculty additions (or subtractions) across disciplines (or majors).

The estimating processes and data requirements we have been discussing in the context of tuition revenue budgeting all come together in what is called a student flow model. Aspects of the model are captured in the process diagram in figures 04-02a, 04-02b, and 04-02c.

Budgeting undergraduate tuition revenue is typically a top-down or centralized activity, because the undergraduate admission process is typically managed through a central office. Budgeting graduate tuition revenue, however, is bottom-up or decentralized, because graduate enrollments are managed by individual departments. Thus the budget officer needs to work with all the academic departments to determine their enrollment estimates and then sum enrollment and tuition dollars across all programs.

Setting tuition price. Tuition pricing is more art than science. At its most simplistic, tuition is set so that:

tuition (price) × *enrollment* (volume) = *total cost* (direct and indirect) *of instruction.*

For many small colleges or proprietary schools, this is the relevant formula. If enrollments are constant across years, then

increase in tuition (price) = *increase in total cost of instruction,*

where meeting enrollment goals at the new price is subject to the price elasticity of demand, or more simply, the continued willingness of applying and returning students to pay the (new) price. Colleges and universities with endowments or other revenues available to support the instruction budget will have more elaborate formulas and will use these other sources to "subsidize" all students or to subsidize students differentially—according to financial need, academic merit, or other criteria—through financial aid (see the next section).

In any case, changes in costs (salary increases, increases in health benefits costs, high utility bills, needed new programs) are first order considerations in thinking about tuition price increases. Other equally important considerations are

Figure 04-02a

First-year and Transfer Class Enrollment Algorithm

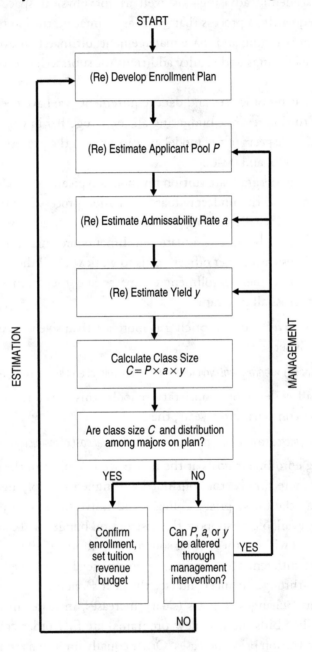

Figure 04-02b

Upper Class Enrollment Algorithm

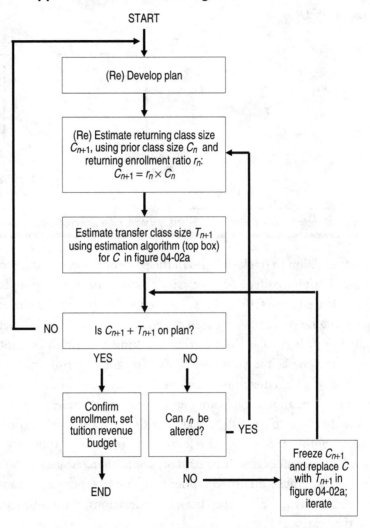

likely changes in nontuition revenues and the students' ability and willingness to pay. Competitive comparisons arise, too. Is the institution's tuition higher or lower than tuitions at peer colleges and universities? Are differences in tuition affecting enrollment, that is, is the enrollment market sensitive to price?

Some institutions take a kind of macroeconomic position when setting tuition price. For example, they look at the Consumer Price Index (CPI) and

Figure 04-02c

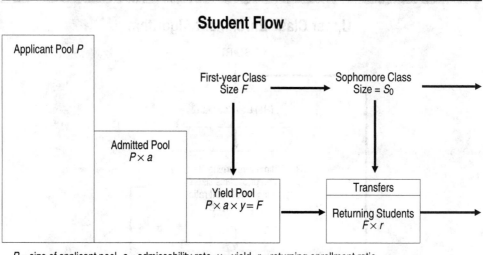

Student Flow

Applicant Pool P

Admitted Pool
$P \times a$

First-year Class
Size F

Yield Pool
$P \times a \times y = F$

Sophomore Class
Size $= S_0$

Transfers

Returning Students
$F \times r$

P = size of applicant pool, a = admissability rate, y = yield, r = returning enrollment ratio

increase tuition to track changes in the price of the goods and services defining the CPI (although a college or university's expenditure "shopping basket" bears little resemblance to the CPI's). This, in essence, is a political position: "Our prices are increasing no faster than those in the economy as a whole." Other institutions may want to proclaim that their tuition is taking a constant percentage of disposable family income across time, hence they might peg tuition changes to growth of that index. Or, redistribution of wealth may be a factor. A college with a large number of qualified applicants and continuing students with "excess" capacity and willingness to pay full "sticker" price may raise tuition price faster than reference to competitors' prices or relevant macroeconomic indices would suggest. The "windfall" revenues from this strategy could then reduce the price (through financial aid) for those qualified students of lesser economic means. Setting tuition prices may involve all of the above considerations, sometimes in ways more intuitive than rational.

Professional school tuitions often differ from those charged to undergraduates. So-called differential tuitions reflect many factors: excess demand for admission, in which case price rations access; or high pay in the profession, in which case comparisons of the present value of the expected career income stream with the investment in tuition (plus income foregone during matriculation) is economically compelling. Here tuition differentials reflect, in part, what the market will bear on the upside. Business, law, and medicine have been examples of professions where tuitions are higher than in other fields and where offsetting financial aid is typically minimal because future earnings can pay off loans.

On the other hand, paying for degrees that admit graduates to vital but typically low-paying professions—in public service, for example—is another consideration. Tuitions in such fields may be lower than the normal undergraduate levels, and in independent universities, access to financial aid will be a major factor in an individual's decision to pursue the professional degree. In such fields, many students will choose to enroll in public institutions where the state appropriation buys down the tuition—often to zero—from levels that an independent institution would have to charge. Moreover, the missions of public institutions include the preparation of students for public service—state teachers' colleges are primary examples.

Setting of tuition and fees at public colleges and universities is almost always a political process, often of enormous symbolic salience, and is very much a function of what appropriation the state makes available (appropriations could be viewed as another revenue source) for the budget under development. Adding to this complexity is the fact that public institutions may charge out-of-state students higher tuitions and/or fees than they charge in-state residents. The ratio of in-state to out-of-state students is a function of individual state policy and politics, as well as the overall student enrollment demand. Budget officers of public institutions are as much engaged in state educational policy and state budget development as they are in the estimation and allocation of resources on their campuses.

Tuition Revenues

The tuition revenue budget is enrollment (measured in head count or credit hours) times tuition (per head or unit). This equation is oversimplified. It assumes every "head" is enrolled full time. Part-time students may be converted to full-time equivalents (FTE) by adding their credit hours and dividing by the number of credit hours constituting full-time status.

Financial Aid

As the tuition revenue budget develops, so should the student financial aid budget. Indeed contemporary accounting standards require that financial aid be subtracted from gross tuition revenues in the institution's audited financial statement of "revenues and other changes;" that is, that revenues exhibit net—some would say, discounted—tuition. Financial aid is a complex subject. For a full exposition, we suggest reading any number of books and papers by McPherson and Schapiro[1], and the article by Lapovsky and Loomis Hubbell.[1]

Aid comes primarily in two forms: need and merit. Many colleges and universities offer need-based financial aid because they want to ensure that students who qualify for admission can afford to enroll. The College Scholarship Service (CSS) of the College Entrance Examination Board provides a national needs assessment tool that calculates how much a family can contribute annually to a college student's total costs, based on the family's size, annual income, financial assets, home equity, and son's or daughter's individual earning capabilities. The difference between the calculated family contribution and the total cost of education or student annual budget (tuition, fees, room, board, travel, books, and spending money) is the annual need:

need = student budget – family contribution

Colleges meet as much need as their policies and financial wherewithal permit through grants and loans. Grants are dollars that students do not have to repay; grants based on academic merit rather than need are usually called scholarships. For some classes of students, both federal and state governments provide grants; similarly, colleges provide grants through either endowments and gifts, or through "recycled" unrestricted revenues. Loans are also part of a financial aid package, and like grants, can be either from governments or the admitting institution. The financial aid package is then the sum of the components needed to meet the student budget: family contribution plus grants plus loans plus self-help, the last of these being an expected amount the student will earn during a year, especially during the summer months. Needless to say, the richer the grant component, and the lesser the loan, the more desirable and competitive a given package is.

The institution's undergraduate financial aid budget is the sum of all the grants the institution provides to qualified students. (This budget does not exhibit grants students acquire on their own or grants provided by agencies external to the college or university.) The aid budget should show as an explicit deduction from gross tuition revenue in both the annual budget and the audited financial statements.

Merit aid serves a different purpose. Institutions offer merit awards to certain kinds of students they wish to enroll. At many colleges and universities, students who do not qualify for need-based aid may qualify for merit aid. For example, the institution may wish to increase the academic quality of its student body and thus will offer a scholarship enticement to applicants with high SAT or ACT scores. If such a student exhibits financial need, an institution may sweeten the aid package with more grant money (and a lesser loan) than would be offered to the "average" admittee. Scholarships are also often offered to students with special skills: quarterbacking, trumpet playing, singing, acting.

Finally, some institutions offer aid to the nonneed student simply to maximize net revenues. For example, consider an admissible applicant to Independent U who also qualifies for admission to the flagship state university, Public U, but who does not qualify for need-based aid. Further suppose that Independent U has some empty seats in the classrooms and empty beds in the residence halls and tends to lose this kind of applicant to Public U. If Independent U offers the applicant a "merit" award equal to the difference between Independent U's and Public U's tuitions, thereby attracting the applicant, then Independent U would realize the residual net tuition (an amount equal to Public U's tuition), plus payments for room, board, and books as additional revenues while incurring few or no marginal costs. In this case net revenue enhancement is the purpose of the award. Awards of this kind are sometimes called characteristic-based aid.[2]

Once again, graduate aid awards are typically offered locally, at the departmental level, and must be budgeted accordingly. At many research universities, graduate student tuition remission is funded in part as direct expenditures from individual principal investigators' grants. Thus there may be strong interactions between estimated direct expenditures for research (see below) and budgeted graduate enrollment.

For budgeting purposes, undergraduate gross tuition and aid should be exhibited and tracked separately from graduate tuition, since they are managed and monitored in very different ways.

Earlier sections characterized the budget officer as the single "condensation point" for all the inputs required to determine the companion tuition revenue and financial aid budgets. Many participants, however, are involved in providing these inputs. An enrollment management committee might bring together the many participants: for example, the admissions and financial aid directors, the directors of housing and dining, deans of undergraduate education and student life, key faculty from representative disciplines, the budget director, and the chief planning officer (perhaps the provost or a vice provost). Guided by an enrollment plan, as part of an overall academic plan, they will work their way through several iterations of the flow models in figures 04-02a, 02b, and 02c. In addition, they may factor into these models various financial aid and housing or dining pricing strategies, since yield is a function of price. The committee would then recommend feasible enrollments, relevant tuition (sticker) prices and financial aid levels, as well as housing and dining charges for the budget under development.

Gifts, Endowment, and Investment Income

Unrestricted revenues and assets (both financial and physical) may be used for any institutional purpose consistent with the mission and articles of incorporation. *Restricted resources* have either their use or locus of control (or both) prescribed by the donor or sponsor; accepting the money is agreeing to comply with conditions.

There is a third colloquial term that is a hybrid: *designated resources* are unrestricted revenues or assets, but senior management or the institution's governing body earmark them for a given unit (e.g., the sciences) or purpose (e.g., financial aid).

Gifts. These come in many guises. They may come through subscription annual giving programs, such as alumni funds, in which case their yearly flow is relatively predictable (based on numbers and dollar levels of the subscriptions). Or they may come through capital campaigns with given goals, in which case their flows may be somewhat less predictable. Least predictable are the gifts that arise due to the entrepreneurship of faculty, department chairs, or deans who seek philanthropic support for their research and instructional programs.

One should budget expected receipts and uses of all gifts, estimating each of the above categories at levels consistent with their predictability (expected value and variability, in statistical terms) within each class. Unrestricted gifts, once estimated and budgeted, can support any institutional expenditure. Restricted gifts cannot. For those gifts designated or restricted only as to purpose (and not to a local jurisdiction), the (central) budget officer can match uses with sources (e.g., gifts designated to student financial aid) and thus develop the budget centrally.

More complex is the budgeting of gifts controlled locally by schools, departments, or individual faculty members. Here the chief academic officer (typically the provost) and the budget officer need first to understand gift balances (that is, gifts accumulated and not yet spent) and flows (that is, likely gift receipts and expenditures) for the given unit and fiscal period being planned. Thus, a particular department's budget proposal might request a new computer from centrally managed unrestricted revenues under the provost's jurisdiction. The provost may know, however, that the department chair has gift balances at his disposal more than sufficient to purchase the computer. Hence, a dialog about the chair's priorities for his own resources versus the provost's priorities for hers should ensue during the budget negotiation process.

Understanding gift flows is important in predicting the year-end balance sheet. For example if deans, department chairs, and faculty members spent more of their gift balances in a budget year than they replenished with new gifts, then there would be a surprise decrease in the institution's net assets if all other expenditures and revenues in the budget were perfectly balanced. This observation is important. Many colleges and universities still budget "gifts used," thus matching revenues to expenditures. Contemporary practice budgets inflows, outflows, and their differences, thus predicting a key change of net assets in the year-end financial statements.

Endowment. Some definitions are in order. If a donor stipulates that a gift is to be held as endowment, state laws require that the gift's principal—its original amount and in some cases, its purchasing power—be preserved in perpetuity. The receiving institution may use (spend) only the yield income and/or the capital appreciation of an invested endowment gift. Donor stipulated endowment is sometimes called true endowment to distinguish it from quasi endowment. The latter term refers to resources—gifts or operating surpluses—which management or the governing board designates to function as endowment. They wish to treat the resource as if it were endowment, thus investing it to preserve the principal. In contrast with true endowment, however, governing boards may choose to reverse decisions creating quasi endowment by withdrawing the principal and spending it.

Governing boards, typically working through their investment committees and the institution's chief investment officer, determine how to invest endowments. Individual endowments are normally pooled and the so-called endowment pool is then invested according to a board-determined asset allocation: the mix of public equities, bonds, real estate, cash, and private equity the board deems likely to have the "right" expected return and "acceptable" level of risk (or volatility). The right asset mix would provide a steady total return, the sum of yield income and capital appreciation, sufficient to support annual budgets and maintain the purchasing power of the principal over time. Individual endowments are configured as shares in the pool; their participation in the pool's total return is proportional to the shares owned.

Endowment return available for budget support each year is usually calculated according to a spending rule. Suppose, for example, that total return on an endowment is 10 percent and that inflation on the "market basket" of services and goods "purchased" each year in the institution's budget is 4 percent. In this case, 4 percent of total return should be retained as invested endowment to preserve purchasing power, while the remaining 6 percent is available for spending. In sum:

$$\text{endowment } \textit{spending}^* \textit{ rate} = \text{total return} - \text{budget inflation}$$

To smooth endowment spending, many institutions use a multiyear trailing average of endowment market value to determine "total return" in this equation. Specifically, the percentage change between successive multiyear (usually three to five year) trailing averages is used for total return.

Here is a sample of endowment spending rules, the first being the one just described:

- *Percent of trailing three-year market average*: For budget year $n + 1$, distribute to spending accounts x percent of the average of 36 months' market values ending December 31 in year n, where x is the difference between expected total return and budget inflation.

- *Snake-in-the-tunnel*: For budget year $n + 1$, distribute to spending accounts last year's amount increased by y percent, where y percent is a function of budget inflation—unless y percent falls below a minimum spending rate or exceeds a maximum rate. (For example, increase last year's distribution by 5 percent unless the amount falls below 3 percent of a three-year trailing market average or above 7 percent of this average.) If y percent falls outside the minimum or maximum, distribute the nearer of the thresholds.

- *Exponentially smoothed rate*: Like the first, but with each month's market value weighted more heavily than its predecessor's in the average. This approach values recent market information more than older return data.

- *Yield only*: Spend only bond yields and stock dividends each year; retain all capital gains.

Endowments, like gifts, may be restricted either as to purpose or to local organizational unit. It follows that budgeting endowment income involves the same considerations as budgeting gifts. However, if total return is based on recent historical data (for example, through the fiscal year just closed or half way through the budget year underway, but preceding by six months the budget being devel-

---

*Endowment spending rate is also called payout rate

oped), then one can budget endowment income with accuracy if the spending rule is predetermined, because market values are known.

The endowment spending rate, while common parlance, is a misnomer. Restricted endowment return distributed via the spending rule may not always be "spent." "Owners" of the restricted endowment may let distributions accumulate in their so-called endowment spending accounts. Knowing these patterns is important for predicting change in net assets through the budget. More on endowment investing and payout formulas is found in chapter 9, Endowment Management. Also see Massy.[3]

Investment income. As we will use the term here, investment income is yield income generated by short- to medium-term investments of working capital; it is usually a combination of yield on short-term bonds and cash instruments. Working capital comprises unspent gift and endowment income balances, gifts for capital projects awaiting expenditure, operating surpluses, and short-term (within-year) favorable variances of operating revenues over expenditures (for example, tuition payments are typically received as a large lump sum at the beginning of a term, whereas the expenditures they support occur evenly over the term). To estimate investment income for budgeting purposes, one starts with the estimated working capital at the start of the budget year and then estimates cash flows throughout the year to determine how balances vary. Expected rates of investment return are applied to expected balances for the appropriate time periods.

Modeling cash flow is very important. Indeed, if cash balances are on average negative, investment income (as defined here) is negative: which is to say, interest payments are flowing from the budget on withdrawals from a bank line of credit. Consequently, the budget officer needs to work with the controller and chief investment officer in the planning of a budget to understand the implied cash flows and their impact on investment income (or its inverse).

This section is especially relevant to predicting the statement of cash flows required by FASB Statement 117 for independent institutions.

Research

Research revenues derive from the grants and contracts that external sponsors award to individual, or teams of individual, faculty members. Sponsors may be federal, such as the National Science Foundation, the National Institutes of Health, the Department of Defense, the National Aeronautics and Space Administration, or the Department of Energy; or they may be private foundations, associations, corporations, and individuals. Grants and contracts come in two parts: direct and indirect.

Direct expenditures. When a faculty member wins an award from a federal agency, it is divided into two parts. One portion supports directly the research activities described in the award application or proposal; it will support some personnel (for example, graduate student tuition payments or a portion of the faculty awardee's salary) and supplies and equipment necessary to perform the requisite research. The faculty awardee, or principal investigator (PI), controls direct grant expenditures, which are restricted both as to purpose and to organizational unit (the principal investigator).

Indirect costs. The PI's academic institution incurs other costs, however, in support of the research conducted through the grant. Such costs are called indirect, and they constitute the other portion of the award. Research takes place in offices and laboratories. Thus, the PI's institution incurs facility costs—depreciation of buildings and equipment, interest payments on construction loans, library costs, utilities costs, maintenance, and repairs. Research projects also require administrative services—accounting, finance, payroll, human resources, information technology, and legal services, among others.

Colleges and universities pool administrative costs and allocate them, primarily between research and instruction, according to federal guidelines found in the Office of Management and Budget (OMB) Circular A-21. The condensed version of these guidelines is this: allocate administrative costs among instruction, research, and other objectives in proportion to direct expenditures incurred by each. For example, suppose that administrative costs for year X are $100 million, that direct expenditures for research are $300 million, for instruction, $200 million, and for other, $0. Then research represents three fifths, or 60 percent, and instruction two fifths, or 40 percent, of total direct expenditures. Sixty percent of the $100 million, or $60 million, of administrative costs would be allocated to research, and $40 million would attach to instruction. The ratio of administrative costs allocable to research to total direct expenditures for research—in our example, $\frac{60}{300} = 20$ percent—is the *administrative indirect cost rate.*

OMB Circular A-21 also guides the allocation of facilities costs to research. In its most simplistic form, the guideline is this: determine the annual costs of facilities used by principal investigators directly for research across the campus, and sum them. This is more easily said than done, however. It requires detailed space surveys, occupancy and usage data by room, depreciation calculations, and operations and maintenance cost data. Continuing the example, suppose that the facilities costs supporting research sum to $120 million and recall that the direct costs of research (that is, the expenditures controlled directly by PIs) total $300. The ratio of facilities costs allocable to research to total direct expenditures for research is $\frac{120}{300} = 40$ percent, the so-called facilities indirect cost rate.

Summing the two rates in the example produces the following result:

$$\text{Total indirect cost rate} = \text{administrative rate} + \text{facilities rate}$$

$$= 20\% + 40\%$$

$$= 60\%$$

Recent editions of OMB Circular A-21 systematically use the term facilities and administration (F&A) rate instead of indirect cost rate, the latter term being less descriptive and often misunderstood, but still common parlance on most campuses.

The grant or contract that the principal investigator receives from the sponsoring agency comprises both direct and indirect costs. As observed earlier, the PI controls direct expenditures to carry out the purpose of the award; the central administration collects the indirect costs from the PI's award through the F&A rate. For each dollar the PI spends (directly), the administration collects an additional amount from the grant equal to the F&A rate *times* $1.00; in our example that is 60 cents. Applied across all contract and grant annual expenditures, this calculation produces unrestricted revenues called indirect cost recovery. In the example,

$$\text{Indirect cost recovery} = 60\% \times \$300 \text{ million} = \$180 \text{ million,}$$

that is, indirect costs recovered *equal* indirect costs incurred.

Estimating indirect cost recovery for budget development purposes is more complex than the example would suggest. First, one needs to know the F&A rate, which is usually negotiated with the cognizant federal agency in advance of the fiscal year being planned, though not always. Rates can change mid-year. Second, one needs to refine estimates of total direct expenditures for research by excluding capitalizable equipment purchases to create the so-called modified total direct cost (MTDC) base. Third, one multiplies the MTDC base by the rate—and yet, it's still not that simple.

Some federal awards involve cost sharing, which for some institutions and some grants may constitute an agreement not to collect the full indirect cost rate. In addition, multiyear awards may have been negotiated years earlier when a different rate was in effect, and that rate may still apply for the budget under development. There are many other contributors that may cause indirect costs recovered to be less than rate times base. Consequently, budget officers and sponsored projects staff need to track and understand this difference in order to forecast indirect cost recovery revenue budgets accurately.

For more information on this complex topic of the F&A rate, see chapter 18, Research and Sponsored Programs. The subject is sufficiently complex that the budget officer needs to call upon the expertise of the sponsored research office staff to develop good research-related budgets.

Research revenue. The following explains why understanding direct and indirect expenditures is necessary for estimating research revenues:

research revenues = research expenditures (costs) *incurred.*

Thus, in theory,

research revenues = direct costs recovered + indirect costs recovered.

= direct costs incurred + indirect costs incurred.

To reiterate earlier examples, indirect costs are recovered (as revenues) by applying the indirect cost rate to grant direct expenditures and billing the sponsoring agency throughout the year. Direct expenditure recovery is budgeted (and accounted for) as restricted; indirect recoveries are budgeted as unrestricted.

The direct component of a grant, even though it is restricted, interacts with the unrestricted budget in ways beyond producing indirect cost recovery. For instance, some portion of faculty salaries (and often all of graduate student stipends) may be paid from the grants. Faculty salaries, at least the academic year portions, are institutional obligations. If a faculty member PI receives a new award, and pays 25 percent of his or her academic year salary therefrom, the PI's academic department or the institution's provost may have a "new" resource to allocate elsewhere. On the other hand, if a PI loses grant support, the department or provost may have a "new" obligation against unrestricted budget dollars. Budget officers need to know sponsoring agencies' and their own institution's policies governing faculty salary "offsets" onto grants and contracts and to monitor, and sometimes attempt to manage, the annual ebbs and flows of offsets across all awards.

Tuition for graduate students may also be paid directly from grants. In this case, budgeted graduate enrollment and gross tuition revenue will be functions of grant support available (among other variables). This is another example of the

Table 04-01

Sample Sponsored Research Award Budget

Salaries and Wages	Percent Effort	Year 1 7/1/00 to 6/30/01	Year 2 7/1/01 to 6/30/02	Year 3 7/1/02 to 6/30/03	Total
Name and/or Title					
Principal Investigator	30	$30,000	$30,900	$31,827	$ 92,727
Research Scientist	40	32,000	32,960	33,949	98,909
Postdoc Associate	50	15,000	15,450	15,914	46,364
*Graduate Research Asst	50	10,000	10,300	10,609	30,909
Total Salaries and Wages		87,000	89,610	92,298	268,908
Employee Benefits @ 20% of salaries		15,400	15,862	16,338	47,600
Non-Salary Costs					
Travel		2,975	3,064	3,156	9,195
**Equipment		5,000	5,150	5,305	15,455
Materials and Supplies		4,000	4,120	4,244	12,364
**Grad Student Tuition		20,000	20,600	21,218	61,818
Total Direct Costs		134,375	138,406	142,558	415,340
Facilities and Admin Costs (F&A) @ 60% (excluding equipment and tuition)		65,625	67,594	69,622	202,840
TOTAL COSTS		$200,000	$206,000	$212,180	$618,180

*Does not incur employee benefit costs
**Does not incur F&A costs

importance of the interplay between restricted and unrestricted resources. Table 04-01 exhibits a sample award budget and shows how F&A and benefit rates work.

This topic is further addressed under Budget Architecture.

Auxiliary Enterprise Revenues

Auxiliary enterprises are retail-like businesses run by colleges and universities for student, faculty, staff, and visitors. Auxiliaries include bookstores, residence halls, dining, student health centers, parking, copy and printing services, and conference centers to name the primary ones. These businesses have the look and feel of their for-profit counterparts, and the standards for operating them are similar: gross sales revenues should cover total operating costs (including allocable indirect costs), and cash flows (net operating revenues, or income from operations) should cover debt service. (See chapter 20, Auxiliary Enterprises and Other Activities, for more on this topic).

These standards might suggest that auxiliary budgets stand alone or are independent of the rest of the annual operating budget. This is not the case. There are crucial interactions with other budgets.

For example, if auxiliaries are not paying for allocable facilities costs or administrative services, then the unrestricted instruction budget is paying those costs (assuming research budgets pay only for research related indirect costs). Such subsidies need to be explicitly understood and managed. Where better business practices can be implemented to improve sales and reduce costs, subsidies can be reduced.

However, there are always howevers. Prices typically cannot be raised beyond external market levels, so pricing one's way out of subsidies may not be possible. Moreover, auxiliary purchases are a part of the student budget, and these affect the financial aid packages of need-based aid recipients. What is gained in auxiliary revenues could be lost in financial aid.

Auxiliaries also often have missions that are not purely business related. For example, the student life office may want apartments in student residences to be available rent-free to encourage faculty to live among students to develop a broader sense of academic community. Or special-event dining programs for students, faculty members, or visiting speakers may be more expensive than pure housing and dining markets would bear.

In these cases, the student life budget should contain the resources required to support community-building expenditures and make explicit transfer payments to the appropriate auxiliaries. This way, all costs are in sight and the business bases and special program activities are properly reflected in the assembly and portrayal of auxiliaries' budgets.

Other auxiliary-like activities include intercollegiate athletics (ticket sales, television revenues, support-group gift revenues) and hospitals and clinical practices (for universities with medical or dental schools). These are complex topics in their own rights. Their budgets need to be developed on a full-revenue/full-cost basis (like all auxiliaries) and any intra-institutional budget subsidies need to be explicitly planned and understood among all budget parties.

To enhance the budget model of auxiliaries, administrators should create shadow balance sheets and cash flow statements so one can understand auxiliary financial performance from a true return-on-net-assets perspective and at least impute investment income or interest on borrowed working capital to them. The practice of allowing auxiliaries to retain their year-end operating surpluses (contributions to net assets) and to repay their year-end operating losses (deductions from their net assets) ties auxiliaries' operations into their balance sheets through standard accounting conventions.

Expenditures

Once revenues are estimated, development of the expenditure budget follows.

If the present year's budget is $100, and it will cost $105 next year to buy the same "market basket" of services and goods, then the inflation increase relevant to budget development is 5 percent. Increasing expenditures by less than 5 percent will require buying less of something in the next year. If one wants to buy more or less of something in next year's budget, say additional or fewer faculty positions, then the change is called a volume increase or volume decrease.

Incremental budgeting. This type of budgeting means just what it says: it involves the annual planning and awarding of (typically small) increments (or sometimes decrements) to last year's budget. The presupposition of incremental budgeting is that the priorities of prior years, represented cumulatively in the current budget, remain appropriate. The other presupposition is sometimes less obvious—namely, that the highest priority proposed new increment is of lesser priority than the lowest priority activity already funded in the present budget! Thus a more refined approach to incremental budgeting is symmetrical incrementalism. Here every increment proposed—both the activity and the budget required to support it—must be compared with an activity of comparable cost already in the budget. Thus the highest priority increment must be prioritized vis-à-vis the lowest priority decrement, then the next highest priority increment with the next comparable dollar-level decrement, and so on up to a certain percent of last year's budget (sometimes called the base). Funding a higher priority proposed increment within present budget levels by eliminating a funded lower priority activity is referred to as growth by substitution.

Zero-based budgeting. This budgeting approach puts everything up for grabs. One starts with $0 at ground zero, and builds a budget activity by activity to fund the program in question optimally at varying resource levels. Each current or proposed activity or function is folded into a "decision package" which includes a description of goals and services. The package describes deliverables at alternate levels of costs and revenues. The sum of all such packages across all activities, prioritized by the unit's budget officer, is a zero-based budget proposal. One then compares the array of activities funded by the program's current budget with the new array and attendant budgets. In the best of worlds, the institution's top budget officers would assemble the expenditure budget from the highest priority decision packages at levels appropriate for the activity. Then, the new budget would be funded, and managers of that budget would add and subtract personnel, and increase or decrease materials, supplies, equipment, and facilities-support levels to create the optimum program delivery capability.

Zero-based budgeting is rare in practice. It's hard to do and presupposes enough rationality to develop "optimal" programs from scratch, when in fact many programs grew incrementally to start with and eventually proved successful, perhaps more by chance than by design. Sometimes one should not tamper with evolution. Zero-based budgeting presupposes the ability to rank activities or functions, often difficult in administrative service units, often impossible in academic departments. It presupposes the courage to implement fundamental changes. Zero-based budget development—especially if constrained to exploring only a few alternatives—is often useful and always enlightening. And it can prove effective if those who prepare the new budgets have the capability to implement the changes that underlie them.

Descriptions of individual categories of expenditures: salaries; benefits; materials, services, and supplies; and capitalizable equipment follow.

Salaries

Most colleges and universities participate in market salary surveys, and compare internal benchmark positions with the market's distribution (mean, median, variance) of salaries for the same jobs. Surveys tell provosts and deans how peer institutions pay faculty according to disciplinary specialization; they tell administrative officers how peer institutions pay for accountants, software engineers, investment officers, information technology specialists, human resource officers, secretaries, and even budget officers. In addition, human resources consulting firms publish their own expectations of how compensation markets will change in coming years.

Salary inflation is the increase in the current budget required to maintain one's current place, usually at some percentile of market mean or median, in the many specialty markets that academic institutions recruit from, and to whom they lose key people. A conscious repositioning of certain classes of faculty or staff in their respective markets will increase or decrease budgets from their inflation-estimated levels. If faculty or staff are added or subtracted from departments (volume changes) according to academic plans, or as a consequence of budget proposals and their attendant negotiations, then the budgets will deviate from salary inflation adjusted levels as well.

A brief note may be useful about turnover savings. A reliable annual phenomenon is senior faculty and staff exiting, and being replaced with junior-level appointments. The difference between the higher pay of the existing senior people and the entering junior replacements is turnover savings, and is available for other use, say, for increasing salaries beyond what is required to sustain market parity, or to hire additional staff, or to contribute to overall budget balance.

This raises the question of how positions are filled, and many colleges and universities focus as much on positions as on salaries during budget development. In extreme cases, numbers of full, associate, and assistant professors are specified during the budget development process, and salary dollars are budgeted for each position. Academic units are controlled as to both budgeted positions and total salaries expended. Position control is as important, here, as expenditure control. Unfilled faculty positions in a department often revert to higher authority: a department's empty positions may revert to a dean, or the dean's empty positions to the provost. Then these positions are available for reallocation (by the higher authority) during annual budget development.

In other institutions, there may be less focus on faculty positions and more on overall expenditures and whether each academic unit is delivering with respect to its agreed-upon plans. Here the focus is more on output measures, whereas position control is more focused on input. Where positions are involved, many institutions, especially public colleges and universities, engage in formula budgeting. Formulas typically determine numbers of faculty positions as a function of total enrollment. Then, too, the formulas sometimes determine attendant support levels, such as numbers of staff, amounts of materials, supplies, equipment, and square footage. Even when formulas are not imposed, they can serve as useful benchmarks in planning. Here, again, revenues (tuition revenues derived from enrollment) interact with expenditures (salaries for faculty positions).

Managing to fill a specific number of faculty positions is structurally identical to maintaining specific enrollments of undergraduate students. Faculty size is a function of faculty flow. Analogous to classes are faculty ranks—assistant, associate, and full professors. Like class size, each of these ranks has a specific number of positions and incumbents. The entering rank, like the first-year class, is filled by recruiting candidates from outside, and there are critical ratios here as well; for example, the so-called hit rate—the number of candidates receiving offers who say yes—is analogous to yield. And finally, the higher ranks are replenished from within through promotions (persistence), and from without through recruitment (transfers). Exits from the full professor rank are analogous to graduation.

Many colleges and universities maintain a faculty flow, or faculty renewal, model to predict and manage faculty size, and to predict and manage faculty salary budgets.

Benefits

Salaries are direct pay, and benefits are indirect pay; their sum is usually called total compensation. Benefits typically include health care, retirement contributions (or guarantees), Social Security taxes, life insurance, tuition remission (for career development or for children attending college), and so on. The sum of all benefit expenditures (on behalf of all employees) is sometimes called the benefit pool. The benefit pool divided by the sum of all salaries and wages is the benefit rate. For example, if all benefits cost $20 million, and salaries and wages equal $100 million, then the benefit rate is 20 percent.

Benefit costs are typically allocated to and recovered from the institution's operating units by applying the benefit rate to salary budgets. Each time a salary dollar is spent directly in the example, a 20-cent charge transfers to the benefit pool to offset expense. The benefits recovered from all budget sources should equal the total benefit costs. Like indirect cost rates, benefit rates allocate costs on average: the faculty and staff of any given unit will not likely incur benefit costs exactly equal to their salaries times the rate. Some institutions, rather than using a rate, allocate benefit costs exactly by summing the actual benefit costs for every employee in a given unit.

Benefit costs are not always easy to forecast. For instance, health insurance costs are notoriously volatile; in addition, participation rates in dollar matching programs, such as an institutional match of individual dollars contributed to a retirement plan, can sometimes change abruptly. The budget officer needs to work with the human resources benefits department to estimate inflation on current benefits; at the same time, changes in the benefit plan may be necessary either to meet competitive pressures or to reduce costs. Once the benefits budget and total budgeted salaries are estimated, the new benefit rate is known.

Benefit rates apply uniformly across unrestricted, designated, and restricted budgets including federally sponsored research grants and contracts. Institutions usually negotiate benefit (and indirect cost) rates with their cognizant agencies in advance, based on cost forecasts.

Materials, Services, and Supplies

This category comprises paper, pencils, and software budgeting, that is, the goods needed to carry out the unit's activities. It also comprises purchased services, such as copying, catering, and telecommunications. Sales of goods and services within the institution are also budgeted here, but with a negative algebraic sign. Internal sales are usually called interdepartmental income and budgeted as negative or contra expense since adding them to revenues would double count those revenues coming into the institution that fund the budgets doing the internal purchasing. Budget officers should ensure that interdepartmental income budgets summed across all units equal the costs of internal services purchased by all units.

Another subcategory applicable primarily to auxiliaries is cost of goods. For example, bookstores buy books to sell. The estimated cost of books to be purchased is budgeted as cost of goods. Food purchased by dining services is also budgeted this way. Cost of goods represents inventory, whereas other auxiliary costs represent the budget required to sell the goods, such as people and rent.

Capitalizable Equipment

Colleges and universities establish capitalization thresholds, often with agreement from external research sponsors and with concurrence of their public accounting firm. A common threshold today is $5,000. Equipment that costs over this threshold and has a useful life of more than one year is capitalizable, which is to say, the cost will show in the annual financial statements as depreciation over the number of years the equipment is deemed useful. For example, suppose a telecommunications department buys a telephone switch for $10 million and its useful life is 10 years. Then the institution's financial statements will credit a $10 million physical asset in the year of purchase (and reduce cash by $10 million unless the money is borrowed, creating a liability) and consume that asset by recording $1 million per year of expenditure under "depreciation" for 10 years (if the typical straight-line depreciation schedule is deployed).

Should institutions budget depreciation or capital outlays? It depends, but they mostly do some of both. For equipment purchased within some reasonable multiple of the capitalization threshold (say multiples of up to 5 or 10), they typically declare the total outlay as budget. As equipment becomes more expensive, however, and as its useful life gets longer, they turn to the capital budget for help. Then the capital budget supplies the money for the purchase, and the unit repays the capital budget with interest through amortization. The unit takes out a mortgage on the equipment.

Let's return to the example of the $10 million telephone switch. The telecommunications department would take out a loan of $10 million from the capital budget (if that were approved in the department's budget request), with an interest rate of, say, 7 percent (this rate should be the overall institution's average cost of capital). The budget of telecommunications would then show an expenditure of over $1.4 million in each annual budget (the "mortgage" payment) for 10 years to amortize the debt. The capital budget would show the source of the loan (either an external loan or an internal loan of working capital) and the amortization payment split into its components of interest and principal. The principal payments are surrogates for depreciation but, of course, will not match a straight-line schedule.

In the case of capital equipment, it may be difficult to budget in such a way as to predict the year-end depreciation expenses. Accurate estimates are theoretically possible if one predicts every purchase and its useful life. But because typical capitalization thresholds are low, it is not always easy. Extrapolation of a given unit's history will often suffice, punctuated occasionally with the large planned equipment acquisition.

Equipment with purchase prices below the capitalization threshold is usually considered materials or supplies and expended through the operating budget.

Bottom Lines

In common parlance, the bottom line equals annual revenues minus annual expenditures. But colleges and universities vary in their determination of which revenues and expenditures qualify for inclusion in the budget. Said another way: institutions vary in how they define operating budgets. For example, some institutions leave restricted gifts and endowments out of budget scope, believing their flows to be difficult to estimate and their deployment difficult to influence. Other institutions do not explicitly budget auxiliaries, believing that revenues will equal expense and ignoring the implied interactions with all other budgets via allocable indirect costs.

There are also ways in which universities interpret operations differently from the for-profit world. For example, universities view endowment payout and investment income as part of operations, yet businesses do not. Businesses and business analysts want to know whether their products are making money. So their financial reports show sales minus costs of production—that is, income from operations. This is the first bottom line. They then add return from investments held and subtract interest on debt to arrive at net revenues.

In the cases of colleges and universities, these kinds of portrayals are revealing, and show just how much revenue the core activities of teaching and research earn on their own. Tuition and fees, plus research revenues, minus the costs of teaching and research would constitute "operating income," and in most colleges and universities this number would be negative. Some would view the supplement provided by endowments and other investments as subsidies. If nothing else, the supplement measures the degree to which an institution does not pass all its costs onto the direct beneficiaries of its programs, primarily students and research sponsors.

Here flows from endowment payout and gifts and their related expenditures, both unrestricted and restricted, are viewed as part of the operating budget.

What Is a Balanced Budget?

This is a big question. Let us define the operating budget broadly as including flows of all resources intended for current consumption—that is, not intended for endowment principal, capital acquisitions, or construction—and including all expenditures that are not capitalizable. Our definition excludes sources and uses reflected in the capital budget (see below), as well as endowment gains not consumed through the endowment spending rule and new gift contributions to endowment. If operating resources, that is, revenues, equal expenditures, then the budget is balanced in a given fiscal year. Differences between revenues and expenses at the end of the year are called *budget variances* and either add to or subtract from net assets. Budget balance in a given year is important but not as important as balance across time. Balance across time has a name: *budget equilibrium.*

Let $R(t)$ be operating revenues at time t and $E(t)$ be expenditures. Balance exists when $R(t) = E(t)$. But equilibrium exists when the *slopes* of these functions, their *rates of change*, are also equal for extended intervals of t, that is, over several fiscal years. In the language of calculus, equilibrium exists when:

$$R(t_0) = E(t_0) \quad \text{and}$$

$$\frac{dR(t)}{dt} = \frac{dE(t)}{dt}$$

where t_0 is the start of a fiscal year, and for all $t > t_0$. To explore this notion, let us look at what might contribute to disequiilibrium. Suppose that the endowment spending rule sets the consumption rate too high, so that the return retained in endowment principal is insufficient to preserve the endowment's budget purchasing power over time. Suppose further that other revenues grow at the natural rate of inflation of expenditures. The budget will trend toward deficits over time since the cost rise on expenditures supported by endowment exceeds the increase available from the endowment payout. Here

$$\frac{dR(t)}{dt} < \frac{dE(t)}{dt}$$

Or consider another, perhaps more complex, contribution to disequilibrium. In periods like the 1970s when inflation dramatically outstripped personal income growth and the returns on stocks and bonds, the natural inflators of expenditures were again higher than those of tuition price and endowment return. Budget deficits were "natural" outcomes unless unnatural forces—like intense management of costs—intervened.

Disequilibrium, usually a pejorative term, is, however, a symmetrical term. In the 1990s, when financial assets grew beyond all expectations and inflation was almost negligible, endowment spending rules generated rapidly growing payouts, well in excess of the "natural" inflation rates of expenditures. Here

$$\frac{dR(t)}{dt} > \frac{dE(t)}{dt}$$

obtains if other growth rates are equal.

During this time, endowed colleges and universities often ran budget surpluses. At the same time, unconsumed gains in endowment market values led to extraordinary growth in net assets.

Let's take a more refined look at balance. Chief academic and financial officers have clear authority over unrestricted resources, and can certainly affect (if modestly) the deployment of restricted funds during the budget process. Consider the following circumstance. Unrestricted revenues (tuition, recovery of indirect costs, unrestricted gifts, and endowment income) fall short of unrestricted expenditures, so there is a deficit in the unrestricted "column" of the budget. But the inflow of restricted resources exceeds the outflow by an amount equal to the unrestricted deficit. The operating budget, as defined broadly, is balanced. Is this a problem? Perhaps not in one or two years. But suppose over time that the unrestricted deficit widens, as does the restricted surplus, say at the same rate.

Then, once again, the institution's budgets are balanced but internal political and ultimately financial problems are growing. In effect, the "owners" of unrestricted resources are living on an increasing line of credit generated (sometimes unknowingly) by the "owners" of restricted resources. To understand this better, let's take the example to the extreme. Imagine a university U with two divisions, P and D, standing for Provost and Department. P controls the unrestricted budget, D controls the restricted. U has no net assets, and lives hand-to-mouth, spending cash as it is received. At the end of the first year of business, U's operations are balanced, as shown in table 04-02, but P's and D's are not.

Division D now wants to spend its surplus, which D claims to "own." D goes to the "bank," but there's no cash, only an IOU from P. In this case, the problem is stark and clear. If, however, U amasses cash balances over time, then interdivisional imbalances can be masked, but probably not for long. Moral of the story for budget officers: know the internal resource flows.

This simple example illustrates another problem. Again to take the extreme case, suppose D's $120 million in revenues come from restricted endowments. The activities supported directly from these sources, and costing $100 million per year, require facilities and administrative services, the latter paid for through P's unrestricted budget. D's need for such indirect support may be the reason P's column is in deficit. Consequently, P should recover F&A (indirect) costs incurred in support of D's activities. If D had to transfer 20 cents to P for every dollar directly expended, the internal imbalance would be corrected. Moral for budget officers: just like federally sponsored research, activities supported from private sponsors through restricted gifts and endowments should pay indirect costs allocable to these activities. Such payments constitute legitimate internal transfers from restricted to unrestricted accounts.

Budget balance is a rich concept, and when viewed as a function of time, becomes still richer, giving rise to the concept of budget equilibrium or sustainable balance. The latter is really the goal, yet it is entirely reasonable that planned strategic short- to medium-term deficits could be the means to future equilibrium. Moreover, there is more than just operating equilibrium: balance sheets, that is, the financial and physical assets and related liabilities, should be managed to maintain or improve their key ratios to operating activities as well. As already shown, excessive consumption of endowment return can create temporary operating balance but longer-term deficits; here financial assets are declining relative to

Table 04-02

Global Balance/Local Imbalance Example (in $000,000)

	P	D	U (= P +D)
Revenues	$100	$120	$220
Expenditures	120	100	220
Surplus (Deficit)	(20)	20	0

the activities they support. Excess consumption of physical capital has a similar effect. If buildings and equipment are not renovated or replaced in a timely way, which is to say depreciation is not offset by new capitalized assets entering the balance sheet, then the institution's ability to attract and retain faculty and students will suffer. Here physical assets are declining relative to the activities they support—for example, research. Maintaining multiyear budget planning and forecasting models that integrate operations with the balance sheet are indispensable to managing long-term financial equilibrium. For a more extensive discussion of equilibrium, see Hopkins and Massy[4].

Who Should Own Budget Variances?

The governing board owns variances. But presidents, provosts, and chief financial offers bear responsibility, and they often delegate their burdens to deans, department chairs, and directors of administrative units. Individual budget units should own their own surpluses and deficits in a very quantitative way: they should retain their year-end surpluses in an internal "bank account" with interest, and they should borrow their deficits from the internal bank and repay them with interest. Excessive negative variances over time may be a sign of bad budgets, bad management, failed plans, or all three. Real quantitative measures matter when assessing financial accountability. (This perspective on "local" ownership of deficits and surpluses is neither universally practiced nor broadly embraced.)

Bottom-line variances are functions of both revenue and expenditure variances, and delegations of responsibility, especially for revenues, are handled very differently across colleges and universities. This topic is also covered in the section on budget architecture.

DEVELOPING THE CAPITAL BUDGET

The capital budget funds equipment, enterprise software development projects, renovations, and new facilities whose costs exceed the capitalization threshold and whose useful lives extend over several years. Like operational budgeting, capital budgeting is a planning and control process. Unlike operational budgeting, however, the capital budgeting process involves planning for expenditures too large and too episodic to be readily incorporated into annual operating budgets. Indeed, in nearly all cases, outlays for capital projects are too large to fund within a single year's operating budget. Capital projects typically require long planning lead times and are implemented over multiple operating budget cycles. They usually require large infusions of capital and have potentially enormous impacts on the balance sheet. Attendant debt service and operating costs can have enormous impacts on operating budgets as well. Accordingly, capital budgets require extraordinary involvement and vigilance of governing boards.

Capital Structures of Colleges and Universities

Capital comes in several forms in colleges and universities. The capital in question may be financial—endowments and so-called working capital. Capital may be physical, such as facilities and equipment. Debt capacity is latent capital, derived from an institution's combination of assets and operating cash flows. Still another form of capital is goodwill. Goodwill is reflected in the strength of the institution—its students, research sponsorship, and philanthropic markets.

An institution's financial capital appears on the balance sheet as investments; and its physical capital under "plant and equipment." Its debt capacity (see below) can be calculated at various credit-rating levels. Its goodwill is less quantitative but will show, among other loci, in the flows of contributions through the operating budget and statement of activities. It will show as well in the ambitiousness and realization of fund-raising goals.

The capital budget may access any or all of these forms of capital.

Equity Capital

Equity capital is defined here as net assets (equity in hand) plus goodwill (equity one can raise in the philanthropic marketplace). Let's consider net assets first.

Net assets comprise financial and physical assets net of liabilities. This section considers financial assets since most physical assets of most colleges and universities are not liquid: they cannot—and would not—be sold to raise cash for other capital projects. The best financial assets are the least restricted and the most liquid. Thus, quasi endowment and working capital (including operating reserves) are the primary sources of equity in hand.

Goodwill underlies the ability to attract external gift funding for capital projects. Individuals and donors give to institutions they trust: they believe in faculty and management's abilities to convert gifts to valuable educational and research outcomes. They value the continuing association with "their" college or university and with the specific project to which they contributed. Indeed, economists would argue that donors are buying an associative good—the opportunity to be associated with a mission of compelling grandeur, people of extraordinary intellect, or programs of unique societal value. They donate to become members of an exclusive club. Goodwill is not manifest explicitly on balance sheets, but it is partly quantifiable by inference.

Gifts for capital projects become equity capital, residing in working capital (and among independent universities, classified as temporarily restricted) until expended for construction. Few capital projects, and hence few capital budgets, are fully funded by gifts. Debt and operating reserves are the other sources.

Debt Capital and Capacity

Debt is borrowed money. If borrowed outside the institution from banks or bondholders, it is external debt, and it is booked as a liability. If borrowed from inside—say from working capital or quasi endowment—it is internal debt, and should be viewed as a liability even through it is not always booked as such in financial statements.

When considering debt, one analyzes its costs. External debt is priced in liquid markets. Short-term debt or working capital lines of credit from banks are negotiated and priced according to amounts required and the borrowing institution's creditworthiness. Colleges and universities can access less expensive debt by issuing tax-exempt bonds, and this is usually preferable to other financing, especially for large-scale projects.

When considering internal loans, one faces opportunity costs, that is, the foregone earnings from the financial asset that is borrowed and converted to new building construction or purchase of equipment. If one borrows from working capital—typically invested in cash or short-term bond funds—the foregone return may be slightly lower than the interest rate on bank loans or taxable bonds. Hence borrowing for smaller projects of relatively short useful lives is often done internally.

Borrowing internally from quasi endowment is another matter. Most endowments are invested between 50 and 80 percent in stocks and the rest in bonds, real estate, and cash. Long-term expected returns on such investments would exceed interest rates on long-term tax-exempt bonds, for example, by several hundred basis points. For large, long-lived capital acquisitions, the opportunity costs are too high to borrow from quasi endowment if the institution's debt capacity allows borrowing the requisite amounts externally.

Let's follow a typical large project through its capital budget life cycle. Tables 04-03a and 04-03b contain the relevant numbers.

At Hypothetical University, the need for a bioengineering laboratory probably grew out of conversations among faculty, then among key department chairs and deans, and then through their convincing the provost and president of the strategic importance of launching a bioengineering initiative. The initiative would involve defining an academic program, recruiting new faculty who would work in this interdisciplinary field, and constructing a building to house offices and laboratories. Out of the planning emerged the goal to raise $100 million for a new laboratory in the upcoming capital campaign.

The board of trustees of Hypothetical University required, by policy, that a donor contribute 50 percent of the project's cost to name the building. In time, a member of the board, an alumna, by name Eponymous, became an enthusiast of the project, and pledged the requisite $50 million—$20 million at the outset and $10 million per year for three years thereafter. The president and her development staff eventually identified an additional $20 million in cash gifts and $5 million in corporate donations of fixed equipment required by the research and instructional programs. The momentum around this project was so strong that the president and board decided to start construction before the remaining $25 million in gifts had been raised.

The budget director and the chief financial officer, confronted with the data in table 04-03b, observed the likely need for project financing in years 03 and 04, and probably thereafter based on their prior experiences with such projects. They presented the cash flows to the board of trustees' finance committee, and argued that internal financing through working capital could carry the project through 03, but that they should lay the groundwork now for long-term tax exempt bond financing. When asked why the university should not just pay off the building with $25 million in quasi endowment, the CFO replied that the likely interest rate on the proposed bond issue was 5 percent, whereas the return on endowment was 10.5 percent. The opportunity cost of "decapitalizing," that is, spending, quasi endowment principal, was too high: future generations would be denied the benefits of the consumed endowment, and balance sheet net assets would be less by $25 million compounded at 5.5 percent per year. (The added assumption is that tuition and indirect cost recovery would pay for the laboratory's operating costs, depreciation, and interest on the loan.)

Another trustee on the finance committee asked, "How much more debt can we afford? Is another $25 million within bounds?" The answer comes from within

Table 04-03a

Eponymous Bioengineering Laboratory
Capital Budget (in $000,000)

Sources	
Naming Gift	$ 50
Other Gifts	25
Debt	25
Total	**$100**
Expenditures	
Planning/Architects Fees	$ 10
Construction	70
Furnishings & Equipment	20
Total	**$100**

Table 04-03b

Eponymous Bioengineering Laboratory Cash Flows

Year	01	02	03	04	Total
Gifts					
Naming	$20	10	10	10	$50
Other	10	5	5	5	25
Total	**$30**	**15**	**15**	**15**	**$75**
Expenditures					
Planning/Architects Fees	$10	0	0	0	$10
Construction	0	20	40	10	70
Furnishings & Equipment	0	0	0	20	20
Total	**$10**	**20**	**40**	**30**	**$100**
Cash Surplus/(Deficit)	$20	(5)	(25)	(15)	$(25)
Cumulative Surplus/(Deficit)*	$20	15	(10)	(25)	$(25)

*To be funded by debt capital

and without the university. Indeed, the capital markets have a lot to say about how much debt is too much; internal comfort levels must be set within external bounds.

Credit analysts calculate several ratios. The two most important are the viability ratio and debt burden ratio. The first is the ratio

$$\frac{expendable\ net\ assets}{long-term\ debt}.$$

The numerator here is the sum of all liquid assets available to pay off the debt. Unrestricted working capital and quasi endowment comprise most of the numerator.

The second ratio,

$$\frac{debt\ service}{total\ expenditures}$$

measures how much of the annual expenditure budget is consumed by debt service and introduces the interdependence between operating and capital budgets. Debt service includes both interest and principal payments; the denominator typically excludes depreciation but includes debt principal payments.

There are no hard and fast rules determining what these ratios must be. The viability ratio should surely exceed 1, and should preferably be multiples of 1. Investment bankers, credit agencies, and bond insurance companies typically do not feel comfortable with debt burden ratios greater than 10 percent, although many other factors may contribute to analysts' comfort levels. Obviously the higher the viability ratio and the lower the debt burden ratio, the higher the credit rating. These and several other ratios along with much more comprehensive coverage of debt capacity measures are found in chapter 6, Managerial Reporting. To determine the amount of debt an institution can afford, analysts compute ratios on a pro-forma basis, assuming additional levels of borrowing and attendant debt service.

The trustee's question about appropriate levels of debt should lead Hypothetical University to develop a debt policy reflecting the trustees' fiduciary comfort levels with leverage, as well as the credit quality they would expect to maintain in the capital markets. For an enlightening treatment of this subject, see Massy.[5]

Linkages between Operating and Capital Budgets

The debt burden ratio introduces the key relationship. If debt is used to finance projects, then debt service becomes an operating obligation. For example, at 5 percent interest per year, the annual interest payment for Eponymous Bioengineering Laboratory is $1.25 million; the debt service is approximately $1.6 million per year if amortized over 30 years. The capital budget needs to ask the operating budget whether it can accommodate an additional expenditure of $1.6 million per year plus annual operating costs of the new lab.

Recall that the hypothetical plan for bioengineering probably postulated new faculty, additional students, and some level of sponsored research. If the plan is coming together, some of the interest on debt plus operating expenditures should be recovered from research sponsors and some from incremental tuition revenues. If, however, the incremental costs cannot be covered through operating revenues or reallocated expenditures, the project lays claim to the university's financial assets: working capital and quasi endowment. If the claim is too large, requiring a material increase in the endowment spending rate, then the CFO's argument for tax-exempt bonds instead of internal financing begins to weaken. This is the reason governing boards take special interest in capital projects and debt financing. Debt capacity is the obverse, the liability side, of their concern about preservation of endowment purchasing power. Indeed, an institution's debt policy is a necessary companion of its endowment asset allocation and spending rule policies: liability management is a function of asset management and vice-versa.

A typical multiyear capital budget would sum all planned projects like the single one in tables 04-03a and 04-03b and would also show interest earnings for positive gift balances and interest payments for bridge and permanent financing. Debt service schedules summed across all projects would also be displayed. The companion, multiyear operating budget would ascertain whether debt service could be accommodated within operating revenues.

One final note about the capital budget. Remember the observation that budgets should predict financial statements? The capital budget is the primary source of facilities renewal, replacement, and additions. New, capitalizable construction adds physical assets—land, buildings, and equipment—to the balance sheet. Associated debt increases liabilities. The capital budget is an important leading indicator of changes in net physical assets.

BUDGET ARCHITECTURE;
RELATED DEVELOPMENT PROCESSES

Budgets and the processes for developing them are designed either by accretion or comprehensively. Development by accretion represents the incremental contributions of many academic and financial "architects" over years. Comprehensive development represents the aesthetic and managerial world views of a few individual leaders at a point in time. The former are like old cities before maps: newcomers can comprehend only a couple buildings or blocks at a time and have to ask city natives how to find their way around; the tools of the cultural anthropologist are required to make sense of the whole. The latter are like designed cities (L'Enfant's Washington, D.C., for example) after maps: newcomers can quickly comprehend the whole, and find their way around on their own.

The next three sections briefly characterize three archetypal designs.

Centralized Unrestricted Budgeting

In this budget archetype, the central administration (president, provost, and chief financial officer) "own" unrestricted revenues—tuition, indirect cost recovery, endowment, and gift income. The goal of the budget process is to divide these revenues "appropriately" among the expenditure budgets of academic and administrative operating units of the campus. The annual budget cycle begins with the central administration estimating revenues, usually on an inertial basis, and then issuing a budget call letter to deans and directors. Such letters typically indicate overall revenue constraints and likely expenditure inflation factors governing the new budget, promulgate any planning priorities that will govern choices among budget proposals, and provide deadlines for proposal submission and budget hearing dates that allow personal discussions among revenue owners and those who would lay claim to their fair share. Revenues, once estimated, act as a constraint and are usually not discussed in hearings. Hearings focus almost exclusively on expenditure budget proposals. The central administration wants to keep the sum of all new budgets within revenue bounds; deans and administrative directors want to maximize their slices of the revenue pie. Negotiation is the behavioral modality.

In this budget archetype, restricted endowment and gifts are mostly off the table, viewed by central administration as "self-balancing," and by deans and directors as off limits. Accounting systems evolve to reify these perspectives.

All-Funds Budgeting

In this archetype, central administration still owns unrestricted revenues, but designated and restricted gifts and endowments are on the table along with unrestricted resources. The budget call letter asks for budget proposals that exhibit the sources and uses of all funds. Thus, the central administration unrestricted allocation is one of the deans' sources, along with their own gift balances and flows, endowment income balances, and new distributions. While deans will still strive to maximize their share of the unrestricted pie, the provost can test requests for her precious incremental resources against the deans' own means (and willingness) to fund them. Moreover, as restricted resources grow relative to unrestricted revenues, the need to recover facilities and administrative service costs supporting restricted activities increases, often severely. Once this issue is addressed formally, by instituting an indirect cost rate applicable to restricted gifts and endowments, unrestricted and restricted resources are structurally linked and must be planned and budgeted together. Accounting systems are redesigned to reveal all sources and their linkages. Table 04-04 presents a typical all-funds budget format. The table shows account fund balances at the end of a fiscal year, then tracks source flows and uses in the new year. The ending balances indicate that the budget unit grew richer by $10 million.

Revenue Responsibility Budgeting

The first archetype formalizes central ownership of unrestricted revenues and represses consideration of restricted sources. The all-funds archetype brings designated and/or restricted resources out into the open, forcing centrally and locally owned revenues simultaneously into play. This approach expands the central unrestricted model; it engages priorities jointly, bringing central and local perspectives into harmony or into dissonance as the case may be.

Revenue responsibility budgeting (RRB) moves still further in the direction of local ownership of revenues. Each school owns the tuition revenue generated by the courses their faculty members teach. Schools own the research recoveries (direct and indirect) their principal investigators win and manage; they also own the facilities and administrative service costs they incur. More specifically, in RRB:

- The schools and auxiliaries are defined as revenue and cost centers: tuition revenues are allocated (belong) to these centers in proportion to credit hours generated by the faculty, research revenues are allocated according to the academic departmental locus of the principal investigator, and so on.

Table 04-04

All-Funds Budget Format ($000,000)

	General	Gifts	Endowments	Research	Total
Beginning Balance		10	5	0	**$15**
Sources					
General (Unrestricted Expenditure Budget)	$100				100
Gifts		20			20
Endowment payout			30		30
Sponsored Research				200	200
Total Sources	**$100**	**20**	**30**	**200**	**$350**
Uses					
Compensation	$70		20	140	$230
Materials, Supplies, Equipment	30	5		40	75
Graduate Tuition Support		10	5	20	35
Total Uses	**$100**	**15**	**25**	**200**	**$340**
ENDING BALANCE	**$0**	**15**	**10**	**0**	**$25**

Indirect costs—facilities and administration—are allocated to, and must be paid by, these centers as well.

- The deans and faculties of these centers have responsibility for developing feasible revenue budgets and total expenditures within revenue constraints.

- There is typically a franchise assessment, participation, on each center, which is combined with other unrestricted revenues such as endowment and gift streams, to form a central redistribution or subvention pool. The pool is redistributed to neutralize differential unit costs (science courses cost more than humanities courses), and to fund institutional (or corporate) priorities.

Revenue responsibility centers' budgets are balanced according to the formula:

revenues − participation + subvention = direct expenditures + indirect expenditures

The total university's budget is the sum of all revenue responsibility centers' budgets.

Budget proposals and formats here are very different from earlier archetypes.

Consistent with overall institutional policy, each center develops enrollment plans, tuition revenue budgets, and faculty course load requirements. Similarly, centers propose research revenue budgets arising from continuing and projected new grants and contracts generated by the PIs whose academic home departments lie within the center, and so on across other locally owned revenue sources. The center then calculates participation (exported revenues), the likely subvention back from the provost (imported revenues), and the F&A (indirect) costs allocable to the center. If additional space is required for the overall program, the attendant facilities costs are factored in. The direct expense budget is total revenues minus total facilities and administrative charges. If this difference is not what the dean and his faculty deem sufficient to support their academic program, they can revisit direct revenues to test the feasibility of increases, reallocate lower priority expenditures to higher priority ones, or return underutilized space to the central pool to reduce facilities costs. Alternatively, they can present their overall plan to the provost, president, and CFO with a case for additional subvention.

The central subvention decision is mostly about the quality of the center's overall plan from a discipline-specific perspective as well as an overall institutional priority perspective. The case for subvention may be based on the school's contribution to the commons, on academic quality, financial need, or negotiation skills. The big resource levers, however, are primarily in the hands of revenue center deans or directors in RRB.

In RRB, all revenues and all expenditures are in play at the center level. There is shared ownership of all revenues, with center and central shares weighted by participation (the franchise assessment) and the indirect cost rates applicable to restricted accounts. The heavy tilt in such systems is toward the centers (schools and auxiliaries).

Also, facilities (space) costs are in active play in RRB. In the first archetype, for example, revenues and facilities costs are the provost's and CFO's problems. Space appears to be free from a dean's point of view. Demand for space will exceed supply at this price. The same is true in the all-funds archetype, except that the dean or provost may bring locally restricted funds into play to fund space renovations—but not to pay rent, unless demand is so intense that leasing commercial space adjacent to campus is required. And then everyone realizes that space isn't free. In RRB, if you use more space, you need to increase revenues to pay the rent; if you use less, revenues can be redeployed to pay for other priorities.

By allocating administrative costs to revenue responsibility centers, RRB also creates pressures on central administration to reduce service costs and improve services (financial, human resources, facilities maintenance, student recruitment and enrollment, library, etc.). Reductions in allocable administrative service costs free up revenues in the individual centers.

Similar, though somewhat less focussed, pressures occur even in the most centralized budget archetype if significant sponsored research dollars are involved. Here facilities and administration costs are reflected in the indirect cost rate. Principal investigators are not bashful about asking why the rate is usurious or the quality of service is dismal. Because such rates are averages, however, a local decision to vacate space will not give rise to commensurate local value: the diminution of the average rate will return the local PIs only pennies on the dollar value of the square feet sacrificed.

Budget architectures should fit institutional contexts. The first archetype is appropriate for a small college or a moderate sized university comprising a liberal arts college and one or two allied professional schools. As institutions grow in size and complexity, and as entrepreneurial research faculty create strong departments able to raise "their own" resources from government and private sponsors and donors, the all-funds model fits. As numbers of professional schools proliferate— operating within very diverse enrollment, research, and philanthropic markets— central leaders are too far removed from the action, and have to master far too much complexity, for a totally centralized budget process to be effective. RRB may work best here. Worthy of note is the fact that some universities have hybrid architectures. The business school, for example, may be a revenue responsibility center, while the centralized unrestricted model is used for all other schools. Budget architectures are accounting-like accountability structures that fall within the broader field of managerial accounting.

For elaboration on these subjects, see Curry,[6] Whalen,[7] and Strauss, Whalen and Curry.[8]

Table 04-05 represents a hypothetical university's budget in RRB format. As shown, the central administration receives $122 million both directly and through participation; the sum goes back to the revenue responsibility centers (all academic here) as subvention. Similarly, central administration spends $250 million directly for facilities and administration, but allocates all of it back to the revenue centers. This table uses the same numbers as in the example in the section on "Research: Indirect Costs." Knowing, in particular, that the facilities rate is 40 percent and the administration rate is 20 percent, what can one infer about relative instructional costs between Schools A and B (use tuition revenues as enrollment measures)?

Table 04-05

Revenue Responsibility Budget Format (in $000,000)

	Administration Centers	Academic Centers		Total
		School A	School B	
DIRECT REVENUES				
Tuition	0	100	50	150
Endowment & Gifts				
Unrestricted	40	0	0	40
Restricted	0	30	50	80
Research				
Restricted	0	100	200	300
F&A recovery	0	60	120	180
INDIRECT REVENUES				
Participation	82	(38)	(44)	0
@20% excluding restricted research				
Subvention	(122)	48	74	0
Total Revenues	0	300	450	750
DIRECT EXPENDITURES				
Instruction	0	100	100	200
Research	0	100	200	300
Facilities	150	0	0	150
Administration	100	0	0	100
INDIRECT EXPENDITURES				
Facilities	(150)	60	90	0
Administration	(100)	40	60	0
Total Expenditures	0	300	450	750

RRB has several aliases: RCM (responsibility or revenue center management, RCB (responsibility center budgeting), and, in the extreme, ETOB (each tub on its own bottom), essentially RRB without the franchise assessment.

BUDGET IMPLEMENTATION AND MANAGEMENT

The quality of a year's budget is measured by whether the plans laid and commitments made are fulfilled. Were the new faculty approved in engineering hired? Did the first-year class meet size and quality thresholds? Were revenues, expenditures, and the bottom line on target? Did administrative services improve? Implementing and managing budgets well lead to affirmative replies to such questions.

Among the clearest and most important postmortems on an annual budget is the audited financial statement. Consequently, budget formats and terminology should comport with financial statement formats and terminology. Once a budget is developed, it is transferred into the institution's financial accounting system where revenues earned and expenditures incurred are recorded throughout the year. To manage outcomes to the budgeted bottom line, one needs to know historical maturation rates of revenues and expenditures, by budget unit and in sum. Moreover, certain key milestones during a year, such as the date fall tuition revenues are recorded, need to remain consistent across time. Thus, for example if one knows that fall tuition revenue is booked on October 1, and fall tuition is typically 55 percent of the annual total, then year-end tuition revenues can be forecast on October 1 and compared with budget. The same is true with expenditures. If salaries are encumbered for the year, then one can also infer year-end total compensation and turnover savings early in the new fiscal year. Such projections should be updated monthly or quarterly depending on the closeness of management levels to the transactions. For example, monthly or even more frequent updates may be necessary at the departmental level, whereas quarterly updates will suffice at the CFO level.

Good budget management should be rewarded and bad management should be penalized. Year-end surpluses should be "banked" (available later for the units that produced them) and deficits should constitute loans repayable over time. Chronic surplus or deficits, however, may indicate ill-formed budgets instead of poor budget management.

Budget management should be a joint effort on several dimensions. Local units should forecast local year-end positions; each hierarchical level up should do the same—but in coordination with their subordinate units. Each quarter, everyone from the provost and CFO down the authority chain should share a common understanding of what revenues and expenditures are problematic and in which areas. They should design joint corrective measures as necessary.

A vital relationship is implied here—that between the budget director and controller. The controller's office should monitor and report budget performance; the budget director should use performance reports to ascertain which assumptions went right and which went awry in budget formulation, especially those that will persist into the new budget year being planned. One way to assure that everyone is appropriately tuned in is to create a budget and finance steering committee co-chaired by the provost and CFO and staffed by the budget director and controller. In this way, the controller understands the inputs to the annual budget and what to look out for during the fiscal year payout. The budget director learns from the controller what is working and what is not working in the budget last developed and can see how these may affect the budget being planned. Top decision makers remain immersed in the context that informs their choices of mid-year corrections or revised planning assumptions and budget allocations going forward.

ROLES OF GOVERNING BODIES

Trustees or regents of colleges and universities are the stewards of long-term viability. Vital players in assessing and blessing strategic direction, they are responsible for the preservation and appropriate growth of financial and physical assets.

Budgets are fiduciary enablers. They predict changes in net assets through operations and through capital budgets. Combined with predictions of total return on investments—crucial to the trustees' approval of endowment spending rates—the operating and capital budgets give comfort (usually) to trustees that net assets are managed and controlled so as to affirm prudent oversight. After a budget is approved, management should provide quarterly budget performance reports to trustees to herald possible problems and to demonstrate active budget monitoring and control. At the same time, trustees need to know how the next year's budget is shaping up.

The Association of Governing Boards of Universities and Colleges (AGB) provides the standard guide to trustee responsibility, and hence to management's obligation to trustees.[9, 10]

MAXIMS TO BUDGET BY

Over many years of budgeting, financial management, financial systems installations, and consulting to all the above, the authors have accumulated some insights that, they believe, have enduring value. They record them here, with brief illustrations and commentary.

Budgets should comport with financial statements. This chapter has stressed that budgets should be developed in the same terms and formats as financial statements and should predict changes in net assets. Language is simpler, and hence communications clearer. Senior management and trustees compare budgets to actuals, where actuals *are* the financial statements. Accountability is served, as is broader fiduciary responsibility.

Yet many institutions defy this maxim. They prepare budgets in one presentation format, maintain a chart of accounts based on fund accounting, and tortuously reconfigure year-end results to comport with new accounting standards for presentation of financial statements. The crosswalk from budget to financial statements, if done at all, is stupefying. And crosswalk talk drives out conversations about the substance of budget performance (a form of Gresham's Law).

Financial information ought to be open and shared rather than hidden and personally brokered. This fosters organizational learning and results in better decisions.

Financial data should reside in one database and should be the source of all budget and financial performance conversations. Data wars deny understanding of financial issues and positions, and they destroy accountability. Colleges and universities should be integrated by a common accounting system. The authors have worked their way through many organizations where *information is power* in the sense that, "I have it, you don't, so I have power over you." A more humane and enabling interpretation of information is power, that is, "*We* have it, and together can make better decisions for our institution." Common, shared data foster understanding of what lies behind the numbers and can mediate opposing perspectives. There is no mediation when opposites use their own shadow system data to support their individual positions.

Never net. Netting masks the dynamics of the components, and denies understanding of them. For example, changes in net tuition revenues do not reveal what is happening with enrollment and financial aid, each of which is governed by its own dynamic. Netting auxiliary revenues against expenses, as some institutions do in budgeting, masks the different markets governing inflation on revenues and expenses.

Budget and financial system hierarchies should be congruent with management responsibility hierarchies. It should be clear who is to be praised and who is to be blamed for most financial management matters. If someone isn't accountable, no one is. Budget directors and CFOs cannot control alone.

Accountability is only as good as the tools that measure it. Some would say, if you don't measure it you won't get it.

Accountability (a) and control (c) are complementary along a continuum and add to 100 percent: a = 100% − c. If people are 100 percent accountable, that is, a = 100%, controls are not necessary, that is, c = 0%. If there is total control (c = 100%), people need not be accountable at all.

Accountability is preferable to control. Processes are simplified and trust is reinforced. If information feedback is accurate, rapid, and monitored by supervisors, most financial related transactions can be completed at the point of origin. No more approval signatures (control points) may be necessary.

People play better budget games when the rules are open, widely understood, and commonly embraced. If you want to change the game, you can challenge the rules that aren't working and alter them. If rules are buried in years of culture, it's hard to know how to address dysfunctionality. "Closed" rules are hostile to newcomers and protect incumbents' administrative roles and territories.

Responsibility should be commensurate with authority—and vice versa. The decoupling of authority and responsibility is common in colleges and universities. For example, faculty have authority over academic standards and the quality and attractiveness of educational offerings. Yet admissions directors have responsibility for delivering the "right" first-year class, and budget officers have the responsibility to present a balanced budget. Organizational bridges can equilibrate authority and accountability. Build bridges! The enrollment management group noted in the section above is an example.

Decentralization of organizations and their budget architectures should be proportional to overall size and complexity. People too far removed from the action don't make the best decisions, and even when they make good decisions, their ability to implement them is inversely proportional to their distance from the action. RRB is one approach to moving authority and responsibility down the organization chart towards the classrooms and laboratories in large, diverse, complex universities. ETOB ("each tub on its own bottom"—essentially an extreme version of RRB without the franchise assessment) is another. Both are imperfect, of course.

Central leverage is required to implement corporate priorities. This is another way of stating the "commons" problem from economics or of restating an operations research theorem that says that the sum of local optimization is not necessarily globally optimal. In universities, the commons include libraries, student life (outside the classroom), streets, lawns, trees, and information systems integration (common database, common platform, and common enterprise software). Central administrations are guardians and sponsors of the commons because calls for budget increases in these areas rarely well up from academic units.

Budget expected values and pool risks by understanding variances around each projection. This is another version of "never net."

College and university budgets should embrace and integrate almost everything. Budget officers, therefore, need to know everything.

NOTES

1. McPherson, Michael S. and Morton Owen Schapiro, *Keeping College Affordable* (Washington, D.C.: The Brookings Institution, October 1991).

2. Lapovsky, Lucie, and Loren Loomis Hubbell, "Positioning for Competition" in *Business Officer,* NACUBO, March 2000.

3. Massy, William F., "Endowments" in *Resource Allocation in Higher Education*, edited by William F. Massy (Ann Arbor, MI: University of Michigan Press, 1996).

4. Hopkins, David S. P. and William F. Massy, *Planning Models for Colleges and Universities* (Palo Alto, CA: Stanford University Press, 1981).

5. Massy, William F., "Optimizing Capital Decisions" in *Resource Allocation in Higher Education*, edited by William F. Massy (Ann Arbor, MI: University of Michigan Press, 1996).

6. Curry, John R., "The USC Experience with Revenue Center Management" in *Responsibility Center Budgeting* by Edward L. Whalen (Bloomington: Indiana University Press, 1991).

7. Whalen, Edward L., *Responsibility Center Budgeting: An Approach to Decentralized Management for Institutions of Higher Education* (Bloomington, IN: Indiana University Press, 1991).

8. Strauss, Jon C., John R. Curry, and Edward L. Whalen, "Revenue Responsibility Budgeting" in *Resource Allocation in Higher Education*, edited by William F. Massy (Ann Arbor, MI: University of Michigan Press, 1991).

9. Zwingle, V. L. *Trustee Responsibilities: A Basic Guide for Governing Boards of Independent (or Public) Institutions. Association of Governing Boards Basics Series, 1997.*

10. Salluzo, Ronald E., and Baroni, Gregory J. "Is Your Board Forgetting the Future?" in *Trusteeship,* Association of Governing Boards of Universities and Colleges, September/October 1998.

REFERENCES AND RESOURCES

Publications and Articles

Curry, John R. "The USC Experience with Revenue Center Management" in *Responsibility Center Budgeting* by Edward L. Whalen. Bloomington: Indiana University Press. 1991.

Hopkins, David S. P., and Massy, William F. *Planning Models for Colleges and Universities.* Palo Alto: Stanford University Press, 1981.

Massy, William F. "Endowments" in *Resource Allocation in Higher Education*, edited by William F. Massy. Ann Arbor, MI: University of Michigan Press, 1996.

Massy, William F. "Optimizing Capital Decisions" in *Resource Allocation in Higher Education*, edited by William F. Massy. Ann Arbor, MI: University of Michigan Press, 1996.

McPherson, Michael S., and Schapiro, Morton Owen. *Keeping College Affordable.* Washington, DC: The Brookings Institution, October 1991.

Strauss, Jon C., Curry, John R., and Whalen, Edward L. "Revenue Responsibility Budgeting" in *Resource Allocation in Higher Education*, edited by William F. Massy. Ann Arbor, MI: University of Michigan Press, 1991.

Whalen, Edward L. *Responsibility Center Budgeting: An Approach to Decentralized Management for Institutions of Higher Education.* Bloomington: Indiana University of Indiana Press, 1991.

Chapter 5

Financial Reporting

by

Herbert Folpe

Sponsors

KPMG, LLP
Contact: Greg J. Baroni
1676 International Drive
McLean, VA 22102
703-747-3004
www.kpmg.com

With over 30 years of serving higher education, KPMG offers a broad range of services that helps our clients analyze their businesses with true clarity, raises their level of performance and delivers the strategic and infrastructural components to support highly dynamic E-business models in colleges, universities, and academic medical centers.

PEOPLESOFT, INC.
Contact: Karen Willett
4460 Hacienda Drive
Pleasanton, CA 94588
925-694-5453
www.peoplesoft.com/highered

PeopleSoft delivers E-business solutions for higher education management needs, including student administration, grants management, finance, human resources, E-procurement, advancement, and more. PeopleSoft also provides comprehensive customer service, consulting, education, and technical support services.

Contents

This chapter provides an overview of general purpose external financial reporting in higher education. Those who want or need a more detailed treatment of the subject should turn to NACUBO's *Financial Accounting and Reporting Manual for Higher Education,* a subscription service. Those who are interested in the history of the subject (and in what reporting standards formerly applied) should refer to Part 5 of the fourth edition of this work (pp. 383–466), to chapter 5 of the fifth edition (pp. 205–235), and to the preface of the third edition (pp. ix–iiix) reprinted in both the fourth edition (pp. xii–xx), and the fifth edition (pp. xxxix–xlv).

GENERAL PURPOSE EXTERNAL FINANCIAL REPORTING—AN OVERVIEW

The purpose and scope of general purpose external financial reporting are set forth by the Financial Accounting Standards Board (FASB) in its Concepts Statement 4, *Objectives of Financial Reporting by Nonbusiness Organizations,* as follows:

> "The aim of that type of financial reporting is limited. It does not attempt to meet all informational needs of those interested in nonbusiness organizations nor to furnish all the types of information that financial reporting can provide . . . . Rather, general purpose external financial reporting focuses on providing information to meet the common interests of external users who cannot generally prescribe the information they want from an organization . . . . The most obvious and important users fitting this description in the nonbusiness environment are resource providers such as members, taxpayers, contributors, and creditors."

General purpose external financial reporting should be distinguished from other types of reporting addressed elsewhere in this book, namely:

- *Managerial Reporting*—Internal reports in a form and containing information tailored to the needs of managers in carrying out their responsibilities. Examples include reports on investment activities, enrollment, and faculty compensation, or any activity that can be measured or benchmarked for activity for management decisions.

- *Regulatory Reporting*—Reports to governmental agencies required by law. Examples include reports filed with state education departments and reports filed with the federal government under OMB Circular A-133. The common characteristic of these reports is that the regulatory user dictates their informational content.

- *Tax Reporting*—This is a specialized form of regulatory reporting and includes IRS Form 990, *Return of Organization Exempt from Income Tax*, and similar types of state filings. Requirements for these reports are established by the Internal Revenue Service and state taxing authorities, respectively.

- *Charitable Solicitation Reporting*—State charitable solicitation regulators require financial reports, usually IRS Form 990 (see above).

General purpose external financial reporting has certain distinguishing characteristics. Financial statements included therein are prepared in accordance with generally accepted accounting principles (GAAP) and generally are subject to audit by independent external auditors. Such financial statements are normally issued on an annual basis and are often included in corporate-like annual reports made available to trustees, donors, and other interested parties inside and outside the institution. Public institutions also provide this information to legislators, state regulatory bodies, and other government entities.

The last 20 years have seen revolutionary changes in the general purpose external financial reporting of colleges and universities.

- In 1984, the standard-setting structure for establishing GAAP for higher education was fundamentally changed, resulting in different standard-setting organizations for independent institutions (FASB) and public institutions (Governmental Accounting Standards Board, or GASB), respectively. As a result, significant differences have been introduced into GAAP for these two segments of higher education.

- In the mid-1990s, independent institutions adopted a new financial reporting model set forth by the FASB in Statements 116, *Accounting for Contributions Received and Contributions Made* (June 1993), and 117, *Financial Statements of Not-for-Profit Organizations* (June 1993). Financial statements required under this model focus on the institution as a whole rather than the previous, longstanding focus on accounting groupings or funds within the institution.

- In 1996, the American Institute of Certified Public Accountants (AICPA) issued a revised *Audit and Accounting Guide, Not-for-Profit Organizations,* (the not-for-profit guide) which applied to all private not-for-profit organizations including independent institutions. The not-for-profit guide provided additional detailed guidance, consistent with FASB Statements 116 and 117, in certain areas (e.g., the reporting of tuition net of most student financial assistance and the accounting and reporting for split interest agreements).

- Public institutions, while still generally following the financial reporting model set forth in the AICPA guide, *Audits of Colleges and Universities* (the audit guide), issued in 1973, have adopted GASB standards that modify aspects of the accounting set forth in that guide. Financial statements required under this model focus on traditional fund groups rather than the institution as a whole.

- Beginning in 1986, GASB has had a project on its agenda to consider a revised financial reporting model for public colleges and universities. That model differed in certain respects from the financial reporting model the board was developing for state and local governments. But in March 1999, GASB decided to abandon the notion of establishing a separate financial reporting model for public colleges and universities. Rather, in November 1999, it issued GASB Statement 35, *Basic Financial Statements—and Management's Discussion and Analysis—for Public Colleges and Universities,* which includes public colleges and universities in the new reporting model developed for state and local governments set forth in GASB Statement 34, *Basic Financial Statements—and Management's Discussion and Analysis—for State and Local Governments,* issued in June 1999. After June 15, 2001, public institutions will generally be required to adopt that reporting model in their first fiscal year. Financial statements required under this model will focus on the organization as a whole, but will differ in many respects from the financial statements required for independent institutions. As a result of these developments, the general unity that existed in the general purpose external financial reporting of independent and public institutions has given way to a number of differences. These differences are explored as follows.

STANDARDS FOR INDEPENDENT INSTITUTIONS

FASB Statement 117 requires that an independent institution's complete set of financial statements include:

- Statement of Financial Position;
- Statement of Activities;

- Statement of Cash Flows; and

- Accompanying Notes to Financial Statements.

Statement 117 also establishes a framework for financial reporting by mandating minimum requirements (i.e., certain information that must be displayed) while permitting flexibility by not prescribing required formats. Such an approach represents a major change for independent institutions, as the audit guide was very prescriptive regarding format. Among the important matters not specified under Statement 117 are:

- degree of disaggregation (although certain totals are required); and

- order of presentation of items of assets and liabilities in Statement of Financial Position or items of revenues and expenses in Statement of Activities.

FASB also indicates that the financial statements should focus on the organization as a whole. That requirement represents a major change from the audit guide's focus on individual fund groups. Disaggregated information may be presented, but is not required. As a result, Statement 117 has led to much more aggregated reporting, particularly in the Statement of Financial position. Statement 117 sets forth certain basic requirements for each of the required financial statements. Those requirements consist of the minimum amounts that must be displayed and certain other information that must be either displayed on the face of the financial statement or disclosed in the notes to the financial statements. In the first required financial statement, the Statement of Financial Position, the following six amounts must be displayed:

- total assets;

- total liabilities;

- total net assets;

- total unrestricted net assets;

- total temporarily restricted net assets; and

- total permanently restricted net assets.

Statement 117 establishes only a few other requirements for this financial statement. Assets and liabilities must be aggregated into reasonably homogeneous groups (e.g., cash, accounts receivable, investments, long-term debt). The statement must also provide information about liquidity using one or more of the following methods.

- sequencing assets according to their nearness to conversion to cash and sequencing liabilities according to the nearness of their maturity and resulting use of cash;

- classifying assets and liabilities as current and noncurrent; and

- including footnote disclosure about liquidity or maturity of assets and liabilities.

The nature and amount of restrictions, distinguishing between permanent and temporary restrictions, must also be disclosed. That information may appear on the face of the Statement of Financial Position or in the footnotes to the financial statements. Institutions are also required to disclose any restrictions on the use of specific assets. Such restrictions (e.g., sinking funds) may also affect the classification of those assets for liquidity purposes.

In applying the flexibility permitted by Statement 117, many institutions have chosen to display certain information not required by the statement. One of the most prevalent of such voluntary disclosures has been to display the components of unrestricted net assets either on the face of the Statement of Financial Position or in the notes to the financial statements. Institutions have included this information to alert users of the financial statements that large balances of unrestricted net assets may not be available for spending. Components disclosed generally include:

- investment in property, plant, and equipment (not liquid and thus not available for spending);

- quasi-endowment (board-designated rather than donor-restricted);

- designated operating funds; and

- realized and unrealized gains on true endowment that is unrestricted under the provisions of the Uniform Management of Institutional Funds Act. (UMIFA) in many states (e.g., New York, Illinois).

Statement format is another area where Statement 117 permits choices. The vast majority of institutions, like most business enterprises, have chosen to use a single-column format for the Statement of Financial Position.

The second required financial statement, the Statement of Activities, must display:

- total change in unrestricted net assets;

- total change in temporarily restricted net assets;

- total change in permanently restricted net assets; and

• total change in net assets.

Statement 117 establishes somewhat more extensive disclosure requirements for other information in this statement than is the case with the Statement of Financial Position. Revenues and expenses must be reported gross and aggregated into reasonably homogeneous groupings. Gains and losses may be reported net. Reclassifications of net assets from temporarily restricted net assets to unrestricted net assets, which arise when purpose or time restrictions on temporarily restricted net assets are met, must be reported separately. The change in net assets reflected in the Statement of Activities must agree with the Statement of Financial Position.

All revenues must be classified as unrestricted unless subject to donor restriction. That requirement, based on FASB's Concepts Statement 6, changed the classification of a number of types of revenue from those followed under the audit guide. The major areas affected are government grants and contracts, and gains and losses on investments and other assets (even if included in endowments). Such gains and losses are reported as increases or decreases in unrestricted net assets unless their use is temporarily or permanently restricted by explicit donor stipulations or by law. That rule has proven to be one of the more controversial in Statement 117 and has been effectively overturned in certain states (e.g., Massachusetts and Maine) by action of the attorney general or by modification of existing law. Statement 117 requires that all expenses be reported as decreases in unrestricted net assets. In addition, expenses must be displayed on a functional basis (e.g., instruction, research, institutional support) either on the face of the Statement of Activities or in the notes to the financial statements. Display or disclosure of expenses by object of expenditure (e.g., salaries, supplies, depreciation) is permitted, but not required.

In practice, the Statement of Activities has proven to be the most diverse in format. Statement 117 illustrates three alternative formats, all of which have been adopted by many institutions. The first of these is the "pancake" format, a single-column format that displays the change in each class of net assets on top of (or below) changes in the two other classes. The second alternative is the "columnar" format, a multi-column format that displays the change in each net asset class in a separate column and includes a total column that displays the components of the change in total net assets. The third and final alternative is a two-statement format, which is similar in many respects to business enterprise reporting. The first of the two statements in this format displays the detail of the change in unrestricted net assets. The second statement displays the detail of the change in the other two classes of net assets, temporarily restricted and permanently restricted, along with a summarized version of the change in unrestricted net assets.

Statement 117 also permits the reporting of an intermediate measure of operations. The statement does not prescribe any definition of operations, but places certain constraints on the use of such a measure. First, an intermediate measure of operations must be displayed in a financial statement that, at a minimum, reports the change in unrestricted net assets for the period. Moreover, if the meaning of "operations" is not clear, a footnote to the financial statements must disclose the nature of the measure and the items excluded from it.

Many independent institutions have taken advantage of this option and included an "operating" measure in their Statement of Activities. Practice, however, has been diverse. The general practice among endowed institutions has been to separate the changes in net assets arising from investment and plant activities from the revenues and expenses related to core mission activities (e.g., instruction and research). Such a separation entails dividing revenues and gains between operating and nonoperating. Items excluded from operations include donor-restricted contributions to endowments, contributions of long-lived assets or cash restricted to the purchase of such assets, and investment returns in excess of the institution's spending rate. All expenses (with the exception of investment-related items) normally arise from core mission activities and, accordingly, have been included in any operating measure. The major difference that has arisen among endowed institutions is in the treatment of temporarily restricted contributions that support core activities. While most institutions generally report the reclassifications that arise from the spending of such contributions in operations, the majority of institutions exclude from that measure the receipt of such contributions from donors.

Practice has not been as uniform for non-endowed institutions, where the motivation for preparing an operating measure has generally been to permit comparison of the general purpose financial statements with the institution's operating budget. As a result, differences in institutional budgetary methods have led to great diversity. Here, general practice has been to exclude items of both revenue and expense from the operating measure. Such items include (1) all changes in temporarily restricted and permanently restricted net assets except for reclassifications funding core activities, (2) unrealized and realized gains and losses on investment, and (3) expenses related to plant (e.g., depreciation, interest on long-term debt, and losses on disposals).

In the third required statement, the Statement of Cash Flows, six amounts must be disclosed:

- total cash flows from investing activities;
- total cash flows from financing activities;
- total cash flows from operating activities;
- net change in cash and cash equivalents;
- cash and cash equivalents, beginning of period; and
- cash and cash equivalents, end of period.

Cash inflows and outflows must be reported gross in the statement. In addition, disclosure is required of (1) an institution's policy on defining cash equivalents, (2) noncash investing and financing activities, and (3) interest and income taxes paid. Statement 117 permits two different formats for displaying the information required, the direct method and the indirect method, which differ in the way they present operating cash flows. The direct method reports major classes of gross cash receipts and gross cash payments and adds them to arrive at the net cash flow from operating activities. In addition, this format must include a reconciliation of change in total net assets to net cash flow from operating activities. Many institutions have not adopted the direct method because it is harder to prepare than the indirect method and may require special subsystems to identify gross cash receipts and/or payments in certain areas (e.g., student receivables). The indirect method reports the same totals as the direct method, but displays cash flows from operating activities in the format of the reconciliation required under the direct method (i.e., reconciliation of changes in total change in net assets to net cash flows from operating activities). Most institutions have adopted this format even though it is generally not considered as useful as the direct format.

Other FASB standards directed at not-for-profit organizations have also had a significant impact on the financial statements included in the general purpose external financial reporting of independent institutions. FASB Statement 116 requires the recognition of unconditional donor promises as an asset. That represents a significant change from the audit guide, which only required disclosure of such pledges. To be recognized, such unconditional promises must be supported by verifiable documentation such as a letter, pledge card, or written agreement. However, such promises are not required to be legally enforceable. Rather, legal enforceability is considered only if there is any uncertainty about whether a communication is a promise. Unconditional promises represent a significant additional asset for some institutions. Statement 116 requires discounting of amounts due in more than one year as well as disclosure of the general payment terms of outstanding unconditional promises (e.g., one to five years, more than five years).

FASB Statement 93, *Recognition of Depreciation by Not-for-Profit Organizations* (August 1987), requires recognition of the cost of using up long-lived assets (i.e., historical cost depreciation). FASB Statement 124, *Accounting for Certain Investments of Not-for-Profit Organizations* (November 1995), requires that investments in equity securities and all debt securities be measured at fair value in the Statement of Financial Position, with both realized and unrealized gains and losses recognized in the Statement of Activities. In addition, other professional literature (i.e., AICPA Statement of Position 94-2) clarified that all other FASB pronouncements apply to private not-for-profit entities, including independent colleges and universities, unless the subject matter is inapplicable (e.g., earnings per share). Among pronouncements that have significantly affected independent institutions have been those applying to pension and postretirement benefits. Finally, the AICPA not-for-profit guide offers detailed guidance that supplements FASB Statements 116 and 117 in a number of areas. In particular, chapter 6 of that guide contains the first definitive guidance on accounting for and reporting of split interest agreements, an area of growing importance to independent institutions.

STANDARDS FOR PUBLIC INSTITUTIONS

GASB Statement 35 will supersede the current authoritative standard, GASB Statement 15, *Governmental College and University Accounting and Financial Reporting Models,* as early as fiscal 2002 for many public institutions, which may adopt GASB Statement 35 earlier if they wish. In light of these changes, this chapter will briefly review the requirements of GASB Statement 15. That statement requires public institutions to follow one of two models—the AICPA college guide model or the governmental model. Because the majority of public institutions have chosen to follow the college guide model, the section below is limited to that alternative.

One of the most important features of the AICPA college guide model is its continuing requirement for fund accounting and reporting. Fund accounting is the procedure by which resources for various purposes are classified for accounting and reporting purposes in accordance with activities or objectives as specified by donors, in accordance with regulations, restrictions, or limitations imposed by sources outside the institution, or in accordance with directions issued by the governing board. Fund reporting requires that all financial statements be presented on a disaggregated fund group basis. Similar funds are combined into:

- current funds;
- loan funds;
- endowment and similar funds;
- annuity and life income funds;
- plant funds; and
- agency funds.

Fund balances must be divided into separate externally restricted and unrestricted balances.

The financial statements required in this model include:

- Balance Sheet;
- Statement of Changes in Fund Balances; and
- Statement of Current Funds Revenues, Expenditures, and Other Changes.

The Balance Sheet reports the assets, liabilities, and fund balances of each fund group. A total column should be used only if all disclosures are made to ensure that totals are not misleading. Institutions have generally used one of two formats when preparing this statement. The vast majority uses a columnar format in which assets, liabilities, and fund balances for each fund are displayed in separate columns. The practice of including a total column in such a format has also increased. In the alternative "pancake" format, each fund group is reported separately, one on top of the other, with no provision for totals of the fund groups.

The second required statement, the Statement of Changes in Fund Balances, reports revenues and other additions, expenditures and other deductions, and transfers among fund groups for each of the fund groups. Revenues are presented in summary form for unrestricted current funds, while the other fund groups report other additions to fund balances in detail. This statement is generally presented in a columnar format. A total column is not required, and most institutions do not display one.

The third required statement, the Statement of Current Funds Revenues, Expenditures, and Other Changes, reports revenues by source, expenditures by function, and other transfers and additions/(deductions) for the current unrestricted and current restricted fund. A total column (current unrestricted plus current restricted) is required and a prior-year total column for current funds is also generally displayed.

Certain other currently effective GASB pronouncements have also significantly affected the general purpose financial statements of public institutions. GASB Statement 3, *Deposits with Financial Institutions, Investments (Including Repurchase Agreements) and Reverse Repurchase Agreements*, requires certain disclosures about deposits with financial institutions, investments, and reverse repurchase agreements (e.g., carrying amounts, market values, and level of credit risk). GASB Statement 14, *The Financial Reporting Entity*, sets forth requirements on what affiliated entities must be included in the institution's financial statements and how they will be displayed. This standard, while specifically applicable to all public colleges and universities, does not offer guidance on how its provisions should be applied by those institutions that follow the AICPA college guide model. As a result, practice has not been uniform, especially regarding the inclusion of "institutionally related entities" in the financial statements of public institutions (e.g., separately incorporated private 501(c)(3) fund-raising foundations). GASB Statement 19, *Governmental College and University Omnibus Statement*, which will be superseded by GASB Statement 35, requires that Pell grants be reported as revenues and expenditures in the current restricted funds. GASB Statement 24, *Accounting and Financial Reporting for Certain Grants and Other Financial Assistance*, requires that grants passed through to other entities be recognized as both revenues and expenditures when any type of administrative responsibility exists for the grant. GASB Statement 31, *Accounting and Financial Reporting for Certain Investments and for External Investment Pools*, requires that certain investments (principally equity securities with readily determinable fair values and debt securities) be reported at fair value and that unrealized gains and losses be reported together with realized gains and losses. In addition, all FASB standards issued through November 30, 1989, as modified by any applicable GASB standards, must also be applied. Among the most important of these pronouncements are FASB Statement 13, *Accounting for Leases*, and the various amendments to that standard, and FASB Statement 34, *Capitalization of Interest Cost*.

GASB Statement 33, *Accounting and Financial Reporting for Nonexchange Transactions*, which is effective for fiscal years beginning after June 15, 2000, will also significantly impact the general purpose financial statements of public colleges and universities. That statement requires that institutions recognize as an asset and revenue certain promises of donors to give resources for restricted and unrestricted "operating" purposes. Other such promises that contain "time requirements" are not recognized when made. Rather, assets and revenues arising from this type of promise are recognized in the period when resources are required to be used or when use may begin, that is, promises having time requirements versus those that do not. Thus cash and securities given for term and permanent endowments are recognized as assets when received, but promises to give such resources are not recognized. Operating and capital appropriations made by state legislatures to public institutions are recognized as assets and revenues on the first day of the state's fiscal year, unless another specific time period (e.g., the university's fiscal year, if different) is explicitly stated in the appropriation.

Reporting Model for Public Institutions

GASB Statement 35 represents a revolutionary change in the general purpose external financial reporting of business-type reporting for public institutions. Statement 35 requires public colleges and universities to report as special-purpose governments under the provisions of GASB Statement 34. The reporting requirements set forth in that statement depend on whether the special-purpose government is engaged only in business-type activities, engaged only in governmental activities, or engaged in both governmental and business-type activities. Business-type activities are any activities for which a fee is charged to external users (e.g., tuition). Given that definition, the majority of public colleges and universities may elect to follow the requirements of GASB Statement 34 for special-purpose governments engaged only in business-type activities, and this section will focus on those requirements. The required elements for those public institutions will include:

- Management's Discussion and Analysis (MD&A), as required;
- Statement of Net Assets or Balance Sheet;
- Statement of Revenues, Expenses, and Changes in Fund Net Assets;
- Statement of Cash Flows;
- Notes to Financial Statements; and
- Required Supplementary Information (RSI) other than MD&A, if applicable.

MD&A, which is required supplementary information, should provide an objective and easily readable analysis of the institution's financial activities based on currently known facts, decisions, or conditions. GASB Statement 34 sets forth the following minimum requirements for MD&A:

- a brief discussion of the basic financial statements, including the relationship of the statements to each other and any significant differences in the information they provide;

- condensed financial information derived from the institution's financial statements comparing the current year to the prior year;

- an analysis of the institution's overall financial position and results of operations to assist users in assessing whether financial position has improved or deteriorated as a result of the year's operations;

- a description of significant capital asset and long-term debt activity during the year; and

- a description of currently known facts, decisions, or conditions that are expected to have a significant effect on financial position (net assets) or results of operations (revenues, expenses, and other changes in net assets).

GASB Statement 35 calls for an aggregated Statement of Net Assets or Balance Sheet prepared on an institution-wide basis. That requirement is a major change for public institutions that have always prepared financial statements disaggregated by fund groups. GASB requires that assets and liabilities be presented on this statement in a classified format distinguishing between current and long-term assets and liabilities. Other ways of displaying liquidity, such as sequencing assets and liabilities as permitted in the private sector FASB in its Statement 117, may not be used. This requirement, along with several others noted below, is indicative of the more prescriptive approach that GASB, as compared with FASB, takes in matters of financial statement display. Institutions may use either a net assets format, where assets less liabilities equal net assets, or a balance sheet format, where assets equal liabilities plus net assets. GASB requires that net assets be displayed in the Statement of Net Assets or Balance Sheet in three broad components:

- invested in capital assets, net of related debt;
- restricted (distinguishing between major categories of restrictions); and
- unrestricted.

GASB's concept of "restricted" net assets is broader than FASB's definition, which is limited to net assets subject to doner-imposed stipulations as to use. Under the GASB concept, net assets should be reported as restricted when constraints placed on net asset use are either:

- externally imposed by creditors (such as through debt covenants), grantors, contributors, or laws or regulations of other governments; or

- imposed by law through constitutional provisions or enabling legislation.

GASB Statement 34 also requires that restricted assets must be reported when restrictions on asset use change the nature or normal understanding of the availability of the asset.

GASB also requires that the Statement of Revenues, Expenses, and Changes in Fund Net Assets be presented on a fully aggregated single-column basis. Display of the changes in the individual components of net assets is not required. Revenues must be reported by source, and expenses may be reported either by object of expenditure or function. GASB Statement 34 requires that an institution distinguish in this statement between operating and nonoperating revenues and expenses and present a separate subtotal for operating revenues, operating expenses, and operating income (i.e., an operating measure). Institutions are required to adopt a policy of disclosure that defines operating revenues and expenses that is appropriate for their activities. A consideration in defining operating revenues and expenses is how individual transactions would be categorized for the purpose of preparing a Statement of Cash Flows using GASB Statement 9, *Reporting Cash Flows of Proprietary and Nonexpendable Trust Funds and Governmental Entities That Use Proprietary Fund Accounting*, which is discussed below. Nonoperating revenues and expenses should be reported after operating income.

Generally, appropriations received from state and local governments would be treated as non-operating revenue. Paragraph 102 of GASB Statement 34 indicates that most revenues considered to be nonexchange or exhange-like, would, under GASB Statement 9, be reported as cash inflows from capital and related financial activities, noncapital financing activities, or investing activities. Therefore, they would generally not be reported as components of operating income. Paragraph 17 of GASB Statement 9, which lists the items that should be included as cash flows from operating activities, is silent on state appropriations. The paragraph, however, does indicate that the only grants that should be included as operating cash inflows are those "that are considered to be operating activities of the grantor government." Such a grant, it concludes, is "essentially the same as a contract for services." Generally, state appropriations to public colleges and universities do not meet this test and, accordingly, are nonexchange transactions that should be classified as nonoperating revenues. Additions to the principal of term or permanent endowments should be reported separately after nonoperating revenues and expenses.

The third required statement, the Statement of Cash Flows, must display cash receipts and payments of a period into four categories.

- cash flows from operating activities;
- cash flows from noncapital financing activities;
- cash flows from capital and related financing activities; and
- cash flows from investing activities.

GASB requires this statement to be prepared using the direct method of presenting cash flows from operating activities (including a reconciliation of operating cash flows to operating income). Use of the indirect method is not permitted. Similar to FASB Statement 117, cash inflows and outflows must be reported gross, not net. Institutions must also disclose noncash investing, capital, and financing transactions, and their policy for determining items treated as cash equivalents.

OUTSTANDING ISSUES

Differences in FASB and GASB Reporting Models

Since the jurisdiction for accounting standard setting for higher education was divided in 1984, business officers and others interested in general purpose external financial reporting of colleges and universities have been concerned about the comparability of the general purpose financial statements of public and independent institutions. With the release of GASB Statement 35 in November 1999, the nature of the differences between the financial statements of independent and public institutions comes into clearer focus. In some ways, GASB's decision to require public institutions to report as special-purpose governments under GASB Statement 34 may serve to narrow those differences and increase comparability. On the other hand, differences in certain other FASB and GASB statements dealing with similar subject matter—for example, FASB Statement 116 and GASB Statement 33, both of which deal with the recognition of gifts from private donors—can impede comparability. The majority of public colleges and universities are expected to fall under the provisions of GASB Statement 34, applicable to special-purpose governments engaged only in business-type activities.

A comparison of the form and content of the financial statements required for such entities with those required of independent institutions by FASB Statement 117 reveals certain differences as well as similarities. Both FASB and GASB require three basic financial statements that provide similar information. GASB also requires an MD&A as part of the general purpose external financial reporting.

Many independent institutions provide some, if not all, of this information in corporate-type annual reports.

The major differences between FASB's Statement of Financial Position and GASB's Statement of Net Assets or Balance Sheet are the methods of displaying liquidity and classification of net assets. GASB is more prescriptive about displaying liquidity, requiring a classified balance sheet, while FASB permits alternative ways of displaying liquidity. In the area of classification of net assets, FASB calls for a threefold breakout of net assets based on the existence of donor stipulations. GASB's breakout is, in part, also based on restrictions, although, as noted above, its definition of "restricted" is broader than FASB's. In addition, GASB requires the breakout of net investment in plant, a disclosure commonly made voluntarily by independent institutions.

The second statement required by each board has the same objective—to display the nature and amount of changes in an institution's net assets. (For GASB, *total* net assets (results of operations) is the objective.) Certain differences between FASB's Statement of Activities and GASB's Statement of Revenues, Expenses, and Changes in Fund Net Assets may limit users' ability to compare the financial performance of independent and public institutions. The most important of these differences may be in the level of aggregation of the statement. GASB Statement 34 illustrates a single column statement that does not break out the change in each net asset class, a requirement under FASB Statement 117. GASB also requires an operating measure and offers guidance on calculating it. Provision of such a measure is optional for independent institutions, and Statement 117 provides no insight on what is to be included in such an intermediate measure. However, many independent institutions include operating measures in their Statement of Activities. How such measures are calculated for independent institutions differs in the absence of any authoritative guidance. The degree to which these differences limit comparability will depend on how uniformly public institutions calculate such measures and whether guidance is issued to make the practice of independent institutions more uniform. A final difference is that independent institutions are required to display expenses on a functional basis either on the face or in the notes, while public institutions may display expenses either by object of expenditure or by function. Again, the degree to which this difference limits comparability will depend on how practice evolves in both sectors of higher education.

On their face, the Statements of Cash Flows required by FASB and GASB are not comparable because the categories into which cash flows are divided in each statement differ. The most important of these differences concern the treatment of cash flows relating to acquisition and disposition of plant assets (capital and related financing flows in the GASB statement and investing flows in the FASB statement). Other important differences also arise in the treatment of student loans and restricted contributions. Users may, however, be able to recast statements of either public or independent institutions to achieve comparability because the concepts underlying the statements (e.g., definition of cash and cash equivalents) are similar.

Other important differences that will affect the comparability of financial statements relate to the treatment of unconditional promises to give gifts permanently restricted to endowments and gifts with time restrictions. GASB Statement 33, unlike FASB Statement 116, does not recognize either of these promises as assets or revenues. Rather, public institutions will recognize such gifts essentially on a cash basis. In addition, these two statements differ in the guidance they offer on when to recognize the expiration of donor-imposed "purpose" restrictions on contributions. Under FASB guidance, such expiration takes place when an expense is incurred for a purpose that meets the donor-imposed restriction even if unrestricted funds are available for such expenditure. GASB is less prescriptive, leaving the question of whether the expenditure was made from unrestricted or restricted funds to the judgment of the institution.

Other Issues

In addition to the question of comparability, two issues remain to be addressed. The first of these, guidance regarding an operating measure, primarily affects independent institutions. The second, the treatment of affiliated organizations, affects primarily public institutions. How these issues are resolved will affect the general purpose external financial reporting of independent and public institutions, respectively.

Given the revolutionary changes that have taken place in the general purpose external financial reporting of both public and independent institutions over the last 20 years, business officers and others responsible for financial reporting in higher education face several challenges in the decade ahead. First, they must implement and explain these changes to their various constituencies. Then they will need to deal with the above issues to ensure the continued credibility of higher education's financial reporting.

REFERENCES AND RESOURCES

Publications and Articles

American Institute of Certified Public Accountants, New York: AICPA.

> *Industry Audit Guide, Audits of Colleges and Universities, With Conforming Changes as of May 1.*

> *AICPA Audit and Accounting Guide, Not-for-Profit Organizations With Conforming Changes as of May 1.*

Anthony, Robert N. *Financial Accounting in Nonbusiness Organizations.* Norwalk, CT: Financial Accounting Standards Board, 1978.

Engstrom, John, H. *Information Needs of College and University Financial Decision Makers.* Norwalk, CT: Government Accounting Standards Board, 1988.

Financial Accounting Standards Board, Norwalk, CT:

> Statement of Financial Accounting Concepts No. 4, *Objectives of Financial Reporting by Nonbusiness Organizations,* (1980).

> Statement of Financial Accounting Concepts No. 6, *Elements of Financial Statements,* (1985).

> Statement of Financial Accounting Standards, No. 116, *Accounting for Contributions Received and Made,* (1993).

> Statement of Financial Accounting Standards, No. 117, *Financial Statements of Not-for-Profit Organizations,* (1993).

> Statement of Financial Accounting Standards, No. 124, *Accounting for Certain Investments Held by Not-for-Profit Organizations,* (1995).

Governmental Accounting Standards Board, Norwalk, CT.

> Concepts Statement No 1, *Objectives of Financial Reporting,* (1987).

> Concepts Statement No. 2, *Service Efforts and Accomplishments Reporting,* (1994).

> Statement No. 14, *The Financial Reporting Entity,* (1991).

> Statement No. 15, *Governmental College and University Accounting and Financial Reporting Models,* (1991).

> Statement No. 19, *Governmental College and University Omnibus Statement,* (1993).

> Statement No. 31, *Accounting and Financial Reporting for Certain Investments and for External Investment Pools,* (1997).

> Statement No. 33, *Accounting and Financial Reporting for Nonexchange Transactions,* (1998).

Statement No. 34, *Basic Financial Statement—and Management's Discussion and Analysis—for State and Local Governments,* (1999).

Statement No. 35, *Basic Financial Statements—and Management's Discussion and Analysis—for Public Colleges and Universities.*

National Association of College and University Business Officers, *Financial Accounting and Reporting Manual for Higher Education,* Washington, D.C.: NACUBO, 1990.

Chapter 6

◆

Managerial Reporting

by

Ron Salluzzo
KPMG

with contributions by

Theresa A. Bachmann, KPMG
Bill Kirby, KPMG

Sponsors

KPMG
Contact: Greg J. Baroni
1676 International Drive
McLean, VA 22102
703-747-3004
www.kpmg.com

With over 30 years of serving higher education, KPMG offers a broad range of services that helps our clients analyze their businesses with true clarity, raises their level of performance and delivers the strategic and infrastructural components to support highly dynamic E-business models in colleges, universities, and academic medical centers.

PEOPLESOFT, INC.
Contact: Karen Willett
4460 Hacienda Drive
Pleasanton, CA 94588
925-694-5453
www.peoplesoft.com/highered

PeopleSoft delivers E-business solutions for higher education management needs, including student administration, grants management, finance, human resources, E-procurement, advancement, and more. PeopleSoft also provides comprehensive customer service.

Contents

Colleges and universities face constant and changing pressures to reinvent themselves, their processes, and operations. Ultimately, the ability of the institution to manage these changes depends on the right people evaluating the right metrics. A well-crafted managerial reporting function provides management the necessary tool not only to assess its current position, but also to make real-time decisions affecting future results. Managerial financial reporting is an administrative discipline that must be dynamic and flexible enough to transform with the institution itself and provide a structure for the evolving informational needs and capabilities of the organization. Key to this transformation is the role of financial professionals (from within the financial office and throughout the organization) to think creatively about "the big picture" and capitalize on the flexibility of today's computing systems to present information in meaningful ways.

This chapter addresses various factors involved in developing and managing an evolving managerial reporting function. It discusses the objectives of managerial reporting, reviews technology's impact on the managerial reporting function, outlines the fundamental elements of an effective reporting function, and considers some possible strategic-level reporting for institutional management.

FINANCIAL ANALYSIS AS A POWERFUL AND STRATEGIC MANAGERIAL TOOL

Change is pervading every aspect of colleges and universities. Colleges and universities face continous pressure to transform as their various constituencies change. Colleges and universities require new approaches to the delivery of higher education. They will have to work smarter; make cost-effectiveness a higher priority; and focus on questions of return on investment, defining key success metrics, benchmarking, and best practices. Advances in technology and other changes are reshaping the industry's landscape. Institutions that do not create (and continue to recreate) competitive advantage will find competitors (old and new) capturing the most attractive segments of the market, and limiting the potential (mission-related and financial) of higher education's traditional institutions.

To help create competitive advantage, the college or university financial office can serve as a powerful strategic element, and managerial reporting can serve as a vital tool for strategic progress. At its best, financial management is an enabling activity that provides an institution not only financial discipline and accountability, but an understanding of the financial consequences of past decisions and a means to predict more effectively the results of future decisions. While managerial reporting focuses on financial performance, its principal value as a management tool lies in highlighting complex managerial interactions and decisions that affect financial performance and align results (or lack thereof) with specific managers, programs, and processes.

Like all operational decisions, a financial reporting function should be shaped by organizational strategy. Arguably, a financial reporting function helps maintain a baseline, or "threshold," for financial discipline and accountability throughout the institution. But if a financial office is to be a strategic element, its deployment of resources and the direction of its managerial reporting must ardently be focused on key performance indicators considered linchpins to the accomplishment of strategic initiatives.

TECHNOLOGY'S IMPACT ON MANAGERIAL REPORTING

Managerial financial reporting must continue to evolve to meet the rapidly changing information needs of college and university management. Such evolving flexibility is possible because of recent advances in technology and software systems such as enterprise resource planning (ERP) systems. Over the past decade, colleges and universities have made enormous investments in their information system infrastructures. Today's challenge is to develop and integrate applications that will increase the return on these investments and help institutions capitalize on their market differentiation. ERP systems integrate information and business processes to enable information entered once to be shared throughout an organization and thus eliminate parallel or repetitive data entry. The capabilities of such systems expand the potential of managerial reporting. Customer resource management (CRM) and other data mining tools have created a whole new realm of potential key performance indicators.

Again, the key to converting available and seemingly disparate information into operational knowledge and strategic advantage is a relentless focus on the mission and strategic objectives of the institution and the measurable factors that will drive those initiatives. Managerial reporting functions and their related reporting models and analytical techniques must adapt and embrace these changes to effectively utilize the new information these systems provide.

But how does one accomplish this? Colleges and universities have amassed volumes of transactional data on students and other constituencies they serve. They have information on buying preferences (from bookstore and on-line university service systems), intellectual interests (based on course and degree selections tracked in the registrar systems), personal information (such as birth date and family financial profile from financial aid systems), and much more. Historically, this transactional data has been stored in the computers of these discrete departments, making it impossible to analyze as a collective whole. Imagine if this transactional data could create actionable knowledge.

Consider the potential for the following scenario on alumni relations. On the 30th birthday of an alumnus, the university-wide reporting system prompts the alumnus's favorite professor (based on automated class evaluation systems) to E-mail the alumnus birthday regards. The message includes a request for any changes to the alumnus's personal records (e.g., job, address, marital changes) and surveys the alumnus's educational needs (e.g., desired additional skills and interests). This information updates the alumnus's personal profile, whose educational interests are now cross-referenced to available and potential continuing education programs. The alumnus's customized quarterly electronic alumni newsletter highlights the available course materials. The alum's recent job promotion also prompts the development office to solicit the individual for an increase in annual giving to the university. This alum has now become a lifetime customer of the university; subscribes regularly to on-line continuing education programs; feels personally compelled to contribute to the university's strategic initiatives; and will strongly convey this loyalty and commitment to the next generation of customers.

The potential of this scenario is notably difficult to accomplish. It is estimated that only 20 percent of an organization's transactional data delivers 80 percent of its action-producing knowledge. Therefore, it is easy to see that computing power and access to information are not enough to harness the potential of such data. Technological advances provide new and improved analytical tools. Such data analysis tools range from commonly used query and reporting tools such as spreadsheets, to on-line analytical processing (OLAP) tools that frame specific questions and investigate particular business assumptions, to sophisticated data mining software applications that use complex artificial intelligence algorithms to identify meaningful patterns and trends.

These advances in technology and analytical tools provide increasing flexibility and sources of operational indicators. However, the key to an effective managerial financial reporting function remains the same—having the "right" metrics evaluated by the "right" people. Therefore, there remains a strong need for sound fundamental elements of a managerial financial reporting function. The following discusses key elements in creating a structure to support the evolving informational needs of a college or university.

FUNDAMENTALS OF AN EFFECTIVE MANAGERIAL REPORTING FUNCTION

Three fundamental elements of a managerial reporting function are:

- effective financial professionals;
- a reliable reporting model; and
- creative analytical techniques.

Effective Financial Professionals

The talent and creativity of financial professionals play an enormous role in the development and delivery of effective managerial reporting systems. Financial professionals who understand the interrelationships between the mechanics of operations and strategic initiatives (e.g., enrollment management and tuition pricing, capital planning and endowment capital development, government relations and grants management) can design and deliver effective managerial financial reports and interpret the operational impact of complex analyses. As such, a fundamental element of a managerial reporting system is a staff of effective financial professionals. This section describes several necessary characteristics of a financial professional. Parrtnerships with the academic leadership are essential to success, as the subjects of these reports are core activities and mission of the institution.

Ability and Willingness to Adapt

Change will continue to be overwhelming. Colleges and universities face the constant pressure of transformation, and their survival will depend almost entirely on the ability to define and execute strategic initiatives differentiating themselves from their competitors. This environment of change is about the only constant that business officers can rely on. Because of the key role finance has in the execution of strategy, financial professionals must be up to the task. They can no longer assume that their jobs are static assignments, processing routine transactions and issuing monthly reporting packages.

Customer Orientation and Consensus-building Skills

One of the greatest challenges to financial management reporting is gaining agreement on what information is relevant. Strong analytical skills are commonly recognized expectations for financial professionals; less readily recognized are customer orientation and the ability to promote consensus and common grounds for communication. The latter skills, however, are ultimately more valuable. Operating managers come to the financial reporting process with differing perspectives on what factors will determine the success of their strategic initiatives. Therefore, financial professionals must be problem solvers, communicators partnering with academic and other operating managers, and believers who see it as a critical professional function to disburse financial management capabilities through operations. In these ways, the voice of finance can be heard (and will be listened to) throughout the organization, helping to dissolve traditional cultural walls that separate finance from the rest of the organization.

Constant Desire to Learn

Because the challenges facing financial professionals change constantly, the need to acquire new skills to master these challenges is ever present. Financial professionals cannot rely on the accounting and finance theory acquired through undergraduate or MBA educations. The business environment changes too quickly and a commitment to continuing education (on the part of the college or university and the individual professional) must be constant. Effective managerial reporting necessitates knowledge of evolving asset-valuation modeling techniques, understanding of changing trends in treasury instruments, and other issues specific to the college and university industry.

An Eye on the "Big Game"

A final characteristic of an effective financial professional should be a continuing awareness and appreciation for the changing competitive playing field for colleges and universities. In his paper, "When Industries Change: Scenarios for Higher Education," David Collis suggests that the higher education industry has been, to date, an attractive business in which to compete, but one in which changing technology, demographics, and other "drivers of change" are significantly shifting the fundamental market forces defining the competitive environment.

Collis argues that without a significant transformation of the business approach, colleges and universities will find competitors (old and new) picking off the most profitable segments of the industry and creating a continuing and spiraling decline in the economics of the traditional higher education industry. Financial professionals who appreciate, analyze, and interpret evolving market forces will contribute significant strategic clout and intellectual capital to the organization.

Financial professionals who demonstrate these characteristics (and business officers who promote them) can spread their "financial IQ" to all management, bettering financial analysis performed throughout the organization and, ultimately, improving the business decisions being made.

Establishing a Reporting Model

For any managerial financial report to have an impact on the institution, it must meet three criteria: it must be relevant, reliable, and readily available. Key to meeting this challenge is the development of a reporting model. Such a model is important because it is the legend or roadmap of important operating indicators management has chosen to drive the strategic success of the institution. It is a schedule of regularly issued management reports with clearly defined issuers, audiences, and reporting periods.

Arguably, advances in computer processing systems and reporting flexibility discussed previously lessen the importance of a reporting model. Today's financial analysts and operating managers have instant access to up-to-the minute operational information from their desktop or laptop computers. Access helps operators respond to trends as they emerge rather than respond to the periodic reporting packages produced by the financial department. However, there is still intrinsic value in a well-thought-out reporting model. All the senior officers play an important role in defining the key performance indicators and objectively assessing progress toward strategic objectives. A reporting model can therefore focus on the most essential of these performance measures and be used to summarize and communicate to a broad population of operators and managers. A reporting model helps provide structure to the managerial financial reporting function and helps maintain the strategic focus of the organization.

Objectives of a Reporting Model

A reporting model should incorporate the following objectives:

Matching metrics and accountability. Everyone in an organization needs to understand the key performance metrics driving mission objectives. More specifically, they need to understand the key performance metrics their performance affects and on which their performance will be assessed. The reporting model (at all its various levels) should align with the metrics outlined as performance indicators during management's annual and long-range goal-setting process. The success of any management report will be measured by its use in current and future decision making.

Consistency. A common reporting model must be built on consistent and generally accepted accounting principles. Consistent information over time is most valuable and, for interinstitutional comparisons, data should be consistent with the reporting practices of other institutions and with the data collection surveys of public agencies, for example, the Department of Education's Integrated Postsecondary Education Data System (IPEDS) and private organizations, for example, the Higher Education Price Index (HEPI).

Summarization. Brevity for its own sake may not be appropriate, but "a picture is worth a thousand words" is a useful criterion in managerial reporting; the key to summarization is to provide what is necessary to convey meaning. The detail should be appropriate to the user's level of responsibility. In any case, and regardless of the user, data overload should be avoided.

Flexibility—critique functions. A reporting model should be subject to a formal process of critical review and enhancement. As such, it should be flexible and should evolve over time as the information needs of its users change. Similarly, the reporting model should be the starting point or locus for additional analytical financial reporting requests. The model's reports should be adequate in detail to allow management to assess quickly trends in key performance indicators, but should frequently elicit ad hoc drill-down inquiries from management.

The Need for a Common Data Model

Another fundamental consideration in the development of a reporting model and the systems underlying the reporting function is an institution wide common understanding and use of data (a common data model), including definitions of data and information elements relevant to the business; periods and cutoffs related to the data-information; currencies and other measurements; definitions of the events triggering data capture; and the required components, structure, and format of data-information.

Accomplishing a common understanding of these elements is not easy. Depending on the complexity of the college or university system (e.g., number of disparate systems and campuses), accomplishing this objective might be a multi-year and/or ongoing objective with major system, process, and personnel implications. However, the objective is fundamental if management plans are to rely on the credibility of the information and the related analyses.

Choosing the Components of a Financial Reporting Model

The reporting model must address several questions, including, Who will use the information? What will the information be used for? and How often must this information be available to be relevant?

These questions will help frame the components and systemic requirements of a reporting model. There is no such thing as an ideal or standard reporting model. A reporting model should be customized to the specific needs of the organization and must be developed in the context of the organization's strategic planning process. Notwithstanding this claim, the following reports are representative of many reporting models, and may help determine what regularly reported information is needed to manage a college or university.

Budget and spending report. Business officers need to regularly understand total spending within the organization. This report typically presents those results by office or department (commensurate with units of accountability) and by object class (e.g., payroll, travel, etc.). The data should be compared to budgeted activity; variances greater than established ranges should be highlighted (see discussion below of important elements of effective variance analysis). For public institutions, the monitoring of cash draws is essential.

Projected sources and uses report. Another common report captures all annual sources of revenue and tracks (at a programmatic level) how they are used. This report makes clear whether the organization is on track to meet current-year budgeted activity. It can provide insight into whether programmatic initiatives are being deployed as scheduled. The report typically includes year-over-year results to provide management another benchmark for operational progress.

Statement of financial position. This report presents the overall financial condition of the institution at regular intervals. It provides important insight into the management of assets and contributing factors to its results of operations.

Fund-raising status report. Given the importance of development activity at colleges and universities, particularly during capital campaigns, another common report is one summarizing fund-raising results. They are typically reported by source (e.g., direct mail campaign, special events, capital campaign solicitations) and should highlight significant individual gifts. The report should also disclose cash receipt activity for pledges outstanding. A supplementary report would show an aging of outstanding pledges.

Cash-flow analysis. This report identifies various sources of current and long-term cash flows, highlighting cash-flow deficiencies, if any. A net current cash-flow analysis pertains to revenues from and on behalf of students that distinguishes among student types, levels of enrollment, and other characteristics unique to the institution and takes into account the effect of student aid grants, loans, and payment delinquencies on cash flow.

Analysis of total return on investments. This report analyzes investment portfolio performance including consideration of interest, dividends, and realized and unrealized gains and losses. Such information, as well as cash-flow data discussed above, is very important to those who make short- and long-term financing and investment management decisions.

These reports are typically prepared regularly throughout the year—in most cases, monthly. Other reports common to the college or university management community, but prepared on a less frequent basis, include the following:

Annual financial management reports. These reports include the annual results of operations and further documentation of programmatic accomplishments and trends that provide a broad overview of the status of the institution.

Annual operating budget. This is the financial expression or plan of an institution's activities for a certain year. It represents the summation as well as the details of divisional and departmental plans.

Short- and long-range capital plans. These plans encompass all of the institution's funds. They should address past, present, and future changes in net assets. In addition, there should be a separate, but integrated, plan for physical capital (equipment and facilities).

Constant-dollar purchasing power of endowment (including new gifts to endowment). This report analyzes the financial condition of endowment funds in relation to the current-dollar costs of programs fulfilling the purposes and objectives of the endowment.

Analysis of endowment payout policies and formulas. This report analyzes the effect of payout policies on the endowment funds and incorporates the analysis of total return into the determination of future spending rates and their effect on the budget.

Summary—Importance of a Reporting Model

A reporting model involves several objectives and considerations and is anything but standard. Establishing a reporting model is an important objective, however, because once a financial function has demonstrated it can foster high-quality data management practices and communicate consistent, valued information across the college or university, operating managers will begin to view financial professionals as strategic partners and value their insights. Sound, widely accepted reporting can minimize the "guesswork" of management, prevent the proliferation of shadow accounting systems, and help provide solid information for making timely corrections to operating plans and assumptions used in strategic planning.

Using Creative Analytical Techniques

This chapter has previously reviewed characteristics to consider in developing the financial acumen of the organization (the "right" people) and factors to consider in determining information appropriate for regular reporting (the "right" metrics). The following section reviews some of the analytical techniques and reporting considerations that may be used by the right people in development and analysis of the right metrics.

Baseline Reporting

Baseline reporting refers to descriptive historical and indicator reporting. Its purpose is to establish norms and to define departure points, trends, and key relationships. Because colleges and universities are composites of complex interactions among numerous activities, managerial reporting must describe relationships between the financial variables and the nonfinancial, which are also indicators of financial activity. Because such a model is not static, reports need to focus on:

- identifying general and unique internal and external environmental variables that affect institutional behavior and financial outcomes;
- locating historical information that may identify trends or cycles for key financial indicators;
- defining the key cause and effect relationships; and
- forecasting future financial outcomes.

Internal Control and Managerial Effectiveness Reporting

Internal control and managerial effectiveness reports should disclose how well specific financial policies and procedures are carried out. Topics covered by these reports may include:

- cash controls;
- payroll and benefit controls (e.g., use of overtime);
- costing targets by cost center and cost minimization or the optimal allocation of resources in specific areas such as utilities, postage, telecommunications, travel, and supplies;
- compliance issues related to restricted funds revenues and expenditures;
- recruitment expenditures in relation to matriculation results (e.g., number and quality of new enrollments, student aid dependency); and
- inventory control and purchasing procedures and outcomes.

Comparative Analysis

Comparative analysis provides an effective performance perspective. Specific internally stipulated objectives (e.g., compensation levels, student achievement scores, revenue and expenditure per student) are measured against achievements at similar institutions using generally accepted or widely used indicators of comparative performance.

Most institutions have peer-group cohort preferences; others have aspiration-group cohorts as well. For specific statistical comparisons, special groupings must be created. Research universities, community colleges, and law and medical schools have their own preferred universes. Objectivity is critical when assembling a comparative sample.

Constant-Dollar Analysis

An important step in managerial reporting is to distinguish between current- and constant-dollar trends. Several states and colleges and universities have developed cost indexes to help them sort out the effect of inflation on institutional budgets. From the standpoint of managerial reporting, constant-dollar budget information is most easily derived by deflating current-dollar budgets by the consumer price index (CPI) or by higher-education industry price indexes such as the HEPI or specific state-developed indexes. Constant-dollar analysis should not be restricted to revenues and expenditures. The institution's capital (plant, endowment, and investment capital) also is affected by inflation. Managerial reporting should include appropriate trend analyses in both current and constant dollars.

Ratio Analysis

Ratio analysis can and should be a major feature of trend analysis, because ratios depicted over time display the inherent stability or instability of key relationships among important institutional financial measures. These ratios communicate information drawn from financial statements in an accessible manner that can aid in assessing the financial health of an institution. Ratio analysis also permits comparison of an institution with an aspiration or peer group. There are several types of ratios, which should focus on four fundamental aspects of financial health.

1. Are resources sufficient and flexible enough to support the mission?
2. Do operating results indicate the institution is living within available resources?
3. Does financial asset performance support the strategic direction?
4. Is debt managed strategically to advance the mission?

Are resources sufficient and flexible enough to support the mission? This question helps policymakers assess the status of the institution's financial resources. Flexibility in making decisions about institutional transformation will depend on the institution's fiscal performance and financial base. Understanding that flexibility will help stewards and external parties determine the institution's risk tolerance during periods of operational transformation. Key ratios to be considered in answering this question include:

Primary Reserve Ratio—comparison of expendable net assets to total expenses. This provides insight into an institution's ability to retain and grow expendable net assets at a rate consistent with, and preferably in excess of, the growth of operations.

Secondary Reserve Ratio—comparison of nonexpendable net assets to total expenses. This provides an assessment of the strength of endowment funds, and is important because endowment funds provide a significant stream of secondary financing for operating and plant requirements.

Do operating results indicate the institution is living within available resources? The allocation of scarce resources is a critical function of stewards in achieving institutional mission. No organization is likely to succeed in all areas, regardless of the amount of resources retained, yet the successful organization in the 21st century must be a superior performer in every area in which it chooses to participate. The challenge posed by this paradigm is measuring the results of choices among alternatives. Several associated questions frame the measurement of resource allocation decisions:

- How are resources used to conduct educational core services?
- How are resources used to conduct educational support services?
- How are resources used to conduct general support services?

Key ratios to be considered in answering these questions include:

Net Income Ratio—comparison of net income (preferably operating net income) to total operating revenues. This indicates the strength of the financial performance of the institution's operations.

Secondary Net Income Ratios—series of ratios showing the results of operations. These may include cash income ratio, operating income ratio, net tuition dependency ratio, net tuition per full-time equivalent (FTE) student ratio, new auxiliary income ratio, net hospital income ratio, contributed income ratio, educational core services ratio, educational support ratio, general support ratio, facilities maintenance ratio, and deferred maintenance ratio.

Does financial asset performance support the strategic direction? Because the long-term future of the institution depends on its ability to replace and enhance the capital base of the enterprise, managing its resource inflow streams is essential to achieving the institution's mission.

Key ratios to be considered in managing these streams include:

Return on Net Assets Ratio—comparison of total net income (i.e., change in net assets) to total net assets, which indicates if an institution is financially better off than in previous years by measuring total economic return including the market performance of the institution's investment portfolio.

Capitalization Ratio—comparison of net assets to total assets. This indicates financial health based on accumulated returns over time.

Composition of Equity Ratio—comparison of financial assets to physical assets. This provides insights into the allocation of equity and the flexibility of the institution's asset structure.

Return on All Investments Ratio—comparison of total investment return to the institution's total asset base (defined as cash, investments, property, plant, and equipment). This quantifies the impact of the potential use of equity as a source of capital.

Is debt managed strategically to advance the mission? Debt is a tool to achieve the desired long-term strategies of the institution, and as such, a debt policy should be linked to the mission and strategic objectives of the institution. A formal debt policy provides the framework through which the institution can evaluate the use of debt to achieve strategic goals.

Key ratios to be considered in the evaluation of an institution's management of debt and its capital structure include:

Viability Ratio—comparison of expendable net assets to long-term debt. This indicates the availability of expendable net assets to cover debt obligations.

Debt Burden Ratio—comparison of debt service to total expenditures. This is an indication of the institution's dependence on borrowed funds as a source of financing for its operations.

Debt Coverage Ratio—comparison of net income to total debt service. This measures the adequacy of net income to cover annual debt service payments.

Leverage Ratio—comparison of unrestricted and temporarily restricted net assets to long-term debt. This includes plant equity in evaluating an institution's ability to meet its long-term debt requirements.

Age of Facilities Ratio—comparison of accumulated depreciation to depreciation expense as a measure of the average age of facilities. This demonstrates if an institution is making necessary reinvestments in facilities.

Trend Analysis

Trend analysis describes the long-range behavior of institutional variables and compares interinstitutional data over time. Data in a trend analysis should span a sufficiently long period to describe turning points, discontinuities, or cycles in the elements that influence financial performance. Institutional rhythms frequently run in multiyear cycles; the specific rhythms should define the trend's length. A three- to five-year trend is appropriate in most instances but will not always be adequate.

Return-on-Investment Analysis

Return-on-investment (ROI) analysis is fundamental to financial analysis. It is sometimes used in a limited fashion in terms of the returns achieved by a short-term cash or long-term endowment investment or, more narrowly, in terms of investment yield. Economists use ROI in a number of ways.

Trade-off analysis is a form of ROI in which the return on a new investment (or expenditure) must be equal to or greater than that of the expenses that it replaces. Plant maintenance, replacement, investment, and improvement expenditures should be subjected to trade-off analysis.

Another type of ROI analysis involves the use of optimization techniques. Optimization formulas attempt to maximize benefits (revenues, cash flow) with a certain amount of resources or to minimize outlays or investments (personnel, physical inputs, costs) for a certain outcome.

Cost-benefit ROI is also widely used. For instance, in the realm of student and faculty morale, the provision of adequate equipment in laboratories or improved facilities in student housing or recreation can be related to the amount of money to be invested. Differences in the amount of capital required could produce significant differentials in perceived quality, which would affect institutional marketability. Thus, in spite of the difficulty of quantifying benefits, cost-benefit analysis is an important tool.

Risk management is also a type of ROI analysis. The problem of liability and the minimization of short- and long-term liability costs and the broader problem of exposure are matters of risk management. Because current and capital budget resources related to risk represent significant percentages in institutional budgets, risk management is a major managerial reporting concern. (See chapter 16, Risk Management and Insurance.)

Variance Analysis

Variance analysis, or exception reporting, is well established in managerial reporting. Its most widespread use occurs with the budget, but it can be applied to many operational phases of financial management. Variance analysis works best within a historical (e.g., compared to the same quarter in the previous year) or a planning (e.g., compared to parameters set forth in a plan) context. Data consistency is crucial for sound variance or exception analysis. An important issue in variance analysis is the degree of deviation considered normal or acceptable. Variance analysis should conclude on the impact of the variances. For example, how do the variances reflect on the standard used? Fundamentally, the user of the report must understand the factors underlying the variance and understand how and if program managers plan to make adjustments to operations based on this insight. A caveat in variance analysis: users should be alert to the possibility of two offsetting variances, which make it appear that what is being measured is on target when, in fact, it is not.

STRATEGIC LEVEL ANALYSIS AND REPORTING

Incorporating Institutional Strategy into Managerial Reporting

As colleges and universities change at an ever-increasing rate, there is a growing need to clarify an institution's market differentiation and to execute strategic initiatives to capitalize on competitive advantage. Two managerial reporting concepts, (1) aligning financial resources and mission, and (2) balancing the budget strategically, address the metrics of strategic analysis directly and suggest tools that can be used to keep colleges and universities on track with their strategic initiatives over extended periods of time. Business officers should consider incorporating such analysis into their managerial reporting model.

Aligning Financial Resources and Mission

Any time a decision on resource allocation is made without consideration of the college or university's mission, the institution risks diffusion of its resources. Ideally, business officers must find a way to deal with resource requests in a consistent and communicative manner so that overall, resources are aligned with institutional goals.

Figure 06-01 is a model that matches revenue allocation decisions to institutional mission. The purpose of the model is to map the financial contribution of some measurable unit of accountability (typically a department) against the department's contribution to strategic imperatives. The vertical axis represents financial performance. The definition of financial performance will depend on what the institution views as critical, and may be a blend of key performance indicators such as operating results, budget size, or return on net assets. Departments must be ranked based on their relative financial performance. The horizontal axis represents the relative contribution of each department to the strategic initiatives of the college or university. By mapping the departments into categories of "Critical," "Very Important," "Important," and "Less Important" to the future, management will have a tool for guiding resource requests. This analysis provides management a tool to determine more objectively the best in line rather than next in line, and helps management direct resources more impartially.

Balancing the Budget Strategically

Colleges and universities are often faced with the dilemma of how to create a "balanced budget." This balancing activity has tended to focus on an accounting

Figure 06-01

Performance Mission Model

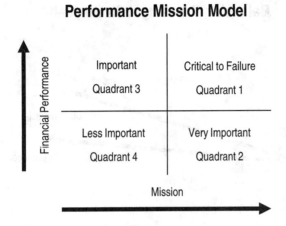

balance of the budget without necessarily focusing on whether the budget is balanced from a strategic perspective. This distinction, which is critical to the long-term success of the institution, relates to the types of investments and reinvestments required by the institution to meet its mission every year. The question of whether a budget is strategically balanced is answered by the ways that the spending patterns implied by the operating budget indicate progress toward strategic objectives. If the operating plan tends to be incremental in nature while the strategic plan represents substantive change, then the governing board, senior managers, and other interested parties should understand that a strategic gap exists in balancing the budget. Generally speaking, this represents a type of deferred obligation that the institution will be forced to make up at a later date, or an increased risk that key strategic initiatives may not be met.

The typical budgetary process provides limited information about meeting strategic objectives. Budgets are generally prepared consistent with reporting lines, usually by departments, and do not capture information according to activity, which is the way most investments are made, particularly in new initiatives. This is a reasonable budgetary methodology, since it aligns accountability and responsibility. A supplement to the budget might well present institutional investments, by special investment, in three categories: physical capital, human capital, and new program initiatives. The investment in human capital, in this

Figure 06-02

Balancing the Budget Strategically

context, is rarely salary support. It often represents the activities necessary for faculty and staff to create new skills that are required by the institutional mission.

Figure 06-02 presents two lines identifying strategic gaps. The top line represents the expenses of an institution that is reinvesting in itself at a rate sufficient to meet the objectives of its strategic plan. If repeatable revenues meet or exceed this amount, the budget is strategically balanced. The second line represents a budget that "gets the job done" but includes little investment in strategic initiatives. If revenue sources meet this line, the budget is financially balanced. Over a period of years, a strategic gap is cumulative in nature. The institution should track the size of that gap, if any, over the period covered by the strategic plan.

THE NATURE, SCOPE, AND PURPOSES OF COSTING

Cost information can serve many purposes and there are numerous cost concepts. It is important to know which concepts are best suited for specific costing objectives. Because higher education costs are increasingly scrutinized by the public, institutional administrators must be prepared to defend the ones they use. On the surface, it might seem advantageous to reduce the multiplicity of approaches to costing and urge adherence to uniform costing formats. However, the variety of costing objectives, coupled with the diversity of colleges and universities, may point away from the use of a single system. Especially where cost information serves internal rather than external purposes, managers should be free to explore and use approaches that they perceive to be best suited for their circumstances.

Types of Accounting and Costs

The meanings of the term "cost" derive from the contexts in which costing takes place. The most commonly used cost definitions are derived from financial accounting, cost accounting, economics, and law.

Financial accounting. Financial accounting defines cost in historical terms as amounts paid or charged for something with a dollar value in the "current" period. Neither future expenses associated with the acquisition of assets nor deferred expenses are included in financial accounting costs. Financial accounting underlies most costing endeavors.

Cost accounting. Cost accounting is concerned with accumulating, classifying, summarizing, interpreting, and reporting the costs of personnel, goods, and services used in institutional operations, as well as the costs resulting from the use and financing of assets (materials) and capital investments (e.g., plant and equipment), including the cost of debt. A major purpose of cost accounting is to determine different types of program, project, activity, and unit or service unit costs.[1] Unit costs often are a prerequisite for setting prices. Cost accounting uses financial accounting information, supplemented by nonfinancial data such as enrollment figures or the number of personnel in key job classifications. Whereas financial accounting stresses institutional costs by organizational *function* and line-item *object* categories, cost accounting normally involves the synthesis of financial accounting and other relevant information and the creation of appropriate costing models.

Economic cost accounting. Economic cost accounting focuses chiefly on the concept of "opportunity costs." Every investment (or expenditure) decision is based on a choice. Choosing A means giving up B. The economic or opportunity cost is the value of what is given up when a specific investment or expenditure is made.[2] Closely related to the concept of opportunity costs is the concept of "cost-benefit" analysis, where the costs and the value of benefits are studied in relation to a specific level of investment or spending.

Costs and the law. The law adds a different dimension to the meaning of costs. Laws and government regulations stipulate cost definitions that may or may not correspond with normal business practice, logic, or current industry convention. Government agencies frequently provide specific cost definitions or guidelines for calculating costs. Colleges and universities with large research components must comply with the limitations imposed by government agencies and others on allowable costs for indirect-cost reimbursement. Sometimes both the law and regulations are vague or overly complex, allowing program officers and auditors to interpret them individually, thus creating uncertainty about the meaning of particular costing requirements.

The types of costs most frequently used in costing terminology follow:

Variable costs. Variable costs vary with the size of enrollment, output, or sales.

Fixed costs. Fixed costs remain the same regardless of changeable elements, such as the size of a class or the amount of a product sold.

Aggregate costs. Aggregate costs, or total costs, are the sum of variable costs plus fixed costs. They encompass a range of otherwise distinct cost elements. For instance, aggregate operating costs might include the total expenditure budget for an entire institution or the budget for a self-supporting professional school, a hospital, and departments.

Average costs. Average costs, or mean costs, are the total costs divided by a number of input or output (e.g., total FTE enrollment, FTE teaching staff, or any other appropriate "unit" measure).

Marginal costs. Marginal costs, also called marginal variable or marginal fixed costs, are the changes in total costs resulting from (unit) changes in input or output.

Direct costs. Direct costs are costs that are directly related to an activity being conducted (e.g., the salary and benefits for a professor are direct costs of the courses he or she teaches).

Indirect costs. Indirect costs, sometimes referred to as "overhead," "prorated," or "marked" costs in the budget, can be charged legitimately to a specific activity that did not necessarily cause them. In higher education, "indirect-cost recovery" for research and educational projects is a topic of intense interest. The indirect-cost concept is an aspect of full costing (see as follows). If a research project is housed in an existing building and occupies a significant portion of a laboratory, maintenance and plant costs do not need to increase to generate indirect costs. However, the same research project may cause laboratory maintenance costs to rise, resulting in "marginal" costs. Colleges and universities must therefore distinguish between marginal or incremental costs and those that are in fact non-incremental.

Historical costs. Historical costs are the monetary value of economic resources acquired by cash disbursements or liabilities incurred; they can be incurred on a cash or accrual basis. The accrual basis is recommended for colleges and universities.

Standard costs. Standard costs are benchmark or predetermined costs that serve as a target or basis of comparison with the actual costs of services rendered. Standard costs are based on historical and/or comparative analysis or cost studies. They can be used in internal pricing and performance evaluation.

Imputed costs. Imputed costs encompass forgone resources (e.g., income) as a cost. For instance, an imputed cost is the interest income forgone when a specific amount of money is spent rather than invested.

Replacement costs. Replacement costs are the financial resources required to replace equipment and/or plant at current or specific future prices. They are different from depreciation.[3]

Projected costs. Projected costs are estimates or forecasts of costs to be incurred in future periods under specific economic and program assumptions.

Committed costs. Committed costs normally derive from contractual commitments to specific expenses or investments without which some funding or other event might not occur.

Discretionary costs. Discretionary costs derive from management decisions or changes in fiscal policy and need not be directly related to any particular service or activity.

Full costing. Full costing is, in a sense, the equivalent of total long-run costs, where an activity's costs include not only variable and fixed operating costs but also equipment and facility costs, debt service, and depreciation.[4]

Common or joint costs. Common or joint costs are associated with "joint-product" costs, as when an expenditure (e.g., a professor's salary) results in two or more outcomes (e.g., a research effort combined with a teaching, a public relations, and/or an administrative outcome).[5]

Ideally, costing is a comprehensive and integrated process encompassing the entire institution. Figure 06-03 depicts this process.

Figure 06-03

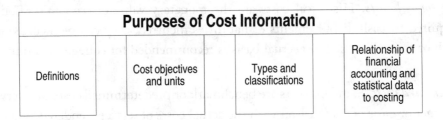

Purposes of Cost Information

| Definitions | Cost objectives and units | Types and classifications | Relationship of financial accounting and statistical data to costing |

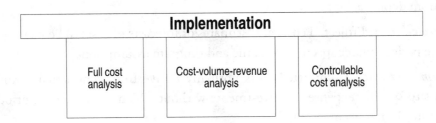

Cost Determination Methods and Approaches

| Specific service method | | | Continuous service method | | |
| Full costing | Variable or direct costing | Standard costing | Full costing | Variable or direct costing | Standard costing |

Implementation

| Full cost analysis | Cost-volume-revenue analysis | Controllable cost analysis |

Source: "Determining Cost of Information in Higher Education." Chapter 4:6 of College and University Business Administration. (Washington, D.C.: NACUBO, 1982.)

Costing Standards

Foremost among the factors affecting the costing process are costing standards. Maintaining consistent costing standards is a key element to establishing a common data model, as previously discussed in this chapter. These standards include:

- clear definitions of costing purposes specify the cost-determination approach to be used;

- cost information is based on the accrual method of accounting;

- cost data is reconciled to supporting financial and other institutional records;

- definitions used in cost determinations are applied uniformly;

- cost information and related costing units cover the same period;

- cost information is consistently determined; cost data, to be comparable, must be consistently collected and recorded; consistency depends on uniform definitions, methods, and interpretations, as well as judgments exercised in the cost-determination process;

- cost is attributed to a cost objective based on a causal or beneficial relationship; all costing endeavors must relate to a specific activity, project, program, or department;

- indirect costs are allocated on the basis of quantitative measures that can be applied in a practical manner; the quantitative measures used represent the relationship of costs to the cost objective, so that indirect costs are equitably distributed;

- common costs incurred to provide two or more services are allocated in an equitable manner; separate costing of jointly produced services can be subjective;

- capital costs reflect the applicable capital costs (i.e., depreciation) for the period, determined on the basis of the estimated useful life of each asset being depreciated; and

- cost information is accompanied by a disclosure statement; disclosures describe the costing method and approach used, the cost definition used, the types of cost included, identification of cost objectives and costing units, and other information pertinent to the cost-determination effort.

Purposes of Costing

Cost information is used both externally and internally. Externally, federal, state, and local government agencies require cost information in relation to appropriation, grant, loan, and legal compliance matters. These agencies usually specify the manner in which cost information is to be provided. Private foundations, businesses, and others who make grants to institutions may request cost information. Banks and other lending agencies are also interested in cost data. When colleges and universities bid for research and other contracts or sell their services, cost information is needed not only to set the prices for these contracts and services but also to document relevant costing details.

Internally, costing is used most frequently for:

- *Annual operations and capital budgeting:* Costing helps determine prices (to generate revenues) and expenditure budget allocations (to minimize or optimize costs).

- *Controlling operations:* Cost analysis verifies and corrects allocations and prices for improved current and future budget construction and management results.

- *Evaluating performance and operational analysis:* Costing in this context focuses on educational, financial, and operational objectives and assists in their implementation.

- *Internal pricing:* Costing acts as both a rationing and a cost allocation device.

- *Indirect-cost recovery:* It is used as a revenue-generating device, defined as reimbursement of overhead costs associated with externally funded research projects.

- *Long-range planning:* A full understanding of the costs of an institution's activities and the long-range behavior of these costs, and knowledge of the cost interactions within an institution are necessary to design an effective long-range plan.

- *Interinstitutional comparisons:* Comparative costing is practiced both within the confines of the current budget and in long-range planning; unless certain precautions are taken, interinstitutional cost comparisons may be based on incompatible or inconsistent methodologies and cost content.

In each instance, one or several cost concepts and costing methodologies may be appropriate and several costing techniques may be applied simultaneously.

Costing Methodologies

Costs can be viewed from a number of management perspectives, and costing methodologies may differ with the nature and purpose of specific costing applications:

- *Costing of broad management systems*—(the institution overall, separate campuses, individual professional schools, and major academic divisions);

- *Costing of discrete organizational subsystems*—(a single academic department or discipline, a single administrative unit, specific academic and administrative programs, and specific academic and administrative activities);

- *Costing project-by-project*—a "from-the-bottom-up" identification of the cost elements. The initial and primary focus should be on the direct costs of the project, followed by consideration of indirect and other capital costs. This is a major difference from costing of discrete organizational subsystems.

In the previously mentioned instances, the cost elements must be clearly articulated. At the same time, specific individuals responsible for carrying out costing tasks should be identified and made accountable for implementing appropriate and sound costing practices. Because each costing application and costing requirement may be carried out in different ways, it is crucial that institutions start the costing process with a clear definition of objectives, an understanding of available methodologies, and appropriate internal communications and decision processes.

Applications of Costing

Allocating Resources

The most important uses of costing in higher education relate to the efficient allocation of resources. In this context, the objective is not merely to determine the cost of services or products but also to allocate limited resources in economically sound ways.

Determining Costs

Because cost accounting normally requires the merging of financial and nonfinancial data, it must be viewed as a separate and distinct accounting activity. A large percentage of cost information, from academic and administrative departments especially, involves joint services (or joint products), which require specialized accounting ledgers that bring together the cost elements from two or more sources.

Budgeting and Analyzing

The operating budget represents a composite of discrete resource allocation and optimization opportunities, for which cost accounting is fundamentally important.[6] Two aspects are worth noting.

- The cost-effective use of utilities, the optimal management of materials and supplies, and the cost-effective management of personnel represent one aspect of the use of cost accounting in budgeting; other examples are cost-effective travel, computer use, data processing, telecommunications, custodial services, security, and all the other routine services normally supervised by the chief financial or business officer.

- A second aspect is the nature of the specific activity whose costs are being determined. For instance, how is the cost of an academic department, a new course to be offered, or a specific student advisement function determined? In terms of costs, what is the real meaning of student services, housing, institutional advancement, instructional support, and academic or institutional research?

Costing and Internal Pricing

Internal pricing provides a direct link to costing by charging departments fees for using the institution's supplies and other resources. When fees are established for the use of central computer services, the consumption of electricity, or the maintenance of facilities, using departments can allocate their budget resources appropriately. At the same time, the institution works with budget information that reflects cost charges where resources are actually used, rather than having to rely on a miscellaneous budget category or simple prorating.

Internal pricing informs users of the cost to the institution of departmental activities. In the economy at large, prices serve the purpose of clearing the shelves; in an institution, internal pricing helps "clear" and often "reallocate" the budget. For instance, departments such as maintenance or computer services may charge fees to user departments, resulting in corresponding debits and credits with respect to the respective line item budget allocations.

In setting internal prices, the costs that they cover must be decided on. The costing standards that underlie internal prices then should be clearly communicated to users. Such communication is especially important when full or indirect-costing standards are adopted. When institutions do not take economies of scale sufficiently into account, even direct-cost internal prices may exceed those charged by the local commercial competition. When internal prices are not competitive, or when they are expected to recover significant internal overhead costs, the manager needs to ensure that users understand what is intended and that the internal pricing system is accepted as fair. Internal pricing should enable both departments and budgets to succeed; it should not create incentives for bypassing the system. A properly conceived internal pricing system is one that is generally accepted within the management hierarchy, does not merely shuffle costs from one department to another, and, most important, contributes to cost-effective management throughout the institution.[7]

COSTS OF SPONSORED PROGRAMS

It is relatively easy to determine the direct costs of the activities of a professor who engages in research under a grant or contract. Salaries, health and other benefits, supplies, travel, and the cost of assistants represent straightforward cost elements.

The determination of other less obvious costs may be somewhat more difficult. How much of the heating and cooling bill, of janitorial services and plant maintenance, should be allocated to the grant? What percentage of general administrative expenditures should be written off against it? How should the depreciation and replacement of capital be accounted for? In other words, exactly what should be included in indirect costs and who should pay for them?

The first formal attempt at establishing guidelines for indirect-cost recovery came with the publication of *Explanation of Principles for Determination of Costs under Government Research and Development Contracts with Educational Institutions*, referred to as the "Blue Book." This publication relied heavily on the principle of averaging. A single indirect-cost rate was applied to all allowable cost categories within the institution. Calculations were based on the audited annual financial report.

In 1957, Bureau of the Budget Circular A-21, "Principles for Costing Research and Development under Grants and Contracts with Educational Institutions," replaced the "Blue Book." Circular A-21 abandoned the single indirect-cost notion, increasing considerably the workload associated with calculating indirect-cost recovery. The audited financial report was no longer the sole source for indirect costing, and henceforth supplemental cost data needed to be collected.

Several subsequent revisions to Circular A-21 have been published. In 1976, the Office of Management and Budget (OMB) assumed jurisdiction over it. Now titled "Cost Principles for Educational Institutions," Circular A-21 was last revised in 1998. Among the more significant changes to Circular A-21 since 1991 are the following:

- The old single "Indirect Cost Rate" has been divided into separate facilities and administrative (F&A) rate components, with the administrative rate component capped at 26 percent.[8]

- A number of costs have been made unallowable for reimbursement and others prescribed as either a direct or indirect cost, usually affecting the capped administrative component.

- Restrictions have been placed on the amount of reimbursement for interest.

- Rules of the government Cost Accounting Standards Board must now be followed in the administration of college and university grants and contracts.

- Additional direction has been prescribed on composition of the research base and on how major cost elements, such as graduate research assistant tuition, are to be distributed.

Indirect and Direct Costs

Section F of Circular A-21 describes each cost category and the allocation base preferred by the federal government. It addresses the following major concepts and concerns.

Identification and assignment of F&A costs. F&A costs are broad categories of costs. "Facilities" is defined as depreciation and use allowances, interest on debt associated with certain buildings, equipment and capital improvements, operation and maintenance expenses, and library expenses. "Administration" is defined as general administration and general expenses, departmental administration, sponsored projects administration, student administration and services, and all other types of expenditures not listed specifically under one of the subcategories of Facilities.

Allocable costs. Allocable costs are costs assignable to a cost objective or sponsored activity, if the assignment can be based on a cause-and-effect relationship, benefit derived, or logic and reason. Allocable costs include direct and indirect costs. A potential allocable cost can be determined by answering the following questions:

- Does the cost serve to advance the work of the final cost objective?
- Does the cost benefit both the project and other objectives of the institution?
- Is the cost necessary and reasonable for the overall operation of the institution?

Reasonable costs. Reasonable costs are incurred within the bounds of prudence, determined by such issues as conflicts of interest, fair value received, the necessity of the costs in question, and adherence to institutional policies.

Allowable costs. Not all allocable or reasonable costs are "allowed" under Circular A-21. Section J describes the costs that are not allowed. The major ones are interest expense (with certain exceptions); fund-raising and investment management costs; intramural student activities costs; cost overruns, general public and alumni relations activities; and entertainment, commencement, and convocation expenses.

Allocation base. The allocation base is the common measurable base used when allocating indirect costs to a major function (e.g., operation and maintenance cost charged to major functions on the basis of net assignable square footage).

Distribution base. The distribution base refers to the base or denominator from which the F&A rate is computed and to which it is applied. The most common base includes salaries and wages, employee benefits, materials and supplies, and services, travel, and certain subgrant and subcontract expenditures.

F&A Rate

In calculating indirect costs, institutions whose total volume of federally sponsored activities does not exceed $10 million in direct cost activity per year may use the simplified method described in Section H of Circular A-21; all others are required to use the "regular" or long-form method. In the simplified method, the institution may use either a salary and wage base or a modified total direct cost base in calculating the F&A rate. Under the long-form method the F&A rate is calculated using a modified total direct cost base consisting of all salaries and wages, benefits, materials and supplies, services, travel, and subgrants and subcontracts up to the first $25,000 of each subgrant or subcontract.

Under both methods, F&A rates are developed in total and not for individual projects. The result of the approval process is an institutional F&A rate.

Once an F&A rate has been calculated, the resulting cost proposal is officially assigned to a "cognizant" federal agency for negotiation and audit. Cost negotiation cognizance is assigned to the Department of Health and Human Services (HHS) or the Department of Defense's Office of Naval Research (DOD), normally depending on which of the two agencies (HHS or DOD) provides more funds to the educational institution for the most recent three years.

Policy Issues

An ongoing dispute between higher education and the Office of Management and Budget (OMB) concerns the adequacy of cost recovery. Colleges and universities argue that Circular A-21 principles fail to provide for full F&A recovery. Government agencies suspect that higher education institutions submit requests for excessive and unjustified cost reimbursements. From time to time, the United States Congress and the national media focus on alleged abuses. There are also significant differences in the F&A recovery rates among institutions. These differences have fueled the perception that the amount of variation is somehow unnatural and likely the result of either inefficient or ineffective management or artificial and inappropriate accounting treatments.

Since 1991 OMB has made a number of changes intended to tighten and standardize the definition and treatment of the costs of sponsored programs, particularly in the area of F&A recovery. These changes, particularly the requirement that college and universities adopt cost accounting standards for estimating, accumulating, and reporting costs, have added to the continuing disagreement between the government and educational institutions about the adequacy of cost reimbursement. While a 1998 study by the Council on Governmental Relations (COGR) ascertained that the range of rates billed to the government has narrowed since 1987, significant variances remain. The report identifies a number of factors that help explain differences. These factors include research volume; research mix; interest rates; cost of energy, heating, and cooling degree-days; age of physical plant; amount of debt; investment in buildings and equipment; and research square footage. Other important factors are also discussed, including an institution's ability to cost share and the government's negotiation practices.

Other Issues

Federal F&A recovery may cause a dilemma for public institutions, depending on how the state views such "revenues." In the eyes of some state authorities, recovery is seen as reimbursement for prior state appropriations in support of federally funded research and educational activities. Thus, the state and not the college or university is entitled to the reimbursement. Indeed, states sometimes recapture all F&A reimbursements. In other instances, anticipated cost recovery is incorporated into the institutional budget and state appropriations are adjusted fully or in part. Some states may provide incentives for leaving a portion of reimbursements at the disposal of the institution. F&A recovery rates, on average, tend to be significantly smaller for public than for independent institutions.

For independent colleges and universities, F&A recovery is supposed to ensure an adequate academic infrastructure by supporting the basic services expected of the institution. However, because such costing relies on judgment, a question of what charges are reasonable and what may be excessive always exists. If business- or government-sponsored research requires an infrastructure, and if without such an infrastructure institutions could not qualify for grants, how much of the infrastructure costs should institutions charge to others? Given the full range of indirect costs, specifically depreciation and use allowances, how do institutions distribute the reimbursed money among their various funds? Specifically, is any money transferred to equipment replacement and plant funds? In most independent institutions, reimbursements are treated as unrestricted revenues and often revert back to the cost-originating departments.

Policy Implications of Costing

Internal Policy Implications

Costing is directly linked to financial policy in two noteworthy aspects. The first concerns the appropriateness of full costing: what it means and when to use it. To the extent that college and university operating and capital budgets incorporate full-costing principles in the long-run sense, they also raise the revenue horizon under which they need to function. Conversely, to the extent that institutions relax their full-costing stance, long-run revenue requirements will appear to become less demanding. If long-run full costing is applied to project, activity, and program costing but not to budgeting and long-range planning, a fundamental policy discrepancy exists. Such inconsistency could damage an institution's long-run financial condition.

The second linkage of costing with financial policy concerns the question of how much current and future revenue should depend on indirect-cost recovery—particularly, how much of it should depend on federal sources. Colleges and universities should answer this question in terms of both academic and financial policy implications.

Internally, costing highlights the comparative costs of academic and operating departments, the latter especially. Many policy concerns may arise from these differences. For instance, where cost differences are the result of more or less efficient uses of resources, management can focus on improving the performance of less-efficient managers. When differences are based on salary and wage discrepancies, questions of equity may arise. Although cost differences alone should not determine which departments or activities survive, very costly operations that cause operating deficits should be scrutinized carefully.

External Policy Implications

The most obvious external policy implication of costing stems from the public's interest in the cost of higher education. The cost of doing business influences the prices that institutions charge and the taxes that citizens pay in support of higher education directly (through appropriations, grants, and contracts) and indirectly (through tax exemptions for philanthropic support).

For public institutions, external policy issues arise from the need to justify annual government appropriations. In this regard, cost information has always been a major factor, with unit and marginal cost data playing special roles in many states' funding practices. Higher education institutions usually derive funding from a variety of governmental and private sources. Private entities that provide funding for colleges and universities, including individual donors, increasingly are requesting certain types of cost information or asking for assurances that resources are used efficiently.

Conclusion

The ultimate objective of costing should be the rational, cost-effective allocation of scarce resources. There is always more than one way to allocate resources or means. What are the procedures used by managers (and by senior management) to ensure that resource allocation is and remains cost-effective? Questions such as this must be addressed continuously, as a function of the technical skills of financial and business officers and of the specific control procedures established to ensure that costing decisions produce value for the institution and its mission.

NOTES

1. "Project" refers to something limited and distinct, for instance, a specific research project or a narrow plant maintenance task reflected in a "job order." "Activity" refers to the management of janitorial and campus security services or other tasks of a relatively homogeneous nature. "Program" (as in program budgeting) is broader and may involve several jurisdictions, for instance, "academic program," "student life program," or "capital development program." "Unit costs" refers to a broad group of "average costs" frequently used by business officers and financial managers in almost ever aspect of the budget.

2. Don R. Hansen, *Management Accounting,* (Boston, MA: PWS-Kent Publishing Co., 1990), p. 31; William A. Koivisto, *Principles and Problems of Modern Economics,* (New York: John Wiley & Sons, Inc., 1957), pp. 595–604.

3. Current revenue deficiencies are prevalent in higher education, as are large amounts of deferred maintenance. Both conditions point to a precarious long-run financial condition, particularly in the chronic underfunding of existing plant and equipment.

4. Variance and multiple regression analyses are favored by some costing experts; similarly, linear and dynamic programming techniques are sometimes advocated. These are sound methodologies but require appropriate depth and quality of data.

5. See National Center for Higher Education Management Systems (NCHEMS) *Resource Requirement Prediction Model;* see also George Wheathersby et al., *Induced*

Course Load Matrix, which assists in allocating costs to individual courses and instructors for calculating or estimating aggregate and unit instructional costs.

6. Efficient resource allocation involves the solution of quantitative optimizations; these are often couched in cost-minimization terms such as "to achieve a specific outcome with as few resources as possible" or "to produce a maximum result with few resources."

7. Occasionally, a college or university may allow academic departments to set internal prices as part of their budget and expenditure control procedures; the chief financial or business officer should participate in the pricing.

8. In 1990–91, indirect-cost ratios as a percentage of direct cost ranged from 40 to 79 percent in independent institutions and from 35 to 43 percent in public institutions. Bill Workman, "Stanford Wants 76% Rate for Overhead . . ." in *San Francisco Chronicle* (July 4, 1991): A 15.

REFERENCES AND RESOURCES

Abowd, John M. *An Econometric Model of Higher Education.* Chicago, Ill.: University of Chicago Press, 1981.

————. *An Econometric Model of the U.S. Market for Higher Education.* New York: Garland Publishing Co., 1984.

Allen, R.H., and Brinkman, P.T. *Marginal Costing Techniques for Higher Education.* Boulder, Colo.: National Center for Higher Education Management Systems, 1983.

Andersen, Charles A. *Conditions Affecting College and University Financial Strength.* Higher Education Panel Report 63. Washington, D.C.: American Council on Education, 1985.

Anderson, Richard E., and Meyerson, Joel W. *Financing Higher Education in a Global Economy.* American Council on Education Series. New York: Macmillan Co., 1990.

Bowen, Howard R. *Investment in Learning: The Individual and Social Value of Higher Education.* San Francisco, Calif.: Jossey-Bass, 1977.

————. *The Costs of Higher Education.* San Francisco, Calif.: Jossey-Bass, 1980.

Brinkman, P.T. "Factors Affecting Instructional Costs at Major Research Universities." *Journal of Higher Education* vol. 52, no. 3 (1981): 265–279.

————. *Instructional Costs per Student Credit Hour: Differences by Level of Instruction.* Boulder, Colo.: National Center for Higher Education Management Systems, 1985.

———. "Marginal Costs of Instruction in Public Higher Education." Ph.D. dissertation, University of Arizona, 1981.

Chaffee, Ellen E. *Rational Decision Making in Higher Education.* Boulder, Colo.: National Center For Higher Education Management Systems, 1983.

Hoenack, Stephen A., and Collins, Eileen A., eds. *The Economics of American Universities: Management, Operations, and Fiscal Environment.* New York: State University of New York Press, 1990.

Hyatt, James A. *A Cost Accounting Handbook for Colleges and Universities.* Washington, D.C.: NACUBO, 1980.

Hyatt, James A., and Santiago, A.A. *Financial Management of Colleges and Universities.* Washington, D.C.: NACUBO, 1986.

James, Estelle, and Hoenack, Stephen A. "Student Financial Aid and Public Policy." *Economics of Education Review* 1 (1988): 127–34.

Jenny, Hans H., Hughes, G.C., and Devine, Richard E. *Hang-Gliding or Looking for an Updraft: A Study of College and University Finance in the 1980s—The Capital Margin.* Wooster, Ohio: College of Wooster, 1981.

Kaiser, Harvey H. "Capital Needs in Higher Education." In *Financing Higher Education: Strategies after Tax Reform.* Edited by Richard E. Anderson and Joel W. Meyerson. San Francisco, Calif.: Jossey-Bass, 1987.

King, George A. "Rethinking Higher Education Capital Finance." Parts 1, 2. *Capital Ideas* 3, nos. 2–3 (1988).

Langfitt, Thomas W. "The Cost of Higher Education: Lessons to Learn from the Health Care Industry." *Change,* November/December 1990, 8–38.

Leslie, Larry L., and Brinkman, Paul T. "Student Price Response in Higher Education: The Student Demand Studies." *Journal of Higher Education* vol. 58, no. 2 (1987), 181–204.

Massy, William F. "A Strategy for Productivity Improvement in College and University Academic Departments." Paper presented at Forum for Postsecondary Governance, Santa Fe, N.M., October 31, 1989.

———. "Productivity Improvement Strategies for College and University Administration and Academic Support." Paper presented at Forum for College Financing, Annapolis, Md., October 26, 1989.

National Center for Higher Education Management Systems. *Costing for Policy Analysis.* Boulder, Colo.: NCHEMS, 1980.

Porter, Michael E. *Competitive Strategy: Techniques for Analyzing Industry and Competitors.* New York: Macmillan Co., The Free Press, 1980.

Robinson, Daniel D. *Capital Maintenance for Colleges and Universities.* Washington, D.C.: NACUBO, 1986.

Chapter 7

Information Technology and Services

Edited by

EDUCAUSE

with contributions by

Carole A. Barone, EDUCAUSE

Robert F. German, University of Virginia

Richard N. Katz, EDUCAUSE

Philip E. Long, Yale University

Barry Walsh, Indiana University

Sponsors

KPMG

Contact: Greg J. Baroni
1676 International Drive
McLean, VA 22102
703-747-3004
www.kpmg.com

With over 30 years of serving higher education, KPMG offers a broad range of services that helps our clients analyze their businesses with true clarity, raises their level of performance and delivers the strategic and infrastructural components to support highly dynamic E-business models in colleges, universities, and academic medical centers.

AT&T

Contact:
295 North Maple Avenue
Basking Ridge, NJ 07920
800-228-7937
www.att.com/campusalliance

An AT&T Campus Alliance offers a full range of integrated communication and network solutions for you and your students—for all the ways you communicate.

ORACLE CORPORATION

Oracle Higher Education
1910 Oracle Way
Reston, VA 20190
888-216-4027
www.oracle.com/industries/highered

Oracle Corporation is the world's leading supplier of software for information management. Oracle currently has over 120,000 customers in 145 countries including major universities, colleges, and community college systems.

BLACKBOARD, INC.
Contact: Lee Wang
1899 L Street, NW, 5th Floor
Washington, DC 20036
202-463-4860 or 800-424-9299
www.blackboard.com

Blackboard Inc. is a leading Internet infrastructure company for E-learning, focused on transforming the Internet into a powerful environment for teaching and learning.

CAMPUS PIPELINE
Contact: Kimberly Woods
155 North West, Suite 400
Salt Lake City, UT 84103
801-519-8191
www.campuspipeline.com

The Campus Pipeline Web Platform—Built to support the connections and interactions that make up your institution's community, Campus Pipeline creates a super-network among students, faculty, staff and administrators.

CARS INFORMATION SYSTEMS
4000 Executive Park Drive, Suite 412
Cincinnati, OH 45241-4009
www.carsinfo.com

The CARS Solution is a rapid implementation, total administrative solution compromised of Student, Financial, Human Resources, Institutional Advancement, and Information Management software.

COLLEGIS
Contact: Melissa Meridith
2300 Maitland Center Parkway, Suite 340
Maitland, FL 32751
800-800-1874
www.collegis.com

COLLEGIS is higher education's strategic technology partner—aligning technology resources and investments with institutional goals. COLLEGIS manages institutional administrative, academic, and communications technology functions.

EDUPRISE
Contact: Joseph C. Costanzo
2000 Perimeter Park Drive, Suite 160
Morrisville, NC 27560
919-376-1339
www.eduprise.com

Eduprise is a leading provider of ASP services, web integration and professional consulting services for enabling rapid transformation of intellectual capital to develop effective E-learning programs. More than a technology company, we are experts in the planning, development and implementation services needed to implement a successful E-learning environment.

NCS
Contact: John D. Schneider
2510 N. Dodge St.
Iowa City, IA 52245
319-339-6644
www.ncs.com

NCS has served the education community with data collection and management services, financial aid processing, testing, instructional management, electronic document management and surveys for 35 years.

THE DOCUMENT COMPANY XEROX
Contact: Ray McClure
80 Linden Oaks Parkway
Rochester, NY 14625
716-383-7668
www.xerox.com

Xerox's Public Sector Organization integrates paper/digital processes to create efficient document networks that maximize productivity and knowledge sharing while minimizing total enterprise operating costs.

Contents

It has been argued that information technology (IT) and information technologists are agents of change. Information technology has long been a major element of higher education's business operations. In fact, the earliest campus investments in mammoth mainframe computers were made to support institutional accounting and budgetary operations.

Until recently, information technology has existed on campus as a necessary evil; a set of tools too complex for general consumption and, therefore, consigned to the stewardship of a somewhat idiosyncratic cadre of specialists. More recently, with the widespread diffusion of personal computers, networks, and the World Wide Web (WWW), information technology and services have become imbedded in the fabric of the institution. What's more, the rapid adoption of key Internet and browser standards is enabling colleges and universities to interconnect with their major constituents—students, parents, alumni, research sponsors, business partners, suppliers, and others. Virtually no area of campus business operation has escaped major impacts by IT. The objectives of this chapter are to:

- identify and highlight areas of critical concern;
- describe institutional frameworks for planning and managing key information technologies, networks, services, and information resources; and
- offer realistic (and constrained) forecasts about the direction, intensity, and speed of changes related to the management and use of information systems, services, and resources on campus.

Caveat emptor: the history of information technology is defined by discontinuities. The greatest futurists of a decade ago could not have anticipated the impact of the World Wide Web on teaching, learning, and institutional management. Managing this essential and mercurial element of institutional life will require leadership, vision, courage, talent—and faith. In this arena, change really is the only constant.

MANAGING INFORMATION TECHNOLOGY RESOURCES

Clark Kerr described a modern university as "a series of individual faculty entrepreneurs held together by a common grievance over parking.[1]" This humorous observation highlights a theme that is particularly important to understanding the management of campus technology resources. Often the only thing that will unite the diverse collection of individuals found at a higher education institution is complaint over a commonly valued resource that is in short supply. These days, technology administrators are managing just such resources, and they experience that otherwise rare unity daily and at loud volume. Their challenge is to find a way to plan and fund their activities so that they are not always reacting to complaints, but anticipating legitimate needs and providing for them.

The challenge is made more daunting by another fact in college and university life: higher education institutions change the way they do things very slowly. This environmental element creates a critical and sometimes paralyzing tension for technology administrators. The pace of fundamental technological change, already dizzyingly rapid, continues to increase. An opportunity that was not imagined six months ago may suddenly appear, then disappear after a brief stay in the realm of the possible. If institutions cannot quickly measure cost against benefit by many standards (not just financial), assess and accept a reasonable level of risk, and then decide and act forcefully before the opportunity disappears, they may find themselves falling behind in effective use of technology. And falling behind in technology use costs institutions faculty, staff, students, and funding because they become less competitive in the contest to demonstrate their connection to and understanding of the rapidly changing world at large. Institutions with the best records for prudent but farsighted technology use often have mechanisms for flexible planning and quick decision making that prominently feature, among other characteristics, good working relationships and mutual respect between technology administrators and financial officers.

Strategic Information Technology Planning

In information technology, strategic planning is uncomfortably close to an oxymoron. Some business leaders have declared that their IT strategic planning has a maximum horizon of 18 months, the result of the high speed of technology change that often renders today's solutions obsolete before they can be implemented. However, it is not only possible for technology administrators to accomplish good IT strategic planning at colleges and universities, but also it is essential that it happen and that it be tied to institutional strategic planning, which in turn is tied to the institutional mission.

Part of effective IT strategic planning in higher education is to remember that the top goals of any IT plan must be to support the top goals of the institution's strategic plan. The institution's goals usually do not change rapidly, even if the IT environment at large is turning somersaults in the years between new strategic plans. The top level of both areas of strategic planning focuses attention on the fundamental elements of institutional character and values, and, for technology administrators, such a planning process offers the opportunity to demonstrate that the technology organization understands the core work of the institution and shapes its plans to support that work. When that common perspective is known and appreciated on all sides, institutional planners invite technology administrators to be important participants in institution-wide planning, and two-way exchange between the planning processes is made easier and its benefits are multiplied.

Some institutions are beginning to make use of the term "enterprise technology architecture" to describe the link between the institution's mission, goals, and major activities and its high-level design of the technology environment. This often is a more productive approach than that associated with the term "information technology architecture," which focuses more on the technology components themselves, not necessarily in the context of what they are there to support.

Effective strategic planning is a multilevel, iterative communication process with many opportunities for feedback and refinement. In addition to being iterative, such a process must be ongoing to allow for introduction of new elements. The pace of technological change means that the life of good answers is short. Technology administrators must be sure that new possibilities are fed responsibly into a fully integrated planning process at appropriate intervals and that technology planning is flexible enough to accommodate the alterations in course that result.

Although it is possible to provide too much technical detail to departmental constituents in the planning process, there is great value in including departmental and unit technology specialists in the detailed planning of the central technology organization. Providing opportunities for building consensus in this way among technology specialists will ensure that esoteric technical questions are resolved in the proper forum and do not unnecessarily become matters of contention in high-level planning.

Organizing to Support Information Technology

In a field that changes so fast, figuring out how to organize human resources to support technology and information resource management is something akin to trying to stand steady during an earthquake—you almost always have to change your footing to maintain your balance. But changing an organizational scheme too frequently confuses and demoralizes the staff involved. Thus many colleges and universities settle on models of staff organization for a period of time, then evaluate and adjust as needed.

Some institutions have elected to bring all computing and telecommunications technology together with information resources under one executive, often called a chief information officer (CIO). Such an executive may be responsible for libraries, broadcast media, printing and copying, information technology, telephone systems, and other related components. Other institutions keep those functions separate or bring together two or three of them. Ultimately, the organizational structure is the least important factor. The most important factors are leadership, shared institutional vision, and sustained communication. When all the components have effective leaders who share a vision of the future for the institution, reporting to the same person is unnecessary. What is essential in such a structure is excellent and sustained communication among all of the units—communication characterized by mutual respect, flexibility, and adaptability. If the leadership, vision, and communication are not present (and often they are not), the institution will be wise to consider consolidation under a single senior officer as a means of achieving a coordinated approach to the complex issues of technology and information resource management. Whatever the reporting structure—and especially when the various technology-related functions do not report within a single organization—having an effective governance structure will go a long way toward ensuring an integrated, cohesive approach to effective information technology resources management.

But struggling with issues of central organization is not the only question in organizing technology support. How much should be centralized, and how much should be in the hands of campus departments and units? The answer to this question seems more intuitive. Support for common infrastructure should be in the central organizations. Support for department- or unit-specific functions should be housed in the departments or units. The problem, of course, is that few functions resolve quite that cleanly. Who should handle support of the history department's server? And who should support the geographic information system software that architecture faculty and environmental science faculty both use? Much of the answer is tied to institutional culture and tradition. In a highly decentralized institution, singling out information technology for a high degree of centralization is inviting a serious cultural conflict. The place for such transformations of institutional culture is in the strategic planning processes described earlier. No technology administrator can effect such changes alone.

Another important question asks for whom a technology support system is being designed. If the answer is every individual in the institution, the support system is doomed from the start. No modern college or university can afford a support system that will meet every individual's needs 24 hours per day. Most technology administrators recognize the wisdom of designing support systems that meet nearly everyone's needs nearly all of the time. This means that priorities must be set. For example, no effort should be spared to ensure that the main telecommunications infrastructure is functioning properly every second of every day and that major administrative applications have no unscheduled "downtimes." But the help desk that provides answers to students about their word processing software may operate only from 9 a.m. to 6 p.m.

Again, technology administrators should not set any such priorities in isolation. They should be the products of iterative and ongoing strategic planning with explicit opportunities for feedback and refinement.

Investing in IT

Colleges and universities face many IT investment challenges, from determining appropriate staffing levels (and then finding the professionals to fill those positions, as well as the means to retain them) and replacement cycles to measuring the return on investment and developing effective funding mechanisms.

Competing for Skilled Staff

By far the largest investment colleges and universities make in technology is in the people who look after it. And in the information age that is the area of greatest risk. Technology administrators in higher education face bigger challenges every day trying to attract and keep highly skilled staff members, because colleges and universities often are not accustomed to aggressively competing for support staff in a labor market where the financial rewards outside higher education are far better than in it. In particular, the continued explosive growth of data networks, particularly in the commercial sector, has created huge demands for qualified network staff, bidding up wages and creating staff scarcities. Market trends suggest this scarcity is not likely to ease in the foreseeable future.

If colleges and universities have any hope of building and maintaining the staff of skilled technology professionals they must have now and in the future, it will come from flexible (and expensive) systems of employee classification and compensation, plus attractive mechanisms for training and retraining, that allow the institutions to compete effectively with the for-profit sector. Ultimately, however, the prospects are shaky for designing any system that can, over the long term, recruit and keep current staff levels of technology professionals at institutions. That is why colleges and universities are looking at outsourcing with greater frequency as a potential answer to the staff drain (see the discussion below on funding mechanisms).

Higher education has a significant advantage to exploit in identifying and cultivating future technology specialists. It can "build its own" from its student populations. While there is a steady outflow on one end of the employment continuum, there is a steady inflow at the other, and that inflow provides continuous refreshments of perspective and of relevant skills to a workforce that must have both.

Life-cycle Budgeting and Replacement

After the realities of today's technology labor market, the most important budget lesson that technology administrators have learned in the past decade or so is that technology expenditures are tending to move from the category of capital investments (often debt-financed) to operating expenditures. The change is tied in part to the migration of computing power from big central machines to distributed servers and desktop machines. It is also due to the related reduction in useful life of most hardware and software, combined with significant drops in the prices of hardware, notably desktop computers.

In the mid-1980s, the average cost of a desktop computer at many institutions was about $2,500, and technologists tried to keep such computers alive for as much as five years. By the late-1990s, the cost of a broadly useful desktop computer had dropped dramatically, and institutions could begin to debate whether replacing them every two years might be prudent.

In fact, studies of total cost of ownership (TCO) of desktop computers suggest that the old $2,500 direct cost was much less than the total that was actually being spent to keep that computer on a desktop for five years. Fixing broken parts, upgrading components, updating software and operating systems, and being unable to incorporate new solutions on campuses because of the aging installed base of desktop environments have real costs, financial or functional. The same studies reveal that the less obvious costs of keeping desktop machines working are greatly reduced when institutions decide to replace them on shorter life cycles.

And "trickling down" old machines to less critical uses almost never proves cost-effective, although it remains a common practice throughout higher education.

Many of the same principles apply to infrastructure components, which usually are longer-lived and more expensive than desktop computers but which are tending downward by both measures.

The primary implications of this lesson are that competent budgeting for technology is a complex effort requiring good understanding of both obvious and nonobvious costs and that institutions need new ways of thinking about technology financing. In the past, central budgeting authorities would hold funds from which "grants" were made to departments or units that made good cases for needing their technology environments refreshed in that particular year; now explicit annual budgeting for technology at the department and unit level often works better. Although debt financing made sense for desktop computers expected to function for five years, leasing may make the best budgetary sense for computers that units will keep for only two years, especially when disposal costs are added to the calculations. And a newcomer to budgeting desktop computing—a concept known as seat management, among other terms—brings the intriguing notion that sometimes it makes sense for the institution to "own" no components of desktop computing. Instead it will simply contract for desktop computing as a service (often billed monthly) from a vendor usually known as an "integrator."

Seat management is already in use by some colleges and universities, and it will grow in popularity as institutions and vendors develop models for adapting the concept for student, faculty, and staff personal use off campus as well.

Of course, there remain major categories of technology expenditure where the old budgeting theories still apply—big-ticket, long-life items such as telephone systems or major administrative applications. But even here there are important new things to know. For example, long-term contracts that specify products and prices in any area of technology, including long-distance services or Internet services, may block institutions from taking advantage of price drops that are common in today's markets. Institutions may find the most cost-effective alternatives are relationship agreements with vendors that feature flexibility that allows them to regularly renegotiate product specifications and prices. Nearly all agreements and contracts should provide for manageable exit from the relationship by the institution under appropriate conditions.

Measuring and Valuing the IT Investment

Many of the current pricing trends in technology mean that colleges and universities get more technical capability for each dollar spent, compared to any previous time (including yesterday). Although institutions are buying more for the same amount of money, it still is not enough. The imperatives to accommodate to some degree the rapid changes in technology and to address the continuing explosion in demand, from PCs on desktops to network connections to Internet bandwidth, still exceed any gains institutions realize from price reductions. As a result, technology administrators must make cases regularly for greater investment in technology, and in doing so they must help the institution understand how to measure and assign value to those investments. This is much easier said than done.

First, the greater part of technology purchases (because of price drops) is now slipping under thresholds of detailed inventory tracking systems or between the cracks of purchasing-system categories at most institutions. Ask a university technology administrator how many PCs his or her institution purchased last year, and the response will likely be an estimate. Ask the same person what proportion of PCs have particular processors, and he or she will probably have to rely on surveys (if available) to answer. For most larger institutions, the capacity to reliably establish a baseline of what currently comprises the technology environment, at least with respect to personal computers, will await the deployment of embedded asset management tools that work across networks, and that day is not yet here for many.

Second, technology administrators face a significant challenge in prioritizing work for their staffs and their equipment. Measuring what you are doing takes time from the task itself, and often asking a machine to track how it is being used reduces its capacity to do its primary work. Because most technology organizations are overwhelmed with demand on both people and equipment, technology administrators must carefully consider when to ask for the kinds of measurement that might generate basic data useful in a return on investment (ROI), total cost of ownership (TCO), or cost/benefit analysis.

Combine those factors with another characteristic of higher education—the challenges inherent in establishing cause-and-effect relationships regarding the "products" of higher education—and technology administrators find themselves in a tough spot. They do have an advantage, however. Their work directly affects some of the core elements of higher education itself, notably the generation, management, and movement of information. Technology administrators known for making effective cases for investment in technology are usually the ones who can effectively draw connections between those investments and functional gains for the activities at the very hearts of their institutions.

Funding Mechanisms

It is a rare higher education technology administrator who gets from central sources all the funding needed to keep his or her environment reasonably current and scaled to demand. The pressure increases constantly to invent more mechanisms to reduce costs, increase efficiency, generate funds, and regulate consumption on commodities or services in short supply. The mechanisms most frequently available are fee-for-service or outsourcing plans.

Associated with these mechanisms is another theme in higher education: for any currently desirable service that is free, demand will grow to infinity. Most institutions learned this while trying to provide their own no-charge, modem-based network access for off-campus faculty, students, and staff. No matter how many new lines they added, demand always exceeded supply. Now most institutions recommend that their populations purchase network access from commercial service providers for a reasonable fee. Unhappiness about this example of outsourcing illustrates one basic problem. It is always harder to charge for something that used to be free than the reverse. University populations, probably no different from the wider world, are quick to assume entitlement for life.

But technology administrators often have good reason to offer new services at no charge. University populations, like their institutions, are extremely slow to change. Often the only way to get them to change a comfortable but outdated technology habit has been to offer the up-to-date alternative at no charge. Bold technology administrators may also establish a fee for the old way of doing things as a disincentive, and they are usually justified in doing so because continuing the obsolete option will be increasingly costly as more users adopt the new way.

Setting a price on a service usually requires knowing what it costs to provide (including the costs of billing for it). As in the cost of ownership of desktop computers, this often is a more complicated calculation than is evident at first. Good technology organizations have made a routine practice out of careful analysis of the costs of providing all of their services, not just considering the people and equipment directly involved but also taking account of the many elements of the organization that contribute to the service indirectly. For a new service, once that information is in hand, a technology administrator (usually working with an institutional finance officer) can evaluate how much of that cost should be passed along to users as a fee.

Sometimes what once seemed good pricing theory goes bad. As prices on certain telephone services dropped, many institutions that charge departments for telephone services elected to fund growing data-network costs by maintaining rates at the previous level and allocating the margins from the telephone fees to the network. This strategy generated funding for major networking projects to the benefit of the institution and all of its populations. But there is a danger in allowing surplus fees charged for one service to fund another. If anything threatens to diminish usage of the first service, the second will suffer. Such is the case in telephones. As Internet-based telephone applications began to appear, and the use of cellular phones, prepaid calling cards, and alternative "dial-around" long-distance carriers increased, technology administrators began to recognize that the decline of usage of some telephone services would mean less revenue for the network. Some institutions have solved the problem by more precisely identifying the charges as related to both telephones and network infrastructure, giving them the opportunity to continue issuing bills for the network component even if usage of the telephone service dwindles.

In the same way that pricing for services deserves careful consideration, a decision to outsource as an option for technology services must follow detailed analysis. Outsourcing options often look more attractive at a glance than they do when all the details are considered. But outsourcing IT still may be the right answer in some cases, and in these days of tight funding it may be the proper choice when an experienced outsource firm can accomplish the task more efficiently and at lower cost than internal staff. It is important to consider the true incremental cost of providing the service with staff from within the institution and to take into consideration customer-service issues, service-level commitments, and compatibility of the outsource firm with the institution's culture. Another important factor is that the cost of managing the outsourcing contractor (a cost not always included in the analysis) may outweigh any dollars directly saved. On the other hand, an organization that has relatively easier access to dollars than to employment positions or skilled candidates to fill them may find that outsourcing is the most feasible way to enable a new activity. Outsource vendors may perform an old or routine function, such as maintenance, freeing up internal staff to move to the development and implementation of new products and services.

No discussion about increasing revenues would be complete without acknowledging that colleges and universities are the sites of many important innovations in technology. Some of those innovations have come from the institutions' technology organizations. Although technology staff do not create marketable products every day in the normal course of their work, technology administrators should always examine products of the staff with that possibility in mind and should have a reward system in place that encourages such work-related creativity, not just for regular staff but for student employees as well.

Standards and Technical Architecture

The more standardized a technology environment is, the lower its costs of support. Faculty, students, and even technology staffs scorned this notion for many years until the burdens of support and the consequences of poor support grew so intense they were impossible to ignore. The near complete ubiquity of the networked environment has driven this point home to everyone in recent years. Once it became easy to share documents or data or images instantly with colleagues across campus or across the globe, *de facto* standards suddenly appeared where they had never been previously. And when it became important to have your desktop computer (no longer a glorified typewriter) connected to the network and working properly every minute of the day and night, the fact that the available technical support staff had no experience troubleshooting your particular brand of network card quickly became a distasteful, and perhaps avoidable, irritant.

Higher education will not soon mirror the absolute standardization common in businesses, but the headaches of managing an unnecessarily diverse environment are driving campus interest in working cooperatively to develop a reasonably limited array of choices to hold down support costs and improve efficiency.

Any notion of standards or choices among limited alternatives is built on the essential foundation of the enterprise technology architecture, in whatever form it exists. Part of that foundation is a high-level description of the main technical components of the architecture. Years ago it made sense to start that description with a listing of discrete elements (big pieces of hardware and major software applications, both oriented around mainframe computers), but now its essence is captured in a campus network diagram.

These days the critical component is the network backbone, to which each building (and the computing devices it contains) on most modern campuses is connected. Fewer campuses each day show mainframe computers connected to that backbone, as physically smaller, less expensive servers with greater capacities and less environmental sensitivity than mainframes take over the role of primary institutional shared-data processors. Through the backbone the campus is connected to the Internet and to special research networks, making accessible an ever-growing worldwide collection of electronic information resources at every campus desktop.

Today few important institutional information resources sit isolated from the campus network, and the old proprietary distinctions between both pieces of hardware and elements of software are made more transparent each day by the broadly accepted technical standards of the Internet and the World Wide Web. In a sense, the widespread adoption of these standards reduces the need for standard hardware and software at the desktop. Communication and work sharing between diverse hardware elements and software packages is easier now than it has ever been. Networked computing is not the most compelling imperative for desktop and workstation standardization; efficiency in support is.

Policy Challenges

Technology administrators and other institutional officials record decisions about many technology matters in policy statements. Colleges and universities use those statements to communicate to their populations their expectations for how those populations will manage and use information resources. Although information resource management policy is important, it is information resource usage policy that attracts the most attention and controversy in higher education institutions. All technology-related policies should be driven by each institution's view of the electronic "culture" it is trying to create and maintain. That view should, in turn, come directly from the institutional and information technology strategic planning processes.

At a minimum, colleges and universities should have written policy, widely disseminated, on such topics as:

- acceptable use (often addressing such issues as "adult" material, harassment, and the definition of "commercial" activity if such activity is against policy, among many other components; this policy should be in harmony with federal and state regulations);

- access and accounts (who can have access to what, and through what account structure);

- official records and their retention (that is, does E-mail or other digital communication/publication constitute an official record? If so, how should it be archived, and how long should it be kept? And who has access to it under what conditions?);

- copyright and conditions of use (including the importance of complying with both copyrights held by others and license provisions limiting the use of information resources to particular populations or geographic areas, outlining how the concept of fair use applies in the digital environment);

- privacy and other user "rights" (what should students, faculty, and staff expect with respect to privacy or other rights or privileges in their use of information resources);

- security, emergency planning, and disaster recovery; and

- enforcement (how compliance with information resource policies will be monitored and enforced).

Usage policy statements are often, by necessity, general and subject to interpretation when applied. Although technology administrators and other institutional officers may wish otherwise, the rules for networked communication are evolving, with each new case pointing out the flaws of a previous theory. The mechanisms for dealing with such cases are evolving too, and successful ones involve some means of rapid discussion of the issues by knowledgeable staff. Some institutions have found that directing complaints to a campus mailing list with a commonly recognized address such as <u>abuse@institution.edu</u> is a way to promote speedy and fruitful discussion among the staff specialists who review incidents and identify actions to be taken.

Security and Disaster Recovery

Among information technology management challenges, security and disaster recovery deserve special mention. As the Internet has become a full-fledged commercial enterprise supporting the routine exchange of huge amounts of money and mission-critical information, it has gained the attention of individuals determined to steal or disrupt this work. At the same time, the Internet community has expanded, including the number of those willing to launch such attacks, and some individuals have developed highly sophisticated tool kits to make such attacks very easy. Every institution has seen a rapid rise in the number of Internet-based security incidents and the losses in machine use, staff time, and data from those incidents. Ongoing attention to machine and network security is now necessary for the entire community of networked machines; without adequate security protection, a network will be subject to complete disruption at unpredictable and certainly inconvenient times.

Security of the networked computing environment is more than ever a shared endeavor between central administration and the system administrators in departments and units. In an environment of distributed computing, system administrators and individual users of computing resources demand and deserve to know the rationale behind security requirements or they may be tempted to ignore them, especially while connecting their machines to the network or putting their own information resources there. This sometimes puts technology administrators into awkward roles as intermediaries between auditors who expect prudent protection of information resources and users who believe in what sometimes is called the battle cry of the Internet: "Information just wants to be free." Developing an appropriately secure environment requires a deep understanding of the vulnerabilities (technical and human/behavioral), common sense, and sense of relative risk.

Decision makers should apply the same balanced thinking to questions of authentication (how a user is recognized as a qualified user of the resource), authorization (analogous to signature-signified approvals on paper documents), and encryption (when to encode information flowing across the network so that unauthorized persons cannot understand or use it). See the more detailed discussion of these concepts in the section on managing institutional information resources.

Likewise, disaster recovery is a changed concept. Contingency planning for data and the machines on which it is housed is no longer a task limited to the central computing organization. All of the principles of backup and recovery previously associated with mainframes need to be applied to the distributed resources. Responsibility for ensuring that important information resources are safeguarded from malicious attack and from accidents now belongs to more people than it did a few years ago. They need to be reminded of that responsibility regularly.

DESIGNING AND MANAGING CAMPUS COMMUNICATIONS NETWORKS[2]

Communications networks are core infrastructure for higher education, providing an essential foundation for all electronic teaching, research, library, and administrative services. How can a school create, manage, and maintain these networks? With continuous advances in technology—real-time video and other services not yet imagined—how can an institution prepare for an unknown future? This section shares some good news: by following some basic guidelines, a campus can ensure a course of network growth and renewal, providing continuous network upgrades and maintaining a position of flexibility to meet expected and unexpected future needs.

The telecommunications industry has developed a standard set of high-level design building blocks and practices that the most basic network shares with the most complex. This substantial experience has enabled the development of a set of guiding principles for designing and managing networks to maximize investment value and promote flexibility to meet changing needs. The key to a campus network that will maintain currency and gracefully accommodate future advanced services is to use these principles to guide ongoing renewals of the standard building blocks to maximize network value, technology, and flexibility to meet campus needs.

Once critical mass is established with a standards-guided campus network, unit costs will level off, even with rapid expansion in connections and bandwidth. Because of rising user expectations and some external factors, however, overall costs for an evolving technology (for example, the data network) are likely to continue to rise at rates substantially above inflation for the foreseeable future. Specialty applications will require specialty equipment and knowledge (but will likely use standard network building blocks and cabling) and thus will come at a premium cost. But those costs need only be incurred when the need emerges locally and justifies the cost.

This section offers a set of principles to guide network planning and design; provides examples of how these principles can be applied to standard building blocks and network design; and discusses the convergence of voice, video, and data networks in the long term, including potential strategies to consider in the immediate future.

Principles to Guide Network Planning and Design

Although the following principles are not inviolable, a network designer or administrator should question exceptions. The principles are illustrated with examples in a follow-on discussion of standard building blocks and data network design.

Planning should be ongoing. Campus needs and network technologies are changing continuously, so planning must be ongoing. Typically there should be a yearly update of the overall network plan and technical standards.

Network designs should be based on standard building blocks. Designing around the standard, replaceable network building blocks is critical but also appropriate and routine. Existing networks likely already conform in most if not all ways to the standard building blocks. Both design and building blocks are standard only at a high level and still need careful mapping to local buildings and campus needs. Commercial products will fit standard designs and building blocks. A corollary to this principle is the principle that *good design minimizes costs.* Networks are extraordinarily complex technical enterprises; bad design (for example, not observing the building blocks) quickly produces high operating and management costs.

Network costs are operating costs, not capital costs. All networks need ongoing renewal; except for pathway and cabling, networking costs are operating, not capital, costs. This is probably the most frequently violated principle. A close corollary to this principle is the *no free lunch principle*, which states that every addition of capacity or function to even a well-designed network does cost something, both to install and to maintain.

Networks should be continuously renewed. Because networks are still growing rapidly in terms of numbers of users, speed and capacity, services, and reliability, they are subject to constant changes in ways small and large. The key to establishing and maintaining a quality network is to use those ongoing changes to provide continuous upgrades within the periodically updated plan.

Networks should grow gracefully. Following these principles initially when constructing small networks allows those networks to evolve more or less seamlessly into more complex higher-speed networks that can fully support advanced services when those services are needed. A corollary to this principle is the *80-percent rule*, which requires upgrading any network component that is running about 80 percent of its capacity for any significant period of time. This rule applies to all the components across the layers, including pathway, cable counts, communications links, switches, routers, and more.

Network investments should be value based. Investment in network building blocks has a significant influence on future flexibility and costs. Investment should be proportional to the expected life span, allow for cost trends, and recognize that opportunity costs can easily dominate marginal cost. The shorter the life span for a particular network element, the closer capacity should be to actual need; the longer the life span, the more overcapacity is appropriate. If costs are dropping over time, investment should be close to actual need; if costs are rising, investment should usually include extra capacity. Opportunity costs may justify overcapacity; for example, marginal materials costs may be quite low to provide extra capacity. Note that the *no free lunch* principle reminds us that all capacity incurs some level of ongoing maintenance, so overcapacity plans should always be related directly to existing or anticipated campus needs and should recognize the carrying costs.

Networks should use commodity goods. Wherever possible, commodity goods should be used; commercial trends drive prices down and encourage innovation to extend the life and utility of common commercial products.

Networks should use open standards. Wherever functional needs can be met, open standards should be adopted and proprietary standards avoided. This is the *commodity goods* principle applied to software. The Internet community will use and develop open standards providing low cost and high innovation, compared to what an individual company or set of companies can do with proprietary protocols.

Networks require active management. A network is a highly complex technical enterprise and can meet predictable service standards only if it is engineered from the ground up to provide management data and error reports and to permit active probing and management by network administrators.

Networks need appropriate redundancy. Network plans should provide for a level of redundancy appropriate for the number of nodes or the amount of capacity that would be disabled by a particular network element failure. Note that as campus expectations for reliability rise, the level of redundancy needed will rise correspondingly. The *no free lunch* principle reminds us that although redundancy may be needed to meet reliability goals, it adds complexity to a network and thus raises costs, so it should be added wisely.

Outsourcing should be used judiciously. A campus should generally have full control over issues that directly affect its programs, but it often makes sense to leave nonprogrammatic issues to others. Data network functions are still critical to the ongoing and rapid development of program-related activities such as providing access to library materials, distance education, and administrative streamlining, so few campuses currently consider outsourcing the core design and management of their data network as they might, for example, their phone network (see further discussion later about voice and video). The use of off-the-shelf components within standard designs provides some benefits similar to outsourcing. And many campuses are outsourcing network services that have standard interfaces to the campus network and are undergoing rapid commercialization or innovation (for example, remote network access). Any outsourcing arrangement requires careful management to ensure that campus program needs drive the services.

Applying the Principles to Standard Building Blocks and Network Design

Functional Layers

At a high level, a campus network consists of precisely defined functional "layers" that build from the physical infrastructure to network applications. Each layer relies on the layer below it (layering is simplified):

- *The physical layer* includes the physical plant that carries electrical signals—the conduit through which the cabling runs (pathway)—and the cable itself.

- *The network layer* includes protocols and electronics that turn electrical signals into messages. For a data network this layer includes: the network hubs, switches, routers, gateways, firewalls, and computer network interface cards that assign names and addresses to devices on the network and that govern how messages are passed.

- *The application layer* includes network applications that turn messages into services. Core data network applications include electronic mail, directories, Web servers and browsers, and so on.

Both the simplest local area network, connecting three machines to a printer, and the most advanced campus networks use these layers and basic building blocks: pathway, cabling, network electronics, and protocols. Each of a network's standard building blocks has a useful life, after which it must be renewed. Guided by an overall plan, individual building blocks can be renewed to upgrade and improve each of the areas over time, providing a gradual improvement in function and capacity across the entire network in the normal course of maintenance.

Pathway

Buried in walls or underground, pathway is the most difficult network element to add or modify, but it has the longest useful life of any network element, on the order of the life of a building, certainly 20 or even 50 years. With respect to the principle of *value-based investment,* pathway entails generally high construction costs, which usually increase at inflation or higher rates, and high opportunity costs for construction (a project is expensive to initiate). However, once construction is under way, marginal costs to provide extra capacity (more pathways) are usually low. For these reasons, constructing adequate buried pathway when the opportunity arises is critical, and it makes sense to overbuild to provide maximum future flexibility. Spare pathway ensures the potential to adjust wired networks to future developments. A rough formula to overbuild pathway is to estimate the maximum concretely foreseeable use and double it. An unfortunate but common problem can occur if construction engineers design pathway as part of a building project and do not adequately anticipate rapidly growing network needs; pathway design needs the attention of network planners who are fully up to date with current and future campus network needs.

Cabling

Both within-building and interbuilding cabling should consider telephone, cable TV, and data needs. Different kinds of cables are often pulled or even bundled together. Cable has a long useful life, 10 years or more, but even so will eventually need to be renewed. A key point is that the most common problem with network planning is misunderstanding or not taking seriously the useful life of cabling (and other components) and failing to plan to renew at the end of that useful life. The application of the guiding principles to cabling is a balancing act between the characteristic of pathway of a very long useful life and the characteristic of network electronics of a short life and frequent technology changes.

Network Electronics

Network electronics are the electrical devices that turn cables into a network; for example, Ethernet hubs and switches. Because these are essentially specialty computers, network electronics evolve quickly, improve in price/performance quickly, and have a correspondingly short useful life, typically three years. In terms of the *value-based investment* principle, network electronics can be quite easily replaced with new electronics to provide faster speed or other improvements, assuming the network protocols do not change. Individual units can be replaced providing new functionality or service to one subset of the campus network without requiring changes to the rest of the network and usually without requiring changes to end user machines.

Protocols

With regard to protocols and the open standards principle, the Internet protocol (IP) wins! Essentially all network-based applications are converting to run over IP networks. There is no need to consider other protocols for the foreseeable future. This provides an excellent example of how quality open standards outperform proprietary standards for mainstream needs. Looking at this industry standard protocol through the lens of the *commodity goods* principle, network electronics are commodity goods, and prices for hubs, switches, bridges, routers, and so forth track along the lines of the fast improvement of hardware price/performance. In terms of the *continuous renewal* principle, a new version of the Internet protocol, IP V6, will gradually phase in to increase capacity and management options in IP networks, but this introduction will coexist with existing networks, allowing network managers to plan this upgrade in the natural course of network renewal.

Possible "killer applications" that could impact network capacity in the future—as did the emergence of the World Wide Web five years ago—include full-motion digital video over the data network or a shift in the underlying network to support guaranteed response, such as is needed for real-time process control. Each of these has the potential to drive new technology and possibly protocols, but each is already in use to a limited degree, and networks are already preparing for their increased demands. By definition, it is difficult to foresee these kinds of applications, but one is likely to emerge again in the next five to ten years. When it does, assuming the standard building block design does not change, pathway needs and cabling demands will not change radically although a new killer application could accelerate a migration from copper to fiber station cabling. What are most likely to change are network electronics, the number of cables used, and possibly network interface equipment in the instruments (computers or phones) themselves. All of these are subject to regular change anyway. A well-designed network should be able to accommodate these changes more or less gracefully, possibly with an extra investment to accelerate turnover of equipment or to add new cables.

The Internet2 effort provides a useful illustration of these principles applied to future developments: national network traffic has been doubling roughly every six months since the early 1990s. The Internet2 project will attempt to develop applications and technologies for next-generation national backbone networks that will be able to accommodate traffic needs for the next decade but that will do so using standard campus connections and technologies. Any new Internet2-style services may require new protocols, but routine upgrades in campus connection bandwidth will be just that: routine.

Voice, Video, and the Specter of Convergence

The guiding principles apply as much to development and management of voice and video networks as they do to data networks. Existing voice and video networks, however, are using mature technology that is changing far less rapidly than data network technology, so the time scales for useful life and continuous renewal are generally far longer than for data. Outsourcing is appropriate for a mature technology when program activities would not be compromised, and both traditional voice networks and video networks based on cable-TV technology may qualify for consideration. Even so, many campuses have historically insourced these networks for either of two reasons: (1) a campus-based service could provide better function and/or lower cost through a local switch or more responsive service than a commercial phone or cable company could; or (2) margins on these services, for example, telephone long distance, were high enough to sustain needed investment in voice, video, and data networking infrastructure.

With maturity in these technologies and commercial competition, full function and responsive service are increasingly available from commercial providers in some geographic areas. Competition has also driven down margins on long distance and cable TV service, eroding a source of network investment whether insourced or outsourced. For these reasons, many campuses that currently insource voice and video are considering the economics and service options of outsourcing.

The outsourcing principle requires that any outsourced service will still require campus-based planning and management. Most outsourcing failures result from a mismatch between campus needs and the outsource service agreements and management plan. While outsourcing voice and video has seemed increasingly attractive over the last few years, a new development is giving pause: the potential for convergence of these networks onto a single network infrastructure.

Technically, voice, video, and data networks will converge: technology exists at this writing to deliver all these services on a data backbone network. However, standards for service and reliability suggest it will be some time, certainly five years, probably longer, before fully functional and reliable voice and video comparable to current analog-based services can be delivered.

Potential advantages of a converged network are compelling. For example:

- a common cabling infrastructure would eliminate costly individual voice circuits in the network core;

- a single qualified installer could efficiently install all three services in a single visit;

- costly traditional specialized telephone and cable electronics would be replaced by highly competitive data network electronics where costs continue to drop rapidly; and

- a single network operations center staff and tool set could diagnose problems across all services.

Realities, however, are likely to temper some of these potential advantages, and experiences with other new technology architectures suggest that some critical issues very likely remain hidden. For example, an equally compelling set of advantages motivated the industry shift from terminal-to-host computer systems to client-server computing. Most industry analysts believe this shift is appropriate and in the end will yield the promised benefits, but the shift has been far more costly and drawn out than industry promoters suggested. Migrating to a converged voice, video, and data network is comparable to the migration to client-server and is likely to incur comparable false starts, hidden costs, and delays.

The biggest impediment to convergence is easily understood: in its 100-year history, the voice industry has achieved the so-called "five-nines" standard of service and reliability, that is, the service works 99.999 percent of the time. Although many individuals will tolerate relatively poor voice service to make a single Internet-based voice call, that does not suggest that institutions could run their business with even a 99-percent voice service standard. The core of any converged network will be data network technology, which today is very far from providing even a 99-percent reliability record. The data network will need massive investments in improved and fully redundant switches before it can approach the reliability of today's voice or even video networks.

Even when data technology can provide high reliability, a converged network will have to consider issues such as how end users can report a problem if the network is down; inventing and acquiring new diagnostic tools; training staff; and much more. No doubt these issues will be solved over time, but experience with massive shifts in core technology in other areas suggests that convergence will take some time to evolve, so campuses will likely need a hybrid plan during this transition. Informed by the guiding principles, such a hybrid plan is likely to include strategies such as:

- piloting converged technology where it makes most sense—in remote locations where the cost of running separate networks is highest and the choice may be service via a converged network or very expensive commercial service (for example, service to a remote building on or off campus);

- using converged technology to address isolated needs within a system where commercial products and successful reference sites exist (for example, trunk lines between separate campuses);

- maintaining a full complement of analog voice and video services but minimizing long-term commitments to major equipment expenses (for example, telephone switches); and

- developing a flexible plan calling for increased use of emerging converged technologies based on service (not technology) milestones.

As always, such strategies need to be informed by how aggressive an institution wishes to be relative to leading-edge technologies. For example, an aggressive campus may prefer to limit voice and video service commitments to five years rather than investing significant capital which might take 10 years to pay back.

Future Technology: Wireless Issues

Cellular technology is certainly not a future issue; it is already on campus today among faculty, students, and staff, but the full implications have yet to unfold. Some trends are already apparent: cellular technology works very well and scales successfully. Some individuals will move away from wired phones completely, but that will not relieve a campus from providing wired phone capability for the indefinite future. Cellular phone plans often provide free long distance and this is likely accelerating the decline in campus long distance revenues, particularly among students. There is also some significant adoption of cellular data services, but data entry, small screen, and bandwidth issues suggest this will not soon become a substitute for a full-function data connection.

Wireless LAN (local area network) data technology is less mature and the prospects are correspondingly less certain. To date most individuals want even their "wireline" data connections to be faster, and current evidence suggests that wireline data connections will provide significantly faster speeds than wireless for the indefinite future. This technology, however, provides significant convenience when wireless speeds are good enough to meet particular needs. Depending on network engineering, current wireless LAN technologies can provide good E-mail and Web browsing service, but most clients will prefer wireline connections to support streaming media and bulk file transfer.

Applications for wireless LAN technology that have already demonstrated success or show great promise include:

- data access for particularly difficult-to-wire locations including, for example, classrooms, laboratories, and library stacks;

- data access for wide open spaces, indoors or out (for example, courtyards); and

- convenient data access everywhere, for example, across an entire campus.

Current wireless LAN data radio spectrum tends to be absorbed by steel, concrete, paper, and books. The future adoption of wireless LAN beyond open spaces will very much depend on future technology developments.

In the next few years, all higher education institutions are likely to adopt wireless LAN in some locations to meet particular needs but it will not be a substitute for a wired infrastructure for the foreseeable future. Between these two extremes, it is not possible to forecast client preference for convenience versus state-of-the-art performance in the face of rapidly developing wireless LAN technology. Commercial practices are also likely to affect speed of adoption; for example, interest would grow rapidly if Internet service providers began to offer wireless LAN services in airports or public spaces.

These various wireless services also raise business opportunities and issues regarding partnering with wireless vendors to provide or ensure campus coverage and potentially to share in risks and rewards. The key is to remember how quickly technology changes and to remember that vendors come and go quickly, as do substantial revenue streams.

In sum, the good news is that there is nothing mysterious about preparing a college or university for a networked future: a campus network can develop and grow according to well-understood principles in an orderly, well-coordinated process of planning and implementation. Today's campus leader, while having little need to be an expert in network technology, must nevertheless take personal interest and provide attention to ensure that this happens.

ADMINISTRATIVE INFORMATION SYSTEMS

Administrative information systems form the basis of much of the institution's core administrative processes. Campus human resources, financial, and student information systems make it possible for institutions to transact business (for example, award credits, pay employees, book grants, etc.), and to assemble and organize the information that campus citizens need for planning and managing their responsibilities. Among the significant challenges that colleges and universities are facing today in the administrative information systems arena, enterprise systems, electronic commerce, decision support systems, user interfaces, and electronic records management stand out. While these are inexorably linked, each presents unique problems and opportunities for institutions.

Enterprise Systems

Student information, financial, and human resources systems form the backbone of campus business operations. These systems are large and complex. These systems are also, in many instances, nearing obsolescence, based often on main-frame computing technology architectures, complex and unfriendly user inter-faces, "batch" processing, and ad hoc integration efforts. Although there has always been a healthy market for commercial administrative information systems packages, the last five years have seen a remarkable escalation in demand for new enterprise resource planning (ERP) vendors and their consulting partners. These ERP systems are used to manage the core business processes in our institutions and include student, human resources/payroll, and fiscal information systems. Chief among the reasons that colleges and universities are acquiring these systems are the desire to effect a re-engineering of business processes in the academy and the ability to more effectively serve new student populations and provide more timely and integrated information to decision makers. (The year 2000 date problem was also a reason prior to that year.)

Not surprisingly, with the shortage of IT workers in the United States today, salaries have risen sharply in the last five years and many institutions find them-selves priced out of the market for quality systems analysts, programmers, database administrators, and systems administrators. This in turn has led a major-ity of institutions to conclude that they cannot support in-house systems develop-ment efforts, and thus vendor-supplied solutions to their administrative systems' needs have become commonplace. This strategy also reflects the complexity and risk inherent in both the reengineering of campus business processes and the replacement of mission-critical technologies.

Understandably, the costs associated with implementing the vendors' prod-ucts, ERP systems, have risen sharply. Today, the cost to implement a single major module such as human resources management, student administration, or financial systems can be more than $20 million for a major research institution. By comparison, these costs were typically less than $5 million in the early 1990s.

One potential risk associated with the widespread move to replace existing enterprise systems is that the commercial market will become saturated. Industry estimates suggest an almost flat growth rate in the baseline ERP market. (Baseline could be defined as back-office operations such as payroll, human resources, pro-curement, manufacturing, and finance). In pursuit of higher revenues, many ven-dors are likely to adjust their priorities into higher growth niches, notably cus-tomer relationship management (CRM) and anything to do with E-business. The result for institutions seeking to acquire and implement an ERP system now may be that the vendor support and commitment is waning in certain niches. Ongoing enhancements and support come from growth in license activity with attendant annual maintenance payments. Some smaller vendors have recently exited the baseline ERP market in order to pursue higher growth opportunities. There is a danger of some retrenchment among the remaining vendors. This could augur badly for higher education, which is perhaps two to four years behind industry in the ERP evolution. On the bright side, as higher education is a relative latecomer to this market, colleges and universities may have a greater impact than they had some years ago and may get the attention of any vendor trying to tap this market. Another positive indicator is that the student administration niche is actually quite robust.

Importantly, traditional ERP vendors may soon come under real pressure from newcomers who do not carry the baggage of a decade of second-generation ERP models and technologies with them. In particular, ERP systems will come under increasing pressure to anticipate new administrative challenges posed by distance education and other nontraditional campus service models. Client-server modeled systems may need to be "rearchitected" to exploit the next revolution known generically as the E-business era.[3]

The institutional executive must consider several enterprise systems issues. For example, how is the college or university going to measure the value or return on these systems? Is it more advantageous to align with one of the existing, but pressured, vendors, or take a riskier approach with one of the newer vendors?

Managing the renewal of a major campus information system, no matter what underlying information technologies you choose, is complex and time consuming. The path to successful enterprisewide system implementation may contain many pitfalls in the form of out-of-control budgets, missed target dates, and projects abandoned or greatly scaled back after major investments are made. The overriding success factor for such projects is having a *project management* architecture that is inclusive, open, and consensus seeking. A number of good management principles and practices should guide projects of this kind.

Establish institutionwide support and commitment to the project, including the support of top campus leadership. Large-scale campus IT implementations are complex and risky endeavors, like the construction and design of major campus facilities. Successful projects depend on actively engaging and communicating with the campus community, particularly the campus leadership. Projects should include steering and advisory structures that will help project staff make complex tradeoff decisions and create realistic expectations about the timeliness of project delivery and the phasing of system features and functions to be released.

Establish a solid framework of vision, principles, and goals for the project. Wherever possible, express project goals in terms directly related to the mission of the institution. The successful implementation of enterprisewide information systems involves, by definition, the redesign of major campus processes. Projects of this nature affect a large portion of the campus community and must be guided by clearly and frequently articulated goals.

Assess the readiness of the campus for change. Most project risk relates to the inability of institutions to bridge the gap between envisioned project results and the organizational, cultural, and behavioral capacity of the campus to change. To bridge this gap, project leaders must assess the capacity of the campus to absorb the anticipated changes. Once this capacity to change is understood, a variety of measures should be taken to lower the barriers to change, or to lower the envisioned goals and outcomes of the project. This activity includes balancing available solutions, prevailing technology architectures and standards, and business needs *before* selecting a solution.

Assess realistically the resources that will be required and secure project funding up front. Confer with colleagues at other comparable institutions to get a clear view about the human and financial resource requirements of these projects. Understand that the acquisition costs of new software often represent a relatively small portion of total project costs. In many cases, the decision to implement new core information systems will require the investment of major resources for renewing the campus network, installed base of workstations, and workforce.

Manage project scope. Principal variables involved in these systems are resources, time, and scope. It is axiomatic that you can control any two of these, but the third will need to be adjusted. As with the more familiar building construction projects, *scope creep* is the nemesis of many major information systems projects. Successful projects are designed to prefer the timely implementation of modest goals to the late implementation of expanded ones.

Develop effective contracts with vendors. Large and complex projects of this kind will likely involve multiple contracts with a variety of software, hardware, and services vendors. Contracts need to be developed with great care and with great specificity regarding vendor performance. Contract administration skills are of enormous importance to the success of these projects.

Provide effective training and especially understand the importance of just-in-time training. Do not attempt to reduce project costs by minimizing training costs. Successful information systems projects are successful because resistance to the changes inherent in these systems is low. Effective and, whenever possible, just-in-time training is the tonic to reduce resistance to change. Resistance to change is borne of fear which is rooted in staff concerns about the possible obsolescence of the knowledge and skill acquired with old systems that are being replaced.

Electronic Commerce

Electronic commerce, E-business, E-learning and other terms refer to the capacity of organizations to effect their business transactions and processes over networks. The very rapid commercialization of the Internet is making it possible for organizations to distribute core activities across time zones and geographical boundaries.

Electronic commerce has tremendous potential to lower institutional costs, to enhance college and university revenues, or to enhance the quality of services provided by a campus.[4] Examples of campus activities that are ripe for E-commerce include:

- online application for admissions and payment of application fees;
- payment of tuition and student bills via the World Wide Web;
- purchase of books, computers, software, logo items, and other merchandise via the Internet;
- business-to-business procurement over the Web;
- electronic access to institutional databases, publications, and other institutionally owned information resources for a fee;
- electronic processing of accounts payable invoices;
- electronic funds transfer (EFT);
- direct deposit of payroll;
- direct deposit of travel reimbursements; and
- electronic grade reporting and transcripts.

These campus activities can be categorized into three basic groups: (1) services aimed at parents and students; (2) services aimed at alumni or the public; and (3) services aimed at internal operations such as procurement, travel, or payroll. How should the institution approach these issues? The temptation to "pave the cowpaths" in the back-office operations of the institution is very strong. It appeals to the "let's not change things too quickly" interests on campus. Studies have suggested that merely digitizing existing processes can be relatively expensive and can produce minimal returns on investment. The quantum leaps in productivity and effectiveness require a transformation of the ways in which we conduct the activities of the institution.

The nature of E-commerce will force institutional governance and leadership issues to the fore. Who, for example, is responsible for campus decision making about E-commerce? Today, at major universities, deans and directors of campus auxiliary service organizations are making independent judgments about E-commerce initiatives, often placing university names, trademarks, and other property into virtual play. Savvy network-based marketing organizations are applying their brands and advertisements to campus Web pages. Business officers and other institutional leaders must immediately begin to develop campuswide strategies and policies for guiding E-commerce or risk both the paving of cowpaths and the atomization of the institution's public presence through willy-nilly E-commerce applications implemented by campus subunits.

E-commerce in higher education is complex, owing to the complexity of the campus governance structures and due to the fact that campus E-commerce architectures will be built on the Internet platform, unlike the private network solutions preferred in industry. Business officers and institutional leaders will need to focus on the unique security requirements inherent in college and university processes or work to change those processes. For example, how will colleges and universities protect the identities of faculty and students who acquire electronic information resources under contracts negotiated by the campus? Librarians have long honored these protections by controlling physical or electronic records in their custody. As E-commerce extends the boundaries of the campus to other suppliers who do not share these cultural values, unique approaches to safeguarding traditions will need to be found, or such traditions will need to be rethought. E-commerce will bind members of the campus community to one another in new ways and will suggest new linkages between the campus and its external constituents, suppliers, regulators, and others. This level of interconnection will force many institutions to reassess a great number of important institutional policies. This interconnection will also foster new and unanticipated opportunities for misuse of institutional resources and for fraud.

Decision Support Systems

One of the most misunderstood aspects of the implementation of administrative information systems (such as student information, payroll, and financial systems) is the balance required between the elements of transaction processing (TP) and decision support (DS). As noted earlier, for the most part, we are implementing these ERP systems to effect some business process change and the focus is on getting electronic forms or the transaction processing component in place. There is, however, much evidence that the longer-term benefit may be on the DS side. Notwithstanding this, the ratio of resources dedicated to DS versus TP is skewed toward the latter. Certainly, if an institution does not already have "the right data" in its existing systems, it will have to endure the lengthy, expensive process of implementing the TP component. But given the right data in the underlying production system, the institution can derive significant benefit from developing a data warehouse or data mart.

Although ERP vendors all have some degree of support for such environments, a significant amount of customization is required for each institution in pursuing decision support systems. That in turn limits what can be presented in the vendors' baseline products. A number of institutions have already put very successful DS systems in place. The University of Minnesota is among the leaders with its Clarity system for financial information, and both the University of California at Davis and Indiana University have very successful efforts in the financial arena.

To some, the pinnacle of the data warehouse concept is the executive information system. Such applications provide tailored, metric-driven reports, or alerts to executives, and also offer elaborate "what if" modeling capability. Very few such systems have shown up in reality yet, but the decision support tools that vendors offer are quite promising with regard to making this kind of functionality available to more than the executive suite. The buzzwords here are OLAP, ROLAP, and so forth, acronyms for online analytical processing and relational online analytical processing, respectively. However, these tools require users who understand the data, the questions being asked, and perhaps even the answer in abstract terms. Before one gets too caught up in this, it is a good idea to ask the proponents if they use "pivot tables" in Excel. Anything other than a strong affirmative is grounds for immediate dismissal of the OLAP idea.

Another major issue being debated in higher education institutions is whether or not to develop an integrated data warehouse or just data marts. The latter can be characterized as subject area datasets, such as financial data or student record data. There is an intuitive appeal to having integration, but the cost/benefit analysis of such an endeavor should be closely evaluated since full integration can be very expensive. It could be said that the need to see a fully integrated view of institutional data is limited to a relatively small number of people who do institutional research or who manage the business analysis of a college or university. In many cases, these are the very people who are characterized as "power users" in their institutions and their need for elaborate tools is relatively low, since they can often integrate the data themselves better than the tools can. The more important issue may be providing easy access to required data for large numbers of faculty, students, and staff who need it. Subject area data marts may provide a better solution for that need. However, this will be a decision that must be made by each institution.

If the solution chosen is leaning toward the data mart approach, then it will be very important to provide metadata to aid in the interpretation and use of the actual data. Put plainly, metadata is information about data. Today's relational systems contain dramatically richer arrays of data than did the previous generation of systems. The result is a lot more data than ever envisioned before. This abundance of information, in turn, requires education about what the data mean and it is here that the metadata approach comes in. This abundance of information suggests new questions of institutional concern, including:

Do you have the right data in your system today? More data does not per se mean better information. As information systems become more powerful, as the cost of data storage declines, and as end users are empowered with better access and niftier tools, the challenges ahead will relate to the complexity inherent in institutional data. In any typical research institution, no fewer than a dozen definitions of a student or of full time equivalent (FTE) may exist. This complexity exists for good historical reason, but will become increasingly problematic as access to data is widened and deepened. This will become most problematic as information becomes available directly to students, their parents, alumni, regulators, and other who do not understand the nuances of institutional data. Simplifying data, maintaining the integrity of data, and developing help resources to explain data will become increasingly important elements of institutional information systems.

Which is preferable—a data mart or integrated data warehouse? This is a fundamental design issue that must be addressed at a level that transcends specific information systems. As mentioned, the decision about data marts and warehouses is a decision about the trade-offs between integration, ease-of-use, and cost.

Metadata—does anyone really understand the data? Increasingly, large volumes of complex data must be tagged with information that explains the data in terms that make sense to end users. Standards must be developed to describe data in consistent fashion in much the same way that librarians have for years developed standards to describe books, photographs, manuscripts, and other information resources.

Do you have the right tools for the users? Tools for mining, extracting, and analyzing data abound. Determining an institutional strategy or framework for deploying the right tools to the right end users is critical. Some tools are ubiquitous (for example, Excel) and are therefore in the institution's mainstream of support, version control, upgrade management, and maintenance. Such commonly available tools accomplish most of the work undertaken by a majority of users. Sophisticated institutional researchers, budget professionals, or research analysts may need to perform complex statistical analyses or to develop models and simulations that will require specialized tools. Selecting a small number of tools and supporting them well is an important element of an overall institutional strategy for decision support.

Will the institution's data anticipate the future? As institutions begin in earnest to deliver distance education and to enter into a variety of consortia and cooperative agreements for the delivery of courses and credits, key data concepts of the institution will be challenged to their limits. Is a distant learner who is enrolled for one course a student? How much full-time equivalency does such an individual merit? How does information about such students get rolled into institutional formulas for state funding or technology support? In short, most of an institution's financial activity is based on assumptions about time and space: seat time, faculty-student ratios, credit hours, and the like. New data constructs will need to be developed to anticipate E-commerce, distance education, and other "virtual" services. Information systems will need to be flexible enough to accommodate these services.

User Interfaces

There no longer seems to be a question about the desired interface for all systems; regardless of their functionality, the World Wide Web has captured the imagination of many users in higher education. Behind this seemingly simple transformation lies a very complex issue related to the behavior of administrative systems. It could be said that there are three levels under which we might deploy systems over the Web. They are:

Web-based access to an application using "thin client" technology. This technology enables a standard client-server system to be "viewed" and operated from a Web browser. It is important to understand that the system is still fundamentally a client-server system. It merely seems to be operated over the Web. This is one approach to deploying an existing client-server application within a browser. One significant advantage of this approach is that it effectively renders the Macintosh versus Windows issue moot since the application is presented in a desktop browser but is in reality running on another server.

Web enabling all of the existing applications' screens. There are some serious scalability issues with this solution having to do with something called "maintaining state" in the Web. In simple terms, this deals with how the application remembers where the user is in the system. Most of the ERP vendors have done some of this but it should be considered an interim solution at best.

Architecting the basic application to be fully "Web aware" and enabled. This involves having the capacity to have large numbers of users log on to an application in a secure and effective manner. Institutions need this for such applications as financial aid or registration processing. This is the Holy Grail for the vendors but for some it requires a complete rearchitecting of their existing applications, as discussed earlier.

A key issue to consider in the user interface arena is: Does the application need to actually "run" in the Web and fully utilize the Web metaphor of links and pages, or is it sufficient for it to be *accessible* over the Web?

Electronic Records Management

In his article on records management, David O. Stephens suggests 10 megatrends in the field. Among these are:

- the shift from paper-based to paperless record-keeping systems;
- the shift from data processing to document processing as the predominant application in computing environments; and
- the shift in life cycle management of electronic records from undefined retention to a retention solution.[5]

Stephens indicates that this field is undergoing a change of "epochal proportions" currently. One of the implied technologies in this paradigm shift is electronic imaging. Vendors in the records management field are increasingly providing solutions that merge storage and retrieval of documents already in electronic form with that of paper-based documents. The likely outcome is that we will no longer see stand-alone imaging application technologies, but rather will see imaging wrapped into the larger document management arena.

The legal and regulatory issues associated with electronic records are still being addressed and may not be fully resolved for some years. Among the issues with which higher education will wrestle is the storage and retention problem for electronic records. One significant difference between visual (paper or microfiche) records and electronic records is that the former are probably going to always be accessible and readable, outside the boundaries of actual physical preservation problems. On the other hand, electronic records created and stored with an early version of a DOS-based word processor may not be readable in 10 years by the then current technologies. One hears of something called "exercising" the records periodically. This implies reading the tape, disk, or other media and rewriting onto a new medium in case the older media should degrade physically or be unreadable with newer technology. This has huge implications for data centers.

TECHNOLOGY IN SUPPORT OF TEACHING AND LEARNING

Technology will serve as the catalyst to bring about massive structural change in higher education. We have only begun to see the effects of technology on teaching and learning. The issues regarding technology in support of teaching and learning raised in this section run deep within our institutions. How a given campus sorts them out is likely to determine its identity, and perhaps its viability, in the 21st century.

New Economic Trends and Models

The education marketplace is changing around higher education, and a new economic model is rapidly emerging. For the business officer, the impact of this shift from the traditional college or university as the focal point of virtually all postsecondary education to a for-profit educational industry has profound implications. This massive restructuring of the economic market will spill over into the traditional educational enterprise.

Along with changes in the modalities of teaching and learning enabled by technology and advanced networking, new providers are entering the market. For-profit entities, such as the Apollo Group's University of Phoenix and Jones International University, the first fully accredited online university offering college degrees entirely online are, for example, gradually increasing their market share.

Wall Street is not ignoring the huge and growing market for lifelong education. Consequently, new corporate educational entities will rapidly emerge. E-commerce in this context becomes both educational and electronic commerce.

Faced with such competition, institutions of higher education will need to identify and carefully analyze the policy and financial issues that must inform their decisions and resulting actions. They can decide to contract their role and focus on what David Collis calls their "core educational products," that is, only those areas in which they possess brand name recognition or specialized market niche. On the other hand, they can decide to "embrace" the new technologies, expand their purpose, and reach out to new markets.[6] In either instance, the leadership needs to understand the conceptual framework within which the decision making will take place and the consequences of such decisions.[7] How does its mission affect the purposes for which an institution considers distributed learning? Is it possible to preserve the institution's unique culture while making fundamental changes in the modalities of teaching and learning? Should the culture be preserved?

Some institutions are more ready than others to address the implications of technology and advanced networking for their future goals, priorities, and economic viability. The hype associated with distance education and the appearance of for-profit competition have led others to enter an ill-defined market without clear institutional goals and without a viable business plan. The higher education community is just beginning to grapple with the policy and cultural barriers to successful entry into the distance learning economy, and some suggest that those barriers will not come down quickly enough to forestall massive structural change.

According to Lee Alley, the roles of many traditional campuses will transition to a focus on providing a venue for "campus life and socialization of the traditional 18-22 age cohort." Others will become providers of core courses to students on other campuses or in remote home and business locations. For-profit vendors will provide locally unique or specialty courses: "Pricing for commodity (core) courses will contract to the lowest level available among a few branded institutions with high-volume and low overhead."[8]

Advanced networks are the enabling forces behind these changes because they allow students to be enrolled simultaneously with multiple educational providers regardless of location. Institutional policies and practices that restrict the acceptance of outside credits have slowed the momentum thus far. However, if these projections are borne out, we will see the rapid unbundling of campus-based student services from per-credit hour pricing, new credit repositories and services, and the emergence of credit brokering and credentialing services.

Terms, Terminology, and Definitions

A muddle of terms, terminology, and definitions permits those who view technology as a threat to divert or shrug off discussion of the consequences: good, bad, and costly. A lack of agreement on terminology further complicates the discourse that must occur on our campuses as we set the direction of a future rich in technology.

Without a conceptual framework and taxonomy within and around which to consider the implications, there is a tendency to treat the various forms of distributed learning as though they are interchangeable. To do so will yield bad academic decisions and bad business plans. Moreover, without a carefully developed business plan, costs are likely to spiral, the educational product may be ignored or rejected by the market, and the viability of the institution in the 21st century may become uncertain.

What exactly are we talking about when we discuss technology in support of teaching and learning? The range of options for where and how the teaching and learning occurs includes the traditional classroom setting (the use of technology to bolster the classroom lecture); distributed learning (the use of technology to support teaching and learning independent of location); distance learning (synchronous or asynchronous learning that is geographically remote from campus); and E-learning (a term generally employed to describe learning that takes place via the Internet). In each instance the objective of the use of technology is different, the target population (market) differs, student ability to deal with the technology varies, and the institutional goals (business, academic, and social) differ.

EDUCAUSE's National Learning Infrastructure Initiative (NLII) is developing a conceptual and decision-making framework, at a sufficient level of detail, to assist higher education leaders in determining how a given institution will position itself in relation to these trends and market behaviors. In addition to the framework, the NLII is developing a taxonomy around which leaders may engage in discussion and decision making about the future identity and economic model for institutions of higher education. These will be useful tools for ensuring that expectations are realistic, the targeted markets are appropriate, and the proper set of issues is addressed.

Impact of Technology on Teaching and Learning

With the realization that the 21st century brings with it a set of social issues related to education, the mission of higher education is expanding to provide access without regard to life circumstances—for example, age, employment status, geography, culture, ethnicity, or family responsibilities. Access takes a number of forms, from physical access to the course material via the Internet or a learning device, to intellectual access in a neutral, nonjudgmental context enabled by network-based learningware.

The classroom lecture, and its concomitant social relationships, is based on "technologies" that prevailed for centuries. Advanced networks and information technology enable the development of a pedagogy that nurtures the learning process among those for whom the traditional classroom model is not a viable form of access or road to academic success. Technology enables students to engage in active learning whether in the traditional campus setting or at a remote location. Faculty acts as mentors and guides in such a learning process.

Knowledge workers require access to lifelong learning. Technology and the Internet enable adult students to acquire the required knowledge at anytime and from anywhere. The for-profit providers have targeted this market segment and have, thus far, shown reasonable success in tapping it. Technology and advanced networking make learning convenient. Convenience appears to be a major motivating factor in choice of learning provider by the nontraditional student. The educational organizations that are addressing the student's desire for convenience are beginning to change the educational landscape.

Access, quality, and productivity are areas in which networking and technology have also made an impact on the traditional campus. Virginia Polytechnic Institute and State University's Math Emporium project offers an elegant example of a felicitous match of advanced networking capability with institutional need and desire to provide access. Faced with burgeoning enrollments in the absence of new funding to accommodate students in the traditional classroom model, the mathematics department embarked on an effort to transform its approach to entry-level mathematics courses. The Math Emporium, a 500-workstation learning center located in a former department store building, provides an active learning environment for more than 10,000 undergraduate students. Using network-based learning modules and diagnostic quizzes, students work at their own pace in mastering the material. Faculty fulfill their "class contact" obligations by spending time in the Math Emporium mentoring students when they encounter difficulty with the material. Ongoing assessment of the learning that is taking place alerts faculty to subject areas where students are experiencing general difficulty, which then prompts them to schedule short tutorial sessions on those topics. According to Anne Moore, "Although a complete set of results has not yet been made publicly available, the failure rate in mathematics at Virginia Tech is down by 39 percent and both student and instructor satisfaction is up."[9]

Enterprisewide transformational change requires more than technology. This type of reconceptualization of the learning environment also calls for radical changes in institutional policy and funding allocation. The Virginia Tech initiative is as much a study of a courageous group of faculty members and administrators who were motivated to change the culture of student/faculty relationships and to reallocate resources, as it is a study of the enabling power of advanced networks. This is an example of decisive, strategic action by an institution that understands its priorities.

Enabling Infrastructures

Recently we have seen the emergence of numerous enabling technologies that offer the infrastructure required for academic transformation: security, authentication, interoperability, and "back-office" integration, that is, the integration of academic support systems with administrative applications such as student records. Faculty and commercial publishers will build courseware upon such infrastructure.

One such project, the Instructional Management System (IMS), was conceived to build a framework of specifications, standards, and definitions around which interoperable products could be developed (see www.imsproject.org). IMS-compliant products will soon enable faculty to execute efficient searches on the Internet for relevant courseware and quickly and easily to create, obtain, and tailor course modules to suit their individual curricular tastes and modes of expression. The IMS holds much promise as the key element of technical infrastructure required to transition gracefully to modalities for teaching and learning that address the issues of quality, access, and affordability.

In addition to its work on an interoperable teaching and learning standards infrastructure, the IMS is geared toward the development of the standards and specifications to record and report the outcomes of the virtual classroom experience.

Other projects, such as the California State University's MERLOT (Multimedia Educational Repository for Learning and Online Teaching), are designed to create both a repository of learning objects that have undergone peer review within the discipline and an electronic community of individuals working with these objects (see merlot.csuchico.edu). Still others, like Indiana University's *Oncourse* system and ANGEL (A New Global Environment for Learning) project, offer seamless links between easy-to-use dynamically created Web applications and administrative systems such as class lists and student profiles. The number of commercial vendors offering similar products and capabilities within a variety of new types of outsourcing options is also growing. Such outsourcing opportunities merit consideration as the costs of in-house development or the purchase of commercial packages escalate and the timeline for implementation lengthens.

Digital Libraries

The aforementioned infrastructure systems and their supporting networks serve also as the enabling technologies for digital libraries springing up around the country. Internet-based instruction tends to assume that the learner has online access to primary library resources. This is generally not the case. Librarians are struggling to augment print publications with appropriate electronic sources and to develop new electronic archiving schemes. Large digital library projects, such as the California Digital Library, are often operated as regional consortia outside the normal library framework to permit the structural, economic, and organizational freedom to experiment with new forms of information and new forms of access to it. Librarians in the future will focus on organizing, defining, and bounding the masses of information available on the Internet. A new information resource profession combining the technical knowledge of the information technologist with the information organization expertise of the librarian is emerginge.

Partnerships and Consortia

Ironically the entry of for-profit competitors into the educational market place has been shadowed by unprecedented initiatives in cooperation among traditional colleges and universities. Small colleges are banding together to offer courses over the Internet that they could never afford to offer to their students on campus. Large universities are collaborating to create a common portal to their Internet course offerings. A growing number of colleges and universities are contracting with commercial service providers to establish Web portals to their campuses, that is, Web sites that are dynamically tailored to individual information tastes (for example, lower division undergraduates, alumni, parents, graduate students, faculty members, and so forth). Often such portals display commercial advertising, a point of contention on some campuses.

Implications for Campus Support Services

Students, whether on or off campus, are coming to expect convenience in their learning experiences. This means the availability of courseware and support on a 7 × 24 basis; it means also that learning is accessible to the student. For some that is the convenience of anytime-anywhere learning; for others it means that the course content is available online in a form that enables the student to become actively engaged with the concepts.

Faculty development and support must keep pace with the ever-changing technology and the student expectations it spawns. To date most campuses offer an uncoordinated array of "boutique" support services, such as a faculty support center, a summer program for faculty training, and departmental support units, intended to address the needs of faculty members who engage in their individual "cottage industries" of courseware development. Such approaches, indeed such independence, are neither functionally scalable nor financially sustainable over the long term as the major portion of the faculty decide to modify their teaching styles.

In an award-winning article published in *CAUSE/EFFECT,* Dorothy Frayer of Duquesne University describes a coherent and coordinated approach to faculty development and support.[10] For such a strategy to be feasible requires the engagement and commitment of institutional leadership, the faculty, and the support units themselves. The Duquesne example typifies the new level of cooperation that is essential to the viability of an institutional strategy.

Instructional design and support services will also change. Such work will require teams consisting largely of faculty members, information technologists, and professionals with formal training in curriculum design and development for interactive, network-based learning in a collaboration that respects and values the critical scrutiny, special insights, and expertise that each contributes to the effort.

MANAGING INSTITUTIONAL INFORMATION RESOURCES

The shift from an operating model characterized by the "marking and parking" of physical objects, to one that promises electronic information "anytime, anywhere," is unprecedented and daunting. To assess the issues associated with the questions of how and by whom institutional information resources will be managed, it may be helpful to review some of the key environmental assumptions on which there appears to be convergence.

The primary form of information resources will be digital. Very soon, institutional information resources will be primarily digital. In the future, they will become increasingly interactive, adding a further premium to the relative value of the electronic word.

The sources of information will continue to increase in number and complexity. The implementation of E-commerce and the proliferation of licensed databases and Web resources are producing literal rivers of information for business and other uses. As the costs of specialized technologies continue to fall, streams of data from packages, utility meters, parking meters, and other sources will become torrents of potential business information resources to be managed at the institutional level.[11]

The volume of institutional information resources and their use will continue to rise. The rapid interconnection of enterprise technologies will fuel a growing demand for information resources. Sophisticated modeling, simulation, and decision support tools will fuel this demand. This demand will likely rise outside the central institutional business and finance units as professionals in distributed campus units and their deans and directors engage in increasingly sophisticated resource management activities such as responsibility center management. Business officers will need to support a likely growing imbalance between sophisticated (and demanding) users of campus business information and an inevitable (and demanding) trailing edge of campus information users.

Access to digital information resources can soon be everywhere. Subject to existing limitations of access based on business and financial literacy, the barriers to the ubiquitous access to institutional information resources will be removed in the near future. Much of the focus of financial information resources management will likely shift to concern over how to build and maintain the network of campus financial managers within a standardized institutional reporting framework and how to protect the integrity of the institution's data and regulating its use.

Information resources themselves and their use will become more complex. Information technology is making it possible and affordable to capture, disseminate, display, model, and simulate information in a variety of forms. Users of institutional information resources will need increasingly sophisticated tool kits to manipulate source data, perform simulations, render numerical data visually, and so forth.

The users of information resources will be increasingly mobile. The promise of distance or distributed learning models, when fulfilled, will reduce further the centrality of the campus as the place where teaching, learning, and research are conducted. Those who manage information resources will need to support electronic infrastructures that mitigate some of the fragmenting tendencies that increased faculty, student, and staff mobility will create.

The stewardship of campus information resources will be increasingly distributed in the short term and potentially centralized in the longer term. The Web is making it easier for members of the campus community to deliver institutional information resources globally. In a networked campus environment, the "central campus" is no longer at the center and is, in fact, only another "node on the network." New management and policy models to govern distributed authority will need to be developed as business officers and others such as campus counsel face new challenges in protecting campus copyrights, trademarks, and intellectual property and in ensuring institutional compliance with state and federal laws and regulations, such as the Family Educational Rights and Privacy Act (FERPA).

Driven by technology and economics, the organizational focus of managing key institutional information resources will shift. As institutional network infrastructures mature, and as the costs of storing electronic media continue to decline, the storage and dissemination of multiple electronic copies will continue to proliferate. Attention may shift from the creation of centrally managed institutional databases to the creation of information confederations that regulate and guide distributed information strategy and inter-enterprise commerce in information resources.[12] Such strategy and policy will be mediated by collaborative agreements for information resources.

Information technologies will blur the boundaries between institutional and personal information resources. Networked information resources are changing profoundly the nature of intellectual property and will likely force a rethinking of the rights to be shared between institutions and their faculties or a rethinking of institutional policies on conflict of interest and commitment.

Who Will Manage Institutional Information Resources?

Managing institutional information resources in the future will require significant changes in economic, technical, legal, and behavioral areas. The network-based model of institutional information delivery will change the political economy of information resources management, and the changing relative influence of those involved in management activities will influence how the economic, technical, legal, and behavioral solutions will evolve.

Figure 07-01

Business Office Centric Model

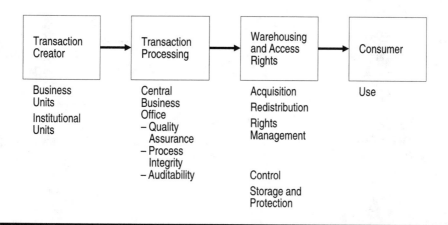

The emergence of the network as a significant and eventually dominant delivery vehicle for campus information resources will likely alter the mix of management roles and responsibilities associated with information resources. Different management models will influence many of the management issues that will arise and these models should be understood. (See figure 07-01.)

While grossly simplified, figure 07-01 describes the dominant practice in higher education. In this scenario, campus institutional and business units complete business transactions and transmit these transactions to institutional systems. These systems add value by testing the validity of transactional data and by moving transactions into the stream of campus business processes (administering student loans, writing payroll, acquiring goods). Central units are then responsible for the production of data warehouses and marts, for mediating campus access to institutional summary information, and for meeting the institution's audit and external reporting requirements. The end users in this model are dependent on centrally defined and mediated information collection, storage, and use policies and practices and their timelines. Too often, these central controls and practices fail to meet "local" information uses and result in the proliferation of so-called "shadow systems." (See figure 07-02.)

Figure 07-02, again grossly simplified, describes an unsettling management model wherein the originators of transactions take back the means of production.

Figure 07-02

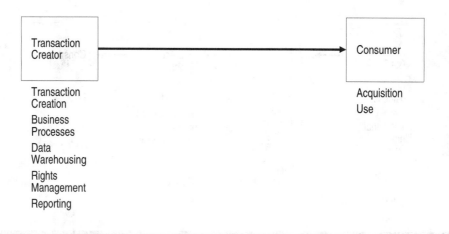

End User Centric Model

In this scenario, campus business units—enabled by technology—avoid the central campus organizations and conduct commerce directly with end consumers over the network. As the price of technologies has fallen and as their use has become simpler, local campus units have used the spreadsheet to assume increasing responsibility for information that they consider "theirs." As E-commerce and the Web make it possible to distribute information and transactions more easily and cheaply, campus business officers are facing new challenges posed by entrepreneurial campus departments that may be tempted to operate outside the framework of institutional processes and controls.

There are many who believe that network technologies will enable such a fully distributed and decentralized marketplace. To a large extent, the devolution of many of the activities associated with the information management "value chain" is occurring as a result of the eased "self reporting" capabilities fostered by the World Wide Web. The end-user-centric model, like much of today's Web environment, is a frontier lacking in the laws, business rules, quality controls, audit requirements, reporting requirements and constraints, and management practices that make it possible for those who acquire information to determine the quality of available information. A world in which everyone can create a transaction, spreadsheet, or file; save it as an HTML (hypertext markup language) file; post this file to a Web site; and broadcast its whereabouts via electronic mailing lists is likely one in which information content is substantially devalued. Such a world may satisfy a transaction creator's short-term needs at the expense of the institution. (See figure 07-03.)

The confederation model, shown in figure 07-03, also greatly simplified, recognizes the unique scale economies that derive from the assumption that the institutional resources to be managed in the near future will be electronic. In electronic form, institutional information resources enjoy the scale economies demonstrated by electronic mass storage generally, including scale economies of disk storage,

Figure 07-03

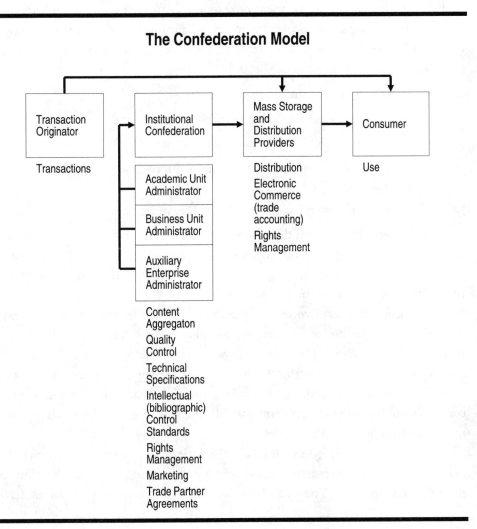

The Confederation Model

systems management, and operations management. For this reason, the management of electronic institutional information resources is likely to become highly centralized and quite possibly commercialized. Firms that currently manage huge data repositories under contract with a variety of public and private organizations are likely to displace the roles of traditional publishers, government agencies, distributors, and institutional libraries in the areas of storing and distributing information resources. As important, centralized and commercialized organizations will likely be early developers and managers of the commercial infrastructure that will be necessary to monitor growing electronic commerce and to account for trade balances between suppliers and consumers.

In a confederated model, the role of the institutional business officer is likely to shift. Future business officers will be responsible for ensuring that departmental infrastructures are robust and secure and that information of institutional importance is identified for appropriate storage, access, archival retention, or legal disposition. This role is manifested through:

- knowledge of institutional business processes;

- management of institutional data standards (charts of account, and so forth);

- training of localized financial and business staff;

- articulation and enforcement of campus quality and accountability standards; and

- oversight and protection of the "official" institutional record.

Such environments will demand a new culture of internal control that relies less on the assumption of direct operational responsibility by central institutional units than on a web of effective partnerships, training, and business agreements throughout (and beyond) the campus.

This scenario is a microcosm of the institution's likely role within the external context of E-commerce. The tendency of networked information environments to foster real-time auction environments will place an accent on institutions' abilities to create market strength. Much of the required market strength will come from the creation of electronic consortia, co-ops, and other leveraging forms. In consortial environments, direct control will likely evolve into the kinds of coordinative controls described.

While the confederation model may become one model of institutional information resource management, the technology underlying the confederation supports other approaches. The creators of institutional information resources, in this technical environment, will continue to be able to produce and distribute institutional information resources independently. Information that is handled in such a fashion will not have the imprimatur of the institution.

Recommended Actions

The discussion of who will manage institutional information resources in the future helps us derive what must be done to assure their effective management in the future. If a model of shared authority evolves, college and university leaders will need to guide campus strategies and investments in a number of key areas.

Set the Course

Campus leaders must craft a vision and finance sustainable strategies for supporting the increasing numbers of community members who will seek remote access to institutional information resources. The vision of a robust environment in which information resources and transactions are exchanged over networks (and between enterprises) will likely change forever the information management practices of the college or university. Electronic commerce, in particular, is likely to force a strategic reassessment of campus information flows, processes, and practices. Business officers should engage the campus in a strategic evaluation of information management practices with a view to identifying new practices, strategies, and policies that anticipate widespread and highly distributed access to institutional electronic information. Such an evaluation should also anticipate the policy and practical implications of integrating institutional data systems with those of external authorities (grantors, K–12, suppliers).

Invest in Campus Networking

William Graves makes the point that a campus intranet, linked to the Internet and based on open Internet standards, can provide a:

- method for enhancing the reach, timeliness, and effectiveness of human communication in every aspect of the institutional mission;

- learning infrastructure to increase the quality of student and faculty institutional work, and access to information resources beyond the campus boundaries; and

- service infrastructure to enable streamlining of institutional management and outreach activities.[13]

The premise that underlies a vision of campus information-dependent processes and resources that are ubiquitously (though selectively) accessible 24 hours a day to students, trading partners, and appropriate members of the campus community is that of robust institutional networks. For this new model to minimize our current dependence on location—to facilitate student access to loan and bill information and so forth—off-campus access to campus business and financial services and information resources must also be robust and secure.

Foster a Culture of Collaboration

The execution of any of the strategies described suggests the need for unprecedented levels of collaboration within colleges and universities and between these institutions and a variety of public and private institutions. Successful business officers will need to foster effective alliances with others on the campus for the acquisition, storage, protection, and distribution of institutional information resources. Campus leaders must create an environment and a set of reinforcing incentives that will encourage deep cooperation. If the challenge of the networked information vision is the challenge of integration,[14] then new levels of intra- and inter-institutional collaboration must be fostered. The creators of new, complex information resources will likely include the faculty, business office, school and departmental administrative professionals, information technologists, auditors, records managers, and others. Professional and other turf barriers to the effective orchestration of such teams must be overcome. In addition, campuses must become increasingly adept at those skills related to the oversight of a variety of outsourcing and shared service arrangements, because campuses will be moving from unified institutional information resource management models to models in which major elements of the resource delivery system may come to be owned and operated by others. The need to collaborate will be heightened by growing shortages of key skills that will be necessary to achieve institutional excellence in these areas of campus endeavor.

Investigate and Invest in the 'Search Engineering' Infrastructure

Key to the creation of distributed information environments is the deployment of technologies that enhance users' ability to find meaningful institutional information in cyberspace. By late 1999, there were more than one million sites and 100 million pages on the Web, and the number continues to double approximately every six months. More than 50 million American adults used the Internet by the end of 1998. In the immediate future, systems will be delivered that provide "visual representations of data, collaborative filters that gather recommendations from users, enterprise software with search capabilities, and advanced Web search engines.[15]" In the longer term, technologies will be available that will answer questions not with lists of documents, but with "multi-dimensional, immersive environments that provide a more intuitive view of large collections of data grouped or clustered by meaning."[16] Colleges and universities must actively monitor the market for search, filtering, personalization, and "agent" technologies, experiment actively with these technologies, and deploy the best of these technologies in campus servers and workstations. These technologies will allow campuses to begin building the compelling virtual environments that will foster user loyalty but that must be bundled with online help services. It is important to note that the costs of creating the levels of integration necessary to support E-commerce are thought to be high.[17] Financial officers will likely participate as members of teams that will configure "personal portals" for members of the campus (and extended) communities. Different members of the community will be given differing views of the institution, depending on those members' rights, authorities, roles, and needs.

Focus on Policy-based Directory Services, Authentication, and Authorization

Campus information technologists are engaged in discussions about the technical authentication and authorization of the users of campus technology and information resources. While the technical aspects of managing authentication and authorization may be esoteric, the policy and economic issues that accompany these technical discussions deserve early attention at the highest campus levels. At the heart of this set of issues is the question of who are the members of the campus community and what authorities and entitlements accrue to such individuals.

The ability to replicate and warehouse institutional financial and business information will raise new and substantial policy issues. Access to information, previously constrained and regulated by limitations of space and photocopiers, will now require the development and oversight of clear policies and the implementation of procedures and guidelines. While information technologies will lower the costs of transactions and information access, rising information use may likely lead to an overall rise in institutional information handling costs. Rising use will also place new and different strains on the campus user support infrastructure. Changing support requirements and economics of access suggest strongly the need for institutions to: (1) develop and implement sound infrastructures for identifying, authenticating, and authorizing information users; and (2) revisit existing assumptions about the nature and size of the "university community."[18]

Many universities, for example, define the boundaries of their communities broadly to include the families of employees, retirees, and alumni. These inclusive boundaries are reasonable as they relate to institutional information resources in the context of self-limiting physical materials. In the context of access via institutional networks and modem pools to university-licensed electronic resources, the policy, economic, technical, and support issues become significantly more complex.[19] These issues will become even more complex as: (1) members of the broader campus community come to expect access to campus printers, content and technical advisers, and other expensive resources; and (2) campuses ponder the complexity and cost of managing the accounting and billing infrastructure that will be needed if costs are to be recovered.

In sum, campus policy makers must begin now to determine who, for the purpose of accessing electronic information resources, shall be deemed a member of the campus community. Campus leaders will need to develop policies that differentiate the rights and authorities among community members and to revisit policies regarding the appropriate use of institutional resources. Campus technologists will have to implement complex campus directory services, determine what levels of support can be offered to which members of the campus community, and develop authentication and authorization solutions that implement the campus policy. None of this will be easy. Finally, in addition to securing access to campus information resources, campus policy makers and technologists will need to revisit institutional policies and practices regarding the protection of the privacy of members of the community. The administration of a robust infrastructure for authenticating and authorizing members of the community along with the powerful accounting environments that will be needed to support electronic commerce in institutional information resources will necessarily demand that institutions maintain significant information about students, faculty, alumni, staff, and others. The administration of this information about campus community members and their network and information predilections will raise significant privacy concerns on campus.

Focus on Standards

As addressed earlier in several sections, today's increasingly complex networked environments and ways of doing campus business require the creation of and adherence to a variety of emerging technical standards and specifications. The

Internet2 initiative, for example, through the Internet Engineering Task Force (IETF) will develop the standards and specifications that will enable differentiated quality of service across the Internet. Campus networks will have to be upgraded to support the protocols that will make these services possible. Other efforts, such as the National Learning Infrastructure Initiative's Instructional Management System (IMS) are bringing together commercial and institutional interests to develop the standards and specifications that will make it possible to develop and share course materials, instructional resources, and institutional processes via networks. Organizations are developing electronic course catalogs for the Western Governors University that will form critical and necessary components of a multi-institutional and global infrastructure that will be needed to share institutional information resources across networks. Campuses should either actively participate in these endeavors to build regional and national infrastructures, or should follow such initiatives closely. When opportunities arise, campuses should invest in their local infrastructures in ways that recognize and leverage national and consortium-based investments.

CONCLUSION

Information technology in the context of higher education's mission and support systems is no longer a luxury. Rather, information technology is now a core element of the institutional infrastructure, an infrastructure whose existence no longer differentiates one institution from another to provide competitive advantage. Higher education's challenge in this new century is no longer to deploy networks and access to computers, but to develop compelling and cohesive technical environments and services that will attract and retain the finest faculty, students, and staff. The challenge, further, is to organize the information within the institution's reach in ways that foster learning and shared sense of community.

Information technology in higher education has moved to "the next level" and must now be managed as an element of an overall institutional approach to risk management. Elements of this approach include the following.

Managing competitive risk. General campus management must now address the question of how information technology contributes to the institution's viability in the market for higher education. Will the information technology infrastructure and suite of IT-enhanced academic and business services differentiate the institution from others? In particular, how will that first generation of college students born in the era of the personal computer (class of 2003) react to unavailable or aging computers, slow networks, poor support, or long lines for services, library materials, and the like? What investments must be made to ensure that the institution's IT environment attracts support for the campus?

Managing technological risk. Information technology is like no other resource on campus. Information technology is in a constant state of rapid evolution and, in the words of Martin Trow, "cuts its own channel" through organizations that deploy it.[20] Campuses will need to develop effective IT planning processes—plans per se—and rapid-deployment capabilities. Institutions will need to remain current with evolving technologies, in experimental mode at least, and will need to adopt and enforce the standards that will be needed to gather in any possible harvests in enhanced productivity and quality that new IT-based services can deliver.

Managing human risk. Colleges and universities are no longer tranquil and idyllic places of employment. We maintain old legacy systems from which young technologists can learn little of lifelong value. We do not pay market salaries or offer stock options. We are rarely the fount of new technological developments. As a result, colleges and universities are now frequently at significant risk of losing their existing IT leadership and are at great disadvantage competing in labor markets for technologists. The campus IT environment can be no better than the planning and engineering that goes into its creation. Planning and engineering depends on people, and campuses must begin to think strategically about how to recruit and retain these people, or how to acquire the needed expertise by other means. Shared services, public-private alliances, outsourcing, and other skill-seeking strategies will grow increasingly important in areas of fierce labor-market competition.

Higher education's success and endurance throughout the ages emanates from our constant ability to renew and rethink ourselves operationally, while remaining true to an enduring mission. The rapid changes in the information technology landscape offer us a set of tools to once again rethink how we deliver our ever-important purpose. Although potentially revolutionary, information technologies are merely the tools to enable change and to mitigate risk. Wisdom, courage, and vision will be the leadership qualities our colleges and universities will need to seize the opportunities presented by these tools.

NOTES

1. Clark Kerr, *The Uses of the University* (Cambridge, Mass.: Harvard University Press, 1982), p. 20.

2. This section was adapted by Philip E. Long from work he previously published in Mark A. Luker, ed., *Preparing Your Campus for a Networked Future* (San Francisco: Jossey-Bass Publishers, 2000).

3. "Rebuilding ERP," *PC Week,* August 23, 1999, pp. 1, 20, 24.

4. Two sources of information on electronic commerce in higher education are Donald Norris and Mark Olson, *E-Business in Education: What You Need to Know* (Washington, D.C.: NACUBO, 1999) and Richard N. Katz and Diana Oblinger, Ed., *The E Is for Everything: E-Commerce, E-Business, and E-Learning in Higher Education* (San Francisco: Jossey-Bass Publishers, Inc., 2000).

5. David O. Stephens, "Megatrends in Records Management," *Records Management Quarterly* (January 1998).

6. David Collis, "When Industries Change: Scenarios for Higher Education," in *Forum Futures 1999* (New Haven, Conn.: Forum for the Future of Higher Education, 1999), pp. 14–17.

7. William H. Graves, "Adapting to the Emergence of Educational Micro Markets," *Educom Review* 32:5 (September/October 1997).

8. Lee Alley, "Cloning the Ivy Tower on Wall Street," a paper presented at the National Learning Infrastructure Initiative Conference, New Orleans, Louisiana, February 1999.

9. "Assessment and Policy," NLII Denver—99 Meeting Notes, July 1999, p. 11.

10. Dorothy Frayer, "Creating a Campus Culture to Support a Teaching and Learning Revolution," *CAUSE/EFFECT* 22:2 (1999): 10–17.

11. See John Gage, "Technology, Change and Opportunity in Higher Education," plenary remarks delivered at the 1997 CAUSE Annual Conference, available as an online video at www.educause.edu/conference/c97/webcast97.html

12. This shift is already well under way in institutional information arenas. See Donald N. Langenberg, "Information Technology and the University: Integration Strategies for the 21st Century," *Journal of the American Society for Information Science* 45 (June 1994): 324. Langenberg argues that "increasingly, new and unanticipated alliances, aided by open, campuswide dialogue on the role of information technology, will greatly advance the integration process. Moreover, not only will this collaboration be institutionwide, it will in some cases also be inter-institutional."

13. William H. Graves, "A Strategy for I/T Investments," in D. Oblinger and S.

Rush, Eds., *The Future Compatible Campus* (Bolton, Mass.: Anker Publishing Company, 1998), pp. 27–28.

14. Langenberg, "Information Technology and the University."

15. Jeff Ubois, "Casting an Information Net," *Upside.com*, February 2, 1998, p. 2.

16. Ibid., p. 5

17. The Gartner Group estimates investments in E-Commerce Web sites ranging from $300,000 (getting on the map) to as much as $20 million to be a "market differentiator." Most of these costs (79 percent) are for labor. See *Inside Gartner Group This Week* XV: 23 (June 9, 1999).

18. Clifford Lynch, "The Changing Role in a Networked Information Environment," in *Library Hi Tech* 15: 1–2 (1997): 30. Lynch describes the authentication and authorization challenge very clearly, arguing: "It has become clear, rather suddenly, that our existing systems of authentication and authorization were not really designed to support the new [networked] environment, and that they can't do so."

19. In several extreme cases, colleges and universities find themselves serving in the role of Internet Service Provider (ISP) to the spouses and children of campus employees, emeriti, alumni, and others. In many of these cases, Internet access is provided at no cost, or at rates that are below campus costs. This situation is not only problematic financially but may be legally unsustainable, vis à vis commercial providers' concerns regarding predatory pricing by non-profits.

20. Martin Trow, "The Development of Information Technology in American Higher Education," *Daedelus* 126:4 (1997): 293–314.

REFERENCES AND RESOURCES

Articles

Adams, Robert McC. "Social Contexts of Technology." *Social Research* 64:3 (Fall 1997): 947–96.

Atkins, Daniel E. "Preparing Information Professionals for Traditional and Emerging Knowledge-Work Environments." Summary of talk presented to the University of Michigan.

Barlow, John Perry. "The Economy of Ideas." *Wired* 2:3 (March 1994).

Berry, Anthony J. "Approaching the Millenium: Transforming Leadership Education." *Leadership & Organizational Development Journal* 18:2 (1997) pp. 86–92.

Brown, John Seeley, and Duguid, Paul. "Organizing Knowledge." (2.21 mb) *California Management Review* 40:3 (Spring 1998): 90–111.

———. "Universities in the Digital Age." (1.90 mb) *Change* 28 (July/August 1996) 11–16.

Drucker, Peter F. "The Age of Social Transformation." (206 kb) *The Atlantic Monthly* 274:5 (November 1994): 53–80.

———. "Infoliteracy." (20 kb) *Drucker Management Magazine* (Spring 1995).

———. "Management's New Paradigms." (4.39 mb) *Forbes* 162:7 (October 5 1998): 152–177.

Evans, Philip B., and Wurster, Thomas S. "Strategy and the New Economics of Information." (6.11 mb) *Harvard Business Review* 75 (September-October 1997): 71–82.

Guskin, Alan E. "Facing the Future: The Change Process in Restucturing Universities." (2.43 mb) *Change* 28 (July/August 1996): 27–37.

Hawkins, Brian L., and Battin, Patricia. "The Changing Role of the Information Resource Professional: A Dialogue." (2.97 mb) *CAUSE/EFFECT* 20:1 (Spring 1997); 22–30.

———. "Creating the Library of the Future: Incrementalism Won't get Us There!" (6.05 mb) *Serials Librarian* 24:3/4 (1994): 17–47.

Higher Education Information Resources Alliance "HEIR Alliance Evaluation Guidelines for Institutional Information Resources." (960 kb) *HEIR Alliance* (July 1995).

———. "What Presidents Need to Know About Evaluating Institutional Information Resources." (494 kb) *HEIR Alliance Executive Strategies Report 6* (July 1995).

———. "Executive Outlook on the Transformation of Higher Education." (584 kb) *HEIR Alliance Executive Strategies Report 7* (July 1996).

Himmelarb, Gertrude. "Revolution in the Library." (1.75mb) *American Scholar* 66:Spring (1997): 197–204.

Jonas, Stephen, Katz, Richard N., Martinson, Linda, Plympton, Margaret F., Relyea, Steven W., Rennie, Edwin D., Rudy, Jilia A., and Walsh, John F. "Campus Financial Systems for the Future." Washington, DC: CAUSE and NACUBO 1996.

Katz, Richard N. "Higher Education and the Forces of Self-Organization: an interview with Margaret Wheatley." (673 kb) *CAUSE/EFFECT* 20:1 (Spring 1997): 18–21.

Nelson, Theodor Holm. "Transcopyright: Dealing with the Dilemma of Digital Copyright." (491 kb) *Educom Review* 32:1 (January/February 1997): 32–35.

Norris, Donald M., and Olson, Mark A. "Preparing for Virtual Commerce in Higher Learning." (955 kb) *CAUSE/EFFECT* 20:1(Spring 1997): 40–44.

Papert, Seymour. "Technology in Schools." (1.94 mb) *Milken Exchange on Educational Technology* 1998.

Rapple, Brendan. "The Electronic Library: New Roles for Librarians." (1.09 mb) *CAUSE/EFFECT* 20:1 (Spring 1997): 45–51.

Rothblatt, Sheldon. "The Place of Knowledge in the American Academic Profession." (3.29 mb) *Daedalus* 126:4 (Fall 1997): 245–264.

Steele, Lowell W. "And the Walls Came Tumbling Down." (4.15 mb) *Technology in Society* 18:3 (1996): 261–284.

"To Publish and Perish." (1.43 mb) *Policy Perspectives* 7:4 (March 1998): 1–12.

Trow, Martin. "The Development of Information Technology in American Higher Education." (2.96 mb)*Daedalus* 126:4 (Fall 1997): 293–314.

Winner, Langdon, "Who Will We Be in Cyberspace?" (1.87 mb) *The Information Society* 12:1 (January/March 1996): 63–72.

Books

Dill, David D., and Sporn, Barbara. "University 2001: What Will the University of the Twenty-First Century Look Like?" (3.12 mb) In *Emerging Patterns of Social Demand and University Reform: Through a Glass Darkly*, 212–236. Oxford: Pergamon for the IAU Press, 1995.

Dyson, Esther. *Release 2.0: A Design For Living in the Digital Age,* NY: Broadway Books, 1997.

Gumport, Patricia J., and Chun, Marc. "Techology and Higher Education: Opportunities and Challenges for the New Era." (5.85 mb) In *American Higher Education in the 21st Century: Social, Political, and Economic Challenges*, 370–395. Baltimore, MD: Johns Hopkins University Press, 1999.

Halal, William E., with Smith, Raymond. *The Infinite Resource: Creating and Managing the Knowledge Enterprise.* San Francisco: Jossey Bass Publishers, 1998.

Hawkins, Brian L., and Battin, Patricia, Eds. *The Mirage of Continuity: Reconfiguring Academic Information Resources for the 21st Century.* Washington: Council on Library and Information Resources and Association of American Universities, 1998.

Hesselbein, Frances, Goldsmith, Marshall, and Beckhard, Richard. *The Organization of the Future.* San Francisco: Jossey Bass Publishers, 1997.

Hope, Jeremey. "Knowledge Management: Leverage Knowledge for Competitve Advantage." (4.55 mb) In *Issue 3: Competing in the Third Wave*, 65–85. Boston: Harvard Business School Press, 1997.

Katz, Richard N., and Associates. *Dancing with the Devil: Information Technology and the New Competition in Higher Education.* San Francisco: Jossey-Bass Publishers, 1999.

Katz, Richard N., and Oblinger, Diana G. *The E is for Everything: E-Commerce, E-Business, and E-Learning in Higher Education.* San Francisco: Jossey-Bass Publishers, 2000.

Norris, Donald M., and Olson, Mark A. *E-Business in Education: What You Need to Know.* Washington D.C.: NACUBO, 1999.

Oblinger, Diana G., and Katz, Richard N., Eds. *Renewing Administration: Preparing Colleges and Universities for the 21st Century.* Bolton, MA: Anker Publishing Co., 1999.

Pearman, Roger R. *Hard Wired Leadership.* Palo Alto, CA: Davies-Black Publishing, 1998.

Rowley, Daniel James, Lujan, Herman D., and Dolence, Michael G. *Strategic Choices for the Academy* San Francisco: Jossey Bass Publishers, 1998.

Tierney, William G. *The Responsive University: Restructuring for High Performance* Baltimore: Johns Hopkins University Press. 1998.

Zusman, Amy. "Issues Facing Higher Education in the 21st Century." (9.57 mb) In *American Higher Education in the 21st Century: Social, Political, and Economic Challenges*, 109–148. Baltimore: Johns Hopkins University Press. 1999.

Magazines and Journals

The EDUCAUSE Quarterly (formerly *CAUSE/EFFECT*). EDUCAUSE, Subscriptions, 4772 Walnut Street, Suite 206, Boulder, Colorado 80301-2508.

The EDUCAUSE Review. EDUCAUSE, Subscriptions, 4772 Walnut Street, Suite 206, Boulder, Colorado 80301-2508.

The ACUTA Journal. ACUTA, Subscriptions, 152 Zandale, Suite 200, Lexington, Kentucky 40503.

Organizations

Association of College and University Telecommunications Administrators (ACUTA)
152 W. Zandale, Suite 200, Lexington, KY 40503
606-278-3338 . . . . www.acuta.org

EDUCAUSE
4772 Walnut Street, Suite 206 Boulder, CO 80301-2538
303-449-4430 . . . . info@educause.edu
1112 16th Street, NW, Suite 600, Washington, DC 20036
202-872-4200 . . . . www.educause.edu

Chapter 8

♦

Treasury Management

by

Dennis Reedy
Indiana University

Jon Speare
Commonfund Treasury, Inc.

with contributions by

Walter Conway, VISA USA

Michael Strauss, Commonfund Treasury, Inc.

Joan K. Thompson, Iowa State University

Sponsor

COMMONFUND

Contact: John S. Griswold Jr.
15 Old Danbury Road
P.O. Box 812
Wilton, CT 06897-0812
203-563-5000
www.commonfund.org

Commonfund provides investment and treasury management services to over 1,350 member colleges, universities and independent schools to maximize risk-adjusted returns for endowment and operation funds.

AT&T

295 North Maple Avenue
Basking Ridge, NJ 07920
800-228-7937
www.att.com/campusalliance

An AT&T Campus Alliance offers a full range of integrated communication and network solutions for you and your students—for all the ways you communicate.

HIGHERMARKETS, INC.

Contact: James Sparkman
1002A O'Reilly Avenue
San Franciso, CA 94117
415-561-4608 or info@highermarkets.com
www.highermarkets.com

HigherMarkets, Inc. brings together higher education institutions and their suppliers. Our mission is to empower our users to communicate and conduct transactions more effectively with each other, focus on their core businesses and realize enormous cost savings.

ASSOCIATION FOR FINANCIAL PROFESSIONALS (AFP)
7315 Wisconsin Avenue
Suite 600
West Bethesda, MD 20814
301-907-2862

AFP, the world's leading association for treasury and financial professionals, supports its membership through research, continuing education, professional certification, publications, representation to key legislators and regulators, and the development of industry standards.

NCS
Contact: John D. Schneider
2510 N. Dodge St.
Iowa City, IA 52245
319-339-6644
www.ncs.com

NCS has served the education community with data collection and management services, financial aid processing, testing, instructional management, electronic document management and surveys for 35 years.

Contents

Treasury management[1] is the discipline of effectively managing cash from the moment a claim for cash is established until an application for disbursement is satisfied. The ultimate objectives of treasury management are to maximize investment income, minimize expenses, and streamline processes associated with cash flows in the most cost-effective manner. Treasury management can be defined as having the right amount of money in the right place at the right time. This definition can be translated into the following formula:

Beginning Cash + Collections – Disbursements
= Investable Balances

An effective treasury management program ensures that funds in transit move safely and economically and, at the same time, are managed to maximize their ability to earn interest. This activity is accomplished within the constraints of liquidity needs, short- and long-term financing requirements, and a college or university's investment and spending policies. The benefits of a good treasury management program can significantly offset the costs of maintaining the program. In their quest for the maximum return on investments and the reduction of costs, treasury managers must look for more efficient means of handling funds as money moves from the payor to the college or university, to the investment vehicle, and out of the investment vehicle for disbursement.

Treasury management should be a key component in every college and university's strategic business plan. Virtually every department on campus has some type of relationship with treasury functions. The management of cash inflows and outflows, information inflows and outflows, financial institution and vendor relationships, working capital management, and the underlying internal processes touch all campus areas. A growing role of the treasury manager is to act as a coordinator/consultant in re-engineering processes in financial and nonfinancial areas as they become more reliant on the effective use of operating assets. The responsibility of the treasury manager has evolved from focusing only on managing cash and short term debt to include: information management, process management, resource management, banking/vendor relationship management, and investment management. All of these responsibilities require specialized expertise, are constantly changing, and are dramatically affected by the evolution of new technologies. Identifying, implementing, and managing technology is becoming a key part of the treasury office's mission of ensuring that the campus is benefiting from the best practices and products available. Overall, the organization's financial health is significantly affected by how well the treasury area manages all of these responsibilities. Before any treasury management system can be effective, however, the appropriate institutional environment must exist.

THE INSTITUTIONAL ENVIRONMENT

An effective program of treasury management relies largely on institutional commitment. Anyone involved with the receipt or disbursement of a college or university's funds must understand the value of the funds, expressed either as a lost opportunity cost, or in terms of the time value of money. Even funds invested overnight can produce revenues. Detrimental to treasury goals is any delay in the cash flow cycle. For example, some institutions pay bills before they are due. Similarly, institutional departments may use an incoming check as an accounting document and delay its deposit to the bank until the accounting and postings are completed. The responsibility of the treasury manager is to create an awareness of the critical relationship of time (the time value of money) and cash value (the cash-flow timeline) throughout the institution. It is important that operations that receive cash on a daily basis, such as bursar, auxiliary enterprises, and the development office, make prompt deposits. Creating a centralized accounts receivable system can also accelerate cash flow. Give departments access to the accounts receivable system and let them input their bills online. This will not only speed up the collection of cash but it will also create a professional image for the college or university. Overall, it is the treasury manager's role to assure that the institution's funds are maximized through process and investment management.

The Cash-Flow Timeline

The cash-flow timeline begins when funds become due and ends when they are available for investment or other uses; the timeline begins again in reverse when funds are disbursed from an investment vehicle and are ultimately presented for payment. Although that sounds simple, it can be complicated because many people in a college or university control the timeline, including the admissions officer, the provost, the financial or business officer, the controller, and the bursar. These individuals can play an important role in delaying or speeding the collection and disbursement process.

Staffing

Appropriate staffing for treasury management varies with institutional size and the complexity of the treasury management program. Regardless of the college or university's size, the use of a single person to act as treasury manager, even on a part-time basis, can have a positive impact on the college or university's financial health. At a smaller institution, one staff member may have full responsibility for all details of the treasury management program, while at larger institutions, the treasury manager acts as a coordinator between the various individuals and departments involved in treasury activities. The treasury manager should pay attention, on a daily basis, to bank balances, receipts, and disbursements. Daily attention provides assurance that cash is being managed correctly, that there is sufficient liquidity to meet requirements, and that surplus funds are being invested. In addition, daily information should be obtained on unexpected incoming funds and disbursements. Meticulous oversight provides knowledge of incoming account receipts and authorized and unauthorized account changes. The treasury manager should give attention to the level of collected funds in the bank accounts, not the deposited cash balance on the institution's records. The level of staffing committed to treasury management should ultimately be based on the economic return gained by additional investment income or reduced borrowing costs.

The evolving responsibilities of the treasury function require that treasury management staff continuously learn new skill sets. External training and networking are necessary in order to obtain and maintain these specialized skills. Associations such as the National Association of College and University Business Officers (NACUBO), the Association of Financial Professionals (AFP), formerly the Treasury Management Association (TMA), and their affiliated regional associations are important resources. Additionally, obtaining and maintaining professional designations, such as the AFP's Certified Cash Manager (CCM), are important to build a knowledge base for this critical function.

Management of Working Capital

Colleges and universities have a unique challenge in managing treasury/operating funds owing to the characteristics of the "higher education industry" and the seasonal demands on their working capital. While there are thousands of colleges and universities in the United States, their cash needs and seasonal trends are similar. The ability to manage working capital while remaining within the constraints of a realistic budget is essential to financial stability. This ability grows ever more important in the higher education industry, where increasing limits on revenue growth are accompanied by steady expense growth.

In the strictest definition, working capital equals current assets minus current liabilities; working capital is the resource available to keep operations running through the short term (less than one year). If an institution depends on resources outside of its working capital cycle to stay afloat, its survival is doubtful in the long term. Cash, inventories, accounts receivable, and any asset that is realizable within the next 12 months constitute working capital. Liabilities include accounts payable, accrued expenses (primarily payroll), and current debt obligations.

Many institutions have two peaks in receiving revenue during the year. These peaks typically occur when tuition payments are received at the start of each term. The finance or business officer and the treasury manager are responsible for managing this variability in operating cash assets.

Smaller institutions with limited resources may manage this variability by actively monitoring balances, investing when the cash level is above a predetermined minimum, and securing a line of credit with a financial institution to maintain the minimum when the cash level falls below this level. The treasury manager must choose among investment alternatives (earnings credit, certificates of deposit, savings accounts, sweep vehicles) including nonbank investment products (money market funds, mutual funds, short-term investment funds).

Larger institutions add another dimension to the working capital dilemma. Operating revenues may rise to such a high level in peak times that the college or university severely limits itself by not utilizing investments with longer maturities. Typically, the annual operating budget incorporates a minimum return on the investable balances. By relying solely on short-term investments, the college or university jeopardizes a large portion of its revenue base. Prudent fiscal management dictates that the treasury officer look to higher returns over time through the use of diverse investment alternatives and strategies.

When reviewing a treasury management plan, the business manager must:

- project cash flow expectations during the year;
- identify both short- and intermediate-term investment levels;
- monitor cash and receivables balances to determine what can be invested, and for how long;
- maximize cash flow by effectively collecting and disbursing funds; and
- protect the institution's operating assets by investing in secure investment

vehicles that have the necessary liquidity for the particular treasury management plan.

An element in managing working capital involves accrual accounting of accounts receivable on the asset side and accounts payable on the liability side. An important aspect of accrual accounting is the management of the turnover ratios that indicate how quickly these accounts are being paid or received by the college or university. Accounts receivable are included in working capital because they represent funds that have been realized or committed because they are expected to be liquidated within a year. The effectiveness of turning receivables into cash in the shortest amount of time has a definite effect on investment balances. Accounts payable need similar management. An institution that pays funds to vendors too quickly depletes its investable balance. Management of these accounts includes separating the discounted invoices for payment within 30 days and then scheduling the remainder within the stated terms, not sooner.

Assume a vendor offers the following terms on a $100,000 invoice: 0.5, 10, net 45 (translated as a one-half percent discount for payments received within 10 days, and full payment for payments received within 45 days). If the institution chooses to remit payment on or before the 10th day, the savings are as follows:

Savings using the discount: $\$100,000 \times 0.005 = \$500$

Assuming an annual return of 5.5 percent on short-term investments:

Opportunity cost of interest income earned:
$$\$100,000 \times 0.055 \times \frac{35}{365} = \$527$$

In this case, the benefit of investing funds longer outweighs the benefit of remitting payment early to receive the stated discount. Although this example does not demonstrate significant savings, the accumulation of savings across outstanding payables can justify cost benefit analysis or working capital decisions.

Again, by properly managing receipts and disbursements, the college or university can maximize investment income. As positive operating surpluses become harder to achieve, the total performance of the treasury management plan will increase in importance, whether it is monitored or not.

Cash Flow Projections

Planning and controlling cash flows are important tasks of the cash manager because cash flow affects the college or university's ability to pay obligations (including salaries and wages), to acquire assets, and to meet unexpected needs. In order to meet liquidity requirements, managers need information about historic cash flows for a given period. An adequate working capital position does not by itself imply an adequate cash position, because working capital may consist of accounts receivable, inventories, and other noncash items. Nor does an adequate cash position imply an acceptable working capital position, as large current liabilities may require more cash than is available.

An analysis of cash flow shows whether the pattern of cash flow from operations will enable an institution to meet its payment schedules properly or whether the institution must arrange for short-term credit. A cash flow statement provides the necessary information to plan effectively for meeting short- and intermediate-range cash needs. The cash flow statement summarizes cash receipts and disbursements by major categories or items, and can point out a net change in cash in a given period. In a computer-based system, it is easy to enter data on receipts and disbursements and to program the computer to prepare a cash flow statement. If such a system is not in operation, the necessary information can be obtained in an analysis similar to that needed to prepare a cash flow projections spreadsheet report (figure 08-01).

The forecasting of cash is critical in developing investment plans. Cash forecasting can range from a simple spreadsheet procedure to the use of a sophisticated treasury workstation. Cash flow analysis is historical in nature, and projections should be based on estimates or pro forma statements. Projection of cash flow is critical to the management of working capital.

THE FINANCIAL ENVIRONMENT

Service Provider Relations

An efficient treasury management program is not possible without a good working relationship between the college or university and its financial service providers. Financial service providers (banks, brokers, third-party processors, etc.) typically provide services that the college or university cannot efficiently provide or chooses not to provide in-house. The treasury manager also must realize that these services involve a cost to the financial provider and require that they earn a reasonable profit.

The college or university should focus on the total package of services provided, rather than on individual service costs. No service is provided for free, even though many financial service providers sometimes tout their products as involv-

Figure 08-01

Sample Cash Flow Projections Spreadsheet Report

Report Period	11/25	11/26	11/27	11/28	11/29	12/01	12/02	12/03	12/04	12/05
Projected cash receipts										
Electronic Transactions (ACH/Wire)										
Card receipts										
Lockbox receipts										
Federal/state Appropriations										
Local deposits										
Working capital drawdowns										
Investment maturities/income										
Total projected cash receipts										
Projected cash disbursements										
Wire transfers										
Payroll										
Vendor										
Purchase of Investments										
Tax payments										
Loan repayments										
Total projected cash disbursements										
Net projected cash flow										
Beginning cash										
Total cash										
Desired cash level										
Surplus/ (borrowings)										

ing no cost to the college or university. While costs should be negotiated, other factors are also important: the quality of service provided; safety of deposits (e.g., FDIC insurance); the promptness of attention given to problems; the willingness and ability of the financial provider to introduce new treasury management techniques, technologies, and services to the institution, and other subjective qualities. As a customer, the institution should meet on a periodic basis to review how well the service provider is performing its service(s). This meeting should include giving the service provider a periodic "report card" on the quality of its services, its effectiveness in improving the treasury management system, and the speed of problem resolution.

Typically, nonbank service providers are compensated for their services via fees. Banks are usually compensated for their services in one of two ways: either fees are paid for each service, or the customer maintains a balance of funds sufficient in size to pay for the services provided by the bank. The compensating balance allows the bank to earn income through investment or lending of idle balances that remain in the institution's accounts. Historically, banks have preferred that customers maintain compensating balances for two reasons: compensating balances are an inexpensive source of money to fund loans, and they ensure liquidity for the bank's balance sheet. Today, a combination of fees and compensating balances is most often used to pay for banking services. When determining the appropriate level of compensating balances remember to discount the earnings rate by the reserve requirement.

Example:

——————— *Average balance maintained* ———————

Ledger balance	$ 1,000,000
Less float	$ 100,000
Collected balance	$ 900,000
Less reserve requirement (10%)	$ 90,000
Investable balance	$ 810,000
Earnings allowance at 5.0%	$ 3,375

In this example, the actual rate of return to the institution is 4.5 percent or $(0.05)(0.90) = (0.045)$, not the stated earnings allowance of 5 percent. The actual earnings rate is reduced by the reserve requirement, therefore, the 4.5 percent rate should be used when comparing investment options. (A further discussion of investment alternatives to earnings credit is discussed in the Short-Term Investment section of this chapter.)

Obtaining Banking and Financial Services

In order to evaluate the total package of services provided by a bank or service provider, treasury managers should consider preparing Requests For Information (RFI) or Requests For Proposals (RFP) for existing or new banking and financial services. The RFI is used to gather information that will help determine whether or not to issue an RFP and what specifications should be included in the RFP. The RFI also assists in identifying which financial institutions or service providers are interested, or capable of providing the desired services. While the RFI is for requesting information, the RFP is a formal request for service providers to submit a bid for the services an institution interested in securing. At its simplest, an RFP is a document that contains/requests:

- a detailed description of the product or service that the institution is seeking and what it hopes to achieve by having this product or service;

- a detailed timetable for the RFP process, for example, when responses are due or when a decision will be made;

- the suggested format of the response;

- the name of the person who may be contacted for any questions;

- a detailed description of the institution's current process as it relates to the RFP;

- additional related products or services in which the college or university is interested; and

- evaluation criteria.

An RFP can also request detailed information from financial institutions on the services they provide and their costs and references. The use of RFIs/RFPs provides a rational, logical, and defensible method for identifying, evaluating, selecting, and negotiating financial services.

Electronic Payment Systems

The two primary types of electronic transactions are wire transfers (FedWire) and automated clearinghouse (ACH) transfers. Under each category are numerous subtypes.

A FedWire transfer is the electronic movement of funds on a real-time basis from the payor bank to the payee bank via transfers among Federal Reserve Bank accounts. A FedWire transfer is initiated when the treasury manager instructs the college or university's disbursement bank to make a transfer. The bank confirms the institution's account balance; if sufficient funds are available, the bank debits the institution's account and credits the payee's account. This transaction is accomplished through one or more banks with the Federal Reserve acting as intermediary to assure absolute same day funding.

ACH transfers use a network of computerized processing centers, typically operated by the Federal Reserve Bank, which transfer funds between ACH member institutions and settle the transactions in a one-to-two-day period. Prearranged instructions are provided by either the payor or payee. ACH transfers differ from FedWire transfers in that they take longer, do not provide for immediate availability of funds, and are significantly less expensive. In addition, ACH transfers may be returned (like a check) whereas FedWire transfers are final.

ACH transfers are most typically used for recurring transactions that have a known due date, such as payroll (direct deposit), interest payments, and rent payments. As with wires, they may be used as a vehicle to send or receive payments. While there is one format for wire transfers, there are multiple formats for ACH transfers.

The different formats of ACH payments relate to the initiator of the payment, the receiver of the payment, and the sophistication of the payment itself, that is, how much invoice or other data are carried along with the transfer of money. For example, a direct payroll deposit, which typically uses the PPD format, contains basic information such as the individual's name and bank account number. This data accompanies the transfer of funds so that the individual's bank can easily identify the recipient. Another ACH format, CTX, is one of the most sophisticated ACH formats and can be processed by only a handful of banks. This type of payment can accommodate thousands of invoices, associated discounts and allowances, and other relevant billing information. Furthermore, a CTX is constructed in such a manner that a bank or financial service provider can transmit this information directly into the recipient's accounts receivable database for automatic receivables updating.

Electronic Commerce

Electronic commerce, or "E-commerce," is the total set of activities that surround the purchase or sale of physical goods or information over information networks. E-commerce is more than just buying and selling. It includes:

- software applications that link buyers and sellers to conduct transactions;
- business strategies to manage and optimize relationships;

- complex business processes such as browsing, shopping, purchasing, selling, order status checking, fulfillment, delivery, customer service, and payment;

- technologies and tools that enable the applications, strategies, and processes to be implemented.

For years, large corporations have conducted E-commerce using Electronic Data Interchange (EDI) over private networks. EDI is used primarily between large corporations and their biggest suppliers, and typically for the largest dollar value and most frequent transactions. Because of high costs and complexity of EDI systems, EDI has not moved significantly beyond this set of high value/high frequency transactions between known and trusted parties.

Several elements are accelerating the use of E-commerce on the Internet by colleges and universities. Foremost is the increased acceptance and use of the Internet as a treasury tool. Complementing this factor is the emergence of packaged software applications that facilitate product selection, approvals, and ordering of goods, services, and information.

Colleges and universities can use E-commerce to reduce their purchasing costs. E-commerce allows institutions to automate low-value manual activities and to better manage their supplier relationships. At the same time, sellers are able to save money by automating their catalogs, inventory management, transaction approval, and order entry, while reducing receivables with the electronic payment.

E-commerce may be implemented several ways, each with its own advantages and disadvantages. First, sellers may create a virtual storefront on the World Wide Web. Buyers access the site using the Internet browsers on their PCs. Transactions generally are secured using channel encryption technology (see Web Payment, below). Institutions need to be assured of at least this basic level of security before they conduct E-commerce with any seller or buyer. A more complex security system called secure electronic transactions (SET) has been developed by a consortium of financial, technology, and computer security organizations. The principal advantage of this technology is the relatively low cost for both buyer and seller.

Alternatively, a buyer can install electronic purchasing software on an internal server, and allow approved sellers to access that server. Sellers post their catalogs, prices, and other terms, and update them directly as conditions change. Buyers access the server through their internal communications network. The internal server is linked to the Internet, but it is protected behind a system called a "firewall" that restricts outside access only to approved sellers. Such a solution is called an intranet. Intranets are secure, but they are very expensive for the buyer to build and maintain, and they limit the choice of sellers to a relatively small number compared to the total available.

A third option is for the institution to participate in an extranet. An extranet is like a hub that links multiple sellers and buyers using a secure, third party server. This approach offers economies of scale to buyers and sellers alike, particularly to smaller institutions that would like to have available to them larger discounts from sellers.

The dominant method of payment for E-commerce on the Web is a payment card. Payment cards include credit, debit, charge, cash, prepaid, chip/smartcards, and purchasing cards. Payment cards offer the buyer convenience and widespread acceptance. For the seller, payment cards reduce float and allow transactions to be completed without prior credit approval, thereby giving suppliers global reach.

Web Payments

Web payments are fundamentally different from face-to-face payments. There are common elements: there is a buyer and a card-issuing financial institution; and there is a seller with a card processor. The difference is that rather than sending the information by swiping the card through a point-of-sale terminal, the payment information must be transmitted over an open and therefore potentially unsecure network—the Internet.

Since the Internet is an open network, payment card information must be protected. Nearly all seller Web sites have a secure transaction area where payment card information is entered. Payment cards should never be used at an unsecure site. The transaction data, including account information, are encrypted most often through the secure sockets layer (SSL) protocol. The encrypted data are then transmitted over the Internet to the seller's Web server.

A second, more sophisticated security protocol is secure electronic transaction (SET). The major advantage of SET over SSL is the addition of digital certificates that link the cardholder and the seller to their respective financial institutions. Therefore, where SSL encrypts the transaction data, SET additionally permits a seller and buyer to verify one another's identity.

Plastic Payment Systems

In addition to the paper payment system and the electronic payment system, payment cards (a plastic payment system) are a third receivables management option for colleges and universities. Payment cards offer a fast, convenient, safe way to be paid. Like all forms of payment, plastic payment cards have direct and indirect costs. These costs will make payment cards a more or less attractive option for each institution—depending on how the card program is implemented.

There are five main categories of payment cards:

- *Credit cards.* The most common type of payment card in the United States. Credit cards allow cardholders to pay their balance in full at the end of the billing period (usually monthly) or revolve the balance into a line of credit.

- *Debit cards.* These cards access the cardholder's demand deposit account (DDA) or checking account directly. Debit cards may be "online," requiring a personal identification number (PIN), or "off-line," and processed like a credit card.

- *Charge cards.* The total amount charged on the account is due at the close of the billing period, usually one month.

- *Commercial cards.* These cards, issued to businesses, corporations, government agencies, and colleges and universities, are used to improve cash management and reduce purchasing costs. Commercial cards are addressed separately at the end of this section.

- *Cash cards or prepaid cards.* These are cards that have preloaded cash value either imbedded in a chip or encoded on a magnetic stripe on the card. Alternatively, these cards may be linked to a prepaid account that is debited when a transaction is processed.

In each payment card transaction, there are the same four roles: the cardholder; the financial institution that issues the card; the seller of the goods or services; and the seller's card processor sometimes called an acquirer.

The other players are the card associations, Visa and MasterCard, and independent companies such as American Express, Diner's Club, or Discover. The associations do not issue cards. Rather, their roles are to define the rules and regulations for the issuance and use of their cards, to promote their brands, to work to eliminate fraud and counterfeit, and—importantly—to operate the high speed processing networks that authorize, clear, and settle transactions between their member financial institutions. Independent card companies such as American Express perform these roles, but also have direct relationships with consumers and merchants—issuing cards, and acting as acquirer.

Most payment card transactions occur in two parts. First the transaction is authorized. During authorization, the seller or merchant sends the transaction (i.e., information such as the card number, expiration date, and amount of purchase) to its card processor. The processor then sends the transaction over a high-speed communications network to the card issuer for approval. The approval is returned to the seller by a reverse process. In most cases, this round trip takes only a few seconds.

At the end of the business day, typically, the seller batches all the card transactions electronically and sends them to the processor for settlement (or an automated closing process does the same thing). The processor clears the transactions according to the procedures for each card brand (Visa, MasterCard, American Express, and other brands each clear and settle their respective transactions separately). At the conclusion of the settlement process, the issuer pays—and the processor receives—the amount of the transaction less a discount amount.

A payment card program will have costs. Direct costs include: the merchant fee charged by the card processor; the cost of point of sale (POS) terminals and PIN pads to authorize and capture card transactions; communications costs; and costs to update internal accounting and reporting systems. The merchant fee depends on a number of factors such as the seller's volume, fraud experience for the seller's industry, and a host of other issues. Sellers can influence the rate they pay by negotiating with competing acquirers or directly with American Express or Discover. Generally, the merchant fee will be a percentage of the transaction amount. Therefore, the absolute dollar cost is more for a large transaction than for a small transaction. In this respect, the costs of plastic card payments are different from check costs, which are relatively independent of the size of the check (before considering bad check costs). However, many processors do charge a transaction fee in addition to percentage discount rates for each transaction.

Interchange

In the case of Visa and MasterCard associations, the merchant fee will be the sum of the interchange reimbursement and fee, the processor's cost to authorize, capture, and settle the transaction, and the acquirer's mark up. There may be additional fees for support services, training, chargeback and copy request processing, and customized reporting, to name a few examples. Of these costs, the largest single element generally will be the interchange amount. The associations set their respective interchange fees. Interchange fees are used to balance the costs between issuers (whose costs include transaction float, credit underwriting, plastic issuance, and customer service) and the processors (whose costs are transaction processing costs). Interchange fees also reflect the associations' marketing priorities. What interchange does not include are a particular issuer's individual program costs such as frequent flyer miles, credit losses, or bankruptcy expense. The acquirer's costs and profit margin are covered by the markup added to the interchange.

Currently, cards are widely used in retail-like operations such as bookstores, auditoriums, and auxiliary enterprises. There is an increasing trend to use cards as a part of re-engineering the accounts receivable process using Web technology and/or telephonic technology. An example is using credit cards as part of a touch tone payment system—also known as pay-by-phone or voice response unit (VRU).

A commercial card is an accounts payable management tool. Commercial cards are issued to and used by faculty and staff. One form of the commercial card is a travel card. Travel cards (sometimes called corporate cards) are used to pay for travel, entertainment, meals, and related costs. Travel cards are the staff member's responsibility. These cards allow the college or university to track expenses among all staff, which can help an institution to negotiate discounts with hotels and airlines. These cards can also minimize the need both for the institution to issue cash advances and for staff to extend their personal credit to conduct official business. Travel cards are issued by all the major card brands, and many programs include sophisticated expense management and reporting systems as well as cardholder benefits.

The second type of commercial card is a purchasing card, sometimes called a procurement card. Faculty and staff use purchasing cards to pay for supplies and other departmental purchases. These cards help institutions reduce costs by eliminating the need for low-value purchase orders, thereby reducing administrative costs (e.g., purchase order preparation, check writing, mailing) significantly. It costs most institutions more than $100 to issue a purchase order, an amount that can exceed the cost of the item purchased. For low value purchases (under $2,500), therefore, purchasing cards are a cost-effective way to manage spending. Purchasing professionals also use purchasing cards to make larger and more frequent purchases. Such cards will have much higher limits.

Purchasing cards are issued in the name of the cardholder (a person or a department), and while they may be used for travel, they are unlike travel cards in that the liability rests with the college or university. Purchasing cards are offered by all major card brands, and there is a wide range of manual and automated reporting and expense tracking systems available from issuers as well as third-party software companies. A variety of limits can be put on each card, including restricting card use to certain merchant categories, limiting the transaction size, and restricting total spending per accounting period.

Purchasing cards are among the fastest growing segments of the payment card industry. Not all of an institution's suppliers are likely to accept payment cards today, but the number of suppliers that do accept them is growing rapidly. Suppliers find that accepting institutions' purchasing cards means reducing their invoicing, credit authorization, and check processing costs. Purchasing cards can also reduce a supplier's float substantially depending on how quickly the institution pays. More suppliers are finding that card acceptance is a key element in their electronic commerce strategy.

Changes in the Cash Flow Environment

Significant changes have taken place over the last few years in the collection of operating cash. Most student-loan payments transitioned to EFT payments from the cumbersome paper system. Federal, state, and local appropriations are made electronically either by a FedWire, or by EDI payment through the ACH network. The use of credit and/or debit (plastic) cards has steadily grown in colleges and universities that have large part-time or nontraditional student programs. Card usage will continue to grow due to the consumer acceptance of replacing checks with some type of card.

On the disbursement side, the transition away from paper began in the 1970s and is continuing into the new millennium. Breaking the institution's disbursements into two categories, payroll and payables, brings to light interesting changes. Today, most payroll transactions are disbursed using the direct deposit electronic payment method. Student payroll has been historically paper generated; however, some institutions are directly depositing these payments to the bank associated with a student "one-card" system, or any bank that the student may choose, which would eliminate the paper. In payables, the transition has been more recent. Small dollar payments represent the majority of volume in payables. Campuses are exploring or implementing the use of purchasing cards. The end result will be one payment for all monthly small dollar payments by the institution while the staff utilizes individual cards for their purchases. Putting together the direct deposit of payroll, a one-card student payroll system and a purchasing card program, a college or university can conceivably move 80 percent of disbursement transactions away from paper processes (figure 08-02).

Figure 08-02

Treasury Tools Used

Cash Flows(1)	% of Inflows	Treasury Tools Used
Federal Appropriation	23	EDI, PC workstation, GL interface, current report via Web
Grants	15	ACH Credit, PC workstation current report via Web
Student Loans	10	FedWire, ACH credit, interface to bursar, deposit reconcilement
Tuition & Fees	27	Lockbox, branch bank support, card acceptance, interactive voice response (IVR), payment module over Web, tuition payment plans, pre-authorized debits
Auxiliary	25	Book transfer, GL interface
	% of Outflows	
Payroll, Staff	50	Maximize Direct Deposit of Payroll (DDP), outsource payroll provider
Payroll, Students	20	Student smart cards, ACH-DDP, paper disbursements
Small $ Purchases	10	Purchasing cards, purchase malls via Web
Large $ Purchases	20	EDI, controlled disbursement, Positive Pay

COLLECTIONS

A collection system should have four objectives:

- to collect receivables in a cost-effective manner;
- to convert collections into available funds as rapidly as possible;
- to identify surplus cash on a daily basis and move it into income-generating investments; and
- to update receivables data quickly and accurately.

An examination of the collection process should begin with identifying all the sources of cash flows into the institution and the typical collection methods used by the college or university. Payments are usually received:

- over-the-counter at various departments, such as the bursar's office, the bookstore, and the dining areas;
- on the Web;

- by mail to the college or university or directly to the institution's bank (lockbox);

- using touchtone technology; or

- electronically contacting the college or university's bank, as initiated by the institution or preauthorized by the payor.

Payments may be in the form of cash, checks, electronic means such as wires, automated clearinghouse transfers, and payment cards. Tuition and fees represent the bulk of inflows for smaller institutions, with endowments, gifts, and bequests playing a lesser role. For larger institutions, the opposite is true, with endowments, gifts, and corporate and governmental research grants making up a larger portion of inflows, and leaving tuition and fees to represent a smaller portion. Large endowment gifts, governmental appropriations, and research grants primarily should be directed to the university in the form of an ACH or wire transfer payment, while tuition and fees lend themselves to collection through lockbox, over the counter, by preauthorized payment, on the Web, or by touchtone phone initiation.

Federal Payments

Institutions receive federal payments from many sources. These may come in the form of contracts, grants, or student financial aid. Since the late 1980s the federal government has mandated that most federal payments come by ACH. The college or university's bank institution may or may not be able to forward all the remittance information to the institution. If the bank is unable to translate the payment-related data contained within the ACH file, it should be asked to contact the Federal Reserve. The Federal Reserve is offering FEDEDI software free of charge to financial institutions and service bureaus with a FedLine or Computer Interface customer. FEDEDI can be used to identify, report, and/or translate payment-related information data contained within ACH files. The job of the cash manager is to educate the areas on campus that receive these funds to notify the treasurer's office in advance of receipt. (This will facilitate the timely reporting and investing of cash receipts. "FEDEDI" is a pending trademark and "FedLine" is a registered trademark of the Federal Reserve.)

Lockboxes

A lockbox is a post office box opened in the name of the institution but accessed and serviced by the bank or remittance processor. A lockbox reduces mail float because remittances are mailed directly to central postal processing centers, bypassing the smaller, less efficient local post office and the institution's mailroom. Special zip codes are used, further speeding delivery to the bank. Typically, an institution receives mail once or, at most, twice a day, while the bank may receive lockbox mail 24 hours a day, seven days a week, with up to 24 pickups each day. Many processors receive the majority of the day's mail by 5:00 a.m. Check processing and collection time is lessened with the use of lockboxes because of highly sophisticated systems and round-the-clock operation. An institution, especially a larger one, may find it beneficial to have more than one lockbox site.

There are two types of lockboxes: wholesale and retail. Wholesale lockboxes are for institutions with moderate item volume and large dollar remittances while retail lockboxes are for institutions with large item volume, and those whose payments are accompanied by machine-readable invoices. The purpose of a retail lockbox is to help manage a high volume of activity and automatically update receivables information. Typically, service charges are higher for wholesale lockboxes than for retail lockboxes because the remittance processing for wholesale lockboxes is less automated and requires faster processing to meet availability deadlines. There is a third type of lockbox that combines the processing methods of both wholesale and retail lockboxes. This combination enables the benefits of both, incorporating the automated processing of the retail lockbox with the quality data capture of the wholesale lockbox.

A lockbox can contribute significantly to several of the objectives of a collection system. For example, a student sends a tuition payment with the tuition invoice to the institution's lockbox. Depending on the bank's lockbox service and the institution's volume of receipts, the processor clears the box several times daily, taking the receipts directly to its processing center, processing the checks, and placing them immediately into the collection system. Photocopies of the checks can be attached to remittance information (such as invoices and correspondence) and dispatched by the provider via courier to the institution. Increasingly, processors are utilizing imaging technology to provide invoice and/or check information to the institution.

If the processor captures invoice information from tuition bills (such as name of the student, Social Security number, semester being paid, and amount being paid), data may be transmitted electronically via personal computer (PC), tape, or data transmission to the institution's data processing system. Typically, this value-added option accelerates the posting of information for matriculation purposes and reduces the amount of internal processing at the institution for posting receivables.

A lockbox can optimize the availability of funds by accelerating the check clearance schedules and meeting availability deadlines set by the Federal Reserve Bank. In contrast, a typical 3:00 p.m. over-the-counter deposit at the local bank is not processed for availability purposes until later that evening, after the availability deadlines have passed. Additionally, in-house clerical expenses for processing remittances and preparing deposits are eliminated by a lockbox, and accounts receivable processing expenses can be reduced through simplified manual posting or eliminated through automatic update via electronic transmission of receivables information. The audit controls of a lockbox system are typically much more elaborate than those found in a bursar's office. The time required to deposit funds into the institution's account may be reduced by two to three days by shortening mail processing, remittance processing, and clearance time. In summary, a lockbox can reduce mail float, minimize remittance processing float, and improve check clearing or availability float.

Choosing a Lockbox Provider

Several issues must be addressed when selecting a lockbox service provider. First, not all processors have the same inter-city mail times—the time it takes an envelope to arrive in one city when mailed from another varies by post office/lockbox location. Independent cash management consulting firms gather and maintain such data. Most major providers will make these data available on request.

Second, availability schedules are very important. The lockbox bank should provide an aggressive schedule of availability when compared to competing banks. The efficiency of the clearance of funds is a significant added value.

Third, the quality of processing, level of customer service, information delivery capabilities, and overall technical facilities should be considered. The quality of processing can be measured by a ratio of errors, such as the number of errors per 10,000 items processed. The quality of customer service can be determined from past experience or references.

Fourth, price should be a consideration, particularly with a retail lockbox. The average value of checks processed should be sufficiently high to improve availability and reduce handling costs to offset the cost of the lockbox. Using a lockbox for low-dollar value items such as student loan payments is often not cost effective. If an institution uses low-cost student labor and a system that deposits over-the-counter checks the same day they are received, it may potentially nullify the availability advantages and the alleged labor savings of lockboxes. Some institutions use lockboxes primarily to save on in-house processing costs.

There are two components to a lockbox price: explicit bank charges, such as fixed monthly maintenance and variable per-item processing charges, and implicit bank charges, known as availability. The following example demonstrates these components.

An average semester tuition remittance is $5,000, and 15,000 students will use the lockbox service.

	Lockbox Processor A	Lockbox Processor B
Aggregate fixed monthly charges	$ 50.00	$ 50.00
Aggregate variable per-item charges*	$ 0.30	$ 0.65

*Includes item processing, photocopying, and daily courier.

On the surface, Processor A appears to offer a more cost-effective system. Preliminary calculations show that $10,500 can be saved each year by awarding the business to Processor A. (15,000 students multiplied by 2 semesters equals 30,000 remittances; $0.65 [Processor B's price] minus $0.30 [Processor A's price] equals $0.35 savings when utilizing Processor A. 30,000 multiplied by $0.35 equals $10,500 per year savings.) However, closer inspection indicates that Processor A accelerates collections by approximately two days while Processor B accelerates collections by three days. In other words, Processor B obtains available funds one day sooner than Proccesor A. Taking this information into consideration, the following savings can be found by using Processor B.

$ 5,000	Average remittance value
250	Business days per year
$ 20	The value of accelerating a single check's availability by one business day
× 5.0 %	Annual interest rate
$ 1.00	Additional interest income earned on a per-check basis due to the one day of accelerated funds availability
× 30,000	Remittances
$ 30,000	Total interest gain
– 10,500	Less incremental cost of the more sophisticated system
$ 19,500	Net total benefit of choosing Bank B

Processor B can accelerate collections faster than Processor A because it uses a primary post office rather than a secondary one, it picks up the mail around the clock rather than during business hours only, and it uses direct sends to move checks directly to distant drawee banks instead of clearing them through the Federal Reserve system, as does Processor A.

The previous example assumes 250 business days a year. Most providers provide payments six days a week and some provide it seven days a week. Therefore, the total net benefit in the example may be overstated.

Payment Plans

In order to accommodate student cash flow needs, many colleges and universities offer short-term payment plans. The plans can be managed internally or outsourced to a vendor, depending on the resources of the institution. To cover the costs of the payment plan, an organization can charge interest and/or fees for this service. The institution can choose any number of months for the payment plan. Payment plans offer the student convenience of payment by check, by money order using a payment coupon, by automatic deduction from student's or parent's bank account, or by credit card. Using payment plan vendors may improve service to your students and families, improve your cash flow, and reduce operating expense. Many payment plan vendors offer online service, whereby you have 24-hour access to all of your account information.

Preauthorized Debit

Preauthorized debit is a collection method used for regularly recurring, typically equal-amount payments within the ACH network. The PPD format is usually used for preauthorized debits. The payor approves the transfer of funds from the payor's bank to the payee's bank on predetermined dates. This collection system can be used for monthly tuition payments, room and board fees, student loan payments, student health plan insurance payments, association dues, computer equipment lease payments, and pledge gifts.

Internet Receipts

The use of the Internet to collect receipts allows universities to process receipts 24 hours a day, seven days a week. This is increasingly important as colleges and universities implement Web registration. Students who have a hold on registration because of delinquent payments can release the hold by making payment on the Web and continue the registration process. The institution will increase cash flow, reduce operating costs, and increase customer service. When outsourcing this service, issues to consider include security, reconcilement, form of payment, and if applicable, interface to mainframe systems.

In regard to Internet usage, the institution must create a policy relating to security, privacy, anonymity, and auditability. Technical areas that need to be addressed include campuswide directory services (privacy and appropriate use of resources), authentication (smart cards, digital certificates, and public and private key technology), payment methods, audit issues, user IDs, and certificate authorities.

International Collections

Colleges and universities increasingly are becoming competitive in recruiting international students in order to create a more global campus climate. However, this practice can create significant issues regarding collecting funds from foreign banks. For example, a prospective French student may send a tuition check drawn on her local bank account in the amount of 30,000 French francs. When the check is finally received, it must be sent back to France for collection and then converted to a United States dollar equivalent. There are numerous risks and costs associated with this procedure, for example:

- the process can take several weeks (lost investment opportunity cost);

- the U.S. dollar equivalent is not known until the item is actually collected (exchange rate fluctuation risk);

- the processing fee for such a remittance may cost the institution $50 (bank transaction cost);

- by the time the item is presented against the account in France, funds may no longer be available or the account may be closed (payment risk); and

- in less developed countries, the payment may not be convertible into U.S. dollars when it is presented because of a foreign currency exchange freeze (foreign exchange conversion risk).

These risks, costs, and time delays are experienced while the student has already enrolled and started classes. International electronic funds transfers are facilitated through SWIFT (Society for Worldwide Interbank Financial Communications) messages, CHIPS (Clearing House Interbank Payment System) settlements, and Tested Telex messages. Payments can be made from most large banks in any country.

The benefits of using electronic funds transfers for international transactions are that:

- funds are transferred and received in a more timely manner thereby accelerating availability;

- payments can be made in U.S. dollars, thereby eliminating exchange rate fluctuation risk;

- the processing fee for international electronic items is only a fraction of the cost of fees for international paper items; and

- stop payments and insufficient fund hassles (payment risk) are eliminated.

The benefits also include the elimination of mail float, reduced processing float, and fewer collection problems. Furthermore, electronic items cannot be "lost in the mail." Electronic transfer offers a reduction in bank processing fees, the potential to update receivables information automatically with the data that accompany the transfer of funds, and the reduction of manual reconciliation.

An additional tool that is becoming increasingly popular is the acceptance of credit cards for foreign transactions. While it does include costs, it is a fast and efficient method to collect international payments.

Concentration of Funds

In a concentration account system, widely distributed funds are gathered into one location and used to fund disbursement requirements. Excess funds can be swept into an investment vehicle to begin earning income rather than sitting idle in a number of different banks and accounts. The process begins when funds in the form of currency and checks are collected at multiple locations and deposited in multiple accounts in field banks. The funds from these relatively small-balance accounts are then transferred to one cash-concentration account.

The mechanisms for concentrating funds are electronic depository transfer checks (DTC), wire transfers, and zero balance accounts (ZBA). DTCs use the ACH mechanism to concentrate funds from field accounts. The electronic funds are usually available the following day. This method is generally used to concentrate recurring or small-dollar payments. Large-dollar or time-critical items are usually concentrated via FedWire to receive same-day availability.

A ZBA is a deposit and/or disbursement account that provides control of balance levels of multiple accounts in the same financial institution. Collection activities of individual schools, divisions, or locations are maintained at the local level, while aggregate cash investments and movement of funds remain closely controlled at the institutional treasury level. When a concentration account ("parent") and subsidiary zero balance ("child") depository accounts are established, balances in the subaccounts are maintained at zero. Daily transactions are posted at the end of each day.

A cash concentration system can be invaluable for institutions with geographically dispersed deposit locations, such as multiple campuses, separate operating units, state university systems, and bicoastal lockbox networks. When developing a concentration system, the treasury manager should examine the number of locations where cash or receivables are handled, the average dollar size of transactions, the availability of funds at the original deposit banks, and the administration needed to oversee the system.

DISBURSEMENTS

The two major types of disbursements in colleges and universities are payroll and vendor payments. As with collections, there are two mechanisms for disbursements: paper and electronic. The primary objective of the disbursement portion of a treasury management program is to reduce costs. This involves:

- timing cash disbursements to maximize discount benefits and avoid early payment;

- minimizing the cost of issuing and processing disbursements;

- knowing when large-dollar disbursements are actually going to clear, to minimize the cost of overdrafts and to retain management control of the disbursement function; and

- maintaining a satisfactory audit trail of payments.

Four disbursement issues warrant close management: the lost opportunity cost of excess funds that remain idle in a disbursement account; the penalty and interest costs of accidental overdrafts resulting from disbursements that exceed account balances; the transfer cost of moving funds into a disbursement account; and the opportunity cost of lost trade discounts. The treasury manager should be familiar with such terms of disbursement as:

- issuance date—the day on which a check is written and mailed;

- payment date—usually considered the postmark date on the envelope;

- funding date—the day funds are deposited to cover the disbursement; and

- presentment date—the day the disbursement, that is, the check, is presented to the institution's bank for payment.

There are usually three ways of funding paper disbursements: commercial demand accounts, zero balance accounts, and controlled disbursements. These differ in the timing and method of funding.

Commercial Demand Accounts

The basic disbursement account is a demand account, which requires immediate funding for all issued disbursement items. Usually the issuance and funding are simultaneous. A check is issued and mailed, and the recipient presents it for payment. The check is returned to the originating bank and then returned as paid to the payor. This process may take up to a week. If the account is funded at the time of issuance, sufficient funds are in the account to cover the presentment whenever it occurs. This type of account can also be "stagger funded," meaning that a series of funding actions are taken in anticipation that checks that were issued will clear on different days. Payroll accounts are a good example of the use of stagger funding: 20 percent may be funded on payday; 60 percent on the day after; and 20 percent two days after.

Zero Balance Accounts

Alternatively an automatic zero balance account (ZBA) transfer can be used to fund the disbursement account. This has the advantage of determining the precise date on which the funds will be deposited in the account. FedWire and ACH transfers can also be used to move funds into a disbursement account.

With ZBAs, separate bank accounts for each of several different institutional entities or disbursement needs can exist in a single bank without leaving any balance. Thus, forecasts are not required for each subaccount, but a forecast for the total funds required in the master account is made. Each evening the required funding for disbursement checks that have cleared that day in the subaccounts is covered or "zeroed out" by funds flowing from the master account.

Controlled Disbursements

Controlled disbursements provide daily notification of the exact dollar amount of disbursements that will be posted against an account that day. For example, at 9:00 a.m. the bank advises the institution that $50,000 is to be posted that day against the account. Thus, $50,000 is transferred, usually by ZBA or FedWire transfers, to cover the requirement. Therefore, no excess balances remain in the account. With a commercial demand account, where there can be multiple daily presentments against the account, the bank cannot provide notification in sufficient time for exact funding needs. In a controlled disbursement account, there are one or two presentments daily (early in the morning). The amount of the residual balance is known early each day so that excess funds can be put to work earning income. If the master account has insufficient funds to cover the checks presented in the controlled disbursement account, a short-term investment can be liquidated and funds transferred to cover the requirement. A line of credit may also be accessed to avoid the penalizing costs of overdrafts. An additional advantage of the controlled disbursement account is that the time and frustration of disbursement forecasting is avoided.

Many banks maintain controlled disbursement accounts for their customers in affiliated banks. With these banks, the controlled disbursement bank accounts are handled like ZBAs and the money is sent from the customer's bank to the affiliated bank automatically. This avoids the cost and labor of sending wires and/or ACH payments.

Generally, all institutions with annual disbursements in excess of $20 million can make effective use of a controlled disbursement account, as well as those that make daily investment and borrowing decisions. This system delays the funding of an account until the check is presented for payment and thus reduces excess balances in the account, optimizes investment opportunities by obtaining disbursement information early in the day, reduces overdraft charges due to inaccurate cash forecasting, and may extend the disbursement float.

The treasury manager should evaluate banking costs, notification time, and service quality. Notification time is important, because the earlier the bank notifies the customer, the sooner the customer knows the funding portion for early-in-the-day investing opportunities. Controlled disbursement accounts generally have higher fees than commercial demand accounts, because of the technology used.

Account Reconciliation

Many banks provide information for managing and reconciling high-volume accounts efficiently and accurately. In a simple version (partial reconciliation), the bank provides the date and the amount of all checks paid in check-numbered sequence. This information may be reported in paper format or electronically. Electronic reporting enables automatic reconciliation of checking accounts by the institution.

Full reconciliation is the reporting of canceled and stopped checks, as well as paid items or paid and outstanding items of regular and controlled disbursement accounts, in various formats. The college or university provides the bank with a list of issued-check information (i.e., the check numbers issued, the date each check was issued, and the dollar amount of each check). The bank merges this information with its data regarding the date paid and amount paid for each check and delivers a fully reconciled statement of the account at the end or each month.

Banks may offer flexible statement cut-off dates to meet monthly, quarterly, and fiscal-year reporting needs. With an account reconciliation system, a college or university can issue online stop payments from its own PC and thus reduce stop-payment costs. There is immediate confirmation of the stop payment and a new check can be issued at once. The most important benefit in establishing an account reconciliation system is the significant reduction in clerical costs.

Check Truncation

Some banks offer check-safekeeping options (check truncation), whereby the bank provides a report whether via paper, or electronically through the Internet (or via CD) with copies of paid checks, eliminating the need to store canceled paper checks. At the bank, mail, delivery, clerical costs, and costs associated with manually sorting checks are eliminated; therefore, bank fees are reduced.

Electronic Disbursements

Electronic mechanisms for disbursements are used to automate disbursement processing and reduce clerical costs.

Preauthorized credits are a disbursement vehicle for recurring payments to employees, vendors, and others via the ACH system, including payroll, travel and expense reimbursements, annuity and pension payments, and intra-institutional transfers. Typical users are institutions with a high volume of recurring payments to a stable payee base, such as employees and pensioners. The most common application is direct deposit of payroll through PPD (prearranged payments or deposits).

The college or university generates a tape or transmission of payroll transactions that contains both the payor's and payee's accounts. The tape or transmission is received by the payroll bank, which transmits the data through the ACH system for distribution to the various payee banks. The institution's account is debited and a credit is made to the payee's account on the payroll date. Savings are achieved in the payroll department because of fewer lost checks, elimination of check-handling costs, and reduction of the cost for printing and storing checks. Bank fees are appreciably less for ACH credits than for check clearing. The substantial costs associated with placing stops on checks are eliminated, and the bank account reconciliation operation is simplified. Benefits for the institution are in the reduction of costs required in preparing and issuing paper payments, elimination of the risk of lost and stolen checks, increased predictability of cash flow, and reduced check handling and clearance costs. Benefits for the payee are convenience and the security of deposits.

Cash concentration and disbursement (CCD) is the transmission of batched electronic payments between a college or university and institutional or corporate receivers. This format is usually used for the payment of pension and health premiums, loans, and investment fees. Payments may be initiated from PC software packages or mainframe ACH systems. CCD has grown in popularity in recent years because of its flexible nature and ease of use.

Personal Computers

PCs are increasingly being used for transaction initiation, performing the following functions:

- ACH transaction—debits and credits;
- online stop payments;
- domestic wire transfers—repetitive and nonrepetitive;
- international wire transfers;
- international foreign exchange drafts; and
- Internet access.

Generally, significant savings in bank service charges can be realized by initiating these transactions on a PC, as compared to manual or telephone initiation. Furthermore, they can be initiated at anytime.

Evaluating a Disbursement System

The treasury manager must consider issues such as centralized versus decentralized disbursement and trade-offs between lengthening the disbursement float and maintaining good vendor relations when evaluating a disbursement system. Treasury management systems work most effectively in a centralized operation. However, a decentralized operation can be made more efficient if all accounts are centralized in one bank, with ZBAs available to each decentralized unit (either geographically or organizationally). If a disbursement system is inefficient and payments are delayed, vendors will become dissatisfied and may institute tighter credit standards for the institution by requiring cash on delivery (COD), payment before delivery (PBD), or interest payment for delayed payments.

Check Fraud

Since the late 1980s, check fraud has become a major issue in college business offices and a problem that all campuses need to address. Many campus disbursement offices ignore the risks of check fraud due to common misconceptions—"it's not a problem on our campus, our financial systems are state of the art, problems only occur in urban areas, and potential fraud losses are minimal." The reality of this epidemic is that check fraud is not limited to large city campuses and that losses can be substantial. Colleges and universities that do not build the appropriate systems to prevent fraud, or are not careful in the oversight of disbursements, become primary targets of the professional check rings that are responsible for the majority of forged checks.

The facts of fraud are that:

- more than 2,000 fraudulent checks are deposited daily;
- fraud is primarily policed by local authorities and federal law enforcement;
- $12 billion was lost to check fraud in 1998;
- recent changes to the Availability Acts make it easier to steal;
- forgery equipment costs only a few thousand dollars; and
- fraud techniques are well publicized nationally.

The types of theft that a college or university can anticipate range from a check stolen from inventory to an image scanned reproduction of check stock. Both types of check fraud are equally dangerous, and equally easy to complete. A number of entities handle a fraudulent check and could share in the liability. The parties include the deposit bank, the presentment bank, the check printers, and the college or university. Liability in the cases of loss is not always clear. The applicable law is under the Uniform Commercial Code, Articles 3 and 4. The business office has the responsibility to use prudent methods in disbursing payments and reconciling its accounts. Financial institutions are required to follow reasonable commercial standards and utilize "ordinary care" in processing checks. Liability is determined by the concept of comparative negligence, which can allocate liability based on the extent that each party's failure contributed to the loss. Overall, check forgery cases are determined on a case-by-case basis, and loss can be allocated to each party involved.

Fraud Prevention Techniques and Treasury Management Tools

A business office is only able to minimize the chance of fraud, never completely eliminate the chance of fraud. The primary goal is to use internal processes and external tools that better control how a campus disburses payments. Establishing tight controls over storage and the distribution of check stock is essential—as is maintaining updated and limited authorizations to who can disburse funds, and who can reconcile payment accounts. Establish and monitor internal processes (dual party signatures, periodic inventory of checks, timely reconcilement, job rotation, controlled vendor lists, etc.). Also establish an effective procedure for identifying a fraudulent check and reporting the crime to the appropriate internal officers and external authorities. (See What to Do in Case of Check Fraud at the end of this chapter.) The disbursement office needs to identify external products and tools that can assist in preventing fraud. This includes check security features such as prenumbered check stock, void pantographs, safety paper, microprinting, artificial watermarks, and warning bands. These products can be obtained from commercial check printers. Banks offer several cash management services for detecting and preventing unauthorized payments. Daily positive pay is an automated check matching service where the college or university sends a check issuance file to the bank every day. The bank matches that information to the checks that are being presented for payment to that account. If a check being presented for payment does not match the issuance information, the college or university is contacted to determine the check's authenticity. Reverse positive pay uses the same matching capability, but the college or university maintains the information database and the bank sends daily information to match presentments with issuance. Stale date control can be added to part of a positive pay-reconcilement program that automatically returns checks after a predetermined date. Positive pay and reverse positive pay are offered by most treasury management service providers.

Alternatives to Paper Disbursements

Campus business officers have moved away from paper disbursement mechanisms in order to gain efficiencies and further minimize fraud. Specifically, colleges and universities are utilizing electronic payment more for large dollar, low volume payables and for payroll payments. Electronic payments allow campus business offices to reduce their exposure to check fraud by reducing the number of checks they issue. Payments are facilitated through electronic commerce (EC) which includes Electronic Data Interchange (EDI). EC is the exchange of business information from one organization to another in an electronic format. The range of electronic commerce goes from totally unstructured messages, such as facsimile (fax) transmissions or E-mail, to highly structured messages, such as EDI. This type of payment provides a vehicle for electronic movement of business data in a standard format from one organization's application system (such as the purchasing system or vendor payable system) to an outside organization's application system. It allows the sender and the receiver to generate and accept business and payment data without the need to re-enter information into each system application. To utilize EDI, the institution and its "trading partners" must agree on a specific format and structure for exchanging data and payment. Common EDI standards have evolved and are maintained and coordinated by the Accredited Standards Committee (ASC) of the American National Standards Institute (ANSI). ACS X12 was formed to develop general EDI standards that could be used in a variety of industries. Educational institutions utilize EDI standards when accepting student loan payments from lenders, establishing trading partner relationships with suppliers, or for healthcare related invoices (for universities that are associated with a hospital). The objective of EDI is to reduce the manual re-entry of large amounts of data in payment of large dollar transactions while reducing the transaction costs.

Educational institutions are also moving away from paper transactions in the processing of low dollar, high volume payments. An effective tool for this is a purchasing card system. Many colleges and universities are implementing or utilizing purchasing card systems for supplies, equipment purchases, or service contracts. The motivations to move to a card-based system include (1) cost savings by eliminating, or greatly reducing, a manual, paper driven purchase-order system; (2) improved control over expenditures by applying spending parameters prior to purchases being made; and (3) improved reporting capability being directly downloaded to the institution's financial applications. By implementing a purchasing card system, the organization distributes precoded cards to staff members who purchase goods on behalf of the organization. The staff person is able to buy goods or services at allowed suppliers and pay for the purchase with the card. Individual cards are embedded with certain controls including spending limits, blocked access to specific categories of merchants, limited single transaction amounts, and restricted access to cash. Detailed purchasing reports can be sent electronically directly into the institution's financial application in order to track and monitor these low dollar, high volume transactions on a timely basis. Most purchasing card systems utilize the Visa, MasterCard, or American Express networks. Programs are offered by larger treasury management providers that have invested in commercial card platforms and enhanced reporting capabilities.

INFORMATION REPORTING SERVICES

Account Analysis Statements

Account analysis statements list the average daily ledger, average daily collected balances, and all account activity, generally on a monthly basis. An account analysis statement allows the cash manager to track funding positions during the month and to know how cash is working. An account analysis statement can be provided through either paper reports or electronic transmissions. This statement represents an invoice, because it recaps the individual services being provided by the bank and details the amount and fee for each transaction. In other words, the account analysis statement also functions as the banking bill. Like all bills, it must be reviewed for invoicing errors before payment. This type of reporting is important because it allows the treasury manager to track banking activity and balance positions over the course of the year, resulting in better analysis and forecasting on a month-to-month basis. It also allows the treasury manager to monitor the bank's service fees.

PC reporting. A basic office computer with specialized software can provide the treasury manager with up-to-date information to make accurate funding and investment decisions. Banks have the capability of providing balance reporting and transaction information on both a previous-day basis and current-day basis for debits and credits. This reporting allows the treasury manager to manage the components of the cash management equation in a timely fashion. It provides the beginning balance, information on incoming credits on a current-day basis, and notification of disbursement needs. Many colleges and universities receive account balance information by a telephone call from the financial institution or a direct PC link to their bank account. The PC link has become the more popular option as the cost of computer hardware continues to decline.

Treasury workstations. In the past, only large universities used treasury workstations. Now even small-to-medium-sized universities can benefit from using them. Treasury workstations allow for the daily collecting or polling of bank information to determine cash positions, verify bank activity, and initiate financial transactions. They allow you to poll banks and have balances waiting when you arrive each morning. A general ledger interface will save treasury staff time and eliminate errors associated with manually entering the data. The open architecture of certain treasury workstations allows both treasury and accounting to gather and manipulate data simultaneously. While bank reporting packages (via PC) may cost less, they are weaker at handling debt, investment, and risk management activities. If you use only one bank and are not involved in complex debt, investment, international, or risk management activities, then bank-provided software might be sufficient. The biggest advantage to using a treasury workstation may be getting into a database environment. Databases allow much better manipulation of data than do spreadsheets, and the options for analysis alone may justify this type of system. The forecasting, trend analysis, and relationship management options are enhanced using a treasury workstation.

Web access. Some financial institutions are moving from providing bank software to handle balance reporting, PC ACH, wire transfer, and stop payment services to providing these services through the Web. This allows more accessibility on a broader network and the ability for the banks to upgrade systems without the cost of replacing software. Users are allowed to view information based on their user ID and password. Transacting business on an "open" highway adds concerns regarding proprietary information and secured transactions. Web-based financial products are new to the treasury area and require security parameters. Detailed security levels are discussed in the E-commerce section. Overall, using the right provider in a secure environment allows a treasury manager to transact business over the Web easily.

SHORT–TERM INVESTMENTS

In the simpler world of the 1950s and early 1960s, institutions often held their cash in non-interest-bearing demand deposits to "pay for a variety of banking services" via compensating balances. However, as interest rates began to rise in the early 1970s, the opportunity cost of holding excess cash in non-interest-bearing accounts became extremely expensive. The effectiveness of investing cash balances became a critical component in an institution's treasury system.

As recently as 10 years ago, Treasury bills, federal agency discount notes, bank certificates of deposit, commercial paper, and banker acceptances comprised the range of the investment products for short-term liquidity funds. Today, the issuance of fixed- and floating-rate asset-backed and mortgage-backed products, combined with the expansion of the interest rate swaps market and the issuance of derivative agency products, has created a new breed of more complicated investment vehicles. Similarly, technological advancements in reducing float, implementing ZBA/auto sweep accounts, and utilizing the Internet to make wire and ACH transfers into and out of selected types of investment vehicles, have fueled the need to take a more active role in the management of an educational institution's operating capital. Accordingly, the simple early 1970s investment strategy of laddering CDs or a series of U.S. Treasuries has given way to more complex yield-enhanced investment opportunities. Although money market funds are widespread investment vehicles today, their birth took place in the 1970s. Moreover, money market accounts did not become household names until the double-digit inflation scare of the late 1970s and the early 1980s, when short-term U.S. interest rates skyrocketed to more than 20 percent.

Why Colleges and Universities Need to Hold Short-Term Investments

The primary reason that many colleges need to hold short-term investments is to maintain reserve liquidity. The cash flows for educational institutions are quite unique. The majority of the inflows are centered around tuition payments early in the fall and spring semesters as well as a stream of loan reimbursements from federal and/or state entities. In contrast, expenses are normally reasonably balanced during the school calendar year, with a slightly higher level of disbursement around the end of the month (payrolls and interest payments). Debt issuance for building projects can throw another wrinkle in the cash flow patterns of an educational institution. A portfolio of short-term investments can help to smooth the peaks and troughs associated with working capital imbalances.

Historically, an educational institution conducts its short-term investment activity in a manner that will provide enhanced liquidity, with returns that exceed the performance of standard bank sweep accounts in a fashion that preserves capital by maintaining a stable $1 par value price. Entities with large working capital pools that dramatically exceed what is required for the management of day-to-day operations may maintain several layers of liquidity protection. Accordingly, a portion of an educational institution's working capital can often be managed with a longer-term focus that may even mirror an endowment allocation structure.

The Role of Treasury

Each individual institution has allocated resources to oversee cash investments. The amount of resources varies from institution to institution. The first role of treasury is to determine the appropriate level of funds to invest, then choose investment alternatives that are manageable with those resources. The overall objectives of investing operating cash balances are, in order of priority: safety, liquidity, and optimal return. Overseeing these objectives, the institution needs to develop a program that includes high-grade investments, and the liquidity to match the cash-flow cycles of the organization.

In determining the appropriate vehicles, the treasury officers may want to analyze a cash investment history of the institution. This analysis is simply a review of periodic cash and operating balances over a several year period. By mapping out the levels of cash held by the organization, the officers can determine the level of cash fluctuation and the amount of cash that has generally been maintained in the institution's accounts. Any cash analysis needs to include all bank accounts, any bank investment accounts, all cash securities held by the institution, and any cash investment vehicles. Figure 08-03 is an example of a cash investment history, which shows this university's cash levels ranging from a low of $10 million to a high of $80 million and depicting seasonal fluctuations. The university can use this information to determine the appropriate vehicles, length of investments, and allocation of cash investments.

Most colleges and universities have a number of options in where to invest cash. Over the past 30 years, the money market has grown from a limited number of traded securities to a significant part of the capital markets. Money funds alone have grown from $0 in 1972 to over $1 trillion in 1997. In 1998, it was estimated that within the education industry there was approximately $64 billion available for investment from operating working capital and endowment cash. The treasury officer now has a complex menu of choices that will match different institutional investment goals. A detailed synopsis of the individual cash-investment security types is included later in this section.

The appropriate investment program is determined by the resources available to oversee the investments, the levels of operating cash invested, and the risk tolerance of the investment opportunities. These include bank commercial products, bank investment products, pooled investment vehicles, separate investment management accounts, and internal management programs.

Figure 08-03

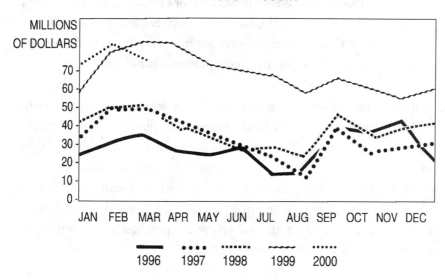

CUBA University
Cash Average Daily Balance
1996–Present

Demand Accounts—Earnings Credit

Most bank cash management providers offer an earnings credit rate on balances maintained in a commercial account. The earnings credit is a proprietary rate determined by the financial institution. The rate is given at the end of the month and is outlined on the monthly analysis statement. There are no underlying investments associated with the earnings credit rate. It is more a pricing decision for the financial institution. The rate is applied to 90 percent of the balances in commercial accounts and can only be used to offset monthly bank charges. Although earnings credit is not based on an investment, it should be analyzed as if it were an investment. Cash funds left in commercial accounts have an associated opportunity cost since they were not invested in more effective vehicles, and 10 percent of the "investment" earns nothing at all.

Sweep Accounts

A commercial bank sweep account is a service that automatically links a commercial bank depository account with an investment product and adjusts the bank account balances to a targeted level by transferring funds to or from the investment vehicle as it is needed, without direct human intervention. In 1991, about $17 billion was held in bank sweep accounts. In contrast, by 1996, more than $110 billion was invested through commercial bank sweep products. Although bank sweep accounts are relatively convenient to set up and easy to use, they are often a very expensive money management method for operating working capital. In 1996, it was estimated that the banking community earned total annual revenues of $1.3 billion from these sweeps, as revenues from fees and spreads averaged more than 100 basis points. That hundred basis points in bank earnings represents lost income to the college or university.

Money market mutual fund sweeps are the fastest growing category of sweep accounts. In 1991, just $2 billion in bank sweeps were placed in money market mutual funds. In contrast, by 1996 this figure had swelled to more than $26 billion. Overall, "sweep account" is a generic term for a type of bank investment product. The individual products vary dramatically in functionality, characteristics, and expense. The treasury manager needs to fully understand the underlying investments and the structure of the sweep being purchased, as well as the expenses that are netted from the investment return.

Money Market Mutual Funds (2a-7 products)

Several educational institutions maintain a portion of their working capital liquidity in money market funds that are defined as Rule 2a-7 funds. Money market funds have several unique investment parameters. These portfolios must maintain a dollar-weighted average portfolio maturity that is 90 days or less. Moreover, the maximum maturity of any single investment is 397 days (13 months). These funds strive to maintain a $1 par value for pricing. For the purpose of calculating a money market fund's net asset value, individual securities are valued by the amortized method of valuation from time of purchase, regardless of the impact of interest rate changes on the market value of the actual investment instrument. Thus money market funds do not "mark to market" the securities in their portfolio. However, if an individual security is sold prior to maturity, then a capital gain or loss adjustment is made to the portfolio. Historically, in order to attempt to hold to the $1 par value pricing, most money funds invest in high quality fixed-income instruments. One misconception of a money fund is that the $1 par value pricing is a guarantee. If the underlying investments of a fund change in value dramatically, the $1 par value can be lowered ("breaking a dollar"). Therefore, using a money fund requires the treasury manager to understand the fund's guidelines, structure, and underlying portfolio.

Commingled Vehicles

Like the 2a-7 funds, a commingled vehicle is an actively managed investment account by one or more investment managers. They differ from the 2a-7 funds in their investment characteristics because they are not limited in average maturity and security selection. The potentially longer weighted average maturity may allow these funds to offer higher returns than the 2a-7 products, but may also change the risk profile of the investment. Although the longer maturity and lesser limitations on security selection allow for more diversified investing, the institution's oversight is heightened due to these funds' ability to invest in more complex securities. Most commingled investment vehicles are either registered SEC mutual funds or common trust accounts. They may have fluctuating unit values, or daily pricing, and each has specific or unique investment goals. Most colleges and universities utilize a commingled vehicle; however, treasury managers need to be familiar with the investment guidelines and maintain confidence in the investment manager.

Separate Investment Accounts

Educational institutions often hire professional money managers to invest cash assets. Segregated account management provides an educational institution with a direct security-specific portfolio, whereby every trade executed has the specific account listed. This approach could increase management costs or limit the ability to invest in longer-dated money market products. Educational institutions with segregated accounts will have to maintain and pay for custodial and/or trustee relationships. Direct "ownership" of security positions may offer a positive level of comfort; however, segregated accounts can suffer from a reduction in certain economies of scale and portfolio diversification that would be available in a commingled management plan. If the day-to-day change in cash assets is volatile, these entities often have liquidation and reinvestment problems.

Internally Managed Investment Accounts

Thirty years ago, internally managed cash accounts were prevalent in educational institutions, and the majority of colleges and universities dedicated enough resources to manage and to trade these accounts. At that time, cash investments were limited to Treasury and Treasury-like securities. The money markets are significantly more complex now, and many more resources are required to manage a cash portfolio. Colleges and universities that do choose to manage their cash internally need to maintain a custodian trust relationship to hold all the securities, and to employ staff that can account for the portfolio daily and oversee trading activity during the day. Because of the complexity of the money markets, the internal staff resembles an investment management staff that is knowledgeable of the sectors, securities, and options. The goal of this type of program is to shift more control over the direction and risk of its cash portfolio to the institution. Internally managed programs should follow detailed investment guidelines approved by the institution's board and have the ability to monitor the portfolio movements through sophisticated analytical systems on an intra-day basis. Unfortunately, these programs are extremely expensive to maintain once all transaction costs and the costs of the resources dedicated are taken into consideration.

Where Higher Education Institutions Go from Here

As discussed earlier, the fixed-income market has experienced some very dramatic improvements over the last 20 to 30 years. The transition to money market accounts and money market mutual funds in the 1970s seemed to pave the way for the explosion in the mortgage-backed, asset-backed, and floating-rate note markets of the 1980s and 1990s. The attached glossary of investment products is a comprehensive review of the different investment security types within the money markets. The investments available for an educational institution's working capital and endowment cash have become much more sophisticated, and the investors in these products need to have the tools and systems to evaluate, monitor, and price these securities. The increased complexity of the products has fueled an expansion in the professional management of working capital. In many cases, educational institutions can use a commingling of assets with other entities to take advantage of the economies of scale offered by professional money managers.

SUMMARY

The roles of the treasury and the treasury manager continue to evolve. Not too many years ago, cash management and investment duties were viewed as being accounting functions. Today it is recognized that, in an ideal situation, the treasury function should be set up as a separate group with their own goals and objectives. It is also clear that treasury staff need different skills from those required in the accounting areas. The treasury function, whether as a stand-alone unit or a specific set of duties and objectives assigned to employees within the business office, plays an important role in achieving and maintaining the financial health of a college or university.

NOTES

1. Treasury Management, previously titled Cash Management, refers to the management of receivables, purchasing, the management of working capital, and working with providers outside of banks. At the majority of higher education institutions, the term *treasury management* is understood also to include endowment and debt management whereas in this chapter, treasury management follows the financial services industry's usage and excludes endowment and debt management.

REFERENCES AND RESOURCES

E-Commerce Sources and Suggested Readings

Klemow, Jason. "Credit Card Transactions Via the Internet," *TMA Journal*, January/February 1999.

President's Management Council's Electronic Processes Initiatives Committee. *Electronic Commerce for Buyers and Sellers.* March 1998 policyworks.gov/epic.

Robinson, Brian. "Attention, Shoppers—Will States Flock to E-Malls?" Civic.com December 1998.

Schooch, William J. "Electronic Purchasing on Every Desktop," *TMA Journal*. May/June 1998.

Shih, C., et al. *Business-to-Business Web Commerce Applications,* Gartner Group, Strategic Analysis Report, August 1998.

U.S. Department of Commerce Secretariat on Electronic Commerce. *The Emerging Digital Economy,* www.e-commerce.gov.

U.S. Office of Management and Budget. *An Assessment of Current Electronic Commerce Activity in Procurement,* March 1998.

Reference Books for Investment Products

Fabozzi, Frank J., and Pollack, Irving M. *The Handbook of Fixed Income Securities.* Homewood, IL: Dow Jones-Irwin, 1987.

Stigum, Marcia, and Robinson, Franklin L. *Money Market & Bond Calculations.* Homewood, IL: Richard D. Irwin, 1996.

Stigum, Marcia. *The Money Market.* Homewood, IL: Dow Jones-Irwin, 1983.

Fabozzi, Frank J. *The Handbook of Mortgage-Backed Securities.* Chicago, IL: Probus Publishing Company, 1988.

Internet Resources

Non-Bank Sites on the World Wide Web

Site Name	Web Address (URL)
Alterna Treasury Management	www.alterna.com/treasury.htm
Bob Browining's Guide to Treasury Technology	www.textor.com/markets/guide
Commerce Net	www.commerce-net
Corporate Finance Network	corpfinet.com
Dun & Bradstreet	www.dbisna.com
Finance.Wat.ch	Finance.Wat.ch
FINWEB	www.finweb.com
KPMG	us.kpmg.com/fs/home.html
Phoenix-Hecht	www.phoenixhecht.com
PricewaterhouseCoopers	www.colybrand.com/industry/finserv/garpsumm.html
Thompson Bank Watch	www.tfn.com/bankwatch
The Treasury Institute for Higher Education	www.treasuryinstitute.org
The Treasury Management Pages	www.mcs.com/-tryhardz/tmp22.html
XRT, Inc.	www.xrt.com

Investment Sites

Commonfund	www.commonfund.org
Dow Jones Indexes	indexes.dowjones.com
Investment News	www.investmentnews.com
Mobius Group, Inc.	www.mobiusg.com
Money Market Directories, Inc.	www.mmdaccess.com
Nelson's Investment Management Network	www.nelnet.com

Association Sites

American Bankers Association (ABA)	aba.com

American Bankruptcy Institute . . . . abiworld.org

American Institute of Certified
Public Accountants (AICPA) . . . . www.aicpa.org/index.html

American National Standards Institute (ANSI) . . . . . . www.ansi.org/home.html

Association for Financial Professionals . . . . www.afp-online.org

Association for Investment Management and Research (AIMR) . . Http://aimr.com

Bank Administration Institution (BAI) . . . . bai.org

Data Interchange Standard Association (DISA) . . . . www.disa.org

EDIBANX . . . . www.edibanx.com

Financial Accounting Standards Board . . . . www.Rutgers.edu/Accounting/
raw/fasb/

Financial Services Technology Consortium . . . . www.fstc.org

International Organization for Standardization . . . . www.iso.ch

National Association of College and
University Business Officers (NACUBO) . . . . www.nacubo.org

National Association of Credit Managers (NACM) . . . . www.nacm.org

National Association of Insurance Commissioners (NAIC) . . . . . . www.naic.org

National Association of Purchasing Managers (NAPM) www.napm.org/napm.html

National Automated Clearing
House Association (NACHA) . . . . www.nacha.org/index.htm

National Investor Relations Institute (NIRI) . . . . www.niri.org

Risk and Insurance Management Society (RIMS) . . . . www.rims.org

Treasury Management Association . . . . www.tma-net.org

Treasury Management Association
of Canada (TMAC) . . . . www.tmac.ca/index.htm1#about

UN/EDIFACT . . . . www.premenos.com/unedifact

Government Sites

Federal Deposit Insurance Corp. (FDIC) . . . . fdic.gov/index.html

Federal Reserve Board of Governors . . . . www.bog.frb.fed.us

FedWorld . . . . www.fedworld.gov

General Accounting Office (GAO) . . . . www.gao.gov

GPO Gate (U.S. Govt. Printing Office) . . . . ssdc.ucsd.edu/gpo

Office of the Comptroller of the Currency (OCC) . . . . www.occ.treas.gov

Securities & Exchange Commission (EDGAR) . . . . . www.sec.gov/edgarhp.htm

U.S. Department of Commerce . . . . www.stat-usa.gov

U.S. Department of Treasury . . . . www.ustreas.gov/treasury

U.S. Library of Congress . . . . www.loc.gov

Financial and Economic Development

Barron's . . . . www.barrons.com/corp link center/index.html

Bloomberg Personal . . . . www.bloomberg.com

CNN Financial News . . . . cnnfn.com/index.html

The Economist . . . . www.economist.com

Financial Times . . . . www.ft.com

International Treasurer . . . . www.intltreasurer.com

New York Times on the Web . . . . www.nytimes.com

Wall Street Journal Personal Edition . . . . bis.dowjones.com/pj.html

Glossary of Investment Products

Asset-Backed Securities (ABS)   Asset-backed securities are short-term investments that contain stable or certain cash flows that are, for example, backed by the payment streams from a variety of loans, leases, or credit card receivables. The first public offering of a security backed by an auto receivable was in 1985, while the first credit card receivable was floated in 1987. Over the last 12 years the ABS market has been the fastest growing segment of the short-end of the fixed income market. By 1998, total asset-backed issuance had surged to $280 billion.

The explosion of the use of the asset backed market reflects in part the positive benefits available via the use of secured financing to lower funding costs and raise capital, especially in the consumer debt market. The overwhelming majority of asset-backed issues are AAA- or AA-rated due to the strong quality of the underlying collateral, the integrity of the payment structure, and the amount of additional credit support.

Asset-backed securities also provide a greater diversification than mortgage-backed securities due to the smaller loan balances and the greater number of consumer receivables. Asset-backed securities have become a major component of short-duration portfolios due to their short average life, high credit quality, and substantial yield enhancement above equivalent maturity U.S. Treasuries.

Bankers' Acceptances   Bankers' acceptances (BAs) are somewhat similar to bank commercial paper in that they are short-term, non-interest-bearing notes that are sold at a discount and redeemed by the accepting bank at full face value at maturity. However, BAs have a major technical difference. A commercial paper transaction is guaranteed by the issuing entity. Bankers' acceptances provide added security in that they are backed by the underlying goods or products that are financed. For the most part, BAs are issued as a byproduct of a foreign trade transaction and incorporate the use of a letter of credit issued against a specific set of imported goods. The big banks through which bankers' acceptances are originated generally sell a portion of these acceptances into the market.

Certificates of Deposit   A certificate of deposit (CD) is a certificate issued by a bank that shows a specific amount of money has been deposited at the issuing institution. CDs are issued by banks to access funds for their finance and lending activities. The CD bears a specific maturity date, interest rate, and denomination. CDs issued in amounts up to $100,000 are insured by the Federal Deposit Insurance Corporation (FDIC). A CD may be issued in either a negotiable or nonnegotiable form. Negotiable CDs provide the investor with the opportunity to sell the CD in the open market prior to the maturity date.

   CD yields are quoted on an interest-bearing basis, versus the discounted basis used for Treasury bills, commercial paper, and bankers' acceptances. A CD with a maturity of one year or less posts interest income at maturity. In contrast, term CDs pay interest on a semiannual basis. The yield on CDs is higher than that on Treasury securities of the same maturity due to the credit rating of the issuing bank, the liquidity of the CD market, and the supply and demand for CDs.

Commercial Paper   Commercial paper (CP) is an unsecured promissory note issued by a corporation for a specific amount and maturing on a specific day that cannot be farther into the future than 270 days. The bulk of the CP issued is for maturities of less than two months. The original purpose of commercial paper was to provide funds for short-term seasonal and working capital needs. In recent years CP has been used for "bridge financing" for plant and equipment expenditures or to temporarily fund a corporate takeover. CP is typically rated by credit agencies that attempt to evaluate the liquidity, cash flow, profitability, and backup credit availability of the entity that is issuing the paper. The minimum lot transaction is $100,000, but most of the paper is bought in million dollar blocks.

Federal Agency Securities   Outside of the Treasury market, the federal agency market is the second most liquid market. These securities carry some form of direct or quasi government backing and can be divided into two sectors: federally sponsored agencies, more commonly called government-sponsored entities (GSEs) and federally related institutions.

   GSEs typically issue two types of securities: discount notes and debentures. The agency discount notes usually range in maturity from five days to 270 days, but some issues go out for as long as one year. The debentures carry maturities similar to U.S. Treasury notes and bonds. In the early 1980s the majority of the larger federal agencies issued straight noncall debentures in accordance to a set calendar issuance cycle similar to the Treasury auction cycle. In the early 1990s the Federal Farm Credit System, for example, issued six- and nine-month debentures for settlement on the first business day of the month, while longer-term coupon debentures were floated eight times a year at approximately six-week intervals.

In recent years, through the expansion of the interest rate swaps and options market, many federal agencies float and redeem paper on an intra-day basis. The majority of these debentures is sold on a spread basis versus Treasuries and may contain a variety of derivative features that can either enhance or reduce the total return to the investor. With the exception of securities issued by the Farm Credit Financial Assistance Corporation, GSE paper is not specifically backed by the full faith and credit of the U.S. government. Nonetheless, it is perceived that it would be highly unlikely that the federal government would allow one of its agencies to default on its obligations. However, while credit risk is limited the actual interest rate risk from these securities can be quite high.

Callable agency paper is a potentially risky derivative product that requires sophisticated analysis to evaluate its embedded option features. Many colleges and universities have bylaws that allow them to invest in agency securities, but these rules were established many years ago, well before these agencies changed their issuance patterns from straight debentures to today's program of largely derivative issuance. In order to evaluate the value of these securities, the proper tools must be available to assess the options-adjusted risk embedded in this product. Direct changes in interest rates and/or changes in current or future market volatility can have a dramatic impact on the overall returns and average life of these securities.

Floating-Rate Notes   The term floating-rate notes (FRNs) includes different types of securities with a similar feature that the interest rate or coupon rate is adjusted periodically to a benchmark or base rate. A simple example of a floating-rate instrument is a Series EE savings bond where the semiannual interest rate is determined in May and November based on 85 percent of the average market return of the five-year Treasury note for the preceding six months.

In theory, floating-rate notes are securities with coupons based on a short-term rate index (such as the three-month Treasury bill or the three-month London InterBank Offered Rate or Eurodollar index (LIBOR) that is reset more than once a year). An adjustable-rate note or variable-rate note is a fixed-income security with coupons that are reset based on a longer index (i.e., the two-year Treasury note). Moreover, adjustable-rate notes are usually reset no more than once a year. Banks and financial institutions have been the largest issuers of variable-rate securities as these institutions attempt to match floating-rate assets with floating-rate liabilities.

Mortgage-Backed Securities (MBS) During the last 15 years, mortgage-backed securities have been one of the fastest growing sectors of the fixed-income securities market. Mortgage-backed securities (MSB) have several unique characteristics, beginning with the payment of interest on a monthly basis. MBSs also differ from standard Treasury investments in that the cash flow pattern is uncertain due to the risk of prepayments or the unscheduled payment of principal. Moreover, a change in the future assumption for prepayments will also affect the rate of return on the investment of a mortgage-backed security.

Mortgage-backed securities are created when mortgage pools are collateralized into interest-bearing securities. This securitization process can be accomplished via either a sale of assets or as a debt obligation of the issuer. In the former, a mortgage pass-through security is created, while in the latter case a mortgage-backed bond is originated.

The collateralized mortgage obligation (CMO) was introduced in June 1983 and was a dynamic innovation that helped to eliminate some of the less desirable monthly interest payment and negative convexity elements of a traditional mortgage-backed security. A group of bonds issued in a CMO deal is called a tranche. The short maturity (one- to two-year average life), enhanced call protection, and conversion to semiannual coupon payments found on many CMO first tranches make them suitable for some operating and endowment cash accounts as either direct investments or as part of an outside managed portfolio.

Repurchase Agreements A repurchase agreement (repo) is a collateralized transaction between a bank or nonbank dealer and an investor. Structurally, a repurchase agreement is the sale of a security with a commitment by the seller to buy back the security from the purchaser at a specified price and on a specified date in the future.

The bulk of repo financing is done on an overnight basis and is called an overnight repo. However, a repo transaction can be set up for longer periods as well. One-week, one-month, and longer term financing positions are called term repos. These longer maturity financing positions should allow for a repricing of the underlying collateral as well as collateral substitution. The seller of a security in a repo agreement continues to receive all the coupon interest income, but will also be impacted by the changes in principal value on the security. The purchaser of a repo transaction receives a set rate of interest on the short-term investment. Repos are viewed as very safe investments because of the direct collateral lending link as well as the creditworthiness of the entity with whom the repo transaction is undertaken. Nonetheless, given the movement in market prices, many purchasers of repos ask for an over-collateralization of the transaction that equates to 102 or 103 percent of the face value of the securities that are on loan. The underlying securities in a term repo position should be repriced on a daily basis, with daily adjustments to collateral positions based on the change in the market's price for the underlying security.

If used properly, repo positions offer investors the opportunity to keep surplus working capital cash invested without facing liquidity, credit, or price risk. However, maintaining an active repo book can be time consuming and can require a variety of safekeeping and security repricing capabilities. Moreover, the interest income derived from repo transactions is usually below other investment alternatives.

The Federal Reserve uses the repo market to implement monetary policy by purchasing or selling collateral (a reverse repo) with its primary dealers. If the Fed opts to buy collateral, it is in effect injecting funds reserves into the financial markets. If the Fed conducts a "matched sale" (a reverse repo), it is selling securities for its own account to drain liquidity from the financial markets. Accordingly, aggressive reserve shifts by the Fed could impact the supply and demand relationship of the repo market, which, in turn, could have an impact on short-term interest rates.

Treasury Securities   Treasury securities are investments issued by the Department of the Treasury that are backed with the full faith and credit of the United States government. Accordingly, Treasuries are viewed as having no default or credit risk. The U.S. Treasury market is the largest and most liquid securities market in the world. Treasury securities are issued in two different forms depending on the length of maturity. Those securities with an original issue maturity of one year or less are issued in a discounted form and are called Treasury bills (T-bills). These holdings are auctioned at a discount from face value and then, at maturity, are redeemed at par. The size of the discount at which a given Treasury bill is auctioned or traded and its time until maturity at par provide an implied yield for investors. Treasury securities of longer maturity are called Treasury notes or bonds.

During the exploding deficit period of the mid-1980s, government bond dealers began to clip the coupons of bonds and sell them as individual securities. In effect a T-bill-like structure was created for Treasuries with maturities from one to 30 years. These products took on "animal like" acronyms as each of the major dealers named its divided Treasury products after various felines. TIGRs, COUGARs, CATs, and LIONs paved the way for the Treasury's own zero coupon bond product called Separate Trading of Registered Interest and Principal Securities, more commonly called STRIPS. Today, all new Treasury notes and bonds with a maturity of 10 years or longer are eligible for the Treasury's zero-coupon STRIPS program.

Many educational institutions use short-dated STRIPS to reinvest the proceeds of a bond financing against the payment schedule for a new building project that may take two to three years to complete. STRIPS solve the issue of the reinvestment of coupon interest and at times can be targeted to a specific payment structure. However, this often comes at the expense of a reduction in the yield, as compared to alternative high-quality fixed-income instruments that are available with returns that are substantially higher than zero coupon bonds. Moreover, the liquidity of short-dated STRIPS is at times limited.

The Treasury yield curve is often viewed as the interest rate differential between Treasury issues from the three-month T-bill to the 30-year T-bond. Market participants will sometimes talk about the Treasury coupon yield curve, which represents the differential on the yield for securities from the current two-year note to the current 30-year bond. During most periods, the yield on U.S. government securities increases with maturity due to the time value of money and the increased inflation and interest rate risk parameters that exist for longer-dated Treasuries. This produces an upward sloping yield curve, which is also termed a normal yield curve. During selected periods when short-term rates are higher than long-term rates, the Treasury yield curve would be downward sloping, and is termed inverted. In recent years inverted yield curves have taken place during periods of aggressive tightening by the Federal Reserve Board (Fed) to moderate inflation and occasionally just prior to the onset of a potential recession.

Glossary of Card/Plastic Terms

Acquirer Obtains merchant's credit card transactions and processes them for payment.

Authorization The process of verifying that the credit card has sufficient funds (credit) available to cover the amount of the transaction. An authorization is obtained for every sale.

Bankcard Such as a MasterCard or Visa credit card.

Batch The collective amount of transactions in the merchant's terminal or point of sale (POS) device that have yet to be settled.

Cardholder Person who uses a credit card to purchase goods and services.

Commercial Card Credit card used by businesses to cover expenses such as travel, entertainment, and purchasing.

Corporate Card Credit card used for business-related expenses such as travel and entertainment.

Debit Card Credit card whose funds are withdrawn directly from the cardholder's checking account.

Discount Rate A collection of fees charged by the acquirer to process the merchant's transaction.

Electronic Cash Register (ECR) A device used for cash sales. Can also be integrated to accept credit cards.

Electronic Draft Capture (EDC) Process of electronically authorizing, capturing, and settling a credit card transaction.

Fleet Card   Private label credit card designed mainly for repairs, maintenance, and fueling of automobiles.

Independent Sales Organizations (ISO)   Companies that independently solicit prospective merchants for acquirers. ISOs may assume either partial or shared financial liability for merchant activity.

Interchange   The fees assessed a transaction by MasterCard and Visa.

Merchant   Customer of acquirer.

Merchant Number   Identifying number assigned to each merchant.

Network   Company used to authorize and capture credit card transactions.

Off-line Transaction   Transaction for which there is no PIN verification; processed like a credit card.

Online Transaction   Transaction requires a personal identification number (PIN).

Private Label   Credit or debit card that can be used only within a specific merchant's store.

Purchasing Card   Credit card used by business to cover purchasing expenses.

Settlement   Process of sending the merchant's batch to the network for processing and payment.

Smart Card   A credit-type card that electronically stores account information in the card itself.

Software   Programming that determines the characteristics and features of the terminal.

T&E Card   Credit card used by businesses for travel and entertainment expenses.

Terminal   Equipment used to capture, transmit, and store credit card transaction.

Value Added Reseller (VAR)   Third party that enhances or modifies existing hardware or software, adding value to the services provided by the processor or acquirer.

What to Do in Case of Check Fraud

The following is a guide as to some of the steps that need to be taken when an instance of check fraud is discovered at your institution.

Notify your institution's chief financial officer.

Notify the bank on which the check was written.

Contact your general banking contacts. They will probably connect you with your bank's Loss Prevention Department (if they have one). It specializes in the handling of check fraud cases.

Be able to provide: check number(s), date(s), amount(s) and endorsement(s). The bank will probably ask to see copies (front and back).

Notify law enforcement agencies. You will probably notify your campus or local police department first. They in turn will contact other agencies such as the state police or the FBI. Your bank will probably also contact the police agencies, but as the victim of the forgery, it is important that you also make this contact.

Notify your internal auditing department.

Document all actions and conversations taken regarding fraud and actions to recover lost funds.

If it appears that the forgery is using your actual check stock, *determine* where the theft of the check stock occurred. If it occurred at your printer or during shipment to you, *notify* the printer and/or the shipping agent.

If the stock came from stock stored at your institution, *take a complete inventory* of the remaining check stock.

Ascertain which specific checks have been stolen. *Place* stop payments against them. *Confirm* with the bank the period of time the stop payment order will be in place.

Take steps to minimize loss to the business community. Even though your institution and your bank, by taking the steps listed above, may be able to minimize losses, the business community that cashes your checks may not be so fortunate.

Notify the major check-cashing institutions in your area, if necessary. This includes banks, grocery and convenience stores, and check-cashing outlets. In many cases, once you notify one institution, it will have its own network within its peer institutions. For example, many grocery stores share information on check forgeries with other grocery stores within the market area.

Promote direct deposit and use positive pay.

Chapter 9

$\blacklozenge$

Endowment Management

Based on Endowment Management chapter from
College and University Business Administration, *Fifth Edition*

by

David A. Salem
The Investment Fund Foundation

with contributions by

Commonfund
Michael T. Dieschbourg, Solomon Smith Barney Consulting Group
Leigh A. Jones

Sponsors

COMMONFUND
Contact: John S. Griswold Jr.
15 Old Danbury Road
P.O. Box 812
Wilton, CT 06897-0812
203-563-5000
www.commonfund.org

Commonfund provides investment and treasury management services to over 1,350 member colleges, universities and independent schools to maximize risk-adjusted returns for endowment and operation funds.

NICHOLAS-APPLEGATE CAPITAL MANAGEMENT
600 West Broadway, 29th Floor
San Diego, CA 92101
619-687-8000

Nicholas-Applegate Capital Management is an independent investment advisory firm and recognized leader in active United States and international equity management. Our institutional clients include major corporations, state and local governments, foundations, endowments, and Taft-Hartley funds. The Nicholas-Applegate group manages over $40 billion in assets and has more than 325 employees with offices in San Diego, New York, and San Francisco. Since inception, our firm has emphasized superior portfolio management and a high level of personal attention to each client. These principles have guided our ongoing success.

SALOMON SMITH BARNEY CONSULTING GROUP

Contact: Michael T. Dieschbourg, CIMA
222 Delaware Avenue, 7th Floor
Wilmington, DE 19801
302-888-4154 or 800-215-9639
www.smithbarney.com/cg

Salomon Smith Barney Consulting Group provides college endowments with full service investment management consulting, including investment and spending policy, asset allocation, manager search and selection, and performance evaluation.

THE VANGUARD GROUP

100 Vanguard Boulevard
Malvern, PA 19355

The Vanguard Group is the nation's second-largest mutual fund company. Founded in 1975, Vanguard offers investment management and other investment-related services to individual and institutional investors worldwide.

Contents

The principles that guide investment management for endowed educational institutions do not differ greatly from those followed by other institutional investors. However, educational endowments do have characteristics that distinguish them from other pools of investable wealth: they are exempt from taxation, they have a very long-term investment horizon (in theory, a perpetual one), and they are supposed to generate a stream of earnings to support current operations that will remain stable (or grow) in real or inflation-adjusted terms. Because other pools of investable wealth share some of these attributes and aims, the similarities between the way educational endowments and other institutional funds are managed outweigh the differences. The investors pursue essentially the same investment policies; they allocate their assets in a similar fashion; and they delegate day-to-day responsibility for investment decision making to many of the same professional investment managers.

It is not surprising that educational institutions pursue investment policies similar to those pursued by other institutional investors, because endowment trustees quite naturally adopt policies and practices that have served them well in other contexts, especially in the management of other institutional funds for which they serve as fiduciaries. Some policies and practices are conducive to investment success regardless of the character of the assets being deployed. Approaches that work well when applied to taxable assets, for example, can also work well when applied to endowment assets. Nevertheless, governing boards and officers must understand fully how endowments differ from other pools of capital, for without such understanding it is unlikely that they will exploit to the maximum extent possible their funds' tax-exempt and perpetual life status.

This chapter provides an overview of endowments, discusses the legal aspects of endowment investing, analyzes alternate endowment investment policies, and describes types of split interest agreement (deferred giving) assets.

TYPES OF ENDOWMENT AND SIMILAR FUNDS

The three principal categories of endowment and similar funds are true endowment funds, term endowment funds, and funds functioning as endowment (sometimes referred to as quasi-endowment funds). *True endowment funds* are funds received from a donor with the restriction that the principal is not expendable. *Term endowment funds* are funds for which the donor stipulates that the principal may be expended after a stated period of time or upon the occurrence of a certain event. *Funds functioning as endowments* are funds that have been established by the governing board to function like an endowment fund but that may be expended at any time at the discretion of the board.

All three types of funds—true endowment funds, term endowment funds, and funds functioning as endowment—are generally commingled for investment purposes and are reported in the net asset (equity) section of the institution's balance sheet by the restrictions or lack thereof which donors have placed on these funds.

Split interest (deferred giving) agreements possess many characteristics of institutional endowment funds for investment and administrative purposes. Institutions may serve as a trustee for various types of split interest agreements (charitable remainder trusts, pooled income trusts, and charitable lead trusts) under which the institution has the fiduciary responsibility to invest the trust assets and make periodic payments (at least annually) of income or stated amounts to a named beneficiary or beneficiaries. Under another type of split interest agreement, the charitable gift annuity contract, assets are transferred to an institution by a donor in return for the institution's promise to pay a stated amount at least annually to a beneficiary or beneficiaries. Sound business practice suggests that the assets of a charitable gift annuity be invested during the term of the contract to earn income that may be used to help meet the stated contractual payments. The assets of split interest agreements should be disclosed separately from the assets of endowment funds on the balance sheet, while their contribution value is included in net assets according to restrictions or lack thereof stipulated by the donor.

Use of Endowment Principal and Earnings

For the purposes of this chapter, the term "spendable return" is used to describe the amount of endowment income or income and appreciation allotted on a regular, periodic basis by the institution for current expenditures. The term "income" is not used, because many institutions have adopted "total return" spending formulas (see following discussion) under which they may expend not only the current yield but also a prudent portion of appreciation. While spendable return for a given institution may be equal to the fund's current yield, the use of a formula usually produces a spendable return that is more than the fund's yield, especially when the current yield is low.

For operational purposes, endowment and similar funds should be classified according to any donor-imposed restrictions placed on the expenditure of their principal and spendable return. For example, if a donor specifies that the principal must be retained but makes no stipulations concerning use of the spendable return, the fund is an *unrestricted endowment fund.* If the donor specifies that the spendable return from the fund is to be used for a certain instructional department or other specific purpose, the fund is a *restricted endowment fund.* Similar situations may exist with respect to use of spendable return from term endowment funds.

If a donor makes a gift to an institution, specifying only that it be used for a specific institutional purpose and not stipulating that the principal of the fund be maintained in perpetuity or for a period of time, and if the governing board elects to invest the fund and expend only the spendable return for the purpose stipulated by the donor, the fund becomes a *restricted fund functioning as endowment.* Similarly, the governing board may create an *unrestricted fund functioning as endowment* by authorizing unrestricted funds to the "endowment and similar funds" group with the intention of retaining the funds on a long-term basis and using only the investment earnings for current expenditures.

Assets of true or term endowment funds must not be hypothecated or pledged for any purpose and normally should not be loaned to or invested in the institution's physical plant. Such conveyances of true or term endowment assets, whether actual or potential, violate the institution's legal obligation to maintain endowment principal inviolate. Funds functioning as endowment, however, can be used for these purposes, because their functional status stems not from donor stipulations but rather from board action.

ACCOUNTING FOR GIFTS

The appropriate accounting for endowment and similar fund gifts depends on the conditions under which funds are accepted and received by an institution. It is therefore essential that these conditions be communicated to the chief financial or business officer, or his or her designee in the accounting office, to ensure proper recording of funds in the institution's accounting records. If conditions of the gift stipulate that the principal is to be retained in perpetuity or for some stated period, the funds received should be accounted for as restricted for endowment. On the other hand, if funds received are not restricted by the donor, they should be accounted for as unrestricted revenue even though the governing board may determine that the funds should be invested and function as endowment.

Historically, endowment and similar funds were accounted for and reported as a separate fund group in the institution's published financial statements. With the adoption of FASB 117 and GASB 35 (see Chapter 5, Financial Reporting), institutions no longer report by funds but on an entity-wide basis. However, most institutions continue to account for their endowment and similar funds in self-balancing sets of accounts to assist with their investment, administration, and stewardship of these funds.

Ensuring Compliance with Fund Restrictions

Compliance with such restrictions is both necessary and expedient. It is necessary because the restrictions carry the force of law, and their violation could trigger private litigation or intervention by state authorities. It is expedient because there is a close and demonstrable link between good stewardship of gifts and bequests and long-term fund-raising success. The officer responsible should therefore have a thorough understanding of the legal environment in which these funds are administered and used.

Every institution should establish policies to ensure compliance with restrictions imposed by donors and designations imposed by the governing board on the use of funds and their spendable return. The chief financial or business officer or designee and independent auditors should periodically examine administrative policies and practices. Such examination should be supplemented from time to time with a review by legal counsel.

A detailed register for endowment and similar funds should be maintained. The register should include such information as:

- name of the donor and members of his or her family, with brief biographical comments;
- amount and date of donation;
- identification of the type of fund;
- restrictions by the donor or designations by the governing board on use of the fund or its spendable return;
- identification of the source of such limitations (donor, grantor, or governing board);
- limitations on investments; and
- reference to formal acceptance and other actions by the governing board.

Donor Relations

Although a register of endowment and similar funds is a useful administrative tool, its limitations should be recognized. It may present terms and limitations in summary form, when in fact they may have been developed through correspondence with a donor over many years. It is therefore essential that an institution maintain complete files of all original gift instruments and related correspondence, as such documents provide an authoritative basis for interpreting donor intent. Fund-raising personnel must ensure that information essential to the administration of an endowment fund is memorialized in a written instrument at the time a gift is made.

Conferences with donors can be especially useful, not only in clarifying and ultimately codifying donor intent, but also in demonstrating the need for unrestricted resources. Such resources are essential to ensure the continued quality of the institution's academic programs and supporting services and to sustain and enhance the institution's financial strength and flexibility. If a donor seeks to restrict the use of a gift or bequest, the institution should, insofar as possible, ensure that such restriction will not prevent effective use of the funds in the future. When a donor is informed that such restrictions are not consistent with the institution's mission, he or she is often willing to grant broad latitude, not only in the use of the fund and its spendable return but also in the manner in which it is invested and administered. Most donors recognize that a gift that unduly hampers an institution's freedom of action is ultimately a poor memorial to their generosity.

A representative of the institution should review gift instruments in draft form to suggest changes in terms or wording that will help the institution comply with the donor's wishes. As defined by the Uniform Management of Institutional Funds Act, a *gift instrument* is a will, deed, grant, conveyance, agreement, memorandum, writing, or other governing document (including the terms of any institutional solicitations from which an institutional fund resulted) under which property is transferred to or held by an institution as an institutional fund. One change in gift instruments commonly suggested by institutional representatives is the inclusion of a "changed conditions" clause permitting the use of funds for purposes other than those initially stipulated by the donor, should future conditions dictate such a change.

Although most gifts to institutions are motivated by charitable impulses, estate planning and tax factors can also be quite important. It is essential, however, that representatives of the institution avoid rendering formal legal or tax opinions or appraising the value of noncash gifts. The value that donors assign to noncash gifts for purposes of computing income tax deductions is in no way binding upon the receiving institution when it assigns its own book value to such gifts. Because tax regulations normally require that receipts for noncash gifts be based on independent appraisals, institutional representatives should avoid rendering their own appraisals of noncash gifts and should refrain from any acts or statements that might be construed as tax or legal advice. The donor should be advised to seek counsel on such matters.

Standard Donor Agreement

Whether or not the administration elects to conduct an internal full-scale review of existing awards and endowments, a standard donor agreement should be created. Figure 09-01 presents a sample donor agreement that is meant to provide a basis for discussion. The draft is basic, brief, and in need of refinement. It is included to illustrate the type of structured questionnaire that should be administered to memorialize fully each donor's wishes. Figure 09-01 is provided for illustrative purposes only.

The objective of a standard donor agreement is to ensure the donor's understanding and acceptance of legal and administrative realities. An agreement should be drafted jointly by the development office, the financial aid office, graduate departments, and other interested departments. The final agreement should be distributed campuswide to the entire community of interest.

Treatment of Noncash Gifts

Educational institutions typically receive many noncash gifts, including gifts of securities in-kind, and the number of issues held by a fund can easily grow beyond reasonable bounds if steps are not taken to routinely liquidate securities not held strictly on investment grounds. The greater the number of issues held by a fund, the higher administrative expenses tend to be. Appropriate diversification of endowment assets can be obtained with a reasonably small number of carefully selected holdings, and maintenance of a large number of small positions in individual issues generally entails costs that are disproportionate to any diversification benefits that their retention provides. To guard against unproductive diversification of fund holdings, many institutions maintain a policy requiring the prompt sale of all securities received by a gift or bequest unless prohibited by the terms of the gift or bequest or unless a particular security is already held in the institution's

Figure 09-01 (also see overleaf)

Standard Donor Agreement

1. Nature of the award contemplated:

    _____

    _____

    _____

2. Type of award

    ☐ Student scholarship   ☐ Student bursary   ☐ Prize   ☐ Research award

    ☐ Graduate student award   ☐ Fellowship   ☐ Other: _____

3.

    Amount of donation/award disbursement: $ _____

    Amount of donation to create capital pool: $ _____

    Envisioned annual disbursement: _____ award(s) × $ _____

    PLEASE NOTE: The university will normally distribute awards on the following basis:

$500	Pooled in faculty or departmental general endowments
$500–$5,000	Normally pooled; individual awards of less than five years' duration considered
$5,000–$25,000	Individual awards with five-year duration
>$25,000	Individual awards in perpetuity (normally 25-year maximum)

    Is this acceptable?   ☐ Yes   ☐ No

    If not, please explain: _____

    _____

    _____

4. Eligible recipient restrictions

    PLEASE NOTE: Awards should be free of criteria based on personal characteristics such as race, ancestry, place of origin, color, ethnic origin, sex, creed, age, marital status, family status, sexual orientation, or handicap. Notwithstanding the above, the university may from time to time establish awards specifically intended to improve the participation of certain groups.

    Is this acceptable?   ☐ Yes   ☐ No

    If not, please explain: _____

    _____

    _____

5. Capital investment restrictions

    PLEASE NOTE: The university is normally obliged to invest only those funds authorized for investment under the Trustee Act. These authorized investments are of a fairly standard, conservative nature.

    Would you consider exempting your donation
    from the restrictions of the Act for investment purposes?   ☐ Yes   ☐ No

Figure 09-01 (concluded)

If not, please explain: _____

_____

_____

6. Capital preservation policy
   PLEASE NOTE: The university's capital preservation policy typically envisions annual spending at a maximum of the average of the past three years' CPI (in %) times the then current market value of the endowment.

   Is this acceptable?   ☐ Yes   ☐ No

   If not, please explain: _____

   _____

   _____

7. Administrative fees
   PLEASE NOTE: The university normally charges an administrative cost recovery equal to $\frac{1}{10}$ of 1 percent of market value monthly, to recognize the costs associated with fund raising and award management. Further, investment manager fees are normally a direct charge to endowment income.

   Is this acceptable?   ☐ Yes   ☐ No

   If not, please explain: _____

   _____

   _____

8. Discretion to university
   PLEASE NOTE: Given changing circumstances and priorities, the right to utilize both the capital and income from a donation would normally revert to the complete discretion of the university 25 years from the date of the donation.

   Is this acceptable?   ☐ Yes   ☐ No

   If not, please explain: _____

   _____

   _____

9. Calendar description/award name
   PLEASE NOTE: Only individually categorized awards normally receive separate calendar descriptions. The nature of the description envisioned:

   In acknowledgment of the terms and conditions and amendments thereto listed above, please sign below:

   Donor Signature _____   Date _____

portfolio or is under consideration as an addition to the portfolio in the near future.

CY PRES

In some instances, a donor may, by the terms of his or her gift, have so limited either the purposes for which an endowment fund may be used or the manner in which it may be invested that the value of the fund to the institution is severely limited. In such cases it is often undesirable, impractical, and sometimes impossible for the institution to continue to comply with the donor's wishes. To gain relief from impractical restrictions, the institution may bring a so-called cy pres action in an appropriate court.

Cy pres ("as near as may be") is a procedure for releasing a limitation on a restricted gift if the donor is no longer living. An institution may seek to depart from the original terms of the gift to make the fund useful while adhering, as nearly as possible, to the donor's original intent. Cy pres is a last resort and often a futile one. It has been attempted in some jurisdictions against living donors, but the courts have refused to approve it in such cases.

The cy pres directive has not been a satisfactory solution and is applied reluctantly in some states. Therefore, the Uniform Management of Institutions Funds Act provides a statutory procedure for the release of restrictions with the consent of the donor. If the donor is deceased, unable to consent, or cannot be identified, the appropriate court may, on application of the institution's governing board, release a limitation shown to be obsolete, inappropriate, or impractical. Many institutions include a "sunset clause" in donative instruments that gives the institution complete discretion to dispose of principal and income after a stated period, typically 25 years. (See figure 09-01, item 8.)

LEGAL STATUS OF ENDOWMENT FUNDS

Endowment funds have been the subject of considerable legal discussion. The most serious question is whether fund appreciation, realized or unrealized, must be treated as principal and therefore considered unexpendable. The answer depends on the extent to which trust law and/or the Uniform Prudent Investors Act (see as follows) is deemed applicable to educational institutions, which are considered charitable corporations under the laws of most states and hence subject to a regulatory framework that combines elements of corporation and contract law with traditional trust principles. Because corporation, contract, and trust law are derived not only from statutes but from centuries of common-law jurisprudence, the regulatory framework in which endowments are managed is at times ambiguous and uncertain. Nonetheless, there are touchstone principles that governing boards and officers can rely on, and there is such widespread acceptance of the legitimacy of certain policies and practices that the institutions following them can be relatively certain that these procedures will withstand legal scrutiny.

There are two generic views of the legal status of endowment funds. The traditional, and by now somewhat discredited, view of an endowment is that it is a trust fund per se, regardless of whether the written instrument establishing it contains the appropriate "terms of art"—specific words or phrases that unambiguously justify the invocation of trust principles. It is inconsequential, to those who insist on viewing endowments only through the prism of trust law, that endowed institutions may hold property in trust for themselves, or that the three-way separation of trustee, life beneficiary, and remainderman—the cornerstone of private trust law—does not exist in an endowment setting. The more modern view, embodied in the Uniform Management of Institutional Funds Act, is that educational institutions hold endowment funds for their own benefit as their absolute property, that the laws applicable to charitable corporations apply, and that principles of private trust law are largely inapposite.

The Traditional View: Endowments Are Trusts

Under the trust fund theory, the principal of an endowment fund must be maintained inviolate in perpetuity. Principal includes:

- the market value of the fund at the moment it was established;
- the market value of any additions to the fund at the moment they were added; and
- realized appreciation in the value of the fund's assets.

For example, assume that an endowment fund of $100,000 was established in Year 1 with the stipulation that all current income be used for faculty salaries. If an additional $60,000 were donated to the fund in Year 5, and if the fund realized investment gains (exclusive of dividends, interest, or rents) of $40,000 in Years 1–10, at the end of Year 10 the entire $200,000 would be deemed inviolate.

Perhaps the most glaring anomaly in treating endowments as trust funds is the nearly universal practice of commingling assets for investment purposes. In private trust law, the rule forbidding trustees from commingling investments of two or more separate trust funds is still strictly applied, at least in theory. In practice, however, this rule is honored more in the breach than the observance, with the assets of many private trusts being invested in commingled investment vehicles such as mutual funds. Also, the anticommingling provisions of trust law have a slightly hollow ring in an era of "certificateless" trading, where the indicia of ownership of most publicly traded securities take the form not of stacks of certificates bearing individual investors' names but rather of a record etched on a silicon wafer in the computer of a custodial bank. (Most custodial banks are members of centralized depository networks that permit them to buy and sell securities without physically exchanging stock or bond certificates. Indeed, most U.S. Treasury obligations do not exist in certificate form.) Banking regulations explicitly permit banks to commingle the assets of trusts for which they serve as trustees, but this is the only exception to the general rule that trust assets cannot legally be commingled.

If endowments are viewed as trust funds, commingling endowment assets for investment purposes is thus not permissible. However, most educational institutions have for many years pooled the assets of the many individual funds (thousands, in the case of a major research university) that collectively constitute their endowments, and this practice has never been challenged. The nearly universal acceptance of the commingling of endowment assets materially weakens the argument that such funds are properly regarded as trusts. (See following discussion of the Uniform Management of Institutional Funds Act and the Uniform Prudent Investors Act.)

Another problem that arises when endowments are viewed as trusts is that trust principles prohibit the governing board from delegating day-to-day responsibility for fund administration to an institution's officers, even if such delegation is the norm with respect to other aspects of the institution's affairs. The extent to which investment discretion can be delegated by an institution's governing board depends on the charter and bylaws under which it operates and the laws of the state in which it is situated; legal counsel should be consulted before the board delegates such authority to others. In some jurisdictions the governing board, or a committee composed of board members, must technically be involved in the selection of individual securities. This is undeniably sound from a legal point of view but perhaps not the most effective means of maximizing investment returns within acceptable volatility constraints, which is the end result that fund fiduciaries seek. Fortunately, the majority of states have adopted the Uniform Management of Institutional Funds Act or variants thereof that permit trustees to delegate considerable discretion to investment and financial professionals who are not members of the board.

The Modern View: Endowments Are Not Trusts

The many states that have rejected the trust theory have opted instead to view educational institutions as charitable corporations that hold endowment funds solely for their own benefit. Investment and administration of such funds is governed by the law of charitable corporations and not the law of private trusts. This does not result in unalloyed gains for educational institutions in these states, however, because the law of charitable corporations is loosely applied and often confusing, drawing on a mixture of corporate, trust, and contract principles. It is possible, for example, for a court in an "absolute ownership" state to reach the conclusion that appreciation must be considered part of principal as in private trust law, contrary to the general rule of corporation law that realized gains may be treated as income and therefore spent.

Depending on the law of the state of incorporation or provisions in an institution's charter, its governing board has some freedom to delegate authority in connection with investment functions to a committee of its members or to appropriate corporate officers. Investment discretion may also be delegated to professional investment managers who are not members of the governing board or officers of the institution, but responsibility for investment activities ultimately rests with the governing board and is thus, in a strictly legal sense, nondelegable. In other words, the governing board may fully delegate the authority to make investment decisions, but it cannot delegate the responsibility it ultimately bears to ensure that endowment assets are invested prudently.

The Uniform Management of Institutional Funds Act

The Uniform Management of Institutional Funds Act (the Uniform Act) is one of a series of nonbinding "model" statutes recommended to individual state legislatures by the National Conference of Commissioners on Uniform State Laws, a private advisory panel that is operated under the auspices of the American Bar Association and the bar associations of individual states and territories. Conceived in the late 1960s and adopted by the National Conference in 1972, the Uniform Act aims to clarify and codify what can and cannot be done by persons administering endowment and similar funds. The Uniform Act prescribes a standard of care and prudence to guide governing boards in exercising their duties. It countermands two important tenets of trust law by specifically permitting endowment trustees to spend a prudent portion of realized endowment gains and to delegate investment discretion to qualified professionals. As of January 1, 2000, the District of Columbia and the following states had adopted the Uniform Act or variants thereof: Alabama, Arkansas, California, Colorado, Connecticut, Delaware, Florida, Georgia, Hawaii, Idaho, Illinois, Indiana, Iowa, Kansas, Kentucky, Louisiana, Maine, Maryland, Massachusetts, Michigan, Minnesota, Missouri, Montana, Nebraska, Nevada, New Hampshire, New Jersey, New Mexico, New York, North Carolina, North Dakota, Ohio, Oklahoma, Oregon, Rhode Island, South Carolina, Tennessee, Texas, Utah, Vermont, Virginia, Washington, West Virginia, Wisconsin, and Wyoming. In addition, Pennsylvania passed a similar act before the Uniform Act was promulgated in 1972.

The Uniform Act provides the following definitions:

Institutional fund is a fund held by an institution for its exclusive use, benefit, or purposes; it does not include a fund held for an institution by a trustee who is a natural person (as distinct from an institution) or a fund in which a beneficiary who is a natural person has an interest other than the rights that could arise on violation or failure of the fund's stated purposes.

Endowment fund is an institutional fund, or any part thereof, not wholly expendable by the institution on a current basis under the terms of the applicable gift instrument. (Implicit in this definition is the continued maintenance of all or a specified part of the original gift.)

Historic dollar value is the aggregate value in dollars of an endowment fund at the time it was established; each subsequent donation to the fund at the time it is made; and each accumulation made pursuant to a direction in the applicable gift instrument at the time the accumulation is added to the fund.

Appreciation is the increase in value over historic dollar value. Therefore, if the market value is below the historic dollar value of the fund, the institution may spend only the current yield ("income" in the traditional trust law sense) that the fund generates in the form of dividends, interest, or rent. If the market value exceeds the historic dollar value of the fund, the institution is free to expend the appreciation in excess of the historic value.

The Uniform Prudent Investors Act (UPIA) is being adopted by many states and guides members of governing boards on grantor trusts (which will become part of the endowment). Legislation in at least one state (Florida) specifically names governing board members in its version of UPIA. The act is being cited by the courts in Employee Retirement Income Security Act of 1974 (ERISA) cases since it is the most recent and specific legislation having to do with prudence of governing board members.

POOLING ENDOWMENT ASSETS

To the extent legally possible, colleges and universities may find it advantageous to commingle investments of endowment and similar funds in an investment pool or pools. An investment pool permits broad diversification of investments with attendant protection of principal and relative stability of revenue. In addition, it permits economies in administration and accounting.

Even though assets are invested as a pool, the identity of separate funds must be maintained. Individual accounts must be kept, usually in subsidiary records, for the principal of each fund in the investment pool. This is particularly important if the pool is administered on a total return basis in conformity with the Uniform Act or other applicable state law. Although the market value of assets of the entire pool may exceed aggregate historic dollar value of the individual funds invested, the value of the proportionate share of the pool's assets related to a particular fund may be greater or less than the historic dollar value of that fund. If the value of the fund's share of the assets is less than its historic dollar value, only the yield may be used.

A consolidated pool may be desirable for investment of endowment funds, term endowment funds, and funds functioning as endowment. However, it is preferable to have separate investment pools for split interest agreements, which have objectives and characteristics different from endowment and similar funds.

The terms of some gift instruments may prohibit pooling or commingling of assets. Legal interpretation of complex language in gift instruments is often necessary, but generally the requirement that a fund be "held separate" is construed as meaning only that the fund balance be separately identified at all times and not that assets of the fund be separately invested. Language to the effect that the fund be "invested separately" or that "its assets shall not be commingled" requires that the fund be separately invested. When it is possible to guide a donor in drafting a gift document, benefits to the fund and to the institution of pooling investments should be explained and the donor's consent sought for participation in the pool.

Separate investment sometimes may be necessary because of special provisions in the gift instrument or because of the nature of gift property. For example, a donor may require retention of a particular investment, limit investments of the fund to certain types of securities or other property, or contribute assets that are unmarketable (restricted stock), not income producing, hard to value, or uncommonly risky. These characteristics might disqualify the gift property as a proper investment for an endowment pool. The only solution is to establish a separately invested fund in the donor's name. That fund alone will suffer the consequences of any change or loss of value occurring because of the nature of the gift property. If the character of the asset changes, as when restrictions on the sale of securities are removed, the fund may then be invested in a pool.

Operating Investment Pools

Operation of an investment pool necessitates procedures permitting equitable distribution of spendable return and assignment of market values of the individual funds invested in the pool.

Investment earnings are distributed to various participating funds on the basis of the assignment to each fund of a number of units calculated on the market value of assets of the pool at the time of entry of each fund into the pool. This procedure is known as the "market value" or "unit" method of accounting for investment pools. Under this method, when an investment pool is inaugurated, or when a change is made from a historic dollar value to a market value method, an arbitrary value is assigned to each share or unit. Each institutional fund then is considered to have the number of units directly proportional to its historic dollar value at the time the market value method is inaugurated. For example, if $100 is assigned for each unit, a fund of $10,000 would have 100 shares.

Thereafter, the pooled assets are valued at specific intervals, usually monthly or quarterly, and a new unit value is determined by dividing the new total market value by total number of units. This new unit value is used to determine the number of units assigned to, or "purchased" by, a new fund as it enters the pool. The new unit value also is used in calculating the value of a fund that may be withdrawn from the pool. For example, the market value of assets of an investment pool having a total of 100,000 units may be $15 million at a given monthly or quarterly valuation date; the value of each unit, therefore, would be $150 ($15 million divided by 100,000 units). A new fund of $30,000 entering the pool on that date would be assigned 200 units ($30,000 divided by $150). A fund holding 300 units that is withdrawn from the pool would have a value of $45,000 (or 300 units multiplied by $150).

Either of two procedures may be followed in admitting funds to or withdrawing funds from the pool. One is to admit or remove funds only on valuation dates. The other is to admit or remove them at any time, with valuation of units being that of the latest valuation date. (Under the provisions of the Tax Reform Act of 1969, the latter method cannot be used for pooled life income funds.) If the latter method is employed, unit values should be determined with sufficient frequency to avoid inequities resulting from variations in unit market value.

A separate account is maintained to which realized gains and losses are charged. No units are assigned and no income is distributed to this account. Regular income (interest and dividends) is prorated to the various funds that compose the total endowment on the basis of the number of units in each fund. The institution may distribute gains and losses to each fund in this pool on a pro-rata basis, but some institutions may not consider the work involved as justified. Realized gains and losses on separately invested funds should be distributed directly to the funds; thus, the fund balance will change each time a gain or loss is realized.

In the past, many colleges and universities followed the historic dollar value method of distributing earnings. When there was little or no change in the valuation of assets held, this method equitably distributed investment revenue. However, because equity securities and other assets that fluctuate in value are of increasing importance to investment pools, the market value method provides a more equitable distribution of income and realized and unrealized gains and losses to each fund. The historic dollar value method is no longer considered acceptable. As a collateral advantage, fluctuations in unit value of the pool provide a useful measure of performance of the investment pool, undistorted by additions or withdrawals of funds.

SETTING ENDOWMENT SPENDING RATES

Endowment management has been significantly affected by the trend toward *total return investing.* Until the 1970s, most educational institutions spent only income (yield) of endowment funds, treating appreciation as an addition to principal. In the early 1970s, several published studies suggested that institutions could enhance the return on their endowment funds by investing more heavily in equities, especially low-yield "growth" stocks. To avoid the immediate reduction in distributable endowment earnings that a redeployment of fund assets from relatively high-yield bonds to lower-yield stocks would have entailed, many institutions moving more heavily into stocks adopted spending policies that permitted the expenditure of both current income and a portion of appreciation. This approach remains the most widely used method of determining annual spending rates, but its risks are better understood than they were when it was first intro-duced, and the importance of diversifying endowment assets is better appreciated.

Alternate Spending Rules

The most common variant of the total return approach in use today links available endowment spending to endowment market values. An example is a per-centage (such as 5 percent) of a moving average of market values (a three-year aver-age is common). The use of a moving average asset base dampens the impact of market fluctuations on available spending, thereby making it easier for an institu-tion to formulate and adhere to annual budgets. In pursuit of even greater cer-tainty in the budgeting process, some institutions have adopted a variant of the total return approach under which distributed endowment earnings are set at a prudent initial dollar level (such as the dollar equivalent of 5 percent of the endowment's market value on the date the formula is adopted) and then permitted to grow at a fixed annual rate equal to the fund's expected long-term real or infla-tion-adjusted rate of return.

Rationale for Spending Rules

Most spending policies aim to balance the need for current income with the need to preserve the purchasing power of both endowment principal and endow-ment earnings. Excessively high spending rates undermine achievement of the lat-ter objective, while reinvesting too large a portion of total return can cause signif-icant program disruptions. The pre-1970s approach of spending all current yield proved acceptable in an era when bonds were the asset of choice for most endow-ments and a policy of spending all income led to a reasonable and sustainable pay-out of 4 to 6 percent per year. High rates of inflation in the 1970s and early 1980s caused stock and bond yields (as distinct from total returns) to rise and put many institutions that had clung to a spend-all-yield rule in the untenable position of spending at unsustainably high rates of 8 percent or more. The moderation of inflation and the strong equity markets of the 1990s caused a rethinking of this strategy. For fiscal year 1999, the average endowment payout rate, or what most institutions label as "spending," was 4.2 percent, while total withdrawals from endowment averaged 5.4 percent (for both public and private institutions).

Striking an appropriate balance between present and future institutional needs can be difficult: to determine what portion of its existing endowment assets an institution can prudently spend each year, its governing board must estimate the endowment's expected long-term real or inflation-adjusted rate of return. By definition, the institution can spend at a rate equal to (but not exceeding) its expected real or inflation-adjusted rate of return without jeopardizing the purchasing power of existing endowment assets. However, to estimate a fund's expected real rate of return, the governing board must make certain assumptions about the endowment's long-term asset mix, which is dependent on the fund's return objectives or desired spending rate. (The higher a fund's long-term return objective, the more aggressively its assets must be invested.)

To escape this vicious circle, most governing boards make defensible assumptions about sustainable spending rates based on capital market history, and then review and if necessary revise spending policies later in the planning process, after appropriate long-term asset mixes have been identified. Over the long term, equities have produced an average annual real total return approximating 6 percent. The corresponding return for long-term high quality bonds has been approximately 2 percent, while cash equivalents have produced a long-term real return of approximately 1 percent. An institution that committed 65 percent to stocks, 30 percent to bonds and 5 percent to cash equivalents (a typical long-term asset mix) might therefore expect to earn a long-term real return of 4.5 percent—perhaps higher if it aggressively invests in "alternative assets" (discussed below) or if the strategies and tactics it employs within conventional asset classes produce incremental returns above a purely passive buy-and-hold approach.

Given the complexities of determining appropriate spending rates and the interrelationship of spending and investment policies, it is not surprising that educational institutions have adopted widely varying endowment spending rules. Selection of an appropriate endowment spending policy is one of the governing board's most important responsibilities, and the typical board spends considerable time ensuring that the policy that it has adopted truly reflects the institution's financial condition and risk tolerances.

INVESTMENT PLANNING

Investing endowment assets effectively is difficult in the absence of a comprehensive investment plan, for several reasons. Endowment management entails the ongoing resolution of many interrelated issues. Modern financial markets are volatile; the natural human tendency when asset prices are fluctuating widely is to act. Without the restraint imposed by a well-prepared and well-understood investment plan action, this sometimes leads to the sale of volatile assets at temporarily depressed prices. Also, in recent years the number of available investment vehicles has proliferated, as have the number and variety of firms professing an ability to invest effectively. This has heightened the need for policies and guidelines that fund fiduciaries can consult as they perform their duties, especially as they evaluate and select investment vehicles and managers. An effective means of preparing a comprehensive investment plan is to divide the planning process into a logically ordered series of discrete tasks.

Identifying Investable Funds

The first step is to identify investable funds. Investment management for an institution of higher education primarily involves true endowment funds, term endowment funds, and funds functioning as endowment. (The investment of split interest agreements is discussed in the section on Split Interest Assets.)

Most educational institutions have funds not needed immediately for operating purposes, as well as other funds earmarked for facilities construction or other capital improvements. These are often invested in high-quality fixed-income instruments that generate high levels of current income. The maturities of such instruments are either very short (to preclude principal losses should interest rates rise) or staggered so that the instruments mature on or about the dates that cash withdrawals must be made to fund expenditures. Although short-term investing is a very important function, long-term funds are the primary subject of this chapter. (For more detail on short-term investment, see chapter 8, Treasury Management.)

Some institutions are responsible for the stewardship of employee pension assets, typically in accordance with policies that differ (albeit not markedly) from those governing investment of endowment assets. As long-term pools of capital exempt from taxation, college and university pension funds have much in common with endowments and can often be invested in similar vehicles, using similar strategies and tactics. Where differences exist, they are often dictated by the distinct contractual and regulatory framework in which pension fund fiduciaries must operate, including the adherence to collective bargaining agreements, ERISA and related regulations, state laws, and other external constraints.

Organizing to Invest

The second step in preparing a comprehensive investment plan is to assign responsibility for the ongoing formulation and implementation of investment policies, strategies, and tactics. For the purposes of this chapter, "policies" refers to the allocation of investable funds across asset classes, based on long-term objectives and risk tolerances. "Strategies" refers to the allocation of funds across asset classes (or outside professional managers) based on short- or medium-term return assumptions. Strategic insights sometimes cause assets to be allocated in proportions that differ from policy norms. "Tactics" refers to the allocation of funds across individual securities based on short-term return assumptions.

For most governing boards, policy formulation is a task that cannot be delegated. Governing boards may choose to delegate policy decisions, but the decisions their designees make are merely *de facto* choices by the governing board. Strategic decisions may be delegated entirely, partly delegated, or retained by the institution's governing board. Tactical decisions may also be delegated or retained, but are almost always delegated to full-time investment professionals. Whatever the amount of an institution's investable funds, these funds must have continuous, enlightened supervision. Each institution should select the form of management organization best suited to its return objectives and to the amount of investable funds that it controls.

Establishing an Investment Committee

Most boards delegate ongoing authority for endowment management to an investment committee, which may be separate from the board's finance committee or subcommittee. Typically, the investment committee is a policy-making body that does not directly manage the institution's investments by attempting to select securities for the portfolio. To facilitate timely decision making and to focus authority, the investment committee should be small. It should be composed of members who understand how modern investment and capital markets function or who can lend other useful skills or perspectives to the committee's work. To ensure that investment committees have the requisite expertise, some institutions appoint as either voting or nonvoting members individuals who are not technically members of the governing board.

It is important to consult legal counsel concerning delegation of investment authority to ensure that such delegation conforms with state laws and institutional bylaws. If the governing board delegates investment authority to an investment committee, the committee may, in turn, delegate to an officer of the college or university or to a portfolio manager the discretionary authority to buy and sell securities and to perform other essential investment functions.

Establishing an Investment Subsidiary

Several institutions with large endowments have created wholly owned subsidiaries to manage their endowment assets under the supervision of an independent board of directors appointed by and responsible to the parent institution's governing board. This arrangement shifts investment decision-making authority (but not ultimate responsibility) to a group of individuals that monitors investment and capital markets on a continuous basis and that has well-defined personal incentives (including, in the case of the subsidiary's professional staff, pecuniary incentives) to deploy investment assets in a manner that comports fully with an institution's return objectives and time horizon.

Obviating Conflicts of Interest

Real or apparent conflicts of interest can and do arise as investment committees go about their work; it is essential that an institution have written policies that define what is and what is not a conflict of interest and that outline procedures to be followed when such conflicts arise. Governing boards and officers do not need to make immediate or certain financial gains for investments to be construed as conflicts of interest; an institution's written policies should compel prompt and complete disclosure of any means by which governing boards or officers could benefit personally from recommended investment decisions.

Formulating and Codifying Investment Policies

Once investable funds have been identified and agreement is reached as to who will make which decisions, the next step in preparing a comprehensive investment plan is to formulate and codify the institution's investment policies. The preparation of a written statement of investment policies is usually the responsibility of the investment committee, but the governing board should confirm these policies through review and ratification of the committee's work.

A comprehensive statement of investment policies and practices addresses the return objective, time horizon, long-term asset allocation guidelines, short-term asset allocation guidelines, and manager selection and evalations criteria.

Return Objective

In most cases, the return objective is to invest funds in a manner that will preserve the purchasing power of income and principal. Alternate objectives are to achieve a prespecified level of income (expressed in either dollar or percentage terms), to maximize current income while ignoring total return, or to maximize capital values while ignoring current income. Regardless of the return objective chosen, the institution should explain the rationale underlying its choice so that all institutional constituents understand clearly what its investment program is designed to accomplish.

Time Horizon

Return objectives are not useful unless they incorporate a specified time horizon. Given the perpetual life status of most endowments, total fund objectives typically have a very long-term time horizon (e.g., 10 or more years). Stated time horizons for individual fund components vary widely: the more volatile and less liquid (i.e., less readily salable) an investment vehicle is, the longer the time horizon should be used to evaluate its results.

Long-Term Asset Allocation Guidelines

Asset allocation guidelines should outline what asset classes and subclasses constitute permissible areas for investment of fund assets and the minimum, maximum, and normal allocation of fund assets to each of these areas. The policy statement should also outline the criteria to be used in determining whether and to what extent funds should be committed to particular areas. These criteria should be as clear and specific as possible, so that all interested parties will understand why certain investments are held and how their performance should be measured and evaluated. Alternate criteria to be used in evaluating proposed investments include enhancing current income, enhancing principal, enhancing liquidity, and reducing market value fluctuations, either generally or in specific economic environments (e.g., deflation, high inflation).

Long-term asset allocation guidelines typically divide endowment assets into at least three parts: a fixed-income component to generate an adequate level of current income and to hedge against deflation; a component that is a multiasset agreement, typically including cash equivalents and other variable income assets, to hedge against high rates of unanticipated inflation; and an equity component to enhance inflation-adjusted returns within acceptable risk parameters. Over time, portions of these components might be allocated to alternate investments such as venture capital, primarily to enhance returns but also to diversify the fund's holdings and hence keep total fund volatility within acceptable bounds. Some institutions further diversify their fixed-income and equity holdings by the addition of international securities. A number of recent studies have shown that these actions tend to reduce volatility.

Evolution of Investment Vehicles Held by Endowments. Until the early 1980s educational endowment funds were invested almost exclusively in established asset classes, primarily domestic common stocks and fixed-income instruments. These traditional investments were held either directly or, especially in the case of smaller endowments, through mutual funds. In recent years, however, educational endowments and other institutional investors have made extensive use of such nontraditional investments as equity real estate, foreign securities, small capitalization stocks, leveraged buyouts, and derivative instruments (options and futures). They have also turned increasingly to professional investment managers who employ highly specialized and aggressive investment approaches.

The results have been mixed. Where success has been achieved, it has been because trustees have recognized that the markets for virtually all investment vehicles, even seemingly long-term assets such as equity real estate, are inherently cyclical. They also recognize that the total return an asset produces is ultimately a function of two variables: entry prices at the time it is acquired and exit prices at the time it is sold. Paying careful attention to investment cycles and avoiding the natural human tendency to extrapolate recent return trends, especially large gains or losses, are crucially important principles for the achievement of investment success, especially with respect to new or unfamiliar asset classes or techniques.

An institution's asset mix should be reviewed continually. An unusually large appreciation in the value of particular types of holdings (whether held directly or through outside managers) should not necessarily dictate an increase in their size, nor should an unusually large depreciation dictate their sale. Rather, asset classes and subclasses in which endowment funds are invested should be reviewed on a case-by-case basis with an eye toward determining whether the original thesis underlying their use remains intact. If it does, the investment should either be retained or perhaps augmented (if its price has fallen) to the extent that fund guidelines permit. The rationale for increasing exposure to an investment that has fallen in price is that it now offers higher expected returns; whether it offers higher risk-adjusted expected returns is the critical question that must be addressed. Clearly, if the policy aims that motivated the institution to make the investment are no longer achievable or desirable, sale of the investment should be considered.

Short-Term Asset Allocation Guidelines

The segregation of assets into discrete segments in accordance with long-term asset allocation guidelines does not address the separate issue of how to exploit temporary opportunities to make asset allocation shifts for total return purposes. These shifts are extremely difficult to make with respect to illiquid investments such as venture capital and equity real estate and can often be counterproductive (because of timing errors) with respect to liquid investments such as stocks and bonds. In practice, most investment committees refrain from making material and frequent shifts themselves. Instead, they either maintain more or less static asset allocations, rebalancing segment weights as needed to offset cash flows or market movements, or they delegate responsibility for short-term asset allocation to full-time investment professionals. Given the difficulties of short-term asset allocation and the risks to an institution of ill-timed shifts, the written statement of guidelines should specify precisely how much flexibility those responsible for short-term allocation decisions enjoy and how their results will be evaluated.

Manager Selection and Evaluations Criteria

Selecting an investment manager or managers is one of the most significant actions taken by the investment committee. Some institutions may have a board member willing to manage the portfolio and serve as chair of the investment committee. The risks of such an arrangement almost always outweigh the potential rewards. Competent talent is rarely available on a continuous and volunteer basis, conflicts of interest may exist, and if returns prove unacceptable, the arrangement may be difficult to dissolve.

Institutions with sufficiently large endowments can achieve continuous supervision by hiring a staff of full-time investment managers and support personnel, often through a wholly owned investment management subsidiary. Under this arrangement, the investment committee retains responsibility for making policy but delegates responsibility for investment strategy and tactics. The committee also retains responsibility for monitoring and evaluating the investment staff's performance.

Most institutions, especially those with small endowments, achieve continuous supervision by retaining external investment advisors. Outside management has many advantages. Modern financial markets are complex and highly volatile, and few investment committees have both the expertise and the time to make profitable strategic and tactical investment choices. Reliance on outside managers also facilitates objective evaluation of performance. The immediate costs of relying on outside managers exceed the costs of relying on volunteers, but the long-term net returns (total return net of manager fees and related expenses) are often higher than they would be in the absence of professional management.

Many consulting firms offer services to institutions to assist in the selection and monitoring of investment managers. To help clients narrow the field and expedite the search and hiring process, the consulting firms conduct ongoing reviews of managers, which may include the manager's investment process, personnel, philosophy, and background. Given the number of professional money managers (more than 26,000), the selection process, if done by the institution without the help of independent consultants, can be an extremely time-consuming and difficult task.

The weights assigned to criteria used in selecting and evaluating investment managers differ, depending on the asset class (or classes) in which prospective managers invest. With respect to active equity managers, for example, the prerequisites for success arguably include a clearly defined investment philosophy, an asset base that is appropriate to this philosophy (neither too small nor too large), and strong incentives to act in the client's long-term interests. These criteria might be applied to managers specializing in other asset classes, but in applying them trustees must carefully consider the distinctive characteristics of the markets in which individual managers will be operating. A proprietary investment philosophy, for example, is not necessarily a prerequisite for success in managing a short-term fixed-income portfolio, nor is asset size as significant a concern for managers of diversified bond portfolios as it is for managers of focused equity portfolios.

While the weights assigned to individual criteria differ depending on the investment vehicles and management approaches being considered, a checklist of aspects of an investment management organization that should be evaluated can be quite useful.

The philosophy underlying the manager's approach. This consideration includes the investment vehicles that will be used, the likely degree of concentration or diversification in a typical portfolio, the economic and industry sectors that will be favored, the criteria to be used in selecting individual holdings, the portfolio's expected performance during rising and falling markets, and the past and expected evolution of the philosophy.

An important question trustees must address in evaluating alternate investment philosophies is where, along the spectrum of risk or diversification, they believe a fund component should lie. This spectrum is quite broad: it ranges from extremely passive approaches, such as those employed to manage stock index funds, to extremely active approaches, such as those employed by commodity traders. When determining the position of a desired approach along the risk spectrum, trustees must consider many variables, including the "efficiency" of the markets in which a prospective manager operates. An efficient market is one in which the widespread availability and rapid dissemination of data affecting asset prices make it impossible for investors to earn superior returns through intensive research or skilled trading. Many studies suggest that the United States stock market is highly efficient, a hypothesis that is supported by evidence suggesting that active equity managers on average tend to underperform passive stock portfolios. Unfortunately, however, the statistical techniques used to measure the market's efficiency do not work very well, because the professional life spans of managers do not generate a sufficient number of data points to produce valid results. Also, while there is universal agreement that the returns a manager produces should be adjusted for risk, there is no agreement on how investment risk should be defined or measured.

The widespread use of approaches lying all along the risk spectrum underscores the diversity of opinions regarding the issue of market efficiency. However diverse these opinions might be, there is no question that most investment markets, including the United States stock market, are becoming increasingly efficient in a valuation sense. Approaches that have worked well in the past could continue to add value, but trustees should be prepared to adjust their return expectations downward to reflect the sophistication and competitiveness of most present-day investment markets. If the search for potentially remunerative approaches causes trustees to doubt the efficacy of active techniques, the trustees should employ passive or semipassive managers. Retaining an active manager in whom trustees have less than total confidence is extremely dangerous, because temporary setbacks caused by normal portfolio volatility can induce skittish trustees to terminate the relationship when the assets a manager has selected are trading at temporarily depressed prices.

The manager's performance. Measuring a manager's performance includes comparisons of the manager's returns with the performance of (in order of significance):

- other managers espousing a similar philosophy;
- other managers specializing in the same asset class or investment vehicles; and
- a benchmark index (passive portfolio) for the asset class or subclass in which the manager invests.

Results should be measured over sufficiently long time periods: rolling three-to-five-year intervals, in the case of most stock and bond managers.

Other variables. Other variables to consider in evaluating managers include the following:

- *Organization,* including the breadth and depth of a firm's overall product line, the depth, experience, and retention of key individuals, the allocation of responsibilities within the firm, and its compensation and ownership structure. The number and type of portfolios for which key investment decisionmakers are responsible should be carefully analyzed, as should the percentage of their time spent on noninvestment activities such as administration and marketing. If the institution has a separately managed account, as distinct from units in a commingled pool or mutual fund that the firm offers, the importance of the institution's account in relation to the firm's other portfolios should also be considered, as should the firm's method of supervising individual portfolio managers to ensure their adherence to stated account objectives and guidelines.

- *Asset size,* including recent trends and the reasons underlying them. Some institutions have experienced difficulties with firms that have grown too fast. Declining assets can indicate that clients have lost confidence in a firm.

- *Research* conducted by the organization, including the character and quantity of research, the degree of reliance on outside sources, the extent to which a firm has harnessed available technologies to the research function, and the degree to which successful implementation of its approach requires extensive and perhaps proprietary analytical tools.

- *Trading history,* including the organization's ability to execute purchase and sale orders promptly and economically, taking into account both commissions and price impact.

- *Control,* including the organization's supervision of portfolio managers and their results, and adherence to stated objectives and institutional policy.

- *Lines of communication,* including the organization's frequency and manner of reporting and past success at retaining accounts.

When applying these criteria, the governing board should recognize that it is impossible to select the one best manager. It is possible to identify a manager who has performed well historically, but there is no assurance that superior performance will continue, and considerable evidence that superior managers' returns tend to regress to the mean. Given these facts, many institutions have sought to limit manager-selection risk through the hiring of multiple managers or by delegating responsibility for manager selection and evaluation to a consultant or a "manager of managers."

MANAGER RELATIONS

The investment authority granted to managers should be as broad as legally possible to provide managers with the flexibility that they need in order to make timely and profitable decisions.

Controlling Manager Actions

Few institutions require prior committee approval of individual purchase and sale decisions, because such a requirement inhibits effective portfolio management. Some institutions maintain "approved lists" of permissible investments, but in practice the lists are either extremely broad (to encompass all issues a manager is likely to consider) or revised periodically to include issues that may already have been purchased. As an alternative to prior committee approval of decisions or approved lists, most institutions formulate written guidelines for managers to follow in deploying portfolio assets. The topics covered in a set of guidelines differ with the asset class and manager approach in question.

Equity manager guidelines may include limits on the size and number of individual investments or the exclusion of socially unacceptable investments. Percentage limits may be set for total equity positions in any industry or group classification, over-the-counter securities, securities in foreign issues, and outstanding shares of any one company. Fixed-income manager guidelines may include percentage limits on the total issues in any one industry or group, on securities of any one issuer, and on the amount of private placements. Such guidelines may also specify any maturity or quality limits to which managers must adhere. Regardless of their exact content, managerial guidelines should be flexible and should be reviewed periodically to ensure their continued appropriateness in light of available investment opportunities and the committee's ongoing assessment of the institution's return objectives and risk tolerances.

Reviewing Manager Actions

Regular reports to the investment committee concerning investment strategies and tactics are extremely helpful, especially if the manager's approach is very active and entails a high degree of volatility. Periodic face-to-face meetings can be quite useful also, although trustees should recognize that time spent traveling to and attending client meetings is time a manager might otherwise spend on investment functions. The committee's principal concern should be to ensure that managers are faithfully implementing the philosophies that they espouse. Manager performance should be evaluated in accordance with a timetable that is specifically suited to the investment vehicles and approach being employed. As a general rule, managers of longer-term vehicles such as stocks and bonds should be evaluated on a three-to-five-year basis, unless it becomes obvious at an earlier date that they are not implementing faithfully or successfully the philosophy of the board.

Investment managers should provide the institution with written reports, preferably monthly but at least quarterly, analyzing recent performance, performance since inception, and diversification and income characteristics. Detailed analyses of holdings showing cost and market values may also be provided by the investment manager but are typically supplied by custodial banks. The institution's expectations regarding the frequency and content of reports and the methods that will be used to evaluate manager results should be codified in writing, typically in the investment advisory contract executed in accordance with relevant state or federal securities laws.

Investments in mutual funds simply involve a purchase of a share in the fund. The advisory agreement is entered into by the manager with the fund itself, not its shareholders/investors. The investment program is specified in the fund prospectus, and operation of the fund is subject to an extensive array of protective safeguards, including requirements of a minimum number of independent directors available to protect the interests of investors. Use of registered mutual funds does not insulate the institution from fiduciary liability, but it does afford an additional layer of regulatory protection not available outside the mutual fund setting.

The burdens associated with controlling and reviewing managers can be discharged by internal staff or by outside consultants or managers if cost and benefit considerations suggest that is preferable.

Using an Investment Consultant

A number of organizations offer consulting services designed to assist governing boards in the preparation and implementation of comprehensive investment plans. In selecting an investment consultant, the investment committee or governing board should probe carefully for any conflict of interest that might prevent the consultant from acting solely in the institution's best interest.

Consideration should be given to the reputation of the investment consultant's firm and the investment consultant's relevant experience and education. Professional designations, such as Certified Investment Management Analyst (CIMA), are strong indicators of a consultant's knowledge and interest in the area of endowments.

ENHANCING ENDOWMENT RETURNS
THROUGH SECURITIES LENDING

To enhance earnings, some colleges and universities lend securities to broker-dealers. A security loan is a transaction in which the owner of securities gives up physical possession of certificates to the borrower and in return receives cash or other collateral equal to the full current market value of the securities. While continuing to receive the equivalent income from the securities, the lender also has the unrestricted use of collateral, representing the full value of the securities for the period they are on loan.

Several firms make a specialty of servicing large portfolio accounts by generating security loan arrangements. Although the practice of securities lending is well established, any institution contemplating participation should first learn all of the procedures, including protective controls. In contracting for security loans, care should be exercised to evaluate the financial stability of the broker-dealers involved. Lending institutions should continuously monitor the market values of securities loaned and require the borrower to maintain the cash or other collateral at levels specified in the agreement.

MEASURING TOTAL FUND RESULTS

An important responsibility of the governing board is to ensure that endowments and other funds of the institution are invested to produce stated objectives. Productivity depends on many factors, such as the degree of volatility and risk the governing board is prepared to accept in the market value of investments, restrictions imposed on investments by donors, and the relative emphasis on current income versus long-term growth. Whatever criteria are used to judge the return on investments, it is essential that the rate of return be properly measured and that timely reports be made to the governing board. Time-weighted rates of return are generally used in these reports because this method of calculating investment performance eliminates the effect of cash flows on the fund during a period thus making the returns comparable to published indices and/or to investment performance of other institutions.

A fund's gross return has two components: yield and market value change. Yield is the income earned on investments from dividends, interest, and net rental income for the period, stated as a percentage of the fund's market value during the period. Market value change is the net increase or decrease in market value over a designated period, allowing for cash added to or taken away from the pool during the period, expressed as a percentage of the beginning market value. The combination of yield and market value change is the total gross return on the fund. It is important that both components of gross total return be computed and reported to the governing board at regular intervals and that a net total return also be reported that reflects the deduction of all expenses incurred in the safekeeping and investment of assets.

Costs of investment management include direct expenses, such as costs of supervision of securities, investments in real estate, and other types of investments, plus the cost of consultant and custodial arrangements. Indirect costs also may be included. Each fund may bear its proportionate share as a charge against income, or an institution may choose to accept such costs as part of general institutional expense. Proportion of market value is a method used for indirect cost allocation of this type; proportion of activity is another.

Significant cash flows into or out of invested funds can seriously affect the rate of return earned on the total fund. Use of a time-weighted rate of return makes it possible to compute measurements that eliminate the effect of cash flows. The time-weighted rate of return, as opposed to the dollar-weighted rate, is the appropriate measure of results achieved by the fund's investment manager. In averaging rates of return over successive periods, arithmetic averages (adding the rates of return and dividing by the number of periods) should be avoided. A geometric average return (the nth root of a compound over n periods) is the best measure of how profitably the portfolio has been managed.

Many institutions are interested in comparing their investment results with the rate of return achieved on widely quoted indexes, such as Standard & Poor's 500 Stock Index. In making such comparisons, governing boards should employ indexes that are appropriate to the assets whose performance is being measured. Stock indexes are appropriate benchmarks for the measurement of equity managers' performance, but they are inappropriate for the measurement of total fund results, which by definition also reflect the performance of nonequity holdings. Evaluation of total fund results can be made by constructing a composite benchmark that weights the performance of individual asset class benchmarks, such as stock or bond indexes, in accordance with their representation in the overall endowment. This measure is the total fund alpha. A more appropriate measure of total fund return is relative to an absolute return defined by spending policy and strategic planning that will allow the board to measure their progress toward fulfilling their mission. The UPIA defines the fiduciary's central consideration as the management of risk. A return target should be established that funds the mission at the lowest possible risk (deviation from target return). The best measurements adjust both the portfolio and the selected indexes on a risk–adjusted basis. A more comprehensive review of performance may also include measurements of the variability of returns and comparisons of turnover rates on individual fund components.

Many organizations offer performance measurement services. These services measure total fund returns and returns produced by individual fund components; they also categorize managers by investment philosophy and compare managers' returns to returns produced by competing firms with similar investment philosophies.

The National Association of College and University Business Officers (NACUBO) annually publishes a comprehensive endowment study that contains performance, asset allocation, and other data on endowment management practices supplied by participating institutions. Participants typically include institutions that represent the vast majority of the total endowment of American higher education. The study has become an important resource for governing boards and administrators seeking to compare their policies and practices to those employed by peer institutions.

In computing rates of return for purposes of evaluating the quality of investment management, it is important to exclude unappraised or unmanaged investments, as well as investments not under control of the governing board or the firms to whom the board has delegated investment discretion. Unmanaged investments include such items as unregistered or "letter" stock, gifts of securities that donors require to be held in the portfolio as a condition of such gifts, or funds invested in institutional buildings. It may be useful to report earnings on all investments, including such items, but they should not be included for purposes of evaluating investment management prowess.

SOCIAL RESPONSIBILITY

The objective of managing endowment and other funds is to seek maximum long-term investment return without incurring excessive risk. However, the governing board should be aware that social responsibility might also be considered. Advocates of investment responsibility have called on educational institutions to be concerned with social, moral, and ethical considerations in their investments.

Traditionally, institutional investors have tended to follow the "Wall Street rule"—they may support positions taken by corporate management unless there is disagreement, in which case that particular stock is sold. However, in recent years, the trend has moved away from strict adherence to this rule. The more thoughtful investor now makes choices beforehand as to the desirability of involvement with individual portfolio companies.

Many institutions accept the premise that corporations have a moral obligation not to inflict injury on society. As investors and therefore owners of the corporation, institutions have an obligation to communicate their concern to corporations and to seek the prevention of social injury. In addition, some institutions may expect corporations to contribute time, talent, materials, or money to social activities. An investor can encourage or attempt to alter a corporation's practices in at least three ways:

- through the purchase or sale of stock or other securities;
- through the use of a proxy, available to the owner of voting stock; and
- through correspondence or other forms of communication.

In exercising an institution's freedom to invest, the board or its agents should bear in mind that this freedom is subject to certain legal and fiduciary responsibilities. For example, state law may prohibit the use of institutional investments to support a particular political point of view.

When analyzing a corporation's level of social responsibility, it is wise to separate those issues that are mandated by law from those that truly represent the corporation's actions within society. Minimal societal involvement should not be construed as lack of interest. Rather, consideration should be given to the nature and size of the business and to the level of involvement that is justified. Conversely, magnanimous corporate activity may raise questions about objectives and values. What may appear to be a "sound social investment" may, on review, produce neither tangible nor intangible returns.

These are but a few of the concerns that the governing board should consider in assessing the complex issue of an institution's social responsibility. Serious consideration should be given to adopting a separate policy concerning issues of social responsibility in investment management. Institutions lacking such a policy may be open to the accusation that such issues are of little or no concern to them. If a policy statement on investor responsibility is adopted by a governing board, it should describe responsibilities of officers and committees, and the decision-making process related to social and political issues in investment decisions.

Colleges and universities may find it helpful to use the services of organizations whose purpose is to provide impartial and timely analysis, without recommendations, of corporate social responsibility.

CUSTODIAL, SAFEKEEPING, AND EXECUTION SERVICES

A custodial or safekeeping arrangement with a bank, trust company, or broker/dealer is essential to implement an institution's investment program safely and efficiently and to monitor results. Services performed by a custodian typically include preparing up-to-date portfolio appraisals, timely exercise or sale of stock rights, presenting called bonds for payment, converting or selling convertible securities, handling and depositing dividends and interest income, and carrying out policies related to proxy voting. Service can be extended to include use of the custodian's nominee name. A nominee is an individual, partnership, or other legal entity established for the limited purpose of facilitating the transferability of record ownership of securities without regard to beneficial ownership or interest. This device facilitates compliance with the requirements of the organized securities markets: the custodial nominee typically is a member of automated clearinghouses for securitied transfers, and as such, acts as an agent for its custodial clients in delivering and receiving securities.

Custodial services should be specified by written agreement and, in addition to the items mentioned above, may include classification of securities holdings, amount of interest and dividends received, accrued interest schedules, and amortization schedules. Under certain arrangements, verified custodial reports may serve as subsidiary records for the institution. If all security transactions flow through the custodian, computer-to-computer transmission may be possible and relatively inexpensive.

Under custodial arrangements, receipt and delivery of securities usually are from or to brokers against payments charged or credited to a designated bank account or received or remitted by check or wire transfer.

The arrangement for buying and selling investments varies with the nature of the portfolio and form of management organization. When an institution has its own internal investment organization, the full-time manager employed by the institution should be responsible for executions. When an independent adviser is employed—whether a bank, trust company, or investment management firm—it should have its own trading department, staffed with persons whose principal responsibilities are executing transactions, checking markets, and identifying prospective sellers or purchasers of particular securities. This arrangement provides for the most advantageous purchases and sales.

It is important to select investment banking and brokerage firms that execute orders promptly and efficiently and that invest idle cash quickly; that have research divisions capable of providing investment information; that are active in underwriting new issues or in managing private placements; and that make a market for, or deal in, certain securities. An investment performance measurement service is also necessary.

Split Interest Agreement Assets

Prior to passage of the Tax Reform Act of 1969, deferred giving arrangements with donors were often informal and were referred to as life income and annuity funds. Many institutions sought to avoid a trust relationship, as defined by local law, by use of "life income agreements" and scrupulous avoidance of the word "trust." The Tax Reform Act of 1969 clearly established the existence of a trust relationship when educational institutions issue qualified split interest (deferred giving) agreements. The act stipulates that gifts or bequests subject to life income must be made to qualified pooled life income trusts or charitable remainder unitrusts or annuity trusts (as defined in the act) in order to qualify for income, estate, or gift tax charitable deductions. Definitions of these methods of deferred giving prepared for the information of donors must include detailed provisions governing administration of various types of trusts. Donors may make additional gifts to existing pooled life income trusts or unitrusts. However, additions to annuity trusts are not permitted under the act.

Institutions that administer or plan to administer deferred-giving agreements should seek advice from counsel to ensure compliance with relevant provisions of federal and state laws. The officer responsible for deferred-giving agreement administration and investments should be thoroughly familiar with the legal, tax, and accounting complexities of deferred-giving programs, and should analyze carefully the utility to the institution (and to potential donors) of various sizes and types of deferred gifts.

Guidelines should be established by the governing board with respect to methods of deferred giving accepted by the institution. These guidelines could include:

- suitability of each type of agreement to the institution's needs and operating capabilities;

- minimum gift amount required to establish the type of trust in question;

- maximum number of life beneficiaries permitted;

- minimum age for beneficiaries; and

- cost of investment management and whether to charge a fee to cover these costs.

Many institutions refrain from charging beneficiaries for investment management. Because of this, many donors recognize that entering into a split interest agreement may produce an income stream somewhat greater than other alternatives; it is important that an institution consider carefully how management costs will be allocated. Management costs are associated with any investment fund, and such expenses should be recognized and accounted for. The institution should consider whether such costs will be charged to specific accounts or offset by general operating resources.

Five types of split interest agreements qualify the donor for federal income tax benefits: charitable gift annuity contracts, pooled life income trusts, charitable remainder unitrusts, charitable remainder annuity trusts, and charitable lead trusts.

Charitable Gift Annuity Contracts

A gift of cash or other assets may be given to an institution by a donor in return for an agreement by the institution that it will pay the donor and/or named beneficiaries periodic annuity payments for the donor's and/or beneficiaries' lifetime. The full faith and credit of the institution stand behind these contracts. The cash or assets donated become the assets of the institution and can be used for any purpose the institution wishes or any restricted purpose the donor specifies. Even though the assets are technically available for immediate use and are not legally required to be set aside for income-producing purposes, most institutions do set these assets aside in a separate account to produce income until the donor and/or beneficiaries have died. Some institutions have accepted non-income-producing real estate (private homes) in return for charitable gift annuity contracts. In these cases the cash used to cover the periodic payments is drawn from operating funds until the asset is sold.

The rates of return paid to the donor and/or beneficiaries are generally based on their respective ages. The American Council on Gift Annuities, an organization that comprises many of the charitable organizations that issue charitable gift annuity contracts, has established payout rates using actuarial methods that presumably leave the institution a residual of 50 percent of the original value of the assets given to the institution. Most colleges and universities that issue charitable gift annuity contracts follow the rates established by the Committee on Gift Annuities.

Pooled Life Income Trusts

A pooled life income fund is a trust, defined in Section 642(c)(5) of the Internal Revenue Code, to which donors make irrevocable gifts of money or securities that are commingled with the property of other donors who have made similar transfers. Each donor retains a life income interest, as do named beneficiaries living at the time the gift is made. Each beneficiary is entitled to a pro rata share of the pooled fund's earnings each year for his or her lifetime. At the death of the last beneficiary, the charitable organization severs the donor's share of the pooled fund and uses it for charitable purposes.

Assets of pooled life income trusts may be commingled with assets of other institutional funds—such as assets of an endowment pool. However, institutions must carefully consider using a consolidated pool, as certain legal restrictions, such as those concerned with self-dealing and investments in tax-exempt securities, may apply. If an institution adopts a total-return spending policy for its pooled endowment and similar funds, pooled life income funds must be invested in a separate pool under the requirements of the Tax Reform Act of 1969. Institutions not using the total-return method may continue to invest pooled life income funds in a pool with other institutional funds as long as adequate accounting records are maintained that specifically identify the life income portion of the pool and the income earned by and attributable to that portion. Any institution with a significant number of life income funds should establish one or more separate life income pools to facilitate compliance with the stringent operating rules established by the act. Tax law requires that the market-value unit-method of accounting be used for all pooled life income funds, whether or not the assets are commingled with assets of endowment funds.

The institution may delegate its trustee responsibility for the investment management of a pooled life income fund to a bank, as long as the institution retains the power to change trustees. Moreover, a bank may use a common trust fund as an investment vehicle; by using this device, it may be possible for smaller institutions to effect considerable cost savings and achieve greater diversification of their pooled life income funds. As noted, responsibility for investing pooled life income fund assets may also be delegated to a registered investment advisor.

Management of a pooled life income fund presents no unique problems, but as with any investment pool, the institution should articulate clearly the fund's return objectives. Institutions operating only one pooled income fund often opt for a balanced fund aimed at moderate income and some growth. Larger institutions may wish to operate more than one life income pool in order to give donors a wider array of income and growth options; an individual donor's selection of an option will depend on his or her charitable objectives for the institution and the ages of beneficiaries and their financial circumstances.

Charitable Remainder Unitrusts

There are four variations of the charitable remainder unitrust (CRUT).

In a "standard" unitrust a donor irrevocably transfers money, securities, or property to a separate trust that has a charitable remainderman, with payments to be distributed to named beneficiaries at least annually in an amount equal to a fixed percentage (not less than 5 percent under the act) of the net fair market value of trust assets determined annually. On the death of the last beneficiary, the trust terminates and assets are distributed to the charitable remainderman. The donor may designate him- or herself and/or other beneficiaries to receive these payments as long as designated beneficiaries are alive at the time the trust is created and payments are made for their lifetimes or for a term not to exceed 20 years.

In a standard unitrust, a stated percentage of the market value of trust assets must be distributed annually regardless of whether this amount is earned by the trust. To meet the payout obligation, tax law specifies that the trustee must first pay all ordinary income from the current year or prior years, then pay realized capital gains from the current year or prior years, and finally return principal to the beneficiary, if necessary. Moreover, the payments retain their character in the hands of the beneficiaries and the beneficiaries are taxed accordingly. Hence the standard unitrust is primarily of interest to donors in high tax brackets who seek maximum appreciation and minimum ordinary income. This dictates an active, closely supervised, growth-oriented investment program.

The "net income" unitrust is similar to a straight unitrust except that payments to beneficiaries are limited to the actual income earned by the trust up to but not exceeding the fixed percentage stated in the trust agreement. Once the initial investment is made, investment activity in such a trust must be executed with care to ensure that income payments are not reduced.

A "net income with makeup" unitrust pays only the trust's income if the actual income is less than the stated percentage multiplied by the trust's fair market value. Deficiencies in distributions (i.e., where the unitrust income is less than the stated percentage) are made up in later years if the trust income exceeds the stated percentage. This option usually is chosen by younger donors seeking capital appreciation until retirement and maximum income thereafter. The investment strategy therefore is similar to that for a standard unitrust initially and shifts to a net income strategy at a later date. The development office is responsible for informing the investment officer of the donor's objectives in such cases.

Administratively, several options are available for managing unitrusts. The institution can, in effect, run a small "trust department," making individual decisions with respect to the investment of each standard unitrust. This is difficult and costly for a large number of trusts. It may be possible, however, for the institution's investment advisor to prepare a list of a limited number of low-yield, growth-oriented securities in which all standard unitrusts will be invested. These ordinarily will be issues held in the institution's regular portfolio. Such a list should be monitored closely and reviewed regularly.

An institution may elect to have a bank serve as trustee of its unitrusts, in which case the investment vehicle for all but the largest trusts ordinarily is the bank's growth-oriented common trust fund. Such an arrangement may permit an institution to accept smaller standard unitrusts than it could afford to accept if it retained direct investment responsibility. An institution also may elect to invest its standard unitrusts in a minimum number of growth-oriented mutual funds.

Charitable Remainder Annuity Trusts

A charitable remainder annuity trust (CRAT) is defined in Section 664(d)(1) of the Internal Revenue Code as one created by a donor irrevocably transferring money or securities for the benefit of a charitable organization in exchange for a fixed dollar amount (at least 5 percent of the initial fair market value of the transferred property) to be paid at least annually to a designated beneficiary or beneficiaries for their lifetimes or for a fixed term not to exceed 20 years. At the death of the donor or the last surviving beneficiary, the trust terminates and assets of the annuity trust are transferred to the charitable organization for which the trust was created.

Except that the dollar amount of annual payment is fixed at the outset, the annuity trust is essentially similar to a unitrust; the same "tiered" payout rule applies to annuity trusts and straight unitrusts. Because of the fixed annual payment, the donor has an interest in how trust assets are invested only to the extent that it affects the character of the payments and the trustee pursues a strategy that, at a minimum, preserves sufficient assets to make required payments for the life of the beneficiary.

Two variants of annuity trusts are the term-of-years trust and the tax-free trust. A term-of-years trust pays the donor income over a period of years rather than over a lifetime. Scheduling payments for the years when the donor's children will be in college is one popular use of this trust. Tax-free trusts are identical to other annuity trusts but are funded with cash or municipal bonds, the income from which is exempt from federal tax.

Charitable Lead Trusts

A charitable lead trust is an arrangement in which a donor establishes and funds a trust with specific distributions to be made to a designated nonprofit charitable organization over a specified period. The donor may restrict the organization's use of the assets distributed. The distributions may be for a fixed dollar amount, an arrangement called a charitable lead annuity trust (CLAT), or for a fixed percentage of the trust's fair market value as determined annually, a charitable lead unitrust (CLUT). Upon termination of the trust, the remainder of the trust assets revert to a noncharitable beneficiary (such as a child or grandchild) designated by the donor.

REFERENCES AND RESOURCES

Publications

Arnott, Robert, and Fabozzi, Frank J., eds. *Asset Allocation: A Handbook of Portfolio Policies, Strategies, and Tactics.* Chicago, Ill.: Probus Publishing Co., 1988.

Biggs, John H. *The Investment Committee.* Washington, DC: Association of Governing Boards of Universities and Colleges, Board Basics Series, 1997.

Bodie, Zvi, Kane, Alex, and Marcus, Alan J. *Investments.* 4th ed. Homewood, Ill: Richard D. Irwin, Inc., 1999.

Cambridge Associates. *1999 NACUBO Endowment Study.* Washington, D.C.: National Association of College and University Business Officers, 2000.

Cary, William L., and Bright, Craig B. *The Law and the Lore of Endowment Funds.* New York: The Ford Foundation, 1969.

Ellis, Charles D., and Vertin, James R., eds. *Classics: An Investor's Anthology.* Homewood, Ill.: Dow-Jones Irwin, 1989.

Ellis, Charles D. *Winning the Loser's Game: Timeless Strategies for Successful Investing.* New York: McGraw-Hill, 1998.

Ennis, Richard M., and Williamson, J. Peter. *Spending Policy For Educational Endowments.* Westport, CT: The Common Fund, 1976.

Endowments & Foundations. Wilmington, DE: Salomon Smith Barney Consulting Group, 1999.

Fabozzi, Frank J. *Fixed Income Portfolio Strategies.* Chicago, Ill.: Probus Publishing Co., 1988.

Financial Analysts Federation. *Performance Presentation Standards.* Adopted as amended by the Committee for Performance Presentation Standards, Charlottesville, Va., April 1990.

Fogler, H. Russell, and Bayston, Darwin M. *Improving the Investment Decision Process: Quantitative Assistance for the Practitioner and for the Firm.* Charlottesville, Va.: Institute of Chartered Financial Analysts, 1984.

Frantzreb, Arthur. *Not on this Board You Don't—Making Your Trustees More Effective.* Chicago, IL: Bonus Books Inc.

Fry, Robert P., Jr. *Creating and Using Investment Policies: A Guide for Nonprofit Boards.* Washington, DC: Association of Governing Boards of Universities and Colleges, 1997.

Golding, Stephen T., and Momjian, Lucy S.G. *Endowment-Spending Policies.* New York, NY: Morgan Stanley Investment Management, 1998.

Investment Counsel Association of America. *The Standards of Measurement and Use for Investment Performance Data.* New York: ICAA, 1988.

Kittell, Cathryn E., ed. *The Challenges of Investing for Endowment Funds.* Charlottesville, Va.: Institute of Chartered Financial Analysts, 1987.

Levine, Sumner N., ed. *The Financial Analyst's Handbook.* 2d ed. Homewood, Ill.: Dow-Jones Irwin, 1988.

Massy, William F. *Endowment: Perspectives, Policies, & Management.* Washington, DC: Association of Governing Boards of Universities and Colleges, 1990.

Panas, Jerold. *Mega Gifts: Who Gives Them, Who Gets Them.* Chicago, IL: Bonus Books, Inc., 1984.

Principles of Real Estate Investment. Wilton, CT: Commonfund, 2000.

Principles of Successful Endowment Management. Wilton, CT: Commonfund, 2000.

Rosenberg, Claude N. *Investing with the Best.* New York: John Wiley & Sons, 1986.

Selected Policies for the Management of Long-Term Financial Assets of Colleges and

Universities. Washington, DC: National Association of College and University Business Officers, 1992.

Sharpe, William F., and Alexander, Gordon J. *Investments.* 4th ed. Engelwood Cliffs, N.J.: Prentice-Hall, 1989.

Short Takes: Investing. Washington, DC: National Association of College and University Business Officers, 1998.

Spitz, William T. *Endowment Management.* Washington, DC: Association of Governing Boards of Universities and Colleges, Board Basics Series, 1997.

Spitz, William T. *Selecting and Evaluating an Investment Manager.* Washington, DC: National Association of College and University Business Officers, 1992.

Succeed in Private Capital Investing. Wilton, CT: Commonfund, 1999.

The Yale Endowment. New Haven, CT: Yale University Press, 1995.

The Yale Endowment, Updates 1996–1999. New Haven, CT: Yale University Press, 1996–1999.

Wagner, Wayne H., ed. *The Complete Guide to Securities Transactions.* New York: John Wiley & Sons, 1989.

Williams, Arthur, III. *Managing Your Investment Manager.* 2d ed. Homewood, Ill.: Dow-Jones Irwin, 1986.

Williamson, J. Peter. *Funds for the Future: College Endowment Management for the 1990's.* Westport, CT: The Common Fund in cooperation with Association of Governing Boards of Universities and Colleges, and National Association of College and University Business Officers, 1993.

Periodicals

Financial Analysts Journal

Forbes

Institutional Investor

Journal of Portfolio Managment

Money Management Letter

Pensions and Investments

Chapter 10

Debt Financing and Management

by

Eva Klein
Eva Klein & Associates, Ltd.

John H. Augustine
Lehman Brothers

Sponsors

J.P Morgan
Contact: Diana Hoadley
60 Wall Street
New York, NY 10260
212-648-4396
www.highereddebt.com/highered

For over a century, J.P. Morgan has provided financial services, advice amd products to the higher education community. Through J.P. Morgan Securities Inc., the firm provides active debt management innovations for colleges and universities.

GEORGE K. BAUM & CO.
Contact: Lee White
717 17th Street, Suite 2500
Denver, CO 80202
303-292-1600 or 800-722-1670
www.gkbaum.com

George K. Baum & Co. is a national investment banking firm with successful history of higher education finance. In 1999 the firm was ranked 2nd in the United States in the number of senior managed college and university bond issues. In particular the firm is the leading underwriter of privatized student housing transactions. The Firm sponsors the Annual NACUBO/NACAS Survey of Campus Auxiliary Activities.

LEHMAN BROTHERS
Contact: John Augustine
3 World Financial Center, 20th Floor
New York, NY 10285
212-526-5436
www.lehman.com

Founded in 1850, Lehman Brothers is a global investment bank with leadership positions in tax-exempt finance, corporate finance, advisory services, securities sales and trading, research, and distribution to institutions and individuals.

MORGAN STANLEY DEAN WITTER
Contact: Patrick J. Hennigan
1221 Avenue of the Americas, 30th Floor
New York, NY 10020
212-762-8262

Morgan Stanley Dean Witter structures tax-exempt and taxable financings and provides strategic financial advice for higher education clients; manages and underwrites new issues; and is an active dealer and market-maker.

SALOMON SMITH BARNEY CONSULTING GROUP
Contact: Michael T. Dieschbourg, CIMA
222 Delaware Avenue, 7th Floor
Wilmington, DE 19801
302-888-4154 or 800-215-9639
www.smithbarney.com/cg

Salomon Smith Barney Consulting Group provides college endowments with full service investment management consulting, including investment and spending policy, asset allocation, manager search and selection, and performance evaluation.

Contents

Nationally, higher education is experiencing a period of profound change, brought about by the combined multiple challenges of the global knowledge economy, expanding use of virtual technologies for instruction, increased competition, an aging physical plant, a baby boomlet, and continuing pressures to improve productivity. Capital facility development needs may be greater now than at any time before or since the huge post-World War II expansion of access to higher education that led to the creation of many new institutions and to massive growth of and investment in existing ones. Today, the three compelling factors that are driving needs for new capital investment are:

- *Renewal*—correction of long-accumulated capital renewal needs for aging facilities;

- *Technology*—achievement of the technological capabilities required in facilities to serve needs of learners preparing to live and work in the global knowledge economy; and

- *Growth*—accommodation, in some states and regions, of expected growth in traditional 18-year old student enrollments and, in all regions, expansion of learning opportunities for working adults—the new traditional learner.

Deferred Maintenance and Capital Renewal

By now, it is well understood that higher education campuses are aging. Approximately one-third of all campus space was built before 1960 and 60 percent was in place before 1970. Another billion square feet of space was added in the 1970s, to reach a cumulative total of 3.1 billion gross square feet by 1980. Thus, by the last formal estimate (1994), almost 80 percent of 4 billion total square feet was considered to be more than 20 years old and the median year of construction was estimated to be 1967.

With this large a portion of facilities built during the 1950s, 1960s, and 1970s, and some certainly much older, many higher education institutions neglected reinvestment in existing physical plant during the 1970s and 1980s. Estimates of the cumulative problem published during the 1990s ranged as high as $26 billion for deferred maintenance and renewal needs, on a national basis. It is possible that those estimates were low.

For a great number of independent institutions, resources have been limited by several factors, including inflation, enrollment declines, and other operating budget pressures. Public systems typically have suffered from legislative preferences for new buildings, rather than renovations. For many institutions and systems, deferred maintenance now has reached serious proportions, and a number of major financing initiatives to address renewal are emerging nationally. For example, Connecticut recently developed a debt program to fund $2 billion of modernization needs at The University of Connecticut alone. Also, a recent comprehensive study of the 16 public universities in North Carolina yielded a total of close to $3 billion in renovation, modernization, and replacement needs, with replacement needs being primarily for science buildings. The state is evaluating alternatives for meeting these needs.[1]

Impact of Technology and the Global Knowledge Economy

We have entered the era of the global knowledge economy, in which technological demands are requiring massive redesign of curricula, retraining of faculty, and wholesale, ongoing investments in telecommunication utilities and technological capacities of buildings. Technology today is pervasive in all disciplines of instruction, although nowhere is its impact more critical than in the sciences and engineering. Thus, even if funding is applied to restore buildings to original condition, the demands of technology have rendered even good buildings functionally obsolete if they were built more than a few years ago. As one observer of the growing problem put it recently, "What good does it do to have a well-maintained horse and buggy?" Indeed, a vast number of instructional and research facilities, even if in good repair, do not have the technology capacities to meet today's instructional and research needs, much less tomorrow's.

Growth of Traditional and New
Traditional Learner Populations

Beginning now, higher education will need to address significant expansion of its traditional student base, resulting from the baby boom echo that will increase 18-year old college enrollments dramatically, with effects felt more in some states and regions than in others. Also, as the nature of work and occupational demands in the global knowledge economy dictate, routine returning for additional education, sometimes called life-long learning, will cease to be an exception. Working, professional adults rapidly are becoming the new traditional learners, again placing increased demands on facilities, even with the application of online, distance learning technologies.

Overall, as we face the new millenium, capital facilities challenges in higher education are of an order of magnitude perhaps rivaled only by the great expansion of the post-war and baby-boom years of the 1950s and 1960s. The magnitude of the needs makes capital formation and maximum prudent use of both internal and external methods of financing even more important and more complex than they have been in the past. In the coming decade, colleges and universities, with their public and private sponsors, must meet these daunting challenges of moderniza- tion and expansion, or find themselves at risk of being replaced by corporate-spon- sored, virtual, technology-intensive new knowledge institutions. For the first time ever, the quality of a campus's facilities may be a major factor in whether that institution will continue to be a preferred educational option for many potential students.

Thus, many institutions that did not need to do so in the past have under- taken or are planning for debt financing programs, in combination with internal resources, public funding, and aggressive private fund-raising programs. It is a time when creativity and the use of all reasonable means to achieve the resources needed are required.

Overview of the Chapter

This chapter provides a primer-style overview of debt securities, debt financ- ing, and debt management.[2] It begins with a general introduction to institutional debt policy and management in higher education. Because the chapter is intended for nonfinancial professionals, the material then includes a general introduction and overview of debt securities markets and structures, describes higher education finance markets, explains typical debt vehicles, explains common standards and measures of creditworthiness, and outlines the bond issuance and rating processes. Most of the chapter's material deals with new money issues, that is, debt issuance for new projects; one section deals with refunding of existing debt. The current legal, tax, and regulatory environments, which are subject to continuous change, are treated only generally. For a more detailed understanding of such issues, which are integral to the structuring and implementation of a borrowing, institutional administrators should seek the advice of an investment banker and bond attorney. Student loan financing is not covered; for a discussion of this topic, readers are referred to the *NACUBO Guide to Issuing and Managing Debt*.

DEBT CAPACITY AND POLICIES

Debt Capacity

The debt capacity, that is, the level of debt an institution can bear prudently, depends on a variety of legal, policy, financial management, market, and rating factors. Conservative financial policies on the part of state governments and private governing boards have tended to prevail in higher education. Borrowing is not always considered an appropriate financial strategy because it reduces financial flexibility for institutions that may experience fluctuations in demand for their services or unexpected increases in costs. On the other hand, there may be an opportunity cost of not borrowing, especially using the tax-exempt market, when there are real needs that, if unmet, may harm an institution's performance.

A college or university's prescribed debt limits can be set statutorily by state governments, by a governing board, or by management. In these cases, the debt limits are, *de facto*, the institution's debt capacity. However, the market itself, often as represented by the decisions of investors, the rating agencies, and financial intermediaries effectively dictates debt limits. The market's debt limits for a borrower may be different from the institution's own internal perception of its debt capacity, and the market's perceptions of appropriate limits may be either more conservative or less conservative than the institution's.

Although the debt capacity of any institution is a function of numerous specific factors, such as the strength of state support, student demand, and unrestricted assets, many colleges and universities may have some degree of unused debt capacity; some may have significant potential to add debt to their balance sheets without loss of financial flexibility.

Debt Policy

Institutions have both externally imposed limitations and internal choices to make about whether and how much to incorporate debt into strategic and capital finance policies.

Limited Debt

Historically, a few independent colleges and universities had charter or endowment provisions that precluded them legally from engaging in borrowings; today, this is no longer the case. Other institutions, while not legally prohibited from borrowing, have had historical policies of avoiding debt to which they have been able to adhere without much difficulty.

Statutory Debt Limits

A number of public institutions have debt limits prescribed by statute or other legal bases; these institutions usually also have restrictions on what kinds of projects they may use their debt capacity to finance. Such debt limits may be expressed as an upper limit for the ratio of debt service to unrestricted current fund expenditures. Alternatively, for auxiliary systems, debt limits may be expressed as the relationship between system net revenues and debt service.

Institutionally Established Debt Policy

A number of public and independent institutions that are active issuers of tax-exempt debt have developed nonstatutory internal debt policies that govern the level of debt liability they intend to incur. Normally, such policies are developed with professional assistance and approved in formal resolutions by the governing board of the institution. Elements of the debt policy may be developed separately for revenue-generating auxiliary facilities and for non-revenue-generating academic facilities. Some colleges and universities have specific policies for other aspects of debt management. For example, an institution might decide to use debt only for auxiliaries that generate revenue or only for major renovations and maintenance, reserving new facilities construction for donor gifts or internal funds.

Capital Planning and Budgeting

Long-range capital planning and budgeting is a difficult but necessary art form in colleges and universities. An institution that has a strong, ongoing strategic planning process tied directly to its operating and capital budgeting processes is in the strongest position to evaluate debt opportunities and to build them successfully into a broad capital development plan.

With a multiyear framework of strategic needs and priorities, a capital budget that incorporates estimates of both new building needs for growth and renovation costs for modernization and technology enhancement should be developed. As time passes, the capital budget must be updated to reflect completed projects, changing priorities, and cost differences.

A complete capital development plan also addresses alternatives for financing that may include:

- appropriations;
- internal/operating funds (pay-as-you-go);
- focused fund-raising or capital campaigns;

- bank debt;

- tax-exempt debt in public markets;

- taxable debt in public markets; and

- private sector development, via ground lease or joint ventures with a real estate developer.

Analyses must be made as to which financing methods are feasible for, or best suit, each planned project. To some extent, these decisions are self-evident, based on statutory debt authority of state-supported institutions, some of which have authority to borrow only for revenue-producing auxiliaries. Even without legal restrictions, revenue-generating projects are often considered to be good candidates for debt financing. In other cases, potential donors are interested only in certain types of facilities. Many capital financing plans are embedded in capital campaign plans. Inevitably, some projects are neither attractive to donors nor fundable from operating funds and may lend themselves only to debt financing. (For more information, see chapter 4, Budgeting.)

Weighing External Borrowing Versus Funding from Internal Cash Flow

Colleges and universities frequently face the decision of whether to fund a project internally with cash flow or whether to incur bank or bond debt. Traditionally, many institutions often preferred to support projects from cash flow because it was simpler, normally requiring only management's decision and the approval of the institution's governing board, and did not entail restrictive commitments to external parties. It is not, however, the most cost-effective alternative, if tax-exempt financing is viable. A simple rule of thumb to consider is that an institution should not use internal funds for capital acquisitions or development that are appropriate for debt issuance if the average rate of return on invested funds exceeds the expected all-in cost of financing (interest plus transaction costs) of bond debt. If an institution uses invested funds earning higher interest rates than the institution would pay on debt, then the difference in lost interest earnings may be considered an opportunity cost. For example, if an institution can achieve an all-in cost of financing of 6.5 percent and is able to earn an average of 7.5 percent on taxable investments, it would be more expensive to use internal or invested funds than to borrow externally. In this example, the opportunity cost of borrowing internally is 1.0 percent multiplied by the amount borrowed.

Choosing Between Bank Debt and Public Debt Markets

Another major consideration is whether a project is of the type and size to warrant the effort and expense of a publicly offered bond issue. In many cases, colleges and universities should explore bank debt alternatives, particularly with local banks where they maintain account relationships and particularly for debt that will be less than $5 million. Although the interest rates may be higher, for smaller borrowings, conventional term loans or mortgage loans may have the advantage of timeliness, simplicity, and minimal transaction costs. In some instances, a private placement of bonds may be a good alternative to either the options of a bank mortgage or a public bond sale. A private placement widens opportunities for potential lenders without all the complications of a public bond sale. (See definitions and descriptions as follows.)

Borrowing Versus Doing Without

A college or university may have a project suitable for bond financing, sufficiently strong credit, and available debt capacity, but may prefer not to borrow for reasons of fiscal policy, lack of familiarity with bond financing, or internal institutional politics. One alternative is to forego the needed facility or renovations. In such cases, an analysis of the comparative costs of borrowing with the potential hidden costs or opportunity costs of not doing the project can be useful.

Quantifying hidden costs is more difficult than comparing internal and external borrowing alternatives, but it is not impossible. In many cases, institutional managers already know intuitively that inadequate facilities are precluding them from attracting or retaining resources—research funding, new faculty, or more students—but may find the addition of a debt-service burden difficult to defend to various internal constituents, especially to faculty.

For example, an institution with severe maintenance problems in its student housing facilities may have reason to believe that it is losing potential freshmen and/or suffering enrollment attrition in part because of the negative impression that deterioration of the housing facilities makes on students and their parents. If this case needs to be made on the basis of something more than intuition, informed judgment, and anecdotal data, then the institution could conduct a survey of current students and parents and departed students and their parents, to determine the extent to which poor residential facilities are or were a factor in their dissatisfaction. Admitted students who chose not to attend also might be surveyed. The resulting data can lead to an estimate of the hidden costs of not performing major renovations to student residences. Perhaps the cost of lost tuition and fees over time would far exceed the annual debt service cost of financing the renovations.

Similar analyses may be made of the impact of inadequate research facilities on research grant volume or on faculty and graduate student recruitment.

It is likely that this kind of analysis will become more common because of the huge amounts of major maintenance that colleges and universities have deferred. Donors generally are not very interested in providing naming gifts for new roofs and underground utility lines, and there are limits to the amount of funds that unrestricted annual giving can contribute to facilities maintenance. There is also the matter of intergenerational equity—the question of whether current operating funds, including student tuition, should be used to fund long-term capital facilities improvements that will be used by future students during several decades.

Often involved in these considerations are the concerns of governing boards about incurring long-term obligations. Institutional leadership needs to work with board members to achieve a balanced evaluation of the risks of borrowing versus the risks of not accomplishing the needed projects. Boards need to be encouraged to undertake soundly planned, long-term financing, so that they do not merely pass on problems to successive generations of governors. An ideal perspective is that a well-planned and well-managed debt program can be a primary resource for resolving many of the plant renewal, growth, and technology enhancement challenges that the institution faces.

Impact of Debt Programs on Institutional Management

Taking on a debt program has both positive and negative implications that should be well understood by governing boards and senior management. A well-conceived debt management program broadens options, affording opportunities for facilities acquisition and development that may not be available by other financing methods. It also provides some budgetary discipline, because when a college or university funds major maintenance with debt, it no longer can yield to the annual temptation to reallocate maintenance budget lines to other budget categories; the debt service that enabled upgrade of the physical plant is now a fixed cost. Debt-financed maintenance and renewal projects also can be accomplished immediately, while their cost is distributed over their useful life.

On the other hand, taking on debt has potential negative consequences that need to be evaluated, including consequences for operating budgets, restrictions imposed by bond indenture covenants, and increased management requirements and workload. Also, institutions contemplating debt financing for the first time should be aware of current accounting rules for the treatment of debt.

Impact on Operating Budget

Many colleges and universities must weigh carefully both the real impact of adding debt service to their fixed cost of operations and the political impact on internal constituencies of doing so. While debt service imposes the discipline of funding plant-related needs and spreads the cost over the useful life of facilities, it also can diminish operating budget flexibility. For many institutions, there is the additional problem of achieving an appropriate balance between funding debt service for facilities and funding faculty salary increases, student financial assistance, and other major budget priorities. The realities of conflicting priorities and campus perceptions about those priorities, especially among faculty, must be considered. If debt issuance seems appropriate, steps should be taken to educate internal constituencies to the advantages for them of the improved facilities, prior to undertaking the financing.

Bond Covenants

A bond covenant or restrictive covenant is a legally enforceable commitment made by the issuer to perform or not to perform some act. Covenants typically are stated in the bond resolution or bond indenture. (See discussions later in this chapter for definitions.) Common covenants include such commitments as:

- maintaining use charges for the financed facility so that they provide sufficient pledged revenues to maintain the prescribed debt service coverage ratio, called a rate covenant;
- completing, maintaining, and operating the project financed;
- maintaining liability and other insurance coverage on the facility financed;
- issuing parity bonds only if the additional bonds test is met;
- taking no action that would violate Internal Revenue Code restrictions on invested proceeds earnings, causing the bonds to become arbitrage bonds;
- segregating and accounting for funds; and
- not selling or encumbering the financed facility or project.

Colleges and universities contemplating debt issuance must consider how such covenants would affect institutional management. Removal of a covenant that at one time may have been acceptable or unavoidable but that since has become onerous or avoidable for the institution may be an occasion for an advance refunding, if the refunding bonds can be issued without a similar restrictive covenant.

Staff and Management Requirements

In addition to the financial and legal restrictions imposed by bond indebtedness, colleges or universities that contemplate a single bond offering or a sustained debt management program must be prepared to allocate the human resources and time required for this financial activity. Additional staff may be required, contributing marginally to the cost of debt.

The process of planning and executing a publicly sold bond issue is time consuming and labor intensive. The most direct effects are felt by the institution's chief financial or business officer and/or treasurer and their staff. The chief business officer will lead planning of the financing, select the team of financing advisors, make recommendations to the governing board on critical issues of structure and timing, and oversee the process. In addition, the chief business officer probably will have the responsibility of educating internal constituents about the financing purposes and outcomes.

The institution's president, other officers, and board members also are involved to a lesser extent. This intensive process may last a few or many months. No matter how small the institution's financial staff is, at least one person must be familiar enough with debt financing to be able to work effectively with underwriters, financial advisors, bond attorneys, issuing authorities, and others, as well as with internal constituents.

Sustained debt management programs, including those with mixes of fixed and variable-rate debt, require continual monitoring to ensure that:

- timely and accurate payments are made;
- all records and relationships with the trustee, paying agent, and remarketing agent are maintained;
- changes and expected changes in variable rates are monitored;
- investment matches with liabilities are maintained;
- opportunities for refunding or use of hedge products and techniques are integrated into debt management; and
- arbitrage rebate calculations are performed.

(Many of these terms are defined later in this chapter.)

INTRODUCTION TO DEBT SECURITIES
AND THE MUNICIPAL MARKET

The Economics of Borrowing and Lending

In the United States, the nonfinancial business sector and the government sector generally are net borrowers of funds in the economy while consumers and, to a lesser extent, financial institutions generally are net lenders of funds. That is, while all types of entities may engage in both borrowing and lending, typically consumers (through savings) and banks (through lending) put more funds into the economy than they borrow, while businesses and governments borrow more than they lend.

The economic purpose of borrowing is to change the timing of an individual's or an organization's expenditures to better match the timing of its income or revenues. A borrower uses someone else's funds for a needed purpose today, rather than deferring the expenditure until the income is available in the future. For making the funds available, the lender is entitled to a return in the form of interest.

For a college or university, the question of the timing of expenditures for capital facilities in relation to the timing of future tuition, fees, research overhead, gift income, or other revenues (borrowing versus pay-as-you-go financing) has special implications. Students avail themselves of the benefits of the college's capital facilities for only a few years; thus, a college or university that pays for facilities from its current resources, on a cash basis, does not distribute the cost of those facilities to the many generations of students who will use them. In contrast, a 20-year or 30-year bond issue distributes costs into future years, presumably over the useful life of the facility and for the several generations of students and faculty who will use them. In this sense, debt financing better matches the timing of expenditure with the actual use of the assets.

Capital Formation

By issuing corporate debt securities, a business entity can raise needed capital without diluting ownership or equity interest in its assets and earnings capability; debt actually increases return on equity. Typically, most corporations have capital formation plans that call for a mix of equity and debt financing. The mix is often highly sophisticated and closely managed. Modern financial management principles suggest that colleges and universities, like business corporations, should have capital formation and management plans in which debt is a legitimate element.

For colleges and universities, debt is an alternative not to ownership equity but to internal funding from gifts, reserves, or current revenues; and, in the tax-exempt municipal market, debt often is the most cost-effective alternative. Unlike the capital formation plans of corporations, those of higher education institutions also include a component for philanthropic fundraising. Many institutions raise funds and apply them directly to capital development projects to which they are designated.

Capital Markets

The domestic United States (and increasingly global) markets for the buying and selling of capital in various forms are called capital markets. In addition to currencies and commodities, there are three basic forms of securities that make up the capital markets: the stock market (equity securities); the bond market (debt securities); and the money market (wholesale market for high-quality, short-term debt securities). The municipal bond market or tax-exempt bond market is a subset of the bond market. Colleges and universities issue debt primarily, though not exclusively, in the tax-exempt municipal bond market, which differs distinctly from the taxable or corporate bond market and from the government bond market (U.S. Treasury securities) in issuance volume, security structures, issuance processes, liquidity, types of investors, and yield behavior.

Bonds

A bond is a promise to repay a specified sum (principal) plus compensation (interest) to a lender for use of the lender's money. Payments of principal and interest are made on specified dates. The terms interest, rate, and coupon denote the percentage rate of compensation to bondholders during the life of the bond. Interest is expressed commonly as a nominal annual rate, although actual payments may be made semiannually, quarterly, monthly, weekly, or daily.

The maturity of a bond is the date when the principal amount becomes due and payable. A serial bond has a series of maturities, with partial amounts of the total principal coming due annually or semiannually during a period of several years. The par value of a bond is the principal amount that is due at maturity. A bond that is traded at a price below its par value is a discount bond; a bond that is traded at a price above its par value is a premium bond.

Historically, bonds came in one of two forms, bearer bonds and registered bonds. Bearer bonds were negotiable by anyone who held them. Bearer bond certificates included interest coupons that the bondholder clipped at payment dates and presented for payment at a bank; payment was made by the paying agent of the borrower to whomever held and submitted the coupons. Registered bonds also are issued as bond certificates but are registered with respect to ownership; consequently, they provide greater security against theft as well as the option of automatic payments made to the bondholder. With widespread automation in the capital markets, all bonds now are issued as book-entry bonds. These are registered bonds whose ownership is recorded in an automated central system by a depository such as Depository Trust Company, a depository owned by a consortium of banks and brokers. Physical bond certificates are not issued in book-entry bond issuances.

Bond Yields

The yield on a bond is the annualized rate of return, expressed as a percent, that the investor will earn on the investment. Although nominal yield may be used to indicate the stated interest rate or the coupon, the return to an investor is described typically in terms of different calculations of bond yields.

Current yield, which describes current income on a bond earned from interest payments, is calculated as follows:

$$\frac{Coupon\ Interest\ Payment}{Annual\ Price\ of\ Bond} = Current\ Annual\ Yield$$

As the equation indicates, the price and the current yield of a bond are inversely related. When the price of the bond rises, the yield goes down, and vice versa. Essentially, the current price of a bond is the sum of the present value of future payments on the bonds, with yield as the determinant of those present values.

Investors typically analyze bonds in terms of their yield to maturity or their yield to call. Yield to maturity is the annual rate of return, compounded semiannually, earned from all payments of principal and interest, assuming that the investor holds the bond to maturity. Unlike current yield, yield to maturity takes into account the time value of money. There are four variables involved: the bond price, the coupon rate, the maturity in years, and the yield to maturity. When the first three are known, yield to maturity can be derived; conversely, when the last three are known, the price of the bond can be derived. The calculations formerly involved the use of bond value tables and interpolation, but now bond calculators or computer programs compute results instantly.

Another yield calculation of interest to bond investors is the yield to call.

Municipal securities typically are issued with call provisions, which give the issuer the right to redeem (or prepay) the bonds after a specified period of time has passed and at an established call price, expressed as a premium over par value. Yield to call is the rate of return to the investor if the bonds are called by the issuer on a call date. When dealers sell bonds to investors, they generally also must quote the yield to call, if it is lower than the security's yield to maturity.

Interest Rate Behavior

Interest rates in the economy generally are driven by business cycles, the inflation expectations of borrowers and lenders, monetary policy, and risk. It is useful to have a basic understanding of these dynamics, as watching the trends can be an important factor in the decision of a college or university about when to issue debt.

The Business Cycle

As the economy grows, demand for borrowing by corporations and municipal borrowers typically increases and interest rates usually rise. However, the experience of recent years has been unusual, in that the United States has had a strong economic growth cycle with very little upward change in interest rates. Typically, when the business cycle turns down, demand for borrowing tends to decline, and interest rates follow suit.

Inflation Expectations

Interest rates are composed of two components, one of which is a factor for the time value of money, which represents the cost to the lender associated with the unavailability of the funds for the duration of the loan. This is referred to as the real rate of interest and represents the cost of the use of money, assuming there is never inflation in prices. The other component of interest rates is a factor for inflation, reflecting the change in purchasing power the lender expects to experience when the money is repaid. When lenders expect inflation to increase, they require higher rates of interest; at the same time, borrowers are willing to pay higher rates when they expect prices to rise, because they expect to repay the obligation with inflated dollars. Consequently, inflation expectations of lenders and borrowers combine to affect interest rates and inflation projections are a factor in interest rate forecasts.

The Federal Reserve Board and Monetary Policy

One of the major central banking functions of the Federal Reserve Board (the

Federal Reserve or the Fed) and its 12 regional Federal Reserve Banks is to control the supply of money in the economy, thereby influencing both inflationary expectations and the level of interest rates. The Federal Reserve sets the interest rate (the discount rate) at which banks may borrow money from it and establishes reserve requirements for banks that, in turn, drive their cost of funds. The Federal Reserve influences the federal funds rate, the rate at which banks borrow readily available funds from each other. By directly influencing short-term rates, the Fed can indirectly have an effect on long-term rates. Most important, however, are the policy actions of the Federal Reserve's Open Market Committee, by which the Fed buys or sells government securities, specifically in order to increase or to reduce the money supply available in the banking system.

Risk

Lender's perceptions of their risk will affect interest rates. The greater the risk of a bond's default, the greater will be the default premium included in the bond's interest rate. Thus, the riskier the bond, the higher interest rate it will have to pay.

Interest rates, then, are determined largely by the supply and demand for funds in the economy or the availability of and demand for credit. The interest rate is the price that will cause supply and demand for money to come into balance. The Flow of Funds reports published by the Federal Reserve trace the flow of funds in the economy. Using data from these reports, analysts can attempt to ascertain the relative historical and current activity of various categories of borrowers and lenders, as well as project future demand for credit and the potential supply of funds that will be available to meet that demand.

The Term Structure of Interest Rates and the Yield Curve

In choosing among different securities, investors consider risk, liquidity, and return. In addition to credit risk or default risk (the risk that the borrower may be unable to make timely principal and interest payments on the debt), investors also face price risk. This is the risk that the price of the bonds will fall because of an increase in the general level of market interest rates. The longer an investor must wait for repayment, the greater the risk of fluctuations in the value of the bond investment, because there is more time for variations in interest rates to occur. Therefore, securities with longer maturities typically carry higher rates of interest, specifically to compensate for this increased risk, although this relationship can be reversed under certain conditions, as described as follows. This is called the term structure of interest rates and is portrayed commonly as a graph called the yield curve, with maturities plotted on the X-axis and interest rates or yields plotted on the Y-axis.

Because of the inherent meaning of the yield curve, in a normal interest rate environment, the normal yield curve is upward sloping, or positively-sloped, reflecting higher yields for longer maturities. When unusual securities market conditions cause short-term rates to exceed long-term rates, the yield curve is inverted. When short-term and long-term rates are close to equivalent, the yield curve is flat. And, when intermediate term rates are higher than short-term or long-term rates, the yield curve is hump-backed.

Figure 10-01 is a hypothetical example of a normal, that is, positively sloped yield curve. In this entirely hypothetical example, rates range from 3 percent for 30-day maturities to 6 percent for 30-year maturities.

Like the yield curve for other classes of debt securities, the yield curve for municipal or tax-exempt securities normally is positively sloped, but its shape does vary sometimes, under conditions like those described previously.

Understanding yield curve behavior is important to both occasional issuers of bonds and to managers of sustained debt issuance programs; it is a major factor in

Figure 10-01

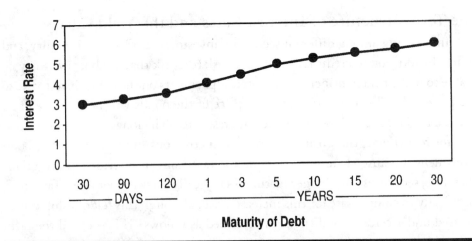

Hypothetical Illustration of Term Structure of Interest Rates
(The Yield Curve)

decisions about when to borrow (new money) or to refund existing debt, and also in how to structure the maturities of a bond issue.

Municipal Securities and the Tax Exemption

Municipal bonds or securities—the debt obligations of state or local governments—have been issued since the early part of the 19th century. The securities market changed dramatically in 1913, when the Sixteenth Amendment to the Constitution established the federal income tax. Income earned on municipal securities was exempted from federal income taxation. As a result, yields on these securities fell dramatically and the municipal securities market became distinctly separate from the corporate bond market. The municipal securities market expanded continuously throughout the 20th century, especially since World War II.

Municipal securities today include many classes of debt obligations issued by states or political subdivisions of states, which may be local governments, agencies of state governments, or special statutory authorities created by state governments for the purpose of debt issuance. This includes public universities and university systems that are considered agencies of their state governments and higher education debt issuance authorities, established as state agencies, which issue debt for private colleges and universities.

Municipal securities differ from corporate debt securities in that the interest income on these obligations is exempt from gross income for federal income tax purposes. The basis for the federal tax exemption arose from the constitutional doctrine of reciprocal immunity, under which the federal government and state governments cannot interfere in each other's affairs, including by means of taxation. In U.S. tax law, this has been interpreted to mean that the federal government cannot tax as income the interest paid on the debt of nonfederal governmental entities. To do so, it is argued, would impair the ability of the states to finance operations.

The Internal Revenue Code, Section 103, provides statutory exemption from federal taxation of interest earned on municipal securities. This section of the Code is amended from time to time to change the manner and degree to which the exemption from taxation is granted. Recent court actions have weakened the reciprocal immunity concept and have advanced conceptually the ability of the United States Congress to control the issue of tax exemption.

Furthermore, most states also exempt from taxation the interest they pay state resident investors on their own securities issues and on municipal bonds issued by obligors within their borders, although most do tax the interest earnings on securities issued by other states. A few states exempt from taxation the interest on all municipal bonds. A triple tax-exempt security is one that is exempt from federal, state, and city income taxes; for example, a bond issued by a New York City entity purchased by a New York City resident would be exempt from federal, New York State, and New York City income taxes.

Taxable Yield Equivalent

This tax exemption privilege is the principal advantage that public borrowers, including higher education institutions that can use this privilege, have over corporate borrowers. An investor who is not required to pay federal and other income taxes on interest earned is willing to accept a lower rate of interest on the investment than would be required for an equivalent taxable investment. This difference is called the taxable yield equivalent of municipal securities. It is computed as follows:

$$\frac{Tax\text{--}Exempt\ Yield}{100\%\ Marginal\ Tax\ Bracket} = Taxable\ Yield\ Equivalent$$

For example, an investor who earns \$200,000 and is hypothetically in a 40 percent marginal tax bracket and who buys a tax-exempt municipal bond with a 7 percent yield earns a taxable yield equivalent of 11.7 percent. Using these hypothetical numbers, a college or university borrower would pay 7 percent as its cost to borrow, whereas a corporate borrower of equivalent creditworthiness would pay 11.7 percent. The higher the investor's tax bracket and taxable yield equivalent, the greater the value of the tax exemption and the lower the interest rates that tax-exempt borrowers must pay to induce that investor to buy their bonds. It is for this reason that changes in federal income tax rates can greatly affect interest rates in the municipal tax-exempt bond market.

Tax-Exempt and Taxable Yield Curves

Municipal market borrowers need to be aware of the relationship or ratio between tax-exempt and taxable interest rates. The relationship changes as a result of a variety of factors. The relationship is important for college and university borrowers that need to consider borrowings in both the tax-exempt and taxable markets as part of their financing programs.

In the long run, municipal market rates generally move in tandem with rates in the corporate and government bond market. In the short run, however, municipal market rates move independently of other fixed-income interest rates and are subject to their own technical or indigenous factors. Most of these factors are aspects of supply and demand. They are important considerations in a college's decisions about when to issue large debt offerings.

Overall Supply and Demand of Securities

Price and yield can be affected by simple fluctuations in the amount of debt issuance flowing into the market at a given time in relation to demand. For example, in December 1985, numerous higher education issuers brought securities to market at the same time, to avoid tax law changes that were to go into effect in 1986. Bond yields and costs to the borrower rose to offset this temporary surge in supply. A more recent example of a time when there was a relatively large supply of higher education debt in the market was in 1998, after the restrictive cap on private college and university issuance was lifted.

If timing is not urgent, financial advisors normally attempt to bring a higher education issue to market when supply for higher education bonds and/or for other competing municipal securities in general is low, relative to normal demand levels.

Credit Quality Preferences

The municipal market can be subject to different demand for issues of varying credit quality, depending on whether investors, as a whole, are more or less risk-averse at a given time. An extremely risk-averse market can drive up prices and drive down yields for even the highest-rated securities. Thus, the yield curves for securities of different credit rating classes can have different shapes.

Tax Law Changes

The municipal market is susceptible to changes in tax law that modify eligibility for issuance in ways that affect supply; that raise or lower individual or corporate tax rates; or that modify provisions for tax deductions or other aspects of the incentive to invest in tax-exempt securities. The Tax Reform Act of 1986 provided several major examples of how tax law can affect demand and investor behavior that, in turn, causes interest rates to rise or fall. For example, commercial bank appetite for tax-exempt debt diminished radically as a result of elimination of a deduction they had been allowed previously for 80 percent of the interest costs on funds they used to purchase tax-exempt securities. Second, the 1986 introduction of the alternative minimum tax (AMT) made certain classes of municipal securities subject to some taxation. Yields on AMT bonds must generally be slightly higher than yields on non-AMT bonds.

A profound change occurs when there is a major increase or decrease in the maximum individual or corporate tax rates, because the yield relationship between taxable and tax-exempt investments is affected directly. Suppose that our hypothetical investor, who had a 40 percent marginal tax bracket, now has a marginal tax rate of only 30 percent. Recalculation of that investor's taxable yield equivalent would bring very different results. If our investor, who is now in a 30 percent tax bracket, buys the same tax-exempt municipal bond yielding 7 percent, he or she now would have a taxable yield equivalent of 10 percent (instead of 11.7 percent, when the marginal tax bracket was 40 percent). Now the 7 percent tax-exempt investment is compared with a taxable investment of only 10 percent rather than 11.7 percent. To the extent that desirable taxable investment alternatives are available at 10 percent or more, yields on tax-exempt investments will have to rise to induce investors to buy them. From the perspective of the higher education borrower, therefore, a tax rate reduction can mean a rise in the tax-exempt interest rates a college or university will have to pay.

COLLEGES AND UNIVERSITIES AS ISSUERS OF MUNICIPAL SECURITIES

Because the municipal tax exemption is restricted to public issuers and public purposes, the legal status or type of entity that issues the bonds is fundamentally important in determining whether the borrower is eligible to issue tax-exempt debt. It also determines the application of regulatory restrictions on uses or eligible projects, treatment of arbitrage (earnings on unspent bond proceeds), financing of costs of issuance, and other related matters. There are differences in bond issuance powers and in limitations on those powers between public and independent higher education institutions, although these differences are much less important today than they were in the past.

As agencies of state governments, public higher education institutions are subdivisions of state government and, as such, can be public issuers of tax-exempt debt, depending on state law. Where state laws permit, a public university may issue bonds directly in the name of the institution. In many states, public colleges and universities are not accorded direct bond issuance powers by the state. In these jurisdictions, the states themselves typically are the issuers of debt for higher education capital projects.

In contrast, independent nonprofit colleges and universities are issuers of qualified 501(c)(3) bonds, a special category of municipal security issued by or on behalf of nongovernmental, tax-exempt, 501(c)(3) entities, to meet various public purposes. (See also chapter 11, Taxation.)

Higher Education Facilities Authorities

To make tax-exempt issuance of securities available to nonpublic entities that develop facilities with public purposes, various state, county, and local special agencies or authorities are created by statute, to serve as the legal municipal issuer of such debt. These are referred to as conduit issuers and such financings sometimes are referred to as conduit financings.

Numerous state and local authorities have been created specifically to issue debt for higher education or for higher education and health care borrowers. They share the common function of serving as the legal entity for bond issuance, but the range and scope of their activities vary considerably. In some states, higher education facilities authorities have extensive policies on credit strength requirements, as well as large staffs to provide substantial assistance to, if not total direction of, the selection of financial intermediaries, capital finance planning, and the conduct of financing transactions. In other states, authorities have smaller staffs or no staff at all, and their roles may be limited to establishing policies and procedures and to reviewing and approving specific financing requests from higher education borrowers.

A few states, such as Massachusetts, have two or more state-level agencies or authorities that have legal powers to issue debt for higher education institutions. In addition, city or county authorities also have been created to issue debt on behalf of one or more colleges or universities within their jurisdictions. Typically, these local authorities are found in states where the municipal legal structure includes charter cities. Examples of states in which there are multiple city or county issuance authorities and where these authorities have issued bonds on behalf of higher education borrowers include New York and California. Finally, industrial development authorities (IDAs) may have the power to issue bonds on behalf of not-for-profit institutions.

Independent colleges and universities located in jurisdictions that include more than one legal entity through which they can issue debt should explore their options; the programs, requirements, flexibility, and levels of assistance provided may vary considerably between issuing authorities.

Growth in Higher Education Bond Issuance

Compared with other industry groups, colleges and universities historically have used debt financing conservatively. The oldest, most well established inde-pendent higher education institutions have tended to rely heavily on private fund-raising, including major gifts from alumni, for capital construction. Smaller pri-vate institutions with less wealthy donor bases often have funded facilities from internal resources. Public institutions have relied heavily on state appropriations, although the state may rely, in turn, on its general obligation debt to fund capital projects. Some colleges and universities have had internal policies that precluded incurring debt.

Thus, until the 1980s and 1990s, issuance of publicly sold bonds and use of complex debt financing structures typically were undertaken only by the larger, better-endowed, or more financially sophisticated institutions; smaller institu-tions, when they borrowed, relied more typically on tax-exempt loans directly from local banking institutions. Beginning in the 1980s, numerous changes in federal tax laws, bank lending programs, and institutional management capacity, combined with continuing fiscal pressures, led increasing numbers of colleges and universities to enter the public tax-exempt debt market.

Figure 10-02 shows that the volume of higher education bond issuance has increased markedly since 1980. Overall higher education volume, including both publicly sold debt and private placements and short-term notes, has risen more or less steadily from $1.046 billion in 1980 to about $14.5 billion in 1999.[3] Exclud-ing private placements and short-term notes, the publicly sold volume has increased from $778 million in 1980 to $13.2 billion in 1999. In fact, higher edu-cation annual dollar volume has nearly doubled since 1990.

In 1980, there were only 65 publicly sold higher education bond issues and a total of 76 reported bond issuances. At that time, the publicly sold volume of $778 million (excluding private placements and short-term notes) represented 1.7 percent of the total municipal tax-exempt market. And, at that time, it was esti-mated that only about 10 percent of the nation's approximately 3,500 colleges and universities had issued publicly sold debt. By 1999, there were 537 publicly sold issues, and a total of 595 issues including private placements. Higher education volume from 1980 through 1999 totaled more than $143 billion, in nearly 6,500 issuances. Higher education now represents about 6 percent of the total municipal market. Many more institutions now are occasional or regular public borrowers.

Figure 10-02 also illustrates clearly the effects of market conditions, includ-ing those relating to tax law as noted. Although the trend line has been rising steadily, there were three noticeable peak years during this 20-year period. They were in 1985, when borrowers rushed to market in advance of the Tax Reform

Figure 10-02

Increase in Dollar Volume of Higher Education Bonds Since 1980
All Issues—Publicly Sold, Privately Placed, and Short-Term Notes

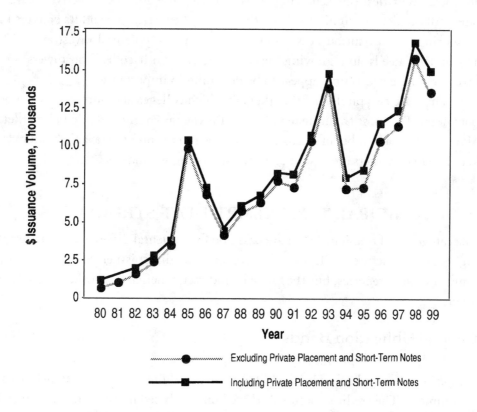

Act of 1986 and the volume was $10.2 billion; 1993, when market interest rates were unusually favorable and volume was $14.5 billion; and 1998, after the tax-exempt volume cap for independent institutions was eliminated and volume was $16.4 billion.

Historically, constraints of credit strength, lack of name recognition, lack of financial sophistication, and the small size of some borrowing needs had kept many colleges and universities out of the public tax-exempt debt market or confined their borrowings to participation in large pooled financings. Because higher education had been a relatively minor player in the tax-exempt bond market, investors did not always understand higher education debt as well as other types of tax-exempt bonds. In fact, higher education is regarded as having a good track record in creditworthiness; defaults on higher education debt generally are believed to be infrequent. Major institutional investors today know how to evaluate these securities, but achieving successful issuance and cost-effective interest rates still can depend significantly on the skill of the institution and its bankers in presenting the institution's case—telling its story—to potential investors. With accelerating needs and growing sophistication of both college borrowers and investors, these constraints appear to be declining in importance.

There are two public debt markets in which colleges and universities can be borrowers. The most traditional and typical is the tax-exempt municipal market. More recently, a number of institutions have begun to enter the taxable bond market. The two markets are described in the following sections.

MUNICIPAL TAX-EXEMPT DEBT STRUCTURES

The categories of municipal debt are based on fundamental differences in underlying security structure. Colleges and universities are direct issuers of bonds in only some of these categories, but they may be indirect beneficiaries of the proceeds of others.

General Obligation Bonds

In the tax-exempt municipal market, general obligation bonds are long-term obligations that are backed by the full faith and credit of the issuer, a state or local government. The credit structure of these bonds is based on the general financial strength and taxing authority of the issuer, without limitation. General obligation bonds are the original and most basic form of municipal debt.

Colleges and universities, like hospitals and other nongovernmental entities, have no taxation powers; by definition, therefore, they cannot be issuers of general obligation bonds in the true sense. (This is not to be confused with the fact that a college or university bond issue can be secured by a general obligation pledge of all the institution's revenues.)

In many states, the state itself issues general obligation bonds, the proceeds of which are designated to fund construction of facilities for the state's higher education system. Illinois, North Carolina, and California are examples of states that periodically finance higher education facilities through state general obligation debt.

Revenue Bonds

Revenue bonds are a relatively newer form of municipal financing than general obligation bonds. Revenue bonds once constituted a small fraction of the total municipal market, but today dominate the market, representing in 1999, 68 percent of the total par amount of tax-exempt issuance.

Revenue bonds are not secured by the general revenues and taxing powers of the issuer; rather, they are issued to support specific projects, the revenues of which are pledged to repay the indebtedness to bondholders. Based on the concept of user fees, revenue bonds have allowed municipal issuers to expand their indebtedness without creating greater burdens on general tax revenues. In the 1950s, highways and utilities were the major purposes for which user fees were charged and revenue bonds were issued. Today, revenue bonds are issued commonly for colleges and universities, hospitals, housing, public power projects, small industrial development projects, pollution-control facilities, and many other public purposes.

With the exception of state general obligation bonds issued by a state to finance college or university facilities, higher education bonds generally are classified as revenue bonds. Tuition and fees that institutions collect may be thought of as roughly equivalent to other types of user fees. As noted previously, however, college and university revenue bonds may carry general obligation pledges of institutional revenues.

For higher education issuers, revenue bond issues may be a consolidation of numerous projects as system revenue bonds, such as for dormitories, food service facilities, or parking.

Special Tax Bonds

Special tax bonds are like general obligation bonds in that they do not depend on specific fee revenues for repayment to bondholders; however, they are supported by a specific dedicated tax or taxes rather than by the full taxing authority and general revenues of the issuer. As an example, Florida's motor vehicle tag tax is pledged by the state of Florida to repay bond issues for higher education institutions, as is a gross receipts tax on utilities.

Double Barreled Bonds

A double-barreled bond is secured legally by both specific user fee revenues from a facility financed and by the taxing power of the issuing governmental entity.

Moral Obligation Bonds

A hybrid form of general obligation bonds and revenue bonds is a moral obligation bond. This type of bond is secured technically by the fees or revenues from the facility financed, but with the additional moral but not legally binding commitment on the part of a governmental entity to pay bondholders from tax revenues in the event that project revenues fall short. Such payments usually are made through appropriation of general state revenues to replenish depleted reserves for the bond issue in question. These types of funds must be appropriated by the legislature.

Often, a moral obligation bond may be a matter of market perception. For example, if a state with a very strong credit rating and conservative fiscal practices issues forms of debt other than general obligation bonds for important state purposes, investors may perceive that the state in question would back the obligation from other sources, if the primary security pledge were inadequate.

Private Activity Bonds and Qualified Private Activity Bonds

Revenue bonds are categorized as either governmental use or private activity bonds. Private activity bonds are revenue bonds, the interest income on which is subject to taxation unless they are qualified (for the tax exemption) private activity bonds. Under current tax law, the tests that are applied to determine whether or not an issue is qualified significantly limit private sector involvement in tax-exempt financed projects. Even private activity bonds that are qualified to be tax-exempt are still subject to more limitations than are governmental use bonds. Issued by or through a public entity to support a private activity with public purposes, qualified private activity bonds are possible in such undertakings as pollution-control facilities, multifamily and single-family housing, stadiums, and small industrial development projects, and are subject to state volume caps.

Qualified 501(c)(3) Bonds

Private colleges, universities, nonprofit hospitals, and other tax-exempt organizations are issuers of an additional subcategory of qualified private activity bond called qualified 501(c)(3) bonds. The term 501(c)(3) refers to Internal Revenue Code provisions that define entities that are exempt from federal income tax. Qualified 501(c)(3) bonds are exempted from the tests applied to other qualified private activity bonds and are not subject to state volume cap limitations; however, these bonds are more limited in their treatment than are governmental use bonds.

Pooled Bond Issues

Numerous states have undertaken, through their higher education facilities authorities, to sell bonds to create a pool of funds from which to make small loans to qualifying colleges and universities. The advantages of pooled financing are significant to small borrowers. For example, pooled financing makes it possible for the small borrower to gain access to funds at tax-exempt rates. This might otherwise not be feasible because the small size of the borrowing would make a stand-alone issue too costly or because the small size of the institution or limited market recognition of its name would make marketing its bonds difficult and expensive.

Until 1986, it was legally possible to issue blind pools, a pooled financing for which the borrowers and their projects were not identified in advance. When the proceeds of the sale of bonds were received, the bond program administrator invested them at taxable returns and earned arbitrage on the invested proceeds until loans were made to qualified borrowers. Since 1986, regulations have precluded blind pools and related arbitrage earnings.

Pools remain a viable form of financing, primarily in states where the education facilities authorities have sufficient resources to survey participants for needs and to organize the complexities of pooled financings. However, the use of pools has been declining somewhat as more individual college issuers are coming to market on their own. The California Educational Facilities Authority, the Dormitory Authority of the State of New York, and the Massachusetts Health and Educational Facilities Authority are among the authorities that have issued pooled debt programs to finance projects at numerous colleges in their states.

LONG-TERM TAX-EXEMPT DEBT

Fixed-Rate Bonds

The most conventional form of tax-exempt debt is the long-term, fixed-rate bond, in which interest rates are fixed for a single or multiple maturities. The final maturity is the period when the final principal is due to bondholders. Final maturities of 20 or 30 years are common and, in some cases today, final maturities as long as 60 years or more are possible.

Most issuances are structured with serial maturities and in par amounts calculated to include the costs of the capital project or projects and the costs of issuance of the bonds, including reserves for debt service. Sometimes, reserves for repair and maintenance of the facilities to be built also are included in the par amounts of the borrowing. Several separate issuances or a series of bond issues may be issued under a single bond resolution and may be treated as a system of facilities, or issuances may be under separate bond resolutions. In higher education, dormitory system or dining system or parking system bonds are common.

Investors in fixed-rate bonds have two advantages: a fixed rate of return and the possibility of appreciation, an increase in value. When market interest rates decline, holders of bonds at higher rates of interest benefit because their bonds appreciate in value. Conversely, colleges and universities that issue fixed-rate debt have the advantage of fixed interest and principal payments, permitting the institution to budget for debt service with great certainty. The risk to the borrowing institution is that, if interest rates decline significantly, the institution then may be paying more than current market interest rates; however in most instances, there eventually are opportunities to call or refund (refinance) outstanding issues.

Call Provisions or Callable Bonds

Long-term, fixed-rate bonds typically have call provisions that enable the borrower to repay bondholders ahead of schedule, at fixed call dates and at fixed call premiums over the par value. For example, 30-year callable bonds issued with serial maturities typically will have a call provision of 10 years, at a premium of 101. This means that if the college chooses to exercise the call provision, the bondholders are repaid 101 percent of the amount then outstanding; the original debt is extinguished and usually is replaced with new debt at prevailing rates.

Term and Serial Bonds

Term bonds have a single maturity at which the entire principal becomes due. Normally, term bonds will have a sinking fund structure, by means of which the borrower sets aside funds, so that the entire principal amount is accumulated for redemption of the bonds at maturity. Serial bonds are issued with portions of the bonds scheduled to mature each year or in selected years, during a period of many years. Serial bonds permit an overall reduction in interest costs because the bonds with shorter maturities pay lower rates of interest than do those with the longer maturities. Serial bond issues can be structured to provide for level debt service or for level principal payments, while allowing the borrower to amortize or reduce the borrowing slowly over time. Typically, an issuance will be structured with both term bonds and serial bonds, that is, a combination of serial maturities and a single term or balloon maturity. Alternatively, a single bullet maturity, without any sinking funds, can be issued.

Lease Structures

Lease certificates of participation are units of ownership in debt that is repaid from lease payments, often on major equipment financing. The investors receive portions of the lease payments in proportion to the lease certificates they own.

Lease structures can be especially effective for colleges and universities that are financing major equipment acquisitions, such as high-technology telecommunications systems, major computer acquisitions, and significant scientific and research instruments. An important feature of many lease financings is that security for the debt is contingent on annual appropriations of funds and not on a general obligation of the issuer.

Zero Coupon Bonds (Capital Appreciation Bonds)

Capital appreciation bonds or zero coupon bonds have a coupon interest rate of 0 percent. When issued, they are sold at a deep discount from the par amount. Upon maturity, the investor receives a return in the form of appreciation, a portion of which represents tax-exempt interest. In higher education finance, zero coupon bonds have been used to finance tuition savings plans and are useful also for specific instances in which the borrower can benefit significantly from having no interest payments to make for a certain time.

SHORT-TERM AND VARIABLE-RATE, TAX-EXEMPT DEBT

Because of the term structure of interest rates, short-term debt normally carries lower interest rates than long-term debt. Long-term variable-rate debt, which emulates the interest rate and maturity features of short-term debt, provides opportunities for flexibility and reduced financing costs.

Notes

Notes are short-term obligations, generally with maturities of one year or less, although there is no entirely accepted standard definition for what constitutes a note. Tax-exempt notes of various kinds, including tax anticipation notes (TANs) and revenue anticipation notes (RANs) enable a governmental borrower to smooth out or anticipate irregular future cash flow. Alternatively, bond anticipation notes (BANs) permit a borrower to finance a construction project temporarily until long-term financing is put in place. Used widely by municipal governments, tax-exempt notes are not used as often by college and university issuers, although several states recently have undertaken initiatives of this type.

Variable Rate Demand Bonds

Variable-rate demand bonds (VRDBs) blend some features of long-term fixed-rate bonds and some features of short-term debt (notes). The bond issuance has a long-term nominal maturity, for example, 30 years; however, the securities have a demand or put feature whereby the bondholder may put the bonds back to the issuer, that is, require the issuer to repurchase the obligation at par value plus accrued interest. VRDBs also bear an interest rate that is reset on a yearly, semiannual, monthly, weekly, or daily basis, based on market conditions. Thus, investors in VRDBs are able to hold long-term investments with the benefit of reduced interest rate risk. If market interest rates rise, the rate that is paid on the VRDBs also will rise. Normally, resetting the interest rate to match the yield required by current market conditions makes it unlikely that investors will exercise the demand option. If a demand or put is exercised, however, the issuer's remarketing agent then must remarket the bonds to new investors. For this contingent service, the issuer of VRDBs pays an ongoing annual remarketing fee to the remarketing agent.

Because of potential rate volatility and exercise of demand features, VRDBs generally are structured with a commercial bank's letter of credit or a standby bond purchase agreement (SBPA), to serve as a liquidity back-up facility. If an investor demands repurchase and the bonds cannot be remarketed immediately, the letter of credit is drawn down for payment of the repurchase price plus accrued interest to the initial bondholder. Letters of credit typically are provided by commercial banks, which charge an initial and ongoing annual fee for providing this liquidity backup. Some VRDB issues have credit support in the form of bond insurance, with a letter of credit or standby bond purchase agreement structured to provide liquidity only.

The college or university borrower faces interest rate risk with VRDBs that it does not face with fixed-rate bond obligations. An issuer of VRDBs must have enough financial liquidity and flexibility to be able to cover increased payments if necessary. On the other hand, the lower (essentially short-term) rates at which VRDBs are sold have enabled a number of institutions to lower their cost of borrowing successfully. With legal restrictions on advance refunding (see the section on Management of Existing Debt), variable-rate debt also provides the flexibility of optional calls or redemptions by the issuer on very short notice, for example, 30 days for a monthly VRDB. In contrast, fixed-rate debt normally has a no-call period of five to 10 years.

VRDBs normally have a one-time fixed-rate conversion option whereby the issuer can, with certain required notices, convert the VRDB to fixed-rate debt. Upon conversion, the bonds become long-term, fixed-rate obligations. Conversions to other forms of interest rate fixing (e.g. monthly to daily to weekly) may be permitted, subject to approval by bond counsel.

Multimodal Bonds

Multimodal bonds permit the issuer to select and change the mode of interest rate resetting periodically to take advantage of changing yield curves. While periodic notice, additional documents, and a marketing period are all required, the advantage is that the mode resetting is not considered a new issuance when the interest rate is changed, thus leaving available the one-time opportunity for refunding, as allowed under federal rules.

Tender Option Bonds

Tender option bonds are similar to VRDBs, but differ in the length of the tender period and the periodic interest-rate resetting. Tender option bonds give the investor the right to sell or put the bonds back to the issuer at par regardless of market conditions. Initially, a tender option bond is structured with the first tender date set at six months to 10 years from the date of issuance. Subsequent tender dates occur periodically thereafter. Between tender dates, the interest rate on the bonds remains fixed.

Tax-Exempt Commercial Paper

Tax-exempt commercial paper is an unsecured promissory note issued in registered or bearer form with a maturity that does not exceed 270 days. Tax-exempt commercial paper is the municipal market's counterpart to taxable commercial paper, which is the short-term unsecured debt typically sold only by corporate entities with very strong credit. Tax-exempt commercial paper usually is backed by a line of credit or letter of credit. Common maturities are 30 days and 60 days.

Tax-exempt commercial paper has been used effectively as a structure for pooled financings initiated by state authorities on behalf of numerous college borrowers. Although this financing mode used to be relatively rare in higher education, its use has been growing, and tax-exempt commercial paper now generally is considered one of the many viable options available to those colleges and universities with credit enhancement and strong underlying credit.

FEDERAL TAX LAW RESTRICTIONS ON TAX-EXEMPT FINANCING

Higher education bond issues are subject to federal and state taxation and securities laws and regulations, as well as to the internally imposed legal and policy restrictions of the institution itself. A comprehensive discussion of the legal framework for bond issuance is beyond the scope of this chapter; however, a number of general limitations under federal tax law are basic to understanding bond issuance in the current environment. A few are discussed here.

Since Section 103 of the Internal Revenue Code was enacted in 1968, successive legislation has placed restrictions on the tax-exempt borrowing privilege. Legislated reductions in applicability of the tax exemption generally are responses to concern that the exemption drains revenues unnecessarily from the U.S. Treasury. This concern is sharpened by a perception that Treasury revenue losses may exceed the interest cost reductions made possible for issuers through use of tax-exempt borrowings.

Prohibition of Arbitrage

Arbitrage arises from the difference or spread between taxable and tax-exempt interest rates. When the proceeds of a tax-exempt issue are invested, prior to being expended, in taxable securities with yields higher than the interest being paid on the tax-exempt bonds, the issuer earns arbitrage profits. Under the Internal Revenue Code and ensuing regulations, municipal borrowers are precluded from earning arbitrage profits in most circumstances and, where such arbitrage is earned, it usually must be rebated, that is, paid to the federal government. The preclusion is implemented in two ways. The majority of bond proceeds are yield restricted; and, where yield restriction does not apply, rebate usually is effective in transmitting arbitrage earnings back to the federal government.

There are six-month, 18-month, and two-year rebate exceptions that have specific spending guidelines and timetables, as well as a variety of penalty options in the event that guidelines and timetables are not met. Also, debt service reserve funds are limited to the lesser of 10 percent of bond proceeds or maximum annual debt service, unless prior bond indentures require larger reserves. When bonds are secured with larger reserves, the investment yield on the reserves is restricted to the yield on the bonds. Because the regulations governing arbitrage are exceedingly complex and change periodically, prospective debt issuers are advised to consult bond counsel for current information.

Reimbursement Regulations

Complex regulations govern the ability of an issuer to use the proceeds of a tax-exempt bond issue to reimburse itself for project-related expenditures made prior to the date of issuance of the bonds. Generally, the regulations require that the issuer declare reasonable official intent to reimburse the prior expenditures with bond proceeds. A college or university's governing board or the issuing authority, or both, must adopt resolutions of intent with certain prescribed characteristics. The intent also must be reasonable in terms of the institution's financial resources, and timing of the expenditures is a factor.

Limitations on Advance Refunding

New money bond issues sold after January 1986 may be advance-refunded only once. Bonds issued earlier may be advance-refunded twice, with certain exceptions. (Advance refunding is discussed in the section on Management of Existing Debt.)

Use of Proceeds Test

The proceeds of a bond issue must be used for the exempt purpose of the issuer. In higher education, this means that proceeds of a tax-exempt bond issue must be used for projects that are related to the educational purposes of the institution. Ninety percent of proceeds of bonds issued by public higher education institutions and 95 percent of proceeds of bonds of independent colleges and universities must be so used. As an example, this restriction may preclude the use of tax-exempt financing for inclusion of space for privately owned and operated retail space in a student union building.

Independent Institution Volume Cap

From 1986 through 1997, a tax-exempt volume issuance cap was in effect for private higher education institutions, limiting their bond issuance to a total amount outstanding of $150 million. This cap was, for some time, a severe constraint on borrowing for those institutions that would have issued larger amounts of tax-exempt debt. In August 1997, the cap limiting the amount of allowable outstanding tax-exempt debt for independent nonprofit colleges and universities was lifted with respect to par amounts outstanding of future debt issues. This change in federal tax legislation allows universities to fund all tax-exempt eligible future capital needs on a tax-exempt basis. Debt issued while the cap was in place still is restricted to the $150 million cap. This means that, if a college or university wants to advance refund pre-1997 debt, both the existing debt and the new debt count toward the cap, until the existing debt is redeemed. This has restricted the ability of many institutions to take advantage of the recent historic lows in the tax-exempt interest rates of the late 1990s. However, in general, the repeal of the tax-exempt volume cap is enabling a number of independent colleges and universities to better address their needs for financing new facilities.

Limitations on Costs of Issuance

Independent colleges and universities may only capitalize (include in the par amount of the borrowing) costs of issuance of the bonds up to a limit of 2 percent of tax-exempt bond proceeds. Costs subject to this limitation include most transaction costs, including underwriting spreads (bond discounts); legal fees, including underwriter's counsel, issuer's counsel, and bond counsel; financial advisory fees; rating agency fees; trustee and paying agent fees; and accounting services fees. (The services these parties provide are discussed in the section on Accessing the Capital Markets, under The Participants.) An exception is made for the fees associated with credit enhancements, that is, bond insurance or letter of credit fees.

TAXABLE DEBT

Intended uses of facilities and various legal and regulatory restrictions on use of tax-exempt debt occasionally require colleges and universities to venture into the taxable debt markets. As colleges and universities begin to engage in complex real estate development strategies, either alone or in alliances with private sector partners, taxable financing is becoming more common. Sometimes, a small borrowing need may not justify the transaction costs involved in public tax-exempt borrowing. And, in some circumstances, institutions have issued taxable debt with options to exchange all or a portion of such bonds for tax-exempt bonds bearing lower interest rates, if and when access to the tax-exempt market became available to them. The categories of taxable debt differ not only in source of funds but also in debt structure and means of market access.

Taxable Bank Debt

Term Loans

A term loan is a loan made by a commercial bank for a defined period or term and bearing a fixed or floating rate of interest. Loan terms (duration) may be brief, such as 90 days, or long-term, such as 10 years. A term loan often is secured by a mortgage, in which real property (land and/or buildings) is pledged as collateral or security for the loan. Banks perform a credit analysis to decide whether or not to make a loan and to determine what features, including term, interest rate, and payment provisions, to offer.

Although reliable estimates of the annual borrowing or total outstanding volume of term loans made by banks to colleges and universities are not readily available, the volume is undoubtedly large, and most colleges and universities are familiar with this kind of financing. An institution often has one or more significant banking relationships in its community; the degree to which it may be able to obtain competitive or favorable terms on a term loan may be tied to the extent of its relationships with local banks.

Line of Credit

A line of credit is an amount of funds made available, usually by a bank, to a borrower; it is sometimes referred to as a credit facility. When funds actually are needed, the borrower exercises or draws down on the line of credit. Upon exercise, the original credit facility often may be converted to a term loan. Lines of credit are used commonly to provide liquidity and can be extremely useful in managing cash flows.

Letter of Credit

A letter of credit is a form of credit facility sold by banks, although it may be provided by other entities. Letters of credit are discussed as a technique for credit enhancement.

Taxable Debt in the Capital Markets

The single major advantage of taxable debt is that it does not bear the restrictions as to issuer, purpose of issuance, and other regulatory limitations to which tax-exempt debt is subject. Essentially, taxable borrowings are much simpler to structure. The single but quite major disadvantage is that the cost of funds, by definition, is higher. Before the private institution volume cap was lifted, taxable bonds were increasingly a viable choice for those university issuers who had reached their tax-exempt cap. Today, with the cap no longer presenting a problem, taxable debt still is used only in cases where the nature of the projects does not constitute a tax-exempt purpose or use. This is the case, for example, with certain kinds of real estate development projects in which universities are the sole sponsors or partners in financing, including research park facilities for commercial tenants, conference centers and hotels, or commercial retail developments.

Capital Leasing or Lease-Purchase Agreements

In a capital lease, the lessee makes a series of lease payments, at the end of which the lessee owns the asset. Capital leases often are a financing option for major equipment acquisitions and may be offered by banks, leasing companies, or equipment vendors. Capital leases are common, for example, in major computer acquisitions.

Commercial Paper

Taxable commercial paper is unsecured promissory notes of corporations, issued for short-term financing or working capital purposes. The paper is issued at a discount and redeemed at face value. Normally, commercial paper programs are issued only by strong credits in large par amounts and rolled over each time the issue matures. A commercial paper program can be credit-enhanced by means of an irrevocable bank letter of credit.

Because of program size and credit requirements, taxable commercial paper has not been used frequently in higher education. It has been used to generate the funding for special pooled financing programs. It is likely that taxable commercial paper, because of its relatively low cost and flexibility, will be used more often in higher education, most likely for large pooled financings.

Medium-Term Notes

Medium-term notes or bonds (MTNs) are taxable securities with intermediate-length maturities, typically from two to 10 years, which, unlike longer-term bonds, are not callable by the issuer. They are a good taxable alternative for higher education borrowers because of the large size of the MTN market and because they can achieve an interest rate lower than that required by long-term bonds while allowing the borrower to avoid the volatility of short-term rates.

Taxable Fixed-Rate Bonds

Taxable fixed-rate bonds are similar in structure to their tax-exempt counterparts, with maturities of 10 to 30 years, but are sold either as public offerings in the taxable United States corporate bond market or as private placements. Private placement of long-term fixed-rate bonds is, in certain situations, a useful alternative to public offering and sale. Private placements can have maturities as long as 30 years, but 15 to 20 years is the common final maturity. Because of their narrower distribution, private placements generally have higher yields than do public offerings by issuers of comparable credit strength. The college or university borrower pays a higher interest rate. The advantages are that issues as small as $5 million may be economically viable; credit enhancement typically is not used; less well-known names can be placed; and the transaction is surrounded by privacy. These bonds are purchased most frequently by investors such as insurance companies, pension funds, and certain mutual funds that intend to hold them to maturity.

Publicly offered taxable fixed-rate bonds can be viable for smaller institutions that are, for various reasons, unable to gain access to the tax-exempt market. Although lack of familiarity of market investors with higher education names is a drawback to smaller or lesser-known issuers, bond insurance may be available to enhance the credit of certain issues.

Foreign Currency Denominated Bonds

The most significant difference between foreign currency denominated bonds and conventional fixed-rate taxable bonds is that principal and interest transactions are made in a foreign currency. When interest rates are more favorable outside the United States, an issuer can consider whether access to a foreign capital market can be used as a means to reduce borrowing costs. The issuer must be aware, however, of the possibility of a gain or loss on payments due to changing currency exchange rates. In higher education, the limited name recognition abroad of many institutions makes it difficult to find foreign investors. Larger well-known public and independent universities, pooled higher education financings, or issues credit-enhanced by a well-recognized commercial bank or bond insurer are most likely to avail themselves of international market opportunities for capital.

Taxable Variable-Rate Demand Bonds

Taxable variable-rate demand bonds (VRDBs) are similar in maturity and rate structure to tax-exempt VRDBs, except that rates are taxable interest rates. The market for taxable VRDBs is relatively small, but they may have applications for specific circumstances in higher education. For example, a few such financings have been accomplished in connection with university-related research parks.

SECURITY STRUCTURES, CREDITWORTHINESS, AND CREDIT ENHANCEMENT

Higher education bond issues are by definition revenue bonds, except when a state's general obligation debt is issued for a higher education purpose. Security structures for higher education debt therefore involve variations on revenue pledges of the institution, that is, pledges of general credit (general revenues) or pledges of specific revenue streams. In addition, through use of a credit enhancement product, the credit strength of a credit enhancement provider can substitute for the credit of the issuer or the issuance.

Forms of Security

Physical Collateral

Physical assets pledged by a borrower to a lender constitute physical collateral. If the borrower defaults on debt service payments, the collateral may be taken by the investor, who then is free to dispose of the property. Normally, the lender sells the collateral to repay the loan. Facilities acquired or constructed with the proceeds of bond funds commonly are pledged as physical collateral to secure the interests of the bondholders. Commercial bank term loans often are structured as mortgages, in which the real property or buildings are collateral for the lending bank.

In the case of corporate debt, physical collateral can be quite meaningful as security. If a corporation defaults on its bonds, bondholders usually can liquidate the corporation's property and recover most or all of their funds. In the case of college and university financing, however, physical collateral, other than undeveloped land in locations with development potential, is typically far less meaningful as security to bondholders. It is not likely that bondholders would be able to convert an academic building, dormitory, student center, or athletic facility located in the core of a university campus to another profitable use. In the case of lease financing of major computer systems or other high technology equipment, physical collateral can be more meaningful, as the assets are suitable to disposition, if necessary.

Collateralization with Endowment and Other Assets

A borrower can collateralize a loan with assets other than physical assets. Securities and invested funds are common forms of collateral. In the past, colleges and universities commonly collateralized bond issues with quasi-endowment. There was no cost associated with doing so, as the collateralized funds could continue to earn returns. Tax law now requires that the yield earned on invested funds held as collateral for bond issues be restricted to the rate of interest paid on the bond issue, although there are some technical steps that can be taken to make partial collateralization useful. This requirement has changed the implications for this type of collateralization, making it virtually unusable as a form of security.

Pledge of General Institutional Credit

Higher education bonds classified as revenue bonds (those other than state general obligation bonds, issued for higher education) can be secured by a pledge of general institutional resources and, consequently, represent general obligations of the institution, a common form of security generally used by public colleges and universities. A pledge of the institution's general credit means that all revenues and resources of the institution that are not restricted legally to another use or purpose can be tapped to meet payments to bondholders in the event of imminent or actual default. As an important practical matter, true endowment funds, that is, endowment that has been restricted as to use by the donor, never can be subject to this or any other kind of pledge of use. Therefore, this form of security pledge is sometimes called a legally available funds pledge. The meaning of such a pledge and its value in terms of the quality of the credit of the borrower depend on the degree of flexibility the institution has in reallocating resources, if necessary, to pay debt service. Policy issues, specific terms of endowments, state requirements, diversity of revenues, size of funds functioning as endowment, and other factors determine the strength of a pledge of general institutional credit.

Pledge of Tuition and Fees

Another common form of security pledge is a pledge of tuition and fee revenues. This kind of security can be either a limited or unlimited pledge. This structure logically provides less security to the bondholder than does a general obligation pledge because funds other than tuition and fees cannot be tapped to pay bondholders. When tuition and fees form the security pledge, the credit analysis focuses closely on the competitive strengths of the institution, strength of student demand, the history of enrollments, and the levels of tuition and fees charged. Minimum coverage of debt service on the bonds most likely will be specified.

Pledge of a Specific Revenue Source

Alternatively, an institution can issue project revenue bonds, the repayment of which is backed only by the specific revenues of the project being financed. In higher education financing, security pledges for auxiliary facilities involve pledges of all or portions of the revenue streams from the auxiliary projects being constructed or, collectively, the revenues from the system of auxiliary facilities. Auxiliary facility financings include student or faculty housing, food services, campus retail stores, parking, stadiums, research facilities, and other financings for which user fees are charged or, as in the case of research, overhead receipts for research facilities, for which a specific stream of revenues is relevant. Bond indentures include pledges of a given portion of the revenues for repayment of the indebtedness of those facilities. In many publicly supported colleges and universities, state or governing board policy establishes a required ratio of debt coverage. In other cases, institutional financing policy, rating agencies, or the market itself drives the amount that can be borrowed against a specific stream of revenues. For example, a policy requirement might be that net project revenues, after costs of operations, must equal 1.2 times debt service, where debt service is defined as the highest annual amount that must be paid during the life of the bond issue.

Credit Ratings (Creditworthiness)

The method by which capital market investors are able to make relatively simple judgments about the credit quality of alternative debt securities is the application of credit ratings to these securities. In the absence of a standard process of ratings that enables relative comparisons and establishes classes or categories of credits, each investor would have to analyze, in exhaustive detail, the underlying business operations, financial strength, and security structure of each bond investment under consideration. While the credit ratings provided by the rating agencies obviate the need for this kind of analysis by investors, the reader should be aware of the fact that major institutional buyers of bonds also perform their own credit analyses.

A credit rating is a measure of the likelihood of timely and complete repayment of principal and interest on debt. Credit ratings are designed to provide investors and other interested parties with a complete system of gradation by which the relative investment quality of bonds can be judged readily. Commercial bank lenders and other financial institutions perform internal credit analyses and assign ratings for their own credit decision purposes. The public debt markets are served for this purpose by independent rating agencies that develop credit standards, formulate and apply credit analysis techniques, and establish and maintain published credit ratings on issuers and issues. In addition to published credit ratings, rating agencies provide other types of rating services, such as credit assessments and underlying ratings. These services can be particularly useful for institutions contemplating debt issuance for the first time.

Normally, a bond or note issue is rated prior to its sale, although some issues are sold as unrated. Based on the judgment of the financial advisor or underwriter about marketing considerations, credit ratings may be sought for the issue. After a rated bond issue is sold, the rating agency or agencies review the credit on a periodic basis and may amend the rating, based on changes in the issuer's financial condition. The rating assigned, both initially and upon amendment, directly affects the marketability and the yields on the bonds.

The three independent rating agencies are Standard & Poor's Corporation (S&P), Moody's Investors Service, Inc. (Moody's), and Fitch IBCA (Fitch).

Long-Term Bond Ratings

Long-term credit ratings fall into two categories—investment grade and noninvestment grade. Long-term investment grade ratings assigned by the rating agencies are as shown in figure 10-03.

Short-term debt ratings

Short-term ratings emphasize the liquidity of the borrower and short-term cyclical elements, rather than long-term credit risk.

Moody's categories for short-term ratings are:

VMIG-1: Best quality—strong protection by established cash flows, superior liquidity support or demonstrated broad-based access to the market for refinancing.

Figure 10-03

Investment Grade Long-Term Bond Ratings
Assigned by Standard & Poor's, Moody's and Fitch IBCA

Capacity to Pay	Standard & Poor's	Moody's	Fitch IBCA
Strongest/Gilt-Edged	AAA	Aaa	AAA
Very Strong/High Grade	AA+	Aa1	AA+
Very Strong/High Grade	AA	Aa2	AA
Very Strong/High Grade	AA–	Aa3	AA–
Strong/Upper Medium Grade	A+	A1	A+
Strong/Upper Medium Grade	A	A2	A
Strong/Upper Medium Grade	A–	A3	A–
Adequate/ Medium Grade	BBB+	Baa1	BBB+
Adequate/ Medium Grade	BBB	Baa2	BBB
Adequate/ Medium Grade	BBB–	Baa3	BBB–

Source: Credit rating agencies

VMIG-2: High quality—margins of protection are ample although not as large as the MIG-1 group.

VMIG-3: Favorable quality—all security elements are accounted for but there is lacking the undeniable strength as MIG-1 and MIG-2. Liquidity and cash flow protection may be narrow and market access for refinancing is likely to be less well established.

VMIG-4: Adequate quality—protection commonly regarded as required of an investment security is present and although not distinctly or predominantly speculative, there is specific risk.

S&P's categories for short-term ratings are:

SP-1: Very strong or strong capacity to pay principal and interest. Issues possessing overwhelming safety characteristics are given a plus (+) designation.

SP-2: Satisfactory capacity to pay principal and interest.

SP-3: Speculative capacity to pay principal and interest.

Fitch's categories for short-term ratings are:

FIN-1: Strongest degree of assurance for timely payment.

FIN-2: A degree of assurance for timely payment only slightly less in degree than the highest category.

FIN-3: A satisfactory degree of assurance for timely payment.

FIN-4: The degree of assurance for timely payment is minimal and is susceptible to near term adverse change.

Credit ratings are assigned to issues, not to issuers, of bonds. They evaluate the institution's capacity to repay a specific bond obligation given the security structure of that issue. Nonetheless, the process of analyzing the creditworthiness of the bond issue includes a comprehensive analysis of the issuer's overall credit characteristics and resources.

Credit Analysis

Credit analysis in corporate finance relies heavily on the use of financial and operating ratios, norms for those ratios, and qualitative factors. Similarly, the financial condition of colleges and universities can be measured by standard ratios established by the rating entity.

Important ratios include balance sheet, operating, demand, contribution, and creditworthiness ratios. Figure 10-04 provides more detail about these ratios.

Figure 10-5 summarizes critical characteristics that credit rating agencies consider in their ratings of colleges and universities. For public institutions, the analysis extends to the state that supports the institution.

Even though a rating is applied to the specific debt obligation, the credit analysis covers the entire institutional entity. The analysis takes into account total revenues and total debt of an entire system or all projects. In auxiliary revenue pledges, the key factor can be how essential the auxiliary facility is to the institution. In rating variable-rate debt, S&P analyzes three hypothetical debt service scenarios to test the institution's vulnerability to rate changes:

- expected level of debt service;

- maximum level of debt service; and

- put scenario, assuming a high rate of interest, plus any demand or put options that may be exercised within the first year.

In addition, rating analysts determine whether the institution's investments are well matched to the put mode of the debt, to ensure that the borrower will have the liquidity to repay bondholders if the demand or put feature is exercised. For example, a bond issue with a 30-day demand feature should be matched by investments with 30-day maturities, held by the institution.

Figure 10-04

Financial Ratio Analysis for Colleges and Universities

Independent Colleges and Universities		Public Colleges and Universities	
Market Demand	Selectivity Matriculation Net tuition per student Educational expenses per student Total tuition discount	Market Demand	Selectivity Matriculation Net tuition per student State appropriation per student Educational expenses per student Total tuition discount

Capital	Unrestricted financial resources
	  to debt
	Expendable financial resources to
	  debt
	Total financial resources to debt
	Actual debt service to operation
	Peak debt service to operations
	Age of plant
		Capital	Unrestricted operating resources
			  to debt
			Expendable resources to debt
			Total resources to debt
			Gross debt service to operation
			Peak debt service to operations

Balance Sheet	Unrestricted financial resources
	  to operations
	Expendable resources to
	  operations
	Total financial resources to
	  student
	Debt per student
		Balance Sheet	Unrestricted operating resources
			  to operations
			Expendable resources to
			  operations
			Unrestricted operating resources
			  to total resources
			Total resources per student

Operating	Operating margin Actual debt service coverage Peak debt service coverage Return on net assets Return on financial assets	Operating	Operating margin Gross debt service coverage Peak debt service coverage Gift and investment reliance Return on resources
Contribution	Net tuition and fees Auxiliary enterprises Grants and contracts Investment income Gifts and pledges	Contribution	State appropriations Net tuition and fees Auxiliary enterprises Grants and contracts Investment income Gifts and pledges

Source: Credit rating agencies

Demand

Credit analysts consider student demand to be perhaps the single most critical factor in creditworthiness; they analyze demand for a college or university's enrollment in light of national and regional demographic and college enrollment trends. Rating agency factors for analysis of public and independent institutional student demand vary, as summarized in figure 10-06.

Student demand analysis also takes into account market competition, in

Figure 10-05

Critical Ratings Considerations for Higher Education Bonds

Public Colleges/Universities	Independent Colleges/Universities
State Characteristics	*State Characteristics*
State general obligation rating	Not applicable
State support for higher education	Not applicable
State support for specific institution	Not applicable
University Characteristics	*University Characteristics*
Legal	Legal
Demand	Demand
Financial	Financial
Debt	Debt

Source: Credit Rating Agencies

terms of competitor institutions, effects of tuition levels on applications, college or university marketing and external relations activities, and volatility of enrollment and related extraneous factors. Given the extreme importance of student demand and enrollment levels, it is important for any institution contemplating long-term debt obligations to make a full and sophisticated analysis of historical enrollment trends and projections of future enrollment. Such analyses should use statistical

Figure 10-06

Student Demand Analysis Factors for Public and Independent Colleges and Universities

Independent Colleges/Universities	Public Colleges/Universities
Application trends	Application trends
Acceptance rates	State acceptance mandates
Matriculation rates	Hierarchy of schools
Student quality	Student selectivity and quality
Geographic diversity	Geographic diversity
Part-time, full-time, and graduate students	Match of legislative priorities for programs with student application trends

Source: Credit rating agencies

Figure 10-07

College and University Revenue Factors in Credit Analysis

Categories of Revenues	Parameter(s) Evaluated
State appropriations	Percentage of total and trends
Tuition	Percentage of total and elasticity
Gifts and grants	Composition of and dependence on
Endowment and investment income	Spending policy
Auxiliary operations	Nature, extent, essentiality

Source: Credit Rating Agencies

forecasting techniques to test various possible scenarios and their potential impact on debt service obligations.

Financial Performance

Factors in the analysis of financial condition include revenues, expenditures, unrestricted net assets balance, operating margins, and endowment. Critical factors in revenue strength are diversity and flexibility. Rating agencies examine revenue categories by the parameters shown in figure 10-07.

The principal factor in analyzing expenditures is the mix of fixed versus variable costs. Expenditure categories reviewed include instructional services, student services, plant maintenance and operations, and mandatory transfers. Because fixed costs are of great concern, factors such as the percentage of tenured faculty, the portion of student services costs that are fixed, and other items of budget inflexibility are reviewed closely.

In analyzing endowment, key factors considered are the total value of endowment, which may differ significantly for public and independent institutions; historical trends in endowment growth; and the percent of quasi-endowment to total endowment. In analyzing unrestricted funds, analysts consider the unrestricted operating net assets, unrestricted plant net assets, quasi-endowment, institution-designated net assets, and institution-restricted funds for debt service (reserves).

Debt Structure and Capacity

In evaluating debt structure, analysts examine the security pledge intended for the bond issue being rated and legal requirements such as the additional bonds test or reserve requirements. In assessing debt capacity, analysts evaluate overall debt as a percentage of total operating budget and as compared to endowment and unrestricted funds. Further, they consider the debt financing philosophy and plans of the college or university, including such factors as matching of long-term debt with long-term assets.

Management

Rating agencies increasingly are relying also on their evaluation of the quality of the institution's management, in assessing credit strength. Various factors or indicators of management performance may be considered.

Typical Higher Education Ratings

Very few college and university bonds have natural (that is, unenhanced) AAA ratings, although many higher education bonds achieve the AAA rating with credit enhancement. In 1991, S&P assigned an AAA rating to only six universities. As of 2000, there now are 11 natural AAA colleges and universities. Most higher education ratings fall in the A range, with a distribution of ratings over the spectrum. Ratings for public universities are tied closely to the credit ratings of their states; these institutions typically have ratings that are one to three rating grades below the state's rating, with the exception of a few flagship research universities that may have ratings equivalent to or even above that of their state.

Credit Enhancement Techniques

Because bond investors are compensated for greater credit risk by higher interest rates, in a given interest rate environment, the credit quality of a bond issue is one of the most significant factors in the cost of borrowing. A major innovation in the modern municipal securities market has been the creation of techniques and products sold by banks and financial guarantee insurance companies that enhance a bond issue's credit standing. In effect, a credit enhancement provider commits to paying bondholders if a borrower cannot make principal and interest payments, thereby assuming the credit risk that the bondholder normally would bear. The bond issue thus assumes the credit rating of the credit enhancement provider, rather than that of the borrower. A borrower whose credit rating on an issue would be in the A range without credit enhancement could pay much lower interest rates based on the AAA credit rating of the credit enhancement provider. For such a borrower, the critical issue is whether the cost of the credit enhancement will lower interest costs sufficiently to result in net savings on the financing, after paying the costs of the credit enhancement.

For borrowers at the margins of being able to issue investment-grade securities based on their own credit, credit enhancement may be the critical factor that makes a bond issue marketable. For such borrowers, the cost-benefit analysis is clear: without the credit enhancement, the borrower would not gain access to tax-exempt funds.

The credit enhancement provider is compensated for assuming risk by means of fees or premiums. In credit-enhanced issues, rating agencies typically assign a rating based on the credit-enhancement provider's rating. The credit-enhancement provider performs an exhaustive credit analysis of the borrower. Readers should be aware that, even with credit enhancement, many investors still will take into account the underlying credit or intrinsic credit of the bonds when evaluating the acceptability of the bonds for their investment. Also, the rating agencies may rate both the underlying credit and the credit enhancement.

The following three credit-enhancement techniques are used:

Guarantees

A third party may provide a guarantee of the payment obligation of a borrower. The guarantor is usually a corporation or other entity related to the borrower. In higher education, 501(c)(3)-related foundations or corporations, or a religious organization could guarantee the debt of a related college. An example would be when an institution guarantees the debt of a related corporation that undertakes a commercial real estate project. Conversely, a related corporation or foundation can guarantee the debt of its related institution.

A guarantee may be collateralized with cash, securities, or other assets capable of being liquidated if the borrower and the guarantor both fail to honor the payment obligations.

Letters of Credit

Letters of credit (LOCs) are issued by commercial banks and other financial institutions to provide for the payment of debt if the borrower fails to make the required payments. The borrower then is obligated to repay the LOC provider, in which case the borrower's obligation to the LOC provider may be converted to a term loan. Under a direct pay letter of credit, the bond trustee draws on the letter of credit without first looking to the institution for payment. The institution then reimburses the bank.

The term for an LOC may be one to 10 years, with the most common terms being three to five years. An evergreen LOC is one in which the term is extended automatically each year, unless the provider gives formal notice that it will not extend the term. Financially strong institutions can issue variable rate debt without a letter of credit. This technique often is referred to as self-liquidity.

The borrower may pay an initial or up-front fee for the letter, as well as an ongoing annual fee for maintenance of the LOC commitment, which is based on the LOC amount outstanding. LOC fees vary considerably with the credit quality of the issuer and with overall market conditions. United States and foreign commercial banks, including international banks, provide LOCs for higher education bonds. The extent to which commercial banks are active LOC providers depends on their own credit ratings and on the rates of return they can earn on the LOCs.

LOCs are limited in term and subject to both renewal and cost risks; therefore, they are most appropriate for VRDBs. An LOC's value in a variable-rate financing is rarely disputable because, except in rare instances, VRDBs are not marketable without the LOC support—for liquidity reasons alone, even if credit enhancement is not essential.

Bond Insurance

Bond insurance is an insurance policy provided by a state-regulated financial guarantee insurance company. The policy is issued at the time of bond closing and guarantees timely payment of principal and interest to bondholders during the life of the bond issue. An insurance premium is determined by multiplying the premium rate by the total debt service payable. The premium rate charged is determined by the insurer, based on its evaluation of the credit quality characteristics of the insured institution. Bond insurance premiums are usually payable in full at the time of issuance. In certain instances, however, premiums are paid annually on the basis of the outstanding principal amount of the bonds.

Bond insurance is typically the credit enhancement of choice for long-term, fixed-rate bonds because the insurance is for the entire term of the bonds, and is irrevocable, and the entire cost of insurance is known at the time of issuance. Bond insurance is provided by a small number of financial guarantee companies that are structured and capitalized specifically for financial guarantee products for the municipal securities market. The value of bond insurance is indisputable for a borrowing college or university that is creditworthy but at the margins of being able to sell debt successfully in its own name; insurance may make an otherwise unmarketable bond issue marketable. For institutions with stronger credit, bond insur-

Figure 10-08

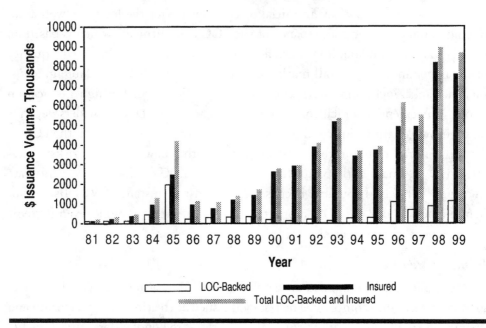

Letter of Credit Backed and Insured Higher Education Volume: 1981–1999

ance may be effective in lowering the overall costs of borrowing. The usefulness of bond insurance in raising a college's credit rating from A or AA to AAA must be analyzed by the financial advisor or underwriter, who can determine whether the cost of the bond insurance premium would be more than offset by the expected savings in interest costs that will be achieved by the AAA rating.

Credit-Enhanced Higher Education Volume

Figure 10-08 shows the growth in LOC-backed and insured higher education volume since 1981. The relative volumes of LOC-backed or insured higher education bonds tend to follow changes in market interest rates. In years when long-term rates are attractive and borrowers tend to favor long-term fixed-rate issuances, bond insurance volume may rise. When short-term rates are more favorable, LOC-backed volume may rise as VRDB issuance rises.

There has been huge growth in the overall use of credit enhancement in higher education finance. Total credit-enhanced volume, which was as little as

$117 million in 1981, or 11 percent of total higher education volume in that year, had climbed to about $8.6 billion in 1999, representing 61 percent of all higher education issuance volume.

There has been noticeable growth since 1996 in the volume of LOC-backed issues. However, the real long-term growth trend has been in the much larger volumes of higher education debt being issued with bond insurance. In 1981, there were two insured higher education issues for a total of only $22.3 million. In 1999, there were 254 insured issues for a total volume of $7.7 billion, representing about half the entire higher education issuance of $14.5 billion that year.

ACCESSING THE CAPITAL MARKETS

Overview of the Financial Intermediation Process

In commercial bank lending, the borrower and lender negotiate directly, without an intermediary. In capital markets, a financial intermediary's services are required. The professionals who specialize in structuring and selling the bonds of municipal entities are public finance or municipal finance bankers. These professionals, who may act either in the role of financial advisor or in the role of investment banker, work with issuers and their bond counsel to structure bond issues, and with investors to sell bonds. They typically are in separate but related departments of investment banking firms, commercial bank securities affiliates, or firms that specialize in financial advisory services to the municipal market.

There are two basic forms of bond sale: private placement and public sale or offering. Each has different structures and requirements.

Private Placement

In a private placement, the banker identifies a limited number of sophisticated investors interested in buying the entire issue of securities to be offered. This method usually is preferred for small issues that would be uneconomical to offer for public sale or for issues with credit weaknesses that may not gain public market acceptance. Private placements usually are simpler than public sales and the costs of issuance are lower; however, the interest rate paid may be higher.

Public Bond Sale

The public offering or sale is used much more often than private placements, especially for large bond issues offered for sale by creditworthy borrowers. Public offerings come in two forms of transaction. A negotiated sale is one in which the

Figure 10-09

Distribution of Competitive, Negotiated, and Private Placement Debt for Higher Education: 1999

Type of Transaction	# of Issues	Volume ($ millions)	Percent Market Share
Competitive sale	106	$ 2,231.6	15.3
Negotiated sale	464	11,939.5	82.1
Private placement	25	378.6	2.6
Totals	595	14,549.6	100.0

Source: Thompson Financial Securities Data. Private placement statistics may be understated.

investment banking firm or bank securities affiliate engaged by the issuer both structures the financing and undertakes to sell the bonds. An issuer may engage a financial advisor as well, in a negotiated sale.

In a competitive sale, an independent financial advisory firm, bank securities affiliate, or investment banker may serve as financial advisor for structuring the bond offering. On a certain date, the financial advisor or the issuer solicits competitive bids from other underwriting firms to purchase and resell the bonds. The financial advisor assists the issuer in selecting the bid that represents the lowest cost financing based on net interest cost or true interest cost. A negotiated or competitive sale of bonds can be accomplished by a single intermediary institution bidding and acting alone, or by a syndicate, a group of intermediaries that divide the bonds among themselves based on their knowledge of customer interest in buying the securities. The process called underwriting indicates that the financial intermediary firm guarantees that the issuer's bonds will be purchased. If the underwriter cannot market all the bonds to investors, the underwriter firm itself buys the bonds.

In general, competitive sale is easier to do when issuers are well known in the market. Higher education bonds more typically are sold by negotiated sale. In 1999, for example, the distribution between competitive sale, negotiated sale, and private placement of higher education debt was as shown in figure 10-09.

The Participants

A number of parties are involved in the conduct of a publicly sold tax-exempt bond issue.

Issuer/Issuing Authority

For independent college and university borrowers, debt issues are conduit financings conducted through special issuing authorities. For public institutions, the issuing function is performed by the state, by an issuing authority, or by the institution itself. The role that the issuing authority plays varies from state to state and within some localities. At a minimum, the board of directors of the issuing authority must review the application of a potential borrower and approve the financing. The board must pass a resolution authorizing the issuance of bonds in its name, on behalf of the borrowing institution. The board, directly and through its staff, maintains fiduciary responsibilities for ongoing management of the debt. In cases where the issuing authority is a large organization, the board and staff may play a far more significant role in organizing and directing the financing. Other authorities are even more active, not only in the structuring and marketing of financings, but also in the actual construction and ongoing management of the facilities financed. States with large numbers of colleges and universities and consequently high volumes of higher education bond activity, such as New York, California, and Massachusetts, tend to have higher education facilities authorities that perform a broad array of financial functions.

Some issuing authorities appoint a standing pool or syndicate of underwriting firms and assign them to conduct various financings. Alternatively, an authority may engage in a proposal competition process to appoint a financial advisor and/or underwriter for each college or university bond issuance.

Underwriter

An underwriter is an investment banking firm or a syndicate of investment banking firms that markets an issuer's bonds to investors. If a single firm is engaged, it is referred to as the sole manager of the underwriting and sale. If a group or syndicate is involved, there is a lead or senior manager and one or more comanagers of the issue's sale. In a negotiated underwriting, the underwriter's public-finance-department bankers work with a college or university, and its financial advisor, if there is one, to plan the financing and to determine when and how it should be brought to market. The underwriter, along with the financial advisor, provides guidance on structuring the bond issue, determines whether credit enhancement is needed, and assists the institution in obtaining credit enhancement. The underwriter is responsible for coordinating the preparation of the Official Statement, which describes the institution and its finances, the project or projects being financed, and the financial structure for security, collateral, and credit enhancements, if any. The municipal securities underwriting and sales department of the underwriter firm works with the public finance department's bankers to structure and ultimately sell the bonds to the final investors.

Underwriter's Counsel

Underwriters are represented in transactions by their own underwriter's legal counsel, who assist the underwriter in coordinating preparation of the Official Statement. Underwriter's counsel also conducts due diligence, to confirm the adequacy of disclosure of required information regarding the issuer and the sale.

Financial Advisor

In a competitive bid bond sale, the team that performs the functions described above up to the point of sale is referred to as the financial advisor. The financial advisor is responsible for all elements of planning and structuring and for the solicitation of competitive bids. The financial advisor assists the issuer in evaluating the comparative costs of bids submitted to select the winning underwriting manager or syndicate. In some cases, bond issuers engaging in a negotiated bond sale employ a financial advisor as well as an underwriter. In this situation, the financial advisor's role is to assist the issuer in structuring the financing; assist in presentations to investors and rating agencies; assist in document preparation; and review the pricing and marketing recommendations of the investment banker and advise the issuer as to their acceptability. In most cases, the investment banker provides these services to the college or university.

Bond Counsel

Bond counsel are attorneys who, representing the interests of future bondholders, prepare an opinion to indicate that the bonds meet all requirements and tests to be issued validly in accordance with law and that the interest earned on them can be excluded from gross income for federal income tax purposes. Bond counsel also render an opinion with respect to state tax law treatment of interest on the bonds. Bond counsel attorneys are an integral part of the financing team and provide ongoing advice on numerous aspects of the transaction.

Obligor's Counsel

Attorneys who represent the interests of the issuer (borrower) in various details of the financing structure are called obligor's counsel. This role may be performed by the institution's general counsel in the case of independent institutions, the state attorney general's office in the case of public institutions, counsel of the issuing education facilities authority, or an outside law firm engaged by the issuer.

Credit Enhancement Provider

If bonds or notes are credit-enhanced, the commercial bank provider of the LOC or the bond insurance company also participates in the development of the financing transaction. The credit enhancement provider plays a significant role in determining the creditworthiness of the borrowing institution and in structuring the security and pledges involved in the transaction.

Credit Enhancement Provider's Counsel

Attorneys typically represent the interests of the credit enhancement provider.

Trustee

The bond trustee, normally a financial institution with trust powers, represents the bondholders in a fiduciary capacity to enforce the terms of a trust agreement or indenture. The trustee bank is paid a fee by the issuer.

Remarketing Agent

In the case of VRDBs, a remarketing agent remarkets bonds when necessary because of demand options exercised by bondholders. The underwriter who manages the initial offering of bonds usually is engaged to serve as remarketing agent and is paid an annual fee for this service.

The Rating Process

The rating process is an extensive, intensive, and formal version of the credit analysis process that should be performed by a potential issuer, with assistance of its bankers, when an institution begins to contemplate a bond issuance. If a credit enhancement is sought, the provider of the enhancement also conducts a full credit analysis prior to the formal rating process. In this case, the rating agency will not rate the underlying or intrinsic credit unless asked to do so, and the primary rating will be based on evaluation of the credit enhancement.

The mechanics of the formal rating process begin with the issuer's application to one or more rating agencies, well in advance of the anticipated date of sale of the bond issue. The issuer decides which and how many ratings to seek, based on the advice of its financial advisor or underwriter.

The issuer then submits detailed information about itself and the proposed debt issue. A Preliminary Official Statement is prepared and submitted to the rating agency with several years of operating statistics, audited financial statements, planning documents, legal documents relating to the security, and other specific information requested by the rating agency. For higher education issues, this information typically covers all aspects of institutional history, management, organization, students, faculty, programs, and finances.

When the rating agency receives the required information, the issue is assigned to an analyst who evaluates the credit strength of the proposed issue, using the institution's data along with statistics from the rating agency's database and other normative measures that the agency has developed from its experience with similar issues and issuers.

During this phase, the principal officers of the issuing institution, its financial advisors, and the rating agency analysts meet. Underwriters for a negotiated sale transaction also may be involved. The meeting affords an opportunity for the institution to present information that is difficult to convey in written form. Sometimes the meeting is in the form of a site visit to the campus. A site visit is required or recommended if the institution has never issued debt before or if it has not issued debt in some time. Decisions about meetings or site visits are made by the rating agency; alternatively, the issuer can request a site visit. An issuer should follow the advice of its underwriter or financial advisor in matters of managing the rating process. Bankers also work with the college or university to prepare and rehearse for rating agency presentations and/or site visits.

Upon completion of meetings or site visits, the credit analysis is completed and a rating recommendation is formulated. The rating committee reviews the analyst's recommendation internally at the rating agency. When the rating is assigned, it is released first to the issuer, who may appeal and present additional information, and then to the public. A credit report then is distributed.

Bond Disclosures

Issuers of debt are expected to disclose all material facts about themselves and the proposed borrowing that may be pertinent to the analysis of the credit quality of the investment. Such information is provided in the Preliminary Official Statement and in the final Official Statement. Investors rely on this information in making their decisions. Responsibility for disclosure lies with the college or university.

The Securities and Exchange Commission (SEC) holds the expectation that colleges or universities and their financial advisors and underwriters should bear responsibility for the completeness and accuracy of disclosures. They are required to exercise due diligence in seeking and making available all possibly pertinent information, including any that may represent present or future adverse conditions.

In higher education, the issue of disclosure has focused recently on concerns relating to debt issued by universities with academic medical centers. Given financial trends in the health care industry and their negative impact on the financial strength of academic medical centers, there has been greater recent emphasis on disclosure of financial information relating to these enterprises.

In July 1995, the Municipal Securities Rulemaking Board (MSRB) required most fixed-rate tax-exempt bond issuers to provide continuing disclosure of material information on an annual basis. Colleges and universities are required to sign Continuing Disclosure Agreements with their underwriters at the closing of each bond issue. These Agreements define which information will be updated each year for the life of the bonds.

Bond Documents

The following basic documents are part of a public tax-exempt bond sale.

Bond Resolution

The first technical and legal document in a bond transaction is the bond resolution, which must be adopted formally by the municipal issuer. For a public institution, the bond resolution is adopted by the institution's governing board. For an independent institution, the bond resolution is adopted by the board of directors of the state or local authority that will issue the debt on behalf of the college or university. The bond resolution sets forth the terms and purpose of the bonds and the financial responsibilities of the parties involved.

Preliminary Official Statement

The Preliminary Official Statement, coordinated by the financial advisor/underwriter, is intended to disclose all information pertinent to marketing bonds to investors. It describes the issuing institution, its programs, its management, and its long-range plans, and it includes historical data. The statement describes the facilities to be financed or other purposes of the financing and the proposed terms of the financing. All significant risks are described. Financial statements and the results of a feasibility study, if performed, are included. This document is the primary vehicle for disclosure of all material information to potential investors.

Trust Agreement or Indenture

At the bond closing, the issuer and the bond trustee execute the trust agreement or indenture, a contract between the issuer and the trustee for the benefit of the bondholders. The indenture sets forth the rights and responsibilities of the issuer and the trustee. In the case of independent institutions, the higher education facilities authority is the issuer that executes the trust agreement with the trustee bank.

Note or Loan Agreement

The note or loan agreement sets forth the terms of the loan and is executed by the borrower and the issuer. In higher education, it usually is an agreement between the borrowing institution and the higher education facilities authority that is issuing the debt on the institution's behalf.

Mortgage or Lien Agreements

If the borrowing is secured by physical collateral (an interest in real property), a mortgage is executed and recorded in the local county clerk's office. If a collateral interest in personal property is pledged, such as computers or other equipment, a security lien agreement granting such interest to the bondholders is executed and recorded.

Credit Enhancement Agreements

Bond issues that are credit-enhanced have additional documentation of the terms and conditions of the LOC or bond insurance. In the case of LOCs, the reimbursement agreement is executed between the borrower and the LOC bank. In the case of bond insurance, the insurance agreement is executed.

Legal Opinions

Each party to the transaction is represented by counsel. The most important opinion document required is bond counsel's opinion that the bonds are validly issued and that the interest on the bonds meets all requirements to be excluded from gross income for federal income tax purposes. All counsel involved in the transaction issue written opinions to indicate that the actions taken in the transaction are duly authorized. Underwriter's counsel also opines on the adequacy of disclosure.

Official Statement

The final version of the Official Statement is prepared immediately after the bonds are sold. The final Official Statement contains the actual interest rate at which the bonds were sold.

Assignment of CUSIP Numbers

The Committee on Uniform Security Identification Procedures (CUSIP), under the auspices of the American Bankers Association, developed a uniform system for numbering and identifying municipal, U.S. government, and corporate securities. A CUSIP number is assigned to each bond in the offering and is its identification throughout its life.

Transcript

All official legal documents pertaining to the bond transaction are bound and preserved as the transcript of the bond issue. The transcript is compiled by bond counsel.

Transaction Costs

A publicly sold bond transaction entails a variety of transaction costs in addition to interest, principally for the many professional services required to bring an issue to market, for credit enhancements and, in the case of variable-rate debt, to maintain the ongoing remarketing function. The basic costs for a publicly sold bond issue include underwriter's spread; fees of bond counsel, underwriter's counsel, issuer's counsel, rating agency, trustee, paying agent, and the issuing authority; and printing and other out-of-pocket expenses. In addition, issues that are insured or supported by an LOC have additional costs for either the bond insurance premium or initial and annual letter-of-credit fee and for legal counsel of the bond insurer or LOC bank.

Underwriter's Spread or Placement Fees

The underwriter's spread compensates the underwriter for buying the issuer's bonds and taking the risk of reselling them to investors. The four components of gross underwriter's spread or underwriter's discount are:

- management fee (for structuring and managing the financing);
- underwriting fee (for assuming the risk of underwriting unsold bonds);
- takedown (cost of selling bonds); and

• expenses (for out-of-pocket outlays for clearly identified services procured by the underwriter).

In private placements, the placement fee includes components for management, selling, and expenses. There is no underwriting fee in private placements, because the intermediary assumes no risk for resale of the bonds.

Transaction costs attendant to a bond issue may be capitalized, that is, included in the par amount of the bond issue and thus do not represent cash requirements for the borrower. For nongovernmental issuers, including independent colleges and universities, capitalized transaction costs are limited to 2 percent of the par amount of the bonds, with the costs of credit enhancement generally excluded from the 2 percent limitation.

Determining the Actual Cost of Interest

For a bond issue with a single maturity, the actual cost of interest is the coupon interest rate, if the bonds are sold at their par value. Because most bond issues are structured with serial maturities, the actual cost of interest is complicated to calculate. The actual cost of interest that the issuer of new money bonds pays is calculated somewhat differently from the rate of return to the bond investor, but is based on similar principles. This calculation must be understood in order to determine, in a competitive bond sale, which bidding underwriter or syndicate is offering the bid that results in the lowest interest cost to the borrowing institution. Calculations of net interest cost (NIC) and true interest cost (TIC) are used to present this figure for comparative purposes. It is important to note that the underwriter's spread, described previously, is incorporated into NIC and TIC calculations.

Net Interest Cost

NIC is a simplified formula that is still used widely but that is no longer an industry standard. It states the total amount of interest that must be paid during the life of a serial bond issue, without regard to the time value of money. To determine the NIC, the sum total of interest payments for the entire bond offering is divided by the product of the amount of bonds outstanding, multiplied by the number of years they are outstanding. The NIC formula is:

$$\textit{Net Interest Cost (NIC)} = \frac{\textit{Total Interest Payments} + \textit{Discount (or} - \textit{Premium)}}{\textit{Bond Year Dollars}}$$

Bond years are the number of bonds outstanding, in $1,000 denominations,

Figure 10-10

A Checklist for Planning a Major Financing

☐ Identify authority to borrow

☐ Identify project(s) to be financed

☐ Engage professional team

☐ Establish qualification for tax-exempt financing (or not). Determine if there are tax-exempt and taxable components

☐ Size the bond issuance (including project costs, capitalized interest, capitalized costs of issuance, reserve fund or surety bonds, interest earnings during draw-down period, and refunding of previous obligations, if any)

☐ Select mode (e.g., fixed or variable, multi-modal, commercial paper, etc.) and term structure(s)

☐ Estimate payment requirements (e.g., level debt service, increasing, decreasing, bullet maturities, etc.)

☐ Identify source of repayment (e.g., departmental budgets, central resources, fee income, gifts, etc.)

☐ Determine call provisions

☐ Determine restrictive covenants, additional bonds test, etc.

☐ Ensure preservation of advance refunding option

☐ Develop investment of proceeds plan and identify arbitrage considerations/effects

☐ Plan reserve funding (with cash proceeds or other source)

☐ Identify qualifications for reimbursement of previously expended project funds, if any

☐ Determine timing of issuance (related to expenditure pattern, project draw-down, and market conditions)

☐ Estimate true interest cost

☐ Educate key internal stakeholders

---

multiplied by the number of years they are outstanding. Bond year dollars are this amount multiplied by $1,000 for each bond.

True Interest Cost

Critics of the NIC method argue that it is misleading to ignore the present value element of the calculation, which results in a distortion of the result of bid comparisons. Unlike NIC, the TIC calculation takes the timing, as well as the total amount, of interest payment, into account. TIC is the rate at which all cash flows must be discounted so that the sum of their present values equals the proceeds of the bond issue. The TIC is computed by an iterative process employing an algebraic formula. Because this is done easily with computers, issuers of debt now can request that bids be expressed with TIC as a basis. TIC now is most often the basis for award of a bond issue to a competing underwriter.

A Checklist for Planning a Financing

Although financing professionals will guide the college or university issuer through the financing process and the rating process also will establish an order of events, it may be useful, particularly for inexperienced institutional issuers, to think in terms of a "checklist" of things to be done in planning an issuance. Figure 10-10 provides a sample checklist.

MANAGEMENT OF EXISTING DEBT

All this discussion pertains to what sometimes is called new money debt, that is, first-time issues of debt for a given project or projects. This section discusses management and refunding of existing debt.

Refunding and Defeasance

A refunding is the issuance of new bonds to replace an outstanding bond issue. Refundings can be done as stand-alone transactions or in combination with new money financings. Refunding is used to:

- reduce the borrower's interest costs if the market is such that new bonds can be issued at interest rates materially lower than that of the currently outstanding bonds;

- remove a restrictive or burdensome covenant imposed by the terms of the existing bond indenture; and

- restructure existing debt, for example, by rescheduling debt amortization.

Because of the transaction costs involved in a refunding, interest rates need to drop considerably to make the cost of refunding worth the benefits.

Defeasance is the termination of the rights and interests of the bondholders and extinguishment of their lien on the pledged revenues of the borrower in connection with a refunding. When final payment on a bond issue is made or when provision is made for all future payments by establishing a risk-free escrow account, bonds are said to be defeased. Defeasance does not always cause the elimination of a liability on the institution's statement of position. Readers should refer to the appropriate accounting literature for details on extinguishment of debt.

Current Refunding

Current refunding is the issuance of new bonds to replace an existing bond issue when the existing issue is callable for redemption at the time of the issuance of the new bonds or will be callable within 90 days of the date of issuance of the new bonds. Because the college or university has the right to call the bonds, an approaching call date is an opportune time to do a current refunding, if it will prove cost-effective. The proceeds of the new bond issue, called the refunding bonds, are used to repay the old bonds, called the refunded bonds. The college or university is left with the refunding bond issue outstanding and, presumably, with more favorable debt-service payments.

Advance Refunding

Bond investors are protected from early repayment of bonds by the no-call period. An institution that wishes to refinance its bonds prior to a call date must do so by means of an advance refunding. Advance refunding entails depositing with the trustee the proceeds of the refunding bonds in a yield-restricted escrow fund, the principal and interest of which is calculated to be sufficient to pay the principal and interest maturing on the refunded bonds until maturity or until the first optional call date. Bonds that are refunded so that the escrowed funds are sufficient to pay all debt service until maturity are called escrowed to maturity. Bonds that are refunded so that the refunding bond proceeds are escrowed until the first call date are called prerefunded bonds. The entire issue then is called for redemption at the call date, normally the first call date.

Special U.S. government securities may be used for the escrow accounts in advance refundings. These State and Local Government Series (SLGS, pronounced "slugs") are sold by the U.S. Treasury through individual subscriptions to states and municipalities. The maturity structures and interest rates on SLGS are tailored to conform to the yield and arbitrage restrictions imposed under Section 103 of the Internal Revenue Code. Open market Treasury securities also may be used in the escrow account but should be employed only when they are more efficient than SLGS.

Institutional planners should consult their professional advisors because of federal limitations on the number of advance refundings allowed. There are two basic types of advance refunding.

Gross refunding and defeasance. In a full cash or gross refunding, the proceeds of the refunding bond issue are sufficient to repay both the principal and interest on the refunded bonds. A gross refunding usually includes a series of special obligation bonds. The proceeds are invested and the interest earnings used to pay the principal and interest on the special obligation bonds. A larger amount of principal outstanding may result, but the annual debt service may be reduced because the special obligation bonds are secured by the earnings on the refunding bonds.

Net cash refunding and defeasance. In a net cash refunding, the size of the refunding bond issue is a principal amount that, with the interest that will be earned on the funds, is sufficient to repay the principal and interest on the refunded bonds. Proceeds of the refunding bonds are invested in SLGS and used to redeem or retire the refunded bonds. A variety of advance funding techniques also are used to accomplish various debt management objectives. Two are mentioned here.

High-to-Low Refunding

The most common refunding structure used by colleges and universities is the high-to-low refunding, in which debt at a higher interest rate is replaced by debt at a lower interest rate. Savings are achieved by the lower-debt service payments on the refunding bonds. This structure is associated with advance refundings when the market affords opportunities for achieving lower interest rates and the escrow is structured for redemption of the refunded bonds at the first optional call date.

Partial Refunding and Defeasance

The economic benefits of refunding tend to be greatest for bonds with the longest maturities and highest interest rates. Shorter serial maturities, noncallable maturities, or low-interest-rate portions of issues may not be good candidates for refunding. In a partial refunding, only selected maturities, generally those offering maximum opportunities for savings, are refunded.

Additional Bonds Test and Parity Debt

Once a college or university has bonds outstanding, issuance of additional debt requires additional analysis of the capacity of the revenues available to be pledged for new obligations. Investors in long-term securities require protection from material changes in the financial capacity of the borrower to repay its obligation. Bondholders are concerned, therefore, about bond issuances subsequent to that of the bonds they hold, especially if a later issue will have claims to the same pledged revenues as those on which they expect to rely. For the protection of bondholders, a legal test, codified in the bond resolution, determines the ability of an issuer to sell additional bonds backed by the same pledged revenues. This additional bonds test is expressed as a ratio of historic revenues to expected future levels of debt service. For example, an additional bonds test might be as follows: additional bonds can be issued only if projected debt service will be less than 12 percent of historical revenues and unrestricted net assets will be at least 70 percent of *pro forma* debt service.

Parity bonds are two or more bond issues in which each bond issue has the same level of priority of claim against pledged revenues. The initial issue is called the prior issue and subsequent issues are called additional parity bonds. The bond indenture of the prior issue normally establishes the requirements to be met before additional parity bonds can be issued.

Hedging Techniques

Hedging is a debt management technique aimed at reducing the borrower's risk and, where possible, achieving economies. Hedging has long been used in corporate finance and is being used increasingly by municipal securities issuers in debt management programs. There are two basic strategies for hedging: investment hedging techniques and derivative hedging products.

Hedging with Investments

A college or university issuer can use investment techniques to take advantage of the lower rates that variable-rate debt normally affords and, at the same time, create a hedge internally to protect against interest-rate risk. Investment hedging is a matter of matching assets and liabilities to achieve a positive correlation between total asset returns and debt-service costs. The institution uses operating funds or other unrestricted funds to make investments so that the interest rate sensitivity on the invested assets mirrors the potential rate volatility of the debt.

Hedging with Derivative Products

In addition to hedging by investment strategies, borrowers can purchase derivative products that provide a hedge against debt risk. Two of many examples of such derivative products are interest rate caps and swaps.

A cap is an interest-rate insurance vehicle in which the seller of the cap, usually a bank or other financial intermediary, agrees to pay the buyer the difference between an agreed-upon index of variable interest rates and a negotiated interest-rate ceiling or cap. For example, a cap is purchased at 7.10 percent. The interest rate in the index, normally selected so that it will closely track the cap-buyer's bonds, rises to 7.25 percent. The college now must pay 7.25 percent on its VRDBs; however, the seller of the cap pays the college the difference of 0.15 percent (15 basis points). Thus, with the cap, the college or university borrower is assured that its interest cost will not exceed 7.10 percent. The borrower and its advisors must evaluate whether the cost of the cap is worth the potential interest rate protection it buys.

An interest-rate swap is an agreement between two parties to exchange interest payments, generally for a period of one to 10 years, or longer. It is typically an exchange of a fixed-rate and a variable-rate cash flow, based on the debt management needs and interest-rate expectations of the two parties. Swaps emerged as a corporate finance tool in the late 1970s. By 1989, worldwide interest-rate swap volume had reached $1.4 trillion, indicating the popularity of the technique. It is estimated that municipal interest-rate swaps outstanding now exceed $50 billion.

A swap allows a college or university to convert temporarily the interest rate paid on variable rate debt to fixed rate, or vice versa, without permanently converting the debt by refunding the existing bonds. Thus, interest rate management can be achieved without the complexities, costs, and limitations attendant to refunding. For the variable rate portion of the swap, payments are keyed to an index such as the Bond Market Association Swap Index, or other published variable rate indexes. The index selected will depend on the nature of the swap. As with caps, there are costs associated with swaps, which must be weighed in determining whether the technique will benefit the institution.

CONCLUDING OBSERVATIONS

As higher education institutions address the strategic and financial challenges of the coming century, one of the costliest challenges—along with faculty and program development—will be the renewal, modernization, and expansion of 21st century college and university campuses. In the last two decades, higher education's sophistication in accessing debt markets has grown considerably. Higher education bond issuance in public markets has grown from about $1 billion in 1980 to more than $14 billion in 1999. Experienced issuers are venturing into newer, more varied, and more sophisticated debt forms and techniques. Many colleges and universities that never had accessed public debt have begun to do so. Many more are likely to include debt in their future capital development programs.

Debt financing and management are complex undertakings, requiring both internal expertise and reliance on the assistance of skilled professionals external to the institution. Professionals who are experienced in higher education finance can provide the nuances, details, and time-sensitive advice that all colleges and universities need when undertaking debt financing.

NOTES

1. Eva Klein & Associates, Ltd., *The University of North Carolina Capital Equity and Adequacy Study*, April 1999.

2. For additional detailed, technical discussions, an important reference is the *NACUBO Guide to Issuing and Managing Debt*, NACUBO, 1994.

3. Statistics including both publicly sold debt and private placements may understate the private placement volume, as the reporting requirements for private placements differ. These debt obligations may not all be recorded and reported.

REFERENCES AND RESOURCES

Publications

Augustine, John. "Cash on Demand: A Framework for Managing a Cash Liquidity Position." *Business Officer*, July 1995, 54–56.

———. "College and University Financial Statements under SFAS Nos. 116 and 117." *The Journal of Financial Statement Analysis*, 1 (Summer 1996).

Calibeo, Thomas. *Public Higher Education Outlook: Boom in Student Demand Underpins Positive Trends as Many Rise to the Needs of the Future*. New York: Moody's Investor Service, December 1998.

Coopers & Lybrand. *Reinventing the University: Managing and Financing Institutions of Higher Education*. New York: John Wiley & Sons, Inc. 1995.

Daley, Joseph C., Carey, Charles E., and King, George A. *A Guide to Municipal Official Statements*. 2d ed. Englewood Cliffs: Prentice Hall, 1990.

Danzig, Lisa, and Gigante, Sharon. "Higher Education Sector Review." *Standard and Poor's CreditWeek Municipal*, July 12, 1999.

Danzig, Lisa, and Neel, Jennifer. "Private College and University Ratio Analysis." *Standard and Poor's CreditWeek Municipal*, November 30, 1998.

Desai, Neelam, Fitzgerals, Susan, and Richman, Naomi (ed.). *Private Colleges and Universities: 1999 Outlook and Medians*. New York: Moody's Investor Service, September 1999.

Dickmeyer, Nathan, and Hughes, K. Scott. *Financial Self-Assessment: A Workbook for Colleges*. Washington, D.C.: NACUBO, 1980.

Fitzgerald, Susan, and Richman, Naomi (ed.). *Rating Methodology, Moody's Rating Approach for Private Colleges and Universities*. New York: Moody's Investor Service, September 1999.

Forrester, Robert T. *A Handbook on Debt Management for Colleges and Universities*. NACUBO Capital Management Series. Washington, D.C.: NACUBO, 1988.

Kaiser, Harvey H. *Crumbling Academe: Solving the Capital Renewal and Replacement Dilemma*. Washington, D.C.: Association of Governing Boards of Universities and Colleges, 1984.

King, George A., Anderson, Richard E., Cyganowski, David M., and Hennigan, Patrick J. *NACUBO Guide to Issuing and Managing Debt*. Washington, D.C.: NACUBO, 1994.

KPMG, LLP and Prager, McCarthy, Sealy, LLC, *Ratio Analysis in Higher Education: Measuring Past Performance to Chart Future Direction*, 4th Edition, New York: KPMG, 1999.

KPMG Peat Marwick. *Ratio Analysis in Higher Education*, 2nd ed. New York: KPMG Peat Marwick, 1987.

Martin, Lisa. *Will Higher Education Follow Healthcare Into Turmoil: Probably Not, But Big Changes Are Underway*. New York: Moody's Investor Service, November 1999.

Massy, William F., and Meyerson, Joel W. Strategy and Finance in Higher Education. Peterson's Guides. Princeton, NJ: Peterson, 1992.

Moak, Lennox L. *Municipal Bonds: Planning, Sale, and Administration*. Chicago, IL.: Municipal Finance Officers Association, 1982.

Moody's Investors Service. *Moody's on Municipals: An Introduction to Issuing Debt*. New York: Moody's Investors Service, 1987.

National Association of College and University Business Officers. *Capital Formation Alternatives in Higher Education*. NACUBO Capital Management Series. Washington, D.C.: NACUBO, 1988.

National Association of College and University Business Officers. *Financial Accounting and Reporting Manual for Higher Education*. Washington, D.C.: NACUBO, published since 1990 and on-going.

National Federation of Municipal Analysts. *Disclosure Handbook for Municipal Securities*. Pittsburgh: National Federation of Municipal Analysts, 1990.

Nelson, John, and Calibeo, Thomas (ed.). *Moody's Approach to Rating Privatized Student Housing Project Financings*, New York: Moody's Investor Service, September 1999.

Oster, Sharon M. Strategic Management for Nonprofit Organizations. London: Oxford University Press, 1995.

Peliquin-Dodd, Mary, and Danzig, Lisa. "Off-Balance Sheet Dormitory Revenue Bonds: A New Financing Choice." *Standard and Poor's CreditWeek Municipal*, July 12, 1999.

———. "Positive Outlook: U.S. Public Higher Education." *Standard and Poor's CreditWeek Municipal*, May 18, 1998.

Public Securities Association. *Fundamentals of Municipal Bonds.* Fourth Edition, New York: Public Securities Association, 1990.

Richman, Naomi, and Nelson, John (ed.). *Rating Methodology, Self-Liquidity Ratings in the Non-Profit Sector: Moody's Approach to Internal Liquidity-Supported Debt of Higher Education and Other Non-Profit Institutions.* New York: Moody's Investor Service, October 1999.

Standard and Poor's Corporation, *Public Finance Viewpoint on Higher Education Vol. 3,* New York: Standard and Poor's, 1998.

Periodicals

The Blue List. A daily list of bond prices used by dealers who trade bonds in the secondary market; the source of information for prices at which an institution's outstanding bonds are trading at any given time.

The Bond Buyer. A daily news publication that provides full coverage of forthcoming negotiated and competitive bond offerings, just sold bond offerings, interest rate trends, market analysis, regulatory news, and other news relating to the municipal bond market. It publishes various indexes of general obligation and revenue bonds.

The Bond Buyer's Directory of Municipal Bond Dealers—"The Red Book". A semiannual directory of financial intermediation service providers; each listing includes municipal bond dealers, municipal bond credit enhancers, government officials, associations, municipal finance consultants, and municipal bond attorneys.

CreditWeek Municipal. Published by S&P; comments on fixed-income topics, news affecting the municipal bond industry, and specific industry/entity credit analyses.

Moody's Bond Record. A monthly listing of all Moody's current debt ratings.

Moody's Municipal & Government Manual. An annual information manual on 20,000 municipalities and more than 1,000 federal, state, local, and regulatory agencies.

Moody's Bond Survey. A weekly publication that covers factors and issues that affect the values of bonds.

Indexes

20-Bond G.O. Index. The Bond Buyer's index of 20 general obligation bonds with 20-year maturities. While the individual ratings of the 20 bonds vary from triple-A to lower investment grades, the overall index has a rating roughly equivalent to single-A. This index is of some interest to higher education issuers as an overall market indicator, but it is an index of general obligation issues, which are not issued by colleges and universities.

11-Bond G.O. Index A subset of the 20-Bond Index that includes those of higher credit quality, approximately equal to a AA.

25-Bond Revenue Index. An index of 25 revenue bonds, the type issued by colleges and universities, with *maturities* of 30 years and with ratings that range from AA to single-A. This index, which is the most pertinent for higher education issuers to follow, occasionally includes a higher education issue.

The Bond Market Association Municipal Swap Index (BMA). Produced by Municipal Market Data, a 7-day high-grade market index comprised of tax-exempt VRDBs from MMD's extensive database. The Index is comprised of actual issues from the most comprehensive source of data on VRDBs available. MMD's database contains extensive information for more than 10,000 active VRDBs. Typically, the Index has included 250 issues in any given week.

Kenny Indices. Provides information about the market environment for variable rate debt and compiles indexes for subscribers and clients on a customized basis. After each repricing, Kenny conveys new index values to remarketing agents, trustees, and issuers.

Rating Agencies

Moody's Investors Service, Inc.
99 Church Street, New York, NY 10007
212-553-0300 . . . . www.moodys.com
Moody's publishes *Moody's Bond Record*; *Moody's Municipal & Government Manual*; *Moody's Bond Survey*; and other specialized publications.

Standard & Poor's Corporation (S&P)
55 Water Street, New York, NY 10041-0003
212-438-2000/2400 . . . . www.standardandpoors.com/ratings
S&P publishes *CreditWeek* and holds occasional one-day seminars on higher education creditworthiness aimed at college and university financial and business officers and investment bankers.

Fitch IBCA (Fitch)
One State Street Plaza, New York, NY 10004
212-908-0500 . . . . www.fitchibca.com
Fitch also rates higher education bonds.

Municipal Bond Industry Organizations

Government Finance Officers Association of the United States and Canada (GFOA)
180 North Michigan Avenue, Suite 800, Chicago, IL 60601
312-977-9700 . . . . www.gfoa.org
GFOA is a professional association of state and local government finance officers
that holds conferences and sponsors activities on topics relating to public finance.

National Federation of Municipal Analysts (NFMA)
P.O. Box 14893, Pittsburgh, PA 15234
412-341-4898 . . . . www.nfma.org
NFMA is a professional association that represents analysts who make credit
recommendations for both issuers and buyers of municipal securities.

Bond Market Association (BMA)(formerly Public Securities Association)
40 Broad Street, New York, NY 10004
212-809-7000 . . . . www.bondmarkets.com
BMA is the national trade organization of dealers and dealer banks that underwrite,
trade, and sell state and local government securities and U.S. government and
federal agency securities.

Municipal Bond Industry Regulatory Body

Municipal Securities Rulemaking Board
1150 18th Street, NW, Suite 400, Washington, D.C. 20036
202-223-9347 . . . . www.msrb.org
The Municipal Securities Rulemaking Board was established by Congress as part of
the Securities Acts Amendments of 1975 to develop rules governing securities firms
and banks involved in underwriting, trading, and selling municipal securities. The
board, which is composed of members of the municipal securities industry and the
public, is a self-regulatory body that sets standards based on the expertise of
industry members.

Higher Education Associations

National Association of College and University Business Officers (NACUBO)
2501 M Street, NW, Suite 400, Washington, D.C. 20037
202-861-2500 . . . . www.nacubo.org
NACUBO publishes material on debt financing and management, sponsors
seminars on debt financing, and contains the Financial Management Center, which
can provide information on debt financing and management.

National Association of
Higher Education Facilities Authorities (NAHEFA) . . . . . www.nahefa.com
NAHEFA is a professional membership organization of the managers of these
authorities. It does not maintain a permanent office address; contact member
authorities for program information.

Data Service Companies

Investment Dealers Digest (IDD)
40 West 57th Street, 11th floor, New York, NY 10019
212-765-5311 . . . . www.sdponline.com
IDD gathers information about municipal bond issues from public sources and
maintains an extensive database.

Thompson Financial Securities Data (Securities Data Company) (SDC)
Two Gateway Center, 11th floor, Newark, NJ 07102
973-622-3100 . . . . www.tfsd.com
SDC is the municipal new issues source for *The Bond Buyer*. It also is a provider of
new issue information to the financial services community, including municipal
underwriters, financial advisors, and bond counsel firms. SDC maintains and can
retrieve data for higher education and teaching hospitals.

Bond Insurers

AMBAC Assurance Corporation
1 State Street Plaza, 17th Floor, New York, NY 10004
212-668-0340 . . . . www.ambac.com
AMBAC is active as an insurer of higher education and related health care bond
issues.

Financial Guarantee Insurance Company (FGIC)
115 Broadway, New York, NY 10006
800-352-0001 . . . . www.fgic.com
FGIC is somewhat less active in higher education bond issues than other companies,
but does consider some financings.

Financial Security Assurance, Inc. (FSA)
350 Park Avenue, New York, NY 10022
212-826-0100 . . . . www.fsa.com
FSA entered the municipal market in 1990, and insures higher education bond
issues.

MBIA Insurance Corporation
113 King Street, Armonk, NY 10504
914-273-4545 . . . . www.mbia.com
MBIA is the largest municipal bond company and is an active insurer of higher
education and related health care bond issues.

Chapter 11

Taxation

by

Kaye B. Ferriter
PricewaterhouseCoopers

Gwen Spencer
PricewaterhouseCoopers

Jocelyn Ceasar
PricewaterhouseCoopers

Sponsors

NCS
Contact: Melanie Barton
4301 Wilson Blvd, Set 200
Arlington, VA 22203
703-284-5615
www.ncs.com

NCS is the leading provider of Taxpayer Relief Act Services to higher education, including 1098-T/1098-E printing and mailing, Web services and toll-free customer service.

WINDSTAR TECHNOLOGIES, INC.
Contact: Janet Chatheld
P.O. Box 800
1540 Providence Highway, Suite 13
Norwood, MA 02062-0800
781-551-5858
www.windstar-tech.com

Windstar Technologies, Inc. develops and distributes the International Tax Navigator, a PC-based software system for nonresident alien tax compliance and case-by-case tax treaty analysis.

Contents

Colleges and universities, though generally exempt from federal income tax, face a panoply of tax issues that are of particular importance and relevance to institutional financial and business officers.[1] These issues include the maintenance, through proper and conscientious organization and operation, of a college or university's tax-exempt status; the treatment and reporting of charitable contributions; the treatment of income derived from activities unrelated to the pursuit of the exempt educational purpose of a college or university (*i.e.*, unrelated business income); the tax reporting responsibilities for nonresident alien students and faculty; the tax treatment of faculty housing and tuition remission; and the compliance responsibilities with respect to employment and state and local taxes. In the burgeoning era of E-commerce, new issues arise in the treatment of all types of transactions via the Internet. Colleges and universities face increased scrutiny from taxing authorities at all levels of government.

This chapter is intended to provide a broad overview of many of the tax-related issues that are of concern to higher education institutions. Many of the following topics are the subjects of entire books. The scope of this chapter does not permit a detailed discussion of any single issue.

OBTAINING AND RETAINING TAX-EXEMPT STATUS

For a college or university to receive recognition of its tax-exempt status from the Internal Revenue Service (IRS), the institution must be organized and operated primarily for exempt purposes as described in Internal Revenue Code (IRC) Section 501(c)(3). Independent institutions must seek recognition under Section 501(c)(3); public institutions, already "passively" exempt as state institutions under Section 115, may choose to apply for recognition under Section 501(c)(3). However, obtaining Section 501(c)(3) status may subject the institution to intermediate sanctions rules and carry with it other tax reporting responsibilities. Exempt purposes recognized by the IRC and the Treasury regulations include educational, literary, and/or scientific objectives.[2] To be exempt as an organization described in Section 501(c)(3), an institution must meet two tests: an organizational test and an operational test.

The organizational test requires that an institution's articles of incorporation limit its purposes to one or more exempt purposes and do not "expressly empower the organization to engage, otherwise than as an insubstantial part of its activities, in activities which in themselves are not in furtherance of one or more exempt purposes."[3] Organizational documents that mandate or allow a substantial involvement in lobbying or activities unrelated to an exempt purpose may preclude an organization from receiving tax-exempt status as a charitable organization or cause an organization to lose its charitable exempt status.

The operational test requires that an institution be "operated exclusively" for one or more of its stated exempt purposes, which is defined by the Department of the Treasury and consistently interpreted by the courts to mean "primarily."[4] Therefore, for example, lobbying and unrelated business activities (discussed below) will not cause an exempt organization to lose its status unless they become substantial in relationship to the overall activities of the organization.

An institution of higher education may be recognized as either a tax-exempt "charitable" organization (insofar as the definition of "charitable" includes the "advancement of education") or an educational organization (which "normally maintains a regular faculty and curriculum and normally has a regularly enrolled body of pupils or students in attendance at the place where its educational activities are regularly carried on").[5] An organization may be educational even though it advocates a particular position or viewpoint, so long as it presents a sufficiently full and fair exposition of the pertinent facts as to permit an individual or the public to form an independent opinion or conclusion.[6] An organization is not educational if its principal function is the mere presentation of unsupported opinion.[7]

Distinction Between Section 501(c)(3) and 501(c)(4) Organizations

As educational organizations, colleges and universities qualify for tax exemption under Section 501(c)(3). Questions often arise as to the distinction between Section 501(c)(3), charitable organizations, and Section 501(c)(4), social welfare organizations. In many ways, the two types of organizations closely resemble one another. Neither may be operated or organized for the benefit of private interests. Both are restricted, to varying degrees, from participating or intervening in political campaigns. Both are liable for unrelated business income tax. Indeed, the promotion of social welfare is one of the definitions of a Section 501(c)(3) charitable organization.[8]

Despite these similarities there are a number of significant distinctions between a charitable organization and a social welfare organization. Social welfare organizations are relatively free to participate in lobbying activities and certain political activities, provided the principal purpose is advancing social welfare. To the contrary, charitable organizations are limited in their lobbying and prohibited from any political activity, as discussed below.

However, there is a trade-off to the political freedoms that Section 501(c)(4) organizations possess. Unlike contributions to Section 501(c)(3) organizations, those to Section 501(c)(4) organizations are not tax deductible by their donors.[9] This is an important distinction for colleges and universities that rely significantly on charitable contributions and the tax deductions such contributions afford their donors. Only Section 501(c)(3) organizations are permitted to receive tax-exempt financing. Furthermore, in general, Section 501(c)(3) organizations are exempt from state sales and property taxes, while Section 501(c)(4) organizations are not.

Private Inurement and Excess Benefit Transactions

As stated, to qualify for and maintain exemption as a charitable organization, an entity must be both organized and operated for exempt purposes. As part of this requirement, the IRC provides that no part of the net earnings of a charitable organization can inure to the benefit of any private shareholder or individual.[10] Moreover, the Treasury regulations state that an organization is not organized and operated exclusively for one or more exempt purposes unless it serves a public rather than a private interest.[11] Thus, to meet this requirement, an organization must prove that it is not organized or operated for the benefit of private interests such as designated individuals, the creator or his or her family, shareholders of the organization, or any other persons.

The concept of private inurement, although it lacks precise definition, is broad. The IRS has stated that "inurement is likely to arise where the financial benefit represents a transfer of the organization's financial resources to an individual solely by virtue of the individual's relationship with the organization, and without regard to accomplishing exempt purposes."[12] The IRS has also stated that the "inurement issue . . . focuses on benefits conferred on an organization's insiders through the use or distribution of the organization's financial resources."[13] The essence of the concept is to ensure that an exempt charitable organization is serving a public and not a private interest.[14]

The IRS has stated that, as a general rule, "an organization's trustees, officers, members, founders, or contributors may not, by reason of their position, acquire any of its funds."[15] Stating the proposition another way, the IRS has observed that "the prohibition of inurement, in its simplest terms, means that a private shareholder or individual cannot pocket the organization's funds except as reasonable payment for goods or services."[16] The existence of private inurement can lead to the revocation of an institution's tax exemption.[17]

Revocation of an exempt organization's favorable tax status is a stiff penalty, and one that the IRS has not imposed except in the most egregious cases, where it was questionable whether the organization meets the definition of a charity.[18] Rather, the IRS is more likely to impose excise tax penalties known as "intermediate sanctions." Neither the private inurement prohibitions nor the intermediate sanction provisions apply directly to state institutions exempt under Section 115. However, they do apply to Section 501(c) affiliates of state institutions.

Intermediate sanctions are penalties imposed on transactions similar in nature to private inurement known as "excess benefit transactions." An excess benefit transaction is defined as a transaction where a "disqualified person" receives excess economic benefits (the amount by which a transaction exceeds fair market value) from an organization.[19] A "disqualified person" is defined as an individual who is in a position to exercise substantial influence over a tax-exempt organization's affairs and engages in a transaction with such organization. There is a five-year look back period for determining disqualified persons. Therefore, a trustee who resigns from the board of a charity is considered to be a disqualified person for the next five years.[20]

There is a two-tier excise tax penalty imposed on Section 501(c)(3) organizations that engage in excess benefit transactions. The first tier of the penalty tax is 25 percent of the amount of the excess benefit. This tax is imposed on the disqualified person, as defined above. Further, each organization manager who knowingly participates in an excess benefit transaction will be taxed at 10 percent of the excess benefit up to $10,000 per violation.[21]

The second tier of the penalty tax is 200 percent of the excess benefit, which is imposed on a disqualified person if the excess benefit is not corrected within a certain period of time. Correction requires that the institution be made whole (i.e., the excess benefit is repaid with interest).[22]

As a safe harbor for exempt organizations, proposed intermediate sanction regulations establish a rebuttable presumption that payments under a compensation arrangement between a disqualified person and a tax-exempt organization are reasonable if the organization meets the following three requirements. First, the compensation arrangement must be approved by the tax-exempt organization's governing board, which must be comprised of persons who do not have a conflict of interest. Second, the governing board must rely on "appropriate data" in deciding whether to approve of the compensation. Third, the governing body must document its actions.[23]

Employees of educational institutions are entitled to reasonable compensation for services rendered; such payments do not constitute inurement. However, excessive compensation can result in the IRS imposing either intermediate sanctions and/or revoking an organization's tax-exempt status. The question of whether compensation is reasonable is a question to be decided in the context of each case, taking into account the experience, skills, and services provided by the individual, as well as the compensation paid to employees performing comparable services elsewhere. In making the determination of whether compensation is reasonable, all elements of the compensation package must be considered, including salary and benefits, such as automobiles, employee benefit plans, below-market loans, and relocation allowances. Compensation arrangements must be carefully evaluated. It is important to report all items of compensation including taxable benefits. Failure to do so could result in the benefits being treated as excess compensation. If uniform performance standards are used to evaluate employees and to justify compensation, private inurement generally does not exist. Moreover, an educational institution making grants and providing scholarships may wish to review procedures for awarding them to ensure that certain individuals do not receive preferential treatment and, therefore, directly or indirectly receive a private benefit.

Political Campaign Activities

A college or university cannot qualify for or maintain tax-exempt status as a charitable organization if it participates or intervenes in any political campaign on behalf of, or in opposition to, any candidate for public office. This prohibition has been interpreted by the IRS to be absolute.[24]

A political expenditure is any amount paid or incurred by a college or university in connection with any participation or intervention in any political campaign on behalf of or in opposition to any candidate for public office. "Intervention" includes the publication or distribution of statements opposing or supporting a candidate. ("Intervention" does not include the participation by students in a political campaign of their choosing in satisfaction of the requirements of a political science course, nor does it include positions taken by a student newspaper that is run by students as an educational endeavor.[25]) An institution that participates in a political campaign on behalf of or in opposition to a candidate for public office, in addition to losing its tax-exempt status, exposes itself to tax liability in the amount of an initial tax equal to 10 percent of the amount of the political expenditure.[26]

An expenditure may be "corrected" by recovery of the expenditure to the extent possible, establishment of safeguards to prevent future political expenditures, and other additional action provided for under Treasury regulations.[27] If the political expenditure is not corrected within a prescribed period, the institution may face an additional tax equal to 100 percent of the amount involved in the political campaign expenditure.

In addition to the revocation of an institution's exemption for participating in political campaign activities, severe penalties may be imposed on the individuals involved in approving or participating in political campaign activity on behalf of the institution. A college or university administrator who knowingly agrees to such expenditure may be subject to a tax equal to 2.5 percent of the political expenditure. This tax is paid by the administrator. There is a reasonable cause exception to this general rule.[28]

A second tax in the amount of 50 percent of the political campaign expenditure may be assessed if the administrator refuses to agree to a correction of the initial expenditure. Again, this tax is paid by the administrator. The maximum taxes are $5,000 and $10,000, respectively, for the first and second levels of liability.

Lobbying

A college or university cannot qualify as, and may lose its status as, a tax-exempt charitable organization if it engages in more than an insubstantial amount of lobbying activities. The term "insubstantial" has never been defined precisely by either the courts or the IRS.

In reaction to this uncertainty, Congress enacted Section 501(h) in 1976 to help clarify the situation. Institutions may elect to be governed by the provisions of Section 501(h). These guidelines define permissible ranges of legislative activities in terms of expenditures of funds and sliding scales of percentages. Entities that do not make the election provided for in Section 501(h) continue to be governed by the "insubstantial part" test. Because lobbying is usually insignificant in terms of the overall programmatic activities pursued by a college or university, it may be in the interest of most institutions to choose to be governed by the insubstantial part test, notwithstanding its inherent uncertainty.

"Safe harbor" guidelines under Section 501(h) are set out in terms of declining percentages of total expenditures. (In this case, the safe harbor guidelines describe acceptable types and amounts of an activity or activities; if the guidelines are not adhered to, an organization will face a penalty—taxes.) The annual level of expenditures for legislative activities is fixed at 20 percent of the first $500,000 of an organization's exempt purpose expenditures, 15 percent of the next $500,000, 10 percent of the next $500,000, and 5 percent of any remaining expenditures. However, in no event may the expenditures in any one taxable year for legislative activities made by a public charity exceed $1 million. Grass roots lobbying (i.e., lobbying of the general public as opposed to lobbying of a legislative body or regulatory agency) expenditures are limited to 25 percent of the amounts derived under the above formula.

A charitable organization that has made the election under Section 501(h) and that exceeds the limitations is subject to an excise tax of 25 percent of the excess lobbying expenditures. If an electing organization's lobbying expenditures exceed 150 percent of either the lobbying limit or the grass roots limit over a four-year period, it may lose its tax-exempt status.

The term "influencing legislation" is defined to mean any attempt to influence any legislation through an effort to affect the opinions of the general public or segments thereof, and through communication with any member or employee of a legislative body or any other governmental official or employee who participates in formulation of the legislation. For organizations that have made the Section 501(h) election, exclusions from the definition of influencing legislation are provided for five types of activities:

- making available the results of nonpartisan analysis, study, or research;
- providing technical advice to a governmental body in response to a written request;
- appearing before or communicating with any legislative body with respect to a possible decision of that body that may affect the existence of the organization, its powers, duties, and its tax-exempt status, or the deduction of contributions;
- communicating with the organization's *bona fide* members with respect to legislation or proposed legislation of direct interest to them, provided that the communication does not directly encourage the members to influence legislation or directly encourage the members to urge nonmembers to influence legislation; and
- communicating with nonlegislative government officials or employees.

Payments to Communities in Lieu of Taxes

Communities once considered the presence of colleges and universities as desirable because of the benefits their educational mission offered the community as well as the jobs they provided to members of the community. Today, in addition to their educational offerings, communities may also regard their colleges and universities as untapped revenue resources. Because of their tax-exempt status, resentment can build over higher education institutions' not paying taxes while concurrently reaping the benefits others' tax dollars provide them, including fire and police protection. To preempt negative attitudes from influencing an institution's favorable tax position, one option is to voluntarily offer to repay the government a mutually agreed-upon amount for services the community furnishes to the organization. Some communities have taxed facilities owned by institutions that are not used for tax-exempt purposes. Other communities have negotiated to keep certain properties on the tax rolls in exchange for permitting an institution to expand.

Aside from voluntary payments, certain communities have been deriving income more aggressively from exempt organizations via state audit enforcement programs that focus on abandoned or unclaimed property. "Abandoned property" can be defined as any item of income or liability that a taxpayer has on its books and records that it cannot prove belongs to them. Such items include uncashed payroll and vendor checks, account receivable credit balances, security deposit accounts, and other liability balances. All of these items will be presumed to be abandoned under a state audit and frequently result in sizable assessments. A substantial portion of presumed abandoned property is, in reality, the result of inaccurate or incomplete accounting practices. A review and correction of these accounting practices can significantly reduce prior period exposure.

CHARITABLE CONTRIBUTIONS

Charitable contributions are a key source of revenue for many colleges and universities.[29] Therefore, it is important for institutions to be aware of the charitable contribution reporting and documentation requirements that affect their donors. The IRS has focused on three areas recently that are of particular concern for charitable donors—rules of substantiation, the impact of taxes on their charitable donations, and deferred giving.

Substantiation Rules

For donors to receive the benefit of a tax deduction from a charitable contribution, they must meet certain substantiation requirements. No deduction will be allowed for any contribution in excess of $250 that is not acknowledged by the charitable organization. The substantiation statement must indicate the amount of the contribution and the value of any goods or services provided to the donor. A canceled check will no longer be considered a valid form of substantiation. When a quid pro quo contribution exceeds $75, the charitable organization is required to inform the donor of the value of any goods or services received. A "quid pro quo contribution" is a payment made partly as a contribution and partly for goods and services, such as a dinner dance or golf tournament.[30] There is a penalty of $10 for each contribution for which there was a failure to disclose, up to $5,000 per event or mailing.[31]

Any charitable deduction claimed in connection with the contribution of property valued in excess of $5,000 ($10,000 for gifts of closely held stock) from an individual, closely held corporation, partnership, or S corporation must be supported by a qualified appraisal. The appraisal must be summarized and attached to the donor's tax return in order to substantiate the deduction.[32] Furthermore, if an individual or partnership donates noncash property worth more than $500, the donor is obligated to complete and attach IRS Form 8283, Non-cash Charitable Contributions, to his or her tax return to claim a contribution deduction. Corporations making noncash contributions of $5,000 or more are also subject to this requirement. In addition, a noncash contribution by any taxpayer in excess of $5,000 requires acknowledgment of receipt by the institution on Form 8283 and, in many cases, requires certification by a qualified appraiser. The donee's signature on Form 8283 merely acknowledges receipt of the donation and does not constitute agreement with the donor's stated valuation. Institutions may carry the donated property at whatever value they choose.

Charitable organizations, including colleges and universities, that dispose of noncash contributions worth more than $500 within two years of receipt are required to file IRS Form 8282, Donee Information Return. The form is due within 125 days of disposition, and the donor must receive a copy of the form. An exception to this filing requirement is property that is given away or used by the institution in furtherance of its tax-exempt purpose. A disposition of property that occurs within two years of receipt by the institution, for an amount substantially less than that claimed by the donor on the occurrence of the original donation, may cause the IRS to challenge the original valuation of the gift.

Colleges and universities are advised to exercise caution when accepting gifts of property that may have significant costs, either in the form of recurring costs such as insurance and real property taxes or in the form of huge one-time outlays, such as the cost of cleaning up a hazardous waste site. They should also be aware of potential unrelated business income when accepting gifts of partnership interests and S corporations.

The IRS is concerned about fund-raising practices that allow contributors the opportunity to obtain something of value while taking a charitable deduction for the full amount paid. Under federal tax law, a charitable contribution deduction must be reduced by the fair market value of any benefit received. For example, if a college or university holds a raffle, a raffle ticket purchaser may be tempted to claim a deduction for the amount paid for the ticket because the payment is made to a charitable organization. However, no deduction would be allowed in that instance because the purchaser is buying a chance to win something. Alternatively, where an amount paid exceeds the value of the thing received, the taxpayer may take a deduction for the difference. For example, if a taxpayer pays $75 for a ticket to a benefit dinner and the actual value of the dinner is $50, the taxpayer is entitled to a deduction for the amount that exceeds the $50 value of the meal, in this case $25.

The IRS has issued guidelines that govern the issue of providing a token item in return for a contribution. Generally, items costing $5 or less are covered by a *de minimis* rule and need not be used to reduce the amount of a donation. Moreover, items bearing the college or university's logo, such as T-shirts, calendars, or key chains, do not generally reduce the amount of the deductible contribution if the donation is $25 or more. In addition, the amount of the donation is not reduced if the fair market value of the benefit received in the form of a token gift does not exceed the lesser of 2 percent of the donation or $50. These amounts were set in 1990 and are indexed each year for inflation.[33]

In order to meet the IRS rules for token benefits, colleges and universities are required to communicate both the deductible and nondeductible portion of donations in all solicitations, including written, broadcast, and telephone materials. In situations where only insubstantial benefits are provided by the institution, the IRS suggests that the following disclosure statement be provided in any solicitation materials: "Under Internal Revenue Service guidelines, the estimated value of the benefits received is not substantial; therefore, the full amount of your payment is a deductible contribution."

Tax Rates on Charitable Donations

Donors who are able to substantiate their full donations to colleges and universities often are surprised to find out that the Internal Revenue Code places limitations on the amount donors may take as deductions. These limits are based on an individual's annual contribution base, generally calculated as a percentage of the individual's adjusted gross income (AGI), and vary depending on the type of gift given to the college or university. An individual may deduct annually cash gifts up to 50 percent of the donor's AGI.[34] If appreciated stock or securities are donated, the annual deduction is limited to 30 percent of the donor's AGI.[35] For ordinary income property, such as inventory, depreciable property, and short-term capital gain property, the donor may deduct the lesser of fair market value or adjusted basis of the gift, again limited to 50 percent of the donor's AGI. Finally, for gifts of appreciated long-term capital gain property, the donor may deduct fair market value except for gifts of personal property not related to the college or university's tax-exempt purpose. For this exception, the donor may take a deduction limited to his or her adjusted basis in the property. Gifts of appreciated long-term capital gain property are subject to a limitation of either 30 or 50 percent of the donor's AGI, depending on whether the donor elects to apply the 50 percent of AGI limitation by decreasing the deductible amount for any potential long-term capital gain. This election applies to all gifts given that year by the donor. Charitable contributions made by corporate donors are limited to 10 percent of pretax income before the deduction for contributions.

Deferred Giving

Deferred giving has become more widespread among institutions. It is possible for a donor to receive current tax deductions for gifts of assets and still receive income from those assets during his or her life. Popular deferred giving vehicles include charitable remainder trusts, pooled income funds, and charitable gift annuities. Very wealthy donors may pass on assets to future generations through the use of charitable lead trusts, which provide income to the institution for a period of time after which the corpus reverts to designated beneficiaries.

UNRELATED BUSINESS INCOME TAX

Colleges and universities, though otherwise tax-exempt, are required to pay federal income tax on their unrelated business income.[36] There may also be a state tax liability. For the unrelated business income tax (UBIT) to apply, the following three conditions must be met:

- the activity earning income must be a trade or business;
- the trade or business must not be substantially related to the college or university's exempt purposes; and
- the trade or business must be regularly carried on.

For UBIT purposes, a trade or business includes any activity undertaken to produce income, regardless of whether it is profitable. However, if an activity that would otherwise be unrelated fails to generate a profit over a number of years, the IRS may disallow the losses, claiming that the activity was not engaged in for profit (the "hobby loss rule"). In order to counteract this argument the institution should have budgets or operating plans that show when it is anticipated that the activity will become profitable.

Whether an activity is "regularly carried on" depends on the frequency and continuity with which the activity is conducted. An activity is not substantially related to a college or university's exempt purpose if there is no causal relationship between the activity and the achievement of the institution's exempt purpose. The fact that proceeds from the activity are used to further the exempt purpose of the organization does not prevent the application of the unrelated business income tax.

There are a number of "UBIT exceptions," for which certain income-producing activities are statutorily exempt from the imposition of UBIT, notwithstanding that the activities are, in fact, unrelated.[37] These include the following:

- *The volunteer exception:* This occurs when substantially all of the work performed in pursuit of the unrelated activity is done by volunteers.

- *The donated goods exception:* This occurs when the unrelated income derived from a particular activity is from the sale of merchandise, substantially all of which was donated to the college or university.

- *The convenience exception:* This occurs when the trade or business is conducted by the college or university primarily for the convenience of its students, staff, and employees.[38]

In addition, unrelated business revenue does not include passive income such as dividends, interest, royalties, capital gains and securities, and rents from real property. An exclusion also exists for income from the performance of basic research[39] and research conducted by colleges and universities.[40]

In situations that give rise to UBIT, taxable income generally is gross income from all of an organization's unrelated trade or businesses, less allowable deductions directly connected with the conduct of these activities. In addition, there are several other allowable deductions:

- a specific deduction of $1,000;
- a deduction for net operating loss carryforwards; and
- a deduction for charitable contributions.

If facilities and personnel are used for both exempt functions and unrelated business activities, then expenses, depreciation, and similar items such as overhead must be allocated between the exempt and the taxable activities. This allocation is necessary to determine the net income from the unrelated business activity. There are many different ways reasonably to allocate expenses between exempt and non-exempt activities. One of these methods may be to allocate expenses that have a causal relationship to labor based on the percentage of time spent on the unrelated activity. For example, if an employee of a college or university spends 10 percent of his or her time on an unrelated business activity, 10 percent of his or her salary and benefits should be allocated as a deduction against the unrelated activity.

Where dual use of a facility occurs, the expenses associated with operating the facility must be allocated between both uses, according to the following formula:

$$\frac{\text{Number of hours facility used for unrelated purposes}}{\text{Total number of hours facility used for unrelated and related purposes}} \times \text{Expenses associated with operating the facility}$$

Although there is authority for this position in *Rensselaer Polytechnic Institute v. Commissioner*,[41] the IRS believes the proper method to allocate fixed expenses is based on a 24-hour-a-day, 12-month-a-year period, using a ratio of hours used for unrelated activities to total hours in the year.

Debt-financed Property

Income received from debt-financed property is generally subject to UBIT. This includes dividends, interest, royalties, and rents derived from property that is subject to an indebtedness, as well as gains from the sale of a capital asset that is subject to an indebtedness at any time during the 12 months prior to the sale. The amount of debt-financed income recognized as UBIT is determined by the ratio of debt outstanding during the year and the tax basis for a property. The following are specifically excluded from treatment as "debt-financed property":

- any property that is substantially related to the college or university's educational purpose;

- any property that is already treated as unrelated business income; or

- any property that is used in a trade or business in a manner covered by one of the exceptions discussed previously, including the volunteer exception, the research exception, the convenience exception, and the donated property exception.[42]

There is an exception to the debt-financed income rule for real property that is leased by colleges and universities.[43] Generally, property subject to a normal commercial mortgage will not be subject to the debt-financed income rules. However, the rules surrounding this exception are complex and need to be reviewed where appropriate.

Investments in Partnerships / Joint Ventures

The investment in a partnership by a college or university may give rise to unrelated business income, regardless of the tax status of the other partners. The test here, as in all other unrelated business income determinations, goes to the nature of the activity pursued by the partnership. If the partnership is involved in an activity that would be an unrelated trade or business activity if it were directly carried on by the college or university, the participation by the college or university in such a partnership does nothing to change the character of the activity carried on by the partnership. Therefore, an institution's allocable share of gross income from a partnership pursuing an unrelated activity constitutes unrelated business taxable income. Even if the income earned by a partnership would otherwise be exempt from UBIT, it will not be exempt if the income is earned by a "publicly traded partnership" and if it has interests that are traded on an established securities market or on a secondary market. Partnerships must report unrelated business income information to all tax-exempt partners.

If the IRS finds that a Section 501(c)(3) organization is no longer operated for exempt purposes when partnering with for-profit corporations, then the organization could risk losing its exempt status, in addition to being liable for UBIT on partnership income. In Revenue Ruling 98-15[44], the IRS discussed the criteria for determining whether a participant in a whole hospital joint venture loses its exempt status. It appears that the IRS will look at exemption issues when the joint venture activity constitutes a substantial portion of the institution's activities. For smaller auxiliary ventures, such as food services or bookstores, the IRS will most likely simply analyze the venture for UBIT. Although the rules have not yet withstood the test of time and court proceedings, an organization should follow certain guidelines to protect its exempt status when entering into a joint venture. First, a college or university should control the joint venture's assets and activities. Second, the for-profit purpose of the joint venture must be secondary to the charitable purpose. Finally, the for-profit management company cannot be guaranteed a future management contract from the joint venture. Essentially, these guidelines ensure that an exempt organization acts "exclusively in furtherance of its exempt purpose and only incidentally for the benefit of the for-profit partners."[45]

Auxiliary Enterprises

Revenue from auxiliary enterprises does not generate unrelated business income if they serve the educational purposes of the institution. As alluded to above, if a college or university opens its auxiliary enterprises to the public, it should be aware of the existence of potential generation of unrelated business income.

For-profit Subsidiaries

Many institutions have wholly owned, for-profit subsidiaries that operate unrelated activities. If a college or university causes a wholly owned for-profit subsidiary to incorporate and capitalize a network of taxable subsidiaries, the activities of the subsidiaries do not jeopardize the parent's exempt status. Institutions that have multiple for-profit subsidiaries should consider having them all owned by a single for-profit holding company, so that losses of one subsidiary might offset the income of another. Moreover, the existence of any number of financial relationships may give rise to unrelated business income in the parent. As discussed as follows in more detail, the fact that a subsidiary may be allowed to use the parent's name and logo in return for royalty payments, and may pay interest on loans made by the parent, will generate unrelated business taxable income in the parent charitable organization to the extent that the subsidiary is able to benefit from the deduction of these amounts.

Advertising

Income from advertising is generally taxable as unrelated business income. Colleges and universities typically solicit and feature advertising in their periodicals and sports programs. One court has held that advertising in collegiate sports programs for events that are conducted for only a few weeks each year, such as the National Collegiate Athletic Association basketball tournament, is not regularly carried on and, therefore, does not result in unrelated business income.[46] However, it should be noted that the IRS has publicly disavowed the court's holding.[47] Income from a publication is categorized either as gross advertising income or circulation income. Circulation income is all income other than advertising income realized from the publication, its circulation, or its distribution. Expenses are divided into direct advertising costs and readership costs. If direct advertising costs exceed gross advertising income, the loss is recognized for tax purposes and may be used to offset other sources of unrelated business income. If gross advertising income exceeds direct advertising costs, the institution may compare circulation income to readership costs. If circulation income is greater than readership costs, the taxable income is the gross advertising income less direct advertising costs. If readership costs exceed circulation income, the excess readership costs may decrease, but not below zero, the previously computed income from advertising.

Corporate Sponsorship

Legislation enacted in 1997 exempts qualified sponsorship payments from UBIT.[48] "Qualified sponsorship payments" are made by a payor who has no expectation of any substantial return benefit other than the use or acknowledgment of the payor's name, logo, or product lines. Importantly, qualified sponsorship payments do not include payments made for messages that contain qualitative or comparative language, price information, an endorsement, or an inducement to purchase, sell, or use the payor's product or services. In addition, they do not include payments that are contingent upon attendance, broadcast ratings, or other factors. Allocations between qualified sponsorship and other revenue are permitted in appropriate situations.

Many colleges and universities have entered into exclusivity contracts with major vendors. The issue here is whether this activity is sponsorship income (passive) or advertising income, or does it represent participation in another trade or business and therefore is subject to tax. The IRS has indicated that it will focus on this area in the near future.

Rental Income

Many colleges and universities rent housing, tennis facilities, skating rinks, stadiums, and chapels to alumni and others. Although rental income is specifically excluded from unrelated business income tax, it is taxable if:

- the rent is tied in whole or part to the net income or profits derived by the lessee;

- the property is debt-financed property and not used in an exempt activity (There is an exception to this rule for debt-financed real property owned by a college, university, or pension trust;

- significant services are provided; or

- fifty percent or more of the rent is for personal property.

In general, the lease or rental of real property to the general public is excluded from UBIT as passive income. Rents based on a fixed percentage of net income or profits are not excluded from UBIT. (Otherwise, an institution could use a net profit rental agreement to operate an unrelated trade or business and disguise taxable profits as tax-free rents.) However, rents based on a fixed percentage of gross receipts or sales are excluded. If a substantial portion (more than 10 percent but less than 50 percent[49]) of rental income is from the rental of personal property, the proceeds attributable to the use of personal property are unrelated business income.

For purposes of the rental exclusion, certain services may be provided without adverse tax implications as long as they are customarily rendered in connection with the lease of the facility. Such services include:

- furnishing of heat, light, and other utilities;

- provision of security;

- the cleaning and maintenance of public areas; and

- the collection of trash.

If additional services are provided that are primarily for the convenience of the user and not customarily rendered, the entire amount received from the party receiving the services is considered unrelated business income because the institution is viewed as conducting a service business. Some examples of services that may give rise to unrelated business taxable income are:

- maid service;

- extensive grounds and playing field maintenance;

- the provision of towels, linens, or laundry service;
- the provision of food, beverage, or other catering services;
- video or audio production services;
- valet parking;
- the resurfacing of an ice rink; and
- lifeguard services at swimming pools.

Royalties

A royalty is a fee for the license of a property right such as a patent, copyright, or mineral interest. Royalties are generally excluded from UBIT. However, a distinction must be made between royalties and personal property rents. Royalty agreements are typically seen in the transfer of technology and the use of the institution's name in connection with someone else's trade or business. Royalties associated with the use of an institution's name in connection with the issuance of bank credit cards and the transfer of mailing lists have recently received a lot of attention.

Credit Cards (Affinity Cards)

Some colleges and universities offer specially designed bank credit cards, called "affinity cards," to alumni. The institution receives payments from the issuing bank, in the form of either a flat fee or a percentage of purchases charged by the user of the affinity credit card. The IRS has contended that such arrangements are analogous to providing memberships lists to a commercial organization and, thus, are taxable transactions.

The Tax Court continues to rule that the income received in connection with the affinity card programs is royalty income and exempt from unrelated business income tax. In *Sierra Club, Inc.* v. *Commissioner,* the Tax Court rejected the IRS's position that the affinity card arrangement was a joint venture between the Sierra Club and American Bancard Service (ABS) or that ABS was the Sierra Club's agent in selling financial services. In either of these cases, the income would be taxable. Instead, the Tax Court found that the arrangement (whereby ABS had access to the Sierra Club's members and the use of its name and logo in exchange for a percentage of the monthly sales charges) was for the use of its name under Section 512(b)(2). As such, this income does not represent unrelated business income.[50]

The Sierra Club case is one of many where the IRS has lost on this issue. For example, in 1997, the Tax Court, in *Mississippi State University Alumni, Inc.* v. *Com-*

missioner, ruled that a university alumni association's income from the affinity credit card program is not subject to UBIT.[51] This decision is consistent with the ruling in *Sierra Club*. The IRS has recently indicated that it will no longer pursue these cases.

Mailing List Rentals

The Tax Court has held in recent cases that payments derived from an organization's rental of its mailing list constituted royalties rather than unrelated business income.[52] The IRS has not appealed these cases and the time to do so has expired.

Mailing list income was also an issue in the Sierra Club case. In the case of the Sierra Club, the Ninth Circuit Court of Appeals, a higher level court than the Tax Court, reviewed the Tax Court's ruling and handed down its decision to sustain the Sierra Club's nontaxable passive income classification of its mailing list rental receipts. Thus, the Tax Court's earlier classification of the mailing list rental income as excludable was upheld.[53] However, services in conjunction with the rental of a mailing list could generate UBIT. In recent Tax Court cases, the IRS unsuccessfully argued that the services performed by the exempt organization tainted *all* the rental income. However, in light of its recent losses, it appears that the IRS might apply some type of allocation approach in determining what portion of the list rental is unrelated business income. Therefore, to avoid UBIT completely, services should not be provided along with rental of a mailing list.

Transactions with Related Entities

If an institution receives rent, interest, annuity, or royalty payments from related organizations, the income may be deemed unrelated income. A "related organization" is defined as an organization that is controlled by an individual or another organization. "Control" is defined, for the purposes of an exempt organization, as ownership of more than 50 percent of the beneficial interests in the entity.[54] Unless the income of the related organization would have been exempt function income if realized directly by the recipient, it will be considered unrelated business income to the extent the related organization reduces its taxable income by the amount of the payment (if a for-profit entity) or its unrelated business income (if a tax-exempt entity).[55]

Bookstores

Net income from the operation of a college or university bookstore is generally not unrelated business income because it serves the educational purposes and programs of the institution or is protected under the convenience exception. However, employing the "fragmentation rule," the IRS will analyze the overall operation of the bookstore as well as each activity and product line to determine whether or not it is related to the accomplishment of the institution's exempt purposes. For example, sales of computers by a college bookstore may generate unrelated business income if the sales are not limited to students, staff, and faculty members or if multiple purchases are allowed. Moreover, the convenience exception has been held by the IRS to be limited to nondurable goods (for example, soap and toothpaste) with a useful life of one year or less, rendering sales of certain items, such as stereos and nonlogo clothing, as tax-generating events.

Athletic Facilities

Many colleges and universities lease their athletic facilities to outside promoters for athletic and other entertainment events. In a situation where a college or university rents its sports facilities to an outsider and the use of the facility includes operation by employees of the institution's athletic department, the college or university is engaged in an unrelated trade or business. As alluded to above, the provision of substantial services by institutional employees would render this situation a taxable event, not covered by the general UBIT exclusion for income received from the rental of real property. Alternatively, if an institution leases facilities for a fixed fee to an unrelated individual or entity who operates a club for the public, but the institution provides no services (such as food, security, maintenance, or laundry), the rental income is excluded from UBIT under the general exception for rent from real property.

Another common activity of colleges and universities that may be subject to UBIT is the provision of health club facilities to those beyond the student, faculty, and employee population, such as alumni and the general community. Although most institutions would not agree, alumni are considered by the IRS to be the "general public" for purposes of determining whether users are members of the college or university community covered by the convenience exception.

Day Care

Income from the operation of a day-care center may qualify for exclusion from UBIT if the center is operated primarily for the convenience of institutional employees, faculty members, and students, or if it is operated as an integral part of the institution's educational program. On the other hand, if an institution runs a day-care center for unrelated third parties (and none of the other exceptions apply), the income generated is probably subject to UBIT, unless it can be proved under Section 501(k) that substantially all of the care provided is for the purposes of enabling individuals to be gainfully employed and the services are available to the general public.

Radio and Television

A college or university may operate a radio or television station as an activity in furtherance of its exempt, educational purpose, if the purpose of such a station is to offer students education and training in the broadcasting industry and it is not run in a commercial way. The revenue generated by a radio or television station operated in such a manner does not constitute unrelated business taxable income. However, the operation of a radio or television station by a college or university may be an unrelated trade or business if the station is operated purely as a commercial enterprise with little teaching or training involved.

Securities Lending

In an effort to enhance the growth of endowment, many colleges and universities undertake sophisticated financial transactions, including those involving securities. An issue that frequently arises is whether securities lending creates debt-financed income that is taxable as unrelated business income. Where an institution uses its own assets as collateral to borrow stock that it has sold short, and the value of the collateral equals the fair market value of the borrowed stock, the transaction does not result in unrelated business income. However, if the borrowing is not fully collateralized, the income derived from the short sale is taxable as unrelated business income.

Life Insurance Policies

An institution may receive deductible contributions by being the named beneficiary on a donor's life insurance policy. In this case, the contributor pays the annual premiums on the donated policies. As a means to significantly increase its revenue, the donee institution can withdraw the accumulated cash value, paying approximately 5 percent in interest per year to the insurance company while earning over 10 percent on the reinvestment of this cash in marketable securities.

Ordinarily, passive investment income such as interest and dividends is excluded from unrelated business income and, therefore, is not taxable. However, the IRS has held that because insurance policy loans are generally regarded as a valid form of indebtedness, the income earned through the reinvestment is unrelated business income to a college or university.

Travel Tours

The IRS has issued final regulations under Section 513 addressing whether travel and tour activities of tax-exempt organizations are substantially related to the purposes for which exemption was granted, and thus generally not subject to tax as an unrelated trade or business.[56] The regulations adopted a general facts-and-circumstances approach, where contemporaneous documentation showing how an organization develops, promotes, and operates the travel tour is relevant to the facts-and-circumstances analysis. This will require that each tour be analyzed during the planning process to evaluate how the tour is related to the organization's exempt purposes. The regulations do not enumerate any specific factors that determine relatedness of travel tour activities to exempt purposes. However, they do include new examples intended to provide additional guidance regarding the application of this facts-and-circumstances approach in both educational and noneducational contexts.

Clarifications made in the final regulations include the following:

- Relevant facts and circumstances include (but are not limited to) how a travel tour is developed, promoted, and operated, as illustrated by examples in the final regulations.

- The number of hours spent on any related travel tour activity is only one factor in determining relatedness of the tour as a whole to exempt purposes and is not by itself determinative. Examples in the final regulation clarify that the nature of the related activities, and the practicalities of engaging in such activities (for example, the hours during which the activity normally would be conducted), also must be taken into account.

- No additional recordkeeping requirements are imposed under the regulations, but examples illustrate that contemporaneous documentation showing how an organization develops, promotes, and operates the travel tour is relevant to the facts-and-circumstances analysis.

The IRS rejected a suggestion to address whether income from travel tour activity is a royalty under Section 512(b)(2) where the exempt organization does not operate the tour, but provides member names to a for-profit tour operator. The IRS stated that the question of what constitutes a royalty is beyond the scope of these regulations, and for guidance referred to Section 1.512(b)-1(b) and *Sierra Club* v. *Commissioner*.

In light of the IRS refusing to discuss the tax treatment of royalty payments, colleges and universities still can receive income from travel tours without incurring business risk from such ventures if the income is treated as royalty payments. The IRS considers royalty income to be passive, nontaxable income to tax-exempt organizations.[57] When a college or university gives permission to a for-profit organization to sell certain products using the college or university's name, the college or university can receive a tax-free royalty in exchange for the benefit it provides. In the case of travel tours, royalties are often structured that compensate the institution at a flat rate based on the number of participants.

E-COMMERCE

The Internet and E-commerce are creating new types of transactions and relationships daily. They are impacting the way colleges and universities conduct business. The IRS has not issued any guidance relative to E-commerce but has indicated that this is an area it will be exploring in the future. Currently the tax implications of E-commerce activities have to be analyzed according to existing tax principles.

Many of the E-commerce issues involve unrelated business income. One issue that has been raised is the nature of income received from "banners" or "hotlinks" on an institution's Web site. It is possible that if an institution receives a fixed payment for them, then the income would fall under the sponsorship rules since they merely represent the next generation means of identifying a business. If payment for "banners" or "hotlinks" is tied to the number of times the site is visited from the link, is the revenue from advertising? Is the content of the linked site relevant to the taxability of the payment? If revenue from an institution's sale of an item is not unrelated business if sold in the institution's bookstore because of the convenience exception, should the answer change if it is sold via a Web site? What happens if an institution abandons its bookstore and provides electronic links to an online bookseller to provide course books?

If there is unrelated business generated from the Web site, what are the appropriate expense allocations that should be made?

Fund raising may be done through the Web site. Will the written acknowledgment standards be met if the receipt of the gift is made through E-mail? Will organizations raising funds on their Web site be required to comply with state registration requirements of all states?

If students and faculty are allowed to have personal Web pages, is the institution responsible for the content of those sites? What happens if a student posts political material on his personal Web page? What are the implications if a faculty member provides a link to a bookseller in order to promote sales of his or her book? What happens if someone breaks into the Web site and posts political materials?

These questions are but a partial list of tax issues that arise in connection with use of the Internet. New issues arise as new uses for technology are developed. Currently, analysis of the transaction is based on how the IRS has treated similar situations in the past.

EMPLOYEE BENEFITS

To attract and retain faculty and staff, higher education institutions may offer benefits such as tuition reduction and faculty housing.

Section 403(b) and 457 Plans

Many colleges and universities set up investment plans for their employees. Such plans include annuity plans under Section 403(b). A Section 403(b) plan, generally speaking, is an annuity contract an institution purchases for its employees; the employees' rights are nonforfeitable, and the plan meets certain nondiscrimination policies.[58] Income that the employer contributes to the plan is excluded from the employee's gross income. Both the employer and the employee can make contributions to Section 403(b) plans. In the year 2000 employees may elect to contribute up to $10,500 to a Section 403(b) plan. Employers may contribute up to 25 percent of pay. However, the total contribution by the employer and the employee cannot exceed the lesser of 25 percent of pay or $30,000. There is a catch up provision that allows contributions in excess of this limit up to 20 percent of the employee's compensation multiplied by the amount of years the employee has worked for the employer, less the amount the employer contributed to annuity contracts for prior years.[59] This limit is indexed each year for inflation. Furthermore, if an employee's rights under the plan are nonforfeitable, the benefits will not be taxed until receipt.[60] Nonforfeitability under a Section 403(b) plan requires that the plan benefits belong to and are payable to the employee.[61] Colleges and universities can also use Section 401(k) plans, after December 31, 1996.[62]

Section 457 deferred compensation plans are very restrictive regarding the amount of compensation an employee may contribute. The maximum amount an employee may defer through a Section 457 plan is the lesser of $7,500 or 33⅓ percent of the participant's includible compensation.[63] Employees who participate in more than one plan may not contribute more than $7,500 to their employer's Section 457 plan.[64] Furthermore, compensation will be included in an employee's gross income when a plan is not an eligible deferred compensation plan and the employer requires no substantial additional future services from the employee.[65]

Tuition Reduction

Employees of educational institutions are allowed a "qualified tuition reduction."[66] A qualified tuition reduction is any amount of reduction in undergraduate tuition provided to an employee of a college or university for the education of the employee, spouse, dependent children, and certain retired and disabled employees and surviving spouses. Amounts excluded from the gross income of an employee as a qualified tuition reduction are not subject to monetary limitations.

The tuition reduction benefit may also be provided to graduate students who attend a higher education institution and are engaged in teaching or research activities. Graduate tuition remission is not available to other employees and their families. However, if they do not receive fair compensation for their research or teaching, the tuition reduction may be deemed by the IRS to be disguised compensation.

To meet the qualified tuition reduction tests, the reduction must be provided to an employee or graduate student of a college or university that normally maintains a regular faculty and curriculum and normally has a regularly enrolled body of students in attendance at the place where its educational activities are regularly carried on. Tuition remission to employees is limited to courses below the graduate level. The tuition reduction benefit must be available to employees on a nondiscriminatory basis in order to qualify for the exclusion from gross income of the employee. In the event that the tuition reduction program discriminates in favor of highly compensated employees or officers, such persons cannot exclude such benefits from their gross income.

Faculty Housing

Another benefit for employees of educational institutions is the provision of faculty housing to the employee by the institution. Gross income of an employee does not include the value of qualified campus lodging furnished to that employee by the institution so long as the employee pays rent equal to at least the lesser of 5 percent of the appraised fair market value of the lodging or comparable market rate rents.[67] Qualified campus lodging is lodging that is located on or in the proximity of the institution's campus and that is furnished to an employee, spouse, or any dependent by or on behalf of the institution for use as a residence.

The appraisal requirement does not need to be met annually; however, the appraisal must be reviewed annually. If the rental period involves one year or less, the value of the lodging may be determined at any time during the year in which the rental period begins. If living in campus housing is a condition of employment (e.g., the president of the college is required to live on campus), the value of the housing is not taxable even where no rent payment is received.

Qualified Transportation

Institutions may subsidize employees' parking or transit passes within certain limits on a pretax basis. This is true even if the employee has the option to receive the transportation benefit or additional pay.[68]

Cafeteria Plans

Institutions may adopt cafeteria plans that allow employees to fund certain health benefits and dependent care subject to certain limitations.[69] Payments to these plans are made on a pretax basis. However, payments to these plans are reportable on Form W-2.

Other Benefits

Other noncash benefits such as club memberships, discounted or free tickets, or use of athletic facilities may result in income that is taxable to the employee. Whether the benefit will be deemed compensation needs to be reviewed on a case-by-case basis in light of all of the relevant facts.

REPORTING AND WITHHOLDING REQUIREMENTS

Most independent colleges and universities are required to file IRS Form 990, Return of Organization Exempt From Tax, each year. Public colleges and universities are not required to file Form 990.[70] In addition, every higher education organization that earns more than $1,000 in gross unrelated business income in a year is required to file Form 990-T, Exempt Organization's Business Income Tax Return. State filing requirements may also exist.

Form 990 requires detailed information on a vast variety of activities and functions, ranging from income-producing programmatic activities to the compensation of officers, directors, and trustees (including disclosure of contingent and deferred compensation). Form 990 requires that the revenue of a reporting organization be broken down into the following three categories:

- related or exempt function income;

- unrelated business income; and

- income that is not exempt from tax but that is specifically excluded from treatment as unrelated business income (e.g., dividends, interest, rent, and income from activities performed by volunteers or for the convenience of students or that is derived from the use of donated merchandise).

The degree of detail required to comply with this requirement makes it necessary for institutions to conduct an in-depth review of all revenue accounts. In order to complete Form 990, an institution must segregate all accounts into the three classifications listed above. In addition, an explanation is required to describe how a particular item fits a particular category. An exclusion code (provided by the IRS) is required for each category of excluded income. Unrelated income reported on the Form 990 must agree with that reported on Form 990-T.

Form 990 Disclosure

Final disclosure regulations were issued in April 8, 1999, and became effective on June 8, 1999.[71] Tax-exempt organizations must now follow specific procedures in making various information available to the public. Information that must be available for public inspection includes the three most recently filed Form 990s and the application for recognition of tax-exemption including:

- the prescribed application (IRS Forms 1023 or 1024) and all attachments;

- any statements or other supporting documents submitted by the organization in support of the application; and

- any letter or other document issued by the IRS concerning the application, such as the determination letter or a list of questions from the IRS about the application.

However, if the application was filed before July 15, 1987, and the organization did not have a copy of the application on July 15, 1987, it need not provide the application to the public.

In Person Requests

If a request is made in person, compliance with such request must occur immediately. If "unusual circumstances" surround the request, the organization may provide the copies the next day. Unusual circumstances may include receipt of a large volume of requests, requests received at the close of the business day, or requests received on a day when the organization's managerial staff is conducting special duties.

Written Requests

A written request can be by mail, electronic mail, facsimile, or private delivery service. If the request is made in writing, the organization has 30 days to respond. The organization is permitted to charge reasonable fees for the copies. "Reasonable" is defined as an amount that is not greater than that charged by the Internal Revenue Service for copies. (Currently, the rate allowed by the IRS is $1.00 for the first page and $0.15 for each additional page.) Actual postage costs incurred are also chargeable as a reasonable fee. The regulations permit an organization to require the payment for copies in advance.

Widely Available

The organization may avoid these requirements by making this information "widely available." The regulations indicate that posting the required information on a Web site would satisfy the disclosure requirements. However, this may not be a suitable alternative for most organizations.

Harassment Campaigns

The regulations provide relief from providing copies as requested if the IRS determines that the organization is the subject of a harassment campaign. A harassment campaign exists when there are extraordinary requests for copies by a single coordinated effort that is designed to disrupt the operations of the organization.

Employment Taxes

Colleges and universities are generally required to withhold federal income taxes and employment taxes on employee wages under the Federal Insurance Contributions Act (FICA) and to remit these funds to the federal government. Public colleges and universities may be required to make payments to the state retirement system in lieu of FICA payments. Nevertheless they are required to pay the Medicare tax on employees hired after March 31, 1986. The IRS has stepped up its examination and collection activity in this area, including the use of payroll audits of colleges and universities, in an effort to stem a rising tide of employment tax deficiencies. In addition, certain state and/or local taxes will likely need to be withheld from the pay of an individual determined to be an employee.

The $100,000 Next-day Deposit Rule

If an institution accumulates $100,000 of tax liability on any day during a payroll period (semiweekly or monthly), the tax must be deposited by the next banking day.[72] This rule applies whether the institution is normally a monthly or semiweekly depositor. Once the institution has accumulated at least $100,000 in a deposit period, it should stop accumulating at the end of that day and begin to accumulate anew on the next day. In addition, if the institution is normally a monthly depositor and accumulates $100,000 of tax liability on any day during a month, the institution becomes a semiweekly schedule depositor on the next day and remains so for at least the rest of the calendar year and for the following calendar year.

Employee Versus Independent Contractor

A college or university that utilizes the services of both employees and independent contractors must understand and be able to communicate clearly the difference between an employee and an independent contractor. This can be a difficult determination for institutions because of widespread confusion in defining an employee and an independent contractor. However, although difficult, the distinction is important. The IRS traditionally has been interested in reviewing whether individuals should be classified as independent contractors or employees. They may levy taxes and penalties where individuals who should be classified as employees are paid as independent contractors.

Determining whether an individual is an employee or an independent contractor is based on the degree of control that the employer exercises over an individual's performance. Adjunct faculty, for example, may be more properly classified as employees than as independent contractors. Several factors indicate that a college or university has the right to control and direct individuals in regard to their performance of teaching services, thereby making them employees, including:

- the institution provides equipment and materials;
- the institution provides training;
- the individual and institution have a continuing relationship;
- institutional credit is given for the courses taught by the individual;

- the institution has the ability to select textbooks;
- the institution establishes the hours of instruction;
- courses are taught at regular intervals;
- substitute teachers must be approved by the institution;
- the institution or the employee can terminate the relationship without incurring additional liability for compensation or to perform services;
- the services of the faculty are an integral part of the institution's business; and
- adjunct faculty teach the same courses, with the same books and under the same guidelines, as regular faculty.

The employer need not actually exercise control over the individual, but merely have the right to do so.

Section 530 of the 1978 Revenue Act provides that although an individual may be a common-law employee, in certain circumstances the individual is not treated as an employee for federal tax purposes. Under Section 530, an institution may treat a worker as an independent contractor rather than as an employee subject to payroll tax withholding if the institution has a reasonable basis for doing so. A reasonable basis exists if the institution relies on:

- judicial precedent, a published IRS ruling, or technical advice or a private letter ruling addressed to the institution;
- a past IRS audit that resulted in no assessment as to the institution's employment tax treatment of individuals with positions substantially similar to the position of the individual whose employee status is at issue; or
- a long-standing recognized practice of a significant segment of the industry in which the individual is engaged.

However, the above exceptions to employee status do not apply to a worker if the institution has treated another worker holding a substantially similar position as an employee for tax purposes.

The easiest way for a college or university to check on the proper classification of its workers is to examine both its accounts payable and its payroll. The institution should investigate individuals paid through accounts payable to determine whether they are properly classified as independent contractors. Further, the institution should review the classification of any individual who receives payment through both accounts payable and payroll. If it is not listing its workers accurately, both the institution and its worker will, most likely, file the improper tax forms, leading to potential imposition of IRS penalties.

If the institution properly classifies its workers and the person performing services is deemed to be an employee, the institution must withhold a certain portion of income for federal income taxes and FICA taxes. In addition, certain state and/or local taxes will likely need to be withheld from the pay of an individual determined to be an employee. There are no withholding requirements for independent contractors, however they are subject to the self-employment tax.

Different reporting and withholding rules apply to nonresident alien independent contractors. These rules are discussed later in the chapter.

Student Employees

Where payments constitute wages, students performing services for a college or university are generally subject to federal income tax withholding. Some students may be in a position to eliminate this tax by certifying on an annual Form W-4 that they did not incur a federal income tax liability in the prior year and that they do not anticipate such a liability in the current year. Students who are enrolled in a college or university and are regularly attending classes are not subject to FICA withholding for amounts received for services provided to the institution during the school year.[73]

The IRS issued additional guidance for institutions in Revenue Procedure 98-16.[74] In this document, the IRS set forth a facts-and-circumstances test for determining whether an employee has the status of a student. Prior guidance indicated that to qualify for the Student FICA exemption an individual needed to be enrolled for 12 credit hours and work 20 hours or less per week for the institution. This "12–20" rule proved particularly troublesome.

Under the Revenue Procedure, undergraduate and graduate students qualify for the Student FICA exemption if they are enrolled not less than "half-time" as defined by the institution's own standards and they are not career employees. There is no set limit as to how many hours a student may work. A "career employee" is an employee who is eligible to participate in an institution's retirement plan, is eligible for tuition remission (other than teaching or research assistant) because of the employment relationship, or is classified by the institution as a career employee.

Furthermore, Rev. Proc. 98-16 eliminates the need for FICA to be withheld from students during short school breaks. However, a student does not qualify for the exemption if he or she is not enrolled in classes during school breaks of more than five weeks.

Scholarships and Fellowships

Scholarships and fellowships are excluded from degree candidates' gross income for amounts used for tuition and course-related fees, books, supplies, and equipment; as such, they are not subject to federal income tax or FICA withholding.[75] Colleges and universities that make payments to students are not required to report them to the IRS even if those payments exceed tuition, books, and fees.[76] This exclusion does not apply to any amount received that represents payment for teaching, research, or other services as a condition for receiving the scholarship. Although qualified scholarship payments to nonresident alien students are not taxable, there are special reporting requirements that are discussed below.

The student-recipient is responsible for determining whether the scholarship, in whole or in part, is included in gross income—whether it was used for qualified tuition and related expenses. However, to assist students in understanding their federal tax liabilities, colleges and universities should advise the recipient in writing about the tax treatment of amounts received. For example, the student should be notified that amounts granted are taxable income if the aggregate received exceeds tuition and fees (not including room and board) required for enrollment or attendance at the institution and fees, books, supplies, and equipment required for courses of instruction.

Nonresident Aliens

Generally, all payments for services performed by a nonresident alien within the United States are subject to federal income tax withholding. Wages paid to a nonresident alien are subject to graduated income tax withholding unless the benefit of a tax treaty is available. Nonwage payments are generally subject to withholding at 30 percent. However, the withholding rate is reduced to 14 percent for scholarships and fellowships received by nonresident aliens temporarily in the United States under "F" visas (foreign students) or "J" visas (students, scholars, trainees, teachers, or research assistants).

Payments to nonresident aliens may also qualify for an exemption from or reduced withholding under a treaty between the United States and the nonresident alien's country of residence. Nonresident alien individuals performing services in the United States can claim tax treaty benefits by completing IRS Form 8233, Exemption From Withholding on Compensation for Independent (and Certain Dependent) Personal Services of a Nonresident Alien Individual, and providing it to the college or university prior to receiving payment. Nonresident alien individuals with scholarship or fellowship income can claim tax treaty benefits by completing an IRS Form W-8BEN, Certificate of Foreign Status of Beneficial Owner for United States Tax Withholding, and providing it to the college or university prior to receiving proceeds from the scholarship or fellowship. Payments made to nonresident aliens must be reported and filed with the IRS annually on IRS Form 1042-S, Foreign Person's U.S. Source Income Subject to Withholding.

Many institutions pay the withholding taxes related to the taxable portion of a scholarship on behalf of their nonresident alien students and accordingly gross up the amount of the award. This may create a problem with the National Collegiate Athletic Association for student athletes who are not allowed to receive awards in excess of tuition, books, fees, and room and board.

Foreign Guest Lecturers—Honoraria to B Visa Holders

Guest speakers and lecturers who enter the United States under a B visa can now be paid honoraria. In the past these visitors could not be compensated for services; however, B-1 visaholders could be reimbursed for expenses. Honoraria may be paid for "usual academic activity" that meets the following requirements:

- the activity may last for no more than nine days at any one institution;
- the services must be conducted for the benefit of the paying institution; and
- the visitor cannot have accepted honoraria payments from more than five institutions in the previous six months.

Under this new provision honoraria can be paid by not-for-profit institutions of higher education and affiliated not-for-profit organizations, and not-for-profit governmental research organizations.

Foreign Guest Lecturers—Expense Reimbursements

The IRS has clarified its position on the tax treatment of expense reimbursements that universities pay to nonresident alien visitors involved in lectures or other educational activities. Expense reimbursements in this case are no longer subject to withholding or reporting if they are made under the accountable plan rules of Sections 62 and 274.

Miscellaneous Requirements

Miscellaneous Income

Colleges and universities are required to file IRS Form 1096, Annual Summary and Transmittal of U.S. Information Returns, with the IRS by the last day of February each year. Form 1096 reports the total number of IRS Forms 1099 issued by the institution. Two examples of Form 1099 are Form 1099-DIV for dividend distributions and Form 1099-MISC for miscellaneous items, such as distributions of $600 or more during the calendar year in payment of rents and payments for services to a nonemployee, prizes, and awards. Form 1099-MISC is also used to report gross royalty payments of $10 or more. A Form 1099-MISC must be filed for every noncorporate provider that received $600 or more during the tax year. Thus, colleges and universities are required to file these forms for legal and accounting partnerships that provide services to the institution.

Magnetic Media

Magnetic media reporting may be required to file information returns such as Forms W-2, 1099, and 1042S with the IRS. Acceptable forms of magnetic media are magnetic tapes; tape cartridges; 3½, 5¼, or 8-inch diskettes; and electronic submission. Financial or business officers may obtain a copy of IRS Publication 1220 from their local IRS office; this publication contains specific rules and procedures governing magnetic filing. Magnetic media filing is required if an institution is required to file 250 or more information returns. The 250-or-more requirement applies separately to each type of return.

An institution must request approval from the IRS for magnetic media filing by submitting IRS Form 4419, Application for Filing Information Returns Magnetically/Electronically. This application is applicable for Forms 1098, 1099 Series, 5498, W-2G, 1042S, 8027, 8596, and W-4. For Form W-2, the applicant must contact the Social Security Administration. Form 4419 must be filed at least 30 days before the due date of a return. The IRS will reply with additional instructions within 30 days and will send a package including labels and transmittals.

An institution may request a waiver from the magnetic media filing requirements by submitting IRS Form 8508, Request for Waiver from Filing Information Returns on Magnetic Media. A waiver request must be filed 45 days before the due date of a return. Failure to file information returns through magnetic media without an approved waiver may result in a penalty of $50 per information return.

Expense Reimbursement

In general, an organization must adhere to a policy of adequate record retention. Contemporaneous documentation is critical to the ability to exclude reimbursements from income. For example, a detailed travel record is required when an automobile is provided to an employee. The record must detail business and personal mileage. This record should be submitted by the employee at least annually and retained by the institution for tax purposes. It is not enough for the employee to keep the record in his or her own files. Recently the IRS has raised this issue on examination of a university. The outcome of the examination was disappointing to those employees who had not submitted proper mileage documentation. If the employee did not submit a detailed mileage record, all of the mileage was considered personal and the additional revenue was included in the employee's W-2. However, in many cases the IRS has allowed the institution to pay the additional tax on behalf of its employees.

Hope Scholarship Credit and Lifetime Learning Credit

The education credits introduced in the Taxpayer Relief Act of 1997 impose reporting requirements on higher education institutions. Final regulations have not yet been issued with regard to the reporting requirements, and penalties for lack of compliance will not be imposed until regulations are issued.[77]

Currently institutions are required to file IRS Form 1098-T, Tuition Payments Statement, for each student for each calendar year. Form 1098-T must be sent to the Internal Revenue Service by March 1 of the following year. In addition, the institution must provide a statement to each student by February 1 that contains the same information provided to the Internal Revenue Service. The statement may be a copy of Form 1098-T or an acceptable substitute.[78] The Temporary Regulations filing requirements are in effect at least through 2000.

When the IRS does issue final regulation filing requirements, it is likely that additional information will be required for reporting purposes, including:

- the name, address, and taxpayer identification number (TIN) of the individual (if any) identified by the student as the person who will claim the student as a dependent; and

- the aggregate amount of payments of qualified tuition and related expenses received by the educational institution and the aggregate amount of reimbursements or refunds paid during the calendar year with respect to the student.

A proactive approach should be taken in determining how the information for future years will be gathered since this data may not be readily available.

Student Loan Interest Deduction

Generally, the Taxpayer Relief Act of 1997 allows taxpayers who pay interest on qualified education loans to claim a federal income tax deduction for the interest payments. A "qualified education loan" is a loan used to pay the costs of attending an eligible educational institution. An "eligible educational institution" is defined in Section 481 of the Higher Education Act of 1965 (20 U.S.C. 1088). Generally the definition includes accredited public, nonprofit, and proprietary postsecondary institutions.

The act requires the filing of information returns[79] by those organizations receiving payments of interest of $600 or more that may be deductible by the taxpayer as interest on a qualified education loan.[80] The information return must be provided to the payor by February 1 and filed with the IRS by March 1. The information return must include the following information:

- the name, address, and TIN of the payee;
- the name, address, and TIN of the payor; and
- the aggregate amount of interest received during the year.

IRS AUDITS

In 1993, the IRS developed a new college and university examination program in response to the increasing number of audits performed on these institutions. To more effectively handle such audits, which can be complex in nature and diverse in subject, IRS adapted its college and university examination program to the Coordinated Examination Program (CEP) it also uses in audits of large corporations. A CEP audit consists of a team of tax examiners and IRS specialists working together.

The IRS takes several factors into consideration when determining which colleges and universities should be audited. Institutions with assets or income in excess of $50 million and with related taxable or tax-exempt entities are likely to be audited.[81] Also, institutions with diverse activities, such as hotels, travel tours, and publishing, could be targeted for IRS audit.[82]

In lieu of CEP audits, which cover all areas of a college or university's tax compliance and can be very expensive for all parties involved, the IRS more frequently performs audits that focus on one or two areas of tax compliance. These focused audits commonly involve employment taxes, contributions to the institution, UBIT, and pension plan issues.[83]

TAX-EXEMPT BONDS

Colleges and universities often obtain tax-exempt bonds at favorable interest rates to finance the building and renovation of campus facilities and the acquisition of certain equipment. An institution should monitor "private use" of the "private payments" related to debt-financed facilities as it seeks to assure that the debt retains its tax-exempt status.

Generally, "private use" is use in an unrelated trade or business or in the trade or business of a person who is not tax-exempt. "Private payments" are payments received to support interest payments on the bond from private use. If the private use of bond-financed facilities exceeds 5 percent (10 percent in the case of public institutions), and the private payments exceed 5 percent (10 percent in the case of public institutions), the bonds will not qualify for tax-exempt status. Up to 2 percent of bond proceeds may be used to pay bond issuance costs. If bond proceeds are used for this purpose, the 5 percent private use and private payments are reduced by the percentage of bond proceeds so used. There is a further requirement that any arbitrage (excess interest earned over bond yield) earned on unspent bond proceeds be rebated to the federal government 60 days after the end of each five-year period after the bonds are issued. A final payment, if required, is due 60 days after the bond is retired. There are certain spend-down exceptions to this requirement depending on the length of time it takes to expend bond proceeds.

NOTES

1. Higher education institutions are exempt from federal income tax under the Internal Revenue Code of 1986, as amended, Section 501(a), as charitable organizations described in Section 501(c)(3) or as political subdivisions or instrumentalities described in Section 115. This latter exception is available only for public institutions.

2. I.R.C. § 501(c)(3) and Treas. Reg. § 1.501(c)(3)-1(d)(1)(i).

3. Treas. Regs. § 1.501(c)(3)-1(b)(1)(i)(a) and § 1.501(c)(3)-1(b)(1)(i)(b).

4. Treas. Reg. § 1.501(c)(3)-1(c)(1) and *Better Business Bureau* v. *United States*, 326 U.S. 279 (1945).

5. Trea. Regs. § 1.501(c)(3)-1(d)(2) and § 1.501(c)(3)-1(d)(3)(ii) Example (1).

6. Treas. Reg. § 1.501(c)(3)-1(d)(3)(i)(b).

7. Ibid.

8. Treas. Reg. § 1.501(c)(3)-1(d)(2).

9. I.R.C. §170.

10. I.R.C. § 501(c)(3).

11. Treas. Reg. § 1.501(c)(3)-1(d)(1)(ii).

12. Gen. Couns. Mem. 38,459 (July 31, 1980).

13. Ibid., citing *Kemper Military School* v. *Crutchley*, 273 F. 125 (W.D. Mo. 1921).

14. *Ginsburg* v. *Commissioner*, 46 T.C. 47 (1966); Rev. Rul. 76-206, 1976-1 C.B. 154.

15. IRS Exempt Organizations Handbook (IRM 7751), § 381.1(1).

16. Ibid. at § 381.1(3).

17. The possibility of private inurement also arises if an institution is involved in partnerships or other joint ventures with individuals and other nonexempt entities. Such activities may be impermissible inurement if the nonexempt participant in a joint arrangement with a tax-exempt entity receives an unreasonable and more than incidental benefit at the expense of the college or university.

18. See, e.g., Report to Intermediate Sanctions for Certain Tax-Exempt Organizations, 141 Cong. Rec. H12841. (Intermediate Sanctions Section)

19. I.R.C. § 4958(c).

20. I.R.C. § 4958(f)(1). The effective date of this provision is for a five-year period beginning after September 13, 1995.

21. I.R.C. § 4958(a).

22. I.R.C. § 4958(b).

23. Prop. Treas. Reg. § 53.4958-6(a).

24. *Branch Ministries, Inc., et al.* v. *Margaret Richardson*, 970 F. Supp. 11 (D.D.C. 1997). This does not apply to organizations exempt under I.R.C. § 115.

25. Rev. Rul. 72-512, 1972-2 C.B. 246 and Rev. Rul. 72-513, 1972-2 C.B. 246.

26. I.R.C. § 4955(a)(1).

27. Treas. Reg. § 53.4955-(1)(e).

28. I.R.C. § 4955(a)(2).

29. I.R.C. § 170 and the Treas. Regs. promulgated thereunder provide the statutory and regulatory basis for the acceptance and treatment of charitable contributions.

30. I.R.C. § 6115(b).

31. I.R.C. § 6714(a).

32. Treas. Reg. § 1.170A-13(c)(2).

33. Rev. Proc. 90-12, 1990-1 C.B. 471.

34. I.R.C. § 170(b)(1)(A).

35. I.R.C. § 170(b)(1)(C).

36. I.R.C. § 511-515 and the regulations promulgated thereunder cover the imposition of tax on, definition of exceptions from, and treatment of unrelated business income.

37. I.R.C. § 513(a).

38. I.R.C. § 513(a)(2).

39. I.R.C. § 512 (b)(9).

40. I.R.C. § 512(b)(8).

41. 732 F.2d 1058 (2d Cir. 1984).

42. I.R.C. §514.

43. I.R.C. § 514(c)(9).

44. Rev. Rul. 98-15, 1998-12 I.R.B. 6.

45. Ibid.

46. *NCAA* v. *Commissioner*, 914 F.2d 1417 (10th Cir. 1990).

47. IRS Action On Decision 1991-015, July 15, 1991.

48. I.R.C. §513(i).

49. Treas. Reg. § 1.512(b)-(1)(c)(2)(ii)(b).

50. *Sierra Club, Inc.* v. *Commissioner*, 86 F.3d 1526 (9th Cir. 1996).

51. *Mississippi State University Alumni, Inc.* v. *Commissioner*, T.C.M. 1997-397 (August 28, 1997).

52. *Common Cause* v. *Commissioner*, 112 T.C. 332 (June 22, 1999); *Planned Parenthood Federation of America, Inc.* v. *Commissioner*, T.C.M. 1999-206 (June 22, 1999).

53. *Sierra Club, Inc.*, 86 F.3d 1526 (9th Cir. 1996).

54. I.R.C. §512(b)(13)(D).

55. I.R.C. § 512(b)(13).

56. T.D. 8874 (February 4, 2000), effective February 7, 2000.

57. I.R.C. § 512(b)(2).

58. I.R.C. § 403(b)(1).

59. I.R.C. § 403(b)(2).

60. I.R.C. § 403(c).

61. I.R.C. § 403(b).

62. I.R.C. § 401(k)(4)(B).

63. I.R.C. § 457(b)(2).

64. I.R.C. § 457(c)(1).

65. I.R.C. § 457(f).

66. I.R.C. § 117(d).

67. I.R.C. § 119(d).

68. I.R.C. § 132(f)

69. I.R.C. § 125.

70. Treas. Reg. § 1.6033-2(g)(1)(v).

71. Treas. Reg. §301.6104(a)—(c).

72. IRS Publication 15, Circular E, Employer's Tax Guide, page 18 (January 1999).

73. I.R.C. § 3121(b)(10).

74. Rev. Proc. 98-16, 1998-5 I.R.B. 19.

75. I.R.C. § 117.

76. IRS Notice 87-31, 1987-1 C.B. 475.

77. IRS Notice 97-73, Discussion G, 1997-2 C.B. 355.

78. IRS Notice 97-73, 1997-2 C.B. 355.

79. IRS Form 1098-E, Student Loan Interest Statement.

80. IRS Notice 98-54, 1998-46 I.R.B. 25, IRS Notice 98-7, 1998-3 I.R.B. 54.

81. NACUBO Guide to IRS Audits, pp. 7–8.

82. IRM §342.14.

83. NACUBO Guide to IRS Audits, p. 9.

REFERENCES AND RESOURCES

Publications

Galloway, Joseph M. *The Unrelated Business Income Tax*. New York: John Wiley & Sons, 1982.

Harding, Bertrand M., Jr., *The Tax Law of Colleges and Universities,* John Wiley & Sons, Inc., 1997.

Hill, Frances, and Kirschten, Barbara. *Federal and State Taxation of Exempt Organizations*. Boston, Massachusetts: Warren, Gorham, and Lamont, 1998.

Hopkins, Bruce R. *The Law of Tax-Exempt Organizations*. New York, New York: John Wiley & Sons, Inc., 1998.

National Association of College and University Business Officers, *A Guide to Federal Tax Issues for Colleges and Universities,* Washington, D.C.: NACUBO and Atlantic Information Services, Inc., 2000.

National Association of College and University Business Officers. *Guidelines for Filing 1990 IRS Forms 990 and 990-T*. Washington, D.C.: NACUBO, 1991.

Periodicals

The Exempt Organization Tax Review

Tax Analysts

Chapter 12

Human Resources and Benefits Administration

by

Roosevelt Thomas Jr.
University of Miami

with contributions by

Wilhelmena Black, University of Miami

Beth Malray, University of Miami

William J. Walsh, University of Miami

John Zanyk, University of Miami

Sponsors

EDUCATIONAL MANAGMENT NETWORK/A DIVISION OF WITT/KIEFFER

Contact: Paula Carabelli
2015 Spring Road, Suite 510
Oak Brook, IL 60523
949-851-5070
www.emnwittkieffer.com

Educational Management Network/A Division of Witt/Kieffer, is the nation's leading executive search firm conducting executive search assignments for colleges, universities, community service, cultural, philanthropic and other not-for-profit organizations.

PEOPLESOFT, INC.

Contact: Karen Willett
4460 Hacienda Drive
Pleasanton, CA 94588
925-694-5453
www.peoplesoft.com

PeopleSoft delivers E-business solutions for higher education management needs, including student administration, grants management, finance, human resources, E-procurement, advancement, and more. PeopleSoft also provides comprehensive customer service, consulting, education, and technical support services.

TIAA-CREF
Contact: Participant Inquiries
730 Third Avenue
New York, NY 10017-3206
800-842-2776
www.tiaa-cref.org

TIAA-CREF, with $240 billion in assets, offers pension/insurance and mutual fund products to 2 million employees at 8,800 colleges, universities, and related nonprofit education and research institutions nationwide.

Contents

One of the most critical issues facing organizations in the new millennium is the strategic deployment of human resources into human capital. Strategic plans are by definition long term and contain bold visions for the future. Such plans are incomplete if they do not anticipate the important need for human capital management. While colleges and universities have escaped much of the workforce turbulence in the business world, such as downsizing, mergers, and acquisitions caused primarily by globalization, they are not immune from the challenges of attracting, managing, and retaining skilled employees.

Human resource management in colleges and universities has extended its sphere of influence beyond the traditional yet still important functions of recruitment, recordkeeping, labor relations, equal employment opportunity (EEO) and affirmative action, employee relations, and compensation and benefits. New functions include training and development, employee assistance programs (EAP), workforce diversity, work/life programs, management development (succession planning), strategic planning, employee education on core competencies of the organization and how individual employees influence outcomes, total quality management or continuous improvement, customer service, and internal consulting, among others. All of these functions contribute directly to the bottom line. According to Mark Huselid,[1] "an investment in sophisticated human resource practices contributes to greater financial performance and productivity" and reduces turnover.

Human resource department leaders must be seen as among senior management in making vital business decisions—including those involved in acquiring, deploying, and utilizing the organization's most vital resources—to best meet the needs of the business.[2]

This chapter provides a comprehensive overview of the human resources function in American colleges and universities. Affirmative action is presented as part of the human resources umbrella although, in many institutions, this area reports directly to the president or chancellor or to an executive other than the chief business and/or financial officer. Although the scope of human resource management is quite broad, a brief summary of the various functions will be presented in this chapter.

EMPLOYMENT

Recruitment and Selection

The recruitment and selection processes are two of the most regulated and scrutinized functions in human resource management. Universities with a large volume of government funded research are particularly vulnerable to audits and investigations from the Office of Federal Contract Compliance Programs (OFCCP) in the U.S. Department of Labor and from the Office for Civil Rights (OCR) in the Department of Education. Fairness and the absence of discrimination in the recruitment and hiring process are of paramount concern. Failure to conduct proper reference checks prior to hiring has led to the introduction of a new concept of "negligent hiring."

The recruitment process begins with a well-developed job description that accurately describes the duties and responsibilities of a position. The job description is normally prepared by a unit supervisor and is approved by the human resource office. The recruitment process varies depending on whether the position is classified as exempt (faculty, research, executive, administrative, or professional) or nonexempt as described in the Fair Labor Standards Act (see section on Federal Laws Affecting Human Resource Management). Typically, nonexempt jobs can be filled in a few days from the local community, while exempt level positions require more extensive recruitment efforts.

The standard recruiting process for nonexempt positions requires a supervisor to complete a detailed requisition form that serves as authorization for human resources to proceed with the posting process. Notice of vacant positions may be placed in various places including bulletin boards throughout the campus, on the Internet, and in local newspapers. The process for exempt positions is longer and varies from the use of an outside executive search firm (headhunter) to advertising on the Internet and in trade journals and newspapers along with posting on campus bulletin boards. Colleges and universities are encouraged to announce vacancies through various minority, community, and governmental publications. Posted positions generally contain an application deadline.

Applicants for nonexempt positions typically apply by visiting the human resources office and completing an application form or using an automated process. Some institutions allow for applications to be completed via the Internet. Applicants may be interviewed, tested, and/or screened by human resources staff before being referred to the hiring department for further interviews. Some institutions use automated processes for screening applicants, which eliminates the initial interviewing and/or screening process, and applicants are sent directly to the hiring department for interviews.

Applicants for exempt-level positions typically apply by sending a resume to the address provided in the announcement or advertisement, unless contacted first by an executive search firm. In some institutions, the human resources office coordinates the interviewing process for certain exempt level positions, but in most universities the process is more decentralized, with the decision for hiring faculty resting in the office of the chief academic officer. Depending on the nature of the position, the selection process may be handled solely by the hiring authority or by a group or committee.

All units involved (the hiring department, human resources, and the office of academic affairs) must adhere to applicable federal, state, local, and college or university requirements when interviewing applicants and extending job offers. The selection of applicants for interviewing and the interviewing process must be free of discrimination based on race, color, religion, national origin, sex, age, disability and in some municipalities, sexual orientation. The procedure outlined in this section describes the process for hiring an outside applicant. The concepts of fairness and nondiscrimination are also important in the recruitment and selection process for internal applicants considered for promotion.

The candidate of choice must undergo a reference check, an extremely important element because of an increase in litigation due to charges of "negligent hiring."[3] In some instances the candidate is also subject to background checks, TB/drug tests, degree and certification verification, physical examination, and so forth. By law, newly hired employees must complete the Employment Eligibility Verification (INS Form I-9) prior to beginning work. The completed form must be in the appropriate university office within three business days of the hire date or the employee becomes ineligible for employment.

Training and Development

Employee training and development efforts, including orientation, continue to exert critical influence on organizations' bottom lines. Success continues to hinge on employees' ability to perform appropriately and at levels that protect the institution's interests. Given the current "full employment" status in the country, most organizations face a shallow pool from which to recruit new hires. At the same time, they must enhance skills and abilities among current employees. Colleges and universities are increasingly encouraging employees to learn and continue growing throughout their careers. Ideally employees are supported through training and development opportunities that enhance individual performance and capability, even beyond their current position.

What Is Training and Development?

In *Behavior in Organizations*, Jerald Greenberg and Robert A. Baron state, "Training is the process through which people systematically acquire and improve the skills and knowledge needed to improve job performances. Just as students learn basic educational skills in the classroom, employees must learn job skills. Training is used not only to prepare new employees to meet the challenges of the jobs they will face, but also to upgrade and refine the skills of existing employees. In fact, according to the American Society for Training and Development, American companies spend over $44 billion on training annually".[4]

Richard C. McCullough, writing for *Training and Development Handbook, third edition*, describes professional development as "the process by which individuals increase their understanding and knowledge and/or improve their skills and abilities, to perform better in their current positions or to prepare themselves for a position to which they can realistically aspire in the near future.".[5]

Organizations continue to face the challenge to make training and development relevant, timely, and cost effective. To meet these criteria, successful training and development activities evolve through a series of steps, including:

- assess training and development needs;
- identify outcomes expected to result from the training or development activity;
- develop goals for the training or development activity;
- identify learning objectives for each goal;
- write a plan for the total program;
- write a lesson plan for each part of the program; and
- write an evaluation plan.

Orientation Comes First

In seeking to turn their new hires into the best trained, most productive employees, most colleges and universities start by introducing those employees to the institution through an orientation process. Orientation helps new employees answer the multitude of questions they face on coming into a new position. New employees must learn the norms of the new workplace at the same time they are learning how they are expected to perform their jobs. The quality of the orientation process can positively affect the quality of the new employee's performance and job satisfaction.

Orientation programs vary according to the goals of the organization. They also vary in length: some are as brief as a few hours; others expand over several days; still others run over weeks or even months of periodic sessions. However, they all should cover the following subjects:

- the organizational culture;
- key policies and procedures;
- job-specific standard operating procedures;
- compensation and benefits;
- safety and accident prevention; and
- physical layout of the workplace.

Career Management and Development

Career management and development can be defined as the effort a college or university makes to establish and implement programs that cultivate and promote short- and/or long-term career goals for its employees.

Successful institutions know that their employees are their strength. Today, many higher education employers are helping employees build careers that make them more valuable. Institutions achieve this in a variety of ways, the most common of which is through career management and development.

Higher education institutions are built on the foundation of strategic planning, which usually is conducted by top management for purposes of defining the organization's mission or vision. The institution then uses this mission to develop its long-range plan. Out of the long-range plan, it extracts its human resource needs. From this list of needs, the organization can determine who needs to be trained for which job in the future. When the analysis is completed, an employee training and development system can be developed to prepare employees to produce at a maximum level now and in the future.

To assess employees' development needs and to determine skill and knowledge levels, an analysis of employees' past experiences is necessary. This information is critical in helping employees make sound career development decisions. The needs assessment process can be facilitated through use of job history assessments, life history assessments, and preferences and skills level testing.

Other factors such as knowledge-based assessments and employee perception assessments are important in developing a career management and development program. Perhaps the most critical factor is the performance appraisal system. When properly done, a performance appraisal is a resource that can help identify employees' needs and strengths. It provides information about their current status and projected futures, and identifies areas for improvement.

Immigration

Over the last decade the United States has received the largest number of immigrants in history, close to 10 million. What are the rights of people from other countries to work in the United States? Employers and governmental agencies have faced these issues for many years.[6]

Of the alphabetical array of visa types, the most common acceptable visas affecting higher education are NAFTA, TN, H-1, H-1A, H-1B, H-2, H2B, H-3, F-1, J-1, R, O, P, and K.[7] While employers can sponsor or petition immigrants to work for them, this is an involved and costly process to be done only with legal advice and counsel.

The Immigration Reform and Control Act of 1986 (revised in 1990) makes visa controls less burdensome while adding another government-ordered form and recordkeeping requirement. IRCA makes it illegal for an employer to discriminate in recruiting, hiring, or terminating employment based on an individual's national origin or citizenship. IRCA also requires employers to examine identification documents (the original—not photocopies) for new employees and for current employees with expired documents.

A list of acceptable documents and instructions for the I-9 form is found in the *INS Handbook for Employers*.[8] Promptness in completing I-9 forms is paramount and the completion timetable, as well as reverification issues and retention periods, are identified in the *Handbook*. (Also see section on Federal Laws Affecting Human Resource Management.)

COMPENSATION, WAGES, AND SALARIES

Compensation Plan

A compensation plan includes all forms of pay and rewards received by employees for the performance of their jobs.[9] Direct compensation refers to basic wages and salaries and other forms of added pay including bonuses, commissions, and incentives, among others. The term "wages" generally refers to pay provided to nonexempt employees, as defined under the Fair Labor Standards Act. Some institutions use the term "salaried" when referring to exempt employees. Indirect compensation refers to the benefits provided such as pension, tuition remission, and various forms of insurance overages. Together, direct and indirect compensation provide employees with tangible rewards for their services and a way of recognizing their importance to the institution.

A compensation plan must be designed to meet the unique needs of a particular college or university. Some of the more important goals of a compensation plan include the ability to:

- reward employees' past performance;
- remain competitive in the labor market;
- maintain salary equity among employees;
- motivate employees' future performance;
- maintain the budget;
- attract new employees; and
- reduce unnecessary turnover.

Job Analysis and Evaluation

The development of a compensation plan begins by determining the positions required in order to achieve the institution's mission and objectives and assessing the value of each position to the institution. The first step is to collect information on each position using a data-gathering process called job analysis, a step usually performed by a person referred to as a job analyst. The analyst obtains information about jobs by determining their duties, tasks, or activities.[10]

The most common methods used to collect data are interviews and questionnaires with occasional use of observation and employee diaries. The data may be collected and evaluated by staff in human resources or by using an outside consultant. Once the information is collected and evaluated, a summary of the findings is presented in a written report. The data will then be used to prepare job descriptions and job specifications, which are customarily reviewed by the jobholders and managers. Some institutions use a compensation review committee to assist with proper classification of positions. The position description and specifications can then be used to develop a compensation plan, assess employees' performance and training needs, and reveal employees' pay adjustments. Position descriptions can change over time because of adjustments in duties, introduction of technology, and consolidation of functions, and will need reassessment.

There is no standard format for job descriptions, but they tend to contain a job title, name of department, date, occupational title, EEO/AAP category, job summary, supervision received and given, work performed, job requirements (knowledge, skills, abilities, and education), and work environment.[11] It is imperative that great attention be given to the "essential functions" to be performed in each position to avoid charges of discrimination in recruitment, hiring, performance assessment, disciplinary actions, and dismissals.

The two major problems a college or university may face with position descriptions are that they are poorly written and outdated. These problems weaken the supervisor's or institution's defense against a grievance or lawsuit and also can lower productivity.

Pricing the Pay Structure

The development of a pay structure is a difficult yet critical component in determining the compensation program for a college or university. It is extremely costly to have a direct and indirect compensation program equal to or greater than the market from which institutions recruit. Historically, colleges and universities have offered richer than market benefits to offset lower than market pay. However, unemployment rates in America are now the lowest in nearly 30 years and competition for qualified job applicants is very intense. In order to be more competitive, colleges and universities are forced to reassess the cost structure and mix of salary and benefits.

The wage and salary component of total compensation is addressed using a pay structure containing grades and salary ranges. This structure is used to determine appropriate classification and pay grade for each position. Traditional job evaluation methods used to determine classification are ranking, job classification, factor comparison, point rating, and Hay Guide Chart-Profile used for management positions.[12] More modern and flexible pay structures used in industry but not so prevalent in higher education are incentive-based pay, skill-based pay, and pay-for-knowledge/multiskills pay. These methods are technical and will not be described in this text.

Classification is based on the relative value of each position to the institution. In determining the value, careful consideration must be given to the practice of equal pay for equal work and to internal equity. The value, or worth, of a position should be based solely on position requirements and not the person performing the duties. Before determining pay ranges, the institution should determine the institution's level of desired competitive capability and benchmark the positions with those in the recruitment market.

From benchmark data, the level of external equity and minimum and maximum pay ranges can be established. In developing ranges, consideration should be given to accommodating salary growth for incumbents without the need for promotion and to reduce the tendency to reclassify employees in order to obtain additional pay. A wider pay range and periodic adjustments of the minimum and maximum should reduce the need to "red circle" employees, that is, freeze pay when an employee reaches the top of the range.

A common problem experienced in implementing a pay plan is that of hiring new employees above the normal starting pay range, in some cases above the salary of incumbent employees. In times of labor shortage and low unemployment rates, it may become necessary to hire an applicant at a higher salary. Colleges and universities do not typically have funds to make across-the-board adjustments to incumbents and therefore may have to provide explanations. In unionized settings, collective bargaining agreements generally prohibit hiring new employees above the starting rate for incumbent union members.

Intermediate Sanctions

Prior to passage of the Taxpayer Bill of Rights 2 in 1996, the only sanction that the IRS could impose on nonprofit entities (including colleges and universities) that violated statutory prohibitions regarding tax liabilities was revocation of tax-exempt status. The IRS was somewhat reluctant to enforce revocation because it was considered too severe a punishment except in egregious cases.

On August 4, 1998, the Internal Revenue Service (IRS) issued proposed regulations implementing the provisions of Internal Revenue Code (IRC) section 4958 under the Taxpayer Bill of Rights 2. At issue is the IRS's concern about "excess benefit transactions" involving individuals categorized as "disqualified persons" under the law. A disqualified person is considered to be an individual who receives an economic benefit that exceeds the fair market value of the goods or services that the organization received in return.[13] Those excess transactions could become taxable. The proposed regulations provide additional definitional certainty to the term "disqualified person," meaning those in a position to exercise substantial influence over the affairs of an institution.

The proposed rules are designed to provide guidance to public charities and social welfare organizations regarding their tax liabilities. The proposed intermediate sanctions also make clear to trustees, officers, and others that the privilege of overseeing or managing a charitable organization is accompanied by potentially significant personal tax liabilities as described in the regulations.[14] Charitable organizations are those that are tax-exempt as described in sections 501(c)(3) or (4) of the IRS Code. State-sponsored colleges and universities that are exempt from tax under section 115 of the Code and have not formally applied for recognition under section 501(c)(3) tax-exempt status will not be subject to intermediate sanctions.

Among those unquestionably considered disqualified persons are the governing board along with the president or chancellor, chief executive officer, chief operational officer, and treasurer and/or chief financial officer. For a large university with a medical school and law school, the definition of a disqualified person reaches farther down the organizational chart and could include positions such as medical school dean, department chair or medical director, and dean of the law school.

Individuals deemed not to have substantial influence include employees:

- as defined in the pension rules of section 414(q);

- with salaries below $85,000; and

- who are not substantial contributors to the institution, or a family member or controlled entity of the disqualified person.

All other employees are evaluated under an IRS "fact-and-circumstances test."

The proposed regulations define an "organization manager" as any individual designated in organizational documents as an officer, director, or trustee, as well as any person who regularly exercises general authority to make administrative or policy decisions on behalf of the institution. The definition also covers someone who is not an officer, director, or trustee, but who serves on a committee of the institution's governing body that is invoking the "rebuttable presumption of reasonableness" as described below.

Rebuttable Presumption of Reasonableness on Executive Compensation Packages

Colleges and universities are allowed to establish a presumption that compensation paid to disqualified individuals or transactions affecting them are reasonable or at fair market value. To establish the presumption, the institution must meet the conditions that follow.

- The compensation arrangement or transaction is approved by the institution's governing body or a committee of the governing body;

- the board or committee must be composed entirely of individuals who do not have a conflict of interest with respect to the arrangement or transaction;

- the governing body, or committee thereof, obtains and relies on appropriate comparability data prior to making its determination; and

- the governing body, or committee thereof, adequately documents the basis for its determination concurrently with making that determination.[15]

In instances where the governing body determines that reasonable compensation should be higher than comparative survey data, it must record the basis for its determination. The proposed regulations spell out in detail the format to be used in recording the determination and steps in approving the final action.

Revenue Sharing Arrangements in Employment Contracts

Revenue sharing transactions in contracts are payments to disqualified persons based in whole or in part on the income of the tax-exempt organization.[16] Under the proposed regulations, such transactions may be considered excess benefits in their entirety if at any point the arrangement allows a disqualified individual to receive additional compensation without providing proportional services that contribute to the institution's achieving its tax-exempt purpose. The IRS refuses to bifurcate a two-part transaction where one part of the transaction is compensatory and reasonable and the other is revenue sharing. Revenue sharing agreements will receive careful scrutiny from the IRS.

Performance Evaluation and Salary Increases

The primary purpose of an employee appraisal is to evaluate the performance of the employee by providing prompt constructive feedback on how well that employee has met the employer's expectations.[17] While accepted as both necessary and beneficial by senior level college and university officials, implementation of an effective performance appraisal system is just as difficult to achieve as it is in industry. The process tends to evoke strong feelings and conflicts in the workplace, particularly between supervisors and employees, and typically results in only a half-hearted effort toward achieving its stated purpose. Performance management is not an exact science, and appraisal systems come with numerous models, methodologies, and controversies.

Some common reasons for conducting performance appraisals follow.

- to provide opportunity for open communication regarding job duties and responsibilities and individual strengths and weaknesses;

- to provide performance feedback;

- to identify individual and institution training and development needs;

- to determine possibility for promotion, demotion, or reassignment;

- to meet legal requirements; and

- to determine pay distribution.

The controversy with performance appraisal systems exists primarily because of its linkage to individual pay. At center stage is the age-old debate over intrinsic versus extrinsic motivation. Merit pay is the traditional extrinsic approach to rewarding employees for good performance and is strongly criticized by those advocating a more intrinsic approach. Other forms of pay such as bonuses, individual and team-based incentives, and gainsharing are not widely used in higher education. While substantial research indicates that merit pay and employee attitudes are positively related, it also shows that little or no relationship exists between merit pay and subsequent performance and motivation.[18] Yet, merit pay is the favored approach used in higher education and industry. For more on the debate over pay for performance, see the paragraph on Motivation in the Current Issues section of this chapter.

Performance management systems today require more than the traditional once-a-year assessment where human resource sends out appraisal forms to supervisors, many of whom call a hasty meeting to review it with the employee. Performance appraisal is a subjective process where supervisors attempt to measure individual skills, achievement of goals and objectives, and various personality traits.

To be effective, a performance appraisal process should be developed in which expectations are linked to the institution's business objectives, performance is planned, people are motivated and coached, and individual and team results, along with competencies, are rewarded. Such a process should be owned and managed by line managers and should include a broad range of evaluators.[19] This growing belief is leading many organizations to use processes similar to the well-known 360-degree assessment methodology. The idea is to obtain input from others, including internal and external customers, regarding performance of an employee, unit, or team.

College and university leaders must give a great deal of consideration to the performance management system in use at their institutions. Positive results can lead to greater morale, trust, productivity, caring, and cooperation. Mutual accountability is critical to the success of an institution.

EMPLOYEE BENEFITS

The two basic forms of payment provided to employees for work performed in a college or university are direct and indirect compensation, commonly referred to as pay and benefits. This section addresses numerous features of a benefits administration program found in higher education institutions. Benefits administration is typically a major component of the human resources department.

Employee benefits came into prominence in the 1920s when more companies began offering a wider array of fringe benefits in an attempt to prevent unionization. They soon became items for collective bargaining; today benefits are generally considered rights to which all employees are entitled and have become one of the fastest growing areas of employment law and litigation.[20] Benefits are generally exempted from personal income tax when paid for by the institution. A host of government regulations and agencies oversee the implementation of benefits administration.

The three legally required benefits that all employers must provide are employer contributions to Social Security, unemployment compensation insurance, and workers' compensation insurance. Together the three account for approximately 25 percent of an employee's benefit package. Some states may require that additional benefits, such as short-term disability, be offered.

Under Titles I and IV of the Employee Retirement Income Security Act (ERISA) and under the Internal Revenue Code, colleges and universities are required to file an annual report with the U.S. Department of Labor regarding their pension and other welfare benefit plans. These annual reporting requirements can be satisfied by filing IRS Form 5500, revised in 1998. It contains information concerning the operation, funding, assets, and investments of pension and welfare plans. The form serves as an important disclosure document for plan participants and beneficiaries and as a source of information and data for use by various federal agencies, Congress, and the private sector in assessing employee benefit, tax, and economic trends and policies. This once onerous reporting requirement was simplified in 1998 by the consolidation of several forms in the 5500 series into one. In 2000, it is expected that employers will be able to submit Form 5500 via computer scanable forms and electronic filing technologies.

Colleges and universities should consider using benefits consultants to help perform cost-benefits analysis and to structure a flexible benefits plan. There are additional costs incurred in communicating the technicalities of a flexible benefits program and counseling employees.

Flexible Benefits Programs

Internal Revenue Section 125

This program enables employees to make benefits selections and to pay for the benefits they choose on a pretax basis. Common section 125 plans include premium conversion plans for health care benefits, flexible spending accounts for health care and dependent care expenses, and full choice, menu-style cafeteria plans.[21] In a cafeteria plan, employees may choose between cash and qualified non-taxable benefits. The taxable cash option is valuable to employees who have the option of obtaining the coverage through another means, such as a spouse, or who may want to forgo the benefit for more money in their paychecks. In the interest of assuring that employees have a health care policy, an institution may request evidence of coverage before allowing someone to opt out of its health care plan.

Three kinds of flexible benefits plans are available.

1. *Premium-only or premium conversion plans,* through which employees' premium contributions to employer-sponsored health and welfare plans are made on a pretax basis. Eligible benefits include health, dental, group long-term disability, and group life insurance.

2. *Flexible reimbursement or flexible spending accounts* to which employees contribute and are reimbursed on a pretax basis for qualified unreimbursed medical or dependent care expenses. Institutions generally limit the predetermined annual amount of dollars an employee can place in either account. Unused funds cannot be returned to employees after the end of the plan year per the IRC.

3. *Full flex or full cafeteria plans,* from which employees select from a menu of benefit selections and have the option of choosing cash instead. Eligible benefits include those in number one above plus unused vacation time for the plan year only. Institutions typically restrict the use of the cash option to its portion of health and dental premiums and require employees to produce evidence of health care coverage through some other means.

Tuition can be included as a section 125 pretax benefit but only on a cash equivalent basis. Colleges and universities offer tuition remission or tuition waiver programs that are not covered under section 125 but are covered in section 117 of the IRC. Under section 117(d), institutions may offer free undergraduate tuition benefits to their employees and dependents. The graduate tuition benefit is taxable to the employee.

Institutions must adhere to the nondiscriminatory provisions of section 125 benefits, or participants will be taxed on the benefits. Two nondiscrimination tests are used to determine if the plan discriminates in favor of highly compensated individuals[22]:

1. The plan benefits of a group of employees described in IRC section 410 (b)(2)(A)(i), and 2—(a) no employee is required to complete more than three years of employment as a condition for participation; and (b) any employee satisfying the employment requirement and who otherwise is entitled to participate does so no later than the first day of the first plan year following completion of the employment requirement, unless that employee has separated from service in the interim.

2. A cafeteria plan must not discriminate in favor of highly compensated participants regarding the contributions and benefits.

Insured Plans

Medical Care

Traditionally, health plans covered only medical, surgical, and hospital expenses. Today's typical health care plan in higher education institutions also covers prescription drugs, optical, and mental health. Some institutions include dental in their health plan while others carve it out and treat it separately.

Rising costs and employee concerns about access have led to increased scrutiny of health care benefits. The growth in health care costs in recent years is attributed to several factors such as changes in Medicare pricing, technological advances in medicine, overuse of costly equipment and services, increased malpractice insurance rates, rising costs of health care labor, and an aging population in need of health care services for a longer period of time.

The type of health care plans offered to college and university faculty and staff include managed care through a health maintenance organization (HMO), preferred provider organization (PPO), point-of-service (POS), and traditional indemnity plans. Institutions generally outsource the administration of health care plans. In order to contain or control costs, some institutions have opted for self-insurance and greater cost sharing with faculty and staff. Most plans now have deductibles, co-payments, coordination of benefits (with other insurance providers), and subrogation of claims. Efforts by health care providers to minimize costs in order to make a profit have led to accusations of poor coverage and access for plan participants.

Health Maintenance Organizations

HMOs are organizations of physicians and other health care professionals that provide a wide range of services to subscribers and their dependents on a pre-paid basis.[23] A provision in the federal HMO Act of 1973 requiring employers to offer an HMO as an option to employees was repealed in 1995 in order to make them more competitive and receptive to employers.[24]

Employees usually must select a primary-care physician (PCP) from the HMO's pool of doctors and pay a small fixed amount for each visit. Typically, the PCP must approve any trips to specialists and nonemergency visits to HMO network hospitals.

Preferred Provider Organization

PPOs are organizations of physicians and other health care professionals that provide a wide range of services to subscribers and their dependents on a prepaid basis.[25] Institutions contract with a PPO directly, or indirectly through an insurance carrier, to secure medical services from health care providers (physicians, labs, hospitals, etc.) to plan participants on a discounted basis. Employees usually do not need a PCP's authorization to visit an in-network specialist.

Point-of-Service Plans

These plans are administered by insurance companies or HMOs and allow employees to go to doctors and hospitals out of the network, for a price. Employees usually need a referral to see a network specialist. POS plans offer the coordinated care of an HMO with a safety net that allows participants to go to nonmember doctors whenever they want.

Traditional Indemnity Plans

Under an indemnity plan, the insured can see any physician, use most hospitals, and be reimbursed after satisfying a deductible. As health care costs began to escalate in the 1970s and 1980s, HMOs were introduced to help control the speed at which costs were increasing. Thus, indemnity plans became less popular in the American marketplace because they were more expensive than competing products such as HMOs. In an indemnity plan, employees select their own doctors and hospitals, pay on a fee-for-service basis, and do not need a referral to see a specialist.

Dental Insurance and Optical Coverage

Dental care plans are becoming more popular and are often separated from medical plans. The primary purpose is to encourage regular visits to the dentist as a preventative measure. Such plans helps pay for dental cost but often fall short of covering catastrophic expenses. Dental plans are provided through insurance companies, dental maintenance organizations (DMOs), and groups of dental care providers. Optical care is offered as part of a regular medical plan or as a stand-alone benefit. Plans generally include eye exams and discounts on lenses and frames.

Short-term Disability Plans

Pay continuation during a period of absence due to a nonjob related illness or injury is generally covered by accrued sick time. An extended period of absence may cause an employee to deplete accrued sick time and vacation time and to experience the need for short-term disability coverage. Some colleges and universities offer such coverage, on an insured or self-insured basis, to fill the time gap until the employee returns to work or goes on long-term disability. Plan features vary depending on costs, maximum benefit provided, and coordination with the institution's long-term disability plan.

Long-term Disability Plans

Long-term disability plans provide a form of pay to faculty and staff who are no longer able to perform their duties because of medical problems projected to last for a long period of time. Coverage may be provided free of charge to employees or through cost sharing, and the plan may include a waiting period before employees become eligible for participation. Plan features generally include a three- or six-month waiting period, a percent of final salary (usually 60 to 70 percent), a monthly maximum income, and a provision to terminate the benefit on death or at normal retirement. The plan may also include a Social Security offset, which reduces the amount paid by the institution, and a "residual" provision that allows the individual to perform some level of work while receiving a reduced monthly benefit.

Life Insurance

Life insurance is one of the oldest and most popular employee benefits. Colleges and universities generally provide employer-paid group term life insurance to faculty and staff with a death benefit equaling one or two times salary. The plan may include a maximum amount. Such insurance is provided on employment, or after a brief waiting period, without medical certification and is convertible upon termination. The value of the premiums paid for group life insurance in excess of $50,000 is subject to Social Security and federal income taxes. The fact that some employees are highly compensated while others are not is not a matter of consideration with respect to the tax issue.

Supplemental Life Insurance

Colleges and universities commonly provide group voluntary participation life insurance plans. Such plans vary in the amount of death benefit depending on design and are paid by employees through payroll deduction. Some plans are straight term while others have cash accumulation features making them more expensive. Supplemental plans generally have a feature allowing for coverage of spouse and children.

Accidental Death and Dismemberment Coverage

Accidental death and dismemberment insurance (AD&D) is commonly offered in two forms: employer paid and voluntary. Colleges and universities generally provide an established amount of blanket coverage to employees in the event of accidental deaths or loss of limb(s) or the irrecoverable loss of sight. Also commonly provided is an established amount of travel accident insurance for employees traveling on institutional business. Institutions commonly provide an insurance plan for employees to purchase additional AD&D coverage for themselves and family members at inexpensive group rates, payable through payroll deductions.

Retiree Medical Plans

Subsidizing medical coverage for retirees in any form is very costly to those colleges and universities providing such a benefit. In addition to inflationary increases in health care costs, the Financial Accounting Standard Board (FASB) Statement of Financial Accounting Standards of 1982 requires institutions to include in their financial statements the costs accrued during employees' working years. For public institutions, the Government Accounting Standards Board (GASB) should be consulted. Medicare is the medical plan available to retirees on reaching the age of 65. Through special retirement agreements, an institution may allow retirees to continue participation in the regular health plan until they reach Medicare eligibility age.

Statutory Programs

Given the plethora of benefits offered today by colleges and universities, it is important to reiterate that only three government required (statutory) benefits must be provided to employees: Social Security, workers' compensation, and unemployment compensation. Social Security is discussed in the Retirement Program Administration section of this chapter.

Workers' Compensation

Workers' Compensation is defined as federal or state-mandated insurance provided to workers to defray the loss of income and cost of treatment due to work-related injuries or illness.[26] Coverage is provided through a state-operated insurance pool, by private companies, or by employers certified by the state to administer their own program without any type of insurance. Workers' compensation benefits include a percentage of salary or wage paid for a preestablished period of time, up to a certain amount, cost of medical treatment, and a death benefit provided to survivors. The 1990s witnessed skyrocketing increases in workers' compensation costs, prompting many institutions to examine causes and devise ways to reduce the expenditure.

To the employer, an advantage of workers' compensation is that the employee usually cannot sue for negligence and punitive damages for injuries covered under this plan. Thus, potentially disastrous monetary awards are avoided by the employer, but the employee still receives some compensation.[27]

Unemployment Compensation

Unemployment compensation benefits are paid to employees who leave an institution involuntarily due to layoff or termination of employment for reasons other than gross misconduct. Upon being determined eligible, terminated employees generally receive payments for a period of 26 weeks. In some cases, payments may extend beyond the 26-week period for various reasons as determined by the state. The payments are taxable to recipients. The Social Security Act of 1970 stipulates that unemployment compensation programs be administered jointly by federal and state governments. Contributions from institutions vary from state to state based on the number of unemployed people drawing from the fund.

Contributions to unemployment compensation are made by the employer in one of two ways, although there are themes and variations to these models: In one method, the employer remits a monthly premium to the state unemployment compensation administrator. The premium is calculated based on the payroll and on the numbers of employees in different occupational titles that have a known risk of injury. The cost, or premium, is calculated as a number of pennies per $100.00 of salary. This particular method is commonly referred to as "insured" because an agency of state government covers the liability.

In a second method, the employer remits a quarterly premium to the state unemployment compensation administrator. The premium is calculated based on the actual number of claims paid during the quarterly billing period. This particular method is commonly referred to as "self-insured" because the employer pays the total cost of the actual claims which were approved for payments.

Noninsured Plans

Historically, colleges and universities have been rather generous with benefits provided to faculty and staff to offset the disparity of pay between their employees and those in business and industry. Some of the benefits provided as noninsured plan benefits include paid vacation, holidays, sick leave, personal leave, funeral leave, educational or sabbatical leave, jury duty or court testimony, and tuition remission or scholarship plans. Federal nondiscrimination laws enacted in the 1990s, such as the Family and Medical Leave Act (FMLA) and Americans with Disabilities Act (ADA), along with recent trends to provide domestic partner benefits, have created some complications in administering these benefits.

Vacations

The number of vacation days or hours accrued annually vary depending on employee category and length of service. Accrual schedules range from very generous granting of maximum benefit days after the first year of employment to accrual schedules requiring employment for 10 to 15 years before being eligible for maximum vacation benefit. Vacation is generally not given in advance, and institutions may place a cap on the maximum number of days vacation can be carried over from one fiscal year to the next. Eligible accrued vacation days or hours is an earned benefit payable on termination of employment. The FASB now requires colleges and universities to include accrued vacation time in the institution's financial statements.

Holidays

The average number of holidays given to employees nationwide is nine, varying from as few as six by small employers to more than 11 by many large employers.[28] Colleges and universities traditionally provide holidays in excess of the national average, some with as many as 13 or 14 per year. Some of the days may be referred to as "floating holidays" to accommodate employees' personal or religious needs.

Sick Leave

Sick leave allows employees to take time off with or without pay for illness suffered by the employee or certain family members. A typical accrual schedule for colleges and universities is one day per month, but the benefit may be more generous for exempt staff. Administration of sick leave has become more complex due to passage of FMLA (see section on Federal Laws Affecting Human Resource Management). FMLA requires institutions to provide up to 12 weeks of unpaid, job-protected leave to eligible employees for certain family and medical reasons. States and municipalities may extend the length of leave required as well as the benefit to other members of the extended family such as grandparents. Institutions with domestic partner benefits may extend paid sick leave benefits to cover illness of such partners.

Sick leave abuse is a common problem in colleges and universities mirroring that in business and industry. Frequently, employees tend to view the sick time benefit as an entitlement and use the time for reasons other than illness. To address the problem, some institutions allow for some kind of conversion of sick time into pay or additional vacation time.

Funeral Leave

Colleges and universities generally provide employees with up to three days of paid funeral leave on the death of an employee's immediate family member. Institutions may also provide this benefit to employees with domestic partners.

Jury Duty and Court Testimony

Institutions must allow employees to report for jury duty or participate in court testimony when called but do not have to pay them for the time they serve. Some states, such as New York, require partial payment of wages for some period of time. Some institutions allow for participation without loss of pay, and some will offset employees' pay by the amount received for services rendered.

Personal and Other Leaves

Colleges and universities may offer other leave periods, including those for educational, sabbatical, maternity/pregnancy, paternity, personal, administrative, and military purposes. Except for administrative and sabbatical leave, which could be with or without pay, the other leaves are generally without pay unless employees are allowed to use accrued vacation time and floating holidays to remain in paid status. Benefits may or may not be continued depending on institutional policy.

Scholarship Plans and Tuition Remission

Colleges and universities commonly waive tuition payments for faculty and staff who work for the institution. Many also grant partial or full tuition waiver for spouses and dependents to pursue an education at the institution. Some institutions pay partial or full cost of dependent undergraduate tuition at other institutions either through a reciprocal agreement or as an out-of-pocket cost. Section 117(d) of the Internal Revenue Code allows colleges and universities to provide free undergraduate tuition benefits to their employees. Any graduate benefits are taxable to the employee. The tuition benefit is a major recruitment tool for most institutions.

Domestic Partners

Perhaps the most controversial benefits issue in higher education during the 1990s and continuing into the 21st century is the provision of benefits for domestic partners. Domestic partners are defined as two individuals of the same or opposite sex who are unmarried, not related by blood, age 21 or older, and live together in a committed relationship. Commitment to the relationship is demonstrated through evidence of joint financial responsibility for common household expenditures. The most sought after benefit is health care.

By 1999, approximately 100 colleges and universities had extended health care coverage to domestic partners of employees.[29] More than a dozen other institutions extended nonhealth care benefits to domestic partners. Of the approximately 100 institutions with health care benefits for domestic partners, about 40 percent extend coverage to couples of the opposite sex as well as to those of the same sex. Other benefits commonly extended are tuition remission and waivers, dental (if not part of medical plan), library privileges, medical leave, and event discounts. Institutions offering tuition remission or waivers to domestic partners need to include the value of the tuition waiver in the employee's compensation and withholding tax. The tax code does not recognize domestic partners, therefore colleges and universities cannot provide tuition benefits on a tax-free basis.

Many institutions are in the discovery and debate phase regarding this issue.

Empirical data indicate that cost is insignificant. Enrollment ranges from one-tenth of 1 percent to slightly more than 1 percent. Enrollment is highest in institutions that extend the benefit to heterosexual couples. Concerns about additional health care costs have proved to be a nonissue since costs for domestic partners of employees have not exceeded those of traditional dependents according to data compiled by Human Rights Campaign, Towers Perrin, and the University of Miami. Other than costs, there are two other issues that must be addressed when considering benefits for domestic partners. One is the question of inclusion of partners of the opposite sex. Many people view exclusion of opposite sex partners as discriminatory and will subject the institution to legal challenge. Others view inclusion as being fair and equitable. For these reasons among others, many colleges and universities have extended coverage to opposite sex partners.

The other issue is one of perception. There appears to be a belief by faculty that the extension of domestic partner benefits will be perceived positively in the national faculty and administrative marketplace. However, benefits for domestic partners could be perceived as damaging charitable giving to the institution, and could affect the support of governmental entities and others. Anecdotal evidence appears to indicate that providing domestic partnership benefits creates minimal negative impact.

Going forward, there appears to be a growing acceptance to extending benefits to domestic partners of college and university employees. The issue remaining is litigation over the exclusion of opposite sex coverage by institutions limiting the benefit to same sex couples.

New Concerns

More than 60 million people in the United States were born between 1946 and 1964. These individuals are commonly referred to as "Baby Boomers" and more recently, the "sandwich generation," because they are caring for their own children as well as their parents. Meanwhile, the single-parent employee is concerned about survival issues such as job retention, child care, transportation, and security. Many employees are under tremendous stress trying to balance work and family pressures. In recognition of this dilemma, many employers have responded by offering some or all of the following:

- access to or information about child care and elderly care services;
- alternative work arrangements such as flextime, compressed work weeks, job sharing, reduced work weeks, and telecommuting;

- wellness and stress management programs;

- flexible spending accounts to assist with dependent care reimbursement;

- access to employee assistance programs;

- long-term care insurance for employees and their parents and grandparents;

- car pooling arrangements;

- on-site medical facilities; and

- financial planning programs.

Colleges and universities offer many of the benefits provided by business and industry to their employees, not only to meet the needs of employees, but also in order to remain competitive in an era of very low unemployment. Like their cash counterparts, today's benefits can help motivate performance, support behavioral change, reinforce new values and business goals, and reflect and fortify the institution's evolving culture.[30]

RETIREMENT PROGRAM ADMINISTRATION

Retirement planning is becoming an increasingly important activity in higher education. Fortunately, colleges and universities are stable institutions with a tradition of providing generous benefits to faculty and staff, including pension plans of various types. The different plans will be described in the sections to follow. While the "three legged stool" approach to retirement planning will be presented, the leg requiring individual initiative and which holds the key to achieving the desired lifestyle, is personal savings and investments. According to the *Wall Street Journal,* "Retirement is like a long vacation in Vegas. The goal is to enjoy these years to the fullest, but not so fully that you run out of money. It is a dicey endeavor, involving tricky issues of longevity and investment returns."[31]

There is an abundance of literature and guides available to assist individuals in retirement planning. TIAA-CREF is perhaps the best known pension organization to employees in higher education institutions. Several insurance companies such as VALIC and UNUM and numerous mutual fund companies are fairly well known in colleges and universities. A typical retirement planning guide includes the following steps:

- determine your income needs in retirement;

- review your retirement income portfolio;

- make sure you have enough insurance for your needs; and

- consider your estate planning needs.

Traditionally, financial advisors have recommended using an estimate of 70 to 80 percent of final preretirement salary as the basis for determining one's yearly retirement income goal. Some planners are now suggesting 90 to 100 percent in order to maintain the desired lifestyle for an anticipated longer life expectancy. Retirement planning is a more sophisticated, time consuming, and serious matter today than in the past.

Objectives of Retirement Programs

A retirement program is a formally designed plan or methodology used by an employer to save and/or invest money on behalf of individual employees to enable them to continue an income stream when they retire from the workforce.

To achieve postretirement income of approximately 70 percent of preretirement income, an employee generally must have a productive work life of about 35 years and retire at age 65. Post-retirement income is derived from three sources. The first source, and the largest portion, is the employee's retirement plan. Because faculty members tend to be mobile, portability is an important and attractive feature in their plan. Portability simply means that employees takes the retirement plan account with them when they change jobs. Many in higher education have relied on a specific type of defined contribution plan that operates under section 403(b) of the tax code, called a 403(b) plan. Vesting, the right of ownership, is an important component of portability, and most 403(b) plans have immediate vesting.

The second largest portion of retirement income typically comes from Social Security. When factoring in the percentage of retirement income that should be made up by Social Security, a common view is that Social Security will constitute 20 percent of the replacement ratio of final average salary. This is a vast overgeneralization but one that does have an impact on retirement plan design.

The third largest portion of retirement income should come from personal investments and savings. Employees of colleges and universities can save voluntary amounts under section 403(b) of the tax code, in a tax-deferred annuity (if the employer offers this plan) or an IRA on a before-tax basis. Some public sector employees may have the choice of a 457 deferred compensation plan. Recently, Congress added Roth IRAs to the range of longer-term savings vehicles that have special tax benefits; in this case an exemption from tax for earnings under specific conditions.

Early and Phased Retirement

Normal retirement age is traditionally 65 in the United States. Faculty and staff will often retire between 60 and 70 with 65 historically being the age most frequently selected. In the last decade, retirement patterns have spread more broadly across the range. At some institutions early retirement at age 55 is possible, provided the employee has the requisite years of service. However, early retirement raises other considerations with which an employee must be concerned, including medical, dental, vision, life insurance, and similar benefits.

Because of these considerations and the genuine complexity of the body of laws that regulate equity, informed consent, due diligence, and access to information, institutions often find it beneficial to employ a specialist to provide pre- and sometimes postretirement counseling. Often such assistance goes beyond helping to understand and include other benefits such as medical and dental, which will be particularly important to the early retiree. Even where the institution arranges for a defined contribution plan or employs a third party administrator for pension administration, it may be necessary to have institutional staff who are trained to advise employees at the time of retirement because of other benefits.

For a brief period of time between the mid-1970s and late 1980s, phased-retirement appeared poised to emerge as an accepted variant to the otherwise abrupt end to work that normal retirement suggests. While phased retirement is not a scientific term and has as many variations as there are colleges and universities that use it, it always involves a gradual separation from work and integrates the amount of pension income with active work income over some time period until only pension income is received. The idea was greeted initially with enthusiasm in the academic community and was embraced as an option to meet specific needs. According to research by Jay Chronister,[32] an option to continue part-time work can dramatically increase the attractiveness of a retirement incentive plan.

Developing a Retirement Policy

Developing a retirement policy is driven more today by fiscal considerations than it is driven by an objective, specified outcome. In the past, an employee typically commenced his or her career with one institution and retired with that same institution 35 years later. Consequently, it was important for that institution to design a retirement plan built on a workforce demographic that included long service as an essential element.

Today, employees are more likely to have multiple, consecutive employers during their productive work years. Thus, a retirement plan that fails to accommodate employee mobility, and produces a value only for employees who stay for the long haul, will lose its competitive edge in recruiting top talent.

Making the issue still more complex is the fact that some employees continue to pursue lifetime careers at colleges and universities. Two workforce types are co-mingled. One type will remain for a lifetime career. The other type will remain for several years, making his or her work at each institution only part of the career.

In defined benefit plans the employee multiplies total years of employment by a specified percentage such as 1, 1.5, or 2 percent. The product is then the percentage of final pay that can be expected at retirement. The employer must fund the plan during the working years to ensure that the money is there when the employee decides to retire. The employer invests the money and is in a position to actually reduce its own contribution to the plan if investments do well. Of course, the opposite can occur or the assumptions about future earnings might be understated and then the plan would be underfunded.

It is axiomatic that investment returns, generally, over the long haul tend to balance out the ups and downs, which may be experienced on an annual basis. Since some employees in a college or university are there for a career, a defined benefit plan is a good retirement vehicle. With these commitments, an investment manager can plan on having the money for many years. Conversely, in the case of employees following a career path that allows them to stay at each institution for only part of a career, an institution may not be well served with a defined benefit plan. In this latter case the institution must form a plan of action that allows it to attract, capture, and hold the employee for a limited time. Here is where the defined contribution plan comes into play. Under a defined contribution plan, an employer has a known, measurable, and set cost for each individual account. Examples include institutions that contribute 6 to 14 percent of salary toward retirement. That cost remains stable unless the employer chooses to change the contribution rate, so the employer is in a position to plan around this "fixed" cost. To the employer with a defined contribution plan it makes no difference what happens in the business economy. The employer does not have excess accumulated interest to reduce later premium costs, nor does it have any risk of greater cost in the event of a downturn in the economy. The cost is set in a defined contribution plan.

In this scenario of permanent and migratory employees, the college or university must mark its narrow path, ensuring that the needs of each population are met.

Program Design

Beyond the choice of which type of pension plan, a number of factors influence the plan design, including cost sharing, benefit or contribution limits, and target level of benefit adequacy. When employees are asked to share the cost of the investment plan, it is contributory. This aspect can be voluntary, or in the case of most public pensions, mandatory. If the college or university pays the full cost, the plan is noncontributory.

"Rules of thumb" serve quite nicely to understand some basic principles of pension plan design. One such rule is that a pension plan will produce a retirement income of about 60 percent of final average pay after 35 years of contributions if the contributions are between 11 percent to 12 percent of income during each of the 35 employment years. For institutions that wish to compete for talent in the defined contribution market, it will be important to determine the amount of contribution that will be required to keep the institution competitive as well as whether or not to make the plan contributory. There are consequences to each decision.

Defined contribution plans have become increasingly popular over the past 20 years. The rules for a specific type of defined contribution plan available only in the public education or nonprofit 501(c)(3) sector are set forth in section 403(b) of the Internal Revenue Code. In the 1980s, a corresponding defined contribution plan for the private, for-profit sector was created in section 401(k). Independent colleges and universities can now offer 401(k) plans to their employees, but the special provisions under section 403(b) may be more attractive for their retirement savings. While the defined contribution pension program is portable, the employee must understand that even if successive employers offer comparable plans, the level of institutional contribution and cost sharing may differ from one employer to another and that some plans are contributory while others are not. The employee must consider whether the new institution offers the same 403(b) product in their inventory of retirement plan vehicles.

While an employer can target a certain level of replacement income in either a defined benefit or a defined contribution plan, the employee participating in a defined benefit plan has greater assurances of reaching the goal as long as all of his or her years of service are with the same employer. If he or she changes employers during his or her career, the benefit from the defined benefit plan will be frozen based on the final earnings and years of service. Most defined benefit plans have a delayed vesting period, and employees who leave too soon forfeit their benefits. Thus, defined benefit plans lack full portability features. The employer's cost of a defined benefit plan is determined based on the level of benefits as well as the demographic makeup of the employee group. In the public sector, employees often share in the cost of providing the benefits that can be made on a pretax basis by using an employer pickup under section 414(h) of the code. Defined benefit plans at independent colleges and universities are qualified plans under section 401(a), and these plans are noncontributory. Very few defined benefit plans allow an employee to withdraw the value of the retirement benefit in a lump sum.

The entire equation of plan design boils down to several simple observations:

First, a defined benefit plan is a cost efficient vehicle for institutions with a workforce that is more or less stable. It is not valuable to employees who may be transient. From the employee's viewpoint, it can be valuable to a workforce that is more stable/permanent and long service.

Second, a defined contribution plan is a cost-effective vehicle for institutions with a workforce that is transient especially in the early years.

Third, the cost associated with either type of plan will be about the same over the long run, although a defined benefit plan offers an employer the opportunity to offset the cost by excess interest income and investment profits.

Several requirements associated with pension plan management are important to note. These plans are labor-intensive, require attention to detail in the extreme, and are highly regulated. Volumes of federal rules and regulations apply to pension plans. These requirements pertain to such issues as plan solvency, fiduciary responsibility, due diligence, financial reporting, and nondiscrimination. The bottom line is that plan design should occur only with assistance from pension management consultants, an actuary, and legal counsel.

Among these requirements are a plan document where all of the benefits, conditions, terms, features, calculation methodologies, application of interest, eligibility, and virtually every aspect of the plan are recorded. The Internal Revenue Service should review and approve the plan document. A summary plan description must also be distributed to each plan participant. In addition, as laws, rules, and regulations change over time, the changes must be incorporated into the plan, and the plan must be amended to accommodate each change. Plan documents can be expensive to maintain and usually require the advice and service of an attorney or pension plan consulting firm.

Law requires that a report of plan contributions and liabilities based on the IRS Form 5500 filing be made annually to participants. It is also common practice today for an employer to provide annually a written projection of retirement income based on the member's length of service to date and his or her anticipated service until normal retirement. Often these reports include projections of more than the retirement plan distribution, such as Medicare, Social Security, and life insurance. Reports like these have become so popular over the past 15 years that virtually all defined contribution plans provide quarterly reports on contributions and earnings to each individual participant.

Periodic Program Review and Management

Regardless of whether an institution has a defined benefit plan or a defined contribution plan and regardless of whether or not the institution utilizes a third party administrator, the institution is responsible for periodic program review. The Internal Revenue Service and U.S. Department of Labor have established rules and regulations for plan fiduciaries. The purpose of a review is to ensure that the plan is sound in its objectives, that plan design features meet the needs for which they are intended, and that plan administration is effective. It is important to distinguish this review from an audit. An audit is an internal review that examines the actions taken to administer the plan and compares that action to the plan document. Periodic program review, on the other hand, is a review of all or part of the plan's objectives and the content of the plan document.

Qualified plan audits occur annually. They involve random samples of plan administration. The common practice is to identify the number of retirement calculations that were performed within a defined time period. From that number, a sample is drawn. An auditor will calculate the benefit and compare it against the actual transaction, looking for differences. The IRS is developing an audit process for 403(b) retirement plans to check for compliance with the rules of these plans.

Retirement Income Planning

Social Security

The Social Security Act of 1935 created a program that assures qualified participants of a very modest income at the time of their retirement. Most colleges and universities participate in the mandatory program, although in some states public institutions are exempt.

Social Security is generally the second largest portion of retirement income planning and has several components. Those components are:

- a monthly retirement income;
- health insurance benefits under Medicare; and
- disability insurance.

Monthly Retirement Income

To be eligible to receive Social Security retirement benefits, a participant must have earned 40 quarters of work credit. Income benefits generally begin at age 65, although they can be claimed at age 62, permanently reducing the income benefit. After age 70 a worker can claim his or her Social Security benefits without any reduction in benefits-based earned income.

The Social Security Act was amended in 1983, increasing the normal retirement age for Social Security purposes from 65 to 67 in graduated steps. Under current rules, by the year 2027, the normal retirement age will be 67. Early retirement is available at age 62 but the level of benefit reduction is greater for these retirees.

An employee who participates in Social Security for 30 years and retires at normal retirement age should expect to receive roughly 15 percent of his or her retirement income from this government program. This statement is a vast generalization, and it can only be regarded as a general planning indicator.

Medicare Benefits

Medical insurance in the United States is most commonly obtained by individuals through their employment. In most cases, when work ends, medical insurance ceases. If work ends at Social Security's normal retirement age, Medicare coverage may be obtained. Retirement before age 65 leaves a gap except in certain disability situations. Medicare has two parts—physician reimbursement and hospital reimbursement. Medicare supplement plans that offer coverage for costs not covered by Medicare are becoming increasingly popular.

Disability Benefits

In 1965, Congress expanded Social Security benefits to include certain serious physical and mental disabilities. Persons who are medically unable to perform any kind of work for 12 months or more are the target group for this benefit.

Financing

Social Security and Medicare are funded jointly by the employer and employee. Since 1991 the Federal Insurance Contributions Act (FICA) tax liability has remained at 7.65 percent for both the employer and the employee for a total of 15.3 percent of income. However, the 7.65 percent rate is composed of two parts: 6.2 percent is collected for retirement from each party, 1.45 percent is collected for medical and disability from each party. The larger part, 6.2 percent, is applicable only to earnings up to a certain limit. In 2000, the limit is $76,200, which is indexed. The smaller part, 1.45 percent, is applicable to all earnings.

The Pension Plan

As noted earlier the two types of pension plans in common use today are the defined benefit plan and the defined contribution plan.

Defined Benefit Plan

This type of plan uses a formula comprised of years of service and a participant's average salary, normally over three or five years, for the years immediately preceding retirement when salary is typically at its highest. This type of plan may be contributory or noncontributory, and it is found most frequently in the public higher education sector. The advantages of a defined benefit plan include:

- *Predictability.* A participant will know with reasonable certainty the approximate amount of retirement income he or she will receive.

- *Security.* A participant can rely on the fact that national economic ups and downs have little effect on his or her future income under the plan.

- *Protection.* Benefits of a defined benefit plan are insured under the Pension Benefit Guaranty Corporation (PBGC). In the event of a plan default, the PBGC could step in to ensure solvency. PBGC coverage does not apply to defined benefit plans of public employers.

Another feature of defined benefit plans is worthwhile to note. The amount of time that a participant spent in the military is added to the total years of eligible service that will be counted toward retirement. Since pension income in this type of plan is a product of the number of years of participation, the addition of military service can be an extremely attractive enticement. There is typically a four-year cap on the amount of military service that may be added.

Some state-sponsored defined benefit plans will allow participants to purchase credit for years of service in a state-sponsored defined benefit plan from another state. Under such an arrangement, participants work for a set number of years with their current public employer. After crossing that threshold, they are permitted to "buy" some of the service from the other state and apply it to their current plan. Often the employee must pay some amount to his or her current retirement plan. Formulas are as numerous as are the states that permit this. Most public defined benefit plans that cover educators have vesting periods that range between five and 10 years before the benefits become owned by the employee.

Disadvantages of the defined benefit plan include its lack of portability. However, often multiple agencies within one state will participate in one plan. Thus, a faculty member may move from one in-state institution to another without a disruption or change in pension plan. No such option is available in defined benefit plans covering independent higher education institutions.

A second disadvantage of defined benefits plans is that, in exchange for the security of a predictable, secure and protected retirement plan, participants forego a chance for obtaining a significantly larger retirement income, which might be achieved by higher investment returns of their defined contribution plans.

Defined Contribution Plans

Currently, the most popular type of retirement plan is the defined contribution plan. This type of plan uses the employee's salary only as a basis to determine the amount of contribution made to an account.

The plan may be contributory or noncontributory. Retirement income will depend on:

- the total amount contributed;
- performance of the investments that are selected; and
- the compounding effect of contributions and investment returns, mortality assumptions, retirement age, and the payout option chosen by the participant.

The single greatest advantage of a defined contribution plan is its portability. Many educational institutions across the country offer the same annuity or insurance company products. They differ from institution to institution only by their eligibility, participation, and contribution requirements.

The second advantage is that the return on investment can be high. That is, intelligent choice of investment options, attention to investment performance, and strong market conditions can enable a participant to realize a substantial return and growth. One must have the time, skill, and ability to do this along with the willingness to accept investment risk. Research has shown that statements of benefit account help employees appreciate the value that the defined contribution plan adds to their compensation.

Investment risk may also be a disadvantage. Participant-directed investments place responsibility squarely on the shoulders of the plan member. A participant can lose money as well as gain money.

A second disadvantage for participants in a defined contribution plan is the uncertainty in estimating future benefits on retirement. Sharp market fluctuations can have marked affect on future estimates.

Optional Plans

While virtually all educational institutions, public and independent, have a retirement plan, many of them will offer a new member of the faculty or staff a choice between a defined benefit plan and a defined contribution plan. This matter of choice began to creep into public sector plans in the late 1950s and early 1960s. At that time the only common retirement vehicle in public higher education was the defined benefit plan. Its inherent lack of portability was inhibiting the movement of academicians from state to state.

While some state colleges and universities had defined contribution plans early in the century, in the 1960s it became evident to some educational administrators that the presence of a defined contribution plan could assist materially in attracting out-of-state faculty and staff. Therefore, several state legislatures such as West Virginia and much later, Pennsylvania, created the Optional (Alternate) Retirement Plan. Many states have a defined benefit plan, frequently called the State Employees Retirement System. They also have a defined contribution plan, frequently called the Optional Retirement System.

Supplemental Plans for Personal Savings

One of the most popular benefits to arrive in the educational community has been the supplemental retirement plan. Participation in this type of plan is entirely voluntary and entirely contributory. In a few cases, an institution may offer a small percentage of salary or portion thereof to encourage participation. By and large, however, membership is at the exclusive option of individual faculty and staff. The amount that can be contributed before tax is based on a detailed formula that takes into account the retirement plan contribution and has annual limits.

One incentive to participation in this type of plan is the tax-saving advantage. In 2000, an employee can shelter up to $10,500 annually in such a plan. Tax is deferred until the retirement income stream begins to flow. Presumably, at that time, (postretirement) gross income will diminish and the employee will be in a lower tax bracket. Thus, it will cost the individual less in taxes to receive it postretirement than it would cost in taxes to receive it currently.

Pension Plan Management

Generally pension plan management may take either of two forms: internal or external.

Internal Management

Internal management is when the institution fully assumes the management of the plan. It requires investment staff, money managers, accountants, actuaries, audit staff, legal counsel, benefit counselors, and a wide array of talents at senior levels of management.

Internal management of a pension fund requires the same level of knowledge and skill whether 800 or 12,000 employees are involved. Internal management will command the attention of several senior executives and require periodic attention of the governing board. Indeed, the stability of the institution as a corporate entity has some risk in this scenario. Fiduciary responsibility, due diligence, and oversight are legal concepts that have precise meaning in pension self-management. The probability is that the smaller the institution, measured in terms of number of employees, the less attractive it is to self-manage.

External Management

External pension management can be done two ways. The first is the employment of a third party administrator to manage the plan. It reduces some burden of investment management, and of employing technical expertise, accountants, and day-to-day functionaries that the institution would otherwise need, but the overall responsibility and oversight will continue to remain the direct responsibility of senior executives and the governing board.

The other form of external management is the engagement of an insurance company or mutual fund company to provide the pension. Typically, this includes agreements with multiple plan providers to provide pension benefits. This model, most often associated with defined contribution plans, allows the institution to retain less involvement in plan administration. Audit staff, accountants, actuaries, legal counsel, and consultants are needed only periodically. The institution simply makes its monthly electronic fund transfer on behalf of each participant. This is not to say that the institution eliminates responsibility altogether. There is still a responsibility to ensure that the plan providers are stable institutions and that they perform to the specifications of the payroll agreement as well as to make sure that the operations of the plan comply with the law. This model requires much less internal supervision than does self-administration.

There are two critical differences between internal and external management. Internal management is time-intensive for some of the senior executives. It also has financial risk as well as potential for financial reward if administering a defined benefit plan. External management is less time-intensive for senior management. It is also less financially risky, has no potential for financial reward but has predictable and known cost implications.

Retirement Support

Retirement planning is an individual, personal responsibility. Pension plans are becoming more difficult to understand because of continually changing laws and regulations and the complexities of investments, payouts, and distribution options. Institutions traditionally assist in employee decision making by providing information. Institutions should strive to ensure that participants have enough facts to make sound pension investment choices. It is critical to remember the distinction between information and advice. Presenting information in a fashion that enables the listener to draw only one conclusion can be construed as advice. Institutional benefits managers and legal staff need to provide information to employees without dispensing advice. If a listener depends on that advice and suffers some loss, the advisor and the institution may share liability for the loss. This is especially true if it can be shown that the advisor was not qualified or trained to provide advice and did not caution the listener about the potential loss that could result from following the advice. Institutions have an affirmative duty to make it clear to their agents that offering investment "advice" to plan participants is prohibited.

Counseling provided by a college or university employer should consist of assisting an employee in identifying and weighing all relevant personal and family information against all relevant plan information, such as investment matters, asset transfer matters, distribution matters, and payout options.

Communication

Law or administrative regulation requires communication of certain types of pension plan information, such as a Summary Plan Description and a Summary of Material Modification that publicizes plan changes. Annual reports of plan income and plan expenditures are also required.

Although quarterly reports are not required to be issued with respect to 403(b) and 401(k) pension plans, it has become a common standard practice for defined contribution plans.

Responsibilities of Retirement Plan Providers

The Employee Retirement Income Security Act and Internal Revenue Code set forth certain legal responsibilities for retirement plan providers. Retirement plan providers can be fiduciaries and as such have obligations to individuals who are purchasing their products. ERISA and IRC establish the standards of care and levels of expectation to which participants are entitled.

Product Lines

Investment performance differs from provider to provider, but some products are similar among companies. Flexibility in fund transfer will differ from provider to provider, as will policies on fees, charges, and the costs that are passed on to participants. Detailed product and service information must be disclosed by the provider, understood by the institution, and made available to participants.

Support Services

Support services focus on enrollment and maintenance. Enrollment services to solicit interest in the product are workshops, benefit fairs, open enrollment, and new employee orientation. Most providers, depending on the volume of business they have with an institution, are quite willing to provide these services.

Another service that is expected is recordkeeping. It is an institutional responsibility to complete IRS Form 5500 based on timely and accurate information received from the provider(s).

Legal Considerations

Internal Revenue Code

Numerous Internal Revenue Code provisions govern qualified retirement plans. They are complex and require costly legal and actuarial assistance. Some of the regulations of great concern to higher education institutions are covered below.

Employee Retirement Income Security Act

Federal laws and regulations under the Employee Retirement Income Security Act of 1974 govern pension plans of independent institutions. ERISA was designed to protect the interest of employees especially when a plan promises a certain monthly dollar amount upon retirement (defined benefit). Over the years a number of changes to ERISA have occurred. While ERISA does not apply to public institutions, many of its features are present in both private and many public plans.

ERISA generally requires that an employee be eligible for participation in a pension plan after one year of service or at age 21 with special provisions for employees of teaching institutions who have immediate vesting in their plan. It also establishes provisions for employee vesting rights in a pension plan. The Retirement Equity Act revised ERISA vesting standards, shortening the period allowed for delayed vesting. The basic options for vesting are:

- full vesting after five years of service;

- twenty percent vesting after three years of service, with 20 percent additional vesting for years four to seven when all employees must be 100 percent vested; and

- a special rule for multiemployer plans with collective bargaining.

ERISA has numerous other provisions including guidelines pertaining to the use of pension funds for operating purposes, unfunded pension programs, soundness of actuarial assumptions, and accommodations for transferred employees who want to transfer funds (portability).

ERISA compliance is monitored by the Department of Labor (DOL) and the Pension Benefit Guaranty Corporation. Internal Revenue Code requirements are monitored by the IRS. The IRS's primary concern is with qualified retirement plans that offer employers and employees favorable income tax treatment. DOL focuses on protection of participants' rights. The PBGC insures pension benefits for employees in private defined benefit pension plans. Institutions with defined benefit plans are required to pay annual premiums to the PBGC. If an institution terminates a defined benefit plan, guaranteed minimum benefits are paid to all participants.

Retirement Equity Act (REA)

The Retirement Equity Act of 1984 amends ERISA and IRC and is designed to provide greater equity in private pension plans for participating employees and their spouses. Consideration is given to the role of the spouse, taking into account the changes in work patterns of men and women and recognizing the status of marriage as an economic partnership with substantial contributions made to the marriage by both spouses. For these and other reasons, REA brought about changes in ERISA regarding eligibility and vesting provisions, parental leave, spouse survivor benefits, and distribution of benefits in divorce cases, among others. In instances where an employee declines to elect survivors' benefits, the institution is required to inform the prospective beneficiaries and obtain written agreement from the beneficiaries authorizing the declination.[33]

Nondiscrimination Requirements

Retirement plans must meet the IRC requirements that contributions or benefits provided do not discriminate in favor of highly compensated employees. The definition of a highly compensated employee was changed in the Small Business Job Protection Act of 1996. Final nondiscrimination regulations became effective January 1, 1994, for qualified private plans and January 1, 1996, for qualified plans maintained by tax-exempt organizations. Until 403(b) regulations are issued, 403(b) plans are subject to good faith testing, including safe harbors. Nondiscrimination does not generally apply to retirement plans of public employers.

There are three basic nondiscrimination requirements: contributions or the benefits provided must be nondiscriminatory in amount; plan benefits, rights, and features provided must be made available to employees in a nondiscriminatory manner; and the effect of plan amendments (including grants of past service credit) and plan terminations must be nondiscriminatory. The nondiscrimination availability requirement applies to any feature of the plan that is of more than insignificant value and any other optional forms of benefits (retirement annuities and single sum payments). Rights and features include ancillary benefits (disability) and other features such as plan loans and investment options.[34]

The two basic testing alternatives for determining nondiscrimination in the amount of contributions or benefits are safe-harbor and general testing. Safe harbor focuses primarily on uniformity of provisions and plan designs. General testing focuses on actuarial results under the plan, i.e. comparison of actual allocation or accrual rates provided to employees. As described earlier, assistance from attorneys and actuaries is important in complying with this requirement.

Cap on Compensation and Contributions

Over the years tax law has placed limits on the amount of contributions a tax-exempt institution can make to a qualified or 403(b) pension plan. The Tax Reform Act of 1986 defined a highly compensated employee, and the Small Business Job Protection Act of 1996 simplified this definition.

A highly compensated employee in the year 2000 is one who:

- is a 5 percent owner at any time during the year or the preceding year; or

- receives compensation in excess of $80,000 in 1999 (indexed to $85,000 for calendar year 2000) and, if the institution so elects, was in the "top paid group" of employees for the preceding year. The "top paid group" for a given year is the top 20 percent of employees ranked on the basis of compensation received during that year.[35]

The law limits the total amount contributed to a defined contribution plan to $30,000 and 25 percent of salary with additional limits on 403(b) through the maximum exclusion allowance. One key provision reduced the absolute limit on the amount of compensation an institution can use to determine contributions to a plan on behalf of an employee from $235,000 to $150,000 (indexed). That figure is $170,000 for calendar year 2000.[36]

Limitations placed on benefits for highly compensated employees are of concern to colleges and universities. Many have responded by exploring and/or establishing nonqualified deferred compensation plans (under IRC section 457).

The Small Business Job Protection Act amended the definition of includable compensation for determining the limit under 457 and 403(b) to include elective deferrals such as contributions to or benefits from section 401(k) plans, section 403(b) tax-sheltered annuities, section 457 deferred compensation plans, and section 125 cafeteria plans.

Lump Sum Distributions

Many college and university retirement plans allow participants to elect a full or partial lump sum distribution from the plan to the extent permitted by the funding vehicle. In order for the participant to be eligible to receive post-1988 salary reduction contributions to a 403(b) annuity contract or any contribution to a 403(b) mutual fund, the employee must meet one of the following conditions:

- is at least 59½ years old;

- is deceased;
- is totally disabled; or
- is separated from the service of the employer.[37]

To avoid the 10 percent penalty on early withdrawals, the participant must further:

- be at least 59½ years old;
- take a life annuity;
- be terminated after age 55;
- be disabled; or
- be deceased.

Employees wanting to exercise "lump sum distribution" rights in qualified retirement plans that contain the option will have to adhere to new IRC rules beginning in 2000. The requirement for a five-year minimum period of service for a qualified plan distribution to be considered a lump sum distribution for income averaging purposes was eliminated under the Small Business Job Protection Act of 1996. In 2000 and beyond, a lump sum distribution for averaging purposes must meet three criteria:

- it must be received within one taxable year;
- it must be "the balance to the credit of an employee"; and
- it must be made for one of the following reasons:
  - the death of the employee,
  - the attainment of age 59½ by the employee,
  - separation from service, or
  - disability, as defined by IRC Section 72(m)(7).[38]

There is no favorable tax treatment for lump-sum distributions from 403(b) plans.

FEDERAL LAWS AFFECTING HUMAN RESOURCE MANAGEMENT[39]

The Family and Medical Leave Act of 1993 requires covered employers to provide up to 12 weeks of unpaid, job-protected leave each year to "eligible" employees for certain family and medical reasons. Employers with 50 or more employees are covered by the act. This statute is enforced by the Department of Labor, Wage and Hour Division (P.L. 103-3 and P.L. 104-1).

The Executive Order 11246 of 1965 prohibits discrimination against employees and job applicants based on their race, sex, color, religion, and national origin by first- and second-tier government contractors whose contracts are in amounts exceeding $5,000. In addition, the order requires government contractors to implement affirmative action plans to increase minority and female participation in the workplace when they have contracts of $50,000 or more a year and have 50 or more employees. This statute is enforced by the Office of Federal Contract Compliance Programs (OFCCP) (41 C.F.R. 60-1 and 2).

Title VI of the Civil Rights Act of 1964 prohibits discrimination on the basis of race, color, or national origin in programs and activities receiving federal financial assistance. The term "program or activity" includes all the operations of an educational institution, government entity, or private employer that receives federal funds. This statute is enforced by the Equal Employment Opportunity Commission (EEOC) (42 U.S.C. 2000d and P.L. 103-382).

Title VII of the Civil Rights Act of 1964 prohibits employment discrimination and harassment in employment activities such as recruitment, selection, promotion compensation, and termination of all forms based on race, color, religion, sex, and national origin. It also prohibits retaliation against employees or individuals who exercise their rights under the act. Employers with 15 or more employees are covered by the law. This statute is enforced by the EEOC (42 U.S.C. 2000e and P.L. 104-1).

The Civil Rights Act of 1991 amended the 1964 Act to provide for compensatory and punitive damages and jury trials in cases of intentional employment discrimination. Employers with 15 or more employees are covered by the act. This statute is enforced by the EEOC (P.L. 102-166 and P.L. 104-331).

The Age Discrimination in Employment Act of 1967 prohibits discrimination in employment against persons 40 years of age or older and prohibits retaliation against employees for exercising their rights under the act. It is unlawful for an employer to fail or refuse to hire or to discharge any individual or otherwise discriminate against any individual with respect to compensation, terms, conditions, or privileges of employment based on age. Employers with 20 or more employees are covered by the act. This statute is enforced by the EEOC (29 U.S.C. 621 and P.L. 104-208).

Fair Labor Standards Act (FLSA) of 1938 establishes minimum wage, overtime pay, equal pay, recordkeeping, and child labor standards for employees who are covered by the act, and who are not exempt from specific provisions. Initially, the FLSA applied only to private employers directly engaged in commerce. Government employees were added to FLSA coverage by amendments to the act in 1966 and 1974. In 1966, coverage was extended to school, hospital, nursing home, and local transit employees.

The FLSA includes an important distinction between employees who are not covered by the act and those who are exempt from any or all of the act's provisions. Employees who are not covered (exempt) are outside the authority of the FLSA. Exempt employees are still subject to the equal pay provisions, even if they are exempt from the minimum wage and overtime provisions. Each exemption is narrowly defined under the law, and employers should exercise caution when exempting employees.

Other important features of the law, as it pertains to pay and overtime calculations for nonexempt employees, are definitions of working time, that is, waiting time, on-call time, rest periods, meal time, sleeping time, training time, travel time, and starting and quitting times. The administration and enforcement of the FLSA and related statutes are the responsibility of the U.S. Department of Labor. Within DOL, the Wage and Hour Division of the Employment Standards Administration has authority for the FLSA. This division issues rules, regulations, and interpretations under the act and conducts inspections and investigations to determine compliance.[40]

The Equal Pay Act of 1963 prohibits sex-based wage discrimination between men and women in the same establishment who are performing substantially equal work requiring equal skill, effort, and responsibility. The act establishes exceptions for wage differentials based on seniority or merit systems for employers that measure earnings by quantity or quality of production, or for differentials based on any other factor than sex. There is no minimum number of employees for employers to be covered by the act. This statute is enforced by the EEOC (29 U.S.C. 206d).

Title IX of the Education Amendments of 1972 prohibits sex discrimination in educational programs or activities that receive federal financial assistance. The Office for Civil Rights (OCR) enforces this statute (20 U.S.C. Chapter 38, Section 1681-1688).

Title IX has been an integral part of the educational process of high schools, colleges, and universities in an attempt to bring about parity for women and men, specifically in athletics. Title IX regulations subpart E does prohibit sex discrimination in employment in education programs and activities; however, most sex discrimination in employment issues are referred by OCR to the EEOC for investigation.

Vietnam Era Veterans Readjustment Assistance Act of 1974 prohibits employment discrimination and requires federal contractors with contracts or subcontracts of $10,000 or more to take affirmative action to employ and advance in employment qualified special disabled and Vietnam-era veterans. This statute is enforced by the OFCCP (41 C.F.R. 60-250).

The Rehabilitation Act of 1973 (Sections 503 and 504) prohibits employment discrimination and requires federal contractors with contracts or subcontracts of $10,000 or more to take affirmative action to employ and advance in employment qualified individuals with disabilities. This act is enforced by the OFCCP (41 C.F.R. 60-741).

The Americans with Disabilities Act of 1990 prohibits discrimination against qualified individuals with disabilities in employment, public service, public accommodations, and telecommunications. It requires employers to provide "reasonable accommodation" to such individuals who can perform the essential function of the position, unless doing so would cause an undue hardship on the business or alter the essence of the position. The act defines "individuals with disabilities" as meaning any person who: has a physical or mental impairment that substantially limits one or more major life activities, has a record of impairments, or is regarded as having an impairment. Employers with 15 or more employees are covered by the act. The EEOC enforces this statute (ADA 424 SC 12101 and P.L. 104-1).

The Pregnancy Discrimination Act of 1978 prohibits employment discrimination on the basis of pregnancy, childbirth, or other related conditions. It requires employers to treat pregnant employees on an equal basis with employees who have other medical conditions. It prohibits discrimination in hiring, promotion, and termination of employment, as well as protects reinstatement rights of women on leave for pregnancy-related reasons. In 1990, the EEOC issued a policy statement concluding that employers that offer parental leave to female employees must also grant parental leave to males. This law applies to employers with 15 or more employees and is enforced by the EEOC (P.L. 95-555).

Federal Privacy Act (1974) applies to federal government records and prohibits federal agencies from revealing certain information without permission from employees and provides protection, procedures for requests for records, requests for correction, fees, penalties, and specific exemptions (29 CFR 1611 et seq. and 5 U.S.C. 552a). The Office of Management and Budget (OMB) provides guidelines, regulations, and continuing assistance to the act.

Williams-Steiger Occupational Safety and Health Act of 1970 (OSH Act) states that each employer has a "general duty" to provide a place of employment "free from recognized hazards." Employers also have the "special duty" to comply with all standards of safety and health established under this act. OSHA has issued a large number of detailed standards covering numerous workplace hazards. Items covered include power tools, machine guards, compressed gas, materials handling and storage, and toxic substances such as asbestos, cotton dust, silica, lead, carbon monoxide and bloodborne pathogens. Although OSHA is federal law, the act allows states to develop and administer their own programs if they are approved by the secretary of labor. There are many criteria for approval, but the most important is that the state program must be judged "at least as effective" as the federal program. Currently 23 states have approved plans in operation (29 CFR 1903.2 (a) (1)).

Consolidated Budget Reconciliation Act (COBRA) of 1985 requires employers of 20 or more employees to make available health care coverage for terminated employees and for the widows, ex-spouses, and dependents of employees, effective for plan years beginning after June 30, 1986. All private sector employers, except employers maintaining church plans (under Sec. 414(e)), are covered under the act. States and any political subdivision, agency, or instrumentality of such states are covered by parallel COBRA provisions in Title XXII of the Public Health Service Act (P.L. 99-272).

Immigration Reform and Control Act of 1986 (IRCA), as amended, applies to every employer in the United States. It also applies to every employee—whether full-time, part-time, temporary, or seasonal. IRCA makes the enforcement of national immigration policy the job of every employer. While its provisions are complex, the basic features of the law fall into four broad categories:

- employers may not hire or continue to employ "unauthorized aliens";
- employers must verify the identity and work authorization of every new employee; employers may not require a particular document but must accept any of the documents listed on the INS Form I-9;

- employers may not discriminate on the basis of citizenship or national origin; and

- certain aliens have amnesty rights; those who can prove U.S. residence continuously from January 1982 to November 1986 are eligible for temporary, and ultimately permanent, resident status.

Penalties for noncompliance include fines for failure to comply with verification rules, criminal sanctions for employers who engage in a pattern or practice of violations, and prohibitions from receiving federal contracts for knowingly hiring illegal aliens.[41] Compliance with the law and inspection of the INS Form I-9 may be monitored by officials of the Immigration and Naturalization Services (INS), the Department of Labor and the Office of Special Counsel for Immigration Related Unfair Employment Practices Office (P.L. 99-603, 8 U.S.C. 132 4a).

The Drug-Free Workplace Act of 1988 requires all institutions that are federal grant recipients and those with federal contracts of $25,000 or more to certify that they will provide a drug-free workplace. Covered employers must issue a statement prohibiting the illegal manufacture, distribution, dispensation, possession or use of any controlled substance in the workplace and must specify the consequences for violating the policy. In addition, the statement must require employees engaged in contract-related work to notify the institution of any criminal conviction. Institutions that receive those notices must, within 30 days, either take appropriate action against the employee, up to and including termination, or require the employee to participate in a rehabilitation program approved by a federal, state, or local health, law enforcement, or other appropriate agency (41 U.S.C. 701 et seq.). This law is enforced by OMB.

RECORDS MANAGEMENT

Human resources departments maintain employment records in order to preserve history, process personnel actions, and comply with myriad legal requirements imposed by both federal and state law.

Legal requirements for employment records in the United States are found primarily in regulations implementing a variety of federal laws. State statutes and regulations generally parallel their federal counterparts with a few variations. Institutions should review the legal record retention requirements for the state in which they reside.

Federal Laws Affecting Personnel Records

Federal employment laws specify standards of conduct for employers and empower federal agencies to implement these laws through regulations.

Records Retention Requirements

Federal and state laws regarding recordkeeping of employment records vary depending on the nature of the document as described below. Generally, institutions should use the longest retention period specified in the event of litigation. Retention periods vary from one year to as many as 30 years dependent on the law and employment issue.

Payroll Records

Payroll records usually include information such as the name, Social Security number, hours worked, compensation rate, federal and state tax withholdings and other deductions, and total wages paid to each employee. These records are often derived from timesheets, timecards, and copies of pay stubs. Various laws require payroll records to be maintained to accomplish specific goals, generally for a period of three years.

Employment Applications and other Preemployment Records

Employment applications and other preemployment records such as job applications, resumes, and advertising should be maintained for one year; two years for federal contractors.

Employment Actions

These records document promotions (tenure and tenure-denial), demotions, transfers, selection for training, layoffs, recalls, or other related employee actions for one year; two years for federal contractors.

Injuries and Illnesses

OSHA requires employers to maintain a summary log and detailed records regarding each occupational injury and illness for five years from the end of the current year.

Employee Medical Records and Hazardous Exposure Records

OSHA requires employers to keep employee medical records while the employee is active (term of employment) plus 30 years. Health insurance claims, however, can be destroyed at the discretion of the employer. This is, perhaps, the most arduous records retention requirement from all the federal agencies. However, OSHA does not reach to all employers. In those cases another federal agency and law may have the controlling language or a state law may be the proper frame of reference. In any case the employing institution is best served by making a determination on every form/type/style of health (medical/dental) record concerning the length of time it should be retained.

Employee Pensions and Benefits

The regulations implementing the Age Discrimination and Employment Act specify that employers must maintain records of pension and benefit plans, seniority system plans, and merit pay plans for the time the plan is in effect plus one year. This requirement applies specifically to the plans and not the employment service or contribution records that determine the eligibility of an individual to participate or benefit from the plan.

The Employee Retirement Income and Security Act does specify the statute of limitations during which an employee can bring a civil suit against an employer for not properly applying the plan.

A defensive strategy adopted by some institutions is to maintain records for long periods, out of a concern for litigation. The decision to maintain records in case of litigation versus the right to destroy them should be carefully reviewed by counsel.

Title VII of the Civil Rights Act

All personnel or employment records must be kept for one year from the date the record was made or personnel action was taken. Records relevant to EEOC actions must be kept until final disposition of the charge or action.

Executive Order 11246

Written affirmative action plans and supporting documents must be maintained for one year and must include data from the previous year.

Age Discrimination in Employment Act (ADEA)

Records containing employee's name, address, date of birth, occupation, pay rate, and weekly compensation must be kept for three years.

Immigration Reform and Control Act (IRCA)

The INS Form I-9 for each employee must be kept for three years after date of hire or one year after date of termination, whichever is later.

Fair Labor Standards Act (FLSA)

Records on employee information, payroll, contracts, or collective bargaining agreements must be kept for three years.

Americans with Disabilities Act (ADA)

All personnel or employment records must be kept for one year from date record was made or personnel action was taken. Records relevant to EEOC actions must be kept until final disposition of the charge or action.

Family Medical Leave Act (FMLA)

All records and documents related to each FMLA-related leave for each employee must be kept for three years.

Occupational Safety and Health Act (OSHA)

Log of all occupational illnesses and accidents, and all other OSHA-related records, must be retained for five years. Copies of medical examinations required by the law and exposures and medical records of potential toxic substances must be retained for 30 years.

Scanned Records and Electronic Imaging Systems

Institutions using electronic imaging systems should carefully establish and follow procedures designed to ensure the trustworthiness of the image information and provide a detailed audit trail. Colleges and universities can capitalize on the benefits of this new technology if the system is properly designed and implemented to meet the anticipated legal requirements of tomorrow.[42]

CURRENT ISSUES

Supervision, Management, and Leadership

In the academic setting, human resource management must partake of the culture and climate of higher education in order to be effective; it must reflect a leadership style keyed to the institution's most demanding and far-reaching goals. At the very least, human resource management needs to encourage by example, at all levels of management, a willingness to take charge, to be out front, and to accommodate differences. Perhaps its most important role is to adapt to change and assist in making changes acceptable. A discussion of some issues in the area of supervision, management, and leadership follow.

Conflict Management

Given the needs of the various units within an institution and the natural goals of good leaders to provide a broad scope of high-quality services, there is bound to be conflict over allocation of resources, particularly in tough economic times. Further, dynamic organizations face conflict over objectives, goals, policies, and practices. Some degree of conflict between faculty and administration, unionized staff, and management, and other groups in an educational community can be expected. The role of leadership and good human resource management is to provide a climate that encourages discussion, communication, respect for others' opinions, and goodwill. In this type of climate, conflicts can be met.

Motivation

T.R. Mitchell defines motivation as "the psychological processes that cause the arousal, direction, and persistence of voluntary actions that are goal directed."[43] Each approach to understanding motivation affords valuable insight necessary for designing and implementing work plans and a human resource development program. Since motivation is an individual behavior, the debate in the workplace is whether an employee is motivated more by intrinsic (personal recognition) rewards or extrinsic (monetary) ones.

Human resource administrators must recognize that various types of motivation techniques should be employed at different times for different individuals and units. In addition to compensation, and sometimes more important than dollars, are such things as recognition and praise of work effort; opportunities to handle new and challenging tasks; invitations to serve on professional committees and task forces; and invitations to attend informal group meetings and social functions. Nonmonetary "psychic income" is as essential as monetary recognition and compensation.

Time Management

As part of training, employees at all levels should be encouraged to practice good time management. Supervisors often can recommend changes that make better use of employees' abilities and of their time. Consultants can be employed to suggest time-saving changes in organization, policies, and practices as well.

Employee Stress

Often the demands of workload, inadequate resources and staffing, poor organization, inadequate policies and procedures, the organization's culture, and the style of leaders and supervisors lead to significant employee stress. Concerned human resource administrators should focus on these matters; they should provide counseling and training to employees in handling stress as a means of increasing job satisfaction and morale, preventing illness, and possibly reducing absenteeism and turnover while increasing productivity. There should also be concern about correcting the organizational leadership and supervisory issues that lead to stress on employees.

Employee Burnout

Burnout frequently results from working under stress for such a long time that the employee is mentally, psychologically, and physically exhausted. Basically the same approaches can be taken to combat burnout as for stress.

Employee Topout

The employee may have reached his or her ceiling in the employment ladder. The realization that he or she is unlikely to advance further can have significant impact on the employee's morale and productivity; if there are opportunities available outside the organization, this realization can lead to focusing on getting a new job. Employees and supervisors should be counseled to detect the signs of topout and to seek ways to overcome it by providing new assignments or tapping other skills.

Employee Boredom

The routine of performing the same job year in and year out can lead to boredom. This affects an employee's morale, productivity, and relationships with coworkers and others who interact with the employee. Managers need to be aware of signs of boredom and seek to combat this problem through counseling, career development, and motivational and supervisory techniques.

Communications

No aspect of human resource management is so pervasive as communication.[44] The scope of communications begins with an array of information disseminated to the public regarding position vacancies, followed by interviewing of qualified candidates, information presented at new employee orientation sessions, and sharing of information about compensation, performance expectations, counseling, and labor relations, to cite a few.

Human resource departments play the lead role in the preparation of managers and materials for effective communication. Managers spend their time communicating with employees, their bosses, people outside the institution, and others within. The effectiveness of their communication determines the effectiveness of their work unit.[45]

Communication today requires a manager to be more sensitive to the diversity of the workforce and the legal ramifications that might occur resulting from poor dissemination of important information and inappropriate communication methods. Human resources departments, through their training units, are strategically positioned to provide the necessary training to an institutions' managers.

Human resources departments communicate with employees more than any other unit within a college or university. The degree of success in communicating determines to a great extent the perception employees develop regarding the institution's commitment to effective interaction with them. Employees want to know about such things as the institution's personnel policies and procedures, pay practices, benefits, grievance procedures, and personal and professional development opportunities. Among the numerous ways to communicate with the workforce, depending on the purpose, are face-to-face interaction, employee handbooks and manuals, videos, multimedia, newspapers, newsletters, bulletin boards, suggestion programs, attitude surveys, committees, electronic mail, and the Internet.

Confidentiality and Privacy

Privacy refers to the interest employees have in controlling the use that is made of their personal information and in being able to engage in behavior free from regulation or surveillance. The difficulty lies in maintaining a proper balance between the common good and personal freedom, between the legitimate business needs of employees and an institution's values. Safeguards to protect personal privacy are more important than ever because of expanding use of electronic communications and potential of increased litigation.

Most employers have confidentiality and privacy practices for the employment application and hiring process, testing, medical files, promotion, tenure, discipline, performance, salary, employment references, benefits data, biographical data, and personnel file maintenance and access. Surprisingly, fewer than one in five employers has a written policy regarding electronic privacy—that is, employee computer files, voice mail, electronic mail, or other networking communications.[46]

Other issues of concern to employers and employees are monitoring of employees' telephone conversations, desk drawers, file cabinets, lockers, computer disks, and files as well as other general workplace "expectations" of privacy. Institutions should develop guidelines on these also.

Perhaps a general rule of thumb an institution might follow would be to balance its interest in preventing inappropriate and unprofessional actions or comments, or even illegal activity, against the privacy interests or the expectation of privacy of employees. Ethics, good business sense, and sensitivity regarding today's litigious society should guide institutions as they determine policies related to confidentiality and privacy matters. Public institutions have somewhat different rules to follow than independent colleges and universities. Records at public institutions are generally more open to public scrutiny. Both public and private employers should provide access to written policies and procedures and communicate with employees as appropriate.

Comparable Worth

The comparable worth theory promotes the concept that jobs should be paid commensurate with their value. The theory contends that while the "true worth" of nonidentical jobs may be similar, some jobs (often held by women) are paid at a lower rate than others (often held by men).[47] Advocates of the theory believe that the national pay differential in entry-level wages reflects wage discrimination. The Equal Pay Act of 1963 prohibits sex-based wage discrimination between men and women in the same establishment who are performing substantially equal work requiring equal skill, effort and responsibility. The practice of paying jobs traditionally held by women less than ones traditionally held by men is what critics call "institutional sex discrimination."[48]

With a few exceptions, comparable worth has not been a major wage and salary issue for colleges and universities, perhaps because so many receive federal funds and implement affirmative actions programs. However, human resource professionals in higher education must remain vigilant in their pursuit of equal pay for equal work for all employees across sex and racial lines.

Equal Employment Opportunity

The objective of equal opportunity is to provide balanced employment opportunity through the recruitment, employment, and promotion of individuals at all levels within a college or university's employment structure without regard to race, color, sex, age, disability, veteran status, religion, national origin, or sexual orientation. A sample nondiscrimination/equal opportunity policy is as follows:

> No citizen of the United States, or any other person within the jurisdiction thereof, shall on the grounds of race, color, sex, age, disability, veteran status, religion, national origin or sexual orientation be excluded from participation in, be denied the benefits of, or be subjected to discrimination or harassment in employment or under any educational program or activity of the institution.

> *and*

> No person in the United States shall, on the basis of sex, be excluded from participation in, be denied the benefits of, or be subjected to discrimination under any educational program or activity receiving federal financial assistance.

> *and*

> No person shall be subject to sexual harassment in employment or educational programs and activities. Sexual harassment includes, but is not limited to, physical or verbal abuse of a sexual nature including graphic commentaries about an individual's body, sexually degrading remarks used to describe an individual, or unwelcome propositions and physical advances of a sexual nature. Sexual harassment also includes the threat or insinuation that the lack of sexual submission will be used as a basis for employment or educational decisions affecting or interfering with an individual's salary, academic standing or other conditions of employment, academic or career development.[49]

Institutions generally seek to prohibit discrimination and promote affirmative action in educational and employment policies and practices implemented in compliance with applicable federal, state and local nondiscrimination and affirmative action laws and regulations.

The affirmative action or equal employment opportunity office on campus is responsible for coordinating into an effective, organized system, the institution's commitment to equal opportunity, developing the affirmative action plan, monitoring those policies and practices affecting employment that are covered by government guidelines, and reviewing all complaints alleging discrimination.

Affirmative Action

Affirmative action is a set of tools used to give qualified individuals equal access and opportunity through positive steps to promote inclusion and eradicate discrimination in employment, education, and business contracting as described below. Affirmative action is a general term usually assigned to three specific purposes:

- increasing the participation of qualified women and minorities in all levels and fields of employment by enhancing hiring and promotional practices;

- providing educational opportunities for women and minorities, particularly in higher education, to involve women and minorities in fields where they have not traditionally been represented; and

- availing businesses owned by women or minorities of contracting opportunities through federal and state governments from which they might otherwise be excluded.

There are two types of affirmative action plans, voluntary and court ordered, which can be implemented in one of three different ways—through executive order 11246, court order, or voluntarily.

Executive Order 11246 mandates employers who are federal contractors to develop, implement, and maintain a written affirmative action plan. The affirmative action plan requirements of the Executive Order cover nonconstruction employers who are recipients of $50,000 in federal contracts and who have 50 or more employees.

A court-ordered plan only applies where there is proof of pervasive and systemic discrimination. An institution may be required by court order to implement an affirmative action program if a court finds discrimination. The program must be narrowly tailored, flexible, temporary, and cannot impose an unacceptable burden on nontargeted groups.

An affirmative action program should be implemented voluntarily. A voluntary plan is valid under Title VII provided that it meets the standards established by the Supreme Court. If an institution adopts a voluntary affirmative action plan designed to meet the standards, it must identify a manifest imbalance in traditionally segregated job categories. The plan must also be designed to break down patterns of race and sex discrimination.[50]

The Supreme Court, in 1994, ruled that quotas are illegal. Empirical and anecdotal evidence have shown that race and gender continue to be major barriers for minorities and women in their quest for employment, quality education, housing, and business opportunities.

Allegations that affirmative action promotes the use of quotas and reverse discrimination have subjected it to rigorous legal challenges. Beginning in the 1980s, efforts by the Reagan-Bush administration to repeal Executive Order 11246 were unsuccessful. Legal challenges in the 1990s were more vigorous and resulted in several actions. For example:

- In 1994, in *Adarand Constructors, Inc.* v. *Pena*, the Supreme Court held that federal affirmative action programs remain constitutional when narrowly tailored to accomplish a compelling government interest such as remedying discrimination.

- In 1995, the Regents of the University of California voted to end all affirmative action programs at the University of California campuses. The universities are no longer allowed to use race, gender, ethnicity, or national origin as a factor in admissions decisions.

- In 1996, citizens of California approved Proposition 209 that abolished all public-sector affirmative action programs in employment, education, and contracting.

- In *Hopwood* v. *Texas* (1996), the Supreme Court ruled against the University of Texas deciding that its law school's policy of considering race in the admission process was a violation of the constitution's equal-protection guarantee.

- In 1998, the state of Washington passed a proposition similar to California's Proposition 209 that banned all state affirmative action programs for women and minorities in education, contracting, and employment.

In addition to various state initiatives to repeal affirmative action programs, legislation has been introduced in Congress seeking to dismantle all federal affirmative action programs. The affirmative action challenge for the 21st century is to affirm the national value of providing to all Americans the opportunity to make the most of their potential to work, learn, and participate in business enterprises.

Diversity Programs

Diversity is inclusive; it is not something that is defined by race or gender. It extends to age, personal and corporate background, education, function, and personality. It includes lifestyle, sexual orientation, geographic origin, tenure with the organization, exempt or nonexempt and management or nonmanagement status. A commitment to diversity is a commitment to all employees, not an attempt at preferential treatment or a replacement for affirmative action.[51]

The American workforce of the future will look different, and the number of employees under the age of 40 will shrink. Employers will have to compete heavily to recruit and retain this talented new workforce. Affirmative action and human resource managers, and staff who are responsible for ensuring equal access and equal opportunity for employment, training programs, compensation, and other employment activities, must be trained to manage cultural and individual differences.

Affirmative action and human resource managers play a key role in minimizing conflict and providing a positive working environment that respects diversity and promotes inclusion. Managing diversity effectively will allow individuals to contribute their unique qualities to improve business outcomes.

Not only do employers need to manage gender, ethnic, and racial cultural differences, they must also address workers seeking a balance between family (traditional and nontraditional) and professional life, flexible work schedules, and accommodation for alternative work sites. Recent legislation such as the Americans with Disabilities Act and the Family Medical Leave Act will require employers to be more flexible in responding to the needs of the future workforce.

Drug-free Workplace

If a college or university contracts with the federal government for the procurement of property or services valued at more than $25,000, it must certify that it will provide a drug-free workplace. The certification must set forth a plan for ensuring a drug-free workplace, including providing employee education, establishing compliance with the program as a condition of employment, and taking appropriate disciplinary action against employees who violate the policy.

In addition to the Drug-Free Workplace Act of 1988, the Department of Transportation and the Department of Defense have issued regulations that require covered employers to conduct drug tests (including random) and maintain certain records.

Drug Testing

In most states, preemployment drug testing is acceptable (for private employers), as is testing related to workers' compensation claims. Preemployment drug testing for state employment is dependent on state law. States with drug testing laws vary in their approach to postemployment drug testing among public employers. In some states, random drug testing of employees is permissible. In many states, reasonable suspicion drug testing is permitted. Reasonable suspicion exists when an employer has reached an independent conclusion that an employee's ability to function in the workplace is impaired. This is usually done by having more than one supervisor observe an employee for objective signs of an impairment.[52]

Government guidelines for lab certification, collection and testing procedures, and test review must be precisely followed. Preemployment drug tests are also covered by the Fair Credit Reporting Act, U.S.C. 1681 et seq. (1997) (FCRA) and appropriate compliance steps should be taken with regard to acknowledgment forms and follow-up on positive results.

Employee Counseling/Employee Assistance Programs

David Ulrich[53] sees the role of human resources as one of employee advocate, servicing the workforce by providing the many services employees expect, such as flexible work arrangements, benefits flexibility, retirement planning, career growth and development counseling, and employee assistance programs.

Being an employee advocate means ensuring that employees receive fair treatment and have adequate means to voice concerns without fear of reprisal. If managers have violated operational policies and procedures or situations exist that adversely affect employee morale, it becomes human resources' responsibility to investigate and rectify the situation. Often misunderstanding or misinformation about management practices and policies causes perceptions of unfair treatment or discrimination. In such instances, active listening and good counseling by a human resources professional or ombudsman can ameliorate the matter. Providing employees access to quality counseling and consultation also help an institution achieve its equal opportunity objectives by demonstrating that the institution cares about the concerns of every employee.

Many employees in colleges and universities need counseling that goes far beyond that which is provided by human resource personnel. Specialists may be provided through an employee assistance program. EAPs are designed to assist employees with chronic personal problems that hinder their job performance. Typically, an EAP refers employees to in-house counselors or outside professionals. Such programs address employee concerns such as personal crises, emotional problems, alcoholism, and abuse of drugs. Among the most prevalent problems among employees are personal crises involving marital, family, financial, or legal matters.[54]

Employee assistance programs have proved very successful in addressing work performance problems. Unfortunately, employees often fail to use an EAP unless faced with the alternative of being fired. Supervisors should be trained to identify an employee who may need assistance from an EAP long before work performance deteriorates to the point of possible termination of employment.

EAPs help address the view of an employee as a "whole person" in need of personal counseling in addition to health care plans and wellness programs such as exercising, smoke cessation, eating disorders, and stress relief. While such programs can mean substantial gains in employee job performance and reduction in absenteeism, institutions must prudently address the financial expenditures and quality concerns regarding the operation of an EAP.

Sexual Harassment

Harassment on the basis of sex is a violation of Section 703 of Title VII of the Civil Rights Act of 1964.

Sexual Harassment, Defined

Unwelcome sexual advances, requests for sexual favors, and other verbal or physical conduct of a sexual nature constitute sexual harassment when (1) submission to such conduct is made either explicitly or implicitly a term or condition of an individual's employment, (2) submission to or rejection of such conduct by an individual is used as the basis for employment decisions affecting such individual, or (3) such conduct has the purpose or effect of unreasonably interfering with an individual's work performance or creating an intimidating, hostile, or offensive working environment. This statute is enforced by the EEOC.

Types of Sexual Harassment

Among the types of sexual harassment are the following:

- *Quid pro quo.* Where the granting or denying of a job benefit is conditioned on submission to or rejection of unwelcome sexual advances, requests for sexual favors, or other verbal or physical conduct of sexual nature.

- *Hostile work environment.* Where the conduct is severe or pervasive enough to alter the conditions of employment and to create an abusive working environment.

- *Third party.* Where employment opportunities or benefits are granted because of an individual's submission to the employer's sexual advances or request for sexual favors. The employer may be held liable for sex discrimination against other persons who were qualified for but denied that employment opportunity or benefit.

- *Nonemployees.* The employer may also be responsible for acts of nonemployees with respect to sexual harassment of employees in the workplace where the employer (or its agents or supervisory employees) knows or should have known of the conduct and fails to take immediate and appropriate corrective action. In reviewing these cases the EEOC will consider the extent of the employer's control and any other legal responsibility which the employer may have with respect to the conduct of the nonemployees.

Sexual harassment is one of the most volatile employment issues. Colleges and universities must take a proactive role in preventing and avoiding claims of sexual harassment. A clear policy, including grievance procedures and an investigation process, should be clearly communicated throughout the institution. Victims of sexual harassment should have several recourses to bring their claims of sexual harassment internally to the attention of management (i.e., appointed counselors, human resources or affirmative action, and managers, even if from another department). Every employee, staff as well as management, needs to understand that sexual harassment is a serious matter and will not be tolerated.

Colleges and universities must also concern themselves with possible cases of sexual harassment of students by employees, supervisors, and faculty. The same types of sexual harassment mentioned earlier can happen to students; therefore, the same kinds of proactive activities are needed in preventing and avoiding claims. Institutions should have in place policies outlining their position on sexual harassment of students and procedures students can follow if they experience it in the workplace or in the classrooms. Vividly stated in the policy should be a statement that each dean and chair is responsible for reporting and/or taking immediate action on becoming aware of the existence of a sexual harassment complaint from a student.

Job Satisfaction

Human resource departments need to be concerned about the job satisfaction of employees. Each employee has individual needs and concerns, and these differences are factors in job satisfaction. In general, areas that management might focus on include:

- problems the employee deals with (the mixture of assignments and challenges);

- policies (the institution's policies, practices, and procedures that enable employees to accomplish their tasks);

- people (the importance of interpersonal relationships); and

- place (the culture and climate of the organization).

Management should be encouraged to recognize and reward individual needs and achievements.

EMPLOYEE RELATIONS

Employee relations refers to the relationship between an institutional administration and the employees of the institution, whether or not they are unionized. Unionization requires more formal relationships and procedures, but many of the same good employee relations practices are applicable, whether employees are organized or not.

The relationship between employees and their supervisors greatly affects employee morale and performance and thus the operation of an institution. Personnel policies, procedures, and programs must be communicated clearly and concisely. In the development of policy, it may be advantageous for the administration to establish advisory committees of administrators, clerical and technical staff, and faculty to allow representatives from each unit to contribute to policy formation. Decision-making processes need to be continually evaluated to ensure appropriate involvement by those who have an interest in the outcome of decisions. If there is no collective bargaining agreement for a particular category of employee, it may be wise to have a grievance procedure involving the human resource department and representatives of the employee group. An advisory group composed of representatives from the employee group may also be advisable.

Communication up, down, and across employee echelons is critically important in maintaining good employee relations. Most supervisors can benefit from training in communication skills, which include listening well, understanding others' concerns, and acknowledging messages, regardless of how or from whom conveyed. Employees need to feel that they can communicate freely with all levels of management and have their concerns understood and, if possible, addressed. Although an effective supervisor might be expected to express ideas well, handle conflicts forthrightly and fairly, and demonstrate exemplary personal integrity, the role often calls for even more subtle virtues: openness, sensitivity, flexibility, empathy, and courage. These, too, are communication skills, and when employees hear the message they convey, they are unlikely to take adversary postures toward the institution itself.

Employee Handbooks

Each institution must decide whether it needs or wants to develop an employee handbook. If so, provisions must be tailored to the institution's individual characteristics, such as size, public versus private, secular versus religious, unionized versus nonunionized, industrial, professional, or service oriented. For example, certain rights and privileges may be available under state law to public employees that are not applicable to employees in independent institutions (disability and pension funds, civil service laws, etc.). The following guidelines, however, are relevant to most institutions.

- Avoid making contractual obligations. An attorney should evaluate language for any terms or phrases that could give rise to enforceable contract rights that the institution may not intend to make. The handbook should also contain clear and conspicuous contract disclaimer language.

- Use clear and concise language. The provisions should be expressed so as to clearly and accurately describe the institution's practices and personnel policies and avoid interpretations the institution does not intend. Benefits should be explained in broad terms only.

- Expressly allow for flexibility and modification.

- It is neither possible nor practical to address in a handbook every policy or employment situation that could arise. Institutions should specifically state that the handbook as a whole is not all inclusive and contains only general statements of policies, and that any or all provisions may be modified at the employer's discretion in accordance with applicable law. Moreover, certain individual provisions (for example, discipline rules) should also specifically retain management flexibility.

Disclaimers

Every employee handbook, policy manual, or any written materials distributed to employees should contain a clear, prominently displayed and unmistakable "disclaimer" of any promise of job security. Courts in several states have specifically ruled that such disclaimers may be used as an absolute defense against breach of contract actions. A disclaimer is most likely to be held effective when it appears in a formal written employment document.

Review of Handbook

Handbooks should be reviewed periodically, updated when necessary, and distributed to all employees upon revision. Any promises or guarantees in a handbook should be eliminated unless the institution is prepared to be bound to its promises and guarantees.[55]

Performance Appraisal

When carefully conceived and implemented, performance appraisal can be a key to higher productivity and overall organizational effectiveness. With up to 70 percent of an institution's budget typically allocated to human resources, maintaining and developing the job performance and productivity of those resources should be of central importance to human resources management. Virtually all human resource functions, and arguably the process of management itself, are based to some degree in the appraisal process. Every institution goes through a process of identifying, measuring, communicating, and using performance-related information, either implicitly or explicitly.

By using performance appraisal, an institution can obtain:

- evaluative information, using information from an individual's past performance as the basis for various personnel actions; and

- developmental information, using information generated by performance appraisals to help the individual prepare for improved levels of job performance and/or the demands of future positions.

Colleges and universities differ greatly in the ways they use information generated through the performance appraisal process. Some only use performance appraisal for one or two purposes, such as to support compensation or internal staffing decisions. Others use performance appraisal for purposes such as skills training, compensation, productivity, and separation programs. Regardless of how the appraisal process is used, any performance appraisal program should accomplish the following objectives:

- identify critical job elements, expectations, and performance goals;

- establish agreement on the job's objectives and the criteria that will be used for evaluation;

- provide feedback on job performance, strengths, and weaknesses;

- identify means for improving performance;

- identify realistic job and career opportunities; and

- provide valid information for personnel decisions that will affect the employee.

The information generated by the appraisal process is equally important from the individual employee's point of view. Feedback generated within the appraisal process can provide the employee with critical information, which, in turn, can help the individual make decisions about his or her future.

Discipline and Dismissal

Employees should be counseled when their performance is unsatisfactory. They should be informed of precisely what is expected of them, both in regard to the quality of their work and basic institutional policies.

Employers should keep written records of employee absences, errors, disciplinary problems, or any other information that may be necessary to justify the disciplining and dismissal of an employee. The employer should share such documentation with the employee periodically, in accordance with institutional policies on discipline and dismissal, before a final discharge action is taken. Such documentation is essential to the employer in case a dismissal is challenged.

Mediation

Mediation is a form of Alternative Dispute Resolution (ADR) that is offered by the U.S. Equal Employment Opportunity Commission as an alternative to the traditional investigative or litigation process for allegations of EEOC violations. Mediation is an informal process in which a neutral third party helps the opposing parties reach a voluntary, negotiated resolution of a charge of discrimination.[56] The decision to mediate is completely voluntary for the charging party and the employer. Mediation gives the parties the opportunity to discuss the issues raised in the charge, clear up misunderstandings, determine the underlying interests or concerns, find areas of agreement and, ultimately, incorporate those areas of agreement into solutions. A mediator does not resolve the charge or impose a decision on the parties. Instead, the mediator helps the parties to agree on a mutually acceptable resolution. The mediation process is strictly confidential.

The Process

An EEOC representative will contact the charging party and employer concerning their participation in the program. If both parties agree, a mediation session conducted by a trained and experienced mediator is scheduled. While it is not necessary to have an attorney or other representative in order to participate in

EEOC's mediation program, either party may choose to do so. Persons attending the mediation session must have the authority to resolve the dispute. If mediation is unsuccessful, the charge is investigated like any other charge. Information disclosed during mediation will not be revealed to anyone—including other EEOC employees.

Retaliation

Like most other major federal labor laws, Title VII contains a prohibition against retaliation. Title VII protects individuals who file a charge or participate in an EEOC investigation. Therefore, institutions may not retaliate in any way against any individual who has filed a discrimination complaint.

Labor Relations

Labor relations differs from traditional relationships of "employee relations" by the intercession of an outside entity and process. This entity (unions) and process (collective bargaining and contract administration) alter the traditional purview of management rights and adds a bureaucracy to management direction and controls.

Employees have been organized in academic organizations since the late 1930s with the vast majority being in the public sector at four-year institutions. The landmark court case of *NLRB* v. *Yeshiva* University in 1980 has seriously limited union growth in independent institutions. At issue in the Yeshiva case was the question of whether the shared joint-governance process between the university and faculty in matters such as hiring, tenure and promotion, and so forth, was to the level that they would be classified as managerial employees. If this were so, no coverage of NLRA (National Labor Relations Act) existed for the faculty. The National Labor Relations Board (NLRB) ruled this was not the case, however the U.S. Appeals Court, Second Circuit and ultimately the U.S. Supreme Court (5–4) disagreed with the NLRB. Unionization of faculty has not been a major factor in independent and religious institutions since the Yeshiva decision; however, there have been challenges leading to four NLRB rulings granting bargaining rights. The most recent case involved a 1999 decision by a regional NLRB office that faculty members at Manhattan College have the right to bargain collectively.[57] The office determined that professors at the college were employees, not managers. The decision is under appeal.

By 1995, approximately 40 percent of full-time faculty in American higher education, primarily but not exclusively in the public sector, were represented by labor unions for the purposes of collective bargaining. It is estimated that upwards of 60–70 percent of labor, clerical, engineering, technical, and related nonfaculty personnel are unionized in the United States.

While unionization in higher education is not growing, the possibility always exists at nonunionized institutions. The following good business principles that leaders in higher education should exemplify in managing their workforce also tend to discourage unionization[58]:

- trust and openness;

- union-free policy;

- effective first-line supervisors;

- effective communication;

- effective human resource planning, recruitment and selection;

- employee development programs;

- effective compensation programs;

- effective employee and labor relations;

- effective human resource research;

- a healthy and safe work environment;

- employee involvement and participation in working conditions (to the extent permitted by law and circumstances); and

- job security.

The magnitude of importance of any unionization attempt is certainly such that an anti-organizing campaign cannot be undertaken without legal counsel. A general sequential scenario is as follows[59]:

- early signs of union activities:
  - employees speaking in groups,
  - employees question authority,
  - employee complaints increase,
  - employees become argumentative,
  - employee new leaders appear,
  - employee discussions of benefits, and
  - employee union terminology appears; such terms as seniority, grievance, bumping, security and job postings appear in the vocabulary;

- union authorization cards:
  - only 30 percent of employees need to sign cards in order for the union to petition for an election;

- union organizing techniques:
  - electronic media (television, radio, etc.) broadcast the union message,
  - "Union Yes" campaigns,
  - organizing committees within the organization (unions know they cannot effectively organize from the outside—they must do it from the inside),
  - community campaigns,
  - joint organizing by two or more unions,
  - messages directed at minorities and women;

- solicitation and distribution of union materials:
  - employee meetings,
  - distribution of advertising materials, handbills;

- unfair labor practice claims:
  - claims of management promises,
  - claims of management threats,
  - claims of management discrimination,
  - claims of management unwarranted discipline,
  - claims of management surveillance of employees, and
  - claims of management improper questioning of employees.

Once organized, ongoing relationships revolve around contract administration, conflict resolution, and periodic renegotiations. A history of collegial joint-governance in faculty matters and no strike arrangements (especially in public institutions) assist in ameliorating adversarial relationships.

The Bargaining Unit

When the union has gathered sufficient signatures to petition for an election, the NLRB will identify the bargaining unit, the group of employees that will be represented by the union. The bargaining unit must be truly representative and contain a mix of the legitimate interests of the group.

To ensure the fullest freedom of collective bargaining, legal constraints and guidelines constrain which groups can be included in bargaining units. Professional and nonprofessional groups cannot be included in the same unit, and a craft unit cannot be placed in a larger unit unless both units agree to it. Physical location, skill levels, degree of ownership, collective bargaining history, and extent of organization of employees are also considered.

From the union's perspective, the most desirable bargaining unit is one whose members are prounion and will help win certification. The unit also must have sufficient influence in the organization to give the union some power once it wins representation. Institutions generally want a bargaining unit that is least beneficial to the union; this maximizes the likelihood of failure in the election and minimizes the power of the unit.[60]

Mandatory Issues

Those issues that are identified specifically by labor laws or court decisions as being subject to bargaining are mandatory issues. If either party demands that issues in this category be bargained over, then bargaining must occur. Generally, mandatory issues relate to wages, benefits, nature of jobs, and other work-related subjects.

Virtually all labor contracts include management rights, which are those rights reserved to the institution to manage, direct, and control its business. By including such a provision, management is attempting to preserve its unilateral right to decide or make changes in any areas not identified in a labor contract. As would be expected, management representatives want to have as many issues defined as management rights as they can.[61]

Union Security Agreements

When a labor organization is certified by the NLRB as the exclusive bargaining representative of all employees in a bargaining unit, by law it must represent all employees in the unit, nonunion and union members alike. A standard union security provision is dues checkoff, which gives the employer the responsibility of withholding union dues from the paychecks of union members.

Other common forms of union security found in labor agreement include the following:

- The *closed shop* states that employers will hire only union members. The closed shop is generally illegal in the United States.

- The *union shop* provides that any employee not a union member upon employment must join the union within thirty days or be terminated.

- The *agency shop* provides for voluntary membership. However, all bargaining unit members must pay union dues and fees.

- The *maintenance-of-membership shop* requires that employees who voluntarily join a union must maintain membership during the life of the agreement. Membership withdrawal is possible during a designated escape period.

- The *open shop* allows employees to join the union or not. Nonmembers do not pay union dues.

Few issues in collective bargaining are more controversial than the negotiation of these agreements. The most popular union security clause, the union shop, is illegal in 21 states having right-to-work laws. Right-to-work laws ban any form of compulsory union membership.[62]

Preparation

Employer and industry data concerning wages, benefits, working conditions, management and union rights, productivity, and absenteeism are gathered. Once the data are analyzed, each side identifies what its priorities are and what strategies and tactics it will use to obtain what it wants. Each tries to allow itself some flexibility in order to trade off less important demands for more critical ones.

Initial Demands

In colleges and universities, traditional issues such as pay, work hours and conditions, benefits, safety, grievance process, job security and training will be addressed—particularly in the nonfaculty groups. Faculty and other professionals will also strive for governance, respect, teaching/patient loads, productivity assessment, evaluation issues, research/consulting opportunities, equipment and technology needs.

Good Faith

Provisions in federal labor law require that both employer and employee bargaining representatives negotiate in *good faith*. In good faith negotiations, the parties agree to send negotiators who can bargain and make decisions, rather than people who do not have the authority to commit either group to a decision.

Settlement and Contract Agreement

After an initial agreement has been made, the two sides usually return to their respective constituencies to determine if what they have informally agreed on is acceptable. A particularly crucial stage is ratification of the labor agreement by union. Prior to the ratification vote, the union negotiating team explains the agreement to the union members and presents it for a vote. If approval is voted, the agreement is then formalized into a contract. The agreement also contains language on the duration of the contract.

Bargaining Impasse

Regardless of the structure of the bargaining process, labor and management do not always reach agreement on the issues. If an impasse occurs, then the disputes can be taken to conciliation, mediation, or arbitration.

In conciliation or mediation, an outside party attempts to help two dead-locked parties to continue negotiations and arrive at a solution. In *conciliation,* the third party attempts to keep union and management negotiators talking so that they can reach a voluntary settlement but makes no proposals for solutions. In *mediation,* the third party assists the negotiators in their discussions and also suggests settlement proposals. In neither conciliation nor mediation does the third party attempt to impose a solution. The process of *arbitration* is a means of deciding a dispute in which negotiating parties submit the dispute to a third party to make a decision. It can be conducted by either individual or a panel of individuals. Arbitration is used to solve bargaining impasses primarily in the public sector.[63]

Contract Administration

Once signed, the collective agreement becomes "the basic legislation governing the lives of the workers."[64] The daily operation and activities in the institution are subject to the conditions of the agreement. Because of the difficulty of writing an unambiguous agreement anticipating all the situations that will occur over its life, disputes will inevitably occur over the contract's interpretation and application. The most common method of resolving these disputes is a grievance procedure.

Grievance Issues

Grievances can be filed over any issue relating to the workplace subject to the collective agreement, or they can be filed over interpretation and implementation of the agreement itself. The most common type of grievance involves discipline and discharge, although many grievances are filed over other issues.

In resolving these sources of conflict, the grievance procedure should serve three separate groups: the institution and unions, by interpreting and adjusting the agreement as conditions require; the employees, by protecting their contractual rights and providing a channel of appeal; and society at large, by keeping industrial peace and reducing the number of disputes in the courts.

Conflict Resolution

Although the desired outcome of collective bargaining is agreement on the conditions of employment, on many occasions negotiators are unable to reach such an agreement at the bargaining table. In these situations several alternatives are used to break the deadlock. The most dramatic response is the strike or lockout, but third-part interventions such as mediation and arbitration are also common.

Decertification

Employees who have a union and no longer wish to be represented by it can use the election process call decertification. This process is similar to the unionization process. Decertification authorization cards must be signed by at least 30 percent of the employees in the bargaining unit before an election may be called. If a majority of those voting in the election want to remove the union, the decertification effort succeeds.[65]

In about one out of four union campaigns, unions are unable to secure a first contract after winning an election. This is an opportunity for a decertification process to be initiated by employees who no longer feel the need to be represented by the union.

Basically, the same employer/union activities, restrictions and issues concerning unfair labor practices apply to the decertification process as they do to the organizing and recognition process.

Employee Relations Consultants and Labor Attorneys

The complexities of a unionization or decertification campaign are such that few colleges or universities have the expertise to proceed without the assistance of consultants and law firms specializing in union matters or the latest best practices of benefits and human resources management. The uniqueness of faculty, research, or medical-related specialties require a technical knowledge of nationwide trends in negotiation strategies, contract language, and cost forecasting of bargaining options.

NOTES

1. Mark Huselid, "Documenting the HR's Effect on Company Performance," *HR Magazine* 39, 1 (1994): 79–85.

2. Randall S. Schuler and Vandra L. Huber, *Personnel and Human Resource Management* (St. Paul, MN: West Publishing Co., 1993).

3. Haynsworth, Baldwin, Johnson, and Greaves, *Florida Employment Law Manual* (Tallahasee, FL: ACCP, 1999), p. 36.

4. Jerald Greenberg and Robert A. Baron, *Behavior in Organizations* 6th ed. (Upper Saddle River, NJ: Simon & Schuster, 2000), p. 76.

5. Richard C. McCullough, "Professional Development," in *Training and Development Handbook,* Third Edition (NY: McGraw-Hill), p. 37.

6. Robert L. Mathis, and John H. Jackson, *Human Resources—Essential Perspectives.* (Cincinnati, OH: South-Western College, 1999.)

7. *The Human Resources Yearbook, 1997/98* (Englewood Cliffs, NJ: Prentice Hall Publishing, 1997), pp. 14.4–14.7.

8. *INS Handbook for Employers* (1998), pp. 1–2.

9. Austin T. Fragomer, Jr., and Steven C. Bell, *Immigration Employment Compliance Handbook* (St. Paul, MN: West Group, 1998), pp. 1–42.

10. A. Sherman, G. Bohlander, and S. Snell, *Managing Human Resources* (Cincinnati, Ohio: South-Western College Publishing, 1996) p. 127.

11. Schuler & Huber, *Personnel and Human Resource Management.*

12. Ibid.

13. National Association of College and University Business Officers, "Intermediate Sanctions Regulations Proposed," *NACUBO Special Action Report, 98-3,* September 30 (1998).

14. James J. McGovern, "Exempt Organizations Update: What's Hot in Washington," *KPMG Washington National Tax,* (1998).

15. Ibid.

16. Ibid.

17. *The 1998 Executive File: Hot Employment Issues* (Brentwood, TN: Lee Smith Publishers LLC), p. 9.

18. R. Heneman, *Merit Pay* (Reading, MA: Addison-Wesley, 1992).

19. T.P. Flannery, D.A. Hofrichter, and P.E. Platten, *People, Performance, & Pay* (New York: The Free Press, 1996).

20. Sherman et al.

21. Spencer's Research Reports, "Internal Revenue Section 125, Flexible Benefits Programs," (1997).

22. Ibid.

23. Sherman et al.

24. Schuler and Huber.

25. Sherman et al.

26. Ibid.

27. Schuler and Huber, "Hay Guide Chart—Profile Used for Management Positions" (1993).

28. Business & Legal Reports, Inc., "Happy Holidays—Paid Time Off," *The HR Professional* #31503010 (1999), p. 5.

29. *Human Rights Campaign,* Colleges & Universities That Offer Domestic Partner Health Benefits, August 5 (1999), http://www.hrc.org/issues/workplac/dp/coll.html.

30 Flannery et al.

31. Jonathan Clements, "Getting Going—Playing the Right Retirement Cards," *The Wall Street Journal* Tuesday, November 16 (1999), p. C1.

32. Jay Chronister, and T.O. Collier, Jr., *Supervisor's Guide to Labor Relations,* (Society for Human Resource Management, 1998).

33. Sherman et al.

34. Spencer's Research Reports.

35. Ibid.

36. Price Waterhouse Coopers, "2000 Cost-of-Living Adjustments," *GHRS Insight* 99/5–October 20 (1999).

37. Spencer's Research Reports.

38. Ibid.

39. BNA's Human Resources Library. [computer software]. Selected Labor Regulations: 29 U.S.C. 206d; 42 U.S.C. 2000e and P.L. 104-1; 41 C.F.R. 60-1 and 2; 29 U.S. 621 and P.L. 104-208; 20 U.S. Chapter 38; Section 1681-1688; ADA 424 SC 12101 and P.L. 104-1; P.L. 102-166 and P.L. 104-331; P.L. 103-3 and P.L. 104-1; 41 C.F.R. 60-250; 41 C.F.R. 60-741; P.L. 95-555; 42 U.S.C. 2000d and P.L. 103-38; and 29 C.F.R. 1604. Provo, UT: Folio Bound VIEWS, Version 3.11.4 (Bureau of National Affairs Resource Library, 1996–1998 & 1999).

40. Gilbert J. Ginsburg, Daniel B. Abrahams, and Sandra J. Boyd, *Fair Labor Standards Handbook* (Washington, DC: Thompson, 1997).

41. Wayne F. Cascio, *Managing Human Resources Productivity, Quality of Work Life, People* (New York, NY: McGraw Hill, 1998).

42. Donald S. Skupsky, *Record Keeping Requirements* (Denver, CO: Information Requirements Clearing House, 1991).

43. T.R. Mitchell, "Motivation: New Directions for Theory, Research, and Practice," *Academy of Management Review* 7 (1982), p. 81.

44. Sherman et al.

45. Ibid.

46. Cascio.

47. Jackson and Schuler.

48. Sherman et al.

49. University of Miami (1999). **Is this the Hagan reference? If not, what?**

50. Roger B. Jacobs, and Cora S. Koch, *Legal Compliance Guide to Personnel Management* (Englewood Cliffs, NJ: Prentice Hall, 1993).

51. R. Roosevelt Thomas, Jr., *Beyond Race and Gender: Unleashing the Power of Your Total Work Force by Managing Diversity* (New York: AMAOM, 1992).

52. Mike Deblieux, *Legal Issues for Managers* (West Des Moines, IA: American Media, 1997).

53. D. Ulrich, M.R. Losey, and G. Lake, *Tomorrow's HR Management* (New York: John Wiley & Sons, 1997).

54. Sherman et al.

55. Seyfarth, Shaw, Fairweather, and Geraldson, *Federal Employment Law and Regulations* (Chicago, IL: HR Comply Co., 1999).

56. U.S. Equal Employment Opportunity Commission, *Get the Facts Series: Mediation* (Miami, FL, 1999).

57. *Chronicle of Higher Education* (1999).

58. Wayne R. Mondy, and Robert M. Noe, *Human Resource Management* (Upper Saddle River, NJ: Prentice Hall, Inc., 1996).

59. Chronister and Collier. **is this right?**

60. Jackson and Schuler.

61. Mathis and Jackson.

62. Sherman et al.

63. Mathis and Jackson.

64. Schuler and Huber.

65. Mathis and Jackson.

REFERENCES AND RESOURCES

Publications and Articles

"*AFL-CIO Organizes on the Web,*" USA Today. October 11, 1999.

A World of Difference Institute. *A World of Difference: Train the Trainers Manual.* New York: Anti-Defamation League, 1996.

Americans United for Affirmative Action. [Online communication]. 1997. *Affirmative Action News, The Legislative Branch.* Atlanta, Georgia: http://www.auaa.org/news/legis.html, 1997.

Bassett, Lawrence C. *Reinventing the Management Wheel.* Internet at http://www.bassettgroup.com/articles/reinventing.htm

BNA's Human Resources Library. [computer software]. Selected Labor Regulations: 29 U.S.C. 206d; 42 U.S.C. 2000e and P.L. 104-1; 41 C.F.R. 60-1 and 2; 29 U.S. 621 and P.L. 104-208; 20 U.S. Chapter 38; Section 1681-1688; ADA 424 SC 12101 and P.L. 104-1; P.L. 102-166 and P.L. 104-331; P.L. 103-3 and P.L. 104-1; 41 C.F.R. 60-250; 41 C.F.R. 60-741; P.L. 95-555; 42 U.S.C. 2000d and P.L. 103-38; and 29 C.F.R. 1604. Provo, UT: Folio Bound VIEWS, Version 3.11.4, 1996–1998 & 1999.

Cascio, Wayne F. *Managing Human Resources Productivity, Quality of Work Life, People.* McGraw Hill, New York, NY, 1998.

Chronister, Jay, and Collier, T.O., Jr. *Supervisor's Guide to Labor Relations.* Society for Human Resource Management, 1998.

Craig, Robert L. *Training and Development Handbook,* Third Edition, McGraw-Hill Book Company, New York, NY, 1987.

Cummings, Thomas G., and Worley, Christopher. *Organizational Development and Change,* Sixth Edition, South-Western College Publishing, Cincinnati, OH, 1997.

Deblieux, Mike. *Legal Issues for Managers.* American Media, West Des Moines, IA, 1997. Drug Free Workplace section.

Deci, E.L., and Ryan, R.M. *Intrinsic Motivation and Self-Determination in Human Behavior.* New York: Plenum Press, 1985.

DeSimone, R.L., and Harris, D.M. *Human Resource Development.* (2nd ed.). Orlando, Florida: The Dryden Press, 1998).

E.A. Winning Associates. "Downsizing Continues: Is the Solution a 32-Hour Workweek?" Internet at http://www.ewin.com/articles/downs.htm

Financial Accounting Standard Board. "Statement of Financial Accounting

Standards No. 43: Accounting for Compensated Absences." December 1980.

Flannery, T.P., Hofrichter, D.A., and Platten, P.E. *People, Performance, & Pay.* The Hay Group. New York: The Free Press, 1996.

Fragomer, Austin T., Jr., and Bell, Steven C. *Immigration Employment Compliance Handbook.* West Group, St. Paul, MN, 1998.

Ginsburg, Gilbert J., Abrahams, Daniel B., and Boyd, Sandra J. *Fair Labor Standards Handbook.* Thompson, Washington D.C., 1997 (1997).

Greenberg, J., and Baron, R.A. *Behavior in Organizations.* (6th ed.). Upper Saddle River, N.J.: Simon & Schuster, 2000.

Hagan, Christine M. "Employee Top Out." Interview. University of Miami School of Business Administration. November 1999.

Heneman, R. *Merit Pay.* Reading, MA:Addison-Wesley, 1992.

Herman, Roger E. *Keeping Good People Strategies for Solving the Dilemma of the Decade.* Oakhill Press, Summerfield, NC, 1997.

Hirschman, Carolyn. "Concerns Dog Cash Balance Conversions." *HR News.* Vol. 18, No. 11, November, 1999.

How to Discipline. Business and Legal Reports. Madison, CT, 1997

Human Rights Campaign, Colleges & Universities That Offer Domestic Partner Health Benefits. August 5, 1999. http://www.hrc.org/issues/workplac/dp/coll.html

Huselid, Mark. "Documenting the HR's Effect on Company Performance," *HR Magazine,* 1994, *39,*no.1, 79–85.

Jackson, Susan E., and Schuler, Randall S. *Managing Human Resources: A Partnership Perspective.* (7th ed.) Cincinnati, Ohio: South-Western College Publishing, 2000.

Jacobs, Roger B., and Koch, Cora S. *Legal Compliance Guide to Personnel Management.* Prentice Hall, Englewood Cliffs, NJ, 1993.

Jette, Richard D., and Wertheim, Edward G. "Performance Appraisal", Human Resources Management Handbook, Second Edition, AMACOM, New York, NY, 1994.

Julius, Daniel. *The Current Status of Graduate Student Unions and a Prognosis for the Future.* Written for Proceedings, Twenty-eighth Annual Conference, National Center for the Study of Collective Bargaining in Higher Education. Bernard M. Baruch College, City University of New York, NY, 2000.

Kaufman, Bruce E. "Evolution and Current Status of University HR Programs." *Human Resource Management,* Summer 1999, *38,* no.2, John Wiley & Sons, Pp. 103–110.

Kelley, Kronenberg, Kelly, Gilmartin, and Fitchel, P.A. *Employment Notes: Federal Record Keeping Requirements.* Miami, Florida, 1995.

Kohn, Alfie. *Punished by Rewards: The Trouble With Gold Stars, Incentive Plans, A's, Praise, and Other Bribes.* New York: Houghton Mifflin, 1993.

Lawyers' Committee for Civil Rights Under Law. *An Affirmative Action Resource Kit.* Washington, D.C. 1996.

Losey, Michael R. "Human Capital: A Guide for the New Millennium." *HR Director: The Arthur Andersen Guide to Human Capital.* New York: Arthur Andersen, 1998/1999 Edition, p.10.

Mathis, Robert L., and Jackson, John H. *Human Resources—Essential Perspectives.* South-Western College, Cincinnati, OH, 1999.

McGovern, James J. "Exempt Organizations Update: What's Hot in Washington." *KPMG Washington National Tax,* 1998.

Milkovich, George T., and Boureau, John W. *Human Resource Management.* Irwin Publishing, Chicago, IL, 1997.

Mitchell, T.R. "Motivation: New Directions for Theory, Research, and Practice. *Academy of Management Review, 7,* 1982, p. 81

Mondy, Wayne R., and Noe, Robert M. *Human Resource Management.* Prentice Hall, Inc., Upper Saddle River, NJ, 1996.

National Association of College and University Business Officers. "Intermediate Sanctions Regulations Proposed." *NACUBO Special Action Report, 98-3,* September 30, 1998.

Potter, Beverly. *Overcoming Job Burnout: How to Renew Enthusiasm for Work,* Ronin Publishing, 1998.

Quinn, Jane B. "A Generation Topped Out." *Newsweek,* September 20, 1993.

Schuler, Randall S., and Huber, Vandra L. Personnel and Human Resource Management. West Publishing Co., St. Paul, MN, 1993).

Seyfarth, Shaw, Fairweather, and Geraldson. *Federal Employment Law and Regulations.* HR Comply Co., Chicago, IL, 1999.

Sherman, A., Bohlander, G., and Snell, S. *Managing Human Resources.* Cincinnati, Ohio: South-Western College Publishing, 1996.

Shuler, R.S., and Huber, V.L. *Personnel and Human Resource Management.* (5th ed.). New York: West Publishing, 1993.

Skupsky, Donald S. *Record Keeping Requirements.* Information Requirements Clearing House, Denver, Co, 1991.

Smith, Adam. *The Wealth of Nations.* Internet at www.bibliomania.com/NonFiction/Smith/Wealth/index.html

Spencer's Research Reports. Internal Revenue Section 125, Flexible Benefits Programs, 1997.

Steptoe and Johnson. "Employee Appraisal Systems: Why They Often Fail and How They Can Succeed." *Executive File.* Brentwood, TN: M.Lee Smith Publishers, 1997, p.9.

Thomas, R. Roosevelt, Jr. *Beyond Race and Gender: Unleashing the Power of Your Total Work Force by Managing Diversity.* New York: AMAOM, 1992.

Tracey, William R. *Human Resources Management and Development Handbook, Second Edition,* AMACOM, New York, NY, 1994.

U.S. Equal Employment Opportunity Commission. *Get the Facts Series: Mediation.* Miami, Florida, 1999.

Ulrich, D., Losey, M.R., and Lake, G. *Tomorrow's HR Management.* New York: John Wiley & Sons, 1997.

Vikesland, Gary. *Preventing and Curing Employee Burnout.* http://www.employer-employee.com.

Workplace Visions, #6. Society for Human Resource Management, Alexandria, VA, 1999.

Journals

Academe

Business Officer

CUPA Journal

EEOC Compliance Manual

ERISA Bulletin

Employment Practices Guide

Fair Employment Practices

Labor Relations Reporter

Organizations

College and University Personnel Association (CUPA)
1233 20th Street, NW, Suite 301, Washington, DC 20036-1250
202-429-0311 . . . . www.cupahr.org

National Association of College and University Business Officers (NACUBO)
2501 M Street, NW, Suite 400, Washington, DC 20037-1308
202-861-2500 . . . . www.nacubo.org

National Center for the Study of Collective Bargaining in Higher Education and the Professions
Baruch College, City University of New York, 17 Lexington Avenue, Box 322, New York, NY 10010, 212-802-6751

Chapter 13

Facilities Management

by

Harvey H. Kaiser
Harvey H. Kaiser Associates, Inc.

Eva Klein
Eva Klein & Associates, Ltd.

Sponsors

SIEMENS BUILDING TECHNOLOGIES, INC.
Contact: Sylvia Rainey
1000 Deerfield Parkway
Buffalo Grove, IL 60089-4547
847-215-1050 ext. 5586
www.sbt.siemens.com/SmartU

Siemens Building Technologies is a world leader providing cost effective, facility performance solutions for the comfort, life safety, security, and energy efficiency of your campus. We also provide training and management leadership to maximize operations while increasing staff productivity.

ADAMS CONSULTING GROUP
Contact: Matt Adams
1097 Lynmorr Drive, N.E., Suite 2104
Atlanta, GA 30319-4124
404-636-5531
www.adams-grp.com

Adams Consulting Group is a management consulting firm that provides the technical services required to effectively outsource virtually any service function or department. We determine the feasibility of outsourcing any service function and provide a detailed cost benefit analysis.

JOHNSON CONTROLS, INC.
Contact: Michelle Tanem
507 East Michigan Street
Milwaukee, WI 53201
414-524-5574
www.johnsoncontrols.com/cg

Johnson Controls is a world leader in creating safe, comfortable, attractive, and productive learning environments while reducing operating costs.

JONES LANG LASALLE

Contact: Herman Bulls
1401 Eye Street, N.W., Suite 800
Washington, DC 20005
202-222-1510
www.am.joneslanglasalle.com

Jones Lang LaSalle provides comprehensive real estate services and investment management to clients worldwide. Our public institutions professionals meet the unique needs of higher education clients.

Contents

T he management of a college or university's facilities—buildings, grounds, utilities, and equipment—involves significant physical, financial, and human resources; a large portion of the institution's total assets; and a significant share of its annual operating budget. Traditionally, the business officer supervised the several discrete units responsible for facilities planning and acquisitions, buildings and grounds, utilities, and equipment; now these functions are more often assumed by a comprehensive facilities management entity.

A comprehensive facilities management program centralizes and coordinates the management of all institutional physical resources. The program:

- administers and integrates facilities planning and capital asset acquisition with other institutional planning;

- directs the design and construction activities on behalf of the institution;

- operates and maintains buildings, grounds, and related support services;

- administers space assignments and utilization; and

- manages real estate.

To be effective, facilities managers must be involved in strategic planning, and they need to establish policy that coordinates the organization's short- and long-term activities with the institution's overall academic, financial, and human resource goals and implementation procedures. Facilities management must operate under clearly delineated policies and procedures for its organizational responsibilities and functional activities. These responsibilities and activities, in turn, should be monitored for necessary adjustment to changes in the institution's mission and resources.

The condition of institutional facilities reflects the vitality, leadership, and interest of the academic community in providing quality education. Recruitment and retention of faculty, students, and staff are strongly influenced by adequate and attractive facilities. Deteriorating and/or inadequate facilities deter achievement of institutional mission. In *A Foundation to Uphold: A Study of Facilities Condition in U.S. Colleges and Universities*[1], a comprehensive national survey (1995) reported an estimated $26 billion in estimated accumulated deferred maintenance, of which $5.7 billion was urgent needs. Approximately 4 billion gross square feet of space showed the effects of age, neglect, and modernization needs for more than 80 percent of total campus space built before 1980.

In addition to funding new construction and modernization, it is necessary to ensure that plant operations and maintenance are adequately funded to avoid deferred maintenance, which can jeopardize the long-term financial stability of the institution. Communicating capital renewal needs, including deferred maintenance, to senior administrators, faculty, students, alumni, governing boards, and legislators is a key responsibility of the facilities management organization.

This chapter presents the concept of facilities as capital assets and discusses the components of comprehensive facilities management, as well as its organizational and administrative aspects. The basic principles discussed can be applied to all institutions, although their functional organization and means of delivery may differ, based on the size of the institution.

FACILITIES AS A CAPITAL ASSET

Optimizing the capital assets of colleges and universities provides the context for comprehensive facilities management. "Capital asset" usually means invested capital in buildings or other facilities that have been purchased, modified, operated, and maintained by the institution. Maintaining this investment demands integrated financial and facilities planning for annual operations and for their periodic renewal and replacement. Higher education's practice of inadequately integrating financial and facilities planning is evidenced by problems of capital renewal and deferred maintenance.

The concept of capital assets management expands the scope of facilities management by adding the dimension of financial planning. The business officer must understand the larger concept of capital assets management and its implications for the organizational structure and functional activities of comprehensive facilities management.

Capital Asset Terminology

Several terms are common in facilities management with distinctions between facilities management (which is technical) and capital asset management (which is strategic).

New Construction Versus Repairs

New construction should be distinguished from repairs. New construction typically is defined as capitalized work that includes new facilities and/or major additions. Repairs are routine physical improvements and include planned, preventive, and emergency maintenance. Major repairs, alternatively defined as capital renewal, are usually large in scope and performed less frequently than repairs accomplished during general building and equipment maintenance. As repairs increase in complexity and cost, they may require special funding allocations or they may be deferred until funds are available. A portion of the cost of major repairs may be capitalized as an addition to plant.

Renovation/Modernization/Upgrade

The terms renovation, modernization, and upgrade are interchangeable to describe functional modifications to portions or all of a facility, and they may extend to the partial or complete replacement of building operating systems and components. Renovations that are driven by program change or conversion of use should be coordinated with upgrades for information technology, life safety systems, and deferred maintenance work. Renovations are driven by institutional program change and/or code or regulatory requirements and should be separated in the budget from work intended to extend the useful life of a facility. Although they are essential to support institutional mission, renovations do not necessarily contribute to maintaining and extending the useful life of capital assets. An important principle of capital asset management is that the cost of functional modifications is a basic fiduciary responsibility and differs from the cost of keeping the physical plant in good condition for its expected useful life.

Capital Renewal

Capital renewal is a systematic approach to planning and budgeting for known future cyclic repair and replacement requirements that extend the life and retain the usable condition of campus facilities and systems. Expenditures for capital renewal are not normally contained in the annual operating budget; they are major repairs intended for building systems and components with a life cycle in excess of one year and are satisfied by introducing an annual renewal allowance to be allocated as required. Capital renewal requirements are normally predictable through life-cycle analysis for components such as roofing, heating and cooling systems, and electrical switchgear. Funding for capital renewal can be provided by special allocations from plant funds or an annual renewal allowance included in the operating budget. (See "Integrated Financial and Facilities Management" in this section.)

Deferred Maintenance

Deferred maintenance is defined as maintenance work deferred on a planned or unplanned basis to a future budget cycle, or postponed until funds are available. Simply stated, deferred routine maintenance work and cyclic capital renewal accumulate into a backlog of deferred maintenance that often requires a capital expenditure. Careful definition and a mutual understanding of the concept within the institutional community are necessary to ensure that estimated backlogs are differentiated between (1) capital renewal of a major maintenance nature and (2) routine maintenance work. Deferred maintenance relates to capital expenditures. Backlog is estimated as major maintenance work prioritized in an annual budget request and postponed from the current to a future budget year. Major maintenance identified for future year's capital renewal should not be included in the deferred maintenance backlog. Institutions should avoid significant accumulations of deferred maintenance. The deferred maintenance account should be reviewed and amended each year before the start of the annual budget process. Delays in funding may erode not only the physical fabric of the institution but also its fiscal structure. The postponement of deferred maintenance for temporary financial relief may solve an immediate budget problem, but the longer the required funds are not made available, the higher the costs for remedying the situation as physical conditions worsen over time.

Depreciation Requirements

The Financial Accounting Standards Board's (FASB) Statement of Financial Accounting Standards No. 93, *Recognition of Depreciation by Not-for-Profit Organizations*[2] requires colleges and universities to recognize the cost of using up long-lived assets depreciation in their general-purpose external financial statements.

In supporting its conclusion that depreciation is to be recognized by colleges and universities, FASB developed three theoretical bases that impact financial planning for facilities renewal:

- depreciation is an allocation of cost, and there is a need to match expenses with revenues to produce net income;

- recognition of depreciation is necessary for an organization to obtain an accurate measurement of the reduction of capital (net assets) and to reach the ultimate goal of overall capital maintenance; and

- depreciation is a means, however indirect, of providing for the replacement of assets.

FASB guidelines follow accounting principles that stipulate depreciation accounting, a process of cost allocation and valuation, to better understand and protect the value of capital assets. Depreciation recognition merges the transactions of separate fund groups by relating operating revenues to the depletion of physical plant resources.

Introducing depreciation into current fund operations has had several important benefits. Useful information on resource management is now available to assist in evaluating organizational performance, and institutions now have the opportunity to strengthen asset management by requiring improvements in fixed-asset management, space management, and capital budget systems. The formal integration of financial and facilities management systems that operated independently in the past (perhaps not properly developed or maintained) provides many benefits.

In addition to systems improvements, depreciation has the potential to change the way senior managers perceive their responsibility for protecting the physical plant of the institution. In their role as stewards, facilities managers will want to maintain facilities for optimum current use and to assure the facilities' availability, value, capacity, and potential for future use.

The funding of an annual depreciation charge (or annual renewal allowance) provides an indirect means of asset replacement. An annual renewal allowance in the operating budget provides a predictable funding source for renewal and replacements. The annual depreciation charge can play a useful role in financial planning for capital renewal.

- Depreciation accounting facilitates the projection of depreciation streams over the useful lives of fixed assets and the adjustment of such streams to present-value dollars. This helps determine minimum cash flow requirements for capital maintenance and for some renewal projects. This information can help form the basis for longer-term asset maintenance programs.

- The depreciation technique selected, as well as the determination of a particular asset's useful life, can and should reflect factors such as obsolescence and special usage requirements, which can affect the magnitude of annual depreciation charges. In this regard, depreciation accounting is helpful in the capital budgeting process. This is because it highlights those classes of assets that are more quickly exhausted than others by assigning them a greater annual expense charge.

- Depreciation accounting can provide a constant flow of dollars to meet interest expenses and sometimes the retirement of debt.

- Depreciation schedules can merge funding requirements for renewal and replacement formulas.

Financial and facilities administrators must recognize the FASB depreciation requirements as a component of capital maintenance and renewal. Complete financial planning for capital asset management must incorporate adequate reserves for:

- an annual depreciation charge or renewal allowance for renewal of building systems and components;

- functional improvements to adapt facilities to institutional changes; and

- deferred maintenance incurred by previously inadequate plant renewal funding.

Integrated Financial and Facilities Management

A primary goal of facilities management is the integration of the fiscal requirements of operating and maintaining capital assets with overall institutional budgeting and planning. Facilities management's ultimate goals are to maintain both a balanced budget and acceptable conditions of capital assets. The balance between achieving goals for deferred maintenance operations and acquiring necessary resources depends on the level of integration of financial and facilities management.

Business officers and facilities administrators must have a close working relationship to interpret strategic plans, agree on acceptable levels of funding for regular maintenance, and recommend allocations for plant renewal, replacements, and functional improvements. The business officer must rely on the facilities administrator's assessments of plant conditions and assurances of effective and efficient plant operations. In turn, the facilities administrator requires the business officer's assistance in gaining support for maintenance and plant renewal funding requests.

FASB's depreciation requirements support concepts long espoused in the facilities management field. Growing concern over capital renewal issues and reduced resources have led to planning for renewal and maintenance on the basis of a life-cycle concept. Empirical models that more precisely define annual funding needs for plant renewal have been developed. The process of defining needs has emphasized distinctions between plant renewal, renovations, and deferred maintenance funding requirements and planning processes.

At the heart of a new language that integrates the descriptive terms of facilities administrators and business officers is the "facilities equilibrium" theory of capital asset management. This theory views facilities as a portfolio of assets that must be managed in a clearly defined state of equilibrium. The goal of facilities portfolio management is the maintenance of the functional and financial value of the facilities as may be required by the institution over the long term.[3]

Life-cycle Costing

The core of the life-cycle concept[4] is that the value of a facility does not depreciate uniformly but by the life of its systems and components. Various components or systems, such as roofs, plumbing, electrical, heating/ventilating/air conditioning (HVAC) systems, and equipment, have identifiable useful lives and require replacement after predictable time periods. The replacement costs at the expiration of a life cycle for components and systems approximates the annual reinvestment necessary to maintain the physical plant. The life-cycle method satisfies generally accepted accounting principles for depreciation as a systematic and rational allocation of plant costs over the life of the plant.

Once the life cycles and replacement costs are established for a facility, business officers and facilities administrators have an accurate and effective tool for evaluating future renewal and replacement requirements for the physical plant.[5] Typical annual renewal and replacement funding needs based on life-cycle analysis range from 1.5 to 3.0 percent of current replacement value, adjusted by investments made for remodeling and renovations.

Facilities Audit

With their technical skills and knowledge of the physical plant, facilities administrators can provide information to support financial management requirements for capital asset funding needs. To meet this challenge, facilities administrators need to assess physical conditions and functional adequacy of facilities, current plant replacement values, projections of costs for regular maintenance, major repairs and renovations, and capital renewal and replacements. They also need to measure the changing condition of the physical plant over time in comparison to other institutions.

A tool for evaluating the physical condition and functional adequacy of the physical plant is a facilities audit.[6]

Such an audit is based on a systematic inspection of facilities by component and subsystem, using a standardized method for recording observations. A properly conducted audit can identify building elements that require varying levels of attention—normal maintenance, major repairs, renewal, or replacement. The audit includes an assessment of the adequacy of facilities to support programs and can assist in the identification of renovation needs. In-house staff, consultants, or a combination of the two can perform the audit. The method of approach is based on goals of the audit, available staff time, and resources. Computerized database systems using digitized photographic records and floor plans have proven valuable in performing and maintaining facilities audits.

The outcomes of a facilities audit are a comprehensive listing of the facility deficiencies, a recommendation of projects by priority, and an estimate of the costs necessary to correct each deficiency. An effective audit includes a structured review and assessment of detailed information collected during facility inspections conducted as visual observations, typically, on three-year cycles of all facilities. By sorting and analyzing data for each facility, business officers and facilities administrators can provide decision makers with a comprehensive and clear understanding of overall facility conditions. Governing boards, executive officers, financial and business officers, institutional planning staffs, the development office, and operations and maintenance personnel can use the audit.

Facilities audit information can be used to:

- provide the basis for evaluating deferred maintenance and funding requirements;

- plan a deferred maintenance program;

- compare conditions between facilities and with other institutions;

- establish a facility condition baseline for setting goals and tracking progress;

- develop cost estimates and priorities for capital renewal and replacement projects;

- improve communication of facility conditions to campus constituencies;

- provide accurate and supportable information for budget planning and project justification;

- develop funding analysis and strategies; and

- demonstrate to external groups the institution's ability and commitment to managing an important resource.

Facility Condition Index

A facility condition index (FCI) is a useful tool that measures the relative condition of a single facility or a group of facilities. The FCI is the ratio of the cost of deficiencies to the current replacement value (CRV) of the physical plant.

$$FCI = \frac{Cost\ of\ Deficiencies}{CRV}$$

The cost of deficiencies is the total dollar amount of existing maintenance and repair deficiencies. It does not include scheduled major repairs and renovations, functional improvements, or new construction. An indicator of improvement or deterioration of the physical plant can be determined by annually recalculating the FCI. Suggested condition ratings assigned to FCI ranges are:

FCI range	Condition rating
Under 0.05	Good
0.05–0.10	Fair
Over 0.10	Poor

These are subjective ratings based on observations of comprehensive condition inspections at a large sample of institutions.

The results of a facilities audit should be incorporated into an estimate of short- and long-term capital renewal needs and, if necessary, into a deferred maintenance reduction plan. The FCI provides a guide for policies on overall capital expenditures for the mix of new construction, renovations, and plant renewal.

COMPREHENSIVE FACILITIES MANAGEMENT PROGRAMS

A comprehensive facilities management program is guided by four management plans: (1) a strategic facilities plan; (2) a capital plan; (3) a facilities management plan; and (4) an operations and maintenance plan. Many of the components of the plans are recognizable as traditional tasks conducted in separate departments. The comprehensive nature of a facilities management program draws these tasks together into a centralized organization guided by the plans outlined in figure 13-01.

Strategic Facilities Plan

A strategic facilities plan outlines the use of current capital assets (and how they may be adapted) and future requirements needed to support the institutional mission. The plan provides guidance for policies ensuring that assets are effectively

Figure 13-01

Comprehensive Facilities Management Program

Management Plans	Components
Strategic facilities plan	Campus master plan/physical development policy
	Facilities information database
	Planning assumptions
	Capital improvement plan
Capital plan	Capital planning process
	Capital plan development
	Capital plan review process
Facilities management plan	Goals and objectives
	Organizational structure
	Facilities management components
	Policies and procedures
Operations and maintenance plan	Organizational structure
	Standards and performance criteria
	Maintenance management audit
	Contracted services
	Energy management planning

---

and efficiently utilized and that the most appropriate facilities are available when needed, at an appropriate cost, in the right location, and at the desired time. The four components in a strategic facilities plan are: (1) campus master plan/physical development policy; (2) facilities information database; (3) planning assumptions; and (4) capital improvement plan.

Campus Master Plan/Physical Development Policy

A master plan[7] for campus development is traditionally presented graphically, with physical improvements visualized in various ways. Where there is less perceived need for graphic detail and more need for a planning tool that is integrated with strategic planning, physical development policy statements are favored to guide future campus development. Selection of the appropriate technique depends on campus preferences for consensus building, specific planning needs, resources available for the process, and time for delivery of necessary guidance for specific projects.

At a minimum, a campus master plan should identify the existing and preferred arrangements of institutional land uses, buildings, landscaping and open space features, pedestrian and vehicular circulation systems, campus infrastructure, and the proposed sequence of improvements when these can be determined. It is a regularly updated policy statement with a planning horizon of at least 10 years.

The campus master plan should be informative and concise. Lengthy discourses of planning philosophies and use of jargon are unnecessary and reduce the value of the policy as a reference document. There should be an easily apparent connection between the goals and objectives and each element of the policy statement. For example, institutions that have extensive land holdings or that require expansion space should define a geographical area of interest. This leads to policies of delineating limits to campus lands, with considerations for acquisition or divestiture to create contiguous or consolidated existing holdings.

The physical development policy is integrated with an overall institutional strategic plan that outlines goals and objectives, future land use, building locations and use, traffic circulation and parking, infrastructure, and capital improvements.

The difference between this form of policy guidance and a typical campus master plan is the realism incorporated through oversight by the institution's senior administration and integration with its financial plan, as well as its academic, administrative, auxiliary, enterprises, and human resource plans.

A physical development policy is characterized by consensus building with campus constituencies, including the governing board. Planning criteria are based on the institution's mission, kind and number of students served, faculty and staff employment, existing facilities' conditions and utilization, and resources required for new facilities or modifications to existing facilities.

Although comprehensive physical planning is a challenging task for a new college or university, it is even more so for an established institution, where the plan must contain a pattern for growth that is integrated with the past. Historic preservation, along with campus appearance, has become an increasingly important factor in institutional planning. Plans often must be revised because of changes in educational objectives, teaching techniques, new technologies, regulatory mandates, and funding. Thus, planners must schedule regular reviews and revisions of the facilities plan. The physical development policy may be subdivided into small geographic areas or precincts requiring early and detailed attention because of an immediacy of implementation.

Facilities Information Database

A facilities information database includes three components that provide sources for routine audits and analyses of the effectiveness and efficiency of the use of capital assets and resources.

Space inventory. A space inventory includes all campus space and serves as the main database for evaluating utilization and conditions. A thoroughly prepared and automated space inventory is essential for fiscal control as well as for facilities management. It can be used to assign classes, assist in calculation of overhead recovery, and to program building maintenance. Although campus space inventories may be conducted to conform to the requirements of the Integrated Postsecondary Education Data System (IPEDS), they should be evaluated for the consistency of approach and opportunities for integration into institutional administrative operations.

Space inventories should be supported by documentation of all existing facilities. The inventory should include narrative descriptions of building history, working and as-built drawings, specifications, surveys, property deeds and titles, operating manuals, and maintenance records. The material should be stored in archives for protection. Microfilming of drawings and duplicate copies of print material are advisable. Space inventory systems should use the space taxonomy outlined in the *Postsecondary Higher Education Facilities Inventory and Classification Manual*[8] to provide a statistical basis for inter-institutional comparisons and exchange of information.

A facilities audit. Surveys of building conditions, routine practice on most campuses, may lack the systematic organization necessary to assist in the development of a comprehensive facilities management program. Such a piecemeal evaluation of needs for new construction or renovation does not allow a thorough assessment of alternatives. Facilities audits provide the basis for decisions about allocating resources for new construction, renovations, and deferred maintenance. Audits also support operating budget needs for maintenance and utility expenditures.

Space utilization. Utilization of space in higher education traditionally measures only data and patterns of use for regularly scheduled classrooms and teaching laboratories. Space utilization data can be used in comparative analyses of the efficient use of space and planning new facilities. The data can also be used in feasibility studies of alternative uses of space or in maintenance planning and scheduling. Many states have introduced space utilization standards to evaluate annual budget allocations for operations and maintenance, with adjustments for different institutional missions.

Planning Assumptions

Certain assumptions must be made in strategic facilities planning. Foremost among these are assumptions made from the external environment, including forces likely to affect the institution in future years. (For a fuller discussion of these planning assumptions, see chapter 2, Planning.) Internal assumptions include:

- academic and nonacademic programs;
- student enrollment;
- staffing;
- research activity;
- other special initiatives;
- funding alternatives; and
- financial resources.

Capital Plan

A capital plan provides the details for implementing institutional physical development policies. The plan is a summary of all capital projects and should anticipate needs for a five-to-ten-year period. It should include a priority listing and a description of individual capital projects for major repairs and renovations, new construction, and functional modifications. The plan should be updated annually to incorporate program changes, revisions to institutional planning assumptions, new or revised regulatory mandates, and cost escalation due to inflation.

The capital plan, by incorporating information on possible sources of funding, provides an opportunity for integrated financial planning. The plan also assists cash flow planning by projecting annual expenditures on capital additions and renovations. When projects are organized into categories of funding sources, a note on the potential source, such as plant funds, reserves, gifts, or grants, should be included.

The introduction to the capital plan should describe the priority selection criteria and define terms to improve readability and usefulness as a campuswide reference. Summaries of projects by cost center, project budgets, and schedules make up the core of the plan. Careful attention should be given to individual project descriptions to ensure that they are reliable sources of information. The use of a project description in a capital plan may be the basis for funding and places an obligation on the facilities administrator to provide correct estimates. The estimates included in the plan should encompass contingencies for inflation and other factors.

Project schedules, organized by types of projects and priorities, should include:

- new buildings and major additions (new construction);
- repairs and renovations (over an established cost limit);
- major maintenance (capital renewal and deferred maintenance);
- regulatory mandates (health and safety, environmental quality, and accessibility for the disabled);
- functional improvements to adequately support programs;
- energy conservation improvements;
- infrastructure improvements (utilities, data, telephone, etc.);
- grounds improvement (including roads and parking); and
- acquisition of land and/or commercially offered facilities.

Individual project descriptions can be organized as appendixes to the overall cost center summaries, for instance, academic facilities, residence and dining halls, or the bookstore. They should be concise but provide enough information for decision makers to evaluate priority, costs, and schedules. Each project description should include a program justification statement and a summary of major spaces to be occupied. Cost estimates should outline major components of work, and "soft costs" for fees, equipment, and contingencies. Such soft costs can range from 30 to 40 percent of direct construction costs. These estimates can be provided by the facilities planning department or by consultants. A project schedule should indicate major components. These include feasibility studies; design, development, and preparation of contract documents; competitive bidding (or other approaches such as design-build); and construction periods to completion. The schedule serves as the basis for summarizing annual capital project budget summaries. Methods of recommended project construction delivery may also be included in the description.

Capital Planning Process

A capital plan outlines capitalized expenditures for new construction, major repairs and renovations, and major equipment. The criteria for defining capitalized projects may be provided for public systems of higher education in published standards. Independent institutions may define capitalized projects on the basis of generally accepted accounting principles and internally adopted standards for minimum levels of value and expected life. Although capitalized expenditures are usually budgeted separately from operating expenditures, they should be integrated with the operating budget to determine the impact of facilities on needs for maintenance personnel, material, equipment, and utilities. (For a full discussion of budgeting, see chapter 4, Budgeting.)

The capital plan displays projects and summarizes annual funding and cash flow requirements for a specified period of time. Periods vary from one to five years, depending on a system or institution's budgeting practices. The plan should begin with guidelines for the capital budgeting process and criteria for project priority selection. It should briefly describe projects by name, with costs for each project year from the beginning of planning through final payment. Finally, a total of each year's expenditures should indicate the institution's cash flow requirements, annual capital needs, and cash management strategies. Projects should have footnotes or be listed by funding source to show the method of funding and financing.

The capital plan, which incorporates programmatic needs, capital renewal, structural improvements, and major deficiencies of existing facilities, is the principal source for the institution's strategic financial plan. It is essential that the total costs of new or expanded programs reflect any required capital expenditure; it is equally important to anticipate major building repairs, functional improvements, and equipment replacement for continuing programs.

The capital plan also draws on the program plans and operating budget requests from academic, administrative, and auxiliary departments. Data collection forms should be developed to solicit the departments' capital expenditure requirements. These forms could include program goals, completion and occupancy goals, estimated costs, priority ranking, projected operating costs, suggested funding sources, and cost-benefit analysis, when appropriate. From these data, the final capital budget can be compiled for presentation to the governing board for approval.

Priority criteria are critical in capital planning. Two concepts influencing final priority decisions affecting capital projects are need and risk. Each project must be assessed to balance the risks entailed in life safety or protection of capital assets with less tangible criteria. For example, do projects that improve the quality of the environment come before life safety or operating economy projects? Principles that guide the priority selection process include the following.

- Major repairs and renovations in the annual operations and maintenance budget should be reserved only for projects that offset facility deterioration and extend the life of plant assets.

- Functional program improvements should be funded separately from major repairs and renovations. Cost-effectiveness may combine system or component renewals with program-driven functional improvements to be done at the same time.

- Capital renewal and deferred maintenance should be funded as special appropriations on a project-by-project basis.

The capital planning process should begin with a preliminary evaluation that classifies projects by possible funding sources. At this time, self-amortizing projects, typically auxiliary cost centers, are separated and evaluated on their own merits. Capital construction should be defined and set aside from the priority selection process under criteria different from major repairs and renovations and functional improvements. Program scope, complexity, and costs usually define capital construction projects for new structures or major additions. Distinguishing between noncapitalized and capitalized projects eases the task of prioritizing major maintenance and functional program improvements to be funded by the annual operating budget.

Capital Plan Review

Academicians' views on facilities improvements, the personal preferences of senior administrators, the influence of donors, and campus community sentiments come into play in the capital budgeting process. A capital plan review committee to select priorities should include the institution's president and chief academic, financial or business, budget, research, student affairs, and facilities administrators. To minimize the vicissitudes of the capital planning process, the committee should monitor progress on major maintenance and capital renewal and special allocations on a quarterly or semiannual basis. This schedule permits a routine opportunity for emergency budgeting and the introduction of new priorities, and it permits cash flow to adjust to such changes. Reports provided by the facilities administrator should summarize the status of authorized and funded projects and list proposed projects for the next budget year. An additional report summarizing anticipated projects for a rolling five-year period can assist in long-range planning.

The capital plan review committee should meet near the close of each fiscal year to provide the formal approvals to be incorporated into the following year's operating and capital budgets. The president should make recommendations to the governing board concerning priorities and the best methods of implementation. This process should afford a balanced meshing of new construction and additions, major maintenance, functional improvements, and capital renewal. Where deferred maintenance programs have been established, they should be included in the overall institutional fiscal management responsibilities of the committee.

Facilities Management Plan

A facilities management plan describes in broad terms the organizational structure, functions, policies, and procedures of the facilities management organization. The plan should be concise and comprehensive and should briefly outline the facilities management organization, including:

- goals and objectives;
- organizational structure;
- primary responsibilities;
- support services and resources from other departments;
- operating policies and procedures; and
- operating budgets.

Operations and Management Plan

An operations and maintenance plan describes the system for staffing, organization, and procedures for managing facilities maintenance: the processes of budgeting, planning, scheduling, executing, and reporting. Performance measures and cost accounting systems designed for controlling effectiveness and efficiency and optimizing expenditures for labor, material, and equipment should be included in the plan.

Organizational Structure

The organizational structure described in the operations and maintenance plan depends on the size, complexity, location, and number of facilities, and an institution's operations and maintenance practices. The specific nature of the facilities to be maintained, required maintenance skills, levels of utilization, age, and condition of facilities also affect the organizational structure. A critical issue guiding organizational structure is whether operations and maintenance services are to be centralized for all campus facilities in one organization at a single location, decentralized into several locations, or divided among cost centers for separate service units. The use of in-house staff versus contracted services is another major consideration.

Standards and Performance Criteria

Reports on standards and the costs of maintaining and operating facilities and records of maintenance work can be developed as part of building histories and used for performance comparisons. Standards for performance provide senior management with benchmarks to measure the effectiveness and efficiency of plant operations and maintenance and assist in the evaluation of management performance.

Contracted Services (Outsourcing, Partnering, and Alliances)

Outsourcing services is an alternative for provision of services in a cost-effective[9] manner. An institution may contract for management services, for operation of the entire facilities management department, or for special tasks. Contracted services can be a preferable alternative to in-house staff when meeting peak workload demands or providing capital-intensive or highly specialized facilities services. Business officers should be aware of the potential benefits, possible pitfalls, and contracting procedures involved in contract services. A wide range of issues should be considered for an effective program of service contracting. Services to be provided must be clearly defined; potential sources must be researched; the terms and conditions must be written soundly for reliable contract administration, and, above all, the quality of the current level of service must be maintained or enhanced. The ultimate goal is "better, faster, and cheaper." Regardless of how services are provided, ongoing institutional management is essential.

Energy Management Planning

Increasing costs, threats of interruptions of energy and fuel supplies, deregulation of utilities, and vastly increased energy consumption have combined to make energy management a major function of comprehensive facilities management. A complete energy management program has four components: delivering energy reliably and at a minimum cost; achieving energy conservation objectives; integrating the energy management program into the institutional structure; and a compliance plan. The interests of the budget officer, business officer, and facilities administrator must be combined in assigning responsibility for institutional energy management.

Energy management includes considering new construction and renovations, recommending retrofitting existing facilities, establishing standards for monitoring energy consumption, and monitoring for regulatory compliance. These efforts need to be coordinated with building users and the departments involved in managing the use of space and monitoring energy conservation activities.[10]

An energy compliance plan coordinates the activities of facilities management with an environmental, health, and safety unit. The plan identifies applicable environmental and code compliance requirements, and testing, reporting, and emergency procedures. It should also be coordinated with a local disaster plan.

FACILITIES MANAGEMENT ORGANIZATION

Facilities management organizations share similar functional activities, regardless of the size of the institution.[11] Of course there are as many ways of organizing as there are colleges and universities. Facilities at a small institution with little activity in new construction and modest property holdings are typically under the direction of a business officer and a physical plant director. More complex organizational structures are necessary as construction activity increases and the institution must accommodate operations and maintenance of larger property holdings.

An effective facilities management organization develops from a clear definition of the basic functions assigned to the unit. Activities may routinely shift from strategy and policy making to specific tasks involving property management, facilities planning, design and construction, operations and maintenance, and support services. Specific conditions and requirements vary widely among institutions; the facilities management organization that can most effectively support an institution will vary just as widely.

Several factors affect the assignment of responsibilities in the facilities management organization. The traditions and size of an institution dictate the number of levels and distribution of responsibilities. Location and size of facilities—urban, suburban, rural, number of buildings, campus setting—affect the number of operating departments and staff. An institution's traditional arrangement of functions and availability of outsourcing certain functions also influence the facilities management operating structure, which can include:

- strategic facilities planning;

- capital budgeting;
- facilities planning, design, and construction;
- facilities maintenance;
- space management and planning; and
- property management.

These functional activities can be organized by operating components at large and medium-size institutions, as illustrated in figure 13-02. These components accomplish the daily activities of managing property, planning to acquire or

Figure 13-02

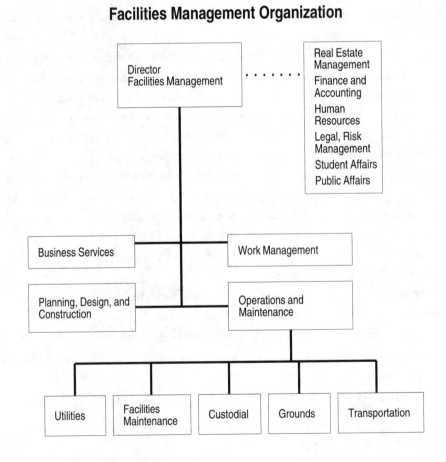

Facilities Management Organization

utilize existing facilities (buildings, grounds, utilities, and equipment), and operating and maintaining physical resources.

Management Control

To be effective, a facilities management program should have a strong management group, which can range in size from a small administrative support unit consisting of a physical plant director and administrative assistant to a collection of departments performing staff functions under the direction of a chief facilities officer. The shape of the organizational structure will depend on whether certain activities are included in the facilities management organization or are provided elsewhere. The management group, headed by the facilities administrator, directs the activities of the functional components.

Business services, for example, can include administrative services, cost accounting and budgeting, human resources, procurement, and management information systems; these may be a part of facilities management, or they may be located in other departments of the institution.

Work management is responsible for work identification, planning, management, coordination, and reporting. The unit performs its major function by the use of work orders. An effective computerized maintenance management system (CMMS) is useful for coordinating and monitoring maintenance activities. Among a work management unit's principal functions are:

- work reception (telephone service calls and written or electronic requests for services);

- planning and estimating;

- maintenance inspection programs;

- work assignment (service calls, preventive maintenance work orders, general work orders);

- priority assignment;

- workload planning;

- maintenance service contracting;

- performance monitoring and evaluation; and

- reporting.

FACILITIES PLANNING, DESIGN, AND CONSTRUCTION

A facilities planning, design, and construction[12] unit is normally included within a facilities management organization for facilities planning and programming for the institution, architectural and engineering planning of new construction, and construction project management. Sometimes, the unit is organized separately from the facilities operations and maintenance services unit, but provides technical assistance.

The size and the necessary staff skills of a facilities planning, design, and construction unit are related to an institutional cycle of capital construction. The levels of real estate activity, program changes, new construction, renovations, interior space planning, and consulting for other institutional departments influence the size and capabilities of in-house staff. In smaller institutions, where resources for developing staff are limited, facilities planning staff may not be appropriate to meet occasional requirements for new construction and renovations. Medium-sized and large institutions that engage in more frequent facilities development activities should develop a facilities planning, design, and construction department as part of a comprehensive facilities management organization.

Regardless of an institution's size, extent of facilities, or stage of development, basic responsibilities of a facilities planning department include:

- advising on institutional strategic facilities planning for capital assets (the group can provide advice on long-range physical development, acquisition or disposal of property, feasibility studies, and selection of consultants);

- programming and designing new construction, renovations, or functional improvements (tasks can be accomplished by in-house staff, outside consultants, or a combination of both);

- supervising construction to ensure quality, schedules, and costs;

- managing space by evaluating current utilization, maintaining a space inventory, and managing assignments;

- consulting within the institution on technical requirements for operations and maintenance, energy management, acquisition of equipment, and facilities-related technologies; and

- controlling costs and managing the development and supervision of information systems for staff operations and project management.

Organization

The facilities planning, design, and construction department is an integral component of the facilities management function. Staff, outside consultants, or a combination of both can accomplish basic responsibilities. A single architect or engineer may meet the planning and design needs of a small or medium-sized institution, serving as an advisor to senior administrators, supervising consultants' design and construction, coordinating space planning, and consulting with other departments. In contrast, large multicampus institutions may require departments at each site that report to a central facilities planning, design, and construction group.

In-house staff should be regularly reviewed to determine if they need training in changing technical standards. Consultants can provide specialized talents and skills that may not be regularly utilized by an institution. The selection of consultants should be based on the specific needs of a project and qualifications of firms. Other institutions that have performed similar projects can be a source for preparing a list of consultants for consideration. Although a disadvantage of hiring consultants is cost, retaining an in-house staff with total planning and design capability may result in false economies over the long term and greater cost, project by project, than use of a consultant. Each institution must make its own evaluation of these options.

Responsibility for reviewing and revising the facilities development plan should be assigned to a facilities planning advisory committee. This committee should include faculty, a governing board representative, members of the administration, staff specialists, and students. It also may include local planning agencies and representatives of surrounding neighborhoods. This may have the additional benefit of enhancing town-gown relations.

Facilities Planning

Facilities planning is a comprehensive process for acquiring space (by construction, purchase, or leasing), modifying existing space, and improving the condition of existing facilities to accommodate changing mission and program requirements. The dynamic nature of academic programs and both internal and external influences on academic and support programs require an integrated approach to coordinate financial and human resources planning with facilities planning.

New construction, renovations, and the buying, selling, or leasing of property should be considered in the context of an overall institutional facilities development policy. The capital plan, in combination with the campus master plan, determines when and where a new facility should be built. The use of a proposed or existing facility, its relationship to the capital plan and to other facilities, and special requirements are issues that must be considered before the facilities administrator begins programming and design. Critical issues that are pertinent to facilities planning include:

- land use;
- enrollment and staffing projections;
- academic, support, research, and service space;
- transportation—vehicular and pedestrian traffic;
- infrastructure—roads, walks, parking, utilities, and services;
- building and site design guidelines;
- historic preservation;
- regulatory standards and codes; and
- campus-community issues.

Capital plans often must be revised because of changes in educational objectives, teaching techniques, and funding. Thus, planners must schedule regular reviews with academic, administrative, student life, and auxiliary units to update and revise the plan. The president or chancellor should periodically review changing conditions and seek approvals from the governing board concerning priorities of construction and renovation projects and the best methods for implementation.

Facility Programming and Design

Facility Program

The design process for any type of construction or renovation work begins with the preparation of a facility program. The facility program defines the scope of a project and includes a project description, budget, space allocation program, and schedule for completion. Initial program development can guide facilities improvements through the design and construction stages.

The programming phase should be guided by the facilities planning department. Facility users should prepare an initial program statement. Early in the process, a decision should be made on whether it is necessary to retain consultants to study alternatives for location, contextual impacts of a building, and special facility requirements. The facility program is a statement of user requirements. In addition to a listing of required spaces and characteristics, the program should include a project justification, a financing plan, an estimate of the impact on operations and maintenance costs, and a schedule.

Descriptions of functional requirements should be obtained and tentative schedules for completing the design and construction phases should be developed. Much information comes from interviews with intended space users; these interviews require thorough preparation and documentation. Institutions may want to use a design and construction standards handbook that outlines administrative and planning information, space standards for typical uses, specification documentation, design and construction requirements, and materials.

Although some institutions work with documents such as notes from planning conferences, such records are seldom as effective as formal program documents. Formal documents help architects and provide guidelines in areas such as the institution's educational philosophy, academic and research programs, planning criteria, and projected growth, developed from institutional planning documents; specific features of the building; and data pertinent to the project gathered from technical information prepared by the facilities planning office.

Pertinent data include special building needs, property and topographic surveys, utility locations, mechanical and electrical system characteristics, test borings, energy conservation measures, safety requirements, and means for accommodating accessibility for the disabled. In addition to these considerations, how the proposed new building will fit into the context of the total environment must be stated.

Defining the project budget is an important component of the programming phase. An institution may prematurely establish a budget for purposes of expediency to launch a project and leave little latitude to satisfy a refined program for required space and equipment and funding delays. To avoid this problem, preparation of a preliminary budget and schedule with adequate total project costs, including all institution's or owner's costs, allowances for inflation, and design and construction contingencies, is needed. This may require a feasibility study. A study of this nature can confirm site alternatives, design concepts, and selection of materials and construction methods, and may more accurately establish budgets and schedules. When engaging consultants for this task, it is advisable to negotiate fees that can later be included in the overall project design fee.

Building Committee

Once a facilities project is approved, a building committee should be appointed to guide project programming and design. The committee, headed by a project director, should be composed of building users, facilities planning personnel, and operations and maintenance staff.

Recommendations from future building users should be submitted to the committee with an accompanying rationale. Some tension between prospective users of a proposed facility and the facilities planning staff responsible for controlling the use of resources should be expected. It should be welcomed as a healthy exchange leading to thorough consideration of the facility's functions and its specific requirements during design development. The operations and maintenance department can provide technical data concerning the site and utilities and, later, evaluations of various structural, electrical, and mechanical systems recommended by designers. It can also provide operating cost estimates for the new facility. It is helpful for members of the committee and the consulting architect, if selected to assist in programming, to visit recently built facilities similar to those planned. Thus, they can avoid unsatisfactory features and incorporate suitable features into the project design.

Project Design Team

A project design team guides the technical development and the design work of a project. The team may comprise one member of the facilities planning staff, an independent architect or engineer, or a team of professionals. Projects with complex equipment or environmental requirements may require a team of skilled specialists to assist the facilities planning staff in designing and preparing construction documents. Large, complex projects may dictate that a professional firm with specific qualifications is commissioned. Cost consultants are useful in establishing or confirming the initial project budgets and providing guidance in budget adjustments, if later plans and designs so dictate. Consideration of staff capabilities for an assignment is necessary to assure that their design skills are appropriate and that the facilities planning department can maintain its responsiveness to other institutional needs as they may occur.

Selection of Designers

An important element in planning for new construction is the selection of project designers (architects and/or engineers). The appearance, usefulness, and cost of a building—including operation and maintenance expenses—are largely a result of the design.

The process of selecting architects and engineers varies among institutions and may be guided by specific requirements defined by the building committee. The building committee should review project requirements and qualifications for desired services and develop a potential list of firms for interviews. Direct selection can follow, although it is preferred that a minimum of three firms be invited to submit qualifications and be interviewed before final selection. Some institutions may include the governing board in the selection process.

Important qualities to look for in selecting a designer are a firm's relevant experience and qualifications, and quality of design work, as well as its ability to work closely with the client and contractors, to design within a budget, and to meet schedules. As with other service providers, it is important to check references. The project manager should also be identified at this time.

Once the designer is chosen, the parties should sign a contract that delineates the assistance that the institution will render, the services that the designer will provide, and the remuneration to be received. A wide variety of contracts are available, including those prepared by architectural and engineering associations. Understandably, these are designed to protect their members' interests and should be thoroughly reviewed by the institution's attorneys. Small institutions may find assistance from states or lending agencies that have developed standard contracts for professional services. Design fees are usually not a consideration in the final selection of firms and are determined in contract negotiations.

Architects and engineers may recommend engaging consultants to solve complicated problems in special-purpose buildings and for specialties such as information technology, acoustics, interior design, food services, and landscape architecture. The designer and institutional representative should interview a potential consultant, state what is desired, and require a memorandum that delineates services to be provided and their cost. The institution—not the designer—should have final approval of consultants added to the design team. If a consultant is approved, the cost of the consultant may be included in the designer's fee or handled by a separate contract with the institution.

Project Manager

Regardless of the design and construction process selected, success or failure (in terms of satisfying functional requirements and meeting goals of design quality, cost, schedule, and economy of operations) depends on effective project management. The facilities planning department provides the leadership for the design team and acts as the authorized institutional representative responsible for approvals. In medium-sized and large institutions, the facilities administrator manages the process in its initial stages with the assistance of a project manager. This task may be completely the responsibility of the facilities administrator in a small institution. Continuity must be established through the design and construction phases to ensure institutional representation to project completion.

With many persons working on the same project, close coordination of their work is important. As the project moves from schematic drawings to final working drawings, the designer, engineers, and consultants must meet frequently with the institution's building committee and facilities planning staff. The project manager acts as the liaison between the building committee, pertinent departments within the institution, consultants, and external agencies involved in project reviews. Architects and engineers need firm decisions from the institution's planners as early as possible to perform expeditiously. The project manager can be especially helpful as a conduit between academic or administrative planners and professional designers.

Approval by the project manager, acting as the authorized representative of the institution, should be required for each phase of the design and construction process. During the review process, the building committee or responsible institutional officer should require that the plans be examined by the operations and maintenance director and other appropriate staff members. A thorough plan review considers local building code compliance, life safety requirements, institutional representative, environmental health issues, parking needs, and future development.

Design Development and Project Cost Estimates

The facilities planning department has a challenging assignment in assuring that development of a design is compatible with the project budget and avoids redesign and/or requests for additional project funding. A budget prepared before programming is complete, or that inadequately defines all project costs, can derail a project and cause bitter disputes among the institution, the funding source, and the designers. A firm statement of the project budget should be provided to the designer, who is responsible for informing the institution of any difficulties in complying with the cost limits and program requirements during design development.

Cost estimates are developed during the design and construction document phases of a project. The initial step in determining project costs occurs in the schematic design phase. At this point, the architect or engineer must become thoroughly familiar with the range of needs the project must meet. At the conclusion of the schematic design phase, the architect or engineer provides cost estimates on the basis of area and volume calculations and outline specifications, rather than on detailed itemized cost-estimating procedures.

The next step in developing project cost estimates is the design development phase, when spaces are drawn and delineated to scale, wall thickness is shown, and size of utilities is indicated. The design development phase should produce floor plans; building elevations; cross sections; statements of types of mechanical, electrical, and structural systems; explanatory sketches of interior spaces; specifications with suggested finished materials; and comprehensive cost estimates. Large projects may benefit from the services of an independent cost consultant.

After institutional review and when approval is obtained for the design development phase, the designer should proceed with the construction document phase. This includes plans, specific details, and other construction information to define the design and method of constructing the entire facility. At the completion of this phase the project designer is responsible for producing a final project cost estimate. This estimate includes the costs of materials, labor, and possible increases for labor and materials through the construction period, as well as profit, overhead, general conditions (expenses for the general contractor and any subcontractors), and various unforeseen contingencies.

The facilities planning department must compile all "soft costs" and add these to the construction cost estimate to confirm that the total estimated project cost will meet the budget. Soft costs include design fees, property transfer fees, land surveys, bidding costs, program construction, service connection fees, and furnishings. A typical figure for soft costs is 30 to 40 percent of "hard costs."

Specifications

An important and complicated step in the design process is the preparation of final specifications. Although the designer is responsible for this task, facilities planning staff must be closely involved and carefully review the designer's work. The institution and the designer must decide which specifications are appropriate for the building.

In addition, although the designer is liable for his or her work, it is prudent for the institution to provide as much review of technical and legal documents as possible.

Technical review is advisable because many designers rely heavily on manufacturers for help in writing specifications. Problems may arise with this method in competitive bidding. In such a case, the documents should be examined by institutional representatives to ensure that specifications are not so restrictive that they eliminate all products except those supplied by the manufacturer that provides the specification information.

The institution's legal counsel should review nontechnical portions of the general and supplementary general conditions before final approval is given. Sections of particular legal importance include insurance coverage and its relation to the institution's overall insurance program, conditions for release of liens, guarantees, and performance and payment bonds.

Fixed equipment, such as laboratory hoods, cooking equipment, dishwashers and similar items that are connected to a building, and building services may be included in the building construction contract. Inclusion of fixed equipment in the contract is important to maintain a single source of responsibility.

Although movable furniture and furnishings also require specifications, these are usually excluded from the general contract. Their acquisition may be a responsibility of the institution's purchasing officer, who should work closely with the designer and the building committee during the period of specifications, preparations, bids, and installation of equipment. If the designer can provide acceptable interior design services, a separate contract could be used for these services.

Procurement Procedures

The construction documentation phase generally leads to construction procurement through competitive bidding. The following general features of lump-sum competitive bidding are also appropriate for alternative procurement methods. Alternative models for capital project procurement as cost-effective methods are discussed as follows.

Bidding Documents

Bidding documents usually include:

- working drawings;
- specifications, including general and supplementary conditions;
- a bid proposal form, including information on total cost, breakdown by trades, any alternate and unit prices requested, and affirmative action; and
- time needed for completion (optional).

A list of alternates to be subtracted from the base bid ("deduct alternates") in the order of the institution's priority can act as a safeguard against bids exceeding project budgets. Items that may be desired but included as contingencies if bids are lower than budget ("add alternates") can be included in the bid proposal. The project designer provides recommendations on the selection of add or deduct alternates. Bids exceeding the designer's estimates, in the absence of adequate alternates or contingencies, create a possible contractual dispute over responsibilities and reimbursement for redesign. In the contract with the designer, careful definition of the institution's responsibilities, the project budget, and the approvals required during design development can avert or reduce these problems.

A contractor usually must put down a refundable deposit for the loan of bidding documents; if the contractor wishes additional copies, they must be purchased. Adequate sets of the drawings and specifications should be on file in the facilities planning office, the designer's office, and such other offices as may be required by state or local laws.

Upon submission of bid proposals, the following may be required from the bidder as part of the package of bidding documents:

- a bid bond signed and returned by the contractor, or a deposit as a guarantee to enter into a contract if selected;

- the contractor's affirmative action commitments;

- a list of subcontractors;

- evidence of liability and workers' compensation insurance; and

- a list of projects of comparable size successfully completed by the contractor.

The following items are usually required at the time the contract is signed, if they are not required as a bidding document:

- a performance bond ensuring that, if the contractor is unable to complete the job, a bonding company will do so;

- a payment bond, often combined with the performance bond, ensuring payment of subcontractors; and

- builders' risk insurance to cover the value of the construction as it progresses.

Three weeks is considered the minimum time that contractors should have for preparing bids for complex projects; one week is adequate for projects of $100,000 or less. If other similar jobs are out for bid in the area at the same time, or the project is of major complexity or size, four to six weeks are more appropriate. Bid dates and delivery locations should be specified in the bid invitation and strictly adhered to. The designer should prepare a tabulation of all bids and distribute it to all the bidders.

Contractor Selection

Complete contractor qualification statements are essential for a thorough contractor selection process. Investigation of contractors and the subcontractors they will employ should include queries into their quality of construction; their financial standing, past performance, reputation, and integrity; and the experience of the proposed construction superintendent. Such an inquiry should also reveal the contractor's ability to work well with designers and project coordinators representing the institution.

To aid the investigation, contractors should provide:

- current audited financial statements;

- a schedule of projects currently under contract, a list of those completed within the last five years, an estimate of their value, and names and addresses of clients and designers involved;

- a statement of experience with projects similar to the one that is under consideration;

- number, names, and qualifications of the supervisors proposed for the job;

- name of bonding company; and

- affirmative action policy.

A "Contractor's Application for Prequalification" is recommended to screen potential contractors and can shorten the bid period. Such a form can produce a complete record of the experience, capabilities, organization, and financial condition of all the companies that apply. Some public institutions may ask for this information to be included with the bid.

Prebid Meeting

A prebid meeting is advisable for large and complex projects. An invitation from the institution to prospective bidders and subcontractors to meet with the designers at least two weeks before bids are due provides an opportunity to review the project. An agenda should provide a description and details of the project, contract documents, and any unusual requirements of the project, including coordination of traffic and utilities. The designers should be prepared to issue an addendum to contract documents resulting from questions raised at the prebid meeting.

Competitive Bidding

To ensure economy and avoid corrupt practices and favoritism, most federal and state agencies require competition on projects they fund. However, independent and some public institutions may find it less expensive in certain circumstances to negotiate a construction contract with only one company. Furthermore, capable contractors, when participating as members of the building team with facilities planners, designers, and engineers, can assist in the design process.

On those projects funded totally or in part by public money, such as state or federal agencies, open bidding without prequalification among bidders normally is required. In situations where closed bidding is allowed, an institution should invite at least three contractors to submit bids to make bidding competitive and to avoid appearances of impropriety. There is a danger that some qualified companies may prefer negotiated work and may not risk bid preparation costs when a large number of bidders lowers their probability of award. Local conditions may help determine how many contractors to invite; for example, some already may be committed to their full bonding capacity.

Although competitive bidding determines the low bidder, an award is never automatic or immediate. Before announcing a decision, the designer and a representative of the institution should analyze all bids for the best combination of alternatives and for certain danger signs, such as an extraordinarily low bid. Since most bids in a competitive market normally fall within a range of 10 to 15 percent of project estimates, a contractor whose bid falls below this range may have developed a particular efficiency or may have made a serious mistake. If a mistake has been made, the contractor should inform the institution promptly, advising whether he or she intends to forfeit bid bond or proceed with the contract as bid. When such circumstances arise, legal counsel should be sought by the institution.

Notice of Award

A formal contract award is announced by a notice of award, followed by the preparation of the contract and submission of the performance bond and insurance certificates by the contractor. However, this does not authorize the start of construction, which may not begin until the contract is executed and the institution issues a notice to proceed. When it is necessary to authorize the purchase of materials or the mobilization of the project prior to issuing a notice to proceed, a letter of intent can be issued.

Alternative Models for Capital Project Delivery

Alternative models for capital project delivery include the following.

Negotiated Contract Awards

Institutions not bound to competitive bidding may wish to negotiate with one general contractor or with several subcontractors. Advantages include greater speed, economy, and quality, but these advantages can be maintained only if the contract is carefully administered. The key is selecting reliable firms. The major types of contracts are outlined below.

Guaranteed Maximum Price (GMP)

A GMP arrangement requires the institution to reimburse the contractor for managing the project if permitted to perform construction work and for labor and materials. The builder guarantees that the cost of the project will not exceed an agreed-on maximum. Speed of construction is considered by some institutions to be the primary advantage of a negotiated contract. By reaching a GMP agreement with a builder, an institution can "fast-track" a project, eliminating the two-to-four-week bidding period and the one-to-two-week bid analysis. On these projects, the process can be further accelerated by beginning site preparation, excavation, and foundation work and purchase of major equipment before detailed working plans for the later stages of construction have been completed. (However, this method can have major risks if design changes occur during preparation of contract documents.)

Cost-plus

A cost-plus arrangement is similar to a GMP agreement but without a guaranteed maximum price for the builder.

Owner-builder

Under an owner-builder arrangement, the institution authorizes an administrator (usually the financial or business officer or facilities administrator) to act as general contractor and designates an experienced staff member as construction project manager. This system allows the institution to contract separately with subcontractors and to eliminate the general contractor's overhead and profit, but it places an added liability and a great time demand on staff and should be attempted only when an experienced project manager is available.

Design Build (or Turnkey)

Design-build contracts can be used when an institution issues a request for proposals that encompasses both the design and construction of a facility into a single contract (rather than the traditional breakdown of architects, engineers, and contractors). Drafting of proposals requires careful development to ensure that a program is satisfied and that standards for materials and building systems are acceptable. Construction management contracts can also be used, where a construction manager is retained at the start of design development to complete the facility for a guaranteed maximum price or to award and manage separate contracts for different elements of the work.

Third-party Financing

Another procurement alternative involves third-party financing through a developer who either leases the facilities to the institution or owns and operates the facility, title to which may revert to the institution after costs are reimbursed to the financing source through regular payments over a fixed period of time. In this contractual relationship, the developer takes all responsibility and risk for delivering the agreed-upon plans. An advantage of third-party financing is that a project is considered "off the books" and bypasses amassing funds in advance of construction through use of institutional funds or fund raising. Another advantage is that it bypasses various procurement processes and should result in a quicker project completion.

Construction

Construction administration is a complex task that assures that a project will be delivered in accordance with drawings and specifications, within budget, and on schedule. The institutional construction administrator plays the key role as the institution's representative in coordinating institutional oversight of a project, with the assistance of the project designer. However, these roles may vary, with the construction administrator acting as the authorized representative and the designer's responsibilities increased or diminished by contractual agreement. Staffing a project for construction administration requires a careful evaluation by facilities planning staff. Careful delineation of a discrete number of projects may by placed under contract with a construction manager to provide construction administration services with termination of services at the completion of an assignment.

Preconstruction Conference

The preconstruction conference is an on-site coordinating meeting. The construction administrator organizes this meeting to resolve any last-minute questions of contractors, suppliers, subcontractors, and institutional representatives. Important details such as responsibility for administration of the project, lines of communication, and timing of work are discussed to eliminate confusion and causes for delay. It is essential that the institution clearly designate the construction administrator as the source of clearing project correspondence, processing of requests for payment, authorization for change orders, and acceptance of the work for overall project coordination and construction in progress. The contractor should submit insurance certificates, performance bonds, and other requirements in the contract documents at this time. The construction administrator should explain procedures regarding method of payment, change orders, and shop drawings, as well as factors related to the site, access to the site, and parking. Names and phone numbers of all official contact persons should be provided, including those to be called in case of emergency.

Notice to Proceed

A written notice to proceed formally establishes the beginning of construction, sent by the institution to the contractor. The notice is sent after the contractor submits all required documents, including the signed contract, insurance certificates, performance bond, affirmative action plan, and list of subcontractors. Work should not be permitted on the site without bonding and insurance in effect or before the contractor is authorized to proceed.

Construction Schedule

The contractor should submit a detailed financial breakdown, a schedule of payments, and a proposed construction schedule soon after the contract is executed. The financial breakdown may take the form of a bar chart or a critical-path diagram. It should include estimates of the contractor's monthly billings to the nearest thousand dollars.

Project Coordination

The contract states the authority that controls construction. The institution, which provides the site and bears the cost, is the ultimate authority, but the contract can empower the designer or a construction manager to act as the institution's agent in matters related to construction. Depending on the contract's terms, the authorized institutional representative can observe the contractor's work, reject unacceptable materials, or order the contractor to maintain the schedule. The institutional representative can condemn portions of the work that are poorly executed, and order the contractor to rebuild. However, the designer cannot interfere with the way the contractor manages the job or deal directly with subcontractors or workers under the contractor's control.

The institution should never bypass the designer if the contract gives the designer the authority to deal directly with the contractor. If the institution approves work, equipment, or materials that the designer disapproves, it may have no legal recourse against the designer or builder should problems develop during the warranty period.

This does not mean that the institution should ignore a project during the construction period; an experienced staff member or consultant should be appointed to act as the institution's representative. The designer may employ a representative for reporting purposes and the contractor may have a project supervisor performing a similar function, but the institution should also have a representative who stays informed of the progress of the work. Some larger institutions find it effective to employ their own inspectors and do not require the designer to perform construction administration. This could result in a reduction of the designer's fee, but may create additional liability for the institution.

Construction in Progress

One of the institutional representative's duties is to keep all parties informed about the status of the work. The best way to do this, especially on complex projects, is to hold weekly progress meetings and to issue regular field reports. Field reports should provide information on such items as work completed, financial situation to date, problems, cost revisions, and change orders.

During construction, the institutional representative should periodically observe the project. If any work is not being accomplished in accordance with the plans and specifications, the designer should undertake to have the contractor correct the problem. Facilities planning representatives should also observe the work for the institution and report any possible problem directly to the institutional representative to be resolved.

Change Orders

While change orders should be avoided, they may be necessary for any of the following reasons:

- errors or omissions in the contract documents;

- problems with delivery of materials as ordered and/or scheduled;

- field or site conditions that were not anticipated during the planning process for construction and alterations (like unforeseen ground conditions or internal design problems, not always discernible before the start of construction);

- connection and alignment problems that may be discovered after the contract is awarded, during shop drawing preparation and review stages (some requiring changes to construction documents);

- building features not shown on record drawings that come to light during preparatory demolition;

- changes that are dictated by regulatory agencies (such as the fire marshal's office) during final field review; and

- changes requested by building users to satisfy new program requirements (since, during the program development stage, it usually is not possible to foresee and describe exactly every item necessary to accommodate evolving programs or program changes.

The best way to control the number of changes is to engage competent designers and to conduct rigorous reviews during design development, using the original program as the control document. Bidding documents should comprehensively cover the process for change orders with conditions for acceptance of changes, methods of determining costs, and necessary authorization(s). The institution must expect change orders and never sign a contract that leaves this expensive issue unresolved. An adequate contingency fund for changes should be provided in the project budget. All change orders represent modifications to the original contract and must be in writing and approved by authorized personnel prior to beginning the work. An allowance of 3 percent for new construction and 5 percent for major renovations in the construction phase of a project should be adequate as a construction contingency. Care should be taken when issuing change orders to ensure that the quality of work and materials are acceptable to the owner and that time extensions do not later become contractor delay claims.

Substantial Completion

When construction is almost complete, architects, engineers, and institutional representatives inspect the project and make a "punch list" of uncompleted items. The only items on the institution's punch list that the institutional representative is bound to include in the final punch list are those that fall within the requirements of the construction contract. The punch list should be sent to all interested parties to inform them that the job will be complete as soon as the contractor finishes the remaining items satisfactorily. The time period between substantial completion and final completion should be agreed on by all parties and is normally 30 to 90 days.

When the contractor notifies the institutional representative that all items on the punch list have been completed, all principals convene for a tour of the facility. If, because of this tour, the institution agrees that the contractor has met all the stipulations of the contract, they can collect any remaining releases of liens and accept the building. When disputes about the work occur between the institution and contractor, the authorized institutional representative usually acts as mediator. Most contracts also include an arbitration clause.

Acceptance and Occupancy

Even in amicable situations, the "final inspection" often is not final. The contractor is responsible for preparing and collecting all certificates of inspection from public agencies and professional testing laboratories and delivering them to the institutional representative as closeout documents.

The contractor should also deliver, through the institution's representative, all warranties to the institution. The warranty period usually begins at substantial completion, but it is vital that the institution specifies the start of each warranty period in the contract documents.

For efficient use of equipment, the contract should require the contractor, as part of the closeout documentation, to compile for the institution a manual that includes manufacturer's literature, catalog cuts, and specifications sheets for each piece of equipment—all the technical data and instructions necessary for the operation and maintenance of the building. The designer should approve this manual.

Testing of equipment and balancing of mechanical systems are important parts of the "turnover" of a facility to the institution. Testing and balancing may be performed under separate contract to a specialized firm to assure that operating equipment fulfills contract requirements. If test operations are included in the contract, it is recommended that the designer designate the time for them. This usually occurs after the institution has accepted the building as substantially complete. One method of testing is to have the contractor supply the skilled personnel necessary to operate the building for five consecutive eight-hour days. During this period the contractor will demonstrate the operation of all equipment to the designer, physical plant staff, and other interested persons.

One of the last contract details, and one of the most important, is the final set of as-built drawings. Because the process of construction inevitably requires changes from the original working drawings, it is essential that the institution acquire at least one set of revised, reproducible drawings that incorporates these alterations. It is usually the designer's responsibility to provide such drawings, and a stipulation to that effect should be included in the contract. Release of the final contractor's retainer should be withheld until an acceptable set of as-built drawings is provided. Final payment should not be made without lien waivers for all contractors, subcontractors, and material suppliers as specified in the contract. When a building is accepted, it should be included in the institution's schedule of insurance for buildings and contents. In addition, a complete description of the intended use of the building on a room-by-room basis, including square footage, should be furnished to the finance or business office for use in indirect cost studies and to update the space inventory.

Commissioning Process

Increasing complexity of institutional buildings and inadequacies in traditional acceptance and occupancy practices is addressed by the building commissioning process. The principal benefit of a formal commissioning process and retaining a commissioning agent is cost avoidance and compliance with specified building systems performance (typically, mechanical and electrical systems). The commissioning process can vary from project to project with roles in some or all project phases, from design through project acceptance. Contract documents for the process can include provisions in agreements with designers, construction delivery sources, and commissioning agent. Cost of a commissioning agent can vary between 2 and 4 percent of the mechanical system construction contract cost, plus 1 to 2 percent of the electrical construction cost.

Space Planning and Management

The goals of space planning and management are to make the best possible use of existing space and to plan for future needs.[13]

The space planning and management process seeks to determine what space exists, how it is being used, who uses the space, how the space should be used, what additional space may be needed or what space may be eliminated, and the most economical way to provide space.

Organization

The assignment of responsibility for gathering information on space and for making decisions about space varies widely among institutions. However, the necessary management tools remain the same, whether the function resides in a special office for space planning and management, in the business office, with facilities management, or in another office. Regardless of the placement in the organizational structure, space planning and management should be considered as key input to facilities planning. For the purposes of this chapter, the term "space manager" describes the person responsible for the space planning and management function in any college or university.

A space manager should maintain close ties with academic administrators, finance or business office staff, the facilities administrator, the classroom scheduling office, and directors of auxiliary enterprises. Space needs and uses are based on decisions concerning academic programs (developing new ones or phasing out or modifying existing ones), enrollment levels and mix of students (such as graduate versus undergraduate and variety of program areas), emphasis on research, and policies on auxiliary enterprises and other service activities. An advisory group or committee composed of representatives of various constituencies is used at some institutions and may be helpful in gaining insights from users and obtaining broader support for decisions. The presence and involvement of the institution's senior academic officer is often valuable when the space manager is seeking a broad institutional perspective on space assignment policies, priorities, and procedures.

Space managers should conduct and manage an inventory of space, analyze utilization, project how space should be used (realignment and remodeling), recommend if space should be reduced, and plan when and how much additional space will be needed. It is recommended that these functions be incorporated into one central office. Without centralization, problems may arise in space planning, allocation, scheduling, construction, maintenance, and operation. At multicampus institutions, it is desirable to have consistent space planning and management procedures and standards for all campuses in the system. This may be accomplished through coordination with a central planning office, which may also establish priorities among the space needs of individual campuses.

Space studies and plans may lead to the determination that certain space is no longer needed for institutional purposes. The institution must then decide whether the space will remain vacant or whether an attempt will be made to rent, lease, sell, or raze it. Vacant space can be an attraction to vandals, and a closed building may create a sense of involuntary retrenchment on the part of the institution. Where there is no potential renter or purchaser for the space, dealing with it effectively may require considerable attention.

Facilities Inventory

A comprehensive facilities inventory includes all institutional property: land, buildings, and infrastructure. Availability of software and vendor services enables an institution to develop a comprehensive relational database, including integration with a computer-aided facility management (CAFM) program. The program provides electronic reference to property, building, and infrastructure drawings, and access by authorized institutional departments. With availability of personal computers and relatively inexpensive statistical and graphics programs, most institutions can conduct, store, edit, and manipulate a computer-assisted space inventory. Information can easily be arranged to generate periodic and special reports. The level of detail and sophistication in reports can be tailored to the institution's size, requirements, and resources. If resources are limited, a simple basic inventory can be designed at first, to be enhanced and extended later.

Minimal requirements for a facilities inventory are a tabulation and description of all buildings and rooms. This inventory is a prerequisite to examining all other aspects of space management. While the inventory should be complete, administrators are cautioned against gathering excessive information. *The Postsecondary Education Facilities Inventory and Classification Manual (PEFIC Manual)* provides detailed instructions for establishing an inventory; definitions of room types, building areas, and program classifications; and a glossary of technical terms. Since the classification system in this manual is widely used, it can provide a basis for interinstitutional comparisons as well as internal management.

Analyzing Use

Once an accurate picture of available space is obtained, a space manager may consider how the space is being used. Two types of space can be analyzed: scheduled space (instructional facilities and many general-use facilities) and allocated space (offices, laboratories, libraries, and some auxiliary enterprises). Procedures for measuring the use of these two types of space begin with a database that includes a room-by-room space inventory, a headcount of the number of full-time equivalent (FTE) students, an evaluation of the distribution of students (by level and program), a count of the number of FTE faculty and staff by department (this should include an indication of office and research space requirements), and a description of course facilities requirements. The last item should be broken down to indicate each course taught by each department, the type of instruction (lecture, laboratory, etc.), the desirable class size, the hours per week per class, and the type of facility used, such as lecture hall, laboratory, or classroom.

Space use analysis studies can be effective tools for decision making. When appropriately used, they highlight a broad range of factors that affect the total resources of a college or university. A space inventory and analysis can reveal many different kinds of space available to serve a variety of programs with distinctly different and unique criteria for use. Care must be taken when examining departmental utilization studies to recognize these varied needs and to employ criteria that are specifically cognizant of them.

It is necessary to distinguish between an institutional analysis of use and the commonly accepted practice of "space utilization studies." The traditional practice in higher education is to limit space utilization studies to the use characteristics of scheduled classrooms (HEGIS Code 110) and teaching laboratories (HEGIS Code 210). This typically represents 15 to 20 percent of an institution's total space inventory.

When considering an institution as a whole, there is danger that a utilization study will be viewed not as a means to an end but as an end in itself. Improved use of space by itself does not necessarily result in an overall improvement in efficiency or even in cost reduction. Focusing on narrow use criteria as ends in themselves may set up unrealistic efficiency goals that conflict with class or program requirements. There is an additional danger that significant differences among institutions will not be considered and that "standardized" criteria and average data for an institution of one size or type will be inappropriately imposed on other institutions.

Space Planning Standards

Space planning standards are guidelines that differ for distinct levels of *macro* and *micro* space planning. *Macro*-level standards, generally used by coordinating agencies in the capital project funding allocation process, compare space available to space required at an institution as part of project evaluation. A subset of macro-level guidelines is utilization standards. Standards with a microlevel of detail are used to guide programming and design for a specific facilities project.

The macro-level guidelines are typically organized for space categories defined by the *Postsecondary Education Facilities Inventory and Classification Manual*. Each category has a specific guideline that requires input measures (e.g., student enrollment, faculty and staff, library volumes, etc.). A space required calculation is compared to the space available reported in each category in a space inventory to determine either a category surplus or deficit. The calculation is useful to measure whether an institution is in need of space or is in excess. This macro-level evaluation should incorporate consideration of facilities adequacy (physical condition deficiencies and ability to support programs) to ensure that the calculations are not treated as an absolute indicator of capital need.

Micro-level guidelines are sufficient in detail for facility programming at the project level. Specific guidelines allocate space requirements for a functional activity to accommodate occupants and equipment.

Space managers should carefully evaluate the sources of standards and their application for current conditions. Many standards in use are an accumulation of experience predating the introduction of information technologies and changes in pedagogy, such as the introduction of student-centered learning and problem-based learning. It is important to understand the relation of any set of standards to the mission of the institution using them. Space standards must be flexible enough to accommodate institutional differences, including size, programs, location, and goals.

OPERATIONS AND MAINTENANCE

The role of the operations and maintenance department is to provide an appropriate physical environment in support of an institution's mission.[14] The department is concerned with timely service operations, maintenance, alterations, and related activity pertaining to the facilities portion of the total institutional environment. The organization affects all segments of the institution and must provide the necessary level of service to maintain facilities and extend their useful lives in a manner that is cost-effective and compatible with institutional objectives. This activity requires efficient, courteous, and dedicated staff who possess technical and professional capability.

Responsibilities

The responsibilities of the department can be performed under various organizational titles: buildings and grounds, physical plant, or operations and maintenance. For the purposes of this chapter, "operations and maintenance," or "O&M," is used to describe these functional activities and their organizational structure within a comprehensive facilities management organization. "Maintenance" is defined as the work required to preserve buildings, grounds, utilities, and equipment or to restore them to their original condition or to such condition that they can be effectively used for their intended purpose. "Operations" includes maintenance, inspections, repairs, and replacement of building operating systems and equipment, central utility plants, and utility distribution systems.

The specific goals of an O&M department are:

- to extend the life of facilities and improve their capability to perform at their maximum potential;

- to reduce operating interruptions and failures of equipment and structures;

- to increase the productivity of O&M personnel;

- to improve work methods and procedures;

- to select the most cost-effective methods of O&M;

- to reduce and eliminate fire and safety hazards;

- to improve and maintain the aesthetic qualities of facilities;

- to manage a work control system that allows analysis and audit of O&M functions;

- to implement programs to conserve energy; and

- to ensure the personal safety and security of building occupants.

The public relations function of O&M employees should not be underestimated. O&M employees should be visible on a regular basis in all departments, to maintain good rapport. There is a correlation between the levels of maintenance and custodial service in buildings and the respect shown facilities by users.

The facilities administrator has an obligation to communicate and interpret the mission of the department to other senior administrators and to the institutional community. For example, the level of institutional budget support chiefly determines the level of custodial and maintenance service; thus, if O&M budgets are reduced or not increased to keep pace with rising costs, service is likely to decrease. This must be communicated to the institutional community. At the same time, such issues should not be used in defense of poor judgment or the ineffective management of resources.

Organizational Structure

The organizational structure of the O&M department depends on the number, complexity, and types of facilities to be maintained and the institution's traditional organizational practices. The specific nature of the maintained facilities, the required maintenance skills, levels of utilization, and the age and condition of the facilities affect the organizational structure. An institution's location (urban or rural), area size, population size, student body (residential or commuting), and climate also affect the services required of O&M. For example, a small college may have maintenance contracts for special equipment in lieu of in-house staff. Larger institutions may be more self-sufficient and maintain machine shops, woodworking shops, and other such facilities.

Differences in the type of institution, whether a two-year college or a research university, affect the complexity and extent of the O&M department. Whether or not an institution is state-supported or independent may be another important factor. Personalities and management styles, availability and capabilities of skilled trades, and unique assignments of responsibilities all affect configurations of an O&M department. Relationships between organizational structure and staffing also depend on management's attitudes toward desired levels of maintenance services and available funds.

Major variables in organizational structures are in the size of the building and equipment maintenance unit, involvement in major repairs and renovations, and use of outside contractors. At small institutions, skilled tradespeople and semiskilled support staff can perform emergency, routine, and preventive maintenance. At larger institutions, these maintenance functions can be organized into separate units. A typical organizational configuration may have separate units for preventive maintenance, emergency and routine maintenance, construction crews, and building operating systems. A construction crew drawn from skilled trade units may perform major repairs and renovations.

The extent of renovations and minor remodeling performed by in-house staff depends on the traditional practices of the institution and the availability of local competitive contracting. The cost-effectiveness of diverting in-house staff from emergency or planned maintenance work to perform what may be more appealing construction work is often debated. The use of in-house staff requires full costing, including overhead, for an accurate comparison to the alternative of contracting for renovations and minor remodeling.

The responsiveness, performance, and reputation of the O&M department can be improved by decentralization of services into maintenance zones. This entails the assignment of small groups of key tradespeople capable of simple repairs and equipment adjustments to clusters of buildings or designated areas. Work is outlined daily by work orders and supplemented by observations of field conditions that need correction. Employing building coordinators who have direct contact with building users and can monitor maintenance needs encourages prompt responses and performance of work.

For convenience and for more effective service in large institutions, certain central services, such as purchasing and human resources management, may have personnel located in the O&M organization. Other services that are sometimes found in the O&M organization are communications (telephone, telegraph, campus mail, and messenger service), waste recycling, trash collection and disposal, pest control, fire protection, and trucking and moving.

Administration

The O&M department is responsible for developing policy for use within the department, as well as developing operating guidelines that conform to institutional policies. The O&M administrative office is responsible for preparing and controlling the budget; preparing the payroll; billing; ordering materials and supplies; work order management; and records management. The director must have timely reports available for effective performance control, cost control, and analysis, which require rapid reporting with more detailed information than is available on typical institutional accounting reports.

O&M can represent 6 to 12 percent of an institution's education and general budget. A director responsible for this large share of institutional resources requires special skills in budget management and financial controls, as well as leadership abilities for a diverse work force. A graduate degree in engineering, business administration, or a related field is becoming a common requirement for this position.

The O&M budget should provide for normal and recurring operation and maintenance of general institutional facilities. Funds for other purposes, such as major nonrecurring maintenance or building alterations for a particular department, should come from other sources, such as the budget of the unit making the request, a special O&M account provided for such projects, or other appropriations.

Certain services required by auxiliary enterprises, such as maintenance and construction, may be performed by O&M on an institutionwide basis, while other services, such as housekeeping, may be performed by the auxiliary itself, by O&M, or by contractors. Auxiliary enterprises should be charged for services rendered by the O&M department. Where services are available from O&M, they should be used by all institutional entities. Duplicate O&M units for auxiliaries or other cost centers are less cost-effective than centralized services and can create inconsistencies in maintenance methods.

The O&M director participates in long-range planning for facilities by being involved in ongoing programs of building condition inspections (facilities audits) and by developing projects for major maintenance and repairs, capital renewal and replacements, utilities, security and safety measures, accessibility for the disabled, and energy conservation.

Another task for the director and staff is the preparation of maintenance standards listing estimated hours for performance of repetitive tasks, to assist in the estimate of labor and material for work orders. These standards help to ensure accurate estimates and to provide documentation on performance that is necessary to satisfy departments requesting services.

The O&M director should participate in the development of written guidelines to ensure that new facilities, additions, or renovations designed by consultants can be economically maintained. The director and staff should also have input on specifications for contracted services.

Effective communication between O&M personnel and users of facilities is necessary to ensure that buildings serve their intended purpose. To accomplish this, building or department representatives from the academic staff should act as a liaison between the building users or department and the O&M department. Requests for services can originate from building users, O&M staff, other interested staff, students, and members of the surrounding community. These requests can reach the attention of the O&M department by telephone, face-to-face conversations, or written or electronic communications.

Personnel Administration

The O&M director must be aware of government regulations and institutional policies concerning employees, such as affirmative action, occupational safety and health regulations, accessibility for the disabled, wage and hour provisions, collective bargaining, age discrimination, and equal employment opportunities. Wage administration is a major concern, since the O&M department typically has many wage levels, reflecting the diversity of jobs for which it is responsible. This is usually handled through the human resources department and may include labor union contract negotiations. (See chapter 12, Human Resources and Benefits Management.)

If employees are covered by one or more union contracts, the director must be fully cognizant of all contract details. The office that administers the labor relations function should have the active cooperation of the director of O&M.

Training

The advancement and training of employees should be encouraged, and employees should be made aware of relevant courses offered by the institution. Courses to improve supervisory skills, for example, usually are available at large institutions. Suppliers and factory representatives, many of whom sponsor workshops on such subjects as carpet maintenance, central chilled water systems, and HVAC repair, are an excellent source of training. Institutional seminars are often available on pertinent subjects, and national and regional associations offer courses and workshops at various levels. Apprenticeship training programs are a growing trend to meet the sophisticated requirements of equipment and building operating systems at colleges and universities. All training, along with job performance evaluations, should be documented in an employee's records.

Work Order System

O&M departments that only respond to emergencies, face large backlogs of routine maintenance, and engage in occasional minor renovations are neither cost-effective nor efficient. An O&M work order management system should be developed, if one does not exist, to record data that reflect performance, to increase productivity of personnel, and to monitor use of materials and contractors to reduce costs.

An O&M work order system is a comprehensive management tool that should include documentation of staffing, organization, and procedures for managing operations and maintenance through the processes of budgeting, initiating, planning, scheduling, executing, and reporting of work. A difficult but important task is coordinating work requests with labor, materials, and work assignments. A work-order system establishes priorities and schedules job requests accordingly. This system should also monitor work requests and performance to advise requesting parties when their requests will be filled. Computerized maintenance management systems (CMMS) for accurately recording work requests, scheduling tasks, generating work orders, and monitoring results are invaluable tools and are available in the marketplace for all sizes of O&M departments.

The work order system should be designed to meet these needs and to provide an accounting device for costing specific jobs. The work order system should include the preparation of a work order form for each work request. This form is used to record any approvals required, to initiate the ordering of necessary materials, and to notify the appropriate personnel who will perform the work. Cost accounting systems are based on completed work orders, and use information on hours worked, labor rates, and material costs to provide payroll information, material control, and accumulations of daily work into weekly, monthly, quarterly, and annual reports of expenditures against budgeted funds.

Managing a work order system requires a process to control the flow of requests initiated by O&M staff and requesters of services. At larger institutions, a work control center staffed by estimators, planners, and schedulers performs this function.

Budgeting, Cost Accounting, and Cost Controls

An operating plan and budget for O&M usually should be prepared at least one year in advance. The plan should include revenues and all projected expenditures for personnel and operations. Supervisors charged with budget responsibilities should participate in budget preparation and accountability for their areas. For this reason, they should fully understand any special organizational formats (such as billing for services for special work) and reporting procedures.

The most common budgeting method is incremental budgeting, in which changes are made to the budget of the prior period. Another method compares a proposed budget to available work standards, providing for internal review and justification of programs and costs. Some states have developed formulas for allocating plant funds to public higher education institutions. These are often based on such data as enrollment, square feet, or credit hours. (See chapter 4, Budgeting.)

The three largest categories of expenditure in O&M budgets are typically labor, purchased goods and services, and utilities. Factors affecting an institution's O&M budget are area wage rates; the age, condition, and hours of use of buildings; and standards of performance and maintenance. Within these parameters, normal housekeeping, preventive maintenance, and replacement can be budgeted fairly accurately. Extraordinary repair and replacement (special nonrecurring items such as roofing) can be requested in the budget as an annual replacement allowance and expended as required. Funds for emergency repair and replacement, however, are often external to the O&M budget and must be transferred from other sources.

Cost accounting systems for O&M departments require timely information and detail not usually produced by a college or university accounting system. An internal cost accounting system is needed to gather and record data for day-to-day operations management and to report information to the institutional accounting system. Included in such a system would be maintenance, capital projects, and reimbursable costs charged back to users of O&M department services. The two systems should be compatible.

Institutional policy determines the extent to which the costs of O&M operations are recovered; they may be fully or partially recovered or not recovered at all. To determine the costs of the various activities of the institution, it is essential that the cost accounting system be designed to include direct, indirect, vendor, and contractor costs. In this way, the costs of activities can provide a sound basis for budgeting.

Allocation of costs for maintenance, utilities, and custodial and other services to other departments, to funded research, and to auxiliaries of the institution should be based on gross costs. The work order system is an essential part of the calculation that includes overhead costs for administration, supervisory time, and other indirect costs that the O&M department must recover from auxiliaries or other reimbursable customers.

Cost control is most effective when the cost accounting system is designed to be consistent with the budget, and vice versa. Accounts in the cost accounting system should match each line item in the budget so that a direct comparison can be made. Comparison of actual costs to the budget is the most important tool available to the O&M director. Performance measurements should also use nonfinancial standards to measure and compare actual performance, such as levels of work backlog, variance of project labor costs to estimates, and time for performing a task within established ranges. Performance standards can be established from internal experience or from published standards.

Building and Equipment Maintenance

Terms commonly used to define types of maintenance include the following.

Emergency Maintenance

Emergency maintenance is unscheduled work that requires immediate action to restore services or remove problems that could interrupt activities. Examples include loss of electrical power, water, heating, or cooling; excessive accumulation of ice or snow; and building failures representing hazards to personnel or equipment.

Service Work

Service work is unplanned maintenance requiring low skill levels for correction. The need for service work is usually identified and reported by facilities users. Examples are replacing lamps, adjusting doors, repairing hardware, and tightening plumbing connections.

Preventive Maintenance

Preventive maintenance is a planned and controlled program of periodic inspection, adjustment, lubrication, replacement of components, and performance testing and analysis. Examples of items that require preventive maintenance include mechanical equipment, motors, filter replacements, emergency generators, the cooling tower, and detection equipment. An institution should have an annual or biennial maintenance schedule that provides for a periodic, thorough inspection of facilities. Especially critical is work involving heating, air-conditioning, power, and water shutdowns, which must be arranged with facilities users.

Routine Maintenance

Routine maintenance is repair or replacement of obsolete, worn, broken, or inoperative building components or systems. This type of work may be scheduled, repetitive work or may be a request of a nonemergency nature initiated by a building user. Examples include building repairs (masonry, hardware, glazing, painting, floor and ceiling finishes), grounds maintenance, equipment adjustments, and contract services.

Major Repairs and Renovations

A variety of terms are used to describe maintenance tasks of a major nature that must be accomplished but are not normally funded for maintenance in the annual operating budget cycle, and are typically treated as capitalized expenditures. Used interchangeably for capitalized maintenance work are capital renewal, repairs and renovations, repairs and replacements, alterations and improvements, and alterations and renovations. This work can be for capital equipment only or for system repairs and replacements or can include renovations or upgrades of space.

Depending on the size of the institution, the O&M department may have service-oriented vehicles of various sizes, from small electric carts to heavy-duty trucks. For institutions that occupy a substantial area, some vehicles may be used to provide a delivery service to skilled workers assigned to outlying job sites, so that the workers will not be required to waste time obtaining supplies.

For dispatch of personnel, equipment, and materials, the O&M department should have its own two-way radio system; the radio frequency may be obtained through federal application. Key O&M personnel should be accessible after normal work hours. For some purposes, especially communications, it may be advantageous for the O&M department to have a joint operation with the campus security or law enforcement department.

When extensive repair or renovation projects must be completed quickly, typically during vacation periods, additional help may be employed on a temporary basis or the projects may be performed under contract. If a particular project requires skills or costly equipment not available at the institution, the services and equipment should be obtained from outside sources on the basis of competitive bids using clear, precise specifications. Where licensed personnel are required to perform work to correct code violations, it may be more economical to have such persons on staff than to hire contractors for the work. (However, consideration must be given to long-term needs and to the cost of such employees.)

Many older buildings contain inefficient, uneconomical systems and obsolete operating components. Inspections may reveal needs for improved heating systems, addition of air-conditioning, new office equipment, improved lighting, and increased electrical capacity. Maintenance analysts or professional engineers should review all proposed changes, and practical solutions should be developed before decisions are made regarding replacements, modifications, and renovations.

Custodial Services

The custodial, or housekeeping, function of O&M includes routine duties to keep building interiors in a presentable condition. Custodial operations may include the use of specialized crews for some operations, such as carpet cleaning or floor stripping and waxing. Whatever their duties, custodians must be given work assignments that are clearly written and explained in a job description. In addition to regular tasks, custodians should report deficiencies such as cracked windows, leaking faucets, and defective plumbing valves, doors, and locks.

To reduce high labor costs, supervisors must be aware of new methods, products, and equipment. In addition to readily available published material, seminars or workshops are sources of current information; also, sales people perform a valuable service in presenting new products and services. Custodial supervisors should be consulted on design and materials under consideration for new construction or alteration projects; their advice to a facilities planning staff and designers and engineers can be valuable in averting "built-in" maintenance and expenses.

To schedule work effectively, and to gain the most efficient use of staff, supervisors must carefully evaluate each building in light of the academic and administrative calendar and seasonal considerations. Supervisors should prepare work assignments based on square footage, adjusted by occupancy or some other equitable, objective measure.

The training of new employees and periodic retraining directly influence the quality and efficiency of custodial service. Training and safety sessions on a regular basis are especially important where high turnover exists. A manual provided to each custodian is also helpful.

Shift work depends on the requirements of the institution's energy conservation program, building schedules, and bargaining unit regulations, as well as commuter and security considerations. There must be a balance between energy conservation and work efficiency. For example, it is more efficient to clean facilities when they are unoccupied, usually in the evening hours; however, lighting the areas where custodians are working may waste energy.

The work assignment for each custodian and the cleanliness requirements of each building will vary, depending on the building's use. Each building should have individual cleaning priorities by specific area. This ensures the cleaning of critical areas regardless of daily worker fluctuation or building traffic. If contractors are used for all or a part of custodial services, the quality of performance should be as closely controlled as though the custodians were on the staff of the institution.

When it is possible to record the hours worked by custodians at their work assignments, time spent to clock in and out at the O&M department can be eliminated. During periods when buildings are not in use, such as between semesters, some institutions employ custodians in other areas of O&M, such as landscape and grounds maintenance. (This may not be permissible in some jurisdictions or bargaining units.) Students may also be employed to support the work of regular custodial staff.

Standards for planning and budgeting custodial work are highly variable. Work criteria for supervisors and custodians should be evaluated carefully to fit variations in types and use of space, types of surface finishes, and desired level of cleaning. Availability of appropriate cleaning materials and equipment, access to spaces, and bargaining unit standards may influence custodial standards.

An alternative to in-house custodial staff is complete or partial contract services. Evaluating contract proposals requires a detailed set of specifications for comparisons to in-house costs. A special form of contract services is, more precisely, contract management. In this approach, custodial staff remains on the institutional payroll and the contract service company provides management for a fee.

Utilities

The utilities component's responsibilities include central plants, which convert fuels to energy and energy to different utilization forms, and utility distribution systems, which transport utilities from central plants or distribution points to a building or point of utilization. The operation and maintenance of institution-wide production and distribution systems, such as central heating and cooling plants, and electrical, water, and sewage distribution systems should be considered part of utilities operations. Building mechanical and electrical systems, except for fuel and purchased electricity, should be considered part of building maintenance.

The landscape of options available for energy purchasing and institutional utility operations is changing dramatically with utility deregulation. It is advantageous to examine opportunities for direct purchase of electricity and natural gas from suppliers, bypassing local energy companies. Innovative "performance contracting" methods range from commitments from a vendor to reduce energy costs at a guaranteed performance level to the acquisition of an institution's utility infrastructure. These methods can include vendor replacement of utility infrastructure capital assets, including building systems, as "off-budget" financed improvements with eventual reversion of improvements to the institution.

The organizational structure and staffing for utilities operation and maintenance depends on the institution's methods for supplying facility needs. In traditional arrangements where utilities are purchased directly from a municipal system and distribution systems are of a limited nature, all needs can be met by the O&M department. At institutions with central energy plants and extensive distribution systems for various utilities, a separate utilities operations and maintenance unit is appropriate.

Regardless of the utility delivery method, there should be a master plan for utility systems, which should be projected as far into the future as possible. This plan depends on the overall physical development policy and the schedule of facilities improvements of the institution. Voltages, steam pressures, and pipe and cable sizes must anticipate growth. Utility loads must be projected continuously for at least five to 10 years. Utilities must be planned not only to meet expected maximum demands, but also to provide standby capacity as a backup for equipment failure and to allow for equipment shutdown for mandatory inspection, maintenance, and overhaul.

Cogeneration (cogenerating electricity in addition to heat) involves weighing the economics of the relatively simple heating system against the more complicated total energy system. It is difficult to balance electrical demand with the need for steam. For example, a turbogenerator may produce electricity at the same time it reduces the pressure of steam, although no economy results if no use for the reduced steam exists. Electrical interconnections with utility companies provide a backup source of electricity and a means of selling excess electricity to the utility company.

For the purchase of electricity, it is more economical to have one electric meter for the entire institution so that charges are based on total demand (the maximum kilowatt-hours used during a specific period). Peak demand also is a factor in determining rates, and such demand should be kept as low as possible. Installation of submetering for individual buildings and energy management control systems are useful to measure demand and evaluate energy performance. Monitoring and management systems can sense demand conditions and take corrective actions. Available power can be limited by shutting down noncritical energy-consuming equipment. Also, capacitors can be installed to improve poor power factors and thus reduce the charges for peak demands.

Utility charges, which may be determined by the use of separate meters, can be made to each auxiliary enterprise and to any other entity. The power requirements of some research laboratories also may justify the use of separate meters to ensure proper charges for power consumed. Records should indicate the locations and dimensions of all utility distribution systems. The locations and functions of shutoff valves and switches also should be indicated.

The water supply must be tested to ensure that the chemical characteristics of the water will not adversely affect the plumbing system or laboratory apparatus through corrosion or deposit of solids, especially in boilers and cooling towers. The water supply also must be checked frequently to ensure purity and to guarantee a consistently acceptable product. Water supply and distribution planning and evaluation should also include fire protection needs.

Sewage or wastewater treatment normally is purchased from a municipal plant. If the institution handles the treatment of sewage, federal standards for the addition of chemicals must be observed. It is desirable to review the use of water frequently and to implement water conservation programs to prevent waste. Water and sewage treatment charges should be separate, so that the latter are based only on outflow. For example, separate water meters should be installed for lawn watering.

Energy Management

O&M administrators, as well as facilities administrators, have an important role in energy conservation. There must be high-level recognition of conservation, with resulting enforcement of energy policies. An institutionwide energy committee is recommended to make users aware that excessive energy use is a problem. Some aids to awareness are bulletins and conservation tips, which can be communicated through institutional publications.

Energy management is an evolutionary process that is vital to the efficient distribution of utilities. Institutions that have succeeded in energy conservation and cost reduction have done so by following carefully planned and coordinated programs, moving from the most elementary conservation steps to levels of increasing sophistication. Effects of deregulation described offer new opportunities for energy management through "performance contracting."

Energy audits and other sources of basic data are essential in implementing an energy management program. Such data enable management to determine priorities for action, to monitor and evaluate the success of a program as it proceeds (i.e., prove that energy consumption reductions have been cost-effective), to share information with the campus community and create awareness, and to discuss energy management problems and opportunities with consultants and others. Energy audits may be advisable to obtain necessary information for specific facilities. However, the cost benefit of an energy audit should be carefully assessed before the decision is made to undertake such a study.

Thorough energy audits require extensive amounts of time and can be costly. Because of this, audits should be prioritized, beginning with facilities that have high energy use. Many larger institutions have in-house capability to analyze energy data; however, facilities planning engineers, schools of engineering, and other such resources may not be available to smaller institutions. In these cases, it may be necessary to use consultants who specialize in energy problems. Before retaining outside consultants or firms, it is important to inquire about their qualifications and potential cost benefits.

A multistep approach to effective energy management separates energy modifications into three categories, based on reduction of consumption and payback.

Quick-fix Modifications

Quick-fix modifications are energy consumption reduction measures that achieve rapid and significant energy savings at negligible cost or at a cost that can produce a return on investment in no more than one year.

Retrofit Modifications

Retrofit modifications are energy consumption reduction measures that require modest capital investment but can yield an additional 10 to 15 percent in energy savings, with payback in a period of one to seven years.

Systems-convert Modifications

Systems-convert modifications require substantial capital investment to convert or replace existing systems, generally involving major changes in systems design. Payback periods often range from seven to 10 years.

A key consideration in any energy management program is the establishment of priorities. Because quick-fix measures have a low cost, they can be implemented without the delay of budget consideration. Also, technical studies are generally not necessary for these measures. Retrofit and system-convert modifications should be determined on the basis of engineering feasibility and cost benefit, coupled with the availability of funding.

No matter how much time, effort, and ingenuity is expended in quick-fix, retrofit, and systems-convert modifications, an energy management program cannot be effective without the understanding and support of the entire campus community. The organization and effect of such a program differs among institutions; each must tailor its program to fit its special needs and circumstances.

Landscape and Grounds Maintenance

Attractive landscaping and grounds maintenance contributes to a safe, pleasant, functional outdoor environment and increases the respect shown the institution by students, staff, and the public. A master plan for landscaping incorporates the overall campus design philosophy. Landscape design provides a positive image of a campus and continuity between architectural and open-space features. Design should be prepared by a landscape architect, with the participation of institutional facilities planning staff and grounds maintenance supervision. The plan should define open spaces and include projections of the locations of permanent features such as buildings, roads and walkways, site furniture, parking lots, lighting, security communications, outdoor art work, and playing fields. A landscape master plan is also important for the location of vegetation, so it does not have to be moved later. The plan should include the location of subsurface utilities and give consideration to the practical aspects of maintaining landscape features.

Some institutions use local nurseries for all grounds maintenance work, others use contract services for the supervision of groundskeepers, and others provide all grounds maintenance services directly. If grounds maintenance supervisors are on the staff, they should study and comment on any capital project site plan and modifications before adoption. After a plan has been adopted, all planting of trees, plants, grass, and shrubs should proceed according to the plan in order to ensure consistent development. Supervisors must be familiar with restrictions on the use of toxic materials and with environmental health regulations.

In addition to regular grounds maintenance services, other work requiring the services of institutional or contract personnel includes road and sidewalk maintenance, snow removal, trash pickup, and care of large trees. The grounds staff may also provide the labor for moving furniture, special events support, and heavy equipment services. When appropriate, procedures and specifications for these services should be drawn up by institutional architects and engineers or physical plant personnel.

Major Repairs and Renovations

Major repairs and renovation is a classification of accounts for work that may be supervised by either O&M or facilities planning, or design and construction. Assessment of responsibility will vary by institutional traditions, staff capability and volume activity. Work of this category is occasionally necessary to maintain facilities in proper condition and to meet safety standards. Examples of major repairs and renovations are road surfacing and the replacement of roofs, walls, floors, ceilings, and electrical and mechanical equipment. These projects should be listed separately in the physical plant accounts. Special funding allocations for major repairs and renovations to supplement current funds usually require a high level of authorization because of the financial impact on the institution generally.

The dollar threshold at which a project becomes a major repair or a renovation project is determined by the institution. Because of the high cost, there is danger that major repair and renovation projects will not be funded, the result being deferred maintenance and subsequent higher costs. A portion of the cost of major repairs and renovations may be capitalized as an addition to plant. Costs should be capitalized if the asset value of the building changes, as indicated by an anticipated increase in insurance, because of improvements.

Alterations change the purpose or use of a facility and involve the institution's facilities planners and space managers. Such changes are made when academic departments or administrative offices request modification of their facilities because of a change in program or function. This work is identified separately from major repairs and renovations as "functional improvements." Funds for functional improvements are often provided in the budgets of departments or offices making a request, depending on the scope of the project.

Incidental or minor repairs and replacements, such as the replacement of doors, are provided for in the regular O&M budget. Such recurring work to maintain facilities can be predicted from experience and included in the annual O&M plan and budget.

Major projects often require design and engineering plans and specifications, accompanied by formal estimates that are provided by the facilities planning department or outside consultants. Estimating procedures that have proved to be most reliable are those that use costing standards, which can be acquired or developed in accordance with the local market.

An effective approach to performing major repairs and renovations at large institutions is to develop a construction branch within the O&M department. When such a construction branch exists, its size and workload should be periodically evaluated to determine if maintenance activities are being deferred or if some projects can be performed more efficiently by outside contractors. Projects not assigned to the O&M staff should be awarded to an outside contractor selected on the basis of the lowest acceptable bid and such factors as timeliness, quality, and aesthetic considerations.

Regardless of who performs the work, responsibility for the project still resides with the institution, which must comply with construction specifications. A successful method of organizing the work process to accomplish major projects is that of appointing a project supervisor. This places responsibility with a staff member and provides a specific source for both decision making and coordination.

Building standards should be developed to provide basic institutional requirements for all major repairs and renovations and compliance with applicable federal, state, and local codes. This ensures that the structural and architectural integrity of the buildings and utilities will be maintained at a high level and provides for special needs concerning life safety, accessibility for the disabled, and energy conservation. Without such standards, new buildings can lose functional and aesthetic value in a short time. Major repair and renovation plans should take into consideration any standardized building and operating system components, including keying systems, doors, and inventoried replacement items. (See the "Facilities Planning, Design, and Construction" section in this chapter.)

Physical Plant Shops

Physical plant shops can provide competent support for maintenance and repair to facilities only if adequately sized and equipped with the basic tools and machines required. Shops may include such specialties as carpentry, electrical work, pipe and plumbing, painting, sheet metal work, vehicle maintenance, and locksmithing. In addition, there may be shops for elevator maintenance, and air-conditioning and refrigeration. Some institutions maintain shops to test materials for such physical and chemical properties as fire resistance and durability.

A centralized shop building should house the offices of the O&M director and staff and serve as staff headquarters. It is beneficial to have a stores-supply operation and a salvage function near the shops because of the large volume of supplies used. An alternative configuration that supports a "zone maintenance" program distributes small service shops throughout a campus and at a campus periphery provides space for the administrative unit and specialized staff and equipment.

A storeroom or warehouse for supplies used in plant operation and maintenance is essential to physical plant services in the alternative configurations of centralized or zone maintenance. Preferably, the O&M department has its own stores operation or the purchasing department's stores are located near the O&M shops.

FACILITIES SUPPORT SERVICES

Several support service activities may be grouped under the organizational structure of a comprehensive facilities management organization. These include security, environmental health and safety, telecommunications, traffic, parking, transportation, and mail services. The nature and size of a college or university dictate the assignment of these activities to a facilities management department or to another location or department in the institution.

Support services usually belong in the area of financial, human resources, or facilities management. The following factors influence management decisions regarding the creation of a facilities support services department, staffing versus contracting for services, department size, and assignment in the facilities management organization:

- an institution's overall building space;

- number of buildings;

- operational practices and traditional alignment of functions;

- geographic location;

- convenience of control of dispersed facilities;

- resource limitations;

- legal requirements;

- quality of available management; and

- land area.

An estimate of required staffing should be made after reviewing the types of services to be performed and the desired levels of service. Consultants can provide guidelines for supervision, staffing, equipment, and procedures. These same guidelines can be used as the basis of specifications when soliciting competitive bidding from outside contractors.

For a full discussion of safety issues, see chapter 14, Environmental Health and Safety. For a full discussion of support services, see chapter 20, Auxiliary Enterprises and Other Services.

REAL ESTATE OWNERSHIP AND FINANCE

Public and independent colleges and universities own title to vast amounts of developed and undeveloped land. In their early history, many independent colleges obtained land assets from private charitable bequests and religious institutions and by purchase. Most public institutions control land assets that have been set aside for educational purposes by states from early in America's history and certainly since the Morrill Act established the concept of the land-grant college in 1862. In recent years, as institutions have adopted increasingly business-oriented approaches to asset and resource management, land assets have taken on increasing strategic importance in long-term financial decisions.

For a higher education institution, appreciated land assets may represent a substantial portion of balance sheet assets, even though the typical accounting practice of carrying these assets in the balance sheet at acquisition value often obscures their true current market value. Moreover, decisions about disposition of real estate resources are long-term, and often permanent, decisions. For these reasons, proper stewardship of these assets, aimed at realizing their financial potential without sacrificing future educational needs, should be a primary consideration for governing boards and senior management. Leaders and managers in colleges and universities should have a basic understanding of commercial real estate ownership, development, and finance and use that knowledge to undertake long-range land-use planning initiatives.

Real Estate Ownership

Fee or Fee Simple

The terms *fee* and *fee simple*, used interchangeably, denote the most direct and absolute form of estate or ownership of land, which includes, but is not limited to, the right to lease and mortgage.

Lease

A lease is a contract between a landlord (lessor) and a tenant (lessee) that enumerates the conditions under which the tenant may occupy and use the property. Basic terms of leases include the term of occupancy, restrictions on use, assignment of responsibilities (for insurance, maintenance, taxes, etc.) between the owner and the tenant, and the payments. If the tenant is responsible for insurance, maintenance and taxes, the lease is referred to as a triple net lease.

Partnership

Partnerships are a predominant entity form for ownership of investment real estate. The principal advantage of the partnership form is that, although the partnership files a tax return, it pays no taxes; rather, partners report their share of the partnership financial results on individual tax returns. In a general partnership, each partner has a voice in decisions and any one can bind the others to a commitment; moreover, each partner is individually liable for the debt or other liabilities of the entire partnership.

In a limited partnership, the general partners have partnership responsibilities for control and liabilities. Limited partners may have little or no participation in decisions, but their liability is limited to the amount of their initial capital contribution. The limited partnership is a vehicle that offers the possibility of raising large sums of capital for development and for extending ownership to numerous categories of investors who have no professional expertise in real estate. For the limited partner in a large partnership, the investment more closely resembles holding a security than it does owning physical property.

Corporate Ownership

Real estate can be owned by a corporation whose charter includes real estate ownership, development, or management as a permitted activity. Real estate corporations may be subject to varying state rules and taxes. The corporate structure limits liability to the assets of the corporation; also, ownership can be extended to many investors and shares of ownership are transferable. Disadvantages of corporate ownership typically concern the fact that losses from real estate cannot be passed through to shareholders and both the corporation and the individual shareholder are taxed on profits (double taxation). The *Subchapter S corporation* affords the corporate advantage of limitations on liability along with some tax advantages of a partnership; thus it does not have the disadvantage of double taxation although the number of shareholders is limited.

Limited Liability Corporation

Limited liability corporations (LLCs) are a relatively new form of entity. They provide both the advantages of protection from liability and favorable tax treatment, in that they are taxed in the manner of partnerships; however, regulations on the creation and operation of LLCs vary from state to state.

In general, tax law regarding treatment of active versus passive loss and income must be considered carefully by both tax-exempt and for-profit entities. Colleges and universities may be general partners in development or they may invest in real estate assets as limited partners. Some colleges and universities may find it appropriate to create real estate corporations or limited liability corporations for their development activities.

Real Estate Finance

A distinctive feature of real estate investments is the accepted practice of borrowing a significant portion of the total value of the property. In real estate, it is common for a purchaser to provide 20 to 30 percent equity and to borrow the balance of the property's cost of acquisition and/or construction. Generally, the alternatives available to finance a particular land transaction or development project are a function of:

- the relative appetite of lenders for adding real estate loans to their portfolios;
- the current types of loan products available from lenders and through intermediaries;
- the nature of and user demand for the project to be financed;

- the income that the project is likely to generate;
- the legal entity that is the borrower;
- the credit quality of the borrower;
- prevailing credit market conditions; and
- the state of the local real estate market in general.

Mortgage financing techniques for real estate are familiar to most colleges and universities, especially to those that have not turned to the sale of tax-exempt bonds in public capital markets. A mortgage is a legally recognized instrument by which real property is pledged to serve as security for the repayment of a debt obligation, usually (but not always) assumed for purposes of acquiring, building, or otherwise improving the mortgaged property.

Lenders active in real estate include banks offering traditional construction and permanent loans as well as conduit programs, federal agencies, insurance companies, pension funds, wealthy individuals or families, and real estate investment trusts. (REITS are typically borrowers, but can also be lenders).

Overview of Financing Structures

As a very basic overview, typical financing sources that might be available for various types of university-related real estate development projects include:

- investor/developer's equity (of a private partner);
- internal investment (equity) funds of the institution (for example, from excess cash flow or gifts, or as endowment investments);
- short term/construction financing (banks);
- mortgage/permanent financing (banks, insurance companies, pension funds, or commercial mortgage-backed securities);
- tax-exempt bonds;
- taxable bonds; and
- federal, state, and local government grants or loans (for example, for projects with scientific or economic development purposes).

Complexity of Modern Financing Approaches

Always, the major consideration for a potential commercial project is whether the revenues from the planned uses will be adequate to cover debt service and operating costs and, eventually, net revenues or profits. For this reason, financing for many of these projects typically requires a market feasibility analysis (discussed below).

In the past, private real estate projects often were financed in a fairly conventional mix of owner's equity and debt, for example 20 to 30 percent equity and 70 to 80 percent debt. In today's environment, in contrast, the range of financing approaches is much more varied. Debt structures can range from full "general obligation" full recourse debt to "no-recourse" debt, to variations in between. Many intermediate forms of obligation (and risk levels) are used in the private sector and, with care, have applications in public and private higher education.

In many cases, higher education real estate projects, with or without private partners, may involve a mixed or "leveraged" financing strategy—essentially using funding from multiple sources for a single project. For example, a facility in a university research park that will include university research uses and private company uses could be financed with a mix of tax-exempt university debt and taxable commercial debt. Debt for such facilities typically would be secured by the rents of the facilities but, in some cases, universities also have pledged other revenue streams, such as their indirect cost recovery from research or gift income, to support projects.

As another example, many important projects with economic development purposes might be financed with a mix of federal government grants, state grants or favored loans, state tax credits, and private equity or philanthropy. Some of these projects may, in addition, have public operating subsidies.

Defining Real Estate Development Activities for Colleges and Universities

For colleges and universities, a hypothetical distinction may be made between typical capital facilities development projects that are purely related to the achievement of an institution's mission (those that, from a tax perspective, are part of the tax-exempt purposes of the institution) and those that are discussed below as commercial real estate development projects. In practice, many innovative real estate development projects are intended to serve traditional facilities needs or new mission-related activities, such as technology transfer, in addition to serving commercial purposes. These are referred to here as hybrid projects that have both institutional and commercial purposes.

For purposes of this discussion, real estate development describes the process of building or causing someone else to build projects that are either entirely commercial in purpose or that may be for hybrid (mission-related and non-mission-related) purposes on sites that typically are not integral to the institution's campus. Often, a real estate development entity in the private sector is involved, and the project is considered a "joint venture" or "public-private partnership." Sources of financing used may be those that are typical for commercial real estate, rather than those associated with collegiate facilities financing.

Using these definitions, typical real estate development projects are:

- faculty and staff housing;
- research parks and incubators;
- student housing;
- hotels and conference centers;
- shopping centers and malls;
- commercial office developments;
- cultural, educational, and recreational facilities;
- retirement communities; and
- new academic or "knowledge communities."

Faculty and Staff Housing

A number of colleges and universities that are located in areas where the cost of residential housing has become disproportionate to the average faculty income have undertaken to build for-sale or rental housing for faculty with private sector or nontraditional partners. For-sale faculty housing developments typically require the faculty member purchaser to resell the home to the institution upon departure from employment, at a pre-established price. In this method, the housing stock remains affordable to future faculty buyers. Another type of project involves a joint effort between the institution and a state housing development agency to build affordable rental units. Some colleges and universities have leased land to developers who have, in turn, developed rental units for faculty and staff housing. If housing costs continue to escalate in certain regions of the United States, and more and more institutions in those regions will need to find ways to make affordable housing available to faculty and staff.

Research Parks and Incubators

Many public and independent universities have begun or are beginning development of university-related research parks and technology incubators. A research park is a commercial development, affiliated with a university or with a group of universities, which is intended to attract corporate research and development tenants that have reasons to locate near a university. An incubator is a facility, sometimes but not always in a research park, where start-up or young companies are able to lease low-cost space and benefit from shared overhead and substantial business and technology development support services. There are today more than 150 university-related research parks under development in the United States, and many hundreds of university-related incubators.

Student Housing

Changing student preferences about living styles have induced a number of institutions to engage private developers to build residential, apartment-style student housing. These projects most often are located off campus on adjacent properties, although some institutions may permit private development for housing purposes on their campus property. The use of standard apartment units for student housing allows flexibility; when student demand declines, units can, if necessary, be rented to other users. The ability of developers to finance such projects is enhanced because of the promise of full occupancy with a focused market. The institution benefits in that it can acquire additional housing resources without the need to finance the project directly or manage it when built. The drawback is that revenues that otherwise might be captured by the institution go to the developer. Whenever a college or university is in a position to provide a low-risk, high-occupancy residential market to a private developer, the institution is in an excellent position to negotiate an agreement in which it maintains some control and possibly an equity position, to benefit from the rental income.

Hotels and Conference Centers

Typically, hotels and conference centers are developed on land leased from the institution from which the institution receives income; the facility is developed and owned by a developer and the hotel is managed for the developer by a company in the hospitality industry. The college or university may be a major but not exclusive user of the facility and the financing often is secured on the project revenues with a form of use contract from the institution. Conference centers and hotels are becoming increasingly popular, as institutions begin to focus on the huge potential higher education market for executive and professional continuing education and as they seek to be regional partners in economic development. Some of these facilities are being developed as part of the core facilities in university-related research parks.

Shopping Centers and Malls

In both urban and suburban locations, institutions have leased land to developers for construction of retail shopping centers. Projects have been undertaken in some cases purely for income-generating purposes. In other cases, the focus of the project is to provide retail and service businesses at or adjacent to the campus, in large part to serve the needs of students, faculty, and staff.

Commercial Office Development

A number of institutions have successfully developed commercial office buildings for purely investment purposes (as opposed to those in research parks, which presumably have technology development purposes), from which they derive endowment income. A college or university may take advantage of its land assets in prime commercial locations to develop commercial buildings for a variety of private, not-for-profit, and governmental tenants.

Cultural, Educational, and Recreational Facilities

Colleges and universities occasionally can find potentially profitable projects that have educational or cultural uses. These might include theme parks, recreational and fitness centers open to public users, golf or tennis facilities, museums, theater and arts centers, and satellite educational facilities. University alumni club facilities, away from the campus, also may fall into this category. Some graduate business schools have developed executive education centers—upscale instructional and conference facilities aimed specifically at corporate continuing education markets.

Retirement Communities

As the U.S. population ages, there is increasing demand for housing suitable for older people, ranging from recent empty-nesters to the elderly who require medical and living-support facilities. College and university campuses are, in many respects, ideal locations for such communities. They have a peaceful environment, the presence of young people, the opportunity of academic classes, libraries, recreational facilities, and, in many cases, clinical programs in medicine, nursing, gerontology, and other relevant disciplines. Such developments may be interesting components to consider in long-range land-use plans.

New Academic or "Knowledge Communities"

Some institutions have undertaken projects for major campus expansion or redevelopment that purposefully mix academic, commercial, and residential uses in a new form of planned academic community or knowledge community. Such projects normally involve a major college or university, a state or local government, partners from the private sector, and possibly a local economic development agency in a large land-use master plan, intended to be implemented in phases over a long time period. They might be considered more elaborate variations of the university-related research park.

Development Strategy and Financing Alternatives

There is no one correct development strategy for colleges and universities to adopt in plans to use land assets. The appropriate strategy is a function of many factors, including:

- the nature of the project to be undertaken;
- the financial resources of the institution and its related foundations;
- the management and real estate expertise resident at the institution or acquired by the institution for the purpose;
- the availability of appropriate private and/or public sector partners;
- the potential impact of the financing obligation, direct or indirect, on the institution's balance sheet and credit ratings; and
- the degree of risk-aversion of the institution, balanced with the relative strength of its desire to make a profit and control the development.

Each situation is unique; each plan needs a unique solution designed as a variation of one of the following three basic alternatives.

The College or University as Developer

Institutions that wish to own, manage, and control a project to achieve certain programmatic or rate-of-return objectives can act as developers themselves. For tax status reasons, discussed below, it is often better to do so through a separate real estate development entity created as a related corporation of the institution. In fact, great numbers of public institutions have "related corporations" or "real estate foundations" through which they acquire, own, develop, and manage various properties. In actuality, most institutions have considerable experience in planning, construction, and management of real property. They may lack experience in certain aspects of zoning, environmental approvals, commercial financing vehicles, real estate marketing, sales, leasing, and other aspects of commercial development, but these skills are not impossible to develop or acquire. This is especially true if the institution creates a related corporation and staffs it with personnel with the requisite expertise.

Master Development or Ground-lease Agreements

An institution may convey control of property by means of a long-term ground lease to a private developer who, in turn, builds and owns the leasehold improvements, undertakes all marketing, leasing, and management, and receives the entire return on the development. The college or university receives ground lease rental payments, which may or may not be tied to revenues generated by the project. For the institution, this is a form of investment that, like stocks and bonds, is entirely passive, requires little to no management, and has a fixed base return (the rental payment) and the potential to share in profits (the payment tied to revenues). Risk is reduced to the risk that the project will fail entirely and the developer might default on ground rent payments. In addition, there is image risk in that, if the development is tied to the institution's name, its failure will be a public relations failure for the institution. One of the most interesting features of this kind of development is that ownership of all the leasehold improvements typically reverts to the institution at the end of the land-lease term. This can be particularly useful for rental housing, conference centers, and research facilities. Again, research parks provide an example of this approach. Also, a number of urban universities own central city property that has been developed via ground lease and provides ground-lease income for years. Hotel developments typically follow this model, as do retail shopping centers and other purely commercial types of projects.

In general, an institution should assess the potential value that a private developer adds to a project before deciding to engage one and, if participation of a developer seems the best option, the terms of the long-term agreement must be considered very carefully. Research parks provide an interesting example. While a number of such projects were undertaken during the 1980s by developers in affiliation with a university, others are being developed directly as projects of the university. Time has shown that a number of the 1980s-era master development agreements did not sufficiently consider the eventual risks, the specific responsibilities of the two parties, and the general pitfalls of a partnership between two such culturally different business entities. Consequently, a great number of these relationships have failed, largely due to mismatched expectations.

Joint Venture Development

A third and very diverse category includes cases where the college or university participates in development with private-sector and/or public entities through a corporate or partnership structure. With variations, this alternative usually includes an equity position or an investment and an active role for the institution in financing and marketing activities. The developer typically may be engaged in development planning, some of the financing, marketing, and project management. Various models for public-private partnerships have been used by colleges and universities with varying degrees of success. Although joint venture partners share objectives, their relative emphasis on objectives can vary. Also, the developer, public-sector agency, and college or university can have different time horizons for quantifiable accomplishments. Thus, opportunities for a conflict in a complex joint venture are myriad, so a carefully structured joint venture contract is essential to long-term success. Nonetheless, joint venture is likely to be optimal in cases where shared control, risk, and rewards are the institution's preference.

A Note on Risk

In any of the above scenarios, it is important to remember that engaging a private development partner—whether under a master development agreement, project-by-project basis, or joint venture—will not necessarily insulate an institution from financial impact or risk. While a private developer might abandon a project that is failing, a college or university is highly unlikely to do so. For example, if a private developer develops a commercial facility in a university's research park, and that facility fails to lease adequately, causing actual or potential default on debt service, it is highly likely that the university will feel compelled to step in to support the project by leasing the facility itself, or otherwise finding a means to avert a default. As another example, if a private party develops student or faculty housing, it is likely that the institution will have to provide some guarantees of demand and occupancy. For this reason, institutions should never assume that involvement of a private partner obviates their risk entirely. And, with respect to credit analysis, the rating agencies generally will consider off-balance sheet financing of a college or university in their evaluations of credit capacity and credit strength.

A Framework for Real Estate Development

Institutions that have little experience in developing land assets other than for capital facilities need to consider several issues when they contemplate turning undeveloped land assets into productive investments. Even institutions that have experience with real estate projects could benefit from a structured framework for assessing investment opportunities. The framework involves five levels of planning and consideration of numerous interrelated issues.

Mission and Long-range Institutional Plan

Planning for a choice of land-use alternatives begins, of necessity, with a comprehensive, very long-range, strategic vision for the future of the institution itself. It is necessary to establish firmly that certain land assets truly are in excess of what may be needed for future core educational purposes. The institution's strategic plan and an ongoing strategic planning process must be in place in order for prudent decisions to be made about reserves of land for future mission-related facilities development. (For a full discussion of this subject, see chapter 2, Planning.) The strategic plan also is the correct vehicle for identifying possible mission-related needs that could be combined with commercial objectives in projects, such as the need to improve the range and quality of student housing or near-campus retail and service businesses.

Administrators must determine if any contemplated real estate projects support or, at a minimum, do not risk interfering with accomplishment of core institutional missions. For example, a decision to convert an existing student residence hall to a retirement community should be made only after careful analysis and strategic planning lead to a determination that the student units will be permanently unnecessary or, conversely, that they could be replaced without great pain in some other way if need arises.

Strategic Resource Management Plan

Within the context of a long-range vision of institutional mission and strategic plans, the next level of analysis in land development must address land use in the context of strategic management of all institutional resources. Given finite financial and human resources and various strategic needs for funding core activities ranging from faculty salaries to new program development, the institution must determine that it has time and money available to devote to real estate asset development.

Comprehensive Strategic Land-use Plan

With outside assistance as needed, administrators should develop a comprehensive strategic land-use plan that addresses all available land parcels and all potential uses for them, even if only a single project is contemplated for the immediate future. The land-use plan also should identify partnership opportunities, development strategy preferences, skills needed, and overall preliminary concepts for financing.

Land Banking

Some institutions, and some groups or consortia of institutions, have undertaken land banking as a long-term land acquisition and development strategy. Land banking, which has been most important in urban areas, involves acquisition of parcels of property over time in a given neighborhood or area—typically the neighborhood surrounding the institution or institutions—until the institutions have significant control of the neighborhood. The purposes can be to have land available for future institutional needs, for institution-sponsored commercial or residential development, or to prevent harmfully incompatible development by others in adjacent areas. Land banking strategies are invaluable for providing for very long-range future expansion of institutional campuses and for enabling institutions to undertake or sponsor supporting, compatible developments. In undertaking land banking, however, institutions should avoid extreme strategies that will discourage high-quality private investment in the designated neighborhood.

Physical Master (Site) Plan

Once a conceptual plan that defines excess land and potential uses has been developed, a physical master plan or site plan is needed. At this stage, preliminary site studies, soil studies, environmental impact studies, and engineering studies may be appropriate to determine if certain uses and sites are compatible or to establish the best disposition of elements for a large site. Master plans can be changed, but it is best to begin development with one in place. The land-use plan and the physical master (site) plan should identify phases of development with approximate timing of the phases.

Asset Business Plan

Real estate development projects, especially large-scale phased plans, can take so long to complete that they may survive transitions in management and governing bodies. The institution may be able to save wasted time and effort and to continue projects more efficiently if a business plan for each asset or related series of assets is prepared that summarizes the partnership relationships, market and financial feasibility, operating plans, *pro forma* financial statements, and other aspects of the development strategy. In some cases, such a plan may be required by some or all project participants, especially those providing any portions of financing. In an appropriate asset management strategy, the business plan for the property must be updated periodically, to reflect current business conditions and expectations.

Development Considerations

Having progressed through strategic planning, land-use planning, master planning, and the development of an asset business plan, actual development must be planned and undertaken with consideration given to a number of issues.

The Risk-return Relationship and Development Strategies

Risk and reward are directly related. The higher the potential risk, the higher the potential reward. Colleges and universities, by their core nature, tend to be risk-averse entities. However, contemplation of a real estate development provides a good opportunity for a fresh consideration of the institution's actual tolerance for some risk. To some extent, the nature of possible projects determines the most appropriate development strategy; however, institutional administrators must examine institutional policies and preferences with respect to overall investment strategies, endowment growth, and risk position when making decisions about what role they should play in land development.

Taxation and Tax Status

Real estate projects with mixed or pure commercial uses are subject to property taxes, which must be considered in development of operating cost estimates. More importantly, projects not considered "exempt" for the purposes of the college or university are subject to taxes on income. Therefore, when a college or university undertakes development of a real estate project directly, it may have to determine the implications for payment of unrelated business income taxes (UBIT) on the revenues generated. At the extreme, if a tax-exempt entity engages in substantial unrelated business activity, it may become vulnerable to review of its tax-exempt status by the Internal Revenue Service. (For a full discussion of this subject, see chapter 11, Taxation.) A major argument in favor of creating a separate corporate entity for real estate development is that the entity may be a tax-paying private entity, and thus clearly segregated from the tax-exempt activities and status of the institution.

Governance and Corporate Organization Structures

For tax status and other reasons, if an institution decides to consider development by any strategy other than passive ground-lease transactions, it must examine governance and corporate structure issues to determine if new or modified forms are required to engage in real estate projects, either alone or with a developer. In the case of public institutions, public agency status virtually dictates that a separate but related real estate entity will be needed. Depending on the circumstances of the transaction, the entity may be a not-for-profit corporation or foundation. Issues can arise as to the ability of the state and or institution to transfer land to such an entity. Alternatively, such an entity may purchase land or receive land as gifts on behalf of the public institution. A number of public universities have created entities for such purposes; others have real estate activities centered in entities that also have other roles, such as fund-raising and endowment management. If an active development role is envisioned, it is also possible that a for-profit land development entity may be required.

Market and Financial Feasibility Analysis

As internal facilities development proceeds from a careful assessment of the internal needs, commercial or hybrid projects also require an assessment of the needs of whatever constituencies or markets the project will meet. These studies, referred to as market feasibility or market and financial feasibility studies, seek to measure the size and nature of the potential market for a given project. Location, project characteristics, transportation, parking, amenities, and numerous other features are considered, as are the nature and quantity of competing projects. For a hotel, for example, the number, quality, type, and rates of existing and planned hotel rooms in the pertinent location would be studied closely to determine if the contemplated project can compete in meeting present and future demand.

Market feasibility is tied closely to financial feasibility. Projections of the rate of absorption, the annual rate at which leasable space is likely to be leased, together with the achievable rental rates, are key variables in cash flow projections and assessments of potential profitability. A project is financially feasible if it is expected to generate at least enough revenues to cover debt service, operating costs (including a factor for vacancies and reserves) and a 20 to 30 percent margin over debt service for profit, over a reasonable period of time.

The financial feasibility analysis uses data generated from market feasibility analyses, including lease rates and estimated absorption rates, preliminary construction cost estimates, financing assumptions, and operating cost estimates, to develop *pro forma* financial statements that demonstrate project feasibility. The *pro forma* statements are prepared for a number of years; in a typical project, there will be less cash flow in the early years that will be made up in later years. *Pro forma* financial statements also are subject to sensitivity analysis, to test the effects of changes in core assumptions on the results. The greater the dependence of a project's financial outcomes on optimistic assumptions, the greater the degree of risk inherent in the project.

Management and Skills

Numerous institutions with small finance staffs and limited development experience should consider their development alternatives to be limited to engaging a developer. In fact, this often may be the most practical choice available, but it is not the only one. It usually is possible to employ someone with suitable skills to enable a more direct development role; alternatively, the institution can engage consultants to represent the institution in development planning and management. In fact, even with a developer-run project, it is important for the institution to have the appropriate internal skills for negotiating project terms in which the institution's interests are addressed adequately.

Community Partnerships and Community Relations

Except in rare cases, community support is necessary for institutional real estate development projects. For a college or university, which is a permanent member of the community, community acceptance goes well beyond the formal regulatory matters of zoning and environmental approvals that developers typically must obtain. The institution should seek the participation of appropriate community leaders in deliberations of possible uses for the land from the outset.

In some communities, the local college or university is the largest entity in the area. It may have the largest land holdings, the highest number of employees, and the greatest economic impact on that community. In other communities, institutions are major if not overwhelming economic forces. In the current economic development environment, higher education institutions are increasingly being recognized as major economic resources, or magnets, by the communities in which they are located. Many are working with local governments and economic development agencies to develop projects that have a potential beneficial impact on the surrounding community. This is often true of colleges or universities located in disadvantaged urban communities or in downtown areas in need of major redevelopment and renewal. Even in cases where the institution is undertaking a project with express purposes of improving a community and providing jobs to its residents, there can be immense implications for community relations.

Sometimes colleges and universities may be regarded not as golden resources but rather as non-tax-paying drains on the local economy. A few large and well-endowed independent universities pay fees "in lieu of taxes" to city governments as a means of compensating for the vast acreage of land that is permanently off the city's property tax rolls. In other jurisdictions, the issue of property taxes has been raised periodically; thus colleges and universities sometimes need to justify their economic posture in their communities. These sensitive issues must be taken into account in strategic land-use planning for all institutions.

A final major community-relations issue is that of potential charges of unfair business competition. In a number of cases, colleges and universities that engage in developments of certain kinds of commercial projects have been accused of competing unfairly with local businesses that, unlike the institution, are subject to taxes and other financial disadvantages. All plans for business-oriented real estate development in which the college or university will be a partner require careful consideration of their impact on small businesses and the consequences of this impact on community relations.

Pitfalls to Avoid

The range of financial gains or losses that can occur in real estate projects makes it important for prudence and skilled judgment to prevail over wishful thinking or reactive decision making. Major resources are at stake. Some of the pitfalls that higher education institutions should seek to avoid follow.

Sale of Land

There probably are only rare cases in which it would be prudent to sell college- or university-owned land assets that are part of or adjacent to the campus. Institutions almost always should consider leasing, including long-term leases, as the preferred alternative for campus property and, indeed, also for many non-campus properties. On the other hand, when institutions receive bequests of property not suited for their use or development, sale of such assets may be most appropriate. Timing, of course, should be such that the assets are sold when they can achieve a price that makes their disposition worthwhile to the institution.

Time Horizon Differences

Higher education institutions typically do not conduct business quickly and have very long life expectancies. Real estate developers, on the other hand, cannot afford to wait interminably for returns on their investments. This is a fundamental difference in time horizon and in business culture that affects behavior and can lead to differing expectations and, ultimately, unsatisfactory relationships. Again, in the last 15 years, a great number of university-developer partnerships for research parks suffered from such differing time horizon expectations and business cultures. When engaging in a project with a developer, the institution should articulate its objectives and expectations plainly and seek to be responsive to its developer partner. The greatest difficulty is crafting a business relationship in which the institution balances correctly between asserting its rights (for example for control or portions of the expected return) and, at the same time, not placing unrealistic business or time horizon demands on its private sector partner.

Business Versus Nonbusiness Objectives

Land development should be undertaken for sound and long-term mission or business reasons: that is, it should be undertaken because the project can be conceived, financed, and built to meet needs and generate income. Real estate projects should not be administrative monuments, nor should they be undertaken to maintain status with peer institutions. An ill-conceived project not rooted in sound business judgment can be a financial drain on the institution as well as a public relations or legal problem.

Bad Market Timing

After the development and lending excesses of the 1980s, many commercial markets throughout the United States were overbuilt, and it took much of the 1990s for the real estate industry to recover. Real estate supply and demand is cyclical, and the factors driving the cycles are becoming more complex, more diverse, and more global in nature. Market data and business planning must be accurate and current and decisions must be made in a timely fashion in order to take advantage of a good market or avoid a bad one. Many institutions establish decision-making bodies that can react more quickly to this requirement than the normal academic procedures.

Environmental and Archaeological Considerations

Land development will entail costs for environmental studies and, in some cases, for prevention and remediation measures. In a few cases, there even may be archaeological factors. These issues should be studied early on in any land use planning to avert problems later in the planning process.

A Long-range Perspective

For colleges and universities, land is a permanent and exceptionally valuable strategic resource. It is incumbent on all institutions that wish to strengthen their financial independence, as well as their long-term ability to weather weak economic conditions, inflation, enrollment dips, and other threats to quality and solvency, to evaluate the long-range and strategic possibilities of their land assets to generate income. Often this can be done in ways that also contribute to the programmatic resources or quality of life at the institution. Land-use decisions are, however, complex and create outcomes that may be difficult or impossible to reverse. Consequently, institutions should proceed cautiously, perform comprehensive analyses, and establish clear plans and appropriate expectations. A project or master plan must be well enough designed and constructed to be able to withstand challenging financial and economic scenarios in the future. It may be better to wait until the next "cycle" rather than undertake a project that might weaken, rather than strengthen, the institution; college and university lands are, after all, a permanent resource that institutions should expect to own and benefit from in perpetuity.

NOTES

1. Harvey H. Kaiser and Jerry Davis. *A Foundation to Uphold: A Study of Facilities Conditions at U.S. Colleges and Universities.* A collaboration effort by APPA: The Association of Higher Education Facilities Offices, the National Association of College and University Business Officers, and Sallie Mae (Alexandria VA, 1996).

2. For a thorough discussion of FASB Statement of Financial Accounting Standards No. 93, see *Recognition of Depreciation by Not-for-Profit-Institutions* (Washington, DC: NACUBO, 1988).

3. See Sean Rush and Applied Management Engineering, P.C., *Managing the Facilities Portfolio: A Practical Approach to Institutional Facility Renewal and Deferred Maintenance* (Washington, DC: NACUBO, 1991).

4. See detailed discussion of life cycle analysis is available in *Life Cycle Cost Analysis* (Washington, DC: American Institute of Architects, 1977).

5. See Facilities Management: *A Manual for Plant Administration, Part II: Maintenance and Operations of Building and Grounds, Chapter 20 Facilities Condition Assessments* (Alexandria VA: APPA: The Association of Higher Education Facilities Officers, 1997).

6. Harvey H. Kaiser, *The Facilities Audit Workbook: A Process for Improving Facilities*

Conditions (Alexandria VA: APPA: The Association of Higher Education Facilities Officers, 1993).

7. See *Facilities Management: A Manual for Plant Administration, Part IV: Maintenance and Operation of Buildings and Grounds, Chapter 52 Campus Master Planning* (Alexandria VA: APPA: The Association of Higher Education Facilities Officers, 1997).

8. See *Post Secondary Education Facilities Inventory and Classification Manual* (Washington, DC: U.S. Department of Education, 1992).

9. See *Facilities Management: A Manual for Plant Administration, Part I: General Administration and Management, Chapter 17 Contracting for Services* (Alexandria VA: APPA: The Association of Higher Education Facilities Officers, 1997); Council of Higher Education Management Associations, *Contract Management or Self-Operation* (Alexandria, VA, : APPA: The Association of Higher Education Facilities Officers, 1993); and National Association of College and University Business Officers, *Contracting for Services* (Washington, DC, NACUBO, 1982).

10. See *Facilities Management: A Manual for Plant Administration, Part III Energy and Utilities Systems, Chapter 40 Energy Management and Conservation* (Alexandria VA: APPA: The Association of Higher Education Facilities Officers, 1997).

11. See *Facilities Management: A Manual for Plant Administration, Part I General Administration and Management,* Chapter 3 Organization (Alexandria VA: APPA: The Association of Higher Education Facilities Officers, 1997).

12. See *Facilities Management: A Manual for Plant Administration, Part IV Facilities Planning, Design, Construction, and Administration and Management* (Alexandria VA: APPA: The Association of Higher Education Facilities Officers, 1997).

13. See *Facilities Management: A Manual for Plant Administration, Part IV Facilities Planning, Design, Construction, and Administration and Management,* Chapter 66 Space Management (Alexandria VA: APPA: The Association of Higher Education Facilities Officers, 1997).

14. See *Facilities Management: A Manual for Plant Administration, Part II: Maintenance and Operations of Buildings and Grounds* (Alexandria VA: APPA: The Association of Higher Education Facilities Officers, 1997).

REFERENCES AND RESOURCES

Publications and Articles

Adams, Matthew C. *Successful Funding Strategies for Facility Renewal*. Alexandria, Va.: APPA, 1999.

American Society of Heating, Refrigeration, and Air Conditioning Engineers. *ASHRAE Handbook*. Atlanta, Ga.: ASHRAE, 1999.

Associated General Contractors of America, American Subcontractors Association, Inc., and Associated Specialty Contractors. *Guidelines for a Successful Construction Project*. Washington, DC: Associated General Contractors of America, American Subcontractors Association, Inc., and Associated Specialty Contractors, 1989.

——. *Building Construction Contracting Methods*. Washington: DC: Associated General Contractors of America, American Subcontractors Association, Inc., and Associated Specialty Contractors, 1991.

American Institute of Architects and Associated General Contractors of America. *Recommended Guide for Competitive Bidding Procedures and Contract Awards for Building Construction*. American Institute of Architects and Associated General Contractors of America, 1982.

Association of Physical Plant Administrators. *Facilities Management: A Manual for Plant Administration*. Alexandria, Va.: APPA, 1997.

——. *Comparative Costs and Staffing Report for College and University Facilities*. Alexandria, Va.: APPA, Biannual.

——. *Case Studies in Environmental Health and Safety*. Alexandria, Va.: APPA, 1990.

Bareither, Harlan D., and Schillinger, J. L. *University Space Planning*. Urbana, Ill.: University of Illinois Press, 1968.

Bent, James A., and Thumann, Albert. *Project Management for Engineering and Construction*. Lilburn, Ga.: Fairmount Press, 1989.

Building Officials and Code Administrators International. *BOCA Codes and Manuals*. Homewood, Ill.: BOCA, 1999.

Callender, John. *Time-Saver Standards*. 5th Ed. New York: McGraw-Hill Book Company, 1994.

Castaldi, B. *Educational Facilities*. Boston: Allyn & Bacon, 1987.

Clough, Richard H, and Sears, Glenn A. *Construction Contracting*. New York: John Wiley & Sons, 1994.

Collins, Stephen J., and Forrester, Robert T. *Recognition of Depreciation by Not-for-Profit Institutions*. Washington, DC: NACUBO, 1988.

De Chiara, Joseph, and Koppelman, Lee E. *Site Planning Standards*. New York: McGraw-Hill Book Company, 1978.

DeGoff, Robert A., and Friedman, Howard A. *Construction Management: Basic*

Principles for Architects, Engineers, and Owners. New York: John Wiley & Sons, 1985.

Dell'Isola, Alphonse J., and Kirk, Stephen J. *Life Cycle Costing for Design Professionals*. New York: McGraw-Hill Book Company, 1995.

Dober, Richard P. *Campus Planning*. Cambridge, Mass.: Reinhold Publishing, 1963: reprinted 1996 by the Society for College and University Planning.

Dunn, John A., Jr. *Financial Planning Guidelines for Facility Renewal and Adaptation*. Ann Arbor, Mich.: Society for College and University Planning, 1989.

Financial Accounting Standards Board. *Recognition of Depreciation for Non-Profit Organizations*. FASB Statement No. 93. Stamford, Conn.: FASB, 1987.

Foxhall, William B. *Professional Construction Management and Project Administration*. New York: American Institute of Architects with Architectural Record Books, 1972.

Haviland, David (Ed.). *The Architect's Handbook of Professional Practice*. Washington, DC: American Institute of Architects Press, 1994.

Kaiser, Harvey H., and Davis, Jerry. *A Foundation to Uphold: A Study of Facilities Conditions in U.S. Colleges and Universities*. Alexandria, VA: APPA, 1996.

————. *Crumbling Academe: Solving the Capital Renewal and Replacement Dilemma*. Washington, DC: Association of Governing Boards, 1984.

————. *The Facilities Audit Work: A Process for Improving Facilities Conditions*. Alexandria, VA.: Association of Physical Plant Administrators, 1987.

————. *Facilities Manager's Reference*. Kingston, MA: R. S. Means Company, 1989.

————. and Applied Management Engineering. *Maintenance Management Audit Workbook*. Kingston, MA: R. S. Means Company, 1991.

————. *Managing Facilities More Effectively*. New Directions for Higher Education Quarterly, No. 30. San Francisco, CA: Jossey-Bass, 1980.

Klein, Eva, "Technology Parks and Incubators: A Nexus Between University Science and Industrial Research and Development," in C.R. Haden, and J.R. Brink (eds), *Innovative Models for University Research*. Amsterdam: Elsevier Science Publishers, 1992.

Liske, Roger W. *Means Facilities Maintenance Standards*. Kingston, Ma: R. S. Means Company, 1988.

Magee, Gregory H. *Facilities Maintenance Management*. Kingston, MA: R. S. Means Company, 1988.

McGraw-Hill Cost Information Systems. *Dodge Construction Systems Costs*. Princeton, NJ: McGraw-Hill Book Company, 1991. (This source is updated annually.)

Meisinger, Richard R., Jr., and Dubeck, Leroy W. *College and University Budgeting.* Washington, DC: NACUBO, 1984.

National Association of College and University Business Officers. *Managing the Facilities Portfolio.* Washington, DC: NACUBO, 1991.

National Fire Protection Association. *Codes, Standards, Recommended Practices, and Manuals.* Quincy, MA: NFPA, issued periodically.

Qayoumi, Mohammad H. *Electrical Distribution and Maintenance.* Alexandria, VA.: Association of Physical Plant Administrators, 1989.

R. S. Means. *Building Construction Cost Data.* Duxbury, MA: R. S. Means Company, 1999. (This source is updated annually.)

Turner, Paul Venable. *Campus.* Cambridge, MA: MIT Press, 1984.

Turner, Wayne C. *Energy Management Handbook.* New York: John Wiley & Sons, 1982.

U.S. Department of Education. *Postsecondary Education Facilities Inventory and Classification Manual.* Washington, DC: U.S. Government Printing Office, 1992.

Organizations

Association of University Real Estate Officials (AUREO)
c/o Cornell Real Estate, Box DH—Real Estate, Ithaca, NY 14853,
607-266-7875 . . . . www.aureo. org

APPA: The Association of Higher Education Facilities Officers (APPA)
1643 Prince Street, Alexandria, VA
703-684-1446 . . . . www.appa.org

Association of University Related Research Parks (AURRP)
1730 K Street, NW, Suite 700, Washington, DC 20006
202-828-4167 . . . . www.aurrp.org

Chapter 14

◆

Environmental Health and Safety

by

Matthew Finucane
University of Pennsylvania

Donald A. Robinson
University of Massachusetts at Amherst

with assistance from

Lawrence Davis, University of Massachusetts at Amherst

Robert T. Forrest, University of Pennsylvania

James P. Fox, University of Massachusetts at Amherst

Robert Laford, University of Massachusetts at Amherst

Edward Mientka, University of Massachusetts at Amherst

Valerie I. Steinberg, University of Massachusetts at Amherst

Note: This chapter draws heavily on the material contained in the 5th edition. Therefore it is appropriate to acknowledge with appreciation those individuals that contributed to that edition. The previous authors who are not acknowledged elsewhere, include Emery E. Sobottka, Louis Mitchell, and Gregory P. Crouch, from Iowa State University and George H. Reed, Jr. and Susan M. McDonald from the University of Massachusetts.

Contents

Environmental health and safety (EH&S) in a college or university setting is a professional service delivery organization that provides injury and illness prevention and safety and health regulatory compliance services to the entire campus community. EH&S, to best serve the campus community, should be viewed as a core value of the institution and not the sole responsibility of any one organizational entity. The EH&S organization is typically located within the administration and finance or the academic affairs structure. Nationally, the trend is to have the EH&S function report directly to a chief administrative officer such as the vice president for administration or provost. This direct reporting line helps assure that, when necessary, essential and critical EH&S matters are brought directly to the attention of the principle administrative officers. This reporting structure is also necessary to minimize the potential conflicts of interest that might arise if EH&S were reporting elsewhere in the organization. The EH&S operation typically encompasses a number of program specialties including: biological safety, environmental health, chemical safety, hazardous materials, environmental management, occupational safety, fire safety, industrial hygiene, occupational medicine, and radiation safety. There is a clear and distinct role for an EH&S organization, although how the EH&S services are delivered, the mix of services, and the terminology used varies greatly between institutions. The structure of the EH&S program should be proportional to the size, complexity, and nature of the institution. At a small institution EH&S may be assigned as a collateral duty supplemented by outside assistance, while at a major research institution there is a greater need for a formal organization structured to deliver a broad range of EH&S services.

EH&S is also faced with undertaking a number of initiatives aimed at reducing institutional vulnerability. The Environmental Protection Agency (EPA) has placed increased attention on environmental compliance at universities and colleges. These efforts have resulted in aggressive enforcement actions and significant penalties. The tragic January 19, 2000, Seton Hall University residential fire has focused increased national emphasis on campus residential life safety programs. The potential misuse of radioactive materials demands the need for strong radiation safety measures to comply with state and federal regulations. The heightened concern over the safe handling of blood and body fluids requires an institutional biological safety program that includes compliance with the Occupational Safety and Health Administration (OSHA) bloodborne pathogen standard. Growing concerns related to ergonomics and the associated workers' compensation costs and human suffering have increased the need for EH&S to evaluate potential repetitive motion activities and develop needed injury prevention programs. Other issues such as indoor air quality, building ventilation, pedestrian safety, and building code compliance are placing increasing demands on EH&S resources.

Regardless of the size of an EH&S "department," the institution must clearly communicate to the campus community the importance of this function. This is accomplished in part through the development of an institutional EH&S policy statement and appropriate policy manuals, which designate the appropriate levels of management responsibility and the authority to implement effective safety programs (see figure 14-01). Ultimately, the head of the institution is responsible for the EH&S program, but he or she usually delegates authority and responsibilities through appropriate directors, deans, and managers. The administrative head of each department or organizational unit in turn bears the primary responsibility for safety, accident prevention, health protection, and compliance with regulations for the persons affected in his or her jurisdiction. The EH&S department acts in partnership with other campus units, developing appropriate safety programs, providing technical assistance, monitoring the delivery of safety programs, and exercising emergency control in cases of imminent danger. The most effective safety policy manuals and statements incorporate a teamwork philosophy that coordinates activities and cooperation at all levels.

This chapter provides an overview of the principal EH&S program areas and emphasizes the complex, technical nature of this rapidly expanding and vital area of college and university administration. Further information and assistance can be obtained from the Campus Safety Health and Environmental Management Association (CSHEMA). CSHEMA, as a division of the National Safety Council (NSC), is the leading association of campus EH&S professionals.

BIOSAFETY AND ENVIRONMENTAL HEALTH

Animal Safety and Health

Many important scientific and medical advances have been made using experimental animals. Institutions that care for and use animals in research, testing, or educational programs must assume responsibility for the well being of the

Figure 14-01

A Sample University Environmental Health & Safety Policy Statement

It is a policy of the University to maintain, insofar as it is reasonable and within its control, an environment for its faculty, staff, students, and visitors that does not adversely affect their health and safety. In support of this policy the University will give high priority, appropriate support, and steady implementation to eliminate where possible, or to reduce to acceptable limits, environmental and occupational hazards that are a threat to the health and safety of personnel or to property.

The ultimate responsibility for the campus safety and environmental health rests with the Chancellor. The Chancellor has delegated to each dean, director, chairperson, and supervisor the responsibility for safety performance within their respective unit. Everyone with supervisory responsibility will be expected to take the initiative so that safe working conditions are maintained, and to request the assistance of the Department of Environmental Health and Safety to expedite action when necessary. Each supervisor must take the initiative to train the employees and students under his/her supervision in safe work practices. In particular, supervisors should ensure that employees and students know (a) all potentially hazardous conditions associated with the operation and the method established to control them, (b) all safety regulations for the area of operation. In addition, supervisors are expected to promote a safety attitude and awareness that will lead employees and students working under their supervision to take a safe course when faced with situations which are not covered by established regulations and practices.

It is incumbent upon each member of the faculty, staff, and student body to provide the constant vigilance necessary to avoid unsafe acts on his/her part. Faculty, staff, and students have an obligation to take all reasonable precautions to prevent injury to themselves or to their fellow employees or students. They are expected to learn and to follow approved standards and procedures that apply to their activities, and to check with their supervisors when they have any doubts concerning potential hazards.

The President has delegated to the Director of Environmental Health and Safety the responsibility and authority for assuming overall compliance with applicable* health and safety standards on campus. The Director shall adopt as guides applicable health and safety standards promulgated by Federal and State agencies in establishing campus regulations and policy. Published standards of nationally recognized professional health and safety groups may serve as guidelines in the absence of appropriate statutes and governmental regulations. The Department of Environmental Health and Safety is responsible for working with and through academic and service units by identifying and assisting in resolving health and safety problems, recommending standards, evaluating and reporting on the status of compliance with standards, providing technical and support services, recommending necessary modifications, recording, analyzing and reporting accident experience, and developing training resources.

In emergency situations and when required to do so by code, regulation, or licensure agreement, the Director of Environmental Health and Safety or his/her representative, in consultation with the appropriate Dean or Director, may require the immediate halt or control of practices or conditions that have been determined to constitute an immediate and serious risk of death or serious harm to members of the campus community. Such actions may be appealed to the President who will make the final determination as to whether the practices may be reinstated.

Specific faculty committees on Radioisotope Use, Biological Hazards, Chemical Hazards, Animal Care, and Biohazards shall be responsible for reviewing and recommending operational policies and practices within their area of expertise. In addition, they may advise the Director of Environmental Health and Safety regarding the application of relevant standards for hazard control.

*Source: Donald Robinson, Director of Environmental Health and Safety, University of Massachusetts at Amherst

animals and the staff caring for them by establishing an animal care and use program. Animals may include traditional laboratory animals, farm animals, or wildlife or aquatic animals studied in natural settings. The animal care program and facilities must meet accepted professional standards and standards specified in the Guide for the Care and the Use of Laboratory Animals (NRC 1996), Animal Welfare Regulations (CFR 1985), Public Health Service Policy on Human Care and Use of Laboratory Animals (PHS 1996), and other federal, state, and local laws and regulations. The goals of such a program should be to:

- ensure humane treatment of the animals by employing staff with adequate professional qualifications and training;

- provide proper facilities for the feeding and housing of animals;

- provide an occupational health and safety program for animal care workers; and

- monitor the care and use of animals (including work with hazardous agents).

Institutional animal care and use committees (IACUC) should be established, with academic and research involvement, to assist in auditing and monitoring the program.

The humane treatment of animals requires scientific and professional judgment that is based on knowledge of each species of laboratory animal and special requirements of the research, teaching, or educational programs. Thus, it is important for the animal care staff to include a director with education and experience in laboratory animal medicine, a resident or consulting veterinarian, and support staff with expertise in laboratory animal science. Special qualifications and certifications may be desirable or even necessary for personnel using hazardous biological, chemical, or physical agents.

Administrators should keep in mind that animals need care every day, including weekends and holidays. The animal care facilities should be designed with consideration for the physical and social needs of the animals, the safety and protection of personnel, and research requirements. Special facilities may be needed for animal research with hazardous agents. Ideally, facilities for the study of infectious diseases should be separate from the activities of animal production, quarantine, and patient care.

Work with experimental animals is associated with specific occupational hazards. Animal care providers have an increased risk of contracting certain infectious diseases (e.g., tetanus, rabies, hepatitis), developing allergies, and sustaining physical injury from animals. An occupational health program for personnel working in animal facilities should be established to assess the health risks to employees and to provide the proper immunizations and medical surveillance to prevent disease.

Institutional administrators should be alert to changes in the laws and regulations in this area.

Biological Safety

A biological safety program is necessary to protect personnel, members of the community, and the institutional environment from disease-causing microorganisms and to comply with relevant regulations. The biological safety program should address proper procedures for the safe handling of etiological agents in research and teaching with special attention to genetic engineering research; for the safe handling and disposal of infectious waste; for infection-control procedures in a student health center or hospital; and for animal safety and health. The National Institutes of Health (NIH) and the Department of Health and Human Services (HHS) have issued guidelines governing the conduct of NIH-supported research on recombinant DNA. An institution conducting such research must establish an institutional biosafety committee with representation from the university as well as the general community to evaluate the safety of recombinant DNA and other potentially biohazardous projects.

Microbiology laboratories may pose special infectious disease risks, especially to personnel who must work in the laboratory environment. Safety programs should focus on protecting laboratory-associated personnel and preventing the escape of potentially hazardous agents into the community and the environment.

The types of biological agents used in a laboratory may range from those that present little or no hazard to laboratory personnel or the environment to those that may cause serious or lethal disease. HHS has described biological safety levels to define the risks of each type of microbiological agent and to recommend the proper containment for controlling infectious agents in the laboratory. These recommendations include adherence to proper microbiological techniques, the use of safety equipment, and proper design of facilities. A biological safety expert and other members of an occupational health program should assess the health risk and provide the proper immunizations and medical surveillance for healthcare workers and laboratory personnel who work with microbiological agents.

Healthcare workers, laboratory researchers, emergency medical personnel, and other employees who have contact with human blood, body fluids, or tissues carry an increased risk of infection with hepatitis B virus (HBV), hepatitis C

(HCV), the human immunodeficiency virus (HIV), and other blood-borne pathogens. OSHA has issued regulations that specify measures to eliminate or minimize employee exposures including a written exposure control plan, engineering and work practice controls, housekeeping, hepatitis B vaccination, communication of hazards, information and training, and recordkeeping.

Food, Drinking Water, and Swimming Pool Safety

Food

A food protection and sanitation (FPS) program should have a goal of "quality food": all food is purchased, stored, prepared, and served in a clean environment. The food service workers are responsible for working in an efficient and safe manner to prevent food-borne illnesses by practicing sanitary work procedures. Management (with the help of EH&S staff) is responsible for training personnel and implementing these procedures. The focus of training should include the guidelines on frequent hand washing, sanitary food handling with emphasis on the minimal handling of food, and monitoring time and temperature variables for potentially hazardous food. The basis for an FPS program on campus should be a state department of health food code. Areas of concern include safe sources of food; storage practices (dry, refrigerated, frozen); personal hygiene; food preparation, handling, and holding, including salad bars and self-serve areas; dish washing; cleaning equipment and floors; pest control for roaches, flies, and rodents; and emergencies due to failure of utilities or equipment. Routine inspections and surveys should be made of all operations.

Water

Potable water should be of high quality, meeting the U.S. Environmental Protection Agency (EPA) standards for physical, chemical, microbiological, and radiological characteristics. Depending on the source of the water, it may need to be treated for removal of certain substances (iron, lead) beyond the requirements for drinking water or adjusted for pH to prevent corrosion in the system. Specific treatment may be necessary to accommodate special research projects.

A municipal water supply is generally adequate from standpoints of quality and quantity. Questions that might arise regarding a water supply include the following: What tests are routinely conducted to assure high-quality water? Are the distribution lines adequate to supply water with sufficient pressure, especially in high-rise buildings, during heavy demand? Are booster pumps needed? Are there adequate lines to large buildings to ensure that a break in one pipe will not totally disrupt the supply?

EPA standards indicate the number of samples to be taken monthly for microbiological analysis from distribution systems. This number is usually based on the population utilizing the system. The system is considered to be of good quality if the monitoring shows the continued absence of the coliform group of bacteria (generally called "indicator" bacteria).

Cross connections in institutional piping can present a serious potential hazard. Two conditions can develop: backsiphonage and backflow. Backsiphonage is a loss of pressure below atmospheric pressure (called negative pressure) in the water system (e.g., a hose extended down into a sink). Backflow is a direct connection between two systems above atmospheric pressure where there is a reverse flow caused by differential pressure (e.g., a drinking-water line and a secondary fire-protection line connected directly). These conditions can be controlled by a break tank or air gap, a physical break between lines, a reduced-pressure backflow prevention device, or a nonpressure vacuum breaker on various pieces of equipment. State health regulations and plumbing codes should be consulted for complete requirements for water supplies and cross connections.

Swimming Pool Areas

Swimming pool areas must be properly constructed and operated (following state and/or local regulations) to prevent disease agents from being transmitted and to prevent accidents from occurring.

Water should be continually recirculated through a filtering system (sand, diatomaceous earth, or similar filtering materials), with a pump capacity to recirculate the entire pool volume four times daily. A chemical disinfectant, usually chlorine, should be continually fed to maintain a residual in the pool. Chlorine gas is extremely toxic, and liquid chlorine should be substituted whenever possible. A coagulant may be added to aid filtration. Chemicals are usually needed to control pH, which is a major factor in aiding the effectiveness of chlorine and in controlling the comfort of chlorinated water for swimmers.

Safety features for swimming pool areas should include an appropriately ventilated room in which to handle gaseous chlorine; nonskid surfaces; safe and easy access to the pool; and one or more lifeguards on duty when the pool is open, with adequate safety and rescue equipment available.

Proper operation of a pool is essential. Records should be maintained that show that a check of pH and disinfectant levels, filter backwashing, and chemical addition has been done at least twice daily. Proper residuals should result in adequate microbiological water quality; the water must meet potable standards. A pool operator usually needs specialized training to maintain a pool adequately, including some knowledge of water chemistry, microbiology, and operation of mechanical equipment such as feeder devices and filters.

General Sanitation

State health department and/or plumbing codes form the basis for the installation, operation, and maintenance of a sewage system, including the collection and disposal of liquid waste (sewage) on a campus as part of normal sanitary functions. On most campuses, the sewage system is likely to be a part of a municipally operated system. A small rural campus (or a larger campus in an "isolated" area) might need to install a large septic system or a series of septic systems. Proper design and careful installation of facilities are critical to the performance of such a system.

Campus housing frequently consists of dormitory rooms and apartments for students and staff. On some campuses, housing is provided to fraternities, sororities, and other special living groups. State health codes usually regulate standards protecting the health, safety, and well being of occupants. State health codes are meant to achieve and maintain levels of quality that are considered adequate for occupants' protection and that provide for essential living needs. The owner's responsibility is to maintain the property, and the tenant's responsibility is to keep a dwelling or rooming unit in a clean and safe condition. Some problems that may occur in housing include the removal of asbestos; the testing for and removal of lead paint; the testing for and mitigation of radon; the control of pests such as roaches, silverfish, and rodents; excessive noise; and mildew due to poor ventilation.

Pests on a campus can include insects (especially roaches), rodents, pigeons, bats, and mammals (such as skunks). The use of pesticides and the licensing of pest-control operators are regulated by EPA and state agencies. On a small campus, a pest-control operator contracted to provide routine service to food operations and to other buildings on a complaint basis may be the most desirable approach to pest control. On a larger campus, with housing units and considerable research activity, it may be more advantageous for pest control to be accomplished in-house. In general, especially with insects and rodents, the primary emphasis should be on good sanitation, with chemicals used to complement this approach.

Development of educational materials for the campus community is also useful to a pest-control program.

Campus housekeeping services should provide and maintain a clean, safe, and orderly environment for students, faculty, staff, and visitors. It is important that all areas of the campus appear clean, not only for aesthetics but also to avoid hazards. Cleaning must be done not casually or haphazardly but in an efficient manner that warrants critical examination of the organization, methods, machines and other equipment, and materials involved. Good work plans are essential and workers must be properly trained in handling hazardous cleaning chemicals, disposing of waste, buffing asbestos tile floors, and general safety routines.

With millions of pets sharing living quarters with humans in the United States, health and safety issues concerning dogs, cats, and other pet animals may occur on a campus. Problems created by pets can be classified into three main categories: health (allergies, diseases), sanitation (excreta), and nuisance (noise, odor, damage to furnishings, abandonment). Depending on the needs of a campus, administrators may issue a general pet policy statement regarding prohibition (on the entire campus or certain areas), enforcement, and leash regulations, including licensing of dogs. Proper pet restraint and enforcement of a campus policy can control health and safety problems arising from pets.

Solid Waste and Recycling

Handling, processing, and disposing of solid waste on a campus can be a formidable task. Inadequate waste handling has been linked to disease transmission and to injuries. Most states have regulations promulgated by health and/or environmental agencies governing solid waste. Many communities also have recycling plans that include colleges and universities. Campus officials should be aware of new requirements that prohibit landscaping and yard waste from licensed landfills.

Solid waste or refuse includes unwanted, useless, discarded materials, ranging from food waste (garbage), combustible rubbish (organic matter such as paper and plastics), noncombustible rubbish (cans, metal, glass), and ashes from incineration of biological waste (dead animals and laboratory and medical waste).

With the exception of biological and hazardous waste, most of the other solid waste may be disposed of in a landfill (used in conjunction with a community facility or run by the campus). An alternative disposal method is incineration, which, depending on the design, could accommodate biological waste. Depending on the size of the incinerator, a campus or city could install a cogeneration facility from the heat generated. This type of disposal would probably entail the installation of expensive air pollution control equipment. Incineration is being downgraded as an acceptable general method of disposal in many areas of the country.

Recycling has "come of age." Campus administrators should develop master plans to deal with recyclable materials, which constitute a large percentage of solid waste. The EPA has estimated that about 75 percent of an office building's waste consists of marketable material, including high-grade office paper, computer paper, and cardboard. If these materials are properly separated, collected, and taken to a recycling center, the campus may receive minor revenue from recyclables. Recycling also reduces landfill disposal (tipping) fees. The major costs usually involved in setting up a recycling program involve the purchase of collection containers, the hiring of vendors to cart material, when appropriate, the hiring of additional staff, and the construction of a transfer station (on a large campus). Fire safety and sanitation concerns must be incorporated into the program's operations. An effective educational campaign is critical to the success of a recycling program. Some states, such as California, require agencies to purchase recycled paper as a percentage of the total amount of paper purchased.

Medical and Infectious Waste

Medical and potentially infectious waste is generated in hospitals and in healthcare, research, and production facilities. This waste includes biological waste containing viable microorganisms that may cause disease in humans; anatomical and pathological waste, including human blood, body fluids, or tissues; animals (and their bedding) infected with pathogenic disease agents; sharp instruments (including hypodermic needles, glass, and scalpel blades); and materials incidental to the production of biological products made with pathogenic microorganisms (e.g., vaccines).

Laboratory workers and others who handle this waste may be directly exposed to infectious agents. These people can be protected by appropriate waste handling and treatment procedures in which the waste is contained and the infectious agent is inactivated. The general public should not be exposed to infectious waste generated by an institution. Modern sanitation practices of sanitary landfilling and a sanitary sewer system in which sewage is conveyed to a waste treatment plant minimize the transmission of infectious agents indirectly to the public through food, air, and water.

Every institution should establish a waste management plan with procedures for the identification and segregation of infectious waste, the proper containment and labeling of infectious waste, and the development of appropriate methods for decontamination of waste. Appropriate treatment may include chemical disinfection, steam autoclaving, or incineration. Administrators must decide if waste will be treated on-site or packaged and handled by a waste hauling company. Personal protection of employees handling the waste must also be considered. Most important for employees are the wearing of protective gloves and clothing and washing their hands. Mixed waste, which includes radioactivity or toxic chemicals in addition to infectious waste, may pose special problems. A careful assessment must be made of the hazards of mixed waste before treatment or disposal.

Waste management plans must comply with all federal, state, and local regulations. Congress passed the Medical Waste Tracking Act in 1988, which directed the EPA to establish a pilot medical waste program. This program included implementing a tracking system for medical waste and a management program to ensure that waste is properly segregated, packaged, labeled, and stored prior to transport. The EPA is in the process of evaluating the pilot program and will report to Congress. In addition, individual states have different requirements that regulate medical waste generators, transporters, and treatment and disposal.

Carcinogens and Teratogens

Cancer is the second most common cause of death in the United States; one in four Americans will suffer from cancer during his or her lifetime. Chemical carcinogens are a type of hazardous chemical used often in healthcare facilities and in biological and chemical research laboratories. Other hazardous chemicals affect reproductive health (reproductive toxins) or the development of the fetus (teratogens). Because these chemicals tend to be hazardous even in very small quantities, it is important to limit employees' exposure to such substances by the engineering of facilities, safety equipment, and proper procedures.

The federal OSHA Laboratory Standard, "Occupational Exposures to Hazardous Chemicals in Laboratories," regulates the use of carcinogens and reproductive toxins as hazardous chemicals (see the Industrial Hygiene section in this chapter). Information on carcinogens is available from the National Toxicology Program and the International Agency for Research on Cancer. The National Cancer Institute of the NIH and the National Research Council have made recommendations for the handling of carcinogens and reproductive toxins.

General Environment (Air, Water, Land)

Air Quality

Air supply, both exterior and interior, should be as free of health hazards as possible. Federal and state authorities have promulgated standards, including the Clean Air Act, and specific regulations from states, cities, and sometimes air quality districts, on exterior air quality. These standards require the control and maintenance of air pollution sources. Sources of air pollution on a campus might be a power plant, incinerators, or chemical fume-hood exhausts from science complexes. Air quality permits are required for some of these sources of air pollution.

Lighting

Illumination can be a complex subject of great importance to any environment. Good exterior lighting is essential to the prevention of accidents and to the security of persons crossing a campus and its parking lots. Emergency lighting that meets the standards of the National Fire Protection Association (NFPA) should be installed in buildings. Indoor lighting fixtures must meet varying comfort and work requirements; appropriate lighting levels are recommended by the Illuminating Engineering Society. Poor lighting can result in fatigue, increases in accidents and injuries, and poor housekeeping. With energy costs escalating, a review of lighting needs, the possible installation of more efficient lighting units, and promotion of better conservation actions are desirable.

Noise

Noise is an unwanted and disturbing sound. In a campus work or study environment, it can be a source of irritation, distraction, and emotional stress and can contribute to inefficient or disruptive performance in a job situation. In a dormitory area, excess noise can interfere with rest, relaxation, and sleep. Increased noise levels can arise from the poor maintenance of mechanical and electrical equipment, coupled with lightweight construction materials that make poor sound barriers. Other sources of noise on a campus can include heating systems, air-conditioning and ventilation equipment, grounds equipment, compactor trucks, and vehicular traffic. The loudness and the frequencies of sounds can be measured by specific instruments. Excessive noise levels (in decibels) have been determined by agencies such as OSHA and the American Industrial Hygiene Association, and criteria for hearing protection and conservation have been established.

CHEMICAL SAFETY, HAZARDOUS MATERIALS, AND ENVIRONMENTAL MANAGEMENT

Chemical safety, the disposal of hazardous materials, and institutional environmental management continue to be high on the list of public concerns and a focal point for government attention. The past couple of years have seen a rise in federal inspections and enforcement actions against higher education institutions for failure to comply with strict interpretations of environmental regulations. Region I of the EPA launched an aggressive inspection program[1] of New England institutions, resulting in costly fines, management changes, and supplementary environmental projects at a number of institutions. Other EPA regions are following suit. Additionally, state regulatory agencies are increasing their efforts and enforcement.[2]

Laws and Regulations

A host of federal laws regulates the production, use, and disposal of hazardous materials. Disposal of hazardous chemical waste is governed by the EPA-administered Resource Conservation and Recovery Act of 1976 (RCRA) and its amendments, designed to prevent future contamination from currently generated hazardous waste. The Comprehensive Environmental Response, Compensation, and Liability Act (CERCLA) of 1980, also known as Superfund, deals with the cleanup of hazardous waste sites. The Superfund Amendments and Reauthorization Act (SARA) of 1986 established requirements regarding emergency planning and community right-to-know reporting on hazardous and toxic chemicals. OSHA, which is charged with worker protection, implemented a Hazard Communication Standard and a Laboratory Safety Standard. Educational institutions of all sizes are faced with an array of complex, sometimes contradictory, and often overlapping regulations. State and local governments often supplement these federal regulations, further complicating the situation. Inspections and citations by government agencies are becoming routine. The concept of multiregulatory review by a single inspector or team appears to be gaining popularity, expanding the possibilities for problem finding. Potential fines for noncompliance can run into tens of thousands of dollars per day. Criminal penalties against executive-level personnel are also being applied more frequently. Thus, it is incumbent upon institutional administrators to have in place programs that meet at least minimum standards.

Chemical Inventory Control

Chemical inventory control strengthens environmental protection programs in a number of ways, while providing materials and cost control. Cost control does not apply only to the purchase of chemical products. The disposal of many waste chemicals is often much more costly than their original purchase price. Since many chemicals have shelf lives, a "first in, first out" method is cost effective. A good inventory control program can ensure that this objective is met.

Organization of the inventory control system ideally starts with a centralized data system. This does not necessarily mean one central source of supply, although for some this may be the choice. Computerized bar-code systems are widely available to assist in this area. When connected to the purchasing department, these systems can substantially improve inventory control by reducing excessive chemical inventories, with a subsequent improvement in safety and hazardous waste disposal.

A centralized system also enables the monitoring of chemicals of concern. SARA Title III (discussed in detail below) requires inventory data. Hazard communication and right-to-know laws require the availability of safety data for hazardous chemicals. Chemical inventory control can assist in ensuring that emergency planning is current and that proper information gets to chemical users.

Transportation of hazardous chemicals on the campus often involves movement within and between buildings. Policies and procedures should be established for both types of movement. For example, double containment (where the first container is surrounded by a second container to control spillage if the first container breaks) for carrying small containers within buildings is prudent; a prohibition against the use of passenger elevators for moving hazardous chemicals may be necessary. Transportation between buildings, especially on public roadways, should be carried out by trained personnel. Knowledge of U.S. Department of Transportation (DOT) and EPA rules on packaging, shipping documents, placarding, and other tasks and procedures is required. DOT CDL-HazMat endorsement licensing is required for drivers of vehicles requiring hazardous material placards.

Superfund Amendments and Reauthorization Act (SARA)

The Emergency Planning and Community Right-to-Know Act of 1986, also known as SARA Title III, sets forth requirements for emergency planning and community right-to-know reporting on hazardous and toxic chemicals. The purpose of SARA is to provide information to the public on chemical-related issues within the community. There are four major provisions: emergency planning, emergency notification, community right-to-know reporting, and toxic chemical release reporting. The act requires the establishment of a local emergency planning committee and the development of an emergency response plan. The planning district is usually a city or county. If the release of a hazardous substance exceeds the reportable quantity for that substance, both the local planning committee and the state emergency response commission should be notified. Any facility that stores more than the "threshold planning quantity" (TPQ) or releases more than the "reportable quantity" to the environment is required to notify emergency planning offices at both the state and local levels. For example, storing 500 pounds or more of ammonia or 10 pounds or more of phosgene (found in some academic laboratories), or releasing one pound of phosphorous triggers regulatory compliance. The local emergency planning committee also uses this information in its emergency preparedness and response planning.

Compliance with SARA requires the collection of inventory data for a list of about 400 substances. If a centralized chemical inventory is not available, a survey of appropriate operations will likely be necessary. The burden may be small for some institutions with limited research activities, and it is likely that many facilities will have none of the regulated substances or will be below the TPQ. Once the data are obtained, however, it is prudent to monitor all chemical purchases for these substances.

Chemical Hazardous Waste

Management of chemical waste on the college or university campus is a major challenge. Many scattered and diverse operations, among them print shops, paint shops, automotive shops, photo labs, and many laboratories generate hazardous waste. Not all personnel who work with chemicals may realize that the waste the department generates requires special handling. Failure to manage hazardous waste properly subjects an administration to potential compliance and liability difficulties, as well as extra costs. Training, then, becomes essential.

Hazardous Waste Regulations

Hazardous wastes are regulated by federal and state authorities. At the federal level, the regulatory authorities include DOT, OSHA, and EPA. DOT deals with the packaging and transportation and OSHA deals with employee protection, right-to-know, and emergency response to spills or leaks. EPA determines what is a regulated hazardous waste and how it is managed from generation to treatment.

To ensure compliance with hazardous waste regulations, administrators must determine the institution's "generator" status. There are three categories of hazardous waste generator:

Regulatory Status	Qualifying Amount
Conditionally Exempt Small-Quantity Generator	less than 100 kilograms per month
Small-Quantity Generator	100 and greater but less than 1,000 kilograms per month
Large-Quantity Generator	1,000 and more kilograms per month or one kilogram or more of acutely hazardous waste

Requirements are more restrictive for large-quantity generators. For example, they must provide formal training, develop emergency procedures, and have a contingency plan. State law may add to this list. Generator status dictates what kind of minimum program is required. Determination of generator status is based on EPA regulations, the facility, and its operations. A committee representing academic, facilities, and EH&S personnel can be helpful in coordinating generator information and can also serve in developing hazardous waste management policies for the institution.

The determination of generator status depends on the accuracy of data collected regarding the amounts of hazardous waste generated. Such a decision may have to be based on projections and represent a best estimate. Some uncertainty factors may also have to be applied to allow for variables if detailed data are not available. This fact alone points out the importance of developing good centralized data acquisition on generated wastes. Besides the obvious added cost control, data can be used to determine priorities for reducing hazardous wastes.

Hazardous Waste Accumulation

Size (generator status) and complexity of the facility often determine the extent of inventory control required to manage hazardous wastes and often dictate the storage method as well. Small generators may allow accumulation at the point of generation. Large generators may pick up and accumulate wastes at a single site. A combination of the two methods may be advantageous for others. In all cases, however, inventory data are necessary and desirable: necessary, because detailed information is required by regulatory agencies and all vendors who handle hazardous wastes; desirable, because the information can be used as a management tool in reducing wastes and minimizing costs. The data can be as simple as a written log of types of hazardous wastes and amounts. Many hazardous waste management vendors keep such a log at the time of waste pickup. More complex needs may benefit from computerized bar-code systems, which are coming into wider use at large institutions.

Transportation of hazardous waste on campus is affected by safety and economic considerations. Safety concerns encourage the timely removal of hazardous waste from work areas to nonoccupied, centralized storage. Economic benefits can be derived from characterizing and consolidating scattered wastes before a vendor picks them up. Compliance with DOT and EPA can complicate the matter, however. For most small facilities, direct pickup for disposal by a vendor is probably the most cost-effective choice.

Waste Reduction

An important policy decision for any institution is its commitment to reducing hazardous waste. Benefits of waste reduction include cost avoidance and reduced liability. Ideally, a written statement defining goals should be published by each institution. The goals may include improving safety by substituting less hazardous materials, avoiding costly off-site disposal, and reducing the long-term liability of the institution. Here again, a broad-based committee can assist in developing such a policy. Support by the highest level of administration can help achieve desired results. Simple waste-treatment methods such as neutralization, evaporation, oxidation, and reduction should be considered, where allowed.

Disposal

Use of the term "disposal" is rare in hazardous waste management today. The familiar 55-gallon lab pack drum, with many small chemical bottles in a bed of vermiculite going into a landfill is rare because of federal bans on land disposal of hazardous waste. The alternative is treatment (destruction of the hazardous component). Eventual environmental benefits are the goal of the federal landfill bans, but the cost is high; treating hazardous waste can raise the disposal cost by 500 percent or more for affected wastes. Long-term liability, however, does decrease.

Strategies to deal with the high cost of hazardous waste management should start with a waste reduction program, as mentioned above. For smaller institutions that qualify, a possible option may be the transfer or pooling of their hazardous waste with larger or other institutions to take advantage of economies of scale. Nearby manufacturing may also be open to transfer of institutional hazardous wastes. Consortia are another possibility. Both large and small institutions can benefit by combining specifications and competitive bidding.

Polychlorinated Biphenyls

Polychlorinated biphenyls (PCBs) are a class of chemical compounds that are regulated by the EPA under the Toxic Substances Control Act of 1976. Concerns about health and pollution effects resulted in a manufacturing ban and restrictions on use of PCBs. Now, PCBs are allowed only as a dielectric (insulating fluid) in existing electrical transformers, capacitors, and related items. PCB transformers are a significant liability and compliance problem; the EPA required the removal, downgrading, or electrical ground fault protection for public access buildings by October 1, 1990. The most recent major changes to management practices can be found in the June 1998 *Federal Register* (63 FR 35383 to 35474).

To comply with regulations, a management plan for PCBs must be in place. If an institution has PCBs but has not instituted a plan, it faces major liabilities in the form of citations and fines. The physical plant department and EH&S should be key contributors to this plan. The plan should include the identification of all PCB transformers and a risk assessment of each transformer and its location. Locations must be marked, and the local fire response personnel must be informed of the inventory. Small PCB-containing transformers and other electrical and mechanical systems can also be found in the lab. A policy dealing with this potential liability should be in place to deal with discarded electrical and hydraulic equipment.

Risk assessment can help in establishing priorities. Priorities might include regulating PCB transformers by removing or downgrading them. Factors that determine such an order might include type of occupancy of the building, fault protection, fire- and heat-sensing equipment, potential smoke paths, and spill containment. By evaluating these and other factors, EH&S personnel can come up with a numerical assessment for each location. These scores then help set priorities for work.

Inspections and off-site management are also necessary adjuncts to a PCB management plan. The inspection schedule should comply with federal regulatory requirements. For safety's sake, inspections should be carried out only by personnel trained in high-voltage operations. Federal record-keeping requirements must also be met. Institutions have been heavily fined for failure to keep accurate records despite adherence to all other regulations. Likewise, off-site management requires compliance with strict storage provisions on-site as well as complete record keeping for each PCB item shipped for treatment.

Underground Storage Tanks and Oil Pollution Prevention

Most college campuses probably have underground storage tanks (USTs) for fuels. If the facility has greater than 42,000 gallons of underground petroleum storage or aboveground storage (AST) of more than 1,320 gallons of oil (a single AST of 660 gallons or more also applies), it is required to have a spill prevention control and countermeasures plan. It is important to check with your regional EPA and state regulatory agencies on what is included under the "oil" definition. Cooking and other seemingly nonhazardous oils may be included.

Leaks from these tanks and their piping pose a large liability for any campus. For example, one gallon of gasoline lost to groundwater can contaminate 1 million gallons of drinking water. Cleanup costs associated with leaks can run into the hundreds of thousands of dollars. With 50 percent of the U.S. population reliant on groundwater for drinking purposes, it is not surprising that the EPA regulates USTs. Regulations required that all USTs comply with all leak prevention and detection technology by 1998 or be removed from service, including pump-out. The regulations further require owners of USTs to prevent, find, and fix leaks. Financial responsibility insurance requirements also exist. Any campus management program for USTs and ASTs should address these key areas.

Decisions regarding upgrading or replacing existing tanks can be aided by comprehensive inventory data risk and cost-benefit analyses. When replacing a tank, EH&S personnel should consider above-ground installations rather than USTs if codes and facility layout allow.

Other Hazardous Waste Issues

Land Disposal Restrictions

In August 1990, the RCRA land disposal restrictions became effective. These restrictions prevent certain hazardous wastes from land disposal unless they meet specified treatment or performance-based standards. Any generator of hazardous waste, including colleges and universities, must determine if its wastes exhibit any of the characteristics of hazardous waste and specify the treatment for that waste. This virtually restricts all hazardous wastes subject to RCRA from direct land-based disposal. These land disposal restrictions create unique challenges to managers of hazardous waste because they require that all wastes subject to the restrictions be treated before being disposed in a landfill.

The Clean Water Act and NPDES

The Clean Water Act of 1987 (CWA) and its subsequent revisions continue to impact colleges and universities as the various programs under this law are implemented by the EPA. The permit programs administered by the EPA under the National Pollution Discharge Elimination System (NPDES) require permits for discharges into the "waters of the United States." Colleges and universities are involved in some of the activities that are or may be covered under the NPDES permit. Such activities include but are not limited to print shops, publishing, photographic equipment and supplies, and operation of steam electric power plants.

Most colleges and universities are affected by the NPDES program through participation in the industrial wastewater pretreatment programs administered by the various publicly owned treatment works. However, recent amendments to the CWA that require dischargers of storm waters to receive NPDES permits for those discharges may affect colleges and universities significantly, depending on how such programs are implemented by the EPA. One such implementation can be seen in the proposed Phase II storm water regulations issued by EPA in November 1999. Compliance with these amendments could require more information gathering, sampling, testing, and reporting.

GENERAL SAFETY

The field of environmental health and safety comprises several areas of specialization, such as industrial hygiene, radiation, occupational health and medical surveillance, and chemical and biological safety. Additional aspects that typically concern a college or university are often grouped into the category of general safety. For the purposes of this chapter, general safety includes lab and facility safety, incident investigation, emergency response, safety inspections, OSHA regulations, ergonomics, first aid, and other code responsibilities.

Components of general safety that develop the knowledge, skills, and abilities to provide for a safe work environment and a healthy and safe employee do not stop when the employee leaves his or her workplace. A safe employee at work is a safer person at home, as well. This focus on individual responsibility and understanding of safety issues do help reduce injuries and associated costs at work. This focus will also have associated cost savings because that person is safe at home and may lead to reduced use of personal sick time, because of accident prevention and safety at home.

Many resources and references are available through the Internet as listed at the end of this chapter.

Facility Safety, Inspections, and Audits

Supervisory staff should conduct safety audits, surveys, and inspections of facilities and equipment on an ongoing basis throughout their area of responsibility. In addition, qualified persons should conduct surveys for compliance with codes and standards. Inspections should include reviews of laboratories and other locations where radioisotopes, biohazards, and hazardous chemicals are present. Some local and state regulations specifically spell out the frequency of required formal inspections. Surveys should include a scrutiny of practices and procedures as well as the physical environment. Inspection results should be recorded and quickly communicated to persons in charge of the areas being surveyed. Department heads, supervisors, and employees should be included in the formulation of recommended corrective action.

Performance of facility safety inspections should go beyond just supervisors and safety professionals. All employees should be involved with safety of the facilities they work in on a daily basis. Routine safety inspection will help determine what items and conditions need to be monitored or changed. Those people involved in the actual work tasks will know their job and area the best and are a valuable resource in safety inspection and incident prevention.

Surveys vary in frequency according to the type and condition of the area surveyed and may range from a daily "walk-through" of residence hall living spaces to formal surveys of all facilities once or twice a year. Additional surveys and random observations should be scheduled for more hazardous areas such as laboratories. By their nature, laboratories contain a great variety of potential hazards. A typical lab has electrical, physical, biological, and chemical hazards. Special labs may contain unusual hazards—radiological, laser, microwave, recombinant DNA, and carcinogens. These require appropriate control and frequent review to assure safety and compliance with relevant regulations. (See the Industrial Hygiene section in this chapter.)

Incident Investigation and Workers' Compensation

Incident prevention is the key to eliminating possibility of injury to employees and property loss. Learning from past incidents is one of the important elements in incident prevention. Procedures must be established for reporting, investigating, analyzing, and recording incidents, injuries, occupational illness, and exposure to hazardous agents. Analysis of incidents provides data for assigning resources to the areas of greatest need and cost benefit. All college and university personnel should be responsible for keeping track of all injuries, incidents, and unsafe conditions.

Incident investigation is an important mechanism for determining direct and indirect incident causes. Information on causes is important when developing strategies to prevent future incidents of a similar nature. "Near hits" are often taken for granted and do not receive the attention they might demand. Many times near hits later result in serious incidents because of a lack of investigation and correction of problems. Therefore, all near hits and minor incidents should be considered for investigation along with major incidents.

Responsible departmental personnel should initiate, complete, and distribute required incident reports and ascertain that corrective action has been started. Follow-up on the progress or success of corrective actions should be the responsibility of the program director or the EH&S department. These reports may become the basis for legal protection of the institution or an employee if court actions arise. OSHA, comparable state plans, and some insurers require that specific records be maintained on prescribed forms. Fines may be imposed for noncompliance with requirements.

Workers' compensation is an insurance system that provides coverage for certain work-related conditions; it results in reimbursement to the employee for lost wages and costs of medical care due to job-related injury or illness. The system provides financial incentives for employers to operate safety programs that decrease the frequency and severity of accidents. The costs of the program are allocated among employers and industries according to the extent to which they are responsible for losses. This presumably rewards good safety practices and penalizes dangerous operations.

Employers, including those in higher education, should work towards a systems approach to incident prevention by developing an occupational injury management program. This type of approach to employee injury management works with all components of the employees' work experience. Included in this would be initial training, supervisor training, job hazard analysis, and training, as well as case management when an employee is injured. By working closely with supervisors and employees, it is possible to develop a job specific training program that helps an employee grow within his or her job safely.

Occupational injury management also helps track an employee's progress through treatment and rehabilitation. This may also include the need to provide the employee with occupational training or retraining, reduced workload, or a temporary reassignment for an injured employee returning to work.

Emergency Response and Preparedness

The emergency operations or action plan provides an overview of procedures for dealing with major campus emergencies. It explains the roles of key campus positions having major responsibilities during an emergency and explains the activation of the Emergency Operations Center (EOC). Both the EOC and the field emergency response organizations are activated and should operate according to principles of the Incident Command System (ICS). Emergency plans should describe the supportive relationship between response and planning components of the campus that are activated during major emergencies.

Department heads must be able to respond with autonomy to a rapidly escalating event. The potential of these events (such as a natural disaster, fire, civil disturbance, chemical emergency, or bomb threat) should be assessed and reviewed in the campus emergency operations or action plan. Included in the campuswide preparedness plan, each department should develop a written emergency plan on how best to use their own personnel and resources to deal with response to each event. Emergency action plans should cover such issues as communication, organizational control, notification procedures, and dealing with the media and the campus community.

Proper planning for emergencies is necessary to minimize employee injury and property damage. The effectiveness of the response during an emergency event depends on the amount and completeness of planning and training performed before the emergency event. Although you cannot prepare for every incident that may occur in a campus setting, it is possible to begin planning for the response needed to help during most situations. If the campus has a plan, that plan can also help respond to those unpredictable situations by giving emergency response and planning personnel a blueprint for organizational direction. Without any advanced planning for potential problems, needed resources, and possible solutions, the campus and the students, faculty, and staff served are going to be left without the service they need and should expect.

When emergency action plans are required by a particular OSHA standard, the plan must be in writing. The plan must include, at a minimum, the following elements:

- emergency evacuation procedures and emergency escape routes (this may include maps showing the location of an assembly area outside of the building);

- procedures to be followed by employees (e.g., power plant personnel) who must remain to perform or shut down critical plant operations;

- procedures to account for all employees after the evacuation has been completed;

- a description of rescue and medical duties (this may include building floor plans showing emergency evacuation routes and the location of emergency equipment like fire extinguishers, fire alarm stations, fire hose cabinets, and disaster response kit);

- the preferred means for reporting emergencies;

- names or regular job titles of persons or departments to be contacted for further information or explanation of duties under the plan; and

- appropriate preplanning and coordination with emergency response agencies.

OSHA Regulations

The Occupational Safety and Health Act of 1970 (OSH Act) established the Occupational Safety and Health Administration within the Department of Labor to promulgate and enforce health and safety regulations. In general, coverage of the OSH Act and regulations extends to all employers and their employees in the 50 states, the District of Columbia, Puerto Rico, and all other territories under federal government jurisdiction. Coverage is provided either directly by OSHA or through an OSHA approved state program.

The following are not covered by the OSH Act:

- self-employed persons;

- farms at which only immediate members of the farm employer's family are employed; and

- working conditions regulated by other federal agencies under other federal statutes.

OSHA regulations cover most occupational hazards including materials handling, personal protective equipment, exposure to harmful chemicals, fall protection, construction safety, ergonomics, and total workplace safety. Employers with fewer than 10 employees are exempt from some of the record-keeping requirements under OSHA rules, but as employers must still adhere to other regulations and requirements.

The enforcement aspects of the OSH provisions do not apply to all state and local governments in their roles as employers. The OSH Act does provide that any state desiring to gain OSHA approval for its private sector occupational safety and health program must provide a program that covers its state and local government workers and is at least as effective as its program for private employees. State plans may also cover only public sector employees. Occupational health and safety requirements for public sector employees vary from state to state. Public universities and colleges should work with their state Department of Labor (or equivalent) to determine what agency and regulations have authority over the institution.

The penalties imposed on an employer for noncompliance with OSHA standards and other safety regulations go far beyond the direct costs associated with severe fines, shutdown of project and facilities, and possible prison sentences. Indirect costs and penalties include lost time from work by injured employees, lost productivity, health care costs, litigation costs, and the pain and suffering and ill health-effects endured by injured employees. Moreover, institutions negotiating contracts with federal agencies may be required to comply with OSHA standards with or without state plan approval.

Even when an institution does not legally fall under OSHA regulation or a comparable plan, the institution may be held to that standard during litigation. This is because OSHA regulations are "nationally accepted minimum standards."

As OSHA continues to develop regulations that affect colleges and universities, compliance with regulations becomes increasingly difficult. The diversity of academic and service-related activities on campus makes administering OSHA mandates very demanding. To meet OSHA's expectations properly, administrators must be cognizant of their responsibilities and ensure that their individual units are in compliance.

Ergonomics

Ergonomics is the science of fitting jobs to people. Ergonomics encompasses the body of knowledge about physical abilities and limitations as well as other human characteristics that are relevant to job design. Ergonomic design is the application of this body of knowledge to the design of the workplace (i.e., work tasks, equipment, environment) for safe and efficient use by workers. Good ergonomic design makes the most efficient use of worker capabilities while ensuring that job demands do not exceed those capabilities.

Work-related musculoskeletal disorders (W-RMSD) currently account for one-third of all occupational injuries and illnesses reported to the Bureau of Labor Statistics (BLS) by employers every year. These disorders thus constitute the largest job-related injury and illness problem in the United States today. In 1997, employers reported a total of 626,000 lost workday W-RMSDs to the BLS, and these disorders accounted for $1 of every $3 spent for workers' compensation in that year. Employers pay $15–$20 billion in workers' compensation costs for these disorders every year, and other expenses associated with W-RMSDs may increase this total to $45–$54 billion a year. Workers with severe W-RMSDs can face permanent disability that prevents them from returning to their jobs or handling simple, everyday tasks like combing their hair, picking up a baby, or pushing a shopping cart.

First Aid and CPR Training

First aid is the immediate, temporary treatment given in the case of accident or sudden illness. First aid is usually given before the services of a physician are available. Adequate availability of first aid is an important part of every work site. Immediate treatment reduces the possibility of more serious health problems and facilitates the probability of recovery. Statistics show that the care rendered during a medical emergency through the actions of trained bystanders (coworkers) is often essential for the potential of full recovery by the injured person.

The Emergency Medical Services (EMS) System is a network of community resources in which bystanders and coworkers play an important role. The EMS system is like a chain made up of several links. Links include citizen response and involvement, notification of emergency resources, first aid care, prehospital care, hospital care, and rehabilitation. Each link depends on the others for success.

The system begins when a responsible citizen, such as an employee, recognizes that an emergency exists and decides to take action, report the emergency, and render care if appropriate. All the links in the chain must work together to provide the best possible care to victims of injury or illness.

OSHA requires that an employer have medical personnel available for advice and consultation on matters of workplace health. In the absence of a health care facility near the workplace, at least one person in each site should be adequately trained to render first aid. First aid supplies approved by a consulting physician should also be readily available.

Employees should be informed of procedures to follow in case of emergencies and rules for first aid, including approved methods of resuscitation. All campus safety officers and related emergency response personnel should be trained in first aid and cardiopulmonary resuscitation (CPR). In addition, OSHA requires those employees working on communication or electrical supply equipment or lines to be regularly instructed in CPR. Some states also require, through public health regulations, that food service providers be provided with basic first aid training.

OSHA further requires that any employee whose job includes responding to medical emergencies or rendering first aid must have annual training in blood-borne pathogen and infection control. OSHA does say that employees acting as "Good Samaritans" by rendering first aid are not covered by the bloodborne pathogens standard. Only an employee trained in first aid and designated by the employer as responsible for rendering medical assistance as part of his or her job duties, is covered by the requirements of the standard, including postexposure incident follow-up, training, and personal protective equipment.

The OSHA regulation on bloodborne pathogens (1910.1030) also says that if employees have occupational exposure to bloodborne pathogens in the workplace, the employer must have a written exposure control plan. This exposure control plan is designed to eliminate or minimize employee exposure.

Even when employees are not expected to perform first aid services within their job, there is a benefit from first aid training. Most people who have to render first aid or perform CPR do so on a family member or someone they know. This type of training, and true concerns over employee health and safety, help to promote a good attitude and positive work relationship between the employer and the employee.

Safety Training

Employees need to be given appropriate information, training, and feedback to accomplish new tasks in their workplace. New employees need to be oriented into the workplace so they can adapt to that culture. Included in that new employee indoctrination should be the concept of employee safety training. Subjects would include their personal responsibility for safety, emergency reporting and evacuation procedures, incident reporting, and workplace hazards. Information needed for an employee to be safe on the job should be shared, even though it may seem that the subject matter is very simple and straightforward. If employees are not given the information in a way that they can understand, they may not comprehend what is needed to work safely.

Through hazard evaluations of the workplace, employers and employees can develop a job-hazard analysis (JHA) for each task performed by employees. JHAs can be used as step-by-step instructional guides when training employees. The hazard analysis lists the specific tasks that are needed to complete a job, the potential hazards in doing them, and the procedures to do them safely. This training adds to general safety training by providing safety knowledge, skills, and abilities that are specific to the job. Training provides the needed information for an employee to be part of a safe work environment.

FIRE SAFETY

Fire often strikes with little warning and quite frequently produces devastating results. Few people realize how relatively easy it is for a fire to get started, how quickly it can change from a small incipient stage to a major, life threatening condition, or how devastating the aftermath can be. Because of this, fire prevention programs are a critical part of any institutional safety program. The goals of a fire prevention program are to protect people and property, and must be established regardless of the size of the institution. This section presents key concepts in fire prevention and in controlling the potential losses that can result from a fire.

Design Review and Code Compliance

College and university EH&S staff should interact with facility, design, and construction departments. Such consultation should include a review of working drawings and specifications to ensure that appropriate standards and codes are specified and met and that any other necessary safeguards are included in new procurements, renovations, and repair of facilities or gifts of equipment. Fire safety and EH&S staff should also develop a relationship with the appropriate institutional departments such as planning, physical plant, security, and risk management. It is much less expensive to avoid a hazard during the planning stage than to correct it after a project is complete. It is imperative that construction or renovation by design meets all applicable building codes, fire prevention regulations, and fire protection standards. These may include state or local building codes, state or local fire codes or fire safety regulations, OSHA regulations, referenced National Fire Protection Association (NFPA) standards, handicapped accessibility standards, national engineering standards, and insurance carrier requirements. Locations using hazardous materials may require special safety features such as fire detection, fire suppression, specifically designed electrical equipment, exhaust ventilation, fire alarm, and spill control systems. Emergency and stand-by power needs should be reviewed for emergency lighting, exit lighting, fume hoods, and fire alarm systems.

Other special uses and occupancies, such as assembly areas, present a high level of concern and will require specific fire protection design. Attention must be given to the use of fire-resistant building materials and furnishings, adequate means of egress, automatic fire sprinkler systems, approved fire alarm systems, handicapped accessibility, and emergency power.

Designing and constructing facilities with an emphasis on fire-safe designs that will contain fire and smoke to a predetermined area is a key concept in building code application. Fire separation walls, fire doors, fire rated assemblies, and fire stopping are all important considerations. Major emphasis is to provide a protected means of egress (corridors, stairways, exitways) and compartmentation.

Fire Protection Concepts

Automatic Sprinkler Systems

It is widely known among fire safety professionals that the proper design, installation, and maintenance of automatic fire sprinkler systems will afford the greatest value not only to property protection, but also to life safety from fire as well. By design, a sprinkler system controls fire at its early stage, thus limiting the amount of heat and smoke produced. New technologies in sprinkler-head design have increased the speed of activation and have proven to be extremely effective in residential occupancies. Contrary to popular belief, sprinkler systems rarely have inadvertent discharges. Sprinkler systems are very reliable and minimize damage by activation only of those heads that are necessary. Technology also allows sprinkler activation to provide activation of the fire alarm system. Many institutions have realized these values and have chosen to go beyond code required installation by installing or retrofitting their facilities with automatic sprinkler protection.

Fire Alarm Systems

A well-designed and maintained fire alarm system will provide early warning of fire to building occupants and can facilitate fire department response. Many factors will dictate the level of detection and system design. Smoke detection is critical in residential occupancies. Most often a combination of smoke detection and heat detection will be utilized in nonresidential areas. System sophistication along with type and location of initiating devices and audio-visual devices will be affected by building construction, occupancy type, audibility requirements, and requirements for people with disabilities. Since the 1970s civilian fire deaths in the United States have dropped from more than 12,000 per year to fewer than 5,000 per year. Two main contributing factors are technological advances and the use of fire and smoke detecting equipment.

Fire Extinguishers

Fire extinguishers deserve a special note because they are such an important element in fire protection control on most college and university campuses. Many states have laws that require fire extinguishers in each campus building. The NFPA also requires that all laboratories be equipped with portable fire extinguishers. Furthermore, OSHA requires fire extinguishers where welding is done, where liquid petroleum gas is stored and used, and for crane operations. Fire extinguishers consist of a fixed type, such as is used over fryolators within a kitchen, or the portable type found in many locations throughout a facility. Portable fire extinguishers must be chosen, installed, inspected, hydrostatically tested, and serviced in accordance with NFPA 10 and OSHA standards. Extinguishers must be easily accessible, clearly marked, and in working order. They are usually placed along a means of exit and should only be used on incipient fires or fires of limited size. Many fires on college and university campuses have been minimized by the quick use of a portable fire extinguisher. Extinguishers can instill a false sense of confidence and should never be a substitute for good fire prevention practices.

Fire Safety Education

Fire safety education is a major component of any fire safety management program. All employees and building occupants should be made aware of potential building fire hazards and control methods. This training and education may be presented in a variety of formats:

- properly posted signs, evacuation plans, and emergency reporting procedures, all serve to increase knowledge of building occupants during a fire emergency; and

- fire evacuation drills will familiarize occupants with the sound of the fire alarm and evacuation procedures.

Formal fire education programs should be presented to all new employees and should be provided periodically for other staff or building occupants. Included should be types, use, and limitations of fire extinguishers; common fire ignition sources and their prevention; compartmentation concepts; hazards to means of egress; fire evacuation procedures; fire reporting (fire alarm activation, pull station locations, and emergency phone numbers); and recommended steps should a fire be encountered.

Regular newsletters, newspaper articles, bulletins, or brochures can all serve to increase fire safety awareness. Special seasonal topics such as winter heating, Fourth of July, Halloween, and the winter holiday season provide important fire and life safety messages.

All employees who are expected to use portable fire extinguishers must have training in their use and understand the basic principles of fire behavior. This includes knowledge of fire classifications, extinguisher types and proper selection. Occupants must know how to properly and safely operate extinguishers, and know the locations of extinguishers within their facility. Hands on training, when properly designed and planned, can be extremely valuable in developing familiarization with extinguisher use. Occupants must also understand the limitations of fire extinguishers and should be cautioned never to place themselves in danger attempting to extinguish a fire.

On-the-job fire safety activities are very effective in building good employee relations. Fires away from campus can have a significant impact on campus staff and students. Institutions should consider development of programs that are built on a total fire safety approach. Such programs could include National Fire Prevention Week activities, assistance with community fire safety efforts, and home fire safety messages.

Routine fire inspections conducted by designated staff, facility managers, and supervisors serve to identify potential fire hazards and areas of concern. Such inspections can be conducted jointly with fire department personnel and can serve as an excellent learning experience for all involved.

Fire Safety Enforcement

Hazard Recognition and Assessment

The majority of fires arise from inherently hazardous situations, such as overheated electrical equipment; equipment chemical reactions and spills; unsupervised experiments and activities without built-in safety or fire control; and lack of knowledge of safety codes or safe methods. Other sources of ignition include equipment in poor condition or not being used as designed, careless use of smoking materials, spontaneous ignition of oily wastes, hot works such as welding and cutting, and static electricity. A critical aspect of fire prevention is assessing and recognizing possible fire hazards, and then implementing and enforcing controls.

Inspections

Fire safety inspections may be of several types. Supervisors and employees should be constantly on the lookout for unsafe conditions and take corrective action as necessary. Formal inspections may be periodic or irregular depending on occupancy and type of facility. Special attention will be given to hazardous materials, storage, housekeeping, and means of egress. Inspections may be conducted internally by the institution or may be conducted by outside agencies such as the local fire department, insurance carriers, or accrediting organizations. State or federal agencies such as OSHA, DOT, and EPA may also conduct them.

Once fire safety inspections have been conducted, results should be communicated where needed within the institution. Appropriate follow-up must occur to correct identified deficiencies. Underlying causes should be determined to prevent recurrence. Follow-up may include a process redesign, relocation of a use or activity, use of alternative products or equipment, improved training, improved maintenance procedures, or improved security. Although fire inspections help to enforce fire safety requirements, they should not be viewed strictly as a compliance issue but as a key component to life safety and good business.

Policies and Procedures

The above methods can only be effective when they are routinely implemented. This requires frequent audits and checks to assure the proper operation of equipment and the proper training and knowledge of the people who will carry out the procedures when an emergency strikes. Established safety policies and procedures must be appropriately enforced to assure protection of life and property from fire and to minimize a fire's effects. Maintaining an emergency response capability to quickly respond to fires during the first moments after a fire starts can be critical in terms of saving lives and controlling losses.

Available Resources

Colleges and universities have a wealth of fire safety resources available to them. Local fire departments can provide information on local codes and regulations as well as general fire safety education. A working relationship with the fire department can serve the institution not only as an emergency response resource, but in fire preplanning and fire prevention and education as well. Beyond the information available through ongoing cooperation and interaction between higher education facilities and the local fire department, professional trade journals from both the fire science spectrum and that of engineering studies can provide valuable information. There is also a wealth of information available on the Internet from thousands of individual fire departments, and state and federal agencies, as well as from universities and colleges that are online. A few key resources with Web sites are listed at the end of this chapter.

INDUSTRIAL HYGIENE

The American Industrial Hygiene Association (AIHA) defines "industrial hygiene" as the science and art devoted to the anticipation, recognition, evaluation, and control of environmental factors or stresses arising in or from the workplace that may cause sickness, impaired health and well-being, or significant discomfort and inefficiency among workers or the citizens of the community.

AIHA defines an "industrial hygienist" as a person having a college or university degree or degrees in engineering, chemistry, physics, or medicine and related biological sciences who, by virtue of special studies and training, has acquired competence in industrial hygiene. An industrial hygienist must be able to:

- recognize the environmental factors and stresses associated with work and work operations and understand their effect on people and their well-being;

- evaluate, on the basis of experience and with the aid of quantitative measurement techniques, the magnitude of these stresses in terms of their ability to impair people's health and well-being; and

- prescribe methods to eliminate, control, or reduce such stresses to alleviate their effects.

Many environmental factors that affect people in the workplace result from the inhalation or ingestion of toxic gases and particulates or by skin contact with these materials. Academic and research environments present numerous opportunities for human contact with harmful agents. In fact, by its very nature, the research environment almost invites this kind of problem. It is easy to understand how faculty, staff, and students may be exposed to hazardous materials in laboratories, but custodians and maintenance personnel who enter the same laboratories should not be forgotten. Other areas such as clinics, theaters, art and photography studios, maintenance shops, and kitchens present opportunities for exposure to hazardous materials. Thus, industrial hygiene plays a very important role in monitoring and controlling human exposure to potentially harmful agents in a college or university environment.

General Control Methods

The industrial hygienist normally evaluates each particular circumstance to ascertain the most logical method of control of harmful agents in materials, equipment, operations, or the building itself. There are usually several options available, and numerous factors dictate the choice of the proper solution. The three major factors are usually worker health and safety, cost effectiveness, and compliance with regulatory requirements and/or consensus standards. In controlling environmental stresses and worker health, the industrial hygienist may:

- substitute a less toxic or less hazardous material for one that is dangerous to health;

- change or alter the process to minimize exposure;

- enclose or isolate the operation so that exposures are eliminated or the number of employees involved is reduced;

- introduce methods that will reduce or eliminate exposures (for example, wet methods to control dusty environments);

- provide local exhaust ventilation at the point of generation of toxic fumes or materials to minimize their circulation;

- provide general or dilution ventilation with clean air to generate a safe environment;

- provide personal protective equipment such as masks, respirators, earplugs, goggles, protective boots, and other special clothing;

- improve housekeeping by providing proper waste disposal, a clean workplace, adequate washing, toilet, and eating facilities, safe drinking water, and control of vermin;

- develop monitoring programs to implement special monitoring devices dictated by unusual or specific hazards (such programs may include the use of film badges or noise dosimeters, air pumps that collect samples in the breathing zone, or continuous monitors with preset alarm levels);

- initiate medical controls surveillance with the aid of an occupational physician, normally as an outgrowth of an occupational medicine program and the resulting tests and evaluation; and

- implement administrative controls, which can include training and education, reducing exposure time, rotating workers, and other methods to eliminate or reduce exposures (administrative controls are normally used to supplement engineering controls or substituted when engineering controls fail or are temporarily out of use).

Ventilation

A primary method used to control toxic materials and thereby control health hazards is ventilation. "Ventilation" is defined as the process of supplying or removing air by natural or mechanical means. From a practical standpoint, the desire is to remove foul air and supply fresh air. Ventilation can further be described by the type of ventilation that is used to control workplace hazards.

Local Exhaust Ventilation

Local exhaust systems are used to capture contaminants at their source, thereby containing the material before it can get into the breathing zone of the worker or into the general environment. A local exhaust is generally preferred to dilution ventilation for toxic materials because it provides a safer and healthier work environment. It also handles a smaller volume of air, which translates into lower heating and air-conditioning costs and smaller blowers and ductwork. The laboratory fume hood is a good example of local exhaust used in the academic setting.

The importance of the fume hood as a safety device in the laboratory should not be underestimated. Laboratory workers think of the fume hood as a primary safety device to protect personnel from exposure to hazardous chemicals and agents used in the laboratory. Laboratory fume hood systems require careful preventive maintenance programs. Because fume hoods are primary safety devices in the laboratory, they must receive priority when repairs are necessary. Laboratory workers must be notified when fume hoods are out of service.

General or Dilution Ventilation

Dilution-ventilation systems add or remove air to keep the concentration of a contaminant below hazardous levels. They can be as uncomplicated as opening doors and windows or using roof ventilators and chimneys. Dilution ventilation is more commonly accomplished, however, by installing systems that artificially move the air with fans and blowers. Dilution ventilation is feasible and appropriate only when the degree of air contamination is very low and the contaminant is released at a substantial distance from the breathing zone of workers. Dilution ventilation should not be used for major sources of contamination or highly toxic materials.

It is common to see both types of ventilation systems in most buildings today, where general ventilation is used to provide comfort to building occupants and local exhaust ventilation is used to control hazardous and toxic materials. Ventilation systems are very complex and require the services of engineers and industrial hygienists to design and maintain them. Ventilation problems are among the most frequent industrial hygiene issues; therefore, a thorough understanding of ventilation principles (air pressures, capture velocities, and reentrainment) is critical to solving ventilation problems.

Indoor Air Quality

Indoor air quality problems (commonly referred to as "sick building syndrome" or "building-related illness") are a very important issue today. Occupants of buildings are quick to complain of discomfort related to the air quality in their work environments. Sick building syndrome (SBS) is a set of nonspecific complaints including eye, nose, and throat irritation, headaches, and fatigue; SBS is diagnosed when at least 20 percent of a building's occupants report these symptoms. Although a specific causative factor has not been discovered, SBS is often related to the ventilation system in a building and can usually be corrected with changes in the system. The most effective changes almost always entail the addition of more fresh air, with better distribution or faster turnover of the air. Building-related illness (BRI) is the occurrence of symptoms as a result of exposure to a specific biological, chemical, or physical entity. It can be caused by air contaminants as diverse as molds, microbiological organisms, chemical vapors, and dusts, and only one or a few occupants may be affected. The cause of BRI may be obvious (e.g., a new carpet) but more frequently is difficult to find. In some cases, a building may have to be evacuated while a team of experts searches for and corrects the problem.

The emphasis on energy efficiency in new construction and remodeling has resulted in the use of extra insulation, airtight windows, and recirculating air systems. The hazards of closed systems are exacerbated by the many sources of air pollution within buildings, including carpeting, furniture, paints, construction glues and caulks, copy machines, tobacco smoke, and even people themselves with perfumes and new clothes. The result is what amounts to a giant air-pollution trap. Indoor air-quality problems can range from simple nuisances, such as a headache or sore throat, to full-fledged diseases, such as pneumonitis. ASHRAE (American Society of Heating, Refrigerating and Air Conditioning Engineers) established criteria that renders acceptable indoor air quality as "air in which there are no known contaminants at harmful concentrations and with which a substantial majority (usually 80 percent) of the people exposed do not express dissatisfaction."

Personal Protective Equipment

Personal protective equipment (PPE) includes any items worn to prevent a hazardous material or harmful physical agent from gaining access to the human body by the three routes of entry—inhalation, ingestion, and skin contact. Typical items include hearing protection, eye protection, respiratory protection, foot protection, protective clothing and gloves, and special items such as air-conditioned suits for heat stress, insulated clothing for cold, protective shields for explosions, and barrier creams. Personal protective equipment should only be considered as a secondary defense for toxic materials and conditions that are impractical or impossible to control in any other way. PPE must never be a substitute for good engineering, housekeeping, and properly trained and informed workers. Policies and work practices should be adopted that will ensure the proper selection, maintenance, and use of personal protective equipment. The selection of PPE must be based on an adequate risk assessment process. This risk assessment may be best accomplished by conducting an inventory of the chemicals used, physical agents present or generated by the process, and directly observing the task or work process. The use of some personal protective equipment (e.g., respirators and eyeglasses) requires a preplacement examination by an occupational physician.

Important Standards and Issues

The field of industrial hygiene encompasses various industry standards and governmental regulations that are too numerous to cover or even list in this overview. However, to provide perspective on the breadth of knowledge and coverage that is expected from industrial hygienists, several important issues are briefly discussed. These topics are chosen because of their importance in workplace safety considerations and their probable influence on college and university safety programs.

Worker Right-to-Know

The worker right-to-know programs are an outgrowth of the federal Hazard Communication Standard. Effective hazard communication programs are the cornerstones of comprehensive safety and health management programs. The purpose of the worker right-to-know laws is to assure that information concerning chemical hazards is provided to affected employers and employees. This transmittal of information is accomplished by means of comprehensive hazard communication programs, which include container labeling and other pertinent forms of warning, material safety data sheets (MSDSs), and employee training. The employee training should include initial training as well as an annual refresher course.

Laws require chemical manufacturers, importers, or distributors to assess the hazards of the chemicals they produce or distribute and provide that information (in the form of MSDSs or container labels) to any buyer of the chemical. Employers in turn must develop a written hazards communication program that outlines the safety program covering hazardous chemicals. This program must include labeling of containers and other forms of warning; a description of employee access to MSDSs; and the process whereby information on the program and training is provided to employees.

In addition to the worker right-to-know rules, many state regulations include requirements for public access to this information and the provision of hazard information to local public safety agencies, such as the fire department or police. Quirks in the federal Hazard Communication Standard (HCS), administered by OSHA, may exempt certain public institutions unless the state has adopted specific agreement status with the federal government. HCS is a performance-based standard that establishes goals for compliance while providing minimal specifications for how employers should reach these goals. The performance-based nature of HCS requires the use of professional judgement in determining how to comply in a particular workplace. EH&S personnel should study and comply with all prevailing state and federal regulations.

Laboratory Standard (Chemical Hygiene Plan)

An OSHA regulation known as "Occupational Exposure to Hazardous Chemicals in Laboratories," the Laboratory Standard, effective May 1, 1990, gave employers until January 31, 1991, to develop and implement a chemical hygiene plan. If no chemical hygiene plan has been adopted, substance-specific industry standards must be met. This plan must protect employees from health hazards associated with all hazardous chemicals in laboratories; keep employee exposures below the limits specified in the OSHA standards; be readily available to employees, employee representatives, and OSHA inspectors; and include the following elements:

- standard operating procedures for uses of hazardous chemicals in the lab;
- designation of a Chemical Hygiene Officer (CHO), that is, an employee who is qualified by training or experience to provide technical guidance in the

development and implementation of the provisions of the chemical hygiene plan;

- control measures used to reduce exposures to hazardous chemicals;

- fume hoods and other containment or protective equipment used in labs;

- training and information about hazardous chemicals and the content of the chemical hygiene plan;

- circumstances under which a particular laboratory operation, procedure, or activity shall require prior approval from the employer, and a list of procedures that assure "prior approval" before starting lab operations;

- medical exams and consultations for employees using hazardous chemicals; and

- appropriate and proper employee protective measures for particular hazardous chemicals.

All colleges and universities are subject to OSHA regulation except public institutions in states without federal-state OSHA agreement plans. However, good safety practice dictates similar procedures and practices for everyone. Administrators should remember that OSHA enforcement actions can target any plan they write, so the plan should be simple, easy to understand, and easy to implement. The Lab Standard is a performance-based standard that establishes goals for compliance while providing minimal specifications for how employers should reach these goals. The performance-based nature of the Lab Standard requires the use of professional judgement in determining compliance in laboratories.

Ergonomics

The National Institute for Safety and Health defines "ergonomics" as the science of fitting workplace conditions and job demands to the capabilities of the working population. Ergonomics is an approach or solution to deal with a number of problems—including work-related musculoskeletal disorders. It is an applied science concerned with the human characteristics that are considered in designing and arranging objects that people use so that people and the objects interact effectively and safely. Ergonomics is also called "human factors engineering." Machinery, chairs, and equipment must fit the different sizes of the people who operate and use them.

The human body can endure considerable stress and discomfort and can perform many awkward and unnatural movements for a limited time when required to do so. However, when these same motions are continued over a long time period, they invariably result in psychological and physiological stress. Many painful conditions and disabling injuries are now associated with poor ergonomic factors in the workplace. Repetitive-motion injuries are among the most common occurrences with workers in manufacturing and are also showing up more frequently on college campuses, particularly among those people who spend many hours using a computer keyboard. Any job that includes repetitive motion or mechanical vibrations should be carefully reviewed and monitored. Prevention of repetitive-motion injuries is much more effective than treatment. In fact, even after treatment for such disorders as carpal tunnel syndrome and tenosynovitis, employees can rarely return to the same work routine.

Confined Spaces

A confined space is any work area that is difficult to enter and leave, is poorly ventilated, and is not intended for full-time occupancy. OSHA regulations that became effective in February 1991 require a written confined space entry program. Asphyxiation and exposure to toxic gases are the primary dangers associated with confined spaces, but other hazards such as noise, mechanical equipment, and flammable and explosive atmospheres can also threaten workers. On agricultural campuses, silos and manure pits are classic examples of confined spaces; other examples include manholes and tanks.

The steps for developing a confined space entry program are:

- *Identify the space.* Identification requires a complete tour of the facility with the help of workers. Whenever a space is entered through unconventional means, it has the potential to be defined as confined space. Such confined spaces include tanks, manholes, vaults, attics, and tunnels.

- *Develop written policies and procedures.* At a minimum, an effective confined space safety program contains the following elements: purpose, scope, and definitions of a confined space program; permit and permit system; operating procedures; contractors; emergencies; duties and responsibilities; and equipment.

- *Develop a permit system.* A permit system defines the exact confined space and designates who can enter the space, under what conditions, and for how long. The permit should only be valid on the date it is issued.

- *Establish a training program.* Training must take place for all people involved in the confined space entry program, including people preparing and recording permits.

- *Develop rescue procedures.* Rescue procedures that are effective and executable must be developed. A large number of fatalities occur when rescuers see someone in trouble and respond without thinking of the consequences.

Despite the dangers, every worker who enters a confined space can work in it and exit safely if proper procedures are developed and followed.

Asbestos

The term "asbestos" identifies a group of naturally occurring fibrous minerals that are mined and processed to produce flexible fibers that can be woven and mixed with a wide variety of media. Asbestos has been used extensively in building materials; the strong fibers are resistant to heat and chemicals and make excellent insulation. However, when the material is disturbed or damaged, small invisible asbestos fibers may be released. When released, asbestos fibers remain in the air for more than 24 hours, posing a lung hazard when inhaled. The inhalation of asbestos can cause diseases of the lungs, including asbestosis, lung cancer, and mesothelioma. The Clean Air Act of 1970 required the EPA to regulate asbestos, making it one of the first hazardous air pollutants to be regulated. The National Emission Standards for Hazardous Air Pollutants (NESHAP) for asbestos was promulgated by the EPA to minimize the release of asbestos during handling.

The health hazards of asbestos and the frequent utilization of the material in construction require that a comprehensive asbestos management program be implemented wherever asbestos is present. To prevent exposure to asbestos fibers that would place personnel at risk, institutional buildings should be inspected to assess the condition of the asbestos. If the buildings are asbestos free, no further action is required. If asbestos-containing material (ACM) is found, an asbestos management program should be implemented to assess whether asbestos removal or asbestos maintenance is appropriate to protect workers and building occupants.

In 1986, the Asbestos Hazard Emergency Response Act (AHERA) was signed into law as part of the Toxic Substance Act. AHERA requires K–12 schools to perform a physical and visual inspection of their buildings to assess the ACM's condition and potential for damage. AHERA requires that a single asbestos coordinator be chosen to oversee implementation of any asbestos activities. AHERA also requires the preparation of an inspection and management plan, training for all custodial and maintenance employees, reinspections, labeling, informing all workers and building occupants of asbestos-related activities, and informing service personnel of relevant ACM information.

The AHERA regulations can serve as a guideline for colleges and universities when preparing their own inspection and management plans, even though colleges and universities are not covered by the regulations.

A comprehensive asbestos management plan consists of the following major elements.

Asbestos Inventory and Assessment

Qualified personnel should conduct a thorough inventory to determine the scope of the asbestos problem, including the amount of asbestos present, its location and condition, and any corrective materials that might be needed. The analysis of the suspected material should be carried out by an accredited laboratory.

Protection of Employees and Building Occupants

People whose work brings them into contact with asbestos can possibly disturb asbestos in the course of routine activities. These employees must be adequately trained and protected, either in house or by attending an EPA-accredited training course.

Asbestos Abatement Action

Abatement action is required if asbestos is determined to be in a condition or location that releases fibers or where they could easily be disturbed. The field of asbestos abatement suffers from a poor reputation; its history is rife with citations, fines, and lawsuits. Studies by government agencies have shown that many asbestos abatement projects have been done improperly and incompetently.

Thus, a critical decision for a building owner in any abatement project is the selection of monitoring and abatement contractors. A poorly executed job can be avoided by prequalifying bidders. A standard and well-written contract reduces the possibility of litigation and increases the possibility of winning a legal challenge.

Asbestos Worker Protection and Work Site Safety

OSHA and EPA regulations govern worker protection, worker medical exams, personal protective equipment, respiratory protection, site enclosure, asbestos containment, removal procedures, and decontamination and cleanup procedures for work involving asbestos. Both the EPA and OSHA must be given advance notification prior to demolition of buildings containing ACM. In addition, many states have enacted their own regulations that may be more rigid than the federal regulations. Colleges and universities should periodically check with the appropriate federal, state, and local authorities to determine whether any new asbestos regulations have been developed. Current federal regulations that affect asbestos-related tasks or workers are:

- OSHA Construction Industry Standard for Asbestos;
- OSHA General Industry Standard for Asbestos;
- OSHA Respiratory Protection Standard;
- EPA Worker Protection Rule;
- EPA National Emission Standards for Hazardous Air Pollutants (NESHAP); and
- EPA Asbestos Hazard Emergency Response Act (AHERA) Regulations.

Proper management of ACM can prevent the occurrence of hazardous and costly fiber releases and limit potential liability for colleges and universities. Properly trained personnel should be selected to inventory, assess, manage, and remove ACM.

OCCUPATIONAL HEALTH MEDICINE

Occupational medicine is the medical field's interaction with the worker and the workplace to assure safe and healthy working conditions and, as a result, healthy employees. The complex workplace in modern institutions contains the potential for disabling injuries and illness. In the academic and research environment, potential hazards include the use of highly toxic chemicals; the study of animal and human diseases; research with lasers, microwaves, or other high-energy sources; the use of radioactive materials; the design and use of unusual and innovative equipment; microelectronic research; and a host of problems that arise because of the desire to enlarge the body of knowledge. Human health and safety can be maintained and protected with proper planning and monitoring. Occupational health medicine plays an important role in determining when, where, and how humans can safely interface with workplace hazards while maintaining personal health and well being.

Numerous regulations require that occupational medicine programs be provided to employees who are accidentally exposed to hazards or who routinely work under conditions or with materials that have identified risks. Examples of possible occupational hazards include asbestos, toxic chemicals, noise, lasers, microwaves (not ovens), pesticides, high voltage, heavy lifting, and repetitive motion. Most of these items or conditions are covered by regulations promulgated by agencies such as OSHA, EPA, and the Nuclear Regulatory Commission (NRC) and by state laws. In most instances, the laws and regulations are very specific and require regular physical examinations and other medical monitoring of employees exposed to these conditions. However, the employer must determine who should be involved and to what extent.

Regulations and good practice philosophies place a strong obligation on the employer to provide a safe workplace and to monitor and protect the health and safety of its employees. An occupational health medicine program is an important element in this process and enhances the effectiveness of existing safety programs. It also minimizes the employee's risks of working with hazardous materials and provides a degree of liability protection for employers, supervisors, and the institution.

The prevention of injury and illness in the workplace is cost effective. Good occupational health medicine programs increase employee morale, increase productivity, and help avoid illness and injury. Potential occupationally related health and safety problems must be identified in their infancy and managed or eliminated before they become debilitating. Occupational medicine personnel should coordinate activities and work closely with safety departments to optimize resources and results.

Health Assessments

Some occupational health medicine programs cover all employees at an academic institution; however, this policy tends to be the exception rather than the rule. Typically, participation in an occupational health medicine program is determined by regulatory requirements and the potential for specific occupational exposures in the workplace.

An occupational exposure is defined as on-the-job contact with any physical, chemical, or biological material that is a potential risk to humans, or exposure to conditions considered to be an occupational risk. In some instances, the determination of an employee's exposure can be subjective and requires the review of supervisors, the occupational physician, and other safety experts.

A proper and complete health assessment involves several elements; it is fairly critical that these be done in proper order. The assessment consists of the following:

- personal health and medical history;
- workplace history and hazard-exposure evaluation;

- complete and comprehensive physical examination; and
- follow-up tests, immunizations, and evaluations.

The employee must complete a personal health and medical history form. This form is usually shared only with the occupational physician. It often contains sensitive and privileged information, and protecting the doctor-patient relationship is of utmost importance. The employer does not have the right to see this form without employee consent and release.

The workplace history and hazard evaluation form is also a private document but, unlike the history form, is available to the employer for evaluation. In fact, several people may be affected by the contents of this form, including the employee, supervisors, and department head, personnel in the safety office, and the occupational physician. The workplace history and hazard evaluation, in conjunction with the medical history, determines and directs further medical evaluations and the placement of an employee in the workplace.

The physical examination and associated tests are reviewed by the occupational physician; by law, the occupationally related items must be revealed to the employer. It is then the employer's responsibility to use this information to assess and correct the health and safety problems existing in the workplace.

Because the purpose of an occupational medicine program is to protect employee health and to improve workplace safety, the evaluation, interpretation, and communication of the health assessment process is critical. The occupational physician, the employee, the supervisors, the health and safety department and top institutional administrators must coordinate activities and work together as a team. If any of the elements present barriers or make unreasonable demands, the purpose of the program can be lost.

Physical Exams

The occupational physician is the final arbiter of the exams and tests to be administered, but these will usually have a direct relationship to the employee's medical history and occupational exposures. Some typical routines including the following.

Baseline Physical Examinations

This exam is provided to all new employees in a workplace. Administrators must determine if all baseline exams should include the same elements or if they should be tailored to the workplace hazards or exposures. For example, should an employee whose only workplace hazard is noise exposure be required to take a whole battery of other tests?

Periodic Examinations

The recall frequency of examinations is often dictated in regulatory requirements. When it is not, the occupational physician must decide how often exams will occur; the decision is usually determined by factors such as age of the employee and frequency and degree of hazard exposure.

Reexamination for Specific Hazards

Employees with existing or developing health problems may require frequent examinations. The occupational physician must determine if the problem is work-related. If it is not work-related, the employee should be referred to his or her personal physician.

Separation Physical Examination

When an employee leaves the institution, he or she should have an examination that certifies this fact. An employee who transfers from areas with workplace hazards or no workplace hazards should have a similar separation examination.

Appropriate Medical and Laboratory Tests

Certain jobs have inherent risks and should include medical testing that is specific to evaluating exposure to hazards. Some examples of possible hazards include:

- animal bites;
- rabies virus research;
- puncture wound potential;
- radiation (ionizing and nonionizing);
- infectious organisms including zoonotic agents;
- cholinesterase inhibiting chemicals; and
- highly toxic chemicals and carcinogens.

Workplace Placement and Accident Investigation

An occupational health medicine program identifies preexisting medical conditions and then uses that information to place employees in the proper workplace. For example, an occupational medical program might keep employees with back injuries from doing jobs with heavy lifting or keep people with allergies away from jobs involving dust or known allergens. An occupational physician can tailor an employee's work schedule to a known medical condition.

The ongoing evaluation and repetitive medical screening of existing employees can help identify potential workplace problems and bring about solutions at an early stage. Solutions may involve changing the workplace safety features, prescribing personal and protective safety equipment for employees, or reassigning workers to a more desirable and correct workplace environment for them. Regardless of the reasons, the early detection of medical problems will ultimately result in less negative impacts (suffering as well as costs) for both the employee and the employer.

The occupational medicine department should be actively involved in certain accident investigations. Medical evaluations frequently provide evidence or information that leads to better understanding of the causes of accidents. In turn, this dictates changes that help prevent accidents. In the case of disabling injuries or accidents, the medical input is almost mandatory. Medical input also can help ascertain that the workplace was not the causative agent in an accident.

RADIATION SAFETY PROGRAMS

Radioactive materials and radiation-producing devices have become extremely valuable tools in modern research, medical diagnosis and therapy, and teaching. The ionizing radiations emitted by these materials and devices, however, have long been recognized as potentially hazardous to human health. Concern over radiation-related hazards led to recommended exposure limits early in this century and, ultimately, to mandatory limits and strict regulatory controls governing the possession and use of all sources of ionizing radiation. Colleges and universities that use radioactive materials or radiation-producing devices are not only obliged in principle but required by law to develop and implement sufficient institutional controls to ensure that the use of such radiation sources does not adversely impact the health of students, staff, visitors, or the general public. Collectively, the administrative and operational controls implemented toward this end constitute the institution's radiation safety program.

Licensing and Registration Requirements

Before radioactive materials can be used at a college or university, the institution must have a license for this use, granted from the appropriate regulatory agency. Depending on the state in which the institution resides, this agency may be the NRC or a state agency such as the department of health (which is usually the state's department of environmental protection).

The type and scope of a radioactive material license issued to a college or university depends on the institution's particular needs, as described in the license application. For most colleges and small universities that have limited uses for radioactive materials, the exact types and quantities of materials to be used, the manner in which they will be used, and the individuals who will use them are designated in a specific license issued to the institution. Larger universities with more varied uses of radioactive material may apply for and be granted a specific license of broad scope.

All types of radioactive material licenses require the development and implementation of numerous administrative and operational components that comprise a radiation safety program, including designation of a radiation safety officer. Institutions that have a broad-scope license must, in addition, establish a radiation safety committee (RSC). The committee consists of the radiation safety officer, a representative of the institution's management, and various members of the faculty or staff who have experience or training in the use of radioactive materials. The RSC has the authority and responsibility to review and approve all uses of radioactive material (and generally radiation-producing devices) at the institution. In addition, the RSC sets the institution's overall policies on the use of ionizing radiation and audits the operation of the radiation safety program.

X-ray–producing devices are found in medical and dental facilities and in many science and engineering research laboratories. Regulatory control over the use of X-ray–producing devices in the United States generally resides with state health departments. State requirements usually include the registration of each X-ray device, the incorporation and maintenance of safety features for the device, periodic radiation surveys, and personnel monitoring.

Personnel Training

Federal regulations mandate the minimum training that must be provided to any individual likely to receive in a year an occupational dose in excess of 100 mrem. Most states have adopted similar regulations governing the training of individuals working with or near radiation sources under their control. The types of personnel requiring training at a typical academic institution likely include such diverse groups as laboratory personnel, custodians, maintenance personnel, and construction workers, as well as various emergency personnel.

Accountability for Materials and Devices

Institutions that utilize radioactive materials and radiation-producing devices are required by state and federal regulations to maintain an accurate account of the types and quantities of these radiation sources in their possession at any given time. For large institutions with diverse uses of radiation sources, this generally requires the development and maintenance of sophisticated systems for accountability and control.

Radiation Surveys and Personnel Dosimetry

Institutions that utilize radiation sources are required by state and federal regulations to perform periodic surveys of all areas in which such sources are used or stored. The frequency of surveys is determined by the degree of hazard posed by the type and use of radiation sources in a particular area.

Dosimetry is the assessment of radiation doses received by individuals who work with sources of ionizing radiation and consists of practices for measuring both externally and internally derived doses. Regulations specify the limits for external radiation doses for individuals who work with radiation sources and further require that individuals likely to receive doses equaling 10 percent or more of these limits be monitored for radiation exposure.

Colleges or universities may also be required by federal regulation and by the conditions of their radioactive material licenses to assess internal radiation doses in personnel through the establishment and maintenance of some form of bioassay program. In this sense, bioassay means the testing of human body fluid for radioactive content to determine if internal radioactive exposure has occurred. The most widely used method of bioassay is urinalysis. Bioassay (radiobioassay) means the determination of kinds, quantities, concentrations, and (in some cases) locations of radioactive material in the human body, whether by direct measurement (in vivo counting) or by analysis and evaluation of materials excreted or removed from the human body. For colleges and universities, the most widely used method of bioassay is thyroid counting for intakes of radioactive iodines.

Radioactive Waste Management

For academic institutions that use large amounts of radioactive materials, the most time-consuming and expensive component of a radiation safety program is likely to be radioactive waste management. As is true for other hazardous wastes, the costs of commercially disposing of radioactive wastes have increased dramatically in recent years. This has resulted in greater efforts to maximize the use of local treatment and disposal options to reduce the total volumes requiring commercial disposal. These options, however, are labor and capital intensive.

The disposal of radioactive wastes is strictly controlled by federal regulations. Recent federal regulations administered by the EPA, under the RCRA, have placed further restrictions on the disposal of radioactive wastes that have hazardous chemical components (i.e., mixed wastes). Under the framework of these regulatory requirements, options for local treatment and disposal of radioactive wastes are limited to volume-reduction methods, such as compaction and decaying short-lived materials in storage, and methods involving small releases to the environment, such as incineration and disposal by way of the sanitary sewer. Disposal methods involving radioactive releases to the environment, however, are strictly controlled by federal and state regulations and must often be specifically approved in the institution's license.

Other Radiation Safety Issues

Radon

In addition to the various radiation safety issues already discussed, colleges and universities may have to address health and safety issues not directly related to the use of radioactive materials or radiation-producing devices on campus. Foremost in this category is the issue of indoor radon.

Radon is a naturally occurring radioactive gas that is formed continuously in virtually all soil and rock. A portion of the radon formed near the earth's surface migrates to the surface, where it is diluted in the atmosphere to very low levels. Radon can also enter buildings and, in certain instances, build up to relatively high concentrations. Prolonged exposure to elevated levels of radon and its radioactive breakdown products is believed to increase an individual's risk of lung cancer.

The EPA has been the principal agency addressing the indoor radon issue. It has established guidelines for maximum indoor radon concentrations and has promoted radon measurement and reduction strategies. Although the initial emphasis of the EPA's program was on homes, the program has been expanded to include schools and other public buildings and workplaces. Currently, the EPA's radon program is not mandated by federal law. However, based on the EPA's guidance, some states have either passed or are considering legislation that would mandate radon testing of public buildings, including colleges and universities.

The degree of radon testing required for large campuses in order to characterize their potential for radon problems can be very substantial. The testing involves, at a minimum, the measurement of radon levels at a number of locations in the lowest habitable levels of a certain percentage of campus buildings. The costs of such a program include not only the price of detectors but also the personnel used for placing and retrieving the detectors and recording the results of analyses. For reasons of health and safety and public relations, however, a basic radon-testing program of this type may be prudent whether or not it is required by local or state law.

Nonionizing Radiation

Radiation safety programs have traditionally been concerned with the control of hazards associated with the use of ionizing radiation. More recently, the control of potential hazards related to the use of sources of nonionizing radiation have been included in the responsibilities of these programs. Sources of nonionizing radiation in colleges or universities may include lasers, microwave ovens, microwave antennae, radio-frequency (RF) induction furnaces, ultraviolet radiation sources, magnetic resonance devices, and sputtering devices. Other more common sources of extremely low frequency RF such as video display terminals have been the subjects of recent attention.

The potential risks to health posed by various forms of nonionizing radiation are far more difficult to assess than those posed by ionizing radiation. For this reason, there has been no comprehensive effort, to date, to control the use of nonionizing radiation sources by regulation. Various related standards and guidelines, however, have been issued. For example, the American National Standards Institute has issued standards on Safe Use of Lasers and Safety Levels with Respect to Human Exposure to Radio Frequency Electromagnetic Fields. Many institutional radiation safety programs have adopted these standards as the basis for safety programs for lasers and RF devices. Such programs generally require, at a minimum, inventorying and periodically inspecting the devices.

Records

All the components of a radiation safety program have associated requirements for the maintenance of records. The type and extent of information to be recorded may, in some cases, be specifically prescribed by regulation or license condition or, in other cases, be inferred from the need to demonstrate compliance in particular areas of the program. The length of time for which records must be maintained varies considerably among program areas. Certain types of records, for example, such as those documenting survey procedures, may be required for only three years. Other records, such as those documenting personnel exposures, may be required in perpetuity. For institutions with substantial uses of radioactive materials and radiation-producing devices, the resources required for the maintenance of these records and record systems may be significant.

NOTES

1. March 15, 1999; Release # 99-3-16: EPA Launches Compliance Initiative Aimed at 258 New England Universities; Fines University of New Hampshire for Hazardous Waste Violations

2. State of Connecticut DEP Consent Order (State and University of Connecticut), 10/23/97, regarding violations of RCRA-equivalent state regulations.

REFERENCES AND RESOURCES

Publications and Articles

American Conference of Governmental Industrial Hygienists, Inc. *Industrial Ventilation.* 23th ed. Cincinnati, Ohio: ACGIH, Publication 2092 (also available on CD-ROM), 1998.

American Society of Heating, Refrigeration and Air Conditioning Engineers. *HVAC Applications Handbook.* Atlanta, Ga.: ASHRACE, 1999.

Association of Physical Plant Administrators of Universities and Colleges. *Regulatory Compliance for Facility Managers.* Alexandria, Va.: APPA, 1989.

Benenson, A. S., ed. *Control of Communicable Diseases in Man.* 16th ed. Washington, D.C.: American Public Health Association, 1995.

Blumenthal, D.S., and Ruttenber, A. A. *Introduction to Environmental Health* 2nd ed. NY: Springer, 1995.

Brewster, R. E., ed. *Environmental Health Guidelines for Child Care Facilities.* Denver, Colo.: National Environmental Health Association, 1986.

Environmental Protection Agency. *National Toxicology Program Fifth Annual Report on Carcinogens: A Summary.* Washington D.C.: EPA, 1989

Fleming, D.O. et al. *Laboratory Principles and Practices.* Washington, D.C., ASM Press., 1995.

Godbey, F. W., and Hatch, L. L. *Occupational Safety and Health Program Guidelines for*

Colleges and Universities. Department of Health, Education, and Welfare Publications, No. 79-108. Cincinnati, Ohio: National Institute for Occupational Safety and Health, 1978.

Government Institutes. *Environmental Law Handbook.* 10th ed. Rockville, Md.: Government Institutes, 1989.

Koren, H., and Bisesi, M. *Handbook of Environmental Health and Safety: Principles and Practices.* 2 vols., 3rd ed., Boca Raton, FL: Lewis Publishers, 1995.

Marriott, N.G. *Principles of Food Sanitation.* Gaithersburg, Maryland: Aspen Publishers, 1994.

Michigan Environmental Health Association. *Environmental Health Ready Reference Manual.* 4th ed., Lansing, Michigan: Michigan Environmental Health Association, 1995.

National Academy of Sciences. *Prudent Practices in the Laboratory.* Washington, D.C.: National Academy Press, 1995.

National Association of College and University Business Officers. *Hazardous Waste Management at Educational Institutions.* Washington, D.C.: NACUBO, 1987.

National Fire Protection Association. *Fire Protection Handbook.* 18th ed. Boston, Mass.: NFPA, 1997.

National Institute for the Foodservice Industry. *Applied Foodservice Sanitation.* 3d ed. Dubuque, Iowa: Wm. C. Brown Publishers, 1985.

National Research Council. *Biosafety in the Laboratory: Prudent Practices for the Handling and Disposal of Infectious Materials.* Washington, D.C.: National Academy Press, 1989.

National Research Council. *Guide for the Care and Use of Laboratory Animals.* Washington, D.C.: National Academy Press, 1996.

National Research Council. *Occupational Health and Safety in the Care and Use of Laboratory Animals.* Washington, D.C.: National Academy Press, 1996.

National Safety Council. *The Fundamentals of Industrial Hygiene.* 4th ed. National Safety Council, Itasca, IL, 1996.

Office of Technology Assessment Task Force. *Reproductive Health Hazards in the Workplace.* Philadephia, Pa.: J. B. Lippincott Co., 1988.

PHS (Public Health Service). *Public Health Service Policy on Humane Care and Use of Laboratory Animals.* Washington, D.C.: U.S. Department of Health and Human Services, 1996.

PHS (Public Health Service). *Biosafety in Microbiological and Biomedical Laboratories.*

4th ed. U.S. Department of Health and Human Services. Washington: D.C., 1999.

PHS (Public Health Service). *The Public Health Implications of Medical Waste: A Report to Congress.* No. PB 1-100271., U.S. Department of Health and Human Services, Washington: D.C., 1990.

Salvato, J.A. *Environmental Engineering and Sanitation.* 4th ed. NY: John Wiley, 1992.

Wilson, R., and Crouch, E. "Risk Assessment and Comparisons: An Introduction." *Science* 236 (1987): 267–270.

Regulations

Relevant regulations include, but are not limited to, the ones listed below. Copies are available from the appropriate agency or the U.S. Government Printing Office.

CFR (Code of Federal Regulations). 1985. Title 9 (Animals and Animal Products), Subchapter A (Animal Welfare). Washington, D.C.: Office of the Federal Register.

CFR 1990. Title 49 (Department of Transportation), Parts 100 through 199 (Transportation of Hazardous Materials). Washington, D.C.: Office of the Federal Register.

CFR 1989. Title 40 (Environmental Protection Agency), Parts 260 through 272 (Hazardous Waste Regulations). Washington, D.C.: Office of the Federal Register.

CFR 1989. Title 40 (Environmental Protection Agency), Parts 280 and 281 (Underground Storage Tanks). Washington, D.C.: Office of the Federal Register.

CFR 1989. Title 40 (Environmental Protection Agency), Part 355 (Emergency Planning and Notification). Washington, D.C.: Office of the Federal Register.

CFR 1990. Title 40 (Environmental Protection Agency), Part 761 (PCB Regulations). Washington, D.C.: Office of the Federal Register.

CFR 1990. Title 29 (OSHA), Part 1910 (General Industry Standards). Washington, D.C.: Office of the Federal Register.

CFR 1991. Title 29 (OSHA), Part 1910.1030 (Occupational Exposure to Bloodborne Pathogens: Final Rule). Washington, D.C.: Office of the Federal Register.

Organizations

American Biological Safety Association (ABSA) . . . . www.absa.org
1202 Allanson Road, Mundelein, IL 60060
Professional organization; association has local affiliates and holds an annual
conference. Education, communication and exchange of information is encouraged
by forums, meetings, and preconference courses.

**American Conference of Governmental
Industrial Hygienists (ACGIH)** . . . . www.acgih.org
P.O. Box 1937, Cincinnati, OH 45201
ACGIH is a source for over 400 technical and scientific publications. Publishes a
monthly peer-reviewed journal, *Applied Occupational and Environmental Hygiene,* and
conduct numerous professional conferences and workshops each year.

American Industrial Hygiene Association (AIHA) . . . . www.aiha.org
2700 Prosperity Ave., Suite 250, Fairfax, VA 22031
Founded in 1939, AIHA is an organization of more than 13,000 professional
members dedicated to the anticipation, recognition, evaluation, and control of
environmental factors arising in or from the workplace that may result in injury,
illness, impairment, or affect the well-being of workers and members of the
community.

American National Standards Institute (ANSI) . . . . web.ansi.org/
11 West 42nd Street, 13th Fl., New York, New York 10036
ANSI has served in its capacity as administrator and coordinator of the United
States private sector voluntary standardization system for 80 years. Founded in 1918
by five engineering societies and three government agencies, the Institute remains a
private, nonprofit membership organization supported by a diverse constituency of
private and public sector organizations.

American Public Health Association (APHA) . . . . www.apha.org
800 I. St., NW, Washington, DC 20001-3710
The American Public Health Association (APHA) is the oldest and largest
organization of public health professionals in the world, representing more than
50,000 members from over 50 occupations of public health.

Canadian Centre for Occupational Health and Safety (CCOHS) . www.ccohs.ca
250 Main Street East, Hamilton ON L8N 1H6, Canada
CCOHS is Canada's national centre for occupational health and safety (OH&S)
information. The web site provides an excellent internet directory of US and
Canadian safety and health resources.

**Campus Safety, Health and Environmental Management Association
(CSHEMA)** . . . . www.safety.utoledo.edu/cshema/home.html
The campus safety division of National Safety Council (NSC) . . . . . www.nsc.org
1121 Spring Lake Drive, Itasca, IL 60143-3201
Founded in 1954, CSHEMA is an organization of campus environmental health and
safety professionals that sponsors a yearly national conference on campus safety and
health; publishes monographs of these conferences; and provides a benchmarking
service. Source of many other books and safety-related materials.

International Association for Food Protection (IAFP) www.foodprotection.org
Formerly: International Association of Milk, Food and Environmental Sanitarians
(IAMFES), 6200 Aurora Avenue, Suite 200W, Des Moines, IA 50322-2863
The Association provides this information network through its two monthly
scientific journals, its Annual Meeting, and other Member benefits, as well as
interaction with other food safety professionals.

National Environmental Health Association (NEHA) . . . . . www.neha.org
720 S. Colorado Boulevard, Suite 970, South Tower, Denver, CO 80246-1925
Has state affiliates; publishes the *Journal of Environmental Health* six times a year; has
developed a series of continuing education modules with emphasis on practical
skills and on-the-job performance. Also makes available educational materials,
including videos, audiocassettes, and reference textbooks. Promotes professional
development by offering the opportunity to obtain nationally recognized
credentials. Holds an annual and midyear conference.

National Fire Protection Association (NFPA) . . . . www.nfpa.org
1 Batterymarch Park, PO Box 910, Quincy, MA 02269-9101
NFPA is an international, nonprofit, membership organization founded in 1896 to
protect people, their property and the environment from destructive fire. More than
65,000 strong, NFPA's membership represents nearly 100 nations and is open to all
individuals interested in promoting a safer world.

National Institute for Occupational
Safety and Health (NIOSH) . . . . www.cdc.gov/niosh
Hubert H. Humphrey Bldg., 200 Independence Ave., SW,
Room 715, Washington, DC 20201
NIOSH was established by the Occupational Safety and Health Act of 1970.
NIOSH is part of the Centers for Disease Control and Prevention (CDC) and is the
only federal Institute responsible for conducting research and making
recommendations for the prevention of work-related illnesses and injuries.

Occupational Safety and Health Administration (OSHA) . . . . www.osha.gov
U.S. Department of Labor,
Occupational Safety and Health Administration (OSHA)
200 Constitution Avenue, N.W., Washington, D.C. 20210
The mission of the Occupational Safety and Health Administration (OSHA) is to
save lives, prevent injuries and protect the health of America's workers. To
accomplish this, federal and state governments must work in partnership with the
more than 100 million working men and women and their six and a half million
employers who are covered by the Occupational Safety and Health Act of 1970.

United States Centers for Disease Control and Prevention (CDC) www.cdc.gov
Atlanta, GA 30333
Federal agency; publishes the *Morbidity and Mortality Weekly Report,* which gives
information on outbreaks of diseases (illnesses) related to food, water, chemicals in
occupational settings, pesticides, medical facilities (nosocomial).

United States Fire Administration (USFA) . . . . <u>www.usfa.fema.gov</u>
16825 S. Seton Ave., Emmitsburg, MD 21727
As an entity of the Federal Emergency Management Agency, the mission of the
USFA is to reduce life and economic losses due to fire and related emergencies,
through leadership, advocacy, coordination, and support. USFA also operates the
National Fire Academy (NFA). Through its courses and programs, the NFA works
to enhance the ability of fire and emergency services and allied professionals to deal
more effectively with fire and related emergencies.

United States Food and Drug Administration (FDA) . . . . . . <u>www.fda.gov</u>
State Training and Information Branch (HFC-153)
5600 Fishers Lane, Room 12-07, Rockville, MD 20857
Federal agency; issues *Catalog of Courses and Training Materials* yearly, listing
training courses, lending library of training materials, and bibliography of training
materials.

Other Information Sources

Any PCB transformer involved in a fire must be reported to the National Response
Center at 800-424-8802 or 202-426-2675. For further information on PCBs, contact
EPA's Office of Toxic Substances at 202-554-1404.

The EPA's Office of Underground Storage Tanks has a summary of regulations
that can be obtained from EPA's Office of Asbestos and Small Business Ombudsman
(OASBO) at 800-368-5888 or 703-557-1938. Also, EPA's RCRA/CERCLA Hotline
at 800-424-9346 or 703-920-9810 should be consulted regarding chemicals that are
hazardous.

Chapter 15

Security and Law Enforcement

by

John Carpenter
San Diego State University

Contents

The responsibility for the safety and protection of individuals and property on college and university campuses falls within two broad categories. The campus establishes either a law enforcement department or a security department. Law enforcement departments are staffed by police officers—trained, sworn, law officers with legal authority to carry weapons and arrest criminals. Security departments, on the other hand, are staffed by security guards whose primary function is to prevent theft, fire, and other incidents by their presence, vigilance, and adherence to proper security procedures. Regardless of the category selected by the institution, the primary responsibility of protecting life and property applies to each. This chapter will discuss many of those responsibilities.

ADMINISTRATION OF THE CAMPUS POLICE OR SECURITY DEPARTMENT

The police or security department has the challenging responsibility of enforcing local, state, and federal laws on campus. The administration, with input from professionals and members of the campus community, needs to determine what type of enforcement department is best suited to its community; provide adequate funds; define the department's mission, goals, and objectives; and communicate its purpose to all members of the campus community. The department's mission must be compatible with the institution's mission. Important aspects of this process are defining the police or security officers' duties and responsibilities and providing full support for this department.

The campus police or security departments of today, regardless of their areas of responsibility, must not simply react to incidents, but must function proactively to prevent violence and theft. Clearly the level of security in any jurisdiction is often reactive and at times crisis driven, but administrators and parents alike expect police or security officers to be proactive in preventing such crises from occurring. This proactive planning must take into account the department's mission and its administrative philosophy before embarking on security strategies.

The mission of a college or university police or security department is to provide as safe an environment as possible, thereby protecting the life and property of members of its community. Whether a college or university operates its own department, contracts for this purpose, or depends on local law-enforcement agencies, the institution's responsibilities include:

- protection of constitutional rights;
- enforcement of local, state, and federal laws and specific institutional regulations;
- maintenance of security in the community;
- identification and elimination of hazards and opportunities for crime;
- establishment of effective crime prevention programs, including education of the institutional community; and
- maintenance of protective patrols to deter and detect crime, to detect fire and safety hazards, and to prevent traffic accidents and congestion.

Although the provision of safety and security in a college or university is ultimately the responsibility of the institution's president, the demanding field of campus law enforcement requires the attention of a trained professional. Creating a safe environment requires strong administrative decisions as well as a competent police or security force.

The form and extent of the security needed by a college or university depends on its unique circumstances. The size of the institution, its location, its facilities, and its populations dictate the services to be rendered by the police or security department. Many larger institutions have staff members who specialize in various areas. In smaller institutions, a single individual may perform multiple tasks.

Campus Police, Municipal Police, and Security Personnel

The decision as to whether to establish a campus police force or rely on the local police department to enforce all laws on campus may depend on the needs of the campus and the relationship with local law enforcement officials. Some independent colleges and universities in states not granting special police authority to campuses have sought such authority through the city police chief or county sheriff. Aside from the method of securing such authority, the quality and training of officers must be no less than any police officer, regardless of the jurisdiction.

The similarities and differences between municipal police officers and campus police officers are rather striking. For the most part the standards for police training in most states would apply to all "sworn officers" certified by that state. The distinctions that separate the two may be influenced by the overall law enforcement philosophy of the institution. While some individuals think that campus police officers are less qualified than municipal officers, the opposite is most often true. With qualifications and training being equal, the difference falls within the area of community relations (people skills). Within our academic environment police officers must be extremely sensitive to situations that may not rise to the level of being a crime (i.e., classroom disruption or assistance with an employee termination). However, when a crisis or criminal incident occurs, the officers must be ready and able to respond appropriately.

It is possible to employ sworn police officers to handle the law enforcement duties and nonsworn security officers trained in campus security techniques to handle premises security issues. Each has a different role and should be selected and trained for their specific responsibilities. These officers should have different job descriptions and different duties, but they can operate under the administration of a single department. Security officers are generally less expensive since they have less training and authority than sworn police officers.

Some campuses have increased the level of security officers' enforcement responsibilities with no corresponding legal authority to enforce laws. This clearly places the officers at personal risk and creates potential liability for the institution. Although some institutions have both police officers and security personnel, campuses should not attempt to establish a hybrid of these two. There should be a clear distinction between the duties and appearance of security officers and police officers, so that there is no confusion within the campus community. Security officers should have clear guidelines and directives as to what they are expected to do in various situations, such as when confronted with violent criminal activity. Expecting security officers, with no training or official arrest authority, to confront or arrest violent criminals would place the officer and campus community in general at risk.

Institutions that employ security officers and expect local law enforcement officers to come to campus when called should have a clear understanding of what is expected when law officers do respond. This understanding should be in the form of a mutual aid agreement. There should also be a system in place so that all officers who may have to respond know exactly where to go on campus. The effectiveness of off-campus police officers is greatly reduced if there is no quick way for them to determine where a particular building or area is located. If the institution has decided to employ police officers rather than security officers, then those officers must be equipped as police officers; this includes weapons. If the issuance of weapons is abhorrent to members of the academic community, they should hire security officers and have the city police respond with their weapons when needed. Not to issue a weapon to police officers endangers the officers. The issuance of firearms is also a liability issue, so qualification and periodic requalification are mandatory.

In the United States, as in other parts of the world, some campuses deploy a combination of full-time employed security officers and police officers. In some cases, contract security guards can be used as the "eyes and ears" of the full-time, trained police or security officers. Because guards are typically paid less than officers, the campus could contract for additional guards to create a higher-profile security presence to deter criminals. In doing so, however, there must be a clear distinction between the police or security officers and the guards.

The level and type of campus security or law enforcement and the method in which it is provided will vary by institution. The police or security department should solicit the support of every individual on a campus, including students, in providing security. The whole institution benefits by making security "everybody's business."

Policy Statement for the Department

Institutions should develop a policy statement that outlines the responsibilities of the police or security department. The statement should include:

- the department's mission;

- the department's authority and jurisdiction;

- code of officer conduct;

- standards of discipline;

- handling complaints;

- recruitment, selection, and training;

- promotion and career development;

- coordination with other departments, specifically student affairs and housing; and

- emergency notification.

A comprehensive review of the campus safety and security needs is critical. An analysis should be prepared of the campus community's opinions and attitudes about general safety issues and the police or security department itself. Some campuses have used experienced members of the university, but it may be more objective to have an outside peer review conducted by experts in the field.

In 1991, the International Association of Campus Law Enforcement Administrators (IACLEA) initiated a peer review program called LEMAP (Loaned Executive Management Assistance Program) to provide management consulting and technical assistance to institutions of higher education. LEMAP provides an opportunity for campus administrators to avail themselves of a professional review of their department's organization, operations, and management systems. The program also provides assistance in evaluating the institution's level of security in terms of crime prevention through environmental designs. The goal of LEMAP is to provide campus law enforcement and security administrators the opportunity to take a critical look at their organization through the eyes of a group of peer professionals.

DEPARTMENTAL ORGANIZATION

Legal Authority of Police and Security Forces

The high level of campus security today is a far cry from the responsibilities faced by security officers of the recent past. Prior to the 1970s, most campuses that contracted or employed security forces to protect their facilities paid little attention to the department's training and job responsibilities. It was assumed that their uniformed presence was simply a deterrent for would-be thieves.

In the past, campuses that contracted for security guards did so through the lowest bid process, and guards' training consisted of an orientation at their agency and a briefing at the contract site. Frequently, the security guard's job was to sit at a desk at the entrance to the specific building and to walk through the building periodically checking for fire hazards and unlocked doors.

Protecting our academic environment today has become a challenge for campus administrators. Contracting for security services should be carefully evaluated before making any commitment. Whether the institution contracts for security officers or employs its own security staff, their responsibilities and liabilities are extensive. The potential for their over-reaction during a crisis or physical confrontation with emotional individuals or even their failure to react when required may well become a political and financial nightmare for the university.

Police Departments

State laws govern campus police departments, outlining their responsibilities, the quality of protection provided, and training required. Campus police also enforce rules and regulations that are unique to the campus, such as student behavior codes.

Police officers are sworn to uphold the oaths they take upon employment. These oaths usually include requirements of the institution to perform in a certain manner. Police officers generally take an oath of office to perform duties in a prescribed manner, as well as an oath of allegiance to the state in which they serve and to the national government. The oath of office is a process that results in the term "sworn" officer. Likewise, an officer who is deputized takes an oath of office and is sworn into office as a deputy, duty-bound to perform services in a manner prescribed by the sheriff of the county in which he or she serves.

"Sworn officers" have greater flexibility in performing their duties in specific areas than those who are not sworn. In some states, a sworn campus police officer operates with the same authority and limitations as a municipal police officer or deputy sheriff. In most instances, because the office of sheriff is an elected office accountable to the people, it is upheld as the highest law enforcement office in a county. Moreover, the various state constitutions allow greater freedom for the office of sheriff than for any other law enforcement office. Thus, the county sheriff can usually exercise greater freedom in the investigation of crimes than local police, despite the fact that a single county may have several police jurisdictions. If campus officers are deputized, the power and authority of the sheriff's office is applicable. It is therefore important for campus officers operating in a deputized status to have specific guidelines regarding how they are expected to utilize their new and expanded power.

Security Departments

Laws that govern security forces are somewhat different from the laws that govern a police force. Campus security forces may not have the authority or flexibility necessary to carry out certain functions (i.e., arrests for crimes not committed in their presence), but their quality and training must meet the level of their assigned responsibilities. Security forces do not have direct access to the FBI Criminal Information Network and Uniform Crime Report, but they should establish protocols for gathering appropriate intelligence from their local police agency. If a security officer is required to make an arrest for a minor offense, such an arrest is considered a "citizen's arrest" and therefore subject to false arrest suits. Police officers are immune to such suits if they acted within the scope of the law, while security officers and citizens making such arrests do so at their own risk—and at the risk of the institution.

Staff Selection and Identification

The objective of campus police or security officer recruitment and selection is to find candidates who are qualified in terms of professional talents, ethics, drive, and emotional stability. A process for selecting officers should include extensive interviews, and psychological and fitness testing, as well as additional testing that provides an accurate measure of skills needed by the department.

The benefits of positive recruitment and selection policies should be manifested in a low rate of personnel turnover, few discipline problems, high morale, good community relations, and effective services. The selection process is generally acknowledged as the key activity in determining operational effectiveness of a department.

The hiring process for police or security officers should include passing a certified or otherwise approved test; completing a physical or medical examination; undergoing a psychological test, followed by an interview with a psychologist; passing an agility test; giving an oral interview; and having a final interview with the department head. The oral interview should be conducted by members of the department, human resources personnel, and others from the campus community that can discuss and present common campus situations that the candidates may have to address.

A comprehensive background investigation must be conducted before a final offer of employment is made. Background investigations should not be conducted solely by letters or phone calls. A person trained in conducting such investigations should personally visit prior employers and talk with coworkers. To allow for an open, honest, and effective discussion with prior supervisors, the applicant should sign and have notarized a waiver that allows full access to personnel records and indemnifies past employers from liability when talking about an applicant's work history.

Officers who were once college students themselves have a better understanding of the academic environment and the nature of the college community. At supervisory and management positions, it is even more important to have a highly educated workforce. Failure to staff the police or security officers' ranks with college educated officers will make it more difficult to promote internal personnel with the desired levels of education to supervisory and management positions.

The chief or director of the department must be thoroughly trained and experienced in campus security and law enforcement. Required qualifications might include graduation from approved state or federal training programs (e.g., FBI National Academy) and certification in accordance with state law. Individuals assuming the position of chief or director of a police or security department may be given an opportunity within a certain time frame to become certified in all necessary areas required by state law.

When a campus police or security department is organized, administrators must give thought to the uniform appearance of the officers who represent the institution. Many institutions outfit officers with standard uniforms, accented with identification patches. In years past, institutions wishing to have a lower profile security presence have dressed security personnel in blazers with pocket patches identifying them as officers of the institution. However, the general public is not accustomed to security personnel dressed this way and, particularly in crowds, officers in blazers are hard to distinguish from other people. Today, the public demands and expects a highly trained and visible police or security department to provide a sense of safety. The standard uniform, which includes a cap or hat, allows the officer to be more readily identifiable in emergency situations. Uniforms may range from standard law enforcement colors to a color scheme that reflects the tradition of the institution. Color schemes of this nature can help instill pride in the officers, through identification with the college or university.

Community-Oriented Policing

Community-oriented policing (COP) is a new way of doing business for law enforcement. It is a partnership between law enforcement officials and the community that aims to put police officers in close contact with the communities they serve and to decrease crime in the process. COP is a major program being incorporated within the police functions throughout the country. Many campuses have been used as models by city police departments when developing such programs. This program is spreading rapidly within police organizations across the country, not because it is a new fad, but rather because it is very effective in reducing crimes and building community support for the police.

Community policing on a college campus entails the full cooperation of students, faculty, and staff. Faculty and staff actively work with police or security officers to identify and understand the most pressing problems on campus and devise solutions together. Through meetings, campus surveys, analysis of citizen complaints, and conversations with students, faculty, and staff, officers learn what issues most concern various segments of the campus community. This information enables officers to better respond to the community's needs. Community-oriented policing gives officers on patrol more leeway to adapt their duties as they identify new ways to prevent crime and promote a safe campus environment.

The 1994 federal crime bill focused national attention on the community-oriented policing philosophy. The act encourages local law enforcement agencies to hire officers for the sole purpose of implementing community-oriented policing in their communities. In 1998 and 1999, many campuses were successful in gaining additional police officers through the Federal COPS Grant program. This program allowed municipal police departments and campuses with sworn officers to hire new officers, with the federal government paying part of their salaries for the first three years.

According to most national surveys, crime remains among the top concerns of Americans, and to fight it, cities and campuses across the nation are turning to community policing. Community policing is a strategy that builds on fundamental policing practices with an emphasis on crime prevention and lasting solutions to problems. It requires new resolve from citizens and new thinking from police or security officers.

Community policing has been shown to reduce crime and fear, while restoring a sense of order. It can also rebuild the bond between citizens and government. Police or security officers, as public servants who interact with citizens on a daily basis, have a unique opportunity to demonstrate the importance of citizen involvement in the community. In turn, they realize that their authority and effectiveness are linked directly to the support they receive from citizens.

Under community policing, citizens may volunteer their time and services to assist the police or security department. They may attend meetings with police or security officers to brainstorm solutions to a recurring problem. Such partnerships can boost the campus community's confidence in the department and foster mutual respect. Community policing encourages officers and citizens to look beyond surface issues to find lasting solutions to crime. Community policing officers collect information from a variety of sources to help identify patterns leading to recurring crimes. Then they work with citizens to set priorities and develop tailor-made responses.

Staffing Levels

The issue of adequate staffing for campus police or security departments has been and will continue to be a significant concern for chiefs and directors. While no one formula or system is applicable to all institutions, there are national standards that can be used to evaluate reasonable minimum staffing levels.

Sample data from the Bureau of Justice Statistics, Campus Law Enforcement Agencies, 1995 state:

> The average operating expenditures for campus law enforcement agencies ranged from $4.3 million on campuses with an enrollment of 30,000 or more to $481,000 on campuses with an enrollment of 2,500 to 4,999. Among all four-year campuses of 2,500 or more students, about two-thirds of the law enforcement employees worked at public institutions.
>
> Public institutions average 2.4 officers per 1,000 students. However, private institutions overall had nearly twice as many law enforcement employees per 1,000 students (4.5 versus 2.4).

A staffing plan developed by the International Association of Chiefs of Police measures "calls for service" to determine the number of patrol posts and staff needed to fill those posts. Graphs, charts, and formulas dealing with officers' activities can be found in *Proactive Police Management*.[1]

Aside from surveys and staffing formulas, it is important to recognize that each campus environment is unique—rural versus urban, residential versus commuting, for example—and the number of police or security staff may vary. Size of physical plant and its nature will also dictate the number of officers. The department is often the only unit, or one of the few units, on campus that work 24 hours a day, seven days a week, 52 weeks a year. Overtime may be required to cover vacations and sick leave. What is important to consider, however, is the level of protective service needed. Since the police or security function tends to be crisis driven, if crime is low and the campus feels relatively safe, it would be difficult to justify additional staffing. This, however, is when such staffing considerations should be made, rather than waiting for a crisis.

Staffing is not limited to officers. Investigators and others are necessary for follow-up, crime prevention, and other tasks. Dispatchers and clerks are necessary for the department to function. Duties assigned to officers outside of patrol, report taking, and responding to other calls diminishes their effectiveness.

Hiring Versus Contracting for Services

Each institution must decide whether to employ its own security staff or to contract for its security needs, based on a variety of factors. Because of each institution's unique identity, there is no specific model for how every campus should "serve and protect" its students, faculty, staff, and guests. Only a careful analysis of the campus environment, administrative philosophy, local law enforcement, and applicable laws will determine what is best for each campus. The level in overall safety of individuals and the campus community's confidence in the police or security department should carry utmost weight in the decision-making process. The least appropriate factor to consider should be budgetary concerns, yet, all too often, budget is the driving force.

The institution must examine the quality of services to be provided before signing the contract. Companies that provide security should supply records of their performance with other businesses and educational institutions. Institutional administrators should examine these performance records to determine if services provided are in line with those desired by the institution. Where state laws require minimum levels of training for security guard certification, the contractor must demonstrate the ability to comply.

The institution should notify the company that training must be an integral part of the ongoing operation of the security program. The company would then be required to perform most of the administrative process related to employment, training, evaluating, testing, and supervision. A clear understanding must exist between the company and the institution regarding services desired and the personnel necessary to deliver those services.

The vendor must provide liability insurance in the amount specified by policy or law. The contract should also be reviewed by legal counsel to ensure that nothing in it is contrary to state law or holds the institution liable if a company employee is found to be negligent.

Jurisdictional Relationships

A college or university campus has boundaries that usually dictate the jurisdiction of the security or law enforcement department. In some states, the jurisdiction of the college or university extends beyond the geographical boundary of the campus, because many institution-related problems spill over to the surrounding community. Some states have laws that give a campus police or security force jurisdiction to operate for a distance of up to one mile or more from the property boundaries of the campus. This action legally extends the jurisdiction of the campus security or law enforcement force into adjacent areas that may be regularly policed by a city or a county police department. Jurisdictions must be well defined, and in their training, officers must be made aware of the geographical boundaries. These limits must also be made known to the local law enforcement agency, and any conflicts should be quickly addressed.

In cases where the jurisdiction extends beyond the geographical boundaries of the campus and concurrent jurisdiction exists, the college or university usually defers to the local police department in matters that occur in the area of concurrent jurisdiction. The exercise of authority in these areas is usually based on the threat level of the incident to the general public. Flagrant violations of law or life-threatening situations, such as robberies or assaults, occurring within the jurisdiction of the campus but outside its geographic boundaries, are often responded to by both the campus police or security department and the local police department. The college or university should have a plan of action so that community law enforcement agencies can expect a certain level of cooperation on a consistent basis.

Mutual aid agreements outline when and how campus departments and municipal departments will work together in providing services to the entire community. However, mutual aid agreements are not permitted in some states because of liability concerns. When they are permitted, they allow an opportunity for both departments to address critical issues such as who will assume command in certain situations, what reporting relationship will exist, and what general orders or policies will be followed. If a local police department provides assistance to a campus police or security department inside the geographical boundaries of the campus, the campus department is usually in charge, as provided by the mutual aid agreement. The reverse is true when the campus department provides assistance to a local department outside the boundaries of the campus.

Law enforcement agencies from external jurisdictions must have confidence in the personnel who are charged with supervising the activities of the campus police or security department. Efforts should be made to work together to develop a relationship that can prove effective during crisis. Joint projects afford personnel opportunities to examine and become familiar with tactics, techniques, and proficiency levels of other agencies. When officers of different departments interact with one another, whether in the investigation of a criminal act or in a training program, they exchange knowledge and gather information that will allow for smoother operations in the future. Special methods of addressing similar problems may also be discussed during cross-training situations.

Record Keeping

Efficient recording and flow of information are essential to the successful operation of any police or security agency. The chief task of the records unit includes filing and indexing police or security paperwork by various classification systems so that this information is accessible for future use. The records function is important in retrieving and using information about accidents, crimes, events, investigations, and rendered services. It is a critical management tool for allocating and documenting departmental resources and for filing state and national reports.

The department should have a record retention schedule and a policy for maintaining all records. Many departments use computer-based records management software; however, accurate and timely input of data is critical to proper retrieval of meaningful information from these systems. Dispatchers and records personnel should be properly trained in acceptable data entry and retrieval procedures. In addition to internal record keeping, the department should have a written policy establishing a procedure for collecting and submitting crime data to a national uniform crime reporting program and national incident-based reporting system. The department records should be maintained in a centralized location and available on a 24-hour basis. All dispatchers who operate the records system should be able to accurately and consistently access all phases of the program. It should be noted that criminal record information is confidential, and state laws mandate a prescribed level of security. Some parts of a file may be withheld from open record requests if they are part of a criminal investigation.

The daily operation of a police or security department requires detailed and systematic record keeping. Records must be kept to reflect the type of activity or service performed across the institution. They document continuity of effort, as well as actions implemented to achieve goals and objectives established by the institution. For example, records of building checks ensure that proper security measures are used and they are also used to define the approximate time of a theft. These records are also useful to many institutions in complying with insurance requirements. Records reflecting calls for assistance provide valuable information in determining services offered.

One of the most important records kept by a security department is the daily activity log. Such a log is useful in determining productivity and workload. For purposes of budget discussion or the allocation of personnel, the daily activity log provides substantial information concerning work performed by officers. Colleges and universities that maintain a police or security department are required under provisions of the Higher Education Amendments of 1998 to make a daily crime log available for public inspection. Information on any crime reported within the jurisdiction of the department must be included in the log within two business days. Information that would jeopardize an investigation or the confidentiality of a victim does not need to be disclosed. Institutions should have policies about the posting of information to the crime log and review by responsible administrators.

Records should also be maintained documenting training activities of personnel. Personnel training is an integral part of day-to-day operations, and training time must be scheduled for those assigned to other than a day shift. Officers are routinely retrained in the proper use of department-issued equipment (e.g., guns, mace, baton, handcuffs). Supervisory personnel must be vigilant to ensure that individuals are afforded opportunities to become proficient with equipment and that the training is properly documented. Training records can be made available for inspection and, quite often, are requested for presentation in civil or criminal court. Campus security departments are routinely confronted with questions concerning quality of training. Training provided by certified instructors or professionals should be documented.

Uniform Crime Statistics

Uniform crime statistics are an important element of records maintained by a police or security department. These statistics categorize incidents by type of crime. The categories are established in accordance with the FBI Uniform Crime Reporting system.

The FBI Uniform Crime Report (UCR) is a compilation of statistical information regarding incidents of crime gathered from law enforcement departments nationwide. However, statistical information is not collected from college or university security departments. For a campus security department's information to be tabulated as a part of the Uniform Crime Report, an official police report must be filed with a recognized law enforcement agency that has jurisdiction. However, campus police departments can and do file reports with the FBI, and there is a section in the annual UCR devoted to universities and colleges. This is a good resource for comparing institutions on the number of criminal incidents that occur.

Campus Crime Reports

Campuses must also publish an annual report of campus security policies and crime statistics. These reports have been required since 1990, when Congress passed the Student Right-to-Know and Campus Security Act, requiring institutions of higher education that are recipients of Title IV financial aid, whether public or independent, to report crime statistics and disclose campus security policies.

The law is intended to provide the general public with an overall assessment of criminal activity on the campus, as well as the institution's policies regarding crime-related issues. Unlike the FBI Uniform Crime Reports, campus crime statistics must be provided to the general public on demand. The act was a direct result of pressure from parent groups concerned about how certain campuses provided protection to their children. The act requires all institutions to develop policies on how they address security, to collect statistical data on incidents of crime, and to distribute an annual report of campus security policies and crime statistics to students, employees, and applicants for enrollment or employment.

TYPES OF SECURITY

Security of Persons

The safety of citizens is of utmost concern to a police or security department, and protection of life is always the first priority of a quality safety program. The daily activities of a campus present a variety personal safety problems.

In providing personal security, an important step is to reduce potential conflicts through effective planning and design. For example, where a major traffic corridor is also a gathering place for students conflicts will arise between people, vehicles, bicycles, skateboards, roller blades, and other recreational devices that may result in personal injury or even death. Rules such as speed limits, limitation of vehicles to parts of the campus, bike paths, or overhead walkways for pedestrian traffic can be used to reduce conflict.

A visible security presence helps to limit disturbances such as robberies, physical attack, and verbal abuse. Routine police or security patrols should combine the use of officers on foot, or bikes, in addition to utilizing patrol cars to provide assurances to those who are threatened and deterrence to those who would commit a crime.

Parking Enforcement

Most campuses experience a high level of frustration over the limited number of parking spaces, the location relative to specific buildings, and the price associated with purchasing a parking permit. There is no standard practice as to whether parking enforcement is within the police or security department or its own department. However, based on the level of frustration by individuals receiving parking citations and the possibility of physical confrontations, parking enforcement is a function often located within security.

Residential Students

A tremendous amount of attention has been devoted to the protection of students. Parent groups have organized and focused attention on security in residence halls and the campus in general. It is important that students be protected in accordance with reasonable safety standards and laws. Reasonable care and prior experience are the basic guides in determining the lengths to which an institution should go in providing protection.

One option in providing protection for residence halls is to install an access control system to deny entry to unauthorized persons. The most frequent residence hall security breach is the result of actions by residents: propping doors open to let friends or other unauthorized persons into residence halls. To ensure security in residence halls, it is imperative that students be aware of and be involved in the security process and strictly adhere to regulations governing security. There is no substitute for students' initiative in providing security. A security device that is in place but unused or circumvented has no effect on deterring crime. If an incident occurs because residents compromised the security measures, the institution still may be found liable. Institutions must have policies in force for dealing with security breaches by students.

In addition to traditional residence halls, colleges and universities have found it necessary to provide housing of a different nature for older students, families, international students, and other nontraditional groups. Types of housing may range from efficiency apartments to individual homes. The institution must continue to emphasize individual responsibility for security in these situations. The presence of young children and families in campus housing communities makes it even more important for the security or police department to provide a variety of crime prevention and education programs. The families of students residing on campus must also be alert to appropriate security measures and practices. International students, unfamiliar with a new country of residence, may need special programs to alert them to the need for crime prevention.

Off-Campus Residents

Students living off campus may encounter differences between security standards on campus and those in the area where they reside. Residents must be aware of the differences so that proper precautions may be taken. The simple matter of selecting a place to live can be a game of guesswork if the area is unfamiliar. While it is the responsibility of the students to gather information about the safety of the area where they intend to live, police departments can help. The crime prevention unit of most police departments discusses such matters and provides crime statistics and other information on criminal activity to help students making decisions on where to live. Campus crime statistics, required under the Campus Security Act, will also list crimes committed in the area around the campus.

Faculty and Staff

Employees may fail to recognize their vulnerability to crime in their work environment. Crime information presented in newsletters, Web sites and via E-mail messages as well as educational programs, keeps security on the minds of those who might otherwise become victims of criminal activity. Security requires the continuous participation and support of all members of the campus community.

The level of violence in the workplace within the academic environment as well as in society in general, has become a significant concern for many employees and managers. The security or police departments should be actively involved in conducting workplace violence presentations for faculty and staff routinely. All threats of violence should be investigated whether or not they reach the technical level of a crime.

Visitors and Guests

Although a campus activity may take place in a designated area, visitors and guests tend to wander throughout the campus. To protect the campus, yet not offend those who are curious, the police or security department needs an established method of detecting potential criminal activity. Officers should be trained to observe the activity of visitors and guests without being offensive.

In the case of visiting dignitaries and other guests, an organized program of threat analysis, crowd control, and traffic regulations must be established. In such cases, the campus police or security department must work with law enforcement agencies of other jurisdictions and with campus constituents to provide for safety. Agencies most commonly involved in the protection of visiting dignitaries are local law enforcement departments, state law enforcement departments, the FBI, the Secret Service, and the State Department. Security measures to protect dignitaries and VIPs can be quite elaborate. The main challenge associated with security for dignitaries is the planning of a transportation route to the campus and to any points visited on the campus. Planning should include the identification of alternate routes. The plan should also include information on the location and capabilities of nearby medical facilities. Crowd control strategies must recognize a balance between public access to the dignitary and security for the dignitary. When the Secret Service and/or State Department are in charge of an event, security for the dignitary will be their highest priority, and they will alter the itinerary, if necessary, for security reasons. (Also see the section on "Special Events" in this section.)

Personal Property

Individuals are ultimately responsible for the protection of themselves and their property. The open display of valuables in vehicles frequently results in their loss. The simple strategy of locking valuables out of sight often determines a thief's choice to bypass one vehicle in favor of another. Members of the campus community should use common sense and park in well-lighted, well-patrolled areas to reduce the opportunity for theft.

The level of security provided is usually based on what can reasonably be expected and consistently performed. It is not reasonable to expect that valuables left in an unlocked, unattended vehicle or building will remain undisturbed solely because the institution has a security force. Because security cannot be provided to every person in every place at all times, it is imperative that each individual take responsibility for the security of his or her own property.

Outsiders may gain access to the campus by pretending to be employees. At one campus, an individual posing as a janitor collecting trash was able to commit multiple thefts of purses and other valuables located under desks and in unlocked drawers. Procedures in such cases should include having the custodial and maintenance staffs wear identification on their outer garment or wear uniforms with distinctive colors and the college or university logo embroidered on it along with the employee's name. The custodial supervisor should contact the security or police department whenever there is a change in personnel. It is also helpful if members of the campus community know and recognize others who are authorized to be in their area; this applies to office personnel, custodial and maintenance employees, and students. Building relationships within the work environment cannot only prevent crime but also make the work experience more enjoyable.

Building Security

The security of a building does not begin when the building is opened for occupancy. Ideally, building security should begin when the architect commences design of the facility. Protection systems, such as card access control, burglar alarms, fire alarms, and other security devices, should be an integral part of the plan when the facility is designed. Unfortunately, these security items are often omitted for reasons of cost; when it is later determined that they are needed, they have to be added—at a higher cost. Details such as the type of windows to be installed or the quality of the locking hardware on the doors can make a tremendous difference in the total security of a facility. The institution should practice a philosophy of including security in the design phase to provide reasonable protection to buildings. Many campuses are installing "card access" control systems in some or all buildings. As planning for new buildings or remodeling of existing buildings are being discussed, consideration of access control systems should be included. The problem many campus police or security chiefs are experiencing is that, all too often, they are not included in the early stages of the planning. As a result, proper installation strategies may not be included. From a security as well as a financial point of view, it is important that campus security or police administrators be included in early planning and design stages for new or remodeled facilities. It is also important that campus police or security departments be responsible for actively monitoring and responding to card-access and intrusion alerts.

If an alarm system or other device specified by the police or security department is eliminated from a design or is reduced in scope for cost or other reasons, the department should be involved in the redesign. All systems rely on a total approach to their design, and to randomly eliminate detectors without reevaluating the total project could negate its effectiveness.

Training on security devices is available from such organizations as the National Crime Prevention Institute and the American Society for Industrial Security. There are also trade shows where one can see a wide variety of products at one time and ask vendors about them. The types of hardware required to secure windows and doors vary widely. Locksmiths can provide information on the types of locks to be used for the level of security desired. Companies that manufacture locking devices also provide information on state-of-the-art locking hardware. The extra time and expense spent selecting adequate locking hardware and card access systems for new buildings or renovated buildings is well worth the effort.

The issue of key control is important. Institutions should have clear policies about who can have a specific key and what happens when a key is lost. Administrators also need to carefully address the question of where to place responsibility for operating the lock shop, including such matters as determining who has access to the shop and who is responsible for hiring and firing of personnel.

The police or security department of a campus is responsible for patrolling the campus to deter criminal activity. Campuses differ in the methods used to secure buildings through patrolled activities. When security patrols check only the external entry to the building, they may not be able to determine if someone has bypassed the locking mechanism in order to illegally gain entry. In most instances, security personnel make periodic checks of a building, using a passkey to gain entry. Officers on patrol should enter and closely examine a building to minimize theft or damage to the facility. Patrolling is one area in which the use of security officers in addition to police officers can augment the effectiveness of a security program.

Campus "One-Card" Systems

The implementation of a campus one-card identification system should be part of any contemporary campus safety program. In the physical world, the highly visible one-card ID identifies the user and his or her access rights to buildings, areas, activities, and services. It is very important for the police or security department to be involved in the design and implementation of the card system. Design considerations such as network security, terminal workstation placements, automated and personnel response requirements, card media selection, campus policy and procedures, and campus data exchange must be coordinated with campus police or security departments.

In the past, access control and alarms systems ran on dedicated private networks. However, a one-card system requires the use of a shared network and accesses databases from many campus departments, including security. This integration creates inherent vulnerabilities and requires more diligence to protect the infrastructure and databases from unauthorized users and malicious hackers.

Policies for dealing with lost or stolen cards must be considered carefully. If students are required to pay a replacement fee for lost or stolen cards they may be reluctant to immediately report such loss to authorities. The campus must, therefore, recognize that there will be a period of time in which the card could be used illegally.

Equipment Security

In addition to securing the facilities where equipment is housed, many devices are available to secure individual items of equipment. Security solutions range from complex electronic security devices to simple tagging systems. At a minimum, the responsible department should record the identification numbers of all equipment items.

Each department within a college or university should conduct a formal inventory at least annually. Frequent inventories help ensure the presence of equipment and help remind people of its value. The inventory should consist of a visual inspection of equipment by identification number and serial number. For inventory purposes, if equipment is to be transferred from one department to another, the transfer should be recorded.

The police or security department may make an engraving tool available for marking personal equipment. Engraving cannot easily be removed and can be used to identify stolen equipment as belonging to a particular department or individual. In the event of theft, the inventory or property office should provide police with a detailed list of equipment with description, identification number, identification tags, and any other unique markings that may have been affixed by engraving tools. Information of this nature is extremely helpful to law enforcement officers when attempting to retrieve stolen goods and return them to their rightful owner.

Although theft by those outside the institution may receive the most attention of the police or security department, a college or university's policy on theft by those inside the institution should be disseminated to faculty, staff, and students throughout the institution. Sanctions for theft should be resolved within the policy guidelines. If arrest is the sanction, then it must apply to all. If termination is the sanction, it too must apply to all. This helps eliminate charges of discrimination.

Grounds Security

The security of campus grounds presents unique challenges. Many institutions have multiple roadways allowing unrestricted access to the campus while others may have limited and controlled access. Regardless of the access restrictions, campus police or security officers must be both guardians and ambassadors of the institution while on patrol. Concern for personal safety and the security of institutional resources sometimes is relaxed because of a sense of safety within the academic environment. It is important for the police or security department to look for weaknesses in the security system and frequently remind students, faculty, and staff of the dangers of complacency.

Many institutions encourage the general public to enjoy their facilities and athletic fields. Some state laws even require public institutions to allow general public access to various facilities, and independent institutions, while not required to do so, allow public access to some facilities to demonstrate good town-gown relations. This open access clearly helps build a strong community partnership, but it presents increased dangers that must be addressed by the police or security department. To accommodate such open access, yet provide an appropriate level of security, the department should develop proactive planning strategies that take into account the department's mission.

In urban areas, a college or university campus is often no different from the area that surrounds it. Devices such as emergency call boxes are frequently used on urban campuses to provide quick contact with the police or security department. Additionally, escort services are used to reduce the potential for criminal acts. Another option is a night shuttle bus, which may help reduce the number of calls for escorts.

Lighting

The police or security department and physical plant personnel should cooperate to evaluate the level of appropriate lighting and develop an ongoing program to monitor conditions. A system for identifying light standards should be formulated so that officers reporting lights out can advise the physical plant personnel of the exact locations. Adding lighting fixtures or upgrading the existing lighting on campus contributes to the overall feeling of safety to students, faculty, staff, and visitors during the evening hours. The installation of high-pressure sodium lights can dramatically improve night visibility. The routine trimming of shrubbery allows existing lighting to be more effective.

Some institutions hire lighting consultants to create an overall lighting plan; local power companies sometimes provide such a plan free of charge. A professionally developed plan can ensure that national standards are met. In addition, the plan will allow monthly electricity use to be estimated, taking into consideration new, high-efficiency lighting. Regardless of cost savings, developing and implementing a lighting plan will help an institution improve the sense of security on campus and possibly reduce its liability.

Crime Prevention Through Environmental Design

Crime prevention through environmental design (CPTED) is based on a theory that proper design and use of an area can reduce the incidence of crime. CPTED principles incorporate facility design and landscaping while taking into consideration the area's criminal activity and how people perceive their level of safety in that area. It involves a combination of physical design as well as the reaction of people to their environment, therefore addressing the issue of crime and the fear of crime.

Special Events

Many campuses host special events such as lectures by guest speakers, athletic events, fine arts festivals, science fairs, and livestock judging contests. Each event requires security of a different nature, aside from general campus security. The police or security department should work closely with the sponsoring organization to assist in determining the type and level of security for the event. Information gathering about events on campus is extremely important because sponsoring organizations are not always aware of security threats that various events may pose.

Many colleges and universities also host open debates on controversial topics. The exchange of different ideas is expected and encouraged on a college or university campus. Security efforts must be aimed at measures that allow discussion to occur without infringing on participants' constitutional rights. In cases where contrasting opinion results in counter-demonstrations, the counter-demonstrators must be allowed their right to protest peacefully. Cooperation with group leaders often leads to better rapport and fewer problems. Hecklers are often a source of irritation, and some persons are more concerned with disrupting activity and forcefully asserting their own views than with intelligent debate. The police or security department must train personnel to identify disorderly persons and must develop methods to quickly remove them from a function.

Rock concerts and other large gatherings pose additional security problems because they may attract large numbers of students and individuals from outside the campus. Because of the volatile nature of some rock concerts, the police or security department should be included in the preplanning phase of scheduling such events. Although most campuses have conduct regulations regarding alcoholic beverages, some people will bring alcoholic beverages to campus events, or they may leave alcoholic beverages in their vehicles and make frequent trips to consume them. Planning for such events must include rules to limit the consumption of alcohol and to prevent ticket holders from re-entering a facility once they have left.

Fraternity, sorority, and student organization parties also attract individuals from outside the campus community. Usually the student government or interfraternity council, working with the college or university administration, devises rules of conduct for parties. These rules range from limiting the number of guests invited to a party to a ban of alcoholic beverages. For such rules to be effective they must be enforced and penalties must be imposed for infractions. The campus administration must work closely with the police or security chief to formulate strategies to reduce the risk of alcohol-related injuries and subsequent liabilities to the university.

Planning for effective transportation of police or security officers to and from areas of activity is part of the security function, as is the planning for ground transportation of dignitaries, performers, college or university officials, or others that must be moved efficiently and safely during events. This is particularly important for controversial events (e.g., rallies, demonstrations, labor strikes, etc.) where there may be activity at dispersed sites around the campus area. One person from the police or security department should be assigned to coordinate the use of buses, vans, private limousines, and other transport vehicles during special events.

In situations where there is the possibility of mass arrests, preplanning is essential. Mass arrests are complicated and can be dangerous for both police and demonstrators. Training, equipment, and coordination with local law enforcement, the jail, and courts are necessary.

ENFORCEMENT

The campus police or security department is charged with providing the greatest degree of protection possible for life and property within the campus community. It is also charged with enforcing laws to ensure that the rights and privileges of individuals are not infringed upon. In carrying out these assignments, officers must maintain an attitude of cooperation in providing services to the college or university community.

The day-to-day operation of a police or security department, which involves vehicular and foot patrols, investigating reports of criminal activity, and parking enforcement, is usually the barometer used to measure the effectiveness of the department. Visibility of officers on campus is important not only as a deterrent to criminal activity, but also a means for providing reassurance to the community.

The level of law enforcement provided by the campus police or security department will depend on the philosophy of the administration and the relative state laws granting such enforcement authority. While most public universities tend to have sworn police officers with full law enforcement authority, such authority varies tremendously at independent universities and colleges. Some state legislatures have enacted laws granting independent colleges and universities the ability to establish fully sworn police departments or have allowed limited police authority. Institutions have a variety of options when deciding the appropriate level of enforcement authority their officers should have, but it is important not to expect "security officers" to function as "police officers."

Federal and State Codes

Federal and state laws apply to police officers' performance of duties and responsibilities. Officers swear to uphold these laws and to discharge duties in a professional manner. Laws safeguard the general public and require the officer to perform in a specific manner. In situations of arrest, search, seizure, and the use of force, there are laws enacted to safeguard the public. Whenever these laws are broken, the officer and the institution are subject to legal action in order to provide remedy to the injured or aggrieved party.

The enforcement of federal and state laws on campus presents many situations where discretion must be used. Students are expected to behave as reasonable adults, but their life experiences may not have provided enough information or training to make the right decisions. State and federal laws allow for discretion on the part of police or security officers. In the interest of educating the campus community it is sometimes more helpful to exercise that discretion than to evoke the full measure of the law. However, incidents that are serious or life threatening require that discretion be more narrowly defined.

Campus Codes

Most colleges and universities have a code of student conduct. These codes are usually enforced through administrative action in judicial hearings. The enforcement of these codes may, or may not, be the responsibility of police or security officers. Whenever these codes are broken, officers are expected to bring the matter to the attention of the appropriate institutional administrator. Hearings for violations of conduct are administrative in nature but frequently parallel statutory laws of the state and federal government. If statutory laws are broken in addition to student conduct codes, action can be brought in a court of law as well as at a student conduct hearing.

Every college or university has its own method of addressing violations of student conduct. Student judiciary hearings attempt to discern the facts of events surrounding a violation so that appropriate corrective action can be directed at resolving the problem. Student courts may be established to address recurring concerns, such as traffic violations, residence hall violations, and fraternity or sorority violations. A main court may be established to hear more serious infractions of codes of conduct. Student courts are made up of students who are charged with providing fairness and sound judgment in rendering decisions. In some instances, the seriousness of a charge may require a review of the court's decision by a higher authority, such as the president of the institution.

In 1998 Congress amended the Family Educational Rights and Privacy Act (FERPA) that protects educational records from disclosure. The new law does not require colleges or universities to release information, but allows them to disclose information related to disciplinary proceedings in some circumstances. Under Section 99.31(a)(13) and Sec. 99.39, Disclosure of Final Results of Certain Disciplinary Proceedings, a postsecondary institution may disclose the final results of any disciplinary proceeding conducted by the institution against a student who is an alleged perpetrator of a crime of violence. The institution must determine, as a result of the proceeding, that the student committed a violation of the institution's rules or policies with regard to that crime. It also permits disclosure of drug and alcohol offenses to parents of students under age 21.

Campus Security Act / Clery Act

The Campus Security Act of 1990 was modified as part of the Higher Education Amendments of 1998 and renamed the Jeanne Clery Disclosure of Campus Security Policy and Campus Crime Statistics Act (Clery Act). The act requires institutions that participate in Title IV student aid programs to:

- prepare an annual security report that includes statements of current campus policies and procedures covering a number of specified topics and campus crime statistics for the last three years;

- compile annual crime statistics on the occurrence of certain crimes on campus, in noncampus buildings or properties, and on public property adjacent to campus facilities, and a separate compilation of hate crimes by category of prejudice;

- provide timely warnings to the campus community of crimes that represent a threat to students and employees;

- maintain a daily log of crimes that are reported to the campus police or security department, if such a department is maintained, that is available for public inspection; and

- distribute the annual security report to current students and employees, and to potential students and employees on request, and submit a copy to the Department of Education.

One of the more controversial sections of the Clery Act requires all college and university officials with "significant responsibility for student and campus activities" to report incidents for the campus crime statistics. The regulations, found at 34 CFR 668.46, now specify that these activities should include, but not be limited to "student housing, student discipline, and campus judicial proceedings." Additional guidance indicates that "a dean of students, director of athletics, team coach, and faculty advisor to a student group" would be required to report, but due to the numerous titles currently in use across the country does not specify exact job titles. Professional or pastoral counselors are not required to provide reports. Colleges and universities are also expected to make a "good faith" effort to obtain crime report information from local police.

The campus crime reports are of interest to the media, special interest groups, and Congress, as well as to students and their parents. The Department of Education compiles statistics from colleges and universities across the country and posts them on a Web site, and it will report institutions that do not comply to Congress. Senior administrators should ensure that systems and resources are in place to comply fully with the requirements as errors or omissions may be costly, leading to sanctions, legal liabilities, and negative publicity.

Drug and Alcohol Policies

A campuswide policy emanating from the president should provide guidelines related to the use and possession of drugs and alcohol. The chief student affairs officer is often charged with promulgating guidelines for possession and use of drugs and alcohol by students. Policies governing the use of illegal drugs usually follow requirements of law.

Policies governing the use of alcohol tend to pose more difficult problems. Institutions must provide guidelines concerning the use of alcohol that do not infringe on individual freedom and at the same time allow for control. If the decision is made to have "zero tolerance" for alcohol on campus, that message must be clearly defined by the president and distributed widely on campus. One of the more difficult problems regarding students is that of applying state law governing underage alcohol consumption. Institutions are obligated to control the use of legally permitted substances such as alcohol on campus. Underage consumption of alcohol (including the crime of possession) is a serious concern for colleges and universities.

Likewise, the possession and use of illegal drugs are major concerns. Police or security departments must actively pursue individuals who are not in compliance with local laws. Citizens' groups also may become involved by maintaining vigilance over campus activities and reporting findings to the local law enforcement agency.

FERPA has been amended to permit postsecondary institutions to disclose to parents and legal guardians of students under the age of 21, without the student's consent, information regarding the student's violation of any federal, state, or local law, or any rule or policy of the institution governing the use or possession of alcohol or a controlled substance.

In addition to this provision, the statute already provides that postsecondary institutions may disclose certain information from a student's educational records to parents or legal guardians under several exceptions to the prior consent rule. Under Sec. 99.31(a)(8) of the regulations, institutions may release information to parents or guardians, without the student's consent, if the student is a dependent for tax purposes. Also, under Sec. 99.31(a)(10), an institution may release information to a parent or guardian in connection with a health or safety emergency. This provision adds a new exception to the prior consent requirement of FERPA.

Institutions confronted with the problem of drug and alcohol abuse on campus also face the concern of providing help for those who are victims. Many employee benefit plans provide for drug and alcohol rehabilitation programs. These programs place responsibility on the individual to make a genuine effort toward rehabilitation. When individuals fail to seek assistance for their problems, an employer has little choice but to follow the law when a violation occurs. The results of intervention of this type can be disastrous for the individual. Programs for preventive counseling and education (Employee Assistance Program) have been implemented at many institutions as part of overall preventive measures.

Hate Crimes

The issue of hate crimes is a national concern. Hate crimes are crimes motivated by ignorance, bigotry, and prejudice intended to hurt or intimidate a person because of his or her race, religion, ethnic origin, sexual orientation, gender, or disability. This problem has been hard to identify because statistics do not single out criminal violations based on a specific definition for hate crimes. Hate crimes are not separate and distinct offenses, but rather crimes motivated by the offender's bias. Because of the difficulty in determining an offender's subjective motivation in the commission of a crime, sufficient evidence that the offender's actions were motivated, in whole or in part, by bias is needed before an offense is designated a hate crime.

Colleges and universities provide a unique environment that causes an increased vulnerability to bias related conflicts. Because their academic standards encourage free inquiry and expression of viewpoints, campuses often become home to verbal and physical expressions of hate.

The requirements for reporting hate crimes have been significantly expanded under the Act. Institutions must report by category of prejudice (race, gender, religion, sexual orientation, ethnicity, or disability) the crimes they are required to report statistics for, except liquor, drug, or weapons violations, and "any other crime involving bodily injury." The numbers of hate crimes must be included both with the other statistics and in a separate notation dealing exclusively with hate crimes. Guidance for classifying hate crimes can be found in the FBI's Uniform Crime Reports "Hate Crime Data Collection Guidelines."

Crime Prevention and Education

Crime prevention is the most effective form of police work. On campuses where crime prevention is practiced effectively, the absence of crime improves the community's ability to function in many ways. For a crime prevention program to be successful, officers must have training and the institution must provide funds for supplies and materials for distribution to the campus community. The campus radio and TV stations can prepare promotions related to crime issues and crime prevention; this involves students in the process while keeping costs low.

The police or security department should emphasize to the community that items lost because of crime are often never recovered. Through crime prevention, the entire campus can work together to prevent criminal acts. Crime prevention requires the cooperation of students, faculty, and staff in order to be effective. Students can assist by reporting suspicious activity, locking valuables out of sight, refraining from propping doors open, and taking advantage of educational opportunities offered by the crime prevention unit.

Faculty and staff can assist in crime prevention efforts by acting as the eyes and ears of the police or security department. They can take steps to secure equipment and other items provided by the institution: personal computers are common targets of theft on many campuses. An additional effort to identify and secure items by using special cables, locks, or electronic devices can help prevent random theft. Again, the crime prevention unit can usually provide specific instructions regarding security measures that are effective for different types of situations.

The college or university should establish a program of informing freshmen students about the campus environment, in advance of, or early in the first quarter or semester of attendance. Most institutions conduct this informative session as part of orientation. A security presentation must be an integral part of the orientation process. Information such as criminal statistics, campus problem areas, and general personal security should be addressed to heighten the awareness of entering students about their new environment. Programs should be offered on a continuing basis to update and inform students about security on campus. Information concerning victimization, including what losses can be expected and the degree to which property is returned, often help to make students more aware of protecting themselves.

Ongoing crime prevention sessions should be conducted for employees. While many employees are aware of theft occurring around them, they are often not aware of the magnitude of the problem or how the thefts are related. The security department should use student newspapers, posters, and crime prevention leaflets, as well as radio spot announcements, to inform the campus community. Such measures serve to keep the campus community alert to the possibility of crime.

OTHER TRENDS

Campus law enforcement will witness more stringent requirements for staff training and the verification of effective utilization of resources in the next decade. Colleges and universities must seek highly qualified professional police or security personnel to provide the necessary leadership and to direct campus law enforcement or security departments.

Criminal activity, economic constraints, and civil liability judgments will force colleges and universities to evaluate their provision of security more closely in the future. A proactive approach to securing a campus, rather than a reactive approach, will become the norm. This approach will use statistical compilations of criminal activity to justify the assignment of personnel and allocations of funding for security purposes.

Even as the overall national crime rates have decreased through most of the 1990s, secondary schools are increasingly experiencing serious problems with gangs, drugs, and general disregard for authority. According to many law enforcement experts, our juvenile detention facilities are filled with teenagers that have little or no regard for another person's life or property. Some of these teenagers will either attend college or simply prey on the campus community.

There will also be an increasing number of independent universities hiring and training professional officers to protect students, faculty, and staff from the violence around them, including workplace violence. Several states are seeking to establish legislation that would allow independent universities to employ "sworn police officers" with the authority to enforce all laws. But, even security officers must receive extensive training in human or cultural relations, crowd control, and defensive tactics, and so forth.

Computer crimes will certainly continue to be a major problem for campus police or security as technology use increases. Computer crimes are no longer considered pranks, but gaining access to student records, financial aid, and other databases and records systems on campus will continue to be challenging targets for mischievous students and others. Campus police or security departments must either have investigators trained in identifying and investigating such crimes or have direct contact with and assistance from law enforcement officers or private investigators who specialize in computer crime.

Unfortunately, terrorist incidents, both domestic and foreign, may become more frequent on college campuses. During the past several years pipe bombs or similar devices have exploded or have been found on some campuses in the United States. There have been reports of "booby-trapped" envelopes in the mail from persons opposed to animal research, for example. The challenge for law enforcement will be to train officers to recognize such devices and to educate faculty and staff to report suspicious material to the police or security department. Mailroom staff must be informed of bomb identification methods. The campus community will look to the police or security department for advice and expertise in dealing with potential threats. The police or security department will need to have the experts on staff or to have ready access to outside experts.

CONCLUSION

The challenge for campus law enforcement in the future is to develop a high-performing police culture to meet the ever-changing needs of the campus community. To be high performing, a police culture must welcome and encourage the academic freedom of expression and study (which sometimes includes student demonstrations) without preconceived or oppressive attitudes. Such a culture encourages individuals to contribute their energies, talents, and skills to the academic process, regardless of age, mental or physical abilities, sexual orientation, gender, religion, race, or ethnicity.

To be an effective campus police or security officer in the future will require a more educated individual with more law enforcement and diversity training than most municipal officers currently have. In the past, campuses have tended to be satisfied with less training for their officers than their counterparts in the surrounding community. If the purpose of having a campus police or security department is to protect its unique community, the officers responsible for this important task must be of the highest caliber.

NOTES

1. Edward A. Thibault, and R. Bruce McBride, *Proactive Police Management* Chapter Thirteen, "Proactive Planning: Operational and Fiscal." Paramus, NJ: Prentice Hall, 1998.

REFERENCES AND RESOURCES

Publications

American Council on Education. *Achieving Reasonable Campus Security, Vol. 2, Self-Regulation Initiatives: Resource Documents for Colleges and Universities.* Washington, D.C.: American Council on Education, 1985.

Bromley, M., and Territo, L. *College Crime Prevention and Personal Safety Awareness.* Springfield, IL: Charles C. Thomas, 1990.

Dubois, Paul A. *The Basics of Crime Prevention,* Los Gatos, CA: Tomasi-deBois & Associates, 1985.

Nichols, D., ed. *The Administration of Public Safety in Higher Education.* Springfield, IL: Charles C. Thomas, 1987.

Smith, M.C. *Coping with Crime on Campus.* Washington, DC: American Council on Education and Macmillan, 1988.

Thibault, Edward A., and McBride, R. Bruce. *Proactive Police Management* Chapter Thirteen, "Proactive Planning: Operational and Fiscal." Paramus, NJ: Prentice Hall, 1998.

U.S. Department of Education, *Code of Federal Regulations, Volume 34,* Part 668.46 (see also November 1, 1999 *Federal Register, Volume 64,* page 59060).

U.S. Department of Justice, Community Relations Service: *Bulletin: Responding to Hate Crimes and Bias-Motivated Incidents on College/University Campuses.* Washington, DC: Department of Justice, July, 1999.

Organizations

International Association of Campus Law Enforcement Administrators (IACLEA)
342 N. Main Street, West Hartford, CT 06117-2507
860-586-7517 . . . . http://www.iaclea.org/

National Association of College and University Business Officers (NACUBO)
2501 M Street, NW, Suite 400, Washington, DC 20037
202-861-2500 . . . . http://www.nacubo.org/

National Association of Student Personnel Administrators, Inc. (NASPA)
1875 Connecticut Avenue, NW, Suite 4181, Washington, DC 20009-5720
202-265-7500 . . . . http://www.naspa.org

Chapter 16

◆

Risk Management and Insurance

by

Rebecca L. Adair
Iowa State University

Elizabeth J. Carmichael
Five Colleges, Inc.

Jules C. Jacquin
Rensselaer Polytechnic Institute

Glenn Klinksiek
Univerisity of Chicago

Joseph D. Murphy
Northeastern University

John E. Watson
Pepperdine University

Sponsors

UNITED EDUCATORS INSURANCE RISK RETENTION GROUP, INC.

Contact: Janice Abraham
Two Wisconsin Circle, Suite 1040
Chevy Chase, MD 20815
301-907-4908
www.ue.org

United Educators, "Education's Own Insurance Company," offers education-specific, seamless insurance coverage, expert claims management and unique risk management services to more than 1,000 member universities, colleges and related institutions.

UNIVERSITY RISK MANAGEMENT & INSURANCE ASSOCIATION (URMIA)

Contact: Jean Bright
Two Wisconsin Circle, Suite 1040
Chevy Chase, MD 20815
301-718-9711
www.urmia.org

URMIA serves higher education risk management to promote the advancement and application of effective risk management principles and practices.

Contents

What is risk management? In the preface of the NACUBO publication, *Risk Management and Insurance: A Handbook of Fundamentals*, the authors share their view that because risk management is an evolving function, there are varying interpretations of what the term means. That was written in 1983. But rather than being honed over time into a singular fine-tuned definition, the range of meanings is now even broader. In addition to the traditional role of a risk manager, many other professions have adopted the term to mean something quite specific to their field. For example, investors use the term risk management in relation to investment portfolios, while physicians may use the term in reference to patient case management. In these fields, the basic concepts of traditional risk management have been utilized to address the uncertainties associated with those professions.

But what is "traditional" risk management and what does risk management mean in higher education? This chapter is designed to serve as a resource and guide for:

- those responsible for the oversight of risk management;
- those given the charge to directly handle risk management; or
- those who need a better understanding of the purpose of risk management in the 21st century.

The information included will provide a basic overview of the risk management process and the components essential to a college or university risk management program.

RISK MANAGEMENT DEFINED

Risk management evolved from insurance buying when methods other than insurance began to be used to treat exposures to risk. Originally, the scope of risk management was narrowly defined to include only accidents that resulted in a loss. The definition excluded speculative risks, or those risks that might result in either a loss or a gain. In the 1980s, as sophisticated risk financing became an important alternative to insurance, risk management expanded to include other risk transfer and control strategies. Now the evolution continues as the focus of traditional risk management expands into strategic risk management, an even more comprehensive approach that does include investment, business, and political risks. A basic definition can help clarify this transition. *The Essentials of Risk Management,* published by the Insurance Institute of America, currently defines risk management as "the process of making and implementing decisions that will minimize the adverse effects of accidental and business losses on an organization." This current definition of risk management reflects the understanding that risk management principles must be applied to eliminate or reduce more than just accidental risks to fully protect the assets of an organization.

THE ROLE OF RISK MANAGEMENT

Institutional Commitment, Policy, and Philosophy

Commitment to Risk Management

Successful risk management programs start with strong support from the governing board, president, and senior academic and financial administrators. Commitment from upper management to the fundamental goals of risk management is essential if risk management practices are to be effective. In addition, an institution should ensure that its risk management policy is aligned with the institution's mission and objectives. A written policy, consistent with the institutional mission and strategic plan of the college or university, should be signed by the president and endorsed by the governing board.

Risk Management Policy

The risk management policy should simply state the basic institutional philosophy on risk management and give a broad overview of the program responsibilities. It should be communicated to everyone in the institution, routinely referenced as the basis for risk management efforts, and periodically reviewed as the role of risk management in the institution continues to evolve. The policy can be amplified or detailed in a risk management manual or similar document that may include specific job duties of the risk manager, reporting functions, and specific goals and expectations for the program.

Risk Management Philosophy

In addition to making an institutional commitment to managing risk and having a written risk management policy, it is important to establish the philosophy that managing risk is everyone's responsibility. This message should be communicated to all areas of the institution and supported with policies and procedures, training programs, and administrative oversight to back up the program.

The exposure to risk at colleges and universities is limitless. Every aspect of the missions of education, research, and outreach generates the potential for problems that can have significant risk implications for the institution. The risk manager, business officer, or other individual responsible for the risk management function must share the risk management goals, philosophy, and process with others to effectively manage risk.

RISK IN HIGHER EDUCATION

Risk can be defined as the potential for loss, including economic loss, human suffering, or that which may prevent the organization from being able to achieve its goals. Actual losses may include property losses, income or revenue losses, financial losses from third-party claims, and loss of reputation, to name but a few. Institutions need to assess their risks strategically to identify both their sources and their impact on the institution as a whole.

Categories of Campus Risk

Most risk exposures of colleges and universities fall within one or more of the following five categories:

- operating risk;
- legal and regulatory risk;
- financial risk;
- political and reputational risk; and
- technological risk.

Operating Risk

Operating risks are those risks that arise out of the operations of the institution. These operations typically include teaching, research, owning and operating the premises, employment, and the provision of food, housing, transportation, safety, and security. Operating losses may include loss of housing, loss of key employees, inability to provide food, or even the ability to open for classes.

Legal and Regulatory Risk

Legal and regulatory risks arise from the numerous laws and regulations with which institutions of higher education must comply, such as the Occupational Safety and Health Act, Environmental Protection Agency, and Office for Civil Rights regulations, and federal, state, and local laws. Failure to comply with laws and regulations may produce losses through fines, revocation of grants, or the shutting down of a facility or research operation.

Financial Risk

Financial risk is the risk of loss of assets. Examples range from physical damage to institutional facilities, theft of institutional property, payment of assets to third parties as a result of a liability to them (such as from copyright infringement), or a drop in the asset value of the endowment fund.

Political and Reputational Risk

Political and reputational risk is the decrease in stature of the institution in the opinion of lawmakers or the general public. For instance, an unpopular view expressed by the faculty or administration could result in a funding reduction for a state institution or an unfortunate student death from binge drinking could severely affect the reputation of an institution, resulting in reduced new enrollment or fewer alumni donations.

Technological Risk

New areas of risk present themselves daily in the area of technology. Whether it is having a Web site shut down or pirated, electronic invasion or modification of records, the risks of distance education, or E-business transactions, the rapidly changing world of technology is a new risk area for institutions of higher education.

These five categories of risk are areas of concern not only to risk managers but also to administrators and governing boards. They represent the need for an integrated approach to risk management for the institution. Others on campus also ought to be working to address risks in these categories. Risk management issues often overlap with issues in legal services, environmental health and safety, human resources, public safety, and business affairs.

A simple example of a strategic risk evaluation is to look at the risks an institution has if it provides housing for its students. The risks include: operational risks (slips and falls in student housing); legal and regulatory risks (compliance with fire codes); financial risks (loss to the institution in the event of damage to a facility); reputational risk (poor public perception of institution if students are injured on campus); and possibly even technological risks (providing cable, computer, and communications access to the facility). If there is a fire in a student residence, the impact on the institution might be a housing shortage on campus, fines for the institution for being out of compliance, damage to the reputation of the institution, and financial losses to repair the building and pay claims of negligence for injury or death of students.

In another example, serious violation of National Collegiate Athletic Association (NCAA) recruiting regulations can result in exposures in each of the first four categories. Operating revenues may decrease, both from enrollment and from attendance at athletic events. Legal sanctions by the NCAA could prohibit participation in bowl games, resulting in loss of revenue that could be considered a financial risk. Political and reputational risks may occur if a promising recruit decides not to commit to the institution because of the NCAA sanctions, alumni may decrease donations, and the athletic program and institutional reputation can be tarnished. Thus, what might first appear to only be a regulatory risk results in a loss with much broader implications.

Strong communication and collaboration among the institution's administrators is necessary to comprehensively protect the institution. As the aforementioned examples illustrate, legal risks are not just the responsibility of legal services, and likewise, financial risks do not just involve the treasurer or controller. A collective effort to combine resources and knowledge is needed to effectively identify and manage institutional risks.

THE RISK MANAGEMENT FUNCTION

Program Structures

Where Does Risk Management Belong?

The higher the responsibility for risk management in the hierarchy of the institution, the more effective it will be. Ideally, depending on the size of the institution, that could be the president, chief financial officer, or chief academic officer. No matter where the function is located, the senior financial administrator must have some risk management oversight, since it is intrinsically tied to institutional assets.

Colleges and universities handle the risk management function in many different ways, and the program structure depends on several variables. Size and complexity of the institution, the importance the institution places on the risk management function, staffing, and budgets can affect how risk management is structured. Many institutions create a defined risk management department or program. Sometimes the decision on where to place the risk management function depends on who has time, interest, and resources in areas that are tied to risk management. And then there are times when it is assigned purely "by default." A survey of institutions to identify the location of the risk management function could find it as part of business and finance, legal services, environmental health and safety, human resources, purchasing, or public safety; a rationale can be presented that each has links to the risk management process. The strength of any program, however, will depend on both the actual and perceived support that the institution gives to the process, and if it provides a structure to promote individual accountability through interdepartmental communication and collaboration on risk issues.

Who Does Risk Management?

Many institutions create a risk management department with a director of risk management and appropriate staff assistance. Some institutions integrate the risk management function into another department, while others assign the function as part of an administrator's responsibilities along with other job duties. Size of the institution alone does not determine the staffing and responsibilities for the risk management function. Small colleges and universities can have a full-time risk manager, but more often the responsibility falls to the CFO and/or other business officers as only one of many roles they must fulfill. Some small institutions place the function in other locations within the institution such as purchasing or safety, some utilize the services of an outside consultant to manage the program, and increasingly, small institutions are collaborating on risk management through consortium activities.

These same models can be found at large institutions as well, where risk management can range from being a large formalized department to being housed within another departmental function. Having a full-time risk manager can give an institution the resources to focus on risk management issues and coordinate them across the institution. However, many colleges and universities, large and small, do not have or choose not to specifically dedicate resources for someone to handle risk management full time and instead opt for alternative solutions that can still be effective.

On an individual basis, the official title of the individual assigned to do risk management, or where the function reports, is not as important as the assets needed either individually or programmatically for risk management to be successful. A combination of technical skills, such as knowledge of insurance products or basic legal principles, and managerial or leadership attributes, such as strong communication skills or a high level of creativity, are both essential components of an effective program.

KEYS TO A SUCCESSFUL PROGRAM

Communication

A fundamental component of an effective risk management program is communication. This simple objective is often the hardest one to achieve. Like that of a computer network, risk management communication requires a web of information exchange. The risk manager serves as an internal consultant who must first seek to understand the business of the institution before the most effective solutions to manage risk can be recommended. To do this, the risk manager must go to those who know the operation best and utilize the basic techniques of listening and asking good questions in order to gather needed information.

The risk manager is also responsible for communicating the institution's position on managing its risks. Written policies, procedures, and guidelines should be developed to assist others in understanding the role risk management needs to play in campus activities. Effective risk managers seek out every opportunity to create two-way communication channels that can benefit the entire organization. The risk management function is one of support and problem solving, established to ensure that a process can be accomplished without jeopardizing the assets of the institution. Risk management must continually reach out to various constituencies to provide information on the risks associated with new issues such as E-commerce and technology transfer, or changes in laws, regulations, or other issues. In turn, risk managers rely on all entities in the institution to inform them of risks, concerns, and issues they face.

And finally, the risk manager is responsible for keeping senior management apprised of issues, trends, problems, and successes associated with risk management efforts on behalf of the institution. As mentioned earlier, the evolving role of risk management would suggest that administrators are recognizing the need to look at all types of risks in making decisions and that strategic risk management has a role to play in successful academic administration.

Problem Solving

A major role played by risk management is that of problem solver. When a problem is identified, the risk manager acts as an internal consultant to assist in finding a solution that will mean the least exposure to the institution while still accomplishing its mission. Risk cannot be eliminated entirely. But as the treatment of risk has broadened from solely using commercial insurance as a safety net for the institution, the options available to manage risks have increased as well. Recognizing that not all exposures are created equally, effective risk managers know that some techniques work more effectively than others depending on the situation, and that they must be creative and resourceful when it comes to generating solutions. An inherent part of academia is to explore the world, and doing so involves a certain element of risk taking. Successful risk management programs will strive to find solutions to get things done, rather than saying they cannot or should not be done. The next section provides fundamental risk management techniques that can be used to do that.

THE RISK MANAGEMENT PROCESS

The process of risk management need not be complex. It can become so because of the complexities of the institutional environment, but the basic process is always the same.
—Risk Management and Insurance: A Handbook of Fundamentals

Although the scope of risk management in higher education continues to broaden, the process has not changed since these words were written in 1983, and in all likelihood, will not. Fundamentally, it is a decision-making process used by people in everyday life and is not specific just to risk management. Yet those new to understanding the risk management process are often surprised to learn that the basic formula is so simple. Reduced to its most basic level, the five steps in the risk management process are:

- identify;
- analyze;
- select;
- implement; and
- monitor.

Step 1: Identify What Is at Risk

Identifying potential loss exposures is the first step in an effective risk management program. Unless the risks are identified, they cannot be treated. The early process of identifying risks to find out what needed to be insured has evolved into identifying those risks to insure, those to retain, what can be controlled and how, and what should be avoided altogether. There are a variety of ways that risks can be identified and a number of individuals who can do it; however, the identification of risk will be most successful when it is a collaborative effort that involves those most familiar with the operation or process. Who should identify risks and how risks can be identified will be covered in greater detail in the section on risk assessment.

Step 2: Analyze the Feasibility of Options

When risk management was primarily thought to be an insurance-buying function, the two options most frequently considered were to avoid the risk or buy commercial insurance. The option to buy insurance often meant that the ideal policy would be one with very broad coverage and limits high enough to cover everything. If such a policy did exist, its cost would be prohibitive and it would require constant endorsement to keep up with the continual changes in an academic environment. But fortunately, the risk management process has evolved beyond avoiding risk at all cost or treating every exposure commercially. Now, in addition to avoidance or insuring, risks can be treated with loss control efforts, risk financing options, and risk transfer methods.

The second step of the risk management process, then, is to take each option into account and determine the feasibility of treating a particular exposure with that option. What works best in one situation does not necessarily work best in another. External factors, special circumstances, financial considerations, available resources, and even common sense can determine whether or not an option is a feasible solution. In some cases, more than one option works equally well, and sometimes no option other than avoidance seems viable.

Step 3: Select the Best Option

The third step in the risk management process involves selecting the option that works best for the particular situation, entity, or for the institution as a whole. Different types of institutions may have different objectives, which means that in order to be most effective, the risk management option or combination of options selected should be consistent with that organization's objectives. For instance, an institution may select an option to self-insure an exposure since it has institution-ally created a high tolerance for risk, developed an organizational objective to min-imize its insurance premium expense, and has resources readily available to recover from a loss. Another institution, however, facing the same exposure may have fewer resources available to recover from the same loss and organizationally be more concerned with consistent cost, so will elect to buy insurance to treat the loss.

Step 4: Implement the Option Selected

Two approaches can be used in implementing risk management options. One is a technical approach that means risk management uses professional exper-tise to independently implement a solution once a decision has been reached on what option appears most viable. The other is an integration approach that requires risk management to collaborate with and rely on others in order to have an option implemented.

For example, a decision is made that the best option to protect the institution's fine arts collection is to buy insurance. Once this has been deter-mined, a technical approach is all that is needed to finalize the process and imple-ment the option. Usually this means that the risk manager independently uses technical knowledge to decide what to buy (type of coverage), how much to buy (limits), how much can be risked (deductibles), and what insurer to use.

But in order to implement a program designed to reduce vehicle accidents, the risk manager can provide the policies and guidance to help improve vehicle safety, but must then rely on others to actually implement the actions needed to reduce losses. In this case, sound technical knowledge and effective communica-tion skills are critically needed to influence the implementation phase.

Step 5: Monitor the Option Selected

The final step in the risk management process is to monitor the option once it is implemented to see if it is working to achieve the desired results or if it needs to be modified. Any activity is likely to change over time as external conditions evolve. This is especially true of activities involving people or technology. What worked effectively as a risk management solution initially may be less effective or even counterproductive over time. Therefore, ongoing or periodic monitoring is essential. Methods to monitor an option can range from simple review of an action to detailed analysis of data that compares past experience with current activity.

The remainder of this chapter will expand on each of these steps in greater detail; if those who find themselves responsible for risk management approach the issues using this five-step process, it can assist them in more effectively responding to the needs of the institution.

STEP 1:
IDENTIFICATION OF
RISK—THE ASSESSMENT PROCESS

A variety of methods can be used to identify the types of losses an institution could incur. Again, communication plays a major role in the process, as it is essential to work in conjunction with individuals who best know an operation in order to conduct an accurate assessment of the exposures. The following methods can assist in identifying exposures.

Inspection

An actual site visit can be the best opportunity to truly understand an operation and witness first hand what exposures exist. It also provides an opportunity to speak directly with personnel associated with an operation to gain their perspective. This will also work toward establishing good communication that will benefit the implementation process if action is needed. For instance, a great deal of information about playground safety can be obtained without leaving the office, but an on-site visit to the university daycare center will provide an actual look at potential risks from the equipment, the surface and grounds, the level of supervision, or external hazards.

Loss Analysis

Looking at past incidents can provide insight into exposures that may continue to exist. If records are kept on losses that have occurred, then analyzing this data can possibly detect trends that might continue or can pinpoint a particular issue that is consistently generating losses. For example, analyzing the loss history of an institutional fleet may indicate that the majority of accidents involved 15-passenger vans. This information might then lead to a training program specifically designed for drivers of 15-passenger vans. On the other hand, the less frequent but more serious losses may never have occurred at the institution. Using loss data from outside collection sources (insurance carriers, brokers, trade organizations, associations) may provide insight into internal weaknesses.

Checklists

Checklists are a good tool to use, especially in the beginning phase of an assessment. A checklist can be obtained from an external source or generated internally with all the components that a successful program or process should include to effectively manage its risks. Then the results can be used to benchmark where the particular issue or program is in comparison to the checklist. Such an exercise points out both the strengths and weaknesses of what is being assessed, which in turn can assist in a better concentration of resources to resolve problem areas.

Flow Analysis

Flow analysis or creating a flow chart can be a valuable identification process that can depict interrelated operations or processes and create an awareness of the types of exposures that might impede continued progress. Often putting an issue or process into diagram form can serve to emphasize the interdependency of one entity with another and with the overall operation of the institution.

Surveys and Questionnaires

Surveys and questionnaires used to gather information can be simple in design or more complex depending on the issue and the type of data needed. Standardized surveys and questionnaires can be beneficial because the information collected is more consistent; however, such methods may not completely identify all the exposures if there is no option to provide additional information beyond what is asked. For example, a survey might be conducted to identify the extent of exposure to the institution from the use of nonowned aircraft. The survey or questionnaire would be sent to all departments, defining nonowned aircraft use and asking them to identify what type and how often this activity occurs in their department. The results can provide the risk manager with information to make sound decisions on how much, if any, nonowned aircraft insurance coverage is needed.

Financial Statements

A review of financial statements can identify institutional assets that may be at risk. For instance, in reviewing the institution's balance sheet, a risk manager can understand what assets might be reduced by an accidental loss. Financial records can also point out continuing operating expenses, such as mortgages, which would continue even though a loss occurs.

Other Records and Documents

Examination of other institutional records and documents can also assist in identifying potential exposures to risk. Analyzing contracts prior to implementation, for instance, can identify language or omissions that could be detrimental to the institution. Other documents and records might include bid documents, leases, waivers, and policy statements.

Situational and Reactionary Loss

There are times when the identification process occurs as a result of a particular situation or in reaction to an event that has already happened. Soon after an event is often the best time to analyze a loss to determine what went wrong and then to identify what can be done to control and finance that same risk in the future.

Range of Assessments

Just as a variety of methods can be used to conduct a risk assessment, there are varying ways that the process can occur. The type of assessment can be driven by external factors, such as an upcoming inspection by EPA, or can be at the discretion of the risk manager as a routine part of the program. There are basically three types of assessments: targeted, comprehensive, and part of a larger assessment process.

Targeted Assessment

A targeted assessment has a specific issue as its focus. For example, risk management may determine that an assessment is needed to identify the exposures associated with the institution's foreign study program. The assessment process then deals only with the issues related to that program.

Comprehensive Assessment

A comprehensive assessment expands to include the larger picture. For example, a comprehensive assessment of the potential property damage risk from fire takes a look at all facilities on campus in order to identify the total exposure.

Part of Larger Institutional Assessment Process

At times, risk assessments may occur as part of a larger institutional process. An institution may undergo an internal audit process that can also serve to identify risk exposures or may undertake *"process-improvement"* studies or the reengineering of administrative functions that can generate risk issues as well.

Figure 16-01

Risk Exposure Matrix

	High Frequency	Low Frequency
High Severity	Avoid or Reduce Frequency or Severity	Work to Reduce and Insure or Transfer
Low Severity	Work to Reduce and Retrain	Ignore

Scope of Assessments

The scope of risk assessments can also be divided into two categories: a detailed analysis or a broader review. The decision on which type of assessment to conduct and how involved it should be largely depends on the desired end result. An institution may want to know all risks associated with its foreign studies program and may spend many months on the process. Purchasing (or accepting as a gift) a piece of land, however, may warrant only a broad review of the most likely risks (especially environmental), with the assumption that any small risks that exist can be managed.

Frequency of Assessments

The frequency of risk assessments can vary, and again, can be driven by either internal or external factors. Assessments can occur on a scheduled basis, an ad-hoc basis, a reactionary basis, or a continuous basis.

Scheduled Assessments

Many risk managers routinely schedule risk assessments for various components of the program. Insurance companies, especially property and workers' compensation carriers, want to periodically inspect institutional facilities as a regular part of underwriting the account. Many times, assessments coincide with the renewal of commercial insurance coverage so that information can be updated for the next policy year. Other scheduled assessments may revolve around the academic calendar- or fiscal-year operation.

Ad-hoc Assessments

Change in academia is one of the few constants. With change comes the need to anticipate risks that accompany new ideas, programs, and activities. The need to assess such risks often cannot be anticipated, but must occur as the need arises. For example, an institution with no prior aircraft ownership or operation is offered a good price on the purchase of an airplane, but such a purchase has many risk exposures that need to be addressed prior to assuming ownership and use.

Reactionary Assessments

Reactionary assessments are usually only conducted after a loss, when it becomes necessary to go back to see why an incident occurred. As was true in the discussion on reactionary assessments as a risk identification method, the time to conduct a reactionary assessment is immediately following a loss. It is important to evaluate not only what went wrong, but the root cause of the incident so that efforts can be focused on what can be done to prevent the same loss from recurring.

Continuous Assessments

As the name implies, the frequency of this type of assessment is ongoing. Risk managers regularly consider whether new issues require modification to insurance and risk management programs. This involves evaluation of internal processes as well as changes affecting the industry.

Risk Measurement

Once a risk has been identified, it also needs to be evaluated for its significance. Again, not all risks are created equal, so some consideration is necessary to determine to what degree a loss interferes with the operation of the institution in achieving its basic objectives. Two factors can be used in benchmarking a loss—frequency and severity.

Figure 16-01 shows a simple matrix that can be useful in measuring a risk exposure.

Using this type of matrix does not involve sophisticated loss calculations but rather management common sense to determine the basic financial impact. For most risks, frequency and severity tend to be inversely related. For example, a major flood can be highly devastating to an institution, but the likelihood that this will routinely occur is very low. Conversely, property damage to institutional vehicles routinely happens; however, the combined total losses would not be considered catastrophic.

Institutions should be concerned with catastrophic losses, such as a major fire, large liability claim, or severe flood. But it is important to remember that it can often be just as financially detrimental to an institution if numerous small losses that happen frequently combine to total just as much or more than a single major event.

Benefits of Risk Assessments

Colleges and universities can benefit from the risk assessment process by:

- understanding the scope of risk issues;
- understanding the urgency of risk issues;
- recognizing what has been accomplished; and
- determining what still needs to be addressed.

As described in the beginning of the chapter, identifying risks and then analyzing their impact is the first step in the basic risk management process. It is also the first step for institutions that choose to proactively understand what exposures they face and how critical it is to take care of them. A risk assessment can serve as a benchmark for the risk manager or business officer to help in formulating risk management goals and objectives. In addition, assessments can be useful in communicating to the administration what is being done by each unit or department to protect the institution and what issues are still of concern.

STEP 2:
ANALYZING THE OPTIONS

The second step in the risk management process is to determine the best option to use in response to a given exposure. Risk options fall into two major categories: risk control options and risk financing options. Risk control options work to lessen opportunities for losses to occur while risk financing options focus on who pays for losses that do occur.

Risk Control

Minimizing losses can be achieved in many ways and should be a common goal for all areas of an institution. A familiar risk management adage states that "the best time to prevent a loss is before it occurs." Proactive loss control efforts do just this. Risk control should be the first consideration for any exposure and then if the selected methods cannot fully protect the institution from a loss, risk financing options should be combined with risk control. The following methods can be used to control risk exposures.

Avoidance

The easiest way to control risk is to avoid it. An assessment may indicate that the risks associated with a certain activity are just too great, so an institution will decide not to do it. However, avoidance is not often a viable option, especially in an academic environment that is designed to foster exploration and the advancement of knowledge.

Prevention

Since avoiding risk usually is not possible, options to prevent losses through risk control should be the basis of all risk management initiatives. Loss prevention programs are designed to reduce the frequency of losses. Examples of loss prevention efforts include safety training to reduce back injuries, driver training programs, routine equipment maintenance, and facility fire safety inspections.

Proactive loss control is the foundation of a strong risk management program and a large part of the risk management effort should be devoted to activities designed to eliminate, reduce, maintain, or minimize the impact of loss.

Reduction

Reduction efforts are concerned with minimizing the severity of a given loss. For example, following a major flood, quick action to implement protective measures and salvage efforts can limit the extent of the damages and reduce the overall cost of the loss. Likewise, fire sprinklers can prevent the spreading of a fire from its point of ignition, and may actually extinguish the fire.

Separation

Controlling risks using separation means that an institution will organize its activities or disperse its assets so that no single loss can completely disrupt its operation. For example, an institution may have a policy that prohibits key administrators such as the president and senior vice presidents from flying together on the same airplane.

Duplication

Duplication utilizes some type of backup system. Probably the most common example of duplication involves computers. Most institutions recognize the need to have duplicate computer data that is routinely backed up and stored off-site in the event of a system failure. Other examples of duplication might be a backup for a food service supplier or backup electrical supply from a local utility for an institution that generates its own power.

Contractual Transfer

Transferring the risk as part of a contract control risks by specifying both the legal and the financial responsibility for a loss. Contracts should be reviewed to ensure that appropriate language regarding the responsibilities of each party with regard to personal or property losses is included and in the best interest of the institution. Indemnification language and insurance clauses are critical components of a contract that specifies who is responsible legally and financially in the event of a loss.

An indemnification clause or a hold harmless agreement specifies that one party to the contract holds the other party harmless from any claims or losses related to the activities covered by the contract. These clauses usually include the cost of the claim as well as any related costs to defend the claim.

Insurance clauses stipulate the type, amount, and evidence of coverage requirements. Different types of contracts may require different types of insurance. Based on the scope of the contract, a review of the insurance requirements should address:

- what types of coverage are needed;
- what limits are needed;
- proof of insurance—certificate of insurance provision; and
- cancellation or reduction in coverage provisions.

Risk Control Opportunities

There are three different opportunities to control risks: preloss, concurrent with a loss, and postloss. Each opportunity includes specific actions that can improve the overall effectiveness of an institution's loss control efforts.

Preloss Actions

Controlling risk prior to a loss means working to limit the number of losses that occur or to lessen the costs of losses that do happen. Effective preloss practices include the following.

Inspection Programs

Two types of inspections can be conducted to identify potential loss exposures: internal and external. Internal inspections are those coordinated by the institution to look at a process, a facility, or an operation. External inspections are those conducted by an outside agency, as a license requirement, regulation, or part of a service contract.

Internal Inspections. Many institutions regularly conduct internal inspections such as laboratory safety inspections, fire safety inspections, and equipment maintenance inspections. These in-house reviews can be done by personnel within the operation using some type of established inspection criteria, or can be done by personnel from another department such as environmental health and safety or facilities. The goal of an internal inspection can be to protect the assets of the institution, but it might also be a regulatory requirement. For example, research institutions using radioactive materials should have internal inspections to ensure that such operations are taking precautions to protect people and facilities. These assurances are also part of the regulatory compliance required by the Nuclear Regulatory Commission, which must be implemented if radioactive materials are used.

External Inspections. Numerous external inspections are conducted routinely on college and university campuses and can be either voluntary or required by law. Myriad regulatory compliance requirements exist that can mean regularly scheduled inspections or unannounced inspections. Examples of external legal or regulatory inspections include those by the fire marshal, the Occupational Safety and Health Administration, the Environmental Protection Agency, insurance company representatives, and municipal building inspectors. Other types of external inspections can be considered more voluntary, such as those conducted by property insurance companies, which may routinely look at facilities for safety as well as underwriting purposes, or by equipment manufacturing companies as preventive maintenance.

Training

Employee training can be a highly effective loss control method. For example, if during the risk assessment process, workers' compensation data shows a significant frequency of back injury claims, a training program on how to help prevent strains and sprains can be implemented to teach employees proper lifting techniques and fall-prevention methods, which could lower the number of injuries.

Formal Policies and Procedures

Effective polices and procedures can be used to control losses by providing staff, students, and visitors with necessary information that, if followed, will eliminate or reduce the chances of an incident occurring. Formal policies and procedures exist on all college and university campuses from the simple signs that point out "smoke-free environment" to elaborate policies on vehicle use. Two obstacles limit the effectiveness of relying on policies and procedures to control losses. Losses can be eliminated or minimized only if the policies and procedures are followed, and written edicts can be misunderstood, misinterpreted, or ignored altogether. The second obstacle is that not everything can be regulated. To create a policy or procedure for every single situation is not reasonable or even desirable. Promoting the message that risk management is everyone's responsibility can help, but common sense cannot be regulated and risk management cannot save people from their own decisions to act in an unsafe manner.

Outsourcing Activities

As mentioned, one way to reduce losses is to avoid the exposure. However, since many activities or operations that have loss potential must take place, another way to eliminate losses or reduce exposure is to contract to have someone else do it. For example, if the institution has had numerous bus accidents in its fleet, it may choose to contract with a professionally managed bus transportation firm to provide these services.

Conscious Assumption of Risk

Similarly, asking others to assume the risk for an activity that they are involved in on campus can shift some or all of the responsibility to the individual or entity. Explaining the potential risks involved and then asking students to sign a release and waiver of liability before they go on a trip sponsored by the mountain-climbing club can limit the liability to the institution in the event of an accident. The student knows that there are risks involved when climbing mountains, so unless there is a specific negligent action on the part of the institution, the student consciously chooses to participate and accepts the responsibility for any risks that might occur.

Functioning Safety Committee

Safety committees can be a source of risk identification and a resource for implementation for a risk management program, but the key word to this method is "functioning." Active review of campus issues and participation by committee members expand the responsibility for risk management. A risk management representative should be a member of the safety committee and use it as a vehicle to effect change. Some institutions also have a formal risk management committee that serves a similar function.

Actions During a Loss

Controlling risk during a loss focuses on efforts to keep a loss contained. Actions designed to go into effect as soon as a loss occurs can help lessen its severity. The most common example of these is a fire suppression system. Within minutes of detection, a fire suppression system can help contain a fire until fire fighters arrive, minimizing the extent of loss. On a larger scale, once triggered, specific preplanned procedures that are part of an emergency response plan can protect the assets of the institution and keep losses as low as possible.

Postloss Actions

Postloss efforts concentrate on techniques to keep a loss from escalating. These include disaster recovery plans, investigation and documentation of an incident immediately after it occurs, liability management to avoid litigation, and proactive public relations.

RISK FINANCING

Because losses will still happen even with strong efforts to control them, risk financing options can help an organization to determine how to pay for losses that do occur with as little impact on continuing operations as possible. Risk financing options include:

- commercial insurance;
- self-insurance;
- limits and deductibles; and
- risk transfer.

Risk management must work with direction from the governing board, president, and chief financial officer to establish risk financing philosophies that will define how much tolerance for risk an institution has and what options will be used.

Commercial Insurance

Purchasing commercial insurance is a risk transfer option that shifts the responsibility for loss to an insurance company. Many institutions use commercial insurance policies as their risk financing backbone, but may utilize one or more other options in combination with commercial insurance to reduce the overall cost of risk.

Categories of Insurance

There are a number of broad categories of insurance with many different types of policies and coverages under each of them. The major categories are:

Property insurance: Generally provides for the replacement of damaged facilities, contents, and other property owned, leased, or in the care and custody of the institution.

Liability insurance: Covers a wide variety of claims made against the institution by another party.

Title insurance: Guarantees a property owner that no one else should be able to claim ownership to that property.

Surety insurance: Provides a backup to a promise to perform a particular action or service.

Life and health insurance: Provides payment on behalf of the covered individual in the event of an accident or illness or to a beneficiary of a covered individual in the event of death.

Types of Insurance

Another way to distinguish among types of insurance is to divide them into either first-party or third-party coverage. First-party insurance provides protection for property owned by the institution. Examples of first-party insurance include policies that cover buildings and contents or auto physical damage. Third-party insurance provides an institution with protection for claims made against it by others. Some examples of third-party insurance include general liability, educators legal liability, employment practices liability, professional practices liability (health provider, attorney, architect, engineer), workers' compensation, life and health insurance, and excess or umbrella insurance.

Some policies provide both first-party and third-party protection in the same policy, such as auto, aircraft, or watercraft insurance. For example, a marine policy covering a research vessel can include coverage in the event the vessel sustains physical damage as well as coverage for claims made by others if they are injured in an accident involving the vessel.

Self-Insurance

For a variety of reasons, an institution may look at the options available to treat an exposure and decide that it will self-insure rather than buy commercial insurance. These reasons might include high premium costs for a particular type of insurance, unavailability of insurance because of negative loss experiences, or simply because an institution has a high tolerance for risk and has the resources available to establish sufficient reserves. Before an institution determines whether or not to self-insure, the feasibility should be carefully assessed, ideally by an experienced consultant hired to study the risk exposure, to assess the financial implications to the institution, and to recommend appropriate levels of funding. Once the viability of self-insurance is established, funds need to be identified to respond to losses for that particular risk. Institutions can finance a self-insurance program in two ways—a funded reserve or an unfunded reserve. A funded reserve means that the institution has put aside actual dollars into an account that will be used to pay claims. An unfunded reserve means the institution knows that losses may occur and approximately at what level, but will pay for losses out of general operating funds. The estimated loss amount is included in budgetary considerations, but actual funds are not earmarked or set aside. Use of either of these mechanisms is a conscious decision—the initial assessment process is necessary in order to establish the amount that will need to be budgeted and available in the event of a loss.

No matter what funding mechanism is used, institutions that elect to self-insure need to do the following:

- *Establish guidelines for operation of the self-insurance program.* Self-insuring requires many of the same criteria used by commercial insurance companies in order to operate effectively. The types of claims paid, how they are paid, limits to coverage, and how funding is established are some of the components that should be formulated into a written document that will give the program structure.

- *Conduct a periodic external review of the program.* Since losses may be paid many years after an incident, reserves should be established at the time an incident takes place, and then re-evaluated each year until a final resolution occurs. An external actuarial service is usually used to establish these annual reserve amounts.

- *Purchase excess insurance.* An institution that decides to self-insure a particular category of risk (e.g., workers' compensation) should consider the purchase of excess or stop-loss insurance to limit its exposure to catastrophic loss in a particular year. This excess or stop-loss insurance can be specific to one claim or an aggregate for the total category for the year.

The concept of self-insurance is often misunderstood and sometimes may be confused with being uninsured. The assumption of risk may happen because an exposure is either not recognized or not perceived to be a particularly large threat. From this comes the philosophy that says, "it probably won't happen, but if it does, we'll figure out how to pay for it then." This type of response to risk, or lack thereof, can leave an institution highly vulnerable to a loss that can adversely affect its operation, since it must now divert funds originally designated for another purpose to pay for the loss. For example, an institution may not see floods as a major threat to its operation, and not include flood insurance as part of its property coverage. But low probability is not the same as no probability. Assuming a flood will never happen leaves the institution uninsured for flood damage and trying to figure out how to pay for the damage out of current funds or the endowment. A decision to self-insure for a flood, however, would assess the financial impact a flood would have on the institution. Then an established amount sufficient for response would be integrated into the budgetary process or would actually be put into an established reserve account designated for that purpose.

Limits and Deductibles

Two common risk-financing tools are the use of insurance limits and deductibles. These have always been part of commercial insurance policies, but often not used as effectively as they might be to the benefit of an institution. A review of insurance policies can ensure that appropriate limits and reasonable deductibles are used in combination to protect the institution while making the best use of the limited dollars allocated to risk financing.

Limits

Every institution would like to have sufficient limits on each insurance policy so that no loss will ever exceed the amount of coverage, but at the same time does not want to pay excessive premiums for limits higher than necessary. Because of the financial implications of being underinsured, most institutions would like to think that they have erred on the side of too high a limit. Most primary liability policies (general liability, auto, professional, malpractice, etc.) have standardized limits, but many institutions elect to purchase excess or umbrella policies to increase these limits. Often the incremental cost is at a progressively lower rate. There may be times, however, when the excess policies will exclude certain coverages provided by the primary policy. The institution must evaluate the appropriate limit on each of its policies, again basing decisions on tolerance for risk and funding reserve potential.

Deductibles

A deductible is the amount of a loss that the institution pays before the insurance company makes its payment. The deductible on any policy will depend on several factors, including an institution's loss history, appetite for risk, the financial incentive that the underwriter will give in exchange for assumption of the risk, and the willingness of the underwriter to accept certain levels of risk.

Bidding a program at various deductible levels can assist in determining the most cost-effective deductible level to select. This will provide a comparison of the premium cost at each deductible level to see if retaining more of the risk can be cost effective. Insurance companies are usually willing to charge a lower premium if the institution agrees to a higher deductible. Selecting a higher deductible can save premium dollars, but the institution must be willing to realize these savings with the knowledge that it accepts the financial responsibility of all claims that are less than the deductible. If the amount saved is greater than the additional cost incurred due to the higher deductible, then this would be a good business decision. No one can predict exactly what the cost associated with losses will be, but factors such as loss histories within the various deductible ranges, along with the potential effectiveness of loss prevention and control efforts to reduce the frequency and severity of losses, can assist in the decision-making process.

Risk Transfer

Risk transfer has been referenced as a risk control option, but it is also a risk financing option. The transfer of risk can be accomplished in several different ways such as:

- contract language;
- waivers and agreements to participate;

- captives;
- risk retention groups; and
- insurance pools.

Contract Language

One of the best methods of risk transfer is the use of a contract between the institution and a third party to transfer the risk of loss to that third party. Some of the more common uses of this risk transfer method are the outsourcing of services, such as food service, construction work, or bookstore operations. Language used in the contract needs to specify as clearly as possible that the third party is assuming all the financial risk of loss and that the indemnification or hold harmless clause includes the cost of defense. The contract should also be clear regarding losses to the contractor's property no matter who is at fault.

Waivers and Agreements to Participate

Most institutions require participants in certain activities to sign a document that states they are voluntarily agreeing to participate and waiving any right to make claims against the institution if they are injured while taking part in the activity. While these may be useful in a court of law to show that the individual voluntarily assumed the risks inherent in the activity, many states do not consider these agreements and waivers to hold much validity unless they are extremely specific in nature. The more pertinent the agreement and waiver is to the particular activity, the more weight it will carry. For example, such documents for a ski club trip need to very specifically address the dangers inherent in skiing and resulting complications (from transportation to hypothermia), specify the limitations of the institution's responsibility, and provide verification that the individual has read, understood, and voluntarily chosen to participate despite the risks involved.

Captives

Some colleges and universities utilize an alternative risk financing method known as a captive. Although using a captive appears to shift the responsibility for losses to another entity, technically it is a risk retention mechanism. A captive is formed as a subsidiary to finance losses, but theoretically is still a part of the institution financially. There are two types of captives: (1) a traditional or pure captive, which has only one institution involved; and, (2) a group captive, which has several institutions that join together to finance the losses of its members. In either case, captives are designed to operate in the same manner as an insurance company and must conform to the insurance rules and regulations of its location. This is why many captives are located outside of the United States, since locations such as Bermuda or the Bahamas are less regulated. Similar to the decision to self-insure, the decision to either join a captive or form one requires a great deal of study to determine if it is in the best interest of the institution.

Risk Retention Groups

A risk retention group can be formed by like institutions with similar or related liabilities that combine their resources as well as their liability exposures and, in effect, form their own mutual insurance company. Congress passed legislation in 1988 to allow the formation of risk retention groups for entities having difficulty finding commercial insurance. Like a captive, a risk retention group must be licensed to operate as an insurance company; however, the regulations differ with regard to location and licensing requirements from those for captives or commercial insurance companies. Once approved by the insurance regulatory authority in one domiciliary state, a risk retention group may operate in other states without having to be approved by each state's insurance regulatory authority.

Insurance Pools

Insurance pools have some of the same characteristics as both the captive and risk retention group. But unlike these two methods, a pool is not considered to be an insurance company and is generally less regulated, if monitored at all. The type of coverage a pool can offer is not limited, but in most cases a pooling arrangement is established to meet only one or two specific exposures. For example, a group of institutions may form a self-insured pool to cover vehicle liability. Members fund the pool through premiums paid into a central fund that is then used to pay losses and administrative costs. While the operation of a pool requires a great deal of management to be successful, it can be a cost-effective alternative to commercial insurance.

STEP 3:
SELECTING THE BEST OPTION

The risk has been identified and evaluated. The options have been analyzed for effectiveness. Selecting the best option to use in managing the risk is the third step in the process. Two key questions can serve in guiding the process toward the best solution.

- What technique or combination of techniques will be the most effective?

- What technique or combination of techniques will be the most economical?

Developing a response to these questions in conjunction with one another will take into account all the variables that can affect the success of a risk management option. For example, an institution with a large vehicle fleet has several options available for use in managing its auto exposure. It can:

- buy commercial auto insurance;

- self-insure (either or both the physical damage and the liability);

- develop a fleet safety program that includes driver training and motor vehicle record checks;

- outsource its vehicle needs—lease rather than own autos to transfer the exposure;

- form a pool with other institutions; or

- use other means of transportation instead of automobiles.

All of these options, or others, could work. But the best solution for the institution is probably a combination of risk financing and loss control. Buying or self-insuring is dependent on financial resources, and loss control efforts are dependent on both human and financial resources. The final option selected is usually driven by both.

Sometimes, however, only one option is truly viable. For example, a small institution usually will not have the resources necessary to self-insure for general liability. In this case, the best and probably only option is to purchase commercial insurance.

STEP 4:
IMPLEMENTING THE OPTIONS SELECTED

The fourth step in the risk management process is to implement the option selected. However, implementation depends on the nature of the option. Some options require only the person in charge of the risk management program to make decisions because they are more technical in nature. But other options mean that risk management must elicit the cooperation and assistance of other managers and employees at the institution.

Technical Decisions

Risk management usually has the authority to independently implement a technical decision such as the purchase of commercial insurance. For example, if an institution with its own aircraft determines that commercial insurance is the best option to cover the exposure, then risk management will need to use technical knowledge to determine what insurance company to use, what limits and deductibles make the best sense, and to negotiate the purchase. It is important for risk management to communicate these decisions to administrators to keep them informed.

Decisions That Require Others

The implementation of other techniques usually means that the risk manager must collaborate with others to implement good risk management practices. For example, the risk manager may develop and recommend travel guidelines for student organizations to use when driving to events off campus. But the risk manager must rely on student affairs administrators, organization advisors, and the students themselves to follow the guidelines in order for the option to succeed.

STEP 5:
MONITORING THE OPTIONS

Monitoring an option is the final step in the risk management process and is one that is often minimized and sometimes even overlooked. Risk management options can be put in place but still not adequately protect the institution. Following the implementation of an option, a review is needed to evaluate the choice and to determine if any modifications might be needed. Like the other steps in the risk management process, there are a variety of ways to monitor an option for effectiveness. The basic formula, however, includes:

- establishing an acceptable level of performance for the option;
- comparing what actually occurs with the established acceptance level; and
- making adjustments to the option to ensure the established standard is reasonable.

For example, an institution may determine that it wants to reduce the number of employee work-related back injuries. A loss history assessment provides data on the current number of injuries. From this, risk management can establish a goal to reduce the number of back injuries, and then implement options such as training or job function assessment in an effort to meet that goal. At some point, a review of the new data in comparison to the old will provide an indication of the effectiveness of the option. Depending on the results, adjustments may need to be made to the option, or a whole new option selected in order to achieve the established level of performance.

RISK MANAGEMENT PROCESS SUMMARY

The risk management process is designed to be both repetitive and self-reinforcing. At the same time, the very culture of college and universities invites change. The challenge, then, to risk management is to continually assess the activities and operation of the institution to determine if the risk control and risk financing practices in place continue to adequately protect the assets, or if modifications need to take place. Each new initiative comes with associated risks that must be assessed as well. The five-step risk management process comes into play constantly, both as an initial action and then again to ensure that all is going well.

RISK MANAGEMENT PROGRAM ADMINISTRATION

Regardless of who facilitates risk management and whether or not the role is full- or part-time, certain aspects of the program must be managed internally. The range of program administration runs from support for a highly complex operation to having the entire function outsourced. But even if the majority of operational details are handled externally, ultimate decision making needs to reside with the institution and requires administrative oversight.

Similar to other institutional operations, there are common administrative functions such as record keeping, budgets, policies and procedures, reports to management, and personnel issues that are part of doing business. Risk management administration includes these as well as the following that are specific to risk management:

- managing claims;
- negotiating insurance coverage;
- maintaining insurance policies;
- monitoring contracts and certificates of insurance;
- allocating the costs of risk;

- investigating losses; and
- facilitating loss prevention and loss control.

What Should a Risk Management Program Include?

The various aspects of a comprehensive and effective risk management program have been identified in earlier sections of this chapter. Who specifically handles these components and to what degree each is a factor will likely differ from institution to institution, but should always address:

- loss prevention and control;
- alternative risk financing; and
- entity/commercial insurance.

Loss prevention, loss control, and alternative risk financing options have been discussed previously. This section will primarily focus on methods of acquisition and types of commercial insurance an institution might need and a brief description of the exposures related to each corresponding coverage.

Marketing the Insurance Portion of the Risk Management Program

Agents, Brokers, and Consultants

Agents are representatives of the insurance company, and sell that company's products. Agents may be general agents representing several companies, or dedicated to one company. Brokers are representatives of the insurance buyer, and are free to access all insurance markets. Consultants, like brokers, are hired by the institution but are compensated on an hourly or retainer basis to give advice on risk management issues or particular insurance coverages and their compensation is not tied to the actual purchase of any insurance products.

The Importance of Agents and Brokers

The importance of a broker or agent to an institution's insurance program, especially one without a full-time risk manager, cannot be overestimated. Like the role of the risk manager, the role of agents and brokers is also evolving from the seller of insurance to the seller of comprehensive risk management services. In part, this change has been a result of competitive market conditions that meant low premiums were available from multiple sources. Agents and brokers looked for other services to offer clients as service enhancements to increase business and maintain a competitive edge. More important is that agents and brokers recognized that changes were taking place in the sophistication of the organizations they worked with and that the increasing importance of the risk management function meant they needed to expand to meet the needs of their clients. In addition to placing insurance coverages, the majority of agencies and brokerage firms now offer a range of risk management support services from loss control recommendations to claims management. If it is the role of risk management to know the institution, it is the role of the agent or broker to know the technical facets of risk management and insurance. This combination of the institutional expert and industry expert working together can maximize both perspectives to collaboratively provide risk management solutions.

Institutions may use the services of only one agency or brokerage firm, or may opt to use several different sources to meet their needs. Different lines of insurance can require different types of service and expertise, something not every broker possesses. For example, auto insurance is highly regulated, state-specific and demands a lot of hands-on, local service. Institutions with complex liability issues may need a high level of technical skill and market knowledge in their broker. Some key considerations should be made in selecting an agent or broker:

- *What services are needed?* Services such as policy placement, claims management, loss prevention, and control are common but others such as record management, cost analysis, and loss forecasting might be needed as well. The working relationship with the agent's or broker's representative or "key contact" is critical, as well as access to and interaction with other specialists in the firm.

- *What range of knowledge is needed?* Technical knowledge of and the ability to appropriately apply policy language, legal implications, claims expertise, higher education expertise, markets, and specialty markets are some of the types of knowledge important to a risk management program.

- *Is bigger better?* Size considerations such as local, regional, or global can be a factor to an institution. The decision on whether to use a large national brokerage firm or a small local agency often depends on the determination of the services and knowledge needed. Strong support services and technical expertise can potentially be found in either size organization. Therefore, risk management should identify the most important needs and then utilize a system to determine who can best meet those needs. Size may or may not affect the quality of service or the attentiveness of an agent or broker. An institution could be one of the largest clients and receive a level of service based on that distinction. Conversely, a college or university could be only one of dozens or even hundreds of similar-sized clients and find the level of service more limited.

Those responsible for risk management should welcome calls from brokers and agents and meet with them as may be appropriate and also discuss possible choices with colleagues to find out whom they use, and whom they like. What is good about a firm? What is not? Firms with a higher education practice will be keyed into markets (underwriters) with knowledge and expertise in higher education risks. Generally speaking, the better an underwriter understands the risk, the fairer and more consistently stable the pricing will remain.

The best broker may not always come up with the lowest price. The lowest price is not always a bargain, especially if there is little or no service, or where it is difficult to obtain claims payments. It is important to remember that the only value an insurance policy has is in paying claims when they arise.

The Bidding Process

For some institutions, the decision as to the agency or brokerage firm has nothing to do with their capabilities, but has been politically or historically motivated. Whenever possible, use the bidding process to identify quality service providers. Formal bidding can be done in two ways: one is designed only to select an agent, broker, or consultant to provide services and does not include any insurance polices as part of the selection process. The other is designed to combine both the services and the insurance policies into one process.

It is usually beneficial to use a formal request for proposal (RFP) when bidding for insurance products and/or services from brokers or agents. Designing an effective RFP can be challenging, but the more specifically the issues are identified, the more likely it will be that those responding are going to meet the needs of the institution.

The process to select an agent, broker, or consultant to provide services without the inclusion of insurance policies has a narrower focus than the process designed to select both the service provider and insurance products. In the first process, the companies are measured on such criteria as services available, staff expertise, availability, compensation, and size of the organization. The criteria used should be those items of importance to the risk management program and may vary institutionally depending on need.

The second process combines the selection of the broker or agent along with the selection of insurance products. However, if there are an overwhelming number of candidates, an RFP can still be developed for a service proposal only, to reduce the agents and brokers to a reasonable number. The number of available markets can help determine what is a reasonable number of service providers to involve in the process. For example, in auto insurance, 20 markets may be willing to bid on the institution's business and so four agents can each be assigned five markets. However, for directors and officers coverage, only five markets may be available, and no more than two brokers would be used.

Once the brokers who will bid on the program have been determined, each should be asked to submit a list of markets, in order of preference, they would like to approach. The brokers should be advised that markets will be assigned by the institution, and that no markets are to be approached by them until they receive their assignments, on penalty of forfeiture. Generally, the incumbent broker is assigned the incumbent market. Following that, brokers should be assigned their first choice, second choice, and so forth.

The RFP should include a description of the coverages desired, including any options to be bid (such as optional coverages, limits, or deductibles). It can be helpful or even desirable also to invite the participants to submit any changes or options that they think would enhance or improve the program. Responses may give insight into the respondent's creativity, technical skill, or knowledge of and interest in the program.

Some general information may also be included such as a description of the evaluation process, how the contract will be awarded, and the institution's contact. If brokers have not been prequalified, then a clear description of the brokerage services required, with a request for information about their operation, needs to be included as well. Expectations on how the written proposal should be presented also help the respondents focus on the issues that truly matter to the institution.

Underwriting information should include exposure data (the metrics that insurers use for calculating premium), loss history, particulars on any large losses, identification of any loss control or prevention programs relevant to the coverage, and relevant information about the institution. Risk management may also choose to include detailed information about the current program, especially if a comparative coverage analysis is desired. Usually, expiring premiums are not disclosed.

Once the responses are in, they need to be evaluated in the context of each other and the expiring program. For the sole decision maker, the analysis need be only as formal as that person requires. However, if others are involved in the decision-making process, the more the responses are broken down into a comparable format, the easier the decision-making process will be for all.

Frequency of the Bidding Process

An effective bidding process can take much time and effort. Some institutions, especially those in the public sector, have mandated requirements on the bidding frequency and specific procedures that must be followed during the process. However, there are other issues to be considered, even if the institution has no specified requirements. Risk management may elect to market the program to improve coverage, improve service, change service providers, reduce costs, or as a matter of routine to benchmark the program. But unless there are specific mandates on the frequency, it is usually not a good idea to market a program too frequently. Underwriters view frequent bidding with no apparent change negatively and may choose not to bid on a program. Because the bidding process is so labor- and cost-intensive, it makes good business sense to market a program only periodically.

INSURANCE

As previously discussed, purchasing insurance is a risk financing option that transfers the loss exposure from the institution to an insurance company. The insurance policy is a contract that stipulates the company's responsibility to the institution when a loss occurs in exchange for a premium that has been paid in advance. The following are categories of insurance policies that typically can be purchased by colleges and universities: property, casualty, title, surety, and life and health.

Property Insurance

Property insurance covers the institution for damage to or loss of buildings, fixtures, and contents due to such perils as fire, flood, or earthquake. Most property policies are classified as "all risk" contracts that cover damage or loss for any reason unless it is specifically excluded. Most property policies have coverage for the replacement value of the property; however, if for some reason the property is not replaced, then the reimbursement is usually limited to the actual cash value.

Usually property policies also include coverage for "business interruption," which means reimbursement for the loss of revenue as a result of damage to the property, and extra expense, which reimburses the institution for additional expenses incurred due to the loss. For example, if a fire occurs in a dormitory, the property policy would cover the costs of repairing the facility and replacing damaged contents owned by the institution. Business interruption would provide compensation for the loss of rents that normally would have been paid by students to live in the facility. Extra expense would provide reimbursement to the institution for the expenses associated with having to temporarily relocate students to hotels or off-campus apartments.

Builder's Risk Insurance

A builder's risk policy provides coverage for damages during construction of a new facility or the renovation of existing facilities.

Crime Insurance

Crime policies insure against direct loss of money, securities, or other property caused by theft or forgery by an employee of the institution acting alone or in collusion with others. Examples of items covered by a crime policy include: destruction, disappearance, or wrongful abstraction of money or securities within or from the institution's premises, banking premises, or night deposit safe; and forgery or alteration of any check, draft, promissory note, bill of exchange, or similar written document.

Coinsurance

The concept of property coinsurance should not be confused with the coinsurance in a medical insurance policy (the participatory co-payment by the insured). Most property policies contain a coinsurance clause to prevent the institution from intentionally understating their property values to save on premiums. Coinsurance is a penalty that can be exercised by the insurance company if it is determined that the institution has not insured its property to an agreed percentage of full value. Some property insurers will add an "agreed amount clause" to the policy indicating that the insurer agrees that the insurance limit is sufficient, thus eliminating the coinsurance worry.

Other Types of Property Insurance

Other types of property insurance to be considered are:

- fine arts;
- boiler and machinery;
- valuable papers;
- mobile equipment;
- transit and cargo;
- vehicle, watercraft, aircraft; and

- student property (renter's insurance).

Casualty Insurance

Every institution faces potential liability as a result of its activities and operations. Casualty insurance is necessary because the institution faces a high probability of claims, the claims are not predictable, or they are not controllable. Many exposures cannot be fully avoided, since they arise from the activities and operations essential to carrying out the mission of the institution.

There are many different types of casualty policies, but most are designed to provide coverage defense and settlement when a third party claims a loss due to an action or omission of the institution.

General Liability Policies

The most common casualty insurance is commercial general liability. This type of policy provides protection from a third party claiming negligent acts or omissions from operation of the premises and from nonprofessional activities that have resulted in bodily injury or property damage. General liability policies will usually also cover personal injury that includes libel or slander. Two limits are associated with general liability policies: per occurrence and aggregate. Occurrence is the maximum amount that will be paid for a single incident while aggregate is the maximum that will be paid during the entire policy period for all losses. Examples of common general liability claims include slips and falls.

Auto Liability Policies

Auto liability policies provide coverage for losses to third parties arising out of the operation of a motor vehicle or driver insured by the policy. The institution should also be sure that the auto liability extends to nonowned, hired, and borrowed vehicles. A commonly asked question is whether or not an institution's auto liability policy provides coverage if an employee or student uses his or her personal vehicle on business for the institution. In most cases, the employee's or student's personal auto policy will provide the primary coverage and the institution's policy will be secondary, or "excess." Auto liability policies can also provide coverage for property damage to the institutional vehicle; however, many institutions with large fleets tend to self-insure for this physical damage coverage.

Workers' Compensation and Employer's Liability

Workers' compensation and employer's liability insurance are both designed to cover employee claims. The first covers claims by employees under the state's workers' compensation act. These acts usually make an employer responsible for medical care and lost wages for employees who are injured on the job or develop an occupational disease. This coverage is unique because the worker does not need to prove that the institution is at fault to file a claim. The policy usually covers whatever the statute requires without a specific dollar limit. In most states, workers cannot sue for damages in excess of the statutory limits. Many institutions choose to self-insure for workers' compensation, but wisely opt to purchase an excess policy in the event of a catastrophic loss.

The second type of insurance covers liability claims against an employer directly or indirectly made by an employee. For example, an employee may sue the manufacturer of a machine, alleging the machine was defective but the manufacturer may in turn sue the employer, alleging poor maintenance as the cause.

States with monopolistic workers' compensation policies do not have employer's liability included in their coverage, so it must be purchased separately.

Educators Legal Liability

These policies are known by a variety of names including directors and officers, school board liability, and educators legal liability. The function of each, however, is to protect the institution from financial loss as a result of wrongful acts for which the institution, its governing board, officers, or other employees are held liable. Common examples of claims covered by these policies are discrimination, denial of tenure, failure to educate, and wrongful termination. This insurance may be purchased as one policy or in a combination of policies. Many of these policies are written on a claims-made basis rather than on an occurrence basis, which can negatively impact the institution if there is a change in insurance carriers.

Fiduciary Liability

Fiduciary liability covers the institution when claims are made for financial losses arising from the failure to properly act as a fiduciary with regard to its employee benefit plans under the Employee Retirement Income Security Act. The policy can also cover errors in administration of benefits. Exposures to an institution are less if the institution does not self-fund the benefit plan, but there may still be potential liability when any advice is given to employees.

Professional Liability

Professional liability insurance covers claims alleging injury or damage arising from a breach of a professional standard. Institutions may need this insurance for exposures from professional schools such as medical, legal, social work, accounting, architecture, or engineering. Institutions may also need professional liability insurance in order to place interns at other institutions or companies. The institution should consider coverage for other professional services it renders such as the student infirmary, a counseling center, notaries, realty services, and attorneys.

Excess and Umbrella Liability Policies

Excess or umbrella policies can be purchased to protect the institution from liability claims that exceed the limit of the various primary policies. An important benefit of these policies is the "drop down" feature, which means that if the primary aggregate limit is exhausted, the excess or umbrella policy will respond to all new claims, subject to the policy deductible.

For example, if an athletic team traveling in an institutional van is involved in an accident due to the fault of an employee driver and all 14 passengers are severely injured, most likely the loss will exceed the limit of the auto liability policy. The institution would then have to pay the amount not covered by insurance if no excess or umbrella policy exists.

Other Components or Types of Liability Policies

Other components or types of liability policies to be considered are:

- premises;
- products;
- athletic;
- police;
- foreign;
- publishing and broadcasting;
- corporal punishment;
- liquor;
- pollution;
- special event;
- student organizations;
- owner's and contractor's;
- garage and garagekeepers;
- nuclear; and

- aviation and marine.

Title Insurance

Title insurance guarantees a property owner that no one else should be able to claim ownership to that property. When purchasing a building or even vacant land, many institutions will purchase title insurance to be sure that there will be no claims of ownership by third parties.

Surety Insurance

Surety insurance provides a financial backup to a promise to perform a particular action or service. For instance, many times an institution will require contractors to purchase performance and payment bonds in connection with a construction project. These bonds will protect the institution in case the contractor does not complete the project for any reason, including bankruptcy. These bonds include:

- bid bonds;
- performance bonds; and
- notary bonds.

Life and Health Insurance

Life and health insurance provides payment on behalf of the covered individual in the event of a covered accident or illness or to a beneficiary on covered individual in the event of death. Some examples of life and health insurance include:

- student health;
- travel and accident;
- repatriation and medical evacuation;
- athletic accident and illness;
- employee life and health;
- disability;
- long-term care; and
- dental and eye.

Choosing an Insurance Policy

Insurance policies can vary widely in provisions and benefits. A well-qualified insurance agent or broker can assist with the evaluation of policies and compare the scope of coverages. While price may be a compelling consideration, it is only one criterion. The quality of an insurance company can vary, too. Each one has its own financial strength and range of loss control and claims services. Agents and brokers can also check references and the rating of insurers that are published by various agencies such as the A.M. Best Company.

When to Switch Insurers

Although policies are frequently purchased in one- or three-year terms, sometimes purchasers tend to renew with little consideration to changing needs and risks. Loyalty is noble and appreciated by the insurer, but circumstances change. There may be valid reasons for moving a policy from one company to another. The most obvious is if an insurer cancels a policy, which can happen because of poor loss history. In this example, the choice to make a change has not been made by the institution. However, there are times an institution may choose to make a change, such as deteriorating financial condition of the insurer, unacceptable service, or acquisition of the company by another insurer. In addition, risk management should monitor the costs of insurance to determine if the price charged and the coverage provided for that charge are consistent with the competition. If an institution experiences an unreasonable price increase, if the long-term price is above the current market, or if broader coverage for the same price is available in the marketplace, then switching insurers may be a good business decision.

Prior to changing insurers, however, it may be advantageous to see if the existing carrier has the capability to revise the existing policy in response to new needs. Depending on the reason changes are needed, it may be beneficial to remain with the current insurance company since it is already familiar with the institution.

Document Review

Certificates of Insurance

Certificates of insurance provide evidence that insurance policies are in place. They state the types of insurance, the amounts of coverage, and expiration dates of the policies. An institution may need to provide others with a certificate of insurance to prove that the college or university has coverage. For example, an institution may want to hold an activity in an off-campus location and that facility may want to verify that the institution is insured. Similarly, an institution will want to request certificates of insurance from all third parties such as tenants and vendors of services. It is particularly important that the institution receive a current certificate of insurance from any third party where risk is transferred through indemnification or hold harmless language. Only signed originals should be accepted and the document should be carefully checked to ensure that the document includes all the necessary and requested information.

Other issues involving certificates of insurance include who should be responsible for certificate verification, who coordinates the process if changes are necessary or if a renewal certificate is needed, and where the certificates are kept on file.

Contracts

Colleges and universities enter into many types of contracts and agreements for a variety of reasons such as professional service agreements, real estate leases, service contracts, and affiliation agreements. The ideal scenario would be to have risk management involved in the early draft stages of such documents; however, this can be difficult to achieve given the volume of contractual documents at most institutions. At a minimum, risk management should review all contracts and agreements prior to their finalization for:

- indemnification and hold harmless language;
- insurance language;
- risk of loss; and
- limitations to liability.

Claims Management

Claims can come from any area of the institution and are as varied as the insurance or self-insurance programs that cover them. Some of the areas on campus that generate the highest frequency of claims are workers' compensation, automobile liability, and general liability. Areas that generate the highest severity include employment practices and catastrophic athletic injury. Risk management should be responsible for tracking all claims and either manage them or monitor the claims management if handled by a third-party administrator.

Strong advocacy on behalf of the institution is needed to ensure that its best interest is considered. Whoever provides the claims service should explain what the claim handling philosophy and practices are. For example, some insurers will defend general liability until an ultimate court decision. This strategy avoids settlements for nuisance claims but runs high in legal defense bills. Other insurers take the reverse view and work for opposite results. A better strategy is to evaluate each claim on its own merit and then determine whether to defend or settle.

Records Management

A risk management program produces a large volume of records that document program activities. Examples include insurance policies, claim files (especially settlement agreements), certificates of insurance, and policies and procedures. Many records need to be retained for long periods of time and some indefinitely. This is especially true for liability insurance policies since most are written on an occurrence basis. An occurrence-based policy means that the policy covers incidents that occur during the time that the policy is in effect, even though the claim is not filed until years later. Other policies that should be retained indefinitely include crime policies and workers' compensation policies.

Cost Allocation

While some institutions incur the cost of their risk management program centrally, others allocate the cost to affiliates and auxiliaries. The principles for allocating costs are:

- the allocation should reflect relative risk both in premium and deductibles;
- the allocation should be no more than the unit would pay if it were free-standing; and
- the methodology should be designed to minimize budget swings from year to year.

Insurance brokers are often familiar with the pricing options used by insurance companies, and these may be modified to assist an institution in developing an allocation process.

A strong argument can be made that the cost allocation process can serve as an incentive to departments to take a proactive role in reducing risks. If costs are centralized and the various entities are not responsible for premium costs or deductibles, then the concepts of risk management are less real to those who have the best opportunity on a day-to-day basis to exercise loss control and reduce the overall cost of risk. However, not all institutions support this concept, which means that risk management must pursue alternative methods for creating accountability.

Reporting

Those responsible for risk management should prepare periodic reports for management and the governing board. At a minimum, these reports should include:

- a list of insurance policies purchased, their limits, and cost;
- a description of loss history and trends; and
- a discussion of loss prevention initiatives.

The report may contain other information on how risks were identified and analyzed, including any risks that are uninsured and whether it was because the policy cost was too high, the risk was uninsurable, or the risk is minor or self-insured. Benchmarking data can also be an effective tool to use in communicating various risk management issues.

A key role played by risk management is to keep senior management and the governing board apprised of potential issues that can impact the operation of the institution. It is only when these issues are raised to the highest level of awareness possible that the necessary attention and support needed to effect change can happen.

Evaluation

An essential component of the risk management process, monitoring is also important to the risk management program. Ideally, the overall program should be reviewed on an annual basis to ensure that the goals and objectives established by risk management are consistent with the needs of the institution and address current external issues and concerns. A formalized review of risk management operations can help to ensure that new risk exposures have been identified and managed, as well as to evaluate the effectiveness of established risk management practices.

Periodically, some form of external review can also provide an institution with an assessment of the risk management program that can be used to strengthen the efforts of the institution to protect its assets. One form of external assessment is conducted as a peer review. Colleagues from other colleges or universities are asked to conduct a program review and furnish the institution with an evaluation based on general effective practices. External reviews can also be conducted by hiring a consulting firm or independent consultant.

SUMMARY

When the institution embraces risk management as everyone's responsibility, the college or university risk manager is empowered to deal more effectively with these encroaching risks.

—Report on the First Critical Issues Forum for
Higher Education Risk Management, March 1997

In March 1997, the Vermont Insurance Institute convened a group of 23 leading risk managers and business officers to participate in its first Critical Issues Forum. The participants agreed that risk management had taken on more importance during the preceding decade as colleges and universities entered into areas that presented greater risks to the institution. Their list of "encroaching risks" included:

- skyrocketing property values;

- an expanded employee base;

- a more litigious society;

- a growing number of uninsurable risks requiring sophisticated self-funding techniques; and

- more demanding regulatory compliance.

As institutions go forward into the new century and further look to broaden the scope of higher education, new issues and initiatives are generating even more diverse and complex exposures in each of the categories of risk. What were recognized as emerging issues in 1997 still present challenges to risk management, but the list continues to grow in response to the changing dynamics of higher education. Although many of the following issues are not new concerns, they now have increased importance to risk managers and the institutions they represent:

- operating risk:
  - campus construction,
  - transit operations,
  - special events, and
  - student housing (life safety and security);

- legal risk:
  - employment practices, and
  - environmental;

- financial risk:
  - investment management,

– misappropriation of funds (wire transfer, ACH), and
– real estate gifts (pollution);

• political and reputational risk:
– student issues (alcohol),
– athletics, and
– foreign study;

• technological risk:
– intellectual property,
– Internet exposures, and
– distance learning.

A Continuing Evolution

The final report of the Critical Issues Forum concludes that a move toward more strategic risk management is needed if colleges and universities are to effectively manage their risks. Participants recognized that risk management and senior administration must be committed to this more holistic risk management approach for a proactive rather than reactive model of risk management. Since then, this philosophy has continued to spread among collegiate risk management professionals and is beginning to emerge in other areas of the institution. Colleges and universities are increasingly more aware that the old model of reactionary risk management, whose role was to respond to problems only after they had occurred, is much less effective than proactively integrating risk management principles and techniques into institutional activities. The recognition that risk management is becoming an essential position or function within the institution is important. But even more important is that managing risk become an essential philosophy— at all levels of the institution.

REFERENCES AND RESOURCES

Publications

Head, George L., and Horn, Stephen II. *Essentials of Risk Management,* Third Edition, Volume 1. Insurance Institute of America, 1997.

Holinski, Edward. "The Future of Risk Management in Higher Education." *URMIA Journal* 1998.

Holinski, Edward M., and Demchak, D. Jean. "1999 Limits of Liability Report for Higher Education." *URMIA Journal* 1999.

Klinksiek, Glenn, Fowler, Patricia, Goldstein, Larry, and Demchak, Jean. "Risk Management in Higher Education: Meeting Expectations?" *URMIA Journal* 1997.

Madsen, Claudine, and Walker, John Walker. *Risk Management and Insurance: A Handbook of Fundamentals.* Washington, DC: National Association of College and University Business Officers, 1983.

Practical Risk Management—The Professional's Handbook. Lake Forest, CA: Advanced Risk Management Techniques, Inc. (ARMTech), 1998.

Report on the First Critical Issues Forum for Higher Education Risk Management. The Vermont Insurance Institute at Champlain College, 1997.

Sonenstein, Burton, and Kumin, Laura A. *Essentials of Risk Management.* Washington, DC: Association of Governing Boards of Universities and Colleges, 1998.

Associations

University Risk Management and Insurance Association (URMIA)
Two Wisconsin Circle, Suite 140, Chevy Chase, MD 20815
301-718-9711 . . . . http://www.urmia.org

National Association of College and University Business Officers (NACUBO)
2501 M Street, NW, Suite 400, Washington, DC 20037
202-861-2500 . . . . http://www.nacubo.org

Risk and Insurance Management Society
655 Third Avenue, New York, NY 10017
212-286-9364 . . . . http://www.rims.org

Periodicals

Business Insurance (weekly)
Risk Management (monthly)
URMIA Journal

Chapter 17

◆

Procurement

by

John F. Riley
Arizona State University

Sponsors

PEOPLESOFT, INC.
Contact: Karen Willett
4460 Hacienda Drive
Pleasanton, CA 94588
925-694-5453
www.peoplesoft.com

PeopleSoft delivers E-business solutions for higher education management needs, including student administration, grants management, finance, human resources, E-procurement, advancement, and more. PeopleSoft also provides comprehensive customer service, consulting, education, and technical support services.

HIGHERMARKETS, INC.
Contact: James Sparkman
1002A O'Reilly Avenue
San Francisco, CA 94117
415-561-4608
www.highermarkets.com

HigherMarkets, Inc. brings together higher education institutions and their suppliers. Our mission is to empower our users to communicate and conduct transactions more effectively with each other, focus on their core businesses and realize enormous cost savings.

Contents

Threcurement function is an integrated organization, under the direction of a single executive, embracing all activities dealing with the flow of goods and services into and out of an institution.

In the institutional setting, procurement typically includes purchasing, stores (warehousing, inventory management, and distribution), receiving, equipment inventory administration (property accounting), storage, and surplus property disposal. In practice, the function is called materials management, procurement, supply, and logistics, with private business, government, military, and nonprofit sectors each using their favorite terminology.

Whatever procurement is called is far less significant than the concept of a single organizational unit that controls the material flows into, within, and sometimes out of the institution. The unit should view this movement as a system, and resolve material flow concerns in an integrated, systematic way.

The key concept of procurement is that a single, integrated organization is responsible not only for buying products and services but also for receiving and coordinating the management, distribution, and disposal of materials. Concentrating procurement in one organization is the most effective way to control the total costs associated with the acquisition and use of goods and services and to maintain access to useful information about those costs.

This chapter introduces procurement in both theory and practice. First the concepts, objectives, and organization of procurement are discussed, and then each of the major components—purchasing, stores, receiving, equipment inventory administration, and surplus disposal—are discussed in detail. Finally, various infrastructure issues, environmental factors, and business affirmative actions are examined.

THE OBJECTIVES OF PROCUREMENT

The procurement department is a service department; its paramount objective is to provide value-added service to institutional customers. These customers comprise every person or department in the institutional community with an official need to acquire goods or services.

Serving the institution's diverse customer interests effectively can be difficult because of the conflicting nature of the services that are sometimes required. Those internal customers who need to acquire goods and services expect a procurement manager to assist them actively and cooperatively in acquiring what they need, when they need it. Those internal customers from the financial and business interests of the institution expect a materials manager to provide control over institutional resources and to ensure that the institution's materials management policies are enforced. Because these internal customer expectations are not always harmonious, a materials manager's job is challenging. One measure of a procurement department's success is how well it can balance the needs for service on the one hand and control of those services on the other.

Other objectives of procurement are:

- to provide an uninterrupted flow of goods and services to the institution at the lowest feasible overall cost;

- to develop reliable sources of supply, and to promote and maintain good supplier relations based on ethical business practices;

- to develop appropriate policies and procedures to ensure that materials management conforms to overall institutional and governmental policies, regulations, and laws, and that it functions effectively and consistently;

- to acquire the best "value" in the goods and services required—value being determined by a combination of factors, including quality, delivery, service, and contribution to the institution's goals and objectives—at a price that can be certified as reasonable;

- to control inventories of material and equipment, keeping to a minimum losses due to deterioration, obsolescence, and theft;

- to promote and maintain good internal customer relations, based on an effective balance of service and control; and

- to develop professional staff who are competent to serve the needs of each department and the institution.

Organization of Procurement

Reporting Relationship

The director of procurement should report to an official who has the stature and institutional role to assure that the materials manager–director is neither improperly restricted in scope nor impaired in ability to maintain control of the decisions involved in committing and protecting the financial resources of the institution. That official is typically the chief financial or business officer.

Centralized, Decentralized, Distributed

Centralized procurement exists when the authority and responsibility for accomplishing all materials-related functions (i.e., purchasing, receiving, stores, equipment inventory administration, storage, and surplus property disposal) are assigned to organizational units under the control of the director of materials management. Decentralized procurement exists when those functions are delegated to others throughout the institution or when they are accomplished by departments that are not under the materials manager's control. Distributed procurement exists when these functions are centrally controlled but physically distributed within the institution.

Few procurement functions are either 100 percent centralized or 100 percent decentralized. Even in industry, where the materials function is generally much more centralized than in higher education, complete centralization seldom exists. Rather, most institutional materials departments are hybrids, with certain authority and responsibility centralized in the administrative unit and the remainder assigned to operating units. With the advent of computer-assisted methods of acquiring, managing, and disseminating information, some procurement functions centrally control their resources that are distributed to primary customer areas. Thus, computer product buyers may be distributed to the institution's information technology department.

The precise degree of centralization, decentralization, or distribution that should exist in an institution cannot be determined by any standard formula or rule of thumb. An institution's objectives, culture, resources, and operating needs all play a part in determining what should be centralized, decentralized, or distributed. Further, transactions may be completely decentralized at some dollar level, as with the use of a corporate purchasing card for transactions under $1,000 or $2,000.

Most financial or business officers who are concerned with cost containment, internal control, efficiency, and consistency of policies and procedures favor the more controlled centralized and distributed models, rather than the less controlled decentralized model. This is especially true when the need for cost containment and control is evident, such as with purchasing or stores. The use of a centrally managed purchasing activity is recommended by the National Institute of Governmental Purchasing, the National Association of Purchasing Management, the American Bar Association through its Model Procurement Code, the National Institute for Municipal Law Officers through its Model Procurement Ordinance, and the National Association of State Purchasing Officials.[1] Four arguments support centralization.[2]

Specialization

People who must perform two distinctly different functions, such as where purchasing is an incidental function in an academic unit, often let the "lesser" function suffer. Procurement functions require professional staff who continually update their specialized knowledge to best serve the institution. The centralized and distributed models allow specialists to be employed and enable them to continually enhance their skills by practice.

Accountability

The centralized and distributed models enhance accountability. For example, who is responsible for the high cost of copy paper if every department buys it on its own? When purchasing authority is decentralized, it is difficult to assign accountability.

Institutional Viewpoint

Unlike personnel in operating units who, because of their position and responsibilities, usually seek what is best for their units, centrally managed materials management staff are motivated by what is best for the entire institution. They can combine requirements to reduce acquisition prices, and they can integrate functions to reduce operational and administrative costs. Policies and procedures are more consistently applied with a centralized or distributed staff than when materials management is decentralized.

Administrative Convenience

A centralized or distributed procurement can usually interact more effectively with other centrally controlled administrative functions and with outside constituencies, such as suppliers, governmental agencies, and auditors.

Arguments for decentralization can prevail, however, when the transactions involved can be executed without disadvantage to overall institutional objectives. Examples of such cases are: small dollar purchases, purchases compelled by emergency situations, the purchase of library materials delegated to the librarian, and the purchase of design and construction services delegated to an architectural and engineering group or capital projects department.

THE PURCHASING FUNCTION

The purchasing department serves internal customers by acquiring the appropriate products and services that meet quality requirements, in the correct quantity, for delivery at the correct time and place, from the correct source, with the appropriate after-sales service, at a reasonable price.[3]

If the purchasing department fails to meet any of these expectations, or if it fails to establish the appropriate balance among these expectations, it will fail to satisfy some of its many customers. The ability to meet these expectations consistently is not a simple matter.

The Purchasing Department's Functions

The purchasing department must perform many different functions. Some of them are:

- to acquire what campus customers need while assuring that the best value, in terms of price, quality, and service, is obtained;

- to establish sources among qualified suppliers by using the appropriate form of competition and negotiation, as permitted by the institution's policies;

- to administer public service programs, such as those designed to increase dollars spent with disadvantaged businesses or to increase purchases of recycled goods;

- to provide customers with information on new products and services, substitute materials, available alternatives, and price discounts;

- to assist campus customers in preparing appropriate quality specifications and requirements;

- to implement systems that reduce both prices and costs, such as blanket orders, systems contracts, consortium buying, and a variety of systems for handling small orders efficiently;

- to coordinate communications with vendors and act as the institution's contact with the marketplace;

- to ensure that purchase orders and contracts contain all necessary information and the appropriate terms and conditions needed to protect the customer and the institution;

- to coordinate and manage any decentralized purchasing delegations to personnel or units outside of materials management;

- to develop and encourage use of standard specifications for items used widely within the institution to facilitate quantity purchasing discounts, product interchangeability, improved maintenance and support, and reduction in inventory costs;

• to perform purchasing research and product testing to take advantage of market trends and short-term economic conditions, continually establish new sources of supply, perform value analysis, develop improved specifications, and qualify new products and services that are cost-effective; and

• to maintain adequate records and files so as to provide information on sources and products, goods and services usage, transactions for archival and audit purposes, and purchasing performance for management monitoring and control.

Specialized Procurement Functions

Because of the extreme diversity of higher education's needs for goods and services, a large number of specialized commitments are made and managed by the institution. Institutional management should analyze these commitments carefully and make conscious decisions regarding which departments should be responsible for them. Assignments should be based on the needs and circumstances of the institution and the capabilities of the departments that are available to handle them.

The procurement department could perform any of the transactions listed below. However, there are times when assignment of such responsibilities to other departments may be appropriate. In addition, some transactions may also require legal review. (See chapter 21, Legal Issues.)

Subcontracted research. The management of subcontracted research agreements is sometimes delegated to the sponsored programs office. (See chapter 18, Research and Sponsored Programs.)

Maintaining records of hazardous materials received and in use. The purchasing department commonly contracts for hazardous materials, but the safety or risk management office frequently administers usage records. (See chapter 14, Environmental Health and Safety.)

Ordering radioactive materials. For control reasons, ordering is often assigned to the radiation safety function, but the purchasing department is usually responsible for establishing appropriate contracts. (See chapter 14, Environmental Health and Safety.)

Buying design, engineering, construction, and remodeling services. This is sometimes assigned to the architectural and engineering unit or to the facilities planning and management department. (See chapter 13, Facilities Management.)

Contracting for insurance, banking, collection, and other financial services. Contracting for these services is frequently assigned to the insurance and risk management unit or the finance and accounting unit. (See chapter 5, Financial Reporting, chapter 6, Managerial Reporting, and chapter 16, Risk Management and Insurance.)

Contracting for audit and specialized financial consulting services. Contracting for these services is typically assigned to the chief financial or business officer or staff in the business office. (See chapter 1, The Role of the Chief Financial and Business Officer, and Chapter 22, Auditing.)

Contracting for travel and travel management services, including hotels and rental cars. Contracting for these services is typically assigned to a separate travel management function.

Purchasing chemicals and controlled substances, and maintaining licenses and related records. These tasks may be assigned to stores and/or pharmacy services.

Negotiating licensing for software, patented or copyrighted materials, and biological items, and licensing of the institution's name, logos, and emblems. These duties could be assigned to the contracts and grants office and the public affairs office, respectively. (See chapter 18, Research and Sponsored Programs.)

Contracting with performers and artists for concerts and exhibitions. Contracting for these services is frequently assigned to the department responsible for fine arts and public events functions. (See chapter 20, Auxiliary Enterprises and Other Services.)

Chartering transportation services, buses, boats, and aircraft. Chartering is typically assigned to transportation or fleet services. (See chapter 20, Auxiliary Enterprises and Other Services.)

Negotiating agreements for classified advertising. This is often assigned to personnel staff. (See chapter 12, Human Resources and Benefits Administration.)

Negotiating media contracts for coverage of educational, cultural, and sporting events. This could be assigned to the public affairs office, the cultural program office, or the intercollegiate athletics department.

Purchasing and leasing real property, and contracting with the public for use of the institution's facilities by others, including leases of space for advertising purposes. A separate property management department or the facilities management department could take over this function.

Organization of Purchasing

The purchasing department is a staff department within materials management, and the materials and purchasing departments should have the independence necessary to make decisions that favor the institution as a whole.

Work Assignment

It is possible to organize the assignment of work in a variety of ways. The specific method that is selected sets the tone for the internal organization of the department.

The two most common ways to organize a purchasing department are by customer department and by commodity. In the departmental orientation, groups of customer departments are assigned to buyers; in the commodity orientation, groups of commodities and services are assigned to buyers. Most purchasing departments in larger institutions use a commodity orientation, while many purchasing departments in smaller institutions are organized along departmental lines.

The decision of which method to use is important, because the one that is selected will have a pervasive effect on the department's efficiency, its effectiveness in meeting unique institutional goals, and the way it carries out its duties. In general, departmental orientation favors service, while commodity orientation favors efficiency. Because maintaining a proper balance of service and efficiency is essential, the chief financial or business officer should pay special attention to how purchasing is organized.

The commodity orientation emphasizes buyer specialization based on unique product knowledge, and it produces buyers who are expert in a relatively limited spectrum of products and vendors, are good technicians, and are effective at producing savings. This method is less client friendly than the departmental orientation because personnel requiring a wide range of goods and services may have to deal with many different buyers simultaneously. Departmental orientation, on the other hand, produces buyers who are highly loyal to their assigned customer departments, whose expertise and product knowledge are more general, and whose knowledge of customer department business and personnel is highly developed.

A variation that may offer the advantages of both the commodity and the departmental orientation is the distributed model, in which the centrally managed purchasing buyers are assigned specific commodities and physically located in the departments that are primary users of these commodities. Thus, buyers assigned laboratory products could be located in the laboratory science departments. This organization can be very effective at producing both the required customer service and the effectiveness in acquisition.

There are other variations of these orientations. In the "commodity manager" orientation, buyers are assigned to customer departments, but they become commodity experts (commodity managers) for the commodities most frequently needed by those departments. For example, the person who buys for the chemistry or biology departments naturally buys more chemicals and laboratory supplies than do other buyers and therefore becomes more expert in these commodities. That buyer is in an ideal position to develop institution-wide agreements for these items, and he or she can provide advice and assistance to other buyers who may be less expert in the chemical and laboratory supply areas.

In a "customer advocate" system, individual commodity-oriented buyers are also assigned to be primary contacts for groups of customer departments. Thus, although personnel in customer departments may have to deal with a number of different buyers to satisfy their different commodity needs, they know that there is a single individual who can represent their interests in a personalized way and who can give advice and assistance if questions or problems arise.

Signature Delegations

Authority to commit the institution to a contract should be delegated to all personnel involved in buying or approving purchases. The delegations should be in writing and should specify the kinds of acquisitions and the dollar limits that are authorized. The dollar limits are usually apportioned so that those who are qualified by training, experience, and level of position have appropriately higher authority to accomplish their greater responsibilities.

Costs and Benefits of Centralized Purchasing

With every procurement function, "value added" should be assessed. The value of the function should be in appropriate proportion to its cost or it should not be supported by the administration. Value can exist in traditional terms of savings and service, or it can exist when governmentally mandated processes are accomplished, such as observing required guidelines, terms, and conditions. Indeed, the existence of a properly functioning centralized purchasing department is usually considered by the federal government to be a prerequisite to receiving federally sponsored programs.

Purchasing authorities estimate that a centralized purchasing operation can achieve savings of 10 to 15 percent over a decentralized operation.[4] Centralized purchasing reduces duplication of effort and record keeping, allows consolidation of requirements through blanket and systems contracting, and promotes efficiency by assigning specialized purchasing tasks to specialists, where the buyers' specialized knowledge protects the institution from loss and liability.

When the purchasing function is centralized, its true costs are easily determined and controlled. On the other hand, when the function is decentralized, the costs are spread across the institution and are more easily ignored. Under a decentralized purchasing system, individuals can defend shopping around town to find "bargains." However, with this practice, the ignored salary and time lost costs usually exceed the cost of the item being purchased.

When the true costs of purchasing are known, cost/benefit analysis becomes possible. This is often done through savings reporting programs. The attempt to measure cost savings is often challenged by those to whom the data are submitted. Should a savings report measure the difference between the last price paid, the average of all bids, or what a department was about to pay before the purchasing department was contacted? Actually, purchasing professionals welcome the opportunity to measure the value added by the purchasing function. This would include avoiding the costs of protests and claims, misdeliveries, returns, improper invoices, and the like. But if it is difficult to measure costs actually incurred, it is even more difficult to measure costs avoided. Further, the purchasing department does not actually save money anyway. Under fund accounting, and especially in the public sector, any savings generated in one transaction is spent by the using department in another.[5] If savings will be reported, then the purchasing manager, the materials manager, and the chief financial or business officer should establish specific reporting ground rules in a collaborative manner and publish the rules with the savings reports.

Purchasing Policies and Procedures

Purchasing Policies

Purchasing policies should be published both formally in a policy manual and informally in a "how to" booklet for customer departments. Whenever flexibility is possible, purchasing policies should be developed in close collaboration with key administrative and academic personnel. Both the formal policy manual and the informal guides are often placed on a Web site for maximum accessibility.

The formal policy manual should clearly indicate that it has been approved by the chief financial or business officer. The policy manual should answer the following questions:

- What is the purchasing officer's authority to bind the institution, in terms of both dollar value and type of acquisition? Must the approval of others be obtained at a certain dollar threshold? Does the purchasing department acquire construction services, library books, or other categories of specialized goods or services?

- Which parts of the procurement process are to be performed by the purchasing department and which are to be performed by other departments? To what extent is the authority for source and price determination centralized, decentralized, distributed, or collaborative?

- What is the policy on unauthorized purchases, those purchases made by individuals who have no authority to do so? What sanctions apply to violators?

- Which products or services are not to be purchased with institutional funds without special authorization, or are not to be purchased at all?

- Does the institution allow purchasing personnel to make personal purchases for themselves or others in the name of the institution or using institutional time or resources?

- What processes are approved for the purposes of price reductions and cost avoidance, such as consortium purchasing, quick pay procedures, and limited value delegations for departments?

- What are the policies covering source selection, price determination, and competition? Under what circumstances is negotiation allowed? What is the threshold for formal competition? Under what circumstances are sole-source acquisitions or waivers to formal competition allowed?

- What ethical guidelines are purchasing department personnel expected to follow with respect to treatment of suppliers, acceptance of gifts, and conflict of interest? What ethical guidelines are customer department staff to follow?

- Can employees also be vendors? What are the labor relations and conflict of interest guidelines?

- Is reciprocal purchasing encouraged from firms or individuals who are donors to the institution?

- What federal and state laws affect institutional purchasing policies?

- What policies apply to contracting with small businesses, local businesses, or firms that are owned by disadvantaged persons, women, or disabled persons?

- What policies govern offshore purchases, use of import brokers, bonded warehouses, and similar entities?

- What processes are to be followed for handling vendor protests?

Purchasing Procedures

The procedures that are to be followed by the purchasing and customer departments should be detailed in a purchasing manual. Such a manual instructs and standardizes the activities of all involved in the procurement process. Appropriate parts of the procedures manual should be excerpted and expanded to serve as a buyer's desk reference. Purchasing procedures manuals should cover the following subjects.

Development of purchase requirements. How are requirements communicated to the purchasing department? What kind of requisition form is used? What supporting documentation is required? What methods of acquisition are available?

Order processing. What preaward processes are followed? What are the procedures for taking bids and negotiating?

Order award. How are source and price determinations made? What kind of order form and what terms and conditions apply?

Contract administration. What are the procedures for ensuring that vendors will perform? What are the alternatives if they do not?

Follow-up and delivery. What follow-up and expediting procedures are employed? What is done to enforce warranties? What are the invoice approval and payment procedures?

Records access and management. What procedures are in place to ensure that records are secure and that access is controlled?

Purchase Planning

Although it may represent the bulk of the purchasing department's work, unplanned purchasing is reactive and therefore relatively inefficient. Planned purchasing, in contrast, anticipates the requirement for goods and services, and contracts for them before they are needed. Planned purchasing is proactive and very efficient.

Every purchasing department must be able to react to last-minute purchase requisitions. At the same time, purchasing departments must attempt to convert as much purchasing as possible from unplanned to planned. This can be accomplished as managers perform the following activities.

Anticipate and Aggregate Repetitive Requirements in Standing Contracts

When prepriced requirements contracts are established by the purchasing department, customers can order against these agreements when goods and services are needed.

Analyze the Institution's Predictable Use of High-Volume Supplies

High-volume supplies that are regularly needed, such as copy paper, paper towels, restroom supplies, and bulbs, may be periodically delivered under drop-shipment contracts, which require human intervention only to stop or change programmed deliveries.

Make Use of Advance Project Information

Advance project information from the sponsored research office, research centers, and the capital programs office may be used to anticipate and get a head start on acquiring the complex goods and services that will be needed for research and new buildings.

Analyze the Typical Start-up Requirements

Analyze the typical start-up requirements for new semesters or quarters, or new faculty and staff, and provide blanket agreements that permit departments to order directly.

An excellent way to develop lists of goods and services for planned purchasing is to review historical records and identify the 20 percent of the purchases that typically account for 80 percent of the expenditures. Customized purchasing strategies can then be developed and implemented for each specific product or service.

The purchasing department should maintain a master purchasing calendar on which all planned purchasing activities are scheduled. This will ensure that agreements are rebid or extended on time and that there will be no interruption in the supply of goods or services.

Competition and Negotiation

Because competition is considered to be the single most effective determinant of reasonable price, competitive bidding is the preferred method of procurement at most institutions. Also, it is relatively easy to make an award decision on a lowest-price basis, compared to determinations that are based on other criteria. On the other hand, complicated competitive bidding procedures are very time-consuming and costly, compared with more flexible procedures that allow buyers to obtain quotations and negotiate prices that represent the best value to the institution. Award determinations that are based on considerations other than the lowest bid are often more appropriate when complex or highly technical goods or services are involved.

Typically, the requirement for formal competitive bidding is linked to the expected dollar value of transactions, with the more costly and formal competitive bidding procedures linked to transactions carrying higher dollar value. Operational, as opposed to political, considerations favor the establishment of the highest possible threshold for formal competitive bidding. The resulting flexibility allows experienced, professional buyers to put together transactions that feature the best combination of quality, price, and service. Unfortunately, some legislatures and governing bodies traditionally favor low thresholds, which put handcuffs on a professional purchasing staff, limit business affirmative action programs, and increase the time and cost of purchasing. On the positive side, low thresholds provide the appearance of good stewardship of the funds entrusted to institutional administrators by legislators and governing bodies.

Institutions that are not subject to external competitive bidding mandates are advised to select bidding policies that are both cost-effective and flexible. Ideally, and absent legislative barriers, institutions can promote cost-effectiveness by allowing expert staff maximum purchasing latitude.

Price and Cost-Reduction Strategies

The purchasing department needs to commit to the control and reduction of both the prices of goods and services, and of the administrative costs of acquiring these goods and services. Several common strategies that can attain those ends should be considered.

Small-Order Procedures

Small-order procedures shift the responsibility for making limited-value purchases from the professional buyers in the purchasing department to clerical personnel in the ordering department. Advocates for these programs argue that a relatively large number of transactions always account for a relatively small aggregate expenditure of institutional funds, and that the institution's investment in processing those orders should be in proportion to their value. Popular limits for these delegations are $1,000 per day, per vendor, with some institutions allowing significantly higher limits.

Automation of the Purchasing Function

Automation of the purchasing function increases efficiency and substitutes systems with moderate-to-high one-time costs for labor-intensive processes that have high recurring costs.

Supply and Logistics Systems

Supply and logistics systems substitute streamlined, specialized supplies distribution and management systems for conventional labor-intensive purchasing systems.

Blanket Orders, Systems Contracts, and Prime Vendor Agreements

Blanket orders, systems contracts, and prime vendor agreements enable the purchasing department to make one-time source and price determinations and then shift the repetitive ordering responsibility to the user departments.

Quick-Pay Procedures and Check-with-Order Systems

Quick-pay procedures maximize prompt-payment discounts earned; check-with-order systems earn cash discounts and reduce accounts payable costs.

Standing Order and Drop-Shipment Contracts

Standing order and drop-shipment contracts reduce prices through consolidation of volume and reduction of suppliers' costs.

Electronic Commerce

Electronic commerce reduces both prices and costs by providing Web-based ordering and transmittal of shipping documents and invoices, electronic interfaces to post encumbrance and expense data to financial management systems, electronic payment, and computer-to-computer inventory management. Electronic purchasing produces more complete data for both buyers and sellers, saves time, and enhances security.[6] In essence, customer department staff log on to electronic catalogs of suppliers competitively selected and click on the goods and services they wish to order. Such electronic stores can show the institution's discounted prices, and can be set to feature the items in the institution's stores before displaying the items available from the supplier. Electronic purchasing systems also provide E-mail notification of shipping dates and the status of any back orders to the ordering individual.

Purchasing Cards

Commercial purchasing cards function as credit cards for the supplier and as debit cards to the buyer. They offer a wide range of electronic controls, such as the ability to specify the types of suppliers at which the card is valid, the dollar limits for specific transactions, and the dates during which the card is valid. Coupled with an electronic interface to the institution's financial management system, purchasing cards can provide near real-time expenditure posting. Purchasing cards are increasingly used as the preferred method of payment for orders made through Web-based electronic catalogs. Internal automation of purchasing card processes can streamline account reallocation and statement reconciliation.

Consortium Purchasing

Consortium purchasing is one of the means available to colleges and universities to reduce product costs that is not frequently employed by the commercial sector. This technique recognizes that greater volume generally results in lower prices, which the consortium can attain by standardizing specifications of materials and ordering procedures to increase purchase volume. Consequently, group purchasing is a common practice among institutions of higher learning. Such groups can be composed of

- many campuses in a large university system;
- independent campuses within geographic regions or conferences;
- teaching hospitals;
- state universities and state agencies; and
- independent nationwide purchasing cooperatives, such as the Educational and Institutional Cooperative Service, Inc. (the E&I Co-op).

The E&I Co-op is the only nationwide buying cooperative that specifically serves higher education and university-related hospitals. The E&I Co-op shares quarters and common membership with the National Association of Educational Buyers (NAEB) and is considered NAEB's buying arm. The E&I Co-op is owned by its members, who buy $5 shares of stock and each year receive a share of the E&I

Co-op's after-cost earnings, called patronage refunds, in proportion to their participation. The E&I Co-op negotiates contracts for commonly used supplies, equipment, furniture, and services, combining the buying power of more than 1,500 colleges and universities and 240 health care institutions.

Make or Buy Decisions—Outsourcing

Many of an institution's needs for goods and services can be satisfied either by institutionally operated enterprises or by outside businesses. Decisions to "make or buy" involve judgments about which of the two alternatives can best satisfy a need. In the case of goods, for example, both institutionally and commercially operated machine shops can produce research apparatus. The institution can also "make or buy" services, such as debt collections, and the management of bookstores, food service programs, residence halls, and campus facilities. A make or buy decision determines which option conserves the institution's resources, strengthens its managerial and financial capabilities, and, above all, best contributes toward the attainment of institutional goals.

The need for a make or buy decision usually arises from a need for new goods or services or from unsatisfactory performance by an existing commercial or internal provider. Performance problems can involve quality, timeliness of service delivery, or cost, that is, the external operation is not producing the expected revenue, or the internal operation is failing to cover its operational and overhead costs.

The difficulty of a make or buy decision varies in proportion to the implementation costs and risks involved. Typically, the risk and cost are low when the institution already has the expertise and facilities necessary to provide the needed goods or services and the implementation is expected to be simple, as for example, when a small but unique electronic item is required by a researcher and an electronics shop exists within the institution. High-risk, high-cost situations occur in opposite cases, as for example, when the institution needs to establish a rapid transit system to move employees and students around campus and to and from remote neighborhoods and parking areas. In this example the equipment, supplies, and operational costs are high, liability exposure is significant, and experienced rapid transit operators probably do not exist on the institution's staff.

When a buy decision is made and implemented, the purchasing manager sometimes becomes the manager of the function, with the outside source providing the expertise, labor, and material. Thus, purchasing managers may have the same managerial interests toward outside providers of goods and services as other institutional executives have toward the in-house enterprises they manage. In cases where another official becomes the contract administrator, as for example, when a food service contract is managed by an auxiliary services official, the purchasing manager should provide specialized support and assistance. This is why purchasing and materials managers should always participate in make or buy decisions.

The arguments for performing services *in house* are numerous:

- The administration believes that an institutionally operated enterprise will be more effective and/or efficient than a commercial provider.

- Strong procurement and/or contract administration expertise does not exist within the institution.

- A competitive marketplace does not exist. Sometimes the need is so unique, such as a systems science visualization lab or a faculty development center, that no commercial source is available.

- The quality requirements may be so stringent that commercial sources cannot be depended on to meet them consistently.

- It is less costly to make than to buy.

- Buying would require abandoning an in-house enterprise, and the institution may wish to protect its skilled or long-term employees.

- Providing an in-house service with an associated income stream could subsidize another activity for which no resources exist.

- Union pressures prevent contracting out a function now performed in-house.

- Administrators feel that the institution will have more control over an in-house service than over an outside supplier who could avoid competition and thus profit to the institution's long-range detriment.

The arguments to *contract out* for services are also numerous:

- The administration believes that a commercial provider will be more effective and/or efficient than the institutionally operated enterprise.

- The institution lacks the needed staff and/or management expertise.

- A strong competitive marketplace exists to provide the goods or services.

- The institution is better able to concentrate on its own unique mission and leave entrepreneurial activities to the private sector.

- It may be less costly to buy than to make. Commercial providers may have advantages in terms of salary and benefit rates, personnel policies, lower overhead, and so on.

- If revenues are involved, there may be potential for a greater revenue stream if commercial firms are involved.

- The decision may turn on simple goodwill between an established supplier and the institution.

- Buying the service may benefit, and performing the service in-house may hurt, social service programs, such as business affirmative action.

- With institutions located in very small towns, "make" decisions can have adverse economic effects on the community, as they may put local firms out of business.

- It is often difficult to quantify the true costs of an in-house service and avoid subsidizing it to the detriment of other programs that compete for the same resources.

- The in-house service may result in unwanted income tax liability or regulatory problems.

Several states have laws that constrain public agencies, including state-related universities, from operating enterprises that compete with the private sector. These laws obviate many make or buy decisions. Even when such laws are not applicable, however, institutional competition with the private sector can still be a controversial issue. The political ramifications of potential "make" decisions should be factored into the decision-making process before any conclusions are reached. An objective framework for deciding how best to operate any function on campus is published by the National Association of College and University Business Officers (NACUBO).[7]

Contracting for Services

The typical college or university can contract for an extremely diverse range of services. Bookstore management, food services, residence hall management, facilities operations and maintenance, architectural and interior design services, campus safety and security services, personnel programs and management, transportation services, computer programming, computing facilities management, hazardous waste disposal, and many other managerial services can be provided by outside firms. Services are not only extremely diverse but also very difficult to buy. They are unlike goods in several ways:

- Services cannot be stocked; they must be performed in real time, exactly when needed.

- Services cannot be inspected before they are used. If they are not acceptable, it is too late to "exchange" them.

- Services have an intangible dimension that makes them hard to specify.

- The quality and reliability of services are often greatly dependent on human factors, including the personal expertise and the personalities of the providers, and the receptiveness of the recipients.

The goal of buying services is the same as buying materials and equipment: to buy the best value. The following framework for analyzing services may be used when making procurement plans.[8] Institutional differences within the following parameters will mandate different kinds of specifications and different procurement strategies.

Value of the service. Services should be classified in the same way that inventory is classified, under ABC analysis: The "A" services are the relatively few that have the widest institutional impact, the "C" services are the relatively many that have the least impact, and the "B" services are those in between. Attention should be given to the procurement process for each in proportion to its impact.

Degree of repetitiveness. Repetitive requirements demand special procurement processes and may justify provision of the services from within the institution.

Degree of tangibility. Services can be tangible (e.g., data entry services) or intangible (e.g., hospitality services). Intangible services are hard to specify; they are, therefore, hard to control if provided by outsiders.

Direction of the service. Services can be directed to people or to facilities. Services directed to people are similar to intangible services and are difficult to buy effectively.

Production of the service. Service production can be either labor or equipment-intensive.

Nature of the demand. Services may be required continuously, periodically, or on a one-time basis.

Nature of service delivery. The service can be performed on the institution's premises or on the provider's premises.

Degree of standardization. Services can be standard or customized.

Skills required. The delivery of services can require a range of provider skills, from simple to complex.

Recommended Framework

Here is a framework for contracting for services.

Define the need. The goal of this first step is to identify the desired service's characteristics and objectives and to develop performance specifications for the service that is required.

Evaluate service delivery options. A list of the various combinations of service delivery methods should be made. Institutional, governmental, or other constraints on either performing the service in-house or buying it outside should be evaluated. A make or buy decision should be made at this time.

Select a contractor. If the decision is to purchase the service, potential providers should be identified. Providers can be identified from advertisements in trade magazines, exhibits at professional association meetings, direct mail solicitation, referral from other institutions, and over the World Wide Web. A service budget should be developed, and potential providers should be prequalified to provide proposals. Requests for proposals should be developed, proposals should be accepted and evaluated, and a successful proposer should be identified.

Negotiate the contract. Through meetings with the initially successful proposer, the deal is optimized for both parties. Service specifications are finalized, appropriate terms and conditions are agreed on, and final price adjustments, if any, are negotiated.

Make a presentation and recommendation to management. A concise written report should be prepared, indicating the recommended award. This should be provided together with an oral presentation so that decision makers can have all the facts and details concerning the recommendation.

Award and administer the contract. Once the contract is awarded, responsibility for monitoring and evaluating performance must be assigned to an appropriate institutional unit. A good contract and a competent contract administrator are the keys to a successful relationship with a service provider. Authority must be assigned for working with the contractor's representatives to resolve problems, conduct financial reviews and audits, approve payments, and implement contract changes that may affect the price of performance. Authority should also be assigned for terminating the agreement for convenience or cause, if necessary, and for managing the contract closeout at the end of the performance period. If the unit that is assigned these responsibilities is not a materials management unit, the precise supporting role that materials management is to play in this process should be defined.

Buyers should keep in mind that services, especially those that are to be performed on the institution's property, usually involve liability issues, and special insurance may be required to protect the institution from loss. Concern about the obvious perils, such as might arise from the presence of supplier trucks on campus, from operating a campus bus service, or from the service of food or drink to the institution's students, calls for appropriate liability insurance. In the case of many personal services contracts, malpractice or errors-and-omissions insurance must be provided to protect against loss from special perils.

Leasing

Most equipment can be leased on a month-to-month or multiyear basis or on a lease-to-own basis. Lease terms are available from equipment manufacturers or dealers or through banks and leasing companies.

Although private businesses may enjoy corporate income tax advantages from leasing versus buying, those advantages are not a consideration for not-for-profit institutions. Not-for-profit institutions should consider leasing principally when the equipment will be required for a relatively short time and owning the asset would not be cost-effective, or the technology is rapidly changing and continual access to the latest technology is desired, or capital budgets are inadequate to purchase equipment but operating funds are available to cover the lease payments. Departments are usually willing to lease and even to pay a premium for the ability to build equity and acquire equipment over time, when the alternative is that the equipment could not be acquired at all.

Lease Versus Buy Analysis

Usually, but not always, leasing is more expensive than buying. An analysis of "lease versus buy" options can highlight the real costs of both alternatives. In principle, such an analysis defines the total costs of each method of acquisition. The lower cumulative cost defines the preferred method. In practice, however, the analysis can be complicated. Acquiring equipment by leasing or buying involves many costs other than the base price of the item. Lease versus buy analysis requires the identification of all of the costs and their evaluation in relation to the acquisition method involved. A lease versus buy analysis should examine the following questions.

♦

- Who bears the risk of loss during the lease period? What is the cost of insurance?

- Can the lease be easily converted to a purchase? What is the cost of doing so?

- What costs occur if the equipment becomes obsolete during the lease period and must be replaced?

- Are supplies or maintenance covered by the lease and what are the costs?

- What is the real cost of financing over the life of the lease? Is nontaxable financing possible?

- Is there a market for the leased equipment in the event that the original user does not wish to continue the lease or convert it to a purchase?

Internal Leases

It may be possible for departments that need equipment to lease it internally by borrowing funds from the institution's short-term investment pool and paying them back over several years. Even if this "loan" is interest bearing, the interest amount may be less than that charged by commercial leasing companies.

Some materials management departments maintain rental pools. These pools typically rent office machines, microscopes, and/or furniture to departments that have short-term needs for those items. Under appropriate circumstances, it might be possible for such a rental service to act as an internal leasing company and extend "rent-to-own" terms to departments.

Terms and Conditions of Purchase

In order to enforce the agreement, all purchases of goods exceeding $500 in value and services that cannot be performed within one year should be made in writing, either on a standard purchase order form or a custom-written contract. The "schedule" or "statement of work" of every contract or purchase order should clearly describe the goods or services to be provided, the required delivery date, the point at which risk of loss transfers from the seller to the buyer, the agreed-upon price, and the credit or payment terms.

A simple rule of thumb is that "standard" purchases using the institution's general funds may be made on a purchase order that has the normal terms and conditions. Standard purchases can be defined as purchases of off-the-shelf goods and catalog items, even if they are not stocked but must be manufactured to order. For all purchases that do not fit this definition, buyers would be better advised to

♦

identify the special problems that might develop during the purchasing process and then include special terms that address those problems in the contract.

Commercial transactions in the United States that involve goods, but not services, are covered by the Uniform Commercial Code, which comprehensively defines the rights and obligations of both the buyer and the seller. In actual practice, most low-value transactions are handled by telephone, fax, E-mail, and over the Web, and are successfully concluded without the benefit of written terms and conditions. However, this is not standard practice for higher-value or more complex transactions. Most sellers have terms and conditions of sale printed somewhere on their catalogs or quotation forms, and if the buyer does not assert superseding terms and conditions, the seller's might govern. But in case of a dispute between the buyer's and the seller's boilerplate, a court could strike both the seller's and the buyer's terms and could substitute the Code terms.

For those who wish to add standard terms and conditions to their purchase orders, the following kinds of provisions are appropriate:

- a "quality" article, which says that the goods or services shall be in strict compliance with specifications and describes corrective action to be taken, if necessary;

- a "changes" article, which specifies who can make changes to the scope of work, usually specifies that changes shall be made in writing, and covers the subject of payment for changes in scope;

- "termination" articles, which cover the buyer's rights to terminate the contract for its convenience and/or because of the seller's default;

- a "warranty" article, which specifies the express and implied warranty protection that the seller will provide to the buyer;

- an "insurance" article, which specifies the minimum coverage the seller must carry to protect the buyer and third parties from loss, such as that resulting from defective products, negligent or intentional acts of the seller, professional errors and omissions, and so forth;

- an "affirmative action" article, which requires the seller to comply with applicable nondiscrimination laws;

- an "interpretation" article, which specifies that the contract will be interpreted in accordance with the laws of the state in which the buyer is located;

- an "assignment" article, which specifies under what conditions the contract obligations may be assigned to others; and

- an "indemnity" article, which protects the institution against loss or cost due to acts or omissions of the supplier.

Purchases that use contract or grant funds require a completely different set of general terms and conditions, which are based on the specific requirements of the governmental agency whose funds are involved. Federal contracts also often contain special provisions that are to "flow down" to the institution's suppliers. Because these provisions cannot be preprinted, they must be inserted into the body of the contract as needed. Close cooperation between the purchasing department and the sponsored research office is required to ensure that all purchasing requirements of sponsoring agencies are enforced.

Finally, the institution's counsel should participate in the development of all terms and conditions to ensure that they appropriately protect the institution.

Purchasing at Small Institutions

According to purchasing professionals who specialize in smaller arenas, it is counterproductive to attempt to impose large-university policies, procedures, organizational features, and strategies on smaller operations.[9] Although the basic purchasing objectives and principles at both large and small institutions are the same, and the same knowledge and skills are needed, the scale, emphasis, and complexity can be very different.

Staff Size

Small institutions generally require the same wide variety of goods and services as large ones. However, at small colleges there are usually only one or two central purchasing people to handle the load, and often they are responsible for a variety of other administrative functions as well. The purchasing staff's specialty, then, is to be effective generalists. They must be very well trained in purchasing basics. They must identify the 20 percent of the purchasing job that has 80 percent of the impact, and concentrate on that 20 percent. They must have the diplomatic skills to persuade suppliers and user department personnel to help with the less critical 80 percent of the job for which they do not have time. They also must possess exceptional time-management skills. To compensate for a potential absence of strong administrative mandate, they must have the necessary political acumen and communications skills to motivate departments to cooperate and observe approved purchasing policies.

Scale of Expenditures

Small institutions obviously spend less than large ones, and this fact can be a disadvantage in terms of commanding the best prices and motivating suppliers to provide the best service. Although small colleges potentially have the most to gain from purchasing consortia, they typically do not have the resources to start their own, and the group purchasing programs that serve large institutions may not meet small institutions' needs. Their purchasing people must take extra care to negotiate the best possible annual agreements for their volume requirements and to make purchasing consortia work for them. Their top management also should support the use of these "approved" contracts.

Scale of Resources

Although no university administrators would admit to enjoying all the resources they need, the resource problem at small institutions can be exceptionally vexing. It not only makes it difficult to recruit and retain adequate numbers of administrative staff people, it can also preclude the acquisition of sophisticated automated systems; perversely, the very items that can help to make an institution less labor-intensive. Part of the solution lies in knowing how to take advantage, ethically, of suppliers' willingness to provide technical information and consultation in areas where they have special expertise.

Centralization and Delegation

Small institutions tend to be less centralized than large ones. This places greater authority in the hands of the faculty, academic departments, and service departments, and less in the central administration. Thus, it is difficult for "central" purchasing to be truly "centralized" or to enforce even minimal internal control. Without centralization, the challenge for administrators is to develop teamwork among departments, to accomplish necessary training through departmental people with whom they share procurement authority, and to maintain necessary internal control by encouraging cooperation and collaboration and by functioning visibly and authoritatively.

Public/Independent Considerations

Many small institutions are independent and therefore are not required to conform to public procurement codes. They are allowed the luxury of developing policies that are both simple and flexible and that can be tailored to their unique needs. Because purchasing responsibility at small institutions is typically less centralized than at larger, state-related universities, complying with even the most collaboratively developed procurement policies calls for exceptional flexibility, patience, and diplomatic skill.

Research Considerations

The programs of smaller institutions are generally not highly research-intensive and thus are relatively free from many of the complicated and costly procurement policies, procedures, and practices required by intense sponsored-research involvement at large institutions.

The foregoing observation is not intended to imply that materials and purchasing managers at smaller institutions can learn or borrow nothing from their colleagues at larger ones. In fact, the reverse is true: much information and help can be obtained from institutions that have more resources and larger, more specialized staffs. It does mean, however, that whatever is learned and acquired must be carefully adapted and scaled to fit the cultural and operational needs of the smaller institution. Otherwise it will not be effective.

To meet such challenges successfully and to function effectively in their unique environment, purchasing staff at small institutions must first thoroughly understand the institution's mission and purpose and their impact on the procurement process. They must be highly skilled in the basics and exceptionally creative and resourceful, to maximize the effect of their limited resources. They must be clever and quick to learn, compensating for their inability to develop a body of specialized commodity knowledge. They must possess effective interpersonal skills, especially those that are needed to persuade others to help them by assuming responsibility for parts of the procurement job. Finally, they must possess exceptional patience and diplomatic skills to function effectively in a very decentralized environment.

Despite its obvious challenges, being part of the procurement function in a small institution can be rewarding. At small institutions, there can be a much closer relationship between procurement activities and the institution's overall objectives, which can provide a unique sense of professional pride and contribution, as well as a broader personal and professional impact than may be possible in some larger university settings. If properly supported by management, purchasing at smaller institutions can offer a refreshing freedom from bureaucracy. The result is an ability to design flexible, effective policies and procedures, free from the kinds of influences that tend to complicate things at larger institutions.

THE STORES FUNCTION

Role and Functions

As with the purchasing function, the stores function's preeminent role is to provide service to campus customers. It can do this in many ways. The chief financial or business officer should define which methods of operation are most important to the overall objectives of the institution and, therefore, which should be pursued by the materials management staff with the most commitment and vigor.

For example, is the primary role of the stores function to provide quick and convenient service, or is it to provide low-cost, standardized products? Is it to reduce the administrative costs of providing consumable supplies? Is it to be in the "storage" business, maintaining deep stocks of repetitively used supplies, or is it to provide a low-inventory logistics service with major suppliers delivering supplies "just in time" for their redistribution to campus customers by stores personnel?

Stores in institutions located in major metropolitan areas may be minimal to nonexistent, depending on the private sector's ability to deliver directly, quickly, and effectively to user departments. In rural areas, stores may provide full services, to compensate for the commercial sector's inability to serve the institution's supply needs directly and quickly.

Value Added

As is the case with every materials management function, the stores function should add quantifiable value to the institution's supply process or it should not be supported. Potentially, stores can:

- minimize the institution's overall supply management costs;
- achieve high-quality, dependable service levels;
- develop stable, predictable, long-term, institution-wide supply support and distribution programs;
- provide consulting in supply management as well as a variety of automated supply management reports to campus departments;
- create a supply management and distribution process that is fiscally responsible and auditable; and
- keep records of hazardous materials provided to campus customers.

Every stores operation should have an approved business plan. It should also have policies that detail its goals and identify the strategies that it will pursue to reach them, and procedures that detail the conduct of its day-to-day business.

Policies and Procedures

Stores policies and procedures should address the following questions.

- To what extent is the stores operation expected to pay its own way? Should the stores function be 100 percent self-supported, paying all costs (including staff, office space, storage facilities, working capital, and all overhead and support expenses); or should it be subsidized by the institution in either overt or subtle ways? How much is the institution willing to subsidize the operation in recognition of the valuable cost-reduction services stores can provide?

- Who are the customers? Departments only? Students? Allied organizations? How do these customers pay for supplies purchased from stores? May stores sell for cash? If so, to whom and under what circumstances are cash sales allowed?

- Are campus customers required to use the stores function, or must stores compete with commercial businesses for the campus market? If use is mandatory, how is that policy enforced?

- May stores sell to customers outside the institution, such as hospitals, governmental entities, other colleges and universities, and private not-for-profit organizations? What are the unrelated income tax implications of off-campus sales? Are the effects tolerable?

- Does the stores operation supply a standardized product line or does it provide competing product lines? What is stocked? How are stocking decisions made? Is the warehouse open to customers or are only catalog sales made?

- How are goods priced for sale? What markup practices should be followed? What units of issue are sold? Does the stores function break cases and packs? Does it cut products, such as pipe and wire? Should a minimum dollar value be set for orders?

- What order entry methods will be provided? Paper requisition? Order entry by computer? Through an integrated financial management system? By telephone? By fax? By E-mail? Or over the Web?

- What kind of catalog will be provided? Loose-leaf or bound? Electronic? How will the catalog be kept up to date?

- Are back orders maintained when stores are out of stock? How are back orders tracked and controlled?

- Is the return of goods accepted? Under what circumstances? What are the refund policies?

- Will buying to replenish stock be done by the stores function or by the purchasing department? What reorder point and order quantity processes will be used to make reorder decisions?

- Do stores supply items that are not stocked? How are nonstock orders tracked and controlled?

- What inventory control processes are employed? What method of inventory valuation is used? How are the physical and book inventories reconciled? How is dead stock identified and controlled?

- How is stock located in the warehouse? What stock-numbering and location-numbering systems are employed? What order-filling processes are employed? What material-handling equipment is provided?

- How are orders packed and delivered? Do stores personnel or others perform the delivery function? Are will-call or walk-in services provided?

- What campus departments are permitted to operate storerooms? How are they operated and regulated? How do they relate to central stores?

- How are hazardous materials acquired, handled, issued, and disposed of by stores?

Organization

Ideally, the stores manager should be a peer of the purchasing manager, under the direction of the materials manager or equivalent official. Supply and logistics skills are as unique as purchasing skills, and the materials manager should make sure that experts occupy both positions.

The stores function can be self-contained, providing all of the infrastructure needed to assure the delivery of the administrative services for which it is responsible, or it can contract for those services from other institutional units. Examples include purchasing, accounts payable, receiving, and delivery services.

Facilities

All stores operations need some warehousing space, plus sufficient office space to house administrative and support personnel. The amount of warehouse space needed depends on a variety of considerations, including the breadth, depth, and kind of inventory that is to be held, how much "just-in-time" inventory procedures are employed, the configuration of the space, the storage efficiency that can be attained (i.e., the cubic volume that can be efficiently utilized and the density of shelf and rack storage that can be achieved), the number of stock turns that can be realized, and the service objectives (i.e., fill rate) that have been established. The cost to buy or rent the needed facilities must also be determined.

Fully equipped loading docks for both shipping and receiving, safe storage for high-pressure gas cylinders and chemicals, and secure storage for theft-sensitive or hazardous items should be provided. A user-friendly telephone system, including appropriate provisions for campus customers to enter orders by telephone, is a necessity; provisions for automating the entire stores process are essential. Material-handling equipment, including forklifts, pallet jacks, stock-picking carts, and delivery trucks should be provided.

Safety

A warehouse is a relatively hazardous place compared to the ordinary office environment. Stores management should make a special effort to provide the safety training and equipment necessary to protect employees and visitors from injury. Training should be provided in safe operation of vehicles and material-handling equipment, safe handling of chemicals and other hazardous stock items, safe lifting of heavy objects, and first aid skills. Safety equipment that should be provided includes safety shoes for warehouse and dock staff, safety glasses for those who cut stock, and a full complement of protective items for those who handle chemicals.

The institution's safety department should be requested to provide regular safety audits of the stores operation as well as advice to management and training to employees on the latest safety practices.

Finally, the stores should contribute to safe working conditions throughout the institution by processing material safety data sheets (MSDS) for the hazardous materials it distributes, in accordance with institutional policies. (For a full discussion of this subject, see chapter 14, Environmental Health and Safety.)

THE RECEIVING FUNCTION

Role and Functions

Like other materials management functions, the role of the receiving department is to provide service to campus customers. In this context, "service" can mean convenience (to departments ordering goods) or control (to the institution's business interests).

When designing the receiving department or assessing the value that it adds to the supplies acquisition process, it is important to understand the differences between receiving and receiving inspection.

Typically, the receiving functions are:

- to accept delivery of incoming parcels from common carriers and vendor trucks;

- to inspect for external signs of damage;

- to file, or assist in filing, damage claims;

- to sort received parcels and stage them for redelivery to appropriate campus destinations;

- to deliver parcels to campus customers, obtaining appropriate signatures on delivery to relieve the receiving department of accountability; and

- to pick up and ship outgoing parcels, or coordinate shipping, via common carriers.

The receiving inspection function is responsible for all of the receiving functions listed above. In addition, it is responsible for opening and inspecting the contents of incoming parcels for conformance with purchase order requirements and certifying receipt for the purpose of authorizing payment when conforming shipments are received. Receiving is a material forwarding function; receiving inspection is an integral part of the purchasing/accounts payable system.

In the institutional setting, because of the extremely wide range of goods received and the sometimes impossibly difficult task of performing quality and/or functional inspections on all of them, the "material forwarding" type of receiving function is typically provided. In the commercial sector, on the other hand, the "receiving inspection" type of function is almost exclusively employed.

Value Added

The receiving function, like any other materials management function, should add value to the supplies and equipment acquisition process, or it should not continue to be supported by the institution.

The advantages of centralized receiving over a decentralized function involve economies of scale and the elimination of "hidden" costs; the elimination of many accounts payable problems; and the reduction of losses resulting from mishandling of shipments and damage claims by inexperienced personnel. Keeping delivery vehicles off campus is another benefit. In the case of campuses that are congested or that have inadequate loading docks, centralized receiving adds value by reducing the traffic impact of carriers and vendor trucks on campus. For institutions that are under community mandates to reduce traffic to and from campus, an off-campus receiving department may be very valuable.

On the other hand, if the receiving function is of the "material forwarding" variety, it is not unusual to find situations in which it deducts value, instead of adding it. For example, overnight or priority parcels can actually be delayed by processing. In these cases, because delay has a negative customer service value, the institution would do better to require rapid delivery services to deliver directly to addressees and bypass central receiving.

The cost of central receiving in terms of personnel, material handling equipment, and facilities can be high. The cost of receiving inspection, because its processes are more complicated and labor-intensive, can be much higher. In both cases, the chief financial or business officer should make sure that the benefits are in proportion to the costs.

Policies and Procedures

Receiving policies should address the following questions:

- Is a receiving or receiving inspection function provided?

- Does receiving also handle outgoing shipments? Does receiving provide a packing service or are packing supplies carried for customer use?

- What processes are employed to identify poorly addressed packages? How are packages that cannot be identified disposed of?

- What security practices are followed to protect received goods? What processes are employed to transfer accountability to customers for delivered items?

- Does the receiving department accept or reject liability for parcels that are received but that mysteriously disappear or become damaged before they are delivered to their ultimate destinations? What resources are available to compensate for such losses?

- What control processes are employed when hazardous materials are received?

THE EQUIPMENT INVENTORY ADMINISTRATION FUNCTION

Role and Functions

The role of equipment inventory administration is to provide service to campus departments by helping them account for and manage their property. It serves the institution's business interests by establishing and maintaining administrative accountability over the property that is under institutional control. Because physical control of equipment is decentralized among campus departments, each department has actual fiscal accountability.

At some institutions, the equipment inventory administration activity is primarily an accounting function and, therefore, is part of the accounting department. At other institutions it is more appropriately assigned to the materials management department. Where the latter is the case, the equipment inventory administrator should be a peer of the purchasing and stores managers, reporting to the materials manager.

The equipment inventory administration function should help campus departments effectively manage and account for their property, establish administrative control over equipment inventories, help establish a climate of responsibility for preserving the institution's assets, and interact with outside auditors and governmental agencies concerning equipment inventory matters.

Equipment inventory administration typically:

- maintains the official equipment records to reflect the addition of new equipment, modifications of equipment, and changes in its location, condition, and custodianship, removing equipment records as appropriate;

- supervises equipment management activities of campus departments ("custodial" departments), including recording and certifying the correctness of periodic physical inventories, modifying or moving equipment, and disposing of equipment; and

- accomplishes all of the federally required property management activities prescribed by applicable Office of Management and Budget (OMB) circulars and contract and grant requirements, maintaining all necessary government property records, and interacting with government property representatives and auditors.

Policies and Procedures

The equipment inventory administration function's policies and procedures should address the following questions:

- What is the official definition of "equipment" (e.g., "movable property with a useful life of at least two years and an acquisition cost of at least $1,000")?

- What property other than that which meets the equipment definition is recorded and controlled on an exception basis (e.g., theft-sensitive items costing less than the equipment definition amount, very expensive items that have a useful life shorter than the equipment definition useful life)?

- What are appropriate reasons for removing equipment from the property records (e.g., sale, theft, use for parts)?

- What are appropriate reasons for transferring equipment to individuals outside the institution (e.g., transfer to another institution when research projects are transferred, donate to another institution when not cost-effective to sell)?

- How frequently are property custodians required to take physical inventories? What sanctions apply if they do not? What assistance does the equipment inventory administration function provide?

- How frequently, and on what sampling basis, is the equipment inventory administration function required to take physical inventory? What pass/fail ground rules apply? What sanctions apply to departments that do not pass?

- How are property numbers assigned? Who is responsible for applying property tags to equipment?

- How does the equipment inventory administration function interact with other administrative departments, such as purchasing and accounting?

THE SURPLUS PROPERTY DISPOSAL FUNCTION

Role and Functions

The primary roles of the surplus property disposal function are to recycle excess property within the institution and to sell surplus property to private buyers, both on and off campus. In this sense, the surplus property disposal function is really an investment recovery function, providing a valuable service to operating departments and the central administration. An important secondary role is the internal control service the surplus property disposal function can provide by acting as the final link in the institution's property management chain. This is a role that symbolizes the institution's concern for preservation of assets and that emphasizes the need for stewardship and accountability on the part of all equipment custodians.

One of the best ways the surplus property disposal function can help recover the value of an asset that is no longer needed by its original institutional "owner" is to help locate another institutional unit that can reuse the item. Failing this, the surplus property disposal function recovers investment from property that is not needed by any institutional unit by selling it.

The objectives of the surplus property disposal function are:

- to minimize the costs of the property disposal function and maximize the proceeds returned to departments;

- to minimize the loss of surplus assets through misappropriation or improper disposal;

- to preserve the value of excess and surplus property through proper protection and storage;

- to maximize the return on scrap by proper sorting and marketing; and

- to maximize the amount of material entering the program through good marketing and maintenance of good customer relations.

The surplus property disposal function accomplishes these objectives by running a businesslike operation that performs the following tasks:

- picking up excess items from campus departments;

- establishing the potential sales value of items in collaboration with campus departments;

- advertising the availability of items to other campus departments for reuse;

- warehousing items for marketing to potential purchasers;

- selling items to individual and commercial buyers in such a way that return is maximized;

- crediting returns to releasing departments or to the institution's general fund, less commission to defray operating costs, as required by institutional policies; and

- coordinating with the equipment inventory administration function to delete sold equipment from the property records.

Policies and Procedures

The policies and procedures of the surplus property disposal function should address the following questions:

- What official is authorized to declare property excess to an individual department's needs? What official is authorized to declare property surplus to the institution's needs?

- What unit is authorized to dispose of surplus property? If only the surplus property disposal function has this authorization, what is the institution's reaction toward departments that dispose of their property without authorization?

- What is the institution's policy on full use of institutional assets? What incentives does the institution provide to encourage transfer of excess items within the institution?

- What is the institution's position on restricting free campus space for the storage of excess and surplus items so that there is an incentive to dispose of surplus property?

- To what extent is the surplus property disposal function self-supporting? What is the disposition of the proceeds of surplus sales? If a commission is retained by the surplus property disposal function for partial or full recovery of costs, is the remainder credited to departments releasing items or to the institution's general fund?

- What disposal methods are employed? Under what circumstances are formal or informal bids taken? Under what circumstances are prepricing, negotiation, and auctions used?

- How long are items retained for sale? What disposition is made of items that do not sell? Can unsold items be donated to charitable organizations?

Only part of the surplus property disposal function is economic, to pay its own way and/or return sales proceeds to campus customers or to the general fund. Another important part is symbolic. It reinforces the idea that items that are no longer needed have value, that the administration wants those items to be cared for appropriately, and that unauthorized disposal of them may be treated as theft. A common mistake is to overlook the symbolic role and instead treat the surplus property disposal function as a "business" that is expected to cover all of its costs and return a portion of the proceeds to departments or to the general fund. Such thinking ignores the fact that a surplus property disposal warehouse is, in reality, a junk store and that junk stores are only marginally profitable, even in the private sector, where costs can be minimized and controlled more effectively than in the institutional setting. Failure to recognize this can put a surplus property disposal operation out of business, and can prove detrimental to the institution in the long run.

INFRASTRUCTURE ISSUES FOR PROCUREMENT

Staffing and Professional Development

Purchasing and materials management employees should be specialists in purchasing, logistics, and distribution principles and practices. Aside from having appropriate analytical, judgmental, intellectual, human relations, negotiating, and self-management skills, all materials management professional and managerial personnel should know and understand:

- the overall procurement, supply management, and distribution process;
- ethical principles that apply to the purchasing and materials management function;
- commercial markets and how they function;
- business and trade practices, including their effect on manufacturing, distribution, and pricing; and
- the electronic systems that facilitate materials management functions.

Members of the materials management staff must understand and be able to work effectively within the culture that makes colleges and universities different from private commercial businesses.

Purchasing Department

The purchasing department's professional and management staff should know and understand:

- principles and practices of economics as they apply to markets and pricing;
- characteristics and practices of the major marketplaces;
- principles of contract and agency law, including the Uniform Commercial Code, and their effects on institutional procurement;
- traditional, nontraditional, and state-of-the-art purchasing methods, including how and when they should be used;
- how to establish and maintain good customer and vendor relations;

- traditional internal control principles that apply to the procurement function;

- automated systems that are most effective in improving the quality and efficiency of the procurement function;

- government requirements that affect hazardous materials acquisition, use, disposal, and safety requirements (as they relate to equipment and supplies);

- government requirements that affect purchasing and subcontracting under federal grants and contracts (e.g., Federal Acquisition Regulations, OMB circulars that pertain to purchasing and property control functions, Executive Orders, and guidelines that affect business affirmative action and subcontracting plans);

- government requirements that affect business and employment affirmative action;

- customs regulations that affect the import and export of goods used for educational or research purposes;

- the international monetary system, including exchange rates, and principles and practices of offshore procurement; and

- traffic and transportation regulations that affect the cost of shipping goods from suppliers to the institution.

Equipment Inventory Administration

The equipment inventory administration function's professional and management staff should know and understand:

- the general principles and generally accepted practices of property administration;

- government requirements, including OMB circulars that pertain to property control practices;

- automated systems that are most effective in improving the quality and efficiency of the equipment inventory function;

- principles and practices of surplus property disposal;

- used property markets and how to maintain good relations with buyers; and

- how to establish and maintain good customer relations.

Stores Department

The stores function's professional staff should know and understand:

- principles and practices of supply, logistics, and distribution;

- principles and practices of inventory and warehouse management;

- principles and practices of economics as they apply to coverage of fixed and variable costs;

- principles and practices of cost (as opposed to fund) accounting;

- automated systems that are most effective in improving the quality and efficiency of the supply and distribution function; and

- how to establish and maintain good customer relations.

Participation in Professional Associations

College and university procurement and purchasing personnel should be encouraged to join and be active in the National Association of Educational Buyers (NAEB), the premier professional association serving the needs of educational purchasers.

NAEB promotes the use of effective purchasing and purchasing management techniques among its members, which include purchasing and materials management professionals at over 1,700 institutions. NAEB provides specialized technical information, workshops and seminars, regional and national meetings to facilitate professional development and networking, a monthly bulletin featuring news and professional development articles, a quarterly journal, and an E-mail list to more than 2,000 purchasing managers.

With the National Association of Purchasing Management (NAPM), NAEB cosponsors the Accredited Purchasing Practitioner (A.P.P.) and Certified Purchasing Manager (C.P.M.) programs and actively encourages its members to become certified. NAEB also conducts benchmarking activities and disseminates this information to its members.

Other professional associations of interest to materials management professionals are listed at the end of this chapter.

Professional Development Through Formal Education, Seminars, and Conferences

Many valuable seminars and courses are presented by professional associations, extension schools, and private trainers. These are useful not only for the job-related knowledge and skills they teach but also for preparing participants for the certification exams and for the promotional opportunities they present. Some extension schools offer certificates in purchasing and materials management subjects. Because of rapidly changing technology, purchasing personnel must stay up-to-date by attending continuing education programs.

Certification

In 1974, NAPM established the C.P.M. program as a professional designation that signifies that the holder is capable of performing at a professional level of competence. Since then, many other professional purchasing and materials-oriented organizations have endorsed the C.P.M. program; as of 1999, over 32,000 individuals had been certified.

The C.P.M. program embodies a step-by-step training process that prepares the candidate to pass four test modules. The first three modules address specific areas of purchasing knowledge, while the fourth module, which is changed and updated periodically to reflect changes in the "state of the art," covers the need for continuing education. There are also minimum experience and education requirements, and recertification is required every five years.

Although the C.P.M. designation is not a job-related requirement in the same sense that, for example, certain professional engineering licenses may be, the C.P.M. designation does demonstrate that the possessor has the knowledge and motivation necessary to function at a professional level. For that reason, it is an appropriate qualification to be sought when recruiting new purchasing buyers and managers.

The Accredited Purchasing Practitioner (A.P.P.) designation is for entry level buyers who are primarily engaged in the tactical and operations side of purchasing, and for persons who work outside of the institution's purchasing department but who have definite purchasing responsibilities. Applicants must pass two modules of the C.P.M. exam and meet minimum experience and education requirements.

Automation

Considering all the hardware and software that is available commercially, there is little reason for any materials department not to be computerized. Software packages for purchasing, stores, and property administration that have a wide variety of flexible features can be purchased from a large number of sources and can be used as is or modified to incorporate unique needs. Additionally, many institutions have integrated financial management systems that have many materials management functions.

The Purchasing Department

Purchasing systems should be well integrated with using departments, accounting and accounts payable, and receiving. Fully integrated systems allow electronic transmission of purchase requirements from users to the purchasing department, provide for conduct of solicitations, and generate the resultant purchase orders or electronic commerce orders. They also provide for recording receipts of goods and invoices, making the match necessary to approve payment, and writing checks. Typical systems also provide a wide variety of reports for customer information, vendor evaluation, productivity measurement, and management control.

The Stores Operation

To assure that the stores operation remains cost-effective, the most current automated processes should be employed. These include:

- Web-based or electronic catalogs and automated order entry systems featuring customer order entry by computer, with bar code input capability;

- automated inventory control systems, including bar code input features;

- automated administrative processes, such as purchasing, receiving, and accounting, including bar code input features wherever feasible;

- a full range of management information and control reports for use by stores and administrative management;

- a full range of supplies usage and budgetary control reports for use by customers; and

- computerized purchasing systems for stock replenishment, including electronic commerce orders to stores' suppliers.

The potential for cost reduction by employing automated material-handling processes should not be ignored. Examples are automated conveyors, computer-operated picking carts, computer-controlled carousels for picking small parts, and computerized shipment sorting and delivery manifest systems.

The Receiving Department

Automation can help receiving become more efficient. For example, if receiving is linked with the purchasing/accounts receivable system, the transmittal of hard-copy purchase orders to receiving might be unnecessary. Automation can also help receiving personnel arrange parcels in delivery-route order and make manifest documents for delivery workers to use to obtain signatures that transfer accountability of delivered parcels to departments.

Equipment Inventory

Equipment inventory records must provide for quick retrieval of a wide variety of data and quick production of a wide variety of reports in a flexible manner and at a reasonable cost. Automated records are the only ones that can fully meet these needs.

The best systems feature bar code–readable property tags and bar coded room tags. These characteristics allow physical inventories to be taken quickly and inexpensively with hand-held scanner/microprocessors. Software is also available that automatically compares physical inventory with book inventory, printing exception reports that highlight equipment that is missing or is not in the previous location.

Electronic Commerce

Electronic commerce (E-commerce) may be defined as the business-to-business exchange of information over a computer network, usually the World Wide Web. By 2003, E-commerce will encompass 10 percent, some $1.3 trillion, of total business-to-business spending, and the sales of electronic commerce software applications will exceed $2 billion.[10] The primary applications in electronic commerce are procurement and payment.

Electronic commerce as a stand alone system facilitates identifying potential sources of goods and services, conducting solicitations, and transmitting orders. When integrated to the institution's financial management system, an E-commerce system can provide for concept and funding approvals, encumbering funds, sending E-mail status reports to ordering departments, posting expenses to the applicable accounting line in the responsible fund, and electronic payments.

The role of purchasing in E-commerce is to conduct solicitations that lead to prepriced systems contracts with electronic commerce capable suppliers. The electronic catalogs of these contracted suppliers are placed in the E-commerce system. As pricing and other terms have already been negotiated, department staff are free to order from these catalogs without further need for competition, or assistance from either purchasing or accounts payable.

Facsimile (Fax) and Electronic Mail (E-mail) Transmission

The main controversy surrounding fax and E-mail transmission involves its appropriateness for documents that have legal implications, such as bids and purchase commitments. If there is concern about direct reception of bids or transmittal of purchase orders via electronic transmission, the safest course of action is to require confirmation by mail, with original signatures, of all offers and acceptances that exceed the institution's threshold for formal competitive bids. From a practical standpoint, there are few purchasing transactions that require legal enforcement, and a viable strategy may be to assume that such transactions are as valid as if they were made on original signed documents.

The other concern about electronic transmission involves maintaining the confidentiality of faxed bids and proposals until the date and time set for public opening. Electronic lockbox software now allows for secure receipt of such bids and proposals until the established date and time for opening these responses.

Ethics

All professional associations have codes of ethics to establish values and norms concerning the appropriateness of certain actions. The special issues covered by purchasing codes of ethics are all based on three concepts: impartiality, honesty, and loyalty.

- *Impartiality.* Purchasing personnel are expected to play no favorites, to treat all suppliers equally, and not to discriminate for things other than value and the merits of each transaction.

- *Honesty.* Purchasing personnel are expected to tell the truth to suppliers and not to mislead suppliers in hopes of getting a better deal; they should play fair at all times.

- *Loyalty.* Purchasing personnel are expected to be loyal to their employer, keeping their business and personal lives separate and free of conflicts of interest.

Buyers and Ethics

There are several important reasons that buyers should be concerned with ethics. One has to do with protecting sources of supply. The buyer's job is to acquire goods and services at prices and terms that are favorable to the employer. To be able to do this consistently, buyers need to establish healthy long-term relationships with suppliers. Such relationships result from treating suppliers ethically. Unethical treatment drives suppliers away or motivates them to retaliate for being mistreated.

Another important reason has to do with the proper uses of power. Buyers must carefully use their purchasing power. They have the ability to reward or punish suppliers by the way in which they spend their employers' money. They can reward by giving orders, by not being a "tough" negotiator, or by freely granting concessions. They can punish by withholding orders or by abusing suppliers in a variety of ways. Strictly observing ethical guidelines helps buyers guard against abusing their power.

Buyers are agents, and the law requires them to observe higher principles of conduct than ordinary employees. These are called "fiduciary duties." Among them are duties that have ethical ramifications. These include the duty of loyalty, the duty of accountability, the duty to inform, the duty of confidentiality, and the duty to avoid negligent action.

Professional buyers are anxious to protect their employer and their profession from unfavorable publicity. They know that the "bad press" that results when they do not act ethically can be very damaging to professional and corporate reputations and can lead to additional laws and governmental control.

General Principles

In general, buyers should avoid accepting gifts or favors of any kind from suppliers. They should also avoid intentionally misleading a supplier in any way. Buyers should avoid playing favorites among suppliers or treating one supplier differently from another in a competitive situation. They should keep their business and personal lives entirely separate, avoiding conflicts of interest. And they should always avoid intentionally mistreating suppliers in any way.

Different professional purchasing associations have endorsed different but generically similar codes of ethics. NAEB actively works with its members to encourage the development of a strong sense of professional ethics. This helps protect them, their institutions, and the purchasing profession's reputation in the business community. The code advocated by NAEB is included at the end of this chapter. It is annotated to assist readers in understanding the meaning of the individual tenets. Materials and purchasing managers should be encouraged to hold instructional sessions for buyers, both central and departmental, on a regular basis, to assure that they thoroughly understand the code's meaning and to make it clear that they are expected to observe its guidance.

Customer Relations

The customers of procurement are those throughout the institution who use materials management's services. Good customer relations pay off in a variety of ways, including reducing unauthorized purchases, minimizing complaints, and improving the overall effectiveness and efficiency of the procurement process. Techniques that should be used by materials management departments to improve customer relations are:

- viewing each customer contact as an opportunity to obtain feedback on the purchasing department's performance;

- publishing an informative policy and procedures manual, in nonbureaucratic language, preferably on the World Wide Web, designed to inform user departments how to get the most out of the materials management function;

- publishing an informative newsletter, with a copy on the Web, designed to communicate timely procurement information of interest to campus departments;

- establishing a formal customer service visit program that requires key materials management employees to visit user departments on a regular basis to review purchasing performance and discuss future projects that involve purchasing activities;

- implementing procedures that allow materials managers to provide user departments with frequent information on the status of work in process;

- establishing training programs in materials management policies and procedures for user departments, with emphasis on how they can interact with materials management more effectively;

- involving using departments in the collaborative formulation of policies and procedures that will affect them;

- publishing a directory of materials management personnel regularly, again preferably on the Web, with a summary of their duties and their telephone numbers;

- establishing a point of contact, such as a materials management "hotline," that using department personnel can call to ask questions and express concerns; and

- conducting formal surveys.

Vendor Relations

The establishment and maintenance of good vendor relations is a major responsibility of every procurement department. Good vendor relations assure that there will always be a broad range of suppliers who are willing to compete for the institution's business and who are consistently motivated to provide reasonable prices and excellent service. Techniques that should be used by materials management departments to improve vendor relations include:

- employing scrupulous ethical business practices in all dealings with suppliers;

- publishing a vendor information pamphlet or other printed material to assist suppliers in interacting effectively with the institution, preferably on the Web;

- making it easy for suppliers to access buyers, by establishing convenient interviewing hours, providing convenient parking, and training buyers in effective vendor interviewing techniques;

- providing suppliers with "sales leads" and an opportunity to demonstrate their products to using departments;

- providing fair and objective third party review of disputed issues; and

- ensuring prompt payment of invoices.

Evaluation of the Procurement Function

The procurement function is difficult to evaluate because it is more a professional than a vocational activity and many of the measurements and judgments required are qualitative rather than quantitative. Nevertheless, the function must be evaluated. There are seven points on which evaluation is possible.[11]

Analysis of Quantitative Factors

Workload and productivity can be measured. Measurements to reveal the timeliness of processes, savings, shipment rejection rate, and inventory investment are all possible. Collected regularly, such measurements permit comparisons to be made over time to track performance improvement or degradation in the materials management department.

Financial and business officers should understand, however, the pitfalls in attempting to make statistical comparisons among different institutions' materials management functions. Because of differences in the nature of the institutions, the departments' organizational structure, the policies and procedures followed, and the kinds of services rendered, these comparisons are seldom very productive.

Qualitative Comparison with User Expectations

Realistically or not, users expect a certain level of service from materials management. Measurements of how well materials management is meeting their expectations, although necessarily subjective, are important in the overall evaluation of the function. Satisfaction can be measured in a variety of ways by tracking complaints and commendations, by interviewing department personnel, and by taking periodic written customer surveys.

Audit

The findings and recommendations from both internal and external audits provide potentially valuable information about the extent to which materials management is following the institution's policies and procedures.

Objectives and Results

Management by objectives systems work by setting performance goals and measuring how well they are accomplished. Such systems can be either formal or informal, but they should be as simple and practical as possible.

Vendor Performance

How well vendors perform can be a measure of how well materials management is doing its job. Certainly materials management cannot guarantee that vendors will always deliver on time or always deliver conforming products or services, but there is a direct correlation between effective vendor selection and management and good vendor performance.

Peer Review

Evaluation of the materials management function by one or more practitioners from other institutions can be a very effective and relatively inexpensive way to get a quick estimate of the function's strengths and weaknesses. Outside evaluators can be objective observers and, if they are carefully chosen for their professional abilities, their work will be highly credible.

Self-Evaluation

Self-evaluation can be as effective as other techniques if the process is appropriately structured and disciplined.

Based on a research study conducted by the Center for Advanced Purchasing Studies, the following rules should be considered when constructing metrics of the procurement function.[12]

Rule 1: The measurement should follow what the organization itself values: If an institution is focused strictly on financial measures, it is counterproductive to measure relationships or behaviors.

Rule 2: The measurement should be compatible with those in other functional areas. For example, if a goal is to reduce the number of suppliers, does that conflict with a goal of increasing business placed with disadvantaged suppliers?

Rule 3: Do not measure for the sake of measuring. Measurements should be constructed with the intent to improve the area or activity being measured.

Rule 4: Be willing to work to find the best metric rather than settle for the easy things to measure.

Rule 5: Trends are more important than targets.

In 1993 and again in 1997, the National Association of Educational Buyers (NAEB), in cooperation with the Center for Advanced Purchasing Studies, conducted a benchmarking survey of more than 50 member institutions. This initiative compared traditional quantitative measures with the results of a customer satisfaction survey.[13] To identify best practices at the institutions with the highest customer satisfaction ratings, the NAEB conducted a two-day site visit to each of the top 10 institutions.[14] These institutions possessed the following characteristics:

- *Accessibility:* Customers said they like materials management because they could always get in touch with someone who helped them.

- *Automation:* The best systems provided for direct-to-vendor ordering of contract items and allowed customers to see the status of their orders.

- *By-pass mechanisms:* The best materials management programs recognized that buyers should only be engaged in value-added work, and accordingly provided a number of by-pass mechanisms for customers to make their own small-dollar purchases.

- *Feedback:* The best materials management programs sought customer feedback at every opportunity.

- *Teams.* The best acted as if the whole department was a single team.

- *Training.* The best trained customers on how to effectively interact with materials management, and trained materials management staff on how to provide customer service.

OTHER PROCUREMENT ISSUES

Environmental Factors

A large part of environmental management involves what is bought and how it is disposed of. Therefore, the materials management community must be especially sensitive to environmental issues and aware of environmentally sound purchasing practices. This is especially true in the institutional sector, where the public trust is open to scrutiny.

Procurement personnel should be well-informed about their institution's environmental impacts and should understand their own role in helping to minimize them. Even if buyers are not principally responsible for the management of environmental programs, they must understand them or they will not be able to provide appropriate support to those who are responsible. The typical areas for procurement involvement in environmental issues follow.

General Workplace Hazards

Although institutions of higher education are perceived by most people to be safe places to work, countless dangers lurk in research materials; in the paints, solvents, and cleaning supplies that were considered benign in the past; and in the office environments in which employees' eyes, backs, and hands can be injured by improper ergonomic design. Harmful materials could be anywhere, furniture and furnishings are required to be treated for fire resistance, and even carpet, drapes, and upholstery can emit harmful fumes. Procurement employees should have a general knowledge of these hazards and should be able to identify sources of the clothing, supplies, equipment, and services necessary to abate them.

Solid Waste

As the problems of landfill capacity, depletion of natural resources, and pollution become more severe, materials management must become increasingly involved in programs that encourage buying goods that have a longer life, that are biodegradable, that have less packaging to discard, that are reusable, that are made from recycled materials, and that can be recycled themselves. It is estimated that recycling alone has the potential to reduce 25–50 percent of the waste stream.[15] Materials management staff should understand recycling technology, methods, and markets.

Hazardous Waste

Hazardous materials management is complex, but does not need to be perplexing. Procurement managers must recognize that hazardous materials management includes not only purchasing, but also handling, disposal, and demonstrating that the institution has acted in support of environmental protection. Because hazardous materials are potentially dangerous, manufacturers are required to provide health and safety guidance specific to each product. This guidance is in the form of Material Safety Data Sheets (MSDSs). Users are expected to use MSDSs when making handling, storage, use, and disposal decisions. When hazardous materials are no longer needed, they may not be discarded in the trash as other waste materials. There are specific disposal requirements and significant consequences for inappropriate disposal. Materials management staff should understand these issues at least well enough to reference disposal options and sources legally available to campus operations and to work cooperatively with research, plant operations, and health and safety professionals on campus to support waste minimization programs wherever feasible. (See chapter 14, Environmental Health and Safety.)

Radioactive Waste

As the research and medical applications for radioisotopes become greater, the disposal options seem to become fewer. Currently, there are only two low-level radioactive waste disposal sites in the United States.[16] Materials management should work cooperatively with researchers, radiation safety officials, and suppliers to find ways to reduce the amount of radioactive products that are purchased and to identify more effective disposal methods. (See chapter 14, Environmental Health and Safety.)

Medical Waste

To minimize the spread of disease, safe disposal of medical waste can never be neglected. As with radioactive waste and hazardous chemical waste, the materials management staff should appreciate the importance of medical waste management and become familiar with the appropriate disposal methods and resources for generators on campus. (See chapter 14, Environmental Health and Safety.)

Air Quality

The procurement staff should actively participate with plant operations and environmental health and safety personnel in the institution's air quality management programs. The use of incinerators and the need to address such potential pollutants as automobile emissions may require institutional investment in stack scrubbers or alternate transportation options, such as vans or busses. Procurement staff can be instrumental in ensuring that institutional goals for air quality improvement are achieved.

Water Use

As with air quality management, water conservation efforts are aided by new technology. The procurement staff should be familiar with this technology and available equipment, such as water-saver valves and nozzles for laboratory, toilet, and shower use; water-saver timers and sprinkler heads for irrigation use; leak detection equipment; and water purification and recycling systems.

Energy Use

The procurement staff should know how to purchase energy-efficient electrical equipment and appliances, energy-saving lamps and lighting supplies, and alternative fuel conversion systems. Materials management staff should also play a significant role in projects for the development of cogeneration capabilities, solar power conversions, buying natural gas and energy from the source, the purchase of methane from landfill generators, and the negotiation of energy performance contracts in which the savings generated through upgraded energy systems pay for these systems.

Business Affirmative Action

Most colleges and universities, both public and independent, enjoy the use of federal and state funds for a significant part of their support. This subjects them to a variety of governmental regulations regarding the kinds of social programs that should be supported. Colleges and universities also have an important public service role that obligates them to serve the needs and promote the interests of their local and state communities.

Because of these obligations, colleges and universities are especially accountable for the social implications of the ways in which they spend their money. The principal example that affects materials management is business contracting programs that require formal or informal preferences to be extended to special groups of businesses, such as small businesses; businesses owned by socially and economically disadvantaged persons, women, or disabled persons; and, sometimes, businesses located in the institutions' home states. Often such programs are mandated by state or local legislation.

Although helping businesses that are owned by socially and economically disadvantaged individuals to enter the economic mainstream is generally considered to be the "right" thing to do, it is neither easy nor inexpensive to accomplish. Accordingly, it takes a strong legislative mandate or an exceptionally dedicated institutional commitment and robust financial and philosophical backing from the highest levels of the organization to make affirmative action work.

The traditional goal of these programs is to increase awards to the preferred businesses. Since preferred business programs do not increase an institution's overall demand for goods or services, increases in awards to preferred businesses must be accompanied by decreases to businesses that are not so favored. This can be a controversial issue and one that demands commitment, participation, and patience at the highest institutional levels. Current research suggests that the traditional goal of increasing awards to disadvantaged businesses is not sufficient to produce equality in the marketplace, and institutional management assistance may be needed after award for disadvantaged businesses to reach equity.[17] Socially motivated business contracting programs take two principal forms.

Equal Opportunity

All suppliers, regardless of their size or ownership, have the same chance of becoming providers of goods and services to the institution in an equal opportunity program. An equal opportunity policy is a nondiscrimination policy.

Affirmative Action

An affirmative action program requires doing something special to assure that targeted firms will be included in the purchasing process. Affirmative action always requires positive and creative efforts and sometimes calls for policy decisions to be put in writing.

Although most people believe that equal opportunity is the ultimate goal of both these programs, most also believe that until "weaker" targeted businesses can compete on an equal footing with their "stronger" counterparts, affirmative action is necessary. Affirmative action is designed to support targeted businesses while they develop the skills, experience, and economic strength necessary for them to hold their own in the marketplace. Most institutional programs favor the affirmative action approach.

Effective business affirmative action programs are serious, long-term projects. They really involve changing institutional buying habits—the institution's ways of making source and price decisions and its view of its social obligations as a part of the business community. Successful business affirmative action programs require dedication and hard work. They also require strong management commitment and backing, including a willingness to allocate appropriate resources to establish and support a specialized business affirmative action function within materials management. For a review of best practices in business affirmative action programs, see *Purchasing from Minority Business Enterprises: Best Practices.*[18]

Business affirmative action programs have four components: outreach, "inreach," compliance monitoring, and reporting.[19]

Outreach. Outreach is the term for reaching out into the community to identify qualified targeted firms and to encourage them to become part of the institution's vendor base. Outreach is affirmative action's external marketing function. Outreach activities consist of:

- participating in professional associations that represent targeted businesses and area purchasing councils that promote business affirmative action;

- networking with affirmative action specialists in other business sectors;

- holding trade fairs, open houses, and seminars in how to do business with the institution;

- publishing informational literature for targeted businesses;

- visiting targeted firms to verify their identity and competence;

- publishing directories of institutional officials and departmental representatives who are active in the procurement process;

- providing technical and management assistance to targeted firms;

- providing assistance in obtaining financing, bonding, and insurance; and

- providing information on the institution's business affirmative action policies to nontargeted firms.

Inreach. "Inreach" describes the process of reaching inside the institution to train, educate, and motivate those on whom business affirmative action depends for its success. Inreach is the program's internal marketing function. Inreach activities consist of training and motivational activities for both materials management and using department staffs, including:

- encouraging trade fair and "business opportunity day" attendance;

- providing classroom and in-service training;

- holding regular meetings of materials management personnel to discuss business affirmative action projects and performance;

- developing materials management job descriptions and personnel evaluations that promote favorable business affirmative action performance;

- establishing incentive award programs for materials management personnel who demonstrate exceptional business affirmative action performance;

- publishing internal directories of targeted businesses for use by all who play a part in source decisions;

- publishing business affirmative action newsletters for broad distribution within the institution; and

- establishing advisory committees, made up of both internal and external representatives, to provide advice on business affirmative action issues.

Compliance Monitoring. Some business affirmative action programs are legislatively required to be two-tiered, particularly in the construction sector, where most of the work is done by subcontractors rather than prime contractors. Those programs may require prime contractors to develop affirmative action subcontracting plans to accompany their bids. The terms of the invitations to bid often specify a minimum level of business affirmative action subcontracting for bids to be considered. In effect, this practice transfers a significant part of the business affirmative action responsibility from the buying institution to the prime contractor, who may or may not be appropriately aggressive in meeting, or making good-faith efforts to meet, the goals of approved plans. In these cases, the institution's business affirmative action staff need to monitor compliance to assure that prime contractors comply with the terms of their business affirmative action contractual obligations.

Another dimension of compliance monitoring involves the need to verify that targeted firms are, indeed, owned and operated by targeted individuals. To protect the institution from criticism and claims that it is dealing with "fronts," the business affirmative action function should have procedures for certifying or verifying the certification of targeted firms.

Reporting. The objective of reporting is to describe in accurate numeric terms the institution's business affirmative action performance. The need for accuracy and honesty in reporting cannot be overemphasized. If the numbers—both awards to targeted firms and the total base of expenditures—are not accurate or if they have been manipulated in any way to inflate the award percentage "bottom line," the institution's credibility can be seriously damaged.

The most realistic reports are excerpted from the accounts payable records and reflect actual, rather than estimated, expenditures. This requires an automated system in which the vendors are coded to reflect the ethnicity, gender, or other attributes of targeted firms.

Business Affirmative Action Techniques

Numerous techniques can be used to improve business affirmative action performance. A few of the most popular make use of materials management's ability to:

- determine source and price by negotiation instead of formal competition;

- use trial purchases as a means to qualify targeted sources;

- reserve small quantities from high-volume purchases for award to targeted firms;

- reserve certain purchases for competition among targeted firms only;

- keep specifications, quantities, delivery time, insurance, and bonding requirements unrestrictive;

- pay quickly;

- encourage manufacturers to distribute their goods through targeted firms;

- encourage nontargeted firms to "partner" with targeted firms for large or complex projects;

- use formal setasides and bid preferences; and

- count contribution to business affirmative action goals as part of "value" for determining the best source.

Getting Started

The following steps should be accomplished when implementing a new business affirmative action program.[20]

- Develop a business affirmative action policy that is explicit about the administrative and financial support that will be provided by management.

- Place the program in the charge of an official with responsibility and authority to implement an effective program.

- Publicize the program, both inside and outside the institution.

- Define areas of underutilization based on present use of targeted suppliers.

- Set goals and timetables.

- Develop specific procedures for outreach, inreach, compliance monitoring, and reporting.

- Establish a performance monitoring and control program.

- Provide training to program staff and establish appropriate links with the personnel performance evaluation system.

The Future

Here is a forecast of the future for procurement.[21]

The differences among the purchasing, procurement, and logistics functions will become blurred as they are more fully integrated through multi-disciplined commodity sourcing teams to design and manage demand-supply chains.

Online information and decision support systems will allow fewer cross-disciplined and business-trained sourcing teams to manage a drastically reduced supply base effectively through a hybrid centralized/decentralized organizational structure.

Building and managing strategic supply-base relationships will consume almost all of the time of sourcing teams, while day-to-day operational transactions will be delegated to internal customers, key suppliers, and automated expert decision systems using artificial intelligence.

Outsourcing of materials and services will continue to increase, and will include services heretofore thought not to be strong candidates for outsourcing, such as purchasing, personnel, and quality management. In addition, more value-added services relating to materials will be assumed by suppliers.

Commodities traditionally not managed by the purchasing department, such as health care, financial services, consulting, training, or transportation, will be managed by sourcing teams.

Organization-wide initiatives for process time compression and synchronization of processes for product/service design, procurement, production and operations, distribution, and supporting administrative functions will become as important as the movements toward total customer satisfaction and total quality management.

Buyer-supplier partnering and alliances will endure as a major strategic initiative and will encompass the entire supply chain, including second-level and third-level suppliers, and perhaps beyond. Both partners will work to make the relationships "seamless," and continued alliances will depend on joint continuous improvement and shared risks and rewards.

Value-added performance measurement of materials management based on total cost of acquisition and ownership will be routinely measured through automated models whose results will dominate "price" as the primary sourcing decision variable.

Graduate higher education directed toward strategic procurement demand-supply chain design and management will have taken root in several universities and will be recognized as an important discipline by world-class companies.

NOTES

1. Larry N. Wellman, "Centralization of the Procurement Function," *NIGP Technical Bulletin,* (Herndon, VA: National Institute of Governmental Purchasing), September/October (1998), p. 2.

2. Richard L. Mooney, *Purchasing Self Assessment Guide,* (Woodbury, NY: National Association of Educational Buyers, 1985), pp. H-2-H-4.

3. Michiel R. Leenders, and Harold E. Fearon, *Purchasing and Supply Management,* 11th ed. (Chicago: Richard D. Irwin, 1997), p. 34.

4. Donald W. Dobler, Lamar Lee, Jr., and David N. Burt, *Purchasing and Materials Management,* 4th ed. (New York: McGraw-Hill Book Company, 1984), p. 623.

5. John F. Riley, "What is the Cost per P.O.?" *NAEB Journal,* (Haupphauge, NY: National Association of Educational Buyers), Summer (1999), pp. 22–23.

6. Mary Mihaly, "Purchasing in the New Millennium," *Industry Week,* May 17 (1999), p. A4.

7. National Association of College and University Business Officers, *Contract Management or Self-Operation: A Decision-Making Guide for Higher Education,* (Washington, DC: NACUBO, 1993).

8. Leenders and Fearon, *Purchasing and Supply Management,* pp. 602–606.

9. National Association of Educational Buyers, *Small Schools,* (Hauppauge, NY: National Association of Educational Buyers, 1993).

10. Mei C. Morin, "Electronic Commerce," A presentation at the Bank One/MasterCard 6th Annual Commercial Card Services User Conference, (Beverly Hills, CA: MasterCard, October 13–15, 1999).

11. Richard L. Mooney, *Stores Self Assessment Guide* (Woodbury, N.Y.: National Association of Educational Buyers, 1986), pp. I-1, I-2.

12. National Association of Purchasing Management, "Strategic Moves Across the Board," *News and Resources,* (Tempe, AZ:NAPM, 1999), at www.napm.org on the Web.

13. Richard L. Mooney and John F. Riley, "Benchmarking Initiative: The Results," A presentation at the Annual Meeting of the National Association of Educational Buyers, (Phoenix, AZ: NAEB, April 24, 1998).

14. Richard L. Mooney, *A Model Purchasing Department for Creating High Customer Satisfaction,* (Hauppauge, NY: National Association of Educational Buyers, 1998), at www.naeb.org on the Web.

15. "In Our Backyard: Environmental Issues at UCLA, Proposals for Change, and

the Institution's Potential as a Model," in *UCLA Urban Planning Program* (Los Angeles, CA: UCLA, 1989), p. 96.

16. Nuclear Regulatory Commission Office of Public Affairs, *Disposal of Radioactive Waste,* (Rockville, MD: Nuclear Regulatory Commission, September 30, 1999), at www.nrc.gov/OPA on the Web.

17. Eugene F. Fregetto, "Government Purchasing and Disadvantaged Business Enterprises: Are Competitive Disparities Being Reduced? *Journal of Developmental Entrepreneurship,* Spring/Summer (1999), pp. 33–57.

18. Richard J. Auskalnis, Carol L. Ketchum, and Craig Carter, *Purchasing from Minority Business Enterprises: Best Practices,* (Tempe, AZ: Center for Advanced Purchasing Studies, 1995, at www.capsresearch.org on the Web.

19. Richard L. Mooney, *Effective Minority Purchasing Program Management* (Woodbury, N.Y.: National Association of Educational Buyers, 1989), pp. 28–40.

20. Thaddeus H. Spratlen, "The Impact of Affirmative Action Purchasing," *Journal of Purchasing and Materials Management* (Spring 1978), p. 6.

21. Ray T. Jensen, Richard L. Mooney, John F. Riley, Debra Seaman Langdon, and Brian K. Yeoman, "The Future of Purchasing," *NAEB Professional Purchaser* (Hauppauge, NY: National Association of Educational Buyers, Fall/Winter 1996), pp. 3–8.

REFERENCES AND RESOURCES

Publications and Articles

Ammer, Dean S. *Materials Management and Purchasing,* 4th ed. Homewood, IL: Richard D. Irwin, 1980.

Dobler, Donald W., Lee, Lamar, Jr., and Burt, David N. *Purchasing and Materials Management,* 4th ed. New York: McGraw-Hill Book Company, 1984.

Emmelhainz, Margaret A. *EDI: A Total Management Guide.* New York: Van Nostrand Reinhold, 1993.

Farrell, P. V., and Aljian, G. W. *Purchasing Handbook,* 4th ed. New York: McGraw Hill Book Company, 1982.

Fearon, Harold E., and Bales, William A. *Purchasing of Nontraditional Goods and Services.* Tempe, AZ: Center for Advanced Purchasing Studies, 1995.

Fearon, Harold E., and Bales, William A. *Measures of Purchasing Effectiveness.* Tempe, AZ: Center for Advanced Purchasing Studies, 1997.

Fearon, Harold E., and Leenders, Michiel R. *Purchasing's Organizational Roles and Responsibilities.* Tempe, AZ: Center for Advanced Purchasing Studies, 1995.

Housley, Charles E. *Hospital Materials Management.* Rockville, MD.: Aspen Systems Corporation, 1978.

Housley, Charles E., ed. *Hospital Purchasing.* Rockville, MD.: Aspen Systems Corporation, 1983.

Housley, Charles E. *Product Standardization and Evaluation.* Rockville, MD.: Aspen Systems Corporation, 1986.

King, Donald Barnett, and Ritterskamp, James J., Jr. *Purchasing Manager's Desk Book of Purchasing Law.* Paramus, NJ: Prentice Hall, 1998.

Leenders, Michiel R., and Flynn, Anna E. *Value-Driven Purchasing: Managing the Key Steps in the Acquisition Process.* Burr Ridge, IL: Irwin Professional Publications, 1995.

Leenders, Michiel R., and Blenkhorn, David L. *Reverse Marketing.* New York: The Free Press, 1988.

Leenders, Michiel R. and Fearon, Harold E. *Purchasing and Supply Management,* 11th ed. Chicago: Richard D. Irwin, 1997.

Monczka, R. M., Carter, P. L., and Hoagland, J. H. *Purchasing Performance Measurement and Control.* East Lansing, MI: Michigan State University, 1979.

Monczka, Robert M., and Trent, Robert J. *Purchasing and Sourcing Strategy: Trends and Implications.* Tempe, AZ: Center for Advanced Purchasing Studies, 1995.

Mooney, Richard L. *Handling Small Orders Effectively.* Hauppauge, NY: National Association of Educational Buyers, July, 1992.

Mooney, Richard L. *Measuring Procurement's Performance.* Hauppauge, NY: National Association of Educational Buyers, 1995.

Mooney, Richard L. *Effective Minority Purchasing Program Management.* Woodbury, NY: National Association of Educational Buyers, 1989.

National Association of College and University Business Officers. *Contract Management or Self-Operation: A Decision Making Guide for Higher Education.* Washington, DC: NACUBO, 1993.

National Association of Educational Buyers. *NAEB Journal.* Hauppauge, NY: NAEB, Quarterly.

National Association of Purchasing Management. *The Journal of Supply Chain Management.* Tempe, AZ: NAPM, Quarterly.

National Association of Purchasing Management. *Purchasing Today*. Tempe, AZ:
    NAPM, Monthly.

Organizations

Association for Healthcare Resource and Materials Management (AHRMM)
One North Franklin, Chicago, IL 60606-2401
312-422-3840 . . . . www.ahrmm.org

Center for Advanced Purchasing Studies (CAPS)
2055 E. Centennial Circle, P.O. Box 22160, Tempe, AZ 85285-2160
480-752-2277 . . . . www.capsresearch.org

Delta Nu Alpha, Logistics and Transportation Organization (DNA)
530 Church Street, Suite 700, Nashville, TN 37219-2394
615-251-0933 or (800) 453-3662 . . . . www.deltanualpha.org

National Association of College and University Business Officers (NACUBO)
2501 M Street, NW, Suite 400, Washington, DC 20037-1308
202-861-2500 . . . . www.nacubo.org

National Association of Educational Buyers (NAEB)
450 Wireless Boulevard, Hauppauge, NY 11788-3934
631-273-2600 . . . . www.naeb.org

National Association of Purchasing Management (NAPM)
P.O. Box 22160, Tempe, AZ 85285-2160
480-752-6276 or 800-888-6276 . . . . www.napm.org

National Association of State Purchasing Officials (NASPO)
167 West Main Street, Suite 600, Lexington, KY 40507
606-231-1877 . . . . www.naspo.org

National Contract Management Association (NCMA)
1912 Woodford Road, Vienna, VA 22182
703-448-9231 or (800) 344-8096 . . . . www.ncmahq.org

National Institute of Governmental Purchasing (NIGP)
151 Spring Street, Suite 300, Herdon, VA 20170-5223
703-736-8900 or (800) FOR-NIGP . . . . www.nigp.org

National Property Management Association, Inc. (NPMA)
1108 Pinehurst Road, Oaktree Center, Dunedin, FL 34698
727-736-3788 . . . . www.npma.org

National Purchasing Institute, Inc. (NPI)
164 Hubbard Way C1, Reno, NV 89502
775-332-1674 . . . . npi.purchasing.co.harris.tx.us

NAEB CODE OF ETHICS

To give first consideration to the objectives and policies of my institution. When buyers observe this guideline, they put their employer's needs before their own. As long as they remember to do this, they will not mix their business and personal lives and will avoid conflicts of interest.

To strive to obtain the maximum value for each dollar of expenditure. This helps buyers keep aware of their responsibility to be loyal to the institution. To obtain maximum value, buyers must keep their skills sharp, stay well informed of markets and effective buying procedures, and follow appropriate rules and regulations.

To decline personal gifts or gratuities. Those who decline gifts or gratuities will have no trouble maintaining objectivity and freedom from obligation to anyone but their employer. Regardless of the type, value, or source of the gift, buyers should simply say "no thanks" to all such offers.

To grant all competitive suppliers equal consideration insofar as state or federal statute and institutional policy permit. As long as buyers follow this advice, they will treat all suppliers equally, favoring none with special treatment or information. They will show favoritism only when required by law or institutional policy, as in the case of business affirmative action preferences.

To conduct business with potential and current suppliers in an atmosphere of good faith, devoid of intentional misrepresentation. This guideline reminds buyers that they must treat suppliers honestly. Intentional misrepresentation is counterproductive to long-range healthy vendor relationships.

To demand honesty in sales representation whether offered through the medium of a verbal or written statement, an advertisement, or a sample of the product. One of the best ways buyers can assert their own high ethical standards is to refuse to countenance dishonesty or other unethical conduct on the part of those from whom they buy.

To receive the consent of the originator of proprietary ideas and designs before using them for competitive purchasing purposes. Original ideas and designs that may be revealed through the competitive process should be considered the property of the originator. It is unethical to disclose them to other suppliers without the originator's consent.

To make every reasonable effort to negotiate an equitable and mutually agree-

able settlement of any controversy with a supplier and/or be willing to submit any major controversies to arbitration or other third-party review, insofar as the established policies of the institution permit. Buyers recognize a supplier's right to disagree with their procurement decisions, and they respect a supplier's right to a fair, open, and respectful hearing. Whenever possible, buyers believe that compromise and negotiation are appropriate tools to reach agreement in cases of dispute.

To accord a prompt and courteous reception insofar as conditions permit to all who call on legitimate business missions. Buyers recognize the role suppliers play in helping to keep their performance and market knowledge sharp. They also recognize that they must treat suppliers with courtesy and attention if they are to expect like treatment from suppliers.

To cooperate with trade, industrial, and professional associations and with governmental and private agencies for the purposes of promoting and developing sound business methods. Institutional buyers believe that cooperation and information sharing among colleagues are appropriate ways to keep the purchasing profession strong and respected. Buyers understand that they must first recognize their obligation to share their knowledge and expertise if they are to expect others to share with them.

To foster fair, ethical, and legal trade practices. If buyers are to be ethical and be perceived as ethical, they must encourage suppliers' representatives to be ethical by refusing to tolerate unethical behavior from them.

To counsel and cooperate with NAEB members and promote a spirit of unity and a keen interest in professional growth among them. Part of the buyers' ethical behavior is being loyal to their profession and to their professional colleagues.

Chapter 18

Research and Sponsored Programs

by

Julie T. Norris
Massachusetts Institute of Technology

Sponsors

KPMG
Contact: Greg J. Baroni
1676 International Drive
McLean, VA 22102
703-747-3004
www.kpmg.com

With over 30 years of serving higher education, KPMG offers a broad range of services that helps our clients analyze their businesses with true clarity, raises their level of performance and delivers the strategic and infrastructural components to support highly dynamic E-business models in colleges, universities, and academic medical centers.

SIEMENS BUILDING TECHNOLOGIES, INC.
Contact: Sylvia Rainey
1000 Deerfield Parkway
Buffalo Grove, IL 60089-4547
847-215-1050 ext. 5586 or 800-877-7545 ext. 5586
www.sbt.siemens.com/SmartU

Siemens offers: environmental controls and monitoring for bio-tech and chem. labs, animal lab facilities, fume hoods and air quality controls, comprehensive services for critical environments management, building automation/HVAC controls, systems integration and networks, utilities, mechanical systems, and facility management services.

Contents

Sponsored programs are the activities of a college or university that are financed by external funds and that support various instructional, research, or public service functions of the institution. Organizations provide external funds to an institution to support and promote research and other activities; to aid in the development and transmission of new knowledge to society; to train individuals for participating in complex technologies; and to provide support for expanding and building specialized facilities and equipment. This is discussed in greater detail in chapter 2, Planning. When an institution receives external funds, it must manage those funds and support the faculty member responsible for carrying out the program for which funding has been awarded. In this way, the institution is a service provider to a client (the faculty member). In most institutions, management of the funds is provided primarily by the business office. In some organizations, the financial or business officer is responsible for financial and administrative aspects of the program and an academic office is responsible for programmatic aspects; in other institutions all the activities—fiscal, administrative, programmatic—are combined in a single office. How an institution organizes to support its research and sponsored activities depends on a number of factors, including size, volume, organizational philosophy, amount of stewardship demanded (by the institution or the federal government), and people involved.

The growth of sponsored programs offices as specific units within an institution has been because of various pressures, both external and internal, on institutions of higher education. Originally, sponsored programs offices were organized to provide support to faculty in the preparation and submission of research proposals to external sponsors. Twenty or 30 years later (in the 1970s and 1980s) functions that had been focused in accounting offices relative to billing and financial reporting began to find their way into more broadly based sponsored projects offices. The 1990s, clearly, was viewed by many as the decade of compliance, as sponsored projects offices assumed more and more responsibility for developing and managing a wide range of compliance issues. These issues are central to appropriate management and stewardship of sponsored programs and have been joined in importance with the advent of electronic research administration initiatives. In fact, these two issues (compliance and electronic research administration) are the two new complexities that central research administrative offices are dealing with as institutions move into the 21st century.

Sponsored programs demand stewardship and accountability in the management of funds on behalf of the external sponsor. Generally, sponsored-program funds (as distinct from gifts) have extensive reporting and management requirements connected with them, as well as specialized technical reporting and administrative support requirements. The complexity of sponsored-program activities and their impact on the host institution cannot be underestimated. Demands on space, facilities, cash flow, and personnel must be carefully considered. The finance or business officer needs to be aware of these requirements and understand, in detail, the requirements of the sponsor when accepting these funds.

Regardless of the size of the externally funded research and other sponsored programs at an institution, the effect of such funding must be carefully weighed when looking at overall institutional goals and objectives. In light of developments concerning indirect costs at some institutions and the pressures within some states for budget cutting, the amount and type of support in the sponsored-program arena becomes an even more critical element for an institution and one for which careful planning must be made. Sponsored-program funds quickly become interwoven with the fabric of an institution; the loss of such funds can have dramatic negative effects on an institution's academic programs and financial plans.

The college or university financial or business officer has legal and fiduciary responsibility to safeguard all institutional funds, including funds from external sources. Included in this responsibility is the necessity to respond to the growth of sponsored programs and to provide appropriate leadership in the formulation and management of policies that impact the sponsored-program activities of the institution.

This chapter presents general principles and significant procedural requirements applicable to any type of sponsored program. It discusses the complex areas of administration made necessary by an ever-increasing number of sponsored-program requirements. Faculty often need to be reminded that grants, cooperative agreements, memorandums of understanding, contracts, and subcontracts (the basic instruments that authorize an institution to embark on a specific sponsored project) are made to the institution, not to the individual. Consequently, the institution is legally responsible for the projects and for fulfilling sponsor requirements. A faculty member (usually the author of a proposal and generally called the "principal investigator" or "project director") is the individual with the scientific or technical expertise to carry out the proposed activity and the client who receives service and support from the institution. The different roles of the faculty and personnel in the sponsored-programs administrative area are important, and adequate understanding and communication between them are critical. Sound and prudent policies for the administration of sponsored programs must be developed, and the principal investigator must be allowed the maximum flexibility possible in meeting the objectives stated in a proposal and the subsequent award.

An interesting development, in general, is the increasing complexity of awards from nongovernmental organizations. This has presented institutions with issues that heretofore have remained in the purview of federal and corporate sponsors. Stated another way, these organizations—while maintaining their nonprofit status—are making significantly greater demands for administrative, fiscal, and compliance activities than in the past. In many ways these demands are very similar to those mandated by the government and preferred by corporate sponsors. Perhaps the best example of this is in the intellectual property area, where nonprofits are trying to incorporate terms related to revenue sharing and of management of intellectual property licensing. This aspect of university-sponsor relations has increased in complexity over the past several years and presents new challenges to institutions and suggests the need for increasing vigilance in this area.

ADMINISTRATION

The activities associated with sponsored programs generally include functions of stimulating and supporting the development of such programs, supporting recognition and incentive activities, and providing general research administration support. These activities may include functions such as:

- assistance with conceptualization of ideas;
- identification of potential sources of support;
- preparation of the proposal and budget;
- review and submission of the proposal;
- negotiation of the award;
- establishment of an account;
- management of awards, purchasing, and property;
- financial reporting;
- management of intellectual property (generally defined as encompassing

patents, copyrights, software, trademarks, trade secrets, and research know-how);

- technology transfer;

- specialized certifications and assurances, including compliance with federal regulations regarding use of small and disadvantaged businesses, affirmative action, and protection of civil rights;

- ensuring compliance with requirements concerning the use of animals and humans in research;

- biohazard and radiation safety;

- preparation of facilities and administrative cost proposals;

- closeout and audit;

- review and management of subrecipients; and

- archiving of records.

How inclusive an institution is in placing these responsibilities within a sponsored projects office depends on the philosophy of the institution and whether or not the combining of functions in a single office is viewed as positive. Clearly, in recent years the trend has been toward combined (or at least colocated) offices.

ORGANIZATION AND STAFFING

Because sponsored-program activities may span almost every area of an institution, coordination is a vital requirement for effective sponsored-program administration. This coordination should begin with the president. Below this level there may be various organizational structures. As indicated earlier, the appropriate structure depends on the institution's overall management philosophy, volume of the sponsored-program activity, organizational structure, and the quality and experience of personnel involved. There is no single correct way to organize sponsored-program administration; each institution must determine its most effective organization but certainly a close relationship between pre- and postaward is essential.

In any organizational structure, cooperation, communication, and coordination among offices are vital. In managing sponsored programs, however, these needs are especially critical, because functional responsibilities often cross organizational lines. For example, management of intellectual property involves sponsored programs offices (reporting/compliance), technology licensing (marketing), and the finance office (accounting and fiscal management). Responsibility for humans and animals used in research cuts across individual project lines and involves the principal investigator, faculty committees, administrative hierarchies, and often federal and local compliance offices. There is also a need to provide for management on topics such as changes in scope or principal investigator and approval for any budgetary and duration changes in a project. Knowledgeable individuals need to know when institutional and/or sponsor prior approval is required. In addition, interpretation of rules and regulations, management of equipment, and providing assurances and certifications are critical to adequate stewardship of sponsored awards. The penalties for mismanagement may sometimes be severe (e.g., debarment of the institution) but always tend to be embarrassing to the institution and may affect the principal investigator's ability to receive follow-on funding for a project. In addition, sponsored-program administration offices generally have some responsibility in areas such as relationships with subrecipients, accounting, fiscal and administrative reporting, billing of cost-reimbursable contracts, and management of letters of credit. Typically, offices with these responsibilities report to the financial or business officer, although they may report to a vice president for research or a chief academic officer if appropriate controls and communications are in place.

A number of institutions have separate affiliated foundations that accept and carry out sponsored-program administration. Research foundations might support only a part of the sponsored-program activity, such as administering the postaward activities and handling intellectual property matters, or they might, as "full service" foundations, handle preaward proposal development, proposal processing, accounting, and postaward activities, as well as having responsibility for compliance with regulations concerning animal care and human subjects.

TYPES OF SPONSORS

Higher education institutions rely on the federal government as the major funding source for sponsored projects. However, in recent years many large institutions find that industrial sources are increasing their sponsorship of research programs—individual projects for individual faculty and, increasingly, large, multi-activity consortia. On average, however, more than 50 percent (and often much more) of a typical institution's sponsored programs are funded by federal sources. While cabinet-level departments of the federal government have extramural programs that provide such funding opportunities, they are mainly concentrated in the Departments of Agriculture (USDA), Defense (DOD), Education (ED), Energy (DOE), and Health and Human Services (HHS). Independent federal agencies also provide funding opportunities, notably the National Science Foundation (NSF), the National Aeronautics and Space Administration (NASA), and the Environmental Protection Agency (EPA).

As funding from nonfederal sources has become more significant in the last decade, an institution can no longer rely on agencies of the federal government as the predominant sponsors of externally funded activities. Particularly for public institutions, state agencies can be a significant funding source for research and other sponsored activities. Additionally, governments at the county and city levels may be a source of support, particularly when a higher education institution can provide specialized services not otherwise available to the local governmental agency.

Another source institutions look to for at least a portion of their sponsored activity is private foundations or other nonprofit entities. Foundations have traditionally been a small source of support for sponsored programs, but such funding has increased in recent years. These relationships generally do not have as many regulatory or procedural compliance requirements as do grants and contracts from federal or state sources. However, because foundations are often a source of gifts to the institution, these relationships may pose additional challenges if there is a need to coordinate proposals with the development office. Coordination with the development office is also necessary when funding for sponsored programs comes from corporate or industrial sources. A contractual gift or grant relationship with corporate or industry sponsors, particularly for research programs, can pose special difficulties in negotiation, particularly in the areas of intellectual property, publication, and data rights. Other potential sources of external funds are foreign governments, corporations, and other international organizations as well as local and state governments and not-for-profit organizations. Receiving funds from international sources requires special knowledge of international laws, intellectual property rights, and currency exchange.

In seeking support from industrial and corporate sponsors, the institution needs to be aware of the range of significant issues that must be addressed relative to such sponsorship. For example, support from industrial sources is generally of shorter duration and less stable for long-term basic (or fundamental) research projects than from federal sponsors. The work tends to be more directed than funding via grants and cooperative agreements from the federal government (although not much different than the restrictions placed on some contract activities supported by the government) and there tend to be more deliverables required (including more frequent progress reports). Although there are fewer cited regulations than in federal awards, certain terms and conditions (notably related to ownership and management of intellectual property and to restrictions on publication) are far more difficult to negotiate and often cause extensive delays in finalizing research agreements.

TYPES OF SUPPORT

The Federal Grant and Cooperative Agreement Act of 1977 identifies two general categories of federal support: assistance and procurement. Three basic types of instruments—grants, cooperative agreements, and contracts—are used to fund assistance or procurement projects.

Assistance

The legal distinction between "assistance" and "procurement" is important because of the types of regulations that accompany each. A distinction often made between assistance (i.e., grants and cooperative agreements) and procurement (i.e., contracts) is that a grant is awarded for what the institution wants to do and a contract is awarded for what the sponsor wants the institution to do. The principal purpose of assistance is the transfer of money, property, services, or anything of value to accomplish a public purpose of support or stimulation authorized by statutes. The Federal Grant and Cooperative Agreement Act provides that funds for assistance be awarded in the form of grants or cooperative agreements. The purposes of both are similar, but cooperative agreements are defined as the instrument of choice when "substantial involvement" in the research on the part of the funding agency is anticipated. The primary advantages in using assistance awards as the instrument for carrying out research is that the work description is generally written in broad, flexible terms allowing the principal investigator initiative in carrying out the research activities. Although both grants and cooperative agreements are included in the definition of assistance, there are differences between the two. For example, a grant is not likely to carry publication restrictions, and title to equipment purchased with grant funds usually rests with the grantee. Reports are generally more frequent with cooperative agreements and the technical oversight of the activity is far more robust with cooperative agreements.

Procurement

The act states that a contract (which is defined as "procurement" rather than "assistance") should be used as the legal instrument whenever the principal purpose is the acquisition by purchase, lease, or barter of property or services for the direct benefit or use of the federal government. A contract may include clauses based on statutory requirements that are not applicable to basic or applied research activities. Often these clauses are included in error; sometimes they are included because the sponsor is unaware of special circumstances related to certain types of institutions (for example, a state institution may not need to carry some types of insurance that independant institutions must have). Where possible, such clauses should be negotiated out of awards.

SPONSORED-PROJECT MANAGEMENT

Preaward Activities

At most institutions, preaward activities are carried out in a sponsored-programs office or in an academic division or unit on the campus. Many universities have sophisticated funding-search processes to identify potential sponsors for research programs. The processes may include computerized sponsored-programs databases, such as those of SPIN, COS, and IRIS. Once a potential funding source has been identified, the principal investigator prepares a proposal for consideration for funding. In many cases, particularly for foundations and other nonfederal funding sources, the sponsor requests a preproposal and, based on that preproposal, may ask for a formal proposal committing the institution. Preproposals generally are short (three to five pages); they describe in general terms the activities to be undertaken, the goals and objectives of the project, and a general funding level needed to carry out the work, although at this stage there is seldom any detailed budget or budget justification. In most cases, institutional central offices do not request or require signoff of the preproposal, but are available for consultation if the need arises. This will change with the preparation and submission of the final proposal. Although responsibility for preparation of the proposal lies primarily with the principal investigator, sponsored-programs offices generally support the development of the proposal by assisting with preparing proposal budgets, providing certifications and assurances, and ensuring that the proposal meets the guidelines of the institution and the potential sponsor. Major project proposals that may involve special collaborators or subrecipients, space requirements, or funding arrangements are often developed by a team that includes faculty and sponsored-programs administration personnel.

Because a proposal is a formal document that binds an institution to its terms, it must be thoroughly reviewed prior to submission. Depending on institutional organization in general and the program requirements in particular, review may be accomplished at various academic levels, in addition to special reviews performed by financial or business officers or experts in fields such as animal care or hazardous waste. Normally, these specialized reviews are performed in a number of offices (e.g., the business office, the facilities office, the human resources office, the risk management office, the animal care office). Some institutions, however, have centralized this review in the sponsored-programs office, and personnel in that office are responsible for securing approvals, if required, from other institutional offices. This method is often viewed positively by faculty who prefer not to have to seek individual approvals from a number of offices. It also is a process that is likely to change when institutions move to electronic processes since multiple reviews or notifications can be done at the same time.

After the review is complete, an official authorized to commit the institution should sign off on the proposal. If the office responsible for submitting a proposal is not the same as the office responsible for administrative management of the award after it is made, coordination between these offices prior to submission of the proposal is essential.

Administrators should develop some type of internal transmittal document for signature by the appropriate campus officers. This document should include information about:

- the availability of space;
- any special health or safety considerations;
- the use of animals or humans in research;
- the agreement to comply with institutional and sponsoring agency requirements;
- cost-sharing requirements (if any);
- the identification of consultants and subrecipients;
- special restrictions or requirements involving intellectual property, publications, or proprietary information;
- any unusual or special requirements needed to carry out the proposed program successfully; and

- commitments made by the institution that extend after the sponsored funding period ends.

This internal transmittal form serves to document the agreement (concurrence) of all parties and should be signed by the principal investigator, the department chair, the appropriate dean, other responsible individuals (such as the chair of the human subjects committee or the institutional animal care and use committee), and the sponsored-programs officer. An internal approval document is particularly important if the formal proposal does not provide for any signatures other than those of the principal investigator and the person authorized to sign for the institution. Note, however, that requirements for internal signatures are institution-specific. The sponsoring agency does not require multiple signatories and, therefore, institutional practices vary. In fact, the practice may vary between units within the same institution, based on the requirements of individual units.

A proposal should be submitted to a potential sponsor only if the institution is prepared and qualified to undertake the proposed work. The same proposal may be submitted to different sponsoring agencies, but multiple submissions should be made known to each potential sponsor. When an external agency decides to fund the proposal, the institution should communicate with its other potential sponsors and either modify those proposals so that the work is not overlapping or withdraw the proposals.

Automated Systems

In the late 1970s and early 1980s, the fledgling use of automated systems expanded dramatically in the sponsored-projects area. In the preaward area, the SPIN and IRIS systems allowed faculty to perform automated searches on funding sources at the federal level. In the last several years, these two systems have been augmented by the COS and RAMS systems and, more importantly, by automated systems created by almost every federal agency to allow electronic, remote access to research opportunities. While many institutions subscribed to one of the systems, some institutions independently developed their own automated systems. In many instances, these expanded to more comprehensive sponsored-program management systems that tracked proposals and awards, provided postaward management information, and allowed automatic billings on contracts and grants. Such systems have become more sophisticated and, coupled with computer-based financial systems, now allow financial or business and sponsored-program officers significant management information on these activities. (See the section on New Developments, for a more extensive discussion.)

Preaward Compliance Activities

In managing both the preaward and post-award activities of sponsored programs, compliance with institutional and agency policy is essential. Many of these mandated compliance requirements are associated with preaward (i.e., proposal development and submission) functions. These are discussed more fully in the Compliance Issues section.

Negotiation and Award

Negotiations take place at various stages of the process when applying for external support. Quite often (particularly in the case of industrial sponsors) there is informal negotiation between a principal investigator and a program officer concerning the scope of work, outcomes, and time frames for a particular activity. In certain instances, but only when initiated by the potential sponsor, negotiation and discussion between the principal investigator and program officials may occur after the submission of the proposal and before the formal award. Federal regulations on lobbying and procurement integrity, however, either prohibit any contact or proscribe stringent conditions under which any contact between an institution or its personnel and a potential federal sponsoring agency or its personnel may take place. Institutions are cautioned to review such regulations with care before initiating a contact with a federal agency after submission of a proposal.

Because external awards are made to the institution and not to the principal investigator, formal negotiation of contracts and grants should occur between an authorized institutional official and the contract or grants officer of the external organization. It is important that the sponsored-programs officer include the principal investigator in the process, but only the authorized institutional official should have formal contact with the sponsoring agency. Faculty members need to be aware that they cannot commit the institution to an agreement; in addition, they must be cautioned that, although they may reach oral or written agreement with program officers, these agreements and commitments are not binding until approved by both the institution and the contracts or grants officer at the sponsoring agency.

Successful negotiation results from the joint efforts of the principal investigator, the sponsored-programs officer, and the contracts or grants program officer of the sponsoring agency. There is generally only minor negotiation on grant awards, limited in most instances to the funding available and the amount of the proposed activity that can be accomplished with that funding. In the area of contract awards, however, significantly more can and should be negotiated, with emphasis on patents, copyrights, title to equipment, and publication restrictions, if any.

Institutional negotiators must be cognizant of the policies of the institution. Both the principal investigator and the sponsored-programs officer must realize that a proposed reduction in funding, particularly if it is substantial, will result in a reduction in the scope of work. Sponsored-programs administrators should work with principal investigators to provide revised scopes of work and should accept a grant or contract only when the faculty member is confident that the funding is sufficient to carry out the intended work. Major program negotiations involving special financial arrangements, rental of space, and impact on cash flow should include a representative of the financial or business office.

When concluding complex negotiations, particularly with federal sponsors, the sponsored-programs officer should perform a detailed and careful review of the terms and conditions of the award to ensure that all material issues have been addressed. In fact, a review of the terms and conditions should be performed on all awards prior to acceptance. Such a review should provide assurance that:

- the award complies with the policies of the institution;
- the award does not make an undue long- or short-term commitment of institutional resources;
- the scope of work can reasonably be accomplished by the principal investigator; and
- the timely submission of technical and fiscal reports is possible.

Acceptance

Grants

Many grants, particularly from the federal government, are unilateral and thus do not require formal acceptance by the institution. In such cases, the granting agency normally provides an institution with an award letter that states the terms and conditions under which the award is to be administered or incorporates these conditions by reference. In other instances, where formal acceptance of a grant is required, an institutional signature on the award document signifies acceptance of standard terms and conditions incorporated by reference or special conditions, which are normally attached to the signature page. Sponsored-programs officers and/or a financial or business officer should carefully review the terms and conditions of each award to ensure that its acceptance does not violate institutional policy or procedure and that the institution can comply with the terms and conditions of the award. On unilateral awards, the expenditure of funds is viewed as acceptance of the terms of the award.

Contracts

In the case of contracts, particularly those negotiated with the federal government, the institution must take special note of the clauses incorporated by reference as well the clauses attached to a specific award. A contract award is normally effective only once the document has been signed by both parties. An institution should take the initiative in requesting modification of provisions, if necessary, to accommodate institutional policies or procedures. Requests for modifications should be negotiated with the sponsor and should be a condition of acceptance of an award.

As mentioned earlier, it is often more difficult and time consuming to negotiate awards with industrial and corporate firms than with the federal government. Corporate sponsors generally want title to intellectual property created under the award, approval of publication in advance, and title to equipment purchased under the project. Many colleges and universities have policies that often preclude transfer of title to intellectual property, generally do not permit publication approval, and often do not yield equipment back to the sponsor. Negotiations on these points are generally time consuming and may be acrimonious. Many large institutions, therefore, begin negotiations by providing sponsors a "sample" agreement to which they can react. This may lead to speedier and more satisfactory negotiation although there are times that formal policies of the industrial firm and the institution simply will preclude agreement on a project.

Establishment of an Account

Following receipt of an award, the institution should establish an account or a series of accounts, where appropriate, for the project. The account should comply with institutional business processes and at the minimum should indicate:

- project title;
- sponsoring agency (if flow-through funds, both the original sponsor and proximate sponsor should be identified);
- sponsor identification number;
- *Catalog of Federal Domestic Assistance* (CFDA) number, if appropriate;

- institutional budget number;
- grant or contract number;
- principal investigator and coinvestigators;
- department(s);
- beginning and ending dates;
- budget detail (depending on the policies of the institution, the degree of detail might vary considerably from a lump sum with total flexibility to a detailed categorization with no flexibility);
- facilities and administrative cost rate;
- type of agreement;
- billing requirements (letter of credit, advance, progress, cost-reimbursable);
- reporting requirements (technical, financial, intellectual property, property);
- prior approval requirements (if any);
- cost-sharing requirements (if any);
- title to equipment and real property; and
- any other special requirements.

This information should be provided to all parties responsible for the project. In addition, institutions might consider whether—in advance of establishment of an account or even acceptance of the award—it wishes to have the concurrence of the investigator and the investigator's administrative unit to adhere to the terms and conditions of the award.

Postaward Activities

An office in the institution, normally the sponsored-programs office, should act as the liaison between the principal investigator and the sponsoring agency and between the principal investigator and other offices at the institution whose functions include handling or processing sponsored project documents. This office should be responsible for monitoring and approving changes in the award, as well as seeking the sponsor's approval where required. The need for prior approval of changes varies with the type of sponsor and type of project (i.e., research or non-research), but such changes generally encompass a broad range of activities, including:

- change in the scope of work;

- change in the principal investigator;

- change in the budget;

- purchase of equipment;

- foreign travel;

- construction or alteration of facilities;

- subrecipients and major subcontractors;

- consulting arrangements;

- period of performance extensions; and

- carryforward of funds.

Office of Management and Budget (OMB) Circular A-110, *Uniform Administrative Requirements for Grants and Other Agreements with Institutions, of Higher Education, Hospitals, and Other Non-Profit Organizations*, allows recipients of federal funds the right, on research grants, to waive prior approval on most budget changes and to approve carryforwards, no-cost extensions, and preaward costs up to 90 days in advance of a project's starting date. Even with institutional ability to manage most of the heretofore agency approvals, certain approvals—namely change in scope, reduction of time, and change in principal investigator—are reserved to the sponsor. Institutional business, financial, and sponsored programs officers should develop internal systems that provide adequate stewardship of federal funds while permitting principal investigators the same degree of flexibility as is provided by federal agencies.

Because the institution is legally responsible for all aspects of an award, it is in principle responsible for the conduct and progress of research on that award. In practice, however, responsibility for meeting the technical and scientific terms of an award belongs to the principal investigator. A sponsored-programs officer must ensure that the principal investigator submits reports in a timely fashion and in adequate detail to fulfill the award's technical requirements and must ensure that other offices of the institution comply with various requirements imposed by the agency.

A concern in dealing with sponsored programs is the issue of subrecipients. The prime recipient of federal grant funds is responsible for monitoring the activities of subrecipients. A subrecipient is defined as a legally constituted organization or institution that helps the prime grantee carry out the scope of work identified in the proposal. Federal regulations require an institution to distinguish between a subrecipient (which helps to carry out the research program) and a subcontractor (which provides goods and services but does not participate in the scope of the work itself). OMB Circulars A-110, and A-133, *Audits of Institutions of Higher Education and Other Non-Profit Institutions,* require that the prime recipient be responsible for activities of the subrecipients and monitor their performance. In such a relationship, the prime recipient is viewed as the sponsor of the activity and is thus mandated to carry out all of the monitoring functions required of the agency funding the research.

Both circulars are instructive, not only for reviewing the text of the regulation, but also for reviewing the information provided by OMB in the publication of the final rule for each. The full text is accessible in the *Federal Register* and the OMB comments generally provide much information on the thinking of the agency in adopting the regulation. This is particularly true of the subrecipient issue, since OMB Circular A-133 provides an exceedingly useful definition of and rationale for the circular's treatment of subrecipients. In addition, the A-133 compliance supplement provides similarly useful information.

Closeout and Termination

Closeouts of sponsored projects occur regularly and continually throughout the institution's fiscal year. Sponsored projects do not adhere to an institution's standard fiscal year; the institution must allow for orderly closeout of research accounts on an ongoing basis. Care should be taken to ensure that all closeout documentation is completed and submitted to the agency as prescribed in the notice of award or the terms and conditions referenced in that award. Generally, closeouts require submission of final fiscal and technical reports, reports of property and equipment, disposition requests or instructions, and submission of invention statements. Compliance with closeout terms and conditions is normally the responsibility of the sponsored-programs office, which works with the principal investigator on technical reports and invention statements and with the business office on financial, property, and other administrative reports. Care should be taken, even after submission of the final technical and fiscal reports, to maintain all the records relating to a project until all appropriate audits have been performed and the institution is free to dispose of the records. Although institutional practices vary, most institutions maintain all contract and grant records for at least seven years. The issue of retention time is often not seen as important, yet it is vitally important. Disposing of records too early can cause significant problems on audit. On the other hand, if records are kept indefinitely, an institution is required to produce these records (regardless of the retention period) if they are available.

Many institutions keep some records beyond the legal retention period, but identify only the most significant key data items, such as a copy of the award signature page, the funding period and amount, and often the closeout documentation, for indefinite retention.

For both grants and contracts, requirements for retaining financial and technical records may exceed the retention requirements for other types of records. There generally are additional requirements in closing out a research contract, particularly with regard to submission of financial documents. Retention requirements should be recognized and policies should be developed to comply with them. Institutions are often unaware that "records" in the federal vernacular applies to technical records as well as administrative and financial records. These are generally the most difficult to handle since technical records normally include the research notebooks generated by investigators and students, printouts from research experiments, and so forth. Some institutions have addressed this issue by making the principal investigator the custodian of the technical records, requiring him or her to seek approval to destroy the records but, at the same time, allowing an investigator who switches institutions to take research data and notebooks to the new institution.

Termination of a project by a sponsoring agency before its scheduled completion date is quite different from a routine closeout and must be dealt with carefully. On government contracts, terminations are usually the result of either default or mutual agreement to terminate. In either instance, the institution should review OMB Circular A-21, *Cost Principles for Educational Institutions*. The section "Termination Costs Applicable to Research Agreements" outlines what costs will be paid by the agency after termination. To deal effectively with early termination of both grants and contracts, an institution should have clear policies on severance pay and other benefits, since reimbursement of those costs is dependent on having written policies that are institutionwide and not applicable only to sponsored projects.

COMPLIANCE ISSUES

Compliance with Institutional Policies

In a number of areas, compliance with institutional policies is critical. Such compliance is important at the time of proposal submission, as well as during the lifetime of a grant or contract. In reviewing a proposal prior to its sign-off and submission, and in reviewing award documents before acceptance, an institution should examine, at a minimum, the following factors:

Eligibility of the investigator. Is the person initiating the proposal eligible under the rules of the institution to be a principal investigator? (Some institutions permit only tenured or tenure-track faculty to submit proposals; others allow all faculty and staff to submit proposals. Still others allow senior research staff members to be principal investigators.) Is the faculty member eligible to be a principal investigator for the program to which he or she is applying? (Some programs have age or gender restrictions, some require citizenship or permanent immigrant status.)

Academic program. Where required, have the appropriate department chairs and deans certified that the proposal is compatible with the goals of the department and college? Does the proposal contribute to the academic program of the institution? Does the proposal provide training and support for students? Does the proposal anticipate the offering of new courses, programs, or degrees? If so, have they been approved?

Space. Is there sufficient space for the research program? Is the space adequate, not only in square footage but also in terms of utilities, floor loading, or other special requirements of the program?

Salaries. Do the salaries comply with the institution's salary scales? Are adequate increments built in for future years? Are benefit rates appropriate? Do the principal investigator and others connected with the project have sufficient time available to carry out the research being proposed? Will the activity require additional staff? If so, are they included in the proposal budget? Have provisions been made for earned leave? The National Institutes of Health have legislatively imposed salary caps for individuals paid on research grants and contracts utilizing NIH funds. In January 2000, the NIH issued new regulations specifying the various capped levels and restricting reimbursement from NIH funds to the capped amount. This creates a problem for recipients, particularly for medical schools and health science institutions, since the balance of the funding for the effort provided must come from discretionary or institutional funds, and cannot be charged to the NIH project.

Graduate students. Is the requested number of graduate research assistants adequate?

Publications. Is the investigator free to publish his or her research results without restriction?

Procurement. Does the institution have adequate policies in place to manage the acquisition of goods, services, and equipment needed for the project? Most colleges and universities have a procurement or purchasing office responsible for the acquisition of goods and services for the institution, including those required on sponsored-program accounts. The policies and standards adopted for the purchasing department should comply with federal regulations, in that the materials and services are obtained in an effective manner and in compliance with appropriate laws and executive orders. (See chapter 17, Procurement.)

Technical reports. Are the number, frequency, and comprehensiveness of periodic technical reports acceptable?

Sponsor supervision. Is the extent of supervision exercised by the external sponsor within satisfactory limits?

Budget. Is the budget sufficiently detailed? Have all necessary direct cost items been included? Have increments been calculated for all budget categories for future years?

Facilities and administrative costs (F&A Costs). Have the institution's F&A-cost rates been properly applied and included in the proposed budget? If not, is there adequate documentation of a sponsor restriction on recovery of F&A costs? Are approved institutional reductions (i.e., cost sharing) adequately documented and justified?

Human subjects. If the proposed project involves the use of humans as subjects in research, has that research been adequately reviewed by an institutional review board (IRB)? Does the research comply with government requirements?

Use of animals in research. If the proposed project involves the use of live, vertebrate animals, has the research protocol been properly reviewed and approved by the institutional animal care and use committee (IACUC)?

Recombinant DNA. If the proposed project involves recombinant DNA, has the investigator secured appropriate approval from the institution's recombinant DNA (biohazards) committee? Does the research comply with federal requirements?

Insurance. Does the proposed research pose any special property liability or other insurance questions? In the case of contracts, is the appropriate Federal Acquisition Regulation (FAR) insurance clause cited? This is particularly important for state institutions that are self-insured for certain actions.

Cost sharing. "Cost sharing" refers to the institution's bearing a portion of the cost of a project, generally defined as "more than 1 percent of total project costs." "Matching," on the other hand, refers to a substantial contribution (as much as 1:1) toward the cost of a project. Matching funds are normally requested for equipment grants and construction grants.

If cost sharing or matching funds are required, are the necessary review and approvals completed to make such commitments? Have the funding sources been identified? Is cost sharing reasonable in terms of the research being undertaken? If cost sharing is provided through the principal investigator's time and effort, does the principal investigator have sufficient time for other duties?

The issue of cost sharing is perhaps one of the most contentious at the present time. The Office of Science and Technology Policy has issued a report in response to the Presidential Review Directive of 1998 asking that cost sharing problems and issues be resolved. A central issue is the extent to which cost sharing is required in program announcements and whether this places certain institutions at a disadvantage in competing for funds. A corollary problem is that of agency program officers asking for cost sharing when negotiating the award in cases where it has not been indicated previously as a requirement. A third problem is the cost of cost sharing to an institution (particularly with the advent of the cost accounting standards), which has posed new, complicated, and costly problems for institutions seeking funds from the government. In fact, the National Science Foundation tried to address this problem with Important Notice 123, which limits the cost sharing that program officers can require as a condition of an award.

Long-term commitments. Does the proposal contemplate institutional funding beyond the period of sponsor funding? If so, is institutional commitment to that support adequate?

Intellectual property. Do the patent and copyright terms, proposed or agreed to, comply with institutional requirements? Are patent assignment agreements on file for all persons who may be in a position to conceive, make, or reduce to practice inventions, improvements, or discoveries developed under the project? Have the sponsor's copyright and rights-in-data terms been considered? Are they acceptable?

Classified research. Does the proposal contemplate the undertaking of any classified research? Is such work in compliance with institutional policy? Does the institution have facilities that are sufficiently secure for classified work?

Completeness and compliance with sponsor limitations. Is the proposal complete for submission? Have all the requirements of the sponsor and the institution been considered? Are they adequately addressed in the proposal or the proposed agreement? If certain information in the proposal is considered by the institution to be proprietary, are all such pages clearly marked? Is there an indication on the cover that proprietary material is included in the proposal? Have all requirements of the sponsor been met with regard to page length, type size, and so forth?

Compliance with Policies of External Funding Sources

The Office of Management and Budget periodically issues management circulars applicable to agencies that fund activities at colleges and universities. These circulars provide guidance to federal agencies but only become directly binding on an institution when the agency implements the circular guidance. To ensure that the provisions apply with the effect of law to colleges and universities, federal agencies implement the circulars in a variety of ways. In practical terms institutions speak of "compliance with OMB Circular A-21" or "compliance with OMB Circular A-133" when, in fact, they mean "compliance with the implementing regulations that agencies have developed to carry out the mandates of the circulars." This distinction is significant because, in certain circumstances, agencies are permitted to implement regulations that deviate from the language in the circular itself. In managing federal awards, it is important to know which regulations apply to grants, cooperative agreements, and contracts; which apply only to grants and cooperative agreements ("assistance" in federal terms); which apply only to contracts ("procurement" in federal terms); and which apply on an optional basis to grants or contracts.

Applicable to All Federal Awards

OMB Circular A-21 was issued on February 26, 1979, and has been amended many times since then. This circular contains the principles used for determining costs applicable to research, development, and educational services performed by colleges and universities under contracts, grants, and other agreements with the federal government. Circular A-21 also specifies the allowability and allocability of costs and describes the process used in developing facilities and administrative (indirect) cost proposals. The circular also includes, as one of its appendixes, the requirements for compliance with the four cost accounting standards that are applicable to colleges and universities. The circular is used by a variety of institutional offices for purposes ranging from the organization of financial systems to the construction of the F&A proposal to a discussion of specific costs and their allowability.

OMB Circular A-133 was issued in 1990 and revised in 1997 (at the same time OMB Circular A-128, which was the audit circular for state and local governments and thereby applied to some state-supported higher education institutions was rescinded). This circular identifies audit standards and procedures for audits of institutions of higher education and other nonprofit institutions.

Applicable Only to Grants and Cooperative Agreements

OMB Circular A-110 was issued on July 1, 1976, and revised on September 30, 1999. This circular specifies standards for obtaining consistency and uniformity among federal agencies in the administration of grants and other agreements. These standard requirements are intended to prevent the proliferation of varying and often conflicting requirements that had been imposed by federal agencies as conditions of grants and other agreements; exceptions to these requirements for uniformity are granted only in unusual cases. Since the circular is applicable to federal agencies and requires agency implementation to be published prior to being effective for colleges and universities, it is important to review the specific agency implementation of A-110 when determining the administrative applicability of any specific section of the circular. Every major research agency has published its implementation of A-110 and all have Code of Federal Regulation (CFR) citations (with the exception of NSF, which can issue its implementations within its grants manual and not via the CFR process).

Applicable Only to Contracts

Contracts are managed in accordance with the Federal Acquisition Regulations. These regulations were intended to codify established policies and procedures for acquisitions by all federal agencies. They prescribe the policies, procedures, and regulations that apply to all procurement actions of the federal government. Federal agencies are permitted to issue supplements to FAR when statutory regulations require deviation from FAR or when an agency has secured a FAR waiver. When an institution receives a contract, therefore, it is critically important to review that contract for clauses that are agency specific (i.e., published in the agency's FAR supplement) rather than government general regulations (i.e., published only in the FAR itself).

Nonfederal Regulations

Although the largest part of an institution's sponsored-programs activity is with the federal government, institutional management should be knowledgeable about the compliance requirements of nonfederal sponsors. Awards from state and local government normally include requirements somewhat different (and perhaps more restrictive) than those imposed by the federal government. Awards from private or industrial sources may have even more stringent requirements with regard to patents, publications, and rights-in-data, although such awards generally have fewer requirements with regard to specific approvals required to carry out the research.

CERTIFICATIONS AND ASSURANCES

Public policy sets a number of requirements with which institutions must comply, both in applying for and in receiving federal funds. State-level and private funding sources have adopted many of the public-policy requirements in their programs, so institutional management must be aware of these requirements regardless of the funding source. These requirements have been instituted to ensure safety and protection for individuals who are participating in research projects and for the community, when biohazards or other potentially dangerous materials are used in research, and to uphold ethical standards of honesty and fairness.

Certifications provide assurance to the sponsor that the institution carrying out the work is aware of applicable requirements, including restrictions on the use of drugs and alcohol, debt delinquency, lobbying, debarment, scientific misconduct, and financial conflicts of interest. These are just a few examples of the types of certification and compliance statements that must be included in proposals and are reviewed on audit. Generally, certifications are divided into areas of individual rights (antidiscrimination, privacy); protection (environmental protection, protection of living organisms); employee directives; fraud, waste, and abuse; and specific administrative requirements of individual federal agencies. Failure to comply with certification and assurance requirements may subject an institution to fines, reimbursement for awarded funds, and/or debarment and suspension.

In recent years, sponsored-programs offices have recognized the breadth and complexity of the compliance requirements and have identified individuals who, as institutional compliance officers, are responsible for monitoring compliance with all such requirements, whether imposed by governmental or nongovernmental sponsors. Where the size of the sponsored-programs office precludes such specialization, institutional officials should clearly identify which offices at the institution are responsible for ensuring compliance with specific regulations.

Animal Welfare

Higher education institutions have a legal responsibility to ensure that animals used in research and instructional activities receive humane care and treatment. Current law provides for regulating the transport, sale, housing, care, handling, and treatment of such animals. These regulations are codified in the Animal Welfare Act as well as in regulations promulgated by the USDA. In addition, organizations performing research using animals must comply with Public Health Service Policy on Humane Care and Use of Laboratory Animals, which is based on the Health Research Extension Act of 1985. Its intent is expressed in the guidelines of the National Institutes of Health (NIH) publication, *Guide for the Care and Use of Laboratory Animals*. Most federal and nonfederal granting agencies have adopted these regulations by reference in their guidelines. An institution will not be awarded federal funds for research until it files an approved Animal Welfare Assurance with the NIH's Office of Protection from Research Risks (OPRR). Such an assurance is granted on submission by an institution of its policies and procedures relating to the care and treatment of animals used in research, a list of the members of its animal care and use committee, and certification that it will review all animal use protocols prior to the initiation of any research involving those animals.

To implement these regulations, an institution must appoint and maintain a committee (the institutional animal care and use committee) to provide oversight of its animal care program. The committee, furthermore, must be appointed by the institution's chief executive officer and report to a senior institutional officer. It must consist of at least five members, including at least one veterinarian, one outside community member, and three individuals involved in animal research. Annual reports must be submitted to the OPRR and the USDA and must include any change in the program or facilities that would place an institution in a different category from that specified in its NIH assurance, any change in the direction of the animal care and use program, and any change in membership of the committee. The annual reports must also include notice of an agreement to conduct institutional inspections at least semiannually. (See also chapter 14, Environmental Health and Safety.)

The issue of animal care and protection is one that continues to attract attention. Faculty and institutional officials should be cognizant of the tensions and conflicts that can arise and should have clear and precise institutional policies for research using animals as well as policies for communication with the media about animal use issues.

Affirmative Action

Institutions using federal funds must meet standards for affirmative action set forth by the U.S. Department of Labor. (For a full discussion of this subject see chapter 12, Human Resources and Benefits Administration.)

Human Subjects

The Department of Health and Human Services has rules for the involvement of humans as subjects in research activities. Many universities that accept federal funds for research have extended these rules to all projects involving human subjects, regardless of the source of funds. The rules specify the permissible exceptions to the general requirement of reviewing all research projects in which humans are used as subjects, and they include special requirements for dealing with children, prisoners, fetuses, or pregnant women. The regulations extend to the use of human organs, tissues, and body fluids, as well as graphic, written, or recorded information from individually identifiable human subjects. Details about requirements for expedited review of projects, documentation of research activities, criteria for approval of research, and informed consent are included in the regulations, published in the *Federal Register* on June 18, 1991. The regulations are government-wide.

To implement the regulations, an institutional review board must be appointed to review protocols for the use of humans as subjects. This board reviews activities involving human subjects to ensure that the methods and techniques used are adequate to protect the rights of subjects; that the risks to subjects are outweighed by the potential benefits; and that legally effective, informed consent of subjects is obtained. Because the legal and ethical liabilities involved are substantial, the IRB must be well-organized with clear lines of authority and responsibility.

Institutions are required to obtain IRB review and approval of projects before submitting a proposal or within 60 days after its submission. In 1991, NIH revised its regulations to require IRB review on noncompeting applications prior to or concurrent with submission of the proposal. Most large institutions have found that securing a general assurance can facilitate the submission of proposals.

As in the case of animal protection, an institution can receive a general assurance number from the Office of Protection from Research Risks on submission of its policies and procedures relating to the use of humans in research, a list of the members of its IRB, and a certification that it will review all human use protocols prior to the initiation of any research involving those humans. Records of all activities of the IRB must be maintained by the institution, along with copies of all informed-consent documents. Annual reporting is required to OPRR. This information is usually maintained by the chief academic officer, although some large institutions have separate officers for IRB activities; in such institutions, records are maintained in those offices.

Biohazards and Recombinant DNA

In 1976, NIH issued guidelines for research involving recombinant DNA molecules. These guidelines have been revised and now require, in general, that every institution in which research involving recombinant DNA technology is being or will be conducted establish a standing biosafety committee. The names, addresses, and qualifications of the committee members must be provided to NIH. The committee is required to review each proposed recombinant DNA experiment and to certify that the activities, personnel, and facilities are in compliance with the regulations.

Drug-Free Workplace

To meet the requirements of federally funded financial aid programs, institutional officials must certify the existence of policies related to drug and alcohol abuse on campus. The Drug-Free Workplace Act of 1988, which applies to all programs funded by the federal government, is an expansion of those requirements. Under the act, an institution must certify that it will provide a drug-free workplace by:

- publishing a statement notifying employees that the unlawful manufacture, distribution, dispensation, possession, or use of a controlled substance is prohibited in the workplace and specifying the actions that will be taken against employees for violating such prohibitions;

- establishing a drug-awareness program;

- requiring that employees engaged in a federal grant or contract agree, as a condition of employment, to abide by the policy and report any drug statute conviction occurring in the workplace; and

- imposing sanctions on, or requiring the participation in a drug abuse assistance program by, employees convicted of a drug statute violation occurring in the workplace.

In 1989, the Drug-Free Schools and Communities Act Amendments became law, and ED was charged with oversight responsibilities. Under these regulations an institution must adopt and implement a drug-prevention program to prevent the unlawful possession, use, or distribution of illicit drugs and alcohol by all students and employees on institutional premises or as part of any of its activities. Institutions are required to submit certifications of compliance to receive federal funds; to distribute the institutional policy and procedure statement annually to all students and employees; and to carry out a biennial review to determine the effectiveness of and implement changes in the program and to ensure that disciplinary sanctions are consistently enforced.

If an institution receives a contract that involves access to classified information or where the contracting officer has determined that, for reasons of national security or health and safety, more stringent regulations with regard to controlled substances are justified, the contracting officer may impose additional requirements for maintaining a drug-free workforce, as required in the Department of Defense Federal Acquisition Regulation Supplement (DFARS). These regulations are similar to those cited above except that they also require random drug testing and formal supervisory training programs. Many institutions, because of the drug testing requirement, will not accept contracts that include this drug-free work force regulation.

Debarment and Suspension

Under Executive Order 12549 (with implementing regulations published in the *Federal Register* on May 26, 1994, and June 26, 1995, and in the FAR at 52.209), applicants for federal funds are asked to certify to their best knowledge and belief that neither they, their principals, nor their researchers are debarred, suspended, or in the process of being debarred or suspended by any federal agency. In addition, the certification indicates that none of the applicants have been convicted or have had a civil judgment rendered against them for a variety of offenses identified in the regulations; are presently indicted or charged with one or a number of offenses so identified; or have had a public transaction at any governmental level terminated for cause or default.

An applicant's signature on a proposal signifies compliance with these regulations. Institutions should develop appropriate internal procedures to ensure that such certifications are appropriate.

Nondelinquency on Federal Debt

In accordance with OMB Circular A-129, *Managing Federal Credit Programs*, recipients of federal awards must provide information on any delinquency of the institution with regard to repayment of any federal debt, excluding personal income tax payments. Institutions, and in some cases individual principal investigators, are required to certify their nondelinquency on federal debt. When such a certification (called an assurance by some agencies) cannot be made, a proposal may be suspended from review or award until the debt is paid or satisfactory arrangements are made for the payment thereof.

Lobbying

P.L. 101-121 amended Title 31, USC, by adding a new Section 1352 (known as the Byrd Amendment) which requires institutions to certify that they have not used federal funds to lobby or otherwise influence certain federal officials and, if using nonfederal funds for such purposes, will advise the government thereof. The regulation is applicable to proposals or awards over $100,000. It prohibits recipients of federal funds from using such funds for lobbying the executive or legislative branches of the U.S. government in connection with a specific award. In addition, the regulation requires potential recipients of federal funds to disclose any lobbying activities undertaken with nonfederal funds.

Procurement Integrity

The Procurement Integrity Act of 1988 precluded institutional and governmental officials from engaging in certain types of conduct judged detrimental to impartial review and award of federal contract funds. The regulations require that no competing contractor or any officer, employee, representative, agency, or consultant of such contractor knowingly make, directly or indirectly, any offer or promise of future employment to any procurement officer of the agency; offer or give, directly or indirectly, any money, gratuity, or other thing of value to any procurement officer of the agency; or solicit or obtain, directly or indirectly, any proprietary or source selection information regarding the procurement. Although the regulations apply to all contract actions, certification is required prior to an award only if the award or modification exceeds $100,000 per year.

REPORTING REQUIREMENTS

All sponsors generally require some type of reporting with respect to scientific or technical, administrative, and fiscal activities on their awards. The extent of such reporting varies: federal agencies usually require technical, fiscal, property and intellectual property (invention) reporting while corporate sponsors generally limit reporting to technical and fiscal reports.

In the case of federal grants and cooperative agreements, the maximum frequency of reports is specified (by the requirements of OMB Circular A-110) to be limited to quarterly. However, A-110 gives agencies flexibility to require reports on a less frequent basis and many federal agencies have adopted annual reporting (often done electronically), especially for technical reports. In the case of contracts, the reporting requirements are specified in the contract document itself and are found in the appropriate sections of FAR or its agency supplement. This discussion describes general requirements for reporting; specific agency regulations should be consulted for details.

It should be noted that timely reporting is becoming more critical. OMB Circular A-110 (for grants and cooperative agreements) and the FAR (for contracts) specify when reports need to be submitted to sponsoring agencies. Not only is timely submission required as a condition of the award and audited in the annual A-133 audits, but failure to submit required reports (especially technical reports) may result in nonrenewal of the award, discrediting the reputation of the institution and the investigators, and in withholding of *all* awards from a federal agency to the institution.

Technical Reporting

Technical reporting is required on a periodic basis, although the timing of reports varies with the sponsoring agency. Technical reporting is legal and binding as a deliverable of the institution and often specifically of the principal investigator. Some agencies allow a principal investigator to submit a progress report when requesting additional funds, which then serves as the prior year's technical report. Other agencies require a technical report only on completion of the project and may allow an investigator to submit preprints and reprints of articles submitted for journal publication to fulfill the reporting requirements. At least one agency, the Office of Naval Research (ONR), has recently given its program officers the option of not requiring final technical reports, relying on periodic progress reports to provide an adequate summary of the technical progress on the project.

There are instances on contracts where monthly reporting is required; in these instances, the principal investigator should agree to the requirement before the institution accepts the award. One recent innovation of some federal agencies is the implementation of systems providing for electronic progress reports, and this trend is expected to continue.

Periodic technical reports give an agency an idea of how the sponsored activities are progressing and if there are any identifiable problems in carrying out the research. These reports allow for a comparison between actual accomplishments and the goals established in the proposal; they also summarize favorable developments or events that positively or negatively affect the conduct of the research.

Fiscal Reports and Payments

Fiscal reports are generally required by both governmental and nongovernmental sponsors on termination of a grant or contract. In addition, federal sponsors normally require more frequent financial reporting (such as the quarterly requirement of OMB Circular A-110 for assistance awards). Often recipients are required to summarize expenditures, provide data on unexpended federal funds and the status of federal cash advances, and, when the letter of credit system is not used, to request advances and/or reimbursements of expenses incurred to date. Institutional systems need to be capable of meeting the level of detail required.

Expenditures represent charges to a specific project or program and may be reported on a cash or accrual basis depending on the business processes of the institution. In the case of cash-based reporting, expenditures are the sum of the actual cash disbursements for direct charges, the amount of F&A (indirect) expense charged, the value of in-kind contributions provided, and the amount of cash advances or reimbursements made to subrecipients. In the case of accrual reporting, expenditures are the sum of actual cash disbursements for direct charges, the amount of F&A expense incurred, the value of in-kind contributions provided, and the net increase (or decrease) in the amounts owed by the recipient for goods or other property received and for services performed by employees, contractors, subrecipients, and other payees as well as other amounts coming due under programs for which previous services or performance were required.

In the case of contracts, the terms and conditions of the contract specify the content and frequency of fiscal reports. OMB Circular A-110 prescribes specific financial reports required of recipients of grants and cooperative agreements. The reports generally included follow.

Financial status report. The financial status report details the status of funds for all nonconstruction projects or programs. This submission may be waived if an agency determines that the request for advance reimbursement or report of federal cash transactions includes sufficient information.

Report of federal cash transactions. The report of federal cash transactions is used when funds are advanced to recipients through letters of credit or with Treasury Department checks. This report is used by federal agencies to monitor cash advanced to recipients and to obtain disbursement information for each agreement.

Request for advance or reimbursement. The request for advance or reimbursement is used for all nonconstruction projects when letters of credit or predetermined advance payment methods are not used. Such requests may be submitted at least monthly.

Outlay report and request for reimbursement on construction projects. This report is used to request reimbursement for construction programs when letters of credit are not used.

Although the sponsoring federal agency may specify the submission schedule for these reports on grants, they cannot be required more often than quarterly or less often than annually. Institutions may submit invoices and receive payments on a monthly basis if they so desire. The government cannot require monthly submissions. In most cases, continued funding of the project depends on timely submission of fiscal reports.

Equipment Reports

Most universities place management of equipment matters in a property management office, although the reporting responsibilities may be shared with a sponsored-programs office. Regardless of where the function is located, individuals charged with responsibility in this area must become familiar with the regulations on equipment title in both OMB Circular A-110 and the FAR, as well as the specific requirements included in any given award. Title to equipment purchased on contracts and grants may, at the time of acquisition, reside with the recipient organization or with the sponsor, depending on the specific terms and conditions of the award. Some agencies permit institutions to request title to a piece of equipment purchased on the project at the end of a project and specify the period of time in which an institution must do so. In some instances, an institution can request title from a sponsoring agency at the time it seeks approval to purchase the equipment. A-110 allows agencies to declare equipment as exempt, thus allowing recipients with a primary purpose of research to (by default) secure title at the time of purchase with no additional reporting requirements to the government.

To prepare and submit timely equipment reports (normally required by federal agencies on at least an annual basis), an institution should have a property management system that meets governmental requirements (generally those specified in OMB Circular A-110) for acquisition, identification, inventorying, managing, and disposing of equipment. In the case of federal awards, the equipment requirements are clear and precise; in the case of awards from nonfederal (particularly industrial) sponsors, this is often not the case. Institutional procedures should ensure that title to equipment acquired on contracts and grants from nonfederal sponsors is delineated clearly in the award document.

Inventions

If required by the award document, institutions must promptly report to the sponsor all inventions made in the course of any sponsored project. As in many other areas, government agencies are utilizing electronic reporting (such as NIH's EDISON system) to meet these requirements. Annual reporting (including negative reporting where an institution indicates that no inventions have been made) is generally required in the case of federal support. During the closeout of grants and contracts, agencies normally require a certification that all inventions conceived or reduced to practice during the course of work under the project (from its origination date through completion) have been reported to the agency. Such reports generally require the signature of both the principal investigator and the appropriate institutional official.

RECORD KEEPING

Federal sponsoring agencies generally require the maintenance of intact records relating to receipt and expenditure of funds. Other records, such as those relating to equipment acquisitions and maintenance, are also frequently required. These records and other pertinent books, documents, or papers are usually subject to audit by sponsoring agencies or their authorized representatives.

The determination as to when the retention time begins and ends varies with the type of record but, in general, the requirement on federal awards is five years from submission of the final report. Institutions should develop processes to identify the varying retention times and to ensure that all documents are kept for audit and other purposes for the full retention time required under the award.

One of the most difficult areas is that of retention of technical records. Recently, the government has indicated that technical records include research notebooks, machine outputs, and so forth. This is a general problem since most faculty retain their research notebooks and use them on an ongoing basis and, if switching institutions, expect to carry their research notebooks with them. For some institutions the answer in this case is to make the faculty member the custodian of the records and not allow him/her to dispose of those records without written permission from the employing institution at the time the record was generated.

PROPERTY

Property is defined as real property (land, including improvements thereto, and buildings) or personal property (equipment). According to OMB Circular A-110, intellectual property is also defined as property and subject to some of the same requirements as other personal property.

In the case of real property, title generally vests in the recipient, provided that the recipient agrees to use the property, after the project under which it was acquired has terminated, for the authorized purposes of the project or for other federally sponsored projects. When the real property is no longer needed for these purposes, title may be permitted to reside in the recipient, provided that the federal government is compensated for its fair share; it may be transferred to the government or another entity, or the property may be sold and the government properly compensated for its share of the costs.

In OMB Circulars A-110 and A-21, the federal government has set dollar and life-expectancy thresholds for consideration of items as equipment (cost of $5,000 or more per unit and a useful life of more than one year). Of course, institutions may have their own thresholds for items to qualify as equipment, but institutions may not have thresholds greater than those established by the government.

Regulations require recipients of federal funds to maintain records on all equipment acquired with such funds unless the equipment is defined as exempt according to A-110. These records require, as a minimum, the following:

- description of the property;
- manufacturer's serial number or other identifying mark;

- source of the property, including sponsor identification number;
- identity of the title holder;
- acquisition date;
- percentage of federal participation in the acquisition cost;
- location, use, and condition;
- unit acquisition cost; and
- ultimate disposition data.

Federal grant-acquired equipment must be inventoried at least once every two years, and there should be a control system in place to ensure adequate safeguards to prevent damage, loss, or theft of the property.

The circular also specifies conditions under which an institution may dispose of equipment it has acquired under grants or cooperative agreements and stipulates the conditions under which the institution must reimburse the sponsor for its fair share of the original purchase of the equipment.

COST ACCOUNTING

Generally accepted accounting procedures for colleges and universities should be followed in the management and administration of sponsored programs. The accounting system should provide for application of cost principles and standards on a consistent basis as provided in OMB Circular A-21 and the specific policies and regulations of sponsoring agencies. The system adopted by the institution should be responsive to billing and reporting requirements, which vary among agencies and are subject to change. Financial or business officers need to monitor these standards and be alert to proposed changes. One of the most important current costing requirements is the requirement for compliance with the Cost Accounting Standards that were incorporated into OMB Circular A-21 in 1996 and earlier in the FAR for contracts.

Four of the nineteen standards that apply to the corporate environment now apply to colleges and universities. These standards are:

- CAS 501—Consistency in Estimating, Accumulating and Reporting;
- CAS 502—Consistency in Allocating Costs Incurred for the Same Purpose;
- CAS 505—Accounting for Unallowable Costs—Educational Institutions; and

• CAS 506—Cost Accounting Period —Educational Institutions.

Although the requirement to file a CAS disclosure statement (DS-2) does not apply to all institutions, the requirement to be in compliance with these standards is incumbent upon all institutions of higher education. These standards, particularly CAS 501 and 502, are often cited when institutions are revising their organizational affiliations and seeking to combine the preaward, postaward, and accounting offices responsible for stewardship of federal funds.

Receipt and Deposit of Funds

Separate accounts for each project should be established and monthly expenditure statements provided on a timely basis to the principal investigator and the sponsored-program office. Although separate bank accounts are not required for each project, procedures must be established to relate a payment properly on a specific project to that account. The monitoring of cash flow is a specific responsibility of senior management, since it has a direct impact on the financial health of the institution. In reviewing its cash management program, the institution should ensure that it has adequate procedures in place to receive and deposit all money on a timely basis and to invest it, when permitted, in accordance with institutional policies and, where necessary, applicable federal regulations. Federal funds awarded to public and independent nonprofit higher education institutions must be maintained in interest-bearing accounts, and any interest earned on federal advances deposited in such accounts must be remitted at least quarterly to the federal government; $250 per year can be retained for the management of these funds. (See Chapter 11, Cash Management.)

Procedures should be developed for follow-up on delinquent accounts. Aging schedules, which provide the dates payments are due and track late payments, should be maintained, and relevant information should be communicated to responsible institutional officials. A difficult issue institutions face is whether to accept a new award from a sponsor delinquent in its payment on a prior award. If the reason for nonpayment is a cash flow or financial sufficiency problem, taking another award may not be in the best interests of the institution. However, if the reason for nonpayment on one project is the result of missing or late progress reports, or issues surrounding the quality and/or quantity of research, more difficult problems are posed. Decisions should be made only after consultation with senior financial and academic officers.

Allowability and Allocability of Costs

OMB Circular A-21, which is applicable to both assistance and procurement awards, specifies the factors affecting the allowability, allocability, and reasonableness of costs on sponsored programs.

Allowability of Costs

Under the cost principles of OMB Circular A-21, costs are allowed if they are reasonable, if they can be allocated to sponsored agreements, if they can be consistently applied, and if they conform to limitations or exclusions in the specific sponsored agreement or the cost principles of A-21.

Circular A-21 provides guidance on the allowability of certain types of costs for sponsored agreements. Unless there are special provisions in a specific grant or contract, in specific program regulations applicable to an award, or in general agency regulations, the provisions of Circular A-21 govern.

Allocability of Costs

Costs are allocable to specific cost objectives (a specific department, project, or function) if the goods and services involved are chargeable to the cost objective in accordance with the relative benefits each receives. Within this guideline, a cost is allocable to a sponsored agreement when it is incurred to advance the work of the sponsored agreement to which it is charged; it benefits both the sponsored project and other work of the institution in proportions that can be reasonably identified; and it is necessary to the overall activities of the institution.

Although costs may be allocable to two or more sponsored projects, care should be taken to ensure that transfers of costs between projects are made only under guidelines provided by the federal agency and within the time frame specified. Costs cannot be transferred from one sponsored agreement to another solely to cover deficits caused by overruns in one account. However, there was a change to OMB Circular A-21 in the early 1990s, which under certain circumstances (the interrelationship of the work involved) allows the allocation or transferring of expenses to benefited projects on any reasonable basis.

DIRECT AND F&A (INDIRECT) COSTS

For administrative and accounting purposes, the costs that pertain to a specific sponsored project are grouped into two categories: direct costs and F&A (indirect costs).[1] Some costs are easily determined to be direct costs; some are as easily identified as F&A costs; but some costs may be defined, according to institutional policy, as either direct or indirect costs. However, costs incurred in like circumstances must be classified as either direct or indirect; they cannot be both.

Direct Costs

Direct costs are costs that can be identified with a specific sponsored project or that can be assigned to more than one sponsored project relatively easily with a high degree of accuracy. Direct costs usually include:

- salaries and wages of persons employed on specific sponsored project accounts;
- benefits for persons employed on specific sponsored projects (benefits normally include FICA, unemployment insurance, and medical insurance);
- equipment acquired for use on the award(s) to which the acquisition costs are allocated;
- supplies and materials needed to carry out the project;
- travel expenses for domestic and international travel connected with the sponsored project; and
- communication, data processing, and miscellaneous costs.

F&A Costs

F&A costs are perhaps the most contentious area of costs within an institution of higher education. F&A costs are costs that cannot be easily identified with a specific project but that are expended to meet the requirements of the project. They include a share of expenses for items such as operation and maintenance, library, depreciation or use allowance, sponsored-projects administration, and departmental administration. Often faculty exert pressure to reduce F&A-cost rates to increase the funds available for direct costs and to make projects more competitive through lower costs. Governmental agencies exert pressure to reduce F&A costs because they see the growth of F&A costs as a diversion of funds from the direct-cost objectives of the sponsored project.

Most institutions have HHS as their cognizant audit agency, although some large institutions have cognizance vested in the Defense Contract Audit Agency (DCAA) and Office of Naval Research (ONR). The decision as to whether HHS or DCAA is cognizant depends on the amount of funding to the institution from defense agencies (DOD, DARPA, etc.) compared to funding from civilian agencies (HHS, NSF, etc.). Among colleges and universities, fewer than 30 are DCAA/ONR cognizant and the balance are HHS cognizant.

F&A cost rates are normally expressed as a percentage of either modified total direct costs or salaries and wages, although a few institutions have an F&A cost rate based on salaries, wages, and benefits. Each institution with total direct expenditures subject to OMB Circular A-21 of over $10 million per year is required to submit an indirect-cost proposal to its cognizant agency within six months of the close of the institution's fiscal year. The preparation of this "long-form" indirect-cost proposal is complex and time-consuming and should be started before the year's financial statement is completed. If expenditures are less than $10 million per year, an institution may use the simplified method for small institutions, unless this procedure would produce results that would be inequitable to either the institution or the government. Although the rate may differ dramatically between long- and short-form institutions, the actual recovery in either case theoretically reimburses an institution for its F&A costs.

Issues surrounding F&A cost rates and recovery of indirect costs by an institution have become more significant as pressures on budgets, at both the federal and institutional levels, increase. With the issuance of recent revisions to OMB Circular A-21, it is clear that federal officials and institutional officers will continue to face this contentious issue. Institutions can expect more detailed reviews of F&A cost proposals and an increasing number of audits from federal offices. There will be increasing pressure on institutions from faculty to reduce or waive F&A cost recovery in favor of direct cost reimbursement. Business and sponsored-programs officers should educate their campuses as to the structure and purpose of indirect costs and help eliminate the myth that indirect costs are profits to an institution.

AUDITS

Expenditures incurred under grants and contracts, as well as the management systems used to administer the institution, are subject to audit by the cognizant federal agency. In addition, an institution's F&A cost proposal itself is subject to audit, as are the budgetary aspects of proposals when a contract is contemplated and the award or modification thereto is expected to exceed $100,000. (See also chapter 22, Auditing.)

Audit requirements have become more stringent in several areas and should be addressed carefully by recipient institutions. The following areas should be managed by the sponsored-programs office.

Pass-through Awards

Pass-through awards are those that are received by an institution from a source other than that which made an original award. In the case of the federal government, pass-through funds may be awarded to a state agency and then re-awarded to a higher education institution. Another routine source of pass-through funding is from another higher education institution, when the subrecipient (i.e., the recipient of the pass-through funds) is expected to help perform the research for which the original funding was made.

Identification of direct federal awards and "pass-through" awards must be provided so that the auditor will know which of the pass-through awards to test for compliance with federal requirements. In applicable cases, the institution should identify the Code of Federal Domestic Assistance (CFDA) number assigned to each project so that major programs can be grouped together.

Subrecipient Relationships

Under OMB Circular A-133, a recipient of federal funds has the same requirements as the federal government for assurance that subrecipient activity is in compliance with the requirements of the federal award. Institutions must there-fore carefully define subrecipients (as compared to vendors) and develop appropriate institutional procedures for monitoring them. The issue of whether a relationship is a subrecipient one or a vendor relationship for goods and services, and therefore how much of the agreement is subject to overhead charges, is not always clear. If one university involves another in the program of research, it is normally a subrecipient relationship (and overhead to the prime recipient is limited to its negotiated overhead rate on the first $25,000 of the subrecipient agreement); this is fairly easy to ascertain. However, when the subrecipient is a commercial firm and is involved, for example, both in substantively participating in the research program and constructing a prototype piece of equipment, the situation becomes murky. It is certainly advisable to develop institutional procedures for determining how to handle such relationships by, perhaps, constructing a decision tree in which certain questions (such as whether the subrecipient will own intellectual property it develops or whether individuals at the subrecipient organization will be coauthors of research papers) are answered.

Compliance Auditing

Audit compliance under OMB Circular A-133 will go beyond testing of financial systems and will include compliance with regulatory mandates such as the Drug-Free Workplace Act and the various civil rights requirements imposed on recipients of federal funds.

The sponsoring federal agency and the U.S. General Accounting Office retain the right to perform their own audits after the completion of the audit performed under Circular A-133.

INTELLECTUAL PROPERTY AND TECHNOLOGY TRANSFER

Institutional Policies

In the area of sponsored programs, institutions are generally concerned about patents, copyrights, and software. With respect to inventions conceived or reduced to practice with any support from federal or federal flow-through sources, the applicable federal regulations are those expressed in the Patent and Trademark Law Amendments Act (Bayh-Dole Act—P.L. 96-517). Subject to these regulations when federal funds are involved, institutional policies generally indicate the extent to which an institution can exert ownership rights to intellectual property developed by its employees. Most institutions exercise ownership over patentable inventions resulting from the work of their employees; most assert ownership of copyrightable material only when such ownership is dictated by special grant or contract terms or when the copyrightable material has been developed under a contract with an employee for a commissioned work. More and more frequently, institutions are claiming ownership of a separate class of copyrightable material— software.

It is crucial that institutions have an established policy for the administration of inventions, because that policy affects the extent to which an institutional official may negotiate patent clauses in grants or contracts. Generally, such clauses are necessary only when dealing with nongovernmental sponsors and can be the most difficult part of contract negotiation if the sponsor wishes to claim title and institutional policy requires that title remain with the institution. Institutional policies should address, at a minimum, the process by which an invention is disclosed; the right to publish research results; the procedures for review of that invention; the requirements for notification to sponsors; the sharing of any income between

the institution and the inventor(s) that derives from the technology; the requirement for employees to formally assign right and title to any patentable technology
to the employing institution; and the reporting obligations mandated under
Bayh-Dole.

The Bayh-Dole Act was signed into law in 1980 and substantially changed
the relationship between the government and colleges and universities in the handling of patentable technology arising under grants and contracts. The act allows
nonprofit organizations and small businesses (including, by definition, colleges
and universities) to elect to retain, with limited exceptions under "special circumstances," title to inventions made in the course of federally sponsored research and
prohibits the assignment of patents to other than a patent management firm. Federal awards are subject to the Patent Rights (Small Business Firms and Nonprofit
Organizations) clause. Institutions that engage in significant amounts of patent
work generally employ a technology transfer officer, with legal and business support, to manage the patent and licensing program and to ensure compliance with
federal requirements. Failure to move expeditiously to commercialize disclosed
technology or to notify the government at appropriate times can allow the federal
government "march-in" rights to the technology, precluding an institution's handling of the technology for any commercial purposes.

Licensing

An institution usually applies for patent protection on an invention (generally referred to as "technology") after the technology has been reviewed for novelty
and its potential for commercialization. Applying for a patent is only the first step
in commercialization. Many institutions with significant patent and copyright
activity want to actively commercialize that technology to make it available to the
public. To do this, institutions often create a technology transfer office or, in
smaller institutions, identify someone in the institution as the technology transfer
officer. This person should be charged with the responsibility to seek commercial
avenues to market the technology and should have the authority to negotiate
licensing agreements. By law, all commercialization agreements provide the government with a royalty free nonexclusive license for the use of the technology.

Support from the inventor is often critical to marketing technology; the
inventor should work closely with the technology transfer office in seeking a market. Sponsored-programs officers normally are involved in this activity as well,
since in many cases the license arrangements can result in the award of grants or
contracts to develop the technology further.

Although institutions often believe that income from licensing technology is a potentially lucrative source of income, that is more often not the case. The patenting and licensing of technology can be quite expensive (recent estimates are that it costs approximately $15,000 to $20,000 to apply for and receive a domestic patent; international protection, often quite necessary, is more expensive than that). Nonetheless, a strong technology licensing program can be an asset to an institution and senior officers should carefully consider the extent and nature of such activities on their campuses.

Rights in Technical Data

Most federal agencies define data as recorded information, regardless of the form or media on which it is recorded. The term includes computer software and data generated under an award of a scientific or technical nature.

Unless there are specific contract and grant provisions to the contrary, the institution is assumed to have the right, and may grant others the right, to copyright, publish, and/or disclose any data first produced in performance of work under a federal award. At the same time, however, the federal government has a royalty-free, nonexclusive, irrevocable license to use, reproduce, perform, display, and make available to the public any data first produced in performance of work under a federal award.

NEW DEVELOPMENTS

One notable trend in sponsored programs over the last decade has been the marked increase in regulatory and compliance requirements and the resulting pressure on F&A rates. In addition, perhaps the most creative and innovative development has been the advent of electronic research administration, which will undoubtedly be one of the key activities throughout the federal government in the 21st century. Each of these trends is discussed in some detail below as well as some other items that are currently a focus of the federal government.

Compliance Auditing

The federal government has audited colleges and universities for years, conducting both audits of systems and audits of specific contracts. The government continues its review of financial systems and processes with compliance auditing and goes beyond the examination of financial systems to test, or require independent state auditors to test, compliance with administrative regulations such as the

Drug-Free Workplace requirements. This is most clearly seen in the compliance supplement to OMB Circular A-133, which defines several specific areas where formal written compliance procedures are required. The areas are:

- allowable/unallowable activities;

- allowable/unallowable cost principles;

- cash management;

- equipment and real property management;

- matching, level of effort, earmarking;

- period of availability of federal funds;

- procurement and suspension/debarment;

- program income;

- reporting;

- subrecipient monitoring; and

- special tests and provisions.

Pressures on the F&A Rate

The portion of a research agreement that is allocated to direct costs and to indirect costs continues to be an issue that both universities and the federal government struggle with on an on-going basis. Of course, it is also a subject of vital interest to researchers, who often believe that the F&A rate can be a determinant in whether a specific award will or will not be made. F&A costs are reimbursements by the government for expenses already incurred in support of grants and contracts and, theoretically, should reimburse the institution for the share of those costs related to sponsored activities. In practice, however, in recent years there has been pressure from certain segments of the federal government (including at various times both OMB and Congress) to hold or reduce rates at colleges and universities. This has been expressed in actions such as the 3.6 percent allowance for faculty administrative effort, the removal of student services from the pool costs, the calculation of a utility allowance, and the pressures to move from the instructional to the research base the cost of donated faculty effort in support of research grants and contracts. There has been a perception by some federal officials that the F&A portion of an award was increasing faster than the direct cost portion. Statistics collected by organizations such as the Council on Governmental Relations and the American Association of Universities, have shown that the overall F&A rate has not increased and, in fact, the administrative components are in many cases decreasing. One of the reasons for renaming of indirect cost to facilities and administrative costs was to segregate the cost pools and the calculation of the rates to allow individuals to more readily do analyses of the various indirect cost components.

At the present time the area of focus tends to be the impact on the research base of the effect of donated effort of faculty. Government auditors maintain that the regulations require institutions to compute the value of the donated effort of faculty in support of research projects (i.e., that effort toward projects which is not promised in a proposal or reimbursed by the government) and move the dollar value of that effort from the instructional to the research base. This, of course, has the effect of reducing the F&A rate. The Office of Science and Technology Policy's Presidential Review Directive report, which was released in late 1999 and for which implementation strategies are being developed, recognizes this issue in combination with related issues concerning cost sharing requirements being imposed, sometimes *ad hoc*, on grantees. This latter issue (cost sharing) was recently addressed by the National Science Foundation when it issued a policy document stating that cost sharing was to be a condition of eligibility but not a criterion of evaluation.

Electronic Research Administration

Electronic research administration (ERA) is probably best defined as a process for using electronic processes to conduct the research enterprise, from preparing and submitting research proposals to receiving and managing awards to submitting technical and fiscal reports. The concept of using electronics to help support the research administration system has been in existence for many years and, in fact, in the early 1990s NIH was working on an electronic proposal system. In 1994 when the National Science Foundation introduced its electronic proposal development and award management system, FastLane, electronic research administration became a reality for the creation and submission of proposals. Equally exciting is the development of automated sponsored project management systems, which are becoming more and more prevalent at large research universities. These systems allow institutions to provide data electronically to principal investigators, departmental administrative personnel, and central administrative personnel to mange externally funded projects in a more time efficient and effective manner. An example of such a system is the Massachusetts Institute of Technology's

COEUS system, and other systems, created both by universities and for-profit firms, are currently under development.

The Federal Demonstration Partnership (FDP), formerly known as the Federal Demonstration Project, is the institutional focal point for the development of cooperative university-government systems for electronic research administration. The FDP is the focal point for developing and testing electronic processes and for working with the Federal Commons to create user friendly and supportable systems in research administration. Currently there are two parallel initiatives—one utilizing electronic data interchange (EDI) transaction sets to interact with the government in submitting electronic proposals and receiving electronic awards and the other utilizing hypertext markup language (HTML) or other Web-based technologies for the same purpose. Both systems are in their infancy but, now that the government has decided that systems must be electronic by 2002, significant progress should be made. Already electronic, of course, are the payment systems of many federal agencies and, again, every federal agency is mandated to have a computerized payment system functioning before 2003.

One of the most promising areas of future development is the creation of electronic compliance systems. Already institutions have computerized budget creation and checking systems and some institutions are building electronic databases to handle human subjects and animal compliance activities, do reporting for invention reports (EDISON), and allow submission of technical and financial reports electronically. These activities will dramatically increase over the next five to 10 years and this creates a specific challenge for universities in the hiring and retention of research administration personnel with the background and skills to effectively work in this new environment.

The Federal Demonstration Partnership

In March 1986, five federal agencies and 10 higher education institutions in Florida began the Florida Demonstration Project in an attempt to reduce unnecessary administrative burdens on sponsored research and to increase research productivity. After two years and a positive review, these agencies and institutions, joined by six more agencies and 40 institutions, embarked on the Federal Demonstration Project. In its expanded version, this initiative was designed to increase research productivity and to reduce administrative costs within the federal government and at academic institutions by standardizing and simplifying federal arrangements for the support of academic research. The project's primary goal was to demonstrate that the most appropriate decision-making level is as close to the principal investigator as possible, while maintaining, at institutional and governmental levels, adequate controls to assure that federal funds have been spent for the purposes for which they were awarded. One of the real successes of this phase of the FDP was the incorporation of the so-called "expanded authorities" into OMB Circular A-110, which allows institutions of higher education and their faculty members to manage most federal research grants at the institutional level. For example, institutions may initiate preaward spending (at their own risk) up to 90 days in advance of an award, give themselves no-cost extensions for up to one year, carry over funds from one grant year to another, and have most governmental prior approval requirements waived.

The Federal Demonstration Partnership, while continuing to emphasize streamlining activities, is now heavily focused on electronic research administration initiatives, the area that has significant promise for the future.

NOTES

1. The 1996 revisions to Circular A-21 changed the name of "indirect costs" to "facilities and administrative costs" to distinguish between the administrative components of the rate and the facilities portion of the rate. The change responded, in part, to concerns about a perceived growth in the overhead rate due to administrative increases. Separating the rate components provides better data on the growth of the rate components that make up the administrative portion of the rate (which is capped at 26 points in the rate) and the facilities portion (which is not capped).

REFERENCES AND RESOURCES

Publications

Annual Register of Grant Support. Wilmette, Ill.: National Register Publishing Co., published annually.

Catalog of Federal Domestic Assistance. Washington, DC: U.S. Government Printing Office, published annually.

Council on Governmental Relations. *The Bayh-Dole Act: A Guide to the Law and Implementing Regulations,* Washington, DC: COGR, 1999.

Council on Governmental Relations. *Managing Externally Funded Programs at Colleges and Universities: A Guideline to Good Management Practices.* Washington, DC: COGR, 1998.

Foundation Center. *The Foundation Directory*. New York: Foundation Center, published every two years.

National Archives and Records Service. *Federal Register*. Washington, DC: U.S. Government Printing Office, published daily.

National Council of University Research Administrators. *Regulation and Compliance: A Compendium of Regulations and Certifications Applicable to Sponsored-Programs*. Washington, DC: NCURA, 1996.

Taft Group. *Taft Corporate Directory*. Washington, DC: Taft Group, published annually.

Periodicals

Commerce Business Daily

Federal Grants and Contracts Weekly

Issues in Science and Technology

Research Management Review

Science and Government Report

The Society of Research Administrators Journal

OMB Circulars

A-21: *Cost Principles for Educational Institutions*

A-88: *Indirect Cost Rates, Audit, and Audit Follow-Up at Educational Institutions*

A-110: *Uniform Administrative Requirements for Grants and Other Agreements with Institutions of Higher Education, Hospitals, and Other Non-Profit Organizations*

A-129: *Managing Federal Credit Programs*

A-133: *Audits of Institutions of Higher Education and Other Non-Profit Organizations*

Agency Materials

National Science Foundation. *Grant Policy Manual*

National Science Foundation. *Guide to Programs*

U.S. Department of Health and Human Services. *Grants Administration Manual*

U.S. Department of Health and Human Services. National Institutes of Health. *NIH Guide to Grants and Contracts*

U.S. Department of Health and Human Services. Public Health Service. *Grant Policy Statement*

Chapter 19

Student Financial Aid

by

J. Stephen Collins
University of Massachusetts, Lowell

Betsy Hobson
Williams College

Stephanie Lorber Karger
Brandeis University

Philip G. Wick

Sponsors

KPMG
Contact: Greg J. Baroni
1676 International Drive
McLean, VA 22102
703-747-3004
www.kpmg.com

With over 30 years of serving higher education, KPMG offers a broad range of services that helps our clients analyze their businesses with true clarity, raises their level of performance and delivers the strategic and infrastructural components to support highly dynamic E-business models in colleges, universities, and academic medical centers.

PEOPLESOFT, INC.
Contact: Karen Willett
4460 Hacienda Drive
Pleasanton, CA 94588
925-694-5453
www.peoplesoft.com

PeopleSoft delivers E-business solutions for higher education management needs, including student administration, grants management, finance, human resources, E-procurement, advancement, and more. PeopleSoft also provides comprehensive customer service, consulting, education, and technical support services.

ACCESS GROUP, INC.
Contact: School Services
1411 Foulk Road
P.O. Box 7430
Wilmington, DE 19803-0430
800-227-2151
www.accessgroup.org

The Access Group is a nonprofit organization dedicated to providing access to education through affordable financing and related services. Committed to providing competitive loan terms and superior service, Access Group offers federal and private loans for students enrolled in law, medical, dental, business, health, and other graduate programs.

KEY EDUCATION RESOURCES
800 Superior Avenue
Cleveland, OH 44114
800-540-1855
www.key.com/educate

Key Education Resources is a leading provider of education payment plans nationwide. We are an excellent resource affording online services that help business offices.

THE COLLEGE BOARD
Contact: Kathleen Little
11911 Freedom Drive, Suite 300
Reston, VA 20190
703-707-8999
www.collegeboard.org

The College and University Enrollment Services division of the College Board provides a suite of integrated enrollment management solutions that support institutions' recruitment, financing, and retention efforts.

Contents

The 1990s witnessed a number of significant events that directly affected financial aid principles, policies, and practices. Federal aid policy continued to shift away from its 30-year priority of "access" for low-income students to concerns of affordability for the middle class. To this end, the Higher Education Amendments of 1992 eliminated home equity from the federal eligibility formula so that more middle income families would qualify for aid—particularly subsidized loans. Every student, regardless of income, became eligible for either subsidized or unsubsidized federal loans. Appropriations for loans more than doubled while those for Pell Grants remained relatively flat. The Taxpayer Relief Act of 1997 created a number of education tax credits, again aimed primarily at the middle class. This prompted a new set of reporting requirements for institutions, which for the first time were promulgated by the U.S. Treasury rather than the Department of Education.

Unlimited entitlement appropriations, the creation of the William D. Ford Federal Direct Loan Program, and significant business and technological improvements created an unparalleled competitive environment for federal student loans. Application forms were standardized and business procedures streamlined, dramatically reducing processing and disbursement times between lenders and guarantors and lenders and students. Students have benefited from lower interest rates, faster and more reliable servicing, and more flexible repayment options. However, federal borrowing limits have not increased proportionately to the increase in educational costs. Consequently, the private commercial market has responded with a host of alternative loan and financial planning and investment programs. In addition, many states have entered the arena as sponsors of a variety of prepaid tuition and savings plans.

Enrollment management clearly came of age as an attempt to control the desired characteristics and size of the student body while in many cases maximizing tuition revenue. Financial aid is used as a critical tool in efforts to recruit and retain students. Although need-based aid continues to be the predominant form of funding, non-need-based gift aid, mainly to recognize academic, artistic, or athletic achievement or other desired skills, has increased at a much faster rate than need-based gift aid.[1] While federal aid continues to be based almost entirely on need, several states—intent on stemming the flight of their top students across state borders—as well as colleges and universities rely on generous awards to attract the best and the brightest regardless of students' financial circumstances.

In 1992, Congress mandated the creation of the Free Application for Federal Student Aid (FAFSA) and a separate Federal Methodology (FM) to determine eligibility for federal funds. This enabled many institutions, particularly public and others with little funding of their own, to discontinue using independent processors. While this free and simplified service benefits the majority of students, it has created at many institutions a two-tiered system of evaluating family ability to contribute to educational costs. This in turn has broadened the concept of need and principles of equity that long have guided the professional financial aid community while encouraging mainly independent institutions to use whatever methodology they believed would best enable them to achieve their educational mission.

The educational enterprise has moved from being producer-driven to consumer-driven. While some students benefit from this highly competitive environment and the variations in need determination and packaging, there is growing concern that issues of affordability have superseded those of access and that the nation's neediest students are being bypassed.

This highly competitive, complex, and customer-driven environment has placed new and considerable demands on financial aid, admission, and bursar operations. Many institutions have reorganized these three operations, often including the registrar to better achieve their administrative goals. Some have combined financial aid and bursar under what is called student financial services, while others have joined admission, financial aid, bursar, and registrar under student-services or enrollment-management umbrellas. Whatever the structure, most institutions have improved lines of horizontal communication among these functions as well as overarching senior management involvement. A number of institutions have adopted "one-stop shopping" designed to minimize student "office hopping" while improving administrative efficiency. The availability of software packages that have interactive student service modules has greatly influenced and assisted the processes of reorganization and cross training in the effort to make student services as efficient and user friendly as possible.

INSTITUTIONAL CONSIDERATIONS

A vital consumer-oriented service provided by colleges and universities is to assist students and their families with the financing of educational expenses. This includes providing financial aid to those students who meet established federal, state, and institutional criteria as well as providing information about special financial aid or financing programs for students and families who want or require additional assistance or who fall outside traditional financial aid guidelines.

This chapter discusses institutional considerations involved in student financial services, the different forms of financial aid, the award cycle, management issues, loan billing and collection procedures, and new dimensions.

Institutional Policy

A well-defined policy for student financial aid should be incorporated within and support the institution's mission and goals and provide the basis for evaluation and review. This policy should result from a consensus that represents directly affected operations and constituencies, including faculty, trustees, administrative staff, and students. The first step in developing or reviewing such a policy is a detailed assessment of student aid and financial services and their impact on the institution.

Such an assessment should include, but not be limited by, consideration of the effect of the aid-packaging policy on:

- the institution's ability to recruit, retain, and graduate students with the characteristics most desired by the institution;

- enrolled students (for example: student work expectations on academic performance and debt burdens on retention or alumni satisfaction level and giving);

- satisfactory academic progress standards;

- the price setting process, that is, the rationale for and impact of institutional allocations for financial aid; and

- enrollment and course selection patterns, particularly in specialized programs such as nursing or in over- or under-enrolled majors.

Other questions to consider include:

- What are the purpose and requirements of each financial aid program, both internal and external?

- Are senior administrators, the president, the governing board, and faculty informed about institutional commitment and policy regarding financial aid?

- Are there up-to-date and effective written, as well as Web-based, materials and procedures for keeping prospective students and enrolled students and parents well informed about financial aid availability and financing options?

- Are good business practices followed in every step of the financial aid program?

- Are optimal procedures in place to ensure the most efficient cash flow?

- How can the institution's default rate on student tuition and loans be reduced?

- What role does institutional research play in developing and evaluating financial aid policies?

The policy statement that emerges from an assessment of this nature should offer a comprehensive view of how the financial services in general and financial aid programs in particular support institutional objectives. The statement provides the framework for the offices and operations involved to develop appropriate procedures and practices and becomes the basis for modifying policies.

Enrollment management and the policies governing student financial aid and financial services are the responsibility of the academic, admissions, student affairs, financial aid, and business departments. An institution should adopt consistent policies and procedures for awarding and administering such assistance. A coordinated and comprehensive institutional policy is critical to the success of a financial aid program. While the policy must meet current needs, it also must encompass plans that will contribute to the college or university's financial strength to ensure support of future students. Financial aid and services have critical implications for enrollment planning (the recruitment, matriculation, retention, and graduation of students) and directly affect the financial stability of the institution. Attention must be paid to changes in the various sources of aid, especially when tuition discounts and other unrestricted institutional revenues are the major sources of aid funds.

An institution's policies for the allocation of the various funds available for aid programs should be designed carefully, because these policies can have a direct effect on enrollment. While laws and regulations govern state and federal aid programs, institutional sources of aid usually offer some flexibility. Financial aid packaging can be used as a tool for attracting students. For example, a policy of low debt burden in the freshman year or for the lowest income students may be implemented. Work-study opportunities for all students can be structured to facilitate development of marketable employment skills and career networks. Establishing special loan or payment programs for those families who are not eligible for federal grant and subsidized loan programs may be very attractive to middle- and upper-middle-income families, as well as to all families offered less aid than they feel they need.

An institution may also consider merit-based aid as an enrollment management tool. Merit aid is often used to try to raise the caliber of the student body or a particular program by attracting high academic achievers or students with a special skill set. A merit aid program must be carefully designed and monitored. This can be a very expensive policy unless the institution raises special funds for merit awards. Even then, merit aid may be largely used for those who would have matriculated without it or may be quickly matched by the competition. It may make better sense to allocate resources to other areas, such as campus visitation plan programs, summer or term-time career-oriented or research internships, or income-contingent loans. In creating a new merit-based scholarship program, enrollment managers need to consider what defines success and then assess the program results accordingly. (For a full discussion of tuition discounting, see chapter 2, Planning.)

A critical aspect of enrollment management is the importance of financial aid to the retention of students. Administrators need to consider to what extent aid policies that attract freshmen will continue to meet the needs of these students as they progress toward a degree. The retention of students will improve if aid can be guaranteed for the entire course of study—provided the students continue to meet all eligibility criteria—and if counseling and alternative payment arrangements are available to assist families with financial issues not resolved by traditional financial aid.

Financial aid policy and funding mechanisms also can be important tools in enrollment management at the graduate level. The sources of graduate aid vary by type of program and level. However, the basic principles of providing good information, effective counseling, and access to several financing options are equally important there.

Administrative Responsibilities

Because the financial aid office has direct involvement with so many other administrative areas, the institution must endeavor to ensure that lines of communication between the financial aid office and the admissions, bursar, and chief financial officers are always open, and that the offices of the registrar and student affairs, development, information systems, institutional research, and publications departments are involved as necessary. The director of financial aid should be a full partner and active participant on the institution's enrollment planning/management team and included in discussions about pricing and tuition setting.

Sound organizational structure should reflect and encourage effective communication and assist the assignment of well-defined tasks, areas of responsibility, and authority that are essential to the successful administration of student financial services. In view of the importance of financial aid to undergraduate admissions, it is essential that the recruitment and enrollment functions be closely coordinated between those departments and the bursar, including some basic measures of cross-training of staffs, especially if operations are separate from each other or report to different administrators. It is also critical that organizational cooperation, and the use of technology and procedures to provide seamless service delivery from the student's perspective, also comply with strict requirements for federal aid administration: the functions of authorizing awards and of disbursing funds to (or for the benefit of) students must be done by different individuals who are organizationally independent of one another (and do not report to the same individual).[2]

The financial aid operation is responsible for the overall administration of the various need-based (and in many cases, merit-based) programs. It is responsible for notifying prospective and continuing students about their awards and for making revisions as changes in conditions dictate (e.g., changes in family circumstances or receipt of external awards). The business office is responsible for fund disbursement, accounts receivable, and cash management. Therefore the business office must:

- set up disbursement mechanisms for the different financial aid funds;
- closely monitor these disbursements (the Department of Education gives detailed information regarding disbursement and record keeping of federal funds in its publication *The Blue Book*);
- draw down and account for federal, state, and private dollars as needed and permitted;
- establish procedures for student billing and receivables including refunds;
- collect and account for all funds related to student aid; and
- do all this in a manner that optimizes cash flow as well as customer service.

If the institution has a separate office for loan administration and collection, care must be taken to ensure there is proper communication among the financial aid, bursar, and loan offices since each may be responsible for a different segment of the student loan process.

The financial aid and business offices must work together closely to make certain that the needs of students, the goals of the institution, and fiduciary responsibilities are met. This includes coordinating fiscal and other reporting efforts to ensure that data agree in order to comply with federal and state regulations as well as institutional audit requirements. Although the financial aid office is responsible for the implementation and overall administration of aid programs—including the maintenance of individual files—the business office must also monitor the operation of these programs. These offices can also work together to ensure that any additional student aid awarded from any institutional department, office campus organization, or outside source is always included in the student's aid record.

The growth and complexity of student aid programs, as well as the myriad new financing options, require coordination in the administration of all aid funds to ensure the efficient and intelligent distribution of limited resources. There must be reliable procedures in place to prevent "overawarding" (when total student resources exceed the cost of attendance or need-based aid exceeds demonstrated need) or improper disbursement of aid funds. In the case of federal and state funds, where coordination of student aid programs is specifically required in the regulations, the institution may face audit exceptions or program review findings. Such findings can carry financial liability or program cancellation penalties if funds are not properly accounted for in the aggregate as well as in individual student records. Lack of coordination also presents a problem for students, who may be asked to duplicate information already available.

The director of financial aid is responsible for policies and procedures that ensure the successful management of the overall financial aid program, although some of these tasks may be controlled or performed in other offices. These include:

- developing institutional financial aid budget reports;
- keeping the appropriate senior staff informed of relevant governmental, political, or other college actions;
- overseeing all federal and state funding;
- providing financial aid and financing information, including that available through the use of modern technology;
- counseling and supporting students and their parents;
- cooperating in coordination of financial aid systems with accounts admissions, registrar (student records), accounts receivable, accounting, and payroll systems;

- recommending and executing policies and practices governing need analysis, student budgets, and award packaging in accordance with federal and state regulations, donor preferences, and sound professional judgment;

- reviewing annually and recommending the need for additional institutional funds;

- staying abreast of marketplace conditions, especially as they relate to the economy, demographics, technology, alternative financing options, and what peer institutions might be doing;

- submitting annually the federal fiscal operations report and application (FISAP) for new funding for the federal campus-based programs;

- coordinating financial aid deadlines, application materials, and procedures with the admissions/enrollment, bursar, and registrar's offices;

- ensuring proper stewardship of restricted endowments and gifts for scholarships, including any appropriate donor relations;

- monitoring existing policies and practices of the financial aid and financial service operation;

- conducting, or supporting, regular evaluation of policies and practices with professional research and analysis;

- recommending changes that encourage cooperation and effectiveness for the primary benefit of prospective and enrolled students; and

- being professionally involved and networked, always seeking development and improvement.

The success of a financial aid and financial services operation is strengthened by an advisory or policy committee that includes members of the enrollment management team (such as the bursar, registrar, admissions director, and dean of students) and several faculty and students. The financial aid office should be responsible for the overall administration, which includes:

- initiating and updating pertinent information and promotional materials;

- receiving and processing financial aid applications;

- evaluating need and other eligibility criteria;

- packaging (i.e., determining grant/loan/job combinations according to institutional guidelines that may include merit consideration);

- reviewing and revising awards upon request and/or receipt of new family financial information;

- communicating with all departments or areas concerned with any aspect of student aid; and

- maintaining individual student records.

If the financial aid office does not control the selection of recipients and the awarding of funds (e.g., awards based strictly on academic or artistic merit, remission of room and board for dormitory assistants, graduate assistantships), the institution should have data-sharing procedures that ensure the financial aid office prompt access to this information. In this way, the risk of overawards can be minimized. Furthermore, the centralization of all financial-aid awards data facilitates accurate accounting for budget and planning purposes, institutional research, and completing national and consortia surveys.

Budgeting Issues

Financial aid has budgetary implications that go beyond direct assignment of scholarships, grants, and operational costs. Other key issues include the institutional "matching funds" required by the three federal campus-based programs, Supplemental Educational Opportunity Grant, Perkins Loan, and Federal Work Study; expenses for financial aid students who may require special academic programs or services; and costs to replace outside sources of budgeted aid funds that may have been overestimated or did not materialize.

Federal Regulatory Concerns

Under Title IV of the Higher Education Act of 1965 (HEA) as amended, institutions must be authorized by the Department of Education to participate in federal student financial aid programs. Eligibility is determined by submission and acceptance of two documents, the Eligibility and Certification Approval Report (ECAR), and the Program Participation Agreement (PPA).

The Department of Education must also establish that the college or university meets regulatory standards of financial responsibility and administrative capability. (See chapter 2 of *The Blue Book*.) Components of financial responsibility include evidence that the institution has (1) adequate financial resources, (2) technological resources (to use ED's electronic processes), and (3) written policies and procedures to adequately administer the Title IV programs, satisfy minimum retention and maximum default rates, and carry out appropriate internal controls. Internal controls include a strict requirement for separation of functions insuring that the authorization of Title IV awards to students and the actual disbursing or delivery of funds to students (directly or as credits on their tuition bills) be done by "two organizationally independent individuals."[3]

Using appropriate federal and professional handbooks and electronic media, designated staff in the financial aid and business offices must be familiar with and able to reference hundreds, if not thousands, of federal and state laws and regulations pertaining to institutional practices and procedures. Among the most notable regulations are:

- nondiscrimination requirements (Title IV, Title IX, and Americans with Disabilities Act);

- confidentiality of student information and disclosure of student records (Family Education Rights and Privacy Act);

- disclosure of information concerning facilities, student aid, crime on campus, academic programs, graduation and attrition rates, job placement rates, and pass rate for licensing exams, if applicable;

- drug-free environment and workplace;

- federal and state requirements concerning determination of student eligibility such as citizenship and visa status, selective service registration, default on prior Title IV loans or repayment of Federal Pell or SEOG funds, and enrollment status;

- required reports and disclosures on athletic programs;

- refund and return of Title IV fund disclosures for students who withdraw from the institution during the course of a semester; and

- compliance with certain tax reporting guidelines.

With the large number of international students attending United States higher education institutions, there are certain Immigration and Naturalization Service (INS) and Internal Revenue Service (IRS) requirements that colleges and universities must heed.

The mismanagement of federal or state funds has serious implications. For example, federal funds must be repaid if a student receives aid in excess of documented need. If irregularities in the administration of federal programs are discovered through an audit or program review, institutions, as well as individuals (including students), may be subject to fines, civil or criminal action, cuts in federal funding allocations, and/or loss of program eligibility. Consequently, it is incumbent upon the institution to be conscientious about its obligations and aware of its liabilities.

Research

Essential to the development and maintenance of a sound financial aid and enrollment management policy are ongoing efforts to provide timely, pertinent, and consistent research and status reports that relate financial aid to the admission process as well as to the budgetary and fee-setting processes. The initiative and expertise for such efforts may devolve to different administrators depending on the size and management arrangement of the institution. For many institutions, this will be the director of institutional research. However, the director of financial aid has important input because of the complexity of the many different funding sources, their intended purpose (e.g., need versus merit) and packaging requirements. It is important not to underestimate the value of research and reports that compare vital factors, over time, within the institution as well as with peer institutions. The availability of integrated student databases permits unlimited possibilities for defining applicant and admitted student pools, determining yield rates (percent of admitted students who enroll) by student characteristics, retention statistics, and other useful information. Along this line of interest are timeframe (multiple years) comparisons.

Depending on the institution's aid policies, the following may be useful comparisons:

- number and percent of financial aid applicants in the applicant pool, admitted, and enrolled subgroups; these applicant, admit, and yield patterns can be segregated by academic profile, student type, or income level;

- number and percent of students denied admission because they were either aid applicants or appeared to require substantial aid;

- number and percent of students admitted who demonstrated need but who were denied aid or "gapped" (full need not met) because of insufficient aid sources;

- percent of these students who enrolled;

- proportion of need-based aid versus merit-based aid and how this has changed over time; and

- statistical analysis of yield rates of those offered strictly merit-based awards or some form of preferential packaging based on merit or another characteristic.

On the financial side are some indexes that relate financial aid expenditures to specific budget items (that also should be compared over time internally and with peer institutions) as follows.

- expenditures by source of aid as a ratio of tuition and fee revenue or operating (E&G) expenditures;

- average scholarship or grant as a percent of cost of attendance (tuition, fees, room, board, books, and typical personal and travel expenses) or as a percent of average total award (package);[4]

- average self-help (loan and job) levels as a percent of cost of attendance;

- sources of institutional aid funds during the past five to 10 years; for example, restricted and unrestricted endowment, tuition revenue, gifts; and

- budgetary implications of changes in the mix of these funds.

Forms of Student Financial Aid

Institutions typically provide assistance to students through combinations of aid commonly called "packages" or awards. Such packages usually include need- or merit-based scholarships and grants that do not have to be repaid, loans that require repayment, and employment. Adjustments to the amount and composition of the initial award are often made as new information about changes in family circumstances is received or the availability of additional funding resources (internal or external to the institution) changes. Most financial aid programs (and certainly those based on financial need), whether institutional, federal, state, or other, require annual application by students.

The largest source of financial aid is federal Title IV funding, followed by institutional and then state funding. These three primary sources allocate their own scholarship/grant, loan, and employment funds to institutions to distribute to students according to prescribed regulations and guidelines. In addition, many private sources of aid—mostly in the form of scholarships—are available through various corporate and civic organizations.

INSTITUTIONAL AID

The institution, consistent with its mission and objectives, must determine when and if it would be beneficial to the overall educational enterprise to make available additional institutional resources for financial aid. The following are some questions to consider in such an assessment:

- What specific purpose is intended and how will this be monitored?

- How will this use of additional funds fit within the institution's current aid programs and policies?

- What non-aid-related programs could be affected by the decision to increase financial aid; that is, what are the institutional trade-offs for using revenues to support student aid versus other parts of the operation?

- Will such additional financial aid be decided in time to be included in the normal budget cycle and the setting of the following year's tuition?

- What is the institution's "discount rate" compared to early points in its history and what is the long-term trend for future points?

- Do students, faculty, and others understand that some tuition dollars are used for financial aid? For independent institutions with minimal endowments, this could be a significant percentage of tuition revenue.

- Does the institution realize that an additional commitment of resources to fund, for example, a larger-than-planned-for first-year class, may have to be extended for several years until that class graduates?

- Will there be sufficient funds to provide for new as well as returning students?

- Will there be a tradeoff between undergraduate and graduate financial aid programs?

- What are the long-term consequences to the institution's financial stability?

It is important to remember that when tuition is increased by a certain percentage the student aid budget will normally increase at a somewhat higher rate (assuming modest increases in student loan and job expectations) because additional students will become needy with an increase in costs.

Scholarships and Grants

Scholarships and grants are considered gift aid. Scholarships are usually based on scholastic achievement and financial need. However, some scholarships are awarded for academic excellence or special talents in specific areas, regardless of financial need. These are commonly called merit scholarships. Grants, on the other hand, typically are based strictly on financial need.

Since scholarships and grants are considered gifts, recipients are not usually expected either to render service to the institution or to repay the award. However, if the scholarship or grant does impose any service or repayment stipulations, these requirements must be clearly described in the award letter.

Fellowships and Assistantships

Fellowships are a common form of financial assistance awarded to graduate students and may pay all educational expenses as well as a stipend for living expenses. Traditionally, applicants have not been required to demonstrate financial need to be eligible for fellowships. Scholastic excellence has been the primary criterion, but some institutions may also consider need.

Assistantships usually include tuition remission and/or a stipend for graduate students and require performance of services by the student. Direct expenses for assistantships are generally charged to the department in which work is performed.

Under the Tax Reform Act of 1986 and subsequent legislation, *all* scholarship and fellowship awards that exceed tuition, fees, and book charges are treated as taxable income. This sometimes occurs when undergraduates receive large institutional or outside awards, although it is more frequently the case at the graduate level when stipends are provided for living costs in addition to tuition or when services (e.g., teaching or research) rendered by the student are compensated. International students are often required to report even those grants that will not be taxed, and may need help understanding the IRS Form 1042S the institution must provide. While the individual student is responsible for providing the appropriate income information to the IRS, it is the institution's responsibility to be conversant with current tax provisions and IRS reporting requirements, and to alert students to the tax consequences of their awards.[5]

Loan Funds

As indicated previously, there has been increasing reliance on student loans for financing a postsecondary education. Many colleges and universities have established their own loan programs to supplement federal programs and/or to offer more attractive alternatives, guarantees, or interest subsidies for commercial plans. Institutional loan programs may be capitalized from the institution's endowment funds or from a line of credit arranged with a local bank or, in some cases, with proceeds from a special bond issue. The borrower may be the student, the student's parents, or both. The decision to offer an institutional loan program involves a full and sophisticated analysis of the costs and benefits of such a program. These loan plans, if well designed and well managed, can be effective recruiting and retention tools.

Institutional loan funds are typically revolving loan funds, whereby a loan that is repaid by the recipient is available for further lending. Interest on loans is added to funds to help cover administrative costs and defaults and to ensure the perpetuity of the loan fund. Families not eligible for subsidized loans benefit from a rate lower than commercial lenders charge but high enough to provide the college a fair return on its funds.

Additional private loan arrangements, including those that may bear the institution's name, could also be secured. National lenders may be willing to provide attractive terms negotiated on the basis of a customized product determined by the institution's performance and other factors.

Short-term loan funds are also maintained by some institutions to provide immediate funds for students in emergency situations. The amount that can be borrowed is usually small and the repayment period may vary, but it is usually within the year in which the award is made. This can be a meaningful as well as helpful service to provide. Some institutions charge no interest if repayment is made on time; others prefer to use the loan interest or fee to discourage abuse and encourage student planning. All institutional loans and extended payment arrangements should be secured by a simple but legally binding promissory note.

Special Payment Options

The increased costs of higher education have given rise to a number of other options to assist students in meeting their financial obligations to the institution whether or not they receive financial aid. Some of these payment options are relatively new, while others have been available for a number of years but are now exercised more frequently. Although a variety of plans are available, they generally fall into one of three categories: prepaid tuition or advanced savings plans; educational installment or deferred payment plans; and credit card or direct debit payments.

Qualified State Tuition Programs under IRS Code Section 529 (QSTP) and Other Prepaid Tuition and Savings Plans

These plans now exist on a rather wide scale and can be expected to increase in popularity as new tax regulations encourage them at the state level. Prepaid tuition plans are offered by colleges, as well as by states, financial institutions, and nonprofit entities. In a typical plan, the family of an entering student prepays all or a portion of the four undergraduate years at the freshman-year rate, sometimes with the help of a loan through the institution. One variation of this plan allows the family of a younger child to pay for one or more years in advance of the entrance date at a specified discount. Another version combines the announcement of the tuition rate for an entering freshman class with a guarantee that the rate will remain the same for that class until it graduates. In order to be attractive, any plan of this type needs to be flexible in the treatment of cases where students are not accepted at the designated institution, or where they are accepted but do not enter, or do not stay for four years. Tax considerations may also be a factor.

Similar options and risks (for the family and the institution) characterize prepaid tuition plans offered by states or organizations outside the institution, although these arrangements usually offer a wider group of institutions from which to choose. In all cases, however, both the institution and the potential user should evaluate the pros and cons of getting involved with these plans. In particular, they should consider factors such as other investment opportunities, penalties assessed when funds are not used as intended, and the level of insurance needed to provide the necessary guarantees and stability for the plan.

Section 529 savings programs are generally sponsored by a state in partnership with a financial institution and offer a managed portfolio of mutual funds, more aggressive for younger children, becoming more conservative as they approach college age. There is no guarantee of financial return to parents or grandparents—or risk to the institution—as there is with the prepaid tuition program. There is the possibility of earnings exceeding the rate of growth in education costs; the proceeds—taxed at the student's rate when used—may be applied to room and board as well as tuition. It should be noted that under current federal law, prepaid tuition plans are regarded as a direct student resource, technically, as a reduction of the cost of attendance. Savings plans are considered parent assets. It would not be advisable for college staff to offer advice to families about the advantages and disadvantages of particular noninstitutional prepaid tuition or savings plans because there are too many variables involved in the complex decisions to be made for each student. But staff should have enough awareness to recognize parent concerns and refer them to appropriate sources of information. It might also be helpful for institutions to include qualified speakers about Section 529 and other alternative investing and borrowing programs as part of the "financial aid nights" or college financing seminars offered by the financial aid, admissions, or alumni offices. To the extent that families able to save or borrow for education rely on these programs, colleges and universities will have more aid funds available for needier students.[6]

Educational Installment and Deferred Payment Plans

These plans allow the family to spread the cost of the entire academic year over a nine-to-12-month period instead of lump sum payments. Usually, in return for a flat fee or a fee calculated on a sliding scale, the designated organization (or perhaps the institution itself) accepts predetermined monthly payments from the family prior to the due date of the institutional payment or over the academic year. In addition to the fee that it charges, the organization earns interest on the funds it holds before remitting payment to the institution. Sometimes a fee includes life insurance.

As a variation of this arrangement, some institutions offer a direct debit plan or an electronic funds transfer. In these cases, the student or parent's bank account is charged and the institution's account is credited according to a specific schedule.

If financial assistance is necessary for a longer period than is offered by these payment plans, students or parents should be advised to apply for long-term loans. Parents may want to consider home equity, life insurance, and retirement programs.

Although deferred payment plans may be considered part of the institution's student aid program, the plans should be handled through the business office because it is a cash receivable issue. Institutions wishing to restrict deferred payment plans to students demonstrating a genuine financial need for deferment may channel such applications through the student financial aid office for need determination. These plans should be examined carefully by the institution and the potential user before being offered or accepted. If the payment plan is understood by students and administered well by the institution, collection and other problems can be minimized.

Arrangements for all payments should be in writing, and the payment agreement form should be signed by the appropriate parties. The agreement should indicate amounts to be paid, dates on which payments are due, interest rate (if applicable), and penalties incurred if payments are not met on specified dates.

Credit Card Payment

Institutions may choose to allow families to pay all or part of the student account with a credit card. Credit card users can earn incentives, and appreciate the convenience. However, there can be large costs to institutions in transaction fees charged by the credit card company. Institutions should analyze the cost of the program compared with the benefit of receiving payments more quickly from some families. Acceptance of credit card payments is essential for paperless transactions and for making full use of Web-based opportunities. Technology may soon change some aspects of credit card usage, relieving the institution of charges.

Employment

Employment is often incorporated into the student aid package; students seeking aid are usually expected to accept part-time employment, loans, or both, as part of their self-help obligation. Regular (i.e., nonfederal) part-time employment for students, with wages paid using institutional or outside funds (e.g., corporate support for students in a particular major), is available at most institutions. Often, financial need is not a requisite in such cases. Furthermore, non-need-based employment income usually does not have to be counted as a resource in evaluating a student for the federal campus-based programs. However, the institution is obligated to be constructively aware of all payments to aided students, including institutional student employment.

Because the financial aid office must have information on all sources of aid at the institution to administer properly the federal, state, and other need-based programs, it should also be responsible for coordinating all student employment records. However, final selection of students for specific jobs should be the responsibility of supervisors in the departments or areas where students work; this selection is usually based on student interest and job skills.

State Aid

States have programs that provide scholarships, grants, tuition waivers, loans, and/or employment to undergraduate and graduate students who meet specific eligibility criteria. In addition, many states sponsor (but do not directly fund) a variety of prepaid tuition plans or savings plans. The state agency or office responsible for overseeing the programs can have a variety of titles, including student aid commission, higher education assistance authority, department of (higher) education, higher education commission, or higher education services corporation. The programs offered are equally diverse. Eligibility may be based on need, academic ability, or a combination of the two; or it may be restricted to specific groups such as veterans (and their dependents), minorities, the disadvantaged, the disabled or handicapped, or students in certain academic majors. Likewise, some state programs may be limited to students attending in-state institutions, while others may be portable to other states under certain conditions.

Many state aid programs require some kind of reporting or other active involvement by the institution's financial aid or business office. In any case, the financial aid office should receive information on the amount and type of state aid awarded to students at the institution, to ensure accurate record keeping, to allow the inclusion of this information in the evaluation of these students for any aid controlled by the institution, and to meet the requirements that cover students applying for federal student assistance.

Outside Aid

"Outside" sources of financial aid include all the programs not covered by any of the above categories. Examples of this very large and diverse group are organizations such as high schools, associations, clubs, veterans' groups, churches, fraternal groups, labor unions, foundations, trusts and corporations; special-interest groups that seek to help students with a certain nationality or ethnic heritage or students pursuing a particular major; and employers that provide tuition assistance to employees or their dependents. Many institutions encourage students to gain these awards, and provide lists of Web sites, books, and other information sources.

Within limits of confidentiality, student financial aid administrators should cooperate with such organizations since award decisions will be based on information supplied by the institution (for example, certification of costs, enrollment status, other aid, and so forth). However, care must be taken to ensure that eligibility guidelines and other policies of the institution are observed. Also, as in the case of state aid programs, the financial aid office should be the institution's clearinghouse for notification about students who receive funds from these outside sources. If students also receive federal, state, or institutional aid, this information will be used to evaluate their overall financial status and to adjust their financial aid awards as may be necessary. Finally, to improve control, providers of outside aid should be encouraged to make their checks payable to both the institution and the student, rather than to the student alone. If the donor organization insists on making the check payable only to the student, it should be sent to the institution for delivery to the student.

FINANCIAL AID AWARDING CYCLE

The objectives of a financial aid program should include:

- developing operational procedures for application, selection, and notification that will permit students to receive prompt consideration for student aid;
- ensuring selection of those candidates who most closely meet the qualifications for aid;

- attaining the widest possible use of available funds while providing adequate funding for each individual student;

- assisting students and families to become better managers of their financial resources both for higher education and in general, through dissemination of information including counseling; and

- advising student borrowers regarding their rights and responsibilities.

The financial aid awarding cycle consists of several steps: application, need analysis, verification, determination of eligibility, packaging, awarding, disbursement, and adjustment, which will be discussed in this section, and reporting, which will be discussed in the section on Financial Aid Management Issues.

Application

The form that all students must use to apply for federal financial aid is called the Free Application for Federal Student Aid (FAFSA). In addition to the FAFSA, many colleges and universities require students to complete one or more supplemental applications. One of the most common of these is the College Scholarship Service (CSS) Profile. Most states also use the FAFSA for their student aid programs; however, a few have their own supplemental application form.

When determining what type(s) of application(s) an institution will require, consideration should be given to the amount and type of institutional aid available and the criteria for determining eligibility. Achieving a balance between seeking enough data for good decision making and keeping the process as simple as possible is a source of continued tension and needs to be regularly evaluated.

Need Analysis

Currently there are two major need-analysis formulas: Federal Methodology (FM) and Institutional Methodology (IM). FM was established by Congress to determine eligibility for federal funds. It is updated via periodic reauthorization and is subject to political and economic pressures. About 400 institutions establish and use IM as a means for determining the family's ability to pay for college and for awarding institutional funds.

Both formulas attempt to assess a family's ability to pay, using income, assets, family size, and number in college as the primary factors in determining the family contribution. While FM is relatively rigid regarding the calculation of the family contribution, financial aid officers are allowed to exercise their "professional judgment" to adjust certain information. For example, estimated-year income can be used rather than base-year income if a parent has retired or become unemployed. Similarly, FM has clear-cut definitions of whether a student will be considered dependent or independent, but again, if the situation warrants, the aid officer can use professional judgment to consider a dependent student independent in very unusual circumstances. The most important caveats are that professional judgment be exercised on a case-by-case basis and that the reasons for special consideration be well documented and placed in the student's financial aid file.

Verification

There is a formal verification procedure for federal funds. The financial aid office is required to confirm certain data items for students whose applications have been selected for review by the federal processor. Many institutions with significant institutional funds verify all aid applications by requiring federal income tax returns, IRS W-2 forms, and sometimes other forms of documentation from all applicants. Alternatively, the Department of Education has established the Quality Assurance Program, which allows participating institutions to study their populations to determine what errors are most common and among which groups of students. These institutions are then able to adjust their verification process to target areas most prone to error.

Determination of Eligibility

While there is a trend toward merit (nonneed) aid, financial need is a major eligibility criterion for most financial aid programs. To receive Title IV assistance, a student must meet some general eligibility requirements, as well as a number of specific requirements unique to each program. Similar requirements exist for the student aid programs administered by the U.S. Department of Health and Human Services (HHS). The financial aid office is responsible for determining that both the general eligibility requirements and the requirements unique to particular programs are met before disbursing financial aid funds. A number of federal, state, and private educational loans and scholarships are available to students and parents without a financial need consideration.

Packaging

Once a student has demonstrated a need for financial assistance and met the other eligibility requirements, the institution must determine the amounts and types of aid the student will receive. Most aid packages consist of a combination of loans, work (self-help), and, sometimes, scholarships/grants (gift aid).

Packaging techniques or strategies can range from the simple to the complex, depending on the institution's philosophy and preferences, the student's credentials and demonstrated need, the amount and type of funding available, and the overall financial need of the student body. Institutions usually have a self-help expectation for most students, whereby a certain percentage or dollar amount of a student's need is first met with a combination of loans and/or work. Even after this principle is applied, however, there is no guarantee of sufficient scholarship and grant funds to meet all of the remaining need, especially in institutions with a high cost and/or a low endowment. Thus, some portion of the student's need may not be funded from any known source, and the student or family will be required to make up the difference with its own resources, such as additional employment, additional debt, or other financial means. Unmet need is sometimes referred to as a "gap."

Certain federal funds, the Federal Supplemental Education Opportunity Grant (FSEOG) and Perkins Loan program regulations, for example, specify that funds be awarded to students with "exceptional financial need." The FSEOG program has the additional provision that first priority be given to students who are also Federal Pell Grant recipients. These criteria must be factored into an institution's packaging policy.

Despite these overall restrictions, however, most institutions attempt to address the needs of individual students or groups with their approach to packaging. For example, entering students, especially those in a high-risk category, may be funded with a larger portion of scholarship and grant funds during the first year or two, with the understanding that more work or loans will be included as the student progresses toward graduation. Similarly, an aggregate loan limit (e.g., the maximum amount allowed by the Perkins or Stafford Loan program) may be offered to a student at a graduated rate (e.g., 15 percent/25 percent/30 percent/30 percent), rather than at the same rate per year, on the assumption that costs, and therefore the student's need, will increase each year along with increasing ability to repay loans. Statutory limits must be observed for federal loan funds.

Some students (e.g., scholars, athletes, and graduate assistants) may be funded using a disproportionately high amount of scholarship grant money, with or without need as a criterion. Although this is the prerogative of the institution, the effect of such decisions on the rest of the packaging strategy must be considered. For certain athletic programs, other considerations and limitations (e.g., National Collegiate Athletic Association [NCAA]) may apply.

In summary, packaging is an imperfect and challenging activity requiring a delicate balance between the needs of the institution and those of its students. Whenever possible, it is important that financial assistance be awarded in a manner that will not adversely affect the student's educational progress or career choices, as could be the case with undue emphasis on loans and work. Likewise, an institution's packaging ratios ideally should be applied uniformly to all students in the same group. On the other hand, the institution usually has its own priorities that need to be addressed, and the financial aid office should have the discretion to handle unique situations on a case-by-case basis. Whatever the features of an institution's packaging strategy may be, it is important to provide students with a reasonable estimate of the amounts and types of aid likely to be available over the long term. In this way, students can make an informed evaluation of how the institution plans to meet their overall needs. Likewise, families should also be advised as to alternatives for payment and financing.

Awarding

An award letter informs the student of the financial aid that will be provided for the academic year. Award letters do not have to follow a prescribed format, but should contain the following information:

- an indication of the total cost of education, the expected family contribution, and the resulting need;

- amounts and types of aid awarded and the academic period(s) covered;

- terms and conditions (e.g., service or repayment obligations, renewal criteria);

- information on institutional financial aid policies and procedures;

- acceptance and payment procedures;

- provision for student verification of compliance statements; and

- a method to accept or reject the aid offered.

For new students, this notification may accompany the admission acceptance letter or may be mailed separately. Technology allows the use of the Web for both the application and notification process.

Disbursement

Once an award has been finalized and the student arrives on campus, the funds are ready to be disbursed to the student's account. After institutional charges have been satisfied, any credit balance that remains may be remitted to the student by check, direct deposit to the student's bank account, or (with family permission) held to cover anticipated future charges. In the case of Federal Family Education Loan Program (FFELP) loans or other outside scholarships and grants, the business office often receives payment directly. The financial aid office and the business office must have well-established means of communication to ensure that students receive only funds for which they are eligible and to avoid negative reactions from students and parents if adjustments have to be made. Such communication also is needed to ensure that the aid office is fully aware of all assistance being received by each student.

To achieve better control over dollars awarded and disbursed by the institution, regulations governing federal programs are specific about how far in advance funds can be credited to student accounts, when direct payment can be made to students, and how long institutions may hold funds before crediting student accounts. As a result of these requirements, the disbursement system should have some means of encumbering awarded funds without actually disbursing them until the appropriate timing or other conditions have been met. In this way, awarded but undisbursed funds are protected from re-awarding or other use until the original recipient and/or the institution have had an opportunity to meet the necessary requirements. Depending on the system involved, encumbrances prior to disbursement may be done manually or by some electronic means. Institutions should be aware of cash-flow issues related to the drawing down of funds within the time frame allowed.

Overcommitment of Funds

Along with cooperation between the business and the financial aid offices in the areas noted above, institutional policies and procedures for both offices should be in place to cover the amount of initial overcommitment of financial aid funds that will be allowed and the actions to be taken if the amounts accepted by students exceed the amounts available. Initial overcommitment can happen in a number of ways, such as when Perkins Loans are awarded in anticipation of funds not yet collected from previous borrowers.

Although the institution's ultimate goal in these cases should be to disburse only the amount of funds actually available, the pursuit of this goal and the timing problems involved may require that more than 100 percent of currently available funds be awarded initially. To help achieve the goal, relevant policies involving both the financial aid office and business office should indicate the percentage of initial overcommitment that the institution will permit (if any). Likewise, if the yield on the students who were awarded funds is higher than anticipated, other policies should address how the shortfall will be covered. For example, the institution may have to use reserve funds if excess awards occur in an institutional program. In the case of federal funds, however, and assuming that the institution has only limited resources of its own, percentage cutbacks affecting some or all students according to a prioritized scheme may have to be implemented.

Award Adjustments

A number of circumstances, other than institutional overcommitment, may cause adjustments to the aid package of individual students or student groups. Some of the most common causes of adjustments are a change in the financial condition of the student and his or her family (often through the verification process); receipt or cancellation of an outside source of aid for the student; the student's inability to fulfill the conditions of the award; changes in the student's level of enrollment; a change in the amount of funding available from a particular program; and institutional error. For cases in which the student withdraws from the institution before the completion of the term, federal regulations regarding the return of Title IV funds must be followed. The Higher Education Amendments of 1998 (1998 HEA) drastically changed how withdrawals are handled. Institutions must understand the implications of these changes and be prepared for the institutional responsibility required. Clearly, communication among departments, including the student's formal withdrawal date, must be ongoing if the adjustment process is to succeed. While institutions often maintain that students must give notice of withdrawal, regulations actually date withdrawal from the time a student stopped "academic participation"—whether or not notice was given.

Adjustments can be made on an individual basis or according to various formulas or prorating techniques, either simple or complex, consistently applied, depending on the circumstances involved. Good financial aid practices, as well as compliance provisions affecting certain federal programs, dictate that any adjustments to student aid packages be documented in the student's folder or in some other acceptable manner. In addition, the financial aid office should notify the student by a revised award letter or other written or electronic means, request the business office to recover or disburse any funds involved, and re-award any recovered funds to other students if appropriate. For cases involving refund or repayment of certain federal awards, the required institutional refund or repayment policy should specify the return of funds to one or more federal programs. Adjustments to financial aid awards take place on a daily basis in nearly every financial aid office. The relevant institutional policies should be covered in the informational materials that are distributed to students.

FINANCIAL AID MANAGEMENT ISSUES

Responsibility for financial aid management may be spread among several administrative departments, but the major share rests with the financial aid office and the business office. Important institutional management issues include reliance on computer systems, compliance and reporting, cash management, record keeping, financial planning and control, and audits.

Computer Systems

The rapid growth of technology and the increasing desire for information have made individual or networked PCs, as well as mainframe computers, essential tools for record keeping, electronic transmission of data and funds, planning, and reporting at nearly every institution. In student financial aid specifically, computers have been used for years to perform the routine tasks of tracking the receipt and status of application materials, maintaining student information, preparing award letters, monitoring and projecting expenditures, transferring funds, and generating a wide variety of reports for both internal and external audiences.

With the more sophisticated systems currently available, however, and with growing demands from constituents, financial aid information can be linked with data maintained in such offices as business, admissions, registrar, housing, athletics, graduate programs, and alumni affairs. Hardware and software resources to accomplish these tasks can be developed in-house or (more likely) purchased from an outside vendor, but will represent a significant financial and staff commitment either way.

When the financial aid office is connected electronically to other departments—and when the resulting system is properly documented, periodically upgraded, and regularly maintained—errors are reduced and a wide variety of labor-saving improvements are made available. In an integrated system, for example, eligibility criteria involving other departments can be checked automatically; changes in students' institutional charges can be accessed immediately; the awarding of financial aid can create a general ledger encumbrance or credit the student's account; institutional cash flow can be maximized; one or more financial aid packaging routines can be applied to students who meet certain preestablished criteria; electronic fund transfers can occur; loan collections or institutional aid expenditures can be monitored and the information used to modify financial projections; alumni addresses can be used to update loan billing records; and any number of "what-if" simulations can be conducted before committing actual funds.

In recent years, state scholarship offices, state and private loan authorities, and in particular the federal government have become much more active in linking their services or requirements to institutions via computer, either in an on-line or a free-standing mode, and have provided the appropriate software (but not hardware) to the institution at little or no cost. Currently, for example, with the proper software and electronic configuration, the financial aid office or business office can retrieve student information from a federal database, calculate need, and prepare one or more financial aid packages; access an outside loan agency's database to obtain or enter information about the institution's students; create records and report to the Department of Education (ED) on individual Pell Grant recipients; request federal cash and report on federal expenditures via the Internet; prepare and file the annual Title IV application and fiscal operations report; complete the monthly reconciliation process for the Direct Loan program; and report to ED on the enrollment status of Federal Family Education Loan (FFEL) and Federal Direct Loan (FDL) borrowers. For most of the above tasks, electronic communication is the only option available and continued development in this area, particularly using the Internet, can be expected.

The federal government in general and ED in particular deserve recognition for the significant commitment that they have made to the electronic environment. The sophisticated financial aid software is updated often, and a considerable amount of training and written guidance is available, usually at no cost. Because of these factors, however, the various modules available can be very frustrating to use unless the institution is willing to make the essential investment in hardware and, in particular, staff and time. Each institution will need to evaluate its own situation and determine whether to interact directly with ED using its own resources, contract with a third-party servicer to complete the various required tasks using information provided by the institution, or use a combination of these two choices.

In light of the above discussion, and given the nature and characteristics of financial aid as an administrative function, the potential of the computer seems nearly unlimited. While reviewing the management issues below, therefore, the reader should assume that many of the activities described must be done, will be done, or at least could be done using a computer system, the Internet, or other electronic resources.

Reporting

Many financial aid office reports are prepared in response to federal regulations. For most institutions, federal Title IV reporting requirements predominate. Any major institutional activity involving such significant numbers should produce internal reports for all the obvious reasons. Discussion of the major Title IV reports follows.

Application and Fiscal Operations Report (FISAP)—ED Form 646

The most important financial aid report for external aid prepared by an institution, the FISAP, is filed electronically on or about October 1 of each year and represents a historical report on the academic year just ended and an application for campus-based funds (i.e., FSEOG, Federal Work-Study, and Federal Perkins Loan) for the upcoming year. For example, the October 2000 FISAP would include a Fiscal Operations Report for 1999–2000 and an application for funds for 2001–2002. The FISAP contains both financial and nonfinancial data that are critical to the application process (e.g., maximization of funds), and important to the auditor.

Pell Grant Origination and Disbursement Records

Effective July 1, 1999, electronic reporting for Pell is accomplished under the new Recipient Financial Management System (RFMS) and includes preparation and submission of Pell origination and disbursement records. RFMS must accept an origination record for a student before a disbursement record can be processed and disbursements made. An institution must submit a disbursement record within 30 days of becoming aware that a student is eligible for (or requires an adjustment to) a Pell Grant. For both types of records, RFMS will either accept a record without corrections, accept it with corrections, or reject it, and will send the appropriate acknowledgment to the institution. Within RFMS, institutions can request and receive various types of data, including an Electronic Statement of Account (ESOA) and Year-to-Date (YTD) data (a replacement for the former Student Payment Summary). The above procedures combine to provide the means for (1) an ongoing reconciliation of institutional and Pell program records, (2) revisions to the Pell authorization level via the ESOA and concurrent notification to the Grant Administration and Payment System (GAPS), and (3) a Pell authorization and expenditure on the year-end ESOA that reflects the actual Pell expenditure shown on institutional records and Pell YTD data. In general, the institution has until September 30 following the end of the award year to submit valid disbursement records.

Federal Cash Drawdown and Expenditure Report

During the latter part of 1997–98, ED implemented, in place of the former ED Payment Management System (EDPMS), the Grant Administration and Payment System (GAPS), part of a larger Education Central Automated Processing System (EDCAPS). GAPS is an electronic (i.e., Internet and Windows) system that is used with the campus-based, Pell, and Federal Direct Loan programs. For the typical institution, GAPS features ACH/EFT or FEDWIRE cash drawdowns by program (i.e., by grant award number), and includes a procedure whereby the institution completes an electronic certification (each time it draws down funds) that funds will be disbursed to students (or their accounts or parents) within three business days.

Federal Direct Loans (FDL) Monthly Reconciliation Reports

Participating institutions must report FDL disbursements and submit required records to ED via the Loan Origination Center (LOC) on a monthly basis and in an electronic format. The LOC initiates the reconciliation process by creating a data file containing three types of records: the Cash Summary Record, the Cash Detail Record, and the (optional) Loan Detail Record. After receiving the data file, the institution compares the data with its own records and attempts to reconcile any discrepancies by communicating back and forth electronically with the LOC. Any items not reconciled during this process are included in the following month's data file from the LOC until all records are reconciled.

FFEL/FDL Student Status Confirmation Report (SSCR)

The SSCR is a listing of current FFEL or FDL borrowers (including students whose parents obtained PLUS loans) sent to the institution electronically by ED via the National Student Loan Data System (NSLDS), and following a schedule specified by the institution (but within ED's guidelines). The institution is required to provide certain enrollment status information (e.g., currently attending, withdrawn, graduated, etc.) and return the information electronically to ED via the NSLDS within 30 days of receipt. If any errors are noted by ED, the institution must correct them and resubmit the data within 10 calendar days.

The institution must file these Title IV reports according to the specified guidelines, because an auditor will look to determine that reports were complete, accurate, and timely. In fact, the required audit of federal student aid programs is itself a report on many of the aspects of financial aid operations, although it is obviously not completed solely by the financial aid office. There may be additional federal reports for the financial aid or business office to complete, as well as those required by donors, state agencies, and various outside organizations. The institution itself should also summarize at least annually all of its major activities and expenditures as well as produce data for research and analysis of policies.

Beyond communicating with these external sources, the financial aid or business office must be prepared to provide any regular or special reports that may be requested by supervisors or other institutional personnel. Formats for these reports will vary greatly, but the offices should strive to have a record-keeping system that minimizes the difficulties of preparation.

In addition to answering the requests of others, it is advisable for the financial aid office to prepare and issue its own periodic report to the appropriate institutional offices or to the institution as a whole. This report should provide a variety of statistical information, a review of the preceding year, and perhaps a discussion of upcoming issues or events. Since the aid office is (or should be) the central clearinghouse for all financial aid information at the institution, it is good practice to prepare a regular report that gives constituents a more complete view of the office's operations and the impact of financial aid expenditures.

Record Keeping

Information that must be kept on individual students varies with the types and sources of financial aid awarded. The financial aid office normally maintains a permanent record for each student, either in electronic or paper format, along with a folder containing the student's institutional aid applications, need analysis forms or reports, tax returns, federal aid eligibility documents, award letters, financial aid transcripts, copies of promissory notes, records of notifications regarding disbursements, documentation of entrance/exit interviews, and other pertinent or required materials. In the case of academic or other data relative to eligibility, the financial aid office might maintain or have access to various master lists rather than placing information in individual folders.

For each federal aid recipient, an institution must maintain certain other records on a current basis. These records should allow ready identification of each student's account and its status, identifying disbursements of federal funds separately from all other expenditures. In general, for federal purposes the records must show cost of attendance, student resources, student eligibility, amount and type of aid awarded and disbursed, and disbursement dates. Federal regulations also require that the institution retain a number of reports and summary documents. Likewise, the institution should maintain its own reports and summaries.

For federal audit purposes, the institution must keep certain Title IV records pertaining to an award year for a minimum of three years after it files the FISAP report. For Pell and Campus Based funds, this includes data for three years after the end of the award year. For the FFELP/FDL loan programs, all required records must be kept for three years following the last day of the loan period and all reports must be kept for three years following the student's completion date. Similar requirements exist for the HHS programs. In addition, Perkins Loan regulations require that an institution retain all repayment records pertaining to an individual loan for three years from the date of loan assignment, repayment in full, or cancellation. In fact, the Department of Education recommends that institutions retain Perkins promissory notes and repayment information beyond the three year requirement. Records involved in any claim or expenditure questioned by federal audit or program review must be further retained until resolution of such questions. In many cases, institutions may substitute electronically imaged copies for original records as long as data is retrievable into a hard-copy format.

In addition to the federal record-retention requirements, the institution should have a policy that provides for the retention of any historical financial aid information that will be of value. The institution may want to retain some of these records for more than the three-year period mandated by the federal government. Occasionally, this information may be needed to help in securing essential data impacting a student's good credit and the institution's default rate for government loan programs.

AUDITS, PROGRAM REVIEWS, AND OTHER EVALUATIONS

Audits

The federal audit requirements that affect most institutions are the ED provisions that mandate (with some exceptions) an independent annual audit of all Title IV programs on a fiscal-year basis. Related audit provisions exist for the HHS programs. The general objective of the audit is to conduct a comprehensive evaluation of an institution's financial statements and other financial data, its internal control structure, and its compliance with federal laws and regulations in areas such as cash management, reporting, institutional eligibility (financial

responsibility, administrative capability, student consumer information requirements, etc.), student eligibility, disbursements, and refund procedures. In addition to addressing these common compliance requirements, the auditor also determines the institution's compliance with the specific requirements of each federal
aid program.

State and private nonprofit institutions of higher education must have their
federal student financial aid programs audited annually under the general guidelines of the Single Audit Act of 1984, using Office of Management and Budget
(OMB) Circular A-133 (June 1997), *Audits of States, Local Governments, and Non-
Profit Organizations.* Audit guides and other resources (e.g., from ED or the American Institute of Certified Public Accountants) as well as relevant compliance supplements (e.g., from OMB) are available to assist the auditor in conducting the
audit, which covers "major" (as defined) federal programs at the institution
regardless of the federal source of these funds. The reports resulting from a Circular A-133 (single) audit include a report on the audit of the institution's financial
statements, two reports on compliance and internal control, and several supplementary items.

In contrast to state and nonprofit institutions, all for-profit (i.e., proprietary)
institutions must have their annual financial statement audit and their Title IV
compliance "attestation" performed according to the requirements of the most
recent ED audit guide, since proprietary institutions are not covered by Circular
A-133.

Institutions may, but usually do not, have the financial statement audit and
the compliance attestation performed by different accounting firms. In either case,
the resulting report package includes a report on the audit of the financial statements, a report on compliance and internal control, an attestation report covering
management's assertions about compliance, and several supplementary items.

In order to provide audit relief for smaller institutions, Circular A-133
exempts from federal audit requirements for a particular fiscal year any entity that
expends less than $300,000 in (all) federal awards in that same year. In addition,
effective July 1, 2000, in return for a letter of credit, institutions that disbursed
less than $200,000 in Title IV funds during each of the two prior award years may
apply for a waiver that permits them to submit audits on a three-year cycle rather
than annually. Several other conditions apply. When audits are submitted on this
delayed basis, the compliance attestations must cover each prior year not previously audited, and the financial statement must cover the most recent fiscal year.

To perform the audit, an institution should select an auditor or firm that is familiar with the institution, with audits of higher education institutions in general, and with the very detailed regulations governing federal student aid programs in particular. The federal government is extremely concerned about audit quality. It is both costly and embarrassing to the institution when audits are not conducted properly or when institutional problems are overlooked by an auditor in their early stages, only to become serious deficiencies or findings at a later date. (For a full discussion of audits, see chapter 22, Auditing.)

The institution's internal audit staff can participate in the audit on a limited basis under the direction of the independent auditors, but is no longer allowed to perform the entire audit.

Audit findings fall into two categories, those involving procedural omissions or deficiencies at the institution and those involving an unallowable expenditure or overexpenditure of dollars. In either case, the federal government can assess fines in addition to recovering the disallowed expenditures; thus a federal audit should be viewed seriously by institutional personnel at all levels. In fact, the cognizant federal agency usually directs any correspondence regarding these audits to the institution's chief executive officer precisely so that major administrators will be aware of any problems that exist and will respond to them accordingly.

Program Reviews

The purpose of a program review is to ensure the proper administration of a financial aid program and to assess the institution's compliance with its own policies as well as with federal laws and regulations. A program review involves a visit to an institution by an ED or guarantee agency representative to review one or more of the institution's operations or procedures. If any deficiencies are found, the program review may require procedural changes, the return of improperly spent dollars, and/or the payment of fines. Although similar in some ways, audits and program reviews have major differences. For example, reviews are usually shorter and more limited in scope than audits. Also, institutions are selected for reviews based on some predetermined criteria, including a determination by ED that the institution poses a risk of noncompliance. An institution may periodically want to conduct its own program review performed by a representative group or organization with appropriate expertise.

Other Methods of Evaluation

Even though the federal audit is the major oversight activity involving the institution's financial aid programs, other resources are available to evaluate and provide guidance on financial aid operations. For example, the National Associa-tion of Student Financial Aid Administrators (NASFAA) publishes the *Self-Evaluation Guide for Institutional Participation* on a regular basis. This guide can be used by the financial aid director, other institutional personnel, or the auditor to assess the financial aid office's adherence to relevant program regulations or standards of good practice. The guide contains hundreds of questions in checklist format and is an excellent tool for obtaining a preliminary assessment of the financial aid func-tion, the business office function, or the management of a particular program.

Other situations may arise in which the financial aid office requests or needs an independent examination and consultation involving one or more operations to either confirm its validity or obtain suggestions for improvement. Such an exam-ination or operational audit can be conducted by the institution's internal audit staff, by the external accountants who are responsible for the financial aid audit, or by an independent consultant. In any case, the goals would be quite different from those of the traditional compliance audit; specifically, the selected individual(s) would seek to assist the financial aid office on a more proactive basis with proce-dures, controls, record keeping, or other administrative functions in order to achieve a more efficient and effective operation over the long term. Such a review could also provide additional insight beyond the issues typically expected to com-ply with government regulations, but which would be important to the institu-tional mission.

LOAN BILLING, COLLECTION, AND DEFAULT MANAGEMENT

When compared with scholarship and grant or work programs, loan management requires the largest investment of administrative resources of all the financial aid programs because loans involve a period of time beyond the student's graduation or withdrawal. In addition, loans and loan defaults have assumed and will con-tinue to assume greater importance as the cost of attendance rises, whether the loan funding is from federal, institutional, or other sources.

The institution should have a clear understanding of the key issues and con-cerns involved in establishing and maintaining a successful loan program. Although federal loans are emphasized here, these issues are applicable to other loan programs as well. Not only is the long-term integrity of these programs at stake, but also the institution's reputation, eligibility for participation in govern-ment programs, and possibly even its bond rating.

Loan Counseling

Federal regulation continues to require entrance, or initial, and exit loan counseling for students who borrow from the Federal Perkins and Federal Stafford (FFEL and FDL) Loan programs. Loan counseling is thought to be one of the most effective default reduction measures as it enables the college or university to provide basic consumer information to the student and to emphasize the importance and consequences of the loan obligation.

The Higher Education Act, as amended in 1998, no longer requires that the counseling be done "in person." Instead, institutions can choose to use "electronic" means provided that the electronic counseling is interactive (i.e., the student must pass a quiz to move to the certification section) and that a knowledgeable person is available after the counseling to answer questions.

Entrance or initial loan counseling must be provided before the first disbursement can be made to the student borrower. Loan counseling must stress the meaning of the loan obligation—even if the student does not complete the program of study—and explain the consequences of delinquency and default for both the student and the institution. Additionally, the institution should provide information about the terms and conditions of the loan; review deferment, forbearance, and cancellation provisions, student rights and responsibilities, and repayment options; and finally, remind the student to keep the lender informed of name, address, and enrollment changes.

Exit counseling should provide the student with individualized information about his or her loan indebtedness and repayment information. The institution must again provide consumer information similar to the entrance or initial loan counseling but must also collect from the borrower updated reference and personal information that will aid in the collection of the loan, such as driver's license number, expected address and employment information.

Most federal loan programs require that an in-person or electronic exit interview be conducted immediately prior to the departure of the borrower from the institution. If all institutional efforts to conduct this fail, federal regulations require the institution to mail exit interview materials to the borrower with instructions for the return of signed documents, typically including a repayment schedule. If the borrower does not return the completed material, the college or university should retain documentation of its attempt to obtain it.

Due Diligence

According to federal regulations for aid programs administered by ED or HHS, an institution must exercise "due diligence" in the collection of federal loans, with the objective of lowering student loan delinquency rates. Institutions must follow certain procedures in exercising their responsibility to inform borrowers of their rights under a loan program, to notify borrowers of delinquency and its consequences, and to conduct and complete collection efforts. Entrance and exit loan counseling are two of the many extremely detailed due diligence requirements. Due diligence procedures are subject to change and are not identical for each loan program, but there are many similarities.

Perkins Loans

The institution must keep borrowers informed of all changes in the Perkins Loan program that affect their rights and responsibilities, and it must promptly respond to all inquiries from borrowers. The institution also must attempt to recover all money owed to the Perkins Loan fund. In order to meet due diligence requirements, the institution must:

- provide entrance or initial loan counseling;
- execute a binding promissory note;
- conduct exit interviews;
- bill the borrower;
- remind the borrower of the impending beginning of the repayment period during the grace period;
- report payment history and default to a national credit bureau;
- send past-due notices and a final demand letter (if necessary); and
- institute collection procedures and litigation (if necessary).

HPSLs and NSLs

The institution must follow due diligence procedures for Health Professions Student Loans (HPSL) and Nursing Student Loans (NSL) that are at least as extensive and effective as those used in the collection of other student loan accounts and must use the steps prescribed in the regulations in accordance with generally accepted collection practices. These procedures, too, are intended to lower student loan delinquency rates. Each participating institution must:

- conduct and document extensive preloan counseling with the borrower prior to disbursing funds (institutions are required to collect very specific information that is regulated by HHS);

- conduct and document exit loan counseling with the borrower prior to the borrower's leaving the institution;

- contact the borrower at least twice during the grace period;

- perform regular billing procedures while the loan is in repayment status;

- contact each borrower during a deferment period;

- notify a past-due borrower at least four times;

- perform address searches when necessary;

- use a collection agent (which may be an internal agent of the college or university);

- become a member of a credit bureau and report accounts past due by more than 120 days to that bureau;

- litigate (if such action seems cost-effective); and

- perform a periodic review of "collectability" of loans that are delinquent (loans that are three or more years past due must be paid to HHS by the institution; the institution is then responsible for collecting the loan).

Other Billing and Collection Issues

The institution must have an effective billing and collection procedure in place. Depending on the volume of the loan portfolio and the institutional resources available, an institution may choose to handle billing and collection in house or use an outside service. In making this decision, the institution should consider the cost of developing or purchasing an internal billing system (amortized over a period of years), as well as the cost of maintaining a system. Furthermore, an analysis of the cost effectiveness of billing and collection options should be done for several volume levels.

The institution must judge whether borrowers will react more favorably to billings from a third party or from the institution. Some people believe that borrowers take billing from a third party more seriously, making it more effective. Others believe that borrowers respond more favorably to direct billing because of institutional loyalty and a resulting feeling that they should help other needy students by repaying in a timely fashion. A common complaint against contracted billing is the impersonality of the process. However, institutions using a computerized system may also appear to be impersonal if care is not taken to respond to individual situations. Many institutions increase collection success by accessing alumni address and employment files. And if a student leaves with an unpaid tuition account, collection of all unpaid loan and tuition balances should be carefully coordinated.

A collection agency should be chosen with care, to guard against harsh or unethical methods of collection. If a collection agency is used, the institution must determine how much of the loan should be placed with the agency—the full amount or only the delinquent amount. It is important to collect delinquent loans quickly, for reasons other than the obvious one of needing the money for immediate reuse. Prolonged delinquency is expensive, because of account maintenance, repeated billings, postal expense, and the potential for lost interest and principal upon default. Further, the loss of invested funds may discourage the institution (or other lender) from program expansion and may even cause program curtailment.

Student loan collectors should also note that a number of students may take several years to become "responsible adults." Initially they may move frequently, switch (or lose) jobs, transfer to new schools, and "forget" to file address change or deferment forms. "Aggressive" collection work, successful with some students, will drive others to "hide" or seek bankruptcy discharge for "undue hardships." Institutions may achieve their best long term collection results with policies and procedures that emphasize maintaining contact and a mentoring relationship with borrowers, extending hardship deferments and special payment arrangements and providing referrals to the career office or alumni network as appropriate.

In general, the billing service and the collection firm used by an institution must not be legally connected to each other in any way. Federal audit requirements specify that the auditor must obtain sufficient information about the outside billing or collection agency to support the audit work and the conclusions reached at the institution. The auditor may obtain this information directly or by using a qualified service auditor's report.

Bankruptcy

Bankruptcy is a legal proceeding that allows debtors who are unable to pay their creditors to "resolve" their debts through the division of their assets among their creditors according to a court-approved plan. The debtor may voluntarily enter into bankruptcy or may be involuntarily placed in bankruptcy by creditors. According to law, a debtor is not obligated to pay a debt if it is discharged during bankruptcy proceedings. A bankrupt person's debts are discharged together, although some debts, termed "nondischargeable," can only be discharged in bankruptcy under exceptional circumstances.

The bankruptcy provisions (Title 11 of the U.S. Code) provide for several types of bankruptcy proceedings, although student loan borrowers usually fall under either Chapter 7 (a liquidation proceeding, sometimes referred to as "straight bankruptcy") or chapter 13 (a debt readjustment proceeding involving a repayment plan submitted by the borrower). In the past, student loans made or guaranteed under Title IV were nondischargeable in bankruptcy during the first five years of repayment if the borrower filed for relief under Chapter 7, but could be discharged under Chapter 13. The same nondischargeability provision now applies to both Chapter 7 and Chapter 13. Under the Higher Education Amendments of 1998, the primary condition for discharge of nondischargeable loans is now "undue hardship."

Even if a borrower files for bankruptcy, the institution may be able to collect most or all of what the student owes on a federal or other loan after bankruptcy proceedings are finished. Changes in the law, such as those cited above, and various legal interpretations place considerable importance on the responsibility to repay the obligation even though there may be temporary setbacks in the borrower's financial condition. There will also be situations in which a debtor will choose to voluntarily complete payment. When a specific case arises, the institution should consult both the bankruptcy regulations in effect at the time and competent legal counsel experienced in bankruptcy law. (For a full discussion of bankruptcy, see chapter 21, Legal Issues.)

IRS Form 1098-E

The Taxpayer Relief Act of 1997 provides for the deductibility of interest paid on education loans during the first 60 months of repayment based on the borrower's adjusted gross income. The amount of the deduction will be phased in from 1998 through 2001, with the maximum amount increasing each year by $500 from $1,000 to $2,500. Interest paid on all education loans is potentially eligible for this deduction.

Each year institutions or their designated loan servicers are responsible for reporting to borrowers who are within the first 60 months of repayment, the yearly amount of interest paid on educational loans, where the interest amounts to $600 or more. This includes institutional student and parent loans as well as Federal Perkins Loans. Interest paid is reported to the borrower and to the IRS using

IRS Form 1098-E. The student or parent borrower is solely responsible for determining his or her eligibility for the deduction.

Default Management

Cohort Default Rate Calculation

The cohort default rate is the percentage of borrowers who enter repayment during an award year who default on their loans before the end of the next year. This rate, while referred to as the "current" default rate, is always based on data that are a few years old. For example, the Federal Perkins Loan cohort default rate calculated in the 1999–2000 FISAP report is based on students who entered repayment between July 1, 1996, and June 30, 1997 (denominator) and who were in default as of June 30, 1998 (numerator). The calculation is similar for the FFEL and FDL programs except that the rate is calculated by the Department of Education based on data provided by guarantee agencies, lenders, and the Direct Loan Servicing Center to the NSLDS database. Institutions with a small number of borrowers entering repayment (fewer than 30) have their default rate calculated based on the sum of borrowers and defaulters for the past three years.

Criteria on which loans may and may not be considered as part of the calculation are specific and governed by regulation. The Department of Education provides each institution with a "draft" cohort default rate that lists every borrower who will be considered in the calculation and his or her repayment status. This is the only opportunity the institution has to verify the students listed in default and to challenge the information for any necessary corrections. The institution may also proactively expand collection efforts for this group.

Implications of High Default Rates

There are serious consequences related to high official default rates, including the loss of eligibility to participate in the FFEL and FDL programs and the Federal Pell Grant Program for institutions whose three most recent official Stafford Loan cohort default rates are 25 percent or more. Additionally, for institutions with a cohort default rate greater than 40 percent, the Department of Education can choose to limit, suspend, and/or terminate an institution's participation in any or all student financial aid (SFA) programs. High Federal Perkins Loan cohort default rates may result in the loss of the Federal Capital Contribution (annual allocation). An institution with a Perkins cohort default rate greater than

50 percent for the three most recent years becomes ineligible to participate in the program and must liquidate its portfolio.

Colleges and universities are eligible to appeal their default rates but must strictly adhere to Department of Education guidelines that outline this process. It is vital for institutions to be proactive in monitoring their loans in repayment and to use every means available to prevent the loans from reaching the default stage.

Default Reduction Measures

While federal regulations no longer require institutions with high default rates to submit a default reduction plan to the Department of Education, new institutions participating in federal programs are required to develop and implement a plan prior to federal certification to participate in Title IV programs.

To reduce the incidence of default, several general regulations have been established. All institutions must:

- make a General Education Development (GED) program available if they admit students without high institution diplomas;

- disburse Stafford and PLUS loan proceeds in two (or more) equal payments, regardless of the length of the loan period; however, with the 1998 HEA, institutions with Stafford Loan cohort default rates below 10 percent for the three most recent cohort default calculations are allowed to make one disbursement to students for loans that have a loan period equal to one semester, one trimester, one quarter, or are less than four months in length;

- hold disbursement of Stafford Loans to first-time borrowers entering the first year of an undergraduate program until 30 days after the first day of the program; again, the 1998 HEA exempted from this provision institutions with cohort default rates below 9.9 percent for the three most recent cohort default rate calculations;

- provide to the lender or the Direct Loan Origination Center an appropriate disbursement schedule that will meet the above requirements; and

- have a fair and equitable policy regarding the refund of charges to students who withdraw from the institution; additionally, by October 7, 2000, they must comply with the return of Title IV funds policy that was created in the 1998 HEA.

FEDERAL AID PROGRAMS

U.S. Department of Education Aid

Various student and financial assistance programs are authorized by Title IV of the Higher Education Act of 1965 (as amended), the Student Loan Reform Act of 1993, or related legislation. They are administered or monitored by the U.S. Department of Education.

The largest programs are covered in the following section. The Federal Pell Grant program is a program of gift aid for which the federal government establishes eligibility criteria. The government also provides specific guidelines for determining the amount of the grant. Three programs—Federal Supplemental Educational Opportunity Grant (FSEOG), Federal Work-Study (FWS), and Federal Perkins Loan—are referred to as "campus based."

Under these programs, the institution applies for and receives funds from the federal government, then determines the recipients and amounts of student awards within federal guidelines and funding levels. In addition, Perkins Loans are collected by the institution or its designated third-party servicer. The institution's allocation of funds is based on past utilization of funds and the need of the institution (determined by a formula) relative to the needs of other institutions.

The former Guaranteed Student Loan program was renamed the Federal Family Education Program (FFELP) in the Higher Education Amendments of 1992. FFELP includes the Federal Stafford Loan, Federal PLUS (Parent) Loan, and Federal Consolidation Loan programs. The Student Loan Reform Act of 1993 authorized the Federal Direct Loan (FDL) program. Like FFELP, the Direct Loan program also has Stafford, PLUS, and Consolidation Loan components.

Although there are some similarities in the administration of FFELP and FDL, a major difference between the two is that funds for the FFELP program generally involve private lenders such as banks and credit unions, as well as guarantors and servicers, whereas the federal government provides funds directly to borrowers through their institutions in the FDL program.

Most institutions participate in one program or the other, although they are allowed to participate in both simultaneously; a student or parent, however, can borrow from only one program during a specific enrollment period.

Administration of loans in repayment status occurs outside the institution and is accomplished according to federal guidelines, but the institution is still held responsible for excessive loan defaults by its students. To help maintain low default rates, many institutions cooperate with lenders and guarantors, providing

Figure 19-01

ED-Administered Student Aid Programs
Appropriations FY 1992-2000, $millions

Program	FY 1992	FY 1993	FY 1994	FY 1995	FY 1996	FY 1997	FY 1998	FY 1999	FY 2000
Pell Grant	5499	5747	6634	6144	4913	5919	7345	7704	7700
FSEOG	577	583.4	583.4	583.4	583.4	583.4	614	619	631
FWS	615	616.9	616.5	616.5	616.5	830	830	870	934
Perkins	156	168.6	158	158	93.3	158	135	130	130
SSIG/LEAP	72	72.4	72.4	63.4	31.4	50	25	25	40

them with debtor name and address change and employment information. Individual student loan or grant limits, reflecting figures in effect for 1999–2000, are provided in the sections that follow to give the reader some perspective on the programs. Figure 19-01 shows the appropriations for the major programs from fiscal years 1992 through 2000.

When an institution applies for federal funds using the FISAP, it must assess its need for money from the three campus-based programs by considering a number of items, including:

- the optimum mix of funds for the institution;
- the funds that can be transferred between and among programs;
- other available aid sources;
- adequacy of institutional resources to manage the funds properly; and
- institutional dependence on federal financial aid, and the contingency plan if funding for a certain program is reduced or does not materialize.

Federal Pell Grant

The Federal Pell Grant program awards portable, need-based grants to eligible undergraduate students. A Pell Grant is intended to provide a "foundation" of financial aid, although some students receive a Pell Grant only and others receive other types of aid only. The program is administered by ED and postsecondary educational institutions. Students complete paper or electronic applications, which are sent to a central processing system that provides an electronic Institutional Student Information Record (ISIR) to the institution and a paper Student Aid Report (SAR) to the student. The institution then uses a payment schedule to determine award amounts based on the cost of attendance at that institution, the Expected Family Contribution (EFC—a measure of the student/family contribution to education) from the ISIR or SAR, the enrollment status of the student (full time or part time, full year or partial year), and the length or the student's program in relation to the length of the academic year. For 2000–2001, full-time annual awards ranged from a minimum of $400 to a maximum of $3,300. Determination of eligibility for a Pell Grant is a prerequisite, in the case of an undergraduate, for applying for aid from the Perkins Loan, FFEL Stafford Loan, and Direct Stafford Loan programs.

Federal Supplemental Educational Opportunity Grant (FSEOG)

The FSEOG program provides grants to eligible undergraduate students. Students apply directly to the institution for a FSEOG using the Free Application for Federal Student Aid (FAFSA) and are selected as recipients by the institution on the basis of need. The institution decides the amount of the grant, which in 1999–2000 ranged from $200 to $4,000 per academic year (with a slightly higher maximum available to students participating in a study-abroad program). Under current regulations, FSEOG funds must first be awarded to students with exceptional need (i.e., those with the lowest EFCs, who will also receive Pell Grants).

Institutional matching provisions are in effect for the FSEOG program. Matching funds must be from the institution's own resources, including institutional grants and scholarships, tuition and fee waivers, state scholarships, and foundation or other charitable funds. In 1999–2000, the institution had to match FSEOG on a one-institutional-to-three-federal-dollar ratio. There are three options for how to provide the matching, including a commingled fund, or an individual, or aggregate, matching with separate institutionally controlled funds.

An institution may transfer up to 25 percent of its Federal Work-Study (FWS) allocation for a particular award year to FSEOG for the same award year and up to 25 percent of its Perkins allocation for a particular award year to FSEOG and/or FWS for the same award year in any combination. Also, effective July 1, 2000, an institution may carry forward up to 10 percent of its FSEOG allocation to the subsequent award year or carry back 10 percent of the allocation to the prior award year; in addition, for payment periods beginning and ending between May 1 and June 30, the institution may make FSEOG awards from the subsequent award year's allocation. These provisions are designed to provide flexibility to the institution in utilizing its funds.

Federal Work-Study (FWS)

The primary objective of the FWS program is to provide part-time employment in either the public, private nonprofit, or private for-profit sector to undergraduate, graduate, or professional students who need the earnings to meet their educational costs. The wage rate must be at least the current federal minimum wage. A student can work for the institution itself or for an eligible off-campus employer. The program is also intended to broaden the range of job opportunities for qualified students. Within the FWS program, the institution may choose to participate in the (optional) Job Location and Development (JLD) program, which uses a certain portion of the FWS allocation to encourage the development and expansion of off-campus part-time or full-time employment opportunities for all students, regardless of need. Other requirements must also be met. In addition, a limited number of institutions that meet the definition of a "work-college" may apply to ED to participate in the Work-Colleges program. A work-college may transfer funds from its allocation for FWS and/or Perkins to fund its Work-Colleges program.

Students apply for the FWS program using the FAFSA and are selected by the institution on the basis of need. The institution decides the amount of the award, places the student in a job, and pays the student or contracts to have the student paid. Working hours are determined by each institution but are generally limited to 15 to 20 hours per week while classes are in session and 40 hours per week during vacation periods. Effective July 1, 2000, the institution must use at least 7 (formerly 5) percent of its FWS allocation to compensate students employed in community-service activities (as defined), at least one of which must be a reading-tutoring or family-literacy project.

An institution may transfer up to 25 percent of its total FWS allocation for a particular award year to the FSEOG program for the same award year, and up to 25 percent of its Perkins allocation for a particular award year to FSEOG and/or FWS for the same award year in any combination. Also, up to 10 percent of an institution's total FWS allocation for an award year may be carried forward to the subsequent award year, or carried back to the prior award year. Finally, students may be paid for work performed between May 15 and June 30 from the subsequent award year's FWS allocation. These provisions are designed to provide flexibility to the institution in utilizing its funds.

Federal Perkins Loan

The Federal Perkins Loan program, the successor to the National Direct Student Loan and National Defense Student Loan programs, provides long-term, low-interest (5 percent in 1999–2000), deferred-repayment loans to undergraduate, graduate, and professional students who demonstrate need. Students apply by completing the FAFSA. Preference is given to students with "exceptional need," although this term is not specifically defined in the program regulations.

The institution's Perkins Loan fund, which must be maintained in an interest-bearing account, is composed of annual federal allocations in the form of a 75 percent federal capital contribution and a 25 percent matching institutional capital contribution. The institution administers the Perkins Loan fund as a "revolving" fund—at the same time loans are being made to students, the fund is receiving repayments of earlier loans. These annual collections, as well as any previous year's cash carryover, are also added to the institution's Perkins Loan budget. Cancellations or deferments of repayment are granted under certain conditions (e.g., cancellations may be granted for certain teaching, volunteer, or military service as well as for bankruptcy, death, or disability).

The institution is fully responsible for administering the Perkins Loan program, including approving, disbursing, and collecting the loans. There is a 10-year maximum repayment period for a loan following a grace period. The 1999–2000 annual dollar limits for the Perkins Loan program were $4,000 per year for an undergraduate student and $6,000 for a graduate or professional student. Aggregate limits were $20,000 for students who have completed at least two years of a bachelor's degree program, and $40,000 for graduate or professional students. Somewhat higher annual and aggregate amounts are available to students participating in a study-abroad program.

Federal Family Education Loan Program (FFELP)

The Federal Family Education Loan Program (FFELP) includes Federal Stafford (subsidized and unsubsidized), Federal PLUS, and Federal Consolidation loans.

Federal Stafford Loans

The subsidized Federal Stafford Loan program makes need-based loans available to undergraduate and graduate or professional students to pay for the costs of attending eligible postsecondary education institutions at least half time. Stafford Loans are usually made by private lenders and are guaranteed through a state or private nonprofit guarantee agency that receives partial or full reimbursement from the federal government for defaulted loans. Institutions can be lenders if they meet certain qualifications. The federal government pays interest for subsidized Stafford Loan borrowers while they are enrolled in a institution (or during grace and deferment periods), as well as a special allowance to lenders. For students who do not qualify for the full (or for any) amount of subsidized Stafford Loan, the unsubsidized Stafford Loan is available. Unlike subsidized Stafford Loan borrowers, unsubsidized borrowers begin to accrue interest on their loan 60 days after disbursement; the option of capitalizing interest is available if students choose to defer payment. Unsubsidized Stafford applicants must have their eligibility for subsidized Stafford determined before borrowing under the unsubsidized Stafford program. The FAFSA is the application required for both programs. Also, unsubsidized Stafford Loans can be used to substitute for the EFC, but cannot exceed the student's cost of attendance (COA) minus other financial aid.

Maximum repayment period, interest rates, and loan limits are established by law. For 1999–2000, the Stafford interest rate was tied to the 91-day Treasury bill rate plus an additional percentage, not to exceed 8.25 percent. Undergraduate limits were $2,625 for the first year, $3,500 for the second year, and $5,500 per year beyond the second year, with an aggregate limit of $23,000. Graduate or professional limits were $8,500 per year with an aggregate limit of $65,500. Other limits apply for periods of enrollment less than an academic year and for certain specialized programs. Also, students usually receive a net amount that is smaller than the amount they borrow because origination fees and insurance fees are subtracted by the lender. Stafford Loan repayment may be canceled or deferred under certain conditions set by law.

In 1994, at the time that the Supplemental Loan for Students (SLS) program was eliminated, ED made additional borrowing limits for unsubsidized Stafford Loans available to borrowers formerly served by SLS, namely, independent undergraduates, graduate or professional students, and dependent undergraduates whose parents are unable to borrow under PLUS. For 1999–2000, the applicable loan limits, in addition to those given above, were $4,000 per year for each of the first two undergraduate years, $5,000 per year for the remaining undergraduate years, and $10,000 per year for graduate or professional students, with aggregate limits of $23,000 for undergraduates and $73,000 for graduate or professional students. Other limits apply for periods of enrollment less than an academic year and for certain specialized programs. Thus, for students eligible for this additional borrowing, their overall aggregate (subsidized and unsubsidized) Stafford borrowing limits (excluding capitalized interest) are $46,000 for undergraduates and $138,500 for graduate or professional students.

Federal PLUS Loans

The Federal PLUS Loan program makes loans available to the parents of dependent students to enable them to pay for the costs of students attending postsecondary educational institutions at least half time. The primary sources of funds are private lending institutions. Many Stafford lenders also participate in the PLUS program. In addition to obtaining other information from the borrower, the lender must also obtain a credit report that reflects no adverse credit history, but the lender is not required to insist that the borrower have employment or meet standard debt/income ratio tests.

Similar to the Stafford Loan, for 1999–2000 the PLUS Loan interest rate was tied to the 91-day Treasury bill rate plus an additional percentage, not to exceed 9 percent. There is no interest subsidy, and repayment begins within 60 days of disbursement unless the borrower is entitled to certain deferments. Interest capitalization is also available under certain circumstances. As with unsubsidized Stafford Loans, PLUS Loans can be used as a substitute for the EFC, but cannot exceed the student's cost of attendance (COA) minus other financial aid. Otherwise, there are no annual or aggregate limits for PLUS.

Federal Consolidation Loans

The Federal Consolidation Loan program allows a borrower to combine several loans into one to facilitate repayment over an extended period. The loans (including FFELP, Direct, Perkins, Nursing, various Health Professions loans, etc.) may be consolidated if the borrower meets certain conditions. For 1999–2000, the applicable interest rate was a weighted average, not to exceed 8.25 percent (in most cases).

For all three types of FFELPs described above, the federal government makes a substantial financial commitment in the form of student interest subsidies (subsidized Stafford Loans only), special allowances to lenders, and loan guarantees. In these cases, the principal is provided by the lender.

Federal Direct Loan (FDL)

Federal Direct Loans include Direct Stafford (subsidized and unsubsidized), Direct PLUS, and Direct Consolidation Loans. The FDL program was established in 1994 as an alternative to the FFELP program. Interest rates and dollar limits are identical to FFELP and, as noted above, there are some similarities in administration, although the institution has more reporting responsibilities under FDL and is therefore more directly involved with ED in the drawdown, disbursement, and reconciliation process. The distinguishing feature of the FDL program is the fact that the federal government, rather than a bank or credit union, is the lender and therefore provides the principal for the loans as well as interest benefits. In 1999–2000, about 2,000 institutions of all types applied for and were approved to participate in the FDL program. As noted earlier, institutions can participate in FFELP and FDL simultaneously (although this is rare), but a student can borrow from only one program during a particular enrollment period.

Leveraging Educational Assistance Partnership (LEAP)

The LEAP (formerly State Student Incentive Grant—SSIG) program provides funding to state agencies to encourage the establishment and expansion of state grants and work-study assistance to undergraduate students, although graduate students may sometimes be eligible. Funds are then matched and redistributed by state agencies. Students must have substantial financial need (as defined) and may apply directly to a state agency or through an institution. General eligibility criteria and maximum awards ($5,000 for 1999–2000) are established by the federal government; however, each state has flexibility in determining standards and award amounts within the limits of federal regulations.

Robert C. Byrd Honors Scholarship

ED provides a scholarship of up to $1,500 to undergraduates for up to four years of full-time (in most cases) attendance. Recipients must demonstrate outstanding academic achievement and the promise of continued excellence. The Byrd Scholarship program is administered by the states.

Packaging of Byrd Scholarship With Other SFA Funds. Under Byrd regulations that took effect in September 1993, the SEA must ensure that the total amount of financial aid awarded to the Byrd Scholar does not exceed the scholar's total cost of attendance. If any federal loans are part of the scholar's financial aid package, they must be reduced prior to reducing the Byrd Scholarship. If the scholar is receiving a Pell Grant, though, the Byrd Scholarship must be reduced prior to reducing the Pell Grant. Section 419 J of the Higher Education Act, as amended, states that a Federal Pell Grant must not be reduced on the basis of the receipt of a Byrd Scholarship.

Paul Douglas Teacher Scholarship

ED formerly provided a scholarship of up to $5,000 annually, not to exceed the cost of attendance less other assistance, to undergraduates pursuing a program in teaching who ranked (with some exceptions) in the top 10 percent of their high school graduating class. The program is administered by the states, and is limited to four years of funding for each recipient. There is a teaching service obligation of two years for each year of funding, with some possibility of reduction for certain types of teaching. Congress has not authorized new funds for this program since the beginning of the 1996–97 award year, but former recipients must fulfill their teaching obligation or repay the funds.

Gaining Early Awareness and Readiness for Undergraduate Programs (GEAR UP)

GEAR UP replaces the National Early Intervention Scholarship and Partnership (NEISP) program and comprises two programs that provide competitive programs aimed at improving early college preparation for lower-income students. The state grant component provides funding directly to states, and the partnership grant component provides funding to partnerships of colleges, local schools, and at least two community programs.

Special Leveraging Educational Assistance Partnership (SLEAP)

The SLEAP program will be run as an additional component to LEAP when funding levels for LEAP exceed $30 million per year. For 1999–2000, funding was below $30 million.

Department of Health and Human Services Student Aid Programs

Several student financial aid programs are administered by HHS. Figure 19-02 shows the appropriations for these programs from 1991 through 2001. Individual student loan or grant limits are provided in the sections below to give the reader some perspective on the programs, and they reflect the amounts in effect 1999–2000.

Nursing Student Loan (NSL)

The NSL program is awarded from a revolving fund (similar to Perkins) maintained at the institution; in addition to collections, sources of funding include a federal capital contribution and an institutional match. Institutional

Figure 19-02

Appropriations of Funds for HHS Programs

YR	EFN (1)	FADHPS (1)	SDS*	LDS (2)	HEAL (3)	NHSC (4)	SUEPN (5)
91	9.7	6.1	8.2	2.8	265		4.6
92	9.7	6.0	17.2	14.7	286		2.7
93	10.3	6.2	16.9	7.8	330		0
94	10.3	6.1	16.8	7.7	259		
95	10.4	6.1	17.2	7.7	274		
96	9.9	5.9	16.0	0	209		
97	11.0	6.6	18.1	0	140	30	
98	11.0	6.6	18.2	0	85	34.3	
99			38.1	0	0	32.7	
00			38.1	0	0	32.6	
01 (req)			38.1	0	0		

1. EFN/FADHPS—Authority for these programs was repealed in the Health Professions Education Partnership Act of 1998. Prior recipients are eligible for continued funding through SDS.

2. LDS—Though there have been no new appropriated funds for this program, collections are maintained in a revolving fund.

3. HEAL—From Oct. 1, + 1995, to Sept. 30, 1998 HEAL Program was in phase-out status and was not extended in Nov. 1998 in the Health Professions Education Partnership Act of 1998.

4. NHSC—National Health Service Corps Scholarship program

5. SUEPN—Scholarships for the Undergraduate Education of Professional Nurses—Health Professions Education Extension Amendments of 1992 repealed SUEPN

* SDS—$7M has been deferred until FY2001

responsibilities include determining student eligibility, making the loan, and collecting repayments from the borrower. The NSL program, a need-based program, is open to undergraduate or graduate nursing students attending an institution at least half time. Loans have a prescribed (5 percent in 1999–2000) rate of interest, a maximum amount that may be borrowed each year, and an aggregate maximum. For 1999–2000, the annual maximum for the first two years was $2,500 and the annual maximum for the final two years was $4,000, not to exceed the student's need. The aggregate maximum was $13,000.

Health Professions Student Loan (HPSL)

The HPSL program provides need-based loan assistance to full-time graduate and some undergraduate health professions students from a revolving fund maintained by the institution. Like Perkins and NSL, the fund is made up of cash carryover, collections, a federal capital contribution, and an institutional match. The maximum amount that could be borrowed in 1999–2000 was the cost of tuition and fees plus $2,500 (or higher under some conditions). There is no aggregate limit. The loans have a prescribed rate of interest (5 percent for 1999–2000). Institutional responsibilities are similar to those of NSL. Students funded for award years prior to July 1, 1993, can continue to be funded under HPSL; new borrowers must borrow under the Primary Care Loan (PCL) program.

Primary Care Loan (PCL)

This loan is, in effect, the new version of HPSL, for new borrowers on or after July 1, 1993. The terms and conditions of PCL are similar to those of HPSL except that borrowers must commit to practice in the field of primary and family care after graduation until the loan is paid off.

Scholarship for Students of Exceptional Financial Need (EFN)

A limited number of one-year awards for certain health professions students with exceptional financial need (as defined) are funded by an annual allocation to the institution. Renewal is possible but not guaranteed. The scholarship covers tuition and fees, but not living expenses. Recipients must sign a contract agreeing to complete a residency program (if applicable) in a particular field (e.g., primary care) and then to practice in that field for five years.

National Health Service Corps (NHSC) Scholarship

Designed to recruit health professionals in primary care and other specialties to staff shortage areas, the NHSC Scholarship program provides tuition and fees and a monthly stipend to certain health professions students, with priority given to former NHSC and former EFN recipients. Students must apply directly to NHSC and are required to work one year in a designated area for each year of support received, with a two-year minimum.

Financial Assistance for Disadvantaged Health Professions Students (FADHPS)

Scholarship assistance is available to certain health professions students with exceptional financial need (as defined) and from disadvantaged backgrounds.

Renewal is possible but not guaranteed. The scholarship covers tuition and fees, but not living expenses. Recipients must sign a contract agreeing to complete a residency program (if applicable) in a particular field (e.g., primary care) and then to practice in that field for five years.

Loans for Disadvantaged Students (LDS)

Authorized in 1990 by Congress, the LDS program offers low-interest (5 percent in 1999–2000) loans to students with need from disadvantaged backgrounds pursuing careers in certain health professions, including some undergraduates. Loan amounts are similar to those of HPSL.

Scholarships for Disadvantaged Students (SDS)

Authorized at the same time as LDS (see above), SDS provides scholarships in varying amounts to needy full-time students from disadvantaged backgrounds pursuing careers in certain health professions, including some undergraduates. Awards to individual students can be used to cover tuition and other educational expenses, including living expenses.

Other Federal Aid

Other federal agencies or departments are sources of a wide variety of specialized financial aid programs for various categories of students. Two of the more prominent are the Veterans Administration Education Assistance and the Bureau of Indian Affairs Higher Education Grant.

Veterans Administration Education Assistance

The Veterans Administration (VA) provides assistance to veterans or current armed services personnel for education or training. The Montgomery GI Bill has two programs providing monthly benefits. One program pays up to $536 per month (in 1999) to those who are or were on active duty; in some cases, it requires an initial contribution by the participant. The other program pays up to $255 per month (in 1999) to members of the Selected Reserves. The Post-Vietnam Era Veterans Educational Assistance Program (VEAP) is a contributory plan for veterans and service personnel who began active duty between January 1, 1977, and June 30, 1985, and who meet other eligibility criteria. Monthly benefits are funded primarily by contributions from the participant and matching funds from the government, on a two-for-one basis.

There are also vocational rehabilitation benefits for service-disabled veterans and a VA work-study program for veterans who are willing to perform VA-related services in return for hourly wages. In addition, financial aid benefits of up to $485 per month (in 1999) are provided for the education of the dependent children and spouses of deceased or disabled service personnel or service persons missing in action.

Institutional responsibilities are limited and include enrollment verifications and, if applicable, counting VA resources in assessing a student's need for other financial aid. VA programs are established or modified periodically; therefore, potential participants should consult the VA about the eligibility requirements and benefits of specific programs.

Bureau of Indian Affairs Higher Education Grant

The Bureau of Indian Affairs (BIA) provides need-based assistance for students who are enrolled members of an Indian, Eskimo, or Aleut tribe and are pursuing an undergraduate or graduate degree at an accredited postsecondary institution. The student is also expected to apply for Title IV student aid.

Americorps Grants

Students that have completed a term of service with Americorps—including VISTA, NCCC (National Civilian Community Corps), or any other Americorps state or national program—are eligible for an educational award of up to $4,525. The award may be used to pay all or part of the cost of attending a qualified institution of higher education or to repay existing or future educational loans. Generally the education award must be used within seven years of completing service, but extensions are possible.

NEW DIMENSIONS

Demographics suggest an increasing racial and ethnic diversity, as well as more nontraditional, older, and part-time students. Given this reality, it is likely that some of the policies and practices—federal as well as institutional—that prevailed during the 1990s will be revisited with a renewed concern for those least able to cross the bridge to further education. The seismic changes in communication and how business is done will stimulate policy makers to discover better ways to deliver financial aid. Particular attention will be given to federal grant-funding increases and mechanisms, which will encourage low-income students not only to enroll, but, as important, to complete their degrees and graduate. There will be concomitant pressures to resist increases in loan debt levels.

Social justice issues involving affirmative action and need-based aid principles, centered about consistent and equitable formulas for determining family contributions, and tax considerations for college costs, will be widely debated by various political, legal, and institutional entities.

These issues, as well as the technical advances that have fundamentally changed operational mechanisms and practices, offer an opportunity for institutions to review and update their mission statements. Enrollment management, using financial aid as a recruitment tool, is a good example of how institutional objectives can be achieved, at least in the short run. However, it is essential that such enrollment strategies be synchronized with the educational mission of the institution, and not the reverse.

Ethical considerations regarding equitable financial aid treatment and full disclosure, especially in the area of student recruitment and retention, will continue to challenge the higher education community. Institutions must provide information about their programs and practices, both publicly and individually, that is consistent, clear, and fully revealing. For example, financial aid award notices should explicitly indicate such things as indirect as well as direct costs, types and terms of loans, eligibility requisites, and institutional packaging policies for the continuation of need-based, as well as for merit-based, aid.

The entrepreneurial and creative spirit that has fired the technological revolution and fundamentally changed the way people and business entities communicate and conduct their affairs will gain an increasing foothold in the business of higher education. Institutions will be presented with all sorts of interesting initiatives, private as well as government supported, such as student/parent loans, savings, and prepaid tuition programs. The challenge will be in sorting out which best suit the institution and students, which should include:

- the appeal and availability to the institution's primary student markets;
- the level of confidence in the capacity of the program sponsor effectively to market, manage, and operate a complex and long-term plan;
- management costs and future financial risks of long-term participation in and commitment to a guaranteed program;
- the potential constraints on tuition policy;
- state savings and prepaid tuition plan benefits and disadvantages;
- the potential impact on admission policy;

- the potential effect on financial aid expenditures related to how educational savings plans are assessed in the determination of family contribution levels;

- federal and state tax implications of the savings and prepaid tuition plans; and

- alumni participation and admission expectations.

The enrollment management team, and specifically the student financial services areas, must be alert to and knowledgeable about any new financing program so that this resource information can be properly disseminated and coordinated.

Technological giant steps in software applications and memory capacity will enable institutions to have greatly enhanced central control and management flexibility and, at the same time, afford students the benefit of online communication with all student and financial service areas. This will fundamentally change the way colleges and universities conduct their business and interact with students. Since the financial aid operation will continue to have the primary responsibility for coordination and accounting for federal, state, and institutional funding for students, it is essential that it be administered by officers who are highly skilled and well trained, and who are excited by and adaptable to rapidly evolving institutional dynamics and technological developments.

NOTES

1. *Chronicle of Higher Education*, April 13, 2000, cited at www.chronicle.com/daily/2000/04/2000041304n.htm, and *Chronicle of Higher Education*, February 4, 2000, cited at www.chronicle.com/weekly/v46/i22/22a03802.htm

2. U.S. Department of Education, Office of Postsecondary Education, *The Blue Book: Accounting, Recordkeeping, and Reporting by Postsecondary Educational Institutions for Federally-Funded Student Financial Aid Programs* (Washington, D.C.: U.S. Government Printing Office, 1999), p. 2–25.

3. *Ibid.*, p. 2–11 to 2–40

4. The Department of Education now publishes this "IPEDS" information at http://nces.edu.gov/IPEDS/cool/ to help families choose among colleges and universities.

5. Internal Revenue Service (IRS), *Publication 520* (Washington, DC: U.S. Government Printing Office, 1999).

6. Peter Schmidt, "Boom in Savings Plans is Changing the Way Families Pay for College,"*The Chronicle of Higher Education*, April 14, 2000. See also, Joseph Hurley, "Personal Financial Planning: College Saving Made Easy," *Journal of Accoun-*

tancy, November, 1999, p. 27–32. See also, James Bierstaker and Peter Westort, "Investing for Higher Education Costs: Which Alternative is Best?" *Personal Financial Planning*, September/October (1999), p. 28–40.

REFERENCES AND RESOURCES

Publications and Articles

American Institute of Certified Public Accountants. *Audit and Accounting Guide, Not-for-Profit Organizations*. New York: AICPA, 1999. Updated periodically.

Collins, J. Stephen. *Audits of Federal Student Financial Aid Programs (2000 Edition)*. Washington, D.C.: NACUBO, 2000. Updated periodically.

Fingar, Judith. *Student Loan Programs: Management and Collections*. Washington, D.C.: NACUBO, 1997. Updated periodically.

National Association of Student Financial Aid Administrators. *Institutional Guide for Financial Aid Self-Evaluation*. Washington, D.C.: NASFAA. Updated periodically.

National Association of Student Financial Aid Administrators. *The NASFAA Encyclopedia of Student Financial Aid*. Washington, D.C.: NASFAA. Updated annually.

U.S. Department of Education. Office of the Chief Financial and Chief Information Officer. *Payee Guide for the Grant Administration and Payment System (GAPS)*. Washington, D.C.: U.S. Government Printing Office, 1998. Updated periodically.

U.S. Department of Education. Office of Inspector General. *Audits of Federal Student Financial Assistance Programs at Participating Institutions and Institution Servicers*. Washington, D.C.: U.S. Government Printing Office, 2000. Updated periodically.

U.S. Department of Education. Office of Postsecondary Education. *The Blue Book: Accounting, Recordkeeping, and Reporting by Postsecondary Educational Institutions for Federally-Funded Student Financial Aid Programs*. Washington, D.C.: U.S. Government Printing Office, 1999. Updated periodically.

U.S. Department of Education, Office of Student Financial Assistance. *Compilation of Student Financial Aid Regulations*. Washington, D.C.: U.S. Government Printing Office. Updated annually.

U.S. Department of Education, Office of Student Financial Assistance. *Direct Loan*

School Guide. Washington, D.C.: U.S. Government Printing Office. Updated annually.

U.S. Department of Education. Office of Student Financial Assistance. *Pell Grant Payment Schedules*. Washington, D.C.: U.S. Government Printing Office. Updated annually.

U.S. Department of Education. Office of Student Financial Assistance. *Student Financial Aid Handbook*. Washington, D.C.: U.S. Government Printing Office. Updated annually.

U.S. Department of Health and Human Services. Office of Finance. *The DHHS Manual for Recipients Financed Under the Payment Management System (PMS)*. Washington, D.C.: U.S. Government Printing Office, January 1994. Find at www.dpm.psc.gov/downloads.

U.S. Department of Health and Human Services. Public Health Service. *Guidelines for Student Financial Aid*. Washington, D.C.: U.S. Government Printing Office, 1999. Updated periodically.

U.S. General Accounting Office. *Government Auditing Standards*. Washington, D.C.: U.S. Government Printing Office, 1999 (as amended).

U.S. Office of Management and Budget. *Circular A-133 Compliance Supplement*. U.S. Government Printing Office, 2000. Updated periodically.

Organizations

U.S. Department of Education, Office of Student Financial Assistance
7th & D Streets, SW, Washington, DC 20202
1-800-433-3243 . . . . www.ifap.ed.gov

U.S. Department of Health and Human Services
5600 Fishers Lane, Rockville, MD 20857
Division of Student Assistance . . . . www.hrsa.gov
Division of Payment Management . . . . www.dpm.psc.gov

National Association of College and University Business Officers (NACUBO)
2501 M Street, NW, Suite 400, Washington, DC 20037-1308
202-861-2500 . . . . www.nacubo.org

National Association of Student Financial Aid Administrators (NASFAA)
1129 20th Street, NW, Suite 400, Washington, DC 20036
202-785-0453 . . . . www.nasfaa.org

The College Board
11911 Freedom Drive, Suite 300, Reston, VA 20190
703-707-8999 . . . . www.collegeboard.org

◆

Chapter 20

Auxiliary Enterprises and Other Activities

by

Richard D. Wertz
University of South Carolina

with contributions by

Alma Allred, University of Utah

Jim Baker, University of Texas

Deborah Carlson, St. Cloud State University

Norman R. Chambers, University of Utah

John Crawford, University of Utah

Manuel Cunard, National Association of College Auxiliary Services

Murray DeArmond, University of Arizona

Kent Dohrman, Cleveland State University

Lou Eichler, University of Iowa

Peter Givler, Association of American University Presses

Harvey J. Goodfriend, San Diego State University

Carol Walker Jordan, Queens College of Charlotte

Michael Kalinowski, University of New Hampshire

Patricia Kearney, University of California, Davis

Alan Kirby, University of California, Santa Barbara

Jill Lancaster, Association of Conference Events Director

Gene Luna, University of South Carolina

Jamie Miller, University of Tennessee

Louise Pede, Wentworth Institute of Technology

Gary Schwarzmueller, Association of College and University
Housing Officers-International

Connie Corzilius Spasser, National Association of College Stores

Nick Thomas, STA Travel, Inc.

Rick Van Brimmer, The Ohio State University

Patricia A. Wilkinson, Santa Clara University

Ross Willingham, Oklahoma State University

Sponsors

AT&T
295 North Maple Avenue
Basking Ridge, NJ 07920
800-228-7937
www.att.com/campusalliance

An AT&T Campus Alliance offers a full range of integrated communication and network solutions for you and your students—for all the ways you communicate.

FOLLETT HIGHER EDUCATION GROUP
Contact: Bruce Snyder
1818 Swift Drive
Oak Brook, IL 60523
603-279-2330
www.fheg.com

Follet Higher Education Group is the largest management operator of academic bookstores in the United States and Canada. Follett has been a symbol for quality service, innovative technology and contemporary merchandising.

**NATIONAL ASSOCIATION OF CAMPUS CARD USERS
(NACCU)**
Contact: Lyn White
21 Colony West
Suite 180
Durham, NC 27705
919-403-2273
www.naccu.org

The National Association of Campus Card Users (NACCU) is a nonprofit educational association working to provide learning and networking opportunities for campus card and industry professionals.

NATIONAL ASSOCIATION OF COLLEGE STORES (NACS)
Contact: Cynthia D'Angelo
500 East Lorain Street
Oberlin, OH 44074
800-622-7498 ext. 2293 or 440-775-7777 ext. 2293
www.nacs.org

NACS, a nonprofit trade association serving college and university bookstores in the United States, Canada, and 15 other countries, is the only national trade association for collegiate retailers and suppliers.

WALLACE'S BOOKSTORE, INC.
Contact: Tim Prather
928 Nandino Boulevard
Lexington, KY 40511
606-254-8861
www.wallaces.com

With nearly 40 years of excellent customer service experience in college and university bookstore management, Wallace's exceeds traditional expectations with our FlexSmart modular store.

Contents

Auxiliary enterprises are "auxiliary" in that they support the mission of the institution and provide essential services to the campus community of students, faculty, and staff. They are "enterprises" in that they are generally self-supporting, recovering their costs through the fees or prices they charge for their goods or services. Ideally, they may even contribute to the institution's revenue stream. Depending on the operation, they may have special criteria for financial transactions and accounting practices, purchasing, personnel classification, and other items, like their counterparts in the for-profit sector.

This chapter will examine the philosophy of auxiliary enterprises and their importance to the institution, in terms of both service and revenue. Several examples of auxiliary enterprises are discussed in detail, but the topics included are not meant to be exhaustive.

In the early years of higher education in the United States, colleges took the position that, unlike the European universities, where very few student services were provided, they would provide creature comforts and look after student needs and interests. Many colleges in the United States were founded in rural settings or outlying areas, and thus it became incumbent on those institutions to provide sleeping quarters, food service, entertainment and recreational facilities, and other services to meet students' needs. If the local area could not or did not provide a desired or necessary service that students needed, the college would then become the service provider. This trend continued throughout the history of higher education in the United States. The "in loco parentis" philosophy of higher education prevailed for decades and only in modern times has the concept died out. However, court rulings in recent years have tended to require colleges and universities to assume some of the responsibilities they formerly had for students.

Auxiliary enterprises should contribute and relate directly to the mission, goals, and objectives of a college or university. They should not be regarded merely as service activities, profit centers, or businesses, but as active expressions of the institution as well, reflecting its history, style, and relation to its constituencies. Such enterprises should reflect the quality of service that a college or university desires for its students, faculty, staff, and alumni. Senior administrators should ensure that managers of the enterprises understand, adopt, and implement the policies supporting an institution's desired style and quality of life. The services provided by successful auxiliary enterprises can be significant factors in attracting and retaining students, faculty, and staff.

Are students and faculty getting their books and educational supplies when they need them? Do students have adequate sleeping and living quarters? Is high-quality food available? Do students have facilities for studying, recreation, and meetings? Is the campus safe? Is parking available? Is health care or child care available?

EXPANDED ROLE OF AUXILIARY ENTERPRISES

The needs of the institutional community have changed over the years. Auxiliary enterprises have come a long way from providing just living and dining facilities. Now they offer shopping malls, computer stores, golf courses, travel agencies, car rental outlets, movie theaters, food courts, laundry and dry cleaning facilities, arenas, skating and skiing areas, and many of the most modern conveniences available anywhere. Students accustomed to these modern conveniences expect and demand that colleges and universities provide whatever is necessary to meet their needs.

Most colleges and universities already provide the essential services, such as food service, bookstores, housing, coin-operated laundries, vending, copy machines, computer support, transportation, and parking. They are now focusing on adding the nonessential services such as those listed in the paragraph above along with bowling alleys and recreation centers. However, before acting on these demands and adding nonessential services, administrators should ensure that essential services satisfy the customers by being market competitive and providing quality products and services.

Colleges and universities, in an effort to recruit good students, must provide those services requested by students. The role of auxiliary enterprises has taken on an even more important aspect as colleges and universities compete for students through the quality of their academic and support programs.

Auxiliary enterprises have grown so important and so extensive on some campuses that local businesses, even more so now than in the past, are "crying foul" and making claims of unfair business practices or unfair competition. This has led to legislation being passed in some states, limiting what higher educational institutions can provide in the way of services.

Outsourcing of Auxiliary Enterprises

Many institutions operate their own auxiliary enterprises, not because they have always done it that way, but because they have determined that it is to their advantage. Others outsource one of more of these services for a variety of reasons: a private company may offer the expertise to operate a service that the institution does not have; it may be able to operate the service more economically than can the institution; it may offer financial incentives to operate the service; the institution may lack the personnel or capital improvement funds necessary for the service or simply want to eliminate or reduce the burden of providing the service.

Private businesses have responded to this need and have offered their services in operating both traditional and new auxiliary enterprises. "Partnering" with a private business is also occurring. Sometimes institutions form partnerships with private businesses. This differs from a full-fledged contractual takeover of a service by a private company in that only specific elements or limited parts of an operation may be involved. These flexible arrangements with a private company can be tailored to meet the needs of a particular institution.

Colleges and universities have also formed cooperatives to operate auxiliary enterprises. This form may have a separate board of directors and may be affiliated with but not officially part of the institution. A separately incorporated entity is another form for operating auxiliary enterprises. This method would also have a separate board of directors and be associated with, but not actually part of, the institution.

Institutions that consider outsourcing an auxiliary service must consider carefully the possible implications for several areas of the insitution, including taxes and financing. For example, contracts with private sector vendors to either use or manage facilities that were acquired or constructed through tax-exempt financing must be written in a way that will not jeopardize such financing or create bond-related problems for the institution. (For more on the subject of outsourcing, see chapter 3, Implementation Strategies and Outcomes Assessment.)

Revenues, Reserves, and Costs of Auxiliary Enterprises

Institutions face many challenges in regard to optimizing operational effectiveness, maximizing revenues, and enhancing customer satisfaction. Administrators, trustees, legislators, and others are demanding more of auxiliary enterprises. The services must be efficient, ideally self-supporting, often must produce revenue for the institution, and must certainly operate at a level of which the institution can be proud. The funding sources of auxiliary enterprises include student fees, revenue from other customers, bonds, and federal, state, and local grants. Fund reserves play a large part in the operation of those services producing revenue, and they have traditionally been used to update equipment, renovate facilities, add new services, or improve the auxiliary enterprise itself. Reserves should be sufficient to meet maintenance and equity requirements. Auxiliary enterprises should be allowed to develop longer-range plans and reserves without fear of these reserves being appropriated for other institutional purposes. If the institution makes a decision to use a percentage of the budget of an auxiliary enterprise or some of its reserves for other institutional purposes, it should be done with a full realization of the effects of such a strategy on deferred maintenance and availability of equity for the auxiliary enterprise.

Another financial issue that has a strong effect on budgets is campus recharges. It is appropriate to expect an auxiliary enterprise to pay for all direct costs. Indirect costs may be less appropriate, and campus practice varies widely in this area. Institutions should have clear and open discussions of their policy in this area and, when a policy is decided upon, it should be applied equally to all auxiliary enterprises on campus, when feasible. Most institutions charge administrative overhead or levy a charge for centrally provided services in such areas as purchasing, payroll, law enforcement, legal aid, accounting services, and many others. Cost accounting practices form the basis of these charges, and a commonly accepted rate of charge that the institution may require is in the range of 11 percent of the expenditures of the auxiliary service, although there are many variations, depending on the service and depending on the institution. Increasingly, colleges and universities are using these funds for other purposes and are depending on them to help balance the institution's budget.

Professional Preparation of Auxiliary Enterprise Administrators

More emphasis is being placed on the operation of auxiliary enterprises than ever before, as well as on their "image" and the "customer relations" aspects of their service. National associations are actively involved in the professional development and education of administrators responsible for auxiliary services.

More and more, administrators of auxiliary services are professionally prepared to operate the auxiliary service "like a business." The contemporary administrator needs to be customer-service oriented, skilled in effective marketing techniques, armed with technology skills, able to write requests for proposal and contract documents, and knowledgeable about public relations concepts. He or she must also be a skilled financial analyst and a labor negotiator. The administrator very often supervises a private company providing a service as well as institutional staff.

Professional associations for auxiliary enterprise administrators are taking an active role in the continuing education of their members. Workshops, seminars, training institutes, and teleconferencing provide up-to-date information aimed at improving the performance of members.

The text that follows is an overview. Auxiliary enterprises have more breadth and depth than described here and involve many activities important to higher education that go well beyond the samples provided.

TYPICAL AUXILIARY SERVICES

Food Services

The philosophy of an institution's food service program and the methodology for its delivery must relate directly to the objectives of the college or university. Dining should be considered an important component of the educational experience, and it is the responsibility of the institution to determine the best way to accomplish this mission. Several methods can be used. Some institutions have one comprehensive food service department for all food service programs on the campus. In others, food services are segmented according to services performed, such as one department for residents, a separate department for cash operations, and another for food service facilities located in the college union. Variations on these methods are also found.

Once a method of delivery is selected, it is necessary to determine how the services are to be managed. Typically, colleges and universities self-operate the food service program, contract with a private company to operate it, or use a combination of self-operated and outsourced management. In the past few decades, colleges and universities have begun to understand the importance of food service programs for recruitment and retention of students and have dedicated revenue to renovating facilities and making them as attractive as possible. New facilities were built to compete with commercial businesses. The food service programs are designed to meet students' demands for contemporary menu items, sparkling décor, and diversity in products and services.

Some institutions outsource their food services. Private businesses offer the institution commissions or guarantees of specific dollar amounts, and they may also invest money in renovating existing facilities or building new ones. Some offer various levels of consultation as well.

Branding is a concept available to both self-operated food services and those operated by private contractors. National, regional, and manufacturer brands of fast foods and other products are available through franchises, licenses, or agreements. Many institutions have also developed their own in-house brands. The institution is responsible for ensuring that proper business practices, quality standards, and health and safety regulations are followed.

There are two major types of dining programs: dining services provided for students residing on and off campus through a prepaid board plan program and a la carte operations, such as snack bars, restaurants, specialty shops, and convenience stores. Each requires a distinctive and different style of management expertise. The distinction between these two types of programs is blurring as companies use variations and blends of them.

Factors in evaluating customer satisfaction include menu variety, payment options, frequency, portion size, clean and attractive facilities, flexible and timely service hours, dine-in or take-out service, locations accepting meal plans or point exchanges, adjustments for examination schedules and class conflicts, courteous service, attention to special requests and religious observances, and accommodation of special dietary restrictions.

An advantage of prepaid meal plans is that they are exempt from sales tax in many states, thus providing a saving to students. Students who live in residence halls usually pay in advance for their meals. A choice of board plans and flexibility to make plan changes may help ensure student satisfaction through the academic year. The growing number of nontraditional students makes it important to offer a variety of meal plans. Various meal options can be offered at prices that differentiate between levels of service, number of meals, and payment options (e.g., declining balance and standard prepaid).

Labor and food costs are the major expenses of a food service department, with the total ranging from 65 to 75 percent of sales. Food costs can be measured as a percentage of sales or cost per meal/transaction by food service unit, for the entire food service operation, or among peer institutions that offer similar menus and board plans. Use of these methods eliminates the factors of missed meals and fluctuations in sales volume. In operating a prepaid board plan, absenteeism is often programmed into the selling price of meal plans. Computer software is available to analyze food costs and to provide menu planning, pricing, and purchasing assistance. Some of these use a "precost" system that forecasts the number of meals to be served and uses standard recipes and portion sizes to predict the cost of ingredients and supplies. Point-of-sale systems track actual meal plan usage and other sales.

Labor costs can be measured as a percentage of sales, cost per meal, meals per labor hour, or labor hours per hundred meals. The last two eliminate the effect of comparing variable labor costs throughout the country and enable comparison among peer institutions.

Cash or retail sales operations differ from board plan operations in that there is no fixed and advanced allocation of revenue. Even more than residential dining operations, retail operations must create their own markets, be competitive, and anticipate and respond to market demands. Accurate point-of-sale (especially cash) and inventory controls are critical. Expenses are normally reported on a percentage-of-sales basis. Electronic point-of-sale systems are good investments to assist in obtaining necessary financial and other management information.

The role of dining services has expanded through the increase in board plan options, the establishment of the decreasing and/or increasing balance card, the creation of campus convenience stores, and the introduction of marketplace concepts and display cooking. In addition to satisfying its customers, food service, whether self-operated, outsourced, or cosourced, can be a revenue source for institutions.

Training of staff in food safety and HACCP (Harvard Analysis Critical Control Points) is essential to safeguard the well-being of all customers. Training in customer service, food presentation, strategic planning, finances, leadership, and teambuilding are important. The National Association of College and University Food Services (NACUFS), the National and State Restaurant Association, and others provide training programs in these and other areas.

Basic services of a college or university food service operation now include business and finance, purchasing, computer systems (food production, access/point of sale), marketing, human resources, training, conferences, and operations. It is essential that these services be well coordinated and focused on department, division, and institution priorities (as defined and designated in the strategic plan).

The food service operation is big business and needs to be treated as such. Often, a university dining program is the largest food service operation in its city. It is important that the operation provide excellent services with an adequate return to meet department, division, and institutional objectives.

The program needs to be evaluated on a regular basis. NACUFS offers a set of principles and practices in its *Professional Practices Manual* for use by food service operations. The practices provide a framework for developing and/or evaluating the food service program. Following a self-study, the food service operation may request a peer review. NACUFS also provides operating, wage and salary, and customer satisfaction benchmarking surveys. In addition to these periodic studies, ongoing surveys and other evaluations of the food service program are important.

Student Housing

A college or university must determine what role housing services play in the mission of the institution. A statement about that role will form the basis for a variety of decisions about the amount and type of housing needed, target population(s), focus of student program efforts, types of facilities needed, and staffing models. The more central housing services are to the mission of the institution, the more important it is for the institution to directly provide these services.

A significant body of research shows the value of a residence hall experience for first-and (somewhat less powerfully) second-year undergraduate students. On-campus residence halls can be important to recruitment, retention, academic success, and positive identification with the institution. These, as well as other favorable results, require an intentional program to link the residence halls to the academic experience. A number of program models are available to make this link. These include residential colleges, freshman interest groups (FIGs), academic theme and honors floors or buildings, live-in faculty and faculty associates, learning resource centers, computer centers, video productions shown on housing cable systems, enhanced academic advising, and freshman experience programs.

Student housing must be addressed in the campus master plan, physical development policy, and financial plan. A long-range housing plan should provide guidance on the percentage of the student body to be housed on campus and the target populations that have priorities. The plan should also allow for flexibility and be couched in the terms "when financially feasible" to protect the financial viability of this auxiliary. Growth limitations, community relations, and changes in the local economy and housing markets may also strongly influence the housing development plan.

There are a variety of ways to meet the targets outlined in the long-range housing plan. The institution may choose to build, own, and manage all of its housing, or it may contract with private firms to build, finance, or manage this housing. Choices are not mutually exclusive. For example, some institutions have made the strategic decision to use privatized housing for upper-division students, graduate students, and student families while maintaining full control over first-year student housing. The age of facilities, amount of deferred maintenance, and rental rate elasticity may also figure in the decision to selectively use privatization as part of a long-range housing plan.

Components of Student Housing

Student housing typically includes an academic and personal development component, a basic services component, a conference housing component, and a food service component. At some institutions, these activities report to the CFO while at others they report to the chief student affairs officer. Some institutions have a bifurcated model, where the academic and personal development components report through student affairs while the others report through business affairs. If a dual reporting line is used, a coordinating structure and strong expectations for collaboration are needed.

There are a variety of models for programming the residence life or personal development component. These include residence hall student governments and other student clubs and committees, live-in residence hall student and professional staff, and judicial or conduct officers and boards. It is important that individuals involved in residence life programs are committed to making the academic connections that students need; are knowledgeable about student communities and the needs of this age group; and are able to create positive environments where students from a variety of diverse religious, ethnic, and cultural backgrounds may live together in harmony. Staff must be aware of and able to manage risk in terms of building security and preventing personal injury, as well as in the sensitive areas of sexual harassment, racial incidents, and alcohol and drug abuse.

Basic services typically include contracts and assignments, facility maintenance (preventive, operational, and long-term), custodial services, accounts receivable and payable, capital projects (small and new facilities), computer support, personnel, and budget and finance. A variety of patterns are used in organizing basic services. It is essential that these housing services be well-coordinated by being placed under one director or by developing an intentional coordinating structure and expectation. Financial spreadsheet models should be developed that allow decision makers to manipulate rental rates, reserve balances, equity for new projects, funds for major maintenance needs, and debt to develop longer-range plans to meet institutional objectives.

Student housing facility maintenance is strongly affected by federal and state regulations. Renovation or maintenance projects may require compliance with the Americans with Disabilities Act (ADA); regulations governing removal of asbestos, lead, or other hazardous materials; and local fire, seismic, and other building codes. Institutions should compare the costs of renovating older buildings with the alternative of razing them and building new housing that meets students' needs.

Many residence hall and apartment operations provide conference services during the summer. Conference income may help the housing auxiliary to employ staff year-round and reduce the rates charged to students during the regular academic year. The conference program may also assist with outreach and recruitment if used to provide housing to summer enrichment programs and other youth groups. On the downside, full-year operation of facilities challenges staff ability to schedule maintenance projects. It is important for colleges and universities to have a clear policy on the types of groups that may use institutional facilities. To the extent that these uses are not related or less related to the institutional mission, income from conference housing activities may be subject to unrelated business income taxes (UBIT).

Since many housing facilities are not composed of units that allow for cooking all meals, most residence halls provide meal plans as part of a room and board rate. Food service may include regular daily meals as well as late night dining and take-out. Meal plans vary from the traditional 19- or 21-meal fixed plan to full a la carte dining. Many campuses offer a variety of meal plans to meet different student needs. Whether self-operated or contracted, the food service must be fully integrated with the residence hall experience.

The housing program should be evaluated on a regular basis. The Association of College and University Housing Officers—International (ACUHO-I) has a set of standards and a self-study program for use by institutional housing operations. ACUHO-I, in partnership with Educational Benchmarking, Inc. (EBI), also provides an annual benchmarking survey of residence hall programs. The National Association of College and University Business Officers (NACUBO) also sponsors an annual benchmarking study of residence hall financial matters. In addition to these periodic studies, annual surveys and other evaluations of all parts of student housing are important.

Faculty Housing

Faculty housing assistance has become an important component of the recruitment package that many colleges and universities use to attract faculty to their campuses. The high cost of housing and the lack of available housing in many regions of the country have led many institutions to develop rental and for-sale housing units for faculty and to provide various forms of housing assistance programs.

Colleges and universities should consider institutional objectives and the needs of the faculty when developing faculty housing programs. Like the approach recommended for development of student housing, a mission statement for faculty housing should be framed in the context of the mission statement of the institution. Faculty renewal models, which project anticipated faculty turnover due to retirements, death, or terminations and creation of new positions, can be used to project the resources that may be required to meet recruitment objectives. The need to retain faculty should also be factored into a strategic plan for faculty housing.

The determination of need is essential in creating programs that will yield successful results in meeting recruitment and retention objectives. Surveys and focus groups of newly recruited faculty and those who did not accept appointment offers can be used to ascertain the role housing played in the decision to accept or decline employment at the institution. Demographic data, including information on family size, marital status, dual income status, previous housing status (i.e., renter versus owner), current housing status, current monthly housing cost, and satisfaction with current housing, can be used to generate profiles of faculty and provide baseline data from which programs can be conceptualized and assumptions can be tested. Market research should also be used to assess interest in the variety of alternative housing programs being considered for implementation. Once a faculty housing program is established, surveys and focus groups should continue to assess the impact of the programs in meeting institutional objectives, to ascertain the level of satisfaction with the programs among faculty participants, and to tailor programs to meet changing faculty demographics.

Issues such as housing supply and demand, affordability, and institutional resources dictate the variety and types of housing assistance programs that should be considered. A faculty housing assistance program could range from merely providing informational resources to assist faculty in locating housing in the community to providing financial assistance in the form of a relocation allowance, mortgage loan, or interest subsidy to developing a stock of rental and for-sale housing. A multifaceted housing program may include all of these features.

Providing information and referrals to community resources, if these resources are readily available, is typically the least costly approach. Services can include referring faculty to rental housing, providing neighborhood profiles for those relocating from other areas, and helping faculty in locating transitional, temporary housing. Many colleges and universities have community-housing offices that assist students in locating suitable rental housing in the community. Extending this resource to faculty may enable the institution to use existing staff to meet faculty housing needs. Another option is to refer faculty to relocation companies that provide area orientations and home-finding assistance to new employees at little or no cost to the employer or employee. These companies should be carefully screened by institutional management, and the satisfaction of faculty referred to these programs should be closely monitored to ensure that the level and quality of service are consistent with institutional objectives.

Providing actual financial assistance in the form of a relocation allowance, mortgage loan, or interest subsidy may be a costly alternative to meeting faculty housing needs if the number of faculty the institution desires to assist is great. A relocation allowance or interest subsidy involves the outright payment of funds that will never be recouped by the institution. Mortgage loans, on the other hand, return funds to the institution over the term of the loan; thus the funds are available to be reinvested in the recruitment and retention of other faculty or to be reallocated for other institutional needs.

The organizational placement of faculty housing program activities can vary greatly from institution to institution. The housing operation may be the appropriate unit to assume responsibility for faculty rental housing and for the informational resource referrals. In some institutions, the housing operation has also assumed responsibility for the development of faculty for-sale housing, although this responsibility may also be delegated to the campus real estate or property management function. Faculty lending programs are characteristically the responsibility of student loan services, general accounting, or the academic personnel office on many campuses that lack resources for staffing a separate office for the purpose. Wherever these responsibilities fall organizationally, one senior administrator should assume responsibility for coordinating all facets of the faculty housing assistance program. Without an overall vision and direction, it is unlikely that the program will be effective in meeting institutional objectives and that resources will be maximized. Ideally, one organizational unit should assume responsibility for developing the strategic plan for faculty housing and implementing the various aspects of the program. This results in a better-coordinated and more effective approach when dealing with faculty and should minimize duplication of effort.

Campus Stores

Campus bookstores are, first and foremost, retailers—businesses for which the definition of success is satisfying customers while producing a financial return. But campus bookstores differ from other retailers in significant ways. It is important for CFOs to be able to communicate to their constituents what makes college stores different from general retail. The answer can be reduced to two concepts—mission and market.

A campus bookstore's mission is to support the mission of the institution it serves. Its customer base, or market, is the campus community—students, faculty, and staff—as well as alumni and visitors. A bookstore provides the academic community with materials that not only further the institution's educational mission but also enhance campus life. Satisfying customer needs is only part of the store's mission. Bookstores also must fulfill their institutional responsibilities by providing high-quality academic support services while meeting budget projections and revenue goals—objectives that can be obtained only in a supportive business environment. It is important, then, that administrators consider three questions: What can a successful bookstore provide its campus? What does a bookstore require to be successful? How can the institution support and facilitate that success?

A bookstore's responsibility goes far beyond the logistical challenge of setting the right book in the hands of every student at the right moment. For example, it is the responsibility of most campus stores, as the principal campus retail technology outlet, to provide computers, software, peripherals, and supplies at substantial academic discounts. On many campuses, the store's copy facility is responsible for preparation, production, and distribution of customized teaching materials requested by instructors. To provide this service the store often assumes the role of publisher, including securing permissions for the use of copyrighted materials. This service allows faculty to use out-of-print books that the store reproduces with the permission of the publisher. This service goes beyond print media and includes various digitized formats.

Like any enterprise, however, the campus bookstore requires a supportive business environment to achieve its potential. The campus store faces the challenges of shifting demographics, rising costs, the increased need for technological solutions, and an increasingly sophisticated and demanding consumer. The expansion of distance learning, the advent of electronic commerce, the development of new course material delivery methods, and publishing-on-demand technologies compel bookstores to evolve to find new ways to serve their existing customers and develop new markets. At the same time, campus bookstores have never before faced such intense competition for the student dollar. Discount, convenience, and department stores, book and office superstores, and Internet booksellers are vying for a slice of the college market.

To meet these challenges in a competitive market, the campus store must be permitted—even directed—to meet current retailing standards. For example, the store requires sufficient space in a highly visible location that is accessible and convenient to parking. What constitutes sufficient space is determined by institutional enrollment, the store's merchandise mix, and the additional services, if any, it is expected to provide to its customers. Space devoted to required but unprofitable services must be carefully evaluated. These service requirements reduce the amount of space available for salable products and increase operating and capital expenses.

To be successful, the campus bookstore must offer a competitive merchandise mix, even if it requires paying unrelated business income taxes or dealing with local area merchants. In today's market, this means stocking used textbooks, trade books, software, soft goods, and general merchandise—which carry a higher margin and meet customer demand. At some institutions, this may mean forging agreements with computer companies to sell personal computers to students, faculty, and staff. At others, it may mean hosting a store Web site that provides not only information about the store's products, but a secure way to purchase them electronically.

Campus stores must stay technologically current in terms of the merchandise they carry, the inventory and point-of-sale (POS) systems that streamline their operations, and the Web pages and Web sites where they promote and sell their products. One service enhanced by E-commerce and the Internet is textbook reservations and purchasing. After registering for classes, the student visits the bookstore's Web site and requests that the bookstore box all the books and supplies required for the courses. When the order is complete, the store then calls the student. Institutions should evaluate whether a "smart card" or "one card" system would benefit both students and the bookstore. (For more information on this subject, see chapter 7, Information Technology and Services.)

As a retail enterprise, the campus bookstore requires an operating model that is primarily focused on sales, gross margin, and operating expenses. Gross margin is the residual after paying for the cost of goods to be sold, usually including inbound freight expense. The calculation of gross margin is further complicated by trade practices such as rebates, discounts, advertising allowances, markdowns, returns, and other arrangements common to the retail industry. While budgeting is mandatory, daily, weekly, and monthly performance data are critical to successfully managing a dynamic process. To acquire those data requires a sophisticated information system that starts at the point of sale and ends with a full set of timely reports tailored to the needs of merchandise buyers and store managers. Proper monitoring of inventory performance requires the application of the retail method of costing. Without this vital information, inventory shrinkage is difficult to measure accurately. It may be challenging for small stores to afford the technology required to function in the contemporary retail environment.

For college stores to prosper, institutions must strive to understand their accounting needs and the seasonal nature of their cash flow. Unlike institutions, retailers use the retail method of inventory valuation. CFOs must be aware of the importance of ensuring accounting system integration and compatability. Budgeting for retail operations differs significantly from other campus units. For example, the cost of merchandise may exceed the budgeted amount because sales increased—an indication of success, not failure. Retail businesses also must reinvest—for example, by budgeting for capital improvements—to stay competitive in serving the needs of campus constituencies and to remain profitable.

Finally, it is crucial that administrators communicate institutional expectations to campus store management. The institution and the store should work together to set financial goals and priorities and to plan for future growth and improvements. This kind of dialogue affords administrators access to firsthand knowledge of student needs and demands, information on trends in the college publishing and college store industries, and an understanding of market realities that may not be reflected in the store's balance sheet. By the same token, the store director learns about campus perceptions of the store, ways to coordinate with other units on campus, and bottom-line expectations of the administration. All too often, the institution's profitability policy for the bookstore is not clearly articulated and communicated to the campus community

Competition has increased to the point that campus stores have relatively little advantage other than location. Mass-market merchants sell almost everything that stores have traditionally offered and often at much lower prices. Trade and reference books are heavily promoted on the Internet by several major sources. Textbooks are also becoming a commodity as a number of online retailers cut prices and heavily promote their products to capture campus market share.

The trend to outsource store management continues, with a growing number of institutions engaging firms that lease and operate stores under contract. Typically, these contracts assure continued employment of staff; guarantee minimum annual commissions versus a percentage of sales; include remodeling, improvements, and policies; and provide for the purchase of the store's inventory. Coupled with a significant bonus, this often represents a substantial infusion of discretionary funds to the institution. Outsourcing the store requires competent administration by an informed institutional representative to assure that all expectations and contract requirements are consistently met.

The campus bookstore should be considered a long-term institutional asset. Regardless of its structure—institutional, contractual, or independent; for profit or nonprofit—and regardless of its reporting lines, the campus bookstore must be operated using sound business practices.

Retail Sales

The nature of retail sales on college and university campuses has changed dramatically over the past 10 years. Even the definition of what constitutes retail sales has broadened considerably. It was not long ago that a discussion about campus retail sales was restricted to entrepreneurial auxiliary enterprise staff, who were careful not to speak too boldly for fear of alienating the academic community. Next came a gradual acceptance of the campus shopping mall concept designed to offer a variety of services in one convenient location, usually associated with the college union. These campus malls generally included a variety of businesses such as travel agencies, dry cleaners, copy centers, bookstores, food outlets, and music stores. Though there was resistance to this mall concept by some in the academic community, it soon became apparent that students overwhelmingly favored a shopping experience that closely resembled what they had been used to prior to arriving on campus. The next trend in retail sales was the dramatic increase in branded concepts. Though branding has most often been associated with cash retail food sales it has also extended to other products and services.

Areas of campus that historically have been institutionally run now face such strong private competition that many institutionally run services have disappeared only to be replaced by their previous competitors. Campus copy centers have become part of the retail sales scenario as regional and national enterprises have moved onto campus and established a strong retail presence. Does a central stores operation still have validity when a nationally recognized office supply store sits next to the campus offering departmental supplies with a fresh retail approach? Can catalog sales with direct deliveries to departments serve the same purpose? The list of possibilities seems endless.

However, the most dramatic change on the campus retail landscape is without question the introduction of retail sales on the Internet. The electronic commerce industry is sweeping across college campuses just as it is throughout the world. College stores find themselves competing with E-commerce companies. The revelation that retail sales are no longer bound by "bricks and mortar" is one of the most challenging concepts to face retail managers in a very long time. E-commerce companies seem to have extensive advertising budgets and an aggressive approach to marketing that has many retail managers searching for effective countermeasures to retain market share. It is difficult to predict how this struggle for campus retailing dollars will ultimately unfold. One thing is certain: the importance of retail sales of all types continues to grow on college and university campuses.

Vending

The most notable change in the vending industry has been the development and introduction of vending equipment that offers a broader selection of fresh products, from cappuccino brewed on the spot from freshly ground coffee beans to French fries cooked in less than 30 seconds by super-heated air. The quality of products served from vending machines has improved dramatically as vending operators continually search for ways to increase revenue and achieve greater customer satisfaction.

College and university vending operations are not unlike private vending companies in that each seeks to generate revenue while providing its customers with quality merchandise at a reasonable price. However, when colleges and universities operate their own in-house vending operations, they may sometimes be more service-oriented than profit-driven. Institutions should be clear about the objectives for their in-house operation so as to avoid confusion and failure of the department to achieve administrative objectives.

In-House Operations

Institutions choosing to operate vending services internally must be prepared to provide logistical means and human resources to support the operation. The institution should employ an experienced vending manager and an experienced vending machine maintenance technician. The vending department may then serve as a student employment opportunity for warehouse workers, route attendants, clerical support, and others.

The institution must identify and provide reasonable warehouse and office space in a location central to the area of operations. Additionally, vending operations require route service vehicles and vending machines. Each vending machine needs a dollar bill validator. The institution may elect to use debit card technology. The vending manager should develop an adequate depreciation schedule and set aside a portion of gross revenue for replacement of equipment over a given period of time.

Contracting

Contracting allows the institution to pursue a vending program without major capital expenditures. Award of the contract is normally based on four criteria: commissions to be paid by the contracting company to the institution; level of service offered by the company to keep machines stocked, clean, and in good repair; retail price of merchandise offered for sale; and quality of merchandise offered for sale. The institution should expect the contracting company to provide adequate vending equipment and the minimal number of personnel required to properly service the account.

Exclusive Beverage Initiatives

Major soft drink manufacturers have long believed that a consumer exposed to a product on an exclusive basis for several years will likely become a life-long consumer of that product. As a result, soft drink manufacturers are aggressively pursuing exclusive beverage commitments from colleges and universities on a national level.

Such contracts may equate to millions of dollars to the institution; however, students, faculty, and staff lose the freedom of choice of alternate brands. Loss of choice is unacceptable to many and such loss may become a matter of public interest and public record. The administration must be prepared to respond effectively to student, faculty, and staff anxieties and publicity associated with a decision to limit brand choice.

Institutions should expect the exclusive beverage contractor to provide new vending machines, fountain equipment, and debit card technology in addition to a significant signing bonus and annual guaranteed payments for the term of the contract. Such commitments reach far beyond vending and normally include every campus venue including athletics, residence halls, catering, student union, campus convenience stores, and any other food service outlets.

Collegiate Licensing

As part of a comprehensive trademark management program, many institutions operate a trademark licensing program. This includes measures to both protect and promote the institution's name and goodwill through commercially available products that bear its trademarks. (Also see chapter 17, Procurement, and chapter 21, Legal Issues.) The institution licenses rights to its name and symbols to manufacturers who in turn pay royalties on the sale of their products, from T-shirts to puzzles. This type of program is often housed in an auxiliary enterprise operation, although institutions have placed these programs in a variety of administrative units including business and administration, bookstore, finance, legal affairs, athletics, alumni relations, and technology transfer.

Institutions approach collegiate licensing in different ways. Some institutions choose to operate the program entirely on-campus, while others employ outside agencies to facilitate many of the licensing functions. An institution that selects an agency-assisted program can expect to pay a percentage of royalty revenues to the agent in exchange for assistance in administering the program. These percentages vary from 10 to 25 percent or more.

The first step in establishing a licensing program is a comprehensive survey of the institution's indicia and the legal registrations to protect their ownership. Registration of the trademarks, service marks, and trade names can be done on both the state and federal levels. Although the state registration process is much simpler and inexpensive, federal registration, albeit more time-consuming and expensive, is a stronger and more far-reaching protection. A key part of the decision-making process of which marks and what registrations are sought is based on the institution's scope within the community and beyond.

Many institutions operate international licensing programs and have registered their trademarks in various foreign countries. While the market for American college and university goods overseas is still developing, international registrations should be given consideration. The economy is increasingly a global one, and many American universities sponsor overseas educational programs.

The duties of the licensing administrator include:

- selecting and developing products;
- negotiating licensing agreements with manufacturers;
- identifying marketing opportunities for goods;
- accounting for sales and royalties;
- monitoring the marketplace for unauthorized products;
- ensuring quality compliance; and
- coordinating promotional uses of licensed product.

An issue that has recently become important in licensing is requiring a guarantee that sweatshops are not used in the production of goods having college and university logos on them.

License agreements with manufacturers usually contain an advance against future royalties, and some institutions charge an administrative or application fee. In the collegiate market, royalties generally range from 6 to 8 percent of the wholesale price of an item on which the mark appears.

Licensing revenues have become a profitable business venture for many institutions. The collegiate product marketplace is estimated to be more than a $2 billion industry. The rewards are particularly high for institutions that have a high regional or national profile or that enjoy exceptional athletic success, such as a national championship in a high-visibility sport.

As collegiate licensing has matured, it has played an ever-increasing role in the overall marketing of a college or university to the public. Licensing programs have become an important part of a strategic "brand" management implementation on the campus.

Travel Agencies

Travel is an essential part of academic life. However, colleges and universities have two separate and unique requirements for travel services. These need to be clearly understood before developing and implementing a strategy to deal with them.

The first type is business travel of faculty and staff, a large cost to the institution and one that requires considerable management, accountability, and integration. The second is the self-funded travel activities of the college community, predominantly students, which are no less important and can be managed to generate income. These two types of travel require fundamentally different approaches and are rarely, if ever, serviced effectively under the same roof. On the other hand, the two can comfortably coexist without compromising contract commitments and service levels.

Naturally enough, in most institutions, the emphasis is on faculty and staff business travel, because it is a major budget item. On a large campus, business travel may cost as much as $10 million annually, and such levels of expenditure require tight control. Self-funded or leisure travel spending by students is also very significant and can represent at least $2–3 million of business on a medium-sized campus. Accommodating this demand is more of a service issue than a financial one. It is critical to ensure that appropriate programs are made available in a manner that supports the objectives of the institution in broadening student experience through travel and improving the quality and mix of services on campus, all within a budget framework that students can afford. Directing student spending to on-campus travel services can create an attractive revenue stream for the institution from the service provider.

Business and leisure travel may be contracted separately by traditional methods of issuing requests for proposals (RFPs) to appropriate suppliers and managing the ensuing competitive bid process. Selection of both agencies should concentrate on their proven areas of specialization and expertise, their service reputation, and, of course, the financial outcomes. With appropriate solutions in place universities and colleges can control costs and generate income, while providing valuable services to the campus community.

Conferences

Campuses are often ideal locations for gatherings and lend themselves to being natural environments for hosting meetings. Dining and sleeping accommodations are already in place. Large and small meeting rooms are available. Audiovisual equipment is on hand. Swimming pools, gymnasiums, tennis courts, golf courses, and other recreational facilities are often available. Intellectual resources also abound—libraries, laboratories, and science facilities—not to mention the expertise that can be provided by faculty members. Added into this mix is the setting of the institution itself, which is very often a desirable place for the conference to be held. It presents an opportunity for conference attendees to be in one place, in a pleasant location, in a learning environment, away from other distractions.

For the institution, there are many advantages to hosting a conference and bringing people to campus. Conferences generate revenue. Facilities are used that otherwise would be vacant, especially during the summer months. Conference revenue helps defray some of the fixed costs. In addition, conference attendees bring in revenue to food service, bookstores, vending machines, and other businesses on campus.

Another advantage of the conference business is exposure of the campus to individuals who normally would not have visited. Good publicity is a goal of most institutions, and bringing people to the campus for a conference is one way to gain exposure and good will. The institution may be interested in developing a good relationship with an association that benefits the college or university. Hosting the meetings or conferences of an association may be something that would benefit the institution. Many institutions use the conference business for recruiting students. Youth camps and programs for talented and gifted youth introduce good students to the campus and may interest them in attending that college or university. Many institutions sponsor athletic camps for football, basketball, wrestling, swimming, soccer, tennis, and other sports, which may lead to the recruitment of student athletes.

To carry out conference activities, institutions need competent staff. Conference administrative staff must be prepared to handle a population that will often be different from the usual college student population. Youth camps and programs for senior citizens are at the opposite ends of the age scale, and different groups have different needs. The security staff also must be prepared to deal with different age groups, populations, and expectations.

The college or university in the conference business must also be sensitive to the local business community. Many institutions, in deference to local business, will host only those conferences that have an educational purpose or are related to the educational mission. Other conferences are referred to the local community to host through commercial sites in the area.

One of the most important components in a successful conference program is widespread institutional support that is clearly communicated from the top down. Every facet of the campus impacted by conferences should fully understand and endorse the benefits of hosting conferences. With this "buy-in," campus service providers will feel comfortable supplying superior, high-quality service.

Arenas

Colleges and universities often have a very visible arena that is used primarily for basketball and entertainment. These facilities are usually managed by:

- the athletics department, which manages the building and student fees are applied to help cover operational costs; or

- a general manager, who is in charge of the building—athletics pays its share of the costs, and entertainment is aggressively pursued to generate additional income to cover operating expenses and fund reserves.

As privatization gains momentum, a third scenario is emerging:

- the general management of the arena is performed by a private firm under contract to the college or university.

Several major companies are currently in the arena management business. Arena management firms can offer services to the college or university such as:

- promoting the arena within the entertainment industry;

- creating strong communication networks in entertainment, including dealing with promoters, agents, artist management, and artists; and

- providing consulting expertise related to higher education computerized systems, building improvements, and preventive maintenance programs including meeting Occupational Safety and Health Administration (OSHA) standards.

Because arenas are multiuse buildings, it is important for the administration to establish priorities for its use of the building.

Arenas are increasingly used to yield profits and build reserves. Some institutions are expanding their arenas to include practice gyms and conference pavilions. As more entertainment business is attracted to the arena, practice gyms become more critical because there is less time available for teams to practice on the arena floor. Conference pavilions increase revenue, and the use of the arena's conference facilities by faculty increases the appreciation of the arena facilities within the academic community.

In setting rate structures for arena use, internal campus groups usually receive a 10–20 percent reduction from the external group rates that include both for-profit and nonprofit organizations. Rates for external groups are usually set competitively with other local operations offering similar services. This reduces the likelihood of the institution's receiving claims of unfair competition from downtown business operators.

When entering into negotiations with entertainment promoters, careful consideration must be given to covering the labor costs of specialized employees necessary to cover the event, such as electricians, fire and safety, police and security, and stagehands.

As the usage of an arena grows, an institution must review its risk management policies. The institution must carry adequate liability insurance to offset accident and injury claims by patrons and also must require those who rent the facility to offer proof of adequate liability coverage. The institution must provide and manage suitable access and services for patrons with disabilities.

Keeping an arena presentable and continually ready for daily use requires regular maintenance schedules and skilled maintenance personnel. Sophisticated equipment such as sound and lighting systems require special care. A written safety program, employee training, maintenance of equipment including personal fall restraint systems, and routine inspections are required to provide a safe working environment. OSHA has lately begun to pay closer attention to arenas, and in particular to their catwalks and rigging systems.

To ensure a financially successful arena, effective security operations are critical, especially during entertainment events. The arena general manager and director of campus security (or chief of police) must be in agreement regarding crowd management and the safety and security of performers. As much as any other factor, a well-organized security force, particularly in a high-risk environment such as a rock concert, will contribute to requests from other artists and to repeat business.

Stadiums

Many colleges and universities have stadiums that were built in the 1920s and 1930s. These facilities have aged to a point that major capital improvements are necessary to ensure safety and comfort for their fans. Today's college sports fans are sophisticated viewers. They want to be seated comfortably and do not want to miss a play while waiting in line at concession stands or rest rooms. They want to see replays on video boards and to view statistical updates throughout the game. They want to be able to have easy access to their seats and to have nearby parking. In the stadiums of old, such features did not exist.

Stadiums at colleges and universities now have such amenities as:

- stadium suites with catered food service;
- private clubs and seating;
- video replays and electronic matrix scoreboards;
- enhanced food courts;
- convenient parking;
- private entrances;
- more women's restrooms;
- sports museums;
- television monitors throughout the stadium;
- waiter and waitress service in club seating areas;
- replacement of artificial surfaces with natural grass on playing fields; and
- upscale souvenir stores.

Raising stadiums to the high standards of today's sports fans is an expensive undertaking. One way to pay for upgrading is to offer premium seating; another is to procure private gifts from friends and alumni. Stadium suites and club seating revenue can help defray the cost for many facility projects, including bringing stadiums up to Americans with Disabilities Act (ADA) standards, providing additional restrooms, waterproofing, concession stands, electrical and plumbing upgrades, and other patron conveniences. Premium seating revenue can be projected long term and can be dedicated to annual bond payments on construction costs. Private gifts can pay long-term debt as well.

However, some people feel that stadium suites and premium seating should not be part of college and university athletics. Professional sports franchises often can get voters to agree to build stadiums with public funds, and professional teams also derive money from sales of television rights to help pay for their operations. Few colleges and universities have these sources of revenue.

College Health Programs

The majority of colleges and universities provide medical care, counseling, and prevention services for students directly. These health programs have the universal mission of advancing the health of their students. Staffs include full- or part-time physicians, nurse practitioners, physician assistants, psychologists, and health educators. The size of programs ranges from small clinics directed by a single nurse to comprehensive health centers offering the full range of primary care and health promotion services. In some cases, services are provided to other members of the campus community as well. Over the past several decades, most colleges and universities have closed the high-cost overnight (hospital and infirmary) care programs and focus on education, prevention, and ambulatory (outpatient) services. Many college or university health programs include specialists in psychological and psychiatric health, women's health care (gynecology), and sports medicine and may include support services, such as pharmacy, X-ray, physical therapy, and laboratories, to assure students ready access to broad-based diagnostic and treatment capability.

In addition to medical services, college health programs offer a balanced blend of prevention and health promotion programs. These include health education and risk reduction programs designed to promote the overall health of the student population (e.g., epidemiological surveys on the health of the population, interventions to reduce high-risk drinking, health screenings for early detection, and surveillance programs to prevent and control outbreaks of infectious disease).

Institutions frequently offer students a supplemental health insurance program, usually tailored to provide medical benefits that extend beyond those available at the college or university clinic. Coverage often provides for specialty referral service as well as for hospital care. Increasingly, such insurance programs are mandatory for students when they enroll; students who have other health insurance may waive the coverage. Thus, with primary care available on campus and with supplemental insurance coverage, all students are protected against the burdensome cost of medical care and its potentially disastrous impact on academic success. Further, the integrity of the insurance plan is protected against the hazards of adverse selection, which can threaten the integrity of plans with a strictly voluntary method of enrollment.

College health programs traditionally have been funded by a designated health fee that prepays many of the health care services on campus. Alternatively, some programs receive a direct allocation from registration fees or from the institution's general fund. Many programs supplement their prepaid budgets by charging nominal user fees for some services. With the enormous changes in the needs of the student population and in health care delivery, and with the ever-escalating costs of care, college health programs have needed to be creative and flexible in order to keep the cost of services affordable for students and their families. They have entered into a variety of agreements with clinical services and public health departments in their communities to facilitate referral care when necessary.

An increasing number of medical services in college health programs are seeking accreditation as ambulatory care centers from a national accrediting body (e.g., the Accreditation Association for Ambulatory Health Care, Inc. and the Joint Commission for the Accreditation of Healthcare Organizations). Successful completion of the accreditation review recognizes that national standards have been met and that accountability for quality care has been documented. Accreditation permits the organization to more easily integrate its services with managed care organizations and other community provider groups to better provide for and manage continuity of medical care for enrolled students.

Organization of Health Services

College or university health programs often report to the chief student affairs officer and participate with other student services to enhance the quality of campus life by advancing the health of students. A small number of programs are contracted to private firms, and, on a few campuses, the medical services are assigned to the institution's health sciences faculty. In all cases, institutions should seek strong student participation and input. Many programs have active student health advisory councils representing student governments, which oversee insurance programs, support health education activities, assist in evaluating user experiences, and help review candidates for staff positions.

Some colleges and universities have turned to their health programs to play a larger role by extending prevention programs to address faculty and staff needs. In conjunction with human resources departments, some community-oriented centers are seeking creative ways to contribute to a healthy workforce by offering occupational health services and focusing their attention on improving the well-being of all members of the campus community. An increasing number of institutions may commit their college health programs to provide these expanded public health responsibilities in the coming years.

Printing, Copying, and Binding

Printing, copying, and binding are absolutely necessary in an academic setting. For many years, colleges and universities have maintained their own printing facilities as a matter of convenience, because of the volume of material being produced on campus.

The institution maintained control of the operation and kept it busy throughout most of the year; it invested in the printing equipment and staffed the facility. In many instances, to justify the expenditures involved, all departmental printing was required to be done through the printing office on campus. If the printing operation could not handle the job, it could then be "farmed out" to a commercial printer. Regardless of whether it is done on- or off-campus, processing all of this material in an efficient and effective manner is crucial.

The policy of requiring departments to utilize the on-campus printer is maintained by many institutions today, because they have invested large sums of money in expensive, up-to-date printing equipment and must maintain the printing volume necessary to justify its costs. As costs have increased to produce sophisticated printing materials, colleges and universities have faced the question of how to make the printing operation become more self-supporting. This may be done by charging the departments more to cover the costs, leasing equipment, increasing volume through additional business, or possibly outsourcing the entire operation. The last option will be discussed in more detail below.

Copy machines are often part of the printing operation. Quick-copy machines may be available in the printing office for jobs brought in by the various departments. The printing office may also be in charge of the copy machines elsewhere on campus. They may be owned by the institution or owned by a private company that operates them for the institution. Copy machines are placed on campus for the convenience of the faculty, staff, and students and usually are heavily utilized throughout the year. They also have the capability of generating revenue for the institution, whether the institution or a private company owns and maintains them.

Digital copiers are replacing light-lens copiers and should be seriously considered when evaluating the institution's copier program. Since digital copiers also print and fax, ideally, one should evaluate the printing program as well as the copy program.

Outsourcing the Copy Function

When an institution decides to focus more on its core business, then the decision to outsource the copy function or any other service may make sense. By outsourcing some functions to firms that can perhaps deliver the service better than the institution can, the administration is relieved of the stress and strain of everyday responsibilities. Several considerations when negotiating a contract for the function are listed below, many of which also apply to an in-house copy operation:

- *Determine the program structure.* Most institutions will have a centralized copy center where all larger jobs should be produced, supported by satellite copiers located at strategic places across campus (usually in each department).

- *Determine equipment needs.* The institution's vendor can assist with this. What is the volume of copiers on campus? Is there room for consolidation? Does each department need its own copier, or can departments share copiers? Will light lens copiers be kept or will digital copiers be used? Will satellite copiers all be the same model or will different models be used? Are color copiers needed?

- *Determine labor needs.* This will be related to the volume of work done at the copy center and the hours of operation. The use of work-study students in the copy center generally helps to keep costs down. Since the work volume at the copy center will vary depending on the academic calendar, the center will need more labor at the beginning of the fall semester and generally less labor over semester breaks and summers. How to deal with the ebb and flow of the academic year needs to be addressed during the negotiation process.

- *Determine costs.* What will the monthly minimum charge be? It usually includes machines, labor, and standard supplies, such as toner, developer, fuser agent, and staples. How many impressions will be included in the monthly minimum charge? What is the charge per impression above the monthly minimum charge? What are overtime labor charges?

- *Determine peripherals.* For example, Should the contract include paper? What is the pricing? As with most contracts, what are the early termination charges?

- *Discuss and document performance standards.* This usually should be included as an exhibit to the contract, which should list the details of the job. These should include hours of operation, behavior expectations of staff, print expectations, the problem resolution process, report expectations (monthly copier usage by machine), customer satisfaction measures, and other job specifics.

- *Determine the importance of customer service to the institution.* This will help guide decision making throughout the contract selection process.

Charging Back Costs

The purpose of a charge-back system is to control costs and to place the responsibility of budget management with the appropriate departments. It is an easy concept to understand and a valid one. If an institution decides to charge-back departments for copier usage, then it should make sure that in-house rates are competitive with outside vendors; otherwise budget and convenience become the two user factors for copying decisions. Faculty may use a copy shop close to home or a shop across the street, which has lower pricing. Accounts payable then must process more checks and the loss of centralized control may lead to a fragmented copy program as well as reduced leverage with the institution's primary vendor.

Copyright Law

The Copyright Act of 1976 addresses the reproduction of works of authorship. Faculty should be made aware of their responsibilities under the law. A notice of the law should be placed at every machine. Copyright guidelines and related materials can be found through the World Wide Web site http://fairuse.stanford.edu, which is sponsored by Stanford University Libraries and Academic Information Resources in collaboration with the Council on Library Resources and FindLaw Internet Legal Resources.

Laundry Services

In general, colleges and universities have shown more interest in providing laundry services (washers and dryers) than in providing dry cleaning services. However, for the institutions that have provided laundry services from a central service unit, dry cleaning services have been more easily incorporated and provided due to the personnel and equipment issues involved.

Some institutions have a long history of providing this type of service for

their students and faculty because services are not available in the local community; in some cases, institutions provide services for citizens from outside the campus, thereby improving town and gown relations.

Many, if not most, colleges and universities outsource the laundry operation.
The high cost of the machines, advances in technology, and high labor requirements for upkeep, make it attractive for institutions to bring in experienced laundry companies to provide better service.

If an institution is preparing an RFP for outsourcing of laundry services or re-
bidding laundries that are already privatized, several issues need to be addressed in
the proposal and contract.

- *Revenue.* The contract should spell out clearly the manner in which the
  revenue sharing will be based. Usually the contract will include either a
  guaranteed revenue amount to be paid or a percentage of gross receipts.

- *Equipment.* The RFP should include any equipment specifications, such as
  top- or front-load, brand preferred, coin- or card-operated, number of
  machines, new or used, a specified number of machines meeting ADA
  requirements, coin changers, and commercial versus residential equipment.
  Issues related to utility charges, vandalism responsibility, custodial services,
  and ventilation provisions should also be addressed.

- *Service.* Expectations for response time for machines out of order should be
  clearly spelled out. This should also require replacement for any machine
  that cannot be repaired within the allowable service response time. The
  proposal should require that a detailed preventive maintenance program be
  provided and followed. How the vendor will handle refunds and damage
  claims is another issue to be clarified in the contract and publicized to the
  student/customer, as should be the manner in which students can report
  machines being out of order. Expectations regarding the on-site visits by the
  vendor's personnel should also be clear, including the requirement that such
  personnel are in uniform or have company identification in clear view when
  on site for service or collections.

- *Renovations to laundry rooms.* If the laundry rooms in a facility need to be
  created or upgraded before placing the vendor's machines there, the RFP
  should be clear about who is responsible for the construction or upgrades.
  Most laundry vendors are willing to handle this aspect, and will adjust their
  revenue sharing to recoup the investment in these rooms. A college or
  university may choose to manage the room renovations itself to have a
  clearer picture of the revenue potential simply from the use of the laundry
  machines, uncomplicated by the costs of the renovations to the laundry

rooms themselves. In addition to the room finishes, utility provisions, and ventilation requirements, the renovations may also include the provision of tables, chairs, hanger bars, televisions, and other amenities.

- *Coin versus card operations.* The RFP should state whether the institution wants the laundry machines to be operated by coins, by debit cards, or both. If the institution has a one-card system on campus, the details of the system and expectations that the laundry machines be compatible to their use should be stated clearly.

- *Insurance requirements.* Vendors should be required to maintain, at a minimum, adequate general liability insurance, vehicle insurance, and workers' compensation insurance.

- *Collections and accounting.* The contract should be clear about the manner, timing, and auditing of revenue collections from the machines or card accounts. In addition, the pricing structure for washing and drying should be articulated by the institution in its RFP. General market conditions will be the best indicator for appropriate pricing structures in each locality.

- *Contract period.* Most vendors will make their proposals based on what they can expect to earn over the life of the contract, given their first-year capital outlay for machines and other related expenses. For public institutions, the contract period may be limited by state procurement regulations. In any event, a reasonable contract period for both parties is five years, perhaps with renewal options for additional years. In addition, conditions for early cancellation of the contract should be clear in the contract.

- *Other enhancements.* The RFP may also have a clause that allows bidding vendors to offer additional inducements to the college or university considering its proposal, if such is allowed by the institutions' procurement policies and regulations.

- *Current and future trends.* Laundry room management will include the continued integration of debit card technologies as more institutions adopt one-card approaches. Utility conservation has caused more interest in front-loading washers, which reduce water consumption by an estimated 30 percent. Some vendors are offering an automated service that allows students to call the laundry room to ascertain the availability of machines and to be called when their laundry cycle is completed. Future clothes dryers may be microwave-generating machines rather than air and tumbling dryers.

PARKING AND TRANSPORTATION

Other than growth, with its increasing demand on parking resources, the cost of building additional parking is probably the most significant parking-related problem. Rather than continuing to build, institutions should consider creative solutions such as deep-discount bus passes, emergency and guaranteed rides home, car and vanpooling, and parking asset management. Whatever tools used, administrators must be mindful of costs, political and environmental issues, and the numerous resources available to help solve the problems of campus parking.

An institution's off-campus neighbors may have concerns related to traffic congestion, air and noise pollution, and safety. All of these are legitimate and must be addressed. Pollution, congestion, loss of green space and trees, and aesthetics can be on-campus concerns as well. Communications with both the on- and off-campus communities is essential to keep both populations informed about future plans and to provide them with the means to express their views and ideas. A campus parking and transportation committee, composed of students, staff, and faculty, is an excellent way to provide input to the institution's administrators. The committee can be a sounding board for parking and transportation proposals as well as a conduit for ideas, complaints, and concerns from the campus community. Keeping the off-campus community informed of parking and transportation issues and decisions that may affect them can be done by establishing a regular open meeting with neighbors. This line of communications provides the institution with an excellent public relations opportunity and can be used to address concerns and issues the off-campus community has about activities that it believes may have a negative impact on surrounding neighborhoods. Neighborhood councils of various constituencies should be included in discussions about proposals that may affect them.

The cost of building parking is dependent on land values, parking lot design, prevailing local wages, and interest payments on the loan or bonds. Should an institution have enough land and both on- and off-campus support, surface lots are relatively inexpensive to build when compared with parking structures. A surface lot can be built at a cost of $1,500 -$2,000 per stall. On the other hand, building costs can run from $10,000–$25,000 per stall for an aboveground structure to well over $30,000 per space for an underground garage. These approximate costs are for the finished product including aisles, ramps, and landscaping.

Constructing new parking can be problematic since it is often necessary to increase existing parking fees in order to fund the project. Support can quickly disappear when fees need to go up. Competition for limited on-campus space can also limit the options. Since colleges and universities see their missions as education and research, finding suitable land to build parking where it does not compete with future buildings can be difficult. Often, in fact, existing parking lots are viewed as future building sites. As difficult as the problems can be, they do have solutions. The first is parking asset management; the second is using alternate transportation options.

Parking Asset Management

It is hard to generalize about the management of parking assets because of the extreme variability among institutions—rural versus urban, residential versus commuter, those with space to spare versus those with limited space. Regardless of these differences, institutions must assign responsibility for parking enforcement, establish fee structures, and coordinate with security, custodial, maintenance, utilities, and other services.

Parking asset management includes responsibility for management of parking lots and garages, access to parking areas, parking and information kiosks, services for stranded vehicles, and keeping access to parking facilities clear.

Pivotal in asset management of parking facilities is the implementation of appropriate revenue control procedures. Pay parking is reportedly the second largest cash industry in America, second only to gambling. Care should be taken to make sure that preferential parking generates commensurate parking revenue. That revenue, in turn, needs to be safeguarded with consistent and thorough oversight. Management of these resources falls into three primary categories.

Parking Meters

Meters need to be installed in areas where it is important to encourage turnover parking, that is, areas where long-term parking (more than one hour) is detrimental to the business needs of the institution. Many departments need to conduct business with members of the community who are not affiliated with the institution or who may not be familiar with parking permits or transportation alternatives. Meters are intended to encourage brief visits and discourage student use during classes.

Pay Lots

Pay lots are the most efficient method of controlling parking in a high-demand situation. The ability to centralize cash collection, minimize enforcement (issuing of tickets), track revenue, and control customer access all combine to make this a very cost-efficient method of asset management. Administrators should be warned, however, that the existence of a pay lot requires vigilance on the part of experienced staff who have been trained in revenue control procedures. Due to the need for this specific knowledge, some campuses opt to provide the service through a private contractor that specializes in parking lot management.

Permit Lots

Permit lots can be established in areas where very little control is needed. Costs can be minimized by selling permits at the greatest interval possible. For example, if the pool of permit holders rarely changes, permits may be sold yearly or may be issued through a payroll deduction program with no expiration date. A lot serving tenured faculty would have a much lower turnover rate than one occupied by wage service workers. Permits and lot designations might therefore be structured based on rank or years of service. Similarly, some institutions have found it necessary to restrict access to parking permits to those who live at least a certain distance from campus or to students who have completed a certain number of credits.

Alternate Transportation Options

Alternate transportation can be used to combat the increased cost of providing parking. Mass transit passes, on- and off-campus shuttle systems, car pools, and van pools, either alone or accompanied with other incentives, can provide attractive options to driving a single-occupant vehicle (SOV) to campus.

Bus Pass Programs

Deep-discount bus pass programs that provide students, staff, and faculty a subsidized transit pass can be an effective way to reduce the number of vehicles coming to campus and the cost of commuting for students and employees. Naturally, the cost of the service must be negotiated with the local transit service. This can be based on a mutually agreed-upon formula that combines service availability and ridership or a per-passenger cost. The cost of the bus pass can be totally subsidized by parking revenues or a shared percentage between the users and parking services. The program can also be financed as an employee benefit paid for by each employer using pretax revenue and through the use of student fees.

However it is financed, safeguards must be put in place to ensure that only those individuals eligible for the bus pass are using it. Annual permits can be affixed to student and employee identification cards or, if technology allows, a magnetic strip on the identification card can indicate if the card is still valid when swiped through a card reader on the fare box. Another method is to use a monthly transit pass that is sold at a discount to current students and employees.

Campus Shuttle Systems

Establishing a campus-operated shuttle can be a costly undertaking. When starting a system, it is best to concentrate on a limited service area, if possible. The service can be expanded as usage increases, experience in operating a system is gained, and additional funds become available. One way of offsetting capital costs is to purchase or lease buses from the state motor pool. This may work particularly well with a large state university system where several campuses provide shuttle service.

High startup costs may make it impractical for an institution to operate its own system. But, if shuttle service is still desirable, contracted service with the local transit company or other provider can be an option. Advantages are that operating, maintenance, training, and liability costs are negotiated with the service provider and are not a regular concern of the department. Another option is to negotiate with the local transit provider for more frequent on-campus service.

Shuttle service can also be provided to remote park and ride lots and to apartment complexes where large numbers of students reside. Another way to use campus shuttles to reduce the number of vehicles coming to campus is to provide morning and afternoon rush-hour service to major transit hubs, thus allowing members of the institutional community to transfer to a bus that will take them directly to the campus. Service can also be provided over the lunch hour to take students and employees to locations where restaurants and other services are available. This, of course, is designed to answer the concern that people need to drive their cars to work in order to run errands.

Ride Share

Another tool to reduce SOV traffic to campus is the promotion of carpools or vanpools. This can be done alone or in coordination with the local transit authority. In the case of a joint transit and institution program, the institution can refer to the transit company's match lists, which is easier and less costly than trying to duplicate this service. Marketing a ride share program is also easier when working with a transit partner. Usually a transit provider with an aggressive ride-share program will have a strong marketing plan as well.

Additional incentives can be used to encourage the use of alternate transportation and answer the objections of people to using alternatives to the single-occupant vehicle.

Emergency or Guaranteed Ride Program

One of the biggest objections to using alternate transportation is the possibility of being stranded if an emergency arises or unscheduled overtime work is required. An emergency or guaranteed ride program can provide a safety net for alternate transportation users. This program can be set up in several ways. The local transit authority may provide such service, which can be included in contractual arrangements already in place. Or, an institution may make its own arrangements with local taxi companies. In most cases, a voucher number for a taxi fare can be given to the individual. Another method is to provide an overnight rental car or use of a campus vehicle if rules allow. The guaranteed ride program might keep a list of carpool participants and their destinations (with the permission of the carpool) to use for helping stranded riders when a carpool driver must leave work early.

Preferential Parking

Lots can be set aside in a key or centralized area for use by carpools only. The idea behind using a highly visible lot in a prime location is to encourage others to form a carpool so they too can take advantage of preferential parking. If it is not feasible to use an entire lot for this purpose, prime parking stalls near entrances of buildings can also serve the same purpose. Another method is to have the carpool members select a stall that is most convenient for them and assign the stall for a particular carpool permit or for carpools in general on a first-come, first-serve basis. In many cases, the carpool will opt not to ask for a space, thus keeping it in the open parking inventory. This is a particularly good option if parking space is very limited.

On-Site Facility Improvements

Some institutions can encourage the use of alternate transportation by giving the community on-site services they might otherwise have to drive off-campus to obtain. These services could include child care facilities, postal services, bank or credit union offices, automatic teller machines, cafeterias and lunchrooms, health service facilities, and recreational and fitness facilities. In addition, transportation-related services such as bus shelters and transit information at key locations can also help in making the use of mass transit easier and more enjoyable.

OTHER AUXILIARY ACTIVITIES

Sales and Services of Educational Activities

Sales and services of educational activities support instruction, research, and public service and also help to demonstrate classroom or related educational techniques to students. Such activities may generate revenue, but their basic support usually is derived from the institution's general fund. Revenues so generated normally are considered incidental, since these activities are operated primarily for demonstration purposes. Examples of such activities are nursery schools, reading and speech laboratories, demonstration schools, college theaters, hotels or restaurants operated for the instruction of students enrolled in courses in hotel or restaurant administration, and stores that sell products of experimental farms and dairies. The goods or services created by these activities are incidental to the basic instructional or laboratory experience of students. In the instruction or laboratory procedures, expenditures are incurred for raw materials, technical supplies, and service personnel.

Certain educational activities, such as laboratory schools and medical and dental clinics, complement the work of educational departments by providing program support for instruction and research. These activities may provide services, for a charge, to students, faculty, staff members, and the general public.

Because such activities are closely related to education and research, their administration should conform to academic lines of control. However, their management differs somewhat from that of other educational and research activities, because many of them involve more business management than do purely academic departments.

Direction of each activity is generally assigned to a member of the educational department, and normal business controls, accountability, and record systems should be maintained. These activities seldom are combined into a single administrative unit, as in the case of auxiliary enterprises and service departments. In some cases, sales and services of these activities are of such small scope that they are performed as an integral part of normal departmental activity. If revenues result from such activities, they are recorded as sales of the educational department.

An educational activity whose operations are of major magnitude may be shown in financial reports separately from other educational activities. Even though its detailed accounting may be decentralized for purposes of institutional control, there should be central recording of revenues and expenditures. A large activity may justify special supervision within the educational or research department. In this case, the chief financial or business officer should be consulted in the establishment and supervision of detailed accounting records and special operating reports, as warranted by the size and character of the activity.

The successful operation of educational activities that involve sales and services requires cooperation and understanding between the chief financial or business officer and academic officers. The primary objectives must remain the educational process and research activities. When an activity ceases to serve these objectives, it should be reclassified.

College Unions

The union is the community center of the college or university, serving students, faculty, staff, alumni, and guests. By whatever form or name, a college union is an organization offering a variety of programs, activities, services, and facilities that, when taken together, represent a well-considered plan for the community life of the college. The union is an integral part of the educational mission of the college, and its goal is the development of persons as well as intellects.

College unions are adapting their operations and facilities in response to trends in higher education and society. They are faced with changes in consumer habits, new educational approaches, advances in technology, and pressure to contain costs and generate revenues. The response of college unions to these trends is discussed below.

Students Are Sophisticated Consumers

Students are accustomed to shopping at businesses that emphasize customer service, quality, value, and attractive facilities. Therefore, college unions have instituted customer-service training programs and market research programs to assess students' needs and satisfaction levels. To assist college unions with their efforts, benchmarking and external review programs have been established specifically for their operations.

College unions are undertaking several initiatives to attract students into their buildings. They are renovating facilities, expanding retail operations, and situating them in high-traffic areas, and redesigning retail spaces, such as food courts, so that declining retail concepts can be changed with minimal capital investment. Recognizing that students are increasingly brand conscious, unions are polishing the image of in-house and offering popular local and national brands.

And because today's students are more diverse, the variety of food offerings is increasing.

Approaches to Educating Students Have Changed

Today's approach to educating students is based on the realization that the classroom is not the only forum in which to educate students. Learning experiences outside the classroom complement instruction in the classroom; classroom boundaries have blurred.

This educational approach affects both the programs and facilities of college unions. In terms of programs, college unions are collaborating with academic departments to offer community service, leadership development, and cultural awareness programs. In terms of facilities, college unions are being constructed to contain both academic and nonacademic facilities. In addition to traditional union operations, such as an information desk and food court, some unions include academic facilities, such as libraries, computer labs, and classrooms. Revenues from both general and auxiliary enterprise funds are commonly used to construct and operate these facilities.

Technology Supports College Union Operations

Technology is integrated into most college union functions, and like other auxiliary enterprises, college unions must invest resources for computer-support services. Meeting rooms and catering orders are booked using automated scheduling systems. Retail operations support debit-card systems. Web sites support E-commerce. Conferencing facilities provide video, voice, and data access.

Containing Costs and Generating Nonfee Revenue Is Increasingly Important

At most public institutions and some independent institutions, college unions rely on revenues from student fees to support their operations. On some campuses, fees can be increased only by a vote of the student government or student body. To garner student loyalty and support, college unions in this setting must be effective in identifying and responding to students' needs.

On many campuses, college unions are increasingly expected to contain costs and minimize their reliance on fees by developing other sources of revenue. They have pursued outsourcing and privatization in order to contain costs and generate revenues. Other sources for generating nonfee revenue include the following:

- *Lease agreements.* Leasing income is derived from tenants such as bookstores, restaurants, convenience stores, copy centers, hair stylists, and banks. To stimulate foot traffic and increase revenues, some college unions have built minimalls with shops leased to optical centers, computer sales and repair shops, florists, and other merchants. College unions also lease space to campus departments such as student ID centers and career services. Unions may set their lease rates based on those in the surrounding commercial district and the square-foot cost to operate and maintain their facility. Rent can be calculated using a square-foot rate, a percentage of sales, or a combination of both.

- *Retail sales.* Some college unions operate in-house retail operations such as bookstores, restaurants, and copy centers. Historically in many unions, retail dining units have been operated more as a service and less as a profit center, but this orientation has shifted in college unions that are being pressed to increase revenues and reduce costs.

- *Facility rentals and catering.* College union meeting facilities are a source of facility-rental and catering income. Some unions pursue off-campus clients to book events in their meeting facilities. They may have professional meeting planners on staff and serve as the campus's one-stop shopping center for conference services. They may operate guestrooms. At some institutions, unions are limited in their ability to pursue off-campus business because of building policies that give priority to student use and state laws that restrict competition by state agencies. Campus departments are another source of facility-rental income. On some campuses, departments pay for their use of meeting rooms. On other campuses, the use is free in return for a fixed rent paid annually or a reduction in utilities equal to the waived rental fees.

- *Fee for service.* Many college unions operate departments that charge a fee for service. These include outdoor programs, game rooms, box offices, copy centers, and student ID offices.

- *Vending.* Some unions manage vending in their facility and, in some cases, throughout their campus. Vending may range from soda and snack machines to phone card and copying machines.

- *Program admissions.* Unions sponsor programs ranging from concerts to noncredit short courses. Some programs are designed to be self-supporting and include an admission or registration fee. Others are subsidized from other revenue sources to give students free access to them.

Institutional support

College unions at private institutions that charge tuition only and no fees typically receive institutional support. Unions at public institutions that house campus departments or provide free use of meeting facilities to campus departments typically receive support. Institutional support may be in the form of salary support, utilities, cleaning, maintenance, debt service, or coverage of operating deficits.

College Union Administration

The administrative structure of college unions is somewhat different from other auxiliary enterprises. Historically, unions have recognized the educational benefits of student involvement in their operations and the development of their programs. Most have a governing or advisory board that is composed mostly of students. It is important to keep in mind the role of student involvement in college union operations. Compared to other auxiliary enterprises, major initiatives may require more student participation and more time to formulate.

Mail Services

The U.S. Postal Service's move to automation technology has made it imperative that college and university mail services operate as efficiently as possible to achieve maximum postage discounts. Campus mail service operations support an institution's mission by providing delivery, collection, and processing of all institutional mail, including domestic and international mail as well as intra-campus mail. Mail service operations may include processing of student mail and sometimes mail for affiliated off-campus locations, in accordance with U.S. Postal Service regulations. Other responsibilities include the regulation of postage meters, the use of postal permits, and the purchase of postage and stamps. Some large institutions provide bulk mail, courier, messenger, and centralized facsimile services. A college or university's method of providing mail service depends on the volume of mail that is processed.

Federal Code 39 CFR 320.4 regulates the transporting of mail on and between college and university campuses and who may carry this mail. Only official mail of the institution may be carried without payment of postage and only employees of the institution may transport this mail.

The institution may operate a contract station post office for the convenience of faculty, staff, and students under an agreement with the U.S. Postal Service. Contract stations provide full post office services such as stamp sales, registered mail, money orders, and express mail. Although the contract station could be a source of revenue, the fee negotiated with the U.S. Postal Service for the operation of the contract station is often not enough to cover the institutional overhead. An alternative means of providing this service may be leasing of space to the U.S. Postal Service for a post office and the installation of stamp vending machines on campus.

The mail services manager must be familiar with postal regulations and must be prepared to take advantage of all opportunities offered by these regulations for reductions in mailing costs and improving delivery time. The benefits of business reply mail should be factored against the use of stamps or premetered mail when departments wish to prepay postage. The design of all mail has a tremendous impact on whether discounts are possible.

Address standardization for the institution's addresses and address files is the key to maintaining service levels for delivery and discounts earned. The National Association of College and University Mail Services (NACUMS) works with the U.S. Postal Service to aid constituent institutions with address standardization.

The U.S. Postal Service offers postage discounts for operations that bar code outgoing mail. Many institutions utilize off-campus vendors to provide bar-code service. The savings to the institution are significant even when the off-campus vendor shares part of the discount. The institution may consider leasing bar-code equipment to avoid being saddled with obsolete equipment. However, the cost of operation and maintenance must be carefully weighed to ensure financial benefit. Computer-generated mail can be bar coded and presorted to attain maximum discounts without sending to an off-campus vendor. Software and processing capabilities for bar coding computer-generated mail are much simpler and less expensive to maintain.

College and university mail service operations should utilize a charge-back system for outgoing mail so that all institutional departments are responsible for their own postage charges and are therefore more inclined to control outgoing mail expenses. Centralizing the mail service reduces redundancy and allows the institution to take advantage of volume-based postal discounts. The charge-backs are easily handled by multistation electronic meters and scales linked to a personal computer with account capture capabilities. The mail center may recover overhead by adding a surcharge to postage charges or retaining part of earned discounts.

Campus mail pickup and delivery should be as efficient as possible. Routes should be designed to minimize travel time. Mail boxes for the pickup and delivery of mail can be placed in campus buildings rather than providing service direct to departments. Outside mailboxes for pickup only can be strategically located to provide supplemental mail service. Delivery routes should be routinely audited to maintain adequate service levels.

Mail service staff should be aware that mail security is paramount. The physical facility should be reviewed for security needs to determine what measures are warranted.

A well-run mail service can save money by automating functions where possible and using off-campus vendors where needed.

Intercollegiate Athletics

Athletic programs are as varied in scope as the institutions that operate them. At some institutions, intercollegiate athletics are operated for student participation as well as to enhance the public relations of the institution, while at others intercollegiate athletics are conducted solely for student participation. If a college or university's intercollegiate athletic program is largely self-supporting, the operation can be classified as an auxiliary enterprise. When the athletic program is intended primarily for students, the operation should be classified as an "educational and general" activity for expense purposes. Some institutions place it in the "institutional support" category of expenses because of its influence on several constituencies—alumni, current and prospective students, parents, and employees—while others report it as "student services."

Financial transactions for intercollegiate athletic programs must be viewed as similar to all other institutional financial transactions. Implicit in this view are internal controls such as proper authorization, approval, and documentation of transactions. Records must contain sufficient information to allow detailed classification of revenues and expenditures. The financial or business officer must periodically review all expenditures to ensure their proper cost classification. Expenditures for a facility that is entirely devoted to athletics should be categorized in the same manner as are expenditures of the athletic program. For example, a stadium used exclusively for football and soccer should be recorded as an auxiliary enterprise if the athletic program is thus recorded. A facility that is used only or primarily for recreational or intramural activities may be classified as a student service. In addition, the financial or business officer must ensure that classification supports the requirements of the athletic conference or association to which the institution belongs.

It is imperative that the administrators responsible for intercollegiate athletics be familiar with regulations of the athletic association or conference of which the institution is a member and ensure that every effort is made to follow them. Regulations often dictate the number of coaches that can be employed, the number of scholarships that can be offered, and the number of sports in which the institution must participate in order to remain a member of the association or conference. For example, in 1999, National Collegiate Athletic Association (NCAA) regulations required an institution to participate in seven men's sports and seven women's sports to be classified as a Division I institution. Such organizations also regulate how and when student athletes are recruited. An athletics compliance officer, responsible for keeping track of changing regulations, should be assigned to the athletic department.

The NCAA requires most member institutions to have an annual independent audit. Even though not every college and university belongs to the NCAA, the NCAA's audit rules are available to provide general guidance for categorizing athletic program transactions.

The NCAA stipulates that revenues and expenditures must be classified by sport, as well as by source and function. In addition to complying with the NCAA audit requirements, member institutions are required to prepare additional financial information that provides indicators as to the administration of revenues and expenditures and internal controls.

The NCAA identifies the following income sources of athletics programs:

- ticket sales;

- radio and television rights;

- program sales, novelty sales, concessions, and parking;

- student activity fees in support of intercollegiate athletics;

- bowl game proceeds;

- investment and endowment income in support of athletics;

- gifts; and

- state appropriations designated for the direct support of an intercollegiate athletic program.

The NCAA identifies the following sources of expenditures:

- travel;

- financial aid;

- maintenance and general administration;

- equipment purchases; and

- any other expenditures in support of athletics.

These categories provide financial and business officers with guidelines for identifying financial activities in intercollegiate athletic programs.

Intercollegiate athletics have come under increasing public and government scrutiny in recent years. Financial and business officers should be aware of the potential tax liabilities of their institution's athletic program. For further discussion of taxation issues, see chapter 11, Taxation.

Several government agencies have started to exercise oversight in the area of intercollegiate athletics, especially over athletic revenues and expenditures, distribution of financial aid or other gender-based program expenditures, broadcast revenues, and other financial data. The financial or business officer must maintain an effective system of financial reporting and internal controls to be able to provide necessary information to federal agencies. He or she should monitor the intercollegiate athletic department to ensure that all financial records are appropriate and should follow regulations set forth by the conference or athletic association in which the institution participates.

Financial and business officers must also be attuned to potential changes in the nature of intercollegiate athletics. Although the Knight Commission on Intercollegiate Athletics has no rule-making capabilities, it can make suggestions and recommendations to the NCAA. In 1991, the Knight Commission issued *Keeping Faith with the Student Athlete: A New Model for Intercollegiate Athletics,* which provided recommendations (many of which were adopted by the NCAA) concerning the fiscal operation of athletic programs. The report covered the following issues:

- *Cost reductions:* The report urged colleges and universities to monitor expenditures closely and to continue to search for cost reduction measures.

- *Athletic grants-in-aid:* The report recommended expanding athletic grants to include additional costs of attendance, as defined by federal guidelines.

- *Independence of athletic foundations and booster clubs:* The report recommended that all funds for athletics raised by autonomous entities be channeled through the institution's financial system and subjected to the same budgetary controls as are revenues from other departments.

- *Revenue-sharing plans:* The report recommended that institutions review revenue-sharing plans, such as the institutionwide distribution of NCAA revenues.

- *Coaches' income:* The report recommended that external sources of income for coaches be negotiated through the institution if that income involves the institution's function, facility, or name.

- *Coaches' contracts:* The report recommended that long-term contracts be offered to coaches who meet an institution's expectations.

In additional to these recommendations, the Knight Report reemphasized the need for independent audits of intercollegiate athletic programs and the expansion of these audits to include admissions processes, academic progress, and graduation rates.

The goal of the financial or business officer in regard to an institution's intercollegiate athletic program should be to provide effective internal controls and reporting procedures that will enhance the quality of the athletic program without sacrificing the institution's primary mission of instruction.

Child Care

Child care has assumed an increasingly important role on U.S. college campuses as a service to nontraditional students, as a device to recruit and retain faculty and staff, and as a location for observation, teacher training, and research. The historical dichotomy between traditional nursery schools (typically part-day programs offered to the community to provide a laboratory site for teachers in training)— and the relatively new campus day care (usually underfunded, full-day programs offered to student families but located at the very edge of campus) is disappearing. In its place has emerged a great variety of better, more useful, developmentally appropriate options. The best choice for an individual campus is often a mix of options based on the academic mission, demand for child care, sources of funding, and current services available in the community. It is difficult to meet the needs of every current and future potential child care client, and therefore institutions must consider how best to define and meet their most compelling needs.

Types of Services

Institutions can provide both direct and/or indirect services. Direct services include the child care, most frequently provided in campus-based centers, but also in off-campus centers, family day-care homes and home networks, or through initiatives with community-based programs (including Head Start). Preschoolers, toddlers, kindergartners, infants, and before/after school children, in that order, are served. While part-day programs continue to exist and provide valuable assistance to families in selected communities, full-day programs are increasingly more common, many operating 10.5 hours per day, at least 46 weeks per year. A smaller number of programs offer half- and even quarter-time slots, flextime, drop-in care, and evening as well as weekend services.

Indirect services can include campus- or community-based resource and referral services to assist families in locating appropriate child care options. Some institutions offer flexible benefit programs in which child care is one of many choices; others offer vouchers, purchase of slots, or assistance with federal tax-reducing dependent care options.

Standards

Many people assume that child care programs on college campuses exceed the level of quality typically found in community settings. Thus, there is an expectation on the part of parents, the community, and students, faculty, and staff that a campus-sponsored program will provide more than the minimum level of services. Child care licensing, which varies by state, provides only minimal standards; these are frequently weakest in minimum allocations of square footage per child and in teacher-child ratios. Accreditation by the National Association for the Education of Young Children (NAEYC) provides a somewhat more reasonable standard, and includes a self-study component prior to the generation of a report and subsequent visit by a trained evaluator. Programs aspiring to an even higher standard require periodic (e.g., five-year) external peer reviews by a group of comparable directors, for only such a group is likely to provide the most specific feedback for continued improvement.

Management

Child care directors should be professionally trained in early childhood education and have direct experience with young children. At most institutions, child care facilities are operated by academic departments, student services, not-for-profit corporations, auxiliary enterprises, human resources, and outside vendor and management companies. Academically connected, if not operated, programs such as lab schools appear less peripheral and somewhat less vulnerable.

Funding

Most institutions provide a combination of ongoing subsidies to campus child care. The top five, in order, are space, utilities, salaries and benefits, supplies, and cash. It is extremely difficult to offer reasonable child care without providing a subsidy. A few general rules that apply to child care follow.

- the younger the children served, the greater the ongoing (permanent) subsidy, due primarily to teacher-child ratios;

- child care is a labor-intensive enterprise, and there may be an inclination to cut costs in this area; programs receiving insufficient subsidy may be subsidized by underpaid caregivers, leading frequently to turnover, unhappy parents, and increased liability risk;

- the cost of providing a full day of care to one child is always smaller than the cost of providing that same day of care to more children in smaller units (e.g., half-day blocks); and

- there are ethical issues best considered in advance regarding the use of child care fees on behalf of young children to subsidize the costs of training college students.

A part of the Higher Education Amendments of 1998, Child Care Access Means Parents in School (Public Law 105-244), provided grants to support the participation of low-income students in postsecondary education. Institutions may be eligible to apply for up to 1 percent of their Federal Pell Grant disbursement. Two other potential sources of funding for support in serving low-income students are U.S. Department of Agriculture (USDA) food reimbursements and state block grants.

Policies

Prudent policies and procedures regarding such issues as applications, admissions, drop-off and pickup of children, handling emergencies, and the role of the parent advisory board are best established in advance. These should be reviewed frequently, and a history file established to record changes. In regard to liability, child care centers are not seen as particularly hazardous places. Maintaining high quality in programs further diminishes liability. On the other hand, there are a host of special concerns given the tender age of the children served; thus, the institutions should review the insurance liability policy normally applied to office and classroom settings to determine if there are any particular concerns related to child care.

Trends

Average program size is increasing; child care centers should give careful consideration to limiting program growth if growth may reduce the quality of service provided. Care for infants and toddlers may be the current greatest need, because it is the hardest to find in most communities. Many new construction and renovation efforts are underway across the country. Subcontracting occurs in a small percentage of campuses and this is unlikely to substantially change, given the mixed results thus far. The number of programs offering a sliding fee scale to parents is predicted to significantly increase.

Resources

The major professional organization for campus directors is the National Coalition for Campus Children's Centers (NCCCC), which develops publications on starting and operating campus-based care, holds an annual conference, hosts a Web site and a chat room, and provides technical assistance. Other organizations for those working with young children are the NAEYC (mentioned previously) and the Association for Childhood Education International (ACEI).

University Presses

A university press carries the results of a university's research and scholarship to readers throughout the nation and the world. Everywhere the press's publications appear they carry the name of the university with them as well.

A university press's publishing program is devoted primarily to scholarly monographs—reports on the results of postdoctoral research—and may also include journals, textbooks, reference books, scholarly editions, fiction and nonfiction for general readers, and poetry. The director of the press is responsible for day-to-day operations and usually reports to a senior academic officer of the university, often the provost or dean of the graduate school. A faculty editorial board approves projects for publication. Some presses also have a business advisory board to assist the director in reviewing current operations and setting long-range goals.

University presses serve a vital gatekeeping function in scholarly communications by selecting manuscripts for publication on the basis of peer review. That process of selection is one of the significant values added to faculty research by a university press. The press also puts considerable effort into the essential labor of clarifying the work it publishes, making sure it is consistent, accurate, and easy to follow, that it is indexed and searchable, that it can be found, retrieved, bought or borrowed, and that, whether produced in print or electronic form, it is legible, easy-to-read, stable, and long-lasting.

The market for scholarly work is small and specialized, and financial margins correspondingly thin. A university press operates on a nonprofit basis, but as a business it competes with commercial publishers for authors, for display space in bookstores, and for market share from readers and libraries. Therefore, virtually all university presses receive financial assistance from their universities, either as a contribution to operating expenses, or in-kind support, or a combination of both. The smaller the press, the more important such support becomes.

University presses have proved themselves resilient and adaptable in a period of rapidly changing markets, shrinking budgets, and evolving technology. As in many other aspects of university life, the balance between serving an educational mission and exploiting commercial opportunity is a delicate one.

RESOURCES

Association of Collegiate Licensing Administrators. *A CIA Collegiate Licensing Resource Book*. East Lansing, MI: ACLA, 1988.

Association of College and University Housing Officers-International. *Standards for College and University Student Housing*. Columbus, OH: ACUHO-I, 1988.

Association of College Unions—International. *ACU-I The Resource Book*. Bloomington, IN: ACU-I, 1998–99.

"The Life Cycle." In A. W. Chickering & Associates (ed.). *The Modern American College* (pp.16–50). San Francisco: Jossey-Bass, 1981.

Conneely, J. F. "Contract laundry operations: Proposed bid specifications." *Talking Stick*, 13 (November 1995): 6–8.

Fairbrook, Paul. *Managing for Profit in Difficult Times—Guide to Operation of Dining Services*. Staunton, VA: National Association of College Auxiliary Services, 1994.

Goldstein, Philip J., Kempner, Daphne E., and Rush, Sean C. *CHEMA: Contract Management or Self-Operation: A Decision-Making Guide for Higher Education*. Alexandria, VA: APPA, 1993.

Hatchell, M. *Laundry Services on University Campuses*. Unpublished manuscript, 1999.

Hays, C. D., Palmer, J. L., and Zaslow, M. L. (Eds.). *Who Cares for America's Children? Child Care Policy for the 1990's*. Washington, D.C.: National Academy Press, 1990.

James Madison University. *Invitation for bids: Dry cleaning and pick-up services*. (IFB #95-96-20D). Harrisonburg, VA: Procurement and Material Management Services, 1996.

JobPlace, Career and Employment Professionals Discussion List. Dewey, D., List owner, dan@,newsjobweb.org.

Journal of American College Health. Washington, D.C.: Heldref Publications, 1999.

National Association of College Auxiliary Services. *Privatization of Campus Housing in Higher Education*. Staunton, VA: NACAS, 1997.

National Association of College Auxiliary Services. *Privatization in Higher Education, Papers and Presentations, NACAS Symposium and Advanced Workshop*. Stauton, VA: NACAS, 1995.

National Association of College Stores. *NACS Book Buyers Manual*. Oberlin, OH: NACS, 1983.

National Association of College and University Business Officers. *Child Care Services: A Guide for Colleges and Universities*. Washington, DC: NACUBO, 1993.

National Association of College and University Business Officers. *Practical Approaches to Rightsizing*. Washington, DC: NACUBO, 1992.

National Association of College and University Business Officers. *Organizational Paradigm Shifts*. Washington, DC: NACUBO, 1996.

National Association of College and University Food Services. *Administering Food Service Contracts: A Handbook for Contract Administrators in College and University Food Services*. East Lansing, MI: NACUFS, 1999.

National Association of College and University Food Services. *Operating Performance Benchmarking Survey, 2000*. East Lansing, MI: NACUFS, 1999.

National Association of College and University Food Services. *Professional Practices in College and University Food Services, 1998*. East Lansing, MI: NACUFS, 1998.

National Association of Collegiate Directors of Athletics. *Athletics Administration*. Cleveland, Ohio: NACDA, 1999.

National Collegiate Athletic Association. *NCAA Financial Audit Guidelines*. Mission, Kansas: NCAA, 1986.

Perricone, Donald R. *Printing, Copying and Duplicating of Colleges and Universities*. Staunton, VA: National Association of College Auxiliary Services, 1995.

Schuh, John H. (ed.) *Educational Programming in College and University Residence Halls*. Columbus, Ohio: Association of College and University Housing Officers-International, 1988.

Shaw, D. "The Key to the Laundry Room: 99% Service." *Condo Management*, 1988.

United States Postal Service. *Domestic Mail Manual*. Washington, DC: U.S. Government Printing Office, Quarterly. www.usps.com.

United States Postal Service. *Guide to College and University Mail Service Centers*. pe.usps.gov/.

Werring, C. "A Self-operated Laundry Program: One successful Alternative." *Talking Stick*, 1995.

Wertz, R. D., and Denton, R. W. *The Shopping Mall on Campus*. Staunton, VA: National Association of College Auxiliary Services, 1993.

Wertz, R. D. *Outsourcing and Privatization of Campus Services*. Staunton, VA: National Association of College Auxiliary Services, 1997.

Whitebook, Howes, M. C., and Phillips, D. *Who Cares? Child Care Teachers and the Quality of Care in America*. Oakland, CA: Child Care Project, 1989.

White, Ken. *Bookstore Planning and Design*. New York: McGraw- Hill Publishing Company, 1982.

Organizations

American College Health Association (ACHA)
P.O. Box 28937, Baltimore, MD 21240-8937
(410) 859-1500 . . . . www.acha.org

American Management Association (AMA)
1601 Broadway, New York, NY 10019-7420
(212) 586-8100 . . . . www.amanet.org

Association of Academic Health Centers (AHC)
1400 16th Street, NW, Suite 720, Washington, DC 20036
(202) 265-9600 . . . . www.ahcnet.org

Association of American Publishers (AAP)
Professional and Scholarly Publishing Division
220 East 23rd Street, New York, NY 10010
(212) 689-8920 . . . . www.publishers.org

The Association of American University Presses (AAUP)
71 West 23rd Street, Suite 901, New York, NY 10010 . www.aaup.princeton.edu

Association of College and University Housing Officers- International (ACUHO-I)
364 West Lane Avenue, Suite C, Columbus, OH 43201-1062
(614) 292-0099 . . . . www.achuo.ohio-state.edu

Association of College Unions—International (ACU-I)
One City Centre, Suite 200, 120 West Seventh Street, Bloomington, IN 47404-3925
(812) 855-8550 . . . . www.indiana.edu/acui

Association of Collegiate Conference and Events Directors—International (ACCED-1)
Colorado State University, Ft. Collins, CO 80523-8037
(970) 491-5151 . . . . acced-i.colostate.edu

Association of Collegiate Licensing Administrators (ACLA)
342 North Main Street, West Hartford, CT 06117-2407 . . . . . www.aclanet.org

Association of Higher Education Facilities Officers (APPA)
1643 Prince Street, Alexandria, VA 22314-2618
(703) 684-1446 ext. 229 . . . . www.appa.org

Council of Higher Education Management Associations (CHEMA)
2501 M Street, NW, Suite 400, Washington, DC 20037-1308
(202) 861-2577 . . . . www.chema-www.colorado.edu

International Graphic Arts Education Association (IGAEA)
200 Deer Run Road, Sewickley, Pennsylvania 15143-2328
412-749-9165 . . . . www.igaea.org/

Healthcare Financial Management Association (HFMA)
1301 Connecticut Avenue, NW, Suite 300, Washington, DC 20036-3417
(202) 296-2920 . . . . www.hfma.org

In-Plant Printing Management Association (IPMA)
1205 West College Avenue, Liberty, MO 64068-1035
(816) 781-1111 . . . . www.ipma.org

Institute of Transportation Engineers (ITE)
525 School Street, SW, Suite 410, Washington, DC 20004-7167
(202) 554-8050 . . . . www.ite.org

Institutional and Municipal Parking Congress
P.O. Box 7167, Fredericksburg, VA 22404-2729

International Association of Auditorium Managers (IAAM)
4425 West Airport Freeway, Suite 590, Irving, TX 75835
(214) 255-8020 . . . . www.iaam.org

National Association for Campus Activities (NACA)
13 Harbison Way, Columbia, SC 29212-3401
(803) 732-NACA . . . . www.naca.org

National Association of Campus Card Users (NACCU)
21 Colony West, Suite 270, Durham, NC 27705
(919) 403-2273 . . . . www.naccu.org

National Association of College and University Business Officers (NACUBO)
2501 M Street, NW, Suite 400, Washington, DC 20037-1308
(202) 861-2500 . . . . http://www.nacubo.org

National Association of College and University Food Services (NACUFS)
1405 South Harrison Road, Suite 305, East Lansing, MI 48824
(517) 332-2494 . . . . www.nacufs.org

National Association of College and University Mail Services (NACUMS)
P.O. Box 31326, Tucson, AZ 85751-1326,
(520) 298-8680 . . . . www.nacums.org

National Association of College Auxiliary Services (NACAS)
P.O. Box 870, Staunton, VA 24402-0870
(540) 885-8826 . . . . www.nacas.org

National Association of College Stores, Inc. (NACS)
528 East Lorain Street, Oberlin, OH 44074-1298
(216) 775-7777 . . . . www.nacs.org

National Association of Printers and Lithographers (NAPL)
75 West Century Road, Paramus, NJ 07652
(201) 634-9600 . . . . www.napl.org

National Automatic Merchandisers Association (NAMA)
20 North Wacker Drive, Suite 3500 Chicago, IL 60606-3102
(312) 346-0370 . . . . www.vending.org

National Collegiate Athletic Association (NCAA)
6201 College Boulevard, Overland Park, KS 66211
(913) 339-1906 . . . . www.ncaa.org

Printing Industries of America, Inc. (PIA)
100 Dangerfield Road, Alexandria, VA 22314
(703) 519-8100 . . . . www.printing.org

Society for Scholarly Publishing (SSP)
10200 West 44th Avenue, Suite 304, Wheat Ridge, CO 80033
(303) 422-3914 . . . . www.sspnet.org

United States Postal Service . . . . www.usps.gov

Periodicals

American Printer

American School and University

Building Operating Management

The Bulletin

Business Handbook (Association of American University Presses)

Business Officer

Chronicle of Higher Education

College Services Administration

College Store Journal

Educational Record

Facility Management Journal

Facilities Manager

In-Plant Printer

Journal of Career Planning and Employment

Journal of College and University Student Housing

Journal of Higher Education

Journal of the National Association of College and University Food Services

NASPA Journal

Review of Higher Education

School and College

Talking Stick

Chapter 21

Legal Issues

by

Beverly E. Ledbetter
Brown University

Sponsors

CREDENTIALS, INC.
Contact: Jack Weber
550 Frontage Road
Suite 3500 Northfield, IL 60093
847-446-7422 ext. 103
www.degreechk.com

Credentials, Inc. is an Internet-based service that was established to provide a single, trusted source for fast and accurate credential verification to businesses around the globe on behalf of academic and professional institutions.

Contents

T he laws that govern higher education today originate from several sources. The United States Constitution establishes the basic legal relationship between the federal government and the states, and creates the foundation for citizens' individual rights. Both of these directly affect the governance and operation of most higher education institutions. State constitutions do the same at the state level, but also often have specific provisions concerning education. Statutes enacted by Congress and state legislatures, as well as ordinances adopted by local governing bodies, contain specific provisions relative to higher education. In addition, administrative rules and regulations that are not specifically related to colleges and universities may control activities conducted on campuses (i.e., employment, fund raising, telecommunications, and hazardous waste disposal). Decisions rendered by federal and state courts and administrative agencies that resolve disputes on individual campuses may set precedents that influence activities on other campuses. Finally, institutional rules, regulations, contracts, and custom and usage further define and close the gaps left open in the constitutional, statutory, administrative, and judicial framework.

This chapter on legal issues explores significant legal issues that arise for colleges and universities, including business law, torts, and civil rights. These areas and the legal issues within them are not mutually exclusive; they are closely interrelated and often directly affect each other. The intent of the chapter is to highlight significant legal issues arising from legal and business relationships and individual rights. The discussion provides only an overview of the areas as they apply to colleges and universities. It is not intended to be and should not be taken as legal advice. Resolution of specific issues requires analysis of both the law and the facts applicable to the specific matter.

THE LEGAL ENTITY AND GOVERNANCE

Colleges and universities, like corporations, are legal entities, which can sue and be sued. Although today's colleges and universities were established in different ways (many independent institutions as trusts and a few through royal charters and most public colleges and universities under state constitutions or by state legislatures), almost all are nonprofit corporations under both state and federal law. Corporate bylaws provide specific directions for the operation of a corporation. The bylaws usually empower a governing board (board of trustees, regents, or governors) to take action in the name of the corporation. The board in turn delegates most of the day-to-day administrative duties of the corporation to the president or chancellor and other senior administrators.

Notwithstanding their legal status as corporations and despite the legal necessity of imposing corporate existence and structure on higher education, colleges and universities do not easily fit into the mold of most corporations. Their product is knowledge; their service is education; and their shareholders are past, present, and future students. Their commitment to intellectual freedom and independence can place them at odds with those upon whom they rely for support.

State Institutions

The degree of state control over higher education institutions varies widely. A handful created under state constitutions and many more established by laws enacted by state legislatures constitute "public" institutions. These colleges and universities (or in some cases systems of institutions), although controlled by governing boards, are dependent on state funding. Therefore, they must answer directly to the state coordinating board or indirectly to the legislature or executives of the state. Over the years, they have waged fierce battles to maintain their autonomy and independence from the legislatures. Their authority, nevertheless, is derived from the state and they are considered to be arms of the state or operating under "the color of state law." The actions they take are considered to be "state actions." As such, they are subject to both the limitations and privileges of state government. State open meetings and open records laws provide the public with access to the institution's operations and records. Equal protection and due process mandated by state and federal constitutions must be afforded to students and faculty of public institutions. At the same time, the Eleventh Amendment of the United States Constitution may afford public institutions some immunity from liability for violation of federal civil rights laws.

Independent Institutions

Institutions that have been privately established, rather than by state constitution or law, are independent and tend to have greater autonomy than public institutions. While they may receive some form of state financial support and may be subject to the jurisdiction of a state coordinating board for some of their activities, they generally are not considered subsidiaries of the state, are not subject to the state's constitutional restraints on government activities, and may avoid some of the intense public scrutiny often imposed on state colleges and universities by taxpayers and residents. They are nevertheless subject to laws enacted to protect the health, safety, and welfare of the public.

TAXATION

An essential aspect of a college or university's legal existence is the tax-exempt status that nonprofit organizations enjoy. This favorable treatment from federal and state governments comes in several forms. Two are crucial to the continuing financial well-being of the institution: (1) classification under state and federal tax law as "nonprofit organizations" to provide exemption from income and certain other taxes; and (2) designation as a 501(c)(3) charitable organization, which allows individuals and entities making contributions to the organization to reduce their federal taxable income by taking charitable deductions. In addition, colleges and universities often enjoy preferential tax treatment with regard to local property and excise taxes.

Higher education institutions, which are exempt from taxation under federal law, also generally are exempt under state and local law. Because of tightening budgets, stiffer competition for funds, and perceived abuses by some members of the higher education community, local governments and private enterprises frequently have challenged the preferential tax treatment that colleges and universities receive. Instead of attempting to repeal the favorable status given to higher education institutions, the latest attacks on tax relief for colleges and universities include initiatives for new kinds of taxes on such real estate as conference centers, dormitory rooms, and campus inns, or attempts to place property not used directly for education purposes on local tax rolls. Occasionally, local governments attempt to increase their tax base either by freezing the nontaxable property base as of a particular time or by imposing a reduced tax rate on university-owned property that is not used primarily for education purposes. Some institutions form agreements with municipalities, providing for payment to the city in lieu of taxes. These payments are usually significantly less than the amount that would have been paid had the subject property paid taxes at the established rate.

Private businesses frequently lobby for anticompetition legislation at both the federal and state level to try to reduce some of the advantages of campus enterprises that may have questionable "educational purposes" or may compete directly with local private businesses (e.g., bookstores, travel services, athletic and recreational facilities). The federal government has imposed an *unrelated business income tax* (UBIT) on nonprofit institutions. The Internal Revenue Service (IRS) taxes profits on regularly carried-on business activities that are not related to the institution's tax-exempt purpose. The increased pressure from "for profit" enterprises has caused colleges and universities to reexamine and modify many of their business practices.

Since colleges and universities cannot exist without some preferential tax treatment from governments, it is unlikely that such advantages will be taken away. The debate over the extent of the relief will continue, however, until an acceptable balance is achieved that allows universities and colleges to provide nonessential but related services to their constituencies and the community without giving them an unfair competitive advantage.

LEGAL RELATIONSHIPS

Institutions of higher education, like all large corporations, are involved in a complex web of legal relationships with individuals, interest groups, governments, and other corporate entities. Colleges and universities also have several constituencies that play important roles in their operation such as students, employees, alumni, donors, and the public. The institution's role as an employer gives rise to its important relationships with faculty, administrators, staff, and students. While employment relationships involving compensation, individual rights, and labor law are common to most employers, special situations such as tenure and academic freedom make the institutional relationship quite different.

Students may relate to institutions individually or collectively. Individually, institutions provide classes, housing, and numerous support services and facilities. Furthermore, arrangements for financial aid and the payment of tuition and fees create legally binding and enforceable obligations. Financial liability for personal injury arises out of the institution's duty to provide for the health and safety of students while on campus or while involved in institutional activities. Colleges and universities also maintain policies that provide students, faculty, and employees with procedures designed to ensure fairness in grievance or disciplinary hearings. Group relationships include associations such as student governments, fraternities and sororities, and newspapers. Although the existence of these groups is at the discretion of the university, once they are permitted or recognized, the university bears significant responsibility for oversight of their activities, and thus some liability for their activities.

Alumni represent another important group with formal ties to colleges and universities. Alumni associations, which are often separately incorporated, can be closely associated with the institution, both legally and administratively, or they can be virtually independent, operating with little institutional control or influence. Regardless of the formal relationship, activities undertaken by the association may be publicly identified with the institution. Individuals volunteer and are regularly asked to contribute money, time, and effort to support the institution. Legal considerations for both the donor and the institution can influence the nature of these transactions. Colleges and universities must weigh the legal as well as the financial advantages and disadvantages of proposed gifts. Donors wishing to take advantage of all of the tax benefits of making a charitable contribution to an institution may attempt to impose restrictions on the gift or to retain partial control of its use. The latter can give rise to significant legal questions regarding the tax-exempt nature of the gift or the university's independence. The intricacies of planned and deferred giving to institutions often require expert legal advice as well as careful monitoring by those responsible for fund raising.

Legal relationships with governmental entities are extensive and multifaceted. Even more complex than the basic corporate and tax considerations are the innumerable areas in which government regulatory requirements are imposed on institutions. These include accreditation, land use, civil and individual rights, government contracts and grants (including research), financial aid and debt collection, environmental protection, drug and alcohol use by students and employees, open records and meetings, student records, reporting of crimes on campus, graduation rates, reporting of participation rates and expenditure for athletic teams, intermediate sanctions for public charities, and privacy of student records. As institutions play greater and more varied roles with regard to the constituents they serve, the list will grow.

A widening variety of affiliated organizations and auxiliary enterprises also have legal connections to higher education institutions. Some operate within the existing corporate organization of the college or university, some may be separately incorporated by the institution, and others may be legally separate and simply have contractual arrangements with the institution. Joint ventures of all types, such as research or real estate development, also exist. The arrangements for such efforts can range from an informal handshake to a complex legal linkage of corporations and partnerships. Hospitals and health centers, research parks and cooperatives, foundations, bookstores, museums, hotels, day-care centers, retirement homes, farms, international exchanges of faculty and students, and agreements with secondary schools are examples of the types of enterprises and programs that have legal, financial, and administrative consequences for colleges and universities.

SELECTED BUSINESS ISSUES

Business issues on campus are greatly affected by areas of the law relating to commercial transactions. Two basic concepts of law, contracts and agency, form the foundation of many of the commercial activities of colleges and universities.

A contract is a binding compact between parties creating legally enforceable duties and obligations. Generally, a court can enforce the promise by a monetary judgment or, in some instances, by requiring specific performance. A contract does not require bargaining between the parties, does not require an affirmative agreement (sometimes failure to act can form a contract), and does not always have to be in writing (although in many cases it does).

Some basic elements are needed for the formation of a contract. The parties must have the legal capacity to make a contract. Persons under the age of 18 or who are mentally incompetent may not have that capacity. Generally there must be some type of mutual assent between the parties, often described as an offer and acceptance. The timing and nature of responses between the parties affect the legalistic mechanics of offers and acceptances. Some type of response or "consideration" is usually needed to make a promise enforceable. Consideration can be in the form of another promise or an action taken in response to or in reliance on the initial promise. Finally, to be enforceable, a contract must be reasonably definite. If critical terms are left open or omitted, a court's decision on the existence of a contract will turn on the court's ability to discern the intention of the parties and to determine reasonable terms to fill the gaps.

The doctrine of agency is founded on a legal relationship between two parties—a principal and an agent—involving the power of one party to act on behalf of the other. In the relationship, the principal delegates power to the agent while maintaining control of the conduct of the agent. The agent, in turn, assumes the power to affect the legal relations of the principal.

Two different forms of agency are applicable to most legal relationships on college and university campuses:

- *Actual authority* is when the principal, either expressly or implicitly, manifests the intent to have the agent act on his or her behalf. The president, with the approval of the board, can conduct a search for and hire a new chair of the history department. Faculty are given the authority to assign grades to students.

- *Apparent authority* exists when a third person shows, from information given by the principal (not the agent or another person), that the agent was given power from the principal, even if no actual authority was ever given. The reasonableness of the third person's reliance on the apparent authority of the agent may be a factor in determining the existence of apparent authority. For example, problems can arise when a faculty member describes to a student degree requirements that are different from those in the catalog, or a staff member without purchasing authority mistakenly signs documents binding the university to acquire a piece of equipment.

Fundamental issues of contract and agency law can be found beneath the surface of nearly all commercial activities of higher education institutions. Five areas of special interest are discussed as follows: contracting authority, fund raising and development, debt collection, use of facilities, and intellectual property.

Contracting Authority

Institutions usually provide central administrative services for procurement and contracting of institutional goods and professional services. Exceptions may exist for more specialized matters (e.g., sponsored research agreements, library acquisitions) where warranted by administrative efficiency, or where the board retains oversight, such as with property purchases or sales, construction, or major funding transactions. Questions of agency are critical to this process. Clear, written policies are necessary to establish the chain of command in the process outlining, for example, who has authority to execute contracts and purchase orders, who develops specifications and evaluation criteria, who can contact bidders, and who can award contracts. The underlying legal reason for this clarity and specificity is to establish actual authority only in certain departments and individuals, and to reduce the possibility of apparent authority arising elsewhere on the campus.

Competitive bidding is often utilized for certain goods or services or for purchases over a certain dollar amount. Public institutions are often required to adhere to state procedures in this area and may be restricted to purchasing certain goods and services in the state or in the United States. Independent institutions are usually governed by board policy. The requirement for obtaining competitive bids may be waived in cases where there is sufficient economic reason or where there is only one vendor (a "sole source") for the item or services being purchased.

Specifications for bids must be crafted carefully, with particular attention being paid to issues such as delivery terms and time, damaged goods and substitution, insurance and indemnification, compliance with regulatory rules, and the type of award to be made. Both state procedures and board policies or guidelines are designed to secure quality products and services for the best competitive price without undue influence or ethical violations.

Nonprofit institutions frequently encounter ethical problems stemming from conflicts of interest by administrators, governing board members, or others with unique influential relationships with the institution. Institutions of higher education wield tremendous buying power and must monitor their procurement decision-making continually to ensure that vendors or individuals acting on their behalf do not improperly influence the institution's decision. Accepting gifts from vendors, providing additional information to an individual vendor, using information improperly during procurement, using institutional goods or services for personal gain, or dealing with vendors with interests held by institutional officials, family, or friends provides unfair competitive advantages and may be violations of state and/or federal law as well as institutional policies. Administrators should make sure that policies and procedures on these topics are clear, that responsible personnel are well informed about the policies, and that the enforcement of them is firm and fair. Policies requiring disclosure of conflicts of interest for administrators, faculty, researchers, and governing board members are commonplace. Institutional policies, educational efforts, and the effectiveness of monitoring are now the focus of federal and state legislation. For instance, the IRS has issued rules that impose intermediate sanctions on both institutions and individuals who are responsible for, or benefit from, prohibited transactions or unduly privileged relationships.

Affirmative action issues must also be addressed when institutions are reporting policies and procedures related to contracting. Regulations may require institutions to follow guidelines relating to minorities or women in the workforce or selection of contractors. Diversity issues, including minority set-aside programs and preferential hiring, are fraught with hazard and require knowledge of current laws as well as consideration of the context in which the issues arise.

Fund Raising and Development

Institutions should be cognizant of the many legal issues in their development work. They must comply with applicable state laws regarding charitable solicitation, registration, and reporting. While some states do not subject colleges and universities to any disclosure, registration, or reporting requirements concerning solicitation practices, many do have such requirements or only partially exempt higher education institutions from solicitation laws. The laws vary widely from state to state, so institutions need to be familiar with the laws in their jurisdiction and in other states where they have significant fiscal or fund raising operations.

Another basic concern of institutions is the type and value of gifts received. With the advent of tough federal and state environmental laws and closer governmental scrutiny of gifts with potentially illegal restrictions (in particular those that may violate civil rights laws), institutions must ensure that they are receiving assets and not liabilities, both legally and financially. The prohibitive cost and potential fines involved in the cleanup of hazardous waste can turn a gift of real property into a major financial headache and a public relations nightmare. Gifts intended to benefit only certain individuals on the basis of race, gender, national origin, religion, or any other legally protected status may be subject to legal challenge and, if handled improperly, may jeopardize future federal financial assistance to the institution.

Institutions must also be aware of donors' legal concerns. The tax deductibility of a contribution can play a significant part in a donor's decision to give to an institution. The IRS has held that a gift is deductible only to the extent that its value exceeds the fair market value of any benefit received by the donor. Regulations, revenue rulings, and letter rulings, as well as judicial decisions, have addressed a vast array of circumstances which may not result in full tax deductibility for gifts.

Charitable dinners, gifts and banquets, concerts and performances, raffles, and alumni travel tours are among examples previously addressed by the IRS. Many donors are also interested in retaining a financial interest in a gift, perhaps for the remainder of their lives, or for the lives of members of their family, before turning it over to the institution. A variety of legal mechanisms are available for achieving these objectives, including gifts with a retained life estate, trusts, and sale-leaseback arrangements. While institutional representatives should not directly provide legal advice to donors on the specific legal ramifications of their gift, most development programs maintain model forms to inform prospective donors about legal developments pertaining to charitable giving, and work closely with the donor and counsel to achieve the desired result within the limits of the law. (For a full discussion of donor restrictions, see chapter 9, Endowment Management.)

Finally, institutions should be aware of issues concerning the privacy of donor records that are collected by the development office, and which include information about annual income, net worth, and the charitable-giving history of selected alumni and potential donors. Although these records are not covered by the Family Education Rights and Privacy Act, which protects the privacy of student "educational records," they should be treated as confidential information. Administrators of public institutions also need to have a clear understanding of the extent to which state open-records laws may provide access to such information, particularly when it is commingled with other information. The release of such records should be guarded and institutional policies should be in place to prevent casual or inadvertent disclosure. Institutional policies should also restrict appropriately the dissemination of such information to academic officers and volunteer fundraisers.

Debt Collection

At the other end of the financial and legal spectrum from soliciting funds lie procedures for collecting money owed to the institution. The Fair Debt Collection Practices Act (FDCPA) governs creditors' efforts to collect any obligation or alleged obligation of a consumer to pay money for property or services purchased for personal, family, or household purposes. Student loans are included in this definition. The act controls a range of creditor actions in an attempt to restrain practices that can be potentially abusive: attempts to secure location information; communications with the debtor and others concerning the alleged debt; false and misleading representations; and "harassment" and "unfair practices," as defined in the act. Violators of the FDCPA can be held civilly liable for damages, penalties, costs, and fees.

Institutions must comply with comprehensive federal regulations mandating "due diligence" in the management and collection of student loans (specifically Perkins Loans). If all due diligence efforts prove unsuccessful, an institution may assign a defaulted loan to the U.S. Department of Education. (For a full discussion of due diligence, see chapter 19, Student Financial Aid.) Federal regulations also give authority to the U.S. Department of Education to award contracts to specific agencies for the collection of these debts. These agencies have the same authority to collect, including the imposition of liens, as the federal government.

When delinquent borrowers file for bankruptcy, creditors, including universities, must attempt collection through federal bankruptcy laws and courts. Individuals usually have a choice between two types of voluntary bankruptcy. Chapter

7 of the Bankruptcy Reform Act of 1978, otherwise known as "straight" or "liquidation" bankruptcy, mandates that the nonexempt assets of a bankrupt individual be distributed among creditors. Chapter 13, on the other hand, provides that the debtor file a "wage-earner" plan under which creditors are paid from future "disposable income." The relief offered by both types of bankruptcy is that a debtor's "dischargeable debts" (as defined by the law and the courts) are canceled at the end of the proceedings or the plan.

While bankruptcy proceedings are pending, creditors ordinarily are prohibited from attempting to collect debts from a bankrupt person. Chapter 7 contains an "automatic stay" provision protecting the debtor from collection efforts by creditors. Withholding transcripts, denying reenrollment, denying additional loans, or taking any other action because of a student's failure to pay a pre-bankruptcy debt can constitute such collection efforts and is not permitted. In addition, public institutions are subject to an antidiscrimination "fresh start" provision precluding governmental units from discriminating against a debtor because of insolvency and failure to pay debts before, during, and after bankruptcy. Similarly, if a debt has been discharged, the creditor is enjoined from pursuing further activities to collect the debt. However, if the debtor is unsuccessful in having the debt discharged, the college or university may continue attempts to collect the loan at the conclusion of the bankruptcy proceedings.

To ensure that student loans from the institution are not discharged in bankruptcy, petitions in bankruptcy that include student loans demand careful attention and prompt review. Prudent institutions have internal policies and procedures for addressing the many issues related to bankruptcy filings. Included in those policies should be close consultation with legal counsel to ensure representation of the institution's financial interests while complying with bankruptcy laws.

Use of Facilities

Colleges and universities, as owners of property, have the legal right to control the use of their facilities. That right, however, is not absolute. Other legal rights and restrictions (stemming from contracts, state or federal laws, or state or federal constitution) may affect that control. As a rule, public institutions usually are more open and accessible than independent institutions because, as arms of the state, they are subject to constitutional provisions—primarily the First Amendment right to free speech. However, if independent colleges and universities engage in activities that may be considered "state action" or devote some facilities to a "public function," they may be held to the constitutional standards applied to public institutions.

The issue of access is complicated by the assortment of facilities on campuses and the variety of activities that campus facilities are used for by both university and nonuniversity groups. Frequently, legal issues relating to First Amendment rights (freedom of expression, religion, assembly) arise. Noncommercial speeches and acts, such as demonstrating, wearing symbolic armbands, leafleting, and picketing, generally have been subject to First Amendment protection on public campuses. Some types of commercial solicitation in dormitories have not been afforded the same degree of protection by the U.S. Supreme Court. However, the Supreme Court has articulated that speech that represents a "clear and present danger" may not be shielded by the First Amendment at all. All speech may be subject to limitations imposed by the university relating to time, place, and manner.

As most speech on campus, particularly by students, is protected by the First Amendment, the time, place, and manner of the speech will need to be considered. Generally, wider latitude will be given to speech in places designated or viewed as "public forums." This does not mean that totally uncontrolled, unrestricted speech can take place even in these forums. An institution is permitted to impose reasonable limitations to protect its interests, such as the preservation of the educational and residential environment, prevention of crime, protection against consumer exploitation, and limitation of institutional liability. Campus regulations, however, must be unrelated to the content of speech (i.e., no specific groups may be favored or discriminated against because of the message being communicated). Further, regulations must be clear and must be narrowly drawn (i.e., contain reasonable alternatives for expression—perhaps a different time, a different place, or a different method of communications).

The proliferation of various kinds of "hate speech" has added a new dimension of constitutional and statutory civil rights protection against discrimination to the free speech debate. Judicial rulings on this topic have not yet produced definitive rules but have affirmed the primacy of First Amendment protection with respect to speech. Institutions undoubtedly will continue to grapple with these issues as they try to ensure that protected groups and individuals are not exposed to discriminatory and harassing speech while others' rights of free speech are lawfully protected. Legal counsel needs to be involved in the development of clear, specific campus regulations in this area.

Intellectual Property

Ideas and information are the stock in trade of colleges and universities. While free exchange of ideas and information is critical to the mission of higher education, the manner in which the information is accessed, used, and disseminated is often legally controlled by the proprietary rights of other individuals or entities. Those controls are in the form of patent, copyright, and trademark rights, all of which are governed by federal or state law.

Patents

A patent allows the owner to protect inventions by granting a right to exclude others from "making, using, offering for sale, or selling" an invention for a period of 20 years. The U.S. Patent and Trademark Office grants three types of patents: (1) utility patents (referring to any process, machine, composition of matter, or improvements thereof); (2) design patents (referring to a unique ornamental design); and (3) plant patents (referring only to asexually reproductive plants). Objects and ideas such as natural phenomena, principles of science, mathematical formulas, and methods of doing business have been deemed nonpatentable.

Copyright

Copyright protection is provided to authors of "original works of authorship," including literary, musical, dramatic, choreographic, graphic, sculptural, video, audio, and certain other intellectual works. Copyright protection attaches at the moment of creation of a work and exists whether the work is ultimately published or not, although proper notice of copyright should be placed on all publicly disseminated materials. Unlike a patent, registration of a copyright (in the Register of Copyrights, Library of Congress) is not legally required to claim a copyright. However, registration does afford additional statutory remedies in the event of copyright infringement.

The main objective of most university copyright policies is to encourage the creation and generation of new knowledge and to secure its widest possible dissemination to the academic community and the public. Two aspects of copyright law significantly affect practices on college and university campuses. One is the doctrine of *fair use,* which is a gray area permitting limited copying of copyrighted work for the purposes of criticism, comments, news reporting, teaching (the amount of material and number of copies is a source of considerable debate), scholarship, or research. The other is the "work for hire" doctrine, which may place the copyright of a work in the hands of an employer or person who has paid to have a work created.

Trademark

A trademark is a mark, motto, device, or emblem that is stamped, printed, or otherwise affixed to goods so that they may be identified in the market. For colleges and universities, trademarks can include team names, logos, and mascots. (Some designs or statements may be eligible for copyright protection as well.)

Several activities on college and university campuses are significantly affected by the status of these intellectual property rights.

- *Collegiate licensing.* Licensing is a mechanism by which an institution agrees to allow other parties to use its trademarks in return for a license fee and royalties. This kind of agreement can generate revenue (particularly for athletic programs), but it also enables institutions to protect and promote their reputations by controlling the use of their marks. Licensing programs can be administered internally or can be turned over to outside contractors. In either case, trademarks should be registered with the state and, in some cases, with the U.S. Patent and Trademark Offices as well. A licensing agreement should be developed with some standard areas to be negotiated with the licensee, including licensing fee and royalties, time period, nonexclusivity, insurance, quality standards, and reporting requirements. Upon implementation of a licensing program, an institution should also have an enforcement policy and plan. Trademark and licensing litigation can be brought under the Lanham Act at the federal level, under similar state laws, or under several other legal theories involving unfair competition, deceptive trade practices, or misappropriation. Halting the infringement and recovering monetary losses are the primary goals of enforcement efforts, but hefty penalties may be tacked on if an infringer acts intentionally and in bad faith.

- *Music licensing.* Music that is performed on campus, whether it is a rock concert in the arena, a band performance at half-time of a football game, or a theater production, is probably copyrighted. In most cases, public on-campus performances are not considered *fair use* that is exempted from copyright restrictions. Generally royalty payments to the author of copyrighted material are not required if the institution does not pay performers, if there is no commercial purpose, and no admission is charged. For many years, colleges and universities have had blanket licenses with three groups representing music copyright holders: the American Society of Composers, Authors, and Publishers (ASCAP); Broadcast Music, Inc. (BMI);

and SESAC. The structure of the licenses is based on the number of full-time equivalency (FTE) enrollment and the amount of music performed at the institution. Institutions are not obligated to accept the blanket licenses and may negotiate directly with those entities if they so desire.

- *Copying of materials*. Copying takes place in various ways and across different media: photocopying of written materials, and copying music, videotapes, videocassettes, and computer programs. The legal issues are so complex that specific answers are sometimes difficult to discern. Although determining the limits of use and copying is a complex undertaking, the *fair use* doctrine and several *safe harbor* provisions provide some accommodations to the educational user. The *fair use* doctrine, which allows limited copying, considers four factors: the purpose and character of the usage, including whether such use is for a commercial nature or for nonprofit educational purposes; the nature of the copyrighted work; the amount and substantiality of the portion of the work used in relation to the copyrighted work as a whole; and the effect of the use on the potential market for or value of the copyrighted work. Guidelines suggested by the U.S. House of Representatives Committee on the Judiciary ("Agreement on Guidelines for Classroom Copying in Not-For-Profit Educational Institutions with Respect to Books and Periodicals" found in the notes of 17 J.S.C.107) and the American Library Association ("Model Policy Concerning College and University Photocopying for Classroom, Research, and Library Reserve" contained in the *Copyright Primer for Libraries and Educators*) are not legally binding but provide more suggestions for the development of institutional photocopying policies. Publishers' legal battles with photocopy firms over the practice of making course packs of copyrighted materials have also restricted the definition of *fair use* as it is applied to photocopying. There are specific guidelines for off-air recording of broadcast programming for educational purposes. As for computer programs, copyright, trade secret, or patent protection may apply. Rightful owners may make copies for their own use or for archival purposes; beyond that, copying of computer programs may raise legal problems for both individuals and institutions. Copyright law and the *fair use* doctrine also apply to information downloaded from the Internet for educational purposes.

- *Computers*. The discussion concerning computer programs and intellectual property leads to other legal issues involving computers. Many kinds of specialized computer-related contracts exist. Contracts to purchase hardware and software contain terms on product specifications, acceptance, warranties as to performance and intellectual property ownership, backups, and training, among other things. Software licensing agreements should address issues such as duration of the license, exclusivity, restrictions on use, updates, and access to the source or programming code. Maintenance agreements may or may not be part of a purchase agreement or license. Group purchase discount agreements should clearly identify the group involved and establish if certain levels of purchase are necessary. Negotiators of such agreements should also be aware of potential antitrust and anticompetition problems. Contracts with outside consulting companies must describe duties, emphasize the independent contractor status of the consultant, and clarify potential intellectual property ownership.

Unlicensed use of copyrighted software is heavily monitored by the Software and Information Industry Association (SIIA), formerly Software Publishing Association, and violations of copyright have been the subject of litigation with colleges and universities. Institutions represent prime targets for enforcement since universities own and/or control the computers used by employees and thus are at risk when employees violate copyrights by using software without appropriate licenses. In addition to the adoption of policies and practices prohibiting the use of unlicensed software on university computers, the university should have an active program of monitoring software usage to avoid lawsuits and major fines.

Digital Millennium Copyright Act

The Digital Millennium Copyright Act (DMCC), enacted by Congress in 1998, was designed to address issues of copyright in the digital age. Two of the five titles address issues of concern to universities. One principal provision is a limitation on the potential financial liability (damages, court costs, attorney's fees, etc.) that online service providers (OSP), including libraries and educational institutions, could be subject to when they function as a common carrier, allowing online users access to copyrighted material placed there by others. The OSP can avoid significant financial claims for third party infringement of copyright by complying with procedures set forth in the act. The institution must:

- develop and post a policy for termination of repeat offenders and provide network users with information on compliance with copyright laws;

- comply with "take down" and "put back" notice requirements; and

- ensure that its system accommodates industry-standard technical measures.

A special exception for public and nonprofit institutions of higher education provides them with limited protection against financial claims even when the offending user is a faculty member, researcher, or graduate student engaged in teaching or research. A particularly helpful aspect of the law is that it does not require the institution to monitor material on the Internet, but, rather, provides immunity from third party claims provided there is good faith compliance with statutory rules. The recent use of institutional Internet servers to copy MP3 (motion picture or music) files provides an example of the extent to which universities may become embroiled in copyright issues. Certain software programs allow users to download copyrighted music or video files. From the standpoint of those responsible for network services, practical problems, such as the extensive consumption of limited bandwidth, abound. From the standpoint of the owners of the copyrights and the musicians who receive royalties, the university may be complicit in copyright violations if it does not ban the software programs or address the violations. Thus, the DMCC provides limited protection but notice of violation requires action on the part of the institution. Exemptions from liability are in addition to any other defense an OSP might have under copyright law (safe harbors, fair use, etc.) or other laws.

Security and confidentiality raise a host of other issues. Various state laws provide legal rights of privacy and/or confidentiality that should be considered in light of criminal statutes that might be called into play. Institutions need to implement procedures to limit access to computer resources and should have technological safeguards to prohibit and police access. An institution's contractual rights and obligations as a provider of computer services must be viewed in conjunction with potential tort liability for breaches of privacy or harassment. Institutions should continuously review the conduct of students, faculty, and staff in this area.

FEDERAL REGULATIONS

Governmental regulation of the activities of higher education institutions continues to grow. Colleges and universities fall under the auspices of many regulatory agencies, a sample of whose activity follows.

Department of Education Regulations

The Department of Education (ED) oversees many of the regulations that apply to educational institutions. ED's oversight begins with the accreditation process. ED recognizes only those private accrediting agencies that meet its requirements. The agencies, in turn, must accredit higher education institutions in order for them to be eligible for the many forms of federal financial assistance. In addition to oversight of federal student aid programs, ED's Office for Civil

Rights (OCR) monitors many of the civil rights laws that apply to colleges and universities and periodically audits institutions' operations in those areas. OCR also investigates complaints of noncompliance with Title VI of the Civil Rights Act of 1964 and Title IX of the Higher Education Amendments of 1972 prohibiting discrimination in programs and activities that receive federal funding. Since federal funding to any institutional program or activity is deemed to be beneficial to the institution as a whole, compliance monitoring encompasses a full range of campus-based programs and departments including admissions, financial aid, and athletics.

ED is also responsible for administering the Drug-Free Schools and Communities Act Amendments of 1989, which require institutions to maintain programs for substance abuse treatment and to notify students and employees annually of legal sanctions arising from drug and alcohol abuse. ED also assists in enforcing federal anti-lobbying provisions that prohibit recipients of federal grants and contracts from using federal funds for lobbying members of Congress, their staffs, or employees of federal agencies in connection with specific contracts or grants. (ED monitors the use of ED funds; the broader anti-lobbying regulations are coordinated by the Office of Management and Budget.)

ED also has responsibility for regulations relating to student welfare, including compliance with the Family Educational Rights and Privacy Act (FERPA), which protects the confidentiality of students' educational records and grants the student (and parents or guardians of dependent students) access to the student's record.

Several regulations require disclosure of information, such as the Student Right-to-Know and Campus Security Act of 1990. The initial act required disclosure of general graduation rates of students and detailed graduation rates based on gender and race for students receiving athletic scholarships in specified athletic programs. The legislation is best known, however, for the provision relating to campus security, now renamed the Jeanne Clery Disclosure of Campus Security Policy and Campus Crime Statistics Act, which focuses on the collection and disclosure of certain crime statistics and institutional campus security policies. It requires the release of statistical data on crimes occurring on property owned or controlled by the institution and public property adjacent to institutional property, as reported to the law enforcement (city or campus police) and certain specified agents of the university. (See chapter 15, Security and Law Enforcement.) The Equity in Athletics Act of 1994 requires institutions of higher education to disclose participation numbers, number of coaches, and expenditures for men and women's teams.

OMB Regulations

The Office of Management and Budget (OMB) also has jurisdiction over certain areas of higher education. OMB circulars establish guidelines for procedures for audits of the financial affairs of state and local entities and nonprofit organizations that receive federal funds, as well as expenditures of federal financial resources for research. In 1989, following enactment of the Drug-Free Workplace Act, OMB promulgated government-wide regulations for recipients of federal contracts and grants. The act and regulations deal with on-the-job behavior and do not mandate drug testing (in contrast to the Department of Defense rule on a drug-free work-force, noted below). They do, however, require that a recipient of federal funds publish and circulate an antidrug statement, establish a drug-free awareness program, and take certain actions to deal with employees convicted of drug-related, work-related crimes.

Environmental Regulations

Most of the environmental issues affecting colleges and universities come under the auspices of the Environmental Protection Agency (EPA) and the corresponding state environmental regulatory agency, although other federal, state, and local agencies and commissions handle some specialized matters. Real estate or development projects may trigger the National Environmental Policy Act, which requires that an environmental impact statement be prepared; most states also have a corresponding statute.

The Resource Conservation and Recovery Act (RCRA) sets up a "cradle-to-grave" tracking system under which the EPA regulates generators, transporters, and disposers of hazardous waste. Included within the scope of RCRA are extensive EPA regulations governing the storage of petroleum and other hazardous products in underground tanks. Cleanup of hazardous waste sites and spills is performed pursuant to the Comprehensive Environmental Response, Compensation, and Liability Act (CERCLA, commonly known as Superfund), also administered by the EPA. CERCLA, as amended by the Superfund Amendments and Reauthorization Act of 1986 (SARA), sets forth broad-based liability standards for the agency to conduct studies and clean up contaminated sites.

Water and air are two of the primary natural resources regulated by the EPA. The Clean Water Act establishes a permitting system for the discharge of wastewater. In addition, colleges and universities should find out if they are subject to the jurisdiction of the Clear Water Act's detailed requirements for the storage of petroleum products. The Safe Drinking Water Act establishes drinking water standards for various chemicals. The EPA and the Consumer Product Safety Commission also oversee the repair or replacement of lead-contaminated water coolers and drinking fountains under the authority of the Safe Drinking Water Act.

Another important aspect of federal environmental regulation is informing employees and the public about the potential hazards of certain chemicals that may exist on campus and other university-owned property. For example, Title III of SARA requires reporting the presence of certain chemicals. The Occupational Safety and Health Administration (OSHA) has primary responsibility for workplace safety, including employee exposure to environmental hazards. OSHA has issued a "Hazard Communication Standard" to inform employees about chemicals used in their workplace. Most state and local governments have similar provisions. All university activities may be subject to these disclosure requirements, including operations (maintenance, electrical, power plant, and painting), research facilities, art studios, and photo labs. Finally, OSHA has detailed standards involving asbestos in the workplace, and the EPA provides guidance in the control and removal of asbestos.

Pursuant to the Toxic Substances Control Act, the EPA regulates polychlorinated biphenyls (PCBs), which occur most commonly on campuses in electric transformer equipment. The use, service, storage, and disposal of transformers are closely monitored and strictly controlled because of the significant environmental and health risks caused by PCBs. The handling of low-level radioactive materials is supervised by the Nuclear Regulatory Commission (NRC). Specific NRC regulations address disposal by incineration, land burial, and discharge into sewers. (For a full discussion of environmental health and safety, see chapter 14, Environmental Health and Safety.)

The EPA has launched an aggressive enforcement initiative against colleges and universities, targeting higher educational institutions as the agency's top enforcement priority. Already, colleges throughout the country have been inspected by EPA and, in many cases, significant penalties have resulted from those inspections. Inspections focus on all areas of campus life subject to environmental regulation, with particular emphasis on laboratory practices, tank and container management, and emergency planning and preparedness.

Taxation

The IRS requires independent institutions annually to file Form 990, which provides information on compensation and benefits for the highest paid employees, affiliated corporations and partnerships, transactions with other noncharitable exempt organizations, and unrelated business income. This form also discloses the identity of independent contractors paid more than $50,000 during the year. IRS audits of exempt organizations focus on a number of areas: fund raising, employment taxes, payments to nonresident aliens, tax-exempt bonds, compensation and benefit packages, and joint venture and unrelated business income activities.

Many tax issues involving individuals occur in the higher education arena. The taxability of retirement and other benefits (e.g., employee educational benefits, tuition and scholarship waivers, and housing) can be of critical concern for both employees and students. Highly compensated employees are subject to taxation on university paid benefits (such as tuition payments for children), if such benefits are economically discriminatory to other classes of employees. The viability of prepaid tuition plans may depend on whether or when taxpayers have to pay income tax on prepaid tuition. And, as mentioned above, charitable giving is strongly influenced by gift and estate tax treatment. (For a full discussion of tax issues, see chapter 11, Taxation.)

Research

Several agencies, predictably those that provide financial support through grants and contracts, regulate the research area. The Public Health Service and the National Institutes of Health have paid increasing attention to scientific misconduct and conflicts of interest relating to researchers. Extensive regulations promulgated by the Department of Health and Human Services (HHS) and other agencies require the establishment of institutional review boards to supervise research involving human subjects. The Department of Agriculture has detailed regulations dealing with the treatment of animals used for research. Other funding agencies, such as the Department of Transportation and the Food and Drug Administration, have their own regulatory and auditing procedures. The Department of Defense (DOD) not only has strict financial accountability standards, but also has procedures for maintaining a "drug-free workforce." All DOD contractors must administer drug testing programs for employees in "sensitive positions," that is, those who are granted access to classified information or who are determined by the contractor to be involved in national security, certain health and safety positions, or functions requiring a high degree of trust or confidence. Unlike the Drug-Free Workplace Act regulated by OMB, DOD's enforcement of a drug-free workforce makes no distinction between drug use on or off the job. If a drug test reveals any illegal drug use, the employee should be removed from duty.

Two statutes control the export of technical data: the Export Administration Act of 1979 and the Arms Export Control Act. These are administered by agencies within the Department of Commerce and the Department of State, respectively. Classified research information, certain unclassified military information, certain nuclear information, and information subject to a patent secrecy order are examples of information that can be restricted from exportation. The issue generally comes up on campuses in the context of federal contract research, but institutional investigators involved in independent consulting are also subject to applicable export controls and should be familiar with those restrictions.

Other Federal Regulatory Areas

Three examples of miscellaneous federal regulatory areas bear special mention. The Federal Trade Commission (FTC) and the Antitrust Division of the Department of Justice (DOJ) investigate antitrust complaints. These agencies have taken a greater interest in college and university activities as institutions expand. Such diverse issues as the National Collegiate Athletic Association's (NCAA) control of football television broadcasts and institutional policies requiring students to live in university housing have been challenged on antitrust grounds. In the early 1990s, the DOJ initiated an antitrust action with respect to several independent institutions' cooperative efforts and data sharing in awarding financial aid to students. The case resulted in a settlement agreement regarding future sharing of information but no financial damages. Antitrust issues in higher education also include the setting of tuition and faculty and staff salaries.

The impact of Federal Communications Commission regulations on higher education institutions has increased significantly with the expansion of institutional efforts to own or operate telephone systems, cable systems, Internet services, satellite systems, and other communication systems or services. The U.S. Postal Service, which has responsibility for monitoring the uses of the lower mailing rates available to colleges and universities, has increased its efforts to ensure that such rates are used only for the legitimate business of the institution and are not lent to others through cooperative ventures.

State and Local Government Regulations

State and local governments, too, are active in a wide array of regulatory matters. With respect to privacy and disclosure, state open meetings and open-records laws are frequent sources of dispute as the public seeks information about state institutions' activities. Disagreements over access to board meetings, information about presidential searches, animal research, and other matters often escalate into litigation, where courts must interpret state laws. In addition, several states have responded to pressures from the private sector (the same pressures that have spurred congressional examination of the UBIT) and have adopted or are considering anticompetition legislation restricting activities of educational institutions in areas that may compete with private businesses.

State and local governments have become more innovative in attempting to obtain greater financial support from colleges and universities as federal assistance for state and local services diminishes. Some cities have attempted to extend local hotel taxes to rooms at conference centers and unions on campuses. Others have considered a tax on student tuition. Local governments are challenging the tax-exempt status of certain campus facilities with an eye toward placing them on local tax rolls. Zoning ordinances have been used to control campus growth and off-campus housing. In response, colleges and universities have come up with new approaches to these problems, such as financing downtown redevelopment projects, making payments in lieu of taxes, or covering a larger portion of expenses for community services.

Risk Management

The breadth and scope of college and university programs and activities is greater than ever. Healthcare centers, day care centers, athletic and recreational programs, international exchange programs, retirement communities, and museums are just a few examples of the enterprises now commonly associated with higher education. Legal and financial risks are associated with each of these operations. In fact, because loss can so often depend on legal relationships, legal counsel and risk managers should always work closely together to address risk reduction and to control liability and potential loss.

There are four basic elements to proper risk management: identification of the risk; evaluation of exposure; selection of the appropriate risk management tools and methods; and implementation and review of a risk management policy. Proper management of risk requires input from various campus constituencies and a close working relationship with counsel. Legal counsel should review all areas for potential liability. Physical plant administrators should compile information concerning maintenance and replacement of facilities and equipment. Financial or business officers should compile figures on the financial effects of the various losses considered. Academic affairs and public relations administrators should analyze the institutional and public effects of potential losses. (For a full discussion of risk management, see chapter 16, Risk Management and Insurance.)

Research Relationships and Technology Transfer

From a legal as well as an administrative standpoint, there are two aspects to technology transfer. The first focuses on the performance of research itself; the second relates to the methods of making research available for public use.

Sponsorship of university research by industry is extensive and an integral part of the research university. Although individual terms must be negotiated in each relationship, some common parties and elements can be identified. Generally, in arrangements where private industry or the federal government sponsors research, three entities have interests that must be defined: the sponsor, the institution, and the researcher. Among these groups, three broad issues must be resolved: ownership of the intellectual property and the rights to control its development; potential conflicts of interest the researcher may face; and the independence and academic freedom of the institution and the researcher in publishing research results.

Because most university researchers are employees, the question of ownership of intellectual property is usually settled by institutional patent and copyright policies. These policies recognize the institution as the owner of works for hire and other property arising out of the employment relationship and thus the grantor of rights to faculty and researchers. However, between the institution and the sponsor, the question of ownership must ordinarily be negotiated. In federally sponsored research, federal regulations may control this issue and leave little room for negotiation. Institutions naturally wish to retain ownership, to maintain as much control as possible over the research, and to be able to take advantage of the financial value of the research. Private sponsors prefer to own research for many of the same reasons. Sponsors are also interested in keeping potentially lucrative research and trade secrets confidential and out of the hands of competitors, a practice that is frequently at odds with the university's self-professed commitment to openness and sharing of research findings. In many cases, compromises are reached whereby the university holds ownership to research in the patent or copyright and grants a license to the sponsor to develop and market it.

Tax issues will inevitably be a part of the discussion on technology transfer. One related issue is whether the license fees received by the institution from third party licenses will be considered to be tax-exempt royalties or treated as compensation for services rendered by the institution or a partnership distribution. Since many institutions have policies that allow faculty-investors to receive a portion (e.g., 50 percent) of the royalties paid to the institution by third-party licensees, another tax-related issue will be whether the payments to the faculty-inventor will be treated as a royalty (generally reported by many institutions as IRS Form 1099 miscellaneous income) or as additional compensation (subject to W-2 reporting requirements).

Issues involving conflict of interest are another area of importance to institutions. Conflict of interest can exist where a faculty member uses influence within the institution for personal gain. A researcher who promotes a relationship with a private sponsor in which the researcher has a financial stake is an obvious example. Most of these prohibited activities and relationships are defined by institutional policies and, in the case of public institutions, by state law. However, they often need to be referred to and reiterated in institutional agreements with private sponsors.

There has always been institutional and researcher sensitivity about academic freedom and the independence of research done for private sponsors. Sponsors, understandably, feel a proprietary interest in the research: they pay for it, so it is theirs. Researchers feel that obligation but also need to remain independent to retain their professional reputations in the academic community. They want to be free to publish their research results and do not want their research to appear to be influenced by a sponsor. This tends to be an ethical issue for institutions and researchers, but it becomes a legal issue when terms about confidentiality and delay of publication must be negotiated into the research contract.

The desire to transfer research into some type of usable technology for public consumption brings up another set of issues. Several options exist to handle this function. The institution may transfer research internally through an existing organizational unit or may "spin off" a separate entity, either a nonprofit or for-profit subsidiary. Other options are to enter into a joint venture or partnership, or contract with an outside entity for the service. The method chosen depends on the political, financial, and legal climate of the institution.

Many factors need to be examined in evaluating the different vehicles for technology transfer: governance and control of the enterprise; physical location and the possible need for new facilities; financing needed for the effort; different regulatory matters that may affect it (e.g., environmental, research and financial accountability, tax matters, land use, securities, antitrust); personnel issues; potential liability; and insurance needs. Only after a thorough analysis is made can the institution decide which method will best meet its needs.

CONSTRUCTION

Design and Construction Contracts

In design and construction contracts, there are more players, their roles are more complex, and the financial stakes are generally higher than in ordinary purchasing and contracting. The owner of a campus building is usually the institution, although complicated arrangements involving the sale of real estate and leaseback of facilities are sometimes made. Colleges and universities, particularly public institutions, increasingly use nonrecourse financing (off-balance sheet financing). Financial support is often required for construction; financiers (sometimes public bodies, sometimes private corporations or partnerships) must deal with issues involving bonds, collateral, and restrictions on indebtedness. The legal issues in such financing usually require counsel specialized in such matters. Architects and engineers must be employed for the building design, and a construction management organization or general contractor must be chosen to coordinate and supervise the construction, unless the institution chooses to assume that role.

The general format of design contracts that are negotiated with architects usually is derived from the American Institute of Architects (AIA). The AIA and other trade industry groups suggest standard contract provisions that tend to protect the interests of architects and contractors in such arrangements. In response, the National Association of Attorneys General has developed provisions that swing the balance toward the owner, particularly involving a public entity. While many provisions can be accepted as customarily used, the important terms for each deal should be negotiated individually.

Fast-Track Design

The "fast-track design" process is a method of construction whereby the specific design elements of the building develop as the building progresses. While the fast-track process allows construction to get started quickly, it also raises the specter of an unknown and uncontrollable budget. A well-drafted contract with architects or builders is essential for providing complete plans that come within the allotted budget.

Design-Build Process

The "design-build" delivery system allows the owner to contract with a single entity responsible for design and construction. This process, while allowing for speed and sometimes cost savings, may be particularly risky for the owner because of the likelihood of disputes over scope.

Insurance

The availability of errors and omissions insurance and the need for indemnification provisions regarding potential pollution and hazardous waste liability are often contentious points of negotiation. Institutions should educate themselves well so that they are prepared to negotiate realistically on these issues. They should have policies in place whose coverage coincides with relevant statutes of limitations for suits against designers.

Subcontractors

Colleges and universities should have a voice in selecting subcontractors to be used by designers. Operations of mechanical aspects of projects—heating, air conditioning, plumbing, and electricity—often can be more expensive than the overall cost of the design and the construction itself. Institutions need to maintain the right to approve subcontractors, engineers, and other professionals to ensure quality performance by those working on components of the project.

Other Problems

Construction contracts pose other problems. Allocation of risk and compensation arrangements are generally of primary interest to both sides in a contract. Does the agreement provide for a single payment at the conclusion of the project, or are progress payments made as construction proceeds? What kind of retainer fees are required? Who controls amounts paid to subcontractors? Cost-plus provisions, which often accompany fast-track design projects, should be viewed cautiously. Scheduling should be pinned down with penalties and liquidated damages for delay; the institutions should have the right to replace contractors if their performance is inadequate. Provisions for instituting change orders should be clearly spelled out and cost limitations should be explicit. Changes to scope and/or design can have great impact on final costs and should be subject to a formal approval process spelled out in the contract. Responsibility for compliance with governmental regulations—zoning, building permits, wage and nondiscrimination laws, and the costs for compliance or noncompliance with the same—should be defined.

Protections need to be built into the contract to cover potential problems. Performance and payment bonds probably will be required. Contractors ordinarily carry and provide proof of risk insurance for the value of the project, as well as workers' compensation and general liability insurance. If disagreements occur, the contract may provide for internal appeals and arbitration. Although arbitration should permit faster resolution and savings in time and expenses, many institutions are reluctant to pursue arbitration because of perceived bias of construction arbitration organizations in favor of construction industries. Thus, colleges and universities must weigh the wisdom of using the judicial system rather than arbitration for resolving disputes. The pros and cons of the two methods of resolution may vary greatly by state or jurisdiction.

In design and construction contracting, as with all contracting, the parties who may speak for the institution should be clearly identified. Confusion and potential liability should not occur because of mixed messages sent by persons with apparent authority. (For a full discussion of construction issues, see chapter 13, Facilities Management.)

Borrowing and Financing

Institutional borrowing and financing often are required to support projects of colleges and universities. State law usually establishes the legal authority and structure for issuing this financing, whether it is revenue bonds for public institutions (which may limit purpose, terms, use of revenues, and indebtedness), conduit financing for independent institutions (which may be state industrial development bonds issued by a city or county on behalf of the institution), certificates of participation (which are annual appropriation provisions for a governmental entity to lease property from a private lessor), or general revenue bonds secured as general obligations of the institution. Other vehicles, such as variable rate demand bonds and bank letters of credit, offer colleges and universities short-term financing options. Some states and institutions have banded together to create multi-university bonds, whereby proceeds of an issuance are used by more than one institution for more than one project.

A critical consideration in this type of financing is whether the bonds will be taxable or tax-exempt. To obtain tax-exempt status, bonds must be either governmental bonds or private activity bonds. Tests involving *private business use, security interests, related private use, private use, qualified bonds,* and *arbitrage*—terms defined in Internal Revenue Code provisions—require legal and accounting analysis usually provided by outside counsel.

Bond offerings must comply with federal and state securities laws. Under the Securities Act of 1933 and parallel "blue sky" laws in most states, securities must be registered with the Securities and Exchange Commission and its state counterpart, although many bonds issued in conjunction with college and university financing may meet definitions that specifically exempt them from such requirements. Detailed disclosure statements are filed as part of the registration process. Even exempt securities must meet certain antifraud provisions. Section 17 of the Securities Act of 1933 and Rule 10b-5 of the Securities and Exchange Act of 1934 both impose liability for material misstatements or omissions made with *scienter*— intentional misrepresentation, reckless disregard, or gross negligence.

Completion of a project does not end the legal and administrative concerns of a bond issuance. Tax law requirements must continue to be monitored to ensure proper tax-exempt use and management of the project, to determine applicability of arbitrage regulations, and to comply with rebate-of-profits requirements. Other terms of the bond documents, such as rate and insurance covenants, annual reports, and replacement funds, may require periodic attention. The up-front and administrative expenses of this kind of financing can be imposing, but the benefits of a carefully prepared bond issuance can far outweigh the costs. (For a full discussion of debt financing, see chapter 10, Debt Financing and Management.)

LIABILITY ISSUES: FACULTY, STAFF, AND STUDENTS

Liability is the legal responsibility for injury, damage, or loss. It can arise from obligations in contracts or from regulatory requirements, both discussed above, Liability can also arise as a "tort," which is a civil wrong imposing liability on a person or entity for personal injuries or invasion of civil liberties. Torts generally occur in three forms: intentional, negligence, and strict liability.

Intentional torts require a finding that a person intentionally violated another person's protected right. Examples include defamation (libel and slander), invasion of privacy, violation of civil rights, intentional infliction of emotional distress, and assault and battery.

Negligence requires proof of four elements: a legal duty owed to the injured party; a breach of that duty (generally for failure to use a reasonable standard of care); proof that the defendant caused the injury (both factually and proximately, meaning that the injury was reasonably foreseeable and there was no intervening cause of the injury); and proof of damages. However, if the injured party is also negligent, assumed the risk involved, or consented to the activity (and in the case of public institutions, if some type of sovereign immunity is provided by law), then liability may not attach. Colleges and universities face negligence claims in all sorts of situations—athletics, alcohol-related activities, supervision and advising of students, injuries from criminal activities on campus, and maintenance of facilities.

Strict liability torts ordinarily arise in abnormally dangerous or ultrahazardous activities, such as storage of explosives or production of dangerous products. The threat of this type of liability is less common but cannot be ignored.

The division of the discussion into liability issues involving faculty and staff and those involving students is an arbitrary one. Circumstances giving rise to legal questions on campus rarely can be placed neatly into these categories. Furthermore, this section focuses on issues related to faculty, staff, and students that involve contract and tort liability. Liability issues in the regulatory and discrimination areas are covered elsewhere in this chapter.

Faculty and Staff

The employment relationship is the subject of both contract and tort liability claims relating to faculty and staff. Two concepts add to the complexity and uniqueness of these questions: tenure and academic freedom.

Tenure is the common practice of granting teachers and researchers permanent or continuous employment after they have successfully completed a probationary period, customarily about seven years. (Alternatives to tenure, such as rolling contracts, growth contracts, and expanding term appointments have been implemented at a few institutions.) Subject to the institution's guidelines, on receiving tenure, an individual generally can be terminated only for *adequate cause* or because of *financial exigencies,* although the breadth and vagueness of those terms leave much room for interpretation. It is essential that the institution regularly review its policy on tenure to avoid unintended consequences stemming from ambiguous terms.

Academic freedom is another amorphous term. Usually grounded in contract as well as custom and usage, it is often interpreted by courts to define broad constitutional rights and responsibilities of the teaching profession. Questions involv-

◆

ing an institution's power to control faculty speech and conduct both in and out of the classroom often delve into matters of academic freedom. Faculty, individually and collectively, have strong opinions and great influence on this subject. The American Association of University Professors' (AAUP) Statement of Principles on Academic Freedom and Tenure sets forth a common understanding of the issues, but it is not a legal treatise.

Tenure is not easily acquired, nor is it readily relinquished once it is achieved, Thus, most situations in which tenure issues come up involve the denial of tenure, a change in a faculty member's employment responsibilities or rights, or a faculty member's termination. The process for awarding tenure usually requires an evaluation by one's peers. The steps in that process, as well as the criteria for evaluating a candidate for tenure, are commonly contained in faculty handbooks and other institutional policies and procedures and are incorporated by reference into the faculty member's employment contract.

Changes in a faculty member's employment rights and responsibilities can occasionally raise issues related to tenure. The removal of administrative duties and pay, failure to receive merit salary increases, and reduction in laboratory space or research time have been the subject of litigation typically with faculty seeking to retain certain privileges related to tenure. However, it is generally accepted that, within limits, terms of employment such as teaching loads, salary raises, and benefits ordinarily can be revised by the institution without violating rights of tenure.

The termination of tenured faculty provides fertile ground for litigation. The contractual justification for such termination traditionally has been vague; *adequate cause* or some similar term can be defined broadly to fit a variety of circumstances. Other ambiguous terms often used in faculty contracts and accompanying institutional policies to explain adequate cause include *insubordination* (defying institutional rules or orders in performing one's job); *moral turpitude* (certain crimes; improper sexual advances have been found to fit this term); *incompetence* (not performing one's job satisfactorily); and *dereliction of duty* (not performing one's job at all). The lack of specific definitions gives an institution some flexibility in determining grounds for termination, but it also causes disagreement and can jeopardize the legality of the termination. Not all institutions subscribe to the AAUP Statement of Principles on Academic Freedom and Tenure. However, failure by an institution to state clearly its own policies may result in the application of the AAUP Statement and subsequent interpretations of it as indicative of the custom of the higher education industry.

◆

Aside from issues related only to tenured faculty, the same definitional difficulties can occur when terminations of faculty or staff result from *financial exigency, reductions in force, program discontinuance,* or a variety of other reasons. Alternatives such as buyouts or severance packages, leaves of absence, early retirement, salary reductions or furloughs, modified calendars or workweeks, or reductions in benefits may alleviate the need for actual terminations. In any case, clear explanations of those conditions and the procedures needed for dealing with them are required.

The legal bases for objecting to the denial of tenure or to terminations of tenured faculty or staff generally fall into three basic categories:

- the procedures for making the decision were not followed, that is, due process was not provided; at public institutions, employees often have constitutional rights of *property* and *liberty* in their jobs and reputations; constitutional due process must be afforded to persons whose property or liberty interests are affected;

- criteria other than those elucidated in the institution's faculty and human resources policies on tenure, employment practices, or termination were used to evaluate the candidate (in many cases it is also alleged that illegal criteria such as race, religion, sex, or age were used); or

- the criteria or the procedures themselves were unfair, being too arbitrary, vague, or broad.

A variety of tort claims by a faculty or staff member often are tacked on to employment contract disputes. Abusive or retaliatory discharge, interference with business or contract relations, intentional infliction of emotional distress, negligent performance of a contract obligation, and defamation (arising out of the peer review process) are some of the creative tort theories that plaintiffs have used to seek additional damages in connection with their claims of breach of employment contract.

Generally speaking, most causes of action in these areas are brought under state laws. Institutions must pay close attention to their policies and practices to avoid liability for such claims. Remedies in these cases vary. Compensatory money damages are most common. However, in cases where courts find egregious institutional behavior, reinstatement with back pay, granting of tenure and promotion, and even punitive damages and attorneys' fees have been awarded to plaintiffs.

Practical Suggestions

Some practical suggestions may help reduce faculty and staff employment disputes.

Fair and objective criteria for evaluating performance and for granting tenure. Institutional administrators should make sure that the criteria for awarding tenure—typically, evaluations of a teacher's instruction skills, publications, and service to the institution—are as fair and objective as possible and are clearly communicated in writing to those who are being evaluated as well as to those who are doing the evaluating. Administrators should caution all involved against oral statements that alter or amend such criteria.

Confidentiality. Institutions should examine the need for confidentiality in the peer review process. Confidentiality purportedly encourages candor in the evaluation process; many courts, however, have found that it can also cover up illegal discrimination. In 1990, the Supreme Court granted the Equal Employment Opportunity Commission access to certain peer review materials, finding that institutions did not have a special privilege against the disclosure of such materials. The decision does not require institutions to eliminate the confidentiality of the peer review process (although by state law some public institutions may be required to do so), but does indicate that, in the event of litigation, peer review records may be disclosed.

Clearly defined grounds for termination. The various grounds for termination, whether performance related or other, should be included in the institution's written policy. While all possible circumstances can never be predicted or defined and elaborate specificity is not required, the articulated grounds should be broad enough to allow some institutional flexibility.

Clear procedures for termination. The institution must have clearly articulated procedures in place for making decisions to separate or terminate employees. When employees are terminated for cause, the rudiments of constitutional due process should be provided: notice of the action to be taken, an opportunity to be heard before an impartial body, and an opportunity to present evidence on one's own behalf. Because those characteristics of due process are generally accepted to be fundamentally fair, independent institutions would be wise to consider adoption of similar procedures.

Adherence to the criteria. Administrators must make sure that the criteria and procedures in place are followed. In some instances, tenure has been granted *by default* because procedures and timetables for tenure decisions were not met. In addition, both staff and faculty have successfully challenged their terminations because the institution did not follow its own procedures. Even where the challenge is unsuccessful, a failure to follow established procedures allows the challenger to make an issue of the process, thereby obfuscating the merits of the matter.

Students

The relationship between colleges and universities and their students is subject to contract analysis, the terms of which are stated and implied in the various written materials published by the institution: admissions brochures, catalogs, student handbooks, disciplinary procedures, housing contracts or licenses, and other institutional policies and documents. While courts have recognized the contractual nature of this relationship since early in this century, they have also found that strict application of commercial contract doctrines is seldom applicable to the resolution of legal issues arising in this context. Instead, courts tend to review the broader relationship between the institution and the student.

The contractual relationship between students and institutions begins with the admissions process. Institutions must follow their published criteria in deciding which students to admit. Students are required to provide truthful information in applications for admission. False or fraudulent information in an application may permit the institution to expel the student or to revoke a degree on the grounds that the breach voids the contract or that contract is void *ab initio* (never existed) because of the deception.

Modification of the institution-student relationship, such as by raising tuition drastically or during the program year, changing graduation requirements, amending disciplinary procedures, or eliminating an academic or other program, can raise a tangle of contractual questions and should be discussed with counsel before proceeding. Institutions are regularly challenged in court on significant tuition increases or decisions to close a program. To minimize these kinds of problems, institutions should state in relevant bulletins, handbooks, and documents that they reserve the right to make such changes, and they should provide notice when the changes are made. Courts are inclined to require the institution to deliver the program promised but tend to defer to academic expertise on the question of the quality of the program.

Discipline

Student disciplinary matters must be analyzed from several perspectives. Disciplinary procedures at independent institutions are established by contract, and student challenges to the results of a disciplinary proceeding or the procedures themselves must be based on breach of contract. On the other hand, student disciplinary procedures at public institutions (like those for faculty) should be structured around constitutional rights of due process. Academic disciplinary procedures are relatively flexible and informal because they involve questions of academic judgment. Nonacademic disciplinary procedures are more formal and must contain basic elements of due process such as a notice, a hearing before an impartial decision-making body, and an opportunity to present evidence.

Organizations

Liability issues involving student organizations and activities revolve around questions of ownership and/or control. The greater the degree of control exercised by the institution or the more substantial the ownership, the more likely it is that the institution will be held liable for the actions of student organizations. In the area of contracts, the doctrine of agency returns. Is there a principal-agent relationship between the institution and the student group? Does the group have actual or apparent authority to bind the institution contractually? Procedures for institutional recognition or registration of student organizations usually establish this relationship and generally limit the authority a group has to act on behalf of the institution.

No action for negligence can succeed without a finding of a breach of duty. Tort issues also turn on the question of control, although the analysis focuses on the institution's duty to supervise the activities of the group rather than questions of agency and delegation of authority. For instance, incidents involving fraternity and sorority hazing and alcohol-related injuries have plagued many campuses. Injuries have occurred during off-campus field trips, international exchange programs, and cooperative internships. Student newspapers have been sued for defamation. In the past, courts regularly enlisted the doctrine of *in loco parentis* ("in the place of the parents") to find that the institution had the authority and responsibility to oversee student conduct in these situations and thus to hold the institution liable for resulting injuries. More recently, that doctrine has faded as courts have recognized students' rights and responsibilities to control their own behavior. As such, unless it is found that a *special* duty or relationship exists between the institution and a student activity, courts have been reluctant to hold the institution liable for the actions of student groups. Written releases requiring students to assume the risk of an activity or waiving the institution's liability in the event of possible injury may help insulate institutions from legal responsibilities but are not failsafe. Such documents may be against public policy or unenforceable in some cases. Institutions generally cannot waive liability for gross negligence or any obligations imposed on them by law.

Athletics

Most courts consider athletic scholarships to be a component of a contractual relationship. The institution provides the scholarship, proper training, and medical treatment; the student participates in the sport and abides by the rules governing eligibility. Injuries sustained in athletics programs, both intramural and intercollegiate, often give rise to contract and tort issues. Contract claims are based on the written materials of the institution and the oral representations of employees. At the same time, damage claims arising from negligence rely on allegations that the institution negligently failed to perform its duty to provide proper training and/or adequate medical care for the athlete. Again, students are routinely required to sign releases before participating in athletic activities, in an attempt to reduce the institution's exposure to liability for injuries that may occur.

NCAA investigations of alleged rules infractions are quite extensive and often require legal assistance and significant financial expenditures for investigation and representation. By far the most compelling legal issues in the athletic arena relate to gender. Both Title IX of the Higher Education Amendments of 1972 and Title VII cases have loomed large in recent years. Although the Title IX cases challenge the representation of women on teams (frequently referred to as proportionality) or differences in the allocation of resources (equal treatment), there is no doubt that many of these issues relate to funding and budgeting for intercollegiate athletics. Title VII and the Equal Pay Act are frequently the basis for challenges alleging that compensation of coaches of women's sports is discriminatory or inequitable.

Campus Security

One aspect of campus life that continues to receive considerable media attention and has raised a great concern about institutional liability in the last few years is crime on campus. The Student Right-to-Know and Campus Security Act of 1990, recently renamed the Jeanne Clery Disclosure of Campus Security Policies and Campus Crime Statistics Act, requires colleges and universities to collect, publish, and distribute annual statistics on crimes on their campuses. Many states have adopted similar legislation. These data are publicly available and frequently are published by national news media and security watchdog groups. The university should pay particular attention to its own statistics, which could become the basis for an allegation that the university is aware of but has not adequately responded to certain dangerous situations.

Legal action by a student against the institution for injuries that are alleged to be related to security or safety may be brought as a breach of contract action. Even if the contact between the institution and student does not support a contractual obligation on the part of the institution, the student may bring a tort action. Tort liability may be imposed (primarily under the theory of negligence) when an injured person can assert that the institution had a legal duty that was not performed and can show that the failure to perform that duty was the cause of the injury. Several relationships may provide a basis for the institution's duty to the student. The landlord-tenant relationship is such a relationship. A landlord has a duty to provide safe premises for a tenant. Thus, ignorance of or inattention to security or safety issues in university housing may lead to substantial risk. Another is when the institution has assumed a special duty—for instance, by putting a fence around certain areas or providing security patrols.

In analyzing the cause of an injury, foreseeability can be a critical factor. Courts have adopted different standards in attempting to define foreseeability. Some have taken a restrictive approach, requiring similar crimes to have occurred on campus before the courts will impose liability on institutions. Other courts take a more expansive view, finding that simply being located in a high-crime area may be sufficient notice to make a crime on campus foreseeable. Ultimately, public policy may tip the scales of liability one way or the other. If the relative burden of protecting against a crime is minimal compared to the likelihood of the crime's occurring on campus, the institution may be held liable if it has not carried that burden. On the other hand, if the cost of providing protection against a relatively unlikely crime is extremely high, courts may be less likely to saddle the institution with liability in such cases.

Practical Suggestions

Common sense is the cornerstone of these pointers on student liability issues. Administrators should:

- Periodically review and revise institutional documents (admissions criteria, catalogs, student handbooks, etc.) to make sure that institutional statements coincide with institutional practices and comply with applicable laws and regulations (the legal horizon in this area is constantly changing for both public and independent institutions, and periodic review is essential);

- Periodically review and revise student disciplinary procedures to make sure that they are fundamentally fair, that they meet minimal constitutional requirements of due process, and that the stated procedures are actually followed. Failure to do so may be alleged as a breach of contract.

- Establish the degree of control the institution expects to have over student organizations and activities and make sure the relationship is made clear to groups and individuals on and off campus.

- Review the law pertaining to releases from liability to ensure they are used in appropriate circumstances to the extent permitted by law; and

- Be aware of problem crime areas and patterns of crime on campus, stay informed about current practices and procedures in the field of security (e.g., standards for lighting, grounds keeping, scheduling of classes, emergency telephone systems), adopt reasonable standards for security and procedures for responding to reports of crime on campus, and follow those standards and procedures.

INDIVIDUAL RIGHTS

More than a century ago, the federal government began implementing laws designed to eliminate certain types of discrimination against racial minorities in the United States. Since that time, legislation has been enacted to include a broader range of classes of people and types of discrimination. For political, administrative, and legal reasons, Congress has imposed obligations primarily on two basic groups: employers and recipients of federal funds or assistance. Colleges and universities are covered by these laws as both employers and recipients of federal assistance and, thus, must comply with federal antidiscrimination laws and regulations. Although not examined below, state laws in most jurisdictions have extensive nondiscrimination provisions as well.

Laws and regulations prohibiting discrimination cut across virtually all program activities of the institution, including admissions, financial aid, athletics, research, hiring, promotions, terminations, workplace conditions and environment, contracting, and procurement.

Nondiscrimination Employment Laws

Civil Rights Statutes

Shortly after the Civil War, Congress enacted the Civil Rights Act of 1871 to address some of the discrimination issues of the time. Those statutes, which are codified in Title 42 of the United States Code (U.S.C.) are still actively employed today.

Section 1981 of the statute prohibits discrimination in the making and enforcement of private contracts on the basis of race. By judicial interpretation, it does not extend to racial harassment in the course of employment. Individuals and organizations can request a jury trial in such a case and can obtain compensatory, and in some cases punitive, damages as well as attorneys' fees. Actions must be filed within applicable state statutes of limitations for personal injuries.

Section 1983 is the legal source for a major portion of discrimination litigation brought against public colleges and universities. It provides that employers acting "under color of state law" (i.e., public officials) may not discriminate against persons on the basis of race, color, religion, sex, national origin, or any other rights "secured by the Constitution and laws" (e.g., rights pertaining to treatment of prisoners, union activity, and political affiliation). The Eleventh Amendment may provide immunity from suit to the state itself or to state employees in their official, but not their individual, capacities. As with Section 1981 actions, complaints brought under Section 1983 are independent of Title VII and have different rules and remedies. They must be brought within applicable state personal injury statutes of limitations, can be heard by a jury, and can result in awards of compensatory and punitive damages and attorneys' fees.

Title VII of the Civil Rights Act of 1964 (Title VII)

Title VII prohibits an employer with 15 or more employees involved in an activity affecting commerce from discriminating against any individual with respect to compensation terms, conditions, or privileges of employment because of that person's race, color, religion, sex or national origin. This prohibition applies to the hiring, evaluation, promotion, and discharge of employees. However, unlike some of the affirmative action requirements that apply to federal contractors and recipients of federal assistance (discussed below), Title VII does not require written plans to remedy an imbalance in the workforce of a protected group.

Discrimination under Title VII has historically been recognized by the courts in two forms: "disparate treatment," which results from overt, intentional discriminatory acts and "disparate impact," which occurs when acts or policies appear neutral on their face, but in practice have a discriminatory effect on a protected class. In 1989, the U.S. Supreme Court also reviewed a third type of case involving an employer's "mixed motives" (i.e., some legitimate and some discriminatory reasons for an employment decision). The Court found that a Title VII violation could occur if a discriminatory motive played a part in an employment decision and if the employer could not prove that it would have made the same decision without a discriminatory motive. An exception to Title VII permits hiring practices that would otherwise be considered discriminatory in a few limited cases in which religion, sex, or national origin is deemed to be a bona fide occupational qualification for the job (the BFOQ exception). At the same time, an employer is required to make reasonable accommodations for a person's sincerely held religious beliefs.

Employment-related sexual harassment also comes under the authority of Title VII. Historically, there were two types of sexual harassment: "quid pro quo" harassment, the submission to or rejection of unwelcome sexual conduct that is used as the basis for employment decisions affecting an individual; and the more recently recognized "hostile work environment" harassment, which occurs when unwelcome verbal, visual, or physical behaviors of a sexual nature have the purpose or effect of substantially interfering with an individual's welfare or work performance, or create an intimidating, hostile, offensive environment. Two 1998 U. S. Supreme Court decisions blurred the line between quid pro quo harassment and hostile environment. Prior to those decisions, an employer was strictly liable for quid pro quo harassment by a supervisor when the employee suffered some tangible and adverse employment action as a consequence of refusing the unwelcome sexual conduct. Following the 1998 decisions, even though an employee may not have suffered any tangible or adverse employment action, an employer can still be held liable, unless it can present an affirmative defense proving that it exercised reasonable care to prevent and correct sexually harassing behavior and that the complaining employee unreasonably failed to take advantage of the opportunities provided by the employer. In another major 1998 decision, the U.S. Supreme Court held that hostile environment harassment could include same sex harassment.

Title VII enforcement is coordinated by the Equal Employment Opportunity Commission (EEOC) and similar state agencies in most states. Complaints must be filed within a certain time (usually 180 to 300 days following the alleged violation, depending on the procedures in the specific state). If the EEOC investigates and finds reasonable cause, it will attempt to conciliate between the parties and to fashion a remedy. Once an agreement has been reached, neither party may file suit based on the same facts. If reasonable cause is not found, the EEOC will dismiss the complaint and notify the complainant of a private right to sue. In the alternative, the complaining party may request a right-to-sue letter be issued by the EEOC after the expiration of 180 days from the date of the filing. Upon the issuance of a right-to-sue letter by the EEOC, the complaining party has 90 days in which to file suit in federal court and may demand a jury trial. Remedies available under Title VII include hiring, reinstatement (with or without back pay), prejudgment interest, attorneys' fees, costs, and prohibition of future discriminatory acts. Punitive damages have been awarded in particularly egregious situations.

Pregnancy Discrimination Act of 1978 (PDA)

The PDA makes it a violation of Title VII for an employer to discriminate in employment opportunities, sick leave plans, or health or disability plans on the basis of pregnancy. Under Supreme Court interpretation of the PDA, if pregnancy health benefits are provided to female employees, they must also be afforded to spouses of male employees. Again, BFOQ exceptions may permit certain discriminatory practices.

Equal Pay Act of 1963

The Equal Pay Act prohibits gender-based pay discrimination among employees. Employers may not pay employees of one sex less than the rate paid to the opposite sex for equal work that requires equal skill, effort, and responsibility performed under similar working conditions. The act, however, does permit differentials based on a seniority system, merit system, or system that measures earnings by quantity or quality, or a differential based on any factor other than sex. An amendment to Title VII states that differences in pay based on sex that are authorized under the Equal Pay Act are not unlawful under Title VII.

The EEOC enforces this act. Cases must be filed within two years of the accrual of the cause of action (within three years in the case of a "willful" violation). Jury trials are available. Damages may include back pay, attorneys' fees, costs, and liquidated damages in an amount equal to back pay and benefits.

Age Discrimination in Employment Act of 1967 (ADEA)

The ADEA protects employees and job applicants who are at least 40 years of age from discrimination on the basis of their age. A recent U.S. Supreme Court decision held that protection extends to favoritism of a younger employee over an older employee, even if the younger employee is also 40 years of age or older, if the basis for the favoritism is age. Simply stated, age discrimination may be found even if both affected employees are in the protected class.

Amendments to the ADEA in 1986 prohibited mandatory retirement on the basis of age in most professions and positions. Exceptions are permitted under the ADEA: good cause, a BFOQ necessary to the normal operation of a particular business (e.g., mandatory retirement of airline pilots), business necessity, and bona fide seniority systems or benefit plans. The Older Workers Benefit Protection Plan passed in 1990 legislatively reversed a 1989 Supreme Court decision and restored a requirement that employers provide equal benefits or equal costs for age-based differences in employee benefit plans.

Charges of discrimination under the ADEA must first be filed with the EEOC or an equivalent state commission within 180 days after the alleged act. An individual must then wait at least 60 days before initiating a civil suit in court. A civil action must be filed within two years of the act of discrimination and within three years if the act was "willful."

A jury trial is available under the ADEA and awards can include back pay, liquidated damages equal to back pay and benefits, front pay (if reinstatement is inappropriate), and attorneys' fees and costs.

Americans with Disabilities Act of 1990 (ADA)

The ADA prohibits discrimination against "any qualified individual with a disability" in any term and condition of employment, including job application procedures, hiring, training, compensation, advancement, and discharge. It does not force employers to give preference to persons with disabilities, but it does require them to make "reasonable accommodations" for otherwise qualified applicants, unless such accommodation would impose an "undue hardship" on the employer's business. Besides governing private employment, the ADA also applies to public accommodations and services, transportation, and telecommunications. Thus, the ADA covers students as well as their relationships with colleges and universities.

The ADA borrowed much of its substantive framework from the Rehabilitation Act of 1973, which applies to most colleges and universities. The ADA, however, specifically emphasizes the employer's duty to reasonably accommodate otherwise qualified individuals with disabilities. As a consequence, much of the discussion has centered on the meaning of "qualified," what constitutes a "disability," and to what extent an employer must go to reasonably accommodate a disabled individual. In 1999, the Supreme Court narrowed the definition of disability within the meaning of the ADA by concluding that if an individual could fully correct his impairment (e.g., corrective lenses making vision 20/20 or medication that fully alleviates the symptoms of high blood pressure), the individual was not disabled and therefore was excluded from the protection of the ADA. Further, the court assumed, without stating that working in itself is a major life activity, that an individual would have to be excluded from a class of jobs or a broad range of jobs, not just a particular job, before one could be considered substantially limited in "working." In addition to addressing the interface between ADA and the Rehabilitation Act, institutional employers must also comply with state regulations regarding employees with disabilities.

Employers with Government Contracts

Employers who receive government contracts or who subcontract with an entity having a federal contract may be required to develop affirmative action plans covering certain protected groups. These required plans generally apply to organizations with 50 or more employees and federal contracts of $50,000 or more.

Executive Order 11246

Executive Order 11246 prohibits certain federal contractors and subcontractors from discriminating in employment on the basis of race, color, religion, sex, or national origin. It places a duty on federal contractors and subcontractors to take affirmative action to make sure that those factors are not involved in the employment process. Equal employment opportunity clauses must be included in contracts; postaward compliance reports and annual reports are required; and written affirmative action programs must be adopted by certain contractors and subcontractors.

Enforcement of this executive order, and of similar ones concerning employment without regard for age, handicap, or service-related disability is accomplished by the Office of Federal Contract Compliance Programs (OFCCP) of the U.S. Department of Labor. Failure to comply with the requirements of the executive order can bar access to future government contracts.

Vietnam Era Veterans Readjustment Assistance Act of 1974 (VEVRAA)

Under the VEVRAA, certain government contracts require contractors to take affirmative action to employ and advance qualified disabled veterans and veterans of the Vietnam era. Written affirmative action plans are required for larger employers.

Rehabilitation Act of 1973

Under Section 503 of the Rehabilitation Act of 1973, federal contractors and subcontractors must take actions to hire, promote, and provide reasonable accommodations for handicapped individuals. Regulations require a written affirmative action plan and maintenance of records on disabled applicants and employees in conformance with the regulations. The EEOC, OFCCP, and Department of Justice all have enforcement powers under the Rehabilitation Act. The OFCCP normally handles "groups" of employees, while the EEOC handles individual and class cases.

Recipients of Federal Assistance

Title VI of the Civil Rights Act of 1964 (Title VI)

The statute itself is fairly clear: "No person in the United States shall, on the ground of race, color, or national origin, be excluded from participation in, be denied the benefits of, or be subjected to discrimination under any program or activity receiving Federal financial assistance." As recipients of federal assistance in one form or another, almost all colleges and universities come within the purview of Title VI. Recent issues have focused on race-restricted financial incentives and admissions set-asides.

The federal agency that provides financial assistance is in charge of enforcement, which means that in most cases ED's Office for Civil Rights oversees compliance on campuses. Individuals may bring private actions under that statute, but have no right to monetary damages. However, because cancellation of future federal assistance can have potentially significant financial impact, institutions are unlikely to take the requirements of Title VI lightly.

Title IX of the Educational Amendment of 1972 (Title IX)

Title IX prohibits sex discrimination in education programs or activities receiving federal financial assistance (as compared to Title VI, which applies to many types of discrimination in all federally assisted programs). While Title IX, on its face, would appear to be easy to comply with by colleges and universities, it has been the focus of many major lawsuits for institutions in recent years. Title IX affects both public and independent institutions in virtually all areas, including recruiting, admissions, counseling, financial aid, and healthcare insurance. Recent focus has been primarily on two areas: athletics and sexual harassment.

In athletics, Title IX does not prohibit single-sex teams or competitions, but it does require equal opportunities for members of both sexes. Major challenges in courts in the past few years have targeted the number of women athletes compared to the number of men athletes. According to the Department of Education's Office for Civil Rights, colleges and universities can be in compliance with Title IX by:

- having men and women student athlete participation rates in proportion to their populations within the student body;

- demonstrating a history of expansion of opportunities for the underrepresented population; or

- meeting the interests and abilities of the underrepresented population.

Most decisions have relied on the proportionality of student athletes relative to the student population, but have left the determination on how to achieve proportionality—eliminating men's teams, adding women's teams or using some other method—to the discretion of the institution. Reverse discrimination actions involving Title IX have focused on the institution's right to eliminate men's athletic teams to achieve proportionality. A majority of the courts have permitted colleges and universities to impose these cuts or otherwise reduce the number of male student-athletes. It is likely that there will be further regulatory and judicial interpretations in this area. Other factors that ED regulations consider in determining equality include: selection of sports and levels of competition, equipment and supplies; scheduling games and practice times; travel and per diem allowances; coaching and tutoring opportunities; locker rooms; medical and training facilities; practices and competitive facilities; recruitment; scholarships and financial aid; and publicity. In addition to previously covered employment laws, Title IX has also been used to raise issues of coaching assignments and compensation. Both the ED and the EEOC have issued regulations and guidance in this area.

Title IX also prohibits sexual harassment in programs and activities at colleges and universities. There have been numerous court decisions in this area in the last few years. In 1998, the U.S. Supreme Court held that for an institution to be liable for the sexually harassing actions toward a student by its employee, an official with the authority to take action must have actual notice of the harassment and act with deliberate indifference in failing to remedy the harassment. A 1999 decision of the U.S. Supreme Court applied the same standard for student-on-student harassment, adding a fourth test to establish liability—the harassing behavior must be "so severe, pervasive, and objectively offensive that it denies its victims the equal access" to the education Title IX is designed to protect. These decisions make it essential for an institution to have an effective communications policy to enable the university community to become aware of sexual harassment issues and an education program to train university leaders and administrators on how to handle harassment claims.

The ED's Office for Civil Rights has enforcement power over Title IX . Individuals may also bring suit alleging Title IX violations.

Rehabilitation Act of 1973, Section 504 (Section 504)

Subpart E of Section 504, which applies to recipients of federal assistance operating education programs and activities, prohibits discrimination against individuals with disabilities in admission to and participation in those programs and activities. Admissions policies and procedures cannot limit the number or proportion of individuals with disabilities admitted, nor may they rely on admissions tests or criteria that produce unfair results for sensory-impaired individuals or inquire whether an applicant is disabled. Academic programs, housing, financial aid, employment of students by the recipient, physical education and athletics, and counseling and placement must be provided to qualified disabled students. This does not mean an institution must disregard a student's disability or make substantial modifications in its program to allow disabled persons to participate. For instance, in one case it was determined that a student was not discriminated against when a university did not agree to waive an LSAT requirement or adjust the student's GPA when considering the student for admission. In another case, a court upheld a university's decision not to admit a blind student to its medical school because the student would not be able to fully benefit from the medical school's educational experience.

Similar to ADA, Section 504 prohibits discrimination against otherwise qualified individuals with physical or mental impairment that substantially limits a major life activity (including such functions as caring for oneself, performing manual tasks, walking, seeing, hearing, speaking, breathing, learning, and working). Accordingly, a crucial first issue that should always be addressed is whether an individual has a disability that is covered under Section 504. In most cases physical impairment is relatively easily identifiable as a disability (hearing, mobility, sight impairments, etc.). However, certain physical impairments protected under Section 504 may not be readily apparent. For instance, individuals who have contagious diseases, such as AIDS and tuberculosis, are afforded protection under the statute (provided that their condition does not directly threaten the health or safety of others). The more difficult cases involve situations relating to mental impairments or learning disabilities. However, courts have found that bipolar affective disorder, schizophrenia, and attention deficit disorder are covered disabilities. Once it is determined that a person has a disability that affects a major life activity, the next inquiry is whether a reasonable accommodation exists that would make a program or activity of the institution accessible to the student. The extent to which an accommodation of a disabled person is "reasonable" may be difficult to decide. However, in a decision respecting academic accommodations, the court looked at the following factors to determine reasonableness: had the institution considered alternative accommodations, their feasibility, cost, and effect on the programs and would the alternatives have lowered academic standards or substantially altered the program? Interpreters for deaf students, auxiliary aids for students in nondegree programs, transportation for disabled students, and housing arrangements are issues that have raised these questions. One federal appeals court decision indicated that institutions can require a student to seek private funding or vocational rehabilitation funding for auxiliary aids, but if the funding is not available the institution should provide the aid unless it is unduly burdensome. Section 504 predates the ADA, and many of the protections and concepts contained in Section 504 are now contained in the ADA. One significant difference between the ADA and Section 504 is that the ADA also prohibits discrimination against a person who is related to or associated with a person with a disability. Section 504 does not contain such a prohibition.

Age Discrimination Act of 1975

This legislation generally prohibits age discrimination in federally funded programs and activities. It does not, however, apply to any age distinction "established under authority of any law," which includes federal, state, or local statutes. Individual federal funding agencies adopt specific regulations dealing with the act, while HHS has promulgated general regulations for auditing and compliance.

Civil Rights Restoration Act of 1987 (CRRA)

The CRRA amends Title VI of the Civil Rights Act of 1964, Title IX of the Education Amendment of 1972, Section 504 of the Rehabilitation Act of 1973, and the Age Discrimination Act of 1975. Enacted after the Supreme Court issued decisions that Congress found unduly narrow or that cast doubt on the definition of "program or activity" in those statutes, the CRRA unequivocally settled the matter by stating that the entire institution is covered by these four laws if any of its programs or activities receive federal financial assistance.

Affirmative Action

If ED has found violations of Title VI, Title IX, Section 504, or the Age Discrimination Act, institutions must implement the remedial actions ordered. Regulations implementing the four acts also have similar provisions that may permit an institution to take *affirmative action* (or *remedial action* or *voluntary action,* depending on the relevant regulations) to overcome the effects of prior discrimination.

The regulations do not provide precise definitions. *Reverse discrimination* lawsuits recently have arisen in the context of race-restricted fellowships or scholarships, or giving favorable treatment to applicants to state institutional programs based on race. Decisions in these cases do not permit race to be the controlling factor, or major factor, in the institution's procedures.

DELIVERY OF LEGAL SERVICES AND ROLE OF COUNSEL

An attorney should perform two basic functions for a college or university: prevent legal problems and respond to legal problems. The attorney's ability to accomplish both of these functions depends on a number of factors: expertise, time, physical location, commitment by the governing board and administration to the prevention and solution of legal problems, and the extent of the financial and human resources provided for support. Boards and senior administrators must examine these fundamental issues to determine how legal services should be obtained.

Specific Roles

The specific responsibilities of an institution's attorney can vary widely. The most traditional responsibility is that of a litigator. Coordinating and handling compliance with federal, state, and local regulatory requirements is another major role. Institutional counsel is often called upon to wear many less lawyerly and less visible hats as well. Many legal counsel handle nonlegal, administrative duties in addition to their legal responsibilities, acting as advisor-counselor, educator-mediator, manager-administrator, draftsperson, and spokesperson. On occasion, legal counsel also may be responsible for legislative affairs, contract administration, deferred giving, and student and faculty disciplinary matters. The institutional attorney is, in a sense, a specialized generalist, managing a general practice in a corporate setting.

Ethical Considerations

The multiple roles of legal counsel can raise some ethical as well as practical difficulties for attorneys and institutions. A fundamental issue, of which attorneys, administrators, and boards must often remind themselves, is who the client is. The Code of Professional Responsibility, developed by the American Bar Association and applicable to attorneys in most jurisdictions in the United States, states that an attorney representing a corporation or similar entity owes allegiance to the entity itself, not to a director, officer, employee, or any other person connected with the entity. This theoretical statement is of little practical use for an attorney representing a corporation: one cannot advise a legal fiction. But in most instances the attorney serves at the pleasure of the board and the chief executive, and it is those groups that the attorney ultimately advises.

The broad language of the code implies two things for college and university attorneys: (1) counsel must remain independent; the good of the corporation itself must be the guiding concern in giving advice. The attorney must not be the *rubber stamp* of the administration or the board. (2) The attorney must be aware of and avoid legal conflicts of interest among individuals or factions on campus or between the institution and its affiliated entities. If the attorney perceives a potential difference of legal interest among the board, administrators, individual employees, or other organizations, that perception should be raised and resolved so that appropriate arrangements for outside counsel can be made if necessary.

Two issues arise from the basic problem of identifying the *client.* The first involves the attorney-client privilege, which is a rule of evidence intended to preserve the confidentiality of communications between client and attorney. In the institutional setting, the answer to what might be privileged returns to the question of who the client is. Perhaps even more critical is whether the privilege exists at all when counsel is acting in a nonlegal, administrative role.

The second issue is the more practical, administrative question of who should have access to the institutional counsel (which can also give rise to attorney-client privilege issues). The board, the president, and vice presidents presumably will; what about deans, department chairs, individual faculty members, student organizations, individual students, or affiliated organizations? There is no single correct answer, although most counsel probably feel that more rather than less access affords them greater ability to do their jobs. Institutional organization, tradition, size, and specific facts determine the answer in individual cases.

Methods of Delivery

Institutions obtain legal services in many ways: hiring attorneys in private law firms off campus (outside counsel); having an attorney work exclusively for the institution on campus (inside or in-house counsel); using a combination of in-house and outside counsel, depending on the legal problems involved; and, in the case of many public institutions, receiving assistance from the office of the state attorney general. Larger, more complex institutions—those that might be expected to have more legal problems—tend to have in-house counsel, while smaller institutions more often rely exclusively on outside counsel for legal assistance.

The question of the need for and wisdom of having an attorney on campus is usually raised by cost—both the need to control it and the desire to make it more predictable. Senior administrators usually begin to consider in-house counsel when legal expenses at an institution reach the point at which it appears to be more economical to have an in-house attorney handle matters. Salaries and overhead must be examined. The nature of the legal expenses that are being incurred should also be analyzed. Are they regular expenses that represent a trend likely to continue, or an aberration that is unlikely to recur in the near future? Are the legal issues of a kind that an in-house counsel could and should be able to handle (and even prevent), or would outside counsel still need to be consulted?

Another factor that needs to be considered is the comparative quality of legal services an in-house counsel will provide to the institution. The quality can be affected by a number of elements, including time. Administrators are more likely to ask for and receive a quick answer if they can walk down the hall and ask a question, especially if they have the comfort of knowing that they will not be billed for that consultation. Because of in-house counsel's knowledge of and familiarity with the client, the attorney on campus should have insight into the mission and operations of the institution, and thus should be able to foresee and handle potential problems.

Advice from in-house counsel may be more direct and candid than advice from outside counsel, because the in-house attorney has only one client and is relatively secure in keeping the client. Outside counsel, who must constantly be concerned that the client may go elsewhere for legal advice, may be more inclined to tell the client what it wants to hear rather than what it should hear. However, there is also an argument that in-house counsel can lose its objectivity because of loyalty to the institution, collegial relationships with administrators, and involvement in nonlegal aspects of management. Consequently, there may be certain situations in which it may be desirable to maintain greater distance and more independence from administrators responsible for the subject area. It may be argued that outside counsel can more easily maintain the appropriate distance to allow for more independent, objective legal advice. These issues largely depend on the individuals involved, but the debate exists and administrators and counsel should be prepared to discuss the issues as they relate to their institution.

If in-house counsel is retained, administrators should not be surprised if the attorney's services are utilized more than expected. Potential legal problems lurk in all corners of the institution, and counsel will be most effective if other administrators who know those corners are on the lookout for problems. The availability of an attorney often causes administrators to be more sensitive to potential legal problems and to seek advice more frequently. At the same time, the attorney employed by the institution full-time is more likely than part-time outside counsel to discover independently some matters requiring legal attention.

Administrators should understand that bringing an attorney in-house would not necessarily reduce legal expenses. Legal matters, litigation in particular, are unpredictable. The outcome of individual cases can never be assured. Nevertheless, the counsel who is asked to monitor and coordinate the legal affairs of the institution should be able to exercise significant control and more accurately predict legal expenses.

Suggestions for Dealing with Counsel

To paraphrase Benjamin Franklin, the one sure thing about a college or university is that it will need legal advice. With that in mind, some suggestions for dealing with legal counsel on or off campus follow.

Administrators should perform three functions with and for their attorneys

- *Establish, understand, and respect the attorney's role.* Administrators should be aware of ethical considerations and set up ground rules for access to legal counsel; once these rules are established, administrators should be sensitive to them and let the attorney perform the job.

- *Give the attorney as much information as possible as soon as possible.* Prevention should be one of the goals of legal counsel, and the sooner potential problems are spotted, the more likely that they can be avoided.

- *Clarify compensation.* Legitimate questions will come up about bills and budgets.

Administrators should raise and resolve these issues immediately and directly.

Administrators should be able to expect three basic things from legal counsel:

- *Clear, prompt advice in response to questions.* This does not mean immediate answers, but deadlines should be set and met.

- *Honesty, independence, and loyalty to the institution in the provision of legal advice.* Simple yes or no answers to questions are not as useful as alternative solutions to problems.

- *The prevention of legal problems.* Many, though not all legal problems, can be prevented.

Finally, the institution should provide the financial and administrative support necessary to permit those efforts by legal counsel.

REFERENCES AND RESOURCES

The Legal Entity and Governance

Beach, John A. "The Management and Governance of Academic Institutions." *Journal of College and University Law* 12 (1985): 301–341.

Ingram, Richard T., et al. *Governing Independent Colleges and Universities: A Handbook for Trustees, Chief Executives and Other Campus Leaders* San Francisco, CA: AGB and Jossey-Bass, 1993.

Ingram, Richard T., et al. *Governing Public Colleges and Universities: A Handbook for Trustees, Chief Executives and Other Campus Leaders* San Francisco, CA: AGB and Jossey-Bass, 1993.

Weeks, Kent M., and Davis, Derek, Eds. "Legal Deskbook for Administrators of Independent Colleges and Universities." 2d Edition, Center for Constitutional Studies, Baylor University, Waco, TX: 1999.

Taxation

Charitable Organizations, Internal Revenue Code Section 501(c)(3): Unrelated Business Income Tax, Internal Revenue Code Section 511.

Hill, Frances R., and Kirschten, Barbara L. *Federal and State Taxation of Exempt Organizations* New York: Warren Gorman & Lamont, 1994.

Legal Relationships

Bickel, Robert D., and Lake, Peter F. *Rights and Responsibilities of the Modern University* Durham, NC: Carolina Academic Press, 1999.

Selected Business Issues

Agreement for all copyrighted music between colleges & universities and BMI, ASCAP & SESAC, 18 Coll. Law. Dig. 210 (1988).

"Agreement on Guidelines for Classroom Copying in Not-for-Profit Educational Institutions with Respect to Books and Periodical" notes 17 USC 107.

Bankruptcy Reform Act of 1978, 11 USCA 101.

Bruwecheide, Janis H., Ed. "Model Policy Concerning College and University Photocopying for Classroom, Research, and Library Reserve," *Copyright Primer for Libraries and Educators* 2nd edition, Washington, DC: ALA Editions, 1995.

Digital Millenium Copyright Act, Public Law 105-304.

Dorian, James C., and Ward, Diane M. *Student Loan Programs: Management and Collections.* Washington, DC: NACUBO, 1991.

Fair Debt Collection Practices Act, 15 USC 1692.

Farber, Daniel, *The First Amendment.* New York: Foundation Press, 1998.

Hazard, John W., "Copyright Office Circular 21: Reproduction of Copyrighted Works by Educators and Librarians," Appendix 4, of *Copyright Law in Business and Practice* Revised Edition, New York: West Group, 1999.

Hemnes, Thomas M.S. "A Guide to Copyright Issues in Higher Education." Washington, DC: National Association of College and University Attorneys, 1997.

Hopkins, Bruce R. *The Law of Fund Raising.* New York: John Wiley & Sons, 1991.

Szczepanski, Steven Z., and Epstein, David M. *Eckstrom's Licensing in Foreign and Domestic Operations.* New York: West Group, 1997.

Federal Regulations

Arms Export Control Act, 22 USC 2751.

Barber, Charles A. *What to Do When OSHA Comes Calling.* Washington, DC, National Association of College and University Attorneys, 1991.

Bennett, Barbara. *Risky Business: Risk Management, Loss Prevention and Insurance Procurement for Colleges and Universities.* Washington, DC: National Association of College and University Attorneys, 1990.

Clean Water Act, 33 USC 1288.

Coil, James H., III. *The New Supervisor's EEO Handbook: A Guide to Federal Antidiscrimination Law and Regulations.* New York, NY: Executive Enterprises, 1988.

Comprehensive Environmental Response Compensation and Liability Act (CERCLA), 42 USC 9601.

Crockett, Richard B., and Kehl, Shelly Sanders. *Accommodating Students with Learning and Emotional Disabilities: A Legal Compendium.* Washington, DC: National Association of College and University Attorneys, 1996.

Drug-Free Schools and Communities Act 20 USC 7101.

Drug-Free Workplace Act, 41 USC 701.

Export Administration Act of 1979, 50 App. USC 2401.

Family Educational Rights and Privacy Act (FERPA) 20 USC 1232.

Goldstein, Michael B. *Technology Transfer and Risk Management.* Washington, DC, National Association of College and University Attorneys, 1990.

Hajian, Tamar, Sizer, Judith R., and Ambash, Joseph W. *Record Keeping and Reporting Requirements for Independent and Public Colleges and Universities.* Washington, DC: National Association of College and University Attorneys, 1998.

Hustles, Thomas P., and Connolly, Walter B., Jr., Eds. *Regulation Racial Harassment on Campus: A Legal Compendium.* Washington, DC: National Association of College and University Attorneys, 1990.

Jeanne Clery Disclosure of Campus Security Policy and Campus Crime Statistics Act, Public Law 105-244, 486e, 20 USCS 1092.

Leskovac, Helen, *Academic Freedom and the Quality of Sponsored Research on Campus* 13 Review of Litigation 13 (Summer 1994): 401.

Levin, Michael I., *1999 United States School Laws and Rules.* West Group, 1999.

McDonald, Steven J. *The Family Educational Rights and Privacy Act: A Legal Compendium.* Washington, DC: National Association of College and University Attorneys, 1999.

Resource Conservation and Recovery Act (RCRA), 42 USC 6901.

Safe Drinking Water Act, Public Law 104-182, 42 USC 300 f.

Securities Act of 1933, 15 USC 77a.

Securities and Exchange Act of 1934, 15 USC 78a.

Student Right-to-Know and Campus Security Act of 1990, Public Law 101-542, 20 USC 1001.

Superfund Amendments and Reauthorization Act of 1986 (SARA), Public Law 99-499, 42 USC 9601.

Title VI of the Civil Rights Act of 1964, 28 CFR 42.

Title IX of the Higher Education Amendments of 1972, 20 USC 1681.

Toxic Substances Control Act, 15 USC 2601.

Wiltbank, J. Kelley, ed. *The Practical Aspects of Technology Transfer: A Legal Compendium.* Washington, DC: National Association of College and University Attorneys, 1990.

Construction

Sweet, Justin, *Legal Aspects of Architecture, Engineering and the Construction Process*, 5th edition. New York: West Publishing Co., 1994.

Liability Issues: Faculty, Staff and Students

American Association of University Professors. *AAUP Policy Documents & Reports.* Washington, DC: AAUP, 1995.

Bazluke, Francine T. *Defamation Issues in Higher Education.* Washington, DC: National Association of College and University Attorneys, 1990.

Berlongi, Alexander. *The Special Events Risk Management Manual.* Dana Point, California: Alexander Berlongi, 1990.

Brown, Valerie L., *Student Disciplinary Issues: A Legal Compendium.* 2d. Edition, Washington, DC: National Association of College and University Attorneys, 1997.

Coil, James H., III. *The New Supervisor's EEO Handbook: A Guide to Federal Antidiscrimination Law and Regulations.* New York, NY: Executive Enterprises, 1988.

Cole, Elsa Kircher, and Shiels, Barbara L., Eds. *Student Legal Issues.* Washington, DC: National Association of College and University Attorneys, 1991.

Equal Pay Act, 29 USC 206.

Lovely, Linda S., "Beyond the Freedom to Do Good and Not to Teach Evil, Professors' Academic Freedom Rights in Classrooms of Public Higher Education." *Wake Forest Law Review* 27(1991):711.

Kaufman, Hattie E. *Access to Institutions of Higher Education for Students with*

Disabilities." Washington, DC: National Association of College and University Attorneys, 1998.

National Association of College and University Attorneys, *Am I Liable? Faculty, Staff and Institutional Liability in the College and University Setting.* Washington, DC: NACUA, 1989.

Sagan, Jean A., and Rebel, Thomas P., *Employment Issues in Higher Education: A Legal Compendium.* Washington, DC: National Association of College and University Attorneys, 1989.

Student Right-to-Know and Campus Security Act of 1990, Public Law 101-542, 20 USC 1001.

Title VII of the Civil Rights Act of 1964, 20 USC 2000.

Title IX of the Higher Education Amendments of 1972, 20 USC 1681.

Individual Rights

Age Discrimination Act of 1967 (ADEA), Public Law 92-295, 5 USC 501.

Age Discrimination Act of 1975, 42 USC 6101.

Americans with Disabilities Act of 1990, 42 USC 12115.

Burlington Industries Inc. v. *Ellerth,* 524 US 742 (1998).

Civil Rights Restoration act of 1987, Public Law 100-259, 42 USC 2000d.

Crockett, Richard B., and Kehl, Shelly Sanders. *Accommodating Students with Learning and Emotional Disabilities: A Legal Compendium.* Washington, DC: National Association of College and University Attorneys, 1996.

Equal Pay act of 1963, 29 USC 206.

Faragher v. *City of Boca Raton,* 524 US 775 (1998).

Hustoles, Thomas P., and Connolly, Walter B., Jr., eds. *Regulation Racial Harassment on Campus: A legal Compendium.* Washington, DC: National Association of College and University Attorneys, 1990.

Pregnancy Discrimination Act of 1978, 42 USC 2000 (e)(k).

Rehabilitation Act of 1973, 29 USC 794.

Sagan, Jean A., and Rebel, Thomas P. *Employment Issues in Higher Education: A Legal Compendium.* Washington, DC: National Association of College and University Attorneys, 1989.

Title VI of the Civil Rights Act of 1964, 28 CFR 42.

Title VII of the Civil Rights Act of 1964, 20 USC 2000.

Title IX of the Higher Education Amendments of 1972, 20 USC 1681.

Vietnam Era Veterans Readjustment Assistance Act of 1974, Public Law 93-295, 5
    USC 501.

Delivery of Legal Services and Role of Counsel

Block, Dennis J., and Subak, John T. *The Relationship between Inside and Outside
    Counsel.* Englewood Cliffs, NJ: Prentice-Hall, 1990.

Daane, Roderick K. "The Role of University Counsel." *Journal of College and
    University Law* 12 (1985) 399–414.

Organizations

**American Association of Collegiate Registrars and Admissions Officers
(AACRAO)**
One Dupont Circle, Suite 520, Washington, DC 20036-1135
202-293-9161 . . . . www.aacrao.com

American Association of State Colleges and Universities (AASCU)
1307 New York Avenue, Fifth Floor, Washington, DC 20005-4701
202-293-7070 . . . . www.asscu.org

American Association of University Professors (AAUP)
1012 14th Street, Suite 500, Washington, DC 20005-3465
202-737-5526 . . . . www.aaup.org

American Council on Education (ACE)
One Dupont Circle, Suite 800, Washington, DC 20036-1135
202-939-9300 . . . . www.acenet.edu

Association of American Universities (AAU)
1200 New York Avenue, NW, Suite 550, Washington, DC 20005
202-408-7500 . . . . www.tulane.edu/aau/

Association of Governing Boards of Universities and Colleges (AGB)
One Dupont Circle, Suite 400, Washington, DC 20036-1135
202-296-8400 . . . . www.agb.org

Association of Higher Education Facilities Officers (APPA)
1643 Prince Street, Alexandria, VA 22314-2818
703-684-1446 . . . . www.appa.org

College and University Personnel Association (CUPA)
1233 20th Street, NW, Suite 301, Washington, DC 20036-1250
202-429-0311 . . . . www.cupa.org

Council for Advancement and Support of Education (CASE)
1307 New York Avenue, NW, Suite 1000, Washington, DC 20005-4701
202-387-5900 . . . . www.case.org

Council on Governmental Relations (COGR)
1200 New York Avenue, NW, Washington, DC 20005
202-289-6655 . . . . www.cogr.edu

National Association for Equal Opportunity in Higher Education (NAFEO)
8701 Georgia Avenue, Suite 200, Silver Spring, MD 20910
301-650-2440 . . . . www.nafeo.org

National Association of College and University Attorneys (NACUA)
One Dupont Circle, NW, Suite 620, Washington, DC 20036
202-833-8390 . . . . www.nacua.org

National Association of College and University Business Officers (NACUBO)
2501 M Street, NW, Suite 400, Washington, DC 20037-1308
202-861-2500 . . . . www.nacubo.org

National Association of Foreign Student Affairs (NAFSA)
1307 New York Avenue, NW, Eighth Floor, Washington, DC 20005-4701
202-737-3699 . . . . www.nafsa.org

National Association of Independent Colleges and Universities (NAICU)
1025 Connecticut Avenue, NW, Suite 700, Washington, DC 20036
202-785-8866 . . . . www.naicu.edu

National Association of State Universities and Land-Grant Colleges (NASULGC)
1307 New York Avenue, NW, Washington, DC 20005-4701
202-478-6040 . . . . www.nasulgc.org

National Association of Student Financial Aid Administrators (NASFAA)
1129 20th Street, NW, Suite 400, Washington, DC 20036
202-785-0453 . . . . www.nasfaa.org/D

National Association of Student Personnel Administrators (NASPA)
1875 Connecticut Avenue, NW, Suite 418, Washington, DC 20009
202-265-7500 . . . . www.naspa.org/D

National Council of University Research Administrators (NCURA)
One Dupont Circle, Suite 220, Washington, DC 20036-1135
202-466-3894 . . . . www.ncura.edu

Chapter 22

♦

Auditing

by

Rick N. Whitfield
University of Pennsylvania

Victoria S. Escalera
Brown University

J. Michael Peppers
University of Texas Medical Branch

with contributions by

David Aniloff, University of Pennsylvania

Mary Lee Brown, University of Pennsylvania

Stephen G. Colicci, Syracuse University

Sponsors

KPMG
Contact: Ingrid A. Stanlis
600 Clinton Square
Rochester, NY 14604
716-263-4015
www.kpmg.com

With over 30 years of serving higher education, KPMG offers a broad range of services that helps our clients analyze their businesses with true clarity, raises their level of performance and delivers the strategic and infrastructural components to support highly dynamic E-business models in colleges, universities, and academic medical centers.

Contents

Colleges and universities experience a variety of audits. Auditors employed by the institution perform some. Auditors retained by management and the board perform others. Auditors who work on behalf of third parties, primarily federal, state, or local government agencies, perform still others. This complex network of audits serves a variety of stakeholders, both internal and external to the institution. These stakeholders require and need reliable information that can only be assured through an effective system of internal controls—the methods and procedures adopted by an institution to safeguard its assets, to ensure accuracy and reliability of financial data, to promote operational efficiency, to protect human resources, to maintain data integrity, and to help ensure adherence to institutional policies, accounting standards, regulations, and laws. Auditing assists all levels of management to assure internal and external stakeholders that financial resources are being properly managed and reported and that the institution is complying with policies, accounting standards, regulations, and laws.

Auditing continues to experience a highly visible role in the management of institutions. In 1992, the Committee of Sponsoring Organizations of the Treadway Commission (COSO) issued a landmark report on internal controls, *Internal Control—Integrated Framework*, often called "COSO," which provides a sound basis for establishing internal control systems and determining their effectiveness.[1]

This chapter presents internal control concepts from COSO's *Framework*. The chapter discusses internal audits: definition, types and process. It elaborates on information technology in internal auditing and external audits. Finally, the chapter notes some trends that will affect auditing at colleges and universities well into the 21st century.

INSTITUTIONAL RESPONSIBILITIES AND INTERNAL CONTROL

Virtually everyone in a college or university is responsible for internal control.

A college or university's system of internal control is a process designed to provide reasonable assurance regarding the achievement of objectives in:

- effectiveness and efficiency of operations;

- reliability of financial reporting; and

- compliance with applicable laws and regulations.

This definition reflects certain fundamental concepts that internal control:

- is a process; it is a means to an end, not an end in itself;

- is effected by people; it is much more than policies, processes, and forms, it is people functioning throughout the organization;

- is geared to the achievement of objectives in several overlapping categories; and

- can be expected to provide only reasonable assurance regarding achievement of strategic, operational, and financial and compliance objectives.[2]

As college or university administrators provide leadership, control consciousness must be inherent in strategic planning, organizational design, and performance measurement responsibilities. They must own the internal control systems in their areas of responsibility. For example:

- *The president* provides leadership and direction to senior administrators. Together with them, the president shapes the values, principles, and major operating policies that form the foundation of the institution's internal control system.

- *Vice presidents* provide direction to senior administrators responsible for major functional areas such as colleges, departments, auxiliary operations, and support services. This should include an evaluation of objectives, risks, and the associated internal controls.

- *Deans and department heads* have line responsibility for designing and implementing control systems at detailed levels. They are also responsible to execute institutionwide control policies and procedures. These responsibilities should come with authority and accountability to the next higher level.

Other groups also play important roles. Governing boards provide important oversight. Financial and budget officers and their staffs often are involved in developing institutionwide budget and financial plans. Internal auditors contribute to the effectiveness of the controls, but they are not responsible for establishing or maintaining them. Outside parties, such as external auditors, also provide information useful in evaluating and improving internal control.[3]

Internal control consists of five interrelated components derived from basic college and university operations and administrative processes as follows.

- *Control environment.* The core of any educational institution is its people. They are the engines that drive the organization. Their individual attributes (integrity, ethical values, and competence) and the environment in which they operate determine the success of the institution.

- *Risk assessment.* Colleges and universities must be aware of and deal with the risks they face. They must set objectives that integrate key activities so the total organization operates in concert. They also must establish mechanisms to identify, analyze, and manage the related risks.

- *Control activities.* Control policies and procedures must be established and executed to help ensure that actions necessary to achieve the institution's objectives are effectively carried out.

- *Information and communication.* Surrounding these activities are information and communication systems. These enable the organization's people to capture and exchange the information needed to conduct, manage, and control its operations.

- *Monitoring.* The entire process must be monitored and modified as necessary.

Thus, the system can react dynamically to changing conditions.[4]

The "tone at the top" set by the governing board and the president defines the institution's control environment. The underlying systems of internal control are only as effective as the personnel who are charged with their implementation and utilization. The importance of effective systems of internal control and the control consciousness of personnel become ever more critical as an institution becomes more complex, entrepreneurial endeavors increase, and decentralization of traditional centralized control processes occurs with the implementation of new technology.

AUDIT COMMITTEES

Colleges and universities are generally governed by a board of trustees, regents, or directors that provide active and independent oversight. The board's degree of involvement varies at each institution. Its responsibilities are generally carried out through various committees. The board should have an audit committee and management should play an important role and be involved in committee meetings.

Activities Related to Internal Controls

Audit committees should review with internal auditors, and the external auditors, the extent to which their work can be relied on to detect control weaknesses or fraud. They should review their assessment of the effectiveness of, or weaknesses in, internal control systems and the adequacy of information systems controls and security. Audit committees should also review with management the institution's process of assessing risk that financial statements may be materially misstated.

Activities Related to Annual Financial Statements

Audit committees should assess whether financial statements are complete and consistent with information known to them. They should review with management, internal auditors, and the external auditors, as appropriate:

- explanations for significant variations in financial statements from the prior year and from budget or plan;

- the appropriateness of accounting principles followed by the institution, the effect of changes in accounting principles during the year, and the reasons for changes not mandated by standards setters or regulators;

- significant accounting and reporting issues addressed during the year and how they were resolved;

- representation letters given by management to the auditors and any difficulties in obtaining them;

- circumstances causing management to seek a second opinion on a significant accounting or auditing issue;

- the consistency between information in the financial statements and information included in "management's discussion and analysis" or elsewhere;

- the nature and substance of significant reserves or other estimates made by management having a material impact on the financial statements; and

- significant charges against reserves established in prior years.[5]

The audit committee may also provide oversight for interim financial reporting to external third parties on regulatory, legal, and tax matters. Depending on the complexity of the institution, matters such as international programs, environmental exposures, joint ventures, partnerships, and other entrepreneurial ventures may fall under the committee's purview.

The audit committee typically has oversight responsibilities for an institution's internal audit function. (See additional information about internal audit reporting relationships below.) These responsibilities may include activities such as approving annual internal audit plans, reviewing written summaries of internal audit reports, and participating in the hiring decision for an institution's chief audit executive.

The audit committee should meet routinely in executive sessions with the chief internal auditor and the external auditors. This provides the opportunity for the committee and the auditors to discuss matters related to the performance of their duties, the adequacy of resources and other matters of concern.

Institutions that do not have an audit committee in their governing board structure generally look to the business and finance committee to fulfill these responsibilities. Where both committee structures exist, institutions should define the roles of each because some responsibilities may overlap.

INTERNAL AUDITS

The roles and responsibilities of internal auditing professionals in higher education can be as diverse as the many institutions they serve. Over time, these roles have experienced significant change. As in other industries, internal auditing in higher education began as a monitoring function for management. It provided independent evaluations of information relating to significant aspects of institutional operations—primarily whether policies were being followed, objectives were being met, and control systems were functioning effectively. Management's need for information and assistance has grown, however, and the internal auditing function is now expected to make significant additional contributions to the success of academic institutions. Internal auditors' information, insight, skills, and abilities can make them important partners with an institution's management.

The governing and standard-setting body of the internal auditing profession is the Institute of Internal Auditors (IIA). Recognizing the dramatic changes impacting the profession, the IIA established an international Guidance Task Force in 1997 to review the status of guidance provided to audit practitioners and to recommend actions for continually improving and updating such guidance. Two of the first outcomes of that review were a detailed monograph and a proposed new definition of "internal auditing." That definition, approved by the IIA Board of Directors in June 1999, provides a starting point for discussion of this important institutional function:

> Internal auditing is an independent, objective assurance and consulting activity designed to add value and improve an organization's operations. It helps an organization accomplish its objectives by bringing a

systematic, disciplined approach to evaluate and improve the effectiveness of risk management, control, and governance processes.[6]

The retention of the concepts of "independence" and "objectivity" reflects the internal auditor's need to freely determine the scope of his or her work and effectively report the results. The previous restriction that internal auditing be conducted "within an organization" was eliminated to reflect the reality that the needs of some organizations for these services are being met by external providers. Although internal audit services in higher education are overwhelmingly provided by institutional employees, cosourcing and outsourcing arrangements do exist. The previous term "appraisal function" was replaced with "assurance and consulting activity" to convey the shift to a more proactive, customer-focused orientation. The concepts of "adding value" and "helping achieve organizational objectives" lift the focus of the internal auditing function to the organizational level and align it with the organization's critical success factors and core processes.[7]

Some of these elements of change in the practice and definition of the profession have sparked continuing discussion—even debate—among those affected in higher education. These dialogues will prove productive to the advancement and expanding role of internal auditing by members of management and audit committees.

Reporting Relationships

The IIA *Standards for the Professional Practice of Internal Auditing (Standards*[8]) state that an internal auditing department's position within an organization should be sufficient to allow it to be effective and conduct its work freely and objectively. A survey of chief audit executives in higher education conducted by the Association of College and University Auditors (ACUA) in 1999 indicated that the auditing functions at their institutions principally reported to the following.[9]

Board of trustees/directors	21%
President/chancellor	37%
Senior or executive vice president	14%
Vice president	19%
Controller	1%
Other	8%

Sixty-four percent of respondents indicated that their institutions had an audit committee. Of those, virtually all chief audit executives reported having direct access to those committees. Over half of the audit committees met quarterly with another 19 percent meeting every six months.

The combination of the above information yields a general picture of the positioning of internal auditing within an organization (figure 22-01). Internal auditing should operate under policies established by its institution's governing board. Generally, an audit charter should exist that provides a statement of purpose, authority, and responsibility for the internal auditing function, which is consistent with the IIA *Standards*.

Scope of the Internal Auditor's Responsibility

The audit charter should set forth the auditor's responsibility and, as such, grant the internal auditor access to people, records, and property. The charter does not spell out what areas should be audited. The internal auditor should be concerned with every phase of institutional activity. The internal auditor's responsibilities should include:

- working with management to assess institutional risk and developing an audit work plan that considers the results of the risk assessment;

- examining financial transactions for accuracy and compliance with institutional policies;

Figure 22-01

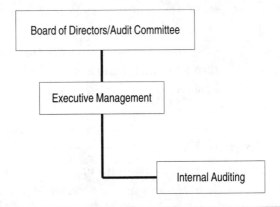

Facilities Management Organization

Board of Directors/Audit Committee

Executive Management

Internal Auditing

- testing the timeliness, reliability, and usefulness of institutional records and reports;

- determining the level of compliance with required internal policies and procedures, state and federal laws, and government regulations;

- evaluating program performance;

- coordinating work with external auditors; and

- reviewing the contractual and project management control for projects.

Coordination with External Auditors

The internal auditor performs an important role for management by interacting with various external-auditing entities (detailed later in this chapter). Generally, oversight of the work and products of external auditors is the responsibility of an institution's governing board; however, the actual coordination of the external auditor's work may be performed primarily by the internal auditor and/or the controller's office. In some instances, internal auditing staff may perform work at the request of the external auditors. The ACUA survey indicated an average of 5 percent of respondents' audit staff time was spent providing assistance to external auditors. Use of internal auditing resources for this purpose should be carefully considered. The cost of using internal versus external resources must be balanced against other priorities of the internal audit function that would be foregone if internal auditors work for the external auditors.

Internal and external audit work should be coordinated to ensure adequate audit coverage and minimize duplicate efforts. The internal auditor can rely on the scope and frequency of the external and/or federal audit work and either reduce the scope of his or her work accordingly or allocate efforts to other areas. Likewise, external auditors will try to rely on internal audit work when it is applicable and will usually ask to see internal auditors' work products as part of their examinations.

Because the federal government requires external audits for several different purposes, internal auditors should remain aware of federal audit requirements. All audits performed on behalf of the government must conform to federal audit standards.

Affiliated Entities

Many institutions have foundations or other entities for which they are fiscally responsible. Although these may be separate legal entities, foundation activities are often intertwined with those of the institution. Foundation personnel may be custodians of institution-owned property and participate in or influence institutional decisions. In addition, some independent colleges and universities have wholly-owned subsidiaries. These may be units held as investments or organizations that provide essential support to the institution, such as a hotel, real estate holding company, or for-profit commercial venture. If these entities are under the control of the institution, they should be considered for inclusion in the audit plan.

Types of Internal Audits and Other Activities

The types of audits and services that internal auditors can provide are comprehensive and varied. Most audits or reviews will have multiple objectives and span two or more of the "types" of audits that follow. Respondents to the ACUA survey indicated that an average of 20 percent of internal audit staff time was spent in the area of operational auditing; 13 percent in management advisory services; 11 percent in financial auditing; 6 percent in investigative activities; and 6 percent in information technology auditing.

Operational Audits

An operational audit evaluates activities of a critical function or process with the objective of giving management assurances about the strengths and success of those activities. These audits can provide an objective examination of operational systems, organizational structures, achievement of goals, control systems, and procedures.

Virtually any department or support function within an institution that has measurable goals and objectives is a candidate for an operational audit. Operations are measured and evaluated against standards set by management. An operational audit should determine whether or not maximum benefit is received for the resources expended. When performing an operational audit of a highly technical or complex activity, the auditor may require the assistance of a consultant or subject matter specialist familiar with the activity being audited.

Management Advisory Services

The advancement of management advisory services (MAS) represents an important example of internal auditors being responsive to management and using their unique skills and abilities to assist in special ways. Advisory services are broadly defined. They may include performing specialized reviews at management's request, serving on special task forces or committees, conducting training sessions for employees of the institution, and consulting. In the course of their overall activities, internal auditors become knowledgeable and gain broad insights that make them particularly capable of performing MAS projects. In addition, the internal auditors' organizational independence and objectivity contribute to their ability to provide direct, unbiased information in the review or consulting activities they perform.

Many internal auditors are providing a valuable management advisory service in the area of coordinating and/or facilitating control self-assessment (CSA) activities at their institutions. CSA equips employees in areas across an institution to conduct assessments designed to provide immediate feedback about the adequacy of controls of various types. With the performance of a CSA, some of the positive benefits of an internal audit–like review can be performed in areas that the limited resources of the internal auditing staff may never reach.

Financial Audits

Financial audits determine whether the financial statements or other reports provide timely, accurate, relevant, reliable, and complete information upon which to base decisions. Financial audits concentrate on accounting controls in the principal areas of control of assets, systems of authorization and approval, and separation of accounting duties from those concerned with operations or custody of assets. In financial audits, the primary concerns are the determination of the reliability and accuracy of financial data, including supporting records, and the evaluation of internal financial controls.

Investigative Audits

Fraud and other financial irregularities may be committed by managers, employees, students, and others who have access to an institution's information and resources. The internal auditing department is often called on to make special investigations when such incidents occur or when there is suspicion of such an occurrence.

The IIA *Standards* set out the internal auditor's responsibilities in the area of fraud: when significant internal control weaknesses are discovered, tests should be performed to determine if an irregularity occurred because of the weakness; when unusual circumstances or transactions occur, the auditor should adopt a skeptical attitude with regard to answers to questions; and the auditor should be alert in thinking how a fraud might take place.

Institutional policy should be established so employees know which office to contact if they become aware of or suspect fiscal improprieties. Often, the internal auditor fills this role. If this is the case, the internal auditor should be properly trained to receive such information and should have clear procedures for contacting appropriate law enforcement agencies at the first indication of criminal activity.

The internal auditor performs three categories of service for the institution in dealing with white-collar crime: he or she recommends means to deter or prevent it, strives to detect it in the conduct of other audit activities, and compiles evidence when conducting investigative reviews.

Compliance Audits

Compliance audits are concerned with adherence to applicable policy, laws, regulations, and other administrative requirements. Internal auditors must spend an increasing amount of time on such audits because of the severe consequences of noncompliance with certain regulations. These consequences can be monetary refunds, loss of future funds, or damage to the institution's reputation. In many cases, compliance audits may help prevent adverse findings in an external audit.

Information Technology and the Internal Auditor

Information, along with the systems and technologies that support its accuracy and integrity, often represents one of the most valuable assets of an organization. Effective management of this information and related information technology (IT) has become critically important to the survival and success of an organization. Many organizations recognize the potential benefits that technology can yield. Successful organizations, however, understand and manage the risks associated with implementing new technologies. Thus management and auditors need to have an appreciation for and a basic understanding of the risks and constraints of IT in order to provide effective direction and adequate controls.[10]

With the widespread use of IT, special problems in the control and security of data demand the attention of management and the internal auditor. The objectives and essential characteristics of accounting control do not change by using IT; however, organizational structures and procedures used in IT systems may differ from those used in manual data processing.

Auditors are often called on to consult and advise on IT security and control-related matters. In many organizations the IT auditors are expected to be involved when major new or upgraded systems are being developed, acquired, or implemented. Through experience, management has recognized the cost benefits of having IT auditors involved on the front-end of new systems initiatives. Recognizing that management and internal auditors need a framework of generally applicable and accepted information technology practices to benchmark their existing and planned IT resources, the Information Systems Audit and Control Foundation designed COBIT® (Control Objectives for Information and Related Technology) as a tool and educational resource for IT control professionals. The COBIT® framework provides precise and clear definitions of a minimum set of controls to ensure effectiveness, efficiency, and economy of each IT process and IT resource utilization.

Traditional IT Controls

Traditional IT controls fall into two categories: general controls and application controls. General controls encompass overall control issues such as planning and acquisition, implementation, operations, data and physical security, and systems software. These controls refer to the overall administration of the management information system area, system development life cycle, and how well the unit is run. Applications controls relate to the methods used to ensure completeness, accuracy, and consistency in an individual application. These controls apply to specific systems, such as the payroll system. For example, a combination lock on computer room doors to bar unauthorized access is a general control. A device that rejects any payroll transaction that does not have an authenticated Social Security number is an application control.

An IT control system must be concerned with evaluating the system's definition, related input, and operating procedures to ensure adequate checks on processing and reporting functions. Effective programming, adequate documentation of programs and systems, separation of responsibilities, security of equipment, programs, data communications, and periodic audits provide the means for achieving internal control in a computerized system. Systems today operate across a wide variety of platforms such as, but not limited to, mainframe computers, midrange computers, client server systems, wide-area and local area networks, desktop workstations (stand-alone or networked), the World Wide Web, or an intranet.

Audits of New Systems

Information systems may be developed by internal staff or external contractors, or may be purchased as a commercial off-the-shelf product. Some development efforts result in large, complex, integrated systems; others in smaller, distributed ones. Management and internal auditors are concerned with the reliability, integrity, and control of these systems. Each type of system requires different expertise for both the information technologists and auditors. Regardless of how the proposed system is acquired, the scope of the audit should assess the functionality and controls that will be in the system and determine their adequacy in safeguarding institutional assets and meeting business needs.

For systems developed internally, the IT auditor should review the systems development life cycle to determine whether the development was documented properly at each particular step and all appropriate development steps were included. The IT auditor also needs to ensure that proper controls are designed and implemented into the system and that sound project management is in place so that business goals are met and the project is delivered on time and on budget.

For purchased systems, the auditor should assess the processes for selecting and evaluating both the vendor and the product. These processes should include, at a minimum, an evaluation of product features versus system requirements, vendor financial stability, availability of documentation, and vendor support. These procedures ensure that appropriate steps were taken in evaluating the software. Purchased systems can be installed with no changes or with extensive modifications. Any type of system must be reviewed to ascertain accountability and reliability.

New Technology

Methods of controlling advanced client/server, Web-based, online and distributed systems can differ; however, the underlying objectives for security and control remain the same. For example, users and transactions require authorization, data and equipment need safeguarding, and applications and systems must be auditable. Operationally, processing results should be accurate and timely, and resources should be used efficiently and effectively.

Organizations have addressed the challenges of distributed systems, advanced networking, communications systems, and powerful workstations by establishing and relying on technical audit personnel and training generalists on the audit staff. Smaller institutions, or institutions where the internal audit function lacks IT audit expertise, should engage consultants to do these reviews.

Audit Tools

New technology includes easy-to-use audit tools and automated workpaper solutions. Computer-assisted audit techniques (CAATS) are available in mainframes, servers, and personal computers. CAATS are particularly effective when used to analyze the vast amount of data that is stored in large systems. With CAATS, an auditor can extract information, compare files, verify counts and values, and perform other functions such as analytical calculations, trend analysis and statistical analysis. Many vendors offer statistical and analytical tools for auditing computer files and records. Other tools useful in auditing include query and ad-hoc report-writing systems, spreadsheet packages, graphics systems, word processors, database systems, scheduling software, and application development tools.

Automated workpaper software was developed to convert the traditional paper-based audit process into a more efficient, automated process. It addresses the needs of an evolving audit department that must deliver high quality audits with fewer resources in a shorter timeframe. Automated workpaper software allows auditors to create risk assessments, planning documents, workpapers, workpaper review comments, audit reports, time reports, and expense reports during the audit process.

Specialized Computer Subjects

Certain areas require a high level of audit expertise. Audits of operating systems or distributed systems in an open systems environment often require specialists. This is particularly true in a rapidly changing environment where it is difficult to keep pace with the staggering variety of new technologies. In large institutions, the internal audit department should assess the adequacy of internal control in these complex areas. In some institutions, consultants may be hired to do these reviews.

Selection of Areas to Be Audited

An integral part of the internal audit function is the development of an audit plan. The relative risk of various activities is the most critical factor in selecting internal audit projects. In determining what to audit, when to audit it, and for what purpose, the auditor must compare the relative benefits expected from the audit to the estimated costs of conducting the audit. The benefits result from recommendations to improve control or various aspects of operations. There is also the benefit of psychological deterrence. When employees know all activities are subject to review, they may follow policies and procedures more closely.

When developing an audit plan, the auditor must:

- develop a comprehensive list of all areas subject to review;

- devise a system (which includes management input) to assess the risk associated with each area;

- rank areas in order of the magnitude of risk to the institution;

- communicate this risk assessment to the institution's key decision makers; and

- select the top-ranked areas as the nucleus of the audit plan.

An annual schedule of activities and functions to be audited should be prepared. Often, a midrange plan of two or more years is also considered when developing the schedule. Sixty-one percent of respondents to the ACUA survey cited earlier in this chapter prepared one-year plans. Eight percent prepared two-year plans, 13 percent prepared three-year plans, and the balance prepared plans longer than three years.

Even with limited information and the subjective nature of risk assessment, the assessment exercises to develop audit plans are useful for two reasons: they give management a framework in which to consider overall risk, and can make management aware of risks it had not considered.

Development of an internal audit plan is important, but the plan must remain flexible, and it must be subject to change as the institution adjusts to changes. The departure of key personnel, changes in laws or regulations, and other factors can affect the auditor's plan. An effective internal audit department is knowledgeable of and sensitive to these changes in the environment.

Performing the Audit Program

Research and Preparation for the Audit Project

To perform an audit, the auditor needs information, accumulated through research and a survey of the area or activity to be audited. This process allows the auditor to develop a profile of the activity to be audited. Thoroughness in conducting preaudit research and the preliminary survey may reduce or eliminate time-consuming audit tests. Adequate research helps the auditor understand the operations of the audited unit to render more informed recommendations. Research findings often direct the auditor's approach in performing the preliminary survey and defining the scope of an audit.

Verification and Evaluation

The audit program should list tests and procedures required for each step of the process to ensure verification and evaluation of the program. Each audit is unique, and it is not always possible or advantageous to develop a standard audit program. Audits require a broad range of techniques for testing activities, such as interviewing, observing, and financial analysis. Care must be taken to ensure that all work performed is relevant to the purpose and scope of the audit. Among the techniques that an auditor may use in the audit process are creating flow charts and statistical sampling.

Communications During an Audit

An area or department is generally made aware of an upcoming audit soon after the annual audit plan is approved. The first specific communication, however, may be an opening or entrance conference with management of the unit to be audited. This meeting provides the opportunity to establish the purpose and scope of the audit and to explain the methods and objectives of the audit process. It is also a time for management to express any specific requests or concerns it may have.

During the course of the audit, a continuous dialogue should be maintained between the auditor and the head and staff of the audited unit. Communicating with and involving the audited unit's staff ensures that they stay informed of the progress on the audit. It also provides a forum for exchanging views on findings as they are developed. Often this approach leads to a resolution of problems before the audit is completed. It also tends to dispel any adversarial attitudes that may be associated with the auditing function.

The Audit Report

The IIA *Standards* provide for three types of reports to management: verbal, interim, and written. Items of a less significant nature may be communicated verbally to management. This informal communication does not, however, provide a means for later follow-up by either management or the auditor. Interim reports are useful when a finding during the audit requires the immediate attention of management. These may be issued verbally or in writing. The traditional report, which may take many forms, is one issued in writing at the conclusion of the audit or review engagement. Usually, a draft of the report is discussed at an exit conference with management of the audited unit. This conference provides an opportunity to clarify points in the report before its formal issuance. Management's responses to any comments or recommendations are generally incorporated into the report.

The audit report should communicate the purpose, scope, and results of the project. It should include the auditor's recommendations for any necessary action or change in operations.

Follow-up

When an institution invests the time and resources necessary to conduct an audit, it is important that any resulting recommendations be acted on by management. After adequate time has passed for implementation of audit recommendations, a follow-up review should be conducted to determine that appropriate actions have been taken by the audited unit. The internal auditor may choose only a subset of all recommendations for actual follow-up. Results of audit follow-up may be reported to executive management or the audit committee as a means of reporting responsiveness to and effectiveness of the audit function.

Staff Qualifications and Training

Historically, great emphasis has been placed on accounting training as a qualification for an internal auditor. As organizations have become more complex, however, the nature and purpose of the internal audit function has expanded. Internal audit staff members may represent a variety of education and experience in areas such as general business, information systems, liberal arts, and technical fields. Audit departments should strive to maintain a staff with the capability to be successful in performing the evolving roles that internal auditing functions are called on to fill.

Both the United States General Accounting Office (GAO) and IIA have adopted minimum continuing education standards for internal auditors. In addition, internal auditors holding professional certifications such as certified internal auditor (CIA), certified information system auditor (CISA), certified fraud examiner (CFE), certified management accountant (CMA), or certified public accountant (CPA) must meet established continuing education to maintain certification.

Staff training is a responsibility of internal auditing management. Since the auditing department may be called on to evaluate a wide range of activities, members of the audit staff should be trained to a high level of proficiency in the use of audit tools such as data extraction and evaluation and sampling software. On-the-job training, departmental training sessions, formal courses, and seminars can be used to meet continuing education requirements. Many professional organizations and associations offer courses for internal auditors. The Association of College and University Auditors provides such opportunities directed specifically at internal auditors in higher education.

EVALUATING THE INTERNAL AUDIT FUNCTION

The audit committee or executive management should ensure a periodic independent review of the audit department. The IIA *Standards* on quality assurance state an external review by a qualified party should be performed at least once every three years. Independent evaluations, referred to as "peer reviews," may be offered or facilitated by the IIA Quality Assurance Review Service, CPA firms, consultants, and ACUA. For institutions that want an evaluation of their internal audit department, ACUA refers internal auditors from other institutions that have been trained in and agree to adhere to the standards prescribed by ACUA in its *Quality Assurance Review Handbook*.[11] The IIA *Business-Focused Quality Assurance Review Manual for Internal Auditing*[12] is an additional guide for conducting such reviews.

EXTERNAL AUDITS

External audits of institutions can be categorized several different ways: by who requests them, the authority that requires them, who performs them, or the subject matter being audited. This section addresses these various categories, starting with the distinctions between self-requested audits that are arranged by the institution itself and involve the selection and engagement of independent auditors to perform the desired or necessary audit services, and those audits that are beyond the institution's control, required and performed by government agencies or sponsors.

Whether self-requested at an independent institution or imposed and performed by a governmental unit at a public institution, the most fundamental, traditional, and important audit of an institution is the independent audit of its annual financial statements. Institutions that expend at least $300,000 in federal funds annually are required to have their financial statement audits conducted in accordance with Office of Management and Budget (OMB) Circular A-133 and generally accepted governmental auditing standards established by the Comptroller General of the United States.

It is still common for higher education institutions to arrange for their financial statements to be audited by a certified public accounting firm in accordance with generally accepted auditing standards established by the American Institute of Certified Public Accountants (AICPA), and for the institution to publish these statements with the auditor's stand-alone opinion on them for most public reporting purposes.

Some public institutions are not required to issue stand-alone financial statements or A-133 reports because their financial and federal award information is included in the statements and reports issued for the higher education system or local or state government through which the institution is governed.

Procurement of Audit Services

When an institution is responsible for making its own arrangements for the required audits, the procurement of audit services should be undertaken in a manner that:

- clearly identifies the scope of the engagement, the services desired, and sufficient, relevant information about the institution to be audited;

- provides for open and fair competition, including opportunities for auditors who qualify as small business or minority enterprises;

- complies with the institution's service procurement policies;

- establishes appropriate criteria related to cost, service, and experience for the evaluation of audit service providers' proposals and qualifications;

- involves those with technical audit competence in the evaluation of proposals and qualifications;

- outlines agreed-upon terms of the audit engagement in a written document; and

- provides opportunities to assess the auditor's performance and communicate that assessment before the next audit cycle.[13]

Most major CPA firms provide a range of consulting as well as audit services. Institutions should exercise caution in engaging the firm that performs the financial statement audit for consulting assignments or other projects that could be performed by institutional employees. For example, when an institution's indirect costs have exceeded $1 million in the prior year, OMB Circular A-133 actually precludes an institution from using the same auditor to audit its financial statements as the one who also prepared the institution's indirect cost proposal or central service cost allocation because of the perception of lack of independence.

OMB Circular A-133

The Office of Management and Budget is a federal administrative agency that develops regulations for other agencies to promote consistency within the government through standard procedures for common functions. The regulations apply to colleges and universities by being passed along as terms of grant and contract agreements from the federal agencies.

Since the issuance in 1990 of **OMB** Circular A-133, applicable to nonprofit organizations receiving federal funding, a higher education institution's financial statements and annual federal funds expenditures are required to be audited by an independent external auditor under the single audit concept. The single audit concept was recognized by the U.S. Congress in 1984 when it passed the Single Audit Act to reduce the audit burden on state and local governmental units. This act was an effort to address the issue of significant time and expense that small government entities had experienced responding throughout each year to different auditors from various sponsoring federal and state agencies as well as from independent CPA firms, many asking similar questions about the entity's policies, practices, and accounts and performing similar transaction tests. It was promulgated for state and local governments in 1988 by **OMB** Circular A-128, *Audits of State and Local Governments.* In 1997, the **OMB** issued revised Circular A-133, *Audits of States, Local Governments, and Nonprofit Organizations* and rescinded Circular A-128.

For most higher education institutions, the total of annual federal financial assistance in the form of student aid and research funding surpasses the $300,000 expenditure threshold that calls for an "A-133 audit." The director of the **OMB** must review this threshold every two years and is permitted to adjust it.

An A-133 audit report includes a schedule of federal awards that lists all federal fund expenditures during the period under audit, by funding agency, pass-through organization, and federal program number from the Catalog of Federal Domestic Assistance (CFDA).

Reports Required of the Independent Auditor

At the conclusion of a financial statement audit, the independent auditor will issue an opinion letter on the institution's basic financial statements and generally provide a management letter. If the audit has been conducted to meet **OMB** Circular A-133 standards, the independent auditor is also responsible for issuing reports about the institution's system of internal control related to the administration of federal programs; compliance with laws, regulations, and specific contract or grant provisions; audit findings and questioned costs pertaining to federal programs (if applicable); and summary information about the audit and the institution's federal funds expenditures on the OMB-prescribed data collection form.

An Opinion on the Institution's Basic Financial Statements

The basic financial statements for all independent colleges and universities and some public institutions include the statement of financial position, the statement of activities, the statement of cash flows, and footnote disclosures. These are the statements often issued in a stand-alone document with the auditor's opinion as to whether or not they are stated "fairly in all material respects in conformity with generally accepted accounting principles." (See OMB Circular A-133.) The auditors will also cite having followed "generally accepted auditing standards" in performance of the audit if they adhere to practice standards of the AICPA. When the financial statement audit has been performed by government auditors or is issued as part of the reporting package required by OMB Circular A-133, the auditors' opinion will state that the audit was conducted in accordance with government auditing standards (issued by the Comptroller General of the United States). In the case of A-133 audits, the financial statements must be accompanied by a schedule of federal awards and the auditors' opinion on the financial statements will include a supplementary paragraph that refers to the audit of the information in the schedule.

Management Letters

Standards of the AICPA require members who conduct audits to communicate to management, the audit committee, or the governing body of an organization any weaknesses in an organization's internal control system that are noted during the audit. This communication is commonly accomplished in writing by means of a "management letter." The management letter contains the auditors' specific findings or comments, recommendations to address any noted problems, and suggestions where opportunities for improvement were evident. There can be two levels of management letter—one addressed to the governing body or audit committee to advise it of the most significant problems or control issues and one containing the less consequential audit findings addressed to a senior member of the organization's management team. Management commonly responds in writing to each of the management letter's comments and recommendations.

When OMB Circular A-133 went into effect, the function of management letters became somewhat controversial. Traditionally, management letters had been provided as confidential documents between an institution's auditors and its executive management. With the advent of A-133, it was suggested by some interpretations of the Circular that management letters were now part of a public reporting package. Subsequent revisions of OMB Circular A-133 have clarified the kinds of audit findings that need to be reported as part of an A-133 audit, and the format for their reporting. Audit findings are classified as material weaknesses or as reportable conditions that are not considered material weaknesses. Where applicable, audit findings and management responses are reported for A-133 purposes in a schedule of current year audit findings, the institution's corrective action plan on those findings, and a summary schedule of prior year audit findings. External auditors' findings or suggestions that do not qualify as material or reportable may still appear in a management letter to the institution, and the auditors will refer to the date of this communication in their report on internal control based on their audit of the financial statements. A copy of the management letter and the auditors' required communication to the audit committee must be provided to federal agencies and pass-through entities that request them.

The Auditor's Report on Internal Control

Audit procedures require the external auditor to gain an understanding of the internal control structure of the organization being audited and to assess control risk so that audit tests can be properly designed to provide sufficient, reliable evidence for the auditor to form an opinion on the financial statements. For A-133 reporting purposes, a separate report on internal control is required wherein the auditor describes the scope and results of the internal control testing related to the financial statements and the institution's federal awards, referring to the schedule of findings and questioned costs (if applicable).

The Auditor's Report on Compliance

Under A-133, the external auditor is also required to report on "compliance with laws, regulations, and the provisions of contracts or grant agreements, the noncompliance with which could have a material effect on the financial statements. . . or . . . each major program" with reference, if applicable, to the schedule of findings and questioned costs. The external auditor may combine the reports on compliance and internal control, or separate them in different ways, for instance, with one report on compliance and internal control over financial reporting (based on testing done for the financial statement audit) and a second report on compliance with major program requirements and internal control over that compliance (based on testing of federal awards and other steps assessing the institution's compliance with relevant laws and regulations).

Data Collection Form

The 1997 revision of OMB Circular A-133 instituted a standard data collection form to accompany all organizations' submissions of A-133 audit reports to the U.S. Census Bureau's federal audit clearinghouse. This form contains information about the audit and lists the federal programs that were audited—by CFDA number, program name, and amount, and noting for each if there were applicable audit findings or questioned costs. This form requires certification statements by the auditors and "a senior level representative of the auditee (e.g., state controller, director of finance, chief executive officer, or chief financial officer)," according to A-133. This certification responsibility often falls, therefore, to the senior business officer at higher education institutions.

Cognizant and Oversight Agencies

Institutions that spend more that $25 million a year in federal awards are assigned a cognizant agency for audit purposes, usually designated as the federal agency that awards the predominant portion of direct funding to that institution. Institutions that do not meet the $25 million threshold and are not assigned a cognizant agency will be under the general oversight of the agency that provides the predominant portion of their federal funding. The great majority of higher education institutions have as their cognizant or oversight agency the U.S. Department of Education, the U.S. Department of Health and Human Services, or the U.S. Department of Defense.

Coordinated Audits

Coordinated audits are audits that implement the single audit concept via distributed and shared efforts among an institution's independent certified public accounting firm or state auditors, its internal auditors, and/or its federal cognizant agency's auditors. When OMB Circular A-133 was first issued, the three-way approach that involved the federal auditors was employed primarily by major research institutions whose federal cognizant agency was the U.S. Department of Defense's Office of Naval Research and where auditors from the Defense Contract Audit Agency were "in residence" at that institution. These resident federal auditors were regularly performing audits of the institution's direct and indirect charges to federal grants, its procurement system, and of other elements pertinent to A-133 requirements. The coordinated audit approach was considered a way to save on the expense of audit fees since institutions would not have to pay independent firms to perform specific audit steps on their campuses where federal and/or internal auditors were still going to do so. However, the coordination of responsibility that was required to perform all A-133 audit steps and to report their results in accordance with A-133 requirements was a more cumbersome task in practice than in theory. Furthermore, the number of institutions assigned to the Office of Naval Research for cognizant agency oversight was reduced in the mid-1990s.

Recent revisions of Circular A-133 do not refer to coordinated audits. Most of the institutions that still use a coordinated audit approach to the A-133 audit involve only the internal and nonfederal auditors, with the external auditors taking responsibility for the audit reports. The coordinated audit approach should be assessed periodically to consider the costs of coordination and to determine that overall audit coverage is neither excessive nor insufficient.

Institutions Exempt from Circular A-133

According to OMB Circular A-133, "Non-federal entities that expend less that $300,000 in federal awards are exempt from federal audit requirements for that year, except as noted, but records must be available for review or audit by appropriate officials of the federal agency, pass-through entity, and General Accounting Office (GAO)." The exception provided in the referenced section specifies that the federal agencies or GAO may still conduct or arrange for additional audits of institutions that are otherwise exempt from A-133.

Institutions that followed a biennial audit cycle in the early 1990s are exempt from the annual audit and reporting provisions of OMB Circular A-133, but must report on a biennial basis. The audit provisions of OMB Circular A-133 are not applicable to non-U.S.-based institutions.

References for A-133 Audits

Government publications available in printed form and on the Internet include:

- OMB Circular A-133 and related OMB compliance supplement, which sets forth the compliance requirements to be tested;

- OMB Circular A-110, *Grants and Agreements with Institutions of Higher Education, Hospitals, and Other Nonprofit Organizations*; and

- OMB Circular A-21, *Cost Principles for Educational Institutions.*

In addition, NACUBO's *Federal Auditing Information Service* is a two-volume subscription publication that provides source documents, extensive information and advice, and regular updates about OMB Circular A-133 and other federal audit requirements and issues.

Other Federal Agency Auditors

U.S. General Accounting Office

The GAO, an arm of the legislative branch and under the direction of the Comptroller General, is charged with ascertaining that both federal agencies and recipients of federal funds are expending funds appropriated by Congress in accordance with congressional intent and in an effective and efficient manner. For instance, the GAO has audited universities' implementation of the Bayh-Dole Act, which involves the transfer of technology developed with government research support into the private sector. An allegation of misspent federal funds or any other issue in higher education that attracts the attention of a member of Congress can become the subject of a GAO audit.

The GAO establishes standards to be followed by GAO, by offices of federal inspectors general, and by nonfederal auditors whose clients are covered by OMB Circular A-133.[14] These government auditing standards are published in a small handbook known as the "yellow book" because of its cover's bright color.

Internal Revenue Service (IRS)

Since the early 1990s, the IRS has focused attention on the nonprofit sector by means of its Coordinated Examination Program (CEP). A CEP audit is a comprehensive review of an institution's potentially taxable and reportable activities. The duration of these audits at various institutions ranges from one to four years. It covers payroll tax and benefit reporting; financial information return filing (IRS Form 990); unrelated business income tax (UBIT) reporting (IRS Form 990T); payments to independent contractors, nonresident aliens, and students; use of tax-exempt bond proceeds; and any practices that could be considered private inurement instead of meeting the public, tax-exempt purpose of the institution. Any one of these topics may also be selected by the IRS as the sole focus of a targeted audit at an institution.

The Environmental Protection Agency (EPA)

In the late 1990s, the EPA started a region-by-region program of audits at institutions of higher education. These audits are unannounced, several days in duration, and intense in their coverage. The EPA auditors focus on finding and correcting any violations of laws or regulations intended to safeguard the environment, visiting campus facilities such as research laboratories, art studios, and storage areas for maintenance supplies and making direct inquiries of those who work in these areas. Substantial costs in fines to the institution can result from these audits.

Intercollegiate Athletics

The National Collegiate Athletics Association (NCAA) requires its Division I members to perform a mandatory self-study and peer review of their intercollegiate athletics programs at least once every 10 years. Institutions must establish a series of committees with broad representation from campuswide constituents. These committees conduct their self-study based on NCAA guidelines and prepare a written report of their findings and recommendations for improvement. An external committee of peer reviewers evaluates the thoroughness and accuracy of the report and makes a recommendation to the NCAA as to whether or not the institution should be certified. This process covers four broad topics:

- governance and commitment to rules compliance;
- academic integrity;
- fiscal integrity; and
- equity, welfare, and sportsmanship.

Under the *governance and commitment to rules compliance* heading, each Division I member institution must have an evaluation of its rules compliance program performed by an authority outside of the athletics department at least once every three years. The NCAA allows institutions and evaluators to determine for themselves the scope and depth of the rules compliance evaluation. While such evaluations can be performed by a variety of qualified on- or off-campus individuals or organizations, institution-based internal audit departments are very often seen as the most appropriate and qualified to conduct them. The Association of College and University Auditors has developed a guide to assist internal auditors in performing these evaluations.

Under the *fiscal integrity* heading, each Division I member institution with an intercollegiate athletics operating budget (excluding staff salaries) in excess of $300,000 must engage a qualified auditor who is not a staff member of the institution to perform an annual financial audit of its intercollegiate athletics activities. The audit is to be performed under certain guidelines developed by the NCAA and the American Institute of Certified Public Accountants. The auditor's report is to be presented no later than 12 months after the fiscal year end to the institution's chief executive officer, and it is intended for internal use only.

The U.S. Department of Education's requirement that a similar financial audit of athletics activities be performed every three years was repealed by Congress effective for institutions' 1999 fiscal years. Instead, colleges and universities that participate in any federal student financial aid program and have intercollegiate athletics programs are required to report certain financial and statistical data annually in compliance with the Equity in Athletics Disclosure Act (EADA) of 1994. The EADA report includes statistical data from the NCAA's Gender Equity Survey, prepared by the institution's athletics department and selected summarized financial data from the audited financial report (required by the NCAA as noted above). The EADA report must be made available by the institution for public inspection.

TRENDS AND DEVELOPMENTS

Tremendous advances in the complexity, power, and variety of computer systems, hardware, and software have revolutionized the way organizations work. Information technology is now an integral part of the strategic direction that organizations take. The future success and growth of many organizations will largely depend on their ability to embrace and understand emerging technologies and use them to improve business processes and attain business goals.

Information technology is constantly evolving, allowing organizations and individuals to work and communicate in ways never before thought possible. The Internet, for example, has created a whole new medium for organizations to communicate and conduct business on a global level. Desktop computer usage continues to grow, and various new hardware, including notebook computers, handheld computers, personal digital assistants (PDAs), cellular phones, and electronic appliances are also being used to communicate, store, and process data. In the coming years, significant change will continue to occur in developmental methodology; storage, processors, communications, database, and interface technologies; and knowledge-based systems. These areas are likely to experience decentralization and changes in standards, communications, operating environments, database management, workstations, and security.

These technologies compel management and auditors to assess the additional risk associated with their development. Risk assessment and the installation of controls are decisions made by management on the collective advice of users, internal auditors, and technical specialists. The risk categories associated with these technologies are similar to the traditional concerns of auditors of management information systems:

- data accuracy and integrity;
- security, including authorization to use systems and physical protection of hardware and software;
- recovery, backup, and error handling;
- compliance with standards and with internal procedures to ensure compatibility; and
- management of the technology risk within the organization.

Developmental Methodology

An effective developmental methodology is critical to ensure that new systems development projects meet business needs and are delivered in a timely, cost-effective manner. Auditors will continue to be concerned about new systems development and should analyze the associated risks and exposures inherent in systems development projects. From a technology perspective, the use of computer-aided software engineering (CASE) tools, rapid application development (RAD) tools, and object-oriented software will enhance systems development. In addition to the traditional concerns about systems development, auditors are also concerned about the consistent and proper use of these tools. "Change management" and "version control" will become more critical concepts of internal control.

Storage Technology

Data storage is at the heart of the worldwide information revolution. Continuing developments in data storage technology allow for more storage capability, longer storage life, and improved error-correction capability and storage mechanisms. Increasing amounts of scientific, technical, and financial data are being created and saved in digital data storage systems, and there is a need to expedite the access and use of this data. Further, a variety of different data and formats need to be addressed, such as images, video, audio, tables, graphics, algorithms, and documents. Storage technologies include floppy disks, hard drives, CD-ROM, digital versatile disk (DVD), optical disk storage, quarter-inch cartridge tape, digital audio tape (DAT), digital linear tape (DLT), and smart cards.

Auditors should be aware of the security risks related to data storage media. Physical security of data storage media is critical, as data will become more subject to theft as the size of the storage medium shrinks and the number of personal digital assistants (PDAs), laptop computers, and other portable devices increases; other risks concern the compatibility of hardware and software as well as technological obsolescence.

Communications Technology

Fast-packet switching, Integrated Services Digital Network (ISDN), Digital Subscriber Lines (DSL), cable modems, fiber optics, and satellites are communications technologies that transmit data at high speeds. Many of these technologies will have the capability to integrate images, voice, data, and video communication through digital switching and transmission. In addition to being used to develop global networks, it is believed that these high-speed communications technologies will soon replace the traditional telephone modem dial-up access to corporate networks and the Internet. High costs and the lack of the necessary infrastructure are obstacles to high-speed communications implementation. Greater acceptance of these technologies can be expected as the cost decreases over the next few years. Auditors should be aware of the capabilities, limitations, and risks of each type of transmission media, as each type is different in terms of cost, performance, and reliability. Heightened scrutiny will be necessary as access and services are expanded.

Database Technologies

Database management systems (DBMS) are software programs that aid in organizing, controlling, and storing the data needed by application programs. They enable data, including sensitive data, to be shared across several locations with improved availability, reduced data redundancy, decreased access time, and enhanced security. These technologies also permit nontraditional documents, such as maps, to be stored and managed.

DBMSs are common components in many of today's emerging applications. For instance, DBMSs are being used to support the data warehouse concept and typically serve as back-end data repositories for Web-based applications. Traditional risks of DBMSs include the lack of coordination of database integrity during network or systems failure, lack of change synchronization between locations, and lack of data security. New risks are associated with the use of databases as a component of Web-based applications.

Interface Technology

Technologies such as image processing, voice recognition products, and computer vision promise improved usage of document storage, processing, problem solving, and the automation of tasks. Concomitant risks of fraud, business interruption, and error should be anticipated. Controls to ensure the integrity and security of data—both image vision and real—are vital. Steps should be taken to ensure that traditional audit and security controls for paper-based systems are not reduced or absent in electronic document workflow. The auditor should review existing controls.

Knowledge-Based Systems

Knowledge-based systems facilitate consistent and efficient quality decisions and enhance personnel productivity and performance. Popular knowledge-based systems include expert systems, rules-based systems, and neural networks. These systems use knowledge and inference procedures to solve difficult problems. This software intensively relies on the establishment and maintenance of the logic used for rule making. The risks lie in improper rule logic, inadequate rule maintenance and rule integrity, and the inability to test all circumstances and conditions.

Internet and Information Systems Security

The growing reliance on networks and the Internet has been the most significant technological development over the last decade. These networks facilitate the storage, processing, and retrieval of programs and data used by a group of people. Unfortunately, there are potential security risks every time an organization builds a network, and even more risks if it is connected to the Internet. These risks are primarily due to the openness and sharing inherent in a networked environment and a lack of security standards. The problem is further complicated by the fact that most networks link multiple computing platforms where the technical nuances of securing each platform are different. In either case, the amount of security controls must be appropriate for the risk and reward environment faced by an organization. Specific security risks include unauthorized access to data, data destruction, denial-of-service attacks, and viruses. Auditors should take steps to ensure that a security policy and baseline security controls are in place to minimize the risk of both internal and external computer security attacks. Auditors should also be aware of emerging security concepts and technologies. Examples of security technologies include firewalls, virtual private networks (VPNs), encryption, digital signatures, and strong authentication.

The auditor must keep a constant vigil because of these expected changes. The number of advances and their greater acceptance suggest a challenging control environment. Audit staffs need training resources in every area. In some of the rapidly changing areas, outside technical assistance should be used.

Compliance Functions

Compliance functions are evolving organizational units within the higher education industry, particularly at large research colleges, universities, and institutes. These functions are being designed as proactive strategies to identify, manage, and mitigate organizational risks to acceptable levels. Formation of these units is being driven by the following factors.

- The changing business environment and increasing complexity of laws and regulations have created a shifting paradigm. Boards and management are expanding their focus to managing enterprisewide business risks (strategic, financial, compliance, operational, and reputational) versus strictly focusing on financial risks.

- Institutions recognize the need to create a proactive mechanism to ensure compliance as well as to identify, manage, and mitigate risks to acceptable levels.

- Financial settlements between institutions and the federal government show adopting an effective compliance program provides a foundation for penalties to be reduced.

- Government oversight and investigative agencies have publicly announced that the higher education industry will encounter increased scrutiny.

Compliance functions are being integrated with audit functions, general counsel, or as stand-alone organizational units reporting to the board and senior management.

Audit Committee Effectiveness

Of emerging interest are two recent reports on increasing the effectiveness of audit committees. The focus has been on how audit committees could be more effective in addressing the unique risks and challenges posed by today's business environment.[15] The *Blue Ribbon Committee on Improving the Effectiveness of Audits,* sponsored by the New York Stock Exchange (NYSE) and the National Association of Securities Dealers (NASD) was charged with developing recommendations to "empower audit committees." As these initiatives moved forward, the National Association of Corporate Directors (NACD) formed a *Blue Ribbon Commission on Audit Committees* to develop guidance on best practices. The outcomes of these initiatives are working their way onto the agendas of all size companies, public and private, for-profit and not-for-profit. They address purpose, composition, process, implementation, and liability of audit committee members. The reports include suggested best practices and sample documents such as audit committee charters and committee self-assessment guides.[16]

NOTES

1. Dennis Applegate and Ted Wills, "Integrating COSO," *Internal Auditor* 56, no. 6 (December 1999): 60–66.

2. Taken from: M. Deverl Cutler, et al., *Internal Control Concepts & Applications.* This publication has adapted, where appropriate, to apply more directly to a college or university, Coopers and Lybrand, et al., *Internal Control Integrated Framework,* (Jersey City, NJ: The Committee of Sponsoring Organizations—COSO—of the Treadway Commission, 1992), p. 3

3. *ibid.,* p. 1.

4. *ibid.,* p. 3.

5. Price Waterhouse, *Improving Audit Committee Performance: What Works Best,* (Altamonte Springs, FL: The Institute of Internal Auditors Research Foundation, 1993), p. 25.

6. Jack L. Krogstad, Anthony J. Ridley, and Larry E. Rittenberg, "Where We're Going," *Internal Auditor* (October 1999), p. 29.

7. *ibid.,* 31–32.

8. Institute of Internal Auditors, *Standards for the Professional Practice of Internal Auditing,* (Altamonte Springs, FL: IIA, 1995).

9. Association of College and University Auditors, *1999 ACUA ABACUS Survey,* (Westerville, OH: ACUA, 1999).

10. Information Systems Audit and Control Foundation, *CoBIT® Framework, Executive Overview,* 2nd Edition, Rolling Meadows, IL: ISACF, April 1998), p. 7.

11. Association of College and University Auditors *Quality Assurance Review Handbook,* (Westerville, OH: ACUA, 1992).

12. Roger Carlolus and Donald Nelson, *The IIA Business-Focused Quality Assurance Review Manual for Internal Auditing*, 3rd Edition, (Altamonte Springs, FL: IIA, 1996).

13. National Association of College and University Business Officers, *Selecting an Auditor,* (Washington, DC: NACUBO, 1992).

14. National Association of College and University Business Officers, *Federal Auditing News for Colleges and Universities,* (Washington, DC: NACUBO, June 1999).

15. Ernst & Young, *Audit Committees—Implementing the New Rules,* (New York: Ernst & Young, January 2000).

16. William G. Bishop, III, Dana R. Hermanson, Paul D. Lapides and Larry E. Rittenberg, "The Year of the Audit Committee," *Internal Auditor* (April 2000): 46–51.

REFERENCES AND RESOURCES

Publications and Articles

Audits of Colleges and Universities With Conforming Changes as of May 1, 1994. Jersey City, NJ: American Institute of Certified Public Accountants.

Committee of Sponsoring Organizations of the Treadway Commission. *Internal Control: Integrated Framework-COSO, Two Volume Addition, 1994.* Jersey City, NJ: American Institute of Certified Public Accountants.

Comptroller General of the United States, Government Auditing Standards, 1994 Revision. Washington, DC: U.S. Government Printing Office, June 1994.

Equity in Athletics Disclosure Act of 1994, Section 405g of the Higher Education Act 1965.

Feidesman, James l., Liefer, Jacqueline C., and Glomb, Michael B. *Federal Auditing Information Service for Higher Education.* Washington DC: National Association of College and University Business Officers in conjunction with Atlantic Information Services, Inc., 1999.

Institute of Internal Auditors Research Foundation. *Standards for the Professional Practice of Internal Auditing.* Altamonte Springs, FL: IIA, 1998.

Institute of Internal Auditors Research Foundation. *Systems Auditability and Control.* Altamonte Springs, FL: IIA, 1991.

Institute of Internal Auditors. *Quality Assurance: Review Manual for Internal Auditing.* 2d ed. Altamonte Springs, FL: IIA, 1990.

Knight Foundation. *Keeping Faith with the Student Athlete: A New Model for Intercollegiate Athletics.* Charlotte, NC: Knight Foundation, 1991.

NCAA Division I Manual, Constitution Articles 6.2 and 6.3, Bylaws Article 23.2.

Root, Steven J. *Internal Auditing Manual.* 1999 Edition. Boston, MA: RIA Group/WG&L.

Sawyer, Lawrence B. *The Practice of Modern Internal Auditing.* Altamonte Springs, FL: The Institute of Internal Auditors, 1981.

Organizations

Association of College and University Auditors (ACUA)
Blendonview Office Park, 5008-03 Pine Creek Drive, Westerville, OH 43081-4899
614-891-7720 . . . . www.acua.org

National Association of College and University Business Officers (NACUBO)
2501 M Street, NW, Suite 400, Washington, DC 20037-1308
202-861-2500 . . . . www.nacubo.org

Institute of Internal Auditors (IIA)
249 Maitland Avenue, Altamonte Springs, FL 32701-4201
407-830-7600 . . . . www.theiia.org

Association of Healthcare Internal Auditors (AHIA)
900 Fox Valley Drive, Suite 204, Longwood, FL 32779-2554
407-786-8200 or (888) 275-2442 . . . . www.ahia.org

American Institute of Certified Public Accountants (AICPA)
Harborside Financial Center, 201 Plaza Three, Jersey City, NJ 07311-3881
201-938-3000 . . . . www.aicpa.org

Index

This index has been compiled from identified key index terms found in CUBA 6. If the word or words you are searching for are not found in this index, please see the book's Table of Contents for the 22 chapters (pages iii, iv, and v), or refer to the specific subject chapter's own Table of Contents.

College and University Business Administration, Sixth Edition
was designed and typeset by
AAH Graphics, Inc. of Fort Valley, Virginia.

Andrea Richards designed the cover.

Text was provided by NACUBO in a variety of word-processing formats,
converted by AAH Graphics into the AAHSET publishing system.
Proofs were posted on the AAH Graphics Internet proofing site
where authors could directly view them without having to produce paper proofs.

The index was generated by the AAHSET system.

The book was printed by Cadmus Professional Communications,
Port City Press Division, Baltimore, Maryland, and
bound by Shortrun Binderies, Medford, New Jersey .

The text of the book is typeset in Garamond 3, which is based
on a type face attributed to Claude Garamont, the first and
one of the most distinguished French letter-cutters and type-founders.
Garamont produced his roman and italic types between
1540 and 1545; however, it is now believed that the type
today called 'Garamond' is actually the work of
Jean Jannon, a French master printer,
who designed this type about 1615.